The Principles of Psychology

The Principles of Psychology

William James

HARVARD UNIVERSITY PRESS
Cambridge, Massachusetts
and London, England
1983

Printed in the United States of America
10 9 8 7 6 5 4 3 2 1

CENTER FOR
SCHOLARLY EDITIONS
AN APPROVED TEXT
MODERN LANGUAGE
ASSOCIATION OF AMERICA

Library of Congress Cataloging in Publication Data

James, William, 1842–1910.
The principles of psychology.

(The Works of William James)
Includes index.
1. Psychology. I. Title. II. Series: James, William, 1842–1910. Works. 1983.
BF121.J2 1983 150 83-8572
ISBN 0-674-70625-0 (pbk.)

Publisher's Note

The Harvard edition of *The Principles of Psychology* provides, for the first time, an authoritative text of this great work. It incorporates the hundreds of changes James made in the eight printings he supervised and also, of key importance, the revisions and new material he inserted in his own annotated copy—alterations and additions too extensive to be made in the plates of the original book. The text thus comes as close as possible to representing James's final intentions. His many quotations, sometimes rendered from memory, have been checked and corrected, and his references to sources have been given full and accurate citations.

The original edition of the *Principles* was reprinted innumerable times over the years, always with the same page numbering regardless of the publisher or the date; thus prior to 1981 all references by page number to passages in the book were to the original pagination. At the end of this volume a pagination key has been provided whereby those citations can be readily equated with the corresponding pages in the present text.

This edition was first published in hard covers in 1981 as part of THE WORKS OF WILLIAM JAMES, a definitive edition of James's published and unpublished writings sponsored by the American Council of Learned Societies. The General Editor is Frederick Burkhardt; the Textual Editor is Fredson Bowers. In the hardcover edition the text is bound in two volumes and a third volume provides extensive annotations, appendixes, and textual information.

Contents

Introduction

George A. Miller

The Principles of Psychology is one of the treasures of American intellectual history, a pioneering exploration of the science of mental life prized for its literary quality as well as for its scientific content. William James possessed, in a more forthright style, much of his novelist brother Henry's gift of expression. As Lewis Mumford put it, "There is a homely elegance in James's writing, a beauty in the presentation of the thought."[1] The *Principles* has survived since 1890, and will live on to charm new generations of readers, because there is art in it.

Although James's prose speaks for itself, the historical role that the *Principles* played does not. How James helped to propel psychology out of its philosophical armchair deserves an introductory account.

Most contemporary psychologists know, because they have been told, that before about 1900 psychology was a branch of philosophy. To understand what that alliance implied—to understand what it meant for psychology that scientific explanation was not even an ambition, much less a criterion—takes an active imagination. A generally Whiggish attitude toward history has made it easy for students of modern psychology to assume that psychologists before 1900 were similar to psychologists today.

[1] *The Golden Day: A Study in American Experience and Culture* (New York: Norton, 1933), p. 255.

If psychology is defined to include every kind of speculative curiosity about mental states or processes, then it has a long history. As a science, however, its history begins in the nineteenth century. It begins around midcentury when a few alert and ambitious men tried to extend to psychology some of the techniques of experimentation that were proving so successful in physiology. Its beginning is usually dated from the time those first attempts were collated and systematized: in Germany in Wilhelm Wundt's *Grundzüge der physiologischen Psychologie* (1874); in America in William James's *Principles of Psychology* (1890). The official birthdate of scientific psychology is often taken to be 1879, the year that the first psychological laboratory was founded by Wundt at the University of Leipzig, although Wundt and James both had demonstrational laboratories as early as 1875.

Why this double birth was necessary is itself an interesting story. The two founders represent two distinct, often contesting, views of man, two schools of thought whose differences have never been resolved. In the seventeenth century the French philosopher and mathematician René Descartes rejected the medieval scholastics' appeal to authority as the basis of all knowledge and proposed an intuitive source instead. Scientific laws, like mathematical theorems, were to be derived by reason alone; reason was said to be innately equipped to comprehend the world. Toward the end of the seventeenth century the English philosopher John Locke followed Descartes's lead in rejecting scholasticism, but objected to innate ideas. Locke claimed that at birth there is nothing in a baby's mind, that all knowledge comes through sensory experience—a claim that was to become central to British empiricism. The German philosopher and mathematician Gottfried Leibniz responded that there is nothing in the mind at birth but the mind itself, and that is a great deal. Leibniz saw the mind as an active, rational unity—a view that became central to German rationalism.

Wundt stands in the rationalist tradition of Leibniz, James in the empiricist tradition of Locke. Wundt's systematization of the new psychology shows the influence of Spinoza, Kant, Humboldt, Hegel, Schopenhauer. James's implicit mentors are Hartley, Hume, James and John Stuart Mill, Condillac, Condorcet. Neither tradition could accept a scientific psychology incorporating the philosophical presuppositions of the other. Each had to work out the significance of the new experimentation in its own terms.

From the beginning, therefore, scientific psychology had philosophical skeletons in its closet. Of course, they were not skeletons to Wundt and James, whose interest in psychology was seen as interest in philosophy. What they wrote was inevitably judged by the prevailing standards of systematic philosophy; their aspiration to be judged also against standards of scientific explanation and proof was a novel and rather daring departure from the dogma of the day, a dogma supported by centuries of precedent. The separation of psychology from philosophy–the creation of separate academic departments, separate professional societies, separate journals and textbooks—was not complete until well into the twentieth century.

Today young psychologists, young American psychologists at any rate, are educated to think of psychology as a discipline independent of philosophy, with its own problems and methods. Even when wrestling with questions that also concern philosophers, psychologists are likely to work alone, apparently on the assumption that you can ignore the skeletons as long as you don't open the closet.

But sometimes the bones rattle. They rattle when empiricist and nativist hypotheses compete. They rattle when behaviorists ignore mental processes, or when cognitive psychologists try to investigate mental representations of knowledge. They rattle when psychologists assume that their working concepts can be (or cannot be) reduced to neurophysiological or biochemical mechanisms. There is so much rattling, in fact, that some psychologists, secure at last in their independence, have begun to open the closet just wide enough for a philosophical peek.

William James was born in New York City, January 11, 1842, to Mary and Henry James. Three brothers and a sister followed, the youngest only six years younger than William.

A fortunate investment in the Erie Canal left the Jameses wealthy enough for William's father to devote himself to theological argumentation and writing, to conversation and correspondence with the leading American and British thinkers of his day, and to the intellectual and spiritual development of his talented children. As a result, William's education was intense, varied, nourishing, and definitely unusual.

The early tutoring of William and his brother Henry was entrusted to a series of women, but, dissatisfied with what Henry later called the "educative ladies," their father sent them next to a series of establishments that endeavored to teach them foreign languages, introduce them to arithmetic, and generally uncover their young talents. Then between 1855 and 1860 William (often with Henry) attended schools in England, France, Switzerland, and Germany. Since the elder James was not easily satisfied, the dominant characteristic of their formal education was continual change.

The James family found few things more interesting than themselves. Their lives and thoughts, and those of their friends, are preserved in voluminous letters and books. Those sources leave a strong impression that one of the most important educational influences on the young Jameses must have been the spirited discourse at their father's dinner table. E. L. Godkin conveys a feeling for it:

> There could not be a more entertaining treat than dinner at the James house, when all the young people were at home. They were full of stories of the oddest kind, and discussed questions of morals or taste or literature with a vociferous vigor so great as sometimes to lead the young men to leave their seats and gesticulate on the floor. I remember, in some of these heated discussions, it was not unusual for the sons to invoke humorous curses on their parent, one of which was, that "his mashed potatoes might always have lumps in them!"[2]

In the autumn of 1861, while other young Americans were going to war, William James went to Harvard, to the Lawrence Scientific School—physical frailty left him unfit for military service. After studying chemistry under Charles William Eliot, he found his interests shifting; he turned next to comparative anatomy and physiology under Jeffries Wyman, who seems to have imparted to him his own scientific conscience and devotion to truth. In 1864 he transferred to the Harvard Medical School, where his studies were sporadic. An ill-fated year with Louis Agassiz on an expedition up the Amazon River exposed him to smallpox and he suffered a "sensitiveness" of the eyes that bothered him intermittently for the rest of his life.

Ill health and an avowed desire to study physiology in Germany sent him off to Europe again in 1867. He took baths for his back,

[2] Quoted in Ralph Barton Perry, *The Thought and Character of William James* (Cambridge, Mass.: Harvard University Press, 1948), p. 23.

studied little physiology but read widely, toyed with thoughts of suicide, and poured out his homesickness in a flood of correspondence. One letter to Henry Bowditch[3] mentions an intention to go to Heidelberg because Helmholtz was there "and a man named Wundt," from whom he hoped to learn something of sensory physiology, but his hopes were thwarted by continued ill health.

In November 1868 James returned to Harvard and in June 1869 he took his medical degree. But his health continued to decline until the spring of 1870 found him in deep melancholy. His biographers have speculated on the significance of this period in his life, for it seems that in these dark months he began to build a personal philosophy that would sustain him against despair. When some essays by Charles Renouvier convinced him that the mind affects the body in ways that can be controlled by deliberate choice, he wrote in his diary, "My first act of free will shall be to believe in free will."[4] He believed he could cure himself by sheer belief. James's condition then began to improve, which fact persuaded him that his personal difficulties had been overcome by philosophical insight.

By 1872 he had recovered sufficiently to accept an offer from President Eliot to teach physiology to Harvard undergraduates. James enjoyed reviving his interest in physiology; having a job to do turned him away from morbid self-examination. In 1875–76 he offered a course entitled "The Relations between Physiology and Psychology" dealing with the new experimental psychology. And in 1878 he agreed to write a textbook on psychology for Henry Holt, which he hoped to finish in two years. That book turned out to be *The Principles of Psychology* and it took, not two, but twelve years of intense work.[5]

Psychology carried James into the Department of Philosophy, where he was to remain. It must be remembered, however, that the author of the *Principles* held posts in physiology (1872–1880), psychology (1889–1897), and philosophy (1880–1907); all three disciplines found their way into its pages.

3 *The Selected Letters of William James*, ed. Elizabeth Hardwick (Boston: Godine, 1980), p. 57.

4 Quoted in Perry, *Thought and Character*, p. 121.

5 A detailed and fascinating account of the interactions between James and the tenacious Holt is given in volume III of the Harvard hardcover edition: Frederick Burkhardt, Fredson Bowers, and Ignas K. Skrupskelis, eds., *The Principles of Psychology* (Cambridge, Mass.: Harvard University Press, 1981), pp. 1532–1579.

James's marriage to Alice Howe Gibbons in 1878 was followed by further improvement in his health; although his health was never really good, for the next thirty years he was able to lead an intensely active life as a teacher, author, and public lecturer. His work did not suffer even in 1882 when, within a span of ten months, both of his parents died, a loss that must have been profoundly felt in so close a family. He had learned how to live with his feelings, with grief as well as with depression.

The loss of his parents may have helped to shape James's much-debated theory of emotion, which was published in 1884 and later developed as Chapter xxv of the *Principles*. According to the 1884 paper:

> Whistling to keep up courage is no mere figure of speech. On the other hand, sit all day in a moping posture, sigh, and reply to everything in a dismal voice, and your melancholy lingers. There is no more valuable precept in moral education than this, as all who have experience know: if we wish to conquer undesirable emotional tendencies in ourselves, we must assiduously, and in the first instance cold-bloodedly, go through the *outward motions* of those contrary dispositions we prefer to cultivate. The reward of persistency will infallibly come, in the fading out of the sullenness or depression, and the advent of real cheerfulness and kindliness in their stead.[6]

As one scholar comments: "The writing of the article may thus have been in part an effort in self-discipline at this critical moment of his life."[7] It is probably no accident that Chapter xxv of the *Principles* begins with a consideration of grief.

After 1890 James devoted most of his thought to philosophy, though he never stopped being a psychologist. In 1907 he resigned his professorship at Harvard. He died at his home in Chocorua, New Hampshire, on August 26, 1910, at the age of sixty-eight.

James's personality has fascinated his biographers, perhaps because his unique combination of innocence and sophistication is so elusive. Ralph Barton Perry distinguished three Willam Jameses: the neurasthenic James, unstable, sometimes morbidly imaginative, moody, and averse to intellectual rigor; the radiant James, vivid, generous, loving, and sensitive; and a third James "in whom

6 "What Is an Emotion?" *Mind,* 9 (1884), 198.

7 Saul Rosenzweig, "The Jameses' Stream of Consciousness," *Contemporary Psychology,* 3 (1958), 250–257.

the second of these is deepened and enriched through being united with the first."[8]

In a letter to his wife some months after their marriage he wrote something that his son Henry called "an unusual bit of self-analysis":

I have often thought that the best way to define a man's character would be to seek out the particular mental or moral attitude in which, when it came upon him, he felt himself most deeply and intensely active and alive. At such moments there is a voice inside which speaks and says: "*This* is the real me!" . . . Now as well as I can describe it, this characteristic attitude in me always involves an element of active tension, of holding my own, as it were, and trusting outward things to perform their part so as to make it a full harmony, but without any *guaranty* that they will. Make it a guaranty – and the attitude immediately becomes to my consciousness stagnant and stingless. Take away the guaranty, and I feel (provided I am *überhaupt* in vigorous condition) a sort of deep enthusiastic bliss, of bitter willingness to do and suffer anything, which translates itself physically by a kind of stinging pain inside my breast-bone (don't smile at this – it is to me an essential element of the whole thing!), and which, although it is a mere mood or emotion to which I can give no form in words, authenticates itself to me as the deepest principle of all active and theoretic determination which I possess.[9]

Take a man who is at his best under the tension of active uncertainty and sign him to a contract to write an introductory textbook. What will he do? Will he merely update the conventional text of his day? Will he accept the guarantee of a successful list of topics and order of presentation? Will he simply try to phrase more felicitously the generalizations already reached by others?

Not William James. Such a man must put his personal stamp on every chapter, or there is no challenge to it, no stinging pain inside the breastbone. The *Principles* was an intellectual adventure, and the spirit of a deeply and intensely active and alive William James still shines through.

Not only did James survive his depression during the 1870s, but some of his fundamental psychological and philosophical ideas began to take shape. Those were the years of the Metaphysical

[8] Perry, *Thought and Character*, p. 385.

[9] *Selected Letters*, p. 109.

Club, founded by Charles Sanders Peirce in 1871. In addition to Peirce and James, the group included Chauncey Wright, Oliver Wendell Holmes, Nicholas St. John Green, and several other defiant young intellectuals around Harvard. Pragmatism, the characteristically American version of empiricist philosophy, originated in a paper that Peirce read to the Metaphysical Club in 1872.

In 1859 the English philosopher Alexander Bain defined belief as "an attitude or disposition of preparedness to act."[10] Peirce later wrote that "From this definition, pragmatism is scarce more than a corollary; so that I am disposed to think of him as the grandfather of pragmatism."[11] To believe that an object is hard, for example, is to be prepared to operate on that object in ways characteristic of such objects. The function of belief, Peirce inferred, is to establish habits of action.

In Peirce's paper, which was not published until 1878, the connection between belief and action was developed into a method for getting at the meaning of our ideas. What a thing means is simply the set of habitual actions it prompts. For example, what does "This block is hard" mean? Peirce said it means that if you operate with the block in such and such ways, such and such experiences will ensue. The whole of our conception of hardness is our conception of its practical effects. A concept with no practical effects is meaningless.

It was William James, not C. S. Peirce, who popularized pragmatism. In 1898, twenty-six years after Peirce explained his theory of meaning to the Metaphysical Club, James, in an address on "Philosophical Conceptions and Practical Results," announced the doctrine publicly, identifying it as the method that British empiricists had followed instinctively. He developed it further in a series of eight public lectures in 1906, published as a book, *Pragmatism*, in 1907.

To Peirce's pragmatic theory of meaning James added a pragmatic theory of truth. What is the meaning of " 'This block is hard' is true"? Does it mean anything more than "This block is hard"?

[10] *The Emotions and the Will* (1859), quoted in Israel Scheffler, *Four Pragmatists: A Critical Introduction to Peirce, James, Mead, and Dewey* (New York: Humanities Press, 1974), p. 58.

[11] Charles Hartshorne and Paul Weiss, eds., *Collected Papers of Charles Sanders Peirce* (Cambridge, Mass.: Harvard University Press, 1931–1958), vol. V, para. 12.

Following Peirce's lead, the statement should be translated: If one acts in the characteristic way, such and such consequences will be experienced. But how can this translation be made? James argued that believing is like acting, that to tell someone "*p* is true" is to tell him to believe *p*. But that is only half the rule: "If you believe *p*, then . . ." Then what? What experiences should ensue? Surely nothing bad can follow from believing *p* if *p* is true. Thus the complete rule is: "*p* is true" means that "If you believe *p*, the effects will be satisfactory."

James's theory of truth provoked violent controversy. Peirce immediately objected that James made truth a personal matter—what one person judges satisfactory may not satisfy another—whereas the truth that science needs is interpersonal. Years later an astute student of James's writings pointed out that "James's references to satisfaction seem to allow for a broad as well as a narrow interpretation. On the narrow interpretation, a belief functions satisfactorily when *it* is satisfied or confirmed by experience. On the broad interpretation, it is not simply a matter of whether the belief is satisfied, i.e., confirmed, but also a matter of whether the believer derives satisfaction consequent upon his believing the proposition in question."[12] James guarded against misuse of the broad interpretation, but many of his critics claimed that he was saying, "Anything that pleases you is true for you."

Although the earliest formulations of James's pragmatic theory of truth date back to 1885, the storm that broke much later need not concern readers of the *Principles*. The *Principles* does, however, exploit the pragmatic principle that meaning depends on practical effects. In Chapter VI, for example, James opposes the view that people are conscious automatons (where conciousness has no mechanical function) by arguing that consciousness evolved because it is efficacious, because it serves a selective function (p. 142)—that is to say, because consciousness has "practical effects." Although James did not invoke Peirce's maxim explictly, this instrumental conception of the mind, often called Darwinian, follows from the same fundamental assumptions. Chapter VII, which treats the "mind-stuff theory," is equally an exercise in pragmatic criticism.

When James takes off in these purely philosophical directions,

[12] Israel Scheffler, *Four Pragmatists*, p. 105.

the argument falls strangely on ears educated to scientific psychology. In other places, however, he becomes purely physiological, or purely psychological. Watching the master weave these strands together adds pleasure to the reading.

Each chapter of the *Principles* is a separate essay that can stand on its own. It almost seems as if the sequence were arbitrary, but closer consideration reveals that the book is much more systematic than a glance at the table of contents might suggest. Because James does not insist on one view as true and preferable to all others but tries to ask questions fairly, assemble facts evenhandedly, and leave the answers open, psychologists of very different schools have been willing to cite him a their intellectual ancestor. But more psychologists have cited the *Principles* than have read it from start to finish. Although the book can be sampled with profit in bits and pieces, the full scope of James's psychology can be appreciated only by a reader willing to follow chapter by chapter as the story unfolds.

After a short essay on the scope of psychology, James launches his masterpiece with two chapters on the brain, followed by a physiologically based theory of habit. This way of introducing psychology was unusual and aroused considerable comment. In those days a standard text would begin with elementary sensations of vision, hearing, taste, smell, and touch, compound those sensations into complex ideas of objects, then compound successive ideas by laws of association, and so gradually build up larger mental structures from the smaller.

James objected to that approach, in part, no doubt, because it *was* the accepted way; in part because he disliked sensory psychophysics; in part because he felt psychology should build from a base in biology; but most of all because it destroyed the unity of conscious experience. In 1900, in his preface to the Italian edition, James wrote:

> So instead of starting with the mind's supposed elements (which are always abstractions) and gradually building-up, I have tried to keep the reader in contact throughout as many chapters as possible, with the actual conscious unity which each of us at all times feels himself to be. This unity is what the classic spiritualism has always fought for against the associationist doctrine that the mind is a mere collection of 'ideas.' But as I wished to disentangle psychology as far as possible from any close alliance with ultimate questions of metaphysics, I have

limited my contention of unity to what is empirically verifiable, namely to the unity of each passing wave or field of consciousness.[13]

The *Principles* starts with the brain. Having opened in his physiological voice, however, James immediately faces a need to distinguish physiology from psychology, that is to say, to treat those ancient and unanswerable questions about the relations of brain and mind. So the philosophical voice dominates the next few chapters, until finally the psychological voice breaks through, almost impatiently: "*The psychologist's attitude towards cognition . . . is a thoroughgoing dualism.* It supposes two elements, mind knowing and thing known, and treats them as irreducible" (p. 214).

But James the philosopher is never really satisfied with dualism. In Chapter XVI, for example, after James the psychologist reviews the experimental work on memory and James the physiologist adds that memory is an important function of the brain, James the philosopher has the last word:

> According to the assumptions of this book, thoughts accompany the brain's workings, and those thoughts are cognitive of realities. The whole relation is one which we can only write down empirically, confessing that no glimmer of explanation of it is yet in sight. That brains should give rise to a knowing consciousness at all, this is the one mystery which returns, no matter what sort the consciousness and of what sort the knowledge may be. (p. 647)

Such philosophical caveats are scattered through the book. James the philosopher seems to be rummaging through all the pockets of psychology, searching for some decisive criterion to distinguish the mental from the physical—and not finding it.

The *Principles* is built of physiology and clinical neurology, with some evolutionary biology thrown in; it is built of introspective, experimental, and clinical psychology; it is built of philosophy enlivened by occasional lay sermons. The gaps and tensions among these sources might have discouraged another man, but they stimulated James.

The *Principles* does not include any discussion of individual differences, any serious account of the cognitive or emotional development of children, or any real appreciation of the social and cultural dimensions of mental life. The first two of these gaps were

[13] Reproduced in volume III of *Principles* (see note 5 above), p. 1483.

inevitable: differential and developmental psychology did not exist in 1890. The third is more interesting.

It is not that James ignored social relations, but that, for such an enormously social and sociable person, his view of them seems curiously restricted. His theory of truth, for example, speaks of truth for the individual, not a socially shared truth. The limitation is illustrated by a famous passage (p. 125) in which he calls habit the enormous flywheel of society, a conservative agent that keeps us all on our individual paths; we become caught in some pursuit early on and habit freezes us there. One scholar has commented that James "seems to fall short of a genuinely *social* perspective. For the notion that possibilities are open or closed to men not simply as a function of increasing personal rigidity but as a function of social organization is one that James never seems to envisage."[14] This social gap in James's psychology is all the more remarkable because, as George Herbert Mead and John Dewey would soon show, James's pragmatic philosophy was well suited for the development of social psychology and for theories of social reconstruction and reform.

It remained for the Chicago school of philosophy and psychology to develop many of the implications of James's ideas. As philosophers, they were pragmatists; as psychologists, they were functionalists. Although the *Principles* provided the inspiration, it was John Dewey who instigated the work of functional psychology, which soon emerged as the major rival of Wundtian psychology. Whereas Wundtians were concerned with the structure of the mind, American psychologists under Dewey's leadership were concerned with the functions it served.

Functional psychologists inherited a pragmatic preoccupation with practical effects, and the practical effect of the mind is to guide behavior. Broadening the definition of psychology to include behavioral as well as mental phenomena enabled functionalism to absorb behavioral observations of animals, of children, of the insane or mentally retarded, of social groups. Mental tests were seen as behavior samples. By the time of Wundt's death in 1920 the introspective science he had founded in Leipzig had been overtaken and overshadowed by the broader, pragmatic American science.

14 Scheffler, *Four Pragmatists*, p. 124.

The functionalists' attention to behavior was so successful, in fact, that the subjective aspect of psychology came to seem unnecessary. In 1913 John B. Watson founded a school of psychology concerned solely with behavior: all mental phenomena were replaced by the behavioral evidence from which they were inferred. The apparent objectivity of this approach was so attractive that behaviorism became a major influence on psychological thought in the United States. It is ironic that James's pragmatic philosophy proved so congenial to these materialistic ideas, since a psychology without consciousness is a psychology without need for James's remarkable introspective talent.

Beginning in the mid-1950s, however, many American psychologists reaffirmed their interest in consciousness and the cognitive representation of reality, and many of the rebels against behaviorism turned back to William James for support. They thumbed the *Principles* ragged to find quotations that lent credibility to a revival of mentalism.

And so it has happened that, even as the very definition of scientific psychology swung violently from functionalism to behaviorism and back to cognitivism, William James's *Principles of Psychology* has continued to hold a living place in everyone's thinking. Such is the genius of the man, and of his work.

The Principles of Psychology

To

my dear friend

François Pillon,

as a token of affection,

and an acknowledgment of what I owe

to the

Critique Philosophique

Preface

The treatise which follows has in the main grown up in connection with the author's class-room instruction in Psychology, although it is true that some of the chapters are more 'metaphysical,' and others fuller of detail, than is suitable for students who are going over the subject for the first time. The consequence of this is that, in spite of the exclusion of the important subjects of pleasure and pain, and moral and æsthetic feelings and judgments, the work has grown to a length which no one can regret more than the writer himself. The man must indeed be sanguine who, in this crowded age, can hope to have many readers for fourteen hundred continuous pages from his pen. But *wer vieles bringt, wird manchem etwas bringen*; and, by judiciously skipping according to their several needs, I am sure that many sorts of readers, even those who are just beginning the study of the subject, will find my book of use. Since the beginners are most in need of guidance, I suggest for their behoof that they omit altogether on a first reading chapters 6, 7, 8, 10 (from page 314 to page 350), 12, 13, 15, 17, 20, 21, and 28. The better to awaken the neophyte's interest, it is possible that the wise order would be to pass directly from chapter 4 to chapters 23, 24, 25, and 26, and thence to return to the first volume again. Chapter 20, on Space-perception, is a terrible thing, which, unless written with all that detail, could not be fairly treated at all. An abridgment of it, called "The Spatial Quale," which appeared in the *Journal of Speculative Philosophy*, vol. XIII, p. 64, may be found by some persons a useful substitute for the entire chapter.

I have kept close to the point of view of natural science throughout the book. Every natural science assumes certain data uncritically, and declines to challenge the elements between which its own 'laws' obtain, and from which its own deductions are carried on. Psychology, the science of finite individual minds, assumes as its data (1) *thoughts and feelings*, and (2) *a physical world* in time and space with which they coexist and which (3) *they know*. Of course these data themselves are discussable; but the discussion of them (as of other elements) is called metaphysics and falls outside the province of this book. This book, assuming that thoughts and feelings exist and are vehicles of knowledge, thereupon contends that psychology when she has ascertained the empirical correlation of the various sorts of thought or feeling with definite conditions of the brain, can go no farther—can go no farther, that is, as a natural science. If she goes farther she becomes metaphysical. All attempts to *explain* our phenomenally given thoughts as products of deeper-lying entities (whether the latter be named 'Soul,' 'Transcendental Ego,' 'Ideas,' or 'Elementary Units of Consciousness') are metaphysical. This book consequently rejects both the associationist and the spiritualist theories; and in this strictly positivistic point of view consists the only feature of it for which I feel tempted to claim originality. Of course this point of view is anything but ultimate. Men must keep thinking; and the data assumed by psychology, just like those assumed by physics and the other natural sciences, must some time be overhauled. The effort to overhaul them clearly and thoroughly is metaphysics; but metaphysics can only perform her task well when distinctly conscious of its great extent. Metaphysics fragmentary, irresponsible, and half-awake, and unconscious that she is metaphysical, spoils two good things when she injects herself into a natural science. And it seems to me that the theories both of a spiritual agent and of associated 'ideas' are, as they figure in the psychology-books, just such metaphysics as this. Even if their results be true, it would be as well to keep them, *as thus presented*, out of psychology as it is to keep the results of idealism out of physics.

I have therefore treated our passing thoughts as integers, and regarded the mere laws of their coexistence with brain-states as the ultimate laws for our science. The reader will in vain seek for any closed system in the book. It is mainly a mass of descriptive details, running out into queries which only a metaphysics alive to the weight of her task can hope successfully to deal with. That will perhaps be centuries hence; and meanwhile the best mark of health that a science can show is this unfinished-seeming front.

The completion of the book has been so slow that several chapters have been published successively in *Mind*, the *Journal of Speculative Philosophy*, the *Popular Science Monthly*, and *Scribner's Magazine*. Acknowledgment is made in the proper places.

The bibliography, I regret to say, is quite unsystematic. I have habitually given my authority for special experimental facts; but beyond that I have aimed mainly to cite books that would probably be actually used by the ordinary American college-student in his collateral reading. The bibliography in W. Volkmann von Volkmar's *Lehrbuch der Psychologie* (1875) is so complete, up to its date, that there is no need of an inferior duplicate. And for more recent references, Sully's *Outlines*, Dewey's *Psychology*, and Baldwin's *Handbook of Psychology* may be advantageously used.

Finally, where one owes to so many, it seems absurd to single out particular creditors; yet I cannot resist the temptation at the end of my first literary venture to record my gratitude for the inspiration I have got from the writings of J. S. Mill, Lotze, Renouvier, Hodgson, and Wundt, and from the intellectual companionship (to name only five names) of Chauncey Wright and Charles Peirce in old times, and more recently of Stanley Hall, James Putnam, and Josiah Royce.

HARVARD UNIVERSITY, August 1890

Contents

Contents

Chapter I

The Scope of Psychology

Psychology is the Science of Mental Life, both of its phenomena and of their conditions. The phenomena are such things as we call feelings, desires, cognitions, reasonings, decisions, and the like; and, superficially considered, their variety and complexity is such as to leave a chaotic impression on the observer. The most natural and consequently the earliest way of unifying the material was, first, to classify it as well as might be, and, secondly, to affiliate the diverse mental modes thus found, upon a simple entity, the personal Soul, of which they are taken to be so many facultative manifestations. Now, for instance, the Soul manifests its faculty of Memory, now of Reasoning, now of Volition, or again its Imagination or its Appetite. This is the orthodox 'spiritualistic' theory of scholasticism and of common-sense. Another and a less obvious way of unifying the chaos is to seek common elements *in* the divers mental facts rather than a common agent behind them, and to explain them constructively by the various forms of arrangement of these elements, as one explains houses by stones and bricks. The 'associationist' schools of Herbart in Germany, and of Hume, the Mills and Bain in Britain, have thus constructed a *psychology without a soul* by taking discrete 'ideas,' faint or vivid, and showing how, by their cohesions, repulsions, and forms of succession, such things as reminiscences, perceptions, emotions, volitions, passions, theories, and all the other furnishings of an individual's mind may be engendered. The very Self or *ego* of the individual comes in this way to be viewed no longer as the pre-existing source of the representations, but rather as their last and most complicated fruit.

Now, if we strive rigorously to simplify the phenomena in either of these ways, we soon become aware of inadequacies in our method. Any particular cognition, for example, or recollection, is accounted for on the soul-theory by being referred to the spiritual faculties of Cognition or of Memory. These faculties themselves are thought of as absolute properties of the soul; that is, to take the case of memory, no reason is given why we should remember a fact as it happened, except that so to remember it constitutes the essence of our Recollective Power. We may, as spiritualists, try to explain our memory's failures and blunders by secondary causes. But its *successes* can invoke no factors save the existence of certain objective things to be remembered on the one hand, and of our faculty of memory on the other. When, for instance, I recall my graduation-day, and drag all its incidents and emotions up from death's dateless night, no mechanical cause can explain this process, nor can any analysis reduce it to lower terms or make its nature seem other than an ultimate *datum*, which, whether we rebel or not at its mysteriousness, must simply be taken for granted if we are to psychologize at all. However the associationist may represent the present ideas as thronging and arranging themselves, still, the spiritualist insists, he has in the end to admit that *something*, be it brain, be it 'ideas,' be it 'association,' *knows* past time *as* past, and fills it out with this or that event. And when the spiritualist calls memory an 'irreducible faculty,' he says no more than this admission of the associationist already grants.

And yet the admission is far from being a satisfactory simplification of the concrete facts. For why should this absolute god-given Faculty retain so much better the events of yesterday than those of last year, and, best of all, those of an hour ago? Why, again, in old age should its grasp of childhood's events seem firmest? Why should illness and exhaustion enfeeble it? Why should repeating an experience strengthen our recollection of it? Why should drugs, fevers, asphyxia, and excitement resuscitate things long since forgotten? If we content ourselves with merely affirming that the faculty of memory is so peculiarly constituted by nature as to exhibit just these oddities, we seem little the better for having invoked it, for our explanation becomes as complicated as that of the crude facts with which we started. Moreover there is something grotesque and irrational in the supposition that the soul is equipped with elementary powers of such an ingeniously intricate sort. Why *should* our memory cling more easily to the near than the remote? Why should it lose its grasp of proper sooner than of abstract names? Such peculiarities seem quite fantastic; and might, for aught we can see *a priori*, be the precise opposites of what they are. Evidently, then, *the faculty does not exist absolutely, but works under conditions*; and *the quest of the conditions* becomes the psychologist's most interesting task.

However firmly he may hold to the soul and her remembering faculty, he must acknowledge that she never exerts the latter without a *cue*, and that something must always precede and *remind* us of whatever we are to recollect. "An *idea*!" says the associationist, "an idea associated with the remembered thing; and this explains also why things repeatedly met with are more easily recollected, for their associates on the various occasions furnish so many distinct avenues of recall." But this does not explain the effects of fever, exhaustion, hypnotism, old age, and the like. And in general, the pure associationist's account of our mental life is almost as bewildering as that of the pure spiritualist. This multitude of ideas, existing absolutely, yet clinging together, and weaving an endless carpet of themselves, like dominoes in ceaseless change, or the bits of glass in a kaleidoscope,—whence do they get their fantastic laws of clinging, and why do they cling in just the shapes they do?

For this the associationist must introduce the order of experience in the outer world. The dance of the ideas is a copy, somewhat mutilated and altered, of the order of phenomena. But the slightest reflection shows that phenomena have absolutely no power to influence our ideas until they have first impressed our senses and our brain. The bare existence of a past fact is no ground for our remembering it. Unless we have seen it, or somehow *undergone* it, we shall never know of its having been. The experiences of the body are thus one of the conditions of the faculty of memory being what it is. And a very small amount of reflection on facts shows that one part of the body, namely, the brain, is the part whose experiences are directly concerned. If the nervous communication be cut off between the brain and other parts, the experiences of those other parts are non-existent for the mind. The eye is blind, the ear deaf, the hand insensible and motionless. And conversely, if the brain be injured, consciousness is abolished or altered, even although every other organ in the body be ready to play its normal part. A blow on the head, a sudden subtraction of blood, the pressure of an apoplectic hemorrhage, may have the first effect; whilst a very few ounces of alcohol or grains of opium or hasheesh, or a whiff of chloroform or nitrous oxide gas, are sure to have the second. The delirium of fever, the altered self of insanity, are all due to foreign matters circulating through the brain, or to pathological changes in that organ's substance. The fact that the brain is the one immediate bodily condition of the mental operations is indeed so universally admitted nowadays that I need spend no more time in illustrating it, but will simply postulate it and pass on. The whole remainder of the book will be more or less of a proof that the postulate was correct.

Bodily experiences, therefore, and more particularly brain-experiences, must take a place amongst those conditions of the mental life of which Psychology need take account. *The spiritualist and the associationist must both be 'cerebralists,'* to the extent at least of admitting that certain peculiarities in the way of working of their own favorite principles are explicable only by the fact that the brain laws are a codeterminant of the result.

Our first conclusion, then, is that a certain amount of brain-physiology must be presupposed or included in Psychology.[1]

In still another way the psychologist is forced to be something of a nerve-physiologist. Mental phenomena are not only conditioned *a parte ante* by bodily processes; but they lead to them *a parte post.* That they lead to *acts* is of course the most familiar of truths, but I do not merely mean acts in the sense of voluntary and deliberate muscular performances. Mental states occasion also changes in the calibre of blood-vessels, or alteration in the heart-beats, or processes more subtle still, in glands and viscera. If these are taken into account, as well as acts which follow at some *remote period* because the mental state was once there, it will be safe to lay down the general law that *no mental modification ever occurs which is not accompanied or followed by a bodily change.* The ideas and feelings, e.g., which these present printed characters excite in the reader's mind not only occasion movements of his eyes and nascent movements of articulation in him, but will some day

[1] Cf. George T. Ladd: *Elements of Physiological Psychology* (1887), pt. III, chap. III, §§ 9, 12.

make him speak, or take sides in a discussion, or give advice, or choose a book to read, differently from what would have been the case had they never impressed his retina. Our psychology must therefore take account not only of the conditions antecedent to mental states, but of their resultant consequences as well.

But actions originally prompted by conscious intelligence may grow so automatic by dint of habit as to be apparently unconsciously performed. Standing, walking, buttoning and unbuttoning, piano-playing, talking, even saying one's prayers, may be done when the mind is absorbed in other things. The performances of animal *instinct* seem semi-automatic, and the *reflex acts* of self-preservation certainly are so. Yet they resemble intelligent acts in bringing about the *same ends* at which the animals' consciousness, on other occasions, deliberately aims. Shall the study of such machine-like yet purposive acts as these be included in Psychology?

The boundary-line of the mental is certainly vague. It is better not to be pedantic, but to let the science be as vague as its subject, and include such phenomena as these if by so doing we can throw any light on the main business in hand. It will ere long be seen, I trust, that we can; and that we gain much more by a broad than by a narrow conception of our subject. At a certain stage in the development of every science a degree of vagueness is what best consists with fertility. On the whole, few recent formulas have done more real service of a rough sort in psychology than the Spencerian one that the essence of mental life and of bodily life are one, namely, 'the adjustment of inner to outer relations.' Such a formula is vagueness incarnate; but because it takes into account the fact that minds inhabit environments which act on them and on which they in turn react; because, in short, it takes mind in the midst of all its concrete relations, it is immensely more fertile than the old-fashioned 'rational psychology,' which treated the soul as a detached existent, sufficient unto itself, and assumed to consider only its nature and properties. I shall therefore feel free to make any sallies into zoology or into pure nerve-physiology which may seem instructive for our purposes, but otherwise shall leave those sciences to the physiologists.

Can we state more distinctly still the manner in which the mental life seems to intervene between impressions made from without upon the body, and reactions of the body upon the outer world again? Let us look at a few facts.

If some iron filings be sprinkled on a table and a magnet brought near them, they will fly through the air for a certain distance and stick to its surface. A savage seeing the phenomenon explains it as the result of an attraction or love between the magnet and the filings. But let a card cover the poles of the magnet, and the filings will press forever against its surface without its ever occurring to them to pass around its sides and thus come into more direct contact with the object of their love. Blow bubbles through a tube into the bottom of a pail of water, they will rise to the surface and mingle with the air. Their action may again be poetically interpreted as due to a longing to recombine with the mother-atmosphere above the surface. But if you invert a jar full of water over the pail, they will rise and remain lodged beneath its bottom, shut in from the outer air, although a slight deflection from their course at the outset, or a re-descent towards the rim of the jar when they found their upward course impeded, would easily have set them free.

If now we pass from such actions as these to those of living things, we notice a striking difference. Romeo wants Juliet as the filings want the magnet; and if no obstacles intervene he moves towards her by as straight a line as they. But Romeo and Juliet, if a wall be built between them, do not remain idiotically pressing their faces against its opposite sides like the magnet and the filings with the card. Romeo soon finds a circuitous way, by scaling the wall or otherwise, of touching Juliet's lips directly. With the filings the path is fixed; whether it reaches the end depends on accidents. With the lover it is the end which is fixed, the path may be modified indefinitely.

Suppose a living frog in the position in which we placed our bubbles of air, namely, at the bottom of a jar of water. The want of breath will soon make him also long to rejoin the mother-atmosphere, and he will take the shortest path to his end by swimming straight upwards. But if a jar full of water be inverted over him, he will not, like the bubbles, perpetually press his nose against its unyielding roof, but will restlessly explore the neighborhood until by re-descending again he has discovered a path round its brim to the goal of his desires. Again the fixed end, the varying means!

Such contrasts between living and inanimate performances end by leading men to deny that in the physical world final purposes exist at all. Loves and desires are to-day no longer imputed to particles of iron or of air. No one supposes now that the end of any activity which they may display is an ideal purpose presiding over the activity from its outset and soliciting or drawing it into being by a sort of *vis a fronte*. The end, on the contrary, is deemed a mere passive result, pushed into being *a tergo*, having had, so to speak, no voice in its own production. Alter the pre-existing conditions, and with inorganic materials you bring forth each time a different apparent end. But with intelligent agents, altering the conditions changes the activity displayed, but not the end reached; for here the idea of the yet unrealized end co-operates with the conditions to determine what the activities shall be.

The pursuance of future ends and the choice of means for their attainment are thus the mark and criterion of the presence of mentality in a phenomenon. We all use this test to discriminate between an intelligent and a mechanical performance. We impute no mentality to sticks and stones, because they never seem to move for *the sake of* anything, but always when pushed, and then indifferently and with no sign of choice. So we unhesitatingly call them senseless.

Just so we form our decision upon the deepest of all philosophic problems: Is the Kosmos an expression of intelligence rational in its inward nature, or a brute external fact pure and simple? If we find ourselves, in contemplating it, unable to banish the impression that it is a realm of final purposes, that it exists for the sake of something, we place intelligence at the heart of it and have a religion. If, on the contrary, in surveying its irremediable flux, we can think of the present only as so much mere mechanical sprouting from the past, occurring with no reference to the future, we are atheists and materialists.

In the lengthy discussions which psychologists have carried on about the amount of intelligence displayed by lower mammals, or the amount of consciousness involved in the functions of the nerve-centres of reptiles, the same test has always been applied: Is the character of the actions such that we must believe them to be performed *for the sake* of their result? The result in question, as we shall hereafter abundantly see, is as a rule a useful one,—the animal is, on the whole, safer under the circumstances for bringing it forth. So far the action has a teleological character; but such mere outward teleology as this might still be the blind result of *vis a tergo*. The growth and movements of plants, the processes of development, digestion, secretion, etc., in animals, supply innumerable instances of performances useful to the individual which may nevertheless be, and by most of us are supposed to be, produced by automatic mechanism. The physiologist does not confidently assert conscious intelligence in the frog's spinal cord until he has shown that the useful result which the nervous machinery brings forth under a given irritation *remains the same when the machinery is altered*. If, to take the stock-instance, the right knee of a headless frog be irritated with acid, the right foot will wipe it off. When, however, this foot is amputated, the animal will often raise the *left* foot to the spot and wipe the offending material away.

Pflüger and Lewes reason from such facts in the following way: If the first reaction were the result of mere machinery, they say; if that irritated portion of the skin discharged the right leg as a trigger discharges its own barrel of a shotgun; then amputating the right foot would indeed frustrate the wiping, but would not make the *left* leg move. It would simply result in the right stump moving through the empty air (which is in fact the phenomenon sometimes observed). The right trigger makes no effort to discharge the left barrel if the right one be unloaded; nor does an electrical machine ever get restless because it can only emit sparks, and not hem pillow-cases like a sewing-machine.

If, on the contrary, the right leg originally moved for the *purpose* of wiping the acid, then nothing is more natural than that, when the easiest means of effecting that purpose prove fruitless, other means should be tried. Every failure must keep the animal in a state of disappointment which will lead to all sorts of new trials and devices; and tranquillity will not ensue till one of these, by a happy stroke, achieves the wished-for end.

In a similar way Goltz ascribes intelligence to the frog's optic lobes and cerebellum. We alluded above to the manner in which a sound frog imprisoned in water will discover an outlet to the atmosphere. Goltz found that frogs deprived of their cerebral hemispheres would often exhibit a like ingenuity. Such a frog, after rising from the bottom and finding his farther upward progress checked by the glass bell which has been inverted over him, will not persist in butting his nose against the obstacle until dead of suffocation, but will often re-descend and emerge from under its rim as if, not a definite mechanical propulsion upwards, but rather a conscious desire to reach the air by hook or crook were the mainspring of his activity. Goltz concluded from this that the hemispheres are not the seat of intellectual power in frogs. He made the same inference from observing that a brainless frog will turn over from his back to his belly when one of his legs is sewed up, although the movements required are then very different from those excited under normal circumstances by the same annoying position. They seem determined, consequently, not merely by the antecedent irritant, but by the final end,—though the irritant of course is what makes the end desired.

Another brilliant German author, Liebmann,[2] argues against the brain's mechanism accounting for mental action, by very similar considerations. A machine as such, he says, will bring forth right results when it is in good order, and wrong results if out of repair. But both kinds of result flow with equally fatal necessity from their conditions. We cannot suppose the clock-work whose structure fatally determines it to a certain rate of speed, noticing that this speed is too slow or too fast and vainly trying to correct it. Its conscience, if it have any, should be as good as that of the best chronometer, for both alike obey equally well the same eternal mechanical laws—laws from behind. But if the *brain* be out of order and the man says "Twice four are two," instead of "Twice four are eight," or else "I must go to the coal to buy the wharf," instead of "I must go to the wharf to buy the coal," instantly there arises a consciousness of error. The wrong performance, though it obey the same mechanical law as the right, is nevertheless condemned,—condemned as contradicting the inner law—the law from in front, the purpose or ideal for which the brain *should* act, whether it do so or not.

We need not discuss here whether these writers in drawing their conclusion have done justice to all the premises involved in the cases they treat of. We quote their arguments only to show how they appeal to the principle that *no actions but such as are done for an end, and show a choice of means, can be called indubitable expressions of Mind.*

I shall then adopt this as the criterion by which to circumscribe the subject-matter of this work so far as action enters into it. Many nervous performances will therefore be unmentioned, as being

2 *Zur Analysis der Wirklichkeit*, p. 489.

purely physiological. Nor will the anatomy of the nervous system and organs of sense be described anew. The reader will find in H. N. Martin's *Human Body*, in G. T. Ladd's *Physiological Psychology*, and in all the other standard Anatomies and Physiologies, a mass of information which we must regard as preliminary and take for granted in the present work.[3] Of the functions of the cerebral hemispheres, however, since they directly subserve consciousness, it will be well to give some little account.

[3] Nothing is easier than to familiarize one's self with the mammalian brain. Get a sheep's head, a small saw, chisel, scalpel and forceps (all three can best be had from a surgical-instrument maker), and unravel its parts either by the aid of a human dissecting book, such as Holden's *Manual of Anatomy*, or by the specific directions *ad hoc* given in such books as Foster and Langley's *Practical Physiology* (Macmillan) or Morrell's *Comparative Anatomy, and Guide to Dissection* (Longman & Co.).

Chapter II

The Functions of the Brain

If I begin chopping the foot of a tree, its branches are unmoved by my act, and its leaves murmur as peacefully as ever in the wind. If, on the contrary, I do violence to the foot of a fellow-man, the rest of his body instantly responds to the aggression by movements of alarm or defence. The reason of this difference is that the man has a nervous system, whilst the tree has none; and the function of the nervous system is to bring each part into harmonious co-operation with every other. The afferent nerves, when excited by some physical irritant, be this as gross in its mode of operation as a chopping axe or as subtle as the waves of light, conveys the excitement to the nervous centres. The commotion set up in the centres does not stop there, but discharges itself, if at all strong, through the efferent nerves into muscles and glands, exciting movements of the limbs and viscera, or acts of secretion, which vary with the animal and with the irritant applied. These acts of response have usually the common character of being of service. They ward off the noxious stimulus and support the beneficial one; whilst if, in itself indifferent, the stimulus be a sign of some distant circumstance of practical importance, the animal's acts are addressed to this circumstance so as to avoid its perils or secure its benefits, as the case may be. To take a common example, if I hear the conductor calling "All aboard!" as I enter the depot, my heart first stops, then palpitates, and my legs respond to the air-waves falling on my tympanum by quickening their movements. If I stumble as

I run, the sensation of falling provokes a movement of the hands towards the direction of the fall, the effect of which is to shield the body from too sudden a shock. If a cinder enter my eye, its lids close forcibly and a copious flow of tears tends to wash it out.

These three responses to a sensational stimulus differ, however, in many respects. The closure of the eye and the lachrymation are quite involuntary, and so is the disturbance of the heart. Such involuntary responses we know as 'reflex' acts. The motion of the arms to break the shock of falling may also be called reflex, since it occurs too quickly to be deliberately intended. Whether it be instinctive or whether it result from the pedestrian education of childhood may be doubtful; it is, at any rate, less automatic than the previous acts, for a man might by conscious effort learn to perform it more skilfully, or even to suppress it altogether. Actions of this kind, into which instinct and volition enter upon equal terms, have been called 'semi-reflex.' The act of running towards the train, on the other hand, has no instinctive element about it. It is purely the result of education, and is preceded by a consciousness of the purpose to be attained and a distinct mandate of the will. It is a 'voluntary act.' Thus the animal's reflex and voluntary performances shade into each other gradually, being connected by acts which may often occur automatically, but may also be modified by conscious intelligence.

An outside observer, unable to perceive the accompanying consciousness, might be wholly at a loss to discriminate between the automatic acts and those which volition escorted. But if the criterion of mind's existence be the choice of the proper means for the attainment of a supposed end, all the acts seem to be inspired by intelligence, for *appropriateness* characterizes them all alike. This fact, now, has led to two quite opposite theories about the relation to consciousness of the nervous functions. Some authors, finding that the higher voluntary ones seem to require the guidance of feeling, conclude that over the lowest reflexes some such feeling also presides, though it may be a feeling of which *we* remain unconscious. Others, finding that reflex and semi-automatic acts may, notwithstanding their appropriateness, take place with an unconsciousness apparently complete, fly to the opposite extreme and maintain that the appropriateness even of voluntary actions owes nothing to the fact that consciousness attends them. They are, according to these writers, results of physiological mechanism pure and simple. In a near chapter we shall return to this controversy again. Let us now look a little more closely at the brain and at the ways in which its states may be supposed to condition those of the mind.

THE FROG'S NERVE-CENTRES

Both the minute anatomy and the detailed physiology of the brain are achievements of the present generation, or rather we may say (beginning with Meynert) of the past twenty years. Many points are still obscure and subject to controversy; but a general way of conceiving the organ has been reached on all hands which in its main feature seems not unlikely to stand, and which even gives a most plausible scheme of the way in which cerebral and mental operations go hand in hand.

The best way to enter the subject will be to take a lower creature, like a frog, and study by the vivisectional method the functions of his different nerve-centres. The frog's nerve-centres are figured in

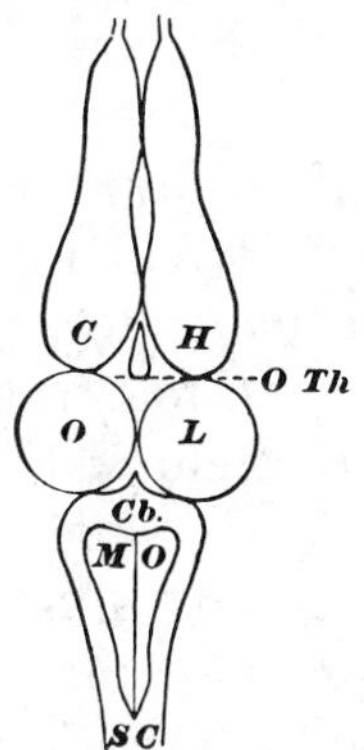

FIG. 1.—*C H*, Cerebral Hemispheres; *O Th*, Optic Thalami; *O L*, Optic Lobes; *Cb*, Cerebellum; *M O*, Medulla Oblongata; *S C*, Spinal Cord.

the accompanying diagram, which needs no further explanation. I will first proceed to state what happens when various amounts of the anterior parts are removed, in different frogs, in the way in which an ordinary student removes them—that is, with no extreme precautions as to the purity of the operation. We shall in this way reach a very simple conception of the functions of the various centres, involving the strongest possible contrast between the cerebral hemispheres and the lower lobes. This sharp conception will have didactic advantages, for it is often very instructive to start with too simple a formula and correct it later on. Our first formula, as we shall later see, will have to be softened down somewhat by the results of more careful experimentation both on frogs and birds, and by those of the most recent observations on dogs, monkeys, and man. But it will put us, from the outset, in clear possession of some fundamental notions and distinctions which we could otherwise not gain so well, and none of which the later more completed view will overturn.

If, then, we reduce the frog's nervous system to the spinal cord alone, by making a section behind the base of the skull, between the spinal cord and the medulla oblongata, thereby cutting off the brain from all connection with the rest of the body, the frog will still continue to live, but with a very peculiarly modified activity. It ceases to breathe or swallow; it lies flat on its belly, and does not, like a normal frog, sit up on its fore-paws, though its hind-legs are kept, as usual, folded against its body and immediately resume this position if drawn out. If thrown on its back it lies there quietly, without turning over like a normal frog. Locomotion and voice seem entirely abolished. If we suspend it by the nose, and irritate different portions of its skin by acid, it performs a set of remarkable 'defensive' movements calculated to wipe away the irritant. Thus, if the breast be touched, both fore-paws will rub it vigorously; if we touch the outer side of the elbow, the hind-foot of the same side will rise directly to the spot and wipe it. The back of the foot will rub the knee if that be attacked, whilst if the foot be cut away, the stump will make ineffectual movements, and then, in many frogs, a pause will come, as if for deliberation, succeeded by a rapid passage of the opposite unmutilated foot to the acidulated spot.

The most striking character of all these movements, after their teleological appropriateness, is their precision. They vary, in sensitive frogs and with a proper amount of irritation, so little as almost to resemble in their machine-like regularity the performances of a jumping-jack, whose legs must twitch whenever you pull the string. The spinal cord of the frog thus contains arrangements of cells and fibres fitted to convert skin-irritations into movements of defence. We may call it the *centre for defensive movements* in this animal. We may indeed go farther than this, and by cutting the spinal cord in various places find that its separate segments are independent mechanisms, for appropriate activities of the head and of the arms and legs respectively. The segment governing the arms is especially active, in male frogs, in the breeding season; and these members alone with the breast and back appertaining to them, everything else being cut away, will then actively grasp a finger placed between them and remain hanging to it for a considerable time.

The spinal cord in other animals has analogous powers. Even in man it makes movements of defence. Paraplegics draw up their legs when tickled; and Robin, on tickling the breast of a criminal an hour after decapitation, saw the arm and hand move towards the spot. Of the lower functions of the mammalian cord, studied so ably by Goltz and others, this is not the place to speak.

If, in a second animal, the cut be made just behind the optic lobes so that the cerebellum and medulla oblongata remain attached to the cord, then swallowing, breathing, crawling, and a rather enfeebled jumping and swimming are added to the movements previously observed.[1] There are other reflexes too. The animal, thrown on his back, immediately turns over to his belly. Placed in a shallow bowl, which is floated on water and made to rotate, he responds to the rotation by first turning his head and then waltzing around with his entire body, in the opposite direction to the whirling of the bowl. If his support be tilted so that his head points downwards, he points it up; he points it down if it be pointed upwards, to the right if it be pointed to the left, etc. But his reactions do not go farther than these movements of the head. He will not, like frogs whose thalami are preserved, climb up a board if the latter be tilted, but will slide off it to the ground.

If the cut be made on another frog between the thalami and the optic lobes, the locomotion both on land and water becomes quite normal, and, in addition to the reflexes already shown by the lower centres, he croaks regularly whenever he is pinched under the arms. He compensates rotations, etc., by movements of the head, and turns over from his back; but still drops off his tilted board. As his optic nerves are destroyed by the usual operation, it is impossible to say whether he will avoid obstacles placed in his path.

When, finally, a frog's cerebral hemispheres alone are cut off by a section between them and the thalami which preserves the latter, an unpractised observer would not at first suspect anything abnor-

[1] It should be said that this particular cut commonly proves fatal. The text refers to the rare cases which survive.

mal about the animal. Not only is he capable, on proper instigation, of all the acts already described, but he guides himself by sight, so that if an obstacle be set up between him and the light, and he be forced to move forward, he either jumps over it or swerves to one side. He manifests sexual passion at the proper season, and, unlike an altogether brainless frog, which embraces anything placed between his arms, postpones this reflex act until a female of his own species is provided. Thus far, as aforesaid, a person unfamiliar with frogs might not suspect a mutilation; but even such a person would soon remark the almost entire absence of spontaneous motion—that is, motion unprovoked by any *present* incitation of sense. The continued movements of swimming, performed by the creature in the water, seem to be the fatal result of the contact of that fluid with its skin. They cease when a stick, for example, touches his hands. This is a sensible irritant towards which the feet are automatically drawn by reflex action, and on which the animal remains sitting. He manifests no hunger, and will suffer a fly to crawl over his nose unsnapped at. Fear, too, seems to have deserted him. In a word, he is an extremely complex machine whose actions, so far as they go, tend to self-preservation; but still a *machine*, in this sense—that it seems to contain no incalculable element. By applying the right sensory stimulus to him we are almost as certain of getting a fixed response as an organist is of hearing a certain tone when he pulls out a certain stop.

But now if to the lower centres we add the cerebral hemispheres, or if, in other words, we make an intact animal the subject of our observations, all this is changed. In addition to the previous responses to present incitements of sense, our frog now goes through long and complex acts of locomotion *spontaneously*, or as if moved by what in ourselves we should call an idea. His reactions to outward stimuli vary their form, too. Instead of making simple defensive movements with his hind-legs, like a headless frog, if touched; or of giving one or two leaps and then sitting still like a hemisphereless one, he makes persistent and varied efforts at escape, as if, not the mere contact of the physiologist's hand, but the notion of danger suggested by it were now his spur. Led by the feeling of hunger, too, he goes in search of insects, fish, or smaller frogs, and varies his procedure with each species of victim. The physiologist cannot by manipulating him elicit croaking, crawling up a board, swimming or stopping, at will. His conduct has become incalculable—we can no longer foretell it exactly. Effort to escape is his dominant reaction, but he *may* do anything else, even swell up and become perfectly passive in our hands.

Such are the phenomena commonly observed, and such the impressions which one naturally receives. Certain general conclusions follow irresistibly. First of all the following:

The acts of all the centres involve the use of the same muscles. When a headless frog's hind-leg wipes the acid, he calls into play all the leg-muscles which a frog with his full medulla oblongata and cerebellum uses when he turns from his back to his belly. Their contractions are, however, *combined* differently in the two cases, so that the results vary widely. We must consequently conclude that specific arrangements of cells and fibres exist in the cord for wiping, in the medulla for turning over, etc. Similarly they exist in the thalami for jumping over seen obstacles and for balancing the moved body; in the optic lobes for creeping backwards, or what not. But in the hemispheres, since the presence of these organs *brings no new elementary form of movement* with it, but only *determines differently the occasions* on which the movements shall occur, making the usual stimuli less fatal and machine-like; we need suppose no such machinery *directly* co-ordinative of muscular contractions to exist. We may rather assume, when the mandate for a wiping-movement is sent forth by the hemispheres, that a current goes straight to the wiping-arrangement in the spinal cord, exciting this arrangement as a whole. Similarly, if an intact frog wishes to jump over a stone which he sees, all he need do is to excite from the hemispheres the jumping-centre in the thalami or wherever it may be, and the latter will provide for the details of the execution. It is like a general ordering a colonel to make a certain movement, but not telling him how it shall be done.[2]

The same muscle, then, is repeatedly represented at different heights; and at each it enters into a different combination with other muscles to co-operate in some special form of concerted movement. *At each height the movement is discharged by some particular form of sensorial stimulus.* Thus in the cord, the skin alone occasions movements; in the upper part of the optic lobes,

[2] I confine myself to the frog for simplicity's sake. In higher animals, especially the ape and man, it would seem as if not only determinate combinations of muscles, but limited groups or even single muscles could be innervated from the hemispheres.

the eyes are added; in the thalami, the semi-circular canals would seem to play a part; whilst the stimuli which discharge the hemispheres would seem not so much to be elementary sorts of sensation, as groups of sensations forming determinate *objects* or *things*. *Prey* is not pursued nor are *enemies* shunned by ordinary hemisphereless frogs. Those reactions upon complex circumstances which we call instinctive rather than reflex, are already in this animal dependent on the brain's highest lobes, and still more is this the case with animals higher in the zoological scale.

The results are just the same if, instead of a frog, we take a pigeon, and cut out his hemispheres as they are ordinarily cut out for a lecture-room demonstration. There is not a movement natural to him which this brainless bird cannot perform if expressly excited thereto; only the inner promptings seem deficient, and when left to himself he spends most of his time crouched on the ground with his head sunk between his shoulders as if asleep.

GENERAL NOTION OF HEMISPHERES

All these facts lead us, when we think about them, to some such explanatory conception as this: *The lower centres act from present sensational stimuli alone; the hemispheres act from perceptions and considerations*, the sensations which they may receive serving only as suggesters of these. But what are perceptions but sensations grouped together? and what are considerations but expectations, in the fancy, of sensations which will be felt one way or another according as action takes this course or that? If I step aside on seeing a rattlesnake, from considering how dangerous an animal he is, the mental materials which constitute my prudential reflection are images more or less vivid of the movement of his head, of a sudden pain in my leg, of a state of terror, a swelling of the limb, a chill, delirium, unconsciousness, etc., etc., and the ruin of my hopes. But all these images are constructed out of my past experiences. They are *reproductions* of what I have felt or witnessed. They are, in short, *remote* sensations; and the *difference between the hemisphereless animal and the whole one* may be concisely expressed by saying that the *one obeys absent, the other only present, objects.*

The hemispheres would then seem to be *the seat of memory.* Vestiges of past experience must in some way be stored up in them, and must, when aroused by present stimuli, first appear as representations of distant goods and evils; and then must discharge into the appropriate motor channels for warding off the evil and securing the benefits of the good. If we liken the nervous currents to electric currents, we can compare the nervous system, *C*, below the hemispheres to a direct circuit from sense-organ to muscle along the line *S* . . . *C* . . . *M* of Fig. 2. The hemisphere, *H*, adds the long

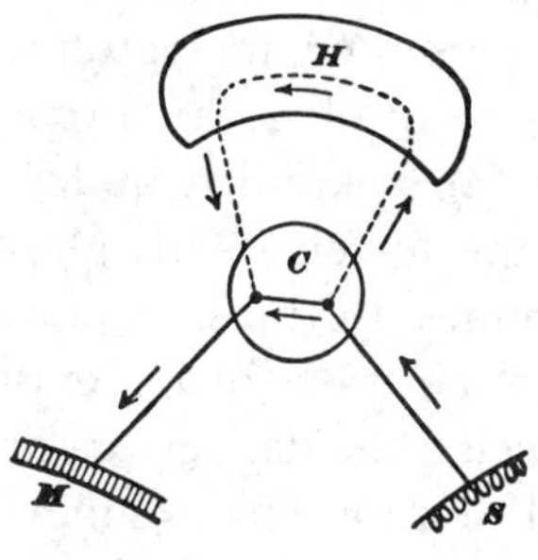

Fig. 2.

circuit or loop-line through which the current may pass when for any reason the direct line is not used.

Thus, a tired wayfarer on a hot day throws himself on the damp earth beneath a maple-tree. The sensations of delicious rest and coolness pouring themselves through the direct line would naturally discharge into the muscles of complete extension: he would abandon himself to the dangerous repose. But the loop-line being open, part of the current is drafted along it, and awakens rheumatic or catarrhal reminiscences, which prevail over the instigations of sense, and make the man arise and pursue his way to where he may enjoy his rest more safely. Presently we shall examine the manner in which the hemispheric loop-line may be supposed to serve as a reservoir for such reminiscences as these. Meanwhile I will ask the reader to notice some corollaries of its being such a reservoir.

First, no animal without it can deliberate, pause, postpone, nicely weigh one motive against another, or compare. Prudence, in a word, is for such a creature an impossible virtue. Accordingly we see that nature removes those functions in the exercise of which prudence is a virtue from the lower centres and hands them over to the cerebrum. Wherever a creature has to deal with complex features of the environment, prudence is a virtue. The higher animals have so to deal; and the more complex the features, the higher we call the animals. The fewer of his acts, then, can *such* an animal perform without the help of the organs in question. In the frog many acts devolve wholly on the lower centres; in the bird fewer; in the rodent fewer still; in the dog very few indeed; and in apes and men hardly any at all.

The advantages of this are obvious. Take the prehension of food as an example and suppose it to be a reflex performance of the lower centres. The animal will be condemned fatally and irresistibly to snap at it whenever presented, no matter what the circumstances may be; he can no more disobey this prompting than water can refuse to boil when a fire is kindled under the pot. His life will again and again pay the forfeit of his gluttony. Exposure to retaliation, to other enemies, to traps, to poisons, to the dangers of repletion, must be regular parts of his existence. His lack of all thought by which to weigh the danger against the attractiveness of the bait, and of all volition to remain hungry a little while longer, is the direct measure of his lowness in the mental scale. And those fishes which, like our cunners and sculpins, are no sooner thrown back from the hook into the water than they automatically seize the hook again, would soon expiate the degradation of their intelligence by the extinction of their type, did not their exaggerated fecundity atone for their imprudence. Appetite and the acts it prompts have consequently become in all higher vertebrates functions of the cerebrum. They disappear when the physiologist's knife has left the subordinate centres alone in place. The brainless pigeon will starve though left on a corn-heap.

Take again the sexual function. In birds this devolves exclusively upon the hemispheres. When these are shorn away the pigeon pays no attention to the billings and cooings of its mate. And Goltz found that a bitch in heat would excite no emotion in male dogs who had suffered large loss of cerebral tissue. Those who have read Darwin's *Descent of Man* know what immense importance in the amelioration of the breed in birds this author ascribes to the mere fact of sexual selection. The sexual act is not performed until every condition of circumstance and sentiment is fulfilled, until time, place, and partner all are fit. But in frogs and toads this passion devolves on the lower centres. They show consequently a machine-like obedience to the present incitement of sense, and an almost total exclusion of the power of choice. Copulation occurs *per fas aut nefas*, occasionally between males, often with dead females, in puddles exposed on the highway, and the male may be cut in two without letting go his hold. Every spring an immense sacrifice of batrachian life takes place from these causes alone.

No one need be told how dependent all human social elevation is upon the prevalence of chastity. Hardly any factor measures more than this the difference between civilization and barbarism. Physiologically interpreted, chastity means nothing more than the fact that present solicitations of sense are overpowered by suggestions of æsthetic and moral fitness which the circumstances awaken in the cerebrum; and that upon the inhibitory or permissive influence of these alone action directly depends.

Within the psychic life due to the cerebrum itself the same general distinction obtains, between considerations of the more immediate and considerations of the more remote. In all ages the man whose determinations are swayed by reference to the most distant ends has been held to possess the highest intelligence. The tramp who lives from hour to hour; the bohemian whose engagements are from day to day; the bachelor who builds but for a single life; the father who acts for another generation; the patriot who thinks of a whole community and many generations; and, finally, the philosopher and saint whose cares are for humanity and for eternity,—these range themselves in an unbroken hierarchy, wherein each successive grade results from an increased manifestation of the special form of action by which the cerebral centres are distinguished from all below them.

In the 'loop-line' along which the memories and ideas of the distant are supposed to lie, the action, so far as it is a physical process, must be interpreted after the type of the action in the lower centres. If regarded here as a reflex process, it must be reflex there as well. The current in both places runs out into the muscles only after it has first run in; but whilst the path by which it runs out is determined in the lower centres by reflections few and fixed amongst the cell-arrangements, in the hemispheres the reflections are many and instable. This, it will be seen, is only a difference of degree and not of kind, and does not change the reflex type. The conception of *all* action as conforming to this type is the fundamental conception of modern nerve-physiology. So much for our general preliminary conception of the nerve-centres! Let us define it more distinctly before we see how well physiological observation will bear it out in detail.

THE EDUCATION OF THE HEMISPHERES

Nerve-currents run in through sense-organs, and whilst provoking reflex acts in the lower centres, they arouse ideas in the hemispheres, which either permit the reflexes in question, check them, or substitute others for them. All ideas being in the last resort reminiscences, the question to answer is: *How can processes become organized in the hemispheres which correspond to reminiscences in the mind?*[3]

Nothing is easier than to conceive a *possible* way in which this might be done, provided four assumptions be granted. These assumptions (which after all are inevitable in any event) are:

1) The same cerebral process which, when aroused from without by a sense-organ, gives the perception of an object, will give an *idea* of the same object when aroused by other cerebral processes from within.

2) If processes 1, 2, 3, 4 have once been aroused together or in immediate succession, any subsequent arousal of any one of them (whether from without or within) will tend to arouse the others in the original order. [This is the so-called law of association.]

3) Every sensorial excitement propagated to a lower centre tends to spread upwards and arouse an idea.

4) Every idea tends ultimately either to produce a movement or to check one which otherwise would be produced.

Suppose now (these assumptions being granted) that we have a baby before us who sees a candle-flame for the first time, and, by virtue of a reflex tendency common in babies of a certain age, extends his hand to grasp it, so that his fingers get burned. So far we have two reflex currents in play: first, from the eye to the extension movement, along the line 1—1—1—1 of Fig. 3; and second, from the

[3] I hope that the reader will take no umbrage at my so mixing the physical and mental, and talking of reflex acts and hemispheres and reminiscences in the same breath, as if they were homogeneous quantities and factors of one causal chain. I have done so deliberately; for although I admit that from the radically physical point of view it is easy to conceive of the chain of events amongst the cells and fibres as complete in itself, and that whilst so conceiving it one need make no mention of 'ideas,' I yet suspect that point of view of being an unreal abstraction. Reflexes in centres may take place even where accompanying feelings or ideas guide them. In another chapter I shall try to show reasons for not abandoning this common-sense position; meanwhile language lends itself so much more easily to the mixed way of describing, that I will continue to employ the latter. The more radical-minded reader can always read 'ideational process' for 'idea.'

finger to the movement of drawing back the hand, along the line 2—2—2—2. If this were the baby's whole nervous system, and if the reflexes were once for all organic, we should have no alteration in his behavior, no matter how often the experience recurred. The retinal image of the flame would always make the arm shoot forward, the burning of the finger would always send it back. But we know that 'the burnt child dreads the fire,' and that one experience usually protects the fingers forever. The point is to see how the hemispheres may bring this result to pass.

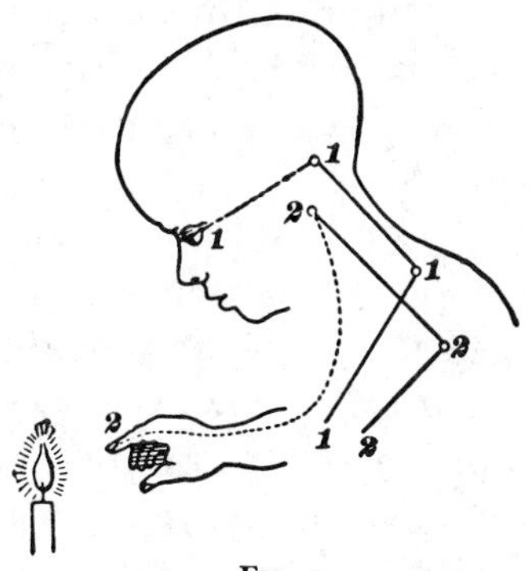

FIG. 3.

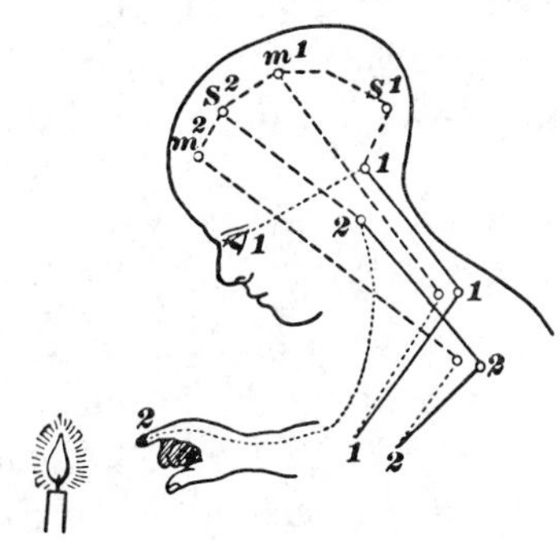

FIG. 4.—The dotted lines stand for afferent paths, the broken lines for paths between the centres; the entire lines for efferent paths.

We must complicate our diagram (see Fig. 4). Let the current 1—1, from the eye, discharge upwards as well as downwards when it reaches the lower centre for vision, and arouse the perceptional process s^1 in the hemispheres; let the feeling of the arm's extension also send up a current which leaves a trace of itself, m^1; let the burnt finger leave an analogous trace, s^2; and let the movement of retraction leave m^2. These four processes will now, by virtue of assumption 2), be associated together by the path s^1—m^1—s^2—m^2, running from the first to the last, so that if anything touches off s^1, ideas of the extension, of the burnt finger, and of the retraction will pass in rapid succession through the mind. The effect on the child's conduct when the candle-flame is next presented is easy to imagine. Of course the sight of it arouses the grasping reflex; but it arouses simultaneously the idea thereof, together with that of the consequent pain, and of the final retraction of the hand; and if these cerebral processes prevail in strength over the immediate sensation in the centres below, the last idea will be the cue by which the final action is discharged. The grasping will be arrested in mid-career, the hand drawn back, and the child's fingers saved.

In all this we assume that the hemispheres do not *natively* couple any particular sense-impression with any special motor discharge. They only register, and preserve traces of, such couplings as are already organized in the reflex centres below. But this brings it inevitably about that, when a chain of experiences has been already registered and the first link is impressed once again from without, the last link will often be awakened in *idea* long before it can exist in *fact*. And if this last link were previously coupled with a motion, that motion may now come from the mere ideal suggestion without waiting for the actual impression to arise. Thus an animal with hemispheres acts in *anticipation* of future things; or, to use our previous formula, he acts from considerations of distant good and ill. If we give the name of *partners* to the original couplings of impressions with motions in a reflex way, then we may say that the function of the hemispheres is simply to bring about *exchanges among the partners.* Movement m^n, which natively is sensation s^n's partner, becomes through the hemispheres the partner of sensation s^1, s^2 or s^3. It is like the great commutating switch-board at a central telephone station. No new elementary process is involved; no impression nor any motion peculiar to the hemispheres; but any number of combinations impossible to the lower machinery taken alone, and an endless consequent increase in the possibilities of behavior on the creature's part.

All this, as a mere scheme,[4] is so clear and so concordant with the general look of the facts as almost to impose itself on our belief; but it is anything but clear in detail. The brain-physiology of late years has with great effort sought to work out the paths by which these couplings of sensations with movements take place, both in the hemispheres and in the centres below.

So we must next test our scheme by the facts discovered in this direction. We shall conclude, I think, after taking them all into

[4] I shall call it hereafter for shortness 'the Meynert scheme'; for the child-and-flame example, as well as the whole general notion that the hemispheres are a supernumerary surface for the projection and association of sensations and movements natively coupled in the centres below, is due to Theodor Meynert, the Austrian anatomist. For a popular account of his views, see his pamphlet *Zur Mechanik des Gehirnbaues*, Vienna, 1874. His most recent development of them is embodied in his *Psychiatry: A Clinical Treatise on Diseases of the Fore-Brain*, translated by B. Sachs, New York, 1885.

account, that the scheme probably makes the lower centres too machine-like and the hemispheres not quite machine-like enough, and must consequently be softened down a little. So much I may say in advance. Meanwhile, before plunging into the details which await us, it will somewhat clear our ideas if we contrast the modern way of looking at the matter with the *phrenological* conception which but lately preceded it.

THE PHRENOLOGICAL CONCEPTION

In a certain sense Gall was the first to seek to explain in detail how the brain could subserve our mental operations. His way of proceeding was only too simple. He took the faculty-psychology as his ultimatum on the mental side, and he made no farther psychological analysis. Wherever he found an individual with some strongly-marked trait of character he examined his head; and if he found the latter prominent in a certain region, he said without more ado that that region was the 'organ' of the trait or faculty in question. The traits were of very diverse constitution, some being simple sensibilities like 'weight' or 'color'; some being instinctive tendencies like 'alimentiveness' or 'amativeness'; and others, again, being complex resultants like 'conscientiousness,' 'individuality.' Phrenology fell promptly into disrepute among scientific men because observation seemed to show that large faculties and large 'bumps' might fail to coexist; because the scheme of Gall was so vast as hardly to admit of accurate determination at all—who of us can say even of his own brothers whether their perceptions of *weight* and of *time* are well developed or not?—because the followers of Gall and Spurzheim were unable to reform these errors in any appreciable degree; and, finally, because the whole analysis of faculties was vague and erroneous from a psychologic point of view. Popular professors of the lore have nevertheless continued to command the admiration of popular audiences; and there seems no doubt that Phrenology, however little it satisfy our scientific curiosity about the functions of different portions of the brain, may still be, in the hands of intelligent practitioners, a useful help in the art of reading character. A hooked nose and a firm jaw are usually signs of practical energy; soft, delicate hands are signs of refined sensibility. Even so may a prominent eye be a sign of power over language, and a bull-neck a sign of sensuality. But the brain behind the eye and neck need no more be the *organ* of the signified faculty than the jaw is the organ of the will or the hand the organ of refinement. These correlations between mind and body are, however, so frequent that the 'characters' given by phrenologists are often remarkable for knowingness and insight.

Phrenology hardly does more than restate the problem. To answer the question, "Why do I like children?" by saying, "Because you have a large organ of philoprogenitiveness," but renames the phenomenon to be explained. What *is* my philoprogenitiveness? Of what mental elements does it consist? And how *can* a part of the brain be its organ? A science of the mind must reduce such complex manifestations as 'philoprogenitiveness' to their *elements.* A science of the brain must point out the functions of *its* elements. A science of the relations of mind and brain must show how the elementary ingredients of the former correspond to the elementary functions of the latter. But phrenology, except by occasional coincidence, takes no account of elements at all. Its 'faculties,' as a rule, are fully equipped persons in a particular mental attitude. Take, for example, the 'faculty' of language. It involves in reality a host of distinct powers. We must first have images of concrete things and ideas of abstract qualities and relations; we must next have the memory of words and then the capacity so to associate each idea or image with a particular word that, when the word is heard, the idea shall forthwith enter our mind. We must conversely, as soon as the idea arises in our mind, associate with it a mental image of the word, and by means of this image we must innervate our articulatory apparatus so as to reproduce the word as physical sound. To read or to write a language other elements still must be introduced. But it is plain that the faculty of spoken language alone is so complicated as to call into play almost all the elementary powers which the mind possesses, memory, imagination, association, judgment, and volition. A portion of the brain competent to be the adequate seat of such a faculty would needs be an entire brain in miniature,—just as the faculty itself is really a specification of the entire man, a sort of homunculus.

Yet just such homunculi are for the most part the phrenological organs. As Lange says:

"We have a parliament of little men together, each one of whom, as happens also in a real parliament, possesses but a single idea which he ceaselessly strives to make prevail"—benevolence, firmness, hope, and the rest. "Instead of one soul, phrenology gives us forty, each alone as enigmatic as the full aggregate psychic life can be. Instead of dividing the latter into effective elements, she divides it into personal beings of peculiar character. . . . 'Herr Pastor, sure there be a horse inside,' called out the peasants to X after their spiritual shepherd had spent hours in explaining to them the construction of the locomotive. With a horse inside truly everything becomes clear, even though it be a queer enough sort of horse—the horse itself calls for no explanation! Phrenology takes a start to get beyond the point of view of the ghost-like soul entity, but she ends by populating the whole skull with ghosts of the same order."[5]

Modern Science conceives of the matter in a very different way. *Brain and mind alike consist of simple elements, sensory and motor.* "All nervous centres," says Dr. J. Hughlings Jackson,[6] "from the lowest to the very highest (the substrata of consciousness), are made up of nothing else than nervous arrangements representing impressions and movements. . . . I do not see of what other 'materials' the rest of the brain *can* be made." Meynert represents the matter similarly when he calls the cortex of the hemispheres the surface of projection for every muscle and every sensitive point of the body. The muscles and the sensitive points are *represented* each by a cortical point, and the brain is nothing but the sum of all these cortical points, to which, on the mental side, as many *ideas* correspond. *Ideas of sensation, ideas of motion* are, on the other hand, *the elementary factors out of which the mind is built up by the associationists in psychology.* There is a complete parallelism between the two analyses, the same diagram of little dots, circles, or triangles joined by lines symbolizes equally well the cerebral and mental processes: the dots stand for cells or ideas, the lines for fibres or associations. We shall have later to criticise this analysis so far as it relates to the mind; but there is no doubt that it is a most convenient, and has been a most useful, hypothesis, formulating the facts in an extremely natural way.

If, then, we grant that motor and sensory ideas variously associated are the materials of the mind, all we need do to get a complete diagram of the mind's and the brain's relations should be to ascertain which sensory idea corresponds to which sensational surface

[5] *Geschichte des Materialismus*, 2d ed., II, p. 344.
[6] *West Riding Asylum Reports*, 1876, p. 267.

of projection, and which motor idea to which muscular surface of projection. The associations would then correspond to the fibrous connections between the various surfaces. This distinct *cerebral localization* of the various elementary sorts of idea has been treated as a 'postulate' by many physiologists (e.g., Munk); and the most stirring controversy in nerve-physiology which the present generation has seen has been the *localization-question.*

THE LOCALIZATION OF FUNCTIONS IN THE HEMISPHERES

Up to 1870, the opinion which prevailed was that which the experiments of Flourens on pigeons' brains had made plausible, namely, that the different functions of the hemispheres were not locally separated, but carried on each by the aid of the whole organ. Hitzig in 1870 showed, however, that in a dog's brain highly specialized movements could be produced by electric irritation of determinate regions of the cortex; and Ferrier and Munk, half a dozen years later, seemed to prove, either by irritations or excisions or both, that there were equally determinate regions connected with the senses of sight, touch, hearing, and smell. Munk's special sensorial localizations, however, disagreed with Ferrier's; and Goltz, from his extirpation-experiments, came to a conclusion adverse to strict localization of any kind. The controversy is not yet over. I will not pretend to say anything more of it historically, but give a brief account of the condition in which matters at present stand.

The one thing which is *perfectly* well established is this, that the 'central' convolutions, on either side of the fissure of Rolando, and (at least in the monkey) the calloso-marginal convolution (which is continuous with them on the mesial surface where one hemisphere is applied against the other), form the region by which all the motor incitations which leave the cortex pass out, on their way to those executive centres in the region of the pons, medulla, and spinal cord from which the muscular contractions are discharged in the last resort. The existence of this so-called 'motor zone' is established by the lines of evidence successively given below:

(1) *Cortical Irritations.* Electrical currents of small intensity applied to the surface of the said convolutions in dogs, monkeys, and other animals, produce well-defined movements in face, fore-limb, hind-limb, tail, or trunk, according as one point or another of the

surface is irritated. These movements affect almost invariably the side opposite to the brain irritations: If the left hemisphere be excited, the movement is of the right leg, side of face, etc. All the objections at first raised against the validity of these experiments have been overcome. The movements are certainly not due to irritations of the base of the brain by the downward spread of the current, for: *a*) mechanical irritations will produce them, though less easily than electrical; *b*) shifting the electrodes to a point close by on the surface changes the movement in ways quite inexplicable by changed physical conduction of the current; *c*) if the cortical 'centre' for a certain movement be cut under with a sharp knife but left *in situ*, although the electric conductivity is physically unaltered by the operation, the physiological conductivity is gone and currents of the same strength no longer produce the movements which they did; *d*) the time-interval between the application of the electric stimulus to the cortex and the resultant movement is what it would be if the cortex acted physiologically and not merely physically in transmitting the irritation. It is namely a well-known fact that when a nerve-current has to pass through the spinal cord to excite a muscle by reflex action, the time is longer than if it passes directly down the motor nerve: the cells of the cord take a certain time to discharge. Similarly, when a stimulus is applied directly to the cortex the muscle contracts two or three hundredths of a second later than it does when the place on the cortex is cut away and the electrodes are applied to the white fibres below.[7]

(2) *Cortical Ablations.* When the cortical spot which is found to produce a movement of the fore-leg, in a dog, is excised (see spot 5 in Fig. 5), the leg in question becomes peculiarly affected. At first it seems paralyzed. Soon, however, it is used with the other legs, but badly. The animal does not bear his weight on it, allows it to rest on its dorsal surface, stands with it crossing the other leg, does not remove it if it hangs over the edge of a table, can no longer

[7] For a thorough discussion of the various objections, see Ferrier's *Functions of the Brain*, 2d ed., pp. 227–234, and François-Franck's *Leçons sur les fonctions motrices du cerveau* (1887), Leçon 31. The most minutely accurate experiments on irritation of cortical points are those of Paneth, in Pflüger's *Archiv für Physiologie*, vol. 37, pp. 523–61.—Recently the skull has been fearlessly opened by surgeons, and operations upon the human brain performed, sometimes with the happiest results. In some of these operations the cortex has been electrically excited for the purpose of more exactly localizing the spot, and the movements first observed in dogs and monkeys have then been verified in men.

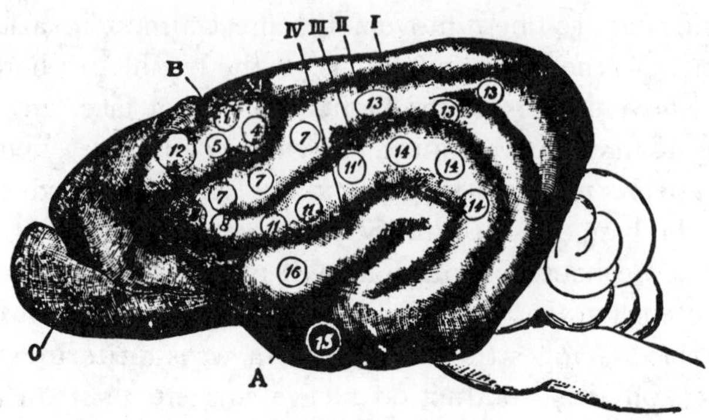

Fig. 5.—Left Hemisphere of Dog's Brain, after Ferrier. *A*, the fissure of Sylvius. *B*, the crucial sulcus. *O*, the olfactory bulb. *I*, *II*, *III*, *IV*, indicate the first, second, third, and fourth external convolutions respectively. (1), (4), and (5) are on the *sigmoid* gyrus.

'give the paw' at word of command if able to do so before the operation, does not use it for scratching the ground, or holding a bone as formerly, lets it slip out when running on a smooth surface or when shaking himself, etc., etc. Sensibility of all kinds seems diminished as well as motility, but of this I shall speak later on. Moreover the dog tends in voluntary movements to swerve towards the side of the brain-lesion instead of going straight forward. All these symptoms gradually decrease, so that even with a very severe brain-lesion the dog may be outwardly indistinguishable from a well dog after eight or ten weeks. Still, a slight chloroformization will reproduce the disturbances, even then. There is a certain appearance of ataxic in-coördination in the movements—the dog lifts his fore-feet high and brings them down with more strength than usual, and yet the trouble is not ordinary lack of co-ordination. Neither is there paralysis. The strength of whatever movements are made is as great as ever—dogs with extensive destruction of the motor zone can jump as high and bite as hard as ever they did, but they seem *less easily moved* to do *anything* with the affected parts. Dr. Loeb, who has studied the motor disturbances of dogs more carefully than anyone, conceives of them *en masse* as effects of an increased inertia in all the processes of innervation towards the side opposed to the lesion. All such movements require an unwonted effort for their execution; and when only the normally usual effort is made they fall behind in effectiveness.[8]

[8] J. Loeb: "Beiträge zur Physiologie des Grosshirns," Pflüger's *Archiv*, xxxix, 293. I simplify the author's statement.

Even when the entire motor zone of a dog is removed, there is no permanent paralysis of any part, but only this curious sort of relative inertia when the two sides of the body are compared; and this itself becomes hardly noticeable after a number of weeks have elapsed. Prof. Goltz has described a dog whose entire left hemisphere was destroyed, and who retained only a slight motor inertia on the right half of the body. In particular he could use his right paw for holding a bone whilst gnawing it, or for reaching after a piece of meat. Had he been taught to give his paw before the operations, it would have been curious to see whether that faculty also came back. His tactile sensibility was permanently diminished on the right side.[9] In *monkeys* a genuine paralysis follows upon ablations of the cortex in the motor region. This paralysis affects parts of the body which vary with the brain-parts removed. The monkey's opposite arm or leg hangs flaccid, or at most takes a small part in associated movements. When the entire region is removed

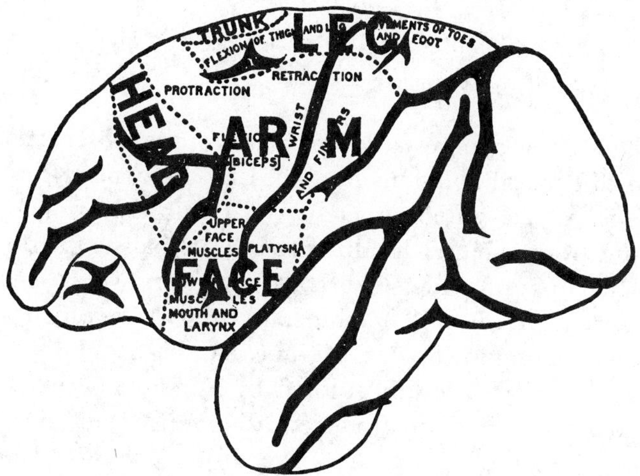

Fig. 6.—Left Hemisphere of Monkey's Brain. Outer Surface.

there is a genuine and permanent hemiplegia in which the arm is more affected than the leg; and this is followed months later by contracture of the muscles, as in man after inveterate hemiplegia.[10] According to Schäfer and Horsley, the trunk-muscles also become paralyzed after destruction of the *marginal* convolution on *both*

9 Goltz: Pflüger's *Archiv*, XLII, 419.
10 'Hemiplegia' means one-sided palsy.

sides (see Fig. 7). These differences between dogs and monkeys show the danger of drawing general conclusions from experiments done on any one sort of animal. I subjoin the figures given by the last-named authors of the motor regions in the monkey's brain.[11]

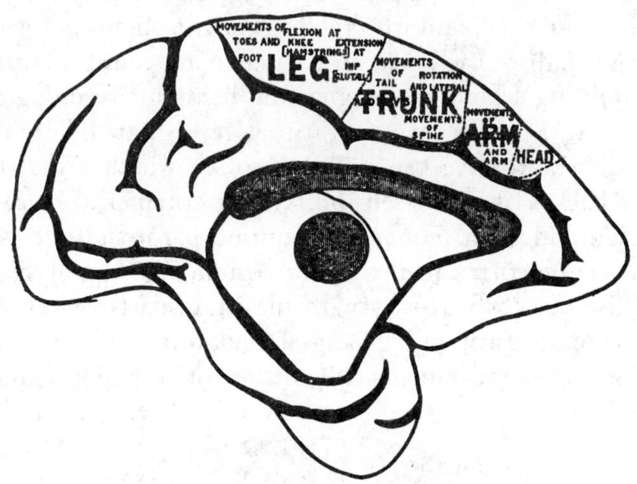

FIG. 7.—Left Hemisphere of Monkey's Brain. Mesial Surface.

In man we are necessarily reduced to the observation *post-mortem* of cortical ablations produced by accident or disease (tumor, hemorrhage, softening, etc.). What results during life from such conditions is either localized spasm, or palsy of certain muscles of the opposite side. The cortical regions which invariably produce these results are homologous with those which we have just been studying in the dog, cat, ape, etc. Figs. 8 and 9 show the result of 167 cases carefully studied by Exner. The parts shaded are regions where lesions produced *no* motor disturbance. Those left white were, on the contrary, never injured without motor disturbances of some sort. Where the injury to the cortical substance is profound in man, the paralysis is permanent and is succeeded by muscular rigidity in the paralyzed parts, just as it may be in the monkey.

(3) *Descending degenerations* show the intimate connection of the rolandic regions of the cortex with the motor tracts of the cord.

11 *Philosophical Transactions of the Royal Society* (B), vol. 179, pp. 6, 10 (1888). In a later paper (*ibid.*, p. 205) Messrs. Beevor and Horsley go into the localization still more minutely, showing spots from which single muscles or single digits can be made to contract.

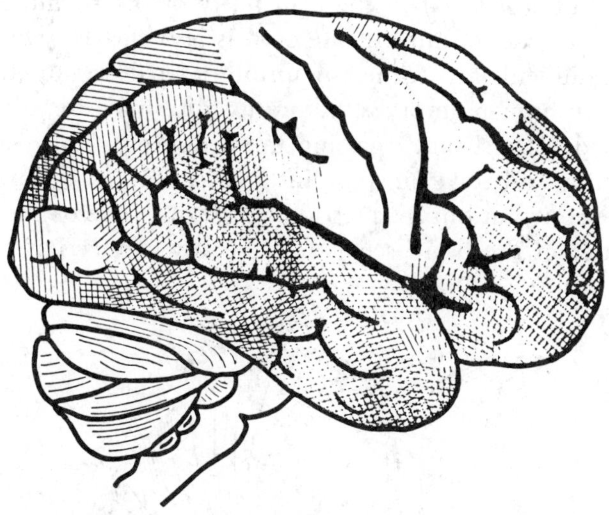

Fig. 8.—Right Hemisphere of Human Brain. Lateral Surface.

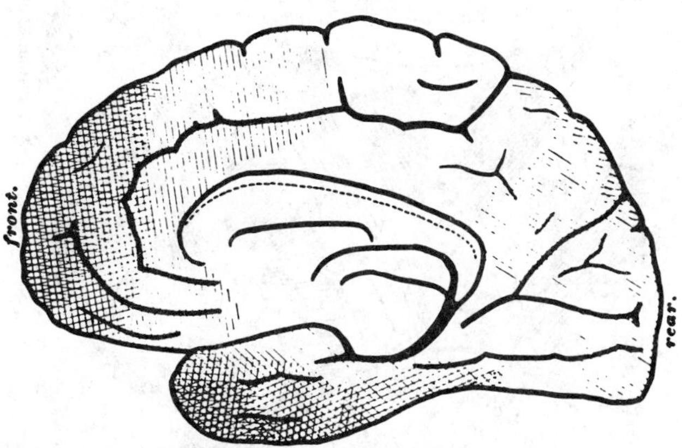

Fig. 9.—Right Hemisphere of Human Brain. Mesial Surface.

When, either in man or in the lower animals, these regions are destroyed, a peculiar degenerative change known as secondary sclerosis is found to extend downwards through the white fibrous substance of the brain in a perfectly definite manner, affecting certain distinct strands which pass through the inner capsule, crura, and pons, into the anterior pyramids of the medulla oblongata, and from thence (partly crossing to the other side) downwards into the anterior (direct) and lateral (crossed) columns of the spinal cord.

(4) *Anatomical proof* of the continuity of the rolandic regions with these motor columns of the cord is also clearly given. Flechsig's 'Pyramidenbahn' forms an uninterrupted strand (distinctly traceable in human embryos, before its fibres have acquired their white 'medullary sheath') passing upwards from the pyramids of the medulla, and traversing the internal capsule and corona radiata to the convolutions in question (Fig. 10). None of the inferior gray matter of the brain seems to have any connection with this

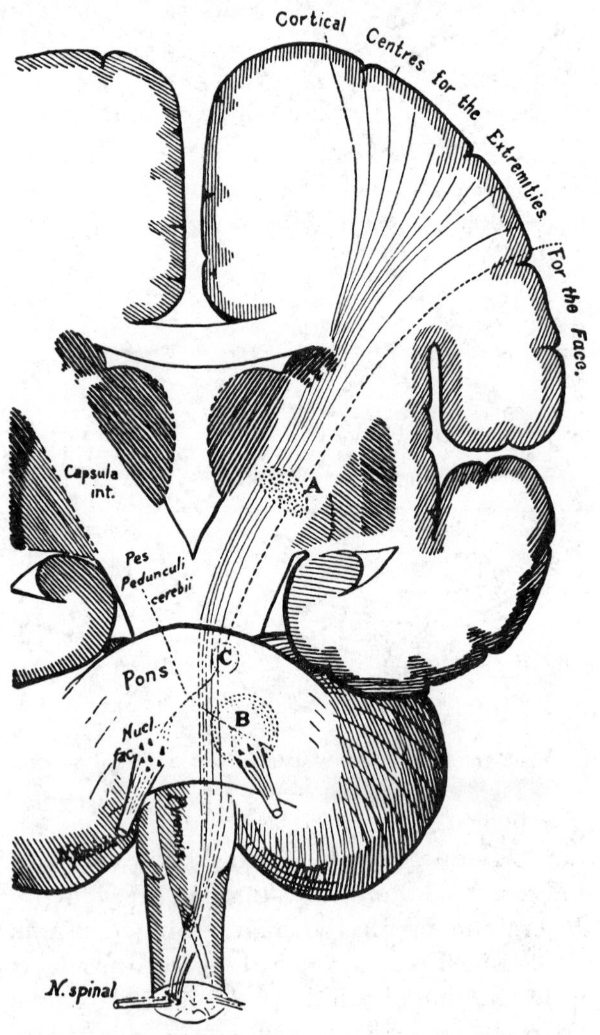

FIG. 10.—Schematic Transverse Section of Brain showing Motor Strand.—After Edinger.

important fibrous strand. It passes directly from the cortex to the motor arrangements in the cord, depending for its proper nutrition (as the facts of degeneration show) on the influence of the cortical cells, just as motor nerves depend for their nutrition on that of the cells of the spinal cord. Electrical stimulation of this motor strand in any accessible part of its course has been shown in dogs to produce movements analogous to those which excitement of the cortical surface calls forth.

One of the most instructive proofs of motor localization in the cortex is that furnished by the disease now called aphemia, or *motor Aphasia.* Motor aphasia is neither loss of voice nor paralysis of the tongue or lips. The patient's voice is as strong as ever, and all the innervations of his hypoglossal and facial nerves, except those necessary for speaking, may go on perfectly well. He can laugh and cry, and even sing; but he either is unable to utter any words at all; or a few meaningless stock phrases form his only speech; or else he speaks incoherently and confusedly, mispronouncing, misplacing, and misusing his words in various degrees. Sometimes his speech is a mere broth of unintelligible syllables. In cases of pure motor aphasia the patient recognizes his mistakes and suffers acutely from them. Now whenever a patient dies in such a condition as this, and an examination of his brain is permitted, it is found that the lowest frontal gyrus (see Fig. 11) is the seat of

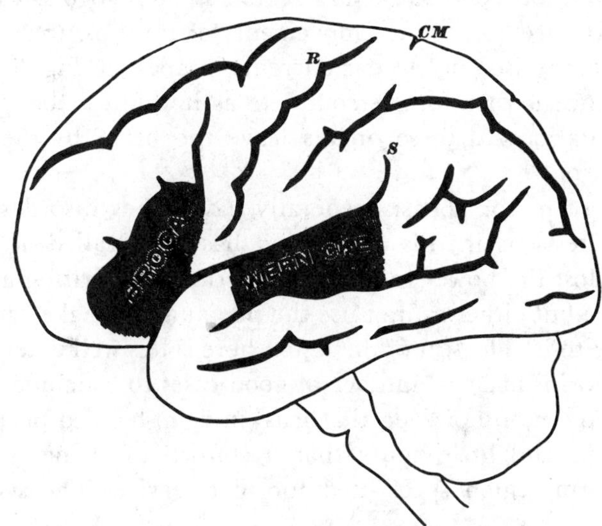

FIG. 11.—Schematic Profile of Left Hemisphere, with the parts shaded whose destruction causes motor ('Broca') and sensory ('Wernicke') Aphasia.

injury. Broca first noticed this fact in 1861, and since then the gyrus has gone by the name of Broca's convolution. The injury in right-handed people is found on the left hemisphere, and in left-handed people on the right hemisphere. Most people, in fact, are left-brained, that is, all their delicate and specialized movements are handed over to the charge of the left hemisphere. The ordinary right-handedness for such movements is only a consequence of that fact, a consequence which shows outwardly on account of that extensive decussation of the fibres whereby most of those from the left hemisphere pass to the right half of the body only. But the left-brainedness might exist in equal measure and not show outwardly. This would happen wherever organs on *both* sides of the body could be governed by the left hemisphere; and just such a case seems offered by the vocal organs, in that highly delicate and special motor service which we call speech. Either hemisphere *can* innervate them bilaterally, just as either seems able to innervate bilaterally the muscles of the trunk, ribs, and diaphragm. Of the special movements of speech, however, it would appear (from the facts of aphasia) that the left hemisphere in most persons habitually takes exclusive charge. With that hemisphere thrown out of gear, speech is undone; even though the opposite hemisphere still be there for the performance of less specialized acts, such as the various movements required in eating.

It will be noticed that Broca's region is homologous with the parts ascertained to produce movements of the lips, tongue, and larynx when excited by electric currents in apes (cf. Fig. 6, p. 45). The evidence is therefore as complete as it well can be that the motor incitations to these organs leave the brain by the lower frontal region.

Victims of motor aphasia generally have other disorders. One which interests us in this connection has been called *agraphia*: they have lost the power to *write*. They can read writing and understand it; but either cannot use the pen at all or make egregious mistakes with it. The seat of the lesion here is less well determined, owing to an insufficient number of good cases to conclude from.[12] There is no doubt, however, that it is (in right-handed people) on the left side, and little doubt that it consists of elements of the hand-and-arm region specialized for that service. The symptom

[12] Nothnagel und Naunyn: *Über die Localisation der Gehirnkrankheiten* (Wiesbaden, 1887), p. 34.

may exist when there is little or no disability in the hand for other uses. If it does not get well, the patient usually educates his right hemisphere, i.e., learns to write with his left hand. In other cases of which we shall say more a few pages later on, the patient can write both spontaneously and at dictation, but cannot *read* even what he has himself written! All these phenomena are now quite clearly explained by separate brain-centres for the various feelings and movements and tracts for associating these together. But their minute discussion belongs to medicine rather than to general psychology, and I can only use them here to illustrate the principles of motor localization.[13] Under the heads of sight and hearing I shall have a little more to say.

The different lines of proof which I have taken up establish conclusively the proposition that *all the motor impulses which leave the cortex pass out,* in healthy animals, *from the convolutions about the fissure of Rolando.*

When, however, it comes to defining precisely what is involved in a motor impulse leaving the cortex, things grow more obscure. Does the impulse start independently from the convolutions in question, or does it start elsewhere and merely flow through? And to what particular phase of psychic activity does the activity of these centres correspond? Opinions and authorities here divide; but it will be better, before entering into these deeper aspects of the problem, to cast a glance at the facts which have been made out concerning the relations of the cortex to sight, hearing, and smell.

Sight

Ferrier was the first in the field here. He found, when the *angular* convolution (that lying between the 'intra parietal' and 'external occipital' fissures, and bending round the top of the fissure of Sylvius, in Fig. 6) was excited in the monkey, that movements of the eyes and head as if for vision occurred; and that when it was extirpated, what he supposed to be total and permanent blindness of the opposite eye followed. Munk almost immediately declared total and permanent blindness to follow from destruction of the *occipital lobe* in monkeys as well as dogs, and said that the angular gyrus had nothing to do with sight, but was only the cen-

[13] An accessible account of the history of our knowledge of motor aphasia is in W. A. Hammond's *Treatise on the Diseases of the Nervous System,* chapter VII.

tre for tactile sensibility of the eyeball. Munk's absolute tone about his observations and his theoretic arrogance have led to his ruin as an authority. But he did two things of permanent value. He was the first to distinguish in these vivisections between sensorial and *psychic* blindness, and to describe the phenomenon of *restitution* of the visual function after its first impairment by an operation; and the first to notice the *hemiopic* character of the visual disturbances which result when only one hemisphere is injured. Sensorial blindness is absolute insensibility to light; psychic blindness is inability to recognize the *meaning* of the optical impressions, as when we see a page of Chinese print but it suggests nothing to us. A hemiopic disturbance of vision is one in which neither retina is affected in its totality, but in which, for example, the left portion of *each* retina is blind, so that the animal sees nothing situated in space towards its right. Later observations have corroborated this hemiopic character of all the disturbances of sight from injury to a single hemisphere in the higher animals; and the question whether an animal's apparent blindness is sensorial or only psychic has, since Munk's first publications, been the most urgent one to answer, in all observations relative to the function of sight.

Goltz almost simultaneously with Ferrier and Munk reported experiments which led him to deny that the visual function was essentially bound up with any one localized portion of the hemispheres. Other divergent results soon came in from many quarters, so that, without going into the history of the matter any more, I may report the existing state of the case as follows:[14]

In *fishes, frogs,* and *lizards* vision persists when the hemispheres are entirely removed. This is admitted for frogs and fishes even by Munk, who denies it for birds.

All of Munk's *birds* seemed totally blind (blind sensorially) after removal of the hemispheres by his operation. The following of a candle by the head and winking at a threatened blow, which are ordinarily held to prove the retention of crude optical sensations by the lower centres in supposed hemisphereless pigeons, are by Munk ascribed to vestiges of the visual sphere of the cortex left behind by the imperfection of the operation. But Schrader, who operated after Munk and with every apparent guarantee of completeness, found that all his pigeons saw after two or three weeks

[14] The history up to 1885 may be found in A. Christiani: *Zur Physiologie des Gehirnes* (Berlin, 1885).

had elapsed, and the inhibitions resulting from the wound had passed away. They invariably avoided even the slightest obstacles, flew very regularly towards certain perches, etc., differing *toto cœlo* in these respects with certain simply *blinded* pigeons who were kept with them for comparison. They did not pick up food strewn on the ground, however. Schrader found that they would do this if even a small part of the frontal region of the hemispheres was left, and ascribes their non-self-feeding when deprived of their occipital cerebrum not to a visual, but to a motor, defect, a sort of alimentary aphasia.[15]

In presence of such discord as that between Munk and his opponents one must carefully note how differently significant is *loss*, from *preservation*, of a function after an operation on the brain. The *loss* of the function does not necessarily show that it *is* dependent on the part cut out; but its *preservation* does show that it is *not* dependent: and this is true though the loss should be observed ninety-nine times and the preservation only once in a hundred similar excisions. That birds and mammals *can* be blinded by cortical ablation is undoubted; the only question is, *must* they be so? Only then can the cortex be certainly called the 'seat of sight.' The blindness may always be due to one of those remote effects of the wound on distant parts, inhibitions, extensions of inflammation,—interferences, in a word,—upon which Brown-Séquard and Goltz have rightly insisted, and the importance of which becomes more manifest every day. Such effects are transient; whereas the *symptoms of deprivation* (*Ausfallserscheinungen*, as Goltz calls them) which come from the actual loss of the cut-out region must from the nature of the case be permanent. Blindness in the pigeons, *so far as it passes away*, cannot possibly be charged to their seat of vision being lost, but only to some influence which temporarily depresses the activity of that seat. The same is true *mutatis mutandis* of all the other effects of operations, and as we pass to mammals we shall see still more the importance of the remark.

In rabbits loss of the entire cortex seems compatible with the preservation of enough sight to guide the poor animals' movements, and enable them to avoid obstacles. Christiani's observations and discussions seem conclusively to have established this, al-

[15] Pflüger's *Archiv*, vol. 44, pp. 175–238. Munk (Berlin Academy *Sitzungsberichte*, 1889, XXXI) returns to the charge, denying the extirpations of Schrader to be complete: "Microscopic portions of the *Sehsphäre* must remain."

though Munk found that all *his* animals were made totally blind.[16]

In dogs also Munk found absolute stone-blindness after ablation of the occipital lobes. He went farther and mapped out determinate portions of the cortex thereupon, which he considered correlated with definite segments of the two retinæ, so that destruction of given portions of the cortex produces blindness of the retinal centre, top, bottom, or right or left side, of the same or opposite eye. There seems little doubt that this definite correlation is mythological. Other observers, Hitzig, Goltz, Luciani, Loeb, Exner, etc., find, whatever part of the cortex may be ablated on one side, that there usually results a *hemiopic* disturbance of *both* eyes, slight and transient when the anterior lobes are the parts attacked, grave when an occipital lobe is the seat of injury, and lasting in proportion to the latter's extent. According to Loeb, the defect is a dimness of vision ('hemiamblyopia') in which (however severe) the centres remain the best seeing portions of the retina, just as they are in normal dogs. The lateral or temporal part of each retina seems to be in exclusive connection with the cortex of its own side. The centre and nasal part of each seems, on the contrary, to be connected with the cortex of the opposite hemispheres. Loeb, who takes broader views than anyone, conceives the hemiamblyopia as he conceives the motor disturbances, namely, as the expression of an increased inertia in the whole optical machinery, of which the result is to make the animal respond with greater effort to impressions coming from the half of space opposed to the side of the lesion. If a dog has right hemiamblyopia, say, and two pieces of meat are hung before him at once, he invariably turns first to the one on his left. But if the lesion be a slight one, *shaking* slightly the piece of meat on his right (this makes of it a stronger stimulus) makes him seize upon it first. If only one piece of meat be offered, he takes it, on whichever side it be.

When both occipital lobes are extensively destroyed total blindness may result. Munk maps out his 'Sehsphäre' definitely, and says that blindness *must* result when the entire shaded part, marked *A*, *A*, in Figs. 12 and 13, is involved in the lesion. Discrepant reports of other observations he explains as due to incomplete ablation. Luciani, Goltz, and Lannegrace, however, contend that they have made complete bilateral extirpations of Munk's Sehsphäre more

[16] A. Christiani: *Zur Physiologie des Gehirnes* (Berlin, 1885), chaps. II, III, IV. H. Munk: Berlin Academy *Sitzungsberichte*, 1884, XXIV.

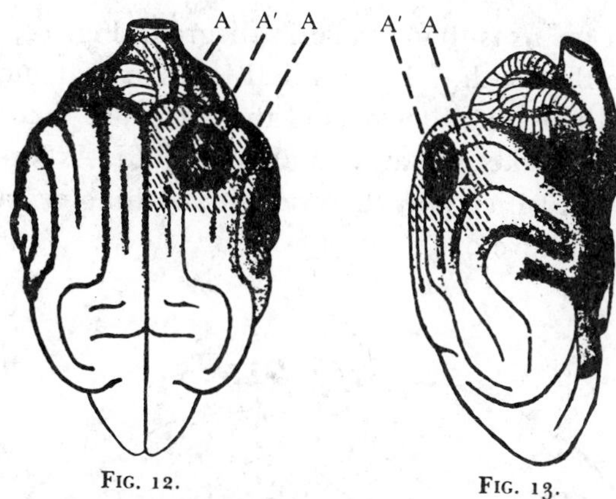

FIG. 12. FIG. 13.

The Dog's visual centre according to Munk, the entire striated region, *A*, *A*, being the exclusive seat of vision, and the dark central circle, *A'*, being correlated with the retinal centre of the opposite eye.

than once, and found a sort of crude indiscriminating sight of objects to return in a few weeks.[17] The question whether a dog is blind or not is harder to solve than would at first appear; for simply blinded dogs, in places to which they are accustomed, show little of their loss and avoid all obstacles; whilst dogs whose occipital lobes are gone may run against things frequently and yet see notwithstanding. The best proof that they may see is that which Goltz's dogs furnished: they carefully avoided, as it seemed, strips of sunshine or paper on the floor, as if they were solid obstacles. This no really blind dog would do. Luciani tested his dogs when hungry (a condition which sharpens their attention) by strewing pieces of meat and pieces of cork before them. If they went straight at them, they *saw*; and if they chose the meat and left the cork, they *saw discriminatingly*. The quarrel is very acrimonious; indeed the subject of localization of functions in the brain seems to have a peculiar effect on the temper of those who cultivate it experimentally. The amount of preserved vision which Goltz and Luciani report seems hardly to be worth considering, on the one hand; and on the other, Munk admits in his penultimate paper that out of 85 dogs he only 'succeeded' 4 times in his operation of producing complete blindness by complete extirpation of his 'Sehsphäre.'[18] The

[17] Luciani und Seppilli: *Die Functions-Localisation auf der Grosshirnrinde* (Deutsch von Fraenkel), Leipzig, 1886, Dogs M, N, and S. Goltz in Pflüger's *Archiv*, vol. 34, pp. 490–6; vol. 42, p. 454. Cf. also Munk: Berlin Academy *Sitzungsberichte*, 1886, VII (pp. 113–121), VIII (pp. 179–188), and Loeb: Pflüger's *Archiv*, vol. 39, p. 337.

[18] Berlin Academy *Sitzungsberichte*, 1886, VII, p. 124.

safe conclusion for *us* is that Luciani's diagram, Fig. 14, represents something like the truth. The occipital lobes are far more important for vision than any other part of the cortex, so that their complete destruction makes the animal almost blind. As for the crude sensibility to light which *may* then remain, nothing exact is known either about its nature or its seat.

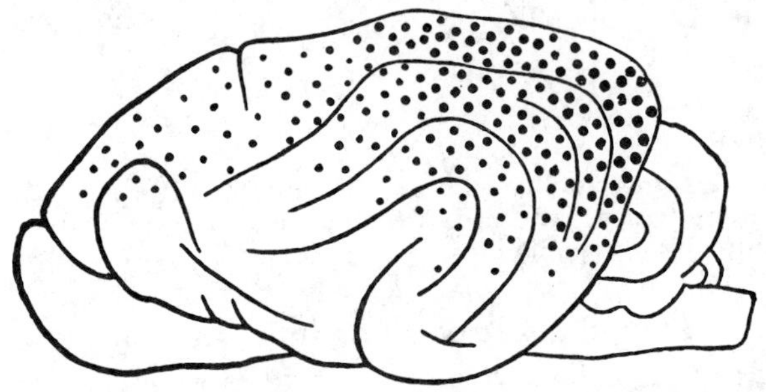

FIG. 14.—Distribution of the Visual Function in the Cortex, according to Luciani.

In the monkey, doctors also disagree. The truth seems, however, to be that the *occipital lobes* in this animal also are the part connected most intimately with the visual function. The function would seem to go on when very small portions of them are left, for Ferrier found no 'appreciable impairment' of it after almost complete destruction of them on both sides. On the other hand, he found complete and permanent blindness to ensue when they and the *angular gyri* in addition were destroyed on both sides. Munk, as well as Brown and Schäfer, found no disturbance of sight from destroying the *angular gyri* alone, although Ferrier found blindness to ensue. This blindness was probably due to inhibitions exerted *in distans,* or to cutting of the white optical fibres passing under the angular gyri on their way to the occipital lobes. Brown and Schäfer got complete and permanent blindness in one monkey from total destruction of both occipital lobes. Luciani and Seppilli, performing this operation on two monkeys, found that the animals were only mentally, not sensorially, blind. After some weeks they saw their food, but could not distinguish by sight between figs and pieces of cork. Luciani and Seppilli seem, however, not to have extirpated the entire lobes. When one lobe only is injured the affection of sight is hemiopic in monkeys: in this all observers agree. On the whole, then, Munk's original location of vision in the occipital lobes is confirmed by the later evidence.[19]

In man we have more exact results, since we are not driven to interpret the vision from the outward conduct. On the other hand, however, we cannot vivisect, but must wait for pathological lesions to turn up. The pathologists who have discussed these (the literature is tedious *ad libitum*) conclude that the occipital lobes are the indispensable part for vision in man. Hemiopic disturbance in both eyes comes from lesion of either one of them, and total blindness, sensorial as well as psychic, from destruction of both.

Hemiopia may also result from lesion in other parts, especially the neighboring angular and supra-marginal gyri, and it may accompany extensive injury in the motor region of the cortex. In these cases it seems probable that it is due to an *actio in distans*, probably to the interruption of fibres proceeding from the occipital lobe. There seem to be a few cases on record where there was injury to the occipital lobes without visual defect. Ferrier has collected as many as possible to prove his localization in the angular gyrus.[20] A strict application of logical principles would make one of these cases outweigh one hundred contrary ones. And yet, remembering how imperfect observations may be, and how individual brains may vary, it would certainly be rash for their sake to throw away the enormous amount of positive evidence for the occipital lobes. Individual variability is always a *possible* explanation of an anomalous case. There is no more prominent anatomical fact than that of the 'decussation of the pyramids,' nor any more usual pathological fact than its consequence, that left-handed hemorrhages into the motor region produce right-handed paralyses. And yet the decussation is variable in amount, and seems sometimes to be absent altogether.[21] If, in such a case as this last, the

[19] H. Munk: *Über die Functionen der Grosshirnrinde* (Berlin, 1881), pp. 36–40. Ferrier: *Functions*, etc., 2d ed., chap. IX, pt. I. Brown and Schäfer: *Philosophical Transactions* (B), vol. 179, p. 321. Luciani und Seppilli: *op. cit.*, pp. 131–138. Lannegrace found traces of sight with both occipital lobes destroyed, and in one monkey even when angular gyri and occipital lobes were destroyed altogether. His paper is in the *Archives de Médecine Expérimentale* for January and March, 1889. I only know it from the abstract in the *Neurologisches Centralblatt*, 1889, pp. 108–10, 420–22. The reporter doubts the evidence of vision in the monkey. It appears to have consisted in avoiding obstacles and in emotional disturbance in the presence of men.

[20] *Localisation of Cerebral Disease* (1878), pp. 117–8.

[21] For cases see Flechsig: *Die Leitungsbahnen in Gehirn und Rückenmark* (Leipzig, 1876), pp. 112, 272; Exner's *Untersuchungen über die Localisation der Functionen*

left brain were to become the seat of apoplexy, the left and not the right half of the body would be the one to suffer paralysis.

The *schema* on this page, copied from Dr. Seguin, expresses, on the whole, the probable truth about the regions concerned in vision. Not the entire occipital lobes, but the so-called cunei, and the first convolutions, are the cortical parts most intimately concerned. Nothnagel agrees with Seguin in this limitation of the

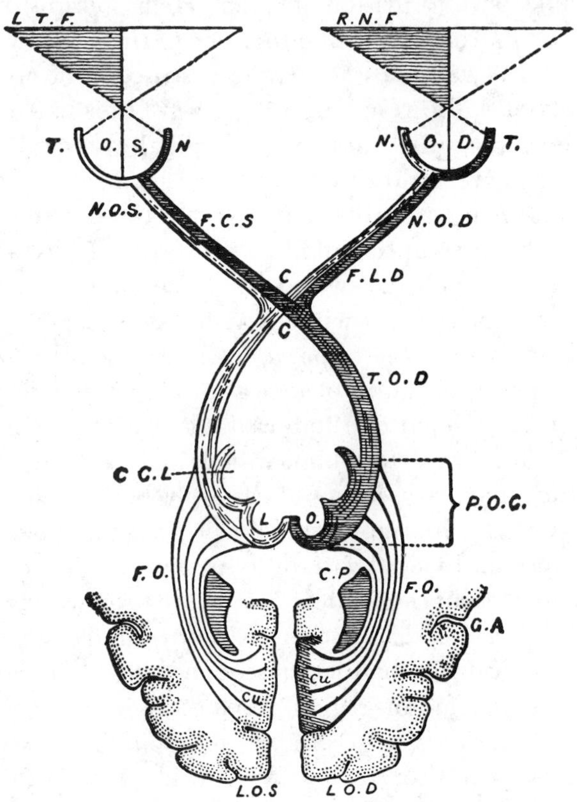

Fig. 15.—Scheme of the mechanism of vision, after Seguin. The *cuneus* convolution (*Cu*) of the right occipital lobe is supposed to be injured, and all the parts which lead to it are darkly shaded to show that they fail to exert their function. *F. O.* are the intra-hemispheric optical fibres. *P. O. C.* is the region of the lower optic centres (corpora geniculata and quadrigemina). *T. O. D.* is the right optic tract; *C*, the chiasma; *F. L. D.* are the fibres going to the lateral or temporal half *T* of the right retina; and *F. C. S.* are those going to the central or nasal half of the left retina. *O. D.* is the right, and *O. S.* the left eyeball. The rightward half of each is therefore blind: in other words, the right nasal field, *R. N. F.*, and the left temporal field, *L. T. F.*, have become invisible to the subject with the lesion at *Cu.*

---

in der Grosshirnrinde des Menschen, pp. 83, 88–125; Ferrier's *Localisation*, etc., p. 11; François-Franck's *Fonctions motrices du cerveau*, p. 63, note.

essential tracts.[22] Henschen (*Brain,* 1893, p. 177) limits it to the cortex of the calcarine fissure. Vitzou: *Archives de Physiologie,* Oct. 1893, finds permanent blindness from loss of both occipital lobes in dogs.

A most interesting effect of cortical disorder is *mental blindness.* This consists not so much in insensibility to optical impressions, as in *inability to understand them.* Psychologically it is interpretable as *loss of associations* between optical sensations and what they signify; and any interruption of the paths between the optic centres and the centres for other ideas ought to bring it about. Thus, printed letters of the alphabet, or words, signify certain sounds and certain articulatory movements. If the connection between the articulating or auditory centres, on the one hand, and the visual centres on the other, be ruptured, we ought *a priori* to expect that the sight of words would fail to awaken the idea of their sound, or of the movement for pronouncing them. We ought, in short, to have *alexia,* or inability to read: and this is just what we do have in many cases of extensive injury about the fronto-temporal regions, as a complication of *aphasic* disease. Nothnagel suggests that whilst the *cuneus* is the seat of optical *sensations,* the other parts of the occipital lobe may be the field of optical *memories and ideas,* from the loss of which mental blindness should ensue. In fact, all the medical authors speak of mental blindness as if it must consist in the loss of visual images from the memory. It seems to me, however, that this is a psychological misapprehension. A man whose power of visual imagination has decayed (no unusual phenomenon in its lighter grades) is not mentally blind in the least, for he recognizes perfectly all that he sees. On the other hand, he *may* be mentally blind, with his optical imagination well preserved; as in the interesting case published by Wilbrand in 1887.[23] In the still more interesting case of mental blindness recently published by Lissauer,[24] though the patient made the most ludicrous mistakes, calling for instance a clothes-brush a pair of spectacles, an umbrella a plant with flowers, an apple a portrait of a lady, etc. etc., he

[22] E. C. Seguin: "Hemianopsia of Central Origin," in *Journal of Nervous and Mental Disease,* vol. XIII, p. 30. Nothnagel und Naunyn: *Über die Localisation der Gehirnkrankheiten* (Wiesbaden, 1887), p. 10.

[23] *Die Seelenblindheit,* etc., p. 51 ff. The mental blindness was in this woman's case moderate in degree.

[24] *Archiv für Psychiatrie,* vol. 21, p. 222.

seemed, according to the reporter, to have his mental images fairly well preserved. It is in fact the momentary loss of our *non*-optical images which makes us mentally blind, just as it is that of our *non*-auditory images which makes us mentally deaf. I am mentally deaf if, *hearing* a bell, I can't recall how it *looks*; and mentally blind if, *seeing* it, I can't recall its *sound or its name*. As a matter of fact, I should have to be not merely mentally blind, but stone-blind, if all my visual images were lost. For although I am blind to the right half of the field of view if my left occipital region is injured, and to the left half if my right region is injured, such hemianopsia does not deprive me of visual *images*, experience seeming to show that the unaffected hemisphere is always sufficient for production of these. To abolish them entirely I should have to be deprived of both occipital lobes, and that would deprive me not only of my inward images of sight, but of my sight altogether.[25] Recent pathological annals seem to offer a few such cases.[26] Meanwhile there are a number of cases of mental blindness, especially for written language, coupled with hemianopsia, usually of the rightward field of view. These are all explicable by the breaking down, through disease, of the *connecting tracts* between the occipital lobes and other parts of the brain, especially those which go to the centres for speech in the frontal and temporal regions of the left hemisphere. They are to be classed among disturbances of *conduction* or of *association*; and nowhere can I find any fact which should force us to believe that optical images need[27] be lost in mental blindness, or that the cerebral centres for such images are locally distinct from those for direct sensations from the eyes.[28]

[25] Nothnagel (*loc. cit.*, p. 22) says: "*Dies trifft aber nicht zu.*" He gives, however, no case in support of his opinion that double-sided cortical lesion may make one stone-blind and yet not destroy one's visual images; so that I do not know whether it is an observation of fact or an *a priori* assumption.

[26] In a case published by C. S. Freund: *Archiv für Psychiatrie*, vol. xx, the occipital lobes were injured, but their cortex was not destroyed, on both sides. There was still vision. Cf. pp. 291–5.

[27] I say 'need,' for I do not of course deny the *possible* coexistence of the two symptoms. Many a brain-lesion might block optical associations and at the same time impair optical imagination, without entirely stopping vision. Such a case seems to have been the remarkable one from Charcot which I shall give rather fully in the chapter on Imagination.

[28] Freund (in the article cited above "Über optische Aphasie und Seelenblindheit") and Bruns ("Ein Fall von Alexie," etc., in the *Neurologisches Centralblatt* for 1888, pp. 481, 509) explain their cases by brokendown conduction. Wilbrand, whose painstaking monograph on mental blindness was referred to a moment ago, gives none

Where an object fails to be recognized by sight, it often happens that the patient will recognize and name it as soon as he touches it with his hand. This shows in an interesting way how numerous the associative paths are which all end by running out of the brain through the channel of speech. The hand-path is open, though the eye-path be closed. When mental blindness is most complete, neither sight, touch, nor sound avails to steer the patient, and a sort of dementia which has been called *asymbolia* or *apraxia* is the result. The commonest articles are not understood. The patient will put his breeches on one shoulder and his hat upon the other, will bite into the soap and lay his shoes on the table, or take his food into his hand and throw it down again, not knowing what to do with it, etc. Such disorder can only come from extensive brain-injury.[29]

The *method of degeneration* corroborates the other evidence localizing the tracts of vision. In young animals one gets secondary degeneration of the occipital regions from destroying an eyeball, and, *vice versa*, degeneration of the optic nerves from destroying the occipital regions. The corpora geniculata, thalami, and subcortical fibres leading to the occipital lobes are also found atrophied in these cases. The phenomena are not uniform, but are indisputable;[30] so that, taking all lines of evidence together, the special connection of vision with the occipital lobes is perfectly made out. It should be added that the occipital lobes have frequently been found shrunken in cases of inveterate blindness in man.

Hearing

Hearing is hardly as definitely localized as sight. *In the dog*, Luciani's diagram will show the regions which directly or indirectly affect it for the worse when injured. As with sight, one-sided

---

but *a priori* reasons for his belief that the optical 'Erinnerungsfeld' must be locally distinct from the Wahrnehmungsfeld (cf. pp. 84, 93). The *a priori* reasons are really the other way. Mauthner (*Gehirn und Auge* (1881), p. 487 ff.) tries to show that the 'mental blindness' of Munk's dogs and apes after occipital mutilation was not such, but real dimness of sight. The best case of mental blindness yet reported is that by Lissauer, as above. The reader will also do well to read Bernard: *De l'aphasie* (1885), chap. v; Ballet: *Le Langage intérieur* (1886), chap. VIII; and James Ross's little book, *On Aphasia* (1887), p. 74. See also Binet in *Revue Philosophique*, XXVI, 481.

29 For a case see Wernicke's *Lehrbuch der Gehirnkrankheiten*, vol. III, p. 554 (1883).

30 The latest account of them is the paper "Über die optischen Centren und Bahnen" by von Monakow in the *Archiv für Psychiatrie*, vol. XX, p. 714.

lesions produce symptoms on both sides. The mixture of black dots and gray dots in the diagram is meant to represent this mixture of 'crossed' and 'uncrossed' connections, though of course no topographical exactitude is aimed at. Of all the region, the temporal lobe is the most important part; yet permanent absolute deafness did not result in a dog of Luciani's, even from bilateral destruction of both temporal lobes in their entirety.[31]

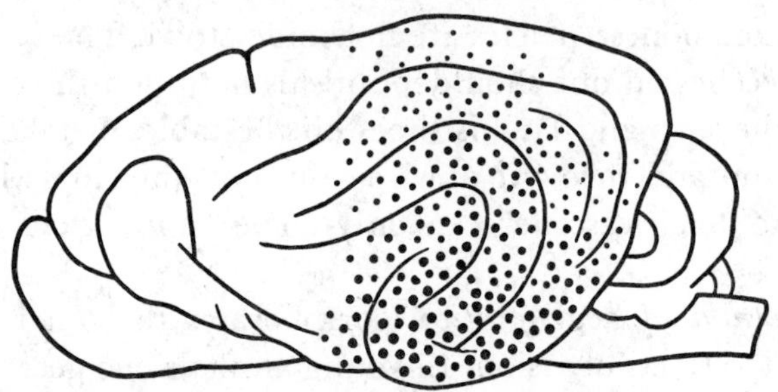

Fig. 16.—Luciani's Hearing Region.

In the monkey, Ferrier and Yeo once found permanent deafness to follow destruction of the upper temporal convolution (the one just below the fissure of Sylvius in Fig. 6) on both sides. Brown and Schäfer found, on the contrary, that in several monkeys this operation failed to noticeably affect the hearing. In one animal, indeed, both entire temporal lobes were destroyed. After a week or two of depression of the mental faculties this beast recovered and became one of the brightest monkeys possible, domineering over all his mates, and admitted by all who saw him to have all his senses, including hearing, 'perfectly acute.'[32] Terrible recriminations have, as usual, ensued between the investigators, Ferrier denying that Brown and Schäfer's ablations were complete,[33] Schäfer that Ferrier's monkey was really deaf.[34] In this unsatisfactory condition the subject must be left, although there seems no reason to doubt that Brown and Schäfer's observation is the more important of the two.

In man the temporal lobe is unquestionably the seat of the hearing function, and the superior convolution adjacent to the sylvian

31 *Die Functions-Localisation*, etc., Dog X; see also p. 161.

32 *Philosophical Transactions* (B), vol. 179, p. 312.

33 *Brain*, vol. XI, p. 10.

34 *Ibid.*, p. 145.

fissure is its most important part. The phenomena of aphasia show this. We studied motor aphasia a few pages back; we must now consider *sensory aphasia.* Our knowledge of this disease has had three stages: we may talk of the period of Broca, the period of Wernicke, and the period of Charcot. What Broca's discovery was we have seen. Wernicke was the first to discriminate those cases in which the patient can *not even understand* speech from those in which he can understand, only not talk; and to ascribe the former condition to lesion of the temporal lobe.[35] The condition in question is *word-deafness,* and the disease is *auditory aphasia.* The latest statistical survey of the subject is that by Dr. M. Allen Starr.[36] In the seven cases of *pure* word-deafness which he has collected (cases in which the patient could read, talk, and write, but not understand what was said to him), the lesion was limited to the first and second temporal convolutions in their posterior two thirds. The lesion (in right-handed, i.e., left-brained, persons) is always on the left side, like the lesion in motor aphasia. Crude hearing would not be abolished, even were the left centre for it utterly destroyed; the right centre would still provide for that. But the *linguistic use* of hearing appears bound up with the integrity of the left centre more or less exclusively. Here it must be that words heard enter into association with the things which they represent, on the one hand, and with the movements necessary for pronouncing them, on the other. In a large majority of Dr. Starr's fifty cases, the power either to name objects or to talk coherently was impaired. This shows that in most of us (as Wernicke said) speech must go on from auditory cues; that is, it must be that our ideas do not innervate our motor centres directly, but only after first arousing the mental sound of the words. This is the immediate stimulus to articulation; and where the possibility of this is abolished by the destruction of its usual channel in the left temporal lobe, the articulation must suffer. In the few cases in which the channel is abolished with no bad effect on speech we must suppose an idiosyncrasy. The patient must innervate his speech-organs either from the corresponding portion of the other hemisphere or directly from the centres of ideation, those, namely, of vision, touch, etc., without leaning on the auditory region. It is the minuter analysis of the facts in the

35 *Der aphasische Symptomencomplex* (1874). See in Fig. 11 the convolution marked WERNICKE.

36 "The Pathology of Sensory Aphasia," *Brain,* July, 1889.

light of such individual differences as these which constitutes Charcot's contribution towards clearing up the subject.

Every namable thing, act, or relation has numerous properties, qualities, or aspects. In our minds the properties of each thing, together with its name, form an associated group. If different parts of the brain are severally concerned with the several properties, and a farther part with the hearing, and still another with the uttering, of the name, there must inevitably be brought about (through the law of association which we shall later study) such a dynamic connection amongst all these brain-parts that the activity of any one of them will be likely to awaken the activity of all the rest. When we are talking as we think, the *ultimate* process is that of utterance. If the brain-part for *that* be injured, speech is impossible or disorderly, even though all the other brain-parts be intact: and this is just the condition of things which, on page 49, we found to be brought about by limited lesion of the left inferior frontal convolution. But back of that last act various orders of succession are possible in the associations of a talking man's ideas. The more usual order seems to be from the tactile, visual, or other properties of the things thought-about to the sound of their names, and then to the latter's utterance. But if in a certain individual the thought of the *look* of an object or of the *look* of its printed name be the process which habitually precedes articulation, then the loss of the *hearing* centre will *pro tanto* not affect that individual's speech. He will be mentally deaf, i.e., his *understanding* of speech will suffer, but he will not be aphasic. In this way it is possible to explain the seven cases of *pure* word-deafness which figure in Dr. Starr's table.

If this order of association be ingrained and habitual in that individual, injury to his *visual* centres will make him not only word-blind, but aphasic as well. His speech will become confused in consequence of an occipital lesion. Naunyn, consequently, plotting out on a diagram of the hemisphere the 71 irreproachably reported cases of aphasia which he was able to collect, finds that the lesions concentrate themselves in three places: first, on Broca's centre; second, on Wernicke's; third, on the supra-marginal and angular gyri under which those fibres pass which connect the visual centres with the rest of the brain[37] (see Fig. 17). With this result Dr. Starr's analysis of purely sensory cases agrees.

[37] Nothnagel und Naunyn: *op. cit.*, plates.

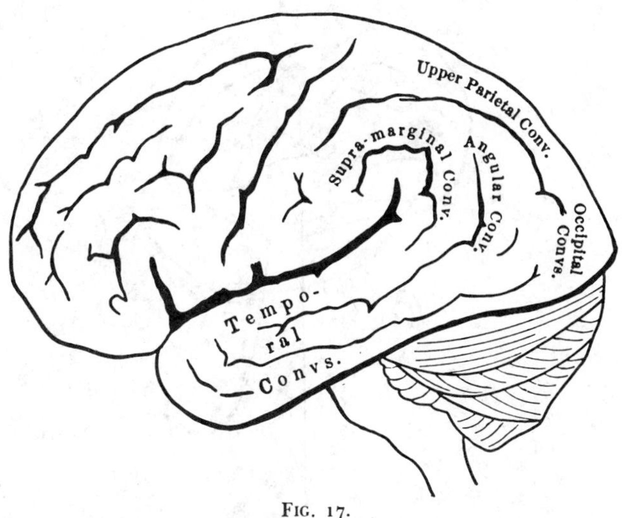

FIG. 17.

In a later chapter we shall again return to these differences in the effectiveness of the sensory spheres in different individuals. Meanwhile few things show more beautifully than the history of our knowledge of aphasia how the sagacity and patience of many banded workers are in time certain to analyze the darkest confusion into an orderly display.[38] There is no 'centre of Speech' in the brain any more than there is a 'faculty' of Speech in the mind. The entire brain, more or less, is at work in a man who uses language. The subjoined diagram, from Ross, shows the four parts most critically concerned, and, in the light of our text, needs no farther explanation (see Fig. 18).

Smell

Everything conspires to point to the median descending part of the temporal lobes as being the organs of smell. Even Ferrier and Munk agree on the hippocampal gyrus, though Ferrier restricts olfaction, as Munk does not, to the lobule or uncinate process of the convolution, reserving the rest of it for touch. Anatomy and pathology also point to the hippocampal gyrus; but as the matter is less interesting from the point of view of human psychology than

[38] Ballet's and Bernard's works cited on p. 61 are the most accessible documents of Charcot's school. Bastian's book on the *Brain as an Organ of Mind* (last three chapters) is also good.

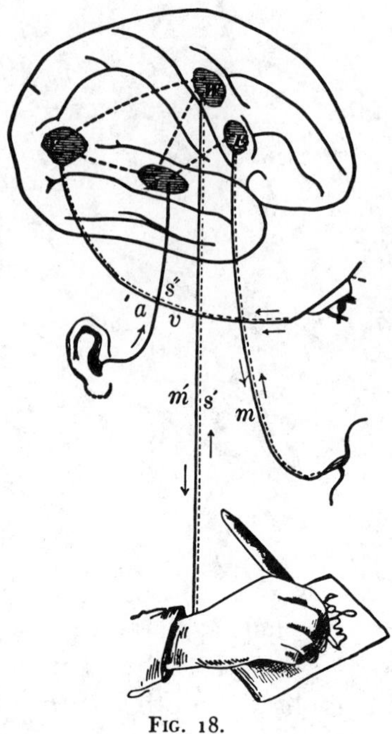

Fig. 18.

were sight and hearing, I will say no more, but simply add Luciani and Seppilli's diagram of the dog's smell-centre.[39] Of

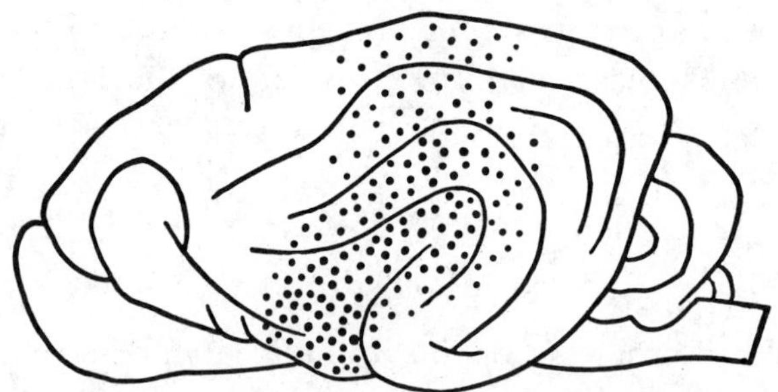

Fig. 19.—Luciani's Olfactory Region in the Dog.

Taste

we know little that is definite. What little there is points to the lower temporal regions again. Consult Ferrier as above.

[39] For details, see Ferrier's *Functions*, chap. ix, pt. iii, and Charles K. Mills: *Transactions of the Congress of American Physicians and Surgeons*, 1889, vol. i, p. 278.

Touch

Interesting problems arise with regard to the seat of tactile and muscular sensibility. Hitzig, whose experiments on *dogs' brains* fifteen years ago opened the entire subject which we are discussing, ascribed the disorders of motility observed after ablations of the motor region to a loss of what he called muscular consciousness. The animals do not notice eccentric positions of their limbs, will stand with their legs crossed, with the affected paw resting on its back or hanging over a table's edge, etc.; and do not resist our bending and stretching of it as they resist with the unaffected paw. Goltz, Munk, Schiff, Herzen, and others promptly ascertained an equal defect of cutaneous sensibility to pain, touch, and cold. The paw is not withdrawn when pinched, remains standing in cold water, etc. Ferrier meanwhile denied that there was any true anæsthesia produced by ablations in the motor zone, and explains the appearance of it as an effect of the sluggish motor responses of the affected side.[40] Munk[41] and Schiff,[42] on the contrary, conceive of the 'motor zone' as essentially sensory, and in different ways explain the motor disorders as secondary results of the anæsthesia which is always there. Munk calls the motor zone the Fühlsphäre of the animal's limbs, etc., and makes it coördinate with the Sehsphäre, the Hörsphäre, etc., the entire cortex being, according to him, nothing but a projection-surface for sensations, with no exclusively or essentially motor part. Such a view would be important if true, through its bearings on the psychology of volition. What is the truth? As regards the fact of cutaneous anæsthesia from motor-zone ablations, all other observers are against Ferrier, so that he is probably wrong in denying it. On the other hand, Munk and Schiff are wrong in making the motor symptoms *depend* on the anæsthesia, for in certain rare cases they have been observed to exist not only without insensibility, but with actual hyperæsthesia of the parts.[43] The motor and sensory symptoms seem, therefore, to be independent variables.

40 *Functions of the Brain*, chap. x, § 14.

41 *Über die Functionen der Grosshirnrinde* (1881), p. 50.

42 *Lezioni di fisiologia sperimentale sul sistema nervoso encefalico* (1873), p. 527 ff. Also *Brain*, vol. IX, p. 289.

43 Bechterew (Pflüger's *Archiv*, vol. 35, p. 137) found *no* anæsthesia in a cat with motor symptoms from ablation of sigmoid gyrus. Luciani got hyperæsthesia coexistent with cortical motor defect in a dog, by simultaneously hemisecting the spinal cord (Luciani und Seppilli: *op. cit.*, p. 234). Goltz frequently found hyperæsthesia of the

In monkeys the latest experiments are those of Horsley and Schäfer,[44] whose results Ferrier accepts. They find that excision of the hippocampal convolution produces transient insensibility of the opposite side of the body, and that permanent insensibility is produced by destruction of its continuation upwards above the corpus callosum, the so-called *gyrus fornicatus* (the part just below the 'calloso-marginal fissure' in Fig. 7). The insensibility is at its maximum when the entire tract comprising both convolutions is destroyed. Ferrier says that the sensibility of monkeys is 'entirely unaffected' by ablations of the motor zone,[45] and Horsley and Schäfer consider it by no means necessarily abolished.[46] Luciani found it diminished in his three experiments on apes.[47]

In man we have the fact that one-sided paralysis from disease of the opposite motor zone may or may not be accompanied with anæsthesia of the parts. Luciani, who believes that the motor zone is also sensory, tries to minimize the value of this evidence by pointing to the insufficiency with which patients are examined. He himself believes that in dogs the tactile sphere extends backwards and forwards of the directly excitable region, into the frontal and parietal lobes (see Fig. 20). Nothnagel considers that pathological evidence points in the same direction;[48] and Dr. Mills, carefully reviewing the evidence, adds the gyri fornicatus and hippocampi to the cutaneo-muscular region in man.[49] If one compare Luciani's

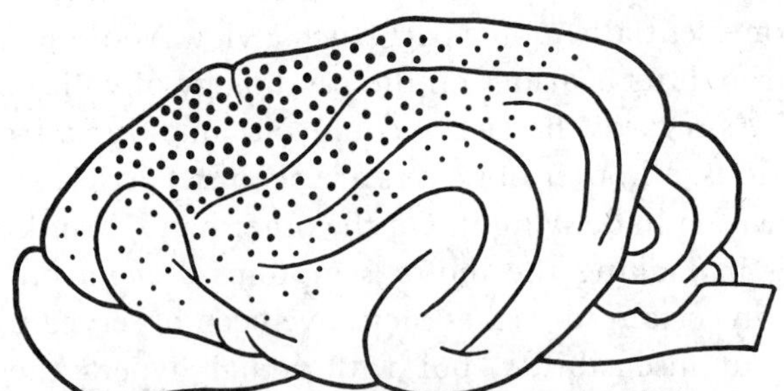

FIG. 20.—Luciani's Tactile Region in the Dog.

whole body to accompany motor defect after ablation of both frontal lobes, and he once found it after ablating the motor zone (Pflüger's *Archiv*, vol. 34, p. 471).

44 *Philosophical Transactions* (B), vol. 179, p. 20 ff.

45 *Functions*, p. 375.

46 Pp. 15–17.

47 Luciani und Seppilli: *op. cit.*, pp. 275–288.

48 *Op. cit.*, p. 18.

49 *Transactions of Congress*, etc., p. 272.

diagrams together (Figs. 14, 16, 19, 20) one will see that the entire parietal region of the dog's skull is common to the four senses of sight, hearing, smell, and touch, including muscular feeling. The corresponding region in the human brain (upper parietal and supra-marginal gyri—see Fig. 17, p. 65) seems to be a somewhat similar place of conflux. Optical aphasias and motor and tactile disturbances all result from its injury, especially when that is on the left side.[50] The lower we go in the animal scale the less differentiated the functions of the several brain-parts seem to be.[51] It may be that the region in question still represents in ourselves something like this primitive condition, and that the surrounding parts, in adapting themselves more and more to specialized and narrow functions, have left it as a sort of *carrefour* through which they send currents and converse. That it should be connected with musculo-cutaneous feeling is, however, no reason why the motor zone proper should not be so connected too. And the cases of paralysis from the motor zone with no accompanying anæsthesia may be explicable without denying all sensory function to that region. For, as my colleague Dr. James Putnam informs me, sensibility is always harder to kill than motility, even where we know for a certainty that the lesion affects tracts that are both sensory and motor. Persons whose hand is paralyzed in its movements from compression of arm-nerves during sleep, still feel with their fingers; and they may still feel in their feet when their legs are paralyzed by bruising of the spinal cord. In a similar way, the motor cortex might be sensitive as well as motor, and yet by this greater subtlety (or whatever the peculiarity may be) in the sensory currents, the sensibility might survive an amount of injury there by which the motility was destroyed. Nothnagel considers that there are grounds for supposing the *muscular* sense to be exclusively connected with the parietal lobe and not with the motor zone. "Disease of this lobe gives pure ataxy without palsy, and of the motor zone pure palsy without loss of muscular sense."[52] He fails, however, to convince more competent critics than the present writer,[53] so I conclude with them that as yet we have no decisive grounds for locating

50 See Exner's *Untersuchungen über die Localisation*, plate xxv.

51 Cf. Ferrier's *Functions*, etc., chap. IV and chap. X, §§ 6 to 9.

52 *Op. cit.*, p. 17.

53 E.g., Charles K. Mills: "Cerebral Localization in Its Practical Relations," *Transactions of the Congress*, etc., p. 272; Leyden: *Beiträge zur Lehre von der Localisation im Gehirn* (1888), p. 72.

muscular and cutaneous feeling apart. Much still remains to be learned about the relations between musculo-cutaneous sensibility and the cortex, but one thing is certain: that neither the occipital, the forward frontal, nor the temporal lobes seem to have anything essential to do with it in man. It is knit up with the performances of the *motor zone and of the convolutions backwards and midwards of them.* The reader must remember this conclusion when we come to the chapter on the Will.

I must add a word about the connection of aphasia with the tactile sense. On p. 51 I spoke of those cases in which the patient can write but not read his own writing. He cannot read by his eyes; but he can read by the feeling in his fingers, if he retrace the letters in the air. It is convenient for such a patient to have a pen in hand whilst reading in this way, in order to make the usual feeling of writing more complete.[54] In such a case we must suppose that the path between the optical and the graphic centres remains open, whilst that between the optical and the auditory and articulatory centres is closed. Only thus can we understand how the look of the writing should fail to suggest the sound of the words to the patient's mind, whilst it still suggests the proper movements of graphic imitation. These movements in their turn must of course be felt, and the feeling of them must be associated with the centres for hearing and pronouncing the words. The injury in cases like this where very special combinations fail, whilst others go on as usual, must always be supposed to be of the nature of increased resistance to the passage of certain currents of association. If any of the *elements* of mental function were destroyed the incapacity would necessarily be much more formidable. A patient who can both read and write with his fingers most likely uses an identical 'graphic' centre, at once sensory and motor, for both operations.

I have now given, as far as the nature of this book will allow, a complete account of the present state of the localization-question. In its main outlines it stands firm, though much has still to be discovered. The anterior frontal lobes, for example, so far as is yet known, have no definite functions. Goltz finds that dogs bereft of them both are incessantly in motion, and excitable by every small stimulus. They are irascible and amative in an extraordinary de-

[54] Bernard: *op. cit.*, p. 84.

gree, and their sides grow bare with perpetual reflex scratching; but they show no *local* troubles of either motion or sensibility. In monkeys not even this lack of inhibitory ability is shown, and neither stimulation nor excision of the prefrontal lobes produces any symptoms whatever. One monkey of Horsley and Schäfer's was as tame, and did certain tricks as well, after as before the operation.[55] It is probable that we have about reached the limits of what can be learned about brain-functions from vivisecting inferior animals, and that we must hereafter look more exclusively to human pathology for light. The existence of separate speech and writing centres in the left hemisphere in man; the fact that palsy from cortical injury is so much more complete and enduring in man and the monkey than in dogs; and the farther fact that it seems more difficult to get complete sensorial blindness from cortical ablations in the lower animals than in man, all show that functions get more specially localized as evolution goes on. In birds localization seems hardly to exist, and in rodents it is much less conspicuous than in carnivora. Even for man, however, Munk's way of mapping out the cortex into absolute areas within which only one movement or sensation is represented is surely false. The truth seems to be rather that, although there is a correspondence of certain regions of the brain to certain regions of the body, yet the several *parts* within each bodily region are represented throughout the *whole* of the corresponding brain-region like pepper and salt sprinkled from the same caster. This, however, does not prevent each 'part' from having its *focus* at one spot within the brain-region. The various brain-regions merge into each other in the same mixed way. As Mr. Horsley says: "There are border centres and the area of representation of the face merges into that for the representation of the upper limb. If there was a focal lesion at that point, you would have the movements of these two parts starting together."[56] The accompanying figure from Paneth shows just how the matter stands in the dog.[57]

I am speaking now of localizations breadthwise over the brain-surface. It is conceivable that there might be also localizations depthwise through the cortex. The more superficial cells are small-

55 *Philosophical Transactions* (B), vol. 179, p. 3.

56 *Transactions of the Congress of American Physicians and Surgeons*, 1889, vol. I, p. 343. Beevor and Horsley's paper on electric stimulation of the monkey's brain is the most beautiful work yet done for precision. See *Philosophical Transactions* (B), vol. 179, p. 205, especially the plates.

57 Pflüger's *Archiv*, vol. 37, p. 523 (1885).

er, the deepest layer of them is large; and it has been suggested that the superficial cells are sensorial, the deeper ones motor;[58] or that the superficial ones in the motor region are correlated with the extremities of the organs to be moved (fingers, etc.), the deeper ones with the more central segments (wrist, elbow, etc.).[59] It need hardly be said that all such theories are as yet but guesses.

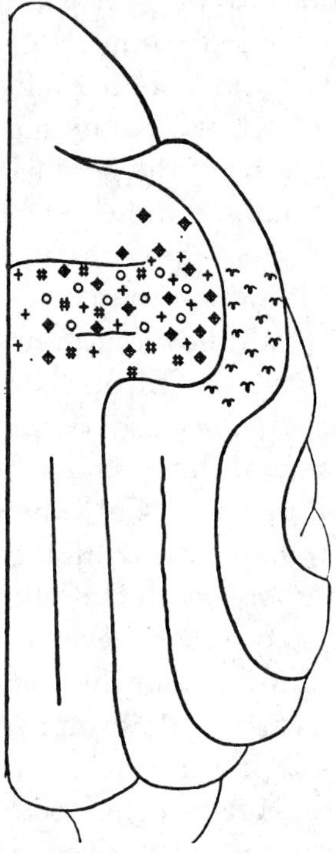

FIG. 21.—Dog's motor centres, right hemisphere, according to Paneth.—The points of the motor region are correlated as follows with muscles: the *loops* with the *orbicularis palpebrarum*; the *plain crosses* with the *flexor*, the *crosses inscribed in circles* with the *extensor, digitorum communis* of the fore-paw; the *plain circles* with the *abductor pollicis longus*; the *double crosses* with the *extensor communis* of the hind-limb.

58 By Luys in his generally preposterous book *The Brain*; also by Horsley.
59 C. Mercier: *The Nervous System and the Mind*, p. 124.

We thus see that the postulate of Meynert and Jackson which we started with on p. 41 is on the whole most satisfactorily corroborated by subsequent objective research. *The highest centres do probably contain nothing but arrangements for representing impressions and movements, and other arrangements for coupling the activity of these arrangements together.*[60] Currents pouring in from the sense-organs first excite some arrangements, which in turn excite others, until at last a motor discharge downwards of some sort occurs. When this is once clearly grasped there remains little ground for keeping up that old controversy about the motor zone, as to whether it is in reality motor or sensitive. The whole cortex, inasmuch as currents run through it, is both. All the currents probably have feelings going with them, and sooner or later bring movements about. In one aspect, then, every centre is afferent, in another efferent, even the motor cells of the spinal cord having these two aspects inseparably conjoined. Marique,[61] and Exner and Paneth[62] have shown that by cutting *round* a 'motor' centre and so separating it from the influence of the rest of the cortex, the same disorders are produced as by cutting it out, so that really it is only the mouth of the funnel, as it were, through which the stream of innervation, starting from elsewhere, pours;[63] consciousness accompanying the stream, and being mainly of things seen if the stream is strongest occipitally, of things heard if it is strongest temporally, of things felt, etc., if the stream occupies most intensely the 'motor zone.' It seems to me that some broad and vague formulation like this is as much as we can safely venture on in the present state of science; and in subsequent chapters I expect to give confirmatory reasons for my view.

60 The frontal lobes as yet remain a puzzle. Wundt tries to explain them as an organ of 'apperception' (*Grundzüge der physiologischen Psychologie*, 3d ed., vol. I, p. 233 ff.), but I confess myself unable to apprehend clearly the Wundtian philosophy so far as this word enters into it, so must be contented with this bare reference.—Until quite recently it was common to talk of an 'ideational centre' as of something distinct from the aggregate of other centres. Fortunately this custom is already on the wane.

61 *Recherches expérimentales sur le mécanisme de fonctionnement des centres psycho-moteurs du cerveau* (Brussels, 1885).

62 Pflüger's *Archiv*, vol. 44, p. 544.

63 I ought to add, however, that François-Franck (*Fonctions motrices*, p. 370) got, in two dogs and a cat, a different result from this sort of 'circumvallation.'

MAN'S CONSCIOUSNESS LIMITED TO THE HEMISPHERES

But is the consciousness which accompanies the activity of the cortex the only consciousness that man has? or *are his lower centres conscious as well?*

This is a difficult question to decide, how difficult one only learns when one discovers that the cortex-consciousness itself of certain objects can be seemingly annihilated in any good hypnotic subject by a bare wave of his operator's hand, and yet be proved by circumstantial evidence to exist all the while in a split-off condition, quite as 'ejective'[64] to the rest of the subject's mind as that mind is to the mind of the bystanders.[65] The lower centres themselves may conceivably all the while have a split-off consciousness of their own, similarly ejective to the cortex-consciousness; but whether they have it or not can never be known from merely introspective evidence. Meanwhile the fact that occipital destruction in man may cause a blindness which is apparently absolute (no feeling remaining either of light or dark over one half of the field of view), would lead us to suppose that if our lower optical centres, the corpora quadrigemina, and thalami, do have any consciousness, it is at all events a consciousness which does not mix with that which accompanies the cortical activities, and which has nothing to do with our personal Self. In lower animals this may not be so much the case. The traces of sight found (*supra*, pp. 55–56) in dogs and monkeys whose occipital lobes were entirely destroyed, may possibly have been due to the fact that the lower centres of these animals saw, and that what they saw was not ejective but objective to the remaining cortex, i.e., it formed part of one and the same inner world with the things which that cortex perceived. It may be, however, that the phenomena were due to the fact that in these animals the cortical 'centres' for vision reach outside of the occipital zone, and that destruction of the latter fails to remove them as completely as in man. This, as we know, is the opinion of the experimenters themselves. For practical purposes, nevertheless, and limiting the meaning of the word consciousness to the personal self of the individual, we can pretty confidently answer the question prefixed to this paragraph by saying that *the cortex is the sole organ of consciousness*

64 For this word, see W. K. Clifford's *Lectures and Essays* (1879), vol. II, p. 72.
65 See below, Chapter VIII.

in man.[66] If there be any consciousness pertaining to the lower centres, it is a consciousness of which the self knows nothing.

THE RESTITUTION OF FUNCTION

Another problem, not so metaphysical, remains. The most general and striking fact connected with cortical injury is that of the *restoration of function.* Functions lost at first are after a few days or weeks restored. *How are we to understand this restitution?*

Two theories are in the field:

1) Restitution is due to the vicarious action either of the rest of the cortex or of centres lower down, acquiring functions which until then they had not performed;

2) It is due to the remaining centres (whether cortical or 'lower') resuming functions which they had always had, but of which the wound had temporarily inhibited the exercise. This is the view of which Goltz and Brown-Séquard are the most distinguished defenders.

Inhibition is a *vera causa,* of that there can be no doubt. The pneumogastric nerve inhibits the heart, the splanchnic inhibits the intestinal movements, and the superior laryngeal those of inspiration. The nerve-irritations which may inhibit the contraction of arterioles are innumerable, and reflex actions are often repressed by the simultaneous excitement of other sensory nerves. For all such facts the reader must consult the treatises on physiology. What concerns us here is the inhibition exerted by different parts of the nerve-centres, when irritated, on the activity of distant parts. The flaccidity of a frog from 'shock,' for a minute or so after his medulla oblongata is cut, is an inhibition from the seat of injury which quickly passes away.

What is known as 'surgical shock' (unconsciousness, pallor, dilatation of splanchnic blood-vessels, and general syncope and collapse) in the human subject is an inhibition which lasts a longer time. Goltz, Freusberg, and others, cutting the spinal cord in dogs, proved that there were functions inhibited still longer by the

66 Cf. Ferrier's *Functions,* pp. 120, 147, 414. See also Vulpian: *Leçons sur la physiologie générale et comparée du système nerveux,* p. 548; Luciani und Seppilli: *op. cit.,* pp. 404–5; H. Maudsley: *Physiology of Mind* (1876), pp. 138 ff., 197 ff., and 241 ff. In G. H. Lewes's *Physical Basis of Mind,* Problem IV: "The Reflex Theory," a very full history of the question is given.

wound, but which re-established themselves ultimately if the animal was kept alive. The lumbar region of the cord was thus found to contain independent vaso-motor centres, centres for erection, for control of the sphincters, etc., which could be excited to activity by tactile stimuli and as readily reinhibited by others simultaneously applied.[67] We may therefore plausibly suppose that the rapid reappearance of motility, vision, etc., after their first disappearance in consequence of a cortical mutilation, is due to the passing off of inhibitions exerted by the irritated surface of the wound. The only question is whether *all* restorations of function must be explained in this one simple way, or whether some part of them may not be owing to the formation of entirely new paths in the remaining centres, by which they become 'educated' to duties which they did not originally possess. In favor of an indefinite extension of the inhibition theory facts may be cited such as the following: In dogs whose disturbances due to cortical lesion have disappeared, they may in consequence of some inner or outer accident reappear in all their intensity for 24 hours or so and then disappear again.[68] In a dog made half blind by an operation, and then shut up in the dark, vision comes back just as quickly as in other similar dogs whose sight is exercised systematically every day.[69] A dog which has learned to beg before the operation recommences this practice quite *spontaneously* a week after a double-sided ablation of the motor zone.[70] Occasionally, in a pigeon (or even, it is said, in a dog) we see the disturbances less marked immediately after the operation than they are half an hour later.[71] This would be impossible were they due to the subtraction of the organs which normally carried them on. Moreover the entire drift of recent physiological and pathological speculation is towards enthroning inhibition as an ever-present and indispensable condition of orderly activity. We shall see how great is its importance, in the chapter on the Will. Mr. Charles Mercier considers that no muscular contraction, once begun, would ever stop without it, short of exhaustion of the system;[72] and Brown-Séquard has for years been accumulating exam-

67 Goltz: Pflüger's *Archiv*, vol. 8, p. 460; Freusberg: *ibid.*, vol. 10, p. 174.

68 Goltz: *Über die Verrichtungen des Grosshirns*, p. 73.

69 Loeb: Pflüger's *Archiv*, vol. 39, p. 276.

70 *Ibid.*, p. 289.

71 Schrader: *ibid.*, vol. 44, p. 218.

72 *The Nervous System and the Mind* (1888), chaps. III, VI; also in *Brain*, vol. XI, p. 361.

ples to show how far its influence extends.[73] Under these circumstances it seems as if error might more probably lie in curtailing its sphere too much than in stretching it too far as an explanation of the phenomena following cortical lesion.[74]

On the other hand, if we admit *no* re-education of centres, we not only fly in the face of an *a priori* probability, but we find ourselves compelled by facts to suppose an almost incredible number of functions natively lodged in the centres below the *thalami* or even in those below the *corpora quadrigemina.* I will consider the *a priori* objection after first taking a look at the facts which I have in mind. They confront us the moment we ask ourselves just *which are the parts which perform the functions abolished by an operation after sufficient time has elapsed for restoration to occur?*

The first observers thought that they must be the *corresponding parts of the opposite or intact hemisphere.* But as long ago as 1875 Carville and Duret tested this by cutting out the fore-leg-centre on one side, in a dog, and then, after waiting till restitution had occurred, cutting it out on the opposite side as well. Goltz and others have done the same thing.[75] If the opposite side were really the seat of the restored function, the original palsy should have appeared again and been permanent. But it did not appear at all; there appeared only a palsy of the hitherto unaffected side. The next supposition is that *the parts surrounding the cut-out region* learn vicariously to perform its duties. But here, again, experiment seems to upset the hypothesis, so far as the motor zone goes at least; for we may wait till motility has returned in the affected limb, and then both irritate the cortex surrounding the wound without exciting the limb to movement, and ablate it, without bringing back the vanished palsy.[76] It would accordingly seem that *the cerebral centres below the cortex* must be the seat of the regained activities. But Goltz destroyed a dog's entire left hemisphere, together with the *corpus striatum* and the *thalamus* on that side, and kept him alive

73 Brown-Séquard has given a résumé of his opinions in the *Archives de Physiologie* for Oct. 1889, 5me. Série, vol. 1, p. 751.

74 Goltz first applied the inhibition theory to the brain in his *Verrichtungen des Grosshirns,* p. 39 ff. On the general philosophy of Inhibition the reader may consult Brunton's *Text-Book of Pharmacology, Therapeutics and Materia Medica,* p. 154 ff., and also *Nature,* vol. 27, p. 419 ff.

75 E.g., Herzen, Hermann und Schwalbe's *Jahresbericht* for 1886, Physiologie Abtheilung, p. 38. (Experiments on new-born puppies.)

76 François-Franck: *op. cit.,* p. 382. Results are somewhat contradictory.

until a surprisingly small amount of motor and tactile disturbance remained.[77] These centres cannot here have accounted for the restitution. He has even, as it would appear,[78] ablated both the hemispheres of a dog, and kept him alive 51 days, able to walk and stand. The corpora striata and thalami in this dog were also practically gone. In view of such results we seem driven, with M. François-Franck,[79] to fall back on the *ganglia lower still,* or even on the *spinal cord* as the 'vicarious' organ of which we are in quest. If the abeyance of function between the operation and the restoration was due *exclusively* to inhibition, then we must suppose these lowest centres to be in reality extremely accomplished organs. They must always have done what we now find them doing after function is restored, even when the hemispheres were intact. Of course this is conceivably the case; yet it does not seem very plausible. And the *a priori* considerations which a moment since I said I should urge, make it less plausible still.

For, in the first place, the brain is essentially a place of currents, which run in organized paths. Loss of function can only mean one of two things, either that a current can no longer run in, or that if it runs in, it can no longer run out, by its old path. Either of these inabilities may come from a local ablation; and 'restitution' can then only mean that, in spite of a temporary block, an inrunning current has at last become enabled to flow out by its old path again—e.g., the sound of 'give your paw' discharges after some weeks into the same canine muscles into which it used to discharge before the operation. As far as the cortex itself goes, since one of the purposes for which it actually exists is the production of new paths,[80] the only question before us is: Is the formation of *these particular 'vicarious' paths* too much to expect of its plastic powers? It would certainly be too much to expect that a hemisphere should receive currents from optic fibres whose *arriving-place* within it is destroyed, or that it should discharge into fibres of the pyramidal strand if their *place of exit* is broken down. Such lesions as these must be irreparable

77 Pflüger's *Archiv,* vol. 42, p. 419.

78 *Neurologisches Centralblatt,* 1889, p. 372.

79 *Op. cit.,* p. 387. See pp. 378 to 388 for a discussion of the whole question. Compare also Wundt's *Physiologische Psychologie,* 3d ed., I, 225 ff., and Luciani und Seppilli: pp. 243, 293.

80 The Chapters on Habit, Association, Memory, and Perception will change our present preliminary conjecture that that is one of its essential uses, into an unshakable conviction.

within that hemisphere. Yet even then, through the other hemisphere, the *corpus callosum,* and the bilateral connections in the spinal cord, one can imagine some road by which the old muscles might eventually be innervated by the same incoming currents which innervated them before the block. And for all minor interruptions, not involving the arriving-place of the 'cortico-petal' or the place of exit of the 'cortico-fugal' fibres, roundabout paths of some sort through the affected hemisphere itself must exist, for every point of it is, remotely at least, in potential communication with every other point. The normal paths are only paths of least resistance. If they get blocked or cut, paths formerly more resistant become the least resistant paths under the changed conditions. It must never be forgotten that a current that runs in has got to run out *somewhere*; and if it only once succeeds by accident in striking into its old place of exit again, the thrill of satisfaction which the consciousness connected with the whole residual brain then receives will reinforce and fix the paths of that moment and make them more likely to be struck into again. The resultant feeling that the old habitual act is at last successfully back again, becomes itself a new stimulus which stamps all the existing currents in. It is matter of experience that such feelings of successful achievement do tend to fix in our memory whatever processes have led to them and Memory is only a matter of paths; and we shall have a good deal more to say upon the subject when we come to the Chapter on the Will.

My conclusion then is this: that some of the restitution of function (especially where the cortical lesion is not too great) is probably due to genuinely vicarious function on the part of the centres that remain; whilst some of it is due to the passing off of inhibitions. In other words, both the vicarious theory and the inhibition theory are true in their measure. But as for determining that measure, or saying which centres are vicarious, and to what extent they can learn new tricks, that is impossible at present.

FINAL CORRECTION OF THE MEYNERT SCHEME

And now, after learning all these facts, what are we to think of the child and the candle-flame, and of that scheme which provisionally imposed itself on our acceptance after surveying the actions of the frog? (Cf. pp. 36–38, *supra.*) It will be remembered that we then considered the lower centres *en masse* as machines for responding to present sense-impressions exclusively, and the hemispheres as equally exclusive organs of action from inward considerations or ideas; and that, following Meynert, we supposed the hemispheres to have no native tendencies to determinate activity, but to be merely superadded organs for breaking up the various reflexes performed by the lower centres, and combining their motor and sensory elements in novel ways. It will also be remembered that I prophesied that we should be obliged to soften down the sharpness of this distinction after we had completed our survey of the farther facts. The time has now come for that correction to be made.

Wider and completer observations show us both that the lower centres are more spontaneous, and that the hemispheres are more automatic, than the Meynert scheme allows. Schrader's observations in Goltz's Laboratory on hemisphereless frogs[81] and pigeons[82] give an idea quite different from the picture of these creatures which is classically current. Steiner's[83] observations on frogs already went a good way in the same direction, showing, for example, that locomotion is a well-developed function of the medulla oblongata. But Schrader, by great care in the operation, and by keeping the frogs a long time alive, found that at least in some of them the spinal cord would produce movements of locomotion when the frog was smartly roused by a poke, and that swimming and croaking could sometimes be performed when nothing above the medulla oblongata remained.[84] Schrader's hemisphereless frogs moved spontaneously, ate flies, buried themselves in the ground, and in short did many things which before his observations were supposed to be impossible unless the hemispheres remained. Steiner[85] and Vulpian have remarked an even greater vivacity in fishes deprived of their hemispheres. Vulpian says of his brainless carps[86] that three days after the operation one of them darted at food and at a knot tied on the end of a string, holding the latter so tight between his jaws that his head was drawn out of water. Later, "they see morsels of white of egg; the moment these sink through the water in front of them, they

81 Pflüger's *Archiv*, vol. 41, p. 75 (1887).

82 *Ibid.*, vol. 44, p. 175 (1888–1889).

83 *Untersuchungen über die Physiologie des Froschhirns*, 1885.

84 *Loc. cit.*, pp. 80, 82–3. Schrader also found a *biting*-reflex developed when the medulla oblongata is cut through just behind the cerebellum.

85 Berlin Academy *Sitzungsberichte* for 1886.

86 *Comptes Rendus de l'Académie des Sciences*, vol. 102, p. 90.

follow and seize them, sometimes after they are on the bottom, sometimes before they have reached it. In capturing and swallowing this food they execute just the same movements as the intact carps which are in the same aquarium. The only difference is that they seem to see them at less distance, seek them with less impetuosity and less perseverance in all the points of the bottom of the aquarium, but they struggle (so to speak) sometimes with the sound carps to grasp the morsels. It is certain that they do not confound these bits of white of egg with other white bodies, small pebbles for example, which are at the bottom of the water. The same carp which, three days after operation, seized the knot on a piece of string, no longer snaps at it now, but if one brings it near her, she draws away from it by swimming backwards before it comes into contact with her mouth."[87] Already on pp. 22–23, as the reader may remember, we instanced those adaptations of conduct to new conditions, on the part of the frog's spinal cord and thalami, which led Pflüger and Lewes on the one hand and Goltz on the other to locate in these organs an intelligence akin to that of which the hemispheres are the seat.

When it comes to birds deprived of their hemispheres, the evidence that some of their acts have conscious purpose behind them is quite as persuasive. In pigeons Schrader found that the state of somnolence lasted only three or four days, after which time the birds began indefatigably to walk about the room. They climbed out of boxes in which they were put, jumped over or flew up upon obstacles, and their sight was so perfect that neither in walking nor flying did they ever strike any object in the room. They had also definite ends or purposes, flying straight for more convenient perching places when made uncomfortable by movements imparted to those on which they stood; and of several possible perches they always chose the most convenient. "If we give the dove the choice of a horizontal bar (*Reck*) or an equally distant table to fly to, she always gives decided preference to the table. Indeed she chooses the table even if it is several meters farther off than the bar or the chair." Placed on the back of a chair, she flies first to the seat and then to the floor, and in general "will forsake a high position, although it give her sufficiently firm support, and in order to reach the ground will make use of the environing objects as intermediate goals of flight, showing a perfectly correct judgment of their dis-

[87] *Comptes Rendus de l'Académie des Sciences*, vol. 102, p. 1529.

tance. Although able to fly directly to the ground, she prefers to make the journey in successive stages. . . . Once on the ground, she hardly ever rises spontaneously into the air."[88]

Young rabbits deprived of their hemispheres will stand, run, start at noises, avoid obstacles in their path, and give responsive cries of suffering when hurt. Rats will do the same, and throw themselves moreover into an attitude of defence. Dogs never survive such an operation if performed at once. But Goltz's latest dog, mentioned on p. 78, which is said to have been kept alive for fifty-one days after both hemispheres had been removed by a series of ablations and the corpora striata and thalami had softened away, shows how much the mid-brain centres and the cord can do even in the canine species. Taken together, the number of reactions shown to exist in the lower centres by these observations make out a pretty good case for the Meynert scheme, as applied to these lower animals. That scheme demands hemispheres which shall be mere supplements or organs of repetition, and in the light of these observations they obviously are so to a great extent. But the Meynert scheme also demands that the reactions of the lower centres shall all be *native*, and we are not absolutely sure that some of those which we have been considering may not have been acquired after the injury; and it furthermore demands that they should be machine-like, whereas the expression of some of them makes us doubt whether they may not be guided by an intelligence of low degree.

Even in the lower animals, then, there is reason to soften down that opposition between the hemispheres and the lower centres which the scheme demands. The hemispheres may, it is true, only supplement the lower centres, but the latter resemble the former in nature and have some small amount at least of 'spontaneity' and choice.

But when we come to monkeys and man the scheme well-nigh breaks down altogether; for we find that the hemispheres do not simply repeat voluntarily actions which the lower centres perform as machines. There are many functions which the lower centres cannot by themselves perform at all. When the motor cortex is injured in a man or a monkey genuine paralysis ensues, which in man is incurable, and almost or quite equally so in the ape. Dr. Seguin knew a man with hemi-blindness, from cortical injury, which had persisted unaltered for twenty-three years. 'Traumatic inhibition'

[88] *Loc. cit.*, p. 216.

cannot possibly account for this. The blindness must have been an 'Ausfallserscheinung,' due to the loss of vision's essential organ. It would seem, then, that in these higher creatures the lower centres must be less adequate than they are farther down in the zoological scale; and that even for certain elementary combinations of movement and impression the co-operation of the hemispheres is necessary from the start. Even in birds and dogs the power of *eating properly* is lost when the frontal lobes are cut off.[89]

The plain truth is that neither in man nor beast are the hemispheres the virgin organs which our scheme called them. So far from being unorganized at birth, they must have native tendencies to reaction of a determinate sort.[90] These are the tendencies which we know as *emotions* and *instincts*, and which we must study with some detail in later chapters of this book. Both instincts and emotions are reactions upon special sorts of objects of *perception*; they depend on the hemispheres; and they are in the first instance reflex, that is, they take place the first time the exciting object is met, are accompanied by no forethought or deliberation, and are irresistible. But they are modifiable to a certain extent by experience, and on later occasions of meeting the exciting object, the instincts especially have less of the blind impulsive character which they had at first. All this will be explained at some length in Chapter XXIV. Meanwhile we can say that the multiplicity of emotional and instinctive reactions in man, together with his extensive associative power, permit of extensive recouplings of the original sensory and motor partners. The *consequences* of one instinctive reaction often prove to be the inciters of an opposite reaction, and being *suggested* on later occasions by the original object, may then suppress the first reaction altogether, just as in the case of the child and the flame. For this education the hemispheres do not need to be *tabulæ rasæ* at first, as the Meynert scheme would have them; and so far from

89 Goltz: Pflüger's *Archiv*, vol. 42, p. 447; Schrader: *ibid.*, vol. 44, p. 219 ff. It is possible that this symptom may be an effect of traumatic inhibition, however.

90 A few years ago one of the strongest arguments for the theory that the hemispheres are purely supernumerary was Soltmann's often-quoted observation that in new-born puppies the motor zone of the cortex is not excitable by electricity and only becomes so in the course of a fortnight, presumably after the experiences of the lower centres have educated it to motor duties. Paneth's later observations, however, seem to show that Soltmann may have been misled through overnarcotizing his victims (Pflüger's *Archiv*, vol. 37, p. 202). In the *Neurologisches Centralblatt* for 1889, p. 513, Bechterew returns to the subject on Soltmann's side without, however, noticing Paneth's work.

their being educated by the lower centres exclusively, they educate themselves.[91]

We have already noticed the absence of reactions from fear and hunger in the ordinary brainless frog. Schrader gives a striking account of the instinctless condition of his brainless pigeons, active as they were in the way of locomotion and voice. "The hemisphereless animal moves in a world of bodies which . . . are all of equal value for him. . . . He is, to use Goltz's apt expression, *impersonal.* . . . Every object is for him only a space-occupying mass, he turns out of his path for an ordinary pigeon no otherwise than for a stone. He may try to climb over both. All authors agree that they never found any difference, whether it was an inanimate body, a cat, a dog, or a bird of prey which came in their pigeon's way. The creature knows neither friends nor enemies, in the thickest company it lives like a hermit. The languishing cooing of the male awakens no more impression than the rattling of the peas, or the call-whistle which in the days before the injury used to make the birds hasten to be fed. Quite as little as the earlier observers have I seen hemisphereless she-birds answer the courting of the male. A hemisphereless male will coo all day long and show distinct signs of sexual excitement, but his activity is without any object, it is entirely indifferent to him whether the she-bird be there or not. If one is placed near him, he leaves her unnoticed. . . . As the male pays no attention to the female, so she pays none to her young. The brood may follow the mother ceaselessly calling for food, but they might as well ask it from a stone. . . . The hemisphereless pigeon is in the highest degree tame, and fears man as little as cat or bird of prey."[92]

Putting together now all the facts and reflections which we have been through, it seems to me that *we can no longer hold strictly to the Meynert scheme.* If anywhere, it will apply to the lowest animals; but in them especially the lower centres seem to have a de-

[91] Münsterberg (*Die Willenshandlung*, 1888, p. 134) challenges Meynert's scheme *in toto*, saying that whilst we have in our personal experience plenty of examples of acts which were at first voluntary becoming secondarily automatic and reflex, we have no conscious record of a single originally reflex act growing voluntary.—As far as conscious record is concerned, we could not possibly have it even if the Meynert scheme were wholly true, for the education of the hemispheres which that scheme postulates must in the nature of things antedate recollection. But it seems to me that Münsterberg's rejection of the scheme may possibly be correct as regards reflexes from the *lower centres*. Everywhere in this department of psychogenesis we are made to feel how ignorant we really are.

[92] Pflüger's *Archiv*, vol. 44, p. 230–1.

gree of spontaneity and choice. On the whole, I think that we are driven to substitute for it some such general conception as the following, which allows for zoological differences as we know them, and is vague and elastic enough to receive any number of future discoveries of detail.

CONCLUSION

All the centres, in all animals, whilst they are in one aspect mechanisms, probably are, or at least once were, organs of consciousness in another, although the consciousness is doubtless much more developed in the hemispheres than it is anywhere else. The consciousness must everywhere *prefer* some of the sensations which it gets to others; and if it can remember these in their absence, however dimly, they must be its *ends* of desire. If, moreover, it can identify in memory any motor discharges which may have led to such ends, and associate the latter with them, then these motor discharges themselves may in turn become desired as *means*. This is the development of *will*; and its realization must of course be proportional to the possible complication of the consciousness. Even the spinal cord may possibly have some little power of will in this sense, and of effort towards modified behavior in consequence of new experiences of sensibility.[93]

All nervous centres have then in the first instance one essential function, that of 'intelligent' action. They feel, prefer one thing to another, and have 'ends.' Like all other organs, however, they *evolve* from ancestor to descendant, and their evolution takes two directions, the lower centres passing downwards into more unhesitating automatism, and the higher ones upwards into larger intel-

[93] Naturally, as Schiff long ago pointed out (*Lehrbuch der Muskel- und Nervenphysiologie*, 1858–59, p. 213 ff.), the 'Rückenmarksseele,' if it now exist, can have no higher sense-consciousness, for its incoming currents are solely from the skin. But it may, in its dim way, both feel, prefer, and desire. See, for the view favorable to the text: G. H. Lewes: *The Physiology of Common Life* (1860), chap. IX. Goltz (*Nervencentren des Frosches*, 1869, pp. 102–130) thinks that the frog's cord has no adaptative power. This may be the case in such experiments as his, because the beheaded frog's short span of life does not give it time to learn the new tricks asked for. But Rosenthal (*Biologisches Centralblatt*, vol. IV, p. 247) and Mendelssohn (Berlin Academy *Sitzungsberichte*, 1885, p. 107) in their investigations on the simple reflexes of the frog's cord, show that there is some adaptation to new conditions, inasmuch as when usual paths of conduction are interrupted by a cut, new paths are taken. According to Rosenthal, these grow more pervious (i.e., require a smaller stimulus) in proportion as they are more often traversed.

lectuality.[94] Thus it may happen that those functions which can safely grow uniform and fatal become least accompanied by mind, and that their organ, the spinal cord, becomes a more and more soulless machine; whilst on the contrary those functions which it benefits the animal to have adapted to delicate environing variations pass more and more to the hemispheres, whose anatomical structure and attendant consciousness grow more and more elaborate as zoological evolution proceeds. In this way it might come about that in man and the monkeys the basal ganglia should do fewer things by themselves than they can do in dogs, fewer in dogs than in rabbits, fewer in rabbits than in hawks,[95] fewer in hawks than in pigeons, fewer in pigeons than in frogs, fewer in frogs than in fishes, and that the hemispheres should correspondingly do more. This passage of functions forward to the ever-enlarging hemispheres would be itself one of the evolutive changes, to be explained like the development of the hemispheres themselves, either by fortunate variation or by inherited effects of use. The reflexes, on this view, upon which the education of our human hemispheres depends, would not be due to the basal ganglia alone. They would be tendencies in the hemispheres themselves, modifiable by education, unlike the reflexes of the medulla oblongata, pons, optic lobes and spinal cord. Such cerebral reflexes, if they exist, form a basis quite as good as that which the Meynert scheme offers, for the acquisition of memories and associations which may later result in all sorts of 'changes of partners' in the psychic world. The diagram of the baby and the candle (see page 37) can be re-edited, if need be, as an entirely cortical transaction. The original tendency to touch will be a cortical instinct; the burn will leave an image in another part of the cortex, which, being recalled by association, will inhibit the touching tendency the next time the candle is perceived, and excite the tendency to withdraw—so that the retinal picture will, upon that next time, be coupled with the original motor partner of the pain. We thus get whatever psychological truth the Meynert scheme possesses without entangling ourselves on a dubious anatomy and physiology.

94 Whether this evolution takes place through the inheritance of habits acquired, or through the preservation of lucky variations, is an alternative which we need not discuss here. We shall consider it in the last chapter in the book. For our present purpose the *modus operandi* of the evolution makes no difference, provided it be admitted to occur.

95 See Schrader's Observations, *loc. cit.*

Some such shadowy view of the evolution of the centres, of the relation of consciousness to them, and of the hemispheres to the other lobes, is, it seems to me, that in which it is safest to indulge. If it has no other advantage, it at any rate makes us realize how enormous are the gaps in our knowledge, the moment we try to cover the facts by any one formula of a general kind.

Chapter III

On Some General Conditions of Brain-Activity

The elementary properties of nerve-tissue on which the brain-functions depend are far from being satisfactorily made out. The scheme that suggests itself in the first instance to the mind, because it is so obvious, is certainly false: I mean the notion that each cell stands for an idea or part of an idea, and that the ideas are associated or 'bound into bundles' (to use a phrase of Locke's) by the fibres. If we make a symbolic diagram on a blackboard, of the laws of association between ideas, we are inevitably led to draw circles, or closed figures of some kind, and to connect them by lines. When we hear that the nerve-centres contain cells which send off fibres, we say that Nature has realized our diagram for us, and that the mechanical substratum of thought is plain. In *some* way, it is true, our diagram must be realized in the brain; but surely in no such visible and palpable way as we at first suppose.[1] An enormous number of the cellular bodies in the hemispheres are fibreless. Where fibres are sent off they soon divide into untraceable ramifications; and nowhere do we see a simple coarse anatomical connection, like a line on the blackboard, between two cells. Too much anatomy has been found to order for theoretic purposes, even by the anatomists; and the popular-science notions of cells and fibres are almost

[1] I shall myself in later places indulge in much of this schematization. The reader will understand once for all that it is symbolic; and that the use of it is hardly more than to show what a deep congruity there is between mental processes and mechanical processes of *some* kind, not necessarily of the exact kind portrayed.

wholly wide of the truth. Let us therefore relegate the subject of the *intimate* workings of the brain to the physiology of the future, save in respect to a few points of which a word must now be said. And first of

THE SUMMATION OF STIMULI

in the same nerve-tract. This is a property extremely important for the understanding of a great many phenomena of the neural, and consequently of the mental, life; and it behooves us to gain a clear conception of what it means before we proceed any farther.

The law is this, that *a stimulus which would be inadequate by itself to excite a nerve-centre to effective discharge may, by acting with one or more other stimuli (equally ineffectual by themselves alone), bring the discharge about.* The natural way to consider this is as a summation of tensions which at last overcome a resistance. The first of them produce a 'latent excitement' or a 'heightened irritability'—the phrase is immaterial so far as practical consequences go; the last is the straw which breaks the camel's back. Where the neural process is one that has consciousness for its accompaniment, the final explosion would in all cases seem to involve a vivid state of feeling of a more or less substantive kind. But there is no ground for supposing that the tensions whilst yet submaximal or outwardly ineffective, may not also have a share in determining the total consciousness present in the individual at the time. In later chapters we shall see abundant reason to suppose that they do have such a share, and that without their contribution the fringe of relations which is at every moment a vital ingredient of the mind's object, would not come to consciousness at all.

The subject belongs too much to physiology for the evidence to be cited in detail in these pages. I will throw into a note a few references for such readers as may be interested in following it out,[2]

[2] Valentin: *Archiv für die gesammte Physiologie,* 1873, p. 458. Stirling: Leipzig Academy *Berichte,* 1874 (*Journal of Anatomy and Physiology,* x [1875], 372). J. Ward: *Archiv für (Anatomie und) Physiologie,* 1880, p. 72. H. Sewall: Johns Hopkins *Studies,* 1880, p. 30. Kronecker und Nicolaides: *Archiv für (Anatomie und) Physiologie,* 1880, p. 437. Exner: *Archiv für die gesammte Physiologie,* Bd. 28, p. 487 (1882). Eckhard: in Hermann's *Handbuch der Physiologie,* Bd. II, Thl. II, p. 31. François-Franck: *Leçons sur les fonctions motrices du cerveau,* pp. 51 ff., 339.—For the process of summation in *nerves* and *muscles,* cf. Hermann: *ibid.,* Bd. II, Thl. II, p. 109, and Bd. I, Thl. I, p. 40. Also Wundt: *Physiologische Psychologie,* I, 243 ff.; Richet: *Travaux du laboratoire de Marey,* 1877, p. 97; *L'Homme et l'intelligence,* pp. 24 ff., 468; *Revue*

and simply say that the direct electrical irritation of the cortical centres sufficiently proves the point. For it was found by the earliest experimenters here that whereas it takes an exceedingly strong current to produce any movement when a single induction-shock is used, a rapid succession of induction-shocks ('faradization') will produce movements when the current is comparatively weak. A single quotation from an excellent investigation will exhibit this law under further aspects:

"If we continue to stimulate the cortex at short intervals with the strength of current which produces the minimal muscular contraction [of the dog's digital extensor muscle], the amount of contraction gradually increases till it reaches the maximum. Each earlier stimulation leaves thus an effect behind it, which increases the efficacy of the following one. In this summation of the stimuli . . . the following points may be noted: 1) Single stimuli entirely inefficacious when alone may become efficacious by sufficiently rapid reiteration. If the current used is very much less than that which provokes the first beginning of contraction, a very large number of successive shocks may be needed before the movement appears—20, 50, once 106 shocks were needed. 2) The summation takes place easily in proportion to the shortness of the interval between the stimuli. A current too weak to give effective summation when its shocks are 3 seconds apart will be capable of so doing when the interval is shortened to 1 second. 3) Not only electrical irritation leaves a modification which goes to swell the following stimulus, but every sort of irritant which can produce a contraction does so. If in any way a reflex contraction of the muscle experimented on has been produced, or if it is contracted spontaneously by the animal (as not unfrequently happens 'by sympathy,' during a deep inspiration), it is found that an electrical stimulus, until then inoperative, operates energetically if immediately applied."[3]

Furthermore:

"In a certain stage of the morphia-narcosis an ineffectively weak shock will become powerfully effective, if, immediately before its application to the motor centre, the skin of certain parts of the body is exposed to

---

Philosophique, t. XXI, p. 564. Kronecker und Hall: *Archiv für (Anatomie und) Physiologie*, 1879 (supplement); Schoenlein: *ibid.*, 1882, p. 357. Sertoli (Hofmann and Schwalbe's *Jahresbericht*, 1882, p. 25). De Watteville: *Neurologisches Centralblatt*, 1883, No. 7. Gruenhagen: *Archiv für die gesammte Physiologie*, Bd. 34, p. 301 (1884).

[3] Bubnoff und Heidenhain: "Über Erregungs- und Hemmungsvorgänge innerhalb der motorischen Hirncentren," *Archiv für die gesammte Physiologie*, Bd. 26, p. 156 (1881).

gentle tactile stimulation. . . . If, having ascertained the subminimal strength of current and convinced one's self repeatedly of its inefficacy, we draw our hand a single time lightly over the skin of the paw whose cortical centre is the object of stimulation, we find the current at once strongly effective. The increase of irritability lasts some seconds before it disappears. Sometimes the effect of a single light stroking of the paw is only sufficient to make the previously ineffectual current produce a very weak contraction. Repeating the tactile stimulation will then, as a rule, increase the contraction's extent."[4]

We constantly use the summation of stimuli in our practical appeals. If a car-horse balks, the final way of starting him is by applying a number of customary incitements at once. If the driver uses reins and voice, if one bystander pulls at his head, another lashes his hind-quarters, and the conductor rings the bell, and the dismounted passengers shove the car, all at the same moment, his obstinacy generally yields, and he goes on his way rejoicing. If we are striving to remember a lost name or fact, we think of as many 'cues' as possible, so that by their joint action they may recall what no one of them can recall alone. The sight of a dead prey will often not stimulate a beast to pursuit, but if the sight of movement be added to that of form, pursuit occurs. "Brücke noticed that his brainless hen, which made no attempt to peck at the grain under her very eyes, began pecking if the grain were thrown on the ground with force, so as to produce a rattling sound."[5] "Dr. Allen Thomson . . . hatched out some chickens on a carpet, where he kept them for several days. They showed no inclination to scrape, . . . but when Dr. Thomson sprinkled a little gravel on the carpet, . . . the chickens immediately began their scraping movements."[6] A strange person, and darkness, are both of them stimuli to fear and mistrust in dogs (and for the matter of that, in men). Neither circumstance alone may awaken outward manifestations, but together, i.e., when the strange man is met in the dark, the dog will be excited to violent defiance.[7] Street-hawkers well know the efficacy of summation, for

[4] *Archiv für die gesammte Physiologie*, Bd. 26, p. 176 (1881). Exner thinks (*ibid.*, Bd. 28, p. 497 (1882)) that the summation here occurs in the spinal cord. It makes no difference where this particular summation occurs, so far as the general philosophy of summation goes.

[5] G. H. Lewes: *Physical Basis of Mind*, p. 478, where many similar examples are given, 487–9.

[6] Romanes: *Mental Evolution in Animals*, p. 163.

[7] See a similar instance in Mach: *Beiträge zur Analyse der Empfindungen*, p. 36, a

they arrange themselves in a line upon the sidewalk, and the passer often buys from the last one of them, through the effect of the reiterated solicitation, what he refused to buy from the first in the row. Aphasia shows many examples of summation. A patient who cannot name an object simply shown him, will name it if he touches as well as sees it, etc.

Instances of summation might be multiplied indefinitely, but it is hardly worth while to forestall subsequent chapters. Those on Instinct, the Stream of Thought, Attention, Discrimination, Association, Memory, Æsthetics, and Will, will contain numerous exemplifications of the reach of the principle in the purely psychological field.

REACTION-TIME

One of the lines of experimental investigation most diligently followed of late years is that of the ascertainment of the *time occupied by nervous events.* Helmholtz led off by discovering the rapidity of the current in the sciatic nerve of the frog. But the methods he used were soon applied to the sensory nerves and the centres, and the results caused much popular scientific admiration when described as measurements of the 'velocity of thought.' The phrase 'quick as thought' had from time immemorial signified all that was wonderful and elusive of determination in the line of speed; and the way in which Science laid her doomful hand upon this mystery reminded people of the day when Franklin first '*eripuit cœlo fulmen,*' foreshadowing the reign of a newer and colder race of gods. We shall take up the various operations measured, each in the chapter to which it more naturally pertains. I may say, however, immediately, that the phrase 'velocity of *thought*' is misleading, for it is by no means clear in any of the cases what particular act of thought occurs during the time which is measured. 'Velocity of nerve-action' is liable to the same criticism, for in most cases we do not know what particular nerve-processes occur. What the times in question

sparrow being the animal. My young children are afraid of their own pug-dog, if he enters their room after they are in bed and the lights are out. Compare this statement also: "The first question to a peasant proves seldom more than a flapper to rouse the torpid adjustments of his ears. The invariable answer of a Scottish peasant is, 'What's your will?'—that of the English, a vacant stare. A second and even a third question may be required to elicit an answer." (R. Fowler: *Some Observations on the Mental State of the Blind, and Deaf, and Dumb* (Salisbury, 1843), p. 14.)

really represent is the total duration of certain *reactions upon stimuli*. Certain of the conditions of the reaction are prepared beforehand; they consist in the assumption of those motor and sensory tensions which we name the expectant state. Just what happens during the actual time occupied by the reaction (in other words, just what is added to the pre-existent tensions to produce the actual discharge) is not made out at present, either from the neural or from the mental point of view.

The method is essentially the same in all these investigations. A signal of some sort is communicated to the subject, and at the same instant records itself on a time-registering apparatus. The subject then makes a muscular movement of some sort, which is the 'reaction,' and which also records itself automatically. The time found to have elapsed between the two records is the total time of that observation. The time-registering instruments are of various types.

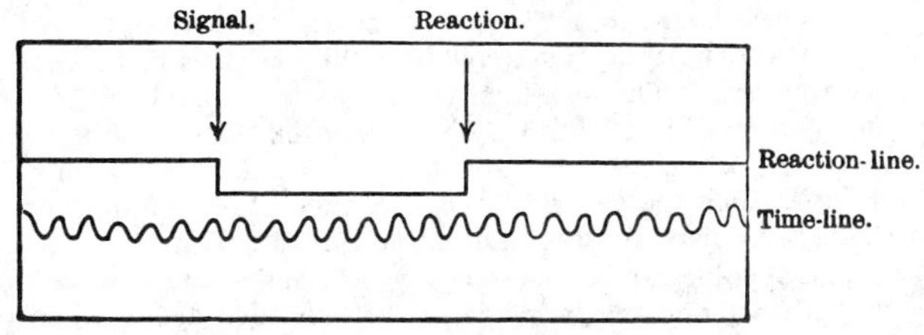

FIG. 21a.

One type is that of the revolving drum covered with smoked paper, on which one electric pen traces a line which the signal breaks and the 'reaction' draws again; whilst another electric pen (connected with a pendulum or a rod of metal vibrating at a known rate) traces alongside of the former line a 'time-line' of which each undulation or link stands for a certain fraction of a second, and against which the break in the reaction-line can be measured. Compare Fig. 21a, where the line is broken by the signal at the first arrow, and continued again by the reaction at the second. Ludwig's Kymograph, Marey's Chronograph are good examples of this type of instrument.

Another type of instrument is represented by the stop-watch, of which the most perfect form is Hipp's Chronoscope. The hand on the dial measures intervals as short as $1/1000$ of a second. The signal (by an appropriate electric connection) starts it; the reaction stops it; and by reading off its initial and terminal positions we have immediately and with no farther trouble the time we seek. A still simpler instrument, though one not very satisfactory in its working, is the 'psychodometer' of Exner and Obersteiner, of which I picture a modification devised by my colleague Professor H. P. Bowditch, which works very well.

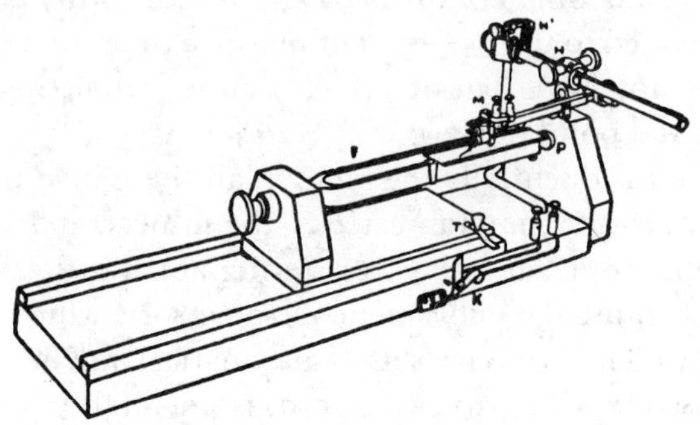

FIG. 22.—Bowditch's Reaction-timer. *F*, tuning-fork carrying a little plate which holds the paper on which the electric pen *M* makes the tracing, and sliding in grooves on the base-board. *P*, a plug which spreads the prongs of the fork apart when it is pushed forward to its extreme limit, and releases them when it is drawn back to a certain point. The fork then vibrates, and, its backward movement continuing, an undulating line is drawn on the smoked paper by the pen. At *T* is a tongue fixed to the carriage of the fork, and at *K* an electric key which the tongue opens and with which the electrical pen is connected. At the instant of opening, the pen changes its place and the undulating line is drawn at a different level on the paper. The opening can be made to serve as a signal to the reacter in a variety of ways, and his reaction can be made to close the pen again, when the line returns to its first level. The reaction time = the number of undulations traced at the second level.

The manner in which the signal and reaction are connected with the chronographic apparatus varies indefinitely in different experiments. Every new problem requires some new electric or mechanical disposition of apparatus.[8]

The least complicated time-measurement is that known as *simple reaction-time,* in which there is but one possible signal and one possible movement, and both are known in advance. The movement is generally the closing of an electric key with the hand. The foot, the jaw, the lips, even the eyelid, have been in turn made organs of reaction, and the apparatus has been modified accord-

[8] The reader will find a great deal about chronographic apparatus in J. Marey: *La Méthode graphique*, pt. II, chap. II. One can make pretty fair measurements with no other instrument than a watch, by making a large number of reactions, each serving as a signal for the following one, and dividing the total time they take by their number. Dr. O. W. Holmes first suggested this method, which has been ingeniously elaborated and applied by Professor Jastrow. See *Science* for September 10, 1886.

ingly.[9] The time usually elapsing between stimulus and movement lies between one and three tenths of a second, varying according to circumstances which will be mentioned anon.

The subject of experiment, whenever the reactions are short and regular, is in a state of extreme tension, and feels, when the signal comes, as if *it* started the reaction, by a sort of fatality, and as if no psychic process of perception or volition had a chance to intervene. The whole succession is so rapid that perception seems to be retrospective, and the time-order of events to be read off in memory rather than known at the moment. This at least is my own personal experience in the matter, and with it I find others to agree. The question is, What happens inside of us, either in brain or mind? and to answer that we must analyze just what processes the reaction involves. It is evident that some time is lost in each of the following stages:

1. The stimulus excites the peripheral sense-organ adequately for a current to pass into the sensory nerve;
2. The sensory nerve is traversed;
3. The transformation (or reflection) of the sensory into a motor current occurs in the centres;
4. The spinal cord and motor nerve are traversed;
5. The motor current excites the muscle to the contracting point.

Time is also lost, of course, outside the muscle, in the joints, skin, etc., and between the parts of the apparatus; and when the stimulus which serves as signal is applied to the skin of the trunk or limbs, time is lost in the sensorial conduction through the spinal cord.

The stage marked 3 is the only one that interests us here. The other stages answer to purely physiological processes, but stage 3 is psycho-physical; that is, it is a higher-central process, and has probably some sort of consciousness accompanying it. What sort?

Wundt has little difficulty in deciding that it is consciousness of a quite elaborate kind. He distinguishes between two stages in the conscious reception of an impression, calling one *perception*, and the other *apperception*, and likening the one to the mere entrance of an object into the periphery of the field of vision, and the other to its coming to occupy the focus or point of view. *Inattentive awareness* of an object, and *attention* to it, are, it seems to me, equivalents for perception and apperception, as Wundt uses the words. To these two forms of awareness of the impression Wundt

[9] See, for a few modifications, Cattell: *Mind*, XI, 220 ff.

adds the conscious volition to react, gives to the trio the name of 'psycho-physical' processes, and assumes that they actually follow upon each other in the succession in which they have been named.[10] So at least I understand him. The simplest way to determine the time taken up by this psycho-physical stage No. 3 would be to determine separately the duration of the several purely physical processes, 1, 2, 4, and 5, and to subtract them from the total reaction-time. Such attempts have been made.[11] But the data for calculation are too inaccurate for use, and, as Wundt himself admits,[12] the precise duration of stage 3 must at present be left enveloped with that of the other processes, in the total reaction-time.

My own belief is that no such succession of conscious feelings as Wundt describes takes place during stage 3. It is a process of central excitement and discharge, with which doubtless some feeling co-exists, but *what* feeling we cannot tell, because it is so fugitive and so immediately eclipsed by the more substantive and enduring memory of the impression as it came in, and of the executed movement of response. Feeling of the impression, attention to it, thought of the reaction, volition to react, *would*, undoubtedly, all be links of the process *under other conditions*,[13] and would lead to the same reaction—after an indefinitely longer time. But these other conditions are not those of the experiments we are discussing; and it is mythological psychology (of which we shall see many later examples) to conclude that because two mental processes lead to the same result they must be similar in their inward subjective constitution. The feeling of stage 3 is certainly no articulate perception. It can be nothing but the mere sense of a reflex discharge. *The re-*

10 *Physiologische Psychologie*, II, 221–2. Cf. also the first edition, 728–9. I must confess to finding all Wundt's utterances about 'apperception' both vacillating and obscure. I see no use whatever for the word, as he employs it, in Psychology. Attention, perception, conception, volition, are its ample equivalents. Why we should need a single word to denote all these things by turns, Wundt fails to make clear. Consult, however, his pupil Staude's article, "Der Begriff der Apperception," etc., in Wundt's periodical *Philosophische Studien*, I, 149, which may be supposed official. For a minute criticism of Wundt's 'apperception,' see Marty: *Vierteljahrsschrift für wissenschaftliche Philosophie*, x, 346.

11 By Exner, for example, Pflüger's *Archiv*, VII, 628 ff.

12 P. 222. Cf. also Richet: *Revue Philosophique*, VI, 395–6.

13 For instance, if, on the previous day, one had resolved to act on a signal when it should come, and it now came whilst we were engaged in other things, and reminded us of the resolve.

action whose time is measured is, in short, *a reflex action pure and simple, and not a psychic act.* A foregoing psychic condition is, it is true, a prerequisite for this reflex action. The preparation of the attention and volition; the expectation of the signal and the readiness of the hand to move, the instant it shall come; the nervous tension in which the subject waits, are all conditions of the formation in him for the time being of a new path or arc of reflex discharge. The tract from the sense-organ which receives the stimulus, into the motor centre which discharges the reaction, is already tingling with premonitory innervation, is raised to such a pitch of heightened irritability by the expectant attention, that the signal is instantaneously sufficient to cause the overflow.[14] No other tract of the nervous system is, at the moment, in this hair-trigger condition. The consequence is that one sometimes responds to a *wrong* signal, especially if it be an impression of the same *kind* with the signal we expect.[15] But if by chance we are tired, or the signal is unexpectedly weak, and we do not react instantly, but only after an express perception that the signal has come, and an express volition, the time becomes quite disproportionately long (a second or more, according to Exner[16]), and we feel that the process is in nature altogether different.

In fact, the reaction-time experiments are a case to which we can immediately apply what we have just learned about the summation of stimuli. 'Expectant attention' is but the subjective name for what objectively is a partial stimulation of a certain pathway, the pathway from the 'centre' for the signal to that for the discharge. In Chapter XI we shall see that all attention involves excitement from within of the tract concerned in feeling the objects to which attention is given. The tract here is the excito-motor arc about to be traversed. The signal is but the spark from without which touches off a train already laid. The performance, under these conditions, exactly resembles any reflex action. The only difference is

[14] "I need hardly mention that success in these experiments depends in a high degree on our concentration of attention. If inattentive, one gets very discrepant figures. . . . This concentration of the attention is in the highest degree exhausting. After some experiments in which I was concerned to get results as uniform as possible, I was covered with perspiration and excessively fatigued although I had sat quietly in my chair all the while." (Exner: *loc. cit.*, VII, 618.)

[15] Wundt: *Physiologische Psychologie*, II, 226.

[16] Pflüger's *Archiv*, VII, 616.

that whilst, in the ordinarily so-called reflex acts, the reflex arc is a permanent result of organic growth, it is here a transient result of previous cerebral conditions.[17]

I am happy to say that since the preceding paragraphs (and the notes thereto appertaining) were written, Wundt has himself become converted to the view which I defend. He now admits that in the shortest reactions "there is neither apperception nor will, but that they are merely *brain-reflexes due to practice*."[18] The means of his conversion are certain experiments performed in his laboratory

[17] In short, what M. Delbœuf calls an '*organe adventice*.' The reaction-time, moreover, is quite compatible with the reaction itself being of a reflex order. Some reflexes (sneezing, e.g.) are very slow. The only time-measurement of a reflex act in the human subject with which I am acquainted is Exner's measurement of winking (in Pflüger's *Archiv für die gesammte Physiologie*, Bd. VIII, p. 526, 1874). He found that when the stimulus was a flash of light it took the wink 0.2168 sec. to occur. A strong electric shock to the cornea shortened the time to 0.0578 sec. The ordinary 'reaction-time' is midway between these values. Exner 'reduces' his times by eliminating the physiological process of conduction. His 'reduced minimum winking-time' is then 0.0471 (*ibid.*, 531), whilst his reduced reaction-time is 0.0828 (*ibid.*, VII, 637). These figures have really no scientific value beyond that of showing, according to Exner's own belief (VIII, 531), that reaction-time and reflex-time measure processes of essentially the same order. His description, moreover, of the process is an excellent description of a reflex act. "Everyone," says he, "who makes reaction-time experiments for the first time is surprised to find how little he is master of his own movements, so soon as it becomes a question of executing them with a maximum of speed. Not only does their energy lie, as it were, outside the field of choice, but even the time in which the movement occurs depends only partly upon ourselves. We jerk our arm, and we can afterwards tell with astonishing precision whether we have jerked it quicker or slower than another time, although we have no power to jerk it exactly at the wished-for moment."—Wundt himself admits that when we await a strong signal with tense preparation there is no consciousness of any duality of 'apperception' and motor response; the two are continuous (*Physiologische Psychologie*, II, 226).—Mr. Cattell's view is identical with the one I defend. "I think," he says, "that if the processes of perception and willing are present at all they are very rudimentary. . . . The subject by a voluntary effort [before the signal comes], puts the lines of communication between the centre for" the stimulus "and the centre for the co-ordination of motions . . . in a state of unstable equilibrium. When therefore a nervous impulse reaches the" former centre, "it causes brain-changes in two directions; an impulse moves along to the cortex and calls forth there a perception corresponding to the stimulus, while at the same time an impulse follows a line of small resistance to the centre for the co-ordination of motions, and the proper nervous impulse, already prepared and waiting for the signal, is sent from the centre to the muscle of the hand. When the reaction has often been made the entire cerebral process becomes automatic, the impulse of itself takes the well-travelled way to the motor centre, and releases the motor impulse." (*Mind*, XI, 232–3.)—Finally, Prof. Lipps has, in his elaborate way (*Grundtatsachen des Seelenlebens*, 179–188), made mince-meat of the view that stage 3 involves either conscious perception or conscious will.

[18] *Physiologische Psychologie*, 3d edition (1887), vol. II, p. 266.

by Herr L. Lange,[19] who was led to distinguish between two ways of setting the attention in reacting on a signal, and who found that they gave very different time-results. In the '*extreme sensorial*' way, as Lange calls it, of reacting, one keeps one's mind as intent as possible upon the expected signal, and 'purposely avoids'[20] thinking of the movement to be executed; in the '*extreme muscular*' way one 'does not think at all'[21] of the signal, but stands as ready as possible for the movement. The muscular reactions are much shorter than the sensorial ones, the average difference being in the neighborhood of a tenth of a second. Wundt accordingly calls them 'shortened reactions' and, with Lange, admits them to be mere reflexes; whilst the sensorial reactions he calls 'complete,' and holds to his original conception as far as they are concerned. The facts, however, do not seem to me to warrant even this amount of fidelity to the original Wundtian position. When we begin to react in the 'extreme sensorial' way, Lange says that we get times so very long that they must be rejected from the count as non-typical. "Only after the reacter has succeeded by repeated and conscientious practice in bringing about an extremely precise co-ordination of his voluntary impulse with his sense-impression do we get times which can be regarded as typical sensorial reaction-times."[22] Now it seems to me that these excessive and 'untypical' times are probably the real 'complete times,' the only ones in which distinct processes of actual perception and volition occur (see above, pp. 95–96). The typical sensorial time which is attained by practice is probably another sort of reflex, less perfect than the reflexes prepared by straining one's attention towards the movement.[23] The times are much more variable in the sensorial way than in the muscular. The several muscular reactions differ little from each other. Only in them does the phenomenon occur of reacting on a false signal, or of reacting before the signal. Times intermediate between these two types occur according as the attention fails to turn itself exclusively to one of the extremes. It is obvious that Herr Lange's distinction between the two types of reaction is a highly important one, and that the 'extreme muscular method,' giving both the shortest times and the most constant

19 *Philosophische Studien*, vol. IV, p. 479 (1888).

20 *Loc. cit.*, p. 488.

21 *Loc. cit.*, p. 487.

22 *Loc. cit.*, p. 489.

23 Lange has an interesting hypothesis as to the brain-process concerned in the latter, for which I can only refer to his essay.

ones, ought to be aimed at in all comparative investigations. Herr Lange's own muscular time averaged 0″.123; his sensorial time, 0″.230.

These reaction-time experiments are then in no sense measurements of the swiftness of *thought*. Only when we complicate them is there a chance for anything like an intellectual operation to occur. They may be complicated in various ways. The reaction may be withheld until the signal has consciously awakened a distinct idea (Wundt's discrimination-time, association-time) and then performed. Or there may be a variety of possible signals, each with a different reaction assigned to it, and the reacter may be uncertain which one he is about to receive. The reaction would then hardly seem to occur without a preliminary recognition and choice. We shall see, however, in the appropriate chapters, that the discrimination and choice involved in such a reaction are widely different from the intellectual operations of which we are ordinarily conscious under those names. Meanwhile the simple reaction-time remains as the starting point of all these superinduced complications. It is the fundamental physiological constant in all time-measurements. As such, its own variations have an interest, and must be briefly passed in review.[24]

The reaction-time varies with the *individual* and his *age*. An individual may have it particularly long in respect of signals of one sense (Buccola, p. 147), but not of others. Old and uncultivated people have it long (nearly a second, in an old pauper observed by Exner, Pflüger's *Archiv*, VII, 612–4). Children have it long (half a second, Herzen in Buccola, p. 152).

Practice shortens it to a quantity which is for each individual a minimum beyond which no farther reduction can be made. The aforesaid old pauper's time was, after much practice, reduced to 0.1866 sec. (*loc. cit.*, p. 626).

Fatigue lengthens it.

Concentration of attention shortens it. Details will be given in the chapter on Attention.

The *nature of the signal* makes it vary.[25] Wundt writes:

[24] The reader who wishes to know more about the matter will find a most faithful compilation of all that has been done, together with much original matter, in G. Buccola's *Legge del tempo*, etc. See also chapter XVI of Wundt's *Physiologische Psychologie*; Exner in Hermann's *Handbuch*, Bd. 2. Thl. II, pp. 252–280; also Ribot's *German Psychology of To-day*, chap. VIII.

[25] The nature of the movement also seems to make it vary. Mr. B. I. Gilman and

"I found that the reaction-time for impressions on the skin with electric stimulus is less than for true touch-sensations, as the following averages show:

	Average	Average Variation
Sound	0.167 sec.	0.0221 sec.
Light	0.222 "	0.0219 "
Electric skin-sensation	0.201 "	0.0115 "
Touch-sensations	0.213 "	0.0134 "

"I here bring together the averages which have been obtained by some other observers:

	Hirsch	Hankel	Exner
Sound	0.149	0.1505	0.1360
Light	0.200	0.2246	0.1506
Skin-sensation	0.182	0.1546	0.1337"[26]

Thermic reactions have been lately measured by A. Goldscheider and by Vintschgau (1887), who find them slower than reactions from touch. That from heat especially is very slow, more so than from cold, the differences (according to Goldscheider) depending on the nerve-terminations in the skin.

Gustatory reactions were measured by Vintschgau. They differed according to the substances used, running up to half a second as a maximum when identification took place. The mere perception of the presence of the substance on the tongue varied from 0".159 to 0".219 (Pflüger's *Archiv,* XIV, 529).

Olfactory reactions have been studied by Vintschgau, Buccola, and Beaunis. They are slow, averaging about half a second (cf. Beaunis, *Recherches expérimentales sur l'activité cérébrale,* 1884, p. 49 ff.).

It will be observed that *sound* is more promptly reacted on than either *sight* or *touch. Taste* and *smell* are slower than either. One individual, who reacted to touch upon the tip of the tongue in

---

I reacted to the same signal by simply raising our hand, and again by carrying our hand towards our back. The moment registered was always that at which the hand broke an electric contact in *starting* to move. But it started one or two hundredths of a second later when the more extensive movement was the one to be made. Orschansky, on the other hand, experimenting on contractions of the masseter muscle, found (*Archiv für (Anatomie und) Physiologie,* 1889, p. 187) that the greater the amplitude of contraction intended, the shorter grew the time of reaction. He explains this by the fact that a more ample contraction makes a greater *appeal to the attention,* and that this shortens the times.

[26] *Physiologische Psychologie,* II, 223.

0″.125, took 0″.993 to react upon the taste of quinine applied to the same spot. In another, upon the base of the tongue, the reaction to touch being 0″.141, that to sugar was 0″.552 (Vintschgau, quoted by Buccola, p. 103). Buccola found the reaction to odors to vary from 0″.234 to 0″.681, according to the perfume used and the individual.

The *intensity of the signal* makes a difference. The intenser the stimulus the shorter the time. Herzen (*Grundlinien einer allgemeinen Psychophysiologie*, p. 101) compared the reaction from a *corn* on the toe with that from the skin of the hand of the same subject. The two places were stimulated simultaneously, and the subject tried to react simultaneously with both hand and foot, but the foot always went quickest. When the sound skin of the foot was touched instead of the corn, it was the hand which always reacted first. Wundt tries to show that when the signal is made barely perceptible, the time is probably the same in all the senses, namely, about 0″.332 (*Physiologische Psychologie*, 2d ed., II, 224).

Where the signal is of touch, the place to which it is applied makes a difference in the resultant reaction-time. G. S. Hall and v. Kries found (*Archiv für (Anatomie und) Physiologie*, 1879 [supplement]) that when the finger-tip was the place the reaction was shorter than when the middle of the upper arm was used, in spite of the greater length of nerve-trunk to be traversed in the latter case. This discovery invalidates the measurements of the rapidity of transmission of the current in human nerves, for they are all based on the method of comparing reaction-times from places near the root and near the extremity of a limb. The same observers found that signals seen by the periphery of the retina gave longer times than the same signals seen by direct vision.

The *season* makes a difference, the time being some hundredths of a second shorter on cold winter days (Vintschgau *apud* Exner, Hermann's *Handbuch*, p. 270).

Intoxicants alter the time. *Coffee* and *tea* appear to shorten it. Small doses of *wine* and *alcohol* first shorten and then lengthen it; but the shortening stage tends to disappear if a large dose be given immediately. This, at least, is the report of two German observers. Dr. J. W. Warren, whose observations are more thorough than any previous ones, could find no very decided effects from ordinary doses (*Journal of Physiology*, VIII, 311). *Morphia* lengthens the time. *Amyl-nitrite* lengthens it, but after the inhalation it may fall to less than the normal. Ether and chloroform lengthen it (for authorities, etc., see Buccola, p. 189).

Certain *diseased states* naturally lengthen the time.

The *hypnotic trance* has no constant effect, sometimes shortening and sometimes lengthening it (Hall, *Mind,* VIII, 170; James, *Proceedings of the American Society for Psychical Research,* 246).

The time taken to *inhibit* a movement (e.g., to cease contraction of jaw-muscles) seems to be about the same as to produce one (Gad, *Archiv für (Anatomie und) Physiologie,* 1887, 368; Orschansky, *ibid.,* 1889, 185).

An immense amount of work has been done on reaction-time, of which I have cited but a small part. It is a sort of work which appeals particularly to patient and exact minds, and they have not failed to profit by the opportunity.

CEREBRAL BLOOD-SUPPLY

The next point to occupy our attention is the *changes of circulation which accompany cerebral activity.*

All parts of the cortex, when electrically excited, produce alterations both of respiration and circulation. The blood-pressure rises, as a rule, all over the body, no matter where the cortical irritation is applied, though the motor zone is the most sensitive region for the purpose. Elsewhere the current must be strong enough for an epileptic attack to be produced.[27] Slowing and quickening of the heart are also observed, and are independent of the vaso-constrictive phenomenon. Mosso, using his ingenious 'plethysmograph' as an indicator, discovered that the blood-supply to the arms diminished during intellectual activity, and found furthermore that the arterial tension (as shown by the sphygmograph) was increased in these members (see Fig. 23). So slight an emotion as that produced by

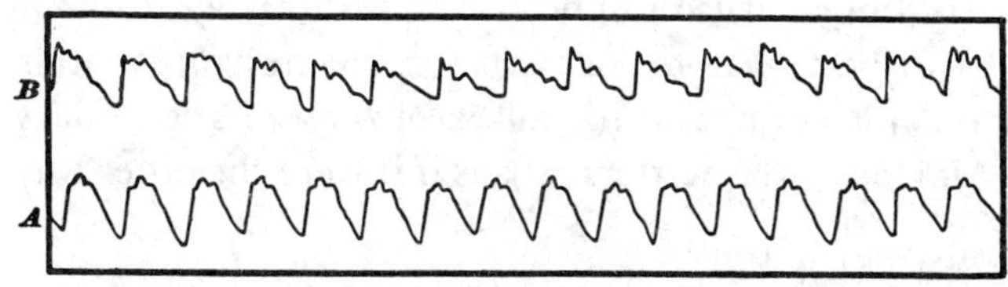

FIG. 23.—Sphygmographic pulse-tracing. *A,* during intellectual repose; *B,* during intellectual activity. (Mosso.)

27 François-Franck: *Fonctions motrices,* Leçon XXII.

the entrance of Professor Ludwig into the laboratory was instantly followed by a shrinkage of the arms.[28] The brain itself is an excessively vascular organ, a sponge full of blood, in fact; and another of Mosso's inventions showed that when less blood went to the legs, more went to the head. The subject to be observed lay on a delicately balanced table which could tip downwards either at the head or at the foot if the weight of either end were increased. The moment emotional or intellectual activity began in the subject, down went the balance at the head-end, in consequence of the redistribution of blood in his system. But the best proof of the immediate afflux of blood to the brain during mental activity is due to Mosso's observations on three persons whose brain had been laid bare by lesion of the skull. By means of apparatus described in his book,[29] this physiologist was enabled to let the brain-pulse record itself directly by a tracing. The intra-cranial blood-pressure rose immediately whenever the subject was spoken to, or when he began to think actively, as in solving a problem in mental arithmetic. Mosso gives in his work a large number of reproductions of tracings which show the instantaneity of the change of blood-supply, whenever the mental activity was quickened by any cause whatever, intellectual or emotional. He relates of his female subject that one day whilst tracing her brain-pulse he observed a sudden rise with no apparent outer or inner cause. She however confessed to him afterwards that at that moment she had caught sight of a *skull* on top of a piece of furniture in the room, and that this had given her a slight emotion.

The fluctuations of the blood-supply to the brain were independent of respiratory changes,[30] and followed the quickening of mental activity almost immediately. We must suppose a very delicate adjustment whereby the circulation follows the needs of the cerebral activity. Blood very likely may rush to each region of the cortex according as it is most active, but of this we know nothing. I need hardly say that the activity of the nervous matter is the primary phenomenon, and the afflux of blood its secondary consequence. Many popular writers talk as if it were the other way about,

28 *La Paura* (1884), p. 117.

29 *Über den Kreislauf des Blutes im menschlichen Gehirn* (1881), chap. II. The Introduction gives the history of our previous knowledge of the subject.

30 In this conclusion M. Gley (*Archives de Physiologie*, 1881, p. 742) agrees with Professor Mosso. Gley found his pulse rise 1–3 beats, his carotid dilate, and his radial artery contract during hard mental work.

and as if mental activity were due to the afflux of blood. But, as Professor H. N. Martin has well said, "that the belief has no physiological basis whatever; it is even directly opposed to all that we know of cell life."[31] A chronic pathological congestion may, it is true, have secondary consequences, but the primary congestions which we have been considering *follow* the activity of the brain-cells by an adaptive reflex vaso-motor mechanism doubtless as elaborate as that which harmonizes blood-supply with cell-action in any muscle or gland.

Of the changes in the cerebral circulation during sleep, I will speak in the chapter which treats of that subject.

CEREBRAL THERMOMETRY

Brain-activity seems accompanied by a local disengagement of heat. The earliest careful work in this direction was by Dr. J. S. Lombard in 1867. Dr. Lombard's latest results include the records of over 60,000 observations.[32] He noted the changes in delicate thermometers and electric piles placed against the scalp in human beings, and found that any intellectual effort, such as computing, composing, reciting poetry silently or aloud, and especially that emotional excitement such as an anger fit, caused a general rise of temperature, which rarely exceeded a degree Fahrenheit. The rise was in most cases more marked in the middle region of the head than elsewhere. Strange to say, it was greater in reciting poetry silently than in reciting it aloud. Dr. Lombard's explanation is that "in internal recitation an additional portion of energy, which in recitation aloud was converted into nervous and muscular force, now appears as heat."[33] I should suggest rather, if we must have a theory, that the surplus of heat in recitation to one's self is due to inhibitory processes which are absent when we recite aloud. In the chapter on the Will we shall see that the *simple* central process is to *speak* when we think; to think silently involves a check in addition. In 1870 the indefatigable Schiff took up the subject, experimenting on live dogs and chickens, plunging thermo-electric needles into the substance of their brain, to eliminate possible errors from vascular changes in the skin when the thermometers were

31 Address before Medical and Chirurgical Faculty of Maryland, 1879.

32 See his book: *Experimental Researches on the Regional Temperature of the Head* (London, 1879).

33 *Loc. cit.*, p. 195.

placed upon the scalp. After habituation was established, he tested the animals with various sensations, tactile, optic, olfactory, and auditory. He found very regularly an immediate deflection of the galvanometer, indicating an abrupt alteration of the intra-cerebral temperature. When, for instance, he presented an empty roll of paper to the nose of his dog as it lay motionless, there was a small deflection, but when a piece of meat was in the paper the deflection was much greater. Schiff concluded from these and other experiments that sensorial activity heats the brain-tissue, but he did not try to localize the increment of heat beyond finding that it was in both hemispheres, whatever might be the sensation applied.[34] Dr. R. W. Amidon in 1880 made a farther step forward, in localizing the heat produced by voluntary muscular contractions. Applying a number of delicate surface-thermometers simultaneously against the scalp, he found that when different muscles of the body were made to contract vigorously for ten minutes or more, different regions of the scalp rose in temperature, that the regions were well focalized, and that the rise of temperature was often considerably over a Fahrenheit degree. As a result of his investigations he gives a diagram in which numbered regions represent the centres of highest temperature for the various special movements which were investigated. To a large extent they correspond to the centres for the same movements assigned by Ferrier and others on other grounds; only they cover more of the skull.[35]

Phosphorus and Thought

Chemical action must of course accompany brain-activity. But little definite is known of its exact nature. Cholesterin and creatin are both excrementitious products, and are both found in the brain. The subject belongs to chemistry rather than to psychology, and I only mention it here for the sake of saying a word about a wide-spread popular error about brain-activity and phosphorus. '*Ohne Phosphor, kein Gedanke,*' was a noted war-cry of the 'materialists' during the excitement on that subject which filled Germany in the '60s. The brain, like every other organ of the body, contains phosphorus, and a score of other chemicals besides. Why the phosphorus should be picked out as its essence, no one knows. It would

34 The most convenient account of Schiff's experiments is by Prof. Herzen, in the *Revue Philosophique*, vol. III, p. 36.

35 *A New Study of Cerebral Cortical Localization* (N. Y., Putnam, 1880), pp. 48–53.

be equally true to say 'Ohne Wasser kein Gedanke,' or 'Ohne Kochsalz kein Gedanke'; for thought would stop as quickly if the brain should dry up or lose its NaCl as if it lost its phosphorus. In America the phosphorus-delusion has twined itself round a saying quoted (rightly or wrongly) from Professor L. Agassiz, to the effect that fishermen are more intelligent than farmers because they eat so much fish, which contains so much phosphorus. All the alleged facts may be doubted.

The only straight way to ascertain the importance of phosphorus to thought would be to find whether more is excreted by the brain during mental activity than during rest. Unfortunately we cannot do this directly, but can only gauge the amount of PO_5 in the urine, which represents other organs as well as the brain, and this procedure, as Dr. Edes says, is like measuring the rise of water at the mouth of the Mississippi to tell where there has been a thunder-storm in Minnesota.[36] It has been adopted, however, by a variety of observers, some of whom found the phosphates in the urine diminished, whilst others found them increased, by intellectual work. On the whole, it is impossible to trace any constant relation. In maniacal excitement less phosphorus than usual seems to be excreted. More is excreted during sleep. There are differences between the alkaline and earthy phosphates into which I will not enter, as my only aim is to show that the popular way of looking at the matter has no exact foundation.[37] The fact that phosphorus-preparations may do good in nervous exhaustion proves nothing as to the part played by phosphorus in mental activity. Like iron, arsenic, and other remedies it is a stimulant or tonic, of whose intimate workings in the system we know absolutely nothing, and which moreover does good in an extremely small number of the cases in which it is prescribed.

The phosphorus-philosophers have often compared thought to a secretion. "The brain secretes thought, as the kidneys secrete urine, or as the liver secretes bile," are phrases which one sometimes hears. The lame analogy need hardly be pointed out. The materials which the brain *pours into the blood* (cholesterin, creatin, xanthin, or whatever they may be) are the analogues of the urine and the bile,

36 *Archives of Medicine*, vol. x, No. 1 (1883).

37 Without multiplying references, I will simply cite Mendel (*Archiv für Psychiatrie*, vol. III, 1872); Mairet (*Archives de Neurologie*, vol. IX, 1885); and Beaunis (*Recherches expérimentales sur l'activité cérébrale*, 1884). Richet gives a partial bibliography in the *Revue Scientifique*, vol. 38, p. 788 (1886).

being in fact real material excreta. As far as these matters go, the brain is a ductless gland. But we know of nothing connected with liver- and kidney-activity which can be in the remotest degree compared with the stream of thought that accompanies the brain's material secretions.

There remains another feature of general brain-physiology, and indeed for psychological purposes the most important feature of all. I refer to the aptitude of the brain for acquiring *habits*. But I will treat of that in a chapter by itself.

Chapter IV[*]

Habit

When we look at living creatures from an outward point of view, one of the first things that strike us is that they are bundles of habits. In wild animals, the usual round of daily behavior seems a necessity implanted at birth; in animals domesticated, and especially in man, it seems, to a great extent, to be the result of education. The habits to which there is an innate tendency are called instincts; some of those due to education would by most persons be called acts of reason. It thus appears that habit covers a very large part of life, and that one engaged in studying the objective manifestations of mind is bound at the very outset to define clearly just what its limits are.

The moment one tries to define what habit is, one is led to the fundamental properties of matter. The laws of Nature are nothing but the immutable habits which the different elementary sorts of matter follow in their actions and reactions upon each other. In the organic world, however, the habits are more variable than this. Even instincts vary from one individual to another of a kind; and are modified in the same individual, as we shall later see, to suit the exigencies of the case. The habits of an elementary particle of matter cannot change (on the principles of the atomistic philosophy), because the particle is itself an unchangeable thing; but those of a compound mass of matter can change, because they are in the

* This chapter has already appeared in the *Popular Science Monthly* for February 1887.

last instance due to the structure of the compound, and either outward forces or inward tensions can, from one hour to another, turn that structure into something different from what it was. That is, they can do so if the body be plastic enough to maintain its integrity, and be not disrupted when its structure yields. The change of structure here spoken of need not involve the outward shape; it may be invisible and molecular, as when a bar of iron becomes magnetic or crystalline through the action of certain outward causes, or India-rubber becomes friable, or plaster 'sets.' All these changes are rather slow; the material in question opposes a certain resistance to the modifying cause, which it takes time to overcome, but the gradual yielding whereof often saves the material from being disintegrated altogether. When the structure has yielded, the same inertia becomes a condition of its comparative permanence in the new form, and of the new habits the body then manifests. *Plasticity*, then, in the wide sense of the word, means the possession of a structure weak enough to yield to an influence, but strong enough not to yield all at once. Each relatively stable phase of equilibrium in such a structure is marked by what we may call a new set of habits. Organic matter, especially nervous tissue, seems endowed with a very extraordinary degree of plasticity of this sort; so that we may without hesitation lay down as our first proposition the following, that *the phenomena of habit in living beings are due to the plasticity*[1] *of the organic materials of which their bodies are composed.*

But the philosophy of habit is thus, in the first instance, a chapter in physics rather than in physiology or psychology. That it is at bottom a physical principle is admitted by all good recent writers on the subject. They call attention to analogues of acquired habits exhibited by dead matter. Thus, M. Léon Dumont, whose essay on habit is perhaps the most philosophical account yet published, writes:

"Everyone knows how a garment, after having been worn a certain time, clings to the shape of the body better than when it was new; there has been a change in the tissue, and this change is a new habit of cohesion. A lock works better after being used some time; at the outset more force was required to overcome certain roughnesses in the mechanism. The overcoming of their resistance is a phenomenon of habituation. It costs less trouble to fold a paper when it has been folded al-

[1] In the sense above explained, which applies to inner structure as well as to outer form.

ready. This saving of trouble is due to the essential nature of habit, which brings it about that, to reproduce the effect, a less amount of the outward cause is required. The sounds of a violin improve by use in the hands of an able artist, because the fibres of the wood at last contract habits of vibration conformed to harmonic relations. This is what gives such inestimable value to instruments that have belonged to great masters. Water, in flowing, hollows out for itself a channel, which grows broader and deeper; and, after having ceased to flow, it resumes, when it flows again, the path traced by itself before. Just so the impressions of outer objects fashion for themselves in the nervous system more and more appropriate paths, and these vital phenomena recur under similar excitements from without, when they have been interrupted a certain time."[2]

Not in the nervous system alone. A scar anywhere is a *locus minoris resistentiæ*, more liable to be abraded, inflamed, to suffer pain and cold, than are the neighboring parts. A sprained ankle, a dislocated arm, are in danger of being sprained or dislocated again; joints that have once been attacked by rheumatism or gout, mucous membranes that have been the seat of catarrh, are with each fresh recurrence more prone to a relapse, until often the morbid state chronically substitutes itself for the sound one. And if we ascend to the nervous system, we find how many so-called functional diseases seem to keep themselves going simply because they happen to have once begun; and how the forcible cutting short by medicine of a few attacks is often sufficient to enable the physiological forces to get possession of the field again, and to bring the organs back to functions of health. Epilepsies, neuralgias, convulsive affections of various sorts, insomnias, are so many cases in point. And, to take what are more obviously habits, the success with which a 'weaning' treatment can often be applied to the victims of unhealthy indulgence of passion, or of mere complaining or irascible disposition, shows us how much the morbid manifestations themselves were due to the mere inertia of the nervous organs, when once launched on a false career.

Can we now form a notion of what the inward physical changes may be like, in organs whose habits have thus struck into new paths? In other words, can we say just what mechanical facts the expression 'change of habit' covers when it is applied to a nervous

2 *Revue Philosophique*, I, 323.

system? Certainly we cannot in anything like a minute or definite way. But our usual scientific custom of interpreting hidden molecular events after the analogy of visible massive ones enables us to frame easily an abstract and general scheme of processes which the physical changes in question *may* be like. And when once the possibility of *some* kind of mechanical interpretation is established, Mechanical Science, in her present mood, will not hesitate to set her brand of ownership upon the matter, feeling sure that it is only a question of time when the exact mechanical explanation of the case shall be found out.

If habits are due to the plasticity of materials to outward agents, we can immediately see to what outward influences, if to any, the brain-matter is plastic. Not to mechanical pressures, not to thermal changes, not to any of the forces to which all the other organs of our body are exposed; for Nature has carefully shut up our brain and spinal cord in bony boxes, where no influences of this sort can get at them. She has floated them in fluid so that only the severest shocks can give them a concussion, and blanketed and wrapped them about in an altogether exceptional way. The only impressions that can be made upon them are through the blood, on the one hand, and through the sensory nerve-roots, on the other; and it is to the infinitely attenuated currents that pour in through these latter channels that the hemispherical cortex shows itself to be so peculiarly susceptible. The currents, once in, must find a way out. In getting out they leave their traces in the paths which they take. The only thing they *can* do, in short, is to deepen old paths or to make new ones; and the whole plasticity of the brain sums itself up in two words when we call it an organ in which currents pouring in from the sense-organs make with extreme facility paths which do not easily disappear. For, of course, a simple habit, like every other nervous event—the habit of snuffling, for example, or of putting one's hands into one's pockets, or of biting one's nails—is, mechanically, nothing but a reflex discharge; and its anatomical substratum must be a path in the system. The most complex habits, as we shall presently see more fully, are, from the same point of view, nothing but *concatenated* discharges in the nerve-centres, due to the presence there of systems of reflex paths, so organized as to wake each other up successively—the impression produced by one muscular contraction serving as a stimulus to provoke the next, until a final impression inhibits the process and closes the chain.

The only difficult mechanical problem is to explain the formation *de novo* of a simple reflex or path in a pre-existing nervous system. Here, as in so many other cases, it is only the *premier pas qui coûte*. For the entire nervous system *is* nothing but a system of paths between a sensory *terminus a quo* and a muscular, glandular, or other *terminus ad quem*. A path once traversed by a nerve-current might be expected to follow the law of most of the paths we know, and to be scooped out and made more permeable than before;[3] and this ought to be repeated with each new passage of the current. Whatever obstructions may have kept it at first from being a path should then, little by little, and more and more, be swept out of the way, until at last it might become a natural drainage-channel. This is what happens where either solids or liquids pass over a path; there seems no reason why it should not happen where the thing that passes is a mere wave of rearrangement in matter that does not displace itself, but merely changes chemically or turns itself round in place, or vibrates across the line. The most plausible views of the nerve-current make it out to be the passage of some such wave of rearrangement as this. If only a part of the matter of the path were to 'rearrange' itself, the neighboring parts remaining inert, it is easy to see how their inertness might oppose a friction which it would take many waves of rearrangement to break down and overcome. If we call the path itself the 'organ,' and the wave of rearrangement the 'function,' then it is obviously a case for repeating the celebrated French formula of '*La fonction fait l'organe*.'

So nothing is easier than to imagine how, when a current once has traversed a path, it should traverse it more readily still a second time. But what made it ever traverse it the first time?[4] In answering this question we can only fall back on our general conception of a nervous system as a mass of matter whose parts, constantly kept in states of different tension, are as constantly tending to equalize their states. The equalization between any two points occurs through whatever path may at the moment be most pervious. But, as a given point of the system may belong, actually or potentially,

3 Some paths, to be sure, are banked up by bodies moving through them under too great pressure, and made impervious. These special cases we disregard.

4 We cannot say *the will*, for, though many, perhaps most, human habits were once voluntary actions, no action, as we shall see in a later chapter, can be *primarily* such. While an habitual action may once have been voluntary, the voluntary action must before that, at least once, have been impulsive or reflex. It is this very first occurrence of all that we consider in the text.

to many different paths, and, as the play of nutrition is subject to accidental changes, *blocks* may from time to time occur, and make currents shoot through unwonted lines. Such an unwonted line would be a new-created path, which if traversed repeatedly, would become the beginning of a new reflex arc. All this is vague to the last degree, and amounts to little more than saying that a new path may be formed by the sort of *chances* that in nervous material are likely to occur. But, vague as it is, it is really the last word of our wisdom in the matter.[5]

It must be noticed that the growth of structural modification in living matter may be more rapid than in any lifeless mass, because the incessant nutritive renovation of which the living matter is the seat tends often to corroborate and fix the impressed modification, rather than to counteract it by renewing the original constitution of the tissue that has been impressed. Thus, we notice after exercising our muscles or our brain in a new way, that we can do so no longer at that time; but after a day or two of rest, when we resume the discipline, our increase in skill not seldom surprises us. I have often noticed this in learning a tune; and it has led a German author to say that we learn to swim during the winter and to skate during the summer.

Dr. Carpenter writes:[6]

"It is a matter of universal experience, that every kind of training for special aptitudes, is both far more effective, and leaves a more permanent impress, when exerted on the *growing* organism, than when brought to bear on the adult. The effect of such training is shown in the tendency of the organ to 'grow to' the mode in which it is habitually exercised; as is evidenced by the increased size and power of particular sets of Muscles, and the extraordinary flexibility of Joints, which are acquired by such as have been early exercised in gymnastic performances. . . . There is no part of the Organism of Man, in which the *reconstructive activity* is so great, during the whole period of life, as it is in the ganglionic substance of the Brain. This is indicated by the enor-

[5] Those who desire a more definite formulation may consult J. Fiske's *Outlines of Cosmic Philosophy*, vol. II, pp. 142–146 and Spencer's *Principles of Biology*, sections 302 and 303, and the part entitled "Physical Synthesis" of his *Principles of Psychology*. Mr. Spencer there tries, not only to show how new actions may arise in nervous systems and form new reflex arcs therein, but even how nervous tissue may actually be born by the passage of new waves of isometric transformation through an originally indifferent mass. I cannot help thinking that Mr. Spencer's data, under a great show of precision, conceal vagueness and improbability, and even self-contradiction.

[6] *Principles of Mental Physiology* (1874), pp. 339–345.

mous supply of Blood which it receives . . . . It is, moreover, a fact of great significance, that the Nerve-substance is specially distinguished by its *reparative* power. For whilst injuries of other tissues (such as the Muscular) which are distinguished by the *speciality* of their structure and endowments, are repaired by substance of a lower or less specialized type, those of Nerve-substance are repaired by a complete reproduction of the normal tissue; as is evidenced in the sensibility of the newly-forming skin which is closing over an open wound, or in the recovery of the sensibility of a piece of 'transplanted' skin, which has for a time been rendered insensible by the complete interruption of the continuity of its nerves. The most remarkable example of this reproduction, however, is afforded by the results of M. Brown-Séquard's[7] experiments upon the gradual restoration of the functional activity of the Spinal Cord after its complete division; which takes place in a way that indicates rather a *reproduction* of the whole of the lower part of the Cord and of the Nerves proceeding from it, than a mere *reunion* of divided surfaces. This reproduction is but a special manifestation of the reconstructive change which is *always* taking place in the Nervous system; it being not less obvious to the eye of Reason, that the 'waste' occasioned by its functional activity must be constantly repaired by the production of new tissue, than it is to the eye of Sense, that such reparation supplies an actual *loss* of substance by disease or injury.

"Now in this constant and active reconstruction of the Nervous system, we recognize a most marked conformity to the general plan manifested in the Nutrition of the Organism as a whole. For, in the first place, it is obvious that there is a tendency to the production of a *determinate type* of structure; which type is often not merely that of the Species, but some special modification of it which characterized one or both of the progenitors. But this type is peculiarly liable to modification during the early period of life; in which the functional activity of the Nervous system (and particularly of the Brain) is extraordinarily great, and the reconstructive process proportionally active. And this modifiability expresses itself in the formation of the Mechanism by which those *secondarily-automatic* modes of Movement come to be established, which, in Man, take the place of those that are *congenital* in most of the animals beneath him; and those modes of Sense-perception come to be *acquired*, which are elsewhere clearly *instinctive*. For there can be no reasonable doubt that, in both cases, a Nervous Mechanism is *developed* in the course of this self-education, corresponding with that which the lower animals inherit from their parents. The *plan* of that *rebuilding* process, which is necessary to maintain the integrity of the

7 [See, later, Masius in van Beneden's and van Bambeke's *Archives de Biologie*, vol. 1 (Liège, 1880).—W. J.]

organism generally, and which goes on with peculiar activity in this portion of it, is thus being incessantly modified; and in this manner all that portion of it which ministers to the *external* life of sense and motion that is shared by Man with the Animal kingdom at large, becomes at adult age the expression of the habits which the individual has acquired during the period of growth and development. Of these Habits, some are common to the race generally, whilst others are peculiar to the individual; those of the former kind (such as walking erect) being universally acquired, save where physical inability prevents; whilst for the latter a special training is needed, which is usually the more effective the earlier it is begun,—as is remarkably seen in the case of such feats of dexterity as require a conjoint education of the perceptive and of the motor powers. And when thus developed during the period of growth, so as to have become a part of the Constitution of the adult, the acquired mechanism is thenceforth maintained in the ordinary course of the Nutritive operations, so as to be ready for use when called upon, even after long inaction.

"What is so clearly true of the Nervous Apparatus of Animal Life, can scarcely be otherwise than true of that which ministers to the automatic activity of the Mind. For, as already shown, the study of Psychology has evolved no more certain result, than that there are uniformities of mental action, which are so entirely conformable to those of bodily action, as to indicate their intimate relation to a 'Mechanism of Thought and Feeling,' acting under the like conditions with that of Sense and Motion. The Psychical principles of *association,* indeed, and the Physiological principles of *nutrition,* simply express—the former in terms of Mind, the latter in terms of Brain—the universally admitted fact, that any sequence of mental action which has been frequently repeated, tends to perpetuate itself; so that we find ourselves automatically prompted to *think, feel,* or *do* what we have been before accustomed to think, feel, or do, under like circumstances, without any consciously-formed *purpose,* or anticipation of results. For there is no reason to regard the Cerebrum as an exception to the general principle, that, whilst each part of the organism tends to *form itself* in accordance with the mode in which it is habitually exercised, this tendency will be especially strong in the Nervous apparatus, in virtue of that *incessant regeneration* which is the very condition of its functional activity. It scarcely, indeed, admits of doubt, that every state of ideational consciousness which is either *very strong* or is *habitually repeated,* leaves an organic impression on the Cerebrum; in virtue of which that same state may be reproduced at any future time, in respondence to a suggestion fitted to excite it. . . . The 'strength of early associations' is a fact so universally recognized, that the expression of it has become proverbial; and this precisely accords with the Physiological principle, that, during the period of growth and development, the formative activity of the Brain will be most amenable to directing influences. It is in this way that what is early 'learned by heart' becomes branded-in (as it were) upon the Cerebrum; so that its 'traces' are never lost, even though the conscious memory of it may have completely faded-out. For when the organic modification has been once *fixed* in the growing Brain, it becomes a part of the normal fabric, and is regularly *maintained* by nutritive substitution; so that it may endure to the end of life, like the scar of a wound."

Dr. Carpenter's phrase that *our nervous system grows to the modes in which it has been exercised* expresses the philosophy of habit in a nutshell. We may now trace some of the practical applications of the principle to human life.

The first result of it is that *habit simplifies the movements required to achieve a given result, makes them more accurate and diminishes fatigue.*

"The beginner at the piano not only moves his finger up and down in order to depress the key, he moves the whole hand, the fore-arm and even the entire body, especially moving its least rigid part, the head, as if he would press down the key with that organ too. Often a contraction of the abdominal muscles occurs as well. Principally, however, the impulse is determined to the motion of the hand and of the single finger. This is, in the first place, because the movement of the finger is the movement *thought of*, and, in the second place, because its movement and that of the key are the movements we try to *perceive*, along with the results of the latter on the ear. The more often the process is repeated, the more easily the movement follows, on account of the increase in permeability of the nerves engaged.

"But the more easily the movement occurs, the slighter is the stimulus required to set it up; and the slighter the stimulus is, the more its effect is confined to the fingers alone.

"Thus, an impulse which originally spread its effects over the whole body, or at least over many of its movable parts, is gradually determined to a single definite organ, in which it effects the contraction of a few limited muscles. In this change the thoughts and perceptions which start the impulse acquire more and more intimate causal relations with a particular group of motor nerves.

"To recur to a simile, at least partially apt, imagine the nervous system to represent a drainage-system, inclining, on the whole, towards certain muscles, but with the escape thither somewhat clogged. Then streams of water will, on the whole, tend most to fill the drains that go towards these muscles and to wash out the escape. In case of a sudden 'flushing,' however, the whole system of channels will fill itself, and the water overflow everywhere before it escapes. But a moderate quantity of water invading the system will flow through the proper escape alone.

"Just so with the piano-player. As soon as his impulse, which has gradually learned to confine itself to single muscles, grows extreme, it overflows into larger muscular regions. He usually plays with his fingers, his body being at rest. But no sooner does he get excited than his whole body becomes 'animated,' and he moves his head and trunk, in particular, as if these also were organs with which he meant to belabor the keys."[8]

Man is born with a tendency to do more things than he has ready-made arrangements for in his nerve-centres. Most of the performances of other animals are automatic. But in him the number of them is so enormous, that most of them must be the fruit of painful study. If practice did not make perfect, nor habit economize the expense of nervous and muscular energy, he would therefore be in a sorry plight. As Dr. Maudsley says:[9]

"If an act became no easier after being done several times, if the careful direction of consciousness were necessary to its accomplishment on each occasion, it is evident that the whole activity of a lifetime might be confined to one or two deeds—that no progress could take place in development. A man might be occupied all day in dressing and undressing himself; the attitude of his body would absorb all his attention and energy; the washing of his hands or the fastening of a button would be as difficult to him on each occasion as to the child on its first trial; and he would furthermore be completely exhausted by his exertions. Think of the pains necessary to teach a child to stand, of the many efforts which it must make, and of the ease with which it at last stands, unconscious even of an effort. For while secondary automatic acts are accomplished with comparatively little weariness—in this regard approaching the organic movements, or the original reflex movements—the conscious efforts of the will soon produce exhaustion. A spinal cord without . . . memory would simply be an idiotic spinal cord . . . . It is impossible for an individual to realise how much he owes to its automatic agency until disease has impaired its functions."

[8] G. H. Schneider: *Der menschliche Wille* (1882), pp. 417–419 (freely translated). For the drain-simile, see also Spencer's *Psychology*, part v, chap. VIII.

[9] *The Physiology of Mind*, p. 154.

The next result is that *habit diminishes the conscious attention with which our acts are performed.*

One may state this abstractly thus: If an act require for its execution a chain, *A*, *B*, *C*, *D*, *E*, *F*, *G*, etc., of successive nervous events, then in the first performances of the action the conscious will must choose each of these events from a number of wrong alternatives that tend to present themselves; but habit soon brings it about that each event calls up its own appropriate successor without any alternative offering itself, and without any reference to the conscious will, until at last the whole chain, *A*, *B*, *C*, *D*, *E*, *F*, *G*, rattles itself off as soon as *A* occurs, just as if *A* and the rest of the chain were fused into a continuous stream. When we are learning to walk, to ride, to swim, skate, fence, write, play, or sing, we interrupt ourselves at every step by unnecessary movements and false notes. When we are proficients, on the contrary, the results not only follow with the very minimum of muscular action requisite to bring them forth, they also follow from a single instantaneous 'cue.' The marksman sees the bird, and, before he knows it, he has aimed and shot. A gleam in his adversary's eye, a momentary pressure from his rapier, and the fencer finds that he has instantly made the right parry and return. A glance at the musical hieroglyphics, and the pianist's fingers have rippled through a cataract of notes. And not only is it the right thing at the right time that we thus involuntarily do, but the wrong thing also, if it be an habitual thing. Who is there that has never wound up his watch on taking off his waistcoat in the daytime, or taken his latch-key out on arriving at the door-step of a friend? Very absent-minded persons in going to their bedroom to dress for dinner have been known to take off one garment after another and finally to get into bed, merely because that was the habitual issue of the first few movements when performed at a later hour. The writer well remembers how, on revisiting Paris after ten years' absence, and, finding himself in the street in which for one winter he had attended school, he lost himself in a brown study, from which he was awakened by finding himself upon the stairs which led to the apartment in a house many streets away in which he had lived during that earlier time, and to which his steps from the school had then habitually led. We all of us have a definite routine manner of performing certain daily offices connected with the toilet, with the opening and shutting of familiar cupboards, and the like. Our lower centres know the order of these movements, and show their knowledge by their 'surprise' if the objects are altered so as to oblige the movement to be made in a different way. But our higher thought-centres know hardly anything about the matter. Few men can tell off-hand which sock, shoe, or trousers-leg they put on first. They must first mentally rehearse the act; and even that is often insufficient—the act must be *performed.* So of the questions, Which valve of my double door opens first? Which way does my door swing? etc. I cannot *tell* the answer; yet my *hand* never makes a mistake. No one can *describe* the order in which he brushes his hair or teeth; yet it is likely that the order is a pretty fixed one in all of us.

These results may be expressed as follows:

In action grown habitual, what instigates each new muscular contraction to take place in its appointed order is not a thought or a perception, but the *sensation occasioned by the muscular contraction just finished.* A strictly voluntary act has to be guided by idea, perception, and volition, throughout its whole course. In an habitual action, mere sensation is a sufficient guide, and the upper regions of brain and mind are set comparatively free. A diagram will make the matter clear:

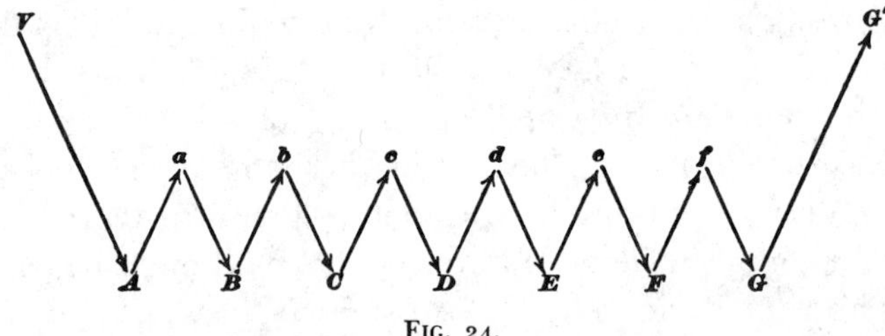

FIG. 24.

Let *A, B, C, D, E, F, G* represent an habitual chain of muscular contractions, and let *a, b, c, d, e, f* stand for the respective sensations which these contractions excite in us when they are successively performed. Such sensations will usually be of the muscles, skin, or joints of the parts moved, but they may also be effects of the movement upon the eye or the ear. Through them, and through them alone, we are made aware whether the contraction has or has not occurred. When the series, *A, B, C, D, E, F, G,* is being learned, each of these sensations becomes the object of a separate perception by the mind. By it we test each movement, to see if it be right before advancing to the next. We hesitate, compare, choose, revoke, reject, etc., by intellectual means; and the order by which the next movement is discharged is an express order from the ideational centres after this deliberation has been gone through.

In habitual action, on the contrary, the only impulse which the centres of idea or perception need send down is the initial impulse, the command to *start*. This is represented in the diagram by *V*; it may be a thought of the first movement or of the last result, or a mere perception of some of the habitual conditions of the chain, the presence, e.g., of the keyboard near the hand. In the present case, no sooner has the conscious thought or volition instigated movement *A*, than *A*, through the sensation *a* of its own occurrence, awakens *B* reflexly; *B* then excites *C* through *b*, and so on till the chain is ended, when the intellect generally takes cognizance of the final result. The process, in fact, resembles the passage of a wave of 'peristaltic' motion down the bowels. The intellectual perception at the end is indicated in the diagram by the effect of *G* being represented, at *G′*, in the ideational centres above the merely sensational line. The sensational impressions, *a*, *b*, *c*, *d*, *e*, *f*, are all supposed to have their seat below the ideational lines. That our ideational centres, if involved at all by *a*, *b*, *c*, *d*, *e*, *f*, are involved in a minimal degree, is shown by the fact that the attention may be wholly absorbed elsewhere. We may say our prayers, or repeat the alphabet, with our attention far away.

"A Musical performer will play a piece which has become familiar by repetition, whilst carrying on an animated conversation, or whilst continuously engrossed by some train of deeply interesting thought; the accustomed sequence of movements being directly prompted by the *sight* of the notes, or by the remembered succession of the *sounds* (if the piece is played from memory), aided in both cases by the guiding sensations derived from the Muscles themselves. But further, a higher degree of the same 'training' (acting on an Organism specially fitted to profit by it) enables an accomplished Pianist to play a difficult piece of music at sight; the movements of the hands and fingers following so immediately upon the sight of the notes, that it seems impossible to believe that any but the very shortest and most direct track can be the channel of the Nervous communication through which they are called forth. The following curious example of the same class of *acquired aptitudes*, which differ from Instincts only in being prompted to action by the Will, is furnished by Robert Houdin:—

"With a view of cultivating the rapidity of visual and tactile Perception, and the precision of respondent Movements, which are necessary for success in every kind of 'prestidigitation,' Houdin early practised the art of juggling with balls in the air; and having, after a month's practice, become thorough master of the art of keeping up *four* balls at once, he placed a book before him, and, while the balls were in the air, accustomed himself to read without hesitation. 'This,' he says, 'will probably seem to my readers very extraordinary; but I shall surprise them still more, when I say that I have just amused myself with repeating this curious experiment. Though thirty years have elapsed since the time I was writing, and though I have scarcely once touched my balls during that period, I can still manage to read with ease while keeping *three* balls up.' "—(*Autobiography*, p. 26.)[10]

We have called *a, b, c, d, e, f,* the antecedents of the successive muscular attractions, by the name of 'sensations.' Some authors seem to deny that they are even this. If not even this, they can only be centripetal nerve-currents, not sufficient to arouse feeling, but sufficient to arouse motor response.[11] It may be at once admitted that they are not distinct *volitions*. The will, if any will be present, limits itself to a *permission* that they exert their motor effects. Dr. Carpenter writes:

"There may still be Metaphysicians who maintain that actions which were originally prompted by the Will with a distinct intention, and which are still entirely under its control, can never cease to be Volitional; and that either an infinitesimally small amount of will is required to sustain them when they have been once set going, or that the will is in a sort of pendulum-like oscillation between the two actions,—the maintenance of the train of *thought*, and the maintenance of the train of *movement*. But if only an infinitesimally small amount of Will is necessary to sustain them, is not this tantamount to saying that they go on by a force of their own? And does not the experience of the *perfect continuity* of our trains of thought during the performance of movements that have become habitual, entirely negative the hypothesis of oscillation? Besides, if such an oscillation existed, there must be *intervals* in which each action goes on *of itself*; so that its essentially automatic character is virtually admitted. The Physiological explanation, that the Mechanism of Locomotion, as of other habitual movements, *grows to* the mode in which it is early exercised, and that it then works automatically under the general control and direction of the Will, can

10 Carpenter's *Mental Physiology* (1874), pp. 217, 218.

11 Von Hartmann devotes a chapter of his *Philosophy of the Unconscious* (English translation, vol. I, p. 72) to proving that they must be both *ideas* and *unconscious*.

scarcely be put down by any assumption of a hypothetical necessity, which rests only on the basis of ignorance of one side of our composite nature."[12]

But if not distinct acts of will, these immediate antecedents of each movement of the chain are at any rate accompanied by consciousness of some kind. They are *sensations* to which we are *usually inattentive*, but which immediately call our attention if they go *wrong*. Schneider's account of these sensations deserves to be quoted. In the act of walking, he says, even when our attention is entirely off,

"we are continuously aware of certain muscular feelings; and we have, moreover, a feeling of certain impulses to keep our equilibrium and to set down one leg after another. It is doubtful whether we could preserve equilibrium if no sensation of our body's attitude were there, and doubtful whether we should advance our leg if we had no sensation of its movement as executed, and not even a minimal feeling of impulse to set it down. Knitting appears altogether mechanical, and the knitter keeps up her knitting even while she reads or is engaged in lively talk. But if we ask her how this be possible, she will hardly reply that the knitting goes on of itself. She will rather say that she has a feeling of it, that she feels in her hands that she knits and how she must knit, and that therefore the movements of knitting are called forth and regulated by the sensations associated therewithal, even when the attention is called away.

"So of everyone who practises, apparently automatically, a long-familiar handicraft. The smith turning his tongs as he smites the iron, the carpenter wielding his plane, the lace-maker with her bobbin, the weaver at his loom, all will answer the same question in the same way by saying that they have a feeling of the proper management of the implement in their hands.

"In these cases, the feelings which are conditions of the appropriate acts are very faint. But none the less are they necessary. Imagine your hands not feeling; your movements could then only be provoked by ideas, and if your ideas were then diverted away, the movements ought to come to a standstill, which is a consequence that seldom occurs."[13]

Again:

"An idea makes you take, for example, a violin into your left hand. But it is not necessary that your idea remain fixed on the contraction

[12] *Mental Physiology*, p. 19.

[13] *Der menschliche Wille*, pp. 447, 448.

of the muscles of the left hand and fingers in order that the violin may continue to be held fast and not let fall. The sensations themselves which the holding of the instrument awakens in the hand, since they are associated with the motor impulse of grasping, are sufficient to cause this impulse, which then lasts as long as the feeling itself lasts, or until the impulse is inhibited by the idea of some antagonistic motion."

And the same may be said of the manner in which the right hand holds the bow:

"It sometimes happens, in beginning these simultaneous combinations, that one movement or impulse will cease if the consciousness turn particularly towards another, because at the outset the guiding sensations must *all* be strongly *felt*. The bow will perhaps slip from the fingers, because some of the muscles have relaxed. But the slipping is a cause of new sensations starting up in the hand, so that the attention is in a moment brought back to the grasping of the bow.

"The following experiment shows this well: When one begins to play on the violin, to keep him from raising his right elbow in playing a book is placed under his right armpit, which he is ordered to hold fast by keeping the upper arm tight against his body. The muscular feelings, and feelings of contact connected with the book, provoke an impulse to press it tight. But often it happens that the beginner, whose attention gets absorbed in the production of the notes, lets drop the book. Later, however, this never happens; the faintest sensations of contact suffice to awaken the impulse to keep it in its place, and the attention may be wholly absorbed by the notes and the fingering with the left hand. *The simultaneous combination of movements is thus in the first instance conditioned by the facility with which in us, alongside of intellectual processes, processes of inattentive feeling may still go on.*"[14]

This brings us by a very natural transition to the *ethical implications of the law of habit.* They are numerous and momentous. Dr. Carpenter, from whose *Mental Physiology* we have quoted, has so prominently enforced the principle that our organs grow to the way in which they have been exercised, and dwelt upon its consequences, that his book almost deserves to be called a work of edification, on this account alone. We need make no apology, then, for tracing a few of these consequences ourselves:

"Habit a second nature! Habit is ten times nature," the Duke of Wellington is said to have exclaimed; and the degree to which

[14] *Der menschliche Wille*, pp. 438, 439–40. The last sentence is rather freely translated—the sense is unaltered.

this is true no one can probably appreciate as well as one who is a veteran soldier himself. The daily drill and the years of discipline end by fashioning a man completely over again, as to most of the possibilities of his conduct.

"There is a story, which is credible enough, though it may not be true, of a practical joker, who, seeing a discharged veteran carrying home his dinner, suddenly called out 'Attention!' whereupon the man instantly brought his hands down, and lost his mutton and potatoes in the gutter. The drill had been thorough, and its effects had become embodied in the man's nervous structure."[15]

Riderless cavalry-horses, at many a battle, have been seen to come together and go through their customary evolutions at the sound of the bugle-call. Most trained domestic animals, dogs and oxen, and omnibus- and car-horses, seem to be machines almost pure and simple, undoubtingly, unhesitatingly doing from minute to minute the duties they have been taught, and giving no sign that the possibility of an alternative ever suggests itself to their mind. Men grown old in prison have asked to be readmitted after being once set free. In a railroad accident to a travelling menagerie in the United States some time in 1884, a tiger, whose cage had broken open, is said to have emerged, but presently crept back again, as if too much bewildered by his new responsibilities, so that he was without difficulty secured.

Habit is thus the enormous fly-wheel of society, its most precious conservative agent. It alone is what keeps us all within the bounds of ordinance, and saves the children of fortune from the envious uprisings of the poor. It alone prevents the hardest and most repulsive walks of life from being deserted by those brought up to tread therein. It keeps the fisherman and the deck-hand at sea through the winter; it holds the miner in his darkness, and nails the countryman to his log-cabin and his lonely farm through all the months of snow; it protects us from invasion by the natives of the desert and the frozen zone. It dooms us all to fight out the battle of life upon the lines of our nurture or our early choice, and to make the best of a pursuit that disagrees, because there is no other for which we are fitted, and it is too late to begin again. It keeps different social strata from mixing. Already at the age of twenty-five you see the professional mannerism settling down on the young

[15] Huxley's *Lessons in Elementary Physiology*, lesson XI.

commercial traveller, on the young doctor, on the young minister, on the young counsellor-at-law. You see the little lines of cleavage running through the character, the tricks of thought, the prejudices, the ways of the 'shop,' in a word, from which the man can by-and-by no more escape than his coat-sleeve can suddenly fall into a new set of folds. On the whole, it is best he should not escape. It is well for the world that in most of us, by the age of thirty, the character has set like plaster, and will never soften again.

If the period between twenty and thirty is the critical one in the formation of intellectual and professional habits, the period below twenty is more important still for the fixing of *personal* habits, properly so called, such as vocalization and pronunciation, gesture, motion, and address. Hardly ever is a language learned after twenty spoken without a foreign accent; hardly ever can a youth transferred to the society of his betters unlearn the nasality and other vices of speech bred in him by the associations of his growing years. Hardly ever, indeed, no matter how much money there be in his pocket, can he even learn to *dress* like a gentleman-born. The merchants offer their wares as eagerly to him as to the veriest 'swell,' but he simply *cannot* buy the right things. An invisible law, as strong as gravitation, keeps him within his orbit, arrayed this year as he was the last; and how his better-bred acquaintances contrive to get the things they wear will be for him a mystery till his dying day.

The great thing, then, in all education, is to *make our nervous system our ally instead of our enemy.* It is to fund and capitalize our acquisitions, and live at ease upon the interest of the fund. *For this we must make automatic and habitual, as early as possible, as many useful actions as we can,* and guard against the growing into ways that are likely to be disadvantageous to us, as we should guard against the plague. The more of the details of our daily life we can hand over to the effortless custody of automatism, the more our higher powers of mind will be set free for their own proper work. There is no more miserable human being than one in whom nothing is habitual but indecision, and for whom the lighting of every cigar, the drinking of every cup, the time of rising and going to bed every day, and the beginning of every bit of work, are subjects of express volitional deliberation. Full half the time of such a man goes to the deciding, or regretting, of matters which ought to be so ingrained in him as practically not to exist for his consciousness at all. If there be such daily duties not yet ingrained in any one of my readers, let him begin this very hour to set the matter right.

In Professor Bain's chapter on "The Moral Habits" there are some admirable practical remarks laid down. Two great maxims emerge from his treatment. The first is that in the acquisition of a new habit, or the leaving off of an old one, we must take care to *launch ourselves with as strong and decided an initiative as possible.* Accumulate all the possible circumstances which shall re-enforce the right motives; put yourself assiduously in conditions that encourage the new way; make engagements incompatible with the old; take a public pledge, if the case allows; in short, envelop your resolution with every aid you know. This will give your new beginning such a momentum that the temptation to break down will not occur as soon as it otherwise might; and every day during which a breakdown is postponed adds to the chances of its not occurring at all.

The second maxim is: *Never suffer an exception to occur till the new habit is securely rooted in your life.* Each lapse is like the letting fall of a ball of string which one is carefully winding up; a single slip undoes more than a great many turns will wind again. *Continuity* of training is the great means of making the nervous system act infallibly right. As Professor Bain says:

> "The peculiarity of the moral habits, contra-distinguishing them from the intellectual acquisitions, is the presence of two hostile powers, one to be gradually raised into the ascendant over the other. It is necessary, above all things, in such a situation, never to lose a battle. Every gain on the wrong side undoes the effect of many conquests on the right. The essential precaution, therefore, is, so to regulate the two opposing powers that the one may have a series of uninterrupted successes, until repetition has fortified it to such a degree as to enable it to cope with the opposition, under any circumstances. This is the theoretically best career of mental progress."

The need of securing success at the *outset* is imperative. Failure at first is apt to dampen the energy of all future attempts, whereas past experience of success nerves one to future vigor. Goethe says to a man who consulted him about an enterprise but mistrusted his own powers: "Ach! you need only blow on your hands!" And the remark illustrates the effect on Goethe's spirits of his own habitually successful career. Prof. Baumann, from whom I borrow the anecdote,[16] says that the collapse of barbarian nations when Europeans come among them is due to their despair of ever succeeding as the new-comers do in the larger tasks of life. Old ways are broken and new ones not formed.

The question of 'tapering-off,' in abandoning such habits as drink and opium-indulgence, comes in here, and is a question about which experts differ within certain limits, and in regard to what may be best for an individual case. In the main, however, all expert opinion would agree that abrupt acquisition of the new habit is the best way, *if there be a real possibility of carrying it out.* We must be careful not to give the will so stiff a task as to insure its defeat at the very outset; but, *provided one can stand it,* a sharp period of suffering, and then a free time, is the best thing to aim at, whether in giving up a habit like that of opium, or in simply changing one's hours of rising or of work. It is surprising how soon a desire will die of inanition if it be *never* fed.

"One must first learn, unmoved, looking neither to the right nor left, to walk firmly on the straight and narrow path, before one can begin 'to make one's self over again.' He who every day makes a fresh resolve is like one who, arriving at the edge of the ditch he is to leap, forever stops and returns for a fresh run. Without *unbroken* advance there is no such thing as *accumulation* of the ethical forces possible, and to make this possible, and to exercise us and habituate us in it, is the sovereign blessing of regular *work.*"[17]

A third maxim may be added to the preceding pair: *Seize the very first possible opportunity to act on every resolution you make, and on every emotional prompting you may experience in the direction of the habits you aspire to gain.* It is not in the moment of their forming, but in the moment of their producing *motor effects,* that resolves and aspirations communicate the new 'set' to the brain. As the author last quoted remarks:

"The actual presence of the practical opportunity alone furnishes the fulcrum upon which the lever can rest, by means of which the moral will may multiply its strength, and raise itself aloft. He who has no solid ground to press against will never get beyond the stage of empty gesture-making."

16 See the admirable passage about success at the outset, in his *Handbuch der Moral* (1879), pp. 38–43.

17 J. Bahnsen: *Beiträge zur Charakterologie* (1867), vol. I, p. 209.

No matter how full a reservoir of *maxims* one may possess, and no matter how good one's *sentiments* may be, if one have not taken advantage of every concrete opportunity to *act*, one's character may remain entirely unaffected for the better. With mere good intentions, hell is proverbially paved. And this is an obvious consequence of the principles we have laid down. A 'character,' as J. S. Mill says, 'is a completely fashioned will'; and a will, in the sense in which he means it, is an aggregate of tendencies to act in a firm and prompt and definite way upon all the principal emergencies of life. A tendency to act only becomes effectively ingrained in us in proportion to the uninterrupted frequency with which the actions actually occur, and the brain 'grows' to their use. Every time a resolve or a fine glow of feeling evaporates without bearing practical fruit is worse than a chance lost; it works so as positively to hinder future resolutions and emotions from taking the normal path of discharge. There is no more contemptible type of human character than that of the nerveless sentimentalist and dreamer, who spends his life in a weltering sea of sensibility and emotion, but who never does a manly concrete deed. Rousseau, inflaming all the mothers of France, by his eloquence, to follow Nature and nurse their babies themselves, while he sends his own children to the foundling hospital, is the classical example of what I mean. But every one of us in his measure, whenever, after glowing for an abstractly formulated Good, he practically ignores some actual case, among the squalid 'other particulars' of which that same Good lurks disguised, treads straight on Rousseau's path. All Goods are disguised by the vulgarity of their concomitants, in this work-a-day world; but woe to him who can only recognize them when he thinks them in their pure and abstract form! The habit of excessive novel-reading and theatre-going will produce true monsters in this line. The weeping of a Russian lady over the fictitious personages in the play, while her coachman is freezing to death on his seat outside, is the sort of thing that everywhere happens on a less glaring scale. Even the habit of excessive indulgence in music, for those who are neither performers themselves nor musically gifted enough to take it in a purely intellectual way, has probably a relaxing effect upon the character. One becomes filled with emotions which habitually pass without prompting to any deed, and so the inertly sentimental condition is kept up. The remedy would be, never to suffer one's self to have an emotion at a concert, without expressing it afterwards in *some* active way.[18] Let the expression be the least thing in the world —speaking genially to one's aunt, or giving up one's seat in a horse-car, if nothing more heroic offers—but let it not fail to take place.

These latter cases make us aware that it is not simply *particular lines* of discharge, but also *general forms* of discharge, that seem to be grooved out by habit in the brain. Just as, if we let our emotions evaporate, they get into a way of evaporating; so there is reason to suppose that if we often flinch from making an effort, before we know it the effort-making capacity will be gone; and that, if we suffer the wandering of our attention, presently it will wander all the time. Attention and effort are, as we shall see later, but two names for the same psychic fact. To what brain-processes they correspond we do not know. The strongest reason for believing that they do depend on brain-processes at all, and are not pure acts of the spirit, is just this fact, that they seem in some degree subject to the law of habit, which is a material law. As a final practical maxim, relative to these habits of the will, we may, then, offer something like this: *Keep the faculty of effort alive in you by a little gratuitous exercise every day.* That is, be systematically ascetic or heroic in little unnecessary points, do every day or two something for no other reason than that you would rather not do it, so that when the hour of dire need draws nigh, it may find you not unnerved and untrained to stand the test. Asceticism of this sort is like the insurance which a man pays on his house and goods. The tax does him no good at the time, and possibly may never bring him a return. But if the fire *does* come, his having paid it will be his salvation from ruin. So with the man who has daily inured himself to habits of concentrated attention, energetic volition, and self-denial in unnecessary things. He will stand like a tower when everything rocks around him, and when his softer fellow-mortals are winnowed like chaff in the blast.

The physiological study of mental conditions is thus the most powerful ally of hortatory ethics. The hell to be endured hereafter, of which theology tells, is no worse than the hell we make for ourselves in this world by habitually fashioning our characters in the wrong way. Could the young but realize how soon they will become mere walking bundles of habits, they would give more heed to their conduct while in the plastic state. We are spinning our own

18 See for remarks on this subject a readable article by Miss V. Scudder on "The Moral Dangers of Musical Devotees," in the *Andover Review* for January 1887.

fates, good or evil, and never to be undone. Every smallest stroke of virtue or of vice leaves its never so little scar. The drunken Rip Van Winkle, in Jefferson's play, excuses himself for every fresh dereliction by saying, 'I won't count this time!' Well! he may not count it, and a kind Heaven may not count it; but it is being counted none the less. Down among his nerve-cells and fibres the molecules are counting it, registering and storing it up to be used against him when the next temptation comes. Nothing we ever do is, in strict scientific literalness, wiped out. Of course, this has its good side as well as its bad one. As we become permanent drunkards by so many separate drinks, so we become saints in the moral, and authorities and experts in the practical and scientific spheres, by so many separate acts and hours of work. Let no youth have any anxiety about the upshot of his education, whatever the line of it may be. If he keep faithfully busy each hour of the working-day, he may safely leave the final result to itself. He can with perfect certainty count on waking up some fine morning, to find himself one of the competent ones of his generation, in whatever pursuit he may have singled out. Silently, between all the details of his business, the *power of judging* in all that class of matter will have built itself up within him as a possession that will never pass away. Young people should know this truth in advance. The ignorance of it has probably engendered more discouragement and faint-heartedness in youths embarking on arduous careers than all other causes put together.

Chapter V

The Automaton-Theory

In describing the functions of the hemispheres a short way back, we used language derived from both the bodily and the mental life, saying now that the animal made indeterminate and unforeseeable reactions, and anon that he was swayed by considerations of future good and evil; treating his hemispheres sometimes as the seat of memory and ideas in the psychic sense, and sometimes talking of them as simply a complicated addition to his reflex machinery. This sort of vacillation in the point of view is a fatal incident of all ordinary talk about these questions; but I must now settle my scores with those readers to whom I already dropped a word in passing (see page 36, note 3) and who have probably been dissatisfied with my conduct ever since.

Suppose we restrict our view to facts of one and the same plane, and let that be the bodily plane: cannot all the outward phenomena of intelligence still be exhaustively described? Those mental images, those 'considerations,' whereof we spoke,—presumably they do not arise without neural processes arising simultaneously with them, and presumably each consideration corresponds to a process *sui generis*, and unlike all the rest. In other words, however numerous and delicately differentiated the train of ideas may be, the train of brain-events that runs alongside of it must in both respects be exactly its match, and we must postulate a neural machinery that offers a living counterpart for every shading, however fine, of the history of its owner's mind. Whatever degree of complication the latter may reach, the complication of the machinery must be quite as extreme, otherwise we should have to admit that there may be mental events to which no brain-events correspond. But such an admission as this the physiologist is reluctant to make. It would violate all his beliefs. 'No psychosis without neurosis,' is one form which the principle of continuity takes in his mind.

But this principle forces the physiologist to make still another step. If neural action is as complicated as mind; and if in the sympathetic system and lower spinal cord we see what, so far as we know, is unconscious neural action executing deeds that to all outward intent may be called intelligent; what is there to hinder us from supposing that even where we know consciousness to be there, the still more complicated neural action which we believe to be its inseparable companion is alone and of itself the real agent of whatever intelligent deeds may appear? "As actions of a certain degree of complexity are brought about by mere mechanism, why may not actions of a still greater degree of complexity be the result of a more refined mechanism?" The conception of reflex action is surely one of the best conquests of physiological theory; why not be radical with it? Why not say that just as the spinal cord is a machine with few reflexes, so the hemispheres are a machine with many, and that that is all the difference? The principle of continuity would press us to accept this view.

But what on this view could be the function of the consciousness itself? *Mechanical* function it would have none. The sense-organs would awaken the brain-cells; these would awaken each other in rational and orderly sequence, until the time for action came; and then the last brain-vibration would discharge downwards into the motor tracts. But this would be a quite autonomous chain of occurrences, and whatever mind went with it would be there only as an 'epiphenomenon,' an inert spectator, a sort of 'foam, aura, or melody' as Mr. Hodgson says, whose opposition or whose furtherance would be alike powerless over the occurrences themselves. When talking, some time ago, we ought not, accordingly, *as physiologists,* to have said anything about 'considerations' as guiding the animal. We ought to have said 'paths left in the hemispherical cortex by former currents,' and nothing more.

Now so simple and attractive is this conception from the consistently physiological point of view, that it is quite wonderful to see how late it was stumbled on in philosophy, and how few people, even when it has been explained to them, fully and easily realize its import. Much of the polemic writing against it is by men who have as yet failed to take it into their imaginations. Since this has been the case, it seems worth while to devote a few more words to making it plausible, before criticising it ourselves.

To Descartes belongs the credit of having first been bold enough to conceive of a completely self-sufficing nervous mechanism which should be able to perform complicated and apparently intelligent acts. By a singularly arbitrary restriction, however, Descartes stopped short at man, and while contending that in beasts the nervous machinery was all, he held that the higher acts of man were the result of the agency of his rational soul. The opinion that beasts have no consciousness at all was of course too paradoxical to maintain itself long as anything more than a curious item in the history of philosophy. And with its abandonment the very notion that the nervous system *per se* might work the work of intelligence, which was an integral, though detachable part of the whole theory, seemed also to slip out of men's conception, until, in this century, the elaboration of the doctrine of reflex action made it possible and natural that it should again arise. But it was not till 1870, I believe, that Mr. Hodgson made the decisive step, by saying that feelings, no matter how intensely they may be present, can have no causal efficacy whatever, and comparing them to the colors laid on the surface of a mosaic, of which the events in the nervous system are represented by the stones.[1] Obviously the stones are held in place by each other and not by the several colors which they support.

About the same time Mr. Spalding, and a little later Messrs. Huxley and Clifford, gave great publicity to an identical doctrine, though in their case it was backed by less refined metaphysical considerations.[2]

A few sentences from Huxley and Clifford may be subjoined to make the matter entirely clear. Professor Huxley says:

1 *The Theory of Practice*, vol. I, p. 416 ff.

2 The present writer recalls how in 1869, when still a medical student, he began to write an essay showing how almost everyone who speculated about brain-processes illicitly interpolated into his account of them links derived from the entirely heterogeneous universe of Feeling. Spencer, Hodgson (in his *Time and Space*), Maudsley, Lockhart Clarke, Bain, Dr. Carpenter, and other authors were cited as having been guilty of the confusion. The writing was soon stopped because he perceived that the view which he was upholding against these authors was a pure conception, with no proofs to be adduced of its reality. Later it seemed to him that whatever *proofs* existed really told in favor of their view.

"The consciousness of brutes would appear to be related to the mechanism of their body simply as a collateral product of its working, and to be as completely without any power of modifying that working, as the steam-whistle which accompanies the work of a locomotive engine is without influence upon its machinery. Their volition, if they have any, is an emotion *indicative* of physical changes, not a *cause* of such changes. . . . The soul stands related to the body as the bell of a clock to the works, and consciousness answers to the sound which the bell gives out when it is struck. Thus far I have strictly confined myself to . . . the automatism of brutes. . . . It is quite true that, to the best of my judgment, the argumentation which applies to brutes holds equally good of men; and, therefore, that all states of consciousness in us, as in them, are immediately caused by molecular changes of the brain-substance. It seems to me that in men, as in brutes, there is no proof that any state of consciousness is the cause of change in the motion of the matter of the organism. If these positions are well based, it follows that our mental conditions are simply the symbols in consciousness of the changes which take place automatically in the organism; and that, to take an extreme illustration, the feeling we call volition is not the cause of a voluntary act, but the symbol of that state of the brain which is the immediate cause of that act. We are conscious automata."

Professor Clifford writes:

"All the evidence that we have goes to show that the physical world gets along entirely by itself, according to practically universal rules. . . . The train of physical facts between the stimulus sent into the eye, or to any one of our senses, and the exertion which follows it, and the train of physical facts which goes on in the brain, even when there is no stimulus and no exertion,—these are perfectly complete physical trains, and every step is fully accounted for by mechanical conditions. . . . The two things are on utterly different platforms—the physical facts go along by themselves, and the mental facts go along by themselves. There is a parallelism between them, but there is no interference of one with the other. Again, if anybody says that the will influences matter, the statement is not untrue, but it is nonsense. . . . Such an assertion belongs to the crude materialism of the savage. The only thing which influences matter is the position of surrounding matter or the motion of surrounding matter. . . . The assertion that another man's volition, a feeling in his consciousness which I cannot perceive, is part of the train of physical facts which I may perceive,—this is neither true nor untrue, but nonsense; it is a combination of words whose corresponding ideas will not go together. . . . Sometimes one series is known better, and sometimes the other; so that in telling a story we speak sometimes of mental and sometimes of material facts. A feeling of chill made a man run; strictly speaking, the nervous disturbance which coexisted with that feeling of chill made him run, if we want to talk about material facts; or the feeling of chill produced the form of sub-consciousness which coexists with the motion of legs, if we want to talk about mental facts. . . . When, therefore, we ask, 'What is the physical link between the ingoing message from chilled skin and the outgoing message which moves the leg?' and the answer is, 'A man's Will,' we have as much right to be amused as if we had asked our friend with the picture what pigment was used in painting the cannon in the foreground, and received the answer, 'Wrought iron.' It will be found excellent practice in the mental operations required by this doctrine to imagine a train, the fore part of which is an engine and three carriages linked with iron couplings, and the hind part three other carriages linked with iron couplings; the bond between the two parts being made out of the sentiments of amity subsisting between the stoker and the guard."

To comprehend completely the consequences of the dogma so confidently enunciated, one should unflinchingly apply it to the most complicated examples. The movements of our tongues and pens, the flashings of our eyes in conversation, are of course events of a material order, and as such their causal antecedents must be exclusively material. If we knew thoroughly the nervous system of Shakespeare, and as thoroughly all his environing conditions, we should be able to show why at a certain period of his life his hand came to trace on certain sheets of paper those crabbed little black marks which we for shortness' sake call the manuscript of *Hamlet*. We should understand the rationale of every erasure and alteration therein, and we should understand all this without in the slightest degree acknowledging the existence of the thoughts in Shakespeare's mind. The words and sentences would be taken, not as signs of anything beyond themselves, but as little outward facts, pure and simple. In like manner we might exhaustively write the biography of those two hundred pounds, more or less, of warmish albuminoid matter called Martin Luther, without ever implying that it felt.

But, on the other hand, nothing in all this could prevent us from giving an equally complete account of either Luther's or Shakespeare's spiritual history, an account in which every gleam of thought and emotion should find its place. The mind-history would run alongside of the body-history of each man, and each point in the one would correspond to, but not react upon, a point in the other. So the melody floats from the harp-string, but neither checks nor quickens its vibrations; so the shadow runs alongside the pedestrian, but in no way influences his steps.

Another inference, apparently more paradoxical still, needs to be made, though, as far as I am aware, Dr. Hodgson is the only writer who has explicitly drawn it. That inference is that feelings, not causing nerve-actions, cannot even cause each other. To ordinary common-sense, felt pain is, as such, not only the cause of outward tears and cries, but also the cause of such inward events as sorrow, compunction, desire, or inventive thought. So the consciousness of good news is the direct producer of the feeling of joy, the awareness of premises that of the belief in conclusions. But according to the automaton-theory, each of the feelings mentioned is only the correlate of some nerve-movement whose *cause* lay wholly in a previous nerve-movement. The first nerve-movement called up the second; whatever feeling was attached to the second consequently found itself following upon the feeling that was attached to the first. If, for example, good news was the consciousness correlated with the first movement, then joy turned out to be the correlate in consciousness of the second. But all the while the items of the nerve series were the only ones in causal continuity; the items of the conscious series, however inwardly rational their sequence, were simply juxtaposed.

REASONS FOR THE THEORY

The 'conscious automaton-theory,' as this conception is generally called, is thus a radical and simple conception of the manner in which certain facts may possibly occur. But between conception and belief, proof ought to lie. And when we ask, 'What proves that all this is more than a mere conception of the possible?' it is not easy to get a sufficient reply. If we start from the frog's spinal cord and reason by continuity, saying, as that acts so intelligently, *though unconscious*, so the higher centres, *though conscious*, may have the intelligence they show quite as mechanically based; we are immediately met by the exact counter-argument from continuity, an argument actually urged by such writers as Pflüger and Lewes, which starts from the acts of the hemispheres, and says: "As *these* owe *their* intelligence to the consciousness which we know to be there, so the intelligence of the spinal cord's acts must really be due to the invisible presence of a consciousness lower in degree." All arguments from continuity work in two ways: you can either level up or level down by their means. And it is clear that such arguments as these can eat each other up to all eternity.

There remains a sort of philosophic faith, bred like most faiths from an æsthetic demand. Mental and physical events are, on all hands, admitted to present the strongest contrast in the entire field of being. The chasm which yawns between them is less easily bridged over by the mind than any interval we know. Why, then, not call it an absolute chasm, and say not only that the two worlds are different, but that they are independent? This gives us the comfort of all simple and absolute formulas, and it makes each chain homogeneous to our consideration. When talking of nervous tremors and bodily actions, we may feel secure against intrusion from an irrelevant mental world. When, on the other hand, we speak of feelings, we may with equal consistency use terms always of one denomination, and never be annoyed by what Aristotle calls 'slipping into another kind.' The desire on the part of men educated in laboratories not to have their physical reasonings mixed up with such incommensurable factors as feelings is certainly very strong. I have heard a most intelligent biologist say: "It is high time for scientific men to protest against the recognition of any such thing as consciousness in a scientific investigation." In a word, feeling constitutes the 'unscientific' half of existence, and anyone who enjoys calling himself a 'scientist' will be too happy to purchase an untrammelled homogeneity of terms in the studies of his predilection, at the slight cost of admitting a dualism which, in the same breath that it allows to mind an independent status of being, banishes it to a limbo of causal inertness, from whence no intrusion or interruption on its part need ever be feared.

Over and above this great postulate that matters must be kept simple, there is, it must be confessed, still another highly abstract reason for denying causal efficacity to our feelings. We can form no positive image of the *modus operandi* of a volition or other thought affecting the cerebral molecules.

"Let us try to imagine an idea—say of food, producing a movement, say of carrying food to the mouth. . . . What is the method of its action? Does it assist the decomposition of the molecules of the gray matter, or does it retard the process, or does it alter the direction in which the shocks are distributed? Let us imagine the molecules of the gray matter combined in such a way that they will fall into simpler combinations on the impact of an incident force. Now, suppose the incident force, in the shape of a shock from some other centre, to impinge upon these molecules. By hypothesis, it will decompose them, and they will fall into the simpler combination. How is the idea of food to prevent this decomposition? Manifestly it can do so only by increasing the force which binds the molecules together. Good! Try to imagine the idea of a beefsteak binding two molecules together. It is impossible. Equally impossible is it to imagine a similar idea loosening the attractive force between two molecules."[3]

This passage from an exceedingly clever writer expresses admirably the difficulty to which I allude. Combined with a strong sense of the 'chasm' between the two worlds, and with a lively faith in reflex machinery, the sense of this difficulty can hardly fail to make one turn consciousness out of the door as a superfluity so far as one's explanations go. One may bow her out politely, allow her to remain as an 'epiphenomenon' (invaluable word!), but one insists that matter shall hold all the power.

"Having thoroughly recognised the fathomless abyss that separates mind from matter, and having so blended the notion into his very nature, that there is no chance of his ever forgetting it, or failing to saturate with it all his meditations, the student of psychology has next to appreciate the association between these two orders of phenomena. . . . They are associated in a manner so intimate that some of the greatest thinkers consider them different aspects of the same process. . . . When the re-arrangement of molecules takes place in the higher regions of the brain, a change of consciousness simultaneously occurs. . . . The change of consciousness never takes place without the change in the brain; the change in the brain never . . . without the change in consciousness. But *why* the two occur together, or what the link is which connects them, we do not know, and most authorities believe that we never shall and never can know. Having firmly and tenaciously grasped these two notions, of the absolute separateness of mind and matter, and of the invariable concomitance of a mental change with a bodily change, the student will enter on the study of psychology with half his difficulties surmounted."[4]

Half his difficulties ignored, I should prefer to say. For this 'concomitance' in the midst of 'absolute separateness' is an utterly irra-

[3] Charles Mercier: *The Nervous System and the Mind* (1888), p. 8.
[4] *Op. cit.*, p. 10.

tional notion. It is to my mind quite inconceivable that consciousness should have *nothing to do* with a business which it so faithfully attends. And the question, 'What has it to do?' is one which psychology has no right to 'surmount,' for it is her plain duty to consider it. The fact is that the whole question of interaction and influence between things is a metaphysical question, and cannot be discussed at all by those who are unwilling to go into matters thoroughly. It is truly enough hard to imagine the 'idea of a beef-steak binding two molecules together'; but since Hume's time it has been equally hard to imagine *anything* binding them together. The whole notion of 'binding' is a mystery, the first step towards the solution of which is to clear scholastic rubbish out of the way. Popular science talks of 'forces,' 'attractions' or 'affinities' as binding the molecules; but clear science, though she may use such words to abbreviate discourse, has no use for the conceptions, and is satisfied when she can express in simple 'laws' the bare space-relations of the molecules as functions of each other and of time. To the more curiously inquiring mind, however, this simplified expression of the bare facts is not enough; there must be a 'reason' for them, and something must 'determine' the laws. And when one seriously sits down to consider what sort of a thing one *means* when one asks for a 'reason,' one is led so far afield, so far away from popular science and its scholasticism, as to see that even such a fact as the existence or non-existence in the universe of 'the idea of a beef-steak' may not be wholly indifferent to other facts in the same universe, and in particular may have something to do with determining the distance at which two molecules in that universe shall lie apart. If this is so, then common-sense, though the intimate nature of causality and of the connection of things in the universe lies beyond her pitifully bounded horizon, has the root and gist of the truth in her hands when she obstinately holds to it that feelings and ideas are causes. However inadequate our ideas of causal efficacy may be, we are less wide of the mark when we say that our ideas and feelings have it, than the Automatists are when they say they haven't it. As in the night all cats are gray, so in the darkness of metaphysical criticism all causes are obscure. But one has no right to pull the pall over the psychic half of the subject only, as the automatists do, and to say that *that* causation is unintelligible, whilst in the same breath one dogmatizes about *material* causation as if Hume, Kant, and Lotze had never been born. One cannot thus blow hot and cold.

One must be impartially *naif* or impartially critical. If the latter, the reconstruction must be thorough-going or 'metaphysical,' and will probably preserve the common-sense view that ideas are forces, in some translated form. But Psychology is a mere natural science, accepting certain terms uncritically as her data, and stopping short of metaphysical reconstruction. Like physics, she must be *naïve*; and if she finds that in her very peculiar field of study ideas *seem* to be causes, she had better continue to talk of them as such. She gains absolutely nothing by a breach with common-sense in this matter, and she loses, to say the least, all naturalness of speech. If feelings are causes, of course their effects must be furtherances and checkings of internal cerebral motions, of which in themselves we are entirely without knowledge. It is probable that for years to come we shall have to infer what happens in the brain either from our feelings or from motor effects which we observe. The organ will be for us a sort of vat in which feelings and motions somehow go on stewing together, and in which innumerable things happen of which we catch but the statistical result. Why, under these circumstances, we should be asked to forswear the language of our childhood I cannot well imagine, especially as it is perfectly compatible with the language of physiology. The feelings can produce nothing absolutely new, they can only reinforce and inhibit reflex currents which already exist, and the original organization of these by physiological forces must always be the ground-work of the psychological scheme.

My conclusion is that to urge the automaton-theory upon us, as it is now urged, on purely *a priori* and *quasi*-metaphysical grounds, is an *unwarrantable impertinence in the present state of psychology.*[4a]

REASONS AGAINST THE THEORY

But there are much more positive reasons than this why we ought to continue to talk in psychology as if consciousness had causal efficacy. The *particulars of the distribution of consciousness,* so far as we know them, *point to its being efficacious.* Let us trace some of them.

It is very generally admitted, though the point would be hard to prove, that consciousness grows the more complex and intense the higher we rise in the animal kingdom. That of a man must exceed

[4a] Cf. *infra* vol. II, 1185–1186.

that of an oyster. From this point of view it seems an organ, superadded to the other organs which maintain the animal in the struggle for existence; and the presumption of course is that it helps him in some way in the struggle, just as they do. But it cannot help him without being in some way efficacious and influencing the course of his bodily history. If now it could be shown in what way consciousness *might* help him, and if, moreover, the defects of his other organs (where consciousness is most developed) are such as to make them need just the kind of help that consciousness would bring provided it *were* efficacious; why, then the plausible inference would be that it came just *because* of its efficacy—in other words, its efficacy would be inductively proved.

Now the study of the phenomena of consciousness which we shall make throughout the rest of this book will show us that consciousness is at all times primarily *a selecting agency*.[5] Whether we take it in the lowest sphere of sense, or in the highest of intellection, we find it always doing one thing, choosing one out of several of the materials so presented to its notice, emphasizing and accentuating that and suppressing as far as possible all the rest. The item emphasized is always in close connection with some *interest* felt by consciousness to be paramount at the time.

But what are now the defects of the nervous system in those animals whose consciousness seems most highly developed? Chief among them must be *instability*. The cerebral hemispheres are the characteristically 'high' nerve-centres, and we saw how indeterminate and unforeseeable their performances were in comparison with those of the basal ganglia and the cord. But this very vagueness constitutes their advantage. They allow their possessor to adapt his conduct to the minutest alterations in the environing circumstances, any one of which may be for him a sign, suggesting distant motives more powerful than any present solicitations of sense. It seems as if certain mechanical conclusions should be drawn from this state of things. An organ swayed by slight impressions is an organ whose natural state is one of unstable equilibrium. We may imagine the various lines of discharge in the cerebrum to be almost on a par in point of permeability—what discharge a given small impression will produce may be called *accidental*, in the sense in which we say it is a matter of accident whether a rain-drop falling on a mountain ridge descend the eastern or the western slope. It is

[5] See in particular the end of Chapter IX.

in this sense that we may call it a matter of accident whether a child be a boy or a girl. The ovum is so unstable a body that certain causes too minute for our apprehension may at a certain moment tip it one way or the other. The natural law of an organ constituted after this fashion can be nothing but a law of caprice. I do not see how one could reasonably expect from it any certain pursuance of useful lines of reaction, such as the few and fatally determined performances of the lower centres constitute within their narrow sphere. The dilemma in regard to the nervous system seems, in short, to be of the following kind. We may construct one which will react infallibly and certainly, but it will then be capable of reacting to very few changes in the environment—it will fail to be adapted to all the rest. We may, on the other hand, construct a nervous system potentially adapted to respond to an infinite variety of minute features in the situation; but its fallibility will then be as great as its elaboration. We can never be sure that its equilibrium will be upset in the appropriate direction. In short, a high brain may do many things, and may do each of them at a very slight hint. But its hair-trigger organization makes of it a happy-go-lucky, hit-or-miss affair. It is as likely to do the crazy as the sane thing at any given moment. A low brain does few things, and in doing them perfectly forfeits all other use. The performances of a high brain are like dice thrown forever on a table. Unless they be loaded, what chance is there that the highest number will turn up oftener than the lowest?

All this is said of the brain as a physical machine pure and simple. *Can consciousness increase its efficiency by loading its dice?* Such is the problem.

Loading its dice would mean bringing a more or less constant pressure to bear in favor of *those* of its performances which make for the most permanent interests of the brain's owner; it would mean a constant inhibition of the tendencies to stray aside.

Well, just such pressure and such inhibition are what consciousness *seems* to be exerting all the while. And the interests in whose favor it seems to exert them are *its* interests and its alone, interests which it *creates*, and which, but for it, would have no status in the realm of being whatever. We talk, it is true, when we are darwinizing, as if the mere *body* that owns the brain had interests; we speak about the utilities of its various organs and how they help or hinder the body's survival; and we treat the survival as if it were an absolute end, existing as such in the physical world, a sort of actual *should-be,* presiding over the animal and judging his reactions, quite apart from the presence of any commenting intelligence outside. We forget that in the absence of some such superadded commenting intelligence (whether it be that of the animal itself, or only ours or Mr. Darwin's), the reactions cannot be properly talked of as 'useful' or 'hurtful' at all. Considered merely physically, all that can be said of them is that *if* they occur in a certain way survival will as a matter of fact prove to be their incidental consequence. The organs themselves, and all the rest of the physical world, will, however, all the time be quite indifferent to this consequence, and would quite as cheerfully, the circumstances changed, compass the animal's destruction. In a word, survival can enter into a purely physiological discussion only as an *hypothesis made by an onlooker* about the future. But the moment you bring a consciousness into the midst, survival ceases to be a mere hypothesis. No longer is it, "*if* survival is to occur, then so and so must brain and other organs work." It has now become an imperative decree: "Survival *shall* occur, and therefore organs *must* so work!" *Real* ends appear for the first time now upon the world's stage. The conception of consciousness as a purely cognitive form of being, which is the pet way of regarding it in many idealistic schools, modern as well as ancient, is thoroughly anti-psychological, as the remainder of this book will show. Every actually existing consciousness seems to itself at any rate to be a *fighter for ends,* of which many, but for its presence, would not be ends at all. Its powers of cognition are mainly subservient to these ends, discerning which facts further them and which do not.

Now let consciousness only be what it seems to itself, and it will help an instable brain to compass its proper ends. The movements of the brain *per se* yield the means of attaining these ends mechanically, but only out of a lot of other ends, if so they may be called, which are not the proper ones of the animal, but often quite opposed. The brain is an instrument of possibilities, but of no certainties. But the consciousness, with its own ends present to it, and knowing also well which possibilities lead thereto and which away, will, if endowed with causal efficacy, reinforce the favorable possibilities and repress the unfavorable or indifferent ones. The nerve-currents, coursing through the cells and fibres, must in this case be supposed strengthened by the fact of their awaking one consciousness and dampened by awaking another. *How* such reaction of the consciousness upon the currents may occur must remain at present unsolved: it is enough for my purpose to have shown that it may not uselessly exist, and that the matter is less simple than the brain-automatists hold.

All the facts of the natural history of consciousness lend color to this view. Consciousness, for example, is only intense when nerve-processes are hesitant. In rapid, automatic, habitual action it sinks to a minimum. Nothing could be more fitting than this, if consciousness have the teleological function we suppose; nothing more meaningless, if not. Habitual actions are certain, and being in no danger of going astray from their end, need no extraneous help. In hesitant action, there seem many alternative possibilities of final nervous discharge. The feeling awakened by the nascent excitement of each alternative nerve-tract seems by its attractive or repulsive quality to determine whether the excitement shall abort or shall become complete. Where indecision is great, as before a dangerous leap, consciousness is agonizingly intense. Feeling, from this point of view, may be likened to a cross-section of the chain of nervous discharge, ascertaining the links already laid down, and groping among the fresh ends presented to it for the one which seems best to fit the case.

The phenomena of 'vicarious function' which we studied in Chapter II seem to form another bit of circumstantial evidence. A machine in working order acts fatally in one way. Our consciousness calls this the right way. Take out a valve, throw a wheel out of gear or bend a pivot, and it becomes a different machine, acting just as fatally in another way which we call the wrong way. But the machine itself knows nothing of wrong or right: matter has no ideals to pursue. A locomotive will carry its train through an open draw-bridge as cheerfully as to any other destination.

A brain with part of it scooped out is virtually a new machine, and during the first days after the operation functions in a thoroughly abnormal manner. As a matter of fact, however, its performances become from day to day more normal, until at last a practised eye may be needed to suspect anything wrong. Some of the restoration is undoubtedly due to 'inhibitions' passing away. But if the consciousness which goes with the rest of the brain, be there not only in order to take cognizance of each functional error, but also to exert an efficient pressure to check it if it be a sin of commission, and to lend a strengthening hand if it be a weakness or sin of omission,—nothing seems more natural than that the remaining parts, assisted in this way, should by virtue of the principle of habit grow back to the old teleological modes of exercise for which they were at first incapacitated. Nothing, on the contrary, seems at first sight more unnatural than that they should vicariously take up the duties of a part now lost without those *duties as such* exerting any persuasive or coercive force. At the end of Chapter XXVI I shall return to this again.

There is yet another set of facts which seem explicable on the supposition that consciousness has causal efficacy. *It is a well-known fact that pleasures are generally associated with beneficial, pains with detrimental, experiences.* All the fundamental vital processes illustrate this law. Starvation, suffocation, privation of food, drink and sleep, work when exhausted, burns, wounds, inflammation, the effects of poison, are as disagreeable as filling the hungry stomach, enjoying rest and sleep after fatigue, exercise after rest, and a sound skin and unbroken bones at all times, are pleasant. Mr. Spencer and others have suggested that these coincidences are due, not to any pre-established harmony, but to the mere action of natural selection which would certainly kill off in the long-run any breed of creatures to whom the fundamentally noxious experience seemed enjoyable. An animal that should take pleasure in a feeling of suffocation would, if that pleasure were efficacious enough to make him immerse his head in water, enjoy a longevity of four or five minutes. But if pleasures and pains have no efficacy, one does not see (without some such *a priori* rational harmony as would be scouted by the 'scientific' champions of the automaton-theory) why the most noxious acts, such as burning, might not give thrills of delight, and the most necessary ones, such as breathing, cause agony. The exceptions to the law are, it is true, numerous, but relate to experiences that are either not vital or not universal. Drunkenness, for instance, which though noxious, is to many persons delightful, is a very exceptional experience. But, as the excellent physiologist Fick remarks, if all rivers and springs ran alcohol instead of water, either all men would now be born to hate it or our nerves would have been selected so as to drink it with impunity. The only considerable attempt, in fact, that has been made to explain the *dis-*

tribution of our feelings is that of Mr. Grant Allen in his suggestive little work *Physiological Æsthetics*; and his reasoning is based exclusively on that causal efficacy of pleasures and pains which the 'double-aspect' partisans so strenuously deny.

Thus, then, from every point of view the circumstantial evidence against that theory is strong. *A priori* analysis of both brain-action and conscious action shows us that if the latter were efficacious it would, by its selective emphasis, make amends for the indeterminateness of the former; whilst the study *a posteriori* of the *distribution* of consciousness shows it to be exactly such as we might expect in an organ added for the sake of steering a nervous system grown too complex to regulate itself. The conclusion that it is useful is, after all this, quite justifiable. But, if it is useful, it must be so through its causal efficaciousness, and the automaton-theory must succumb to the theory of common-sense. I, at any rate (pending metaphysical reconstructions not yet successfully achieved), shall have no hesitation in using the language of common-sense throughout this book.

Chapter VI

The Mind-Stuff Theory

The reader who found himself swamped with too much metaphysics in the last chapter will have a still worse time of it in this one, which is exclusively metaphysical. Metaphysics means nothing but an unusually obstinate effort to think clearly. The fundamental conceptions of psychology are practically very clear to us, but theoretically they are very confused, and one easily makes the obscurest assumptions in this science without realizing, until challenged, what internal difficulties they involve. When these assumptions have once established themselves (as they have a way of doing in our very descriptions of the phenomenal facts) it is almost impossible to get rid of them afterwards or to make anyone see that they are not essential features of the subject. The only way to prevent this disaster is to scrutinize them beforehand and make them give an articulate account of themselves before letting them pass. One of the obscurest of the assumptions of which I speak is *the assumption that our mental states are composite in structure, made up of smaller states conjoined.* This hypothesis has outward advantages which make it almost irresistibly attractive to the intellect, and yet it is inwardly quite unintelligible. Of its unintelligibility, however, half the writers on psychology seem unaware. As our own aim is *to understand* if possible, I make no apology for singling out this particular notion for very explicit treatment before taking up the descriptive part of our work. *The theory of 'mind-stuff' is the theory that our mental states are compounds,* expressed in its most radical form.

EVOLUTIONARY PSYCHOLOGY DEMANDS A MIND-DUST

In a general theory of evolution the inorganic comes first, then the lowest forms of animal and vegetable life, then forms of life that possess mentality, and finally those like ourselves that possess it in a high degree. As long as we keep to the consideration of purely outward facts, even the most complicated facts of biology, our task as evolutionists is comparatively easy. We are dealing all the time with matter and its aggregations and separations; and although our treatment must perforce be hypothetical, this does not prevent it from being *continuous.* The point which as evolutionists we are bound to hold fast to is that all the new forms of being that make their appearance are really nothing more than results of the redistribution of the original and unchanging materials. The self-same atoms which, chaotically dispersed, made the nebula, now, jammed and temporarily caught in peculiar positions, form our brains; and the 'evolution' of the brains, if understood, would be simply the account of how the atoms came to be so caught and jammed. In this story no new *natures,* no factors not present at the beginning, are introduced at any later stage.

But with the dawn of consciousness an entirely new nature seems to slip in, something whereof the potency was *not* given in the mere outward atoms of the original chaos.

The enemies of evolution have been quick to pounce upon this undeniable discontinuity in the data of the world, and many of them, from the failure of evolutionary explanations at this point, have inferred their general incapacity all along the line. Everyone admits the entire incommensurability of feeling as such with material motion as such. "A motion became a feeling!"—no phrase that our lips can frame is so devoid of apprehensible meaning. Accordingly, even the vaguest of evolutionary enthusiasts, when deliberately comparing material with mental facts, have been as forward as anyone else to emphasize the 'chasm' between the inner and the outer worlds.

"Can the oscillation of a molecule," says Mr. Spencer, "be represented side by side with a nervous shock [he means a mental shock], and the two be recognized as one? No effort enables us to assimilate them. That a unit of feeling has nothing in common with a unit of motion, becomes more than ever manifest when we bring the two into juxtaposition."[1]

[1] *Psychology,* § 62.

And again:

> "Suppose it to have become quite clear that a shock in consciousness and a molecular motion, are the subjective and objective faces of the same thing; we continue utterly incapable of uniting the two, so as to conceive that reality of which they are the opposite faces."[2]

In other words, incapable of perceiving in them any common character. So Tyndall, in that lucky paragraph which has been quoted so often that everyone knows it by heart:

> "The passage from the physics of the brain to the corresponding facts of consciousness is unthinkable. Granted that a definite thought, and a definite molecular action in the brain, occur simultaneously; we do not possess the intellectual organ, nor apparently any rudiment of the organ, which would enable us to pass, by a process of reasoning, from the one to the other."[3]

Or in this other passage:

> "We can trace the development of a nervous system, and correlate with it the parallel phenomena of sensation and thought. We see with undoubting certainty that they go hand in hand. But we try to soar in a vacuum the moment we seek to comprehend the connection between them. . . . There is no fusion possible between the two classes of facts—no motor energy in the intellect of man to carry it without logical rupture from the one to the other."[4]

None the less easily, however, when the evolutionary afflatus is upon them, do the very same writers leap over the breach whose flagrancy they are the foremost to announce, and talk as if mind grew out of body in a continuous way. Mr. Spencer, looking back on his review of mental evolution, tells us how "in tracing up the increase we found ourselves passing *without break* from the phenomena of bodily life to the phenomena of mental life."[5] And

[2] *Ibid.*, § 272.

[3] *Fragments of Science for Unscientific People*, 5th ed., p. 420.

[4] Belfast Address, *Nature*, August 20, 1874, p. 318. I cannot help remarking that the disparity between motions and feelings on which these authors lay so much stress, is somewhat less absolute than at first sight it seems. There are categories common to the two worlds. Not only temporal succession (as Helmholtz admits, *Physiologische Optik*, p. 445), but such attributes as intensity, volume, simplicity or complication, smooth or impeded change, rest or agitation, are habitually predicated of both physical facts and mental facts. Where such analogies obtain, the things do have something in common.

[5] *Psychology*, § 131.

Mr. Tyndall, in the same Belfast Address from which we just quoted, delivers his other famous passage:

"Abandoning all disguise, the confession that I feel bound to make before you is that I prolong the vision backward across the boundary of the experimental evidence, and discern in that matter, which we in our ignorance, and notwithstanding our professed reverence for its Creator, have hitherto covered with opprobrium, the promise and potency of every form and quality of life."[6]

—mental life included, as a matter of course.

So strong a postulate is continuity! Now this book will tend to show that mental postulates are on the whole to be respected. The demand for continuity has, over large tracts of science, proved itself to possess true prophetic power. We ought therefore ourselves sincerely to try every possible mode of conceiving the dawn of consciousness so that it may *not* appear equivalent to the irruption into the universe of a new nature, non-existent until then.

Merely to call the consciousness 'nascent' will not serve our turn.[7]

6 *Nature*, as above, 317–8.

7 'Nascent' is Mr. Spencer's great word. In showing how at a certain point consciousness must appear upon the evolving scene this author fairly outdoes himself in vagueness.

"In its higher forms, Instinct is probably accompanied by a rudimentary consciousness. There cannot be co-ordination of many stimuli without some ganglion through which they are all brought into relation. In the process of bringing them into relation, this ganglion must be subject to the influence of each—must undergo many changes. And the quick succession of changes in a ganglion, implying as it does perpetual experiences of differences and likenesses, constitutes the *raw material* of consciousness. The *implication* is that as fast as Instinct is developed, some kind of consciousness becomes nascent." (*Psychology*, § 195.)

The words 'raw material' and 'implication' which I have italicized are the words which do the *evolving*. They are supposed to have all the rigor which the 'synthetic philosophy' requires. In the following passage, when 'impressions' pass through a common 'centre of communication' in succession (much as people might pass into a theatre through a turnstile) consciousness, non-existent until then, is supposed to result:

"Separate impressions are received by the senses—by different parts of the body. If they go no further than the places at which they are received, they are useless. Or if only some of them are brought into relation with one another, they are useless. That an effectual adjustment may be made, they must be all brought into relation with one another. But this implies some centre of communication common to them all, through which they severally pass; and as they cannot pass through it simultaneously, they must pass through it in succession. So that as the external phenomena responded to become greater in number and more complicated in kind, the variety

It is true that the word signifies not yet *quite* born, and so seems to form a sort of bridge between existence and nonentity. But that is a verbal quibble. The fact is that discontinuity comes in if a new nature comes in at all. The *quantity* of the latter is quite immaterial. The girl in *Midshipman Easy* could not excuse the illegitimacy of her child by saying, 'it was a very little one.' And Consciousness, however little, is an illegitimate birth in any philosophy that starts without it, and yet professes to explain all facts by continuous evolution.

If evolution is to work smoothly, consciousness in some shape must have been present at the very origin of things. Accordingly we find that the more clear-sighted evolutionary philosophers are beginning to posit it there. Each atom of the nebula, they suppose, must have had an aboriginal atom of consciousness linked with it; and, just as the material atoms have formed bodies and brains by massing themselves together, so the mental atoms, by an analogous process of aggregation, have fused into those larger consciousnesses which we know in ourselves and suppose to exist in our fellow-animals. Some such doctrine of *atomistic hylozoism* as this is an indispensable part of a thorough-going philosophy of evolution. According to it there must be an infinite number of degrees of consciousness, following the degrees of complication and aggregation of the primordial mind-dust. To prove the separate existence of these degrees of consciousness by indirect evidence, since direct intuition of them is not to be had, becomes therefore the first duty of psychological evolutionism.

---

and rapidity of the changes to which this common centre of communication is subject must increase—there must result an unbroken series of these changes—*there must arise a consciousness.*

"Hence the progress of the correspondence between the organism and its environment, necessitates a gradual reduction of the sensorial changes to a succession; and by so doing *evolves a distinct consciousness*—a consciousness that becomes higher as the succession becomes more rapid and the correspondence more complete." (*Ibid.*, § 179.)

It is true that in the *Fortnightly Review* (n.s., vol. XIV, p. 716) Mr. Spencer denies that he means by this passage to tell us anything about the origin of consciousness at all. It resembles, however, too many other places in his *Psychology* (e.g., §§ 43, 110, 244) not to be taken as a serious attempt to explain how consciousness must at a certain point be 'evolved.' That, when a critic calls his attention to the inanity of his words, Mr. Spencer should say he never meant anything particular by them, is simply an example of the scandalous vagueness with which this sort of 'chromo-philosophy' is carried on.

SOME ALLEGED PROOFS THAT MIND-DUST EXISTS

Some of this duty we find already performed by a number of philosophers who, though not interested at all in evolution, have nevertheless on independent grounds convinced themselves of the existence of a vast amount of sub-conscious mental life. The criticism of this general opinion and its grounds will have to be postponed for a while. At present let us merely deal with the arguments assumed to prove aggregation of bits of mind-stuff into distinctly sensible feelings. They are clear and admit of a clear reply.

The German physiologist A. Fick, in 1864, was, so far as I know, the first to use them. He made experiments on the discrimination of the feelings of warmth and of touch, when only a very small portion of the skin was excited through a hole in a card, the surrounding parts being protected by the card. He found that under these circumstances mistakes were frequently made by the patient,[8] and concluded that this must be because the number of sensations from the elementary nerve-tips affected was too small to sum itself distinctly into either of the qualities of feeling in question. He tried to show how a different manner of the summation might give rise in one case to the heat and in another to the touch.

"A feeling of temperature," he says, "arises when the intensities of the units of feeling are evenly gradated, so that between two elements *a* and *b* no other unit can spatially intervene whose intensity is not also *between* that of *a* and *b*. A feeling of contact perhaps arises when this condition is not fulfilled. Both kinds of feeling, however, are composed of the same units."

But it is obviously far clearer to interpret such a gradation of

[8] His own words are: "Mistakes are made in the sense that he admits having been touched, when in reality it was radiant heat that affected his skin. In our own beforementioned experiments there was never any deception on the entire palmar side of the hand or on the face. On the back of the hand in one case in a series of 60 stimulations 4 mistakes occurred, in another case 2 mistakes in 45 stimulations. On the extensor side of the upper arm 3 deceptions out of 48 stimulations were noticed, and in the case of another individual, 1 out of 31. In one case over the spine 3 deceptions in a series of 11 excitations were observed; in another, 4 out of 19. On the lumbar spine 6 deceptions came among 29 stimulations, and again 4 out of 7. There is certainly not yet enough material on which to rest a calculation of probabilities, but anyone can easily convince himself that on the back there is no question of even a moderately accurate discrimination between warmth and a light pressure so far as but small portions of skin come into play. It has been as yet impossible to make corresponding experiments with regard to sensibility to cold." (*Lehrbuch der Anatomie und Physiologie der Sinnesorgane* (1864), p. 29.)

intensities as a brain-fact than as a mind-fact. If in the brain a tract were first excited in one of the ways suggested by Prof. Fick, and then again in the other, it might very well happen, for aught we can say to the contrary, that the psychic accompaniment in the one case would be heat, and in the other pain. The pain and the heat would, however, not be composed of psychic units, but would each be the direct result of one total brain-process. So long as this latter interpretation remains open, Fick cannot be held to have proved psychic summation.

Later, both Spencer and Taine, independently of each other, took up the same line of thought. Mr. Spencer's reasoning is worth quoting *in extenso*. He writes:

"Although the individual sensations and emotions, real or ideal, of which consciousness is built up, appear to be severally simple, homogeneous, unanalyzable, or of inscrutable natures, yet they are not so. There is at least one kind of feeling which, as ordinarily experienced, seems elementary, that is demonstrably not elementary. And after resolving it into its proximate components, we can scarcely help suspecting that other apparently-elementary feelings are also compound, and may have proximate components like those which we can in this one instance identify.

"Musical sound is the name we give to this seemingly-simple feeling which is clearly resolvable into simpler feelings. Well-known experiments prove that when equal blows or taps are made one after another at a rate not exceeding some sixteen per second, the effect of each is perceived as a separate noise; but when the rapidity with which the blows follow one another exceeds this, the noises are no longer identified in separate states of consciousness, and there arises in place of them a continuous state of consciousness, called a tone. On further increasing the rapidity of the blows, the tone undergoes the change of quality distinguished as a rise in pitch; and it continues to rise in pitch as the blows continue to increase in rapidity, until it reaches an acuteness beyond which it is no longer appreciable as a tone. So that out of units of feeling of the same kind, many feelings distinguishable from one another in quality result, according as the units are more or less integrated.

"This is not all. The inquiries of Professor Helmholtz have shown that when, along with one series of these rapidly-recurring noises, there is generated another series in which the noises are more rapid though not so loud, the effect is a change in that quality of the tone known as its *timbre*. As various musical instruments show us, tones which are alike in pitch and strength are distinguishable by their harshness or sweetness, their ringing or their liquid characters; and all their specific peculiarities are proved to arise from the combination of one, two, three, or more, supplementary series of recurrent noises with the chief series of recurrent noises. So that while the unlikenesses of feeling known as differences of pitch in tones, are due to differences of integration among the recurrent noises of one series, the unlikenesses of feeling known as differences of *timbre*, are due to the simultaneous integration with this series of other series having other degrees of integration. And thus an enormous number of qualitatively-contrasted kinds of consciousness that seem severally elementary, prove to be composed of one simple kind of consciousness, combined and re-combined with itself in multitudinous ways.

"Can we stop short here? If the different sensations known as sounds are built out of a common unit, is it not to be rationally inferred that so likewise are the different sensations known as tastes, and the different sensations known as odours, and the different sensations known as colours? Nay, shall we not regard it as probable that there is a unit common to all these strongly-contrasted classes of sensations? If the unlikenesses among the sensations of each class may be due to unlikenesses among the modes of aggregation of a unit of consciousness common to them all; so, too, may the much greater unlikenesses between the sensations of each class and those of other classes. There may be a single primordial element of consciousness, and the countless kinds of consciousness may be produced by the compounding of this element with itself and the re-compounding of its compounds with one another in higher and higher degrees: so producing increased multiplicity, variety, and complexity.

"Have we any clue to this primordial element? I think we have. That simple mental impression which proves to be the unit of composition of the sensation of musical tone, is allied to certain other simple mental impressions differently originated. The subjective effect produced by a crack or noise that has no appreciable duration, is little else than a nervous shock. Though we distinguish such a nervous shock as belonging to what we call sounds, yet it does not differ very much from nervous shocks of other kinds. An electric discharge sent through the body, causes a feeling akin to that which a sudden loud report causes. A strong unexpected impression made through the eyes, as by a flash of lightning, similarly gives rise to a start or shock; and though the feeling so named seems, like the electric shock, to have the body at large for its seat, and may therefore be regarded as the correlative rather of the efferent than of the afferent disturbance, yet on remembering the mental change that results from the instantaneous transit of an object across the field of vision, I think it may be perceived that the feeling accompanying the efferent disturbance is itself reduced very nearly to the same form. The state of consciousness so generated is, in fact, comparable in quality to the initial state of consciousness caused by a blow (distinguishing it from the pain or other feeling that commences the instant after); which state of consciousness caused by a blow, may be taken as the primitive and typical form of the nervous shock. The fact that sudden brief disturbances thus set up by different stimuli through different sets of nerves, cause feelings scarcely distinguishable in quality, will not appear strange when we recollect that distinguishableness of feeling implies appreciable duration; and that when the duration is greatly abridged, nothing more is known than that some mental change has occurred and ceased. To have a sensation of redness, to know a tone as acute or grave, to be conscious of a taste as sweet, implies in each case a considerable continuity of state. If the state does not last long enough to admit of its being contemplated, it cannot be classed as of this or that kind; and becomes a momentary modification very similar to momentary modifications otherwise caused.

"It is possible, then—may we not even say probable—that something of the same order as that which we call a nervous shock is the ultimate unit of consciousness; and that all the unlikenesses among our feelings result from unlike modes of integration of this ultimate unit. I say of the same order, because there are discernible differences among nervous shocks that are differently caused; and the primitive nervous shock probably differs somewhat from each of them. And I say of the same order for the further reason, that while we may ascribe to them a general likeness in nature we must suppose a great unlikeness in degree. The nervous shocks recognized as such, are violent—must be violent before they can be perceived amid the procession of multitudinous vivid feelings suddenly interrupted by them. But the rapidly-recurring nervous shocks of which the different forms of feeling consist, we must assume to be of comparatively moderate, or even of very slight, intensity. Were our various sensations and emotions composed of rapidly-recurring shocks as strong as those ordinarily called shocks, they would be unbearable: indeed life would cease at once. We must think of them rather as successive faint pulses of subjective change, each having the same quality as the strong pulse of subjective change distinguished as a nervous shock."[9]

INSUFFICIENCY OF THESE PROOFS

Convincing as this argument of Mr. Spencer's may appear on a first reading, it is singular how weak it really is.[10] We do, it is true,

[9] *Principles of Psychology*, § 60.

[10] Oddly enough, Mr. Spencer seems quite unaware of the *general* function of the

when we study the connection between a musical note and its outward cause, find the note simple and continuous while the cause is multiple and discrete. Somewhere, then, there *is* a transformation, reduction, or fusion. The question is, Where?—in the nerve-world or in the mind-world? Really we have no experimental proof by which to decide; and if decide we must, analogy and *a priori* probability can alone guide us. Mr. Spencer assumes that the fusion must come to pass in the mental world, and that the physical processes get through air and ear, auditory nerve and medulla, lower brain and hemispheres, without their number being reduced. Figure 25 will make the point clear.

Let the line *a–b* represent the threshold of consciousness: then everything drawn below that line will symbolize a physical process, everything above it will mean a fact of mind. Let the crosses stand

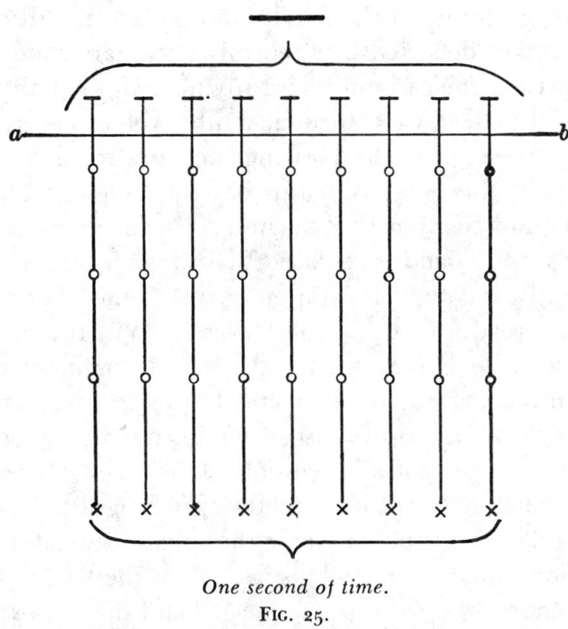

One second of time.

FIG. 25.

theory of elementary units of mind-stuff in the evolutionary philosophy. We have seen it to be absolutely indispensable, if that philosophy is to work, to postulate consciousness in the nebula,—the simplest way being, of course, to suppose every atom animated. Mr. Spencer, however, will have it (e.g., *First Principles*, § 71) that consciousness is only the occasional result of the 'transformation' of a certain amount of 'physical force' to which it is 'equivalent.' Presumably a brain must already be there before any such 'transformation' can take place; and so the argument quoted in the text stands as a mere local detail, without general bearings.

for the physical blows, the circles for the events in successively higher orders of nerve-cells, and the horizontal marks for the facts of feeling. Spencer's argument implies that each order of cells transmits just as many impulses as it receives to the cells above it; so that if the blows come at the rate of 20,000 in a second the cortical cells discharge at the same rate, and one unit of feeling corresponds to each one of the 20,000 discharges. Then, and only then, does 'integration' occur, by the 20,000 units of feeling 'compounding with themselves' into the 'continuous state of consciousness' represented by the short line at the top of the figure.

Now such an interpretation as this flies in the face of physical analogy, no less than of logical intelligibility. Consider physical analogy first.

A pendulum may be deflected by a single blow, and swing back. Will it swing back the more often the more we multiply the blows? No; for if they rain upon the pendulum too fast, it will not swing at all but remain deflected in a sensibly stationary state. In other words, increasing the cause numerically need not equally increase numerically the effect. Blow through a tube: you get a certain musical note; and increasing the blowing increases for a certain time the loudness of the note. Will this be true indefinitely? No; for when a certain force is reached, the note, instead of growing louder, suddenly disappears and is replaced by its higher octave. Turn on the gas slightly and light it: you get a tiny flame. Turn on more gas, and the breadth of the flame increases. Will this relation increase indefinitely? No, again; for at a certain moment up shoots the flame into a ragged streamer and begins to hiss. Send slowly through the nerve of a frog's gastrocnemius muscle a succession of galvanic shocks: you get a succession of twitches. Increasing the number of shocks does not increase the twitching; on the contrary, it stops it, and we have the muscle in the apparently stationary state of contraction called tetanus. This last fact is the true analogue of what must happen between the nerve-cell and the sensory fibre. It is certain that cells are more inert than fibres, and that rapid vibrations in the latter can only arouse relatively simple processes or states in the former. The higher cells may have even a slower rate of explosion than the lower, and so the twenty thousand supposed blows of the outer air may be 'integrated' in the cortex into a very small number of cell-discharges in a second. This other diagram will serve to contrast this supposition with Spencer's. In Fig. 26 all 'integration' occurs below the threshold of consciousness. The fre-

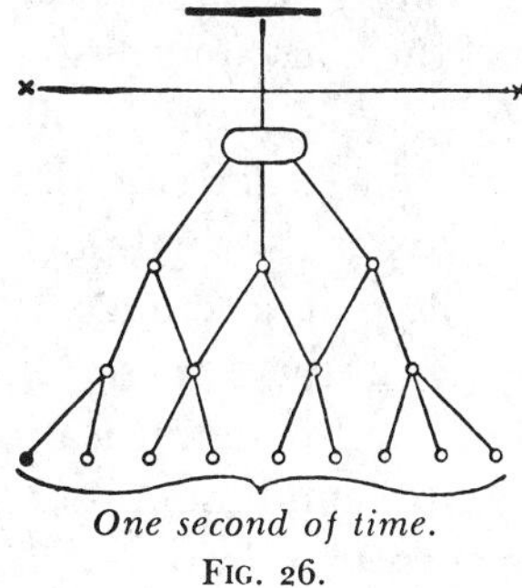

One second of time.
FIG. 26.

quency of cell-events becomes more and more reduced as we approach the cells to which feeling is most directly attached, until at last we come to a condition of things symbolized by the larger ellipse, which may be taken to stand for some rather massive and slow process of tension and discharge in the cortical centres, to which, *as a whole*, the feeling of musical tone symbolized by the line at the top of the diagram *simply and totally* corresponds. It is as if a long file of men were to start one after the other to reach a distant point. The road at first is good and they keep their original distance apart. Presently it is intersected by bogs each worse than the last, so that the front men get so retarded that the hinder ones catch up with them before the journey is done, and all arrive together at the goal.[11]

On this supposition there *are* no unperceived units of mind-stuff preceding and composing the full consciousness. The latter is itself an immediate psychic fact and bears an immediate relation to the neural state which is its unconditional accompaniment. Did each

[11] The compounding of colors may be dealt with in an identical way. Helmholtz has shown that if green light and red light fall simultaneously on the retina, we see the color yellow. The mind-stuff theory would interpret this as a case where the feeling green and the feeling red 'combine' into the *tertium quid* of feeling, yellow. What no doubt really occurs is that a third kind of nerve-process is set up when the combined lights impinge on the retina,—not simply the process of red plus the process of green, but something quite different from both or either. Of course, then, there *are* no feelings, either of red or of green, present to the mind at all; but the feeling of yellow which *is* there, answers as directly to the nerve-process which momentarily then exists, as the feelings of green and red would answer to their respective nerve-processes did the latter happen to be taking place.

neural shock give rise to its own psychic shock, and the psychic shocks then combine, it would be impossible to understand why severing one part of the central nervous system from another should break up the integrity of the consciousness. The cut has nothing to do with the psychic world. The atoms of mind-stuff ought to float off from the nerve-matter on either side of it, and come together over it and fuse, just as well as if it had not been made. We know, however, that they do not; that severance of the paths of conduction between a man's left auditory centre or optical centre and the rest of his cortex will sever all communication between the words which he hears or sees written and the rest of his ideas.

Moreover, if feelings can mix into a *tertium quid*, why do we not take a feeling of greenness and a feeling of redness, and make a feeling of yellowness out of them? Why has optics neglected the open road to truth, and wasted centuries in disputing about theories of color-composition which two minutes of introspection would have settled forever?[12] We cannot mix feelings as such, though we may mix the objects we feel, and from *their* mixture get new feelings. We cannot even (as we shall later see) have two feelings in our mind at once. At most we can compare together *objects previously presented* to us in distinct feelings; but then we find each object stubbornly maintaining its separate identity before consciousness, whatever the verdict of the comparison may be.[13]

SELF-COMPOUNDING OF MENTAL FACTS IS INADMISSIBLE

But there is a still more fatal objection to the theory of mental units 'compounding with themselves' or 'integrating.' It is logically unintelligible; it leaves out the essential feature of all the 'combinations' we actually know.

All the 'combinations' which we actually know are EFFECTS,

[12] Cf. Mill's *System of Logic*, book VI, chap. IV, § 3.

[13] I find in my students an almost invincible tendency to think that we can immediately perceive that feelings do combine. "What!" they say, "is not the taste of lemonade composed of that of lemon *plus* that of sugar?" This is taking the combining of objects for that of feelings. The physical lemonade contains both the lemon and the sugar, but its taste does not contain their tastes; for if there are any two things which are certainly *not* present in the taste of lemonade, those are the lemon-sour on the one hand and the sugar-sweet on the other. These tastes are absent utterly. The entirely new taste which is present *resembles*, it is true, both those tastes; but in Chapter XIII we shall see that resemblance cannot always be held to involve partial identity.

wrought by the units said to be 'combined,' UPON SOME ENTITY OTHER THAN THEMSELVES. Without this feature of a medium or vehicle, the notion of combination has no sense.

"A multitude of contractile units, by joint-action, and by being all connected, for instance, with a single tendon, will pull at the same, and will bring about a dynamical effect which is undoubtedly the resultant of their combined individual energies. . . . On the whole, tendons are to muscular fibres, and bones are to tendons, combining recipients of mechanical energies. A medium of composition is indispensable to the summation of energies. To realise the complete dependence of mechanical resultants on a combining substratum, one may fancy for a moment all the individually contracting muscular elements severed from their attachments. They might then still be capable of contracting with the same energy as before, yet no co-operative result would be accomplished. The medium of dynamical combination would be wanting. The multiple energies, singly exerted on no common recipient, would lose themselves in entirely isolated and disconnected efforts."[14]

In other words, no possible number of entities (call them as you like, whether forces, material particles, or mental elements) can sum *themselves* together. Each remains, in the sum, what it always was; and the sum itself exists only *for a bystander* who happens to overlook the units and to apprehend the sum as such; or else it exists in the shape of some other *effect* on an entity external to the sum itself. Let it not be objected that H_2 and O combine of themselves into 'water,' and thenceforward exhibit new properties. They do not. The 'water' is just the old atoms in the new position, H–O–H; the 'new properties' are just their combined *effects,* when in this position, upon external media, such as our sense-organs and the various reagents on which water may exert its properties and be known.

"Aggregations are organised wholes only when they behave as such in the presence of other things. A statue is an aggregation of particles of marble; but as such it has no unity. For the spectator it is one; in and for itself it is an aggregate: just as, to the consciousness of an ant crawling over it, it may again appear a mere aggregate. No summing up of parts can make an unity of a mass of discrete constituents, unless this unity exist for some other subject, not for the mass itself."[15]

[14] E. Montgomery, in *Mind,* v, 18–19. See also pp. 24–5.

[15] J. Royce: *Mind,* vi, p. 376. Lotze has set forth the truth of this law more clearly and copiously than any other writer. Unfortunately he is too lengthy to quote. See

Just so, in the parallelogram of forces, the 'forces' themselves do not combine into the diagonal resultant; a *body* is needed on which they may impinge, to exhibit their resultant effect. No more do musical sounds combine *per se* into concords or discords. Concord and discord are names for their combined effects on that external medium, the *ear*.

Where the elemental units are supposed to be feelings, the case is in no wise altered. Take a hundred of them, shuffle them and pack them as close together as you can (whatever that may mean); still each remains the same feeling it always was, shut in its own skin, windowless, ignorant of what the other feelings are and mean. There would be a hundred-and-first feeling there, if, when a group or series of such feelings were set up, a consciousness *belonging to the group as such* should emerge. And this 101st feeling would be a totally new fact; the 100 original feelings might, by a curious physical law, be a signal for its *creation*, when they came together; but they would have no substantial identity with it, nor it with them, and one could never deduce the one from the others, or (in any intelligible sense) say that they *evolved* it.

Take a sentence of a dozen words, and take twelve men and tell to each one word. Then stand the men in a row or jam them in a bunch, and let each think of his word as intently as he will; nowhere will there be a consciousness of the whole sentence.[16] We

---

his *Microcosmus*, bk. II, ch. I, § 5; *Metaphysik*, §§ 242, 260; *Grundzüge der Psychologie*, part II, chap. I, §§ 3, 4, 5. Compare also Reid's *Essays on the Intellectual Powers of Man*, essay V, chap. III *ad fin.*; Bowne's *Metaphysics*, pp. 361–76; St. G. Mivart: *Nature and Thought*, pp. 98–101; E. Gurney: "Monism," in *Mind*, VI, 153; and the article by Prof. Royce, just quoted, on "Mind-stuff and Reality."

In defence of the mind-stuff view, see W. K. Clifford: *Mind*, III, 57 (reprinted in his *Lectures and Essays*, II, 71); G. T. Fechner: *Elemente der Psychophysik*, Bd. II, cap. XLV; H. Taine: *On Intelligence*, bk. III; E. Haeckel: "Zellseelen und Seelenzellen" in *Gesammelte populäre Vorträge*, Bd. I, p. 143; W. S. Duncan: *Conscious Matter*, *passim*; F. Zöllner: *Über die Natur der Cometen*, pp. 320 ff.; Alfred Barratt: *Physical Ethics* and *Physical Metempiric*, *passim*; J. Soury: "Hylozoismus," in *Kosmos*, V Jahrgang, Heft X, p. 241; A. Main: *Mind*, I, 292, 431, 566; II, 126, 402; *Id.*, *Revue Philosophique*, II, 86, 88, 419; III, 51, 502; IV, 402; F. W. Frankland: *Mind*, VI, 116; Whittaker: *Mind*, VI, 498 (historical); Morton Prince: *The Nature of Mind and Human Automatism* (1885); A. Riehl: *Der philosophische Kriticismus*, Bd. II, Theil 2, 2ter Abschnitt, 2tes Cap. (1887). The clearest of all these statements is, as far as it goes, that of Prince.

16 "Someone might say that although it is true that neither a blind man nor a deaf man by himself can compare sounds with colors, yet since one hears and the other sees they might do so both together. . . . But whether they are apart or close together makes

talk of the 'spirit of the age,' and the 'sentiment of the people,' and in various ways we hypostatize 'public opinion.' But we know this to be symbolic speech, and never dream that the spirit, opinion, sentiment, etc., constitute a consciousness other than, and additional to, that of the several individuals whom the words 'age,' 'people,' or 'public' denote. The private minds do not agglomerate into a higher compound mind. This has always been the invincible contention of the spiritualists against the associationists in Psychology,—a contention which we shall take up at greater length in Chapter X. The associationists say the mind is constituted by a multiplicity of distinct 'ideas' *associated* into a unity. There is, they say, an idea of a, and also an idea of b. *Therefore,* they say, there is an idea of $a + b$, or of a and b together. Which is like saying that the mathematical square of a plus that of b is equal to the square of $a + b$, a palpable untruth. Idea of a, plus idea of b, are *not* identical with idea of $(a + b)$. It is one, they are two; in it, what knows a also knows b; in them, what knows a is expressly posited as not knowing b; etc. In short, the two separate ideas can never by any logic be made to figure as one and the same thing as the 'associated' idea.

This is what the spiritualists keep saying; and since we do, as a matter of fact, have the 'compounded' idea, and do know a and b together, they adopt a farther hypothesis to explain that fact. The separate ideas exist, they say, but *affect* a third entity, the soul. *This* has the 'compounded' idea, if you please so to call it; and the compounded idea is an altogether new psychic fact to which the separate ideas stand in the relation, not of constituents, but of occasions of production.

This argument of the spiritualists against the associationists has never been answered by the latter. It holds good against any talk about self-compounding amongst feelings, against any 'blending,' or 'complication,' or 'mental chemistry,' or 'psychic synthesis,' which supposes a resultant consciousness to float off from the constituents *per se*, in the absence of a supernumerary principle of con-

no difference; not even if they permanently keep house together; no, not if they were Siamese twins, or more than Siamese twins, and were inseparably grown together, would it make the assumption any more possible. Only when sound and color are represented in the same reality is it thinkable that they should be compared." (Brentano: *Psychologie vom empirischen Standpunkte,* p. 209.)

sciousness which they may affect. The mind-stuff theory, in short, is unintelligible. Atoms of feeling cannot compose higher feelings, any more than atoms of matter can compose physical things! The 'things,' for a clear-headed atomistic evolutionist, are not. Nothing is but the everlasting atoms. When grouped in a certain way, *we* name them this 'thing' or that; but the thing we name has no existence out of our mind. So of the states of mind which are supposed to be compound because they know many different things together. Since indubitably such states do exist, they must exist as single new facts, effects, possibly, as the spiritualists say, on the Soul (we will not decide that point here), but at any rate independent and integral, and not compounded of psychic atoms.[17]

[17] The reader must observe that we are reasoning altogether about the *logic* of the mind-stuff theory, about whether it can *explain the constitution* of higher mental states by viewing them as *identical with lower ones* summed together. We say the two sorts of fact are not identical: a higher state *is* not a lot of lower states; it is itself. When, however, a lot of lower states have come together, or when certain brain-conditions occur together which, *if they occurred separately, would produce* a lot of lower states, we have not for a moment pretended that a higher state may not emerge. In fact it does emerge under those conditions; and our Chapter IX will be mainly devoted to the proof of this fact. But such emergence is that of a new psychic entity, and is *toto cœlo* different from such an 'integration' of the lower states as the mind-stuff theory affirms.

It may seem strange to suppose that anyone should mistake criticism of a certain theory about a fact for doubt of the fact itself. And yet the confusion is made in high quarters enough to justify our remarks. Mr. J. Ward, in his article "Psychology" in the *Encyclopædia Britannica*, speaking of the hypothesis that " 'a series of feelings, can be aware of itself as a series,' " says (p. 39): "Paradox is too mild a word for it; even contradiction will hardly suffice." Whereupon, Professor Bain takes him thus to task: "As to 'a series of states being aware of itself,' I confess I see no insurmountable difficulty. It may be a fact, or not a fact; it may be a very clumsy expression for what it is applied to; but it is neither paradox nor contradiction. A 'series' merely contradicts an individual, or it may be two or more individuals as co-existing; but that is too general to exclude the possibility of self-knowledge. It certainly does not bring the property of self-knowledge into the foreground, which, however, is not the same as denying it. An algebraic series might know itself, without any contradiction: the only thing against it is the want of evidence of fact." (*Mind*, XI, 459). Prof. Bain thinks, then, that all the bother is about the difficulty of seeing how a series of feelings can have the knowledge of itself *added to it*!!! As if anybody ever was troubled about that. That, notoriously enough, is a fact: our consciousness is a series of feelings to which every now and then is *added* a retrospective consciousness that they have come and gone. What Mr. Ward and I are troubled about is merely the silliness of the mind-stuffists and associationists continuing to say that the 'series of states' *is* the 'awareness of itself'; that if the states be posited severally, their collective consciousness is *eo ipso* given; and that we need no farther explanation, or 'evidence of fact.'

CAN STATES OF MIND BE UNCONSCIC

The passion for unity and smoothness is in some . satiate that, in spite of the logical clearness of these reasonin conclusions, many will fail to be influenced by them. They estab-lish a sort of disjointedness in things which in certain quarters will appear intolerable. They sweep away all chance of 'passing without break' either from the material to the mental, or from the lower to the higher mental; and they thrust us back into a pluralism of consciousnesses—each arising discontinuously in the midst of two disconnected worlds, material and mental—which is even worse than the old notion of the separate creation of each particular soul. But the malcontents will hardly try to refute our reasonings by direct attack. It is more probable that, turning their back upon them altogether, they will devote themselves to sapping and mining the region roundabout until it is a bog of logical liquefaction, into the midst of which all definite conclusions of any sort may be trusted ere long to sink and disappear.

Our reasonings have assumed that the 'integration' of a thousand psychic units must be either just the units over again, simply rebaptized, or else something real, but then other than and additional to those units; that if a certain existing fact is that of a thousand feelings, it cannot at the same time be that of ONE feeling; for the essence of feeling is to be felt, and as a psychic existent *feels*, so it must *be*. If the one feeling feels like no one of the thousand, in what sense can it be said to *be* the thousand?[17a] These assumptions are what the monists will seek to undermine. The Hegelizers amongst them will take high ground at once, and say that the glory and beauty of the psychic life is that in it all contradictions find their reconciliation; and that it is just because the facts we are considering *are* facts of the self that they are both one and many at the same time. With this intellectual temper I confess that I cannot contend. As in striking at some unresisting gossamer with a club, one but overreaches one's self, and the thing one aims at gets no harm. So I leave this school to its devices.

The other monists are of less deliquescent frame, and try to break down distinctness among mental states by *making a distinc-*

[17a] If the sensation of *pitch* be ignorant of all such things as *taps*, what sense is there in the declaration that it consists of nothing but things that know taps exclusively?

ion. This sounds paradoxical, but it is only ingenious. The distinction is that *between the unconscious and the conscious being of the mental state*. It is the sovereign means for believing what one likes in psychology, and of turning what might become a science into a tumbling-ground for whimsies. It has numerous champions, and elaborate reasons to give for itself. We must therefore accord it due consideration. In discussing the question:

DO UNCONSCIOUS MENTAL STATES EXIST?

it will be best to give the list of so-called proofs as briefly as possible, and to follow each by its objection, as in scholastic books.[18]

First Proof. The *minimum visibile*, the *minimum audibile*, are objects composed of parts. How can the whole affect the sense unless each part does? And yet each part does so without being separately sensible. Leibnitz calls the total consciousness an '*apperception*,' the supposed insensible consciousness by the name of '*petites perceptions*.'

"To judge of the latter," he says, "I am accustomed to use the example of the roaring of the sea with which one is assailed when near the shore. To hear this noise as one does, one must hear the parts which compose its totality, that is, the noise of each wave, . . . although this noise would not be noticed if its wave were alone. One must be affected a little by the movement of one wave, one must have some perception of each several noise, however small it be. Otherwise one would not hear that of 100,000 waves, for of 100,000 zeroes one can never make a quantity."[19]

Reply. This is an excellent example of the so-called 'fallacy of division,' or predicating what is true only of a collection, of each member of the collection distributively. It no more follows that

[18] The writers about 'unconscious cerebration' seem sometimes to mean that and sometimes unconscious thought. The arguments which follow are culled from various quarters. The reader will find them most systematically urged by E. von Hartmann: *Philosophy of the Unconscious*, vol. I and by E. Colsenet: *La Vie inconsciente de l'esprit* (1880). Consult also T. Laycock: *Mind and Brain*, vol. I, chap. V (1860); W. B. Carpenter: *Mental Physiology*, chap. XIII; F. P. Cobbe: *Darwinism in Morals, and Other Essays*, essay XI, "Unconscious Cerebration" (1872); F. Bowen: *Modern Philosophy*, pp. 429–480; R. H. Hutton: *Contemporary Review*, vol. XXIV, p. 201; J. S. Mill: *An Examination of Sir William Hamilton's Philosophy*, chap. XV; G. H. Lewes: *Problems of Life and Mind*, 3d series, Prob. II, chap. X, and also Prob. III, chap. II; D. G. Thompson: *A System of Psychology*, chap. XXXIII; J. M. Baldwin: *Handbook of Psychology*, chap. IV.

[19] *Nouveaux essais*, Avant-propos.

if a thousand things together cause sensation, one thing alone must cause it, than it follows that if one pound weight moves a balance, then one ounce weight must move it too, in less degree. One ounce weight does not move it *at all;* its movement *begins* with the pound. At most we can say that each ounce affects it in *some* way which helps the advent of that movement. And so each infra-sensible stimulus to a nerve no doubt affects the nerve and helps the birth of sensation when the other stimuli come. But this affection is a nerve-affection, and there is not the slightest ground for supposing it to be a 'perception' unconscious of itself. "A certain *quantity* of the cause may be a necessary condition to the production of *any* of the effect,"[20] when the latter is a mental state.

Second Proof. In all acquired dexterities and habits, secondarily automatic performances as they are called, we do what *originally* required a chain of deliberately conscious perceptions and volitions. As the actions still keep their intelligent character, intelligence must still preside over their execution. But since our consciousness seems all the while elsewhere engaged, such intelligence must consist of unconscious perceptions, inferences, and volitions.

Reply. There is more than one alternative explanation in accordance with larger bodies of fact. One is that the perceptions and volitions in habitual actions may be performed consciously, only so quickly and inattentively that no *memory* of them remains. Another is that the consciousness of these actions exists, but is *split-off* from the rest of the consciousness of the hemispheres. We shall find in Chapter X numerous proofs of the reality of this split-off condition of portions of consciousness. Since in man the hemispheres indubitably co-operate in these secondarily automatic acts, it will not do to say either that they occur without consciousness or that their consciousness is that of the lower centres, which we know nothing about. But either lack of memory or split-off cortical consciousness will certainly account for all of the facts.[21]

Third Proof. Thinking of A, we presently find ourselves thinking of C. Now B is the natural logical link between A and C, but we have no consciousness of having thought of B. It must have been in our mind '*un*consciously,' and in that state affected the sequence of our ideas.

Reply. Here again we have a choice between more plausible ex-

20 J. S. Mill: *Examination of Hamilton*, chap. xv.

21 Cf. Dugald Stewart: *Elements of the Philosophy of the Human Mind*, chap. II.

planations. Either B was consciously there, but the next instant forgotten, or its *brain-tract* alone was adequate to do the whole work of coupling A with C, without the idea B being aroused at all, whether consciously or 'unconsciously.'

Fourth Proof. Problems unsolved when we go to bed are found solved in the morning when we wake. Somnambulists do rational things. We awaken punctually at an hour predetermined overnight, etc. Unconscious thinking, volition, time-registration, etc., must have presided over these acts.

Reply. Consciousness forgotten, as in the hypnotic trance.

Fifth Proof. Some patients will often, in an attack of epileptiform unconsciousness, go through complicated processes, such as eating a dinner in a restaurant and paying for it, or making a violent homicidal attack. In trance, artificial or pathological, long and complex performances, involving the use of the reasoning powers, are executed, of which the patient is wholly unaware on coming to.

Reply. Rapid and complete oblivescence is certainly the explanation here. The analogue again is hypnotism. Tell the subject of an hypnotic trance, during his trance, that he *will* remember, and he may remember everything perfectly when he awakes, though without your telling him no memory would have remained. The extremely rapid oblivescence of common *dreams* is a familiar fact.

Sixth Proof. In a musical concord the vibrations of the several notes are in relatively simple ratios. The mind must unconsciously count the vibrations, and be pleased by the simplicity which it finds.

Reply. The brain-process produced by the simple ratios may be as directly agreeable as the conscious process of comparing them would be. No counting, either conscious or 'unconscious,' is required.

Seventh Proof. Every hour we make theoretic judgments and emotional reactions, and exhibit practical tendencies, for which we can give no explicit logical justification, but which are good inferences from certain premises. We know more than we can say. Our conclusions run ahead of our power to analyze their grounds. A child, ignorant of the axiom that two things equal to the same are equal to each other, applies it nevertheless in his concrete judgments unerringly. A boor will use the *dictum de omni et nullo* who is unable to understand it in abstract terms.

"We seldom consciously think how our house is painted, what the shade of it is, what the pattern of our furniture is, or whether the door opens to the right or the left, out or in. But how quickly should we notice a change in any of these things? Think of the door that you have most often opened, and tell, if you can, whether it opens to the right or left, out or in. Yet, when you open the door, you never put your hand on the wrong side to find the latch, nor try to push it when it opens with a pull. . . . What is the precise characteristic in your friend's step that enables you to recognize it when he is coming? Did you ever consciously think the idea, 'If I run into a solid piece of matter I shall get hurt, or be hindered in my progress,' and do you avoid running into obstacles because you ever distinctly conceived, or consciously acquired and thought that idea?"[22]

Most of our knowledge is at all times potential. We act in accordance with the whole drift of what we have learned, but few items rise into consciousness at the time. Many of them, however, we may recall at will. All this co-operation of unrealized principles and facts, of potential knowledge, with our actual thought is quite inexplicable unless we suppose the perpetual existence of an immense mass of *ideas in an unconscious state*, all of them exerting a steady pressure and influence upon our conscious thinking, and many of them in such continuity with it as ever and anon to become conscious themselves.

Reply. No such mass of ideas is supposable. But there are all kinds of short-cuts in the brain; and processes not aroused strongly enough to give any 'idea' distinct enough to be a premise, may, nevertheless, help to determine just that resultant process of whose psychic accompaniment the said idea *would* be a premise, if the idea existed at all. A certain overtone may be a feature of my friend's voice, and may conspire with the other tones thereof to arouse in my brain the process which suggests to my consciousness his name. And yet I may be ignorant of the overtone *per se*, and unable, even when he speaks, to tell whether it be there or no. It leads me to the idea of the name; but it produces in me no such

[22] J. E. Maude: "The Unconscious in Education," in *Education*, vol. II, p. 401 (1882).

cerebral process as that to which the *idea of the overtone* would correspond. And similarly of our learning. Each subject we learn leaves behind it a modification of the brain, which makes it impossible for the latter to react upon things just as it did before; and the result of the difference may be a tendency to act, though with no idea, much as we should *if* we were consciously thinking about the subject. The becoming conscious of the latter at will is equally readily explained as a result of the brain-modification. This, as Wundt phrases it, is a 'predisposition' to bring forth the conscious idea of the original subject, a predisposition which other stimuli and brain-processes may convert into an actual result. But such a predisposition is no 'unconscious idea'; it is only a particular collocation of the molecules in certain tracts of the brain.

Eighth Proof. Instincts, as pursuits of ends by appropriate means, are manifestations of intelligence; but as the ends are not foreseen, the intelligence must be unconscious.

Reply. Chapter XXIV will show that all the phenomena of instinct are explicable as actions of the nervous system, mechanically discharged by stimuli to the senses.

Ninth Proof. In sense-perception we have results in abundance, which can only be explained as conclusions drawn by a process of unconscious inference from data given to sense. A small human image on the retina is referred, not to a pygmy, but to a distant man of normal size. A certain gray patch is inferred to be a white object seen in a dim light. Often the inference leads us astray: e.g., pale gray against pale green looks red, because we take a wrong premise to argue from. We think a green film is spread over everything; and knowing that under such a film a red thing would look gray, we wrongly infer from the gray appearance that a red thing must be there. Our study of space-perception in Chapter XVIII will give abundant additional examples both of the truthful and illusory percepts which have been explained to result from unconscious logic operations.

Reply. That chapter will also in many cases refute this explanation. Color- and light-contrast are certainly purely sensational affairs, in which inference plays no part. This has been satisfactorily proved by Hering,[23] and shall be treated of again in Chapter XVII. Our rapid judgments of size, shape, distance, and the like, are best explained as processes of simple cerebral association. Certain sense-

23 *Zur Lehre vom Lichtsinne* (1878).

impressions directly stimulate brain-tracts, of whose activity ready-made conscious percepts are the immediate psychic counterparts. They do this by a mechanism either connate or acquired by habit. It is to be remarked that Wundt and Helmholtz, who in their earlier writings did more than anyone to give vogue to the notion that unconscious inference is a vital factor in sense-perception, have seen fit on later occasions to modify their views and to admit that results *like* those of reasoning may accrue without any actual reasoning process unconsciously taking place.[24] Maybe the excessive and riotous applications made by Hartmann of their principle have led them to this change. It would be natural to feel towards him as the sailor in the story felt towards the horse who got his foot into the stirrup,—"If you're going to get on, I must get off."

Hartmann fairly boxes the compass of the universe with the principle of unconscious thought. For him there is no namable thing that does not exemplify it. But his logic is so lax and his failure to consider the most obvious alternatives so complete that it would, on the whole, be a waste of time to look at his arguments in detail. The same is true of Schopenhauer, in whom the mythology reaches its climax. The visual perception, for example, of an object in space results, according to him, from the intellect performing the following operations, all unconscious. First, it apprehends the inverted retinal image and turns it right side up, constructing *flat space* as a preliminary operation; then it computes from the angle of convergence of the eyeballs that the two retinal images must be the projection of but a single *object*; thirdly, it constructs the third dimension and sees this object *solid*; fourthly, it assigns its *distance*; and fifthly, in each and all of these operations it gets the objective character of what it 'constructs' by unconsciously inferring it as the only possible *cause* of some sensation which it unconsciously feels.[25] Comment on this seems hardly called for. It is, as I said, pure mythology.

None of these facts, then, appealed to so confidently in proof of the existence of ideas in an unconscious state, prove anything of the sort. They prove either that conscious ideas were present which the next instant were forgotten; or they prove that certain

[24] Cf. Wundt: *Über den Einfluss der Philosophie*, etc.—Antrittsrede (1876), pp. 10–11;—Helmholtz: *Die Thatsachen in der Wahrnehmung* (1879), p. 27.

[25] Cf. *Über die vierfache Wurzel des Satzes vom zureichenden Grunde*, pp. 59–65. Compare also F. Zöllner's *Natur der Cometen*, pp. 342 ff., and 425.

results, *similar* to results of reasoning, may be wrought out by rapid brain-processes to which no ideation seems attached. But there is one more argument to be alleged, less obviously insufficient than those which we have reviewed, and demanding a new sort of reply.

Tenth Proof. There is a great class of experiences in our mental life which may be described as discoveries that a subjective condition which we have been having is really something different from what we had supposed. We suddenly find ourselves bored by a thing which we thought we were enjoying well enough; or in love with a person whom we imagined we only liked. Or else we deliberately analyze our motives, and find that at bottom they contain jealousies and cupidities which we little suspected to be there. Our feelings towards people are perfect wells of motivation, unconscious of itself, which introspection brings to light. And our sensations likewise: we constantly discover new elements in sensations which we have been in the habit of receiving all our days, elements, too, which have been there from the first, since otherwise we should have been unable to distinguish the sensations containing them from others nearly allied. The elements must exist, for we use them to discriminate by; but they must exist in an unconscious state, since we so completely fail to single them out.[26] The books of the analytic school of psychology abound in examples of the kind. Who knows the countless associations that mingle with his each and every thought? Who can pick apart all the nameless feelings that stream in at every moment from his various internal organs, muscles, heart, glands, lungs, etc., and compose in their totality his sense of bodily life? Who is aware of the part played by feelings of innervation and suggestions of possible muscular exertion in all his judgments of distance, shape, and size? Consider, too, the difference between a sensation which we simply *have* and one which we *attend to*. Attention gives results that seem like fresh creations; and yet the feelings and elements of feeling which it reveals must have been already there—in an unconscious state. We all know *practically* the difference between the so-called sonant and the so-called surd consonants, between D, B, Z, G, V, and T, P, S, K, F, respectively. But comparatively few persons know the difference *theoretically*, until their attention has been called to what it is, when they perceive it readily enough. The sonants are

[26] Cf. the statements from Helmholtz to be found later in Chapter XIII.

nothing but the surds plus a certain element, which is alike in all, superadded. That element is the laryngeal sound with which they are uttered, surds having no such accompaniment. When we hear the sonant letter, both its component elements must really be in our mind; but we remain unconscious of what they really are, and mistake the letter for a simple quality of sound until an effort of attention teaches us its two components. There exist a host of sensations which most men pass through life and never attend to, and consequently have only in an unconscious way. The feelings of opening and closing the glottis, of making tense the tympanic membrane, of accommodating for near vision, of intercepting the passage from the nostrils to the throat, are instances of what I mean. Everyone gets these feelings many times an hour; but few readers, probably, are conscious of exactly what sensations are meant by the names I have just used. All these facts, and an enormous number more, seem to prove conclusively that, in addition to the fully conscious way in which an idea may exist in the mind, there is also an unconscious way; that it is unquestionably the same identical idea which exists in these two ways; and that therefore any arguments against the mind-stuff theory, based on the notion that *esse* in our mental life is *sentiri*, and that an idea must consciously be felt as what it is, fall to the ground.

Objection. These reasonings are one tissue of confusion. Two states of mind which refer to the same external reality, or two states of mind the later one of which refers to the earlier, are described as the same state of mind, or 'idea,' published as it were in two editions; and then whatever qualities of the second edition are found openly lacking in the first are explained as having really been there, only in an 'unconscious' way. It would be difficult to believe that intelligent men could be guilty of so patent a fallacy, were not the history of psychology there to give the proof. The psychological stock-in-trade of some authors is the belief that two thoughts about one thing are virtually the same thought, and that this same thought may in subsequent reflections become more and more *conscious* of what it really *was* all along from the first. But once make the distinction between simply *having an idea* at the moment of its presence and subsequently knowing all sorts of things *about it*; make moreover that between a state of mind itself, taken as a subjective fact, on the one hand, and the objective thing it knows, on the other, and one has no difficulty in escaping from the labyrinth.

Take the latter distinction first: Immediately all the arguments based on sensations and the new features in them which attention brings to light fall to the ground. The sensations of the B and the V when we attend to these sounds and analyze out the laryngeal contribution which makes them differ from P and F respectively, are *different sensations* from those of the B and the V taken in a simple way. They stand, it is true, for the *same letters*, and thus mean the *same outer realities*; but they are different mental affections, and certainly depend on widely different processes of cerebral activity. It is unbelievable that two mental states so different as the passive reception of a sound as a whole, and the analysis of that whole into distinct ingredients by voluntary attention, should be due to processes at all similar. And the subjective difference does not consist in that the first-named state *is* the second in an 'unconscious' form. It is an absolute psychic difference, even greater than that between the states to which two different surds will give rise. The same is true of the other sensations chosen as examples. The man who learns for the first time how the closure of his glottis feels, experiences in this discovery an absolutely new psychic modification, the like of which he never had before. He had another feeling before, a feeling incessantly renewed, and of which the same glottis was the organic starting point; but that was not the later feeling in an 'unconscious' state; it was a feeling *sui generis* altogether, although it took cognizance of the same bodily part, the glottis. We shall see, hereafter, that the same reality can be cognized by an endless number of psychic states, which may differ *toto cœlo* among themselves, without ceasing on that account to refer to the reality in question. Each of them is a conscious fact; none of them has any mode of being whatever except a certain way of being felt at the moment of being present. It is simply unintelligible and fantastical to say, because they point to the same outer reality, that they must therefore be so many editions of the same 'idea,' now in a conscious and now in an 'unconscious' phase. There is only one 'phase' in which an idea can be, and that is a fully conscious condition. If it is not in that condition, then it is not at all. Something else is, in its place. The something else may be a merely physical brain-process, or it may be another conscious idea. Either of these things may perform much the same *function* as the first idea, refer to the same object, and roughly stand in the same relations to the upshot of our thought. But that is no reason why we should throw away the logical principle of identity in psychology, and say that, however it may fare in the outer world, the mind at any rate is a place in which a thing can be all kinds of other things without ceasing to be itself as well.

Now take the other cases alleged, and the other distinction, that namely between *having* a mental state and knowing all *about* it. The truth is here even simpler to unravel. When I decide that I have, without knowing it, been for several weeks in love, I am simply giving a name to a state which previously *I have not named*, but which was fully conscious; which had no residual mode of being except the manner in which it was conscious; and which, though it was a feeling towards the same person for whom I now have a much more inflamed feeling, and though it continuously led into the latter, and is similar enough to be called by the same name, is yet in no sense identical with the latter, and least of all in an 'unconscious' way. Again, the feelings from our viscera and other dimly-felt organs, the feelings of innervation (if such there be), and those of muscular exertion which, in our spatial judgments, are supposed unconsciously to determine what we shall perceive, are just exactly what we feel them, perfectly determinate conscious states, not vague editions of other conscious states. They may be faint and weak; they may be very vague cognizers of the same realities which other conscious states cognize and name exactly; they may be unconscious of much in the reality which the other states are conscious of. But that does not make them *in themselves* a whit dim or vague or unconscious. They *are* eternally as they feel when they exist, and can, neither actually nor potentially, be identified with anything else than their own faint selves. A faint feeling may be looked back upon and classified and understood in its relations to what went before or after it in the stream of thought. But it, on the one hand, and the later state of mind which knows all these things about it, on the other, are surely not two conditions, one conscious and the other 'unconscious,' of the same identical psychic fact. It is the destiny of thought that, on the whole, our early ideas are superseded by later ones, giving fuller accounts of the same realities. But none the less do the earlier and the later ideas preserve their own several substantive identities as so many several successive states of mind. To believe the contrary would make any definite science of psychology impossible. The only identity to be found among our successive ideas is their similarity of cognitive or representative function as dealing with the same objects. Identity of *being*, there is none; and I believe that throughout the rest of this volume the reader will reap the advantages of the simpler way of formulating the facts which is here begun.[27]

So we seem not only to have ascertained the unintelligibility of the notion that a mental fact can be two things at once, and that what seems like one feeling, of blueness for example, or of hatred, may really and 'unconsciously' be ten thousand elementary feelings which do not resemble blueness or hatred at all, but we find that we can express all the observed facts in other ways. The mind-stuff theory, however, though scotched, is, we may be sure, not killed. If we ascribe consciousness to unicellular animalcules, then single cells can have it, and analogy should make us ascribe it to the several cells of the brain, each individually taken. And what a convenience would it not be for the psychologist if, by the adding together of various doses of this separate-cell-consciousness, he could

[27] The text was written before Professor Lipps's *Grundtatsachen des Seelenlebens* (1883) came into my hands. In Chapter III of that book the notion of unconscious thought is subjected to the clearest and most searching criticism which it has yet received. Some passages are so similar to what I have myself written that I must quote them in a note. After proving that dimness and clearness, incompleteness and completeness do not pertain to a state of mind *as such*—since every state of mind must be *exactly* what it is, and nothing else—but only pertain to the way in which states of mind stand for objects, which they more or less dimly, more or less clearly, *represent*; Lipps takes the case of those sensations which attention is said to make more clear. "I perceive an object," he says, "now in clear daylight, and again at night. Call the content of the day-perception a, and that of the evening-perception a^1. There will probably be a considerable difference between a and a^1. The colors of a will be varied and intense, and will be sharply bounded by each other; those of a^1 will be less luminous, and less strongly contrasted, and will approach a common gray or brown, and merge more into each other. Both percepts, however, as such, are completely determinate and distinct from all others. The colors of a^1 appear before my eye neither more nor less decidedly dark and blurred than the colors of a appear bright and sharply bounded. But now I know, or believe I know, that one and the same real Object A corresponds to both a and a^1. I am convinced, moreover, that a represents A better than does a^1. Instead, however, of giving to my conviction this, its only correct, expression, and keeping the content of my consciousness and the real object, the representation and what it means, distinct from each other, I substitute the real object for the content of the consciousness, and talk of the experience as if it consisted in one and the same object (namely, the surreptitiously introduced real one), constituting twice over the content of my consciousness, once in a clear and distinct, the other time in an obscure and vague fashion. I talk now of a distincter and of a less distinct *consciousness* of A, whereas I am only justified in talking of two consciousnesses, a and a^1, equally distinct *in se*, but to which the supposed external object A corresponds with different degrees of distinctness." (Pp. 37–8.)

treat thought as a kind of stuff or material, to be measured out in great or small amount, increased and subtracted from, and baled about at will! He feels an imperious craving to be allowed to *construct* synthetically the successive mental states which he describes. The mind-stuff theory so easily admits of the construction being made, that it seems certain that 'man's unconquerable mind' will devote much future pertinacity and ingenuity to setting it on its legs again and getting it into some sort of plausible working-order. I will therefore conclude the chapter with some consideration of the remaining difficulties which beset the matter as it at present stands.

DIFFICULTY OF STATING THE CONNECTION BETWEEN MIND AND BRAIN

It will be remembered that in our criticism of the theory of the integration of successive conscious units into a feeling of musical pitch, we decided that whatever integration there was was that of the air-pulses into a simpler and simpler sort of physical effect, as the propagations of material change got higher and higher in the nervous system. At last, we said (p. 159), there results some simple and massive process in the auditory centres of the hemispherical cortex, to which, *as a whole*, the feeling of musical pitch directly corresponds. Already, in discussing the localization of functions in the brain, I had said (p. 73) that consciousness accompanies the stream of innervation through that organ and varies in quality with the character of the currents, being mainly of things seen if the occipital lobes are much involved, of things heard if the action is focalized in the temporal lobes, etc., etc.; and I had added that a vague formula like this was as much as one could safely venture on in the actual state of physiology. The facts of mental deafness and blindness, of auditory and optical aphasia, show us that the whole brain must act together if certain thoughts are to occur. The consciousness, which is itself an integral thing not made of parts, 'corresponds' to the entire activity of the brain, whatever that may be, at the moment. This is a way of expressing the relation of mind and brain from which I shall not depart during the remainder of the book, because it expresses the bare phenomenal fact with no hypothesis, and is exposed to no such logical objections as we have found to cling to the theory of ideas in combination.

Nevertheless, this formula which is so unobjectionable if taken vaguely, positivistically, or scientifically, as a mere empirical law of concomitance between our thoughts and our brain, tumbles to pieces entirely if we assume to represent anything more intimate or ultimate by it. The ultimate of ultimate problems, of course, in the study of the relations of thought and brain, is to understand why and how such disparate things are connected at all. But before that problem is solved (if it ever is solved) there is a less ultimate problem which must first be settled. Before the connection of thought and brain can be explained, it must at least be *stated* in an elementary form; and there are great difficulties about so stating it. To state it in elementary form one must reduce it to its lowest terms and know which mental fact and which cerebral fact are, so to speak, in immediate juxtaposition. We must find the minimal mental fact whose being reposes directly on a brain-fact; and we must similarly find the minimal brain-event which will have a mental counterpart at all. Between the mental and the physical minima thus found there will be an immediate relation, the expression of which, if we had it, would be the elementary psycho-physic law.

Our own formula escapes the unintelligibility of psychic atoms by *taking the entire thought* (even of a complex object) *as the minimum with which it deals on the mental side.* But in taking the entire brain-process as its minimal fact on the material side it confronts other difficulties almost as bad.

In the first place, it ignores analogies on which certain critics will insist, those, namely, between the composition of the total brain-process and that of the *object* of the thought. The total brain-process is composed of parts, of simultaneous processes in the seeing, the hearing, the feeling, and other centres. The object thought of is also composed of parts, some of which are seen, others heard, others perceived by touch and muscular manipulation. "How then," these critics will say, "should the thought not itself be composed of parts, each the counterpart of a part of the object and of a part of the brain-process?" So natural is this way of looking at the matter that it has given rise to what is on the whole the most flourishing of all psychological systems—that of the Lockian school of associated ideas—of which school the mind-stuff theory is nothing but the last and subtlest offshoot.

The second difficulty is deeper still. *The 'entire brain-process' is not a physical fact at all.* It is the appearance to an onlooking mind of a multitude of physical facts. 'Entire brain' is nothing but our name for the way in which a million of molecules arranged in certain positions may affect our sense. On the principles of the corpuscular or mechanical philosophy, the only realities are the separate molecules, or at most the cells. Their aggregation into a 'brain' is a fiction of popular speech. Such a fiction cannot serve as the objectively real counterpart to any psychic state whatever. Only a genuinely physical fact can so serve. But the molecular fact is the only genuine physical fact—whereupon we seem, if we are to have an elementary psycho-physic law at all, thrust right back upon something like the mind-stuff theory, for the molecular fact, being an element of the 'brain,' would seem naturally to correspond, not to the total thoughts, but to elements in the thought.

What shall we do? Many would find relief at this point in celebrating the mystery of the Unknowable and the 'awe' which we should feel at having such a principle to take final charge of our perplexities. Others would rejoice that the finite and separatist view of things with which we started had at last developed its contradictions, and was about to lead us dialectically upwards to some 'higher synthesis' in which inconsistencies cease from troubling and logic is at rest. It may be a constitutional infirmity, but I can take no comfort in such devices for making a luxury of intellectual defeat. They are but spiritual chloroform. Better live on the ragged edge, better gnaw the file forever!

THE MATERIAL-MONAD THEORY

The most rational thing to do is to suspect that there may be a third possibility, an alternative supposition which we have not considered. Now there *is* an alternative supposition—a supposition moreover which has been frequently made in the history of philosophy, and which is freer from logical objections than either of the views we have ourselves discussed. It may be called the *theory of polyzoism or multiple monadism*; and it conceives the matter thus:

Every brain-cell has its own individual consciousness, which no other cell knows anything about, all individual consciousnesses being 'ejective' to each other. There is, however, among the cells one central or pontifical one to which *our* consciousness is attached. But the events of all the other cells physically influence this arch-cell; and through producing their joint effects on it, these other cells may be said to 'combine.' The arch-cell is, in fact, one of those 'external media' without which we saw that no fusion or integration of a number of things can occur. The physical modifications of the arch-cell thus form a sequence of results in the production whereof every other cell has a share, so that, as one might say, every other cell is represented therein. And similarly, the conscious correlates to these physical modifications form a sequence of thoughts or feelings, each one of which is, as to its substantive being, an integral and uncompounded psychic thing, but each one of which may (in the exercise of its *cognitive* function) be *aware of THINGS* many and complicated in proportion to the number of other cells that have helped to modify the central cell.

By a conception of this sort, one incurs neither of the internal contradictions which we found to beset the other two theories. One has no unintelligible self-combining of psychic units to account for on the one hand; and on the other hand, one need not treat as the physical counterpart of the stream of consciousness under observation, a 'total brain-activity' which is non-existent as a genuinely physical fact. But, to offset these advantages, one has physiological difficulties and improbabilities. There is no cell or group of cells in the brain of such anatomical or functional pre-eminence as to appear to be the keystone or centre of gravity of the whole system. And even if there were such a cell, the theory of multiple monadism would, in strictness of thought, have no right to stop at it and treat it as a unit. The cell is no more a unit, materially considered, than the total brain is a unit. It is a compound of molecules, just as the brain is a compound of cells and fibres. And the molecules, according to the prevalent physical theories, are in turn compounds of atoms. The theory in question, therefore, if radically carried out, must set up for its elementary and irreducible psychophysic couple, not the cell and its consciousness, but the primordial and eternal atom and its consciousness. We are back at Leibnitzian monadism, and therewith leave physiology behind us and dive into regions inaccessible to experience and verification; and our doctrine, although not self-contradictory, becomes so remote and unreal as to be almost as bad as if it were. Speculative minds alone will take an interest in it; and metaphysics, not psychology, will be responsible for its career. That the career may be a successful one must be admitted as a possibility—a theory which Leibnitz, Herbart, and Lotze have taken under their protection must have some sort of a destiny.

THE SOUL-THEORY

But is this my last word? By no means. Many readers have certainly been saying to themselves for the last few pages: "Why on earth doesn't the poor man say *the Soul* and have done with it?" Other readers, of anti-spiritualistic training and prepossessions, advanced thinkers, or popular evolutionists, will perhaps be a little surprised to find this much-despised word now sprung upon them at the end of so physiological a train of thought. But the plain fact is that all the arguments for a 'pontifical cell' or an 'arch-monad' are also arguments for that well-known spiritual agent in which scholastic psychology and common-sense have always believed. And my only reason for beating the bushes so, and not bringing it in earlier as a possible solution of our difficulties, has been that by this procedure I might perhaps force some of these materialistic minds to feel the more strongly the logical respectability of the spiritualistic position. The fact is that one cannot afford to despise any of these great traditional objects of belief. Whether we realize it or not, there is always a great drift of reasons, positive and negative, towing us in their direction. If there be such entities as Souls in the universe, they may possibly be affected by occurrences in the nervous centres. To the state of the entire brain at a given moment they may respond by inward modifications of their own. These changes of state may be pulses of consciousness, cognitive of objects few or many, simple or complex. The soul would be thus a medium upon which (to use our earlier phraseology) the manifold brain-processes *combine their effects*. Not needing to consider it as the inner aspect' of any arch-molecule or brain-cell, we escape that physiological improbability; and as its pulses of consciousness are unitary and integral affairs from the outset, we escape the absurdity of supposing feelings which exist separately and then 'fuse together' by themselves. The separateness is in the brain-world, on this theory, and the unity in the soul-world; and the only trouble that remains to haunt us is the metaphysical one of understanding how one sort of world or existent thing can affect or influence another at all. This trouble, however, since it also exists inside of both worlds, and involves neither physical improbability nor logical contradiction, is relatively small.

I confess, therefore, that to posit a soul influenced in some mysterious way by the brain-states and responding to them by conscious affections of its own, seems to me the line of least logical resistance, so far as we yet have attained.

If it does not strictly *explain* anything, it is at any rate less positively objectionable than either mind-stuff or a material-monad creed. *The bare* PHENOMENON, *however, the* IMMEDIATELY KNOWN *thing which on the mental side is in apposition with the entire brain-process is the state of consciousness and not the soul itself.* Many of the stanchest believers in the soul admit that we know it only as an inference from experiencing its *states.* In Chapter X, accordingly, we must return to its consideration again, and *ask ourselves whether, after all, the ascertainment of a blank unmediated correspondence, term for term, of the succession of states of consciousness with the succession of total brain-processes, be not the simplest psycho-physic formula, and the last word of a psychology which contents itself with verifiable laws, and seeks only to be clear, and to avoid unsafe hypotheses.* Such a mere admission of the empirical parallelism will there appear the wisest course. By keeping to it, our psychology will remain positivistic and non-metaphysical; and although this is certainly only a provisional halting-place, and things must some day be more thoroughly thought out, we shall abide there in this book, and just as we have rejected mind-dust, we shall take no account of the soul. The spiritualistic reader may nevertheless believe in the soul if he will; whilst the positivistic one who wishes to give a tinge of mystery to the expression of his positivism can continue to say that nature in her unfathomable designs has mixed us of clay and flame, of brain and mind, that the two things hang indubitably together and determine each other's being, but how or why, no mortal may ever know.

Chapter VII

The Methods and Snares of Psychology

We have now finished the physiological preliminaries of our subject and must in the remaining chapters study the mental states themselves whose cerebral conditions and concomitants we have been considering hitherto. Beyond the brain, however, there is an outer world to which the brain-states themselves 'correspond.' And it will be well, ere we advance farther, to say a word about the relation of the mind to this larger sphere of physical fact.

PSYCHOLOGY IS A NATURAL SCIENCE

That is, the mind which the psychologist studies is the mind of distinct individuals inhabiting definite portions of a real space and of a real time. With any other sort of mind, absolute Intelligence, Mind unattached to a particular body, or Mind not subject to the course of time, the psychologist as such has nothing to do. 'Mind,' in his mouth, is only a class name for *minds*. Fortunate will it be if his more modest inquiry result in any generalizations which the philosopher devoted to absolute Intelligence as such can use.

To the psychologist, then, the minds he studies are *objects*, in a world of other objects. Even when he introspectively analyzes his own mind, and tells what he finds there, he talks about it in an objective way. He says, for instance, that under certain circumstances the color gray appears to him green, and calls the appearance an illusion. This implies that he compares two objects, a real color seen under certain conditions, and a mental perception which he believes to represent it, and that he declares the relation between them to be of a certain kind. In making this critical judgment, the psychologist stands as much outside of the perception which he criticises as he does of the color. Both are his objects. And if this is true of him when he reflects on his own conscious states, how much truer is it when he treats of those of others! In German philosophy since Kant the word *Erkenntnisstheorie*, criticism of the faculty of knowledge, plays a great part. Now the psychologist necessarily becomes such an *Erkenntnisstheoretiker*. But the knowledge he theorizes about is not the bare function of knowledge which Kant criticises—he does not inquire into the possibility of knowledge *überhaupt*. He assumes it to be possible, he does not doubt its presence in himself at the moment he speaks. The knowledge he criticises is the knowledge of particular men about the particular things that surround them. This he may, upon occasion, in the light of his *own* unquestioned knowledge, pronounce true or false, and trace the reasons by which it has become one or the other.

It is highly important that this natural-science point of view should be understood at the outset. Otherwise more may be demanded of the psychologist than he ought to be expected to perform.

A diagram will exhibit more emphatically what the assumptions of Psychology must be:

1 The Psychologist	2 The Thought Studied	3 The Thought's Object	4 The Psycholo- gist's Reality

These four squares contain the irreducible data of psychology. No. 1, the psychologist, believes Nos. 2, 3, and 4, which together form *his* total object, to be realities, and reports them and their mutual relations as truly as he can without troubling himself with the puzzle of how he can report them at all. About such *ultimate* puzzles he in the main need trouble himself no more than the geometer, the chemist, or the botanist do, who make precisely the same assumptions as he.[1]

Of certain fallacies to which the psychologist is exposed by reason of his peculiar point of view—that of being a reporter of subjective

[1] On the relation between Psychology and General Philosophy, see G. C. Robertson: *Mind*, vol. VIII, p. 1, and J. Ward: *ibid.*, p. 153; J. Dewey: *ibid.*, vol. XI, p. 1.

as well as of objective facts, we must presently speak. But not until we have considered the methods he uses for ascertaining what the facts in question are.

THE METHODS OF INVESTIGATION

Introspective Observation is what we have to rely on first and foremost and always. The word introspection need hardly be defined—it means, of course, the looking into our own minds and reporting what we there discover. *Everyone agrees that we there discover states of consciousness.* So far as I know, the existence of such states has never been doubted by any critic, however sceptical in other respects he may have been. That we have *cogitations* of some sort is the *inconcussum* in a world most of whose other facts have at some time tottered in the breath of philosophic doubt. All people unhesitatingly believe that they feel themselves thinking, and that they distinguish the mental state as an inward activity or passion, from all the objects with which it may cognitively deal. *I regard this belief as the most fundamental of all the postulates of Psychology*, and shall discard all curious inquiries about its certainty as too metaphysical for the scope of this book.

A Question of Nomenclature. We ought to have some general term by which to designate all states of consciousness merely as such, and apart from their particular quality or cognitive function. Unfortunately most of the terms in use have grave objections. 'Mental state,' 'state of consciousness,' 'conscious modification,' are cumbrous and have no kindred verbs. The same is true of 'subjective condition.' 'Feeling' has the verb 'to feel,' both active and neuter, and such derivatives as 'feelingly,' 'felt,' 'feltness,' etc., which make it extremely convenient. But on the other hand it has specific meanings as well as its generic one, sometimes standing for pleasure and pain, and being sometimes a synonym of '*sensation*' as opposed to *thought*; whereas we wish a term to cover sensation and thought indifferently. Moreover, 'feeling' has acquired in the hearts of platonizing thinkers a very opprobrious set of implications; and since one of the great obstacles to mutual understanding in philosophy is the use of words eulogistically and disparagingly, impartial terms ought always, if possible, to be preferred. The word *psychosis* has been proposed by Mr. Huxley. It has the advantage of being correlative to *neurosis* (the name applied by the same author to the corresponding nerve-process), and is moreover technical and devoid of partial implications. But it has no verb or other grammatical form allied to it. The expressions 'affection of the soul,' 'modification of the ego,' are clumsy, like 'state of consciousness,' and they implicitly assert theories which it is not well to embody in terminology before they have been openly discussed and approved. 'Idea' is a good vague neutral word, and was by Locke employed in the broadest generic way; but notwithstanding his authority it has not domesticated itself in the language so as to cover bodily sensations, and it moreover has no verb. 'Thought' would be by far the best word to use if it could be made to cover sensations. It has no opprobrious connotation such as 'feeling' has, and it immediately suggests the omnipresence of cognition (or reference to an object other than the mental state itself), which we shall soon see to be of the mental life's essence. But can the expression 'thought of a toothache' ever suggest to the reader the actual present pain itself? It is hardly possible; and we thus seem about to be forced back on some *pair* of terms like Hume's 'impression and idea,' or Hamilton's 'presentation and representation,' or the ordinary 'feeling and thought,' if we wish to cover the whole ground.

In this quandary we can make no definitive choice, but must, according to the convenience of the context, use sometimes one, sometimes another of the synonyms that have been mentioned. *My own partiality is for either* FEELING *or* THOUGHT. I shall probably often use both words in a wider sense than usual, and alternately startle two classes of readers by their unusual sound; but if the connection makes it clear that mental states at large, irrespective of their kind, are meant, this will do no harm, and may even do some good.[2]

The inaccuracy of introspective observation has been made a subject of debate. It is important to gain some fixed ideas on this point before we proceed.

The commonest spiritualistic opinion is that the Soul or *Subject* of the mental life is a metaphysical entity, inaccessible to direct knowledge, and that the various mental states and operations of which we reflectively become aware are objects of an inner sense which does not lay hold of the real agent in itself, any more than sight or hearing gives us direct knowledge of matter in itself. From this point of view introspection is, of course, incompetent to lay

2 Compare some remarks in Mill's *Logic*, bk. I, chap. III, §§ 2, 3.

hold of anything more than the Soul's *phenomena*. But even then the question remains, How well can it know the phenomena themselves?

Some authors take high ground here and claim for it a sort of infallibility. Thus Ueberweg:

> "When the mental image as such is the object of my apprehension, there is no meaning in seeking to distinguish its existence in my consciousness (in me) from its existence out of my consciousness (in itself)—for the object apprehended is, in this case, one which does not even exist, as the objects of external perception do, in itself outside my consciousness. It exists only within me."[3]

And Brentano:

> "The phenomena inwardly apprehended are true in themselves. As they appear—of this the evidence with which they are apprehended is a warrant—so they are in reality. Who, then, can deny that in this a great superiority of Psychology over the physical sciences comes to light?"

And again:

> "No one can doubt whether the psychic condition he apprehends in himself *be*, and be *so*, as he apprehends it. Whoever should doubt this would have reached that *finished* doubt which destroys itself in destroying every fixed point from which to make an attack upon knowledge."[4]

Others have gone to the opposite extreme, and maintained that we can have no introspective cognition of our own minds at all. A deliverance of Auguste Comte to this effect has been so often quoted as to be almost classical; and some reference to it seems therefore indispensable here.

Philosophers, says Comte,[5] have

> "in these latter days imagined themselves able to distinguish, by a very singular subtlety, two sorts of observation of equal importance, one external, the other internal, the latter being solely destined for the study of intellectual phenomena. . . . I limit myself to pointing out the principal consideration which proves clearly that this pretended direct contemplation of the mind by itself is a pure illusion. . . . It is in fact

[3] *System of Logic*, § 40.

[4] *Psychologie*, bk. I, chap. I, §§ 2, 3.

[5] *Cours de philosophie positive*, I, 34–7.

evident that, by an invincible necessity, the human mind can observe directly all phenomena except its own proper states. For by whom shall the observation of these be made? It is conceivable that a man might observe himself with respect to the *passions* that animate him, for the anatomical organs of passion are distinct from those whose function is observation. Though we have all made such observations on ourselves, they can never have much scientific value, and the best mode of knowing the passions will always be that of observing them from without; for every strong state of passion . . . is necessarily incompatible with the state of observation. But, as for observing in the same way *intellectual* phenomena at the time of their actual presence, that is a manifest impossibility. The thinker cannot divide himself into two, of whom one reasons whilst the other observes him reason. The organ observed and the organ observing being, in this case, identical, how could observation take place? This pretended psychological method is then radically null and void. On the one hand, they advise you to isolate yourself, as far as possible, from every external sensation, especially every intellectual work,—for if you were to busy yourself even with the simplest calculation, what would become of *internal* observation?—on the other hand, after having with the utmost care attained this state of intellectual slumber, you must begin to contemplate the operations going on in your mind, when nothing there takes place! Our descendants will doubtless see such pretensions some day ridiculed upon the stage. The results of so strange a procedure harmonize entirely with its principle. For all the two thousand years during which metaphysicians have thus cultivated psychology, they are not agreed about one intelligible and established proposition. '*Internal observation*' gives almost as many divergent results as there are individuals who think they practise it."

Comte hardly could have known anything of the English, and nothing of the German, empirical psychology. The 'results' which he had in mind when writing were probably scholastic ones, such as principles of internal activity, the faculties, the ego, the *liberum arbitrium indifferentiæ*, etc. John Mill, in replying to him,[6] says:

"It might have occurred to M. Comte that a fact may be studied through the medium of memory, not at the very moment of our perceiving it, but the moment after: and this is really the mode in which our best knowledge of our intellectual acts is generally acquired. We reflect on what we have been doing, when the act is past, but when its impression in the memory is still fresh. Unless in one of these ways, we could not have acquired the knowledge, which nobody denies us to

6 *Auguste Comte and Positivism*, 3d edition (1882), p. 64.

have, of what passes in our minds. M. Comte would scarcely have affirmed that we are not aware of our own intellectual operations. We know of our observings and our reasonings, either at the very time, or by memory the moment after; in either case, by direct knowledge, and not (like things done by us in a state of somnambulism) merely by their results. This simple fact destroys the whole of M. Comte's argument. Whatever we are directly aware of, we can directly observe."

Where now does the truth lie? Our quotation from Mill is obviously the one which expresses the most of *practical* truth about the matter. Even the writers who insist upon the absolute veracity of our immediate inner apprehension of a conscious state have to contrast with this the fallibility of our *memory* or *observation* of it, a moment later. No one has emphasized more sharply than Brentano himself the difference between the immediate *feltness* of a feeling, and its perception by a subsequent reflective act. But which mode of consciousness of it is that which the psychologist must depend on? If to *have* feelings or thoughts in their immediacy were enough, babies in the cradle would be psychologists, and infallible ones. But the psychologist must not only *have* his mental states in their absolute veritableness, he must report them and write about them, name them, classify and compare them and trace their relations to other things. Whilst alive they are their own property; it is only *post-mortem* that they become his prey.[7] And as in the naming, classing, and knowing of things in general we are notoriously fallible, why not also here? Comte is quite right in laying stress on the fact that a feeling, to be named, judged, or perceived, must be already past. No subjective state, whilst present, is its own object; its object is always something else. There are, it is true, cases in which we appear to be naming our present feeling, and so to be experiencing and observing the same inner fact at a single stroke, as when we say 'I feel tired,' 'I am angry,' etc. But these are illusory, and a little attention unmasks the illusion. The present conscious state, when I say 'I feel tired,' is not

[7] Wundt says: "The first rule for utilizing inward observation consists in taking, as far as possible, experiences that are accidental, unexpected, and not intentionally brought about. . . . *First* it is best as far as possible to rely on *Memory* and not on immediate Apprehension. . . . *Second,* internal observation is better fitted to grasp clearly conscious states, especially voluntary mental acts: such inner processes as are obscurely conscious and involuntary will almost entirely elude it, because the effort to observe interferes with them, and because they seldom abide in memory." (*Logik,* II, 482.)

the direct state of tire; when I say 'I feel angry,' it is not the direct state of anger. It is the state of *saying-I-feel-tired*, of *saying-I-feel-angry*,—entirely different matters, so different that the fatigue and anger apparently included in them are considerable modifications of the fatigue and anger directly felt the previous instant. The act of naming them has momentarily detracted from their force.[8]

The only sound grounds on which the infallible veracity of the introspective judgment might be maintained are empirical. If we had reason to think it has never yet deceived us, we might continue to trust it. This is the ground actually maintained by Herr Mohr.

"The illusions of our senses," says this author, "have undermined our belief in the reality of the outer world; but in the sphere of inner observation our confidence is intact, for we have never found ourselves to be in error about the reality of an act of thought or feeling. We have never been misled into thinking we were *not* in doubt or in anger when these conditions were really states of our consciousness."[9]

But sound as the reasoning here would be, were the premises correct, I fear the latter cannot pass. However it may be with such strong feelings as doubt or anger, about weaker feelings, and about the *relations to each other* of all feelings, we find ourselves in continual error and uncertainty so soon as we are called on to name and class, and not merely to feel. Who can be sure of the exact *order* of his feelings when they are excessively rapid? Who can be sure, in his sensible perception of a chair, how much comes from the eye and how much is supplied out of the previous knowledge of the mind? Who can compare with precision the *quantities* of disparate feelings even where the feelings are very much alike? For instance, where an object is felt now against the back and now against the cheek, which feeling is most extensive? Who can be sure that two given feelings are or are not exactly the same? Who can tell which is briefer or longer than the other when both occupy

[8] In cases like this, where the state outlasts the act of naming it, exists before it, and recurs when it is past, we probably run little practical risk of error when we talk as if the state knew itself. The state of feeling and the state of naming the feeling are continuous, and the infallibility of such prompt introspective judgments is probably great. But even here the certainty of our knowledge ought not to be argued on the *a priori* ground that *percipi* and *esse* are in psychology the same. The states are really two; the naming state and the named state are apart; '*percipi* is *esse*' is not the principle that applies.

[9] J. Mohr: *Grundlage der empirischen Psychologie* (Leipzig, 1882), p. 47.

but an instant of time? Who knows, of many actions, for what motive they were done, or if for any motive at all? Who can enumerate all the distinct ingredients of such a complicated feeling as *anger*? and who can tell offhand whether or no a perception of *distance* be a compound or a simple state of mind? The whole mind-stuff controversy would stop if we could decide conclusively by introspection that what seem to us elementary feelings are really elementary and not compound.

Mr. Sully, in his work on *Illusions*, has a chapter on those of Introspection from which we might now quote. But, since the rest of this volume will be little more than a collection of illustrations of the difficulty of discovering by direct introspection exactly what our feelings and their relations are, we need not anticipate our own future details, but just state our general conclusion that *introspection is difficult and fallible; and that the difficulty is simply that of all observation of whatever kind.* Something is before us; we do our best to tell what it is, but in spite of our good will we may go astray, and give a description more applicable to some other sort of thing. The only safeguard is in the final *consensus* of our farther knowledge about the thing in question, later views correcting earlier ones, until at last the harmony of a consistent system is reached. Such a system, gradually worked out, is the best guarantee the psychologist can give for the soundness of any particular psychologic observation which he may report. Such a system we ourselves must strive, as far as may be, to attain.

The English writers on psychology, and the school of Herbart in Germany, have in the main contented themselves with such results as the immediate introspection of single individuals gave, and shown what a body of doctrine they may make. The works of Locke, Hume, Reid, Hartley, Stewart, Brown, the Mills, will always be classics in this line; and in Professor Bain's *Treatises* we have probably the last word of what this method taken mainly by itself can do—the last monument of the youth of our science, still untechnical and generally intelligible, like the Chemistry of Lavoisier, or Anatomy before the microscope was used.

The Experimental Method. But psychology is passing into a less simple phase. Within a few years what one may call a microscopic psychology has arisen in Germany, carried on by experimental methods, asking of course every moment for introspective data, but eliminating their uncertainty by operating on a large scale and taking statistical means. This method taxes patience to the utmost, and could hardly have arisen in a country whose natives could be *bored*. Such Germans as Weber, Fechner, Vierordt, and Wundt obviously cannot; and their success has brought into the field an array of younger experimental psychologists, bent on studying the *elements* of the mental life, dissecting them out from the gross results in which they are embedded, and as far as possible reducing them to quantitative scales. The simple and open method of attack having done what it can, the method of patience, starving out, and harassing to death is tried; the Mind must submit to a regular *siege*, in which minute advantages gained night and day by the forces that hem her in must sum themselves up at last into her overthrow. There is little of the grand style about these new prism, pendulum, and chronograph-philosophers. They mean business, not chivalry. What generous divination, and that superiority in virtue which was thought by Cicero to give a man the best insight into nature, have failed to do, their spying and scraping, their deadly tenacity and almost diabolic cunning, will doubtless some day bring about.

No general description of the methods of experimental psychology would be instructive to one unfamiliar with the instances of their application, so we will waste no words upon the attempt. *The principal fields of experimentation* so far have been: 1) the connection of conscious states with their physical conditions, including the whole of brain-physiology, and the recent minutely cultivated physiology of the sense-organs, together with what is technically known as 'psycho-physics,' or the laws of correlation between sensations and the outward stimuli by which they are aroused; 2) the analysis of space-perception into its sensational elements; 3) the measurement of the *duration* of the simplest mental processes; 4) that of the *accuracy of reproduction* in the memory of sensible experiences and of intervals of space and time; 5) that of the manner in which simple mental states *influence each other*, call each other up, or inhibit each other's reproduction; 6) that of the *number of facts* which consciousness can simultaneously discern; finally, 7) that of the elementary laws of oblivescence and retention. It must be said that in some of these fields the results have as yet borne little theoretic fruit commensurate with the great labor expended in their acquisition. But facts are facts, and if we only get enough of them they are sure to combine. New ground will from year to year be broken, and theoretic results will grow. Meanwhile the experimental method has quite changed the face of the science so far as the latter is a record of mere work done.

The *comparative method,* finally, supplements the introspective and experimental methods. This method presupposes a normal psychology of introspection to be established in its main features. But where the origin of these features, or their dependence upon one another, is in question, it is of the utmost importance to trace the phenomenon considered through all its possible variations of type and combination. So it has come to pass that instincts of animals are ransacked to throw light on our own; and that the reasoning faculties of bees and ants, the minds of savages, infants, madmen, idiots, the deaf and blind, criminals, and eccentrics, are all invoked in support of this or that special theory about some part of our own mental life. The history of sciences, moral and political institutions, and languages, as types of mental product, are pressed into the same service. Messrs. Darwin and Galton have set the example of circulars of questions sent out by the hundred to those supposed able to reply. The custom has spread, and it will be well for us in the next generation if such circulars be not ranked among the common pests of life. Meanwhile information grows, and results emerge. There are great sources of error in the comparative method. The interpretation of the 'psychoses' of animals, savages, and infants is necessarily wild work, in which the personal equation of the investigator has things very much its own way. A savage will be reported to have no moral or religious feeling if his actions shock the observer unduly. A child will be assumed without self-consciousness because he talks of himself in the third person, etc., etc. No rules can be laid down in advance. Comparative observations, to be definite, must usually be made to test some pre-existing hypothesis; and the only thing then is to use as much sagacity as you possess, and to be as candid as you can.

THE SOURCES OF ERROR IN PSYCHOLOGY

The first of them arises from the Misleading Influence of Speech. Language was originally made by men who were not psychologists, and most men to-day employ almost exclusively the vocabulary of outward things. The cardinal passions of our life, anger, love, fear, hate, hope, and the most comprehensive divisions of our intellectual activity, to remember, expect, think, know, dream, with the broadest genera of æsthetic feeling, joy, sorrow, pleasure, pain, are the only facts of a subjective order which this vocabulary deigns to note by special words. The elementary qualities of sensation, bright, loud, red, blue, hot, cold, are, it is true, susceptible of being used in both an objective and a subjective sense. They stand for outer qualities and for the feelings which these arouse. But the objective sense is the original sense; and still to-day we have to describe a large number of sensations by the name of the object from which they have most frequently been got. An orange color, an odor of violets, a cheesy taste, a thunderous sound, a fiery smart, etc., will recall what I mean. This absence of a special vocabulary for subjective facts hinders the study of all but the very coarsest of them. Empiricist writers are very fond of emphasizing one great set of delusions which language inflicts on the mind. Whenever we have made a word, they say, to denote a certain group of phenomena, we are prone to suppose a substantive entity existing beyond the phenomena, of which the word shall be the name. But the *lack* of a word quite as often leads to the directly opposite error. We are then prone to suppose that no entity can be there; and so we come to overlook phenomena whose existence would be patent to us all, had we only grown up to hear it familiarly recognized in speech.[10] It is hard to focus our attention on the nameless, and so there results a certain vacuousness in the descriptive parts of most psychologies.

But a worse defect than vacuousness comes from the dependence of psychology on common speech. Naming our thought by its own objects, we almost all of us assume that as the objects are, so the thought must be. The thought of several distinct things can only consist of several distinct bits of thought, or 'ideas'; that of an abstract or universal object can only be an abstract or universal idea. As each object may come and go, be forgotten and then thought of again, it is held that the thought of it has a precisely similar independence, self-identity, and mobility. The thought of the object's recurrent identity is regarded as the identity of its recurrent thought; and the perceptions of multiplicity, of coexistence, of

[10] In English we have not even the generic distinction between the-thing-thought-of and the-thought-thinking-it, which in German is expressed by the opposition between *Gedachtes* and *Gedanke*, in Latin by that between *cogitatum* and *cogitatio*.

succession, are severally conceived to be brought about only through a multiplicity, a coexistence, a succession, of perceptions. The continuous flow of the mental stream is sacrificed, and in its place an atomism, a brickbat plan of construction, is preached, for the existence of which no good introspective grounds can be brought forward, and out of which presently grow all sorts of paradoxes and contradictions, the heritage of woe of students of the mind.

These words are meant to impeach the entire English psychology derived from Locke and Hume, and the entire German psychology derived from Herbart, so far as they both treat 'ideas' as separate subjective entities that come and go. Examples will soon make the matter clearer. Meanwhile our psychologic insight is vitiated by still other snares.

'*The Psychologist's Fallacy.*' The *great* snare of the psychologist is the *confusion of his own standpoint with that of the mental fact* about which he is making his report. I shall hereafter call this the 'psychologist's fallacy' *par excellence*. For some of the mischief, here too, language is to blame. The psychologist, as we remarked above (p. 183), stands outside of the mental state he speaks of. Both itself and its object are objects for him. Now when it is a *cognitive* state (percept, thought, concept, etc.), he ordinarily has no other way of naming it than as the thought, percept, etc., *of that object*. He himself, meanwhile, knowing the self-same object in *his* way, gets easily led to suppose that the thought, which is *of* it, knows it in the same way in which he knows it, although this is often very far from being the case.[11] The most fictitious puzzles have been introduced into our science by this means. The so-called question of presentative or representative perception, of whether an object is present to the thought that thinks it by a counterfeit image of itself, or directly and without any intervening image at all; the question of nominalism and conceptualism, of the shape in which things are present when only a general notion of them is before the mind; are comparatively easy questions when once the psychologist's fallacy is eliminated from their treatment,—as we shall ere long see (in Chapter XII).

Another variety of the psychologist's fallacy is the assumption that the mental state studied must be conscious of itself as the psychologist is conscious of it. The mental state is aware of itself only

[11] Compare B. P. Bowne's *Metaphysics* (1882), p. 408.

from within; it grasps what we call its own content, and nothing more. The psychologist, on the contrary, is aware of it from without, and knows its relations with all sorts of other things. What the thought sees is only its own object; what the psychologist sees is the thought's object, plus the thought itself, plus possibly all the rest of the world. We must be very careful therefore, in discussing a state of mind from the psychologist's point of view, to avoid foisting into its own ken matters that are only there for ours. We must avoid substituting what we know the consciousness *is*, for what it is a consciousness *of*, and counting its outward, and so to speak physical, relations with other facts of the world, in among the objects of which we set it down as aware. Crude as such a confusion of standpoints seems to be when abstractly stated, it is nevertheless a snare into which no psychologist has kept himself at all times from falling, and which forms almost the entire stock-in-trade of certain schools. We cannot be too watchful against its subtly corrupting influence.

Summary. To sum up the chapter, Psychology assumes that thoughts successively occur, and that they know objects in a world which the psychologist also knows. *These thoughts are the subjective data of which he treats, and their relations to their objects, to the brain, and to the rest of the world constitute the subject-matter of psychologic science.* Its methods are introspection, experimentation, and comparison. But introspection is no sure guide to truths *about* our mental states; and in particular the poverty of the psychological vocabulary leads us to drop out certain states from our consideration, and to treat others as if they knew themselves and their objects as the psychologist knows both, which is a disastrous fallacy in the science.

Chapter VIII

The Relations of Minds to Other Things

Since, for psychology, a mind is an object in a world of other objects, its relation to those other objects must next be surveyed. First of all, to its

TIME-RELATIONS

Minds, as we know them, are temporary existences. Whether my mind had a being prior to the birth of my body, whether it shall have one after the latter's decease, are questions to be decided by my general philosophy or theology rather than by what we call 'scientific facts'—I leave out the facts of so-called spiritualism, as being still in dispute. Psychology, as a natural science, confines itself to the present life, in which every mind appears yoked to a body through which its manifestations appear. In the present world, then, minds precede, succeed, and coexist with each other in the common receptacle of time, and of their *collective* relations to the latter nothing more can be said. The life of the *individual* consciousness in time seems, however, to be an interrupted one, so that the question:

Are we ever wholly unconscious?

becomes one which must be discussed. Sleep, fainting, coma, epilepsy, and other 'unconscious' conditions are apt to break in upon and occupy large durations of what we nevertheless consider the mental history of a single man. And, the fact of interruption being admitted, is it not possible that it may exist where we do not suspect it, and even perhaps in an incessant and fine-grained form?

This might happen, and yet the subject himself never know it. We often take ether and have operations performed without a suspicion that our consciousness has suffered a breach. The two ends join each other smoothly over the gap; and only the sight of our wound assures us that we must have been living through a time which for our immediate consciousness was non-existent. Even in sleep this sometimes happens: We think we have had no nap, and it takes the clock to assure us that we are wrong.[1] We thus may live through a real outward time, a time known by the psychologist who studies us, and yet not *feel* the time, or infer it from any inward sign. The question is, how often does this happen? Is consciousness really discontinuous, incessantly interrupted and recommencing (from the psychologist's point of view)? and does it only seem continuous to itself by an illusion analogous to that of the zoetrope? Or is it at most times as continuous outwardly as it inwardly seems?

It must be confessed that we can give no rigorous answer to this question. Cartesians, who hold that the *essence* of the soul is to think, can of course solve it *a priori*, and explain the appearance of thoughtless intervals either by lapses in our ordinary memory, or by the sinking of consciousness to a minimal state, in which perhaps all that it feels is a bare existence which leaves no particulars behind to be recalled. If, however, one have no doctrine about the soul or its essence, one is free to take the appearances for what they seem to be, and to admit that the mind, as well as the body, may go to sleep.

Locke was the first prominent champion of this latter view, and the pages in which he attacks the Cartesian belief are as spirited as any in his *Essay*. "Every drowsy nod shakes their doctrine who teach that their soul is always thinking." He will not believe that men so easily forget. M. Jouffroy and Sir W. Hamilton, attacking the question in the same empirical way, are led to an opposite conclusion. Their reasons, briefly stated, are these:

In somnambulism, natural or induced, there is often a great dis-

[1] Messrs. Payton Spence (*Journal of Speculative Philosophy*, XIII, 337; XIV, 286) and M. M. Garver (*American Journal of Science*, 3d series, XX, 189) argue, the one from speculative, the other from experimental grounds, that, the physical condition of consciousness being neural vibration, the consciousness must itself be incessantly interrupted by unconsciousness—about fifty times a second, according to Garver.

play of intellectual activity, followed by complete oblivion of all that has passed.[2]

On being suddenly awakened from a sleep, however profound, we always catch ourselves in the middle of a dream. Common dreams are often remembered for a few minutes after waking, and then irretrievably lost.

Frequently, when awake and absent-minded, we are visited by thoughts and images which the next instant we cannot recall.

Our insensibility to habitual noises, etc., whilst awake, proves that we can neglect to attend to that which we nevertheless feel. Similarly in sleep, we grow inured, and sleep soundly in presence of sensations of sound, cold, contact, etc., which at first prevented our complete repose. We have learned to neglect them whilst asleep as we should whilst awake. The mere *sense-impressions* are the same when the sleep is deep as when it is light; the difference must lie in a *judgment* on the part of the apparently slumbering mind that they are not worth noticing.

This discrimination is equally shown by nurses of the sick and mothers of infants, who will sleep through much noise of an irrelevant sort, but waken at the slightest stirring of the patient or the babe. This last fact shows the *sense-organ* to be pervious for sounds.

Many people have a remarkable faculty of registering when asleep the flight of time. They will habitually wake up at the same minute day after day, or will wake punctually at an unusual hour determined upon overnight. How can this knowledge of the hour (more accurate often than anything the waking consciousness shows) be possible without mental activity during the interval?

Such are what we may call the classical reasons for admitting that the mind is active even when the person afterwards ignores the fact.[3] Of late years, or rather, one may say, of late months, they

2 That the appearance of mental activity here is real can be proved by suggesting to the 'hypnotized' somnambulist that he shall remember when he awakes. He will then often do so.

3 For more details, cf. Malebranche: *Recherche de la vérité*, bk. III, pt. I, chap. I; J. Locke: *Essay Concerning Human Understanding*, book II, ch. I; C. Wolff: *Psychologia Rationalis*, § 59; Sir W. Hamilton: *Lectures on Metaphysics and Logic*, lecture XVII; J. Bascom: *The Science of Mind*, § 12; Théodore Jouffroy: *Mélanges philosophiques*, "Du sommeil"; H. Holland: *Chapters on Mental Physiology*, p. 80; B. Brodie: *Psychological Inquiries*, p. 147; E. M. Chesley: *Journal of Speculative Philosophy*, vol. XI, p. 72; Théodule Ribot: *Les Maladies de la personnalité*, pp. 8–10; H. Lotze: *Metaphysic* (English trans.), p. 533.

have been reinforced by a lot of curious observations made on hysterical and hypnotic subjects, which prove the existence of a highly developed consciousness in places where it has hitherto not been suspected at all. These observations throw such a novel light upon human nature that I must give them in some detail. That at least four different and in a certain sense rival observers should agree in the same conclusion justifies us in accepting the conclusion as true.

'Unconsciousness' in Hysterics

One of the most constant symptoms in persons suffering from hysteric disease in its extreme forms consists in alterations of the natural sensibility of various parts and organs of the body. Usually the alteration is in the direction of defect, or anæsthesia. One or both eyes are blind, or color-blind, or there is hemianopsia (blindness to one half the field of view), or the field is contracted. Hearing, taste, smell may similarly disappear, in part or in totality. Still more striking are the cutaneous anæsthesias. The old witch-finders looking for the 'devil's seals' learned well the existence of those insensible patches on the skin of their victims, to which the minute physical examinations of recent medicine have but recently attracted attention again. They may be scattered anywhere, but are very apt to affect one side of the body. Not infrequently they affect an entire lateral half, from head to foot; and the insensible skin of, say, the left side will then be found separated from the naturally sensitive skin of the right by a perfectly sharp line of demarcation down the middle of the front and back. Sometimes, most remarkable of all, the entire skin, hands, feet, face, everything, and the mucous membranes, muscles and joints so far as they can be explored, become *completely* insensible without the other vital functions becoming gravely disturbed.

These hysterical anæsthesias can be made to disappear more or less completely by various odd processes. It has been recently found that magnets, plates of metal, or the electrodes of a battery, placed against the skin, have this peculiar power. And when one side is relieved in this way, the anæsthesia is often found to have transferred itself to the opposite side, which until then was well. Whether these strange effects of magnets and metals be due to their direct physiological action, or to a prior effect on the patient's mind ('expectant attention' or 'suggestion') is still a mooted question. A still better awakener of sensibility is the hypnotic trance, into which many of these patients can be very easily placed, and in which their lost sensibility not infrequently becomes entirely restored. Such returns of sensibility succeed the times of insensibility and alternate with them. But Messrs. Pierre Janet[4] and A. Binet[5] have shown that during the times of anæsthesia, and coexisting with it, *sensibility to the anæsthetic parts is also there, in the form of a secondary consciousness* entirely cut off from the primary or normal one, but susceptible of being *tapped* and made to testify to its existence in various odd ways.

Chief amongst these is what M. Janet calls 'the method of *distraction.*' These hysterics are apt to possess a very narrow field of attention, and to be unable to think of more than one thing at a time. When talking with any person they forget everything else. "When Lucie talked directly with anyone," says M. Janet, "she ceased to be able to hear any other person. You may stand behind her, call her by name, shout abuse into her ears, without making her turn round; or place yourself before her, show her objects, touch her, etc., without attracting her notice. When finally she becomes aware of you, she thinks you have just come into the room again, and greets you accordingly. This singular forgetfulness makes her liable to tell all her secrets aloud, unrestrained by the presence of unsuitable auditors."

Now M. Janet found in several subjects like this that if he came up behind them whilst they were plunged in conversation with a third party, and addressed them in a whisper, telling them to raise their hand or perform other simple acts, they would obey the order given, although their *talking* intelligence was quite unconscious of receiving it. Leading them from one thing to another, he made them reply by signs to his whispered questions, and finally made them answer in writing, if a pencil were placed in their hand. The primary consciousness meanwhile went on with the conversation, entirely unaware of these performances on the hand's part. The consciousness which presided over these latter appeared in its turn to be quite as little disturbed by the upper consciousness's con-

[4] *L'Automatisme psychologique*, Paris, 1889, *passim.*

[5] See his articles in the Chicago *Open Court*, for July 25, August 1, and November 7, 1889. Also in the *Revue Philosophique* for 1889 and '90.

cerns. This *proof by 'automatic' writing,* of a secondary consciousness's existence, is the most cogent and striking one; but a crowd of other facts prove the same thing. If I run through them rapidly, the reader will probably be convinced.

The apparently anæsthetic hand of these subjects, for one thing, *will often adapt itself discriminatingly* to whatever object may be put into it. With a pencil it will make writing movements; into a pair of scissors it will put its fingers and will open and shut them, etc., etc. The primary consciousness, so to call it, is meanwhile unable to say whether or no *anything* is in the hand, if the latter be hidden from sight. "I put a pair of eyeglasses into Léonie's anæsthetic hand, this hand opens it and raises it towards the nose, but half way thither it enters the field of vision of Léonie, who sees it and stops stupefied: 'Why,' says she, 'I have an eyeglass in my left hand!' " M. Binet found a very curious sort of connection between the apparently anæsthetic skin and the mind in some Salpêtrière-subjects. Things placed in the hand were not felt, but *thought* of (apparently in visual terms) and in no wise referred by the subject to their starting point in the hand's sensation. A key, a knife, placed in the hand occasioned *ideas* of a key or a knife, but the hand felt nothing. Similarly the subject *thought of* the number 3, 6, etc., if the hand or finger was bent three or six times by the operator, or if he stroked it three, six, etc., times.

In certain individuals there was found a still odder phenomenon, which reminds one of that curious idiosyncrasy of 'colored hearing' of which a few cases have been lately described with great care by foreign writers. These individuals, namely, *saw* the impression received by the hand, but could not feel it; and the thing seen appeared by no means associated with the hand, but more like an independent vision, which usually interested and surprised the patient. Her hand being hidden by a screen, she was ordered to look at another screen and to tell of any visual image which might project itself thereon. Numbers would then come, corresponding to the number of times the insensible member was raised, touched, etc. Colored lines and figures would come, corresponding to similar ones traced on the palm; the hand itself or its fingers would come when manipulated; and finally objects placed in it would come; but on the hand itself nothing would ever be felt. Of course simulation would not be hard here; but M. Binet disbelieves this (usually very shallow) explanation to be a probable one in cases in question.[6]

The usual way in which doctors measure the delicacy of our touch is by the compass-points. Two points are normally felt as one whenever they are too close together for discrimination; but what is 'too close' on one part of the skin may seem very far apart on another. In the middle of the back or on the thigh, less than 3 inches may be too close; on the finger-tip a tenth of an inch is far enough apart. Now, as tested in this way, with the appeal made to the primary consciousness, which talks through the mouth and seems to hold the field alone, a certain person's skin may be entirely anæsthetic and not feel the compass-points at all; and yet this same skin will prove to have a perfectly normal sensibility if the appeal be made to that other secondary or sub-consciousness, which expresses itself automatically by writing or by movements of the hand. M. Binet, M. Pierre Janet, and M. Jules Janet have all found this. The subject, whenever touched, would signify 'one point' or 'two points,' as accurately as if she were a normal person. She would signify it only by these movements; and of the movements themselves her primary self would be as unconscious as of the facts they signified, for what the submerged consciousness makes the hand do automatically is unknown to the consciousness which uses the mouth.

Messrs. Bernheim and Pitres have also proved, by observations too complicated to be given in this spot, that the hysterical blindness is no real blindness at all. The eye of an hysteric which is totally blind when the other or seeing eye is shut, will do its share of vision perfectly well when *both* eyes are open together. But even where both eyes are semi-blind from hysterical disease, the method of automatic writing proves that their perceptions exist, only cut off from communication with the upper consciousness. M. Binet has found the hand of his patients unconsciously writing down words which their eyes were vainly endeavoring to 'see,' i.e., to bring to the upper consciousness. Their submerged consciousness was of course seeing them, or the hand could not have written as it

[6] This whole phenomenon shows how an idea which remains itself below the threshold of a certain conscious self may occasion associative effects therein. The skin-sensations unfelt by the patient's primary consciousness awaken nevertheless their usual visual associates therein.

did. Colors are similarly perceived by the sub-conscious self, which the hysterically color-blind eyes cannot bring to the normal consciousness. Pricks, burns, and pinches on the anæsthetic skin, all unnoticed by the upper self, are recollected to have been suffered, and complained of, as soon as the under self gets a chance to express itself by the passage of the subject into hypnotic trance.

It must be admitted, therefore, that *in certain persons*, at least, *the total possible consciousness may be split into parts which coexist but mutually ignore each other*, and share the objects of knowledge between them. More remarkable still, they are *complementary*. Give an object to one of the consciousnesses, and by that fact you remove it from the other or others. Barring a certain common fund of information, like the command of language, etc., what the upper self knows the under self is ignorant of, and *vice versa*. M. Janet has proved this beautifully in his subject Lucie. The following experiment will serve as the type of the rest: In her trance he covered her lap with cards, each bearing a number. He then told her that on waking she should *not see* any card whose number was a multiple of three. This is the ordinary so-called 'post-hypnotic suggestion,' now well known, and for which Lucie was a well-adapted subject. Accordingly, when she was awakened and asked about the papers on her lap, she counted and said she saw those only whose number was not a multiple of 3. To the 12, 18, 9, etc., she was blind. But the *hand*, when the sub-conscious self was interrogated by the usual method of engrossing the upper self in another conversation, wrote that the only cards in Lucie's lap were those numbered 12, 18, 9, etc., and on being asked to pick up all the cards which were there, picked up these and let the others lie. Similarly when the sight of certain things was suggested to the sub-conscious Lucie, the normal Lucie suddenly became partially or totally blind. "What is the matter? I can't see!" the normal personage suddenly cried out in the midst of her conversation, when M. Janet whispered to the secondary personage to make use of her eyes. The anæsthesias, paralyses, contractions and other irregularities from which hysterics suffer seem then to be due to the fact that their secondary personage has enriched itself by robbing the primary one of a function which the latter ought to have retained. The curative indication is evident: get at the secondary personage, by hypnotization or in whatever other way, and make her *give up* the eye, the skin, the arm, or whatever the affected part may be.

The normal self thereupon regains possession, sees, feels, or is able to move again. In this way M. Jules Janet easily cured the well-known subject of the Salpêtrière, Witt., of all sorts of afflictions which, until he discovered the secret of her deeper trance, it had been difficult to subdue. "Cessez cette mauvaise plaisanterie," he said to the secondary self—and the latter obeyed. The way in which the various personages share the stock of possible sensations between them seems to be amusingly illustrated in this young woman. When awake, her skin is insensible everywhere except on a zone about the arm where she habitually wears a gold bracelet. This zone has feeling; but in the deepest trance, when all the rest of her body feels, this particular zone becomes absolutely anæsthetic.

Sometimes the mutual ignorance of the selves leads to incidents which are strange enough. The acts and movements performed by the sub-conscious self are withdrawn from the conscious one, and the subject will do all sorts of incongruous things of which he remains quite unaware. "I order Lucie [by the method of *distraction*] to make a *pied de nez*, and her hands go forthwith to the end of her nose. Asked what she is doing, she replies that she is doing nothing, and continues for a long time talking, with no apparent suspicion that her fingers are moving in front of her nose. I make her walk about the room; she continues to speak and believes herself sitting down."

M. Janet observed similar acts in a man in alcoholic delirium. Whilst the doctor was questioning him, M. J. made him by whispered suggestion walk, sit, kneel, and even lie down on his face on the floor, he all the while believing himself to be standing beside his bed. Such *bizarreries* sound incredible, until one has seen their like. Long ago, without understanding it, I myself saw a small example of the way in which a person's knowledge may be shared by the two selves. A young woman who had been writing automatically was sitting with a pencil in her hand, trying to recall at my request the name of a gentleman whom she had once seen. She could only recollect the first syllable. Her hand meanwhile, without her knowledge, wrote down the last two syllables. In a perfectly healthy young man who can write with the planchette, I lately found the hand to be entirely anæsthetic during the writing act; I could prick it severely without the Subject knowing the fact. The *writing on the planchette*, however, accused me in strong terms of hurting the hand. Pricks on the *other* (non-writing) hand, meanwhile, which awakened strong protest from the young man's vocal organs, were denied to exist by the self which made the planchette go.[7]

We get exactly similar results in the so-called post-hypnotic suggestion. It is a familiar fact that certain subjects, when told during a trance to perform an act or to experience an hallucination after waking, will when the time comes, obey the command. How is the command registered? How is its performance so accurately timed? These problems were long a mystery, for the primary personality remembers nothing of the trance or the suggestion, and will often trump up an improvised pretext for yielding to the unaccountable impulse which possesses the man so suddenly and which he cannot resist. Edmund Gurney was the first to discover, by means of automatic writing, that the secondary self is awake, keeping its attention constantly fixed on the command and watching for the signal of its execution. Certain trance-subjects who were also automatic writers, when roused from trance and put to the planchette,—not knowing then what they wrote, and having their upper attention fully engrossed by reading aloud, talking, or solving problems in mental arithmetic,—would inscribe the orders which they had received, together with notes relative to the time elapsed and the time yet to run before the execution.[8] It is therefore to no 'automatism' in the mechanical sense that such acts are due: a self presides over them, a split-off, limited and buried, but yet a fully conscious, self. More than this, the buried self often comes to the surface and drives out the other self whilst the acts are performing. In other words, the subject lapses into trance again when the moment arrives for execution, and has no subsequent recollection of the act which he has done. Gurney and Beaunis established this fact, which has since been verified on a large scale; and Gurney also showed that the patient became *suggestible* again during the brief time of the performance. M. Janet's observations, in their turn, well illustrate the phenomenon.

"I tell Lucie to keep her arms raised after she shall have awakened. Hardly is she in the normal state, when up go her arms above her head, but she pays no attention to them. She goes, comes, converses, holding her arms high in the air. If asked what her arms are doing, she is surprised at such a question, and says very sincerely: 'My hands are doing nothing; they are just like yours.' . . . I command her to weep, and when

[7] See *Proceedings of the American Society for Psychical Research*, vol. I, p. 548.

[8] *Proceedings of the (London) Society for Psychical Research*, May 1887, p. 268 ff.

awake she really sobs, but continues in the midst of her tears to talk of very gay matters. The sobbing over, there remained no trace of this grief, which seemed to have been quite sub-conscious."

The primary self often has to invent an hallucination by which to mask and hide from its own view the deeds which the other self is enacting. Léonie 3[9] writes real letters, whilst Léonie 1 believes that she is knitting; or Lucie 3 really comes to the doctor's office, whilst Lucie 1 believes herself to be at home. This is a sort of delirium. The alphabet, or the series of numbers, when handed over to the attention of the secondary personage may for the time be lost to the normal self. Whilst the hand writes the alphabet, obediently to command, the 'subject,' to her great stupefaction, finds herself unable to recall it, etc. Few things are more curious than these relations of mutual exclusion, of which all gradations exist between the several partial consciousnesses.

How far this splitting up of the mind into separate consciousnesses may exist in each one of us is a problem. M. Janet holds that it is only possible where there is abnormal weakness, and consequently a defect of unifying or co-ordinating power. An hysterical woman abandons part of her consciousness because she is too weak nervously to hold it together. The abandoned part meanwhile may solidify into a secondary or sub-conscious self. In a perfectly sound subject, on the other hand, what is dropped out of mind at one moment keeps coming back at the next. The whole fund of experiences and knowledges remains integrated, and no split-off portions of it can get organized stably enough to form subordinate selves. The stability, monotony, and stupidity of these latter is often very striking. The post-hypnotic sub-consciousness seems to think of nothing but the order which it last received; the cataleptic sub-consciousness, of nothing but the last position imprinted on the limb. M. Janet could cause definitely circumscribed reddening and tumefaction of the skin on two of his subjects, by suggesting to them in hypnotism the hallucination of a mustard-poultice of any special shape. "J'ai tout le temps pensé à votre sinapisme," says the subject, when put back into trance after the suggestion has taken effect. A man N., . . . whom M. Janet operated on at long intervals, was betweenwhiles tampered with by another operator, and when

[9] M. Janet designates by numbers the different personalities which the subject may display.

put to sleep again by M. Janet, said he was 'too far away to receive orders, being in Algiers.' The other operator, having suggested that hallucination, had forgotten to remove it before waking the subject from his trance, and the poor passive trance-personality had stuck for weeks in the stagnant dream. Léonie's sub-conscious performances having been illustrated to a caller, by a '*pied de nez*' executed with her left hand in the course of conversation, when, a year later, she meets him again, up goes the same hand to her nose again, without Léonie's normal self suspecting the fact.

All these facts, taken together, form unquestionably the beginning of an inquiry which is destined to throw a new light into the very abysses of our nature. It is for that reason that I have cited them at such length in this early chapter of the book. They prove one thing conclusively, namely, that *we must never take a person's testimony, however sincere, that he has felt nothing, as proof positive that no feeling has been there.* It may have been there as part of the consciousness of a 'secondary personage,' of whose experiences the primary one whom we are consulting can naturally give no account. In hypnotic subjects (as we shall see in a later chapter) just as it is the easiest thing in the world to paralyze a movement or member by simple suggestion, so it is easy to produce what is called a systematized anæsthesia by word of command. A systematized anæsthesia means an insensibility, not to any one element of things, but to some one concrete thing or class of things. The subject is made blind or deaf to a certain person in the room and to no one else, and thereupon denies that that person is present, or has spoken, etc. M. P. Janet's Lucie, blind to some of the numbered cards in her lap (p. 204 above), is a case in point. Now when the object is simple, like a red wafer or a black cross, the subject, although he denies that he sees it when he looks straight at it, nevertheless gets a 'negative after-image' of it when he looks away again, showing that the *optical impression* of it has been received. Moreover reflection shows that such a subject must *distinguish the object from others like it in order to be blind to it.* Make him blind to one person in the room, set all the persons in a row, and tell him to count them. He will count all but that one. But how can he tell *which* one not to count without recognizing who he is? In like manner, make a stroke on paper or blackboard, and tell him it is not there, and he will see nothing but the clean paper or board.

Next (he not looking) surround the original stroke with other strokes exactly like it, and ask him what he sees. He will point out one by one all the new strokes, and omit the original one every time, no matter how numerous the new strokes may be, or in what order they are arranged. Similarly, if the original single stroke to which he is blind be *doubled* by a prism of some sixteen degrees placed before one of his eyes (both being kept open), he will say that he now sees *one* stroke, and point in the direction in which the image seen through the prism lies, ignoring still the original stroke.

Obviously, then, he is not blind to the *kind* of stroke in the least. He is blind only to one individual stroke of that kind in a particular position on the board or paper—that is to a particular complex object; and, paradoxical as it may seem to say so, he must distinguish it with great accuracy from others like it, in order to remain blind to it when the others are brought near. He discriminates it, as a preliminary to not seeing it at all.

Again, when by a prism before one eye a previously invisible line has been made visible to that eye, and the other eye is thereupon closed or screened, *its* closure makes no difference; the line still remains visible. But if then the prism be removed, the line will disappear even to the eye which a moment ago saw it, and both eyes will revert to their original blind state.

We have, then, to deal in these cases neither with a blindness of the eye itself, nor with a mere failure to notice, but with something much more complex; namely, an active counting out and positive exclusion of certain objects. It is as when one 'cuts' an acquaintance, 'ignores' a claim, or 'refuses to be influenced' by a consideration. But the perceptive activity which works to this result is disconnected from the consciousness which is personal, so to speak, to the subject, and makes of the object concerning which the suggestion is made, its own private possession and prey.[10]

[10] How to conceive of this state of mind is not easy. It would be much simpler to understand the process, if adding new strokes made the first one visible. There would then be two different objects apperceived as totals,—paper with one stroke, paper with many strokes; and, blind to the former, he would see all that was in the latter, because he would have apperceived it as a different total in the first instance.

A process of this sort occurs sometimes (not always) when the new strokes, instead of being mere repetitions of the original one, are lines which combine with it into a total object, say a human face. The subject of the trance then may regain his sight of the line to which he had previously been blind, by seeing it as part of the face.

The mother who is asleep to every sound but the stirrings of her babe, evidently has the babe-portion of her auditory sensibility systematically awake. Relatively to that, the rest of her mind is in a state of systematized anæsthesia. That department, split off and disconnected from the sleeping part, can none the less wake the latter up in case of need. So that on the whole the quarrel between Descartes and Locke as to whether the mind ever sleeps is less near to solution than ever. On *a priori* speculative grounds Locke's view that thought and feeling may at times wholly disappear seems the more plausible. As glands cease to secrete and muscles to contract, so the brain should sometimes cease to carry currents, and with this minimum of its activity might well coexist a minimum of consciousness. On the other hand, we see how deceptive are appearances, and are forced to admit that a part of consciousness may sever its connections with other parts and yet continue to be. On the whole it is best to abstain from a conclusion. The science of the near future will doubtless answer this question more wisely than we can now.

Let us turn now to consider the

RELATIONS OF CONSCIOUSNESS TO SPACE

This is the problem known in the history of philosophy as the *question of the seat of the soul.* It has given rise to much literature, but we must ourselves treat it very briefly. Everything depends on what we conceive the soul to be, an extended or an inextended entity. If the former, it may occupy a seat. If the latter, it may not; though it has been thought that even then it might still have a *position.* Much hair-splitting has arisen about the possibility of an inextended thing nevertheless being *present* throughout a certain amount of extension. We must distinguish the kinds of presence. In some manner our consciousness is 'present' to everything with which it is in relation. I am *cognitively* present to Orion whenever I perceive that constellation, but I am not *dynamically* present there, I work no effects. To my brain, however, I am dynamically present, inasmuch as my thoughts and feelings seem to react upon the processes thereof. If, then, by the seat of the mind is meant nothing more than the locality with which it stands in immediate dynamic relations, we are certain to be right in saying that its seat is somewhere in the cortex of the brain. Descartes, as is well known, thought that the inextended soul was immediately present to the pineal gland. Others, as Lotze in his earlier days, and W. Volkmann, think its position must be at some point of the structureless matrix of the anatomical brain-elements, at which point they suppose that all nerve-currents may cross and combine. The scholastic doctrine is that the soul is totally present, both in the whole and in each and every part of the body. This mode of presence is said to be due to the soul's inextended nature and to its simplicity. Two extended entities could only correspond in space with one another, part to part,—but not so does the soul, which has no parts, correspond with the body. Sir William Hamilton and Professor Bowen defend something like this view. I. H. Fichte, Ulrici, and, among American philosophers, Mr. J. E. Walter,[11] maintain the soul to be a space-filling principle. Fichte calls it the inner body, Ulrici likens it to a fluid of non-molecular composition. These theories remind us of the 'theosophic' doctrines of the present day, and carry us back to times when the soul as vehicle of consciousness was not discriminated, as it now is, from the vital principle presiding over the formation of the body. Plato gave head, breast, and abdomen to the immortal reason, the courage, and the appetites, as their seats respectively. Aristotle argues that the heart is the sole seat. Elsewhere we find the blood, the brain, the lungs, the liver, the kidneys even, in turn assigned as seat of the whole or part of the soul.[12]

The truth is that if the thinking principle is extended we neither know its form nor its seat; whilst if unextended, it is absurd to speak of its having any space-relations at all. Space-relations we shall see hereafter to be *sensible* things. The only objects that can have mutual relations of position are objects that are perceived coexisting in the same felt space. A thing not perceived at all, such as the inextended soul must be, cannot coexist with any perceived objects in this way. No lines can be felt stretching from it to the other objects. It can form no terminus to any space-interval. It can therefore in no intelligible sense enjoy position. Its relations cannot be spatial, but must be exclusively cognitive or dynamic, as we have seen. So far as they are dynamic, to talk of the soul being 'present' is only a figure of speech. Hamilton's doctrine that the

11 *Perception of Space and Matter*, 1879, part II, chap. 3.

12 For a very good condensed history of the various opinions, see W. Volkmann von Volkmar: *Lehrbuch der Psychologie*, § 16, Anm. Complete references to Sir W. Hamilton are given in J. E. Walter: *Perception of Space and Matter*, pp. 65–6.

soul is present to the whole body is at any rate false: for cognitively its presence extends far beyond the body, and dynamically it does not extend beyond the brain.[13]

THE RELATIONS OF MINDS TO OTHER OBJECTS

are either relations to *other minds*, or to *material things*. The material things are either the mind's *own brain*, on the one hand, or *anything else*, on the other. The relations of a mind to its own brain are of a unique and utterly mysterious sort; we discussed them in the last two chapters, and can add nothing to that account.

The mind's relations to other objects than the brain are *cognitive and emotional* relations exclusively, so far as we know. It *knows* them, and it inwardly *welcomes or rejects* them, but it has no other dealings with them. When it seems to *act* upon them, it only does so through the intermediary of its own body, so that not it but the body is what acts on them, and the brain must first act upon the body. The same is true when other things seem to act on it—they only act on the body, and through that on its brain.[14] All that it *can* do *directly* is to know other things, misknow or ignore them, and to find that they interest it, in this fashion or in that.

Now the *relation of knowing* is the most mysterious thing in the world. If we ask how one thing *can* know another we are led into the heart of *Erkenntnisstheorie* and metaphysics. The psychologist, for his part, does not consider the matter so curiously as this. Finding a world before him which he cannot but believe that *he* knows, and setting himself to study his own past thoughts, or someone else's thoughts, of what he believes to be that same world; he cannot but conclude that those other thoughts know it after their fashion even as he knows it after his. Knowledge becomes for him an ultimate relation that must be admitted, whether it be explained or not, just like difference or resemblance, which no one seeks to explain.

Were our topic Absolute Mind instead of being the concrete minds of individuals dwelling in the natural world, we could not

13 Most contemporary writers ignore the question of the soul's seat. Lotze is the only one who seems to have been much concerned about it, and his views have varied. Cf. *Medicinische Psychologie*, § 10. *Microcosmus*, bk. III, ch. 2. *Metaphysic*, bk. III, ch. 5. *Grundzüge der Psychologie*, part II, ch. 3. See also G. T. Fechner: *Psychophysik*, chap. XXXVII.

14 I purposely ignore 'clairvoyance' and action upon distant things by 'mediums,' as not yet matters of common consent.

tell whether that Mind had the function of knowing or not, as knowing is commonly understood. We might learn the complexion of its thoughts; but, as we should have no realities outside of it to compare them with,—for if we had, the Mind would not be Absolute,—we could not criticise them, and find them either right or wrong; and we should have to call them simply the thoughts, and not the *knowledge*, of the Absolute Mind. Finite minds, however, can be judged in a different way, because the psychologist himself can go bail for the independent reality of the objects of which they think. He knows these to exist outside as well as inside the minds in question; he thus knows whether the minds think and *know*, or only think; and though his knowledge is of course that of a fallible mortal, there is nothing in the conditions that should make it more likely to be wrong in this case than in any other.

Now by what tests does the psychologist decide whether the state of mind he is studying is a bit of knowledge, or only a subjective fact not referring to anything outside itself?

He uses the tests we all practically use. If the state of mind *resembles* his own idea of a certain reality; or if without resembling his idea of it, it seems to imply that reality and refer to it by operating upon it through the bodily organs; or even if it resembles and operates on some other reality that implies, and leads up to, and terminates in, the first one,—in either or all of these cases the psychologist admits that the state of mind takes cognizance, directly or remotely, distinctly or vaguely, truly or falsely, of the reality's nature and position in the world. If, on the other hand, the mental state under examination neither resembles nor operates on any of the realities known to the psychologist, he calls it a subjective state pure and simple, possessed of no cognitive worth. If, again, it resemble a reality or a set of realities as he knows them, but altogether fail to operate on them or modify their course by producing bodily motions which the psychologist sees, then the psychologist, like all of us, may be in doubt. Let the mental state, for example, occur during the sleep of its subject. Let the latter dream of the death of a certain man, and let the man simultaneously die. Is the dream a mere coincidence, or a veritable cognition of the death? Such puzzling cases are what the Societies for 'Psychical Research' are collecting and trying to interpret in the most reasonable way.

If the dream were the only one of the kind the subject ever had in his life, if the context of the death in the dream differed in many particulars from the real death's context, and if the dream led to no action about the death, unquestionably we should all call it a strange coincidence, and naught besides. But if the death in the dream had a long context, agreeing point for point with every feature that attended the real death; if the subject were constantly having such dreams, all equally perfect, and if on awaking he had a habit of acting immediately as if they were true and so getting 'the start' of his more tardily informed neighbors,—we should probably all have to admit that he had some mysterious kind of clairvoyant power, that his dreams in an inscrutable way knew just those realities which they figured, and that the word 'coincidence' failed to touch the root of the matter. And whatever doubts anyone preserved would completely vanish if it should appear that from the midst of his dream he had the power of *interfering* with the course of the reality, and making the events in it turn this way or that, according as he dreamed they should. Then at least it would be certain that he and the psychologist were dealing with the *same*. It is by such tests as these that we are convinced that the waking minds of our fellows and our own minds know the same external world.

The psychologist's attitude towards cognition will be so important in the sequel that we must not leave it until it is made perfectly clear. *It is a thoroughgoing dualism.* It supposes two elements, mind knowing and thing known, and treats them as irreducible. Neither gets out of itself or into the other, neither in any way *is* the other, neither *makes* the other. They just stand face to face in a common world, and one simply knows, or is known unto, its counterpart. This singular relation is not to be expressed in any lower terms, or translated into any more intelligible name. Some sort of *signal* must be given by the thing to the mind's brain, or the knowing will not occur—we find as a matter of fact that the mere *existence* of a thing outside the brain is not a sufficient cause for our knowing it: it must strike the brain in some way, as well as be there, to be known. But the brain being struck, the knowledge is constituted by a new construction that occurs altogether *in* the mind. The thing remains the same whether known or not.[15] And

[15] I disregard *consequences* which may later come to the thing from the fact that it is known. The knowing *per se* in no wise affects the thing.

when once there, the knowledge may remain there, whatever becomes of the thing.

By the ancients, and by unreflecting people perhaps to-day, knowledge is explained as the *passage* of something from without into the mind—the latter, so far, at least, as its sensible affections go, being passive and receptive. But even in mere sense-impression the duplication of the object by an inner construction must take place. Consider, with Professor Bowne, what happens when two people converse together and know each other's mind.

"No thoughts leave the mind of one and cross into the mind of the other. When we speak of an exchange of thought, even the crudest mind recognizes that this is a mere figure of speech . . . . To perceive another's thought, we must construct his thought within ourselves; . . . this thought is our own, and is strictly original with us. At the same time we owe it to the other; and if it had not originated with him it would probably never have originated with us. But what has the other done? . . . This: by an entirely mysterious world-order the speaker is enabled to produce a series of signs which are totally unlike [the] thought, but which, by virtue of the same mysterious order, act as a series of incitements upon the hearer, so that he constructs in himself the corresponding mental state. The act of the speaker consists in availing himself of the proper incitements. The act of the hearer is immediately only the reaction of the soul against the incitement. . . . All communion between finite minds is of this sort. . . . Probably no reflecting person would deny this conclusion; but when we say that what is thus true of perception of another's thought is equally true of the perception of the outer world in general, many minds will be disposed to question, and not a few will deny it outright. Yet there is no alternative but to affirm that to perceive the universe we must construct it in thought, and that our knowledge of the universe is but the unfolding of the mind's inner nature . . . . By describing the mind as a waxen tablet, and things as impressing themselves upon it, we seem to get great insight until we think to ask where this extended tablet is, and how things stamp themselves on it, and how the perceptive act would be explained even if they did. . . . The immediate antecedents of sensation and perception are a series of nervous changes in the brain. Whatever we know of the outer world is revealed only in and through these nervous changes. But these are totally unlike the objects assumed to exist as their causes. If we might conceive the mind as in the light, and in direct contact with its objects, the imagination at least would be comforted; but when we conceive the mind as coming in contact with the outer world only in the dark chamber of the skull, and then not in contact with the objects perceived, but only with a series of nerve changes of which, moreover, it knows nothing, it is plain that the object is a long way off. All talk of pictures, impressions, etc., ceases because of the lack of all the conditions to give such figures any meaning. It is not even clear that we shall ever find our way out of the darkness into the world of light and reality again. We begin with complete trust in physics and the senses, and are forthwith led away from the object into a nervous labyrinth, where the object is entirely displaced by a set of nervous changes which are totally unlike anything but themselves. Finally, we land in the dark chamber of the skull. The object has gone completely, and knowledge has not yet appeared. Nervous signs are the raw material of all knowledge of the outer world according to the most decided realism. But in order to pass beyond these signs into a knowledge of the outer world, we must posit an interpreter who shall read back these signs into their objective meaning. But that interpreter, again, must implicitly contain the meaning of the universe within itself; and these signs are really but excitations which cause the soul to unfold what is within itself. Inasmuch as by common consent the soul communicates with the outer world only through these signs, and never comes nearer to the object than such signs can bring it, it follows that the principles of interpretation must be in the mind itself, and that the resulting construction is primarily only an expression of the mind's own nature. All reaction is of this sort; it expresses the nature of the reacting agent, and knowledge comes under the same head. This fact makes it necessary for us either to admit a pre-established harmony between the laws and nature of thought and the laws and nature of things, or else to allow that the objects of perception, the universe as it appears, are purely phenomenal, being but the way in which the mind reacts against the ground of its sensations."[16]

The dualism of Object and Subject and their pre-established harmony are what the psychologist as such must assume, whatever ulterior monistic philosophy he may, as an individual who has the right also to be a metaphysician, have in reserve. I hope that this general point is now made clear, so that we may leave it, and descend to some distinctions of detail.

There are two kinds of knowledge broadly and practically distinguishable: we may call them respectively *knowledge of acquaintance* and *knowledge-about.* Most languages express the distinction; thus, γνῶναι, εἰδέναι; *noscere, scire*; *kennen, wissen*; *con-*

[16] B. P. Bowne: *Metaphysics*, pp. 403–10. Cf. also Lotze: *Logik*, §§ 308, 326–7.

naître, savoir.[17] I am acquainted with many people and things, which I know very little about, except their presence in the places where I have met them. I know the color blue when I see it, and the flavor of a pear when I taste it; I know an inch when I move my finger through it; a second of time, when I feel it pass; an effort of attention when I make it; a difference between two things when I notice it; but *about* the inner nature of these facts or what makes them what they are, I can say nothing at all. I cannot impart acquaintance with them to anyone who has not already made it himself. I cannot *describe* them, make a blind man guess what blue is like, define to a child a syllogism, or tell a philosopher in just what respect distance is just what it is, and differs from other forms of relation. At most, I can say to my friends, Go to certain places and act in certain ways, and these objects will probably come. All the elementary natures of the world, its highest genera, the simple qualities of matter and mind, together with the kinds of relation that subsist between them, must either not be known at all, or known in this dumb way of acquaintance without *knowledge-about.* In minds able to speak at all there is, it is true, *some* knowledge about everything. Things can at least be classed, and the times of their appearance told. But in general, the less we analyze a thing, and the fewer of its relations we perceive, the less we know about it and the more our familiarity with it is of the acquaintance-type. The two kinds of knowledge are, therefore, as the human mind practically exerts them, relative terms. That is, the same thought of a thing may be called knowledge-about it in comparison with a simpler thought, or acquaintance with it in comparison with a thought of it that is more articulate and explicit still.

The grammatical sentence expresses this. Its 'subject' stands for an object of acquaintance which, by the addition of the predicate, is to get something known about it. We may already know a good deal, when we hear the subject named—its name may have rich connotations. But, know we much or little then, we know more still when the sentence is done. We can relapse at will into a mere condition of acquaintance with an object by scattering our attention and staring at it in a vacuous trance-like way. We can ascend to knowledge *about* it by rallying our wits and proceeding to notice and analyze and think. What we are only acquainted with is only

[17] Cf. John Grote: *Exploratio Philosophica,* p. 60; H. Helmholtz: *Popular Scientific Lectures,* London, pp. 308–9.

present to our minds; we *have* it, or the idea of it. But when we know about it, we do more than merely have it; we seem, as we think over its relations, to subject it to a sort of *treatment* and to *operate* upon it with our thought. The words *feeling* and *thought* give voice to the antithesis. Through feelings we become acquainted with things, but only by our thoughts do we know about them. Feelings are the germ and starting point of cognition, thoughts the developed tree. The minimum of grammatical subject, of objective presence, of reality known about, the mere beginning of knowledge, must be named by the word that says the least. Such a word is the interjection, as *lo! there! ecco! voilà!* or the article or demonstrative pronoun introducing the sentence, as *the, it, that.* In Chapter XII we shall see a little deeper into what this distinction, between the mere mental having or feeling of an object and the thinking of it, portends.

The mental states usually distinguished as feelings are the *emotions,* and the *sensations* we get from skin, muscle, viscus, eye, ear, nose, and palate. The 'thoughts,' as recognized in popular parlance, are the *conceptions* and *judgments.* When we treat of these mental states in particular we shall have to say a word about the cognitive function and value of each. It may perhaps be well to notice now that our senses only give us acquaintance with facts of body, and that of the mental states of other persons we only have conceptual knowledge. Of our own past states of mind we take cognizance in a peculiar way. They are 'objects of memory,' and appear to us endowed with a sort of warmth and intimacy that makes the perception of them seem more like a process of sensation than like a thought.

Chapter IX[*]

The Stream of Thought

We now begin our study of the mind from within. Most books start with sensations, as the simplest mental facts, and proceed synthetically, constructing each higher stage from those below it. But this is abandoning the empirical method of investigation. No one ever had a simple sensation by itself. Consciousness, from our natal day, is of a teeming multiplicity of objects and relations, and what we call simple sensations are results of discriminative attention, pushed often to a very high degree. It is astonishing what havoc is wrought in psychology by admitting at the outset apparently innocent suppositions, that nevertheless contain a flaw. The bad consequences develop themselves later on, and are irremediable, being woven through the whole texture of the work. The notion that sensations, being the simplest things, are the first things to take up in psychology is one of these suppositions. The only thing which psychology has a right to postulate at the outset is the fact of thinking itself, and that must first be taken up and analyzed. If sensations then prove to be amongst the elements of the thinking, we shall be no worse off as respects them than if we had taken them for granted at the start.

The first fact for us, then, as psychologists, is that thinking of some sort goes on. I use the word thinking, in accordance with what was said on p. 186, for every form of consciousness indis-

* A good deal of this chapter is reprinted from an article "On Some Omissions of Introspective Psychology" which appeared in *Mind* for January 1884.

criminately. If we could say in English 'it thinks,' as we say 'it rains' or 'it blows,' we should be stating the fact most simply and with the minimum of assumption. As we cannot, we must simply say that *thought goes on.*

FIVE CHARACTERS IN THOUGHT

How does it go on? We notice immediately five important characters in the process, of which it shall be the duty of the present chapter to treat in a general way:

1) Every thought tends to be part of a personal consciousness.

2) Within each personal consciousness thought is always changing.

3) Within each personal consciousness thought is sensibly continuous.

4) It always appears to deal with objects independent of itself.

5) It is interested in some parts of these objects to the exclusion of others, and welcomes or rejects—*chooses* from among them, in a word—all the while.

In considering these five points successively, we shall have to plunge *in medias res* as regards our vocabulary, and use psychological terms which can only be adequately defined in later chapters of the book. But everyone knows what the terms mean in a rough way; and it is only in a rough way that we are now to take them. This chapter is like a painter's first charcoal sketch upon his canvas, in which no niceties appear.

1) *Thought tends to Personal Form*

When I say *every 'thought' is part of a personal consciousness,* 'personal consciousness' is one of the terms in question. Its meaning we know so long as no one asks us to define it, but to give an accurate account of it is the most difficult of philosophic tasks. This task we must confront in the next chapter; here a preliminary word will suffice.

In this room—this lecture-room, say—there are a multitude of thoughts, yours and mine, some of which cohere mutually, and some not. They are as little each-for-itself and reciprocally independent as they are all-belonging-together. They are neither: no one of them is separate, but each belongs with certain others and with none beside. My thought belongs with my other thoughts, and your thought with your other thoughts. Whether anywhere in the room there be a mere thought, which is nobody's thought, we have no means of ascertaining, for we have no experience of its like. The only states of consciousness that we naturally deal with are found in personal consciousnesses, minds, selves, concrete particular I's and you's.

Each of these minds keeps its own thoughts to itself. There is no giving or bartering between them. No thought even comes into direct *sight* of a thought in another personal consciousness than its own. Absolute insulation, irreducible pluralism, is the law. It seems as if the elementary psychic fact were not *thought* or *this thought* or *that thought*, but *my thought*, every thought being *owned*. Neither contemporaneity, nor proximity in space, nor similarity of quality and content are able to fuse thoughts together which are sundered by this barrier of belonging to different personal minds. The breaches between such thoughts are the most absolute breaches in nature. Everyone will recognize this to be true, so long as the existence of *something* corresponding to the term 'personal mind' is all that is insisted on, without any particular view of its nature being implied. On these terms the personal self rather than the thought might be treated as the immediate datum in psychology. The universal conscious fact is not 'feelings and thoughts exist,' but 'I think' and 'I feel.'[1] No psychology, at any rate, can question the *existence* of personal selves. The worst a psychology can do is so to interpret the nature of these selves as to rob them of their worth. A French writer, speaking of our ideas, says somewhere in a fit of anti-spiritualistic excitement that, misled by certain peculiarities which they display, we 'end by personifying' the procession which they make,—such personification being regarded by him as a great philosophic blunder on our part. It could only be a blunder if the notion of personality meant something essentially different from anything to be found in the mental procession. But if that procession be itself the very 'original' of the notion of personality, to personify it cannot possibly be wrong. It is already personified. There are no marks of personality to be gathered *aliunde*, and then found lacking in the train of thought. It has them all already; so that to whatever farther analysis we may subject that form of personal selfhood under which thoughts appear, it is, and must remain, true that the thoughts which psy-

[1] B. P. Bowne: *Metaphysics*, p. 362.

chology studies do continually tend to appear as parts of personal selves.

I say 'tend to appear' rather than 'appear,' on account of those facts of sub-conscious personality, automatic writing, etc., of which we studied a few in the last chapter. The buried feelings and thoughts proved now to exist in hysterical anæsthetics, in recipients of post-hypnotic suggestion, etc., themselves are parts of *secondary personal selves.* These selves are for the most part very stupid and contracted, and are cut off at ordinary times from communication with the regular and normal self of the individual; but still they form conscious unities, have continuous memories, speak, write, invent distinct names for themselves, or adopt names that are suggested; and, in short, are entirely worthy of that title of secondary personalities which is now commonly given them. According to M. Janet these secondary personalities are always abnormal, and result from the splitting of what ought to be a single complete self into two parts, of which one lurks in the background whilst the other appears on the surface as the only self the man or woman has. For our present purpose it is unimportant whether this account of the origin of secondary selves is applicable to all possible cases of them or not, for it certainly is true of a large number of them. Now although the *size* of a secondary self thus formed will depend on the number of thoughts that are thus split-off from the main consciousness, the *form* of it tends to personality, and the later thoughts pertaining to it remember the earlier ones and adopt them as their own. M. Janet caught the actual moment of inspissation (so to speak) of one of these secondary personalities in his anæsthetic somnambulist Lucie. He found that when this young woman's attention was absorbed in conversation with a third party, her anæsthetic hand would write simple answers to questions whispered to her by himself. "Do you hear?" he asked. "*No,*" was the unconsciously written reply. "But to answer you must hear." "*Yes, quite so.*" "Then how do you manage?" "*I don't know.*" "There must be someone who hears me." "*Yes.*" "Who?" "*Someone other than Lucie.*" "Ah! another person. Shall we give her a name?" "*No.*" "Yes, it will be more convenient." "*Well, Adrienne, then.*" "Once baptized, the subconscious personage," M. Janet continues, "grows more definitely outlined and displays better her psychological characters. In particular she shows us that she is conscious of the feelings excluded from the consciousness of the primary or normal personage. She it is who tells us that I am pinching the arm or touching the little finger in which Lucie for so long has had no tactile sensations."[2]

In other cases the adoption of the name by the secondary self is more spontaneous. I have seen a number of incipient automatic writers and mediums as yet imperfectly 'developed,' who immediately and of their own accord write and speak in the name of departed spirits. These may be public characters, as Mozart, Faraday, or real persons formerly known to the subject, or altogether imaginary beings. Without prejudicing the question of real 'spirit-control' in the more developed sorts of trance-utterance, I incline to think that these (often deplorably unintelligent) rudimentary utterances are the work of an inferior fraction of the subject's own natural mind, set free from control by the rest, and working after a set pattern fixed by the prejudices of the social environment. In a spiritualistic community we get optimistic messages, whilst in an ignorant Catholic village the secondary personage calls itself by the name of a demon, and proffers blasphemies and obscenities, instead of telling us how happy it is in the summer-land.[3]

Beneath these tracts of thought, which, however rudimentary, are still organized selves with a memory, habits, and sense of their own identity, M. Janet thinks that the facts of catalepsy in hysteric patients drive us to suppose that there are thoughts quite unorganized and impersonal. A patient in cataleptic trance (which can be produced artificially in certain hypnotized subjects) is without memory on waking, and seems insensible and unconscious as long as the cataleptic condition lasts. If, however, one raises the arm of such a subject it stays in that position, and the whole body can thus be moulded like wax under the hands of the operator, retaining for a considerable time whatever attitude he communicates to it. In hysterics whose arm, for example, is anæsthetic, the same thing may happen. The anæsthetic arm may remain passively in positions which it is made to assume; or if the hand be taken and made to hold a pencil and trace a certain letter, it will continue tracing that letter indefinitely on the paper. These acts, until recently,

[2] *L'Automatisme psychologique*, pp. 317–18.

[3] Cf. A. Constans: *Relation sur une épidémie d'hystéro-démonopathie en 1861*, 2me ed., Paris, 1863.—Chiap e Franzolini: *L'Epidemia di istero-demonopatie in Verzegnis*, Reggio, 1879.—See also J. Kerner's little work: *Nachricht von dem Vorkommen des Besessenseyns*, 1836.

were supposed to be accompanied by no consciousness at all: they were physiological reflexes. M. Janet considers with much more plausibility that feeling escorts them. The feeling is probably merely that of the position or movement of the limb, and it produces no more than its natural effects when it discharges into the motor centres which keep the position maintained, or the movement incessantly renewed.[4] Such thoughts as these, says M. Janet, "are known by *no one*, for disaggregated sensations reduced to a state of mental dust are not synthetized in any personality."[5] He admits, however, that these very same unutterably stupid thoughts tend to develop memory,—the cataleptic ere long moves her arm at a bare hint; so that they form no important exception to the law that all thought tends to assume the form of personal consciousness.

2) *Thought is in Constant Change*

I do not mean necessarily that no one state of mind has any duration—even if true, that would be hard to establish. The change which I have more particularly in view is that which takes place in sensible intervals of time; and the result on which I wish to lay stress is this, that *no state once gone can recur and be identical with what it was before*. Let us begin with Mr. Shadworth Hodgson's description:

> "I go straight to the facts, without saying I go to perception, or sensation, or thought, or any special mode at all. What I find, when I look at my consciousness at all, is, that what I cannot divest myself of, or not have in consciousness, if I have any consciousness at all, is a sequence of different feelings. I may shut my eyes and keep perfectly still, and try not to contribute anything of my own will; but whether I think, or do not think, whether I perceive external things or not, I always have a succession of different feelings. Anything else that I may have also, of a more special character, comes in as parts of this succession. Not to have the succession of different feelings is not to be conscious at all. . . . The chain of consciousness is a sequence of *differents*."[6]

Such a description as this can awaken no possible protest from anyone. We all recognize as different great classes of our conscious states. Now we are seeing, now hearing; now reasoning, now will-

4 For the Physiology of this compare the chapter on the Will.

5 *Loc. cit.*, p. 316.

6 *The Philosophy of Reflection*, I, 248, 290.

ing; now recollecting, now expecting; now loving, now hating; and in a hundred other ways we know our minds to be alternately engaged. But all these are complex states. The aim of science is always to reduce complexity to simplicity; and in psychological science we have the celebrated 'theory of *ideas*' which, admitting the great difference among each other of what may be called concrete conditions of mind, seeks to show how this is all the resultant effect of variations in the *combination* of certain simple elements of consciousness that always remain the same. These mental atoms or molecules are what Locke called 'simple ideas.' Some of Locke's successors made out that the only simple ideas were the sensations strictly so called. Which ideas the simple ones may be does not, however, now concern us. It is enough that certain philosophers have thought they could see under the dissolving-view-appearance of the mind elementary facts of *any* sort that remained unchanged amid the flow.

And the view of these philosophers has been called little into question, for our common experience seems at first sight to corroborate it entirely. Are not the sensations we get from the same object, for example, always the same? Does not the same piano-key, struck with the same force, make us hear in the same way? Does not the same grass give us the same feeling of green, the same sky the same feeling of blue, and do we not get the same olfactory sensation no matter how many times we put our nose to the same flask of cologne? It seems a piece of metaphysical sophistry to suggest that we do not; and yet a close attention to the matter shows that *there is no proof that the same bodily sensation is ever got by us twice.*

What is got twice is the same OBJECT. We hear the same *note* over and over again; we see the same *quality* of green, or smell the same objective perfume, or experience the same *species* of pain. The realities, concrete and abstract, physical and ideal, whose permanent existence we believe in, seem to be constantly coming up again before our thought, and lead us, in our carelessness, to suppose that our 'ideas' of them are the same ideas. When we come, some time later, to the chapter on Perception, we shall see how inveterate is our habit of not attending to sensations as subjective facts, but of simply using them as stepping-stones to pass over to the recognition of the realities whose presence they reveal. The grass out of the window now looks to me of the same green in the sun as in the shade, and yet a painter would have to paint one part of it dark brown, another part bright yellow, to give its real sensational effect. We take no heed, as a rule, of the different way in which the same things look and sound and smell at different distances and under different circumstances. The sameness of the *things* is what we are concerned to ascertain; and any sensations that assure us of that will probably be considered in a rough way to be the same with each other. This is what makes off-hand testimony about the subjective identity of different sensations well-nigh worthless as a proof of the fact. The entire history of Sensation is a commentary on our inability to tell whether two sensations received apart are exactly alike. What appeals to our attention far more than the absolute quality or quantity of a given sensation is its *ratio* to whatever other sensations we may have at the same time. When everything is dark a somewhat less dark sensation makes us see an object white. Helmholtz calculates that the white marble painted in a picture representing an architectural view by moonlight is, when seen by daylight, from ten to twenty thousand times brighter than the real moonlit marble would be.[7]

Such a difference as this could never have been *sensibly* learned; it had to be inferred from a series of indirect considerations. There are facts which make us believe that our sensibility is altering all the time, so that the same object cannot easily give us the same sensation over again. The eye's sensibility to light is at its maximum when the eye is first exposed, and blunts itself with surprising rapidity. A long night's sleep will make it see things twice as brightly on wakening, as simple rest by closure will make it see them later in the day.[8] We feel things differently according as we are sleepy or awake, hungry or full, fresh or tired; differently at night and in the morning, differently in summer and in winter; and above all things differently in childhood, manhood, and old age. Yet we never doubt that our feelings reveal the same world, with the same sensible qualities and the same sensible things occupying it. The difference of the sensibility is shown best by the difference of our emotion about the things from one age to another, or when we are in different organic moods. What was bright and exciting becomes weary, flat, and unprofitable. The bird's song is tedious, the breeze is mournful, the sky is sad.

[7] *Populäre wissenschaftliche Vorträge*, Drittes Heft (1876), p. 72.

[8] Fick, in L. Hermann's *Handbuch der Physiologie*, Bd. III, Th. I, p. 225.

To these indirect presumptions that our sensations, following the mutations of our capacity for feeling, are always undergoing an essential change, must be added another presumption, based on what must happen in the brain. Every sensation corresponds to some cerebral action. For an identical sensation to recur it would have to occur the second time *in an unmodified brain*. But as this, strictly speaking, is a physiological impossibility, so is an unmodified feeling an impossibility; for to every brain-modification, however small, must correspond a change of equal amount in the feeling which the brain subserves.

All this would be true if even sensations came to us pure and single and not combined into 'things.' Even then we should have to confess that, however we might in ordinary conversation speak of getting the same sensation again, we never in strict theoretic accuracy could do so; and that whatever was true of the river of life, of the river of elementary feeling, it would certainly be true to say, like Heraclitus, that we never descend twice into the same stream.

But if the assumption of 'simple ideas of sensation' recurring in immutable shape is so easily shown to be baseless, how much more baseless is the assumption of immutability in the larger masses of our thought!

For there it is obvious and palpable that our state of mind is never precisely the same. Every thought we have of a given fact is, strictly speaking, unique, and only bears a resemblance of kind with our other thoughts of the same fact. When the identical fact recurs, we *must* think of it in a fresh manner, see it under a somewhat different angle, apprehend it in different relations from those in which it last appeared. And the thought by which we cognize it is the thought of it-in-those-relations, a thought suffused with the consciousness of all that dim context. Often we are ourselves struck at the strange differences in our successive views of the same thing. We wonder how we ever could have opined as we did last month about a certain matter. We have outgrown the possibility of that state of mind, we know not how. From one year to another we see things in new lights. What was unreal has grown real, and what was exciting is insipid. The friends we used to care the world for are shrunken to shadows; the women, once so divine, the stars, the woods, and the waters, how now so dull and common! the young girls that brought an aura of infinity, at present hardly distinguishable existences; the pictures so empty; and as for the books, what *was* there to find so mysteriously significant in Goethe, or in John Mill so full of weight? Instead of all this, more zestful than ever is the work, the work; and fuller and deeper the import of common duties and of common goods.

But what here strikes us so forcibly on the flagrant scale exists on every scale, down to the imperceptible transition from one hour's outlook to that of the next. Experience is remoulding us every moment, and our mental reaction on every given thing is really a resultant of our experience of the whole world up to that date. The analogies of brain-physiology must again be appealed to to corroborate our view.

Our earlier chapters have taught us to believe that, whilst we think, our brain changes, and that, like the aurora borealis, its whole internal equilibrium shifts with every pulse of change. The precise nature of the shifting at a given moment is a product of many factors. The accidental state of local nutrition or blood-supply may be among them. But just as one of them certainly is the influence of outward objects on the sense-organs during the moment, so is another certainly the very special susceptibility in which the organ has been left at that moment by all it has gone through in the past. Every brain-state is partly determined by the nature of this entire past succession. Alter the latter in any part, and the brain-state must be somewhat different. Each present brain-state is a record in which the eye of Omniscience might read all the foregone history of its owner. It is out of the question, then, that any total brain-state should identically recur. Something like it may recur; but to suppose *it* to recur would be equivalent to the absurd admission that all the states that had intervened between its two appearances had been pure nonentities, and that the organ after their passage was exactly as it was before. And (to consider shorter periods) just as, in the senses, an impression feels very differently according to what has preceded it; as one color succeeding another is modified by the contrast, silence sounds delicious after noise, and a note, when the scale is sung up, sounds unlike itself when the scale is sung down; as the presence of certain lines in a figure changes the apparent form of the other lines, and as in music the whole æsthetic effect comes from the manner in which one set of sounds alters our feeling of another; so, in thought, we must admit that those portions of the brain that have just been maximally excited retain a kind of soreness which is a condition of our present consciousness, a codeterminant of how and what we now shall feel.[9]

Ever some tracts are waning in tension, some waxing, whilst others actively discharge. The states of tension have as positive an influence as any in determining the total condition, and in deciding what the *psychosis* shall be. All we know of submaximal nerve-irritations, and of the summation of apparently ineffective stimuli, tends to show that *no* changes in the brain are physiologically ineffective, and that presumably none are bare of psychological result. But as the brain-tension shifts from one relative state of equilibrium to another, like the gyrations of a kaleidoscope, now rapid and now slow, is it likely that its faithful psychic concomitant is heavier-footed than itself, and that it cannot match each one of the organ's irradiations by a shifting inward iridescence of its own? But if it can do this, its inward iridescences must be infinite, for the brain-redistributions are in infinite variety. If so coarse a thing as a telephone-plate can be made to thrill for years and never reduplicate its inward condition, how much more must this be the case with the infinitely delicate brain?

I am sure that this concrete and total manner of regarding the mind's changes is the only true manner, difficult as it may be to carry it out in detail. If anything seems obscure about it, it will grow clearer as we advance. Meanwhile, if it be true, it is certainly also true that no two 'ideas' are ever exactly the same, which is the proposition we started to prove. The proposition is more important theoretically than it at first sight seems. For it makes it already impossible for us to follow obediently in the footprints of either the Lockian or the Herbartian school, schools which have had almost unlimited influence in Germany and among ourselves. No doubt it is often *convenient* to formulate the mental facts in an atomistic sort of way, and to treat the higher states of consciousness as if they were all built out of unchanging simple ideas. It is con-

9 It need of course not follow, because a total brain-state does not recur, that no *point* of the brain can ever be twice in the same condition. That would be as improbable a consequence as that in the sea a wave-crest should never come twice at the same point of space. What can hardly come twice is an identical *combination* of wave-forms all with their crests and hollows reoccupying identical places. For such a total combination as this is the analogue of the brain-state to which our actual consciousness at any moment is due.

venient often to treat curves as if they were composed of small straight lines, and electricity and nerve-force as if they were fluids. But in the one case as in the other we must never forget that we are talking symbolically, and that there is nothing in nature to answer to our words. *A permanently existing 'idea' or 'Vorstellung' which makes its appearance before the footlights of consciousness at periodical intervals, is as mythological an entity as the Jack of Spades.*

What makes it convenient to use the mythological formulas is the whole organization of speech, which, as was remarked a while ago, was not made by psychologists, but by men who were as a rule only interested in the facts their mental states revealed. They only spoke of their states as *ideas of this or of that thing*. What wonder, then, that the thought is most easily conceived under the law of the thing whose name it bears! If the thing is composed of parts, then we suppose that the thought of the thing must be composed of the thoughts of the parts. If one part of the thing have appeared in the same thing or in other things on former occasions, why then we must be having even now the very same 'idea' of that part which was there on those occasions. If the thing is simple, its thought is simple. If it is multitudinous, it must require a multitude of thoughts to think it. If a succession, only a succession of thoughts can know it. If permanent, its thought is permanent. And so on *ad libitum*. What after all is so natural as to assume that one object, called by one name, should be known by one affection of the mind? But, if language must thus influence us, the agglutinative languages, and even Greek and Latin with their declensions, would be the better guides. Names did not appear in them inalterable, but changed their shape to suit the context in which they lay. It must have been easier then than now to conceive of the same object as being thought of at different times in non-identical conscious states.

This, too, will grow clearer as we proceed. Meanwhile a necessary consequence of the belief in permanent self-identical psychic facts that absent themselves and recur periodically is the Humian doctrine that our thought is composed of separate independent parts and is not a sensibly continuous stream. That this doctrine entirely misrepresents the natural appearances is what I next shall try to show.

3) *Within each personal consciousness, thought is sensibly continuous*

I can only define 'continuous' as that which is without breach, crack, or division. I have already said that the breach from one mind to another is perhaps the greatest breach in nature. The only breaches that can well be conceived to occur within the limits of a single mind would either be *interruptions, time*-gaps during which the consciousness went out altogether to come into existence again at a later moment; or they would be breaks in the *quality*, or content, of the thought, so abrupt that the segment that followed had no connection whatever with the one that went before. The proposition that within each personal consciousness thought feels continuous, means two things:

1. That even where there is a time-gap the consciousness after it feels as if it belonged together with the consciousness before it, as another part of the same self;

2. That the changes from one moment to another in the quality of the consciousness are never absolutely abrupt.

The case of the time-gaps, as the simplest, shall be taken first. And first of all, a word about time-gaps of which the consciousness may not be itself aware.

On page 198 we saw that such time-gaps existed, and that they might be more numerous than is usually supposed. If the consciousness is not aware of them, it cannot feel them as interruptions. In the unconsciousness produced by nitrous oxide and other anæsthetics, in that of epilepsy and fainting, the broken edges of the sentient life may meet and merge over the gap, much as the feelings of space of the opposite margins of the 'blind spot' meet and merge over that objective interruption to the sensitiveness of the eye. Such consciousness as this, whatever it be for the onlooking psychologist, is for itself unbroken. It *feels* unbroken; a waking day of it is sensibly a unit as long as that day lasts, in the sense in which the hours themselves are units, as having all their parts next each other, with no intrusive alien substance between. To expect the consciousness to feel the interruptions of its objective continuity as gaps, would be like expecting the eye to feel a gap of silence because it does not hear, or the ear to feel a gap of darkness because it does not see. So much for the gaps that are unfelt.

With the felt gaps the case is different. On waking from sleep, we usually know that we have been unconscious, and we often have an accurate judgment of how long. The judgment here is certainly an inference from sensible signs, and its ease is due to long practice in the particular field.[10] The result of it, however, is that the consciousness is, *for itself*, not what it was in the former case, but interrupted and discontinuous, in the mere time-sense of the words. But in the other sense of continuity, the sense of the parts being inwardly connected and belonging together because they are parts of a common whole, the consciousness remains sensibly continuous and one. What now is the common whole? The natural name for it is *myself, I*, or *me*.

When Paul and Peter wake up in the same bed, and recognize that they have been asleep, each one of them mentally reaches back and makes connection with but *one* of the two streams of thought which were broken by the sleeping hours. As the current of an electrode buried in the ground unerringly finds its way to its own similarly buried mate, across no matter how much intervening earth; so Peter's present instantly finds out Peter's past, and never by mistake knits itself on to that of Paul. Paul's thought in turn is as little liable to go astray. The past thought of Peter is appropriated by the present Peter alone. He may have a *knowledge*, and a correct one too, of what Paul's last drowsy states of mind were as he sank into sleep, but it is an entirely different sort of knowledge from that which he has of his own last states. He *remembers* his own states, whilst he only *conceives* Paul's. Remembrance is like direct feeling; its object is suffused with a warmth and intimacy to which no object of mere conception ever attains. This quality of warmth and intimacy and immediacy is what Peter's *present* thought also possesses for itself. So sure as this present is me, is mine, it says, so sure is anything else that comes with the same warmth and intimacy and immediacy, me and mine. What the qualities called warmth and intimacy may in themselves be will have to be matter for future consideration. But whatever past feelings appear with those qualities must be admitted to receive the greeting of the present mental state, to be owned by it, and accepted as belonging together with it in a common self. This community of self is what the time-gap cannot break in twain, and is why a present thought, although not ignorant of the time-gap, can

10 The accurate registration of the 'how long' is still a little mysterious.

still regard itself as continuous with certain chosen portions of the past.

Consciousness, then, does not appear to itself chopped up in bits. Such words as 'chain' or 'train' do not describe it fitly as it presents itself in the first instance. It is nothing jointed; it flows. A 'river' or a 'stream' are the metaphors by which it is most naturally described. *In talking of it hereafter, let us call it the stream of thought, of consciousness, or of subjective life.*

But now there appears, even within the limits of the same self, and between thoughts all of which alike have this same sense of belonging together, a kind of jointing and separateness among the parts, of which this statement seems to take no account. I refer to the breaks that are produced by sudden *contrasts in the quality* of the successive segments of the stream of thought. If the words 'chain' and 'train' had no natural fitness in them, how came such words to be used at all? Does not a loud explosion rend the consciousness upon which it abruptly breaks, in twain? Does not every sudden shock, appearance of a new object, or change in a sensation, create a real interruption, sensibly felt as such, which cuts the conscious stream across at the moment at which it appears? Do not such interruptions smite us every hour of our lives, and have we the right, in their presence, still to call our consciousness a continuous stream?

This objection is based partly on a confusion and partly on a superficial introspective view.

The confusion is between the thoughts themselves, taken as subjective facts, and the things of which they are aware. It is natural to make this confusion, but easy to avoid it when once put on one's guard. The things are discrete and discontinuous; they do pass before us in a train or chain, making often explosive appearances and rending each other in twain. But their comings and goings and contrasts no more break the flow of the thought that thinks them than they break the time and the space in which they lie. A silence may be broken by a thunder-clap, and we may be so stunned and confused for a moment by the shock as to give no instant account to ourselves of what has happened. But that very confusion is a mental state, and a state that passes us straight over from the silence to the sound. The transition between the thought of one object and the thought of another is no more a break in the *thought* than a joint in a bamboo is a break in the wood. It is a part of the *consciousness* as much as the joint is a part of the *bamboo.*

The superficial introspective view is the overlooking, even when the things are contrasted with each other most violently, of the large amount of affinity that may still remain between the thoughts by whose means they are cognized. Into the awareness of the thunder itself the awareness of the previous silence creeps and continues; for what we hear when the thunder crashes is not thunder *pure,* but thunder-breaking-upon-silence-and-contrasting-with-it.[11] Our feeling of the same objective thunder, coming in this way, is quite different from what it would be were the thunder a continuation of previous thunder. The thunder itself we believe to abolish and exclude the silence; but the *feeling* of the thunder is also a feeling of the silence as just gone; and it would be difficult to find in the actual concrete consciousness of man a feeling so limited to the present as not to have an inkling of anything that went before. Here, again, language works against our perception of the truth. We name our thoughts simply, each after its thing, as if each knew its own thing and nothing else. What each really knows is clearly the thing it is named for, with dimly perhaps a thousand other things. It ought to be named after all of them, but it never is. Some of them are always things known a moment ago more clearly; others are things to be known more clearly a moment hence.[12] Our

[11] Cf. Brentano: *Psychologie,* vol. I, pp. 219–20. Altogether this chapter of Brentano's on the Unity of Consciousness is as good as anything with which I am acquainted.

[12] Honor to whom honor is due! The most explicit acknowledgment I have anywhere found of all this is in a buried and forgotten paper by the Rev. James Wills, on "Accidental Association," in the *Transactions of the Royal Irish Academy,* vol. XXI (1848). Mr. Wills writes:

"At every instant of conscious thought, there is a certain sum of perceptions, or reflections, or both together, present, and together constituting one whole state of apprehension. Of this, some definite portion may be far more distinct than all the rest; and the rest be in consequence proportionably vague, even to the very limit of obliteration. But still, within this limit, the most dim shade of perception enters into, and in some infinitesimal degree modifies, the whole existing state. This state will thus be in some way modified by any sensation or emotion, or act of distinct attention, that may give prominence to any part of it; so that the actual result is capable of the utmost variation, according to the person or the occasion. . . . To any portion of the entire scope here described there may be a special direction of the attention, and this special direction is strictly what is *recognized as* the idea present to the mind. This idea is evidently not commensurate with the entire state of apprehension, and much perplexity has arisen from not observing this fact. However deeply we may suppose the attention to be engaged by any thought, any consider-

own bodily position, attitude, condition, is one of the things of which *some* awareness, however inattentive, invariably accompanies the knowledge of whatever else we know. We think; and as we think we feel our bodily selves as the seat of the thinking. If the thinking be *our* thinking, it must be suffused through all its parts with that peculiar warmth and intimacy that make it come as ours. Whether the warmth and intimacy be anything more than the feeling of the same old body always there, is a matter for the next chapter to decide. *Whatever* the content of the ego may be, it is habitually felt *with* everything else by us humans, and must form a *liaison* between all the things of which we become successively aware.[13]

On this gradualness in the changes of our mental content the principles of nerve-action can throw some more light. When studying, in Chapter III, the summation of nervous activities, we saw that no state of the brain can be supposed instantly to die away. If a new state comes, the inertia of the old state will still be there and modify the result accordingly. Of course we cannot tell, in our ignorance, what in each instance the modifications ought to be. The commonest modifications in sense-perception are known as the phenomena of contrast. In æsthetics they are the feelings of delight or displeasure which certain particular orders in a series of impressions give. In thought, strictly and narrowly so called, they are unquestionably that consciousness of the *whence* and the *whither* that always accompanies its flows. If recently the brain-tract *a* was vividly excited, and then *b*, and now vividly *c*, the total present consciousness is not produced simply by *c*'s excitement, but also by the dying vibrations of *a* and *b* as well. If we want to represent the brain-process we must write it thus: ${}_{a}{}^{b}c$—three different processes coexisting, and correlated with them a thought which is no one of the three thoughts which they would have produced had each of them occurred alone. But whatever this fourth thought

able alteration of the surrounding phenomena would still be perceived; the most abstruse demonstration in this room would not prevent a listener, however absorbed, from noticing the sudden extinction of the lights. . . . Our mental states have always an *essential unity*, such, that each state of apprehension, however variously compounded, is a single whole, of which every component is, therefore, strictly apprehended (so far as it is apprehended), as a part. Such is the elementary basis from which all our intellectual operations commence."

13 Compare the charming passage in Taine on *Intelligence* (N. Y. ed.), I, 83–4.

may exactly be, it seems impossible that it should not be something *like* each of the three other thoughts whose tracts are concerned in its production, though in a fast-waning phase.

It all goes back to what we said in another connection only a few pages ago (p. 227). As the total neurosis changes, so does the total psychosis change. But as the changes of neurosis are never absolutely discontinuous, so must the successive psychoses shade gradually into each other, although their *rate* of change may be much faster at one moment than at the next.

This difference in the rate of change lies at the basis of a difference of subjective states of which we ought immediately to speak. When the rate is slow we are aware of the object of our thought in a comparatively restful and stable way. When rapid, we are aware of a passage, a relation, a transition *from* it, or *between* it and something else. As we take, in fact, a general view of the wonderful stream of our consciousness, what strikes us first is this different pace of its parts. Like a bird's life, it seems to be made of an alternation of flights and perchings. The rhythm of language expresses this, where every thought is expressed in a sentence, and every sentence closed by a period. The resting-places are usually occupied by sensorial imaginations of some sort, whose peculiarity is that they can be held before the mind for an indefinite time, and contemplated without changing; the places of flight are filled with thoughts of relations, static or dynamic, that for the most part obtain between the matters contemplated in the periods of comparative rest.

Let us call the resting-places the 'substantive parts,' and the places of flight the 'transitive parts,' of the stream of thought. It then appears that the main end of our thinking is at all times the attainment of some other substantive part than the one from which we have just been dislodged. And we may say that the main use of the transitive parts is to lead us from one substantive conclusion to another.

Now it is very difficult, introspectively, to see the transitive parts for what they really are. If they are but flights to a conclusion, stopping them to look at them before the conclusion is reached is really annihilating them. Whilst if we wait till the conclusion *be* reached, it so exceeds them in vigor and stability that it quite eclipses and swallows them up in its glare. Let anyone try to cut a thought across in the middle and get a look at its section, and he will see how difficult the introspective observation of the transitive tracts is. The rush of the thought is so headlong that it almost always brings us up at the conclusion before we can arrest it. Or if our purpose is nimble enough and we do arrest it, it ceases forthwith to be itself. As a snowflake caught in the warm hand is no longer a flake but a drop, so, instead of catching the feeling of relation moving to its term, we find we have caught some substantive thing, usually the last word we were pronouncing, statically taken, and with its function, tendency, and particular meaning in the sentence quite evaporated. The attempt at introspective analysis in these cases is in fact like seizing a spinning top to catch its motion, or trying to turn up the gas quickly enough to see how the darkness looks. And the challenge to *produce* these psychoses, which is sure to be thrown by doubting psychologists at anyone who contends for their existence, is as unfair as Zeno's treatment of the advocates of motion, when, asking them to point out in what place an arrow *is* when it moves, he argues the falsity of their thesis from their inability to make to so preposterous a question an immediate reply.

The results of this introspective difficulty are baleful. If to hold fast and observe the transitive parts of thought's stream be so hard, then the great blunder to which all schools are liable must be the failure to register them, and the undue emphasizing of the more substantive parts of the stream. Were we not ourselves a moment since in danger of ignoring any feeling transitive between the silence and the thunder, and of treating their boundary as a sort of break in the mind? Now such ignoring as this has historically worked in two ways. One set of thinkers have been led by it to *Sensationalism*. Unable to lay their hands on any coarse feelings corresponding to the innumerable relations and forms of connection between the facts of the world, finding no *named* subjective modifications mirroring such relations, they have for the most part denied that feelings of relation exist; and many of them, like Hume, have gone so far as to deny the reality of most relations *out* of the mind as well as in it. Substantive psychoses, sensations and their copies and derivatives, juxtaposed like dominoes in a game, but really separate, everything else verbal illusion,—such is the upshot of this view.[14] The *Intellectualists*, on the other hand, unable

[14] E.g.: "The stream of thought is not a continuous current, but a series of dis-

to give up the reality of relations *extra mentem*, but equally unable to point to any distinct substantive feelings in which they were known, have made the same admission that the feelings do not exist. But they have drawn an opposite conclusion. The relations must be known, they say, in something that is no feeling, no mental modification continuous and consubstantial with the subjective tissue out of which sensations and other substantive states are made. They are known, these relations, by something that lies on an entirely different plane, by an *actus purus* of Thought, Intellect, or Reason, all written with capitals and considered to mean something unutterably superior to any fact of sensibility whatever.

But from our point of view both Intellectualists and Sensationalists are wrong. If there be such things as feelings at all, *then so surely as relations between objects exist in rerum naturâ, so surely, and more surely, do feelings exist to which these relations are known.* There is not a conjunction or a preposition, and hardly an adverbial phrase, syntactic form, or inflection of voice, in human speech, that does not express some shading or other of relation which we at some moment actually feel to exist between the larger objects of our thought. If we speak objectively, it is the real relations that appear revealed; if we speak subjectively, it is the stream of consciousness that matches each of them by an inward coloring of its own. In either case the relations are numberless, and no existing language is capable of doing justice to all their shades.

We ought to say a feeling of *and*, a feeling of *if*, a feeling of *but*, and a feeling of *by*, quite as readily as we say a feeling of *blue* or a feeling of *cold*. Yet we do not: so inveterate has our habit become of recognizing the existence of the substantive parts alone, that language almost refuses to lend itself to any other use. The Empiricists have always dwelt on its influence in making us suppose that where we have a separate name, a separate thing must needs be there to correspond with it; and they have rightly denied the existence of the mob of abstract entities, principles, and forces, in whose favor no other evidence than this could be brought up. But they have said nothing of that obverse error, of which we said a word in Chapter VII (see p. 194), of supposing that where there is

---

tinct ideas, more or less rapid in their succession; the rapidity being measurable by the number that pass through the mind in a given time." (Bain: *The Emotions and the Will*, p. 29.)

no name no entity can exist. All *dumb* or anonymous psychic states have, owing to this error, been coolly suppressed; or, if recognized at all, have been named after the substantive perception they led to, as thoughts 'about' this object or 'about' that, the stolid word *about* engulfing all their delicate idiosyncrasies in its monotonous sound. Thus the greater and greater accentuation and isolation of the substantive parts have continually gone on.

Once more take a look at the brain. We believe the brain to be an organ whose internal equilibrium is always in a state of change—the change affecting every part. The pulses of change are doubtless more violent in one place than in another, their rhythm more rapid at this time than at that. As in a kaleidoscope revolving at a uniform rate, although the figures are always rearranging themselves, there are instants during which the transformation seems minute and interstitial and almost absent, followed by others when it shoots with magical rapidity, relatively stable forms thus alternating with forms we should not distinguish if seen again; so in the brain the perpetual rearrangement must result in some forms of tension lingering relatively long, whilst others simply come and pass. But if consciousness corresponds to the fact of rearrangement itself, why, if the rearrangement stop not, should the consciousness ever cease? And if a lingering rearrangement brings with it one kind of consciousness, why should not a swift rearrangement bring another kind of consciousness as peculiar as the rearrangement itself? The lingering consciousnesses, if of simple objects, we call 'sensations' or 'images,' according as they are vivid or faint; if of complex objects, we call them 'percepts' when vivid, 'concepts' or 'thoughts' when faint. For the swift consciousnesses we have only those names of 'transitive states,' or 'feelings of relation,' which we have used.[15] As the brain-changes are continuous, so do all these

[15] Few writers have admitted that we cognize relations through feeling. The intellectualists have explicitly denied the possibility of such a thing—e.g., Prof. T. H. Green (*Mind*, vol. VII, p. 28): "No feeling, as such or as felt, is [of?] a relation. . . . Even a relation between feelings is not itself a feeling or felt." On the other hand, the sensationists have either smuggled in the cognition without giving any account of it, or have denied the relations to be cognized, or even to exist, at all. A few honorable exceptions, however, deserve to be named among the sensationists. Destutt de Tracy, Laromiguière, Cardaillac, Brown, and finally Spencer, have explicitly contended for feelings of relation, consubstantial with our feelings or thoughts of the terms 'between' which they obtain. Thus Destutt de Tracy says (*Élémens d'idéologie*, T. Ier, chap. IV): "The faculty of judgment is itself a sort of sensibility, for it is the

consciousnesses melt into each other like dissolving views. Properly they are but one protracted consciousness, one unbroken stream.

Feelings of Tendency

So much for the transitive states. But there are other unnamed states or qualities of states that are just as important and just as

---

faculty of feeling the relations among our ideas; and to feel relations is to feel." Laromiguière writes (*Leçons de philosophie*, IIme Partie, 3me Leçon):

"There is no one whose intelligence does not embrace simultaneously many ideas, more or less distinct, more or less confused. Now, when we have many ideas at once, a peculiar feeling arises in us: we feel, among these ideas, resemblances, differences, relations. Let us call this mode of feeling, common to us all, the feeling of relation, or relation-feeling (*sentiment-rapport*). One sees immediately that these relation-feelings, resulting from the propinquity of ideas, must be infinitely more numerous than the sensation-feelings (*sentiments-sensations*) or the feelings we have of the action of our faculties. The slightest knowledge of the mathematical theory of combinations will prove this. . . . *Ideas* of relation originate in feelings of relation. They are the effect of our comparing them and reasoning about them."

Similarly, de Cardaillac (*Études élémentaires de philosophie*, Section I, chap. VII): "By a natural consequence, we are led to suppose that at the same time that we have several sensations or several ideas in the mind, we feel the relations which exist between these sensations, and the relations which exist between these ideas. . . . If the feeling of relations exists in us, . . . it is necessarily the most varied and the most fertile of all human feelings: 1° the most varied, because, relations being more numerous than beings, the feelings of relation must be in the same proportion more numerous than the sensations whose presence gives rise to their formation; 2°, the most fertile, for the relative ideas of which the feeling-of-relation is the source . . . are more important than absolute ideas, if such exist. . . . If we interrogate common speech, we find the feeling of relation expressed there in a thousand different ways. If it is easy to seize a relation, we say that it is *sensible*, to distinguish it from one which, because its terms are too remote, cannot be as quickly perceived. A sensible difference, or resemblance. . . . What is taste in the arts, in intellectual productions? What but the feeling of those relations among the parts which constitutes their merit? . . . Did we not feel relations we should never attain to true knowledge, . . . for almost all our knowledge is of relations. . . . We never have an isolated sensation; . . . we are therefore never without the feeling of relation. . . . An *object* strikes our senses; we see in it only a sensation. . . The relative is so near the absolute, the relation-feeling so near the sensation-feeling, the two are so intimately fused in the composition of the object, that the relation appears to us as part of the sensation itself. It is doubtless to this sort of fusion between sensations and feelings of relation that the silence of metaphysicians as to the latter is due; and it is for the same reason that they have obstinately persisted in asking from sensation alone those ideas of relation which it was powerless to give."

Dr. Thomas Brown writes (*Lectures*, XLV, *init.*): "There is an extensive order of our feelings which involve this notion of relation, and which consist indeed in the mere perception of a relation of some sort. . . . Whether the relation be of two, or of many external objects, or of two or many affections of the mind, the feeling of this relation . . . is what I term a relative suggestion; that phrase being the simplest which

cognitive as they, and just as much unrecognized by the traditional sensationalist and intellectualist philosophies of mind. The first fails to find them at all, the second finds their *cognitive function,* but denies that anything in the way of *feeling* has a share in bring-

---

it is possible to employ, for expressing, without any theory, the mere fact of the rise of certain feelings of relation, after certain other feelings which precede them; and therefore, as involving no particular theory, and simply expressive of an undoubted fact . . . . That the feelings of relation are states of the mind essentially different from our simple perceptions, or conceptions of the objects . . . that they are not what Condillac terms *transformed sensations,* I proved in a former Lecture, when I combated the excessive simplification of that ingenious, but not very accurate philosopher. There is an original tendency or susceptibility of the mind, by which, on perceiving together different objects, we are instantly, without the intervention of any other mental process, sensible of their relation in certain respects, as truly as there is an original tendency or susceptibility by which, when external objects are present, and have produced a certain affection of our sensorial organ, we are instantly affected with the primary elementary feelings of perception; and, I may add, that, as our sensations or perceptions are of various species, so are there various species of relations;—the number of relations, indeed, even of external things, being almost infinite, while the number of perceptions is, necessarily, limited by that of the objects which have the power of producing some affection of our organs of sensation. . . . Without that susceptibility of the mind, by which it has the feeling of relation, our consciousness would be as truly limited to a single point, as our body would become, were it possible to fetter it to a single atom."

Mr. Spencer is even more explicit. His philosophy is crude in that he seems to suppose that it is only in transitive states that outward relations are known; whereas in truth space-relations, relations of contrast, etc., are felt along with their terms, in substantive states as well as in transitive states, as we shall abundantly see. Nevertheless Mr. Spencer's passage is so clear that it also deserves to be quoted in full (*Principles of Psychology*, § 65):

"The proximate components of Mind are of two broadly-contrasted kinds—Feelings and the Relations between feelings. Among the members of each group there exist multitudinous unlikenesses, many of which are extremely strong; but such unlikenesses are small compared with those which distinguish members of the one group from members of the other. Let us, in the first place, consider what are the characters which all Feelings have in common, and what are the characters which all Relations between feelings have in common.

"Each feeling, as we here define it, is any portion of consciousness which occupies a place sufficiently large to give it a perceivable individuality; which has its individuality marked off from adjacent portions of consciousness by qualitative contrasts; and which, when introspectively contemplated, appears to be homogeneous. These are the essentials. Obviously if, under introspection, a state of consciousness is decomposable into unlike parts that exist either simultaneously or successively, it is not one feeling but two or more. Obviously if it is indistinguishable from an adjacent portion of consciousness, it forms one with that portion—is not an individual feeling but part of one. And obviously if it does not occupy in consciousness an appreciable area, or an appreciable duration, it cannot be known as a feeling.

"A Relation between feelings is, on the contrary, characterized by occupying no appreciable part of consciousness. Take away the terms it unites, and it disappears

ing it about. Examples will make clear what these inarticulate psychoses, due to waxing and waning excitements of the brain, are like.[16]

---

along with them; having no independent place—no individuality of its own. It is true that, under an ultimate analysis, what we call a relation proves to be itself a kind of feeling—the momentary feeling accompanying the transition from one conspicuous feeling to an adjacent conspicuous feeling. And it is true that, notwithstanding its extreme brevity, its qualitative character is appreciable; for relations are (as we shall hereafter see) distinguishable from one another only by the unlikenesses of the feelings which accompany the momentary transitions. Each relational feeling may, in fact, be regarded as one of those nervous shocks which we suspect to be the units of composition of feelings; and, though instantaneous, it is known as of greater or less strength and as taking place with greater or less facility. But the contrast between these relational feelings and what we ordinarily call feelings, is so strong that we must class them apart. Their extreme brevity, their small variety, and their dependence on the terms they unite, differentiate them in an unmistakeable way.

"Perhaps it will be well to recognize more fully the truth that this distinction cannot be absolute. Besides admitting that, as an element of consciousness, a relation is a momentary feeling, we must also admit that just as a relation can have no existence apart from the feelings which form its terms, so a feeling can exist only by relations to other feelings which limit it in space or time or both. Strictly speaking, neither a feeling nor a relation is an independent element of consciousness: there is throughout a dependence such that the appreciable areas of consciousness occupied by feelings, can no more possess individualities apart from the relations which link them, than these relations can possess individualities apart from the feelings they link. The essential distinction between the two, then, appears to be that whereas a relational feeling is a portion of consciousness inseparable into parts, a feeling ordinarily so-called, is a portion of consciousness that admits imaginary division into like parts which are related to one another in sequence or co-existence. A feeling proper is either made up of like parts that occupy time, or it is made up of like parts that occupy space, or both. In any case, a feeling proper is an aggregate of related like parts, while a relational feeling is undecomposable. And this is exactly the contrast between the two which must result if, as we have inferred, feelings are composed of units of feeling, or shocks."

16 M. Paulhan (*Revue Philosophique*, xx, 455–6), after speaking of the faint mental images of objects and emotions, says: "We find other vaguer states still, upon which attention seldom rests, except in persons who by nature or profession are addicted to internal observation. It is even difficult to name them precisely, for they are little known and not classed; but we may cite as an example of them that peculiar impression which we feel when, strongly preoccupied by a certain subject, we nevertheless are engaged with, and have our attention almost completely absorbed by, matters quite disconnected therewithal. We do not then exactly think of the object of our preoccupation; we do not represent it in a clear manner; and yet our mind is not as it would be without this preoccupation. Its object, absent from consciousness, is nevertheless represented there by a peculiar unmistakable impression, which often persists long and is a strong feeling, although so obscure for our intelligence." "A mental sign of the kind is the unfavorable disposition left in our mind towards an individual by painful incidents erewhile experienced and now perhaps forgotten. The sign remains, but is not understood; its definite meaning is lost." (P. 458.)

Suppose three successive persons say to us: 'Wait!' 'Hark!' 'Look!' Our consciousness is thrown into three quite different attitudes of expectancy, although no definite object is before it in any one of the three cases. Leaving out different actual bodily attitudes, and leaving out the reverberating images of the three words, which are of course diverse, probably no one will deny the existence of a residual conscious affection, a sense of the direction from which an impression is about to come, although no positive impression is yet there. Meanwhile we have no names for the psychoses in question but the names hark, look, and wait.

Suppose we try to recall a forgotten name. The state of our consciousness is peculiar. There is a gap therein; but no mere gap. It is a gap that is intensely active. A sort of wraith of the name is in it, beckoning us in a given direction, making us at moments tingle with the sense of our closeness, and then letting us sink back without the longed-for term. If wrong names are proposed to us, this singularly definite gap acts immediately so as to negate them. They do not fit into its mould. And the gap of one word does not feel like the gap of another, all empty of content as both might seem necessarily to be when described as gaps. When I vainly try to recall the name of Spalding, my consciousness is far removed from what it is when I vainly try to recall the name of Bowles. Here some ingenious persons will say: "How *can* the two consciousnesses be different when the terms which might make them different are not there? All that is there, so long as the effort to recall is vain, is the bare effort itself. How should that differ in the two cases? You are making it seem to differ by prematurely filling it out with the different names, although these, by the hypothesis, have not yet come. Stick to the two efforts as they are, without naming them after facts not yet existent, and you'll be quite unable to designate any point in which they differ." Designate, truly enough. We can only designate the difference by borrowing the names of objects not yet in the mind. Which is to say that our psychological vocabulary is wholly inadequate to name the differences that exist, even such strong differences as these. But namelessness is compatible with existence. There are innumerable consciousnesses of emptiness, no one of which taken in itself has a name, but all different from each other. The ordinary way is to assume that they are all emptinesses of consciousness, and so the same state. But the feeling of an absence is *toto cœlo* other than the absence of a feeling: it is an intense feeling. The rhythm of a lost word may be there without a sound to clothe it; or the evanescent sense of something which is the initial vowel or consonant may mock us fitfully, without growing more distinct. Everyone must know the tantalizing effect of the blank rhythm of some forgotten verse, restlessly dancing in one's mind, striving to be filled out with words.

Again, what is the strange difference between an experience tasted for the first time and the same experience recognized as familiar, as having been enjoyed before, though we cannot name it or say where or when? A tune, an odor, a flavor sometimes carry this inarticulate feeling of their familiarity so deep into our consciousness that we are fairly shaken by its mysterious emotional power. But strong and characteristic as this psychosis is—it probably is due to the submaximal excitement of wide-spreading associational brain-tracts—the only name we have for all its shadings is 'sense of familiarity.'

When we read such phrases as 'naught but,' 'either one or the other,' '*a* is *b*, but,' 'although it is, nevertheless,' 'it is an excluded middle, there is no *tertium quid*,' and a host of other verbal skeletons of logical relation, is it true that there is nothing more in our minds than the words themselves as they pass? What then is the meaning of the words which we think we understand as we read? What makes that meaning different in one phrase from what it is in the other? 'Who?' 'When?' 'Where?' Is the difference of felt meaning in these interrogatives nothing more than their difference of sound? And is it not (just like the difference of sound itself) known and understood in an affection of consciousness correlative to it, though so impalpable to direct examination? Is not the same true of such negatives as 'no,' 'never,' 'not yet'?

The truth is that large tracts of human speech are nothing but *signs of direction* in thought, of which direction we nevertheless have an acutely discriminative sense, though no definite sensorial image plays any part in it whatsoever. Sensorial images are stable psychic facts; we can hold them still and look at them as long as we like. These bare images of logical movement, on the contrary, are psychic transitions, always on the wing, so to speak, and not to be glimpsed except in flight. Their function is to lead from one set of images to another. As they pass, we feel both the waxing and the waning images in a way altogether peculiar and a way quite different from the way of their full presence. If we try to hold fast the feeling of direction, the full presence comes and the feeling of direction is lost. The blank verbal scheme of the logical movement gives us the fleeting sense of the movement as we read it, quite as well as does a rational sentence awakening definite imaginations by its words.

What is that first instantaneous glimpse of someone's meaning which we have, when in vulgar phrase we say we 'twig' it? Surely an altogether specific affection of our mind. And has the reader never asked himself what kind of a mental fact is his *intention of saying a thing* before he has said it? It is an entirely definite intention, distinct from all other intentions, an absolutely distinct state of consciousness, therefore; and yet how much of it consists of definite sensorial images, either of words or of things? Hardly anything! Linger, and the words and things come into the mind; the anticipatory intention, the divination is there no more. But as the words that replace it arrive, it welcomes them successively and calls them right if they agree with it, it rejects them and calls them wrong if they do not. It has therefore a nature of its own of the most positive sort, and yet what can we say about it without using words that belong to the later mental facts that replace it? The intention *to-say-so-and-so* is the only name it can receive. One may admit that a good third of our psychic life consists in these rapid premonitory perspective views of schemes of thought not yet articulate. How comes it about that a man reading something aloud for the first time is able immediately to emphasize all his words aright, unless from the very first he have a sense of at least the form of the sentence yet to come, which sense is fused with his consciousness of the present word, and modifies its emphasis in his mind so as to make him give it the proper accent as he utters it? Emphasis of this kind is almost altogether a matter of grammatical construction. If we read 'no more' we expect presently to come upon a 'than'; if we read 'however' at the outset of a sentence it is a 'yet,' a 'still,' or a 'nevertheless,' that we expect. A noun in a certain position demands a verb in a certain mood and number, in another position it expects a relative pronoun. Adjectives call for nouns, verbs for adverbs, etc., etc. And this foreboding of the coming grammatical scheme combined with each successive uttered word is so practically accurate that a reader incapable of understanding four ideas of the book he is reading aloud, can nevertheless read it with the most delicately modulated expression of intelligence.

Some will interpret these facts by calling them all cases in which certain images, by laws of association, awaken others so very rapidly that we think afterwards we felt the very *tendencies* of the nascent images to arise, before they were actually there. For this school the only possible materials of consciousness are images of a perfectly definite nature. Tendencies exist, but they are facts for the outside psychologist rather than for the subject of the observation. The tendency is thus a *psychical* zero; only its *results* are felt.

Now what I contend for, and accumulate examples to show, is that 'tendencies' are not only descriptions from without, but that they are among the *objects* of the stream, which is thus aware of them from within, and must be described as in very large measure constituted of *feelings* of *tendency*, often so vague that we are unable to name them at all. It is, in short, the re-instatement of the vague to its proper place in our mental life which I am so anxious to press on the attention. Mr. Galton and Prof. Huxley have, as we shall see in Chapter XVIII, made one step in advance in exploding the ridiculous theory of Hume and Berkeley that we can have no images but of perfectly definite things. Another is made in the overthrow of the equally ridiculous notion that, whilst simple objective qualities are revealed to our knowledge in subjective feelings, relations are not. But these reforms are not half sweeping and radical enough. What must be admitted is that the definite images of traditional psychology form but the very smallest part of our minds as they actually live. The traditional psychology talks like one who should say a river consists of nothing but pailsful, spoonsful, quartpotsful, barrelsful, and other moulded forms of water. Even were the pails and the pots all actually standing in the stream, still between them the free water would continue to flow. It is just this free water of consciousness that psychologists resolutely overlook. Every definite image in the mind is steeped and dyed in the free water that flows round it. With it goes the sense of its relations, near and remote, the dying echo of whence it came to us, the dawning sense of whither it is to lead. The significance, the value, of the image is all in this halo or penumbra that surrounds and escorts it,—or rather that is fused into one with it and has become bone of its bone and flesh of its flesh; leaving it, it is true, an image of the same *thing* it was before, but making it an image of that thing newly taken and freshly understood.

What is that shadowy scheme of the 'form' of an opera, play, or book, which remains in our mind and on which we pass judgment when the actual thing is done? What is our notion of a scientific or philosophical system? Great thinkers have vast premonitory glimpses of schemes of relation between terms, which hardly even as verbal images enter the mind, so rapid is the whole process.[17] We all of us have this permanent consciousness of whither our thought is going. It is a feeling like any other, a feeling of what thoughts are next to arise, before they have arisen. This field of view of consciousness varies very much in extent, depending largely on the degree of mental freshness or fatigue. When very fresh, our minds carry an immense horizon with them. The present image shoots its perspective far before it, irradiating in advance the regions in which lie the thoughts as yet unborn. Under ordinary conditions the halo of felt relations is much more circumscribed. And in states of extreme brain-fag the horizon is narrowed almost to the passing word,—the associative machinery, however, providing for the next word turning up in orderly sequence, until at last the tired thinker is led to some kind of a conclusion. At certain moments he may find himself doubting whether his thoughts have not come to a full stop; but the vague sense of a *plus ultra* makes him ever struggle on towards a more definite expression of what it may be; whilst the slowness of his utterance shows how difficult, under such conditions, the labor of thinking must be.

The awareness that our *definite* thought has come to a stop is an entirely different thing from the awareness that our thought is definitively completed. The expression of the latter state of mind is the falling inflection which betokens that the sentence is ended, and silence. The expression of the former state is 'hemming and hawing,' or else such phrases as '*et cetera*,' or 'and so forth.' But notice that every part of the sentence to be left incomplete feels differently as it passes, by reason of the premonition we have that we shall be unable to end it. The 'and so forth' casts its shadow

[17] Mozart describes thus his manner of composing: First bits and crumbs of the piece come and gradually join together in his mind; then the soul getting warmed to the work, the thing grows more and more, "and I spread it out broader and clearer, and at last it gets almost finished in my head, even when it is a long piece, so that I can see the whole of it at a single glance in my mind, as if it were a beautiful painting or a handsome human being; in which way I do not hear it in my imagination at all as a succession—the way it must come later—but all at once, as it were. It is a rare feast! All the inventing and making goes on in me as in a beautiful strong dream. But the best of all is the *hearing of it all at once*."

back, and is as integral a part of the object of the thought as the distinctest of images would be.

Again, when we use a common noun, such as *man,* in a universal sense, as signifying all possible men, we are fully aware of this intention on our part, and distinguish it carefully from our intention when we mean a certain group of men, or a solitary individual before us. In the chapter on Conception we shall see how important this difference of intention is. It casts its influence over the whole of the sentence, both before and after the spot in which the word *man* is used.

Nothing is easier than to symbolize all these facts in terms of brain-action. Just as the echo of the *whence,* the sense of the starting point of our thought, is probably due to the dying excitement of processes but a moment since vividly aroused; so the sense of the whither, the foretaste of the terminus, must be due to the waxing excitement of tracts or processes which, a moment hence, will be the cerebral correlatives of some thing which a moment hence will be vividly present to the thought. Represented by a curve, the neurosis underlying consciousness must at any moment be like this:

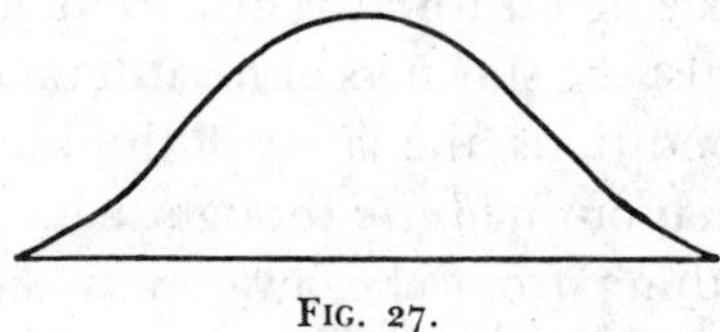

Fig. 27.

Each point of the horizontal line stands for some brain-tract or process. The height of the curve above the line stands for the intensity of the process. All the processes are *present,* in the intensities shown by the curve. But those before the latter's apex *were* more intense a moment ago; those after it *will be* more intense a moment hence. If I recite *a, b, c, d, e, f, g,* at the moment of uttering *d,* neither *a, b, c,* nor *e, f, g,* are out of my consciousness altogether, but both, after their respective fashions, 'mix their dim lights' with the stronger one of the *d,* because their neuroses are both awake in some degree.

There is a common class of mistakes which shows how brain-processes begin to be excited before the thoughts attached to them are *due*—due, that is, in substantive and vivid form. I mean those mistakes of speech or writing by which, in Dr. Carpenter's words, "we mis-pronounce or mis-spell a word, by introducing into it a letter or syllable of some other whose turn is shortly to come; or, it may be, the whole of the anticipated word is substituted for the one which ought to have been expressed."[18] In these cases one of two things must have happened: either some local accident of nutrition *blocks* the process that is *due,* so that other processes discharge that ought as yet to be but nascently aroused; or some opposite local accident *furthers* the *latter processes* and makes them explode before their time. In the chapter on Association of Ideas, numerous instances will come before us of the actual effect on consciousness of neuroses not yet maximally aroused.

It is just like the 'overtones' in music. Different instruments give the 'same note,' but each in a different voice, because each gives more than that note, namely, various upper harmonics of it which differ from one instrument to another. They are not separately heard by the ear; they blend with the fundamental note, and suffuse it, and alter it; and even so do the waxing and waning brain-processes at every moment blend with and suffuse and alter the psychic effect of the processes which are at their culminating point.

Let us use the words *psychic overtone, suffusion,* or *fringe,* to designate the influence of a faint brain-process upon our thought, as it makes it aware of relations and objects but dimly perceived.[19]

If we then consider the *cognitive function* of different states of mind, we may feel assured that the difference between those that are mere 'acquaintance,' and those that are 'knowledges-*about*' (see pp. 216–217) is reducible almost entirely to the absence or presence

[18] *Mental Physiology,* § 236. Dr. Carpenter's explanation differs materially from that given in the text.

[19] Cf. also S. Stricker: *Vorlesungen über allgemeine und experimentelle Pathologie* (1879), pp. 462–3, 501, 547; Romanes: *Mental Evolution in Man: Origin of Human Faculty,* p. 82. It is so hard to make one's self clear that I may advert to a misunderstanding of my views by the late Prof. Thomas Maguire of Dublin (*Lectures on Philosophy,* 1885). This author considers that by the 'fringe' I mean some sort of psychic material by which sensations in themselves separate are made to cohere together, and wittily says that I ought to "see that uniting sensations by their 'fringes' is more vague than to construct the universe out of oysters by platting their beards" (p. 211). But the fringe, as I use the word, means nothing like this; it is part of the *object cognized,*–substantive *qualities* and *things* appearing to the mind in a *fringe of relations.* Some parts–the transitive parts–of our stream of thought cognize the relations rather than the things; but both the transitive and the substantive parts form one continuous stream, with no discrete 'sensations' in it such as Prof. Maguire supposes, and supposes me to suppose, to be there.

of psychic fringes or overtones. Knowledge *about* a thing is knowledge of its relations. Acquaintance with it is limitation to the bare impression which it makes. Of most of its relations we are only aware in the penumbral nascent way of a 'fringe' of unarticulated affinities about it. And, before passing to the next topic in order, I must say a little of this sense of affinity, as itself one of the most interesting features of the subjective stream.

In all our voluntary thinking there is some topic or subject about which all the members of the thought revolve. Half the time this topic is a problem, a gap we cannot yet fill with a definite picture, word, or phrase, but which, in the manner described some time back, influences us in an intensely active and determinate psychic way. Whatever may be the images and phrases that pass before us, we feel their relation to this aching gap. To fill it up is our thoughts' destiny. Some bring us nearer to that consummation. Some the gap negates as quite irrelevant. Each swims in a felt fringe of relations of which the aforesaid gap is the term. Or instead of a definite gap we may merely carry a mood of interest about with us. Then, however vague the mood, it will still act in the same way, throwing a mantle of felt affinity over such representations, entering the mind, as suit it, and tingeing with the feeling of tediousness or discord all those with which it has no concern.

Relation, then, to our topic or interest is constantly felt in the fringe, and particularly the relation of harmony and discord, of furtherance or hindrance of the topic. When the sense of furtherance is there, we are 'all right'; with the sense of hindrance we are dissatisfied and perplexed, and cast about us for other thoughts. Now *any* thought the quality of whose fringe lets us feel ourselves 'all right,' is an acceptable member of our thinking, whatever kind of thought it may otherwise be. Provided we only feel it to have a place in the scheme of relations in which the interesting topic also lies, that is quite sufficient to make of it a relevant and appropriate portion of our train of ideas.

For the important thing about a train of thought is its conclusion. That is the *meaning*, or, as we say, the topic of the thought. That is what abides when all its other members have faded from memory. Usually this conclusion is a word or phrase or particular image, or practical attitude or resolve, whether rising to answer a problem or fill a pre-existing gap that worried us, or whether accidentally stumbled on in revery. In either case it stands out from the other segments of the stream by reason of the peculiar interest attaching to it. This interest *arrests* it, makes a sort of crisis of it when it comes, induces attention upon it and makes us treat it in a substantive way.

The parts of the stream that precede these substantive conclusions are but the means of the latter's attainment. And, provided the same conclusion be reached, the means may be as mutable as we like, for the 'meaning' of the stream of thought will be the same. What difference does it make what the means are? "*Qu'importe le flacon, pourvu qu'on ait l'ivresse?*" The relative unimportance of the means appears from the fact that when the conclusion is there, we have always forgotten most of the steps preceding its attainment. When we have uttered a proposition, we are rarely able a moment afterwards to recall our exact words, though we can express it in different words easily enough. The practical upshot of a book we read remains with us, though we may not recall one of its sentences.

The only paradox would seem to lie in supposing that the fringe of felt affinity and discord can be the same in two heterogeneous sets of images. Take a train of words passing through the mind and leading to a certain conclusion on the one hand, and on the other hand an almost wordless set of tactile, visual and other fancies leading to the same conclusion. Can the halo, fringe, or scheme in which we feel the words to lie be the same as that in which we feel the images to lie? Does not the discrepancy of terms involve a discrepancy of felt relations among them?

If the terms be taken *quâ* mere sensations, it assuredly does. For instance, the words may rhyme with each other,—the visual images can have no such affinity as *that*. But *quâ* thoughts, *quâ* sensations *understood*, the words have contracted by long association fringes of mutual repugnance or affinity with each other and with the conclusion, which run exactly parallel with like fringes in the visual, tactile and other ideas. The most important element of these fringes is, I repeat, the mere feeling of harmony or discord, of a right or wrong direction in the thought. Dr. Campbell has, so far as I know, made the best analysis of this fact, and his words, often quoted, deserve to be quoted again. The chapter is entitled "What is the cause that nonsense so often escapes being detected, both by the writer and by the reader?" The author, in answering this question, makes (*inter alia*) the following remarks:[20]

"That connexion [he says] or relation which comes gradually to subsist among the different words of a language, in the minds of those who speak it, . . . is merely consequent on this, that those words are employed as signs of connected or related things. It is an axiom in geometry, that things equal to the same thing are equal to one another. It may, in like manner, be admitted as an axiom in psychology, that ideas associated by the same idea will associate one another. Hence it will happen, that if from experiencing the connexion of two things, there results, as infallibly there will result, an association between the ideas or notions annexed to them, as each idea will moreover be associated by its sign, there will likewise be an association between the ideas of the signs. Hence the sounds considered as signs will be conceived to have a connexion analogous to that which subsisteth among the things signified; I say, the sounds considered as signs; for this way of considering them constantly attends us in speaking, writing, hearing, and reading. When we purposely abstract from it, and regard them merely as sounds, we are instantly sensible that they are quite unconnected, and have no other relation than what ariseth from similitude of tone or accent. But to consider them in this manner commonly results from previous design and requires a kind of effort which is not exerted in the ordinary use of speech. In ordinary use they are regarded solely as signs, or, rather, they are confounded with the things they signify; the consequence of which is, that in the manner just now explained, we come insensibly to conceive a connexion among them of a very different sort from that of which sounds are naturally susceptible.

"Now this conception, habit, or tendency of the mind, call it which you please, is considerably strengthened both by the frequent use of language and by the structure of it. . . . Language is the sole channel through which we communicate our knowledge and discoveries to others, and through which the knowledge and discoveries of others are communicated to us. By reiterated recourse to this medium, it necessarily happens, that when things are related to each other, the words signifying those things are more commonly brought together in discourse. Hence the words and names themselves, by customary vicinity, contract in the fancy a relation additional to that which they derive purely from being the symbols of related things. Farther, this tendency is strengthened by the structure of language. All languages whatever, even the most barbarous, as far as hath yet appeared, are of a regular

20 George Campbell: *The Philosophy of Rhetoric,* book II, chap. VII.

and analogical make. The consequence is, that similar relations in things will be expressed similarly; that is, by similar inflections, derivations, compositions, arrangement of words, or juxtaposition of particles, according to the genius or grammatical form of the particular tongue. Now as, by the habitual use of a language (even though it were quite irregular), the signs would insensibly become connected in the imagination, wherever the things signified are connected in nature, so, by the regular structure of a language, this connexion among the signs is conceived as analogous to that which subsisteth among their archetypes."

If we know English and French and begin a sentence in French, all the later words that come are French; we hardly ever drop into English. And this affinity of the French words for each other is not something merely operating mechanically as a brain-law, it is something we feel at the time. Our understanding of a French sentence heard never falls to so low an ebb that we are not aware that the words linguistically belong together. Our attention can hardly so wander that if an English word be suddenly introduced we shall not start at the change. Such a vague sense as this of the words belonging together is the very minimum of fringe that can accompany them, if 'thought' at all. Usually the vague perception that all the words we hear belong to the same language and to the same special vocabulary in that language, and that the grammatical sequence is familiar, is practically equivalent to an admission that what we hear is sense. But if an unusual foreign word be introduced, if the grammar trip, or if a term from an incongruous vocabulary suddenly appear, such as 'rat-trap' or 'plumber's bill' in a philosophical discourse, the sentence detonates, as it were, we receive a shock from the incongruity, and the drowsy assent is gone. The feeling of rationality in these cases seems rather a negative than a positive thing, being the mere absence of shock, or sense of discord, between the terms of thought.

So delicate and incessant is this recognition by the mind of the mere fitness of words to be mentioned together that the slightest misreading, such as 'casualty' for 'causality,' or 'perpetual' for 'perceptual,' will be corrected by a listener whose attention is so relaxed that he gets no idea of the *meaning* of the sentence at all.

Conversely, if words do belong to the same vocabulary, and if the grammatical structure is correct, sentences with absolutely no meaning may be uttered in good faith and pass unchallenged. Discourses at prayer-meetings, reshuffling the same collection of cant phrases, and the whole genus of penny-a-line-isms and newspaper-reporter's flourishes give illustrations of this. "The birds filled the tree-tops with their morning song, making the air moist, cool, and pleasant," is a sentence I remember reading once in a report of some athletic exercises in Jerome Park. It was probably written unconsciously by the hurried reporter, and read uncritically by many readers. An entire volume of 784 pages lately published in Boston[21] is composed of stuff like this passage picked out at random:

"The flow of the efferent fluids of all these vessels from their outlets at the terminal loop of each culminate link on the surface of the nuclear organism is continuous as their respective atmospheric fruitage up to the altitudinal limit of their expansibility, whence, when atmosphered by like but coalescing essences from higher altitudes,—those sensibly expressed as the essential qualities of external forms,—they descend, and become assimilated by the afferents of the nuclear organism."[22]

There are every year works published whose contents show them to be by real lunatics. To the reader, the book quoted from seems pure nonsense from beginning to end. It is impossible to divine, in such a case, just what sort of feeling of rational relation between the words may have appeared to the author's mind. The border line between objective sense and nonsense is hard to draw; that between subjective sense and nonsense, impossible. Subjectively, any collocation of words may make sense—even the wildest words in a dream—if one only does not doubt their belonging together. Take the obscurer passages in Hegel: it is a fair question whether the rationality included in them be anything more than the fact

[21] *Substantialism: Or, Philosophy of Knowledge,* by 'Jean Story' (1879).

[22] M. G. Tarde, quoting (in Delbœuf: *Le Sommeil et les rêves* (1885), p. 226) some nonsense-verses from a dream, says they show how "prosodic forms may subsist in a mind from which logical rules are effaced. . . . I was able, in dreaming, to preserve the faculty of finding two words which rhymed, to appreciate the rhyme, to fill up the verse as it first presented itself with other words which, added, gave the right number of syllables, and yet I was ignorant of the sense of the words. . . . Thus we have the extraordinary fact that the words called each other up, without calling up their sense. . . . Even when awake, it is more difficult to ascend to the meaning of a word than to pass from one word to another; or to put it otherwise, *it is harder to be a thinker than to be a rhetorician,* and on the whole nothing is commoner than trains of words not understood."

that the words all belong to a common vocabulary, and are strung together on a scheme of predication and relation,—immediacy, self-relation, and what not,—which has habitually recurred. Yet there seems no reason to doubt that the subjective feeling of the rationality of these sentences was strong in the writer as he penned them, or even that some readers by straining may have reproduced it in themselves.

To sum up, certain kinds of verbal associate, certain grammatical expectations fulfilled, stand for a good part of our impression that a sentence has a meaning and is dominated by the Unity of one Thought. Nonsense in grammatical form sounds half rational; sense with grammatical sequence upset sounds nonsensical; e.g., "Elba the Napoleon English faith had banished broken to he Saint because Helena at." Finally, there is about each word the psychic 'overtone' of feeling that it brings us nearer to a forefelt conclusion. Suffuse all the words of a sentence, as they pass, with these three fringes or haloes of relation, let the conclusion seem worth arriving at, and all will admit the sentence to be an expression of thoroughly continuous, unified, and rational thought.[23]

Each word, in such a sentence, is felt, not only as a word, but as having a *meaning*. The 'meaning' of a word taken thus dynamically in a sentence may be quite different from its meaning when taken statically or without context. The dynamic meaning is usually reduced to the bare fringe we have described, of felt suitability or unfitness to the context and conclusion. The static meaning, when the word is concrete, as 'table,' 'Boston,' consists of sensory images awakened; when it is abstract, as 'criminal legislation,' 'fallacy,' the meaning consists of other words aroused, forming the so-called 'definition.'

[23] We think it odd that young children should listen with such rapt attention to the reading of stories expressed in words half of which they do not understand, and of none of which they ask the meaning. But their thinking is in form just what ours is when it is rapid. Both of us make flying leaps over large portions of the sentences uttered and we give attention only to substantive starting points, turning points, and conclusions here and there. All the rest, 'substantive' and separately intelligible as it may *potentially* be, actually serves only as so much transitive material. It is *internodal* consciousness, giving us the sense of continuity, but having no significance apart from its mere gap-filling function. The children probably feel no gap when through a lot of unintelligible words they are swiftly carried to a familiar and intelligible terminus.

Hegel's celebrated dictum that pure being is identical with pure nothing results from his taking the words statically, or without the fringe they wear in a context. Taken in isolation, they agree in the single point of awakening no sensorial images. But taken dynamically, or as significant,—as *thought*,—their fringes of relation, their affinities and repugnances, their function and meaning, are felt and understood to be absolutely opposed.

Such considerations as these remove all appearance of paradox from those cases of extremely deficient visual imagery of whose existence Mr. Galton has made us aware (see below). An exceptionally intelligent friend informs me that he can frame no image whatever of the appearance of his breakfast-table. When asked how he then remembers it at all, he says he simply '*knows*' that it seated four people, and was covered with a white cloth on which were a butter-dish, a coffee-pot, radishes, and so forth. The mind-stuff of which this 'knowing' is made seems to be verbal images exclusively. But if the words 'coffee,' 'bacon,' 'muffins,' and 'eggs' lead a man to speak to his cook, to pay his bills, and to take measures for the morrow's meal exactly as visual and gustatory memories would, why are they not, for all practical intents and purposes, as good a kind of material in which to think? In fact, we may suspect them to be for most purposes better than terms with a richer imaginative coloring. The scheme of relationship and the conclusion being the essential things in thinking, that kind of mind-stuff which is handiest will be the best for the purpose. Now words, uttered or unexpressed, are the handiest mental elements we have. Not only are they very *rapidly* revivable, but they are revivable as actual sensations more easily than any other items of our experience. Did they not possess some such advantage as this, it would hardly be the case that the older men are and the more effective as thinkers, the more, as a rule, they have lost their visualizing power and depend on words. This was ascertained by Mr. Galton to be the case with members of the Royal Society. The present writer observes it in his own person most distinctly.

On the other hand, a deaf and dumb man can weave his tactile and visual images into a system of thought quite as effective and rational as that of a word-user. *The question whether thought is possible without language* has been a favorite topic of discussion among philosophers. Some interesting reminiscences of his childhood by Mr. Ballard, a deaf-mute instructor in the National College at Washington, show it to be perfectly possible. A few paragraphs may be quoted here.

"In consequence of the loss of my hearing in infancy, I was debarred from enjoying the advantages which children in the full possession of their senses derive from the exercises of the common primary school, from the every-day talk of their school-fellows and playmates, and from the conversation of their parents and other grown-up persons.

"I could convey my thoughts and feelings to my parents and brothers by natural signs or pantomime, and I could understand what they said to me by the same medium; our intercourse being, however, confined to the daily routine of home affairs and hardly going beyond the circle of my own observation. . . .

"My father adopted a course which he thought would, in some measure, compensate me for the loss of my hearing. It was that of taking me with him, when business required him to ride abroad; and he took me more frequently than he did my brothers; giving, as the reason for his apparent partiality, that they could acquire information through the ear, while I depended solely upon my eye for acquaintance with affairs of the outside world. . . .

"I have a vivid recollection of the delight I felt in watching the different scenes we passed through, observing the various phases of nature, both animate and inanimate; tho we did not, owing to my infirmity, engage in conversation. It was during those delightful rides, some two or three years before my initiation into the rudiments of written language, that I began to ask myself the question: *How came the world into being?* When this question occurred to my mind, I set myself to thinking it over a long time. My curiosity was awakened as to what was the origin of human life in its first appearance upon the earth, and of vegetable life as well, and also the cause of the existence of the earth, sun, moon, and stars.

"I remember at one time when my eye fell upon a very large old stump which we happened to pass in one of our rides, I asked myself, 'Is it possible that the first man that ever came into the world rose out of that stump? But that stump is only a remnant of a once noble magnificent tree, and how came that tree? Why, it came only by beginning to grow out of the ground just like those little trees now coming up.' And I dismissed from my mind, as an absurd idea, the connection between the origin of man and a decaying old stump. . . .

"I have no recollection of what it was that first suggested to me the question as to the origin of things. I had before this time gained ideas of the descent from parent to child, of the propagation of animals, and of the production of plants from seeds. The question that occurred to my mind was: whence came the first man, the first animal, and the first plant, at the remotest distance of time, before which there was no man, no animal, no plant; since I knew they all had a beginning and an end.

"It is impossible to state the exact order in which these different questions arose, *i.e.*, about men, animals, plants, the earth, sun, moon, &c. The lower animals did not receive so much thought as was bestowed upon man and the earth; perhaps because I put man and beast in the same class, since I believed that man would be annihilated and there was no resurrection beyond the grave,—tho I am now told by my mother that, in answer to my question, in the case of a deceased uncle who looked to me like a person in sleep, she had tried to make me understand that he would awake in the far future. It was my belief that man and beast derived their being from the same source, and were to be laid down in the dust in a state of annihilation. Considering the brute animal as of secondary importance, and allied to man on a lower level, man and the earth were the two things on which my mind dwelled most.

"I think I was five years old, when I began to understand the descent from parent to child and the propagation of animals. I was nearly eleven years old, when I entered the Institution where I was educated; and I remember distinctly that it was at least two years before this time that I began to ask myself the question as to the origin of the universe. My age was then about eight, not over nine years.

"Of the form of the earth, I had no idea in my childhood, except that, from a look at a map of the hemispheres, I inferred there were two immense discs of matter lying near each other. I also believed the sun and moon to be two round, flat plates of illuminating matter; and for those luminaries I entertained a sort of reverence on account of their power of lighting and heating the earth. I thought from their coming up and going down, traveling across the sky in so regular a manner, that there must be a certain something having power to govern their course. I believed the sun went into a hole at the west and came out of another at the east, traveling through a great tube in the earth, describing the same curve as it seemed to describe in the sky. The stars seemed to me to be tiny lights studded in the sky.

"The source from which the universe came was the question about which my mind revolved in a vain struggle to grasp it, or rather to fight the way up to attain to a satisfactory answer. When I had occupied myself with this subject a considerable time, I perceived that it was a matter much greater than my mind could comprehend; and I remember well that I became so appalled at its mystery and so bewildered at my inability to grapple with it that I laid the subject aside and out of my mind, glad to escape being, as it were, drawn into a vortex of inextricable confusion. Tho I felt relieved at this escape, yet I could not resist the desire to know the truth; and I returned to the subject; but as before, I left it, after thinking it over for some time. In this state of perplexity, I hoped all the time to get at the truth, still believing that, the more I gave thought to the subject, the more my mind would penetrate the mystery. Thus, I was tossed like a shuttlecock, returning to the subject and recoiling from it, till I came to school.

"I remember that my mother once told me about a being up above, pointing her finger towards the sky and with a solemn look on her countenance. I do not recall the circumstance which led to this communication. When she mentioned the mysterious being up in the sky, I was eager to take hold of the subject, and plied her with questions concerning the form and appearance of this unknown being, asking if it was the sun, moon, or one of the stars. I knew she meant that there was a living one somewhere up in the sky; but when I realized that she could not answer my questions, I gave it up in despair, feeling sorrowful that I could not obtain a definite idea of the mysterious living one up in the sky.

"One day, while we were haying in a field, there was a series of heavy thunder-claps. I asked one of my brothers where they came from. He pointed to the sky and made a zigzag motion with his finger, signifying lightning. I imagined there was a great man somewhere in the blue vault, who made a loud noise with his voice out of it; and each time I heard[24] a thunder-clap I was frightened, and looked up at the sky, fearing he was speaking a threatening word."[25]

Here we may pause. The reader sees by this time that it makes little or no difference in what sort of mind-stuff, in what quality of imagery, his thinking goes on. The only images *intrinsically* important are the halting-places, the substantive conclusions, provisional or final, of the thought. Throughout all the rest of the stream, the feelings of relation are everything, and the terms re-

[24] Not literally *heard*, of course. Deaf-mutes are quick to perceive shocks and jars that can be felt, even when so slight as to be unnoticed by those who can hear.

[25] Quoted by Samuel Porter: "Is Thought Possible without Language?" in *Princeton Review*, 57th year, pp. 108–12 (Jan. 1881). Cf. also W. W. Ireland: *The Blot upon the Brain* (1886), Paper x, part II; G. J. Romanes: *Mental Evolution in Man*, pp. 81–83, and references therein made. Prof. Max Müller gives a very complete history of this controversy in pp. 30–64 of his *Science of Thought* (1887). His own view is that Thought and Speech are inseparable; but under speech he includes any conceivable sort of symbolism or even mental imagery, and he makes no allowance for the wordless summary glimpses which we have of systems of relation and direction.

lated almost naught. These feelings of relation, these psychic overtones, halos, suffusions, or fringes about the terms, may be the same in very different systems of imagery. A diagram may help to accentuate this indifference of the mental means where the end is the same. Let *A* be some experience from which a number of thinkers start. Let *Z* be the practical conclusion rationally inferrible from it. One gets to the conclusion by one line, another by

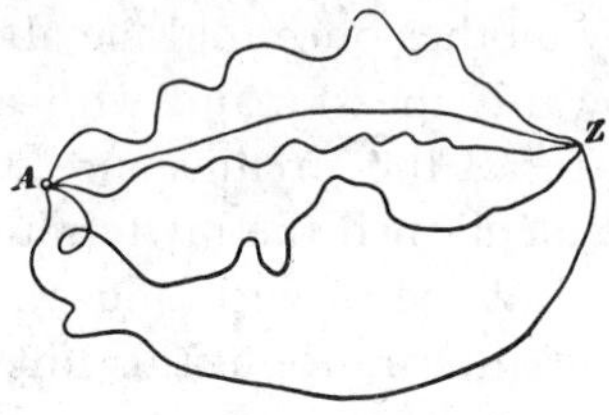

Fig. 28.

another; one follows a course of English, another of German, verbal imagery. With one, visual images predominate; with another, tactile. Some trains are tinged with emotions, others not; some are very abridged, synthetic and rapid, others, hesitating and broken into many steps. But when the penultimate terms of all the trains, however differing *inter se*, finally shoot into the same conclusion, we say and rightly say, that all the thinkers have had substantially the same thought. It would probably astound each of them beyond measure to be let into his neighbor's mind and to find how different the scenery there was from that in his own.

Thought is in fact a kind of Algebra, as Berkeley long ago said, "in which, though a particular quantity be marked by each letter, yet to proceed right it is not requisite that in every step each letter suggest to your thoughts that particular quantity it was appointed to stand for." Mr. Lewes has developed this algebra-analogy so well that I must quote his words:

"The leading characteristic of Algebra is that of operation on relations. This also is the leading characteristic of Thought. Algebra cannot exist without values, nor Thought without Feelings. The operations are so many blank forms until the values are assigned. Words are vacant sounds, ideas are blank forms, unless they symbolise images and sensations, which are their values. Nevertheless it is rigorously true, and of the greatest importance, that analysts carry on very extensive operations with blank forms, never pausing to supply the symbols with values until the calculation is completed; and ordinary men, no less than philosophers, carry on long trains of thought without pausing to translate their ideas (words) into images. . . . Suppose some one from a distance shouts 'A lion!' At once the man starts in alarm . . . . To the man the word is not only an . . . expression of all that he has seen and heard of lions, capable of recalling various experiences, but is also capable of taking its place in a connected series of thoughts without recalling any of those experiences, without reviving an image however faint of a lion—simply as a sign of a certain relation included in the complex so named. Like an algebraic symbol it may be operated on without conveying other significance than an abstract relation: it is a sign of Danger related to fear with all its motor sequences. Its logical position suffices. . . . Ideas are *substitutions* which require a secondary process when what is symbolised by them is translated into the images and experiences it replaces; and this secondary process is frequently not performed at all, generally only performed to a very small extent. Let any one closely examine what has passed in his mind when he has constructed a chain of reasoning, and he will be surprised at the fewness and faintness of the images which have accompanied the ideas. Suppose you inform me that 'the blood rushed violently from the man's heart, quickening his pulse, at the sight of his enemy.' Of the many latent images in this phrase how many were salient in your mind and in mine? Probably two—the man and his enemy—and these images were faint. Images of blood, heart, violent rushing, pulse, quickening, and sight, were either not revived at all, or were passing shadows. Had any such images arisen they would have hampered thought, retarding the logical process of judgment by irrelevant connections. The symbols had substituted *relations* for these *values* . . . . There are no images of two things and three things when I say 'two and three equal five;' there are simply familiar symbols having precise relations. . . . The verbal symbol 'horse' which stands for all our experiences of horses serves all the purposes of Thought without recalling one of the images clustered in the perception of horses, just as the sight of a horse's form serves all the purposes of *recognition* without recalling the sound of its neighing or its tramp, its qualities as an animal of draught, &c."[26]

It need only be added that as the Algebrist, though the sequence of his terms is fixed by their relations rather than by their several values, must give a real value to the *final* one he reaches; so the thinker in words must let his concluding word or phrase be trans-

[26] *Problems of Life and Mind,* 3d Series, Problem IV, chapter 5. Compare also Victor Egger: *La Parole intérieure* (Paris, 1881), chaps. V, VI.

lated into its full sensible-image-value, under penalty of the thought being left unrealized and pale.

This is all I have to say about the sensible continuity and unity of our thought as contrasted with the apparent discreteness of the words, images, and other means by which it seems to be carried on. Between all their substantive elements there is 'transitive' consciousness, and the words and images are 'fringed,' and not as discrete as to a careless view they seem. Let us advance now to the next head in our description of Thought's stream.

4) *Human thought appears to deal with objects independent of itself; that is, it is cognitive, or possesses the function of knowing*

For Absolute Idealism, the infinite Thought and its objects are one. The Objects are, through being thought; the eternal Mind is, through thinking them. Were a human thought alone in the world there would be no reason for any other assumption regarding it. Whatever it might have before it would be its vision, would be there, in *its* 'there,' or then, in *its* 'then'; and the question would never arise whether an extra-mental duplicate of it existed or not. The reason why we all believe that the objects of our thoughts have a duplicate existence outside, is that there are *many* human thoughts, each with the *same* objects, as we cannot help supposing. The judgment that *my* thought has the same object as *his* thought is what makes the psychologist call my thought cognitive of an outer reality. The judgment that my own past thought and my own present thought are of the same object is what makes *me* take the object out of either and project it by a sort of triangulation into an independent position, from which it may *appear* to both. *Sameness* in a multiplicity of objective appearances is thus the basis of our belief in realities outside of thought.[27] In Chapter XII we shall have to take up the judgment of sameness again.

To show that the question of reality being extra-mental or not is not likely to arise in the absence of repeated experiences of the *same*, take the example of an altogether unprecedented experience, such as a new taste in the throat. Is it a subjective quality of feeling, or an objective quality felt? You do not even ask the question at this point. It is simply *that taste*. But if a doctor hears you

27 If but one person sees an apparition we consider it his private hallucination. If more than one, we begin to think it may be a real external presence.

describe it, and says: "Ha! Now you know what *heartburn* is," then it becomes a quality already existent *extra mentem tuam*, which you in turn have come upon and learned. The first spaces, times, things, qualities, experienced by the child probably appear, like the first heartburn, in this absolute way, as simple *beings*, neither in nor out of thought. But later, by having other thoughts than this present one, and making repeated judgments of sameness among their objects, he corroborates in himself the notion of realities, past and distant as well as present, which realities no one single thought either possesses or engenders, but which all may contemplate and know. This, as was stated in the last chapter, is the *psychological* point of view, the relatively uncritical non-idealistic point of view of all natural science, beyond which this book cannot go. A mind which has become conscious of its own cognitive function, plays what we have called 'the psychologist' upon itself. It not only knows the things that appear before it; it knows that it knows them. This stage of reflective condition is, more or less explicitly, our habitual adult state of mind.

It cannot, however, be regarded as primitive. The consciousness of objects must come first. We seem to lapse into this primordial condition when consciousness is reduced to a minimum by the inhalation of anæsthetics or during a faint. Many persons testify that at a certain stage of the anæsthetic process objects are still cognized whilst the thought of self is lost. Professor Herzen says:[28]

> "During the syncope there is absolute psychic annihilation, the absence of all consciousness; then at the beginning of coming to, one has at a certain moment a vague, limitless, infinite feeling—a sense of *existence in general* without the least trace of distinction between the me and the not-me."

Dr. Shoemaker of Philadelphia describes during the deepest conscious stage of ether-intoxication a vision of

> "two endless parallel lines in swift longitudinal motion . . . on a uniform misty background . . . together with a constant sound or whirr, not loud but distinct . . . which seemed to be connected with the parallel lines. . . . These phenomena occupied the whole field. There were present no dreams or visions in any way connected with human affairs, no ideas or impressions akin to anything in past experience, no emotions, of course no idea of personality. There was no conception as to

[28] *Revue Philosophique*, vol. XXI, p. 671.

what being it was that was regarding the two lines, or that there existed any such thing as such a being; the lines and waves were all."[29]

Similarly a friend of Mr. Herbert Spencer, quoted by him in *Mind* (vol. III, p. 556), speaks of "an undisturbed empty quiet everywhere, except that a stupid presence lay like a heavy intrusion *somewhere,*—a blotch on the calm." This sense of objectivity and lapse of subjectivity, even when the object is almost indefinable, is, it seems to me, a somewhat familiar phase in chloroformization, though in my own case it is too deep a phase for any articulate after-memory to remain. I only know that as it vanishes I seem to wake to a sense of my own existence as something additional to what had previously been there.[30]

Many philosophers, however, hold that the reflective consciousness of the self is essential to the cognitive function of thought. They hold that a thought, in order to know a thing at all, must expressly distinguish between the thing and its own self.[31] This is a perfectly wanton assumption, and not the faintest shadow of reason exists for supposing it true. As well might I contend that I cannot dream without dreaming that I dream, swear without swearing that I swear, deny without denying that I deny, as maintain that I cannot know without knowing that I know. I may have either acquaintance-with, or knowledge-about, an object O without think-

29 Quoted from the *Therapeutic Gazette,* by the N. Y. *Semi-Weekly Evening Post* for Nov. 2, 1886.

30 In half-stunned states self-consciousness may lapse. A friend writes me: "We were driving back from——in a wagonette. The door flew open and X., alias 'Baldy,' fell out on the road. We pulled up at once, and then he said, 'Did anybody fall out?' or 'Who fell out?'—I don't exactly remember the words. When told that Baldy fell out, he said, 'Did Baldy fall out? Poor Baldy!' "

31 Kant originated this view. I subjoin a few English statements of it. J. Ferrier: *Institutes of Metaphysic,* Proposition I: "Along with whatever any intelligence knows, it must, as the ground or condition of its knowledge, have some cognisance of itself." Sir William Hamilton: *Discussions on Philosophy and Literature, Education and University Reform,* p. 47: "*We know*; and *We know that we know*:—these propositions, *logically* distinct, are *really* identical; each implies the other. . . . So true is the scholastic brocard:—'*Non sentimus nisi sentiamus nos sentire.*' " H. L. Mansel: *Metaphysics,* p. 58: "Whatever variety of materials . . . may exist within reach of my mind, I can become conscious of them only by recognising them as mine. . . . Relation to the conscious self is thus the permanent and universal feature which every state of consciousness, as such, must exhibit." T. H. Green: *Introduction to Hume,* p. 12: "A consciousness by the man . . . of himself in negative relation to the thing that is his object, and this consciousness . . . must be taken to go along with the perceptive act itself. No less than this indeed can be involved in any act that is to be the beginning of knowledge at all. It is the minimum of possible thought or intelligence."

ing about myself at all. It suffices for this that I think O, and that it exist. If, in addition to thinking O, I also think that I exist and that I know O, well and good; I then know one more thing, a fact about O, of which I previously was unmindful. That, however, does not prevent me from having already known O a good deal. O *per se*, or O *plus* P, are as good objects of knowledge as O *plus me* is. The philosophers in question simply substitute one particular object for all others, and call it *the* object *par excellence*. It is a case of the 'psychologist's fallacy' (see p. 195). *They* know the object to be one thing and the thought another; and they forthwith foist their own knowledge into that of the thought of which they pretend to give a true account. To conclude, then, *thought may, but need not, in knowing, discriminate between its object and itself.*

We have been using the word Object. *Something must now be said about the proper use of the term Object in Psychology.*

In popular parlance the word object is commonly taken without reference to the act of knowledge, and treated as synonymous with individual subject of existence. Thus if anyone ask what is the mind's object when you say 'Columbus discovered America in 1492,' most people will reply 'Columbus,' or 'America,' or, at most, 'the discovery of America.' They will name a substantive kernel or nucleus of the consciousness, and say the thought is 'about' that, —as indeed it is,—and they will call that your thought's 'object.' Really that is usually only the grammatical object, or more likely the grammatical subject, of your sentence. It is at most your 'fractional object'; or you may call it the 'topic' of your thought, or the 'subject of your discourse.' But the *Object* of your thought is really its entire content or deliverance, neither more nor less. It is a vicious use of speech to take out a substantive kernel from its content and call that its object; and it is an equally vicious use of speech to add a substantive kernel not articulately included in its content, and to call that its object. Yet either one of these two sins we commit, whenever we content ourselves with saying that a given thought is simply 'about' a certain topic, or that that topic is its 'object.' The object of my thought in the previous sentence, for example, is strictly speaking neither Columbus, nor America, nor its discovery. It is nothing short of the entire sentence, 'Columbus-discovered-America-in-1492.' And if we wish to speak of it substantively, we must make a substantive of it by writing it out thus with hyphens between all its words. Nothing but this can possibly name its delicate idiosyncrasy. And if we wish to *feel* that idiosyncrasy we must reproduce the thought as it was uttered, with every word fringed and the whole sentence bathed in that original halo of obscure relations, which, like an horizon, then spread about its meaning.

Our psychological duty is to cling as closely as possible to the actual constitution of the thought we are studying. We may err as much by excess as by defect. If the kernel or 'topic,' Columbus, is in one way less than the thought's object, so in another way it may be more. That is, when named by the psychologist, it may mean much more than actually is present to the thought of which he is reporter. Thus, for example, suppose you should go on to think: 'He was a daring genius!' An ordinary psychologist would not hesitate to say that the object of your thought was still 'Columbus.' True, your thought is *about* Columbus. It 'terminates' in Columbus, leads from and to the direct idea of Columbus. But for the moment it is not fully and immediately Columbus, it is only 'he,' or rather 'he-was-a-daring-genius'; which, though it may be an unimportant difference for conversational purposes, is, for introspective psychology, as great a difference as there can be.

The object of every thought, then, is neither more nor less than all that the thought thinks, exactly as the thought thinks it, however complicated the matter, and however symbolic the manner of the thinking may be. It is needless to say that memory can seldom accurately reproduce such an object, when once it has passed from before the mind. It either makes too little or too much of it. Its best plan is to repeat the verbal sentence, if there was one, in which the object was expressed. But for inarticulate thoughts there is not even this resource, and introspection must confess that the task exceeds her powers. The mass of our thinking vanishes for ever, beyond hope of recovery, and psychology only gathers up a few of the crumbs that fall from the feast.

The next point to make clear is that, *however complex the object may be, the thought of it is one undivided state of consciousness.* As Thomas Brown says:[32]

"I have already spoken too often to require again to caution you against a mistake, into which, I must confess, that the terms, which the

[32] *Lectures on the Philosophy of the Human Mind*, Lecture 45.

poverty of our language obliges us to use, might, of themselves, very naturally lead you;—the mistake of supposing, that the most complex states of mind are not truly, in their very essence, as much one and indivisible, as those which we term simple—the complexity and seeming coexistence which they involve being relative to our feeling[33] only, not to their own absolute nature. I trust I need not repeat to you, that, in itself, every notion, however seemingly complex, is, and must be, truly simple—being one state, or affection, of one simple substance, mind. Our conception of a whole army, for example, is as truly this one mind existing in this one state, as our conception of any of the individuals that compose an army: Our notion of the abstract numbers, eight, four, two, is as truly one feeling of the mind, as our notion of simple unity."

The ordinary associationist-psychology supposes, in contrast with this, that whenever an object of thought contains many elements, the thought itself must be made up of just as many ideas, one idea for each element, and all fused together in appearance, but really separate.[34] The enemies of this psychology find (as we have already seen) little trouble in showing that such a bundle of separate ideas would never form one thought at all, and they contend that an Ego must be added to the bundle to give it unity, and bring the various ideas into relation with each other.[35] We will not discuss the ego just yet, but it is obvious that if things are to be thought in relation, they must be thought together, and in one *something,* be that something ego, psychosis, state of consciousness, or whatever you please. If not thought with each other, things are not thought in relation at all. Now most believers in the ego make the same mistake as the associationists and sensationists whom they oppose. Both agree that the elements of the subjective stream are discrete and separate and constitute what Kant calls a 'manifold.' But while the associationists think that a 'manifold' can form a single knowledge, the egoists deny this, and say that the knowledge comes only when the manifold is subjected to the synthetizing activity of an ego. Both make an identical initial hypothesis; but the

33 Instead of saying *to our feeling only,* he should have said, to the *object* only.

34 "There can be no difficulty in admitting that association does form the ideas of an indefinite number of individuals into one complex idea; because it is an acknowledged fact. Have we not the idea of an army? And is not that precisely the ideas of an indefinite number of men formed into one idea?" (James Mill's *Analysis of the Phenomena of the Human Mind* (J. S. Mill's Edition), vol. I, p. 264.)

35 For their arguments, see above, pp. 160–164.

egoist, finding it won't express the facts, adds another hypothesis to correct it. Now I do not wish just yet to 'commit myself' about the existence or non-existence of the ego, but I do contend that we need not invoke it for this particular reason—namely, because the manifold of ideas has to be reduced to unity. *There is no manifold of coexisting ideas*; the notion of such a thing is a chimera. *Whatever things are thought in relation are thought from the outset in a unity, in a single pulse of subjectivity, a single psychosis, feeling, or state of mind.*

The reason why this fact is so strangely garbled in the books seems to be what on an earlier page (see p. 195 ff.) I called the psychologist's fallacy. We have the inveterate habit, whenever we try introspectively to describe one of our thoughts, of dropping the thought as it is in itself and talking of something else. We describe the things that appear to the thought, and we describe other thoughts *about* those things—as if these and the original thought were the same. If, for example, the thought be 'the pack of cards is on the table,' we say, "Well, isn't it a thought of the pack of cards? Isn't it of the cards as included in the pack? Isn't it of the table? And of the legs of the table as well? The table has legs—how can you think the table without virtually thinking its legs? Hasn't our thought then, all these parts—one part for the pack and another for the table? And within the pack-part a part for each card, as within the table-part a part for each leg? And isn't each of these parts an idea? And can our thought, then, be anything but an assemblage or pack of ideas, each answering to some element of what it knows?"

Now not one of these assumptions is true. The thought taken as an example is, in the first place, not of 'a pack of cards.' It is of 'the-pack-of-cards-is-on-the-table,' an entirely different subjective phenomenon, whose Object implies the pack, and every one of the cards in it, but whose conscious constitution bears very little resemblance to that of the thought of the pack *per se*. What a thought *is*, and what it may be developed into, or explained to stand for, and be equivalent to, are two things, not one.[36]

[36] I know there are readers whom nothing can convince that the thought of a complex object has not as many parts as are discriminated in the object itself. Well, then, let the word parts pass. Only observe that these parts are not the separate 'ideas' of traditional psychology. No one of them can live out of that particular thought, any more than my head can live off of my particular shoulders. In a sense a soap-bubble has parts; it is a sum of juxtaposed spherical triangles. But these tri-

An analysis of what passes through the mind as we utter the phrase *the pack of cards is on the table* will, I hope, make this clear, and may at the same time condense into a concrete example a good deal of what has gone before.

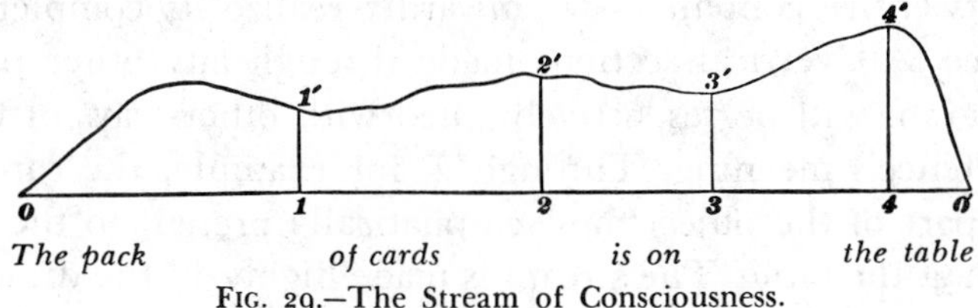

FIG. 29.—The Stream of Consciousness.

It takes time to utter the phrase. Let the horizontal line in Fig. 29 represent time. Every part of it will then stand for a fraction, every point for an instant, of the time. Of course the thought has *time-parts*. The part 2–3 of it, though continuous with 1–2, is yet a different part from 1–2. Now I say of these time-parts that we cannot take any one of them so short that it will not after some fashion or other be a thought of the whole object 'the pack of cards is on the table.' They melt into each other like dissolving views, and no two of them feel the object just alike, but each feels the total object in a unitary undivided way. This is what I mean by denying that in the thought any parts can be found corresponding to the object's parts. Time-parts are not such parts.

Now let the vertical dimensions of the figure stand for the objects or contents of the thoughts. A line vertical to any point of the horizontal, as 1–1′, will then symbolize the object in the mind at the instant 1; a space above the horizontal, as 1–1′–2′–2, will symbolize all that passes through the mind during the time 1–2 whose line it covers. The entire diagram from 0 to 0′ represents a finite length of thought's stream.

Can we now define the psychic constitution of each vertical section of this segment? We can, though in a very rough way. Immediately after 0, even before we have opened our mouths to speak, the entire thought is present to our mind in the form of an intention to utter that sentence. This intention, though it has no simple

angles are not separate realities; neither are the 'parts' of the thought separate realities. Touch the bubble and the triangles are no more. Dismiss the thought and out go its parts. You can no more make a new thought out of 'ideas' that have once served than you can make a new bubble out of old triangles. Each bubble, each thought, is a fresh organic unity, *sui generis*.

name, and though it is a transitive state immediately displaced by the first word, is yet a perfectly determinate phase of thought, unlike anything else (see p. 245). Again, immediately before o′, after the last word of the sentence is spoken, all will admit that we again think its entire content as we inwardly realize its completed deliverance. All vertical sections made through any other parts of the diagram will be respectively filled with other ways of feeling the sentence's meaning. Through 2, for example, the cards will be the part of the object most emphatically present to the mind; through 4, the table. The stream is made higher in the drawing at its end than at its beginning, because the final way of feeling the content is fuller and richer than the initial way. As Joubert says, "we only know just what we meant to say, after we have said it." And as M. V. Egger remarks, "before speaking, one barely knows what one intends to say, but afterwards one is filled with admiration and surprise at having said and thought it so well."

This latter author seems to me to have kept at much closer quarters with the facts than any other analyst of consciousness.[37] But even he does not quite hit the mark, for, as I understand him, he thinks that each word as it occupies the mind *displaces* the rest of the thought's content. He distinguishes the 'idea' (what I have called the total *object* or meaning) from the consciousness of the words, calling the former a very feeble state, and contrasting it with the liveliness of the words, even when these are only silently rehearsed. "The feeling," he says, "of the words makes ten or twenty times more noise in our consciousness than the sense of the phrase, which for consciousness is a very slight matter."[38] And having distinguished these two things, he goes on to separate them in time, saying that the idea may either precede or follow the words, but that it is a 'pure illusion' to suppose them simultaneous.[39] Now I believe that in all cases where the words are *under-*

37 In his work, *La Parole intérieure* (Paris, 1881), especially chapters v and vi.

38 Page 301.

39 Page 218. To prove this point, M. Egger appeals to the fact that we often hear someone speak whilst our mind is preoccupied, but do not understand him until some moments afterwards, when we suddenly 'realize' what he meant. Also to our digging out the meaning of a sentence in an unfamiliar tongue, where the words are present to us long before the idea is taken in. In these special cases the word does indeed precede the idea. The idea, on the contrary, precedes the word whenever we try to express ourselves with effort, as in a foreign tongue, or in an unusual field of intellectual invention. Both sets of cases, however, are exceptional, and M. Egger would probably himself admit, on reflection, that in the former class there is some

stood, the total idea may be and usually is present not only before and after the phrase has been spoken, but also whilst each separate word is uttered.[40] It is the overtone, halo, or fringe of the word, *as spoken in that sentence.* It is never absent; no word in an understood sentence comes to consciousness as a mere noise. We feel its meaning as it passes; and although our object differs from one moment to another as to its verbal kernel or nucleus, yet it is *similar* throughout the entire segment of the stream. The same object is known everywhere, now from the point of view, if we may so call it, of this word, now from the point of view of that. And in our feeling of each word there chimes an echo or foretaste of every other. The consciousness of the 'Idea' and that of the words are thus consubstantial. They are made of the same 'mind-stuff,' and form an unbroken stream. Annihilate a mind at any instant, cut its thought through whilst yet uncompleted, and examine the object present to the cross-section thus suddenly made; you will find, not the bald word in process of utterance, but that word suffused with the whole idea. The word may be so loud, as M. Egger would say, that we cannot *tell* just how its suffusion, as such, feels, or how it differs from the suffusion of the next word. But it does differ; and we may be sure that, could we see into the brain, we should find the same processes active through the entire sentence in different degrees, each one in turn becoming maximally excited and then yielding the momentary verbal 'kernel,' to the thought's content, at other times being only sub-excited, and then combining with the other sub-excited processes to give the overtone or fringe.[41]

We may illustrate this by a farther development of the diagram on p. 269. Let the objective content of any vertical section through the stream be represented no longer by a line, but by a plane figure, highest opposite whatever part of the object is most prominent in consciousness at the moment when the section is made. This part,

---

sort of a verbal suffusion, however evanescent, of the idea, when it is grasped—we hear the echo of the words as we catch their meaning. And he would probably admit that in the second class of cases the idea persists after the words that came with so much effort are found. In normal cases the simultaneity, as he admits, is obviously there.

40 A good way to get the words and the sense separately is to inwardly articulate word for word the discourse of another. One then finds that the meaning will often come to the mind in pulses, after clauses or sentences are finished.

41 The nearest approach (with which I am acquainted) to the doctrine set forth here is in O. Liebmann's *Zur Analysis der Wirklichkeit*, pp. 427–438.

in verbal thought, will usually be some word. A series of sections 1–1′, taken at the moments 1, 2, 3, would then look like this:

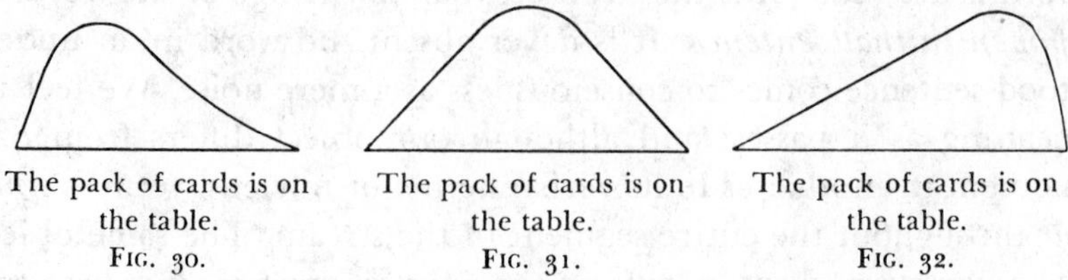

The pack of cards is on the table.
FIG. 30.

The pack of cards is on the table.
FIG. 31.

The pack of cards is on the table.
FIG. 32.

The horizontal breadth stands for the entire object in each of the figures; the height of the curve above each part of that object marks the relative prominence of that part in the thought. At the moment symbolized by the first figure *pack* is the prominent part; in the third figure it is *table*, etc.

We can easily add all these plane sections together to make a solid, one of whose solid dimensions will represent time, whilst a cut across this at right angles will give the thought's content at the moment when the cut is made. Let it be the thought, 'I am the same I that I was yesterday.' If at the fourth moment of time we annihilate the thinker and examine how the last pulsation of his consciousness was made, we find that it was an awareness of the whole content with *same* most prominent, and the other parts of the thing known relatively less distinct. With each prolongation of the scheme in the time-direction, the summit of the curve of section would come further towards the end of the sentence. If we make a solid wooden frame with the sentence written on its front, and the time-scale on one of its sides, if we spread flatly a sheet of India rubber over its top, on which rectangular co-ordinates are painted, and slide a smooth ball under the rubber in the direction from 0 to 'yesterday,' the bulging of the membrane along this

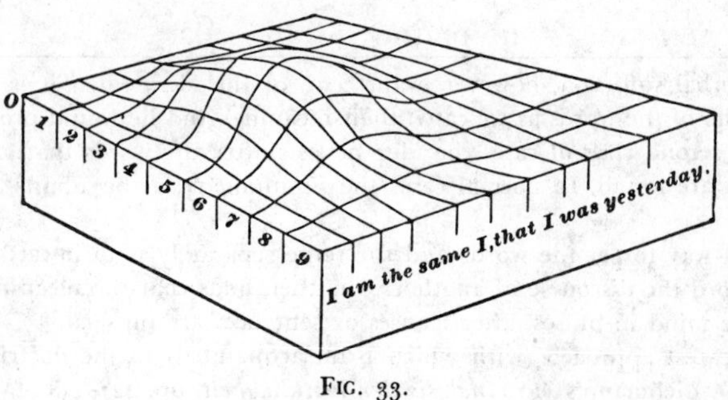

FIG. 33.

diagonal at successive moments will symbolize the changing of the thought's content in a way plain enough, after what has been said, to call for no more explanation. Or to express it in cerebral terms, it will show the relative intensities, at successive moments, of the several nerve-processes to which the various parts of the thought-object correspond.

The last peculiarity of consciousness to which attention is to be drawn in this first rough description of its stream is that

5) *It is always interested more in one part of its object than in another, and welcomes and rejects, or chooses, all the while it thinks*

The phenomena of selective attention and of deliberative will are of course patent examples of this choosing activity. But few of us are aware how incessantly it is at work in operations not ordinarily called by these names. Accentuation and Emphasis are present in every perception we have. We find it quite impossible to disperse our attention impartially over a number of impressions. A monotonous succession of sonorous strokes is broken up into rhythms, now of one sort, now of another, by the different accent which we place on different strokes. The simplest of these rhythms is the double one, tick-tóck, tick-tóck, tick-tóck. Dots dispersed on a surface are perceived in rows and groups. Lines separate into diverse figures. The ubiquity of the distinctions, *this* and *that, here* and *there, now* and *then,* in our minds is the result of our laying the same selective emphasis on parts of place and time.

But we do far more than emphasize things, and unite some, and keep others apart. We actually *ignore* most of the things before us. Let me briefly show how this goes on.

To begin at the bottom, what are our very senses themselves but organs of selection? Out of the infinite chaos of movements, of which physics teaches us that the outer world consists, each sense-organ picks out those which fall within certain limits of velocity. To these it responds, but ignores the rest as completely as if they did not exist. It thus accentuates particular movements in a manner for which objectively there seems no valid ground; for, as Lange says, there is no reason whatever to think that the gap in Nature between the highest sound-waves and the lowest heat-waves is an abrupt break like that of our sensations; or that the difference between violet and ultra-violet rays has anything like the objective importance subjectively represented by that between light and darkness. Out of what is in itself an undistinguishable, swarming *continuum*, devoid of distinction or emphasis, our senses make for us, by attending to this motion and ignoring that, a world full of contrasts, of sharp accents, of abrupt changes, of picturesque light and shade.

If the sensations we receive from a given organ have their causes thus picked out for us by the conformation of the organ's termination, Attention, on the other hand, out of all the sensations yielded, picks out certain ones as worthy of its notice and suppresses all the rest. Helmholtz's work on Optics is little more than a study of those visual sensations of which common men never become aware—blind spots, *muscæ volitantes*, after-images, irradiation, chromatic fringes, marginal changes of color, double images, astigmatism, movements of accommodation and convergence, retinal rivalry, and more besides. We do not even know without special training on which of our eyes an image falls. So habitually ignorant are most men of this that one may be blind for years of a single eye and never know the fact.

Helmholtz says that we notice only those sensations which are signs to us of *things*. But what are things? Nothing, as we shall abundantly see, but special groups of sensible qualities, which happen practically or æsthetically to interest us, to which we therefore give substantive names, and which we exalt to this exclusive status of independence and dignity. But in itself, apart from my interest, a particular dust-wreath on a windy day is just as much of an individual thing, and just as much or as little deserves an individual name, as my own body does.

And then, among the sensations we get from each separate thing, what happens? The mind selects again. It chooses certain of the sensations to represent the thing most *truly*, and considers the rest as its appearances, modified by the conditions of the moment. Thus my table-top is named *square*, after but one of an infinite number of retinal sensations which it yields, the rest of them being sensations of two acute and two obtuse angles; but I call the latter *perspective* views, and the four right angles the *true* form of the table, and erect the attribute squareness into the table's essence, for æsthetic reasons of my own. In like manner, the real form of the circle is deemed to be the sensation it gives when the line of vision is perpendicular to its centre—all its other sensations are signs of this sensation. The real sound of the cannon is the sensation it makes when the ear is close by. The real color of the brick is the sensation it gives when the eye looks squarely at it from a near point, out of the sunshine and yet not in the gloom; under other circumstances it gives us other color-sensations which are but signs of this—we then see it looks pinker or blacker than it really is. The reader knows no object which he does not represent to himself by preference as in some typical attitude, of some normal size, at some characteristic distance, of some standard tint, etc., etc. But all these essential characteristics, which together form for us the genuine objectivity of the thing and are contrasted with what we call the subjective sensations it may yield us at a given moment, are mere sensations like the latter. The mind chooses to suit itself, and decides what particular sensation shall be held more real and valid than all the rest.

Thus perception involves a twofold choice. Out of all present sensations, we notice mainly such as are significant of absent ones; and out of all the absent associates which these suggest, we again pick out a very few to stand for the objective reality *par excellence.* We could have no more exquisite example of selective industry.

That industry goes on to deal with the things thus given in perception. A man's empirical thought depends on the things he has experienced, but what these shall be is to a large extent determined by his habits of attention. A thing may be present to him a thousand times, but if he persistently fails to notice it, it cannot be said to enter into his experience. We are all seeing flies, moths, and beetles by the thousand, but to whom, save an entomologist, do they say anything distinct? On the other hand, a thing met only once in a lifetime may leave an indelible experience in the memory. Let four men make a tour in Europe. One will bring home only picturesque impressions—costumes and colors, parks and views and works of architecture, pictures and statues. To another all this will be non-existent; and distances and prices, populations and drainage-arrangements, door- and window-fastenings, and other useful statistics will take their place. A third will give a rich account of the theatres, restaurants, and public balls, and naught beside; whilst the fourth will perhaps have been so wrapped in his own subjective broodings as to tell little more than a few names of places through which he passed. Each has selected, out of the same mass of presented objects, those which suited his private interest and has made his experience thereby.

If, now, leaving the empirical combination of objects, we ask how the mind proceeds *rationally* to connect them, we find selection again to be omnipotent. In a future chapter we shall see that all Reasoning depends on the ability of the mind to break up the totality of the phenomenon reasoned about, into parts, and to pick out from among these the particular one which, in our given emergency, may lead to the proper conclusion. Another predicament will need another conclusion, and require another element to be picked out. The man of genius is he who will always stick in his bill at the right point, and bring it out with the right element—'reason' if the emergency be theoretical, 'means' if it be practical—transfixed upon it. I here confine myself to this brief statement, but it may suffice to show that Reasoning is but another form of the selective activity of the mind.

If now we pass to its æsthetic department, our law is still more obvious. The artist notoriously selects his items, rejecting all tones, colors, shapes, which do not harmonize with each other and with the main purpose of his work. That unity, harmony, 'convergence of characters,' as M. Taine calls it, which gives to works of art their superiority over works of nature, is wholly due to *elimination*. Any natural subject will do, if the artist has wit enough to pounce upon some one feature of it as characteristic, and suppress all merely accidental items which do not harmonize with this.

Ascending still higher, we reach the plane of Ethics, where choice reigns notoriously supreme. An act has no ethical quality whatever unless it be chosen out of several all equally possible. To sustain the arguments for the good course and keep them ever before us, to stifle our longing for more flowery ways, to keep the foot unflinchingly on the arduous path, these are characteristic ethical energies. But more than these; for these but deal with the means of compassing interests already felt by the man to be supreme. The ethical energy *par excellence* has to go farther and choose which *interest* out of several, equally coercive, shall become supreme. The issue here is of the utmost pregnancy, for it decides a man's entire career. When he debates, Shall I commit this crime? choose that profession? accept that office, or marry this fortune?—his choice really lies between one of several equally possible future Characters. What he shall *become* is fixed by the conduct of this moment.

Schopenhauer, who enforces his determinism by the argument that with a given fixed character only one reaction is possible under given circumstances, forgets that, in these critical ethical moments, what consciously *seems* to be in question is the complexion of the character itself. The problem with the man is less what act he shall now choose to do, than what being he shall now resolve to become.

Looking back, then, over this review, we see that the mind is at every stage a theatre of simultaneous possibilities. Consciousness consists in the comparison of these with each other, the selection of some, and the suppression of the rest by the reinforcing and inhibiting agency of attention. The highest and most elaborated mental products are filtered from the data chosen by the faculty next beneath, out of the mass offered by the faculty below that, which mass in turn was sifted from a still larger amount of yet simpler material, and so on. The mind, in short, works on the data it receives very much as a sculptor works on his block of stone. In a sense the statue stood there from eternity. But there were a thousand different ones beside it, and the sculptor alone is to thank for having extricated this one from the rest. Just so the world of each of us, howsoever different our several views of it may be, all lay embedded in the primordial chaos of sensations, which gave the mere *matter* to the thought of all of us indifferently. We may, if we like, by our reasonings unwind things back to that black and jointless continuity of space and moving clouds of swarming atoms which science calls the only real world. But all the while the world *we* feel and live in will be that which our ancestors and we, by slowly cumulative strokes of choice, have extricated out of this, like sculptors, by simply rejecting certain portions of the given stuff. Other sculptors, other statues from the same stone! Other minds, other worlds from the same monotonous and inexpressive chaos! My world is but one in a million alike embedded, alike real to those who may abstract them. How different must be the worlds in the consciousness of ant, cuttle-fish, or crab!

But in my mind and your mind the rejected portions and the selected portions of the original world-stuff are to a great extent the same. The human race as a whole largely agrees as to what it shall notice and name, and what not. And among the noticed parts we select in much the same way for accentuation and preference or subordination and dislike. There is, however, one entirely extraordinary case in which no two men ever are known to choose alike. One great splitting of the whole universe into two halves is made by each of us; and for each of us almost all of the interest attaches to one of the halves; but we all draw the line of division between them in a different place. When I say that we all call the two halves by the same names, and that those names are '*me*' and '*not-me*' respectively, it will at once be seen what I mean. The altogether unique kind of interest which each human mind feels in those parts of creation which it can call *me* or *mine* may be a moral riddle, but it is a fundamental psychological fact. No mind can take the same interest in his neighbor's *me* as in his own. The neighbor's me falls together with all the rest of things in one foreign mass, against which his own *me* stands out in startling relief. Even the trodden worm, as Lotze somewhere says, contrasts his own suffering self with the whole remaining universe, though he have no clear conception either of himself or of what the universe may be. He is for me a mere part of the world; for him it is I who am the mere part. Each of us dichotomizes the Kosmos in a different place.

Descending now to finer work than this first general sketch, let us in the next chapter try to trace the psychology of this fact of self-consciousness to which we have thus once more been led.

Chapter X

The Consciousness of Self

Let us begin with the Self in its widest acceptation, and follow it up to its most delicate and subtle form, advancing from the study of the empirical, as the Germans call it, to that of the pure, Ego.

THE EMPIRICAL SELF OR ME

The Empirical Self of each of us is all that he is tempted to call by the name of *me*. But it is clear that between what a man calls *me* and what he simply calls *mine* the line is difficult to draw. We feel and act about certain things that are ours very much as we feel and act about ourselves. Our fame, our children, the work of our hands, may be as dear to us as our bodies are, and arouse the same feelings and the same acts of reprisal if attacked. And our bodies themselves, are they simply ours, or are they *us*? Certainly men have been ready to disown their very bodies and to regard them as mere vestures, or even as prisons of clay from which they should some day be glad to escape.

We see then that we are dealing with a fluctuating material; the same object being sometimes treated as a part of me, at other times as simply mine, and then again as if I had nothing to do with it at all. *In its widest possible sense,* however, *a man's Self is the sum total of all that he* CAN *call his,* not only his body and his psychic powers, but his clothes and his house, his wife and children, his ancestors and friends, his reputation and works, his lands and horses, and yacht and bank-account. All these things give him the same emotions. If they wax and prosper, he feels triumphant; if they dwindle and die away, he feels cast down,—not necessarily in the same degree for each thing, but in much the same way for all. Understanding the Self in this widest sense, we may begin by dividing the history of it into three parts, relating respectively to—

1. Its constituents;
2. The feelings and emotions they arouse,—*Self-feelings*;
3. The actions to which they prompt,—*Self-seeking and Self-preservation.*

1. *The constituents of the Self* may be divided into two classes, those which make up respectively—

(a) The material Self;
(b) The social Self;
(c) The spiritual Self; and
(d) The pure Ego.

(*a*) The body is the innermost part of *the material Self* in each of us; and certain parts of the body seem more intimately ours than the rest. The clothes come next. The old saying that the human person is composed of three parts—soul, body and clothes—is more than a joke. We so appropriate our clothes and identify ourselves with them that there are few of us who, if asked to choose between having a beautiful body clad in raiment perpetually shabby and unclean, and having an ugly and blemished form always spotlessly attired, would not hesitate a moment before making a decisive reply.[1] Next, our immediate family is a part of ourselves. Our father and mother, our wife and babes, are bone of our bone and flesh of our flesh. When they die, a part of our very selves is gone. If they do anything wrong, it is our shame. If they are insulted, our anger flashes forth as readily as if we stood in their place. Our home comes next. Its scenes are part of our life; its aspects awaken the tenderest feelings of affection; and we do not easily forgive the stranger who, in visiting it, finds fault with its arrangements or treats it with contempt. All these different things are the objects of instinctive preferences coupled with the most important practical interests of life. We all have a blind impulse to watch over our body, to deck it with clothing of an ornamental sort, to cherish parents, wife and babes,

[1] See, for a charming passage on the Philosophy of Dress, H. Lotze's *Microcosmus*, Eng. tr., vol. I, p. 592 ff.

and to find for ourselves a home of our own which we may live in and 'improve.'

An equally instinctive impulse drives us to collect property; and the collections thus made become, with different degrees of intimacy, parts of our empirical selves. The parts of our wealth most intimately ours are those which are saturated with our labor. There are few men who would not feel personally annihilated if a life-long construction of their hands or brains—say an entomological collection or an extensive work in manuscript—were suddenly swept away. The miser feels similarly towards his gold; and although it is true that a part of our depression at the loss of possessions is due to our feeling that we must now go without certain goods that we expected the possessions to bring in their train, yet in every case there remains, over and above this, a sense of the shrinkage of our personality, a partial conversion of ourselves to nothingness, which is a psychological phenomenon by itself. We are all at once assimilated to the tramps and poor devils whom we so despise, and at the same time removed farther than ever away from the happy sons of earth who lord it over land and sea and men in the full-blown lustihood that wealth and power can give, and before whom, stiffen ourselves as we will by appealing to anti-snobbish first principles, we cannot escape an emotion, open or sneaking, of respect and dread.

(*b*) *A man's Social Self* is the recognition which he gets from his mates. We are not only gregarious animals, liking to be in sight of our fellows, but we have an innate propensity to get ourselves noticed, and noticed favorably, by our kind. No more fiendish punishment could be devised, were such a thing physically possible, than that one should be turned loose in society and remain absolutely unnoticed by all the members thereof. If no one turned round when we entered, answered when we spoke, or minded what we did, but if every person we met 'cut us dead,' and acted as if we were non-existing things, a kind of rage and impotent despair would ere long well up in us, from which the cruellest bodily tortures would be a relief; for these would make us feel that, however bad might be our plight, we had not sunk to such a depth as to be unworthy of attention at all.

Properly speaking, *a man has as many social selves as there are individuals who recognize him* and carry an image of him in their mind. To wound any one of these his images is to wound him.[2] But as the individuals who carry the images fall naturally into classes, we may practically say that he has as many different social selves as there are distinct *groups* of persons about whose opinion he cares. He generally shows a different side of himself to each of these different groups. Many a youth who is demure enough before his parents and teachers, swears and swaggers like a pirate among his 'tough' young friends. We do not show ourselves to our children as to our club-companions, to our customers as to the laborers we employ, to our own masters and employers as to our intimate friends. From this there results what practically is a division of the man into several selves; and this may be a discordant splitting, as where one is afraid to let one set of his acquaintances know him as he is elsewhere; or it may be a perfectly harmonious division of labor, as where one tender to his children is stern to the soldiers or prisoners under his command.

The most peculiar social self which one is apt to have is in the mind of the person one is in love with. The good or bad fortunes of this self cause the most intense elation and dejection—unreasonable enough as measured by every other standard than that of the organic feeling of the individual. To his own consciousness he *is* not, so long as this particular social self fails to get recognition, and when it is recognized his contentment passes all bounds.

A man's *fame*, good or bad, and his *honor* or dishonor, are names for one of his social selves. The particular social self of a man called his honor is usually the result of one of those splittings of which we have spoken. It is his image in the eyes of his own 'set,' which exalts or condemns him as he conforms or not to certain requirements that may not be made of one in another walk of life. Thus a layman may abandon a city infected with cholera; but a priest or a doctor would think such an act incompatible with his honor. A soldier's honor requires him to fight or to die under circumstances where another man can apologize or run away with no stain upon his social self. A judge, a statesman, are in like manner debarred by the honor of their cloth from entering into pecuniary relations perfectly honorable to persons in private life. Nothing is commoner than to hear people discriminate between their different selves of this sort: "As a man I pity you, but as an official I must show you no mercy"; "As a politician I regard him as an ally,

2 "Who filches from me my good name," etc.

but as a moralist I loathe him"; etc., etc. What may be called 'club-opinion' is one of the very strongest forces in life.[3] The thief must not steal from other thieves; the gambler must pay his gambling-debts, though he pay no other debts in the world. The code of honor of fashionable society has throughout history been full of permissions as well as of vetoes, the only reason for following either of which is that so we best serve one of our social selves. You must not lie in general, but you may lie as much as you please if asked about your relations with a lady; you must accept a challenge from an equal, but if challenged by an inferior you may laugh him to scorn: these are examples of what is meant.

(*c*) By the Spiritual Self, so far as it belongs to the Empirical Me, I mean a man's inner or subjective being, his psychic faculties or dispositions, taken concretely; not the bare principle of personal Unity, or 'pure' Ego, which remains still to be discussed. These psychic dispositions are the most enduring and intimate part of the self, that which we most verily seem to be. We take a purer self-satisfaction when we think of our ability to argue and discriminate, of our moral sensibility and conscience, of our indomitable will, than when we survey any of our other possessions. Only when these are altered is a man said to be *alienatus a se*.

Now this spiritual self may be considered in various ways. We

[3] "He who imagines commendation and disgrace not to be strong motives on men . . . seems little skilled in the nature or history of mankind: the greatest part whereof he shall find to govern themselves chiefly, if not solely, by this law of fashion; and, so they do that which keeps them in reputation with their company, little regard the laws of God or the magistrate. The penalties that attend the breach of God's laws, some, nay, most, men seldom seriously reflect on; and amongst those that do, many, whilst they break the law, entertain thoughts of future reconciliation, and making their peace for such breaches: and as to the punishments due from the laws of the commonwealth, they frequently flatter themselves with the hope of impunity. But no man escapes the punishment of *their* censure and dislike who offends against the fashion and opinion of the company he keeps, and would recommend himself to. Nor is there one of ten thousand who is stiff and insensible enough to bear up under the constant dislike and condemnation of his own club. He must be of a strange and unusual constitution who can content himself to live in constant disgrace and disrepute with his own particular society. Solitude many men have sought, and been reconciled to: but nobody that has the least thought or sense of a man about him, can live in society under the constant dislike and ill opinion of his familiars, and those he converses with. This is a burden too heavy for human sufferance: and he must be made up of irreconcilable contradictions, who can take pleasure in company, and yet be insensible of contempt and disgrace from his companions." (Locke's *Essay*, book II, ch. XXVIII, § 12.)

may divide it into faculties, as just instanced, isolating them one from another, and identifying ourselves with either in turn. This is an *abstract* way of dealing with consciousness, in which, as it actually presents itself, a plurality of such faculties are always to be simultaneously found; or we may insist on a concrete view, and then the spiritual self in us will be either the entire stream of our personal consciousness, or the present 'segment' or 'section' of that stream, according as we take a broader or a narrower view—both the stream and the section being concrete existences in time, and each being a unity after its own peculiar kind. But whether we take it abstractly or concretely, our considering the spiritual self at all is a reflective process, is the result of our abandoning the outward-looking point of view, and of our having become able to think of subjectivity as such, *to think ourselves as thinkers.*

This attention to thought as such, and the identification of ourselves with it rather than with any of the objects which it reveals, is a momentous and in some respects a rather mysterious operation, of which we need here only say that as a matter of fact it exists; and that in everyone, at an early age, the distinction between thought as such, and what it is 'of' or 'about,' has become familiar to the mind. The deeper grounds for this discrimination may possibly be hard to find; but superficial grounds are plenty and near at hand. Almost anyone will tell us that thought is a different sort of existence from things, because many sorts of thought are of no things—e.g., pleasures, pains, and emotions; others are of nonexistent things—errors and fictions; others again of existent things, but in a form that is symbolic and does not resemble them—abstract ideas and concepts; whilst in the thoughts that do resemble the things they are 'of' (percepts, sensations), we can feel, alongside of the thing known, the thought of it going on as an altogether separate act and operation in the mind.

Now this subjective life of ours, distinguished as such so clearly from the objects known by its means, may, as aforesaid, be taken by us in a concrete or in an abstract way. Of the concrete way I will say nothing just now, except that the actual 'section' of the stream will ere long, in our discussion of the nature of the principle of *unity* in consciousness, play a very important part. The abstract way claims our attention first. If the stream as a whole is identified with the Self far more than any outward thing, a *certain portion of the stream abstracted from the rest* is so identified in an altogether peculiar degree, and is felt by all men as a sort of innermost centre within the circle, of sanctuary within the citadel, constituted by the subjective life as a whole. Compared with this element of the stream, the other parts, even of the subjective life, seem transient external possessions, of which each in turn can be disowned, whilst that which disowns them remains. Now, *what is this self of all the other selves?*

Probably all men would describe it in much the same way up to a certain point. They would call it the *active* element in all consciousness; saying that whatever qualities a man's feelings may possess, or whatever content his thought may include, there is a spiritual something in him which seems to *go out* to meet these qualities and contents, whilst they seem to *come in* to be received by it. It is what welcomes or rejects. It presides over the perception of sensations, and by giving or withholding its assent it influences the movements they tend to arouse. It is the home of interest,—not the pleasant or the painful, not even pleasure or pain, as such, but that within us to which pleasure and pain, the pleasant and the painful, speak. It is the source of effort and attention, and the place from which appear to emanate the fiats of the will. A physiologist who should reflect upon it in his own person could hardly help, I should think, connecting it more or less vaguely with the process by which ideas or incoming sensations are 'reflected' or pass over into outward acts. Not necessarily that it should *be* this process or the mere feeling of this process, but that it should be in some close way *related* to this process; for it plays a part analogous to it in the psychic life, being a sort of junction at which sensory ideas terminate and from which motor ideas proceed, and forming a kind of link between the two. Being more incessantly there than any other single element of the mental life, the other elements end by seeming to accrete round it and to belong to it. It becomes opposed to them as the permanent is opposed to the changing and inconstant.

One may, I think, without fear of being upset by any future Galtonian circulars, believe that all men must single out from the rest of what they call themselves some central principle of which each would recognize the foregoing to be a fair general description,—accurate enough, at any rate, to denote what is meant, and keep it unconfused with other things. The moment, however, they came to closer quarters with it, trying to define more accurately its precise nature, we should find opinions beginning to diverge. Some would say that it is a simple active substance, the soul, of which they are thus conscious; others, that it is nothing but a fiction, the imaginary being denoted by the pronoun I; and between these extremes of opinion all sorts of intermediaries would be found.

Later we must ourselves discuss them all, and sufficient to that day will be the evil thereof. *Now,* let us try to settle for ourselves as definitely as we can, just how this central nucleus of the Self may *feel,* no matter whether it be a spiritual substance or only a delusive word.

For this central part of the Self is *felt.* It may be all that Transcendentalists say it is, and all that Empiricists say it is into the bargain, but it is at any rate no *mere ens rationis,* cognized only in an intellectual way, and no *mere* summation of memories or *mere* sound of a word in our ears. It is something with which we also have direct sensible acquaintance, and which is as fully present at any moment of consciousness in which it *is* present, as in a whole lifetime of such moments. When, just now, it was called an abstraction, that did not mean that, like some general notion, it could not be presented in a particular experience. It only meant that in the stream of consciousness it never was found all alone. But when it is found, it is *felt*; just as the body is felt, the feeling of which is also an abstraction, because never is the body felt all alone, but always together with other things. *Now can we tell more precisely in what the feeling of this central active self consists,*—not necessarily as yet what the active self *is,* as a being or principle, but what we *feel* when we become aware of its existence?

I think I can in my own case; and as what I say will be likely to meet with opposition if generalized (as indeed it may be in part inapplicable to other individuals), I had better continue in the first person, leaving my description to be accepted by those to whose introspection it may commend itself as true, and confessing my inability to meet the demands of others, if others there be.

First of all, I am aware of a constant play of furtherances and hindrances in my thinking, of checks and releases, tendencies which run with desire, and tendencies which run the other way. Among the matters I think of, some range themselves on the side of the thought's interests, whilst others play an unfriendly part thereto. The mutual inconsistencies and agreements, reinforcements and obstructions, which obtain amongst these objective matters reverberate backwards and produce what seem to be incessant reactions of my spontaneity upon them, welcoming or opposing, appropriating or disowning, striving with or against, saying yes or no. This palpitating inward life is, in me, that central nucleus which I just tried to describe in terms that all men might use.

But when I forsake such general descriptions and grapple with particulars, coming to the closest possible quarters with the facts, *it is difficult for me to detect in the activity any purely spiritual element at all. Whenever my introspective glance succeeds in turning round quickly enough to catch one of these manifestations of spontaneity in the act, all it can ever feel distinctly is some bodily process, for the most part taking place within the head.* Omitting for a moment what is obscure in these introspective results, let me try to state those particulars which to my own consciousness seem indubitable and distinct.

In the first place, the acts of attending, assenting, negating, making an effort, are felt as movements of something in the head. In many cases it is possible to describe these movements quite exactly. In attending to either an idea or a sensation belonging to a particular sense-sphere, the movement is the adjustment of the sense-organ, felt as it occurs. I cannot think in visual terms, for example, without feeling a fluctuating play of pressures, convergences, divergences, and accommodations in my eyeballs. The direction in which the object is conceived to lie determines the character of these movements, the feeling of which becomes, for my consciousness, identified with the manner in which I make myself ready to receive the visible thing. My brain appears to me as if all shot across with lines of direction, of which I have become conscious as my attention has shifted from one sense-organ to another, in passing to successive outer things, or in following trains of varying sense-ideas.

When I try to remember or reflect, the movements in question, instead of being directed towards the periphery, seem to come from the periphery inwards and feel like a sort of *withdrawal* from the outer world. As far as I can detect, these feelings are due to an actual rolling outwards and upwards of the eyeballs, such as I believe occurs in me in sleep, and is the exact opposite of their action in fixating a physical thing. In reasoning, I find that I am apt to have a kind of vaguely localized diagram in my mind, with the various fractional objects of the thought disposed at particular points thereof; and the oscillations of my attention from one of them to another are most distinctly felt as alternations of direction in movements occurring inside the head.[4]

In consenting and negating, and in making a mental effort, the movements seem more complex, and I find them harder to describe. The opening and closing of the glottis play a great part in these operations, and, less distinctly, the movements of the soft palate, etc., shutting off the posterior nares from the mouth. My glottis is like a sensitive valve, intercepting my breath instantaneously at every mental hesitation or felt aversion to the objects of my thought, and as quickly opening, to let the air pass through my throat and nose, the moment the repugnance is overcome. The feeling of the movement of this air is, in me, one strong ingredient of the feeling of assent. The movements of the muscles of the brow and eyelids also respond very sensitively to every fluctuation in the agreeableness or disagreeableness of what comes before my mind.

In *effort* of any sort, contractions of the jaw-muscles and of those of respiration are added to those of the brow and glottis, and thus the feeling passes out of the head properly so called. It passes out of the head whenever the welcoming or rejecting of the object is *strongly* felt. Then a set of feelings pour in from many bodily parts, all 'expressive' of my emotion, and the head-feelings proper are swallowed up in this larger mass.

In a sense, then, it may be truly said that, in one person at least, *the 'Self of selves,' when carefully examined, is found to consist mainly of the collection of these peculiar motions in the head or between the head and throat.* I do not for a moment say that this is *all* it consists of, for I fully realize how desperately hard is introspection in this field. But I feel quite sure that these cephalic motions are the portions of my innermost activity of which I am *most distinctly aware.* If the dim portions which I cannot yet define should prove to be like unto these distinct portions in me, and I like other men, *it would follow that our entire feeling of spiritual activity, or what commonly passes by that name, is really a feeling of bodily activities whose exact nature is by most men overlooked.*

Now, without pledging ourselves in any way to adopt this hypothesis, let us dally with it for a while to see to what consequences it might lead if it were true.

[4] For some farther remarks on these feelings of movement see the next chapter.

In the first place, the nuclear part of the Self, intermediary between ideas and overt acts, would be a collection of activities physiologically in no essential way different from the overt acts themselves. If we divide all possible physiological acts into *adjustments* and *executions*, the nuclear self would be the adjustments collectively considered; and the less intimate, more shifting self, so far as it was active, would be the executions. But both adjustments and executions would obey the reflex type. Both would be the result of sensorial and ideational processes discharging either into each other within the brain, or into muscles and other parts outside. The peculiarity of the adjustments would be that they are minimal reflexes, few in number, incessantly repeated, constant amid great fluctuations in the rest of the mind's content, and entirely unimportant and uninteresting except through their uses in furthering or inhibiting the presence of various things, and actions before consciousness. These characters would naturally keep us from introspectively paying much attention to them in detail, whilst they would at the same time make us aware of them as a coherent group of processes, strongly contrasted with all the other things consciousness contained,—even with the other constituents of the 'Self,' material, social, or spiritual, as the case might be. They are reactions, and they are *primary* reactions. Everything arouses them; for objects which have no other effects will for a moment contract the brow and make the glottis close. It is as if all that visited the mind had to stand an entrance-examination, and just show its face so as to be either approved or sent back. These primary reactions are like the opening or the closing of the door. In the midst of psychic change they are the permanent core of turnings-towards and turnings-from, of yieldings and arrests, which naturally seem central and interior in comparison with the foreign matters, *apropos* to which they occur, and hold a sort of arbitrating, decisive position, quite unlike that held by any of the other constituents of the Me. It would not be surprising, then, if we were to feel them as the birthplace of conclusions and the starting point of acts, or if they came to appear as what we called a while back the 'sanctuary within the citadel' of our personal life.[5]

[5] Wundt's account of Self-consciousness deserves to be compared with this. What I have called 'adjustments' he calls processes of 'Apperception.' "In this development (of consciousness) one particular group of percepts claims a prominent significance, namely, those of which the spring lies in ourselves. The images of feelings

If they really were the innermost sanctuary, the *ultimate* one of all the selves whose being we can ever directly experience, it would follow that *all* that is experienced is, strictly considered, *objective*; that this Objective falls asunder into two contrasted parts, one realized as 'Self,' the other as 'not-Self'; and that over and above these parts there *is* nothing save the fact that they are known, the fact of the stream of thought being there as the indispensable subjective condition of their being experienced at all. But this *condition* of the experience is not one of the *things experienced* at the moment; this knowing is not immediately *known*. It is only known in subsequent reflection. Instead, then, of the stream of thought being one of *con*-sciousness, "thinking its own existence along with whatever else it thinks," (as Ferrier says) it might be better called a stream of *Scious*ness pure and simple, thinking objects of some

we get from our own body, and the representations of our own movements distinguish themselves from all others by forming a *permanent* group. As there are always some muscles in a state either of tension or of activity it follows that we never lack a sense, either dim or clear, of the positions or movements of our body. . . . This permanent sense, moreover, has this peculiarity, that we are aware of our power at any moment voluntarily to arouse any one of its ingredients. We excite the sensations of movement immediately by such impulses of the will as shall arouse the movements themselves; and we excite the visual and tactile feelings of our body by the voluntary movement of our organs of sense. So we come to conceive this permanent mass of feeling as immediately or remotely subject to our will, and call it the *consciousness of ourself*. This self-consciousness is, at the outset, thoroughly sensational, . . . only gradually the second-named of its characters, its subjection to our will, attains predominance. In proportion as the apperception of all our mental objects appears to us as an inward exercise of will, does our self-consciousness begin both to widen itself and to narrow itself at the same time. It widens itself in that every mental act whatever comes to stand in relation to our will; and it narrows itself in that it concentrates itself more and more upon the inner activity of apperception, over against which our own body and all the representations connected with it appear as external objects, different from our proper self. This consciousness, contracted down to the process of apperception, we call our Ego; and the apperception of mental objects in general, may thus, after Leibnitz, be designated as the raising of them into our self-consciousness. Thus the natural development of self-consciousness implicitly involves the most abstract forms in which this faculty has been described in philosophy; only philosophy is fond of placing the abstract ego at the outset, and so reversing the process of development. Nor should we overlook the fact that the completely abstract ego [as pure activity], although suggested by the natural development of our consciousness, is never actually found therein. The most speculative of philosophers is incapable of disjoining his ego from those bodily feelings and images which form the incessant background of his awareness of himself. The notion of his ego as such is, like every notion, derived from sensibility, for the process of apperception itself comes to our knowledge chiefly through those feelings of tension [what I have above called inward adjustments] which accompany it." (*Physiologische Psychologie*, 2te Aufl., Bd. II, pp. 217–19.)

of which it makes what it calls a 'Me,' and only aware of its 'pure' Self in an abstract, hypothetic or conceptual way. Each 'section' of the stream would then be a bit of sciousness or knowledge of this sort, including and contemplating its 'me' and its 'not-me' as objects which work out their drama together, but not yet including or contemplating its own subjective being. The sciousness in question would be the *Thinker*, and the existence of this thinker would be given to us rather as a logical postulate than as that direct inner perception of spiritual activity which we naturally believe ourselves to have. 'Matter,' as something behind physical phenomena, is a postulate of this sort. Between the postulated Matter and the postulated Thinker, the sheet of phenomena would then swing, some of them (the 'realities') pertaining more to the matter, others (the fictions, opinions, and errors) pertaining more to the Thinker. But *who* the Thinker would be, or how many distinct Thinkers we ought to suppose in the universe, would all be subjects for an ulterior metaphysical inquiry.

Speculations like this traverse common-sense; and not only do they traverse common-sense (which in philosophy is no insuperable objection) but they contradict the fundamental assumption of *every* philosophic school. Spiritualists, transcendentalists, and empiricists alike admit in us a continual direct perception of the thinking activity in the concrete. However they may otherwise disagree, they vie with each other in the cordiality of their recognition of our *thoughts* as the one sort of existent which skepticism cannot touch.[6] I will therefore treat the last few pages as a parenthetical digression, and from now to the end of the volume revert to the path of common-sense again. I mean by this that I will continue to assume (as I have assumed all along, especially in the last chapter) a direct awareness of the process of our thinking as such, simply insisting on the fact that it is an even more inward and subtle phenomenon than most of us suppose.

At present, then, the only conclusion I come to is the following: That (in some persons at least) the part of the innermost Self which is most vividly felt turns out to consist for the most part of a collection of cephalic movements of 'adjustments' which, for want of attention and reflection, usually fail to be perceived and classed

[6] The only exception I know of is M. P. Souriau, in his important article in the *Revue Philosophique*, vol. XXII, p. 449. M. Souriau's conclusion is 'que la conscience n'existe pas' (p. 472).

as what they are; that over and above these there is an obscurer feeling of something more; but whether it be of fainter physiological processes, or of nothing objective at all, but rather of subjectivity as such, of thought become 'its own object,' must at present remain an open question,—like the question whether it be an indivisible active soul-substance, or the question whether it be a personification of the pronoun I, or any other of the guesses as to what its nature may be.

Farther than this we cannot as yet go clearly in our analysis of the Self's constituents. So let us proceed to the emotions of Self which they arouse.

2. SELF-FEELING

These are primarily *self-complacency* and *self-dissatisfaction.* Of what is called 'self-love,' I will treat a little farther on. Language has synonyms enough for both primary feelings. Thus pride, conceit, vanity, self-esteem, arrogance, vainglory, on the one hand; and on the other modesty, humility, confusion, diffidence, shame, mortification, contrition, the sense of obloquy and personal despair. These two opposite classes of affection seem to be direct and elementary endowments of our nature. Associationists would have it that they are, on the other hand, secondary phenomena arising from a rapid computation of the sensible pleasures or pains to which our prosperous or debased personal predicament is likely to lead, the sum of the represented pleasures forming the self-satisfaction, and the sum of the represented pains forming the opposite feeling of shame. No doubt, when we are self-satisfied, we do fondly rehearse all possible rewards for our desert, and when in a fit of self-despair we forebode evil. But the mere expectation of reward *is* not the self-satisfaction, and the mere apprehension of the evil *is* not the self-despair, for there is a certain average tone of self-feeling which each one of us carries about with him, and which is independent of the objective reasons we may have for satisfaction or discontent. That is, a very meanly-conditioned man may abound in unfaltering conceit, and one whose success in life is secure and who is esteemed by all may remain diffident of his powers to the end.

One may say, however, that the normal *provocative* of self-feeling is one's actual success or failure, and the good or bad actual position one holds in the world. "He put in his thumb and pulled out a plum, and said what a good boy am I." A man with a broadly extended empirical Ego, with powers that have uniformly brought him success, with place and wealth and friends and fame, is not likely to be visited by the morbid diffidences and doubts about himself which he had when he was a boy. "Is not this great Babylon, which I have planted?"[7] Whereas he who has made one blunder after another, and still lies in middle life among the failures at the foot of the hill, is liable to grow all sicklied o'er with self-distrust, and to shrink from trials with which his powers can really cope.

The emotions themselves of self-satisfaction and abasement are of a unique sort, each as worthy to be classed as a primitive emotional species as are, for example, rage or pain. Each has its own peculiar physiognomical expression. In self-satisfaction the extensor muscles are innervated, the eye is strong and glorious, the gait rolling and elastic, the nostril dilated, and a peculiar smile plays upon the lips. This whole complex of symptoms is seen in an exquisite way in lunatic asylums, which always contain some patients who are literally mad with conceit, and whose fatuous expression and absurdly strutting or swaggering gait is in tragic contrast with their lack of any valuable personal quality. It is in these same castles of despair that we find the strongest examples of the opposite physiognomy, in good people who think they have committed 'the unpardonable sin' and are lost forever, who crouch and cringe and slink from notice, and are unable to speak aloud or look us in the eye. Like fear and like anger, in similar morbid conditions, these opposite feelings of Self may be aroused with no adequate exciting cause. And in fact we ourselves know how the barometer of our self-esteem and confidence rises and falls from one day to another through causes that seem to be visceral and organic rather than rational, and which certainly answer to no corresponding variations in the esteem in which we are held by our friends. Of the origin of these emotions in the race, we can speak better when we have treated of—

3. SELF-SEEKING AND SELF-PRESERVATION

These words cover a large number of our fundamental instinctive impulses. We have those of *bodily self-seeking*, those of *social self-seeking*, and those of *spiritual self-seeking*.

[7] See the excellent remarks by Prof. Bain on the "Emotion of Power" in his *Emotions and the Will*.

All the ordinary useful reflex actions and movements of alimentation and defence are acts of bodily self-preservation. Fear and anger prompt to acts that are useful in the same way. Whilst if by self-seeking we mean the providing for the future as distinguished from maintaining the present, we must class both anger and fear with the hunting, the acquisitive, the home-constructing and the tool-constructing instincts, as impulses to self-seeking of the bodily kind. Really, however, these latter instincts, with amativeness, parental fondness, curiosity and emulation, seek not only the development of the bodily Self, but that of the material Self in the widest possible sense of the word.

Our *social self-seeking*, in turn, is carried on directly through our amativeness and friendliness, our desire to please and attract notice and admiration, our emulation and jealousy, our love of glory, influence, and power, and indirectly through whichever of the material self-seeking impulses prove serviceable as means to social ends. That the direct social self-seeking impulses are probably pure instincts is easily seen. The noteworthy thing about the desire to be 'recognized' by others is that its strength has so little to do with the worth of the recognition computed in sensational or rational terms. We are crazy to get a visiting-list which shall be large, to be able to say when anyone is mentioned, "Oh! I know him well," and to be bowed to in the street by half the people we meet. Of course distinguished friends and admiring recognition are the most desirable—Thackeray somewhere asks his readers to confess whether it would not give each of *them* an exquisite pleasure to be met walking down Pall Mall with a duke on either arm. But in default of dukes and envious salutations almost anything will do for some of us; and there is a whole race of beings to-day whose passion is to keep their names in the newspapers, no matter under what heading, 'arrivals and departures,' 'personal paragraphs,' 'interviews,'—gossip, even scandal, will suit them if nothing better is to be had. Guiteau, Garfield's assassin, is an example of the extremity to which this sort of craving for the notoriety of print may go in a pathological case. The newspapers bounded his mental horizon; and in the poor wretch's prayer on the scaffold, one of the most heartfelt expressions was: "The newspaper press of this land has a big bill to settle with thee, O Lord!"

Not only the people but the places and things I know enlarge my Self in a sort of metaphoric social way. '*Ça me connaît,*' as the

French workman says of the implement he can use well. So that it comes about that persons for whose *opinion* we care nothing are nevertheless persons whose notice we woo; and that many a man truly great, many a woman truly fastidious in most respects, will take a deal of trouble to dazzle some insignificant cad whose whole personality they heartily despise.

Under the head of *spiritual self-seeking* ought to be included every impulse towards psychic progress, whether intellectual, moral, or spiritual in the narrow sense of the term. It must be admitted, however, that much that commonly passes for spiritual self-seeking in this narrow sense is only material and social self-seeking beyond the grave. In the Mohammedan desire for paradise and the Christian aspiration not to be damned in hell, the materiality of the goods sought is undisguised. In the more positive and refined view of heaven many of its goods, the fellowship of the saints and of our dead ones, and the presence of God, are but social goods of the most exalted kind. It is only the search of the redeemed inward nature, the spotlessness from sin, whether here or hereafter, that can count as spiritual self-seeking pure and undefiled.

But this broad external review of the facts of the life of the Self will be incomplete without some account of the

RIVALRY AND CONFLICT OF THE DIFFERENT SELVES

With most objects of desire, physical nature restricts our choice to but one of many represented goods, and even so it is here. I am often confronted by the necessity of standing by one of my empirical selves and relinquishing the rest. Not that I would not, if I could, be both handsome and fat and well dressed, and a great athlete, and make a million a year, be a wit, a *bon-vivant*, and a lady-killer, as well as a philosopher; a philanthropist, statesman, warrior, and African explorer, as well as a 'tone-poet' and saint. But the thing is simply impossible. The millionaire's work would run counter to the saint's; the *bon-vivant* and the philanthropist would trip each other up; the philosopher and the lady-killer could not well keep house in the same tenement of clay. Such different characters may conceivably at the outset of life be alike *possible* to a man. But to make any one of them actual, the rest must more or less be suppressed. So the seeker of his truest, strongest, deepest self must review the list carefully, and pick out the one on which to stake his salvation. All other selves thereupon become unreal, but the fortunes of this self are real. Its failures are real failures, its triumphs real triumphs, carrying shame and gladness with them. This is as strong an example as there is of that selective industry of the mind on which I insisted some pages back (p. 273 ff.). Our thought, incessantly deciding, among many things of a kind, which ones for it shall be realities, here chooses one of many possible selves or characters, and forthwith reckons it no shame to fail in any of those not adopted expressly as its own.

I, who for the time have staked my all on being a psychologist, am mortified if others know much more psychology than I. But I am contented to wallow in the grossest ignorance of Greek. My deficiencies there give me no sense of personal humiliation at all. Had I 'pretensions' to be a linguist, it would have been just the reverse. So we have the paradox of a man shamed to death because he is only the second pugilist or the second oarsman in the world. That he is able to beat the whole population of the globe minus one is nothing; he has 'pitted' himself to beat that one; and as long as he doesn't do that nothing else counts. He is to his own regard as if he were not, indeed he *is* not.

Yonder puny fellow, however, whom everyone can beat, suffers no chagrin about it, for he has long ago abandoned the attempt to 'carry that line,' as the merchants say, of self at all. With no attempt there can be no failure; with no failure no humiliation. So our self-feeling in this world depends entirely on what we *back* ourselves to be and do. It is determined by the ratio of our actualities to our supposed potentialities; a fraction of which our pretensions are the denominator and the numerator our success: thus, $\text{Self-esteem} = \frac{\text{Success}}{\text{Pretensions}}$. Such a fraction may be increased as well by diminishing the denominator as by increasing the numerator.[8] To give up pretensions is as blessed a relief as to get them gratified; and where disappointment is incessant and the struggle

[8] Cf. Carlyle: *Sartor Resartus*, "The Everlasting Yea." "I tell thee, Blockhead, it all comes of thy Vanity; of what thou *fanciest* those same deserts of thine to be. Fancy that thou deservest to be hanged (as is most likely), thou wilt feel it happiness to be only shot: fancy that thou deservest to be hanged in a hair-halter, it will be a luxury to die in hemp. . . . What Act of Legislature was there that *thou* shouldst be Happy? A little while ago thou hadst no right to *be* at all," etc., etc.

unending, this is what men will always do. The history of evangelical theology, with its conviction of sin, its self-despair, and its abandonment of salvation by works, is the deepest of possible examples, but we meet others in every walk of life. There is the strangest lightness about the heart when one's nothingness in a particular line is once accepted in good faith. *All* is not bitterness in the lot of the lover sent away by the final inexorable 'No.' Many Bostonians, *crede experto* (and inhabitants of other cities, too, I fear), would be happier women and men to-day, if they could once for all abandon the notion of keeping up a Musical Self, and without shame let people hear them call a symphony a nuisance. How pleasant is the day when we give up striving to be young,—or slender! Thank God! we say, *those* illusions are gone. Everything added to the Self is a burden as well as a pride. A certain man who lost every penny during our civil war went and actually rolled in the dust, saying he had not felt so free and happy since he was born.

Once more, then, our self-feeling is in our power. As Carlyle says: "Make thy claim of wages a zero, then; thou hast the world under thy feet. Well did the wisest of our time write: 'It is only with *renunciation* that life, properly speaking, can be said to begin.' "

Neither threats nor pleadings can move a man unless they touch some one of his potential or actual selves. Only thus can we, as a rule, get a 'purchase' on another's will. The first care of diplomatists and monarchs and all who wish to rule or influence is, accordingly, to find out their victim's strongest principle of self-regard, so as to make that the fulcrum of all appeals. But if a man has given up those things which are subject to foreign fate, and ceased to regard them as parts of himself at all, we are well-nigh powerless over him. The Stoic receipt for contentment was to dispossess yourself in advance of all that was out of your own power,—then fortune's shocks might rain down unfelt. Epictetus exhorts us, by thus narrowing and at the same time solidifying our Self to make it invulnerable: "I must die; well, but must I die groaning too? . . . I will speak what appears to be right, and if the despot says, 'Then I will put you to death,' I will reply, 'When did I ever tell you that I was immortal? You will do your part, and I mine: it is yours to kill and mine to die intrepid; yours to banish, mine to depart untroubled.' . . . How do we act in a voyage? We choose the pilot, the sailors, the hour. Afterwards comes a storm. What have I to care for? My part is performed. This matter belongs to the pilot. But the ship is sinking; what then have I to do? That which alone I can do; submit to being drowned, without fear, without clamor, or accusing of God; but as one who knows, that what is born, must likewise die."[9]

This Stoic fashion, though efficacious and heroic enough in its place and time, is, it must be confessed, only possible as an habitual mood of the soul to narrow and unsympathetic characters. It proceeds altogether by exclusion. If I am a Stoic, the goods I cannot appropriate cease to be *my* goods, and the temptation lies very near to deny that they are goods at all. We find this mode of protecting the Self by exclusion and denial very common among people who are in other respects not Stoics. All narrow people *intrench* their Me, they *retract* it,—from the region of what they cannot securely possess. People who don't resemble them, or who treat them with indifference, people over whom they gain no influence, are people on whose existence, however meritorious it may intrinsically be, they look with chill negation, if not with positive hate. Who will not be mine I will exclude from existence altogether; that is, as far as I can make it so, such people shall be as if they were not.[10] Thus may a certain absoluteness and definiteness in the outline of my Me console me for the smallness of its content.

Sympathetic people, on the contrary, proceed by the entirely opposite way of expansion and inclusion. The outline of their self often gets uncertain enough, but for this the spread of its content more than atones. *Nil humani a me alienum.* Let them despise this little person of mine, and treat me like a dog, *I* shall not negate *them* so long as I have a soul in my body. They are realities as much as I am. What positive good is in them shall be mine too, etc., etc. The magnanimity of these expansive natures is often touching indeed. Such persons can feel a sort of delicate rapture in thinking that, however sick, ill-favored, mean-conditioned, and generally forsaken they may be, they yet are integral parts of the whole of this brave world, have a fellow's share in the strength of the dray-horses, the happiness of the young people, the wisdom of the wise ones, and are not altogether without part or lot in the

[9] T. W. Higginson's translation (1866), pp. 6, 10, 105.

[10] "The usual mode of lessening the shock of disappointment or disesteem is to contract, if possible, a low estimate of the persons that inflict it. This is our remedy for the unjust censures of party spirit, as well as of personal malignity." (Bain: *Emotions and the Will*, p. 209.)

good fortunes of the Vanderbilts and the Hohenzollerns themselves. Thus either by negating or by embracing, the Ego may seek to establish itself in reality. He who, with Marcus Aurelius, can truly say, "O Universe, I wish all that thou wishest," has a self from which every trace of negativeness and obstructiveness has been removed—no wind can blow except to fill its sails.

A tolerably unanimous opinion ranges the different selves of which a man may be 'seized and possessed,' and the consequent different orders of his self-regard, in an *hierarchical scale, with the bodily Self at the bottom, the spiritual Self at top, and the extracorporeal material selves and the various social selves between.* Our merely natural self-seeking would lead us to aggrandize all these selves; we give up deliberately only those among them which we find we cannot keep. Our unselfishness is thus apt to be a 'virtue of necessity'; and it is not without all show of reason that cynics quote the fable of the fox and the grapes in describing our progress therein. But this is the moral education of the race; and if we agree in the result that on the whole the selves we can keep are the intrinsically best, we need not complain of being led to the knowledge of their superior worth in such a tortuous way.

Of course this is not the only way in which we learn to subordinate our lower selves to our higher. A direct ethical judgment unquestionably also plays its part, and last, not least, we apply to our own persons judgments originally called forth by the acts of others. It is one of the strangest laws of our nature that many things which we are well satisfied with in ourselves disgust us when seen in others. With another man's bodily 'hoggishness' hardly anyone has any sympathy;—almost as little with his cupidity, his social vanity and eagerness, his jealousy, his despotism, and his pride. Left absolutely to myself I should probably allow all these spontaneous tendencies to luxuriate in me unchecked, and it would be long before I formed a distinct notion of the order of their subordination. But having constantly to pass judgment on my associates, I come ere long to see, as Herr Horwicz says, my own lusts in the mirror of the lusts of others, and to *think* about them in a very different way from that in which I simply *feel*. Of course, the moral generalities which from childhood have been instilled into me accelerate enormously the advent of this reflective judgment on myself.

So it comes to pass that, as aforesaid, men have arranged the various selves which they may seek in an hierarchical scale according to their worth. A certain amount of bodily selfishness is required as a basis for all the other selves. But too much sensuality is despised, or at best condoned on account of the other qualities of the individual. The wider material selves are regarded as higher than the immediate body. He is esteemed a poor creature who is unable to forego a little meat and drink and warmth and sleep for the sake of getting on in the world. The social self as a whole, again, ranks higher than the material self as a whole. We must care more for our honor, our friends, our human ties, than for a sound skin or wealth. And the spiritual self is so supremely precious that, rather than lose it, a man ought to be willing to give up friends and good fame, and property, and life itself.

In each kind of self, material, social, and spiritual, men distinguish between the immediate and actual, and the remote and potential, between the narrower and the wider view, to the detriment of the former and advantage of the latter. One must forego a present bodily enjoyment for the sake of one's general health; one must abandon the dollar in the hand for the sake of the hundred dollars to come; one must make an enemy of his present interlocutor if thereby one makes friends of a more valued circle; one must go without learning and grace, and wit, the better to compass one's soul's salvation.

Of all these wider, more potential selves, *the potential social self* is the most interesting, by reason of certain apparent paradoxes to which it leads in conduct, and by reason of its connection with our moral and religious life. When for motives of honor and conscience I brave the condemnation of my own family, club, and 'set'; when, as a protestant, I turn catholic; as a catholic, freethinker; as a 'regular practitioner,' homœopath, or what not, I am always inwardly strengthened in my course and steeled against the loss of my actual social self by the thought of other and better *possible* social judges than those whose verdict goes against me now. The ideal social self which I thus seek in appealing to their decision may be very remote: it may be represented as barely possible. I may not hope for its realization during my lifetime; I may even expect the future generations, which would approve me if they knew me, to know nothing about me when I am dead and gone. Yet still the emotion that beckons me on is indubitably the pursuit of an ideal social self, of a self that is at least *worthy* of approving recognition by the highest *possible* judging companion, if such companion there be.[11] This self is the true, the intimate, the ultimate, the permanent Me which I seek. This judge is God, the Absolute Mind, the 'Great Companion.' We hear, in these days of scientific enlightenment, a great deal of discussion about the efficacy of prayer; and many reasons are given us why we should not pray, whilst others are given us why we should. But in all this very little is said of the reason why we *do* pray, which is simply that we cannot *help* praying. It seems probable that, in spite of all that 'science' may do to the contrary, men will continue to pray to the end of time, unless their mental nature changes in a manner which nothing we know should lead us to expect. The impulse to pray is a necessary consequence of the fact that whilst the innermost of the empirical selves of a man is a Self of the *social* sort, it yet can find its only adequate *Socius* in an ideal world.

All progress in the social Self is the substitution of higher tribunals for lower; this ideal tribunal is the highest; and most men, either continually or occasionally, carry a reference to it in their breast. The humblest outcast on this earth can feel himself to be real and valid by means of this higher recognition. And, on the other hand, for most of us, a world with no such inner refuge when the outer social self failed and dropped from us would be the abyss of horror. I say 'for most of us,' because it is probable that individuals differ a good deal in the degree in which they are haunted by this sense of an ideal spectator. It is a much more essential part of the consciousness of some men than of others. Those who have the most of it are possibly the most *religious* men. But I am sure that even those who say they are altogether without it deceive themselves, and really have it in some degree. Only a non-gregarious animal could be completely without it. Probably no one can make sacrifices for 'right,' without to some degree personifying the principle of right for which the sacrifice is made, and ex-

[11] It must be observed that the qualities of the Self thus ideally constituted are all qualities approved by my actual fellows in the first instance; and that my reason for now appealing from their verdict to that of the ideal judge lies in some outward peculiarity of the immediate case. What once was admired in me as courage has now become in the eyes of men 'impertinence'; what was fortitude is obstinacy; what was fidelity is now fanaticism. The ideal judge alone, I now believe, can read my qualities, my willingnesses, my powers, for what they truly are. My fellows, misled by interest and prejudice, have gone astray.

pecting thanks from it. *Complete* social unselfishness, in other words, can hardly exist; *complete* social suicide hardly occur to a man's mind. Even such texts as Job's, "Though He slay me, yet will I trust in Him," or Marcus Aurelius's, "If gods hate me and my children, there is a reason for it," can least of all be cited to prove the contrary. For beyond all doubt Job revelled in the thought of Jehovah's recognition of the worship after the slaying should have been done; and the Roman emperor felt sure the Absolute Reason would not be all indifferent to his acquiescence in the gods' dislike. The old test of piety, "Are you willing to be damned for the glory of God?" was probably never answered in the affirmative except by those who felt sure in their heart of hearts that God would 'credit' them with their willingness, and set more store by them thus than if in His unfathomable scheme He had not damned them at all.

All this about the impossibility of suicide is said on the supposition of *positive* motives. When possessed by the emotion of *fear*, however, we are in a *negative* state of mind; that is, our desire is limited to the mere banishing of something, without regard to what shall take its place. In this state of mind there can unquestionably be genuine thoughts, and genuine acts, of suicide, spiritual and social, as well as bodily. Anything, *anything*, at such times, so as to escape and not to be! But such conditions of suicidal frenzy are pathological in their nature and run dead against everything that is regular in the life of the Self in man.

WHAT SELF IS LOVED IN 'SELF-LOVE'?

We must now try to interpret the facts of self-love and self-seeking a little more delicately from within.

A man in whom self-seeking of any sort is largely developed is said to be selfish.[12] He is on the other hand called unselfish if he

[12] The *kind* of selfishness varies with the self that is sought. If it be the mere bodily self; if a man grabs the best food, the warm corner, the vacant seat; if he makes room for no one, spits about, and belches in our faces,—we call it hoggishness. If it be the social self, in the form of popularity or influence, for which he is greedy, he may in material ways subordinate himself to others as the best means to his end; and in this case he is very apt to pass for a disinterested man. If it be the 'other-worldly' self which he seeks, and if he seeks it ascetically,—even though he would rather see all mankind damned eternally than lose his individual soul,—'saintliness' will probably be the name by which his selfishness will be called.

shows consideration for the interests of other selves than his own. Now what is the intimate *nature* of the selfish emotion in him? and what is the primary *object* of its regard? We have described him pursuing and fostering as his self first one set of things and then another; we have seen the same set of facts gain or lose interest in his eyes, leave him indifferent, or fill him either with triumph or despair according as he made pretensions to appropriate them, treated them as if they were potentially or actually parts of himself, or not. We know how little it matters to us whether *some* man, a man taken at large and in the abstract, prove a failure or succeed in life,—he may be hanged for aught we care,—but we know the utter momentousness and terribleness of the alternative when the man is the one whose name we ourselves bear. *I* must not be a failure, is the very loudest of the voices that clamor in each of our breasts: let fail who may, *I* at least must succeed. Now the first conclusion which these facts suggest is that each of us is animated by a *direct feeling of regard for his own pure principle of individual existence*, whatever that may be, taken merely as such. It appears as if all our concrete manifestations of selfishness might be the conclusions of as many syllogisms, each with this principle as the subject of its major premise, thus: Whatever is me is precious; this is me; therefore this is precious; whatever is mine must not fail; this is mine; therefore this must not fail, etc. It appears, I say, as if this principle inoculated all it touched with its own intimate quality of worth; as if, previous to the touching, everything might be matter of indifference, and nothing interesting in its own right; as if my regard for my own body even were an interest not simply in this body, but in this body only so far as it is mine.

But what is this abstract numerical principle of identity, this 'Number One' within me, for which, according to proverbial philosophy, I am supposed to keep so constant a 'lookout'? Is it the inner nucleus of my spiritual self, that collection of obscurely felt 'adjustments,' *plus* perhaps that still more obscurely perceived subjectivity as such, of which we recently spoke? Or is it perhaps the concrete stream of my thought in its entirety, or some one section of the same? Or may it be the indivisible Soul-Substance, in which, according to the orthodox tradition, my faculties inhere? Or, finally, can it be the mere pronoun I? Surely it is none of these things, that self for which I feel such hot regard. Though all of them together were put within me, I should still be cold, and fail to exhibit anything worthy of the name of selfishness or of devotion to 'Number One.' To have a self that I can *care for,* nature must first present me with some *object* interesting enough to make me instinctively wish to appropriate it for its *own* sake, and out of it to manufacture one of those material, social, or spiritual selves, which we have already passed in review. We shall find that all the facts of rivalry and substitution that have so struck us, all the shiftings and expansions and contractions of the sphere of what shall be considered me and mine, are but results of the fact that certain *things* appeal to primitive and instinctive impulses of our nature, and that we follow their destinies with an excitement that owes nothing to a reflective source. These objects our consciousness treats as the primordial constituents of its Me. Whatever other objects, whether by association with the fate of these, or in any other way, come to be followed with the same sort of interest, form our remoter and more secondary self. *The words* ME, *then, and* SELF, *so far as they arouse feeling and connote emotional worth, are* OBJECTIVE *designations, meaning* ALL THE THINGS *which have the power to produce in a stream of consciousness excitement of a certain peculiar sort.* Let us try to justify this proposition in detail.

The most palpable selfishness of a man is his bodily selfishness; and his most palpable self is the body to which that selfishness relates. Now I say that he identifies himself with this body because he loves *it,* and that he does not love it because he finds it to be identified with himself. Reverting to natural history-psychology will help us to see the truth of this. In the chapter on Instincts we shall learn that every creature has a certain selective interest in certain portions of the world, and that this interest is as often connate as acquired. Our *interest in things* means the attention and emotion which the thought of them will excite, and the actions which their presence will evoke. Thus every species is particularly interested in its own prey or food, its own enemies, its own sexual mates, and its own young. These things fascinate by their intrinsic power to do so; they are cared for for their own sakes.

Well, it stands not in the least otherwise with our bodies. They too are percepts in our objective field—they are simply the most interesting percepts there. What happens to them excites in us emotions and tendencies to action more energetic and habitual than any which are excited by other portions of the 'field.' What my comrades call my bodily selfishness or self-love, is nothing but the sum of all the outer acts which this interest in my body spontaneously draws from me. My 'selfishness' is here but a descriptive name for grouping together the outward symptoms which I show. When I am led by self-love to keep my seat whilst ladies stand, or to grab something first and cut out my neighbor, what I really love is the comfortable seat, is the thing itself which I grab. I love them primarily, as the mother loves her babe, or a generous man an heroic deed. Wherever, as here, self-seeking is the outcome of simple instinctive propensity, it is but a name for certain reflex acts. Something rivets my attention fatally, and fatally provokes the 'selfish' response. Could an automaton be so skilfully constructed as to ape these acts, it would be called selfish as properly as I. It is true that I am no automaton, but a thinker. But my thoughts, like my acts, are here concerned only with the outward things. They need neither know nor care for any pure principle within. In fact the more utterly 'selfish' I am in this primitive way, the more blindly absorbed my thought will be in the objects and impulses of my lusts, and the more devoid of any inward looking glance. A baby, whose consciousness of the pure Ego, of himself as a thinker, is not usually supposed developed, is, in this way, as some German has said, '*der vollendeteste Egoist.*' His corporeal person, and what ministers to its needs, are the only self he can possibly be said to love. His so-called self-love is but a name for his insensibility to all but this one set of things. It may be that he needs a pure principle of subjectivity, a soul or pure Ego (he certainly needs a stream of thought) to make him sensible at all to anything, to make him discriminate and love *überhaupt*,—how that may be, we shall see ere long; but this pure Ego, which would then be the *condition* of his loving, need no more be the *object* of his love than it need be the object of his thought. If his interests lay altogether in other bodies than his own, if all his instincts were altruistic and all his acts suicidal, still he would need a principle of *consciousness* just as he does now. Such a principle cannot then be the principle of his bodily *selfishness* any more than it is the principle of any other tendency he may show.

So much for the bodily self-love. But my *social* self-love, my interest in the images other men have framed of me, is also an interest in a set of objects external to my thought. These thoughts in other men's minds are out of my mind and 'ejective' to me. They come and go, and grow and dwindle, and I am puffed up with pride, or blush with shame, at the result, just as at my success or failure in the pursuit of a material thing. So that here again, just as in the former case, the pure principle seems out of the game as an *object* of regard, and present only as the general form or condition under which the regard and the thinking go on in me at all.

But, it will immediately be objected, this is giving a mutilated account of the facts. Those images of me in the minds of other men are, it is true, things outside of me, whose changes I perceive just as I perceive any other outward change. But the pride and shame which I feel are not concerned merely with *those* changes. I feel as if something else had changed too, when I perceive my image in your mind to have changed for the worse, something in me to which that image belongs, and which a moment ago I felt inside of me, big and strong and lusty, but now weak, contracted, and collapsed. Is not this latter change the change I feel the shame about? Is not the condition of this thing inside of me the proper object of my egoistic concern, of my self-regard? And is it not, after all, my pure Ego, my bare numerical principle of distinction from other men, and no empirical part of me at all?

No, it is no such pure principle, it is simply my total empirical selfhood again, my historic Me, a collection of objective facts, to which the depreciated image in your mind 'belongs.' In what capacity is it that I claim and demand a respectful greeting from you instead of this expression of disdain? It is not as being a bare I that I claim it; it is as being an I who has always been treated with respect, who belongs to a certain family and 'set,' who has certain powers, possessions, and public functions, sensibilities, duties, and purposes, and merits and deserts. All this is what your disdain negates and contradicts; this is 'the thing inside of me' whose changed treatment I feel the shame about; this is what was lusty, and now, in consequence of your conduct, is collapsed; and this certainly is an empirical objective thing. Indeed, the thing that is felt modified and changed for the worse during my feeling of shame is often more concrete even than this,—it is simply my bodily person, in which your conduct immediately and without any reflection at all on my part works those muscular, glandular, and vascular changes which together make up the 'expression' of shame. In this instinctive, reflex sort of shame, the body is just as much the entire vehicle of the self-feeling as, in the coarser cases which we first took up, it was the vehicle of the self-seeking. As, in simple 'hoggishness,' a succulent morsel gives rise, by the reflex mechanism, to behavior which the bystanders find 'greedy,' and consider to flow from a certain sort of 'self-regard'; so here your disdain gives rise, by a mechanism quite as reflex and immediate, to another sort of behavior, which the bystanders call 'shame-faced' and which they consider due to another kind of self-regard. But in both cases there may be no particular self *regarded* at all by the mind; and the name self-regard may be only a descriptive title imposed from without the reflex acts themselves, and the feelings that immediately result from their discharge.

After the bodily and social selves come the spiritual. But which of my spiritual selves do I really care for? My Soul-substance? my 'transcendental Ego, or Thinker'? my pronoun I? my subjectivity as such? my nucleus of cephalic adjustments? or my more phenomenal and perishable powers, my loves and hates, willingnesses and sensibilities, and the like? Surely the latter. But they, relatively to the central principle, whatever it may be, are external and objective. They come and go, and it remains—"so shakes the magnet, and so stands the pole." It may indeed have to be there for them to be loved, but being there is not identical with being loved itself.

To sum up, then, *we see no reason to suppose that 'self-love' is primarily, or secondarily, or ever, love for one's mere principle of conscious identity*. It is always love for something which, as compared with that principle, is superficial, transient, liable to be taken up or dropped at will.

And zoological psychology again comes to the aid of our understanding and shows us that this must needs be so. In fact, in answering the question what things it is that a man loves in his self-love, we have implicitly answered the farther question, of why he loves them.

Unless his consciousness were something more than cognitive, unless it experienced a partiality for certain of the objects, which, in succession, occupy its ken, it could not long maintain itself in existence; for, by an inscrutable necessity, each human mind's appearance on this earth is conditioned upon the integrity of the body with which it belongs, upon the treatment which that body gets from others, and upon the spiritual dispositions which use it as their tool, and lead it either towards longevity or to destruction. *Its own body, then, first of all, its friends next, and finally its spiritual dispositions,* MUST *be the supremely interesting* OBJECTS *for each human mind.* Each mind, to begin with, must have a certain minimum of selfishness in the shape of instincts of bodily self-seeking in order to exist. This minimum must be there as a basis for all farther conscious acts, whether of self-negation or of a selfishness more subtle still. All minds must have come, by the way of the survival of the fittest, if by no directer path, to take an intense interest in the bodies to which they are yoked, altogether apart from any interest in the pure Ego which they also possess.

And similarly with the images of their person in the minds of others. I should not be extant now had I not become sensitive to looks of approval or disapproval on the faces among which my life is cast. Looks of contempt cast on other persons need affect me in no such peculiar way. Were my mental life dependent exclusively on some other person's welfare, either directly or in an indirect way, then natural selection would unquestionably have brought it about that I should be as sensitive to the social vicissitudes of that other person as I now am to my own. Instead of being egoistic I should be spontaneously altruistic, then. But in this case, only partially realized in actual human conditions, though the self I empirically love would have changed, my pure Ego or Thinker would have to remain just what it is now.

My spiritual powers, again, must interest me more than those of other people, and for the same reason. I should not be here at all unless I had cultivated them and kept them from decay. And the same law which made me once care for them makes me care for them still.

My own body and what ministers to its needs are thus the primitive object, instinctively determined, of my egoistic interests. Other objects may become interesting derivatively through association with any of these things, either as means or as habitual concomitants; *and so in a thousand ways the primitive sphere of the egoistic emotions may enlarge* and change its boundaries.

This sort of interest is really the *meaning of the word 'my.'* Whatever has it is *eo ipso* a part of me. My child, my friend dies, and where he goes I feel that part of myself now is and evermore shall be:

> "For this losing is true dying;
> This is lordly man's down-lying;
> This his slow but sure reclining,
> Star by star his world resigning."

The fact remains, however, that certain special sorts of thing tend primordially to possess this interest, and form the *natural* me. But all these things are *objects*, properly so called, to the subject which does the thinking.[13] And this latter fact upsets at once the dictum of the old-fashioned sensationalist psychology, that altruistic passions and interests are contradictory to the nature of things, and that if they appear anywhere to exist, it must be as secondary products, resolvable at bottom into cases of selfishness, taught by experience a hypocritical disguise. If the zoological and evolutionary point of view is the true one, there is no reason why any object whatever *might* not arouse passion and interest as primitively and instinctively as any other, whether connected or not with the interests of the me. The phenomenon of passion is in origin and essence the same, whatever be the target upon which it is discharged; and what the target actually happens to be is solely a question of fact. I might conceivably be as much fascinated, and as primitively so, by the care of my neighbor's body as by the care of my own. The only check to such exuberant altruistic interests is natural selection, which would weed out such as were very harmful to the individual or to his tribe. Many such interests, however, remain unweeded out—the interest in the opposite sex, for example, which seems in mankind stronger than is called for by its utilitarian need; and alongside of them remain interests, like that in alcoholic intoxication, or in musical sounds, which, for aught we can see, are without any utility whatever. The sympathetic instincts and the egoistic ones are thus co-ordinate. They arise, so far as we can tell, on the same psychologic level. The only difference between them is, that the instincts called egoistic form much the larger mass.

The only author whom I know to have discussed the question whether the 'pure Ego,' *per se*, can be an object of regard, is Herr Horwicz, in his extremely able and acute *Psychologische Analysen*. He too says that all self-regard is regard for certain objective things. He disposes so well of one kind of objection that I must conclude by quoting a part of his own words:

First, the objection:

"The fact is indubitable that one's own children always pass for the prettiest and brightest, the wine from one's own cellar for the best—at

[13] Lotze: *Medicinische Psychologie*, 498–501; *Microcosmus*, bk. II, chap. V, §§ 3, 4.

least for its price,—one's own house and horses for the finest. With what tender admiration do we con over our own little deed of benevolence! our own frailties and misdemeanors, how ready we are to acquit ourselves for them, when we notice them at all, on the ground of 'extenuating circumstances'! How much more really comic are our own jokes than those of others, which, unlike ours, will not bear being repeated ten or twelve times over! How eloquent, striking, powerful, our own speeches are! How appropriate our own address! In short, how much more intelligent, soulful, better, is everything about us than in anyone else. The sad chapter of artists' and authors' conceit and vanity belongs here.

"The prevalence of this obvious preference which we feel for everything of our own is indeed striking. Does it not look as if our dear Ego must first lend its color and flavor to anything in order to make it please us? . . . Is it not the simplest explanation for all these phenomena, so consistent among themselves, to suppose that the Ego, the self, which forms the origin and centre of our *thinking* life, is at the same time the original and central object of our life of feeling, and the ground both of whatever special ideas and of whatever special feelings ensue?"

Herr Horwicz goes on to refer to what we have already noticed, that various things which disgust us in others do not disgust us at all in ourselves.

"To most of us even the bodily warmth of another, for example the chair warm from another's sitting, is felt unpleasantly, whereas there is nothing disagreeable in the warmth of the chair in which we have been sitting ourselves."

After some further remarks, he replies to these facts and reasonings as follows:

"We may with confidence affirm that our own possessions in most cases please us better [not because they are ours], but simply because we know them better, 'realize' them more intimately, feel them more deeply. We learn to appreciate what is ours in all its details and shadings, whilst the goods of others appear to us in coarse outlines and rude averages. Here are some examples: A piece of music which one plays one's self is heard and understood better than when it is played by another. We get more exactly all the details, penetrate more deeply into the musical thought. We may meanwhile perceive perfectly well that the other person is the better performer, and yet nevertheless—at times—get more enjoyment from our own playing because it brings the melody and harmony so much nearer home to us. This case may almost be taken as typical for the other cases of self-love. On close examination, we shall almost always find that a great part of our feeling about what is ours is due to the fact that we *live closer* to our own things, and so feel them more thoroughly and deeply. As a friend of mine was about to marry, he often bored me by the repeated and minute way in which he would discuss the details of his new household arrangements. I wondered that so intellectual a man should be so deeply interested in things of so external a nature. But as I entered, a few years later, the same condition myself, these matters acquired for me an entirely different interest, and it became my turn to turn them over and talk of them unceasingly. . . . The reason was simply this, that in the first instance I *understood* nothing of these things and their importance for domestic comfort, whilst in the latter case they came home to me with irresistible urgency, and vividly took possession of my fancy. So it is with many a one who mocks at decorations and titles, until he gains one himself. And this is also surely the reason why one's own portrait or reflection in the mirror is so peculiarly interesting a thing to contemplate . . . not on account of any absolute '*c'est moi*,' but just as with the music played by ourselves. What greets our eyes is what we know best, most deeply understand; because we ourselves have felt it and lived through it. We know what has ploughed these furrows, deepened these shadows, blanched this hair; and other faces may be handsomer, but none can speak to us or interest us like this."[14]

Moreover, this author goes on to show that our own things are *fuller* for us than those of others because of the memories they awaken and the practical hopes and expectations they arouse. This alone would emphasize them, apart from any value derived from their belonging to ourselves. We may conclude with him, then, that *an original central self-feeling can never explain the passionate warmth of our self-regarding emotions, which must, on the contrary, be addressed directly to special things less abstract and empty of content. To these things the name of 'self' may be given, or to our conduct towards them the name of 'selfishness,' but neither in the self nor the selfishness does the pure Thinker play the 'title-rôle.'*

Only one more point connected with our self-regard need be mentioned. We have spoken of it so far as active instinct or emotion. It remains to speak of it as cold *intellectual self-estimation.*

[14] *Psychologische Analysen auf physiologischer Grundlage,* Theil II, IIte Hälfte, § 11. The whole section ought to be read.

We may weigh our own Me in the balance of praise and blame as easily as we weigh other people,—though with difficulty quite as fairly. The *just* man is the one who can weigh himself impartially. Impartial weighing presupposes a rare faculty of abstraction from the vividness with which, as Herr Horwicz has pointed out, things known as intimately as our own possessions and performances appeal to our imagination; and an equally rare power of vividly representing the affairs of others. But, granting these rare powers, there is no reason why a man should not pass judgment on himself quite as objectively and well as on anyone else. No matter how he *feels* about himself, unduly elated or unduly depressed, he may still truly *know* his own worth by measuring it by the outward standard he applies to other men, and counteract the injustice of the feeling he cannot wholly escape. This self-measuring process has nothing to do with the instinctive self-regard we have hitherto been dealing with. Being merely one application of intellectual comparison, it need no longer detain us here. Please note again, however, how the pure Ego appears merely as the vehicle in which the estimation is carried on, the objects estimated being all of them facts of an empirical sort,[15] one's body, one's credit, one's fame,

[15] Professor Bain, in his chapter on "Emotions of Self," does scant justice to the primitive nature of a large part of our self-feeling, and seems to reduce it to reflective self-estimation of this sober intellectual sort, which certainly *most* of it is not. He says that when the attention is turned inward upon self as a Personality, "we are putting forth towards ourselves the kind of exercise that properly accompanies our contemplation of other persons. We are accustomed to scrutinize the actions and conduct of those about us, to set a higher *value* upon one man than upon another, by comparing the two; to *pity* one in distress; to feel *complacency* towards a particular individual; to *congratulate* a man on some good fortune, that it pleases us to see him gain; to *admire* greatness or excellence as displayed by any of our fellows. All these exercises are intrinsically social, like Love and Resentment; an isolated individual could never attain to them, nor exercise them. By what means then, through what fiction [!], can we turn round and play them off upon self? Or how comes it that we obtain any satisfaction by putting self in the place of the other party? Perhaps the simplest form of the reflected act is that expressed by Self-Worth and Self-Estimation; based and begun upon observation of the ways and conduct of our fellow-beings. We soon make comparisons among the individuals about us; we see that one is stronger and does more work than another, and in consequence, perhaps, receives more pay. We see one putting forth more kindness than another, and in consequence receiving more love. We see some individuals surpassing the rest in astonishing feats, and drawing after them the gaze and admiration of a crowd. We acquire a series of fixed associations towards persons so situated; favourable in the case of the superior, and unfavourable towards the inferior. To the strong and laborious man we attach an estimate of greater reward, and feel that to be in his place would be a happier lot than falls to others. Desiring as we do, from the primary motives of our being, to possess

one's intellectual ability, one's goodness, or whatever the case may be.

The empirical life of Self is divided, as below, into

	MATERIAL	SOCIAL	SPIRITUAL
SELF-SEEKING	Bodily Appetites and Instincts Love of Adornment, Foppery, Acquisitiveness, Constructiveness Love of Home, etc.	Desire to please, be noticed, admired, etc. Sociability, Emulation, Envy, Love, Pursuit of Honor, Ambition, etc.	Intellectual, Moral and Religious Aspiration, Conscientiousness
SELF-ESTIMATION	Personal Vanity, Modesty, etc. Pride of Wealth, Fear of Poverty	Social and Family Pride, Vainglory, Snobbery, Humility, Shame, etc.	Sense of Moral or Mental Superiority, Purity, etc. Sense of Inferiority or of Guilt

good things, and observing these to come by a man's superior exertions, we feel a respect for such exertion, and a wish that it might be ours. We know that we also put forth exertions for our share of good things; and on witnessing others, we are apt to be reminded of ourselves, and to make comparisons with ourselves; which comparisons derive their interest from the substantial consequences. Having thus once learned to look at other persons as performing labours, greater or less, and as realizing fruits to accord; being, moreover ourselves in all respects like our fellows; —we find it an exercise neither difficult nor unmeaning, to contemplate self as doing work and receiving the reward. . . . As we decide between one man and another,— which is worthier, . . . so we decide between self and all other men; being, however, in this decision under the bias of our own desires." A couple of pages farther on we read: "By the terms Self-complacency, Self-gratulation, is indicated a positive enjoyment in dwelling upon our own merits and belongings. As in the other modes, so here, the starting-point is the contemplation of excellence or pleasing qualities *in another person*, accompanied more or less with fondness or love." Self-pity is also regarded by Professor Bain, in this place, as an emotion diverted to ourselves from a more immediate object, "in a manner that we may term fictitious and unreal. Still, as we can view self in the light of another person, we can feel towards it the emotion of pity called forth by others in our situation."

This account of Professor Bain's is, it will be observed, a good specimen of the old-fashioned mode of explaining the several emotions as rapid calculations of results, and the transfer of feeling from one object to another, associated by contiguity or similarity with the first. Zoological evolutionism, which came up since Professor Bain first wrote, has made us see, on the contrary, that many emotions must be *primitively* aroused by special objects. None are more worthy of being ranked primitive than the self-gratulation and humiliation attendant on our own successes and failures in the main functions of life. We need no borrowed reflection for these feelings. Professor Bain's account applies to but that small fraction of our self-feeling which reflective criticism can add to, or subtract from, the total mass.—Lotze has some pages on the modifications of our self-regard by universal judgments, in *Microcosmus*, book v, chap. v, § 5.

THE PURE EGO

Having summed up in the above table the principal results of the chapter thus far, I have said all that need be said of the constituents of the phenomenal self, and of the nature of self-regard. Our decks are consequently cleared for the struggle with that pure principle of personal identity which has met us all along our preliminary exposition, but which we have always shied from and treated as a difficulty to be postponed. Ever since Hume's time, it has been justly regarded as the most puzzling puzzle with which psychology has to deal; and whatever view one may espouse, one has to hold his position against heavy odds. If, with the Spiritualists, one contend for a substantial soul, or transcendental principle of unity, one can give no positive account of what that may be. And if, with the Humians, one deny such a principle and say that the stream of passing thoughts is all, one runs against the entire common-sense of mankind, of which the belief in a distinct principle of selfhood seems an integral part. Whatever solution be adopted in the pages to come, we may as well make up our minds in advance that it will fail to satisfy the majority of those to whom it is addressed. The best way of approaching the matter will be to take up first—

The Sense of Personal Identity

In the last chapter it was stated in as radical a way as possible that the thoughts which we actually know to exist do not fly about loose, but seem each to belong to some one thinker and not to another. Each thought, out of a multitude of other thoughts of which it may think, is able to distinguish those which belong to its own Ego from those which do not. The former have a warmth and intimacy about them of which the latter are completely devoid, being merely conceived, in a cold and foreign fashion, and not appearing as blood-relatives, bringing their greetings to us from out of the past.

Now this consciousness of personal sameness may be treated either as a subjective phenomenon or as an objective deliverance, as a feeling, or as a truth. We may explain how one bit of thought can come to judge other bits to belong to the same Ego with itself; or we may criticise its judgment and decide how far it may tally with the nature of things.

As a mere subjective phenomenon the judgment presents no difficulty or mystery peculiar to itself. It belongs to the great class of judgments of sameness; and there is nothing more remarkable in making a judgment of sameness in the first person than in the second or the third. The intellectual operations seem essentially alike, whether I say 'I am the same,' or whether I say 'the pen is the same, as yesterday.' It is as easy to think this as to think the opposite and say 'neither I nor the pen is the same.'

This sort of *bringing of things together into the object of a single judgment* is of course essential to all thinking. The things are conjoined *in* the thought, whatever may be the relation in which they appear to the thought. The thinking them is *thinking* them together, even if only with the result of judging that they do not *belong* together. This sort of *subjective synthesis*, essential to knowledge as such (whenever it has a complex object), must not be confounded with *objective synthesis* or union instead of difference or disconnection, known among the things.[16] The subjective synthesis is involved in thought's mere existence. Even a really disconnected world could only be *known* to be such by having its parts temporarily united in the Object of some pulse of consciousness.[17]

The sense of personal identity is not, then, this mere synthetic form essential to all thought. It is the sense of a sameness perceived *by* thought and predicated of things *thought-about*. These things are a present self and a self of yesterday. The thought not only thinks them both, but thinks that they are identical. The psychologist, looking on and playing the critic, might prove the thought wrong, and show there was no real identity,—there might have

16 "Also nur dadurch, dass ich ein Mannigfaltiges gegebener Vorstellungen in *einem Bewusstsein* verbinden kann, ist es möglich, dass ich mir die *Identität des Bewusstseins* in diesen *Vorstellungen* selbst vorstelle, d. i. die analytische Einheit der Apperception ist nur unter der Voraussetzung irgend einer synthetischen möglich." In this passage (*Kritik der reinen Vernunft*, 2te Aufl., § 16) Kant calls by the names of analytic and synthetic apperception what we here mean by objective and subjective synthesis respectively. It were much to be desired that someone might invent a good pair of terms in which to record the distinction—those used in the text are certainly very bad, but Kant's seem to me still worse. 'Categorical unity' and 'transcendental synthesis' would also be good Kantian, but hardly good human, speech.

17 So that we might say, by a sort of bad pun, "only a connected world can be known as disconnected." I say bad pun, because the point of view shifts between the connectedness and the disconnectedness. The disconnectedness is of the realities known; the connectedness is of the knowledge of them; and reality and knowledge of it are, from the psychological point of view held fast to in these pages, two different facts.

been no yesterday, or, at any rate, no self of yesterday; or, if there were, the sameness predicated might not obtain, or might be predicated on insufficient grounds. In either case the personal identity would not exist as a *fact*; but it would exist as a *feeling* all the same; the consciousness of it by the thought would be there, and the psychologist would still have to analyze that, and show where its illusoriness lay. Let us now be the psychologist and see whether it be right or wrong when it says, *I am the same self that I was yesterday.*

We may immediately call it right and intelligible so far as it posits a past time with past thoughts or selves contained therein—these were data which we assumed at the outset of the book. Right also and intelligible so far as it thinks of a present self—that present self we have just studied in its various forms. The only question for us is as to what the consciousness may mean when it calls the present self the *same* with one of the past selves which it has in mind.

We spoke a moment since of warmth and intimacy. This leads us to the answer sought. For, whatever the thought we are criticising may think about its present self, that self comes to its acquaintance, or is actually felt, with warmth and intimacy. Of course this is the case with the *bodily* part of it; we feel the whole cubic mass of our body all the while, it gives us an unceasing sense of personal existence. Equally do we feel the inner 'nucleus of the spiritual self,' either in the shape of yon faint physiological adjustments, or (adopting the universal psychological belief), in that of the pure activity of our thought taking place as such. Our remoter spiritual, material, and social selves, so far as they are realized, come also with a glow and a warmth; for the thought of them infallibly brings some degree of organic emotion in the shape of quickened heart-beats, oppressed breathing, or some other alteration, even though it be a slight one, in the general bodily tone. The character of 'warmth,' then, in the present self, reduces itself to either of two things,—something in the feeling which we have of the thought itself, as thinking, or else the feeling of the body's actual existence at the moment,—or finally to both. We cannot realize our present self without simultaneously feeling one or other of these two things. Any other fact which brings these two things with it into consciousness will be thought with a warmth and an intimacy like those which cling to the present self.

Any *distant* self which fulfils this condition will be thought with such warmth and intimacy. But which distant selves *do* fulfil the condition, when represented?

Obviously those, and only those, which fulfilled it when they were alive. *Them* we shall imagine with the animal warmth upon them; to them may possibly cling the aroma, the echo of the thinking taken in the act. And by a natural consequence, we shall assimilate them to each other and to the warm and intimate self we now feel within us as we think, and separate them as a collection from whatever selves have not this mark, much as out of a herd of cattle let loose for the winter on some wide Western prairie the owner picks out and sorts together, when the time for the round-up comes in the spring, all the beasts on which he finds his own particular brand.

The various members of the collection thus set apart are felt to belong with each other whenever they are thought at all. The animal warmth, etc., is their herd-mark, the brand from which they can never more escape. It runs through them all like a thread through a chaplet and makes them into a whole, which we treat as a unit, no matter how much in other ways the parts may differ *inter se*. Add to this character the farther one that the distant selves appear to our thought as having for hours of time been *continuous* with each other, and the most recent ones of them continuous with the Self of the present moment, melting into it by slow degrees; and we get a still stronger bond of union. As we think we see an identical bodily thing when, in spite of changes of structure, it exists continuously before our eyes, or when, however interrupted its presence, its quality returns unchanged; so here we think we experience an identical *Self* when it appears to us in an analogous way. Continuity makes us unite what dissimilarity might otherwise separate; similarity makes us unite what discontinuity might hold apart. And thus it is, finally, that Peter, awakening in the same bed with Paul, and recalling what both had in mind before they went to sleep, reidentifies and appropriates the 'warm' ideas as his, and is never tempted to confuse them with those cold and pale-appearing ones which he ascribes to Paul. As well might he confound Paul's body, which he only sees, with his own body, which he sees but also feels. Each of us when he awakens says, Here's the same old self again, just as he says, Here's the same old bed, the same old room, the same old world.

The sense of our own personal identity, then, is exactly like any one of our other perceptions of sameness among phenomena. It is a conclusion grounded either on the resemblance in a fundamental respect, or on the continuity before the mind, of the phenomena compared.

And it must not be taken to mean more than these grounds warrant, or treated as a sort of metaphysical or absolute Unity in which all differences are overwhelmed. The past and present selves compared are the same just so far as they *are* the same, and no farther. A uniform feeling of 'warmth,' of bodily existence (or an equally uniform feeling of pure psychic energy?) pervades them all; and this is what gives them a *generic* unity, and makes them the same in *kind*. But this generic unity coexists with generic differences just as real as the unity. And if from the one point of view they are one self, from others they are as truly not one but many selves. And similarly of the attribute of continuity; it gives its own kind of unity to the self—that of mere connectedness, or unbrokenness, a perfectly definite phenomenal thing—but it gives not a jot or tittle more. And this unbrokenness in the stream of selves, like the unbrokenness in an exhibition of 'dissolving views,' in no wise implies any farther unity or contradicts any amount of plurality in other respects.

And accordingly we find that, where the resemblance and the continuity are no longer felt, the sense of personal identity goes too. We hear from our parents various anecdotes about our infant years, but we do not appropriate them as we do our own memories. Those breaches of decorum awaken no blush, those bright sayings no self-complacency. That child is a foreign creature with which our present self is no more identified in feeling than it is with some stranger's living child to-day. Why? Partly because great time-gaps break up all these early years—we cannot ascend to them by continuous memories; and partly because no representation of how the child *felt* comes up with the stories. We know what he said and did; but no sentiment of his little body, of his emotions, of his psychic strivings as they felt to him, comes up to contribute an element of warmth and intimacy to the narrative we hear, and the main bond of union with our present self thus disappears. It is the same with certain of our dimly-recollected experiences. We hardly know whether to appropriate them or to disown them as fancies, or things read or heard and not lived through. Their animal heat has evaporated; the feelings that accompanied them are so lacking in the recall, or so different from those we now enjoy, that no judgment of identity can be decisively cast.

Resemblance among the parts of a continuum of feelings (especially bodily feelings) experienced along with things widely different in all other regards, *thus constitutes the real and verifiable 'personal identity' which we feel.* There is no other identity than this in the 'stream' of subjective consciousness which we described in the last chapter. Its parts differ, but under all their differences they are knit in these two ways; and if either way of knitting disappears, the sense of unity departs. If a man wakes up some fine day unable to recall any of his past experiences, so that he has to learn his biography afresh, or if he only recalls the facts of it in a cold abstract way as things that he is sure once happened; or if, without this loss of memory, his bodily and spiritual habits all change during the night, each organ giving a different tone, and the act of thought becoming aware of itself in a different way; he *feels,* and he *says,* that he is a changed person. He disowns his former me, gives himself a new name, identifies his present life with nothing from out of the older time. Such cases are not rare in mental pathology; but, as we still have some reasoning to do, we had better give no concrete account of them until the end of the chapter.

This description of personal identity will be recognized by the instructed reader as the ordinary doctrine professed by the empirical school. Associationists in England and France, Herbartians in Germany, all describe the Self as an aggregate of which each part, as to its *being,* is a separate fact. So far so good, then; thus much is true whatever farther things may be true; and it is to the imperishable glory of Hume and Herbart and their successors to have taken so much of the meaning of personal identity out of the clouds and made of the Self an empirical and verifiable thing.

But in leaving the matter here, and saying that this sum of passing things is all, these writers have neglected certain more subtle aspects of the Unity of Consciousness, to which we next must turn.

Our recent simile of the herd of cattle will help us. It will be remembered that the beasts were brought together into one herd because their owner found on each of them his brand. The 'owner' symbolizes here that 'section' of consciousness, or pulse of thought, which we have all along represented as the vehicle of the judgment of identity; and the 'brand' symbolizes the characters of warmth and continuity, by reason of which the judgment is made. There is found a *self*-brand, just as there is found a herd-brand. Each brand, so far, is the mark, or cause of our knowing, that certain things belong-together. But if the brand is the *ratio cognoscendi* of the belonging, the belonging, in the case of the herd, is in turn the *ratio existendi* of the brand. No beast would be so branded unless he belonged to the owner of the herd. They are not his because they are branded; they are branded because they are his. So that it seems as if our description of the belonging-together of the various selves, as a belonging-together which is merely *represented*, in a later pulse of thought, had knocked the bottom out of the matter, and omitted the most characteristic one of all the features found in the herd—a feature which common-sense finds in the phenomenon of personal identity as well, and for our omission of which she will hold us to a strict account. For common-sense insists that the unity of all the selves is not a mere appearance of similarity or continuity, ascertained after the fact. She is sure that it involves a real belonging to a real Owner, to a pure spiritual entity of some kind. Relation to this entity is what makes the self's constituents stick together as they do for thought. The individual beasts do not stick together, for all that they wear the same brand. Each wanders with whatever accidental mates it finds. The herd's unity is only potential, its centre ideal, like the 'centre of gravity' in physics, until the herdsman or owner comes. He furnishes a real centre of accretion to which the beasts are driven and by which they are held. The beasts stick together by sticking severally to him. Just so, common-sense insists, there must be a real proprietor in the case of the selves, or else their actual accretion into a 'personal consciousness' would never have taken place. To the usual empiricist explanation of personal consciousness this is a formidable reproof, because all the individual thoughts and feelings which have succeeded each other 'up to date' are represented by ordinary Associationism as in some inscrutable way 'integrating' or gumming themselves together on their own account, and thus fusing into a stream. All the incomprehensibilities which in Chapter VI we saw to attach to the idea of things fusing without a *medium* apply to the empiricist description of personal identity.

But in our own account the medium is fully assigned, the herdsman is there, in the shape of something not among the things collected, but superior to them all, namely, the real, present onlooking, remembering, 'judging thought' or identifying 'section' of the stream. This is what collects,—'owns' some of the past facts which it surveys, and disowns the rest,—and so makes a unity that is actualized and anchored and does not merely float in the blue air of possibility. And the reality of such pulses of thought, with their function of knowing, it will be remembered that we did not seek to deduce or explain, but simply assumed them as the ultimate kind of fact that the psychologist must admit to exist.

But this assumption, though it yields much, still does not yield all that common-sense demands. The unity into which the Thought —as I shall for a time proceed to call, with a capital T, the present mental state—binds the individual past facts with each other and with itself, does not exist until the Thought is there. It is as if wild cattle were lassoed by a newly-created settler and then owned for the first time. But the essence of the matter to common-sense is that the past thoughts never were wild cattle, they were always owned. The Thought does not capture them, but as soon as it comes into existence it finds them already its own. How is this possible unless the Thought have a *substantial* identity with a former owner,—not a mere continuity or a resemblance, as in our account, but a *real unity*? Common-sense in fact would drive us to admit what we may for the moment call an Arch-Ego, dominating the entire stream of thought and all the selves that may be represented in it, as the ever self-same and changeless principle implied in their union. The 'Soul' of Metaphysics and the 'Transcendental Ego' of the Kantian Philosophy, are, as we shall soon see, but attempts to satisfy this urgent demand of common-sense. But, for a time at least, we can still express without any such hypotheses that appearance of never-lapsing ownership for which common-sense contends.

For how would it be if the Thought, the present judging Thought, instead of being in any way substantially or transcendentally identical with the former owner of the past self, merely inherited his 'title,' and thus stood as his legal representative now? It would then, if its birth coincided exactly with the death of another owner, *find* the past self already its own as soon as it found it at all, and the past self would thus never be wild, but always owned, by a title that never lapsed. We can imagine a long succession of herdsmen coming rapidly into possession of the same cattle by transmission of an original title by bequest. May not the 'title' of a collective self be passed from one Thought to another in some analogous way?

It is a patent fact of consciousness that a transmission like this actually occurs. Each pulse of cognitive consciousness, each Thought, dies away and is replaced by another. The other, among the things it knows, knows its own predecessor, and finding it 'warm,' in the way we have described, greets it, saying: "Thou art *mine,* and part of the same self with me." Each later Thought, knowing and including thus the Thoughts which went before, is the final receptacle—and appropriating them is the final owner—of all that they contain and own. Each Thought is thus born an owner, and dies owned, transmitting whatever it realized as its Self to its own later proprietor. As Kant says, it is as if elastic balls were to have not only motion but knowledge of it, and a first ball were to transmit both its motion and its consciousness to a second, which took both up into *its* consciousness and passed them to a third, until the last ball held all that the other balls had held, and realized it as its own. It is this trick which the nascent thought has of immediately taking up the expiring thought and 'adopting' it, which is the foundation of the appropriation of most of the remoter constituents of the self. Who owns the last self owns the self before the last, for what possesses the possessor possesses the possessed.

It is impossible to discover any *verifiable* features in personal identity which this sketch does not contain, impossible to imagine how any transcendent non-phenomenal sort of an Arch-Ego, were he there, could shape matters to any other result, or be known in time by any other fruit, than just this production of a stream of consciousness each 'section' of which should know, and knowing, hug to itself and adopt, all those that went before,—thus standing as the *representative* of the entire past stream; and which should similarly adopt the objects already adopted by any portion of this spiritual stream. Such standing-as-representative, and such adopting, are perfectly clear phenomenal relations. The Thought which, whilst it knows another Thought and the Object of that Other, appropriates the Other and the Object which the Other appropriated, is still a perfectly distinct phenomenon from that Other; it may hardly resemble it; it may be far removed from it in space and time.

The only point that is obscure is the *act of appropriation* itself. Already in enumerating the constituents of the self and their rivalry, I had to use the word appropriate. And the quick-witted reader probably noticed at the time, in hearing how one constituent was let drop and disowned and another one held fast to and espoused, that the phrase was meaningless unless the constituents were objects in the hands of something else. A thing cannot appropriate itself; it *is* itself; and still less can it disown itself. There must be an agent of the appropriating and disowning; but that agent we have already named. It is the Thought to whom the various 'constituents' are known. That Thought is a vehicle of choice as well as of cognition; and among the choices it makes are these appropriations, or repudiations, of its 'own.' But the Thought never is an object in its own hands, it never appropriates or disowns itself. It appropriates *to* itself, it is the actual focus of accretion, the hook from which the chain of past selves dangles, planted firmly in the Present, which alone passes for real, and thus keeping the chain from being a purely ideal thing. Anon the hook itself will drop into the past with all it carries, and then be treated as an object and appropriated by a new Thought in the new present which will serve as living hook in turn. The present moment of consciousness is thus, as Mr. Hodgson says, the darkest in the whole series. It may feel its own immediate existence—we have all along admitted the possibility of this, hard as it is by direct introspection to ascertain the fact—but nothing can be known *about* it till it be dead and gone. Its appropriations are therefore less to *itself* than to the most intimately felt *part of its present Object, the body, and the central adjustments,* which accompany the act of thinking, in the head. *These are the real nucleus of our personal identity,* and it is their actual existence, realized as a solid present fact, which makes us say 'as sure *as I exist,* those past facts were part of myself.' They are the kernel to which the *represented* parts of the Self are assimilated, accreted, and knit on; and even were Thought entirely unconscious of itself in the act of thinking, these 'warm' parts of its present object would be a firm basis on which the consciousness of personal identity would rest.[18] Such consciousness, then, as a psycho-

[18] Some subtle reader will object that the Thought cannot call any part of its Object 'I' and knit other parts on to it, without first knitting that part on to *Itself;* and that it cannot knit it on to Itself without knowing Itself;—so that our supposition (above, pp. 290–291) that the Thought may conceivably have no immediate knowledge

logic fact, can be fully described without supposing any other agent than a succession of perishing thoughts, endowed with the functions of appropriation and rejection, and of which some can know and appropriate or reject objects already known, appropriated, or rejected by the rest.

To illustrate by diagram, let A, B, and C stand for three succes-

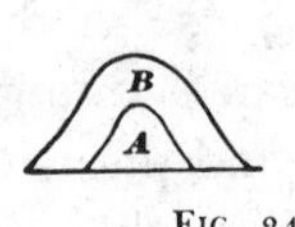

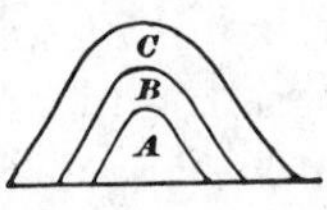

Fig. 34.

sive thoughts, each with its object inside of it. If B's object be A, and C's object be B; then A, B, and C would stand for three pulses in a consciousness of personal identity. Each pulse would *be* something different from the others; but B would know and adopt A, and C would know and adopt A and B. Three successive states of the same brain, on which each experience in passing leaves its mark, might very well engender thoughts differing from each other in just such a way as this.

The passing Thought then seems to be the Thinker; and though there *may* be another non-phenomenal Thinker behind that, so far we do not seem to need him to express the facts. But we cannot definitively make up our mind about him until we have heard the reasons that have historically been used to prove his reality.

THE PURE SELF OR INNER PRINCIPLE OF PERSONAL UNITY

To a brief survey of the theories of the Ego let us then next proceed. They are three in number, as follows:

---

of Itself is thus overthrown. To which the reply is that we must take care not to be duped by words. The words *I* and *me* signify nothing mysterious and unexampled—they are at bottom only names of *emphasis*; and Thought is always emphasizing something. Within a tract of space which it cognizes, it contrasts a *here* with a *there*; within a tract of time a *now* with a *then*: of a pair of things it calls one *this*, the other *that*. I and *thou*, I and *it*, are distinctions exactly on a par with these,—distinctions possible in an exclusively *objective* field of knowledge, the 'I' meaning for the Thought nothing but the bodily life which it momentarily feels. The sense of my bodily existence, however obscurely recognized as such, *may* then be the absolute original of my conscious selfhood, the fundamental perception that *I am*. All appropriations *may* be made *to* it, *by* a Thought not at the moment immediately cognized by itself. Whether these are not only logical possibilities but actual facts is something not yet dogmatically decided in the text.

1) The Spiritualist theory;
2) The Associationist theory;
3) The Transcendentalist theory.

The Theory of the Soul

In Chapter VI we were led ourselves to the spiritualist theory of the 'Soul,' as a means of escape from the unintelligibilities of mind-stuff 'integrating' with itself, and from the physiological improbability of a material monad, with thought attached to it, in the brain. But at the end of the chapter we said we should examine the 'Soul' critically in a later place, to see whether it had any other advantages as a theory over the simple phenomenal notion of a stream of thought accompanying a stream of cerebral activity, by a law yet unexplained.

The theory of the Soul is the theory of popular philosophy and of scholasticism, which is only popular philosophy made systematic. It declares that the principle of individuality within us must be *substantial*, for psychic phenomena are activities, and there can be no activity without a concrete agent. This substantial agent cannot be the brain but must be something *immaterial*; for its activity, thought, is both immaterial, and takes cognizance of immaterial things, and of material things in general and intelligible, as well as in particular and sensible ways,—all which powers are incompatible with the nature of matter, of which the brain is composed. Thought moreover is simple, whilst the activities of the brain are compounded of the elementary activities of each of its parts. Furthermore, thought is spontaneous or free, whilst all material activity is determined *ab extra*; and the will can turn itself against all corporeal goods and appetites, which would be impossible were it a corporeal function. For these objective reasons the principle of psychic life must be both immaterial and simple as well as substantial, must be what is called *a Soul*. The same consequence follows from subjective reasons. Our consciousness of personal identity assures us of our essential simplicity: the owner of the various constituents of the self, as we have seen them, the hypothetical Arch-Ego whom we provisionally conceived as possible, is a real entity of whose existence self-consciousness makes us directly aware. No material agent could thus turn round and grasp *itself*—material activities always grasp something else than the agent. And if a brain *could* grasp itself and be self-conscious, it would be conscious of itself *as* a brain and not as something of an altogether different kind. The Soul then exists as a simple spiritual substance in which the various psychic faculties, operations, and affections inhere.

If we ask what a Substance is, the only answer is that it is a self-existent being, or one which needs no other subject in which to inhere. At bottom its only positive determination is Being, and this is something whose meaning we all realize even though we find it hard to explain. The Soul is moreover an *individual* being, and if we ask what that is, we are told to look in upon our Self, and we shall learn by direct intuition better than through any abstract reply. Our direct perception of our own inward being is in fact by many deemed to be the original prototype out of which our notion of simple active substance in general is fashioned. The *consequences* of the simplicity and substantiality of the Soul are its incorruptibility and natural *immortality*—nothing but God's direct *fiat* can annihilate it—and its *responsibility* at all times for whatever it may have ever done.

This substantialist view of the soul was essentially the view of Plato and of Aristotle. It received its completely formal elaboration in the middle ages. It was believed in by Hobbes, Descartes, Locke, Leibnitz, Wolff, Berkeley, and is now defended by the entire modern dualistic or spiritualistic or common-sense school. Kant held to it while denying its fruitfulness as a premise for deducing consequences verifiable here below. Kant's successors, the absolute idealists, profess to have discarded it,—how that may be we shall inquire ere long. Let us make up our minds what to think of it ourselves.

It is at all events needless for expressing the actual subjective phenomena of consciousness as they appear. We have formulated them all without its aid, by the supposition of a stream of thoughts, each substantially different from the rest, but cognitive of the rest and 'appropriative' of each other's content. At least, if I have not already succeeded in making this plausible to the reader, I am hopeless of convincing him by anything I could add now. The unity, the identity, the individuality, and the immateriality that appear in the psychic life are thus accounted for as phenomenal and temporal facts exclusively, and with no need of reference to any more simple or substantial agent than the present Thought or 'section' of the stream. We have seen it to be single and unique in the sense of having no *separable* parts (above, p. 233 ff.)—perhaps that is the only kind of simplicity meant to be predicated of the soul. The present Thought also has being,—at least all believers in the Soul believe so—and if there be no other Being in which it 'inheres,' it ought itself to be a 'substance.' If *this* kind of simplicity and substantiality were all that is predicated of the Soul, then it might appear that we had been talking of the soul all along, without knowing it, when we treated the present Thought as an agent, an owner, and the like. But the Thought is a perishing and not an immortal or incorruptible thing. Its successors may continuously succeed to it, resemble it, and appropriate it, but they *are* not it, whereas the Soul-Substance is supposed to be a fixed unchanging thing. By the Soul is always meant something *behind* the present Thought, another kind of substance, existing on a non-phenomenal plane.

When we brought in the Soul at the end of Chapter VI, as an entity which the various brain-processes were supposed to affect simultaneously, and which responded to their combined influence by single pulses of its thought, it was to escape integrated mind-stuff on the one hand, and an improbable cerebral monad on the other. But when (as now, after all we have been through since that earlier passage) we take the two formulations, first of a brain to whose processes pulses of thought *simply* correspond, and second, of a brain to whose processes pulses of thought *in a Soul* correspond, and compare them together, we see that at bottom the second formulation is only a more roundabout way than the first, of expressing the same bald fact. That bald fact is that *when the brain acts, a thought occurs.* The spiritualistic formulation says that the brain-processes knock the thought, so to speak, out of a Soul which stands there to receive their influence. The simpler formulation says that the thought simply *comes.* But what positive meaning has the Soul, when scrutinized, but the *ground of possibility* of the thought? And what is the 'knocking' but the *determining of the possibility to actuality*? And what is this after all but giving a sort of concreted form to one's belief that the coming of the thought, when the brain-processes occur, has *some* sort of ground in the nature of things? If the word Soul be understood merely to express that claim, it is a good word to use. But if it be held to do more, to gratify the claim,—for instance, to connect rationally the thought which comes, with the processes which occur, and to mediate intelligibly between their two disparate natures,—then it is an illusory term. It is, in fact, with the word Soul as with the word Substance in general. To say that phenomena inhere in a Substance is at bottom only to record one's protest against the notion that the bare existence of the phenomena is the total truth. A phenomenon would not itself be, we insist, unless there were something *more* than the phenomenon. To the more we give the provisional name of Substance. So, in the present instance, we ought certainly to admit that there is more than the bare fact of coexistence of a passing thought with a passing brain-state. But we do not answer the question 'What is that more?' when we say that it is a 'Soul' which the brain-state affects. This kind of more *explains* nothing; and when we are once trying metaphysical explanations we are foolish not to go as far as we can. For my own part I confess that the moment I become metaphysical and try to define the more, I find the notion of some sort of an *anima mundi* thinking in all of us to be a more promising hypothesis, in spite of all its difficulties, than that of a lot of absolutely individual souls. Meanwhile, as *psychologists,* we need not be metaphysical at all. The phenomena are enough, the passing Thought itself is the only *verifiable* thinker, and its empirical connection with the brain-process is the ultimate known law.

To the other arguments which would prove the need of a soul, we may also turn a deaf ear. The argument from free-will can convince only those who believe in free-will; and even they will have to admit that spontaneity is just as possible, to say the least, in a temporary spiritual agent like our 'Thought' as in a permanent one like the supposed Soul. The same is true of the argument from the kinds of things cognized. Even if the brain could not cognize universals, immaterials, or its 'Self,' still the 'Thought' which we have relied upon in our account *is* not the brain, closely as it seems connected with it; and after all, if the brain could cognize at all, one does not well see why it might not cognize one sort of thing as well as another. The great difficulty is in seeing how a thing can cognize *anything.* This difficulty is not in the least removed by giving to the thing that cognizes the name of Soul. The Spiritualists do not deduce any of the properties of the mental life from otherwise known properties of the soul. They simply find various characters ready-made in the mental life, and these they clap into the

Soul, saying, "Lo! behold the source from whence they flow!" The merely verbal character of this 'explanation' is obvious. The Soul invoked, far from making the phenomena more intelligible, can only be made intelligible itself by borrowing their form,—it must be represented, if at all, as a transcendent stream of consciousness duplicating the one we know.

Altogether, the Soul is an outbirth of that sort of philosophizing whose great maxim, according to Dr. Hodgson, is: "Whatever you are *totally* ignorant of, assert to be the explanation of everything else."

Locke and Kant, whilst still believing in the soul, began the work of undermining the notion that we know anything about it. Most modern writers of the mitigated spiritualistic or dualistic philosophy—the Scotch school, as it is often called among us—are forward to proclaim this ignorance, and to attend exclusively to the verifiable phenomena of self-consciousness, as we have laid them down. Dr. Wayland, for example, begins his *Elements of Intellectual Philosophy* with the phrase "Of the essence of Mind we know nothing," and goes on: "All that we are able to affirm of it is, that it is *something* which perceives, reflects, remembers, imagines, and wills; but what that something *is*, which exerts these energies, we know not. It is only as we are conscious of the action of these energies that we are conscious of the existence of mind. It is only by the exertion of its own powers that the mind becomes cognizant of their existence. The cognizance of its powers, however, gives us no knowledge of that essence of which they are predicated. In these respects, our knowledge of mind is precisely analogous to our knowledge of matter." This analogy of our two ignorances is a favorite remark in the Scotch school. It is but a step to lump them together into a single ignorance, that of the 'Unknowable' to which anyone fond of superfluities in philosophy may accord the hospitality of his belief, if it so please him, but which anyone else may as freely ignore and reject.

The Soul-theory is, then, a complete superfluity, so far as accounting for the actually verified facts of conscious experience goes. So far, no one can be compelled to subscribe to it for definite scientific reasons. The case would rest here, and the reader be left free to make his choice, were it not for other demands of a more practical kind.

The first of these is *Immortality*, for which the simplicity and substantiality of the Soul seem to offer a solid guarantee. A 'stream' of thought, for aught that we see to be contained in its essence, may come to a full stop at any moment; but a simple substance is incorruptible and will, by its own inertia, persist in Being so long as the Creator does not by a direct miracle snuff it out. Unquestionably this is the stronghold of the spiritualistic belief,—as indeed the popular touchstone for all philosophies is the question, "What is their bearing on a future life?"

The Soul, however, when closely scrutinized, guarantees no immortality of a sort *we care for*. The enjoyment of the atom-like simplicity of their substance *in sæcula sæculorum* would not to most people seem a consummation devoutly to be wished. The substance must give rise to a stream of consciousness continuous with the present stream, in order to arouse our hope, but of this the mere persistence of the substance *per se* offers no guarantee. Moreover, in the general advance of our moral ideas, there has come to be something ridiculous in the way our forefathers had of grounding their hopes of immortality on the simplicity of their substance. The demand for immortality is nowadays essentially teleological. We believe ourselves immortal because we believe ourselves *fit* for immortality. A 'substance' ought surely to perish, we think, if not worthy to survive; and an insubstantial 'stream' to prolong itself provided it be worthy, if the nature of Things is organized in the rational way in which we trust it is. Substance or no substance, soul or 'stream,' what Lotze says of immortality is about all that human wisdom can say:

> "We have no other principle for deciding it than this general idealistic belief: that every created thing will continue whose continuance belongs to the meaning of the world, and so long as it does so belong; whilst everyone will pass away whose reality is justified only in a transitory phase of the world's course. That this principle admits of no further application in human hands need hardly be said. *We* surely know not the merits which may give to one being a claim on eternity, nor the defects which would cut others off."[19]

[19] *Metaphysik*, § 245 *fin.* This writer, who in his early work, the *Medicinische Psychologie*, was (to my reading) a strong defender of the Soul-Substance theory, has written in §§ 243–5 of his *Metaphysik* the most beautiful criticism of this theory which exists.

A second alleged necessity for a soul-substance is our forensic responsibility before God. Locke caused an uproar when he said that the unity of *consciousness* made a man the same *person*, whether supported by the same *substance* or no, and that God would not, in the great day, make a person answer for what he remembered nothing of. It was supposed scandalous that our forgetfulness might thus deprive God of the chance of certain retributions, which otherwise would have enhanced his 'glory.' This is certainly a good speculative ground for retaining the Soul—at least for those who demand a plenitude of retribution. The mere stream of consciousness, with its lapses of memory, cannot possibly be as 'responsible' as a soul which *is* at the judgment day all that it ever was. To modern readers, however, who are less insatiate for retribution than their grandfathers, this argument will hardly be as convincing as it seems once to have been.

One great use of the Soul has always been to account for, and at the same time to guarantee, the closed individuality of each personal consciousness. The thoughts of one soul must unite into one self, it was supposed, and must be eternally insulated from those of every other soul. But we have already begun to see that, although unity is the rule of each man's consciousness, yet in some individuals, at least, thoughts may split away from the others and form separate selves. As for insulation, it would be rash, in view of the phenomena of thought-transference, mesmeric influence and spirit-control, which are being alleged nowadays on better authority than ever before, to be too sure about that point either. The definitively closed nature of our personal consciousness is probably an average statistical resultant of many conditions, but not an elementary force or fact; so that, if one wishes to preserve the Soul, the less he draws his arguments from *that* quarter the better. So long as our self, on the whole, makes itself good and practically maintains itself as a closed individual, why, as Lotze says, is not that enough? And why is the *being*-an-individual in some inaccessible metaphysical way so much prouder an achievement?[20]

My final conclusion, then, about the substantial Soul is that it explains nothing and guarantees nothing. Its successive thoughts

[20] On the empirical and transcendental conceptions of the self's unity, see Lotze: *Metaphysic,* § 244.

are the only intelligible and verifiable things about it, and definitely to ascertain the correlations of these with brain-processes is as much as psychology can empirically do. From the metaphysical point of view, it is true that one may claim that the correlations have a rational ground; and if the word Soul could be taken to mean merely some such vague problematic ground, it would be unobjectionable. But the trouble is that it professes to give the ground in positive terms of a very dubiously credible sort. I therefore feel entirely free to discard the word Soul from the rest of this book. If I ever use it, it will be in the vaguest and most popular way. The reader who finds any comfort in the idea of the Soul, is, however, perfectly free to continue to believe in it; for our reasonings have not established the non-existence of the Soul; they have only proved its superfluity for scientific purposes.

The next theory of the pure Self to which we pass is

The Associationist Theory

Locke paved the way for it by the hypothesis he suggested of the same substance having two successive consciousnesses, or of the same consciousness being supported by more than one substance. He made his readers feel that the *important* unity of the Self was its verifiable and felt unity, and that a metaphysical or absolute unity would be insignificant, so long as a *consciousness* of diversity might be there.

Hume showed how great the consciousness of diversity actually was. In the famous chapter on Personal Identity, in his *Treatise of Human Nature*, he writes as follows:

"There are some philosophers, who imagine we are every moment intimately conscious of what we call our SELF; that we feel its existence and its continuance in existence; and are certain, beyond the evidence of a demonstration, both of its perfect identity and simplicity. . . . Unluckily all these positive assertions are contrary to that very experience, which is pleaded for them, nor have we any idea of *self*, after the manner it is here explain'd. . . . It must be some one impression, that gives rise to every real idea. . . . If any impression gives rise to the idea of self, that impression must continue invariably the same, thro' the whole course of our lives; since self is suppos'd to exist after that manner. But there is no impression constant and invariable. Pain and pleasure, grief and joy, passions and sensations succeed each other, and never all exist at the same time. . . . For my part, when I enter most intimately into what I call *myself*, I always stumble on some particular perception or other, of heat or cold, light or shade, love or hatred, pain or pleasure. I never can catch *myself* at any time without a perception, and never can observe any thing but the perception. When my perceptions are remov'd for any time, as by sound sleep; so long am I insensible of *myself*, and may truly be said not to exist. And were all my perceptions remov'd by death, and cou'd I neither think, nor feel, nor see, nor love, nor hate after the dissolution of my body, I shou'd be entirely annihilated, nor do I conceive what is farther requisite to make me a perfect non-entity. If any one, upon serious and unprejudic'd reflection, thinks he has a different notion of *himself*, I must confess I can reason no longer with him. All I can allow him is, that he may be in the right as well as I, and that we are essentially different in this particular. He may, perhaps, perceive something simple and continu'd, which he calls *himself*; tho' I am certain there is no such principle in me.

"But setting aside some metaphysicians of this kind, I may venture to affirm of the rest of mankind, that they are *nothing but a bundle or collection of different perceptions*, which succeed each other with an inconceivable rapidity, and are in a perpetual flux and movement. Our eyes cannot turn in their sockets without varying our perceptions. Our thought is still more variable than our sight; and all our other senses and faculties contribute to this change; nor is there any single power of the soul, which remains unalterably the same, perhaps for one moment. The mind is a kind of theatre, where several perceptions successively make their appearance; pass, re-pass, glide away, and mingle in an infinite variety of postures and situations. *There is properly no simplicity in it at one time, nor identity in different*; whatever natural propension we may have to imagine that simplicity and identity. The comparison of the theatre must not mislead us. They are the successive perceptions only, that constitute the mind; nor have we the most distant notion of the place, where these scenes are represented, or of the materials of which it is compos'd."

But Hume, after doing this good piece of introspective work, proceeds to pour out the child with the bath, and to fly to as great an extreme as the substantialist philosophers. As they say the Self is nothing but Unity, unity abstract and absolute, so Hume says it is nothing but Diversity, diversity abstract and absolute; whereas in truth it is that mixture of unity and diversity which we ourselves have already found so easy to pick apart. We found among the objects of the stream certain feelings that hardly changed, that stood out warm and vivid in the past just as the present feeling does now; and we found the present feeling to be the centre of accretion to which, *de proche en proche*, these other feelings are, *by the judging Thought*, felt to cling. Hume says nothing of the judging Thought; and he denies this thread of resemblance, this core of sameness running through the ingredients of the Self, to exist even as a phenomenal thing. To him there is no *tertium quid* between pure unity and pure separateness. A succession of ideas "connected by a close relation affords to an accurate view as perfect a notion of diversity as if there was *no manner of relation" at all.*

"All our distinct perceptions are distinct existences, and the mind never perceives any real connexion among distinct existences. Did our perceptions either inhere in something simple and individual, or *did the mind perceive some real connexion* among them, there wou'd be no difficulty in the case. For my part, I must plead the privilege of a sceptic, and confess, that this difficulty is too hard for my understanding. I pretend not, however, to pronounce it insuperable. Others, perhaps, . . . may discover some hypothesis, that will reconcile these contradictions."[21]

Hume is at bottom as much of a metaphysician as Thomas Aquinas. No wonder he can discover no 'hypothesis.' The unity of the parts of the stream is just as 'real' a connection as their diversity is a real separation; both connection and separation are ways in which the past thoughts appear to the present Thought;—unlike each other in respect of date and certain qualities—this is the separation; alike in other qualities, and continuous in time—this is the connection. In demanding a more 'real' connection than this obvious and verifiable likeness and continuity, Hume seeks 'the world behind the looking-glass,' and gives a striking example of that Absolutism which is the great disease of philosophic Thought.

The chain of distinct existences into which Hume thus chopped up our 'stream' was adopted by all of his successors as a complete inventory of the facts. The associationist Philosophy was founded. Somehow, out of 'ideas,' each separate, each ignorant of its mates, but sticking together and calling each other up according to certain laws, all the higher forms of consciousness were to be explained,

21 Appendix to book I of Hume's *Treatise of Human Nature*.

and among them the consciousness of our personal identity. The task was a hard one, in which what we called the psychologist's fallacy (p. 195 ff.) bore the brunt of the work. Two ideas, one of 'A,' succeeded by another of 'B,' were transmuted into a third idea of '*B after A*.' An idea from last year returning now was taken to be an idea *of last year*; two similar ideas stood for an *idea of similarity*, and the like; palpable confusions, in which certain facts *about* the ideas, possible only to an outside knower of them, were put into the place of the ideas' own proper and limited deliverance and content. Out of such recurrences and resemblances in a series of discrete ideas and feelings a knowledge was somehow supposed to be engendered in each feeling that it *was* recurrent and resembling, and that it helped to form a series to whose unity the name *I* came to be joined. In the same way, substantially, Herbart,[22] in Germany, tried to show how a conflict of ideas would fuse into a *manner of representing itself* for which *I* was the consecrated name.[23]

The defect of all these attempts is that the conclusion asserted to follow from certain premises is by no means rationally involved in the premises. A feeling of any kind, if it simply *returns*, ought to be nothing else than what it was at first. If memory of previous existence and all sorts of other cognitive functions are attributed to it when it returns, it is no longer the same, but a widely different feeling, and ought to be so described. *We* have so described it with the greatest explicitness. We have said that feelings never do return. We have not pretended to *explain* this; we have recorded it as an empirically ascertained law, analogous to certain laws of brain-physiology; and, seeking to define the way in which new feelings do differ from the old, we have found them to be *cognizant* and *appropriative* of the old, whereas the old were always cognizant and appropriative of something else. Once more, this account pretended to be nothing more than a complete description of the facts. It explained them no more than the associationist account explains them. But the latter both assumes to explain them and in the same breath falsifies them, and for each reason stands condemned.

It is but just to say that the associationist writers as a rule seem

22 Herbart believed in the Soul, too; but for him the 'Self' of which we are 'conscious' is the empirical Self—not the soul.

23 Compare again the remarks on pp. 160–164 above.

to have a lurking bad conscience about the Self; and that although they are explicit enough about what it is, namely, a train of feelings or thoughts, they are very shy about openly tackling the problem of how it comes to be aware of itself. Neither Bain nor Spencer, for example, directly touches this problem. As a rule, associationist writers keep talking about 'the mind' and about what 'we' do; and so, smuggling in surreptitiously what they ought avowedly to have postulated in the form of a present 'judging Thought,' they either trade upon their reader's lack of discernment or are undiscerning themselves.

Mr. D. G. Thompson is the only associationist writer I know who perfectly escapes this confusion, and *postulates* openly what he needs. "All States of Consciousness," he says, "imply and postulate a subject Ego, whose substance is unknown and unknowable, to which [why not say *by* which?] States of Consciousness are referred as attributes but which in the process of reference becomes objectified and becomes itself an attribute of a subject Ego which lies still beyond, and which ever eludes cognition though ever postulated for cognition."[24] This is exactly our judging and remembering present 'Thought,' described in less simple terms.

After Mr. Thompson, M. Taine and the two Mills deserve credit for seeking to be as clear as they can. Taine tells us in the first volume of his *Intelligence* what the Ego *is*,—a continuous web of conscious events no more really distinct from each other[25] than rhomboids, triangles, and squares marked with chalk on a plank are really distinct, for the plank itself is one. In the second volume he says all these parts have a common character embedded in them, that of being *internal* [this is our character of 'warmness,' otherwise named]. This character is abstracted and isolated by a mental fiction, and is what we are *conscious of* as our self—'this stable *within* is what each of us calls *I* or *me*.' Obviously M. Taine forgets to tell us what this 'each of us' is, which suddenly starts up and performs the abstraction and 'calls' its product I or me. The character does not abstract *itself*. Taine means by 'each of us' merely the present 'judging Thought' with its memory and tendency to appropriate, but he does not name it distinctly enough, and lapses

24 *System of Psychology* (1884), vol. I, p. 114.

25 'Distinct only to *observation*,' he adds. To whose observation? the outside psychologist's, the Ego's, their own, or the plank's? *Darauf kommt es an!*

into the fiction that the entire series of thoughts, the entire 'plank,' is the reflecting psychologist.

James Mill, after defining Memory as a train of associated ideas beginning with that of my past self and ending with that of my present self, defines my Self as a train of ideas of which Memory declares the first to be continuously connected with the last. The successive associated ideas 'run, as it were, into a single point of consciousness.'[26] John Mill, annotating this account, says:

"The phenomenon of Self and that of Memory are merely two sides of the same fact, or two different modes of viewing the same fact. We may, as psychologists, set out from either of them, and refer the other to it. . . . But it is hardly allowable to do both. At least it must be said, that by doing so we explain neither. We only show that the two things are essentially the same; that my memory of having ascended Skiddaw on a given day, and my consciousness of being the same person who ascended Skiddaw on that day, are two modes of stating the same fact: a fact which psychology has as yet failed to resolve into anything more elementary. In analysing the complex phenomena of consciousness, we must come to something ultimate; and we seem to have reached two elements which have a good prima facie claim to that title. There is, first, . . . the difference between a fact, and the Thought of that fact: a distinction which we are able to cognize in the past, and which then constitutes Memory, and in the future, when it constitutes Expectation; but in neither case can we give any account of it except that it exists . . . . Secondly, in addition to this, and setting out from the belief . . . that the idea I now have was derived from a previous sensation . . . there is the further conviction that this sensation . . . was my own; that it happened to myself. In other words, I am aware of a long and uninterrupted succession of past feelings going as far back as memory reaches, and terminating with the sensations I have at the present moment, all of which are connected by an inexplicable tie, that distinguishes them not only from any succession or combination in mere thought, but also from the parallel successions of feelings which I believe, on satisfactory evidence, to have happened to each of the other beings, shaped like myself, whom I perceive around me. This succession of feelings, which I call my memory of the past, is that by which I distinguish my Self. Myself is the person who had that series of feelings, and I know nothing of myself, by direct knowledge, except that I had

[26] *Analysis,* etc., J. S. Mill's Edition, vol. I, p. 331. The 'as it were' is delightfully characteristic of the school.

them. But there is a bond of some sort among all the parts of the series, which makes me say that they were feelings of a person who was the same person throughout [according to us this is their 'warmth' and resemblance to the 'central spiritual self' now actually felt], and a different person from those who had any of the parallel successions of feelings; and this bond, to me, constitutes my Ego. Here, I think, the question must rest, until some psychologist succeeds better than any one has yet done in shewing a mode in which the analysis can be carried further."[27]

The reader must judge of our own success in carrying the analysis farther. The various distinctions we have made are all parts of an endeavor so to do. John Mill himself, in a later-written passage, so far from advancing in the line of analysis, seems to fall back upon something perilously near to the Soul. He says:

"The fact of recognising a sensation, . . . remembering that it has been felt before, is the simplest and most elementary fact of memory: and the *inexplicable tie* . . . which connects the present consciousness with the past one, of which it reminds me, is as near as I think we can get to a positive conception of Self. That there is something real in this tie, real as the sensations themselves, and not a mere product of the laws of thought without any fact corresponding to it, I hold to be indubitable. . . . This original element, . . . to which we cannot give any name but its own peculiar one without implying some false or ungrounded theory, is the Ego, or Self. As such, I ascribe a reality to the Ego—to my own Mind—different from that real existence as a Permanent Possibility, which is the only reality I acknowledge in Matter. . . . We are forced to apprehend every part of the series as linked with the other parts by *something in common*, which is not the feelings themselves, any more than the succession of the feelings is the feelings themselves: and as that which is the same in the first as in the second, in the second as in the third, in the third as in the fourth, and so on, must be the same in the first and in the fiftieth, this common element is a permanent element. But beyond this, we can affirm nothing of it except the states of consciousness themselves. The feelings or consciousnesses which belong or have belonged to it, and its possibilities of having more, are the only facts there are to be asserted of Self—the only positive attributes, except permanence, which we can ascribe to it."[28]

Mr. Mill's habitual method of philosophizing was to affirm boldly some general doctrine derived from his father, and then make

[27] J. Mill's *Analysis*, vol. II, p. 174.
[28] *Examination of Hamilton*, 4th ed., p. 262.

so many concessions of detail to its enemies as practically to abandon it altogether.[29] In this place the concessions amount, so far as

[29] His chapter on the Psychological Theory of Matter is a beautiful case in point, and his concessions there have become so celebrated that they must be quoted for the reader's benefit. He ends the chapter with these words (*loc. cit.*, p. 247): "The theory, therefore, which resolves Mind into a series of feelings, with a background of possibilities of feeling, can effectually withstand the most invidious of the arguments directed against it. But, groundless as are the extrinsic objections, the theory has intrinsic difficulties which we have not yet set forth, and which it seems to me beyond the power of metaphysical analysis to remove. . . . The thread of consciousness which composes the mind's phænomenal life, consists not only of present sensations, but likewise, in part, of memories and expectations. Now what are these? In themselves, they are present feelings, states of present consciousness, and in that respect not distinguished from sensations. They all, moreover, resemble some given sensations or feelings, of which we have previously had experience. But they are attended with the peculiarity, that each of them involves a belief in more than its own present existence. A sensation involves only this: but a remembrance of sensation, even if not referred to any particular date, involves the suggestion and belief that a sensation, of which it is a copy or representation, actually existed in the past: and an expectation involves the belief, more or less positive, that a sensation or other feeling to which it directly refers, will exist in the future. Nor can the phænomena involved in these two states of consciousness be adequately expressed, without saying that the belief they include is, that I myself formerly had, or that I myself, and no other, shall hereafter have, the sensations remembered or expected. The fact believed is, that the sensations did actually form, or will hereafter form, part of the self-same series of states, or thread of consciousness, of which the remembrance or expectation of those sensations is the part now present. If, therefore, we speak of the Mind as a series of feelings, we are obliged to complete the statement by calling it a series of feelings which is aware of itself as past and future; and we are reduced to the alternative of believing that the Mind, or Ego, is something different from any series of feelings, or possibilities of them, or of accepting the paradox that something which *ex hypothesi* is but a series of feelings, can be aware of itself as a series.

"The truth is, that we are here face to face with that final inexplicability, at which, as Sir W. Hamilton observes, we inevitably arrive when we reach ultimate facts; and in general, one mode of stating it only appears more incomprehensible than another, because the whole of human language is accommodated to the one, and is so incongruous with the other, that it cannot be expressed in any terms which do not deny its truth. The real stumbling block is perhaps not in any theory of the fact, but in the fact itself. The true incomprehensibility perhaps is, that something which has ceased, or is not yet in existence, can still be, in a manner, present: that a series of feelings, the infinitely greater part of which is past or future, can be gathered up, as it were, into a single present conception, accompanied by a belief of reality. I think, by far the wisest thing we can do, is to accept the inexplicable fact, without any theory of how it takes place; and when we are obliged to speak of it in terms which assume a theory, to use them with a reservation as to their meaning."

In a later place in the same book (p. 561) Mill, speaking of what may rightly be demanded of a theorist, says: "He is not entitled to frame a theory from one class of phænomena, extend it to another class which it does not fit, and excuse himself by saying that if we cannot make it fit, it is because ultimate facts are inexplicable." The class of phenomena which the associationist school takes to frame its theory of the

they are intelligible, to the admission of something very like the Soul. This 'inexplicable tie' which connects the feelings, this 'something in common' by which they are linked and which is not the passing feelings themselves, but something 'permanent,' of which we can 'affirm nothing' save its attributes and its permanence, what is it but metaphysical Substance come again to life? Much as one must respect the fairness of Mill's temper, quite as much must one regret his failure of acumen at this point. At bottom he makes the same blunder as Hume: the sensations *per se*, he thinks, have no 'tie.' The tie of resemblance and continuity which the remembering Thought finds among them is not a 'real tie' but 'a mere product of the laws of thought'; and the fact that the present Thought 'appropriates' them is also no real tie. But whereas Hume was contented to say that there might after all *be* no 'real tie,' Mill, unwilling to admit this possibility, is driven, like any scholastic, to place it in a non-phenomenal world.

John Mill's concessions may be regarded as the *definitive bankruptcy of the associationist description* of the consciousness of self, starting, as it does, with the best intentions, and dimly conscious of the path, but 'perplexed in the extreme' at last with the inadequacy of those 'simple feelings,' non-cognitive, non-transcendent of themselves, which were the only baggage it was willing to take along. One must *beg* memory, knowledge on the part of the feelings of something outside themselves. That granted, every other true thing follows naturally, and it is hard to go astray. The knowledge the present feeling has of the past ones is a real tie between them, so is their resemblance; so is their continuity; so is the one's 'appropriation' of the other: all are real ties, realized in the judging Thought of every moment, the only place where *disconnections* could be realized, did they exist. Hume and Mill both imply that a disconnection can be realized there, whilst a tie cannot. But the ties and the disconnections are exactly on a par, in this matter of self-consciousness. The way in which the present Thought ap-

---

Ego are feelings unaware of each other. The class of phenomena the Ego presents are feelings of which the later ones are intensely aware of those that went before. The two classes do not 'fit,' and no exercise of ingenuity can ever make them fit. No *shuffling* of unaware feelings can make them aware. To get the awareness we must openly beg it by postulating a new feeling which has it. This new feeling is no 'Theory' of the phenomena, but a simple statement of them; and as such I postulate in the text the present passing Thought as a psychic integer, with its knowledge of so much that has gone before.

propriates the past is a real way, so long as no other owner appropriates it in a more real way, and so long as the Thought has no grounds for repudiating it stronger than those which lead to its appropriation. But no other owner ever does in point of fact present himself for my past; and the grounds which I perceive for appropriating it—viz., continuity and resemblance with the present—outweigh those I perceive for disowning it—viz., distance in time. My present Thought stands thus in the plenitude of ownership of the train of my past selves, is owner not only *de facto*, but *de jure*, the most real owner there can be, and all without the supposition of any 'inexplicable tie,' but in a perfectly verifiable and phenomenal way.

Turn we now to what we may call

THE TRANSCENDENTALIST THEORY

which owes its origin to Kant. Kant's own statements are too lengthy and obscure for verbatim quotation here, so I must give their substance only. Kant starts, as I understand him, from a view of the *Object* essentially like our own description of it on p. 265 ff., that is, it is a system of things, qualities or facts in relation. "*Object* is that in the knowledge (Begriff) of which the Manifold of a given Perception is connected."[30] But whereas we simply begged the vehicle of this connected knowledge in the shape of what we call the present Thought, or section of the Stream of Consciousness (which we declared to be the ultimate fact for psychology), Kant denies this to be an ultimate fact and insists on analyzing it into a large number of distinct, though equally essential, elements. The 'Manifoldness' of the Object is due to Sensibility, which *per se* is chaotic, and the unity is due to the synthetic handling which this Manifold receives from the higher faculties of Intuition, Apprehension, Imagination, Understanding, and Apperception. It is the one essential spontaneity of the Understanding which, under these different names, brings unity into the manifold of sense.

"The Understanding *is*, in fact, nothing more than the faculty of binding together *a priori*, and of bringing the Manifold of given ideas under the unity of Apperception, which consequently is the supreme principle in all human knowledge" (§ 16).

30 *Kritik der reinen Vernunft*, 2te Aufl., § 17.

The material connected must be *given* by lower faculties to the Understanding, for the latter is not an intuitive faculty, but by nature 'empty.' And the bringing of this material 'under the unity of Apperception' is explained by Kant to mean the thinking it always so that, whatever its other determinations be, it may be known as *thought by me*.[31] Though this consciousness, that *I think it*, need not be at every moment explicitly realized, it is always *capable* of being realized. For if an object *incapable* of being combined with the idea of a thinker were there, how could it be known, how related to other objects, how form part of 'experience' at all?

The awareness that *I think* is therefore implied in all experience. No connected consciousness of anything without that of *Self* as its presupposition and 'transcendental' condition! All things, then, so far as they are intelligible at all, are so through combination with pure consciousness of *Self*, and apart from this, at least potential, combination nothing is knowable *to us* at all.

But this self, whose consciousness Kant thus established deductively as a *conditio sine quâ non* of experience, is in the same breath denied by him to have any positive attributes. Although Kant's name for it—the 'original transcendental synthetic Unity of Apperception'—is so long, our consciousness *about* it is, according to him, short enough. Self-consciousness of this 'transcendental' sort tells us, 'not how we appear, not how we inwardly are, but only *that* we are' (§ 25). At the basis of our knowledge of our selves there lies only "the simple and utterly empty idea: *I*; of which we cannot even say we have a notion, but only a consciousness which accompanies all notions. In this *I*, or *he* or *it* (the thing) which thinks, nothing more is represented than the bare transcendental Subject of the knowledge $=x$, which is only recognized by the thoughts which are its predicates, and of which, taken by itself, we cannot form the least conception" (*ibid.*, 'Paralogisms'). The pure Ego of

[31] It must be noticed, in justice to what was said above on page 264 ff., that neither Kant nor his successors anywhere discriminate between the *presence* of the apperceiving Ego to the combined object, and the *awareness by* that Ego *of* its own presence and of its distinctness from what it apperceives. That the Object must be known to something which *thinks*, and that it must be known to something which *thinks that it thinks*, are treated by them as identical necessities,—by what logic, does not appear. Kant tries to soften the jump in the reasoning by saying the thought *of itself* on the part of the Ego need only be *potential*—"the 'I think' must *be capable* of accompanying all other knowledge"—but a thought which is only potential is actually no thought at all, which practically gives up the case.

all apperception is thus for Kant not the soul, but only that 'Subject' which is the necessary correlate of the Object in all knowledge. There *is* a soul, Kant thinks, but this mere ego-form of our consciousness tells us nothing about it, neither whether it be substantial, nor whether it be immaterial, nor whether it be simple, nor whether it be permanent. These declarations on Kant's part of the utter barrenness of the consciousness of the pure Self, and of the consequent impossibility of any deductive or 'rational' psychology, are what, more than anything else, earned for him the title of the 'all-destroyer.' The only self we know anything positive *about*, he thinks, is the empirical *me*, not the pure *I*; the self which is an object among other objects and the 'constituents' of which we ourselves have seen, and recognized to be phenomenal things appearing in the form of space as well as time.

This, for our purposes, is a sufficient account of the 'transcendental' Ego.

Those purposes go no farther than to ascertain whether anything in Kant's conception ought to make us give up our own, of a remembering and appropriating Thought incessantly renewed. In many respects Kant's meaning is obscure, but it will not be necessary for us to squeeze the texts in order to make sure what it actually and historically was. If we can define clearly two or three things which it may *possibly* have been, that will help us just as much to clear our own ideas.

On the whole, a defensible interpretation of Kant's view would take somewhat the following shape. Like ourselves he believes in a Reality outside the mind of which he writes, but the critic who vouches for that reality does so on grounds of faith, for it is not a verifiable phenomenal thing. Neither is it manifold. The 'Manifold' which the intellectual functions combine is a mental manifold altogether, which thus *stands between* the Ego of Apperception and the outer Reality, but still stands inside the mind. In the function of knowing there is a multiplicity to be connected, and Kant brings this multiplicity inside the mind. The Reality becomes a mere empty *locus*, or unknowable, the so-called Noumenon; the manifold phenomenon is in the mind. We, on the contrary, put the Multiplicity with the Reality outside, and leave the mind simple. Both of us deal with the same elements—thought and object—the only question is in which of them the multiplicity shall be lodged. Wherever it is lodged it must be 'synthetized' when it comes to be thought. And that particular way of lodging it will be the better, which, in addition to describing the facts naturally, makes the 'mystery of synthesis' least hard to understand.

Well, Kant's way of describing the facts is mythological. The notion of our thought being this sort of an elaborate internal machine-shop stands condemned by all we said in favor of its simplicity on pages 266 ff. Our Thought is not composed of parts, however so composed its objects may be. There is no originally chaotic manifold in it to be reduced to order. There is something almost shocking in the notion of so chaste a function carrying this Kantian hurly-burly in her womb. If we are to have a dualism of Thought and Reality at all, the multiplicity should be lodged in the latter and not in the former member of the couple of related terms. The parts and their relations surely belong less to the knower than to what is known.

But even were all the mythology true, the process of synthesis would in no whit be *explained* by calling the inside of the mind its seat. No mystery would be made lighter by such means. It is just as much a puzzle *how* the 'Ego' can employ the productive Imagination to make the Understanding use the categories to combine the data which Recognition, Association, and Apprehension receive from sensible Intuition, as how the Thought can combine the objective facts. Phrase it as one may, the difficulty is always the same: *the Many known by the One*. Or does one seriously think he understands better *how* the knower 'connects' its objects, when one calls the former a transcendental Ego and the latter a 'Manifold of Intuition' than when one calls them Thought and Things respectively? Knowing must have a vehicle. Call the vehicle Ego, or call it Thought, Psychosis, Soul, Intelligence, Consciousness, Mind, Reason, Feeling,—what you like—it must *know*. The best grammatical subject for the verb *know* would, if possible, be one from whose other properties the knowing could be deduced. And if there be no such subject, the best one would be that with the fewest ambiguities and the least pretentious name. By Kant's confession, the transcendental Ego has no properties, and from it nothing can be deduced. Its name is pretentious, and, as we shall presently see, has its meaning ambiguously mixed up with that of the substantial soul. So on every possible account we are excused from using it instead of our own term of the present passing 'Thought,' as the principle by which the Many is simultaneously known.

The *ambiguity* referred to in the meaning of the transcendental Ego is as to whether Kant signified by it an *Agent*, and by the Experience it helps to constitute, an operation; or whether the experience is an event *produced* in an unassigned way, and the Ego a mere indwelling *element* therein contained. If an operation be meant, then Ego and Manifold must both be existent prior to that collision which results in the experience of one by the other. If a mere analysis is meant, there is no such prior existence, and the elements only *are* in so far as they are in union. Now Kant's tone and language are everywhere the very words of one who is talking of operations and the agents by which they are performed.[32] And yet there is reason to think that at bottom he may have had nothing of the sort in mind.[33] In this uncertainty we need again do no more than decide what to think of his transcendental Ego *if it be* an agent.

Well, if it be so, Transcendentalism is only Substantialism grown shame-faced, and the Ego only a 'cheap and nasty' edition of the soul. All our reasons for preferring the 'Thought' to the 'Soul' apply with redoubled force when the Soul is shrunk to this estate. The Soul truly explained nothing; the 'syntheses,' which she performed, were simply taken ready-made and clapped on to her as expressions of her nature taken after the fact; but at least she had some semblance of nobility and outlook. She was called active; might select; was responsible, and permanent in her way. The Ego is simply *nothing*: as ineffectual and windy an abortion as Philosophy can show. It would indeed be one of Reason's tragedies if the good Kant, with all his honesty and strenuous pains, should have deemed this conception an important outbirth of his thought.

But we have seen that Kant deemed it of next to no importance at all. It was reserved for his Fichtean and Hegelian successors to call it the first Principle of Philosophy, to spell its name in capitals and pronounce it with adoration, to act, in short, as if they were going up in a balloon, whenever the notion of it crossed their mind. Here again, however, I am uncertain of the facts of history,

32 "As regards the soul, now, or the 'I,' the 'thinker,' the whole drift of Kant's advance upon Hume and sensational psychology is toward the demonstration that the subject of knowledge is an *Agent*." (G. S. Morris: *Kant's Critique*, etc. (Chicago, 1882), p. 224.)

33 "In Kant's Prolegomena," says H. Cohen,—I do not myself find the passage,—"it is expressly said that the problem is not to show how experience arises (ensteht), but of what it consists (besteht)." (*Kants Theorie der Erfahrung* (1871), p.138.)

and know that I may not read my authors aright. The whole lesson of Kantian and post-Kantian speculation is, it seems to me, the lesson of simplicity. With Kant, complication both of thought and statement was an inborn infirmity, enhanced by the musty academicism of his Königsberg existence. With Hegel it was a raging fever. Terribly, therefore, do the sour grapes which these fathers of philosophy have eaten set our teeth on edge. We have in England and America, however, a contemporary continuation of Hegelism from which, fortunately, somewhat simpler deliverances come; and, unable to find any definite psychology in what Hegel, Rosenkranz, or Erdmann tells us of the Ego, I turn to Caird and Green.

The great difference, practically, between these authors and Kant is their complete abstraction from the onlooking Psychologist and from the Reality he thinks he knows; or rather it is the absorption of both of these outlying terms into the proper topic of Psychology, viz., the mental experience of the mind under observation. The Reality coalesces with the connected Manifold, the Psychologist with the Ego, knowing becomes 'connecting,' and there results no longer a finite or criticisable, but an 'absolute' Experience, of which the Object and the Subject are always the same. Our finite 'Thought' is virtually and potentially this eternal (or rather this 'timeless'), absolute Ego, and only provisionally and speciously the limited thing which it seems *primâ facie* to be. The later 'sections' of our 'Stream,' which come and appropriate the earlier ones, *are* those earlier ones, just as in substantialism the Soul is throughout all time the same.[34] This 'solipsistic' character of an Experi-

[34] The contrast between the Monism thus reached and our own psychological point of view can be exhibited schematically thus, the terms in squares standing for what, for us, are the ultimate irreducible data of psychological science, and the vincula above it symbolizing the reductions which post-Kantian idealism performs:

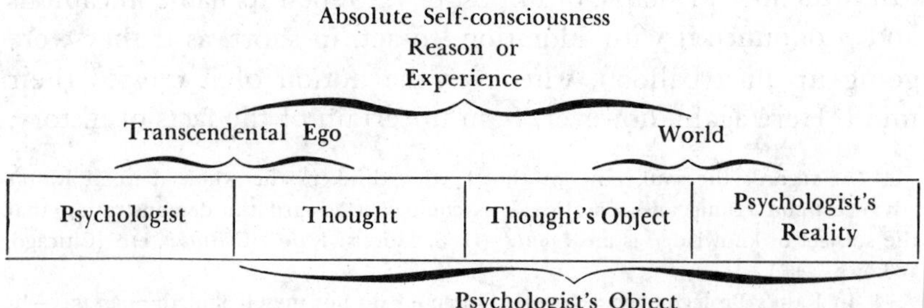

These reductions account for the ubiquitousness of the 'psychologist's fallacy' (bk. II, ch. I, p. 32) in the modern monistic writings. For *us* it is an unpardonable logical

ence conceived as absolute really annihilates psychology as a distinct body of science.

Psychology is a natural science, an account of particular finite streams of thought, coexisting and succeeding in time. It is of course conceivable (though far from clearly so) that in the last metaphysical resort all these streams of thought may be thought by one universal All-thinker. But in this metaphysical notion there is no profit for psychology; for grant that one Thinker does think in all of us, still what He thinks in me and what in you can never be deduced from the bare idea of Him. The idea of Him seems even to exert a positively paralyzing effect on the mind. The existence of finite thoughts is suppressed altogether. Thought's characteristics, as Professor Green says, are

"not to be sought in the incidents of individual lives which last but for a day. . . . No knowledge, nor any mental act involved in knowledge, can properly be called a 'phenomenon of consciousness.' . . . For a phenomenon is a sensible event, related in the way of antecedence and consequence to other sensible events; but the consciousness which constitutes a knowledge . . . is not an event so related nor made up of such events."

Again, if

"we examine the constituents of any perceived object . . . we shall find alike that it is only for consciousness that they can exist, and that the consciousness for which they thus exist cannot be merely a series of phenomena or a succession of states. . . . It then becomes clear that there is a function of consciousness, as exercised in the most rudimentary experience [namely, the function of *synthesis*], . . . which is incompatible with the definition of consciousness as any sort of succession of any sort of phenomena."[35]

Were we to follow these remarks, we should have to abandon our notion of the 'Thought' (perennially renewed in time, but always cognitive thereof), and to espouse instead of it an entity copied from thought in all essential respects, but differing from it in be-

---

sin, when talking of a thought's knowledge (either of an object or of itself), to change the terms without warning, and, substituting the psychologist's knowledge therefore, still make as if we were continuing to talk of the same thing. For monistic idealism, this is the very enfranchisement of philosophy, and of course cannot be too much indulged in.

[35] T. H. Green: *Prolegomena to Ethics*, §§ 57, 61, 64.

ing 'out of time.' What psychology can gain by this barter would be hard to divine. Moreover this resemblance of the timeless Ego to the Soul is completed by other resemblances still. The monism of the post-Kantian idealists seems always lapsing into a regular old-fashioned spiritualistic dualism. They incessantly talk as if, like the Soul, their All-thinker were an Agent, operating on detached materials of sense. This may come from the accidental fact that the English writings of the school have been more polemic than constructive, and that a reader may often take for a positive profession a statement *ad hominem* meant as part of a reduction to the absurd, or mistake the analysis of a bit of knowledge into elements for a dramatic myth about its creation. But I think the matter has profounder roots. Professor Green constantly talks of the 'activity' of Self as a 'condition' of knowledge taking place. Facts are said to become incorporated with other facts only through the '*action* of a combining self-consciousness upon data of sensation.'

"Every object we perceive . . . requires in order to its presentation the *action* of a principle of consciousness, not itself subject to conditions of time, upon successive appearances, such action as may *hold the appearances together,* without fusion, in an apprehended fact."[36]

It is needless to repeat that the connection of things in our knowledge is in no whit *explained* by making it the deed of an agent whose essence is self-identity and who is out of time. The agency of phenomenal thought coming and going in time is just as easy to *understand*. And when it is furthermore said that the agent that combines is the same 'self-distinguishing subject' which 'in another mode of its activity' presents the manifold object to itself, the unintelligibilities become quite paroxysmal, and we are forced to confess that the entire school of thought in question, in spite of occasional glimpses of something more refined, still dwells habitually in that mythological stage of thought where phenomena are explained as results of dramas enacted by entities which but reduplicate the characters of the phenomena themselves. The self must not only *know* its object,—that is too bald and dead a relation to be written down and left in its static state. The knowing must be painted as a 'famous victory' in which the object's distinctness is in some way 'overcome.'

[36] *Loc. cit.*, § 64.

"The self exists as one self only as it opposes itself, as object, to itself, as subject, and immediately denies and transcends that opposition. Only because it is such a concrete unity, which has in itself a resolved contradiction, can the intelligence cope with all the manifoldness and division of the mighty universe, and hope to master its secrets. As the lightning sleeps in the dew-drop, so in the simple and transparent unity of self-consciousness there is held in equilibrium that vital antagonism of opposites, which . . . seems to rend the world asunder. The intelligence is able to understand the world, or, in other words, to break down the barrier between itself and things, and find itself in them, just because its own existence is implicitly the solution of all the division and conflict of things."[37]

This dynamic (I had almost written dynamitic) way of representing knowledge has the merit of not being tame. To turn from it to our own psychological formulation is like turning from the fireworks, trap-doors, and transformations of the pantomime into the insipidity of the midnight, where

"ghastly through the drizzling rain
On the bald street breaks the blank day."[38]

And yet turn we must, with the confession that our 'Thought'—a cognitive phenomenal event in time—is, if it exist at all, itself the only Thinker which the facts require. The only service that transcendental egoism has done to psychology has been by its protests against Hume's 'bundle'-theory of mind. But this service has been ill-performed; for the Egoists themselves, let them say what they will, believe in the bundle, and in their own system merely *tie it up*, with their special transcendental string, invented for that use alone. Besides, they talk as if, with this miraculous tying or 'relating,' the Ego's duties were done. Of its far more important duty of choosing some of the things it ties and appropriating them, to

[37] E. Caird: *Hegel* (1883), p. 149.

[38] One is almost tempted to believe that the pantomime-state of mind and that of the hegelian dialectics are, emotionally considered, one and the same thing. In the pantomime all common things are represented to happen in impossible ways, people jump down each other's throats, houses turn inside out, old women become young men, everything 'passes into its opposite' with inconceivable celerity and skill; and this, so far from producing perplexity, brings rapture to the beholder's mind. And so in the hegelian logic, relations elsewhere recognized under the insipid name of distinctions (such as that between knower and object, many and one) must first be translated into impossibilities and contradictions, then 'transcended' and identified by miracle, ere the proper temper is induced for thoroughly enjoying the spectacle they show.

the exclusion of the rest, they tell us never a word. To sum up, then, my own opinion of the transcendentalist school, it is (whatever ulterior metaphysical truth it may divine) a school in which psychology at least has naught to learn, and whose deliverances about the Ego in particular in no wise oblige us to revise our own formulation of the Stream of Thought.[39]

With this, all possible rival formulations have been discussed. The literature of the Self is large, but all its authors may be classed as radical or mitigated representatives of the three schools we have named, substantialism, associationism, or transcendentalism. Our own opinion must be classed apart, although it incorporates essential elements from all three schools. *There need never have been a quarrel between associationism and its rivals if the former had admitted the indecomposable unity of every pulse of thought, and the latter been willing to allow that 'perishing' pulses of thought might recollect and know.*

We may sum up by saying that personality implies the incessant presence of two elements, an objective person, known by a passing subjective Thought and recognized as continuing in time. *Hereafter let us use the words* ME *and* I *for the empirical person and the judging Thought.*

[39] The reader will please understand that I am quite willing to leave the hypothesis of the transcendental Ego as a substitute for the passing Thought open to discussion on *general speculative grounds*. Only *in this book* I prefer to stick by the common-sense assumption that we have successive conscious states, because all psychologists make it, and because one does not see how there can be a Psychology written which does not postulate such thoughts as its ultimate data. The data of all natural sciences become in turn subjects of a critical treatment more refined than that which the sciences themselves accord; and so it may fare in the end with our passing Thought. We have ourselves seen (pp. 286–291) that the *sensible* certainty of its existence is less strong than is usually assumed. My quarrel with the transcendental Egoists is mainly about their *grounds* for their belief. Did they consistently propose it as a *substitute* for the passing Thought, did they consistently *deny the latter's existence*, I should respect their position more. But so far as I can understand them, they habitually believe in the passing Thought also. They seem even to believe in the Lockian stream of separate ideas, for the chief glory of the Ego in their pages is always its power to 'overcome' this separateness and unite the naturally disunited, *'synthetizing,' 'connecting,' or 'relating' the ideas together* being used as synonyms, by transcendentalist writers, for *knowing various objects at once*. Not the being conscious at all, but the being conscious of *many things together* is held to be the difficult thing, in our psychic life, which only the wonder-working Ego can perform. But on what slippery ground does one get the moment one changes the definite notion of *knowing an object* into the altogether vague one of *uniting or synthetizing the ideas* of its various parts!—In the chapter on Sensation we shall come upon all this again.

Certain vicissitudes in the me demand our notice.

In the first place, although its changes are gradual, they become in time great. The central part of the *me* is the feeling of the body and of the adjustments in the head; and in the feeling of the body should be included that of the general emotional tones and tendencies, for at bottom these are but the habits in which organic activities and sensibilities run. Well, from infancy to old age, this assemblage of feelings, most constant of all, is yet a prey to slow mutation. Our powers, bodily and mental, change at least as fast.[40] Our possessions notoriously are perishable facts.

The identity which the *I* discovers, as it surveys this long proces-

[40] "When we compare the listless inactivity of the infant, slumbering, from the moment at which he takes his milky food, to the moment at which he awakes to require it again, with the restless energies of that mighty being which he is to become, in his maturer years, pouring truth after truth in rapid and dazzling profusion upon the world, or grasping in his single hand the destiny of empires, how few are the circumstances of resemblance which we can trace, of all that intelligence which is afterwards to be displayed; how little more is seen, than what serves to give feeble motion to the mere machinery of life. . . . Every age,—if we may speak of many ages, in the few years of human life,—seems to be marked with a distinct character. Each has its peculiar objects, that excite lively affections; and in each, exertion is excited by affections, which, in other periods, terminate, without inducing active desire. The boy finds a world in less space than that which bounds his visible horizon; he wanders over his range of field, and exhausts his strength in pursuit of objects, which, in the years that follow, are seen only to be neglected; while, to him, the objects, that are afterwards to absorb his whole soul, are as indifferent as the objects of his present passions are destined then to appear. . . . How many melancholy opportunities must every one have had of witnessing the progress of intellectual decay, and the coldness that steals upon the once benevolent heart! We quit our country, perhaps, at an early period of life, and, after an absence of many years, we return, with all the remembrances of past pleasure, which grow more tender as we approach their objects. We eagerly seek him, to whose paternal voice we have been accustomed to listen, with the same reverence as if its predictions had possessed oracular certainty,—who first led us into knowledge, and whose image has been constantly joined, in our mind, with all that veneration which does not forbid love. We find him sunk, perhaps in the imbecility of idiotism, unable to recognize us—ignorant alike of the past and of the future, and living only in the sensibility of animal gratification. We seek the favourite companion of our childhood, whose gentleness of heart, etc. . . . We find him hardened into man, meeting us scarcely with the cold hypocrisy of dissembled friendship—in his general relations to the world, careless of the misery which *he* is not to feel . . . . When we observe all this, . . . do we use only a metaphor of little meaning, when we say of him, that he is become a different person, and that his mind and character are changed? In what does the identity consist? . . . The supposed test of identity, when applied to the mind in these cases, completely fails. It neither affects, nor is affected, in the same manner, in the same circumstances. It, therefore, if the test be a just one, is not the same identical mind." (T. Brown: *Lectures on the Philosophy of the Human Mind*, "On Mental Identity.")

sion, can only be a relative identity, that of a slow shifting in which there is always some common ingredient retained.[41] The commonest element of all, the most uniform, is the possession of the same memories. However different the man may be from the youth, both look back on the same childhood, and call it their own.

Thus the identity found by the *I* in its *me* is only a loosely construed thing, an identity 'on the whole,' just like that which any outside observer might find in the same assemblage of facts. We often say of a man 'he is so changed one would not know him'; and so does a man, less often, speak of himself. These changes in the *me*, recognized by the I, or by outside observers, may be grave or slight. They deserve some notice here.

THE MUTATIONS OF THE SELF

may be divided into two main classes:

1. Alterations of memory; and
2. Alterations in the present bodily and spiritual selves.

1. *Alterations of memory* are either *losses* or false recollections. In either case the *me* is changed. Should a man be punished for what he did in his childhood and no longer remembers? Should he be punished for crimes enacted in post-epileptic unconsciousness, somnambulism, or in any involuntarily induced state of which no recollection is retained? Law, in accord with common-sense, says: "No; he is not the same person forensically now which he was then." These losses of memory are a normal incident of extreme old age, and the person's *me* shrinks in the ratio of the facts that have disappeared.

In dreams we forget our waking experiences; they are as if they were not. And the converse is also true. As a rule, no memory is retained during the waking state of what has happened during mesmeric trance, although when again entranced the person may

41 "Sir John Cutler had a pair of black worsted stockings, which his maid darned so often with silk, that they became at last a pair of silk stockings. Now, supposing those stockings of Sir John's endued with some degree of consciousness at every particular darning, they would have been sensible, that they were the same individual pair of stockings both before and after the darning; and this sensation would have continued in them through all the succession of darnings; and yet after the last of all, there was not perhaps one thread left of the first pair of stockings; but they were grown to be silk stockings, as was said before." (Pope's *Martinus Scriblerus*, quoted by Brown, *ibid.*)

remember it distinctly, and may then forget facts belonging to the waking state. We thus have, within the bounds of healthy mental life, an approach to an alternation of *me's*.

False memories are by no means rare occurrences in most of us, and whenever they occur they distort the consciousness of the me. Most people, probably, are in doubt about certain matters ascribed to their past. They may have seen them, may have said them, done them, or they may only have dreamed or imagined they did so. The content of a dream will oftentimes insert itself into the stream of real life in a most perplexing way. The most frequent source of false memory is the accounts we give to others of our experiences. Such accounts we almost always make both more simple and more interesting than the truth. We quote what we should have said or done, rather than what we really said or did; and in the first telling we may be fully aware of the distinction. But ere long the fiction expels the reality from memory and reigns in its stead alone. This is one great source of the fallibility of testimony meant to be quite honest. Especially where the marvellous is concerned, the story takes a tilt that way, and the memory follows the story. Dr. Carpenter quotes from Miss Cobbe the following, as an instance of a very common sort:

> "It happened once to the writer to hear a most scrupulously conscientious friend narrate an incident of table-turning, to which she appended the assurance that the table rapped when *nobody was within a yard of it*. The writer was confounded by this latter fact, the lady was fully satisfied of its accuracy, but promised to look at the note she had made, ten years ago, of the transaction. The note was examined, and it was found to contain the distinct statement, that the table rapped when *the hands of six persons rested on it*! Nothing could be more instructive, for the lady's memory in all other points beside this one proved to be strictly correct and in this point she had erred in entire good faith."[42]

It is next to impossible to get a story of this sort accurate in all its details, although it is the inessential details that suffer most change.[43] Dickens and Balzac were said to have constantly mingled

[42] *Hours of Work and Play*, p. 100.

[43] For a careful study of the errors in narratives, see E. Gurney: *Phantasms of the Living*, vol. 1, pp. 126–158. In the *Proceedings of the Society for Psychical Research* for May 1887 Mr. Richard Hodgson shows by an extraordinary array of instances how utterly inaccurate everyone's description from memory of a rapid series of events is certain to be.

their fictions with their real experiences. Everyone must have known *some* specimen of our mortal dust so intoxicated with the thought of his own person and the sound of his own voice as never to be able even to think the truth when his autobiography was in question. Amiable, harmless, radiant J. V.! mayst thou ne'er wake to the difference between thy real and thy fondly-imagined self![44]

2. When we pass beyond alterations of memory to abnormal *alterations in the present self* we have still graver disturbances. These alterations are of three main types, from the descriptive point of view. But certain cases unite features of two or more types; and our knowledge of the elements and causes of these changes of personality is so slight that the division into types must not be regarded as having any profound significance. The types are:

(1) Insane delusions;
(2) Alternating selves;
(3) Mediumships or possessions.

1) In insanity we often have delusions projected into the past, which are melancholic or sanguine according to the character of the disease. But the worst alterations of the self come from present perversions of sensibility and impulse which leave the past undisturbed, but induce the patient to think that the present *me* is an altogether new personage. Something of this sort happens normally in the rapid expansion of the whole character, intellectual as well as volitional, which takes place after the time of puberty. The pathological cases are curious enough to merit longer notice.

The basis of our personality, as M. Ribot says, is that feeling of our vitality which, because it is so perpetually present, remains in the background of our consciousness.

"It is the basis because, always present, always acting, without peace or rest, it knows neither sleep nor fainting, and lasts as long as life itself, of which it is one form. It serves as a support to that self-conscious *me* which memory constitutes, it is the medium of association among its other parts. . . . Suppose now that it were possible at once to change our body and put another into its place: skeleton, vessels, viscera, muscles, skin, everything made new, except the nervous system with its stored-up memory of the past. There can be no doubt that in such a

44 See Josiah Royce (*Mind*, vol. 13, p. 244, and *Proceedings of the American Society for Psychical Research*, vol. 1, p. 366), for evidence that a certain sort of hallucination of memory which he calls 'pseudo-presentiment' is no uncommon phenomenon.

case the afflux of unaccustomed vital sensations would produce the gravest disorders. Between the old sense of existence engraved on the nervous system, and the new one acting with all the intensity of its reality and novelty, there would be irreconcilable contradiction."[45]

With the beginnings of cerebral disease there often happens something quite comparable to this:

"Masses of new sensation, hitherto foreign to the individual, impulses and ideas of the same inexperienced kind, for example terrors, representations of enacted crime, of enemies pursuing one, etc. At the outset, these stand in contrast with the old familiar *me,* as a strange, often astonishing and abhorrent *thou.*[46] Often their invasion into the former circle of feelings is felt as if the old self were being taken possession of by a dark overpowering might, and the fact of such 'possession' is described in fantastic images. Always this doubleness, this struggle of the old self against the new discordant forms of experience, is accompanied with painful mental conflict, with passion, with violent emotional excitement. This is in great part the reason for the common experience, that the first stage in the immense majority of cases of mental disease is an emotional alteration particularly of a melancholic sort. If now the brain-affection, which is the immediate cause of the new abnormal train of ideas, be not relieved, the latter becomes confirmed. It may gradually contract associations with the trains of ideas which characterized the old self, or portions of the latter may be extinguished and lost in the progress of the cerebral malady, so that little by little the opposition of the two conscious *me's* abates, and the emotional storms are calmed. But by that time *the old me itself has been falsified and*

[45] *Maladies de la mémoire,* p. 85. The little that would be left of personal consciousness if *all* our senses stopped their work is ingenuously shown in the remark of the extraordinary anæsthetic youth whose case Professor Strümpell reports (in the *Deutsches Archiv für klinische Medicin,* XXII, 347, 1878). This boy, whom we shall later find instructive in many connections, was totally anæsthetic without and (so far as could be tested) within, save for the sight of one eye and the hearing of one ear. When his eye was closed, he said: "*Wenn ich nicht sehen kann, dann* BIN *ich gar nicht*—I no longer *am.*"

[46] "One can compare the state of the patient to nothing so well as to that of a caterpillar, which, keeping all its caterpillar's ideas and remembrances, should suddenly become a butterfly with a butterfly's senses and sensations. Between the old and the new state, between the first self, that of the caterpillar, and the second self, that of the butterfly, there is a deep scission, a complete rupture. The new feelings find no anterior series to which they can knit themselves on; the patient can neither interpret nor use them; he does not recognize them; they are unknown. Hence two conclusions, the first which consists in his saying, *I no longer am*; the second, somewhat later, which consists in his saying, *I am another person.*" (H. Taine: *De l'intelligence,* 3me édition (1878), vol. II, p. 462.)

turned into another by those associations, by that reception into itself of the abnormal elements of feeling and of will. The patient may again be quiet, and his thought sometimes logically correct, but in it the morbid erroneous ideas are always present, with the adhesions they have contracted, as uncontrollable premises, and the man is no longer the same, but a really new person, his old self transformed."[47]

But the patient himself rarely continues to describe the change in just these terms unless new *bodily sensations* in him or the loss of old ones play a predominant part. Mere perversions of sight and hearing, or even of impulse, soon cease to be felt as contradictions of the unity of the me.

What the particular perversions of the bodily sensibility may be which give rise to these contradictions is, for the most part, impossible for a sound-minded person to conceive. One patient has another self that repeats all his thoughts for him. Others, amongst whom are some of the first characters in history, have familiar dæmons who speak with them, and are replied to. In another someone 'makes' his thoughts for him. Another has two bodies, lying in different beds. Some patients feel as if they had lost parts of their bodies, teeth, brain, stomach, etc. In some it is made of wood, glass, butter, etc. In some it does not exist any longer, or is dead, or is a foreign object quite separate from the speaker's self. Occasionally, parts of the body lose their connection for consciousness with the rest, and are treated as belonging to another person and moved by a hostile will. Thus the right hand may fight with the left as with an enemy.[48] Or the cries of the patient himself are assigned to another person with whom the patient expresses sympathy. The literature of insanity is filled with narratives of such illusions as these. M. Taine quotes from a patient of Dr. Krishaber an account of sufferings, from which it will be seen how completely aloof from what is normal a man's experience may suddenly become:

"After the first or second day it was for some weeks impossible to observe or analyze myself. The suffering—angina pectoris—was too overwhelming. It was not till the first days of January that I could give an account to myself of what I experienced. . . . Here is the first thing of which I retain a clear remembrance. I was alone, and already a prey to

47 W. Griesinger: *Die Pathologie und Therapie der psychischen Krankheiten*, § 29.

48 See the interesting case of 'old Stump' in the *Proceedings of the American Society for Psychical Research*, p. 552.

permanent visual trouble, when I was suddenly seized with a visual trouble infinitely more pronounced. Objects grew small and receded to infinite distances—men and things together. I was myself immeasurably far away. I looked about me with terror and astonishment; *the world was escaping from me*. . . . I remarked at the same time that my voice was extremely far away from me, that it sounded no longer as if mine. I struck the ground with my foot, and perceived its resistance; but this resistance seemed illusory—not that the soil was soft, but that the weight of my body was reduced to almost nothing. . . . I had the feeling of being without weight. . . ." In addition to being so distant, "objects appeared to me *flat*. When I spoke with anyone, I saw him like an image cut out of paper with no relief. . . . This sensation lasted intermittently for two years. . . . Constantly it seemed as if my legs did not belong to me. It was almost as bad with my arms. As for my head, it seemed no longer to exist. . . . I appeared to myself to act automatically, by an impulsion foreign to myself. . . . There was inside of me a new being, and another part of myself, the old being, which took no interest in the new-comer. I distinctly remember saying to myself that the sufferings of this new being were to me indifferent. I was never really dupe of these illusions, but my mind grew often tired of incessantly correcting the new impressions, and I let myself go and live the unhappy life of this new entity. I had an ardent desire to see my old world again, to get back to my old self. This desire kept me from killing myself. . . . I was another, and I hated, I despised this other; he was perfectly odious to me; it was certainly another who had taken my form and assumed my functions."[49]

In cases similar to this, it is as certain that the *I* is unaltered as that the *me* is changed. That is to say, the present Thought of the patient is cognitive of both the old *me* and the new, so long as its memory holds good. Only, within that objective sphere which formerly lent itself so simply to the judgment of recognition and of egoistic appropriation, strange perplexities have arisen. The present and the past, both seen therein, will not unite. Where is my old me? What is this new one? Are they the same? Or have I two? Such questions, answered by whatever theory the patient is able to conjure up as plausible, form the beginning of his insane life.[50]

49 *De l'intelligence*, 3me édition (1878), vol. II, p. 461, note. Krishaber's book *(De la névropathie cérébro-cardiaque*, 1873) is full of similar observations.

50 Sudden alterations in outward fortune often produce such a change in the empirical *me* as almost to amount to a pathological disturbance of self-consciousness. When a poor man draws the big prize in a lottery, or unexpectedly inherits an estate; when a man high in fame is publicly disgraced, a millionaire becomes a pauper, or a

A case with which I am acquainted through Dr. C. I. Fisher of Tewksbury has possibly its origin in this way. The woman, Bridget F.,

> "has been insane for many years and . . . always speaks of her supposed self as 'the rat' asking me to 'bury the little rat,' etc. Her real self she speaks of in the third person as 'the good woman,' saying, 'The good woman knew Dr. F. and used to work for him,' etc. Sometimes she sadly asks 'Do you think the good woman will ever come back?' . . . She works—needle work, knitting, laundry etc. and shows her work and says 'Isn't that good for only a rat?' She has during periods of depression hid herself under buildings, and crawled into holes and under boxes. 'She was only a rat and wants to die' she would say when we found her."

2. The phenomenon of *alternating personality* in its simplest phases seems based on lapses of memory. Any man becomes, as we say, *inconsistent* with himself if he forgets his engagements, pledges, knowledges, and habits; and it is merely a question of degree at what point we shall say that his personality is changed. In the pathological cases known as those of double or alternate personality the lapse of memory is abrupt, and is usually preceded by a period of unconsciousness or syncope lasting a variable length of time. In the hypnotic trance we can easily produce an alteration of the personality, either by telling the subject to forget all that has happened to him since such or such a date, in which case he becomes (it may be) a child again, or by telling him he is another altogether imaginary personage, in which case all facts about himself seem for the time being to lapse from out his mind, and he throws himself into the new character with a vivacity proportionate to the amount of histrionic imagination which he possesses.[51] But in the pathological cases the transformation is spontaneous. The most famous case, perhaps, on record is that of Félida X., reported by Dr. Azam of Bordeaux.[52] At the age of fourteen this woman began to pass into a 'secondary' state characterized by a change in her

---

loving husband and father sees his family perish at one fell swoop, there is temporarily such a rupture between all past habits, whether of an active or a passive kind, and the exigencies and possibilities of the new situation, that the individual may find no medium of continuity or association to carry him over from the one phase to the other of his life. Under these conditions mental derangement is no unfrequent result.

51 The number of subjects who can do this with any fertility and exuberance is relatively quite small.

52 First in the *Revue Scientifique* for May 20, 1876, then in his book, *Hypnotisme, double conscience et altérations de la personnalité* (Paris, 1887).

general disposition and character, as if certain 'inhibitions,' previously existing, were suddenly removed. During the secondary state she remembered the first state, but on emerging from it into the first state she remembered nothing of the second. At the age of forty-four the duration of the secondary state (which was on the whole superior in quality to the original state) had gained upon the latter so much as to occupy most of her time. During it she remembers the events belonging to the original state, but her complete oblivion of the secondary state when the original state recurs is often very distressing to her, as, for example, when the transition takes place in a carriage on her way to a funeral, and she hasn't the least idea which one of her friends may be dead. She actually became pregnant during one of her early secondary states, and during her first state had no knowledge of how it had come to pass. Her distress at these blanks of memory is sometimes intense and once drove her to attempt suicide.

To take another example, Dr. Rieger gives an account[53] of an epileptic man who for seventeen years had passed his life alternately free, in prisons, or in asylums, his character being orderly enough in the normal state, but alternating with periods, during which he would leave his home for several weeks, leading the life of a thief and vagabond, being sent to jail, having epileptic fits and excitement, being accused of malingering, etc., etc., and with never a memory of the abnormal conditions which were to blame for all his wretchedness.

> "I have never got from anyone," says Dr. Rieger, "so singular an impression as from this man, of whom it could not be said that he had any properly conscious past at all. . . . It is really impossible to think one's self into such a state of mind. His last larceny had been performed in Nürnberg, he knew nothing of it, and saw himself before the court and then in the hospital, but without in the least understanding the reason why. That he had epileptic attacks, he knew. But it was impossible to convince him that for hours together he raved and acted in an abnormal way."

Another remarkable case is that of Mary Reynolds, lately republished again by Dr. Weir Mitchell.[54] This dull and melancholy young woman, inhabiting the Pennsylvania wilderness in 1811,

[53] *Der Hypnotismus* (1884), pp. 109–15.

[54] *Transactions of the College of Physicians of Philadelphia*, April 4, 1888. Also, less complete, by the Rev. William S. Plumer in *Harper's Magazine*, May 1860.

"was found one morning, long after her habitual time for rising, in a profound sleep from which it was impossible to arouse her. After eighteen or twenty hours of sleeping she awakened, but in a state of unnatural consciousness. Memory had fled. To all intents and purposes she was as a being for the first time ushered into the world. 'All of the past that remained to her was the faculty of pronouncing a few words, and this seems to have been as purely instinctive as the wailings of an infant; for at first the words which she uttered were connected with no ideas in her mind.' Until she was taught their significance they were unmeaning sounds.

" 'Her eyes were virtually for the first time opened upon the world. Old things had passed away; all things had become new.' Her parents, brothers, sisters, friends, were not recognized or acknowledged as such by her. She had never seen them before,—never known them,—was not aware that such persons had been. Now for the first time she was introduced to their company and acquaintance. To the scenes by which she was surrounded she was a perfect stranger. The house, the fields, the forest, the hills, the vales, the streams,—all were novelties. The beauties of the landscape were all unexplored.

"She had not the slightest consciousness that she had ever existed previous to the moment in which she awoke from that mysterious slumber. 'In a word, she was an infant, just born, yet born in a state of maturity with a capacity for relishing the rich, sublime, luxuriant wonders of created nature.'

"The first lesson in her education was to teach her by what ties she was bound to those by whom she was surrounded, and the duties devolving upon her accordingly. This she was very slow to learn, and, 'indeed, never did learn, or, at least, never would acknowledge the ties of consanguinity, or scarcely those of friendship. She considered those she had once known as for the most part strangers and enemies, among whom she was, by some remarkable and unaccountable means, transplanted, though from what region or state of existence was a problem unsolved.'

"The next lesson was to re-teach her the arts of reading and writing. She was apt enough, and made such rapid progress in both, that *in a few weeks* she had readily re-learned to read and write. In copying her name which her brother had written for her as a first lesson, she took her pen in a very awkward manner and began to copy from right to left in the Hebrew mode, as though she had been transplanted from an Eastern soil. . . .

"The next thing that is noteworthy is the change which took place in her disposition. Instead of being melancholy she was now cheerful to extremity. Instead of being reserved she was buoyant and social.

Formerly taciturn and retiring, she was now merry and jocose. Her disposition was totally and absolutely changed. While she was, in this second state, extravagantly fond of company, she was much more enamored of nature's works, as exhibited in the forests, hills, vales, and water-courses. She used to start in the morning, either on foot or horseback, and ramble until nightfall over the whole country; nor was she at all particular whether she were on a path or in the trackless forest. Her predilection for this manner of life may have been occasioned by the restraint necessarily imposed upon her by her friends, which caused her to consider them her enemies, and not companions, and she was glad to keep out of their way.

"She knew no fear, and as bears and panthers were numerous in the woods, and rattlesnakes and copperheads abounded everywhere, her friends told her of the danger to which she exposed herself, but it produced no other effect than to draw forth a contemptuous laugh, as she said, 'I know you only want to frighten me and keep me at home, but you miss it, for I often see your bears and I am perfectly convinced that they are nothing more than black hogs.'

"One evening, after her return from her daily excursion, she told the following incident: 'As I was riding to-day along a narrow path a great black hog came out of the woods and stopped before me. I never saw such an impudent black hog before. It stood up on its hind feet and grinned and gnashed its teeth at me. I could not make the horse go on. I told him he was a fool to be frightened at a hog, and tried to whip him past, but he would not go and wanted to turn back. I told the hog to get out of the way, but he did not mind me. "Well," said I, "if you won't for words, I'll try blows;" so I got off and took a stick and walked up toward it. When I got pretty close by, it got down on all fours and walked away slowly and sullenly, stopping every few steps and looking back and grinning and growling. Then I got on my horse and rode on.' . . .

"Thus it continued for five weeks, when one morning, after a protracted sleep, she awoke and was herself again. She recognized the parental, the brotherly, and sisterly ties as though nothing had happened, and immediately went about the performance of duties incumbent upon her, and which she had planned five weeks previously. Great was her surprise at the change which one night (as she supposed) had produced. Nature bore a different aspect. Not a trace was left in her mind of the giddy scenes through which she had passed. Her ramblings through the forest, her tricks and humor, all were faded from her memory, and not a shadow left behind. Her parents saw their child; her brothers and sisters saw their sister. She now had all the knowledge that she had possessed in her first state previous to the change, still fresh and in as vigorous exercise as though no change had been. But any new acquisitions she had made, and any new ideas she had obtained, were lost to her now—yet not lost, but laid up out of sight in safe keeping for future use. Of course her natural disposition returned; her melancholy was deepened by the information of what had occurred. All went on in the old-fashioned way, and it was fondly hoped that the mysterious occurrences of those five weeks would never be repeated, but these anticipations were not to be realized. After the lapse of a few weeks she fell into a profound sleep, and awoke in her second state, taking up her new life again precisely where she had left it when she before passed from that state. She was not now a daughter nor a sister. All the knowledge she possessed was that acquired during the few weeks of her former period of second consciousness. She knew nothing of the intervening time. Two periods widely separated were brought into contact. She thought it was but one night.

"In this state she came to understand perfectly the facts of her case, not from memory, but from information. Yet her buoyancy of spirits was so great that no depression was produced. On the contrary, it added to her cheerfulness, and was made the foundation, as was everything else, of mirth.

"These alternations from one state to another continued at intervals of varying length for fifteen or sixteen years, but finally ceased when she attained the age of thirty-five or thirty-six, leaving her *permanently in her second state*. In this she remained without change for the last quarter of a century of her life."

The emotional opposition of the two states seems, however, to have become gradually effaced in Mary Reynolds:

"The change from a gay, hysterical, mischievous woman, fond of jests and subject to absurd beliefs or delusive convictions, to one retaining the joyousness and love of society, but sobered down to levels of practical usefulness, was gradual. The most of the twenty-five years which followed she was as different from her melancholy, morbid self as from the hilarious condition of the early years of her second state. Some of her family spoke of it as her third state. She is described as becoming rational, industrious, and very cheerful, yet reasonably serious; possessed of a well-balanced temperament and not having the slightest indication of an injured or disturbed mind. For some years she taught school, and in that capacity was both useful and acceptable, being a general favorite with old and young.

"During these last twenty-five years she lived in the same house with the Rev. Dr. John V. Reynolds, her nephew, part of that time keeping house for him, showing a sound judgment and a thorough acquaintance with the duties of her position.

"Dr. Reynolds, who is still living in Meadville," says Dr. Mitchell, "and who has most kindly placed the facts at my disposal, states in his letter to me of January 4, 1888, that at a later period of her life she said she did sometimes seem to have a dim, dreamy idea of a shadowy past, which she could not fully grasp, and could not be certain whether it originated in a partially restored memory or in the statements of the events by others during her abnormal state.

"Miss Reynolds died in January, 1854, at the age of sixty-one. On the morning of the day of her death she rose in her usual health, ate her breakfast, and superintended household duties. While thus employed, she suddenly raised her hands to her head and exclaimed 'Oh! I wonder what is the matter with my head!' and immediately fell to the floor. When carried to a sofa she gasped once or twice and died."

In such cases as the preceding, in which the secondary character is superior to the first, there seems reason to think that the first one is the morbid one. The word *inhibition* describes its dulness and melancholy. Félida X.'s original character was dull and melancholy in comparison with that which she later acquired, and the change may be regarded as the removal of inhibitions which had maintained themselves from earlier years. Such inhibitions we all know temporarily, when we cannot recollect or in some other way command our mental resources. The systematized amnesias (losses of memory) of hypnotic subjects ordered to forget all nouns, or all verbs, or a particular letter of the alphabet, or all that is relative to a certain person, are inhibitions of the sort on a more extensive scale. They sometimes occur spontaneously as symptoms of disease.[55] Now M. Pierre Janet has shown that such inhibitions when they bear on a certain class of sensations (making the subject anæsthetic thereto) and also on the memory of such sensations, are the basis of changes of personality. The anæsthetic and 'amnesic' hysteric is one person; but when you restore her inhibited sensibilities and memories by plunging her into the hypnotic trance—in other words, when you rescue them from their 'dissociated' and split-off condition, and make them rejoin the other sensibilities and memories—she is a different person. As said above (p. 201), the hypnotic

[55] Cf. Ribot's *Diseases of Memory* for cases. See also a large number of them in Forbes Winslow's *On Obscure Diseases of the Brain, and Disorders of the Mind*, chapters XIII–XVII.

trance is one method of restoring sensibility in hysterics. But one day when the hysteric anæsthetic named Lucie was already in the hypnotic trance, M. Janet for a certain reason continued to make passes over her for a full half-hour as if she were not already asleep. The result was to throw her into a sort of syncope from which, after half an hour, she revived in a second somnambulic condition entirely unlike that which had characterized her thitherto—different sensibilities, a different memory, a different person, in short. In the waking state the poor young woman was anæsthetic all over, nearly deaf, and with a badly contracted field of vision. Bad as it was, however, sight was her best sense, and she used it as a guide in all her movements. With her eyes bandaged she became entirely helpless, and like other persons of a similar sort whose cases have been recorded, she almost immediately fell asleep in consequence of the withdrawal of her last sensorial stimulus. M. Janet calls this waking or primary (one can hardly in such a connection say 'normal') state by the name of Lucie 1. In Lucie 2, her first sort of hypnotic trance, the anæsthesias were diminished but not removed. In the deeper trance, 'Lucie 3,' brought about as just described, no trace of them remained. Her sensibility became perfect, and instead of being an extreme example of the 'visual' type, she was transformed into what in Prof. Charcot's terminology is known as a motor. That is to say, that whereas when awake she had thought in visual terms exclusively, and could imagine things only by remembering how they *looked,* now in this deeper trance her thoughts and memories seemed to M. Janet to be largely composed of images of movement and of touch.

Having discovered this deeper trance and change of personality in Lucie, M. Janet naturally became eager to find it in his other subjects. He found it in Rose, in Marie, and in Léonie; and his brother, Dr. Jules Janet, who was *interne* at the Salpêtrière Hospital, found it in the celebrated subject Witt. . . . whose trances had been studied for years by the various doctors of that institution without any of them having happened to awaken this very peculiar individuality.[56]

With the return of all the sensibilities in the deeper trance, these subjects turned, as it were, into normal persons. Their memories in particular grew more extensive, and hereupon M. Janet spins a

56 See the interesting account by M. J. Janet in the *Revue Scientifique*, May 19, 1888.

theoretic generalization. *When a certain kind of sensation,* he says, *is abolished in an hysteric patient, there is also abolished along with it all recollection of past sensations of that kind.* If, for example, hearing be the anæsthetic sense, the patient becomes unable even to imagine sounds and voices, and has to speak (when speech is still possible) by means of motor or articulatory cues. If the motor sense be abolished, the patient must will the movements of his limbs by first defining them to his mind in visual terms, and must innervate his voice by premonitory ideas of the way in which the words are going to sound. The practical consequences of this law would be great, for all experiences belonging to a sphere of sensibility which afterwards became anæsthetic, as, for example, touch, would have been stored away and remembered in tactile terms, and would be incontinently forgotten as soon as the cutaneous and muscular sensibility should come to be cut out in the course of disease. Memory of them would be restored again, on the other hand, so soon as the sense of touch came back. Now, in the hysteric subjects on whom M. Janet experimented, touch did come back in the state of trance. The result was that all sorts of memories, absent in the ordinary condition, came back too, and they could then go back and explain the origin of many otherwise inexplicable things in their life. One stage in the great convulsive crisis of hystero-epilepsy, for example, is what French writers call the *phase des attitudes passionelles,* in which the patient, without speaking or giving any account of herself, will go through the outward movements of fear, anger, or some other emotional state of mind. Usually this phase is, with each patient, a thing so stereotyped as to seem automatic, and doubts have even been expressed as to whether any consciousness exists whilst it lasts. When, however, the patient Lucie's tactile sensibility came back in the deeper trance, she explained the origin of her hysteric crisis in a great fright which she had had when a child, on a day when certain men, hid behind the curtains, had jumped out upon her; she told how she went through this scene again in all her crises; she told of her sleep-walking fits through the house when a child, and how for several months she had been shut in a dark room because of a disorder of the eyes. All these were things of which she recollected nothing when awake, because they were records of experiences mainly of motion and of touch.

But M. Janet's subject Léonie is interesting, and shows best how with the sensibilities and motor impulses the memories and character will change.

"This woman, whose life sounds more like an improbable romance than a genuine history, has had attacks of natural somnambulism since the age of three years. She has been hypnotized constantly by all sorts of persons from the age of sixteen upwards; and she is now forty-five. Whilst her normal life developed in one way in the midst of her poor country surroundings, her second life was passed in drawing-rooms and doctors' offices, and naturally took an entirely different direction. To-day, when in her normal state, this poor peasant woman is a serious and rather sad person, calm and slow, very mild with everyone, and extremely timid: to look at her one would never suspect the personage which she contains. But hardly is she put to sleep hypnotically when a metamorphosis occurs. Her face is no longer the same. She keeps her eyes closed, it is true, but the acuteness of her other senses supplies their place. She is gay, noisy, restless, sometimes insupportably so. She remains good-natured, but has acquired a singular tendency to irony and sharp jesting. Nothing is more curious than to hear her after a sitting when she has received a visit from strangers who wished to see her asleep. She gives a word-portrait of them, apes their manners, pretends to know their little ridiculous aspects and passions, and for each invents a romance. To this character must be added the possession of an enormous number of recollections, whose existence she does not even suspect when awake, for her amnesia is then complete. . . . She refuses the name of Léonie and takes that of Léontine (Léonie 2) to which her first magnetizers had accustomed her. 'That good woman is not myself,' she says, 'she is too stupid!' To herself, Léontine or Léonie 2, she attributes all the sensations and all the actions, in a word all the conscious experiences, which she has undergone *in somnambulism*, and knits them together to make the history of her already long life. To Léonie 1 [as M. Janet calls the waking woman], on the other hand, she exclusively ascribes the events lived through in waking hours. I was at first struck by an important exception to the rule, and was disposed to think that there might be something arbitrary in this partition of her recollections. In the normal state Léonie has a husband and children; but Léonie 2, the somnambulist, whilst acknowledging the children as her own, attributes the husband to 'the other.' This choice was perhaps explicable, but it followed no rule. It was not till later that I learned that her magnetizers in early days, as audacious as certain hypnotizers of recent date, had somnambulized her for her first *accouchements*, and that she had lapsed into that state spontaneously in the later ones.

Léonie 2 was thus quite right in ascribing to herself the children—it was she who had had them, and the rule that her first trance-state forms a different personality was not broken. But it is the same with her second or deepest state of trance. When after the renewed passes, syncope, etc., she reaches the condition which I have called Léonie 3, she is another person still. Serious and grave, instead of being a restless child, she speaks slowly and moves but little. Again she separates herself from the waking Léonie 1. 'A good but rather stupid woman,' she says, 'and not me.' And she also separates herself from Léonie 2: 'How can you see anything of me in that crazy creature?' she says. 'Fortunately I am nothing for her.' "

Léonie 1 knows only of herself; Léonie 2, of herself and of Léonie 1; Léonie 3 knows of herself and of both the others. Léonie 1 has a visual consciousness; Léonie 2 has one both visual and auditory; in Léonie 3 it is at once visual, auditory, and tactile. Prof. Janet thought at first that he was Léonie 3's discoverer. But she told him that she had been frequently in that condition before. A former magnetizer had hit upon her just as M. Janet had, in seeking by means of passes to deepen the sleep of Léonie 2.

"This resurrection of a somnambulic personage who had been extinct for twenty years is curious enough; and in speaking to Léonie 3, I naturally now adopt the name of Léonore which was given her by her first master."

The most carefully studied case of multiple personality is that of the hysteric youth Louis V. about whom MM. Bourru and Burot have written a book.[57] The symptoms are too intricate to be reproduced here with detail. Suffice it that Louis V. had led an irregular life, in the army, in hospitals, and in houses of correction, and had had numerous hysteric anæsthesias, paralyses, and contractures attacking him differently at different times and when he lived at different places. At eighteen, at an agricultural House of Correction he was bitten by a viper, which brought on a convulsive crisis and left *both of his legs* paralyzed for three years. During this condition he was gentle, moral, and industrious. But suddenly at last, after a long convulsive seizure, his paralysis disappeared, and with it his memory for all the time during which it had en-

57 *Variations de la personnalité* (Paris, 1888).

dured. His character also changed: he became quarrelsome, gluttonous, impolite, stealing his comrades' wine, and money from an attendant, and finally escaped from the establishment and fought furiously when he was overtaken and caught. Later, when he first fell under the observation of the authors, his *right side* was half paralyzed and insensible, and his character intolerable; the application of metals transferred the paralysis to the *left* side, abolished his recollections of the other condition, and carried him psychically back to the hospital of Bicêtre where he had been treated for a similar physical condition. His character, opinions, education, all underwent a concomitant transformation. He was no longer the personage of the moment before. It appeared ere long that any present nervous disorder in him could be temporarily removed by metals, magnets, electric or other baths, etc.; and that any past disorder could be brought back by hypnotic suggestion. He also went through a rapid spontaneous repetition of his series of past disorders after each of the convulsive attacks which occurred in him at intervals. It was observed that each physical state in which he found himself, excluded certain memories and brought with it a definite modification of character.

"The law of these changes," say the authors, "is quite clear. There exist precise, constant, and necessary relations between the bodily and the mental state, such that it is impossible to modify the one without modifying the other in a parallel fashion."[58]

The case of this proteiform individual would seem, then, nicely to corroborate M. P. Janet's law that anæsthesias and gaps in memory go together. Coupling Janet's law with Locke's that changes of memory bring changes of personality, we should have an apparent explanation of some cases at least of alternate personality. But mere anæsthesia does not sufficiently explain the changes of disposition, which are probably due to modifications in the perviousness of motor and associative paths, co-ordinate with those of the sensorial paths rather than consecutive upon them. And indeed a glance at other cases than M. Janet's own, suffices to show us that sensibility and memory are not coupled in any invariable

[58] *Op. cit.*, p. 84. In this work and in Dr. Azam's (cited on a previous page), as well as in Prof. Théodule Ribot's *Maladies de la personnalité* (1885), the reader will find information and references relative to the other known cases of the kind.

way.[59] M. Janet's law, true of his own cases, does not seem to hold good in all.

Of course it is mere guesswork to speculate on what may be the cause of the amnesias which lie at the bottom of changes in the Self. Changes of blood-supply have naturally been invoked. Alternate action of the two hemispheres was long ago proposed by Dr. Wigan in his book on the *Duality of the Mind.* I shall revert to this explanation after considering the third class of alterations of the Self, those, namely, which I have called 'possessions.'

I have myself become quite recently acquainted with the subject of a case of alternate personality of the 'ambulatory' sort, who has given me permission to name him in these pages.[60]

The Rev. Ansel Bourne, of Greene, R. I., was brought up to the trade of a carpenter; but, in consequence of a sudden temporary loss of sight and hearing under very peculiar circumstances, he became converted from Atheism to Christianity just before his thirtieth year, and has since that time for the most part lived the life of an itinerant preacher. He has been subject to headaches and temporary fits of depression of spirits during most of his life, and has had a few fits of unconsciousness lasting an hour or less. He also has a region of somewhat diminished cutaneous sensibility on the left thigh. Otherwise his health is good, and his muscular strength and endurance excellent. He is of a firm and self-reliant disposition, a man whose yea is yea and his nay, nay; and his character for uprightness is such in the community that no person who knows him will for a moment admit the possibility of his case not being perfectly genuine.

On January 17, 1887, he drew 551 dollars from a bank in Providence with which to pay for a certain lot of land in Greene, paid certain bills, and got into a Pawtucket horse-car. This is the last incident which he

59 His own brother's subject Witt. . . . , although in her anæsthetic waking stage she recollected nothing of either of her trances, yet remembered her deeper trance (in which her sensibilities became perfect—see above, p. 205) when she was in her lighter trance. Nevertheless in the latter she was as anæsthetic as when awake. (*Loc. cit.*, p. 619.)—It does not appear that there was any important difference in the sensibility of Félida X. between her two states—as far as one can judge from M. Azam's account she was to some degree anæsthetic in both (*op. cit.*, pp. 71, 96).—In the case of double personality reported by M. Dufay (*Revue Scientifique*, vol. XVIII, p. 69), the memory seems to have been best in the more anæsthetic condition.—Hypnotic subjects made blind do not necessarily lose their visual ideas. It appears, then, both that amnesias may occur without anæsthesias, and anæsthesias without amnesias, though they may also occur in combination. Hypnotic subjects made blind by suggestion will tell you that they clearly imagine the things which they can no longer see.

60 A full account of the case, by Mr. R. Hodgson, will be found in the *Proceedings of the Society for Psychical Research* for 1891.

remembers. He did not return home that day, and nothing was heard of him for two months. He was published in the papers as missing, and foul play being suspected, the police sought in vain his whereabouts. On the morning of March 14th, however, at Norristown, Pennsylvania, a man calling himself A. J. Brown, who had rented a small shop six weeks previously, stocked it with stationery, confectionery, fruit and small articles, and carried on his quiet trade without seeming to anyone unnatural or eccentric, woke up in a fright and called in the people of the house to tell him where he was. He said that his name was Ansel Bourne, that he was entirely ignorant of Norristown, that he knew nothing of shop-keeping, and that the last thing he remembered—it seemed only yesterday—was drawing the money from the bank, etc., in Providence. He would not believe that two months had elapsed. The people of the house thought him insane; and so, at first, did Dr. Louis H. Read, whom they called in to see him. But on telegraphing to Providence, confirmatory messages came, and presently his nephew, Mr. Andrew Harris, arrived upon the scene, made everything straight, and took him home. He was very weak, having lost apparently over twenty pounds of flesh during his escapade, and had such a horror of the idea of the candy-store that he refused to set foot in it again.

The first two weeks of the period remained unaccounted for, as he had no memory, after he had once resumed his normal personality, of any part of the time, and no one who knew him seems to have seen him after he left home. The remarkable part of the change is, of course, the peculiar occupation which the so-called Brown indulged in. Mr. Bourne has never in his life had the slightest contact with trade. 'Brown' was described by the neighbors as taciturn, orderly in his habits, and in no way queer. He went to Philadelphia several times; replenished his stock; cooked for himself in the back shop, where he also slept; went regularly to church; and once at a prayer-meeting made what was considered by the hearers a good address, in the course of which he related an incident which he had witnessed in his natural state of Bourne.

This was all that was known of the case up to June 1890, when I induced Mr. Bourne to submit to hypnotism, so as to see whether, in the hypnotic trance, his 'Brown' memory would not come back. It did so with surprising readiness; so much so indeed that it proved quite impossible to make him whilst in the hypnosis remember any of the facts of his normal life. He had heard of Ansel Bourne, but "didn't know as he had ever met the man." When confronted with Mrs. Bourne he said that he had "never seen the woman before," etc. On the other hand, he told of his peregrinations during the lost fortnight,[61] and gave all sorts

[61] He had spent an afternoon in Boston, a night in New York, an afternoon in Newark, and ten days or more in Philadelphia, first in a certain hotel and next in

of details about the Norristown episode. The whole thing was prosaic enough; and the Brown-personality seems to be nothing but a rather shrunken, dejected, and amnesic extract of Mr. Bourne himself. He gives no motive for the wandering except that there was 'trouble back there' and he 'wanted rest.' During the trance he looks old, the corners of his mouth are drawn down, his voice is slow and weak, and he sits screening his eyes and trying vainly to remember what lay before and after the two months of the Brown experience. "I'm all hedged in," he says: "I can't get out at either end. I don't know what set me down in that Pawtucket horse-car, and I don't know how I ever left that store, or what became of it." His eyes are practically normal, and all his sensibilities (save for tardier response) about the same in hypnosis as in waking. I had hoped by suggestion, etc., to run the two personalities into one, and make the memories continuous, but no artifice would avail to accomplish this, and Mr. Bourne's skull to-day still covers two distinct personal selves.

The case (whether it contain an epileptic element or not) should apparently be classed as one of spontaneous hypnotic trance, persisting for two months. The peculiarity of it is that nothing else like it ever occurred in the man's life, and that no eccentricity of character came out. In most similar cases, the attacks recur, and the sensibilities and conduct markedly change.[62]

3. In *'mediumships'* or *'possessions'* the invasion and the passing away of the secondary state are both relatively abrupt, and the duration of the state is usually short—i.e., from a few minutes to a few hours. Whenever the secondary state is well developed no memory for aught that happened during it remains after the primary consciousness comes back. The subject during the secondary consciousness speaks, writes, or acts as if animated by a foreign person, and often names this foreign person and gives his history. In old times the foreign 'control' was usually a demon, and is so now in communities which favor that belief. With us he gives himself

---

a certain boarding-house, making no acquaintances, 'resting,' reading, and 'looking round.' I have unfortunately been unable to get independent corroboration of these details, as the hotel registers are destroyed, and the boarding-house named by him has been pulled down. He forgets the name of the two ladies who kept it. The ladies were traced later by Dr. Newbold and full corroboration obtained of the boarding-house episode.

62 The details of the case, it will be seen, are all *compatible* with simulation. I can only say of that, that no one who has examined Mr. Bourne (including Dr. Read, Dr. Weir Mitchell, Dr. Guy Hinsdale, and Mr. R. Hodgson) practically doubts his ingrained honesty, nor, so far as I can discover, do any of his personal acquaintances indulge in a sceptical view.

out at the worst for an Indian or other grotesquely speaking but harmless personage. Usually he purports to be the spirit of a dead person known or unknown to those present, and the subject is then what we call a 'medium.' Mediumistic possession in all its grades seems to form a perfectly natural special type of alternate personality, and the susceptibility to it in some form is by no means an uncommon gift, in persons who have no other obvious nervous anomaly. The phenomena are very intricate, and are only just beginning to be studied in a proper scientific way. The lowest phase of mediumship is automatic writing, and the lowest grade of that is where the Subject knows what words are coming, but feels impelled to write them as if from without. Then comes writing unconsciously, even whilst engaged in reading or talk. Inspirational speaking, playing on musical instruments, etc., also belong to the relatively lower phases of possession, in which the normal self is not excluded from conscious participation in the performance, though their initiative seems to come from elsewhere. In the highest phase the trance is complete, the voice, language, and everything are changed, and there is no after-memory whatever until the next trance comes. One curious thing about trance-utterances is their generic similarity in different individuals. The 'control' here in America is either a grotesque, slangy, and flippant personage ('Indian' controls, calling the ladies 'squaws,' the men 'braves,' the house a 'wigwam,' etc., etc., are excessively common); or, if he ventures on higher intellectual flights, he abounds in a curiously vague optimistic philosophy-and-water, in which phrases about spirit, harmony, beauty, law, progression, development, etc., keep recurring. It seems exactly as if one author composed more than half of the trance-messages, no matter by whom they are uttered. Whether all sub-conscious selves are peculiarly susceptible to a certain stratum of the *Zeitgeist*, and get their inspiration from it, I know not; but this is obviously the case with the secondary selves which become 'developed' in spiritualist circles. There the beginnings of the medium trance are indistinguishable from effects of hypnotic suggestion. The subject assumes the rôle of a medium simply because opinion expects it of him under the conditions which are present; and carries it out with a feebleness or a vivacity proportionate to his histrionic gifts. But the odd thing is that persons unexposed to spiritualist traditions will so often act in the same way when they become entranced, speak in the name of the departed, go through the motions of their several death-agonies, send messages about their happy home in the summer-land, and describe the ailments of those present. I have no theory to publish of these cases, several of which I have personally seen.

As an example of the automatic writing performances I will quote from an account of his own case kindly furnished me by Mr. Sidney Dean of Warren, R. I., member of Congress from Connecticut from 1855 to 1859, who has been all his life a robust and active journalist, author, and man of affairs. He has for many years been a writing subject, and has a large collection of manuscript automatically produced.

"Some of it," he writes us, "is in hieroglyph, or strange compounded arbitrary characters, each series possessing a seeming unity in general design or character, followed by what purports to be a translation or rendering into mother English. I never attempted the seemingly impossible feat of copying the characters. They were cut with the precision of a graver's tool, and generally with a single rapid stroke of the pencil. Many languages, some obsolete and passed from history, are professedly given. To see them would satisfy you that no one could copy them except by tracing.

"These, however, are but a small part of the phenomena. The 'automatic' has given place to the *impressional*, and when the work is in progress I am in the normal condition, and seemingly two minds, intelligences, persons, are practically engaged. The writing is in my own hand but the dictation not of my own mind and will, but that of another, upon subjects of which I can have no knowledge and hardly a theory; and I, myself, consciously criticise the thought, fact, mode of expressing it, etc., while the hand is recording the subject-matter and even the words impressed to be written. If *I* refuse to write the sentence, or even the word, the impression instantly ceases, and my willingness must be mentally expressed before the work is resumed, and it is resumed at the point of cessation, even if it should be in the middle of a sentence. Sentences are commenced without knowledge of mine as to their subject or ending. In fact, I have never known in advance the subject of disquisition.

"There is in progress now, at uncertain times, not subject to my will, a series of twenty-four chapters upon the scientific features of life, moral, spiritual, eternal. Seven have already been written in the manner indicated. These were preceded by twenty-four chapters relating generally to the life beyond material death, its characteristics, etc. Each chapter is signed by the name of some person who has lived on earth,—some with whom I have been personally acquainted, others known in history. . . . I know nothing of the alleged authorship of any chapter until it is completed and the name impressed and appended. . . . I am interested not only in the reputed authorship,—of which I have nothing corroborative,—but in the philosophy taught, of which I was in ignorance until these chapters appeared. From my standpoint of life—which has been that of biblical orthodoxy—the philosophy is new, seems to be reasonable, and is logically put. I confess to an inability to successfully controvert it to my own satisfaction.

"It is an intelligent *ego* who writes, or else the influence assumes individuality, which practically makes of the influence a personality. It is *not* myself; of that I am conscious at every step of the process. I have also traversed the whole field of the claims of 'unconscious cerebration,' so called, so far as I am competent to critically examine it, and it fails, as a theory, in numberless points, when applied to this strange work through me. It would be far more reasonable and satisfactory for me to accept the silly hypothesis of re-incarnation,—the old doctrine of metempsychosis,—as taught by some spiritualists to-day, and to believe that I lived a former life here, and that once in a while it dominates my intellectual powers, and writes chapters upon the philosophy of life, or opens a post-office for spirits to drop their effusions, and have them put into English script. No; the easiest and most natural solution to me is to admit the claim made, i.e., that it is a decarnated intelligence who writes. But *who*? that is the question. The names of scholars and thinkers who once lived are affixed to the most ungrammatical and weakest of *bosh*. . . .

"It seems reasonable to me—upon the hypothesis that it is a person using another's mind or brain—that there must be more or less of that other's style or tone incorporated in the message, and that to the unseen personality, i.e., the power which impresses, the thought, the fact, or the philosophy, and not the style or tone, belongs. For instance, while the influence is impressing my brain with the greatest force and rapidity, so that my pencil fairly flies over the paper to record the thoughts, I am conscious that, in many cases, the vehicle of the thought, i.e., the language, is very natural and familiar to me, as if, somehow, *my* personality as a writer was getting mixed up with the message. And, again, the style, language, everything, is entirely foreign to my own style."

I am myself persuaded by abundant acquaintance with the trances of one medium that the 'control' may be altogether different from any *possible* waking self of the person. In the case I have in mind, it professes to be a certain departed French doctor; and is, I am convinced, acquainted with facts about the circumstances, and the living and dead relatives and acquaintances, of numberless sitters whom the medium never met before, and of whom she has never heard the names. I record my bare opinion here unsupported by the evidence, not, of course, in order to convert anyone to my view, but because I am persuaded that a serious study of these trance-phenomena is one of the greatest needs of psychology, and think that my personal confession may possibly draw a reader or two into a field which the *soi-disant* 'scientist' usually refuses to explore.

Many persons have found evidence conclusive to their minds that in some cases the control is really the departed spirit whom it pretends to be. The phenomena shade off so gradually into cases where this is obviously absurd, that the presumption (quite apart from *a priori* 'scientific' prejudice) is great against its being true. The case of Lurancy Vennum is perhaps as extreme a case of 'possession' of the modern sort as one can find.[63] Lurancy was a young girl of fourteen, living with her parents at Watseka, Ill., who (after various distressing hysterical disorders and spontaneous trances, during which she was possessed by departed spirits of a more or less grotesque sort) finally declared herself to be animated by the spirit of Mary Roff (a neighbor's daughter, who had died in an insane asylum twelve years before) and insisted on being sent 'home' to Mr. Roff's house. After a week of 'homesickness' and importunity on her part, her parents agreed, and the Roffs, who pitied her, and who were spiritualists into the bargain, took her in. Once there, she seems to have convinced the family that their dead Mary had exchanged habitations with Lurancy. Lurancy was said to be temporarily in heaven, and Mary's spirit now controlled her organism, and lived again in her former earthly home.

"The girl now in her new home, seemed perfectly happy and content, knowing every person and everything that Mary knew when in her original body, twelve to twenty-five years ago, recognizing and calling by name those who were friends and neighbors of the family from 1852 to 1865, when Mary died, calling attention to scores, yes, hundreds of incidents that transpired during her natural life. During all the period of her sojourn at Mr. Roff's she had no knowledge of, and did not recognize any of Mr. Vennum's family, their friends or neighbors, yet Mr.

[63] *The Watseka Wonder*, by E. W. Stevens. Chicago, Religio-Philosophical Publishing House, 1887.

and Mrs. Vennum and their children visited her and Mr. Roff's people, she being introduced to them as to any strangers. After frequent visits, and hearing them often and favorably spoken of, she learned to love them as acquaintances, and visited them with Mrs. Roff three times. From day to day she appeared natural, easy, affable and industrious, attending diligently and faithfully to her household duties, assisting in the general work of the family as a faithful, prudent daughter might be supposed to do, singing, reading or conversing as opportunity offered, upon all matters of private or general interest to the family."

The so-called Mary whilst at the Roffs' would sometimes 'go back to heaven,' and leave the body in a 'quiet trance,' i.e., without the original personality of Lurancy returning. After eight or nine weeks, however, the memory and manner of Lurancy would sometimes partially, but not entirely, return for a few minutes. Once Lurancy seems to have taken full possession for a short time. At last, after some fourteen weeks, conformably to the prophecy which 'Mary' had made when she first assumed 'control,' she departed definitively and the Lurancy-consciousness came back for good. Mr. Roff writes:

"She wanted me to take her home, which I did. She called me Mr. Roff, and talked with me as a young girl would, not being acquainted. I asked her how things appeared to her—if they seemed natural. She said it seemed like a dream to her. She met her parents and brothers in a very affectionate manner, hugging and kissing each one in tears of gladness. She clasped her arms around her father's neck a long time, fairly smothering him with kisses. I saw her father just now (eleven o'clock). He says she has been perfectly natural, and seems entirely well."

Lurancy's mother writes, a couple of months later, that she was

"perfectly and entirely well, and natural. For two or three weeks after her return home, she seemed a little strange to what she had been before she was taken sick last summer, but only, perhaps, the natural change that had taken place with the girl, and except it seemed to her as though she had been dreaming or sleeping, etc. Lurancy has been smarter, more intelligent, more industrious, more womanly and more polite than before. We give the credit of her complete cure and restoration to her family, to Dr. E. W. Stevens and Mr. and Mrs. Roff, by their obtaining her removal to Mr. Roff's, where her cure was perfected. We firmly believe that had she remained at home, she would have died, or we would have been obliged to send her to the insane asylum, and if so, that she would have died there, and further, that I could not have lived but a short time with the care and trouble devolving on me. Several of the relatives of Lurancy, including ourselves, now believe she was cured by spirit power, and that Mary Roff controlled the girl."

Eight years later, Lurancy was reported to be married and a mother, and in good health. She had apparently outgrown the mediumistic phase of her existence.[64]

On the condition of the sensibility during these invasions, few observations have been made. I have found the hands of two automatic writers anæsthetic during the act. In two others I have found this not to be the case. Automatic writing is usually preceded by shooting pains along the arm-nerves and irregular contractions of the arm-muscles. I have found one medium's tongue and lips apparently insensible to pin-pricks during her (speaking) trance.

If we speculate on the brain-condition during all these different perversions of personality, we see that it must be supposed capable of successively changing all its modes of action, and abandoning the use for the time being of whole sets of well organized association-paths. In no other way can we explain the loss of memory in passing from one alternating condition to another. And not only this, but we must admit that organized systems of paths can be thrown out of gear with others, so that the processes in one system give rise to one consciousness, and those of another system to another *simultaneously* existing consciousness. Thus only can we understand the facts of automatic writing, etc., whilst the patient is out of trance, and the false anæsthesias and amnesias of the hysteric type. But just what sort of dissociation the phrase 'thrown out of gear' may stand for, we cannot even conjecture; only I think we ought not to talk of the doubling of the self as if it consisted in the failure to combine on the part of certain systems of *ideas* which usually do so. It is better to talk of *objects* usually combined, and which are now divided between the two 'selves,' in the hysteric and automatic cases in question. Each of the selves is due to a system of

64 My friend Mr. R. Hodgson informs me that he visited Watseka in April 1890, and cross-examined the principal witnesses of this case. His confidence in the original narrative was strengthened by what he learned; and various unpublished facts were ascertained, which increased the plausibility of the spiritualistic interpretation of the phenomenon.

cerebral paths acting by itself. If the brain acted normally, and the dissociated systems came together again, we should get a new affection of consciousness in the form of a third 'Self' different from the other two, but knowing their objects together, as the result.—After all I have said in the last chapter, this hardly needs further remark.

Some peculiarities in the lower automatic performances suggest that the systems thrown out of gear with each other are contained one in the right and the other in the left hemisphere. The subjects, e.g., often write backwards, or they transpose letters, or they write mirror-script. All these are symptoms of agraphic disease. The left hand, if left to its natural impulse, will in most people write mirror-script more easily than natural script. Mr. F. W. H. Myers has laid stress on these analogies.[65] He has also called attention to the usual inferior moral tone of ordinary planchette writing. On Hughlings Jackson's principles, the left hemisphere, being the more evolved organ, at ordinary times inhibits the activity of the right one; but Mr. Myers suggests that during the automatic performances the usual inhibition may be removed and the right hemisphere set free to act all by itself. This is very likely to some extent to be the case. But the crude explanation of 'two' selves by 'two' hemispheres is of course far from Mr. Myers's thought. The selves may be more than two, and the brain-systems severally used for each must be conceived as interpenetrating each other in very minute ways.

SUMMARY

To sum up now this long chapter. The consciousness of Self involves a stream of thought, each part of which as 'I' can 1) remember those which went before, and know the things they knew; and 2) emphasize and care paramountly for certain ones among them as '*me*,' and *appropriate to these* the rest. The nucleus of the '*me*' is always the bodily existence felt to be present at the time. Whatever remembered-past-feelings *resemble* this present feeling are deemed to belong to the same *me* with it. Whatever other things are perceived to be *associated* with this feeling are deemed to form

[65] See his highly important series of articles on Automatic Writing, etc., in the *Proceedings of the Society for Psychical Research*, especially Article II (May 1885). Compare also Dr. Maudsley's instructive article in *Mind*, vol. XIV, p. 161, and Luys's essay, "Sur le dédoublement," etc., in *L'Encéphale* for 1888. Also Brown-Séquard: *Forum*, August 1890.

part of that me's *experience*; and of them certain ones (which fluctuate more or less) are reckoned to be themselves *constituents* of the me in a larger sense,—such are the clothes, the material possessions, the friends, the honors and esteem which the person receives or may receive. This me is an empirical aggregate of things objectively known. The *I* which knows them cannot itself be an aggregate; neither for psychological purposes need it be considered to be an unchanging metaphysical entity like the Soul, or a principle like the pure Ego, viewed as 'out of time.' It is a *Thought*, at each moment different from that of the last moment, but *appropriative* of the latter, together with all that the latter called its own. All the experiential facts find their place in this description, unencumbered with any hypothesis save that of the existence of passing thoughts or states of mind. The same brain may subserve many conscious selves, either alternate or coexisting; but by what modifications in its action, or whether ultra-cerebral conditions may intervene, are questions which cannot now be answered.

If anyone urge that I assign no *reason* why the successive passing thoughts should inherit each other's possessions, or why they and the brain-states should be functions (in the mathematical sense) of each other, I reply that the reason, if there be any, must lie where all real reasons lie, in the total sense or meaning of the world. If there be such a meaning, or any approach to it (as we are bound to trust there is), it alone can make clear to us why such finite human streams of thought are called into existence in such functional dependence upon brains. This is as much as to say that the special natural science of *psychology* must stop with the mere functional formula. *If the passing thought be the directly verifiable existent which no school has hitherto doubted it to be, then that thought is itself the thinker*, and psychology need not look beyond. The only pathway that I can discover for bringing in a more transcendental thinker would be to *deny* that we have any *direct* knowledge of the thought as such. The latter's existence would then be reduced to a postulate, an assertion that there *must be* a *knower* correlative to all this *known*; and the problem *who that knower is* would have become a metaphysical problem. With the question once stated in these terms, the spiritualist and transcendentalist solutions must be considered as *prima facie* on a par with our own psychological one, and discussed impartially. But that carries us beyond the psychological or naturalistic point of view.

Chapter XI

Attention

Strange to say, so patent a fact as the perpetual presence of selective attention has received hardly any notice from psychologists of the English empiricist school. The Germans have explicitly treated of it, either as a faculty or as a resultant, but in the pages of such writers as Locke, Hume, Hartley, the Mills, and Spencer the word hardly occurs, or if it does so, it is parenthetically and as if by inadvertence.[1] The motive of this ignoring of the phenomenon of attention is obvious enough. These writers are bent on showing how the higher faculties of the mind are pure products of 'experience'; and experience is supposed to be of something simply *given*. Attention, implying a degree of reactive spontaneity, would seem to break through the circle of pure receptivity which constitutes 'experience,' and hence must not be spoken of under penalty of interfering with the smoothness of the tale.

But the moment one thinks of the matter, one sees how false a notion of experience that is which would make it tantamount to the mere presence to the senses of an outward order. Millions of items of the outward order are present to my senses which never properly enter into my experience. Why? Because they have no *interest* for me. *My experience is what I agree to attend to.* Only those items

[1] Bain mentions attention in the *Senses and the Intellect*, p. 558, and even gives a theory of it on pp. 370–374 of the *Emotions and the Will*. I shall recur to this theory later on.

which I *notice* shape my mind—without selective interest, experience is an utter chaos. Interest alone gives accent and emphasis, light and shade, background and foreground—intelligible perspective, in a word. It varies in every creature, but without it the consciousness of every creature would be a gray chaotic indiscriminateness, impossible for us even to conceive. Such an empiricist writer as Mr. Spencer, for example, regards the creature as absolutely passive clay, upon which 'experience' rains down. The clay will be impressed most deeply where the drops fall thickest, and so the final shape of the mind is moulded. Give time enough, and all sentient things ought, at this rate, to end by assuming an identical mental constitution—for 'experience,' the sole shaper, is a constant fact, and the order of its items must end by being exactly reflected by the passive mirror which we call the sentient organism. If such an account were true, a race of dogs bred for generations, say in the Vatican, with characters of visual shape, sculptured in marble, presented to their eyes, in every variety of form and combination, ought to discriminate before long the finest shades of these peculiar characters. In a word, they ought to become, if time were given, accomplished *connoisseurs* of sculpture. Anyone may judge of the probability of this consummation. Surely an eternity of experience of the statues would leave the dog as inartistic as he was at first, for the lack of an original interest to knit his discriminations on to. Meanwhile the odors at the bases of the pedestals would have organized themselves in the consciousness of this breed of dogs into a system of 'correspondences' to which the most hereditary caste of *custodi* would never approximate, merely because to them, as human beings, the dog's interest in those smells would for ever be an inscrutable mystery. These writers have, then, utterly ignored the glaring fact that subjective interest may, by laying its weighty index-finger on particular items of experience, so accent them as to give to the least frequent associations far more power to shape our thought than the most frequent ones possess. The interest itself, though its genesis is doubtless perfectly *natural, makes* experience more than it is made by it.

Everyone knows what attention is. It is the taking possession by the mind, in clear and vivid form, of one out of what seem several simultaneously possible objects or trains of thought. Focalization, concentration, of consciousness are of its essence. It implies withdrawal from some things in order to deal effectively with others, and is a condition which has a real opposite in the confused, dazed, scatterbrained state which in French is called *distraction*, and *Zerstreutheit* in German.

We all know this latter state, even in its extreme degree. Most people probably fall several times a day into a fit of something like this: The eyes are fixed on vacancy, the sounds of the world melt into confused unity, the attention is dispersed so that the whole body is felt, as it were, at once, and the foreground of consciousness is filled, if by anything, by a sort of solemn sense of surrender to the empty passing of time. In the dim background of our mind we know meanwhile what we ought to be doing: getting up, dressing ourselves, answering the person who has spoken to us, trying to make the next step in our reasoning. But somehow we cannot *start*; the *pensée de derrière la tête* fails to pierce the shell of lethargy that wraps our state about. Every moment we expect the spell to break, for we know no reason why it should continue. But it does continue, pulse after pulse, and we float with it, until—also without reason that we can discover—an energy is given, something—we know not what—enables us to gather ourselves together, we wink our eyes, we shake our heads, the background-ideas become effective, and the wheels of life go round again.

This curious state of inhibition can for a few moments be produced at will by fixing the eyes on vacancy. Some persons can voluntarily empty their minds and 'think of nothing.' With many, as Professor Exner remarks of himself, this is the most efficacious means of falling asleep. It is difficult not to suppose something like this scattered condition of mind to be the usual state of brutes when not actively engaged in some pursuit. Fatigue, monotonous mechanical occupations that end by being automatically carried on, tend to produce it in men. It is not sleep; and yet when aroused from such a state, a person will often hardly be able to say what he has been thinking about. Subjects of the hypnotic trance seem to lapse into it when left to themselves; asked what they are thinking of, they reply, 'of nothing particular'![2]

[2] "The first and most important, but also the most difficult, task at the outset of an education is to overcome gradually the inattentive dispersion of mind which shows itself wherever the organic life preponderates over the intellectual. The training of animals . . . must be in the first instance based on the awakening of attention (cf.

The abolition of this condition is what we call the awakening of the attention. One principal object comes then into the focus of consciousness, others are temporarily suppressed. The awakening may come about either by reason of a stimulus from without, or in consequence of some unknown inner alteration; and the change it brings with it amounts to a concentration upon one single object with exclusion of aught besides, or to a condition anywhere between this and the completely dispersed state.

TO HOW MANY THINGS CAN WE ATTEND AT ONCE?

The question of *the 'span' of consciousness* has often been asked and answered—sometimes *a priori*, sometimes by experiment. This seems the proper place for us to touch upon it; and our answer, according to the principles laid down in Chapter IX, will not be difficult. The number of *things* we may attend to is altogether indefinite, depending on the power of the individual intellect, on the form of the apprehension, and on what the things are. When apprehended conceptually as a connected system, their number may be very large. But however numerous the things, they can only be known in a single pulse of consciousness for which they form one complex 'object' (p. 266 ff.), so that properly speaking there is before the mind at no time a plurality of *ideas*, properly so called.

The 'unity of the soul' has been supposed by many philosophers, who also believed in the distinct atomic nature of 'ideas,' to preclude the presence to it of more than one objective fact, manifested in one idea, at a time. Even Dugald Stewart opines that every *minimum visibile* of a pictured figure

"constitutes just as distinct an object of attention to the mind, as if it were separated by an interval of empty space from the rest. . . . It is impossible for the mind to attend to more than one of these points at once; and as the perception of the figure implies a knowledge of the

---

Adrien Léonard: *Essai sur l'éducation des animaux*, Lille, 1842); that is to say, we must seek to make them gradually perceive separately things which, if left to themselves, would not be attended to, because they would fuse with a great sum of other sensorial stimuli to a confused total impression of which each separate item only darkens and interferes with the rest. Similarly at first with the human child. The enormous difficulties of deaf-mute- and especially of idiot-instruction is principally due to the slow and painful manner in which we succeed in bringing out from the general confusion of perception single items with sufficient sharpness." (Waitz: *Lehrbuch der Psychologie als Naturwissenschaft*, p. 631.)

relative situation of the different points with respect to each other, we must conclude, that the perception of figure by the eye, is the result of a number of different acts of attention. These acts of attention, however, are performed with such rapidity, that the effect, with respect to us, is the same as if the perception were instantaneous."[3]

Such glaringly artificial views can only come from fantastic metaphysics or from the ambiguity of the word 'idea,' which, standing sometimes for mental state and sometimes for thing known, leads men to ascribe to the thing, not only the unity which belongs to the mental state, but even the simplicity which is thought to reside in the Soul.

When the things are apprehended by the *senses,* the number of them that can be attended to at once is small, "*Pluribus intentus, minor est ad singula sensus.*"

"By Charles Bonnet the Mind is allowed to have a distinct notion of six objects at once; by Abraham Tucker the number is limited to four; while Destutt de Tracy again amplifies it to six. The opinion of the first and last of these philosophers," [continues Sir William Hamilton] "appears to me correct. You can easily make the experiment for yourselves, but you must beware of grouping the objects into classes. If you throw a handful of marbles on the floor, you will find it difficult to view at once more than six, or seven at most, without confusion; but if you group them into twos, or threes, or fives, you can comprehend as many groups as you can units; because the mind considers these groups only as units,—it views them as wholes, and throws their parts out of consideration."[4]

Professor Jevons, repeating this observation, by counting instantaneously beans thrown into a box, found that the number 6 was guessed correctly 120 times out of 147, 5 correctly 102 times out of 107, and 4 and 3 always right.[5] It is obvious that such observations decide nothing at all about our attention, properly so called. They rather measure in part the distinctness of our vision—especially of the primary-memory-image[6]—in part the amount of association

[3] *Elements of the Philosophy of the Human Mind,* part I, chap. II, *fin.*

[4] *Lectures on Metaphysics,* lecture XIV.

[5] *Nature,* vol. III, p. 281 (1871).

[6] If a lot of dots or strokes on a piece of paper be exhibited for a moment to a person in *normal* condition, with the request that he say how many are there, he will find that they break into groups in his mind's eye, and that whilst he is analyzing and counting one group in his memory the others dissolve. In short, the impression made

in the individual between seen arrangements and the names of numbers.[7]

Each number-name is a way of grasping the beans as one total object. In such a total object, all the parts converge harmoniously to the one resultant concept; no single bean has special discrepant associations of its own; and so, with *practice*, they may grow quite numerous ere we fail to estimate them aright. But where the 'object' before us breaks into parts disconnected with each other, and forming each as it were a separate object or system, not conceivable in union with the rest, it becomes harder to apprehend all these parts at once, and the mind tends to let go of one whilst it attends to another. Still, within limits this can be done. M. Paulhan has experimented carefully on the matter by declaiming one poem aloud whilst he repeated a different one mentally, or by writing one sentence whilst speaking another, or by performing calculations on paper whilst reciting poetry.[8] He found that

"the most favorable condition for the doubling of the mind was its simultaneous application to two easy and heterogeneous operations.

---

by the dots changes rapidly into something else. In the *trance-subject*, on the contrary, it seems to *stick*; I find that persons in the hypnotic state easily count the dots in the mind's eye so long as they do not much exceed twenty in number.

[7] Mr. Cattell made Jevons's experiment in a much more precise way (*Philosophische Studien*, III, 121 ff.). Cards were ruled with short lines, varying in number from four to fifteen, and exposed to the eye for a hundredth of a second. When the number was but four or five, no mistakes as a rule were made. For higher numbers the tendency was to under- rather than to over-estimate. Similar experiments were tried with letters and figures, and gave the same result. When the letters formed familiar words, three times as many of them could be named as when their combination was meaningless. If the words formed a sentence, twice as many of them could be caught as when they had no connection. "The sentence was then apprehended as a whole. If not apprehended thus, almost nothing is apprehended of the several words; but if the sentence as a whole is apprehended, then the words appear very distinct."—Wundt and his pupil Dietze had tried similar experiments on rapidly repeated strokes of sound. Wundt made them follow each other in groups, and found that groups of twelve strokes at most could be recognized and identified when they succeeded each other at the most favorable rate, namely, from three to five tenths of a second (*Physiologische Psychologie*, 2d ed., II, 215). Dietze found that by mentally subdividing the groups into sub-groups as one listened, as many as forty strokes could be identified as a whole. They were then grasped as eight sub-groups of five, or as five of eight strokes each. (*Philosophische Studien*, II, 362.)—Later in Wundt's Laboratory, Bechterew made observations on two *simultaneously* elapsing series of metronome strokes, of which one contained one stroke more than the other. The most favorable rate of succession was 0.3 sec., and he then discriminated a group of 18 from one of 18 + 1, apparently. (*Neurologisches Centralblatt*, 1889, 272.)

[8] *Revue Scientifique*, vol. 39, p. 684 (May 28, 1887).

Two operations of the same sort, two multiplications, two recitations, or the reciting one poem and writing another, render the process more uncertain and difficult."

The attention often, but not always, oscillates during these performances; and sometimes a word from one part of the task slips into another. I myself find when I try to simultaneously recite one thing and write another that the beginning of each word or segment of a phrase is what requires the attention. Once started, my pen runs on for a word or two as if by its own momentum. M. Paulhan compared the time occupied by the same two operations done simultaneously or in succession, and found that there was often a considerable gain of time from doing them simultaneously. For instance:

"I write the first four verses of Athalie, whilst reciting eleven of Musset. The whole performance occupies 40 seconds. But reciting alone takes 22 and writing alone 31, or 53 altogether, so that there is a difference in favor of the simultaneous operations."

Or again:

"I multiply 421 312 212 by 2; the operation takes 6 seconds; the recitation of 4 verses also takes 6 seconds. But the two operations done at once only take 6 seconds, so that there is no loss of time from combining them."

Of course these time-measurements lack precision. With three systems of object (writing with *each* hand whilst reciting) the operation became much more difficult.

If, then, by the original question, how many ideas or things can we attend to at once, be meant how many entirely disconnected systems or processes of conception can go on simultaneously, the answer is, *not easily more than one, unless the processes are very habitual; but then two, or even three,* without very much oscillation of the attention. Where, however, the processes are less automatic, as in the story of Julius Cæsar dictating four letters whilst he writes a fifth,[9] there must be a rapid oscillation of the mind from one to the next, and no consequent gain of time. Within any one

[9] Cf. Christian Wolff: *Psychologia Empirica*, § 245. Wolff's account of the phenomena of attention is in general excellent.

of the systems the parts may be numberless, but we attend to them collectively when we conceive the whole which they form.

When the things to be attended to are small sensations, and when the effort is to be exact in noting them, it is found that attention to one interferes a good deal with the perception of the other. A good deal of fine work has been done in this field, of which I must give some account.

It has long been noticed, when expectant attention is concentrated upon one of two sensations, that the other one is apt to be displaced from consciousness for a moment and to appear subsequent; although in reality the two may have been contemporaneous events. Thus, to use the stock example of the books, the surgeon would sometimes see the blood flow from the arm of the patient whom he was bleeding, *before* he saw the instrument penetrate the skin. Similarly the smith may see the sparks fly *before* he sees the hammer smite the iron, etc. There is thus a certain difficulty in perceiving the exact *date* of two impressions when they do not interest our attention equally, and when they are of a disparate sort.

Professor Exner, whose experiments on the *minimal perceptible succession* in time of two sensations we shall have to quote in another chapter, makes some noteworthy remarks about the way in which the attention must be *set* to catch the interval and the right order of the sensations, when the time is exceeding small. The point was to tell whether two signals were simultaneous or successive; and, if successive, which one of them came first.

The first way of attending which he found himself to fall into, was when the signals did not differ greatly—when, e.g., they were similar sounds heard each by a different ear. Here he lay in wait for the *first* signal, whichever it might be, and identified it the next moment in memory. The second, which could then always be known by default, was often not clearly distinguished in itself. When the time was too short, the first could not be isolated from the second at all.

The second way was to accommodate the attention for a certain *sort* of signal, and the next moment to become aware in memory of whether it came before or after its mate.

"This way brings great uncertainty with it. The impression not prepared for comes to us in the memory more weak than the other, obscure as it were, badly fixed in time. We tend to take the subjectively stronger stimulus, that which we were intent upon, for the first, just as we are apt to take an objectively stronger stimulus to be the first. Still, it may happen otherwise. In the experiments from touch to sight it often seemed to me as if the impression for which the attention was *not* prepared were there already when the other came."

Exner found himself employing this method oftenest when the impressions differed strongly.[10]

In such observations (which must not be confounded with those where the two signals were identical and their successiveness known as mere *doubleness*, without distinction of which came first), it is obvious that each signal must combine stably in our perception with a *different* instant of time. It is the simplest possible case of two discrepant concepts simultaneously occupying the mind. Now the case of the signals being *simultaneous* seems of a different sort. We must turn to Wundt for observations fit to cast a nearer light thereon.

The reader will remember the reaction-time experiments of which we treated in Chapter III. It happened occasionally in Wundt's experiments that the reaction-time was reduced to zero or even assumed a negative value, which, being translated into common speech, means that the observer was sometimes so intent upon the signal that his reaction *actually coincided in time with it, or even preceded it,* instead of coming a fraction of a second after it, as in the nature of things it should. More will be said of these results anon. Meanwhile Wundt, in explaining them, says this:

"In general *we have a very exact feeling of the simultaneity of two stimuli,* if they do not differ much in strength. And in a series of experiments in which a warning precedes, at a fixed interval, the stimulus, we involuntarily try to react, not only as promptly as possible, but also in such wise that our movement may coincide with the stimulus itself. We seek to make our own feelings of touch and innervation [muscular contraction] objectively *contemporaneous with the signal* which we hear; and experience shows that in many cases we approximately succeed. In these cases we have a distinct consciousness of hearing the signal, reacting upon it, and feeling our reaction take place,—all at one and the same moment."[11]

10 Pflüger's *Archiv*, XI, 429–31.

11 *Physiologische Psychologie*, 2d ed., II, p. 240.

In another place, Wundt adds:

"The difficulty of these observations and the comparative infrequency with which the reaction-time can be made thus to disappear shows how hard it is, when our attention is intense, to keep it fixed even on *two* different ideas at once. Note besides that when this happens, one always tries to bring the ideas into a certain connection, to grasp them as components of a certain complex representation. Thus in the experiments in question, it has often seemed to me that I produced by my own recording movement the sound which the ball made in dropping on the board."[12]

The 'difficulty,' in the cases of which Wundt speaks, is that of forcing two non-simultaneous events into apparent combination with the same instant of time. There is no difficulty, as he admits, in so dividing our attention between two *really* simultaneous impressions as to feel them to be such. The cases he describes are really cases of anachronistic perception, of subjective time-displacement, to use his own term. Still more curious cases of it have been most carefully studied by him. They carry us a step farther in our research, so I will quote them, using as far as possible his exact words:

"The conditions become more complicated when we receive a series of impressions separated by distinct intervals, into the midst of which a heterogeneous impression is suddenly brought. Then comes the question, with which member of the series do we perceive the additional impression to coincide? with that member with whose presence it really coexists, or is there some aberration? . . . If the additional stimulus belongs to a different sense very considerable aberrations may occur.

"The best way to experiment is with a number of visual impressions (which one can easily get from a moving object) for the series, and with a sound as the disparate impression. Let, e.g., an index-hand move over a circular scale with uniform and sufficiently slow velocity, so that the impressions it gives will not fuse, but permit its position at any instant to be distinctly seen. Let the clockwork which turns it have an arrangement which rings a bell once in every revolution, but at a point which can be varied, so that the observer need never know in advance just when the bell-stroke takes place. In such observations three cases are possible. The bell-stroke can be perceived either exactly at the moment to which the index points when it sounds—in this case there will be no

[12] *Ibid.*, p. 262.

time-displacement; or we can combine it with a later position of the index— . . . *positive time-displacement,* as we shall call it; or finally we can combine it with a position of the index earlier than that at which the sound occurred—and this we will call a *negative displacement.* The most natural displacement would apparently be the positive, since for apperception a certain time is always required. . . . But experience shows that the opposite is the case: it happens most frequently that the sound appears earlier than its real date—far less often coincident with it, or later. It should be observed that in all these experiments it takes some time to get a distinctly perceived combination of the sound with a particular position of the index, and that a single revolution of the latter is never enough for the purpose. The motion must go on long enough for the sounds themselves to form a regular series—the outcome being a simultaneous perception of two distinct series of events, of which either may by changes in its rapidity modify the result. The first thing one remarks is that the sound belongs in a certain region of the scale; only gradually is it perceived to combine with a particular position of the index. But even a result gained by observation of many revolutions may be deficient in certainty, for accidental combinations of attention have a great influence upon it. If we deliberately try to combine the bell-stroke with an arbitrarily chosen position of the index, we succeed without difficulty, provided this position be not too remote from the true one. If, again, we cover the whole scale, except a single division over which we may see the index pass, we have a strong tendency to combine the bell-stroke with this actually seen position; and in so doing may easily overlook more than 1/4 of a second of time. Results, therefore, to be of any value, must be drawn from long-continued and very numerous observations, in which such irregular oscillations of the attention neutralize each other according to the law of great numbers, and allow the true laws to appear. Although my own experiments extend over many years (with interruptions), they are not even yet numerous enough to exhaust the subject—still, they bring out the principal laws which the attention follows under such conditions."[13]

Wundt accordingly distinguishes the *direction* from the *amount* of the apparent displacement in time of the bell-stroke. The direction depends on the rapidity of the movement of the index and (consequently) on that of the succession of the bell-strokes. The moment at which the bell struck was estimated by him with the least tendency to error, when the revolutions took place once in a second. Faster than this, *positive* errors began to prevail; slower, *negative*

[13] *Physiologische Psychologie,* 2d ed., II, 264–6.

ones almost always were present. On the other hand, if the rapidity went *quickening*, errors became *negative*; if *slowing, positive*. The amount of error is, in general, the greater the slower the speed and its alterations. Finally, individual differences prevail, as well as differences in the same individual at different times.[14]

Wundt's pupil von Tschisch has carried out these experiments on a still more elaborate scale,[15] using, not only the single bell-stroke, but 2, 3, 4, or 5 simultaneous impressions, so that the attention had to note the place of the index at the moment when a whole group of things was happening. The single bell-stroke was always heard too early by von Tschisch—the displacement was invariably 'negative.' As the other simultaneous impressions were added, the dis-

[14] This was the original 'personal equation' observation of Bessel. An observer looked through his equatorial telescope to note the moment at which a star crossed the meridian, the latter being marked in the telescopic field of view by a visible thread, beside which other equidistant threads appear. "Before the star reached the thread he looked at the clock, and then, with eye at telescope, counted the seconds by the beat of the pendulum. Since the star seldom passed the meridian at the exact

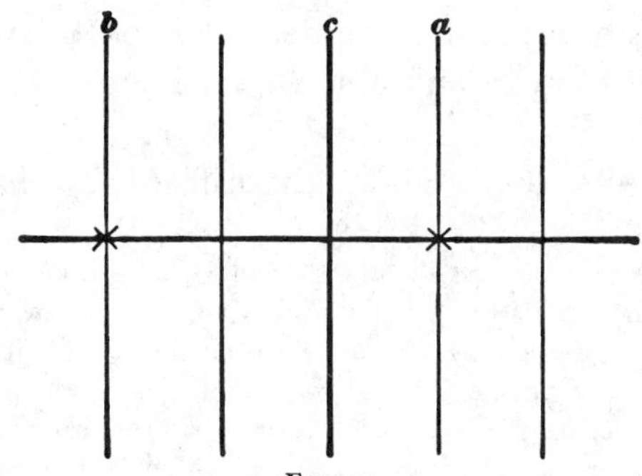

FIG. 35.

moment of a beat, the observer, in order to estimate fractions, had to note its position at the stroke before and at the stroke after the passage, and to divide the time as the meridian-line seemed to divide the space. If, e.g., one had counted 20 seconds, and at the 21st the star seemed removed by *ac* from the meridian-thread *c*, whilst at the 22d it was at the distance *bc*; then, if *ac* : *bc* :: 1 : 2, the star would have passed at 21⅓ seconds. The conditions resemble those in our experiment: the star is the index-hand, the threads are the scale; and a time-displacement is to be expected, which with high rapidities may be positive, and negative with low. The astronomic observations do not permit us to measure its absolute amount; but that it exists is made certain by the fact that after all other possible errors are eliminated, there still remains between different observers a personal difference which is often much larger than that between mere reaction-times, amounting . . . sometimes to more than a second." (*Op. cit.*, p. 269.)

[15] *Philosophische Studien*, II, no. 4, 603.

placement first became zero and finally positive, i.e., the impressions were connected with a position of the index that was too late. This retardation was greater when the simultaneous impressions were disparate (electric tactile stimuli on different places, simple touch-stimuli, different sounds) than when they were all of the same sort. The increment of retardation became relatively less with each additional impression, so that it is probable that six impressions would have given almost the same result as five, which was the maximum number used by Herr von T.

Wundt explains all these results by his previous observation that a reaction sometimes antedates the signal (see above, p. 390). The mind, he supposes, is so intent upon the bell-strokes that its 'apperception' keeps ripening periodically after each stroke in anticipation of the next. Its most natural rate of ripening may be faster or slower than the rate at which the strokes come. If faster, then it hears the stroke too early; if slower, it hears it too late. The position of the index on the scale, meanwhile, is noted at the moment, early or late, at which the bell-stroke is subjectively heard. Substituting several impressions for the single bell-stroke makes the ripening of the perception slower, and the index is seen too late. So, at least, do I understand the explanations which Herren Wundt and von Tschisch give.[16]

This is all I have to say about the difficulty of having two dis-

[16] *Physiologische Psychologie*, 2d ed., II, 273–4; 3d ed., II, 339; *Philosophische Studien*, II, 621 ff.—I know that I am stupid, but I confess I find these theoretical statements, especially Wundt's, a little hazy. Herr von Tschisch considers it impossible that the perception of the index's position should come in too late, and says it demands no particular attention (p. 622). It seems, however, that this can hardly be the case. Both observers speak of the difficulty of seeing the index at the right moment. The case is quite different from that of distributing the attention impartially over simultaneous momentary sensations. The bell or other signal gives a momentary sensation, the index a continuous one, of motion. To note any one *position* of the latter is to *interrupt* this sensation of motion and to substitute an entirely different percept—one, namely, of position—for it, during a time however brief. This involves a sudden change in the manner of attending to the revolutions of the index; which change *ought* to take place neither sooner nor later than the momentary impression, and *fix* the index as it is then and there visible. Now this is not a case of simply getting two sensations at once and so feeling them—which would be an harmonious act; but of *stopping one* and changing it into another, whilst we simultaneously get a third. Two of these acts are discrepant, and the whole three rather interfere with each other. It becomes hard to 'fix' the index at the very instant that we catch the momentary impression; so we fall into a way of fixing it either at the last possible moment before, or at the first possible moment after, the impression comes.

This at least seems to me the more probable state of affairs. If we fix the index before

crepant concepts together, and about the number of things to which we can simultaneously attend.

THE VARIETIES OF ATTENTION

The things to which we attend are said to *interest* us. Our interest in them is supposed to be the *cause* of our attending. What makes an object interesting we shall see presently; and later inquire in what sense interest may cause attention. Meanwhile

Attention may be divided into kinds in various ways.

It is either to

a) Objects of sense (sensorial attention); or to

b) Ideal or represented objects (intellectual attention).

It is either

c) Immediate; or

d) Derived: immediate, when the topic or stimulus is interesting in itself, without relation to anything else; derived, when it owes its interest to association with some other immediately interesting thing. What I call derived attention has been named 'apperceptive' attention. Furthermore, Attention may be either

---

the impression really comes, that means that we perceive it too late. But why do we fix it *before* when the impressions come slow and simple, and *after* when they come rapid and complex? And why under certain conditions is there no displacement at all? The answer which suggests itself is that when there is just enough leisure between the impressions for the attention to adapt itself comfortably both to them and to the index (one second in W.'s experiments) it carries on the two processes at once; when the leisure is excessive, the attention, following its own laws of ripening, and being *ready* to note the index before the other impression comes, notes it *then*, since that is the moment of easiest action, whilst the impression, which comes a moment later, interferes with noting it again; and finally, that when the leisure is insufficient, the momentary impressions, being the more fixed data, are attended to first, and the index is fixed a little later on. The noting of the index at too early a moment would be the noting of a real fact, with its analogue in many other rhythmical experiences. In reaction-time experiments, for example, when, in a regularly recurring series, the stimulus is once in a while omitted, the observer sometimes reacts as if it came. Here, as Wundt somewhere observes, we catch ourselves acting merely because our inward preparation is complete. The 'fixing' of the index is a sort of action; so that my interpretation tallies with facts recognized elsewhere; but Wundt's explanation (if I understand it) of the experiments requires us to believe that an observer like von Tschisch shall steadily and without exception get an hallucination of a bell-stroke before the latter occurs, and *not hear the real bell-stroke afterwards*. I doubt whether this is possible, and I can think of no analogue to it in the rest of our experience. The whole subject deserves to be gone over again. To Wundt is due the highest credit for his patience in working out the facts. His explanation of them in his earlier work (*Vorlesungen über Menschen- und Thierseele*, I, 37–42, 365–371) consisted merely in the appeal to the unity of consciousness, and may be considered quite crude.

e) Passive, reflex, non-voluntary, effortless; or

f) Active and voluntary.

Voluntary attention is always derived; we never make an *effort* to attend to an object except for the sake of some *remote* interest which the effort will serve. But both sensorial and intellectual attention may be either passive or voluntary.

In *passive immediate sensorial attention* the stimulus is a sense-impression, either very intense, voluminous, or sudden,—in which case it makes no difference what its nature may be, whether sight, sound, smell, blow, or inner pain,—or else it is an *instinctive* stimulus, a perception which, by reason of its nature rather than its mere force, appeals to some one of our normal congenital impulses and has a directly exciting quality. In the chapter on Instinct we shall see how these stimuli differ from one animal to another, and what most of them are in man: strange things, moving things, wild animals, bright things, pretty things, metallic things, words, blows, blood, etc., etc., etc.

Sensitiveness to immediately exciting sensorial stimuli characterizes the attention of childhood and youth. In mature age we have generally selected those stimuli which are connected with one or more so-called permanent interests, and our attention has grown irresponsive to the rest.[17] But childhood is characterized by great active energy, and has few organized interests by which to meet new impressions and decide whether they are worthy of notice or not, and the consequence is that extreme mobility of the attention with which we are all familiar in children, and which makes their first lessons such rough affairs. Any strong sensation whatever produces accommodation of the organs which perceive it, and absolute oblivion, for the time being, of the task in hand. This reflex and passive character of the attention which, as a French writer says, makes the child seem to belong less to himself than to every object which happens to catch his notice, is the first thing which the teacher must overcome. It never is overcome in some people, whose work, to the end of life, gets done in the interstices of their mind-wandering.

The passive sensorial attention is *derived* when the impression, without being either strong or of an instinctively exciting nature, is connected by previous experience and education with things that

[17] Note that the permanent interests are themselves grounded in certain objects and relations in which our interest is immediate and instinctive.

are so. These things may be called the *motives* of the attention. The impression draws an interest from them, or perhaps it even fuses into a single complex object with them; the result is that it is brought into the focus of the mind. A faint tap *per se* is not an interesting sound; it may well escape being discriminated from the general rumor of the world. But when it is a signal, as that of a lover on the window-pane, it will hardly go unperceived. Herbart writes:

"How a bit of bad grammar wounds the ear of the purist! How a false note hurts the musician! or an offence against good manners the man of the world! How rapid is progress in a science when its first principles have been so well impressed upon us that we reproduce them mentally with perfect distinctness and ease! How slow and uncertain, on the other hand, is our learning of the principles themselves, when familiarity with the still more elementary percepts connected with the subject has not given us an adequate predisposition!—Apperceptive attention may be plainly observed in very small children when, hearing the speech of their elders, as yet unintelligible to them, they suddenly catch a single known word here and there, and repeat it to themselves; yes! even in the dog who looks round at us when we speak of him and pronounce his name. Not far removed is the talent which mind-wandering school-boys display during the hours of instruction, of noticing every moment in which the teacher tells a story. I remember classes in which, instruction being uninteresting, and discipline relaxed, a buzzing murmur was always to be heard, which invariably stopped for as long a time as an anecdote lasted. How could the boys, since they seemed to hear nothing, notice when the anecdote began? Doubtless most of them always heard something of the teacher's talk; but most of it had no connection with their previous knowledge and occupations, and therefore the separate words no sooner entered their consciousness than they fell out of it again; but, on the other hand, no sooner did the words awaken old thoughts, forming strongly-connected series with which the new impression easily combined, than out of new and old together a total interest resulted which drove the vagrant ideas below the threshold of consciousness, and brought for a while settled attention into their place." [18]

Passive intellectual attention is immediate when we follow in thought a train of images exciting or interesting *per se*; derived, when the images are interesting only as means to a remote end, or

[18] Herbart: *Psychologie als Wissenschaft*, § 128.

merely because they are associated with something which makes them dear. Owing to the way in which immense numbers of real things become integrated into single objects of thought for us, there is no clear line to be drawn between immediate and derived attention of an intellectual sort. When absorbed in intellectual attention we may become so inattentive to outer things as to be 'absent-minded,' 'abstracted,' or '*distraits*.' All revery or concentrated meditation is apt to throw us into this state.

"Archimedes, it is well known, was so absorbed in a geometrical meditation, that he was first aware of the storming of Syracuse by his own death-wound, and his exclamation on the entrance of Roman soldiers was,—*Noli turbare circulos meos*. In like manner, Joseph Scaliger, the most learned of men, when a Protestant student in Paris, was so engrossed in the study of Homer, that he became aware of the massacre of St Bartholomew, and of his own escape, only on the day subsequent to the catastrophe. The philosopher Carneades was habitually liable to fits of meditation so profound, that, to prevent him sinking from inanition, his maid found it necessary to feed him like a child. And it is reported of Newton, that, while engaged in his mathematical researches, he sometimes forgot to dine. Cardan, one of the most illustrious of philosophers and mathematicians, was once, upon a journey, so lost in thought, that he forgot both his way and the object of his journey. To the questions of his driver whither he should proceed, he made no answer; and when he came to himself at nightfall, he was surprised to find the carriage at a stand-still, and directly under a gallows. The mathematician Vieta was sometimes so buried in meditation, that for hours he bore more resemblance to a dead person than to a living, and was then wholly unconscious of everything going on around him. On the day of his marriage, the great Budæus forgot everything in his philological speculations, and he was only awakened to the affairs of the external world by a tardy embassy from the marriage-party, who found him absorbed in the composition of his *Commentarii*."[19]

The absorption may be so deep as not only to banish ordinary sensations, but even the severest pain. Pascal, Wesley, Robert Hall, are said to have had this capacity. Dr. Carpenter says of himself that

"he has frequently begun a lecture, whilst suffering neuralgic pain so severe as to make him apprehend that he would find it impossible to

19 Sir William Hamilton: *Metaphysics*, lecture XIV.

proceed; yet no sooner has he, by a determined effort, fairly launched himself into the stream of thought, than he has found himself continuously borne along without the least distraction, until the end has come, and the attention has been released; when the pain has recurred with a force that has over-mastered all resistance, making him wonder how he could have ever ceased to feel it."[20]

Dr. Carpenter speaks of launching himself by a determined *effort.* This effort characterizes what we called *active or voluntary attention.* It is a feeling which everyone knows, but which most people would call quite indescribable. We get it in the sensorial sphere whenever we seek to catch an impression of extreme *faintness,* be it of sight, hearing, taste, smell, or touch; we get it whenever we seek to *discriminate* a sensation merged in a mass of others that are similar; we get it whenever we *resist the attractions* of more potent stimuli and keep our mind occupied with some object that is naturally unimpressive. We get it in the intellectual sphere under exactly similar conditions: as when we strive to sharpen and make distinct an idea which we but vaguely seem to have; or painfully discriminate a shade of meaning from its similars; or resolutely hold fast to a thought so discordant with our impulses that, if left unaided, it would quickly yield place to images of an exciting and impassioned kind. All forms of attentive effort would be exercised at once by one whom we might suppose at a dinner-party resolutely to listen to a neighbor giving him insipid and unwelcome advice in a low voice, whilst all around the guests were loudly laughing and talking about exciting and interesting things.

There is no such thing as voluntary attention sustained for more than a few seconds at a time. What is called sustained voluntary attention is a repetition of successive efforts which bring back the topic to the mind.[21] The topic once brought back, if a congenial one, *develops*; and if its development is interesting it engages the attention passively for a time. Dr. Carpenter, a moment back, described the stream of thought, once entered, as 'bearing him along.' This passive interest may be short or long. As soon as it flags, the

20 *Mental Physiology,* § 124. The oft-cited case of soldiers not perceiving that they are wounded is of an analogous sort.

21 Prof. J. M. Cattell made experiments to which we shall refer further on, on the degree to which reaction-times might be shortened by distracting or voluntarily concentrating the attention. He says of the latter series that "the averages show that the attention can be held strained, that is, the centres kept in a state of unstable equilibrium for one second" (*Mind,* XI, 240).

attention is diverted by some irrelevant thing, and then a voluntary effort may bring it back to the topic again; and so on, under favorable conditions, for hours together. During all this time, however, note that it is not an identical *object* in the psychological sense (p. 265), but a succession of mutually related objects forming an identical *topic* only, upon which the attention is fixed. *No one can possibly attend continuously to an object that does not change.*

Now there are always some objects that for the time being *will not develop.* They simply *go out*; and to keep the mind upon anything related to them requires such incessantly renewed effort that the most resolute Will ere long gives out and lets its thoughts follow the more stimulating solicitations after it has withstood them for what length of time it can. There are topics known to every man from which he shies like a frightened horse, and which to get a glimpse of is to shun. Such are his ebbing assets to the spendthrift in full career. But why single out the spendthrift when to every man actuated by passion the thought of interests which negate the passion can hardly for more than a fleeting instant stay before the mind? It is like 'memento mori' in the heyday of the pride of life. Nature rises at such suggestions, and excludes them from the view:—How long, O healthy reader, can you now continue thinking of your tomb?—In milder instances the difficulty is as great, especially when the brain is fagged. One snatches at any and every passing pretext, no matter how trivial or external, to escape from the odiousness of the matter in hand. I know a person, for example, who will poke the fire, set chairs straight, pick dust-specks from the floor, arrange his table, snatch up the newspaper, take down any book which catches his eye, trim his nails, waste the morning *anyhow,* in short, and all without premeditation,—simply because the only thing he *ought* to attend to is the preparation of a noonday lesson in formal logic which he detests. Anything but *that*!

Once more, the object must change. When it is one of sight, it will actually become invisible; when of hearing, inaudible,—if we attend to it too unmovingly. Helmholtz, who has put his sensorial attention to the severest tests, by using his eyes on objects which in common life are expressly overlooked, makes some interesting remarks on this point in his chapter on retinal rivalry.[22] The phenomenon called by that name is this, that if we look with each eye upon a different picture (as in the annexed stereoscopic slide),

[22] *Physiologische Optik,* § 32.

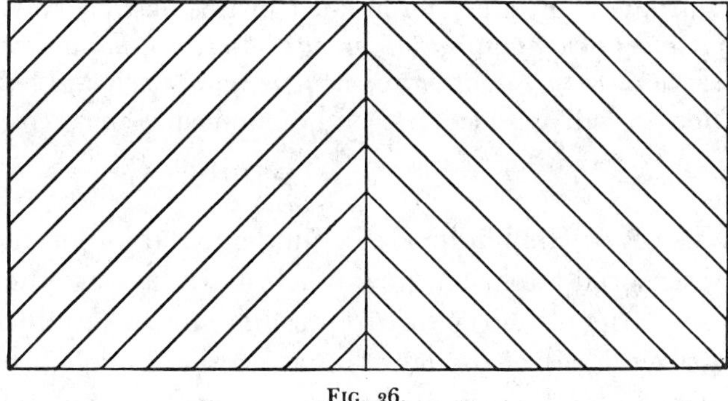

FIG. 36.

sometimes one picture, sometimes the other, or parts of both, will come to consciousness, but hardly ever both combined. Helmholtz now says:

"I find that I am able to attend voluntarily, now to one and now to the other system of lines; and that then this system remains visible alone for a certain time, whilst the other completely vanishes. This happens, for example, whenever I try to count the lines first of one and then of the other system. . . . But it is extremely hard to chain the attention down to one of the systems for long, unless we associate with our looking some distinct purpose which keeps the activity of the attention perpetually renewed. Such a one is counting the lines, comparing their intervals, or the like. An equilibrium of the attention, persistent for any length of time, is under no circumstances attainable. The natural tendency of attention when left to itself is to wander to ever new things; and so soon as the interest of its object is over, so soon as nothing new is to be noticed there, it passes, in spite of our will, to something else. If we wish to keep it upon one and the same object, we must seek constantly to find out something new about the latter, especially if other powerful impressions are attracting us away."

And again criticising an author who had treated of attention as an activity absolutely subject to the conscious will, Helmholtz writes:

"This is only restrictedly true. We move our eyes by our will; but one without training cannot so easily execute the intention of making them converge. At any moment, however, he can execute that of looking at a near object, in which act convergence is involved. Now just as little can we carry out our purpose to keep our attention steadily fixed upon a certain object, when our interest in the object is exhausted, and the purpose is inwardly formulated in this abstract way. *But we can set ourselves new questions about the object, so that a new interest in it arises, and then the attention will remain riveted.* The relation of attention to will is, then, less one of immediate than of mediate control."

These words of Helmholtz are of fundamental importance. And if true of sensorial attention, how much more true are they of the intellectual variety! The *conditio sine quâ non* of sustained attention to a given topic of thought is that we should roll it over and over incessantly and consider different aspects and relations of it in turn. Only in pathological states will a fixed and ever monotonously recurring idea possess the mind.

And now we can see why it is that what is called sustained attention is the easier, the richer in acquisitions and the fresher and more original the mind. In such minds, subjects bud and sprout and grow. At every moment, they please by a new consequence and rivet the attention afresh. But an intellect unfurnished with materials, stagnant, unoriginal, will hardly be likely to consider any subject long. A glance exhausts its possibilities of interest. Geniuses are commonly believed to excel other men in their power of sustained attention.[23] In most of them, it is to be feared, the so-called 'power' is of the passive sort. Their ideas coruscate, every subject branches infinitely before their fertile minds, and so for hours they may be rapt. *But it is their genius making them attentive, not their attention making geniuses of them.* And, when we come down to the root of the matter, we see that they differ from ordinary men less in the character of their attention than in the nature of the objects upon which it is successively bestowed. In the genius, these form a concatenated series, suggesting each other mutually by some rational law. Therefore we call the attention 'sustained' and the topic of meditation for hours 'the same.' In the common man the

23 " 'Genius,' says Helvetius, 'is nothing but a continued attention,' (*une attention suivie*). 'Genius,' says Buffon, 'is only a protracted patience,' (*une longue patience*). 'In the exact sciences, at least,' says Cuvier, 'it is the patience of a sound intellect, when invincible, which truly constitutes genius.' And Chesterfield has also observed, that 'the power of applying an attention, steady and undissipated, to a single object, is the sure mark of a superior genius.' " (Hamilton: *Lectures on Metaphysics*, lecture XIV.)

series is for the most part incoherent, the objects have no rational bond, and we call the attention wandering and unfixed.

It is probable that genius tends actually to prevent a man from acquiring habits of voluntary attention, and that moderate intellectual endowments are the soil in which we may best expect, here as elsewhere, the virtues of the will, strictly so called, to thrive. But, whether the attention come by grace of genius or by dint of will, the longer one does attend to a topic the more mastery of it one has. And the faculty of voluntarily bringing back a wandering attention, over and over again, is the very root of judgment, character, and will. No one is *compos sui* if he have it not. An education which should improve this faculty would be *the* education *par excellence*. But it is easier to define this ideal than to give practical directions for bringing it about. The only general pedagogic maxim bearing on attention is that the more interest the child has in advance in the subject, the better he will attend. Induct him therefore in such a way as to knit each new thing on to some acquisition already there; and if possible awaken curiosity, so that the new thing shall seem to come as an answer, or part of an answer, to a question pre-existing in his mind.

At present having described the varieties, let us turn to

THE EFFECTS OF ATTENTION

Its remote effects are too incalculable to be recorded. The practical and theoretical life of whole species, as well as of individual beings, results from the selection which the habitual direction of their attention involves. In Chapters XIV and XV some of these consequences will come to light. Suffice it meanwhile that each of us literally *chooses*, by his ways of attending to things, what sort of a universe he shall appear to himself to inhabit.

The immediate effects of attention are to make us:

a) perceive—
b) conceive—
c) distinguish—
d) remember—

better than otherwise we could—both more successive things and each thing more clearly. It also

e) shortens 'reaction-time.'

a and *b*. Most people would say that a sensation attended to becomes stronger than it otherwise would be. This point is, however, not quite plain, and has occasioned some discussion.[24] From the strength or intensity of a sensation must be distinguished its clearness; and to increase *this* is, for some psychologists, the utmost that attention can do. When the facts are surveyed, however, it must be admitted that to some extent the relative intensity of two sensations may be changed when one of them is attended to and the other not. Every artist knows how he can make a scene before his eyes appear warmer or colder in color, according to the way he sets his attention. If for warm, he soon begins to *see* the red color start out of everything; if for cold, the blue. Similarly in listening for certain notes in a chord, or overtones in a musical sound, the one we attend to sounds probably a little more loud as well as more emphatic than it did before. When we mentally break a series of monotonous strokes into a rhythm, by accentuating every second or third one, etc., the stroke on which the stress of attention is laid seems to become stronger as well as more emphatic. The increased visibility of optical after-images and of double images, which close attention brings about, can hardly be interpreted otherwise than as a real strengthening of the retinal sensations themselves. And this view is rendered particularly probable by the fact that an imagined visual object may, if attention be concentrated upon it long enough, acquire before the mind's eye almost the brilliancy of reality, and (in the case of certain exceptionally gifted observers) leave a negative after-image of itself when it passes away (see Chapter XVIII). Confident expectation of a certain intensity or quality of impression will often make us sensibly see or hear it in an object which really falls far short of it. In face of such facts it is rash to say that attention cannot make a sense-impression more intense.

But, on the other hand, the intensification which may be brought about seems never to lead the judgment astray. As we rightly perceive and name the same color under various lights, the same sound at various distances; so we seem to make an analogous sort of allowance for the varying amounts of attention with which objects are viewed; and whatever changes of feeling the attention may bring

24 See, e.g., Ulrici: *Leib und Seele*, II, 28; Lotze: *Metaphysic*, § 273; Fechner: *Revision der Hauptpuncte der Psychophysik*, XIX; G. E. Müller: *Zur Theorie der sinnlichen Aufmerksamkeit*, § 1; Stumpf: *Tonpsychologie*, I, 71.

we charge, as it were, to the attention's account, and still perceive and conceive the object as the same.

"A gray paper appears to us no lighter, the pendulum-beat of a clock no louder, no matter how much we increase the strain of our attention upon them. No one, by doing this, can make the gray paper look white, or the stroke of the pendulum sound like the blow of a strong hammer,—everyone, on the contrary, feels the increase as that of his own conscious activity turned upon the thing."[25]

Were it otherwise, we should not be able to note *intensities* by attending to them. Weak impressions would, as Stumpf says,[26] become stronger by the very fact of being observed.

"I should not be able to observe faint sounds at all, but only such as appeared to me of maximal strength, or at least of a strength that increased with the amount of my observation. In reality, however, I can, with steadily increasing attention, follow a diminuendo perfectly well."

The subject is one which would well repay exact experiment, if methods could be devised. Meanwhile there is no question whatever that attention augments the *clearness* of all that we perceive or conceive by its aid. But what is meant by clearness here?

c. Clearness, so far as attention produces it, *means distinction from other things* and *internal analysis or subdivision.* These are essentially products of intellectual *discrimination,* involving comparison, memory, and perception of various relations. The attention *per se* does not distinguish and analyze and relate. The most we can say is that it is a condition of our doing so. And as these processes are to be described later, the clearness they produce had better not be farther discussed here. The important point to notice here is that it is not attention's *immediate* fruit.[27]

d. Whatever future conclusion we may reach as to this, we cannot deny that *an object once attended to will remain in the memory,*

[25] Fechner: *op. cit.*, p. 271.

[26] *Tonpsychologie,* I, p. 71.

[27] Compare, on clearness as the essential fruit of attention, Lotze's *Metaphysic,* § 273.

whilst one inattentively allowed to pass will leave no traces behind. Already in Chapter VI (see pp. 165 ff.) we discussed whether certain states of mind were 'unconscious,' or whether they were not rather states to which no attention had been paid, and of whose passage recollection could afterwards find no vestiges. Dugald Stewart says:[28] "The connexion between attention and memory has been remarked by many authors." He quotes Quintilian, Locke, and Helvetius; and goes on at great length to explain the phenomena of 'secondary automatism' (see above, p. 119 ff.) by the presence of a mental action grown so inattentive as to preserve no memory of itself. In our chapter on Memory, later on, the point will come up again.

e. Under this head, the *shortening of reaction-time*, there is a good deal to be said of Attention's effects. Since Wundt has probably worked over the subject more thoroughly than any other investigator and made it peculiarly his own, what follows had better, as far as possible, be in his words. The reader will remember the method and results of experimentation on 'reaction-time,' as given in Chapter III.

The facts I proceed to quote may also be taken as a supplement to that chapter. Wundt writes:

"When we wait with strained attention for a stimulus, it will often happen that instead of registering the stimulus, we react upon some entirely different impression,—and this not through confounding the one with the other. On the contrary, we are perfectly well aware at the moment of making the movement that we respond to the wrong stimulus. Sometimes even, though not so often, the latter may be another kind of sensation altogether,—one may, for example, in experimenting with sound, register a flash of light, produced either by accident or design. We cannot well explain these results otherwise than by assuming that the strain of the attention towards the impression we expect coexists with a preparatory innervation of the motor centre for the reaction, which innervation the slightest shock then suffices to turn into an actual discharge. This shock may be given by any chance impression, even by one to which we never intended to respond. When the preparatory innervation has once reached this pitch of intensity, the time that intervenes between the stimulus and the contraction of the muscles which react, may become vanishingly small."[29]

28 *Elements*, part I, chap. II.

29 *Physiologische Psychologie*, 2d ed., II, 226.

"The perception of an impression is facilitated when the impression is preceded by a warning which announces beforehand that it is about to occur. This case is realized whenever several stimuli follow each other at equal intervals,—when, e.g., we note pendulum movements by the eye, or pendulum-strokes by the ear. Each single stroke forms here the signal for the next, which is thus met by a fully prepared attention. The same thing happens when the stimulus to be perceived is preceded, at a certain interval, by a single warning: the time is always notably shortened. . . . I have made comparative observations on reaction-time with and without a warning signal. The impression to be reacted on was the sound made by the dropping of a ball on the board of the 'drop apparatus.' . . . In a first series no warning preceded the stroke of the ball; in the second, the noise made by the apparatus in liberating the ball served as a signal. . . . Here are the averages of two series of such experiments:

Height of Fall		Average	Mean Error	No. of Expts.
25 cm.	No warning	0.253	0.051	13
	Warning	0.076	0.060	17
5 cm.	No warning	0.266	0.036	14
	Warning	0.175	0.035	17

". . . In a long series of experiments (the interval between warning and stimulus remaining the same), the reaction-time grows less and less, and it is possible occasionally to reduce it to a vanishing quantity (a few thousandths of a second), to zero, or even to a negative value.[30] . . . The only ground that we can assign for this phenomenon is *the preparation (vorbereitende Spannung) of the attention*. It is easy to understand that the reaction-time should be shortened by this means; but that it should sometimes sink to zero and even assume negative values, may appear surprising. Nevertheless this latter case is also explained by what happens in the simple reaction-time experiments" just referred to, in which, "when the strain of the attention has reached its climax, the movement we stand ready to execute escapes from the control of our will, and we register a wrong signal. In these other experiments, in which a warning foretells the moment of the stimulus, it is also plain that attention accommodates itself so exactly to the latter's reception that *no sooner is it objectively given than it is fully apperceived, and with the apperception the motor discharge coincides.*"[31]

30 By a negative value of the reaction-time Wundt means the case of the reactive movement occurring *before* the stimulus.

31 *Op. cit.*, II, 239.

Usually, when the impression is fully anticipated, attention prepares the motor centres so completely for both stimulus and reaction that the only time lost is that of the physiological conduction downwards. But even this interval may disappear, i.e., the stimulus and reaction may become objectively contemporaneous; or more remarkable still, the reaction may be discharged before the stimulus has actually occurred.[32] Wundt, as we saw some pages back (p. 388), explains this by the effort of the mind so to react that we may feel our own movement and the signal which prompts it, both at the same instant. As the execution of the movement must precede our feeling of it, so it must also precede the stimulus, if that and our movement are to be felt at once.

The peculiar theoretic interest of these experiments lies in their *showing expectant attention and sensation to be continuous or identical processes, since they may have identical motor effects.* Although other exceptional observations show them likewise to be continuous *subjectively,* Wundt's experiments do not: he seems never, at the moment of reacting prematurely, to have been misled into the belief that the real stimulus was there.

As concentrated attention accelerates perception, so, conversely, perception of a stimulus is *retarded by anything which either baffles or distracts the attention* with which we await it.

"If, e.g., we make reactions on a sound in such a way that weak and strong stimuli irregularly alternate so that the observer can never expect a determinate strength with any certainty, the reaction-time for *all* the various signals is increased,—and so is the average error. I append two examples. . . . In Series I a strong and a weak sound alternated regularly, so that the intensity was each time known in advance. In II they came irregularly.

	Average Time	Average Error	No. of Expts.
I. *Regular Alternation*			
Strong sound	0.116″	0.010″	18
Weak sound	0.127″	0.012″	9
II. *Irregular Alternation*			
Strong sound	0.189″	0.038″	9
Weak sound	0.298″	0.076″	15

32 The reader must not suppose this phenomenon to be of frequent occurrence. Experienced observers, like Exner and Cattell, deny having met with it in their personal experience.

"Still greater is the increase of the time when, unexpectedly into a series of strong impressions, a weak one is interpolated, or *vice versâ*. In this way I have seen the time of reaction upon a sound so weak as to be barely perceived rise to 0.4″ or 0.5″, and for a strong sound to 0.25″. It is also matter of general experience that a stimulus expected in a general way, but for whose intensity attention cannot be adapted in advance, demands a longer reaction-time. In such cases . . . the reason for the difference can only lie in the fact that wherever a preparation of the attention is impossible, the time of both perception and volition is prolonged. Perhaps also the conspicuously large reaction-times which are got with stimuli so faint as to be just perceptible may be explained by the attention tending always to adapt itself for something more than this minimal amount of stimulus, so that a state ensues similar to that in the case of unexpected stimuli. . . . Still more than by previously unknown stimuli is the reaction-time prolonged by *wholly unexpected* impressions. This is sometimes accidentally brought about, when the observer's attention, instead of being concentrated on the coming signal, is dispersed. It can be realized purposely by suddenly thrusting into a long series of equidistant stimuli a much shorter interval which the observer does not expect. The mental effect here is like that of being startled;—often the startling is outwardly visible. The time of reaction may then easily be lengthened to one quarter of a second with strong signals, or with weak ones to a half-second. Slighter, but still very noticeable, is the retardation when the experiment is so arranged that the observer, ignorant whether the stimulus is to be an impression of light, sound, or touch, cannot keep his attention turned to any particular sense-organ in advance. One notices then at the same time a peculiar unrest, as the feeling of strain which accompanies the attention keeps vacillating between the several senses.

"Complications of another sort arise when what is registered is an impression anticipated both in point of quality and strength, but accompanied by other stimuli which make the concentration of the attention difficult. The reaction-time is here always more or less prolonged. The simplest case of the sort is where a momentary impression is registered in the midst of another, and continuous, sensorial-stimulation of considerable strength. The continuous stimulus may belong to the same sense as the stimulus to be reacted on, or to another. When it is of the same sense, the retardation it causes may be partly due to the distraction of the attention by it, but partly also to the fact that the stimulus to be reacted on stands out less strongly than if alone, and practically becomes a less intense sensation. But other factors in reality are present; for we find the reaction-time more prolonged by the concomitant stimulation when the stimulus is weak than when it is strong. I made experiments in which the principal impression, or signal for reaction, was a bell-stroke whose strength could be graduated by a spring against the hammer with a movable counterpoise. Each set of observations comprised two series; in one of which the bell-stroke was registered in the ordinary way, whilst in the other a toothed wheel belonging to the chronometric apparatus made during the entire experiment a steady noise against a metal spring. In one half of the latter series (A) the bell-stroke was only moderately strong, so that the accompanying noise diminished it considerably, without, however, making it indistinguishable. In the other half (B) the bell-sound was so loud as to be heard with perfect distinctness above the noise.

		Mean	Maximum	Minimum	No. of Expts.
A (Bell-stroke moderate)	Without noise.....	0.189	0.244	0.156	21
	With noise........	0.313	0.499	0.183	16
B (Bell-stroke loud)	Without noise.....	0.158	0.206	0.133	20
	With noise........	0.203	0.295	0.140	19

"Since, in these experiments, the sound B even with noise made a considerably stronger impression than the sound A without, we must see in the figures a direct influence of the disturbing noise on the process of reaction. This influence is freed from mixture with other factors when the momentary stimulus and the concomitant disturbance appeal to different senses. I chose, to test this, sight and hearing. The momentary signal was an induction-spark leaping from one platinum point to another against a dark background. The steady stimulation was the noise above described.

Spark	Mean	Maximum	Minimum	No. of Expts.
Without noise	0.222	0.284	0.158	20
With noise	0.300	0.390	0.250	18

"When one reflects that in the experiments with one and the same sense the relative intensity of the signal is always depressed [which by itself is a retarding condition] the amount of retardation in these last observations makes it probable that *the disturbing influence upon attention is greater when the stimuli are disparate than when they belong to the same sense.* One does not, in fact, find it particularly hard to register immediately, when the bell rings in the midst of the noise; but when the spark is the signal one has a feeling of being coerced, as one turns away from the noise towards it. This fact is immediately connected with other properties of our attention. The effort of the latter is accompanied by various corporeal sensations, according to the sense which is engaged. The innervation which exists during the effort of attention is therefore probably a different one for each sense-organ."[33]

Wundt then, after some theoretical remarks which we need not quote now, gives a table of retardations, as follows:

	Retardation
1. Unexpected strength of impression:	
a) Unexpectedly strong sound	0.073
b) Unexpectedly weak sound	0.171
2. Interference by like stimulus (sound by sound)	0.045[34]
3. Interference by unlike stimulus (light by sound)	0.078

It seems probable, from these results obtained with elementary processes of mind, that all processes, even the higher ones of reminiscence, reasoning, etc., whenever attention is concentrated upon them instead of being diffused and languid, are thereby more rapidly performed.[35]

Still more interesting reaction-time observations have been made by Münsterberg. The reader will recollect the fact noted in Chapter III (p. 99) that reaction-time is shorter when one concentrates his attention on the expected movement than when one concentrates it on the expected signal. Herr Münsterberg found that this is equally the case when the reaction is no simple reflex, but can take place only after an intellectual operation. In a series of experiments the five fingers were used to react with, and the reacter had to use a different finger according as the signal was of one sort or another. Thus when a word in the nominative case was called out he used

33 *Op. cit.*, pp. 241–5.

34 It should be added that Mr. J. M. Cattell (*Mind*, XI, 233) found, on repeating Wundt's experiments with a disturbing noise upon two practised observers, that the simple reaction-time either for light or sound was hardly perceptibly increased. Making strong voluntary concentration of attention shortened it by about 0.013 seconds on an average (p. 240). Performing mental additions whilst waiting for the stimulus lengthened it more than anything, apparently. For other, less careful, observations, compare Obersteiner, in *Brain*, I, 439. Cattell's negative results show how far some persons can abstract their attention from stimuli by which others would be disturbed. —A. Bertels (*Versuche über die Ablenkung der Aufmerksamkeit*, Dorpat, 1889) found that a stimulus to one eye sometimes prevented, sometimes improved, the perception of a quickly ensuing very faint stimulus to the other.

35 Cf. Wundt: *Physiologische Psychologie*, 1st ed., p. 794.

the thumb, for the dative he used another finger; similarly adjectives, substantives, pronouns, numerals, etc., or, again, towns, rivers, beasts, plants, elements; or poets, musicians, philosophers, etc., were co-ordinated each with its finger, so that when a word belonging to either of these classes was mentioned, a particular finger and no other had to perform the reaction. In a second series of experiments the reaction consisted in the utterance of a word in answer to a question, such as "name an edible fish," etc.; or "name the first drama of Schiller," etc.; or "which is greater, Hume or Kant?" etc.; or (first naming apples and cherries, and several other fruits) "which do you prefer, apples or cherries?" etc.; or "which is Goethe's finest drama?" etc.; or "which letter comes the later in the alphabet, the letter L or the first letter of the most beautiful tree?" etc.; or "which is less, 15 or 20 *minus* 8?"[36] etc. etc. etc. Even in this series of reactions *the time was much quicker when the reacter turned his attention in advance towards the answer than when he turned it towards the question.* The shorter reaction-time was seldom more than one fifth of a second; the longer, from four to eight times as long.

To understand such results, one must bear in mind that in these experiments the reacter always knew in advance in a general way the *kind* of question which he was to receive, and consequently the *sphere within which* his possible answer lay.[37] In turning his attention, therefore, from the outset towards the answer, those brain-processes in him which were connected with this entire 'sphere' were kept sub-excited, and the question could then discharge with a minimum amount of lost time that particular answer out of the 'sphere' which belonged especially to it. When, on the contrary, the attention was kept looking towards the question exclusively and averted from the possible reply, all this preliminary sub-excitement of motor tracts failed to occur, and the entire process of answering had to be gone through with *after* the question was heard. No wonder that the time was prolonged. It is a beautiful example of the summation of stimulations, and of the way in which expectant attention, even when not very strongly focalized, will prepare the motor centres, and shorten the work which a stimulus has to perform on them, in order to produce a given effect when it comes.

36 *Beiträge zur experimentellen Psychologie,* Heft 1, pp. 73–106 (1889).

37 To say the very least, he always brought his articulatory innervation close to the discharging point. Herr M. describes a tightening of the head-muscles as characteristic of the attitude of attention to the reply.

THE INTIMATE NATURE OF THE ATTENTIVE PROCESS

We have now a sufficient number of facts to warrant our considering this more recondite question. And two physiological processes, of which we have got a glimpse, immediately suggest themselves as possibly forming in combination a complete reply. I mean

1. *The accommodation or adjustment of the sensory organs*; and

2. *The anticipatory preparation from within of the ideational centres concerned with the object to which the attention is paid.*

1. The sense-organs and the bodily muscles which favor their exercise are adjusted most energetically in sensorial attention, whether immediate and reflex, or derived. But there are good grounds for believing that even intellectual attention, attention to the *idea* of a sensible object, is also accompanied with some degree of excitement of the sense-organs to which the object appeals. The preparation of the ideational centres exists, on the other hand, wherever our interest in the object—be it sensible or ideal—is *derived* from, or in any way connected with, other interests, or the presence of other objects, in the mind. It exists as well when the attention thus derived is classed as passive as when it is classed as voluntary. So that on the whole we may confidently conclude—since in mature life we never attend to anything without our interest in it being in some degree derived from its connection with other objects—that *the two processes of sensorial adjustment and ideational preparation probably coexist in all our concrete attentive acts.*

The two points must now be proved in more detail. First, as respects the sensorial adjustment.

That it is present when we attend to *sensible* things is obvious. When we look or listen we accommodate our eyes and ears involuntarily, and we turn our head and body as well; when we taste or smell we adjust the tongue, lips, and respiration to the object; in feeling a surface we move the palpatory organ in a suitable way; in all these acts, besides making involuntary muscular contractions of a positive sort, we inhibit others which might interfere with the result—we close the eyes in tasting, suspend the respiration in listening, etc. The result is a more or less massive organic feeling that attention is going on. This organic feeling comes, in the way described on page 289, to be contrasted with that of the objects which it accompanies, and regarded as peculiarly ours, whilst the objects form the not-me. We treat it as a sense of our *own activity*, although it comes in to us from our organs after they are accommodated, just as the feeling of any object does. Any object, if *immediately* exciting, causes a reflex accommodation of the sense-organ, and this has two results—first, the object's increase in clearness; and second, the feeling of activity in question. Both are sensations of an 'afferent' sort.

But in *intellectual* attention, as we have already seen (p. 287), similar feelings of activity occur. Fechner was the first, I believe, to analyze these feelings, and discriminate them from the stronger ones just named. He writes:

"When we transfer the attention from objects of one sense to those of another, we have an indescribable feeling (though at the same time one perfectly determinate, and reproducible at pleasure), of altered *direction* or differently localized tension (*Spannung*). We feel a strain forwards in the eyes, one directed sidewise in the ears, increasing with the degree of our attention, and changing according as we look at an object carefully, or listen to something attentively; and we speak accordingly of *straining the attention*. The difference is most plainly felt when the attention oscillates rapidly between eye and ear; and the feeling localizes itself with most decided difference in regard to the various sense-organs, according as we wish to discriminate a thing delicately by touch, taste, or smell.

"But now I have, when I try to vividly recall a picture of memory or fancy, a feeling perfectly analogous to that which I experience when I seek to apprehend a thing keenly by eye or ear; and this analogous feeling is very differently localized. While in sharpest possible attention to real objects (as well as to after-images) the strain is plainly forwards, and (when the attention changes from one sense to another) only alters its direction between the several external sense-organs, leaving the rest of the head free from strain, the case is different in memory or fancy, for here the feeling withdraws entirely from the external sense-organs, and seems rather to take refuge in that part of the head which the brain fills. If I wish, for example, to recall a place or person it will arise before me with vividness, not according as I strain my attention forwards, but rather in proportion as I, so to speak, retract it backwards."[38]

In myself the 'backward retraction' which is felt during attention to ideas of memory, etc., seems to be principally constituted by the feeling of an actual rolling outwards and upwards of the eyeballs, such as occurs in sleep, and is the exact opposite of their behavior when we look at a physical thing. I have already spoken of this feel-

[38] *Psychophysik*, Bd. II, pp. 475–6.

ing on page 287.[39] The reader who doubts the presence of these organic feelings is requested to read the whole of that passage again.

It has been said, however, that we may attend to an object on the periphery of the visual field and yet not accommodate the eye for it. Teachers thus notice the acts of children in the school-room at whom they appear not to be looking. Women in general train their peripheral visual attention more than men. This would be an objection to the *invariable and universal* presence of movements of adjustment as ingredients of the attentive process. Usually, as is well known, no object lying in the marginal portions of the field of vision can catch our attention without at the same time 'catching our eye'—that is, fatally provoking such movements of rotation and accommodation as will focus its image on the fovea, or point of greatest sensibility. Practice, however, enables us, *with effort*, to attend to a marginal object whilst keeping the eyes immovable. The object under these circumstances never becomes perfectly distinct—the place of its image on the retina makes distinctness im-

39 I must say that I am wholly unconscious of the peculiar feelings in the scalp which Fechner goes on to describe. "The feeling of strained attention in the different sense-organs seems to be only a muscular one produced in using these various organs by setting in motion, by a sort of reflex action, the muscles which belong to them. One can ask, then, with what particular muscular contraction the sense of strained attention in the effort to recall something is associated? On this question my own feeling gives me a decided answer; it comes to me distinctly, not as a sensation of tension in the inside of the head, but as a feeling of strain and contraction in the scalp with a pressure from without inwards over the whole cranium, undoubtedly caused by a contraction of the muscles of the scalp. This harmonizes very well with the German popular expression *den Kopf zusammennehmen*, etc., etc. In a former illness, in which I could not endure the slightest effort of continuous thought, and had no theoretical bias on this question, the muscles of the scalp, especially those of the occiput, assumed a fairly morbid degree of sensibility whenever I tried to *think*." (*Ibid.*, pp. 490–491.) In an early writing by Professor Mach, after speaking of the way in which by attention we decompose complex musical sounds into their elements, this investigator continues: "It is more than a figure of speech when one says that we 'search' among the sounds. This hearkening search is very observably a bodily activity, just like attentive looking in the case of the eye. If, obeying the drift of physiology, we understand by attention nothing mystical, but a bodily disposition, it is most natural to seek it in the variable tension of the muscles of the ear. Just so, what common men call attentive looking reduces itself mainly to accommodating and setting of the optic axes. . . . According to this, it seems to me a very plausible view that quite generally Attention has its seat in the mechanism of the body. If nervous work is being done through certain channels, that by itself is a mechanical ground for other channels being closed." (Wien, *Sitzungsberichte*, mathematisch-naturwissenschaftliche Classe, XLVIII, pt. 3, 297, 1863.)

possible—but (as anyone can satisfy himself by trying) we become more vividly conscious of it than we were before the effort was made. Helmholtz states the fact so strikingly that I will quote his observation in full. He was trying to combine in a single solid percept pairs of stereoscopic pictures illuminated instantaneously by the electric spark. The pictures were in a dark box which the spark from time to time lighted up; and, to keep the eyes from wandering betweenwhiles, a pin-hole was pricked through the middle of each picture, through which the light of the room came, so that each eye had presented to it during the dark intervals a single bright point. With parallel optical axes the points combined into a single image; and the slightest movement of the eyeballs was betrayed by this image at once becoming double. Helmholtz now found that simple linear figures could, when the eyes were thus kept immovable, be perceived as solids at a single flash of the spark. But when the figures were complicated photographs, many successive flashes were required to grasp their totality.

"Now it is interesting," he says, "to find that, although we keep steadily fixating the pin-holes and never allow their combined image to break into two, we can, nevertheless, before the spark comes, keep our attention voluntarily turned to any particular portion we please of the dark field, so as then, when the spark comes, to receive an impression only from such parts of the picture as lie in this region. In this respect, then, our attention is quite independent of the position and accommodation of the eyes, and of any known alteration in these organs, and free to direct itself by a conscious and voluntary effort upon any selected portion of a dark and undifferenced field of view. This is one of the most important observations for a future theory of attention."[40]

Hering, however, adds the following detail:

"Whilst attending to the marginal object we must always," he says, "*attend at the same time* to the object directly fixated. If even for a single instant we let the latter slip out of our mind, our eye moves towards the former, as may be easily recognized by the after-images produced, or by the muscular sounds heard. The case is then less properly to be called one of translocation, than one of unusually wide *dispersion,* of the attention, in which dispersion the largest share still falls upon the thing directly looked at,"[41]

40 *Physiologische Optik,* p. 741.

41 Hermann's *Handbuch,* III, 1, 548.

and consequently directly accommodated for. Accommodation exists here, then, as it does elsewhere, and without it we should lose a part of our sense of attentive activity. In fact, the *strain* of that activity (which is remarkably great in the experiment) is due in part to unusually strong contractions of the muscles needed to keep the eyeballs still, which produce unwonted feelings of pressure in those organs.

2. But if the peripheral part of the picture in this experiment be not physically accommodated for, what is meant by its sharing our attention? What happens when we 'distribute' or 'disperse' the latter upon a thing for which we remain unwilling to 'adjust'? This leads us to that second feature in the process, the '*ideational preparation*' of which we spoke. *The effort to attend to the marginal region of the picture consists in nothing more nor less than the effort to form as clear an idea as is possible of what is there portrayed.* The idea is to come to the help of the sensation and make it more distinct. It comes with effort, and such a mode of coming is the remaining part of what we know as our attention's 'strain' under the circumstances. Let us show how universally present in our acts of attention this reinforcing imagination, this inward reproduction, this anticipatory thinking of the thing we attend to, is.

It must as a matter of course be present when the attention is of the intellectual variety, for the thing attended to then *is* nothing but an idea, an inward reproduction or conception. If then we prove ideal construction of the object to be present in *sensorial* attention, it will be present everywhere. When, however, sensorial attention is at its height, it is impossible to tell how much of the percept comes from without and how much from within; but if we find that the *preparation* we make for it always partly consists of the creation of an imaginary duplicate of the object in the mind, which shall stand ready to receive the outward impression as if in a matrix, that will be quite enough to establish the point in dispute.

In Wundt's and Exner's experiments quoted above, the lying in wait for the impressions, and the preparation to react, consist of nothing but the anticipatory imagination of what the impressions or the reactions are to be. Where the stimulus is unknown and the reaction undetermined, time is lost, because no stable image can under such circumstances be formed in advance. But where both nature and time of signal and reaction are foretold, so completely does the expectant attention consist in premonitory imagination that, as we have seen (pp. 392, note, 404–406, 410), it may mimic the intensity of reality, or at any rate produce reality's motor effects. It is impossible to read Wundt's and Exner's pages of description and not to interpret the '*Apperception*' and '*Spannung*' and other terms as equivalents of *imagination*. With Wundt, in particular, the word *Apperception* (which he sets great store by) is quite interchangeable with both imagination and attention. All three are names for the excitement from within of ideational brain-centres, for which Mr. Lewes's name of *preperception* seems the best possible designation.

Where the impression to be caught is very weak, the way not to miss it is to sharpen our attention for it by preliminary contact with it in a stronger form.

"If we wish to begin to observe overtones, it is advisable, just before the sound which is to be analyzed, to sound very softly the note of which we are in search . . . . The piano and harmonium are well fitted for this use, as both give overtones that are strong. Strike upon the piano first the *g′* [of a certain musical example previously given in the text]; then, when its vibrations have objectively ceased, strike powerfully the note *c*, in whose sound *g′* is the third overtone, and keep your attention steadily bent upon the pitch of the just heard *g′*; you will now hear this tone sounding in the midst of the *c*. . . . If you place the resonator which corresponds to a certain overtone, for example *g′* of the sound *c*, against your ear, and then make the note *c* sound, you will hear *g′* much strengthened by the resonator. . . . This strengthening by the resonator can be used to make the naked ear attentive to the sound which it is to catch. For when the resonator is gradually removed, the *g′* grows weaker; but the attention, once directed to it, holds it now more easily fast, and the observer hears the tone *g′* now in the natural unaltered sound of the note with his unaided ear."[42]

Wundt, commenting on experiences of this sort, says that

"on carefully observing, one will always find that one tries first to recall the image in memory of the tone to be heard, and that then one hears it in the total sound. The same thing is to be noticed in weak or fugitive visual impressions. Illuminate a drawing by electric sparks separated by considerable intervals, and after the first, and often after the second and third spark, hardly anything will be recognized. But

42 Helmholtz: *Tonempfindungen*, 3d ed., 85-9 (English tr., 2d ed., 50, 51; see also pp. 60–1).

the confused image is held fast in memory; each successive illumination completes it; and so at last we attain to a clearer perception. The primary motive to this inward activity proceeds usually from the outer impression itself. We hear a sound in which, from certain associations, we suspect a certain overtone; the next thing is to recall the overtone in memory; and finally we catch it in the sound we hear. Or perhaps we see some mineral substance we have met before; the impression awakens the memory-image, which again more or less completely melts with the impression itself. In this way every idea takes a certain time to penetrate to the focus of consciousness. And during this time we always find in ourselves the peculiar *feeling* of attention. . . . The phenomena show that an *adaptation* of attention to the impression takes place. The surprise which unexpected impressions give us is due essentially to the fact that our attention, at the moment when the impression occurs, is not accommodated for it. The accommodation itself is of the double sort, relating as it does to the intensity as well as to the quality of the stimulus. Different qualities of impression require disparate adaptations. And we remark that our feeling of the *strain* of our inward attentiveness increases with every increase in the strength of the impressions on whose perception we are intent."[43]

The natural way of conceiving all this is under the symbolic form of a brain-cell played upon from two directions. Whilst the object excites it from without, other brain-cells, or perhaps spiritual forces, arouse it from within. The latter influence is the 'adaptation of the attention.' *The plenary energy of the brain-cell demands the co-operation of both factors*: not when merely present, but when both present and attended to, is the object fully perceived.

A few additional experiences will now be perfectly clear. Helmholtz, for instance, adds this observation to the passage we quoted a while ago concerning the stereoscopic pictures lit by the electric spark.

"These experiments," he says, "are interesting as regards the part which attention plays in the matter of double images. . . . For in pictures so simple that it is relatively difficult for me to see them double, I can succeed in seeing them double, even when the illumination is only instantaneous, the moment I strive to *imagine in a lively way how they ought then to look.* The influence of attention is here pure; for all eye movements are shut out."[44]

43 *Physiologische Psychologie,* 2nd ed., II, 208.

44 *Physiologische Optik,* 741.

In another place[45] the same writer says:

"When I have before my eyes a pair of stereoscopic drawings which are hard to combine, it is difficult to bring the lines and points that correspond, to cover each other, and with every little motion of the eyes they glide apart. *But if I chance to gain a lively mental image (Anschauungsbild) of the represented solid form* (a thing that often occurs by lucky chance), I then move my two eyes with perfect certainty over the figure without the picture separating again."

Again, writing of retinal rivalry, Helmholtz says:

"It is not a trial of strength between two sensations, but depends upon our fixing or failing to fix the attention. Indeed there is scarcely any phenomenon so well fitted for the study of the causes which are capable of determining the attention. It is not enough to form the conscious intention of seeing first with one eye and then with the other; *we must form as clear a notion as possible of what we expect to see. Then it will actually appear.*"[46]

In figures 37 and 38, where the result is ambiguous, we can make the change from one apparent form to the other by imagining strongly in advance the form we wish to see. Similarly in those puzzles where certain lines in a picture form by their combination an object that has no connection with what the picture ostensibly represents; or indeed in every case where an object is inconspicuous and hard to discern from the background; we may not be able to

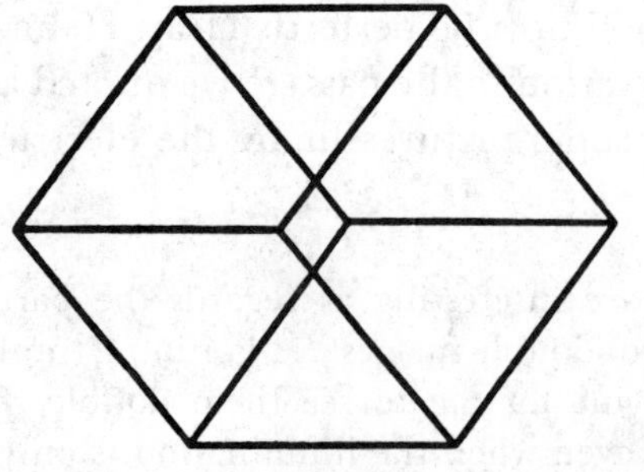

Fig. 37.

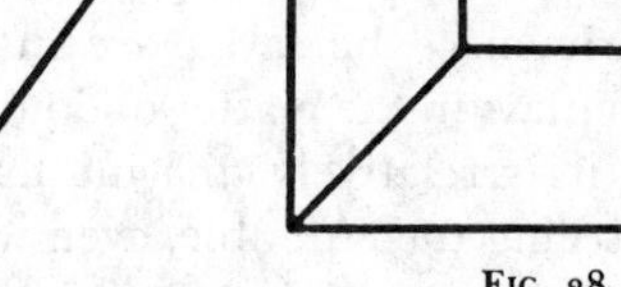

Fig. 38.

see it for a long time; but, having once seen it, we can attend to it again whenever we like, on account of the mental duplicate of it

45 P. 728.

46 *Popular Lectures on Scientific Subjects*, Eng. Trans., p. 294.

which our imagination now bears. In the meaningless French words '*pas de lieu Rhône que nous*,' who can recognize immediately the English 'paddle your own canoe'?[47] But who that has once noticed the identity can fail to have it arrest his attention again? When watching for the distant clock to strike, our mind is so filled with its image that at every moment we think we hear the longed-for or dreaded sound. So of an awaited footstep. Every stir in the wood is for the hunter his game; for the fugitive his pursuers. Every bonnet in the street is momentarily taken by the lover to enshroud the head of his idol. The image in the mind *is* the attention; the *preperception*, as Mr. Lewes calls it, is half of the perception of the looked-for thing.[48]

[47] Similarly in the verses which someone tried to puzzle me with the other day: "*Gui n'a beau dit, qui sabot dit, nid a beau dit elle?*"

[48] I cannot refrain from referring in a note to an additional set of facts instanced by Lotze in his *Medicinische Psychologie*, § 431, although I am not satisfied with the explanation, fatigue of the sense-organ, which he gives. "In quietly lying and contemplating a wall-paper pattern, sometimes it is the ground, sometimes the design, which is clearer and consequently comes nearer. . . . Arabesques of monochromic many-convoluted lines now strike us as composed of one, now of another connected linear system, and all without any intention on our part. [This is beautifully seen in Moorish patterns; but a simple diagram like Fig. 39 also shows it well. We see it

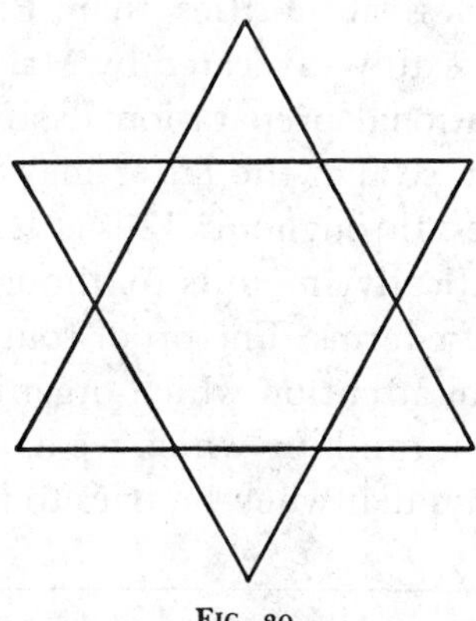

FIG. 39.

sometimes as two large triangles superposed, sometimes as a hexagon with angles spanning its sides, sometimes as six small triangles stuck together at their corners.] . . . Often it happens in revery that when we stare at a picture, suddenly some one of its features will be lit up with especial clearness, although neither its optical character nor its meaning discloses any motive for such an arousal of the attention. . . . To one in process of becoming drowsy the surroundings alternately fade into darkness and abruptly brighten up. The talk of the bystanders seems now to come from indefinite distances; but at the next moment it startles us by its threatening loudness at our

It is for this reason that men have no eyes but for those aspects of things which they have already been taught to discern. Any one of us can notice a phenomenon after it has once been pointed out, which not one in ten thousand could ever have discovered for himself. Even in poetry and the arts, someone has to come and tell us what aspects we may single out, and what effects we may admire, before our æsthetic nature can 'dilate' to its full extent and never 'with the wrong emotion.' In kindergarten-instruction one of the exercises is to make the children see how many features they can point out in such an object as a flower or a stuffed bird. They readily name the features they know already, such as leaves, tail, bill, feet. But they may look for hours without distinguishing nostrils, claws, scales, etc., until their attention is called to these details; thereafter, however, they see them every time. In short, *the only things which we commonly see are those which we preperceive*, and the only things which we preperceive are those which have been labelled for us, and the labels stamped into our mind. If we lost our stock of labels we should be intellectually lost in the midst of the world.

Organic adjustment, then, and ideational preparation or preperception are concerned in all attentive acts. An interesting theory is defended by no less authorities than Professors Bain[49] and Ribot,[50] and still more ably advocated by Mr. N. Lange,[51] who will have it that the ideational preparation itself is a consequence of muscular adjustment, so that the latter may be called the essence of the attentive process throughout. This at least is what the theory of these authors practically amounts to, though the former two do not state it in just these terms. The proof consists in the exhibition of cases of intellectual attention which organic adjustment accompanies, or of objects in thinking which we have to execute a movement. Thus Lange says that when he tries to imagine a certain col-

---

very ear," etc. These variations, which everyone will have noticed, are, it seems to me, easily explicable by the very unstable equilibrium of our ideational centres, of which constant change is the law. We *conceive* one set of lines as object, the other as background, and forthwith the first set becomes the set we *see*. There need be no *logical* motive for the conceptual change, the irradiations of brain-tracts by each other, according to accidents of nutrition, 'like sparks in burnt-up paper,' suffice. The changes during drowsiness are still more obviously due to this cause.

49 *The Emotions and the Will*, 3d ed., p. 370.

50 *Psychologie de l'attention* (1889), p. 32 ff.

51 *Philosophische Studien*, IV, 413 ff.

ored circle, he finds himself first making with his eyes the movement to which the circle corresponds, and *then* imagining the color, etc., as a consequence of the movement.

"Let my reader," he adds, "close his eyes and think of an extended object, for instance a *pencil.* He will easily notice that he first makes a slight movement [of the eyes] corresponding to the straight line, and that he often gets a weak feeling of innervation of the hand as if touching the pencil's surface. So, in thinking of a certain sound, we turn towards its direction or repeat muscularly its rhythm, or articulate an imitation of it."[52]

But it is one thing to point out the presence of muscular contractions as constant concomitants of our thoughts, and another thing to say, with Herr Lange, that thought is *made possible* by muscular contraction alone. It may well be that where the object of thought consists of two parts, one perceived by movement and another not, the part perceived by movement is habitually called up first and fixed in the mind by the movement's execution, whilst the other part comes secondarily as the movement's mere associate. But even were this the rule with all men (which I doubt[53]), it would only be a practical habit, not an ultimate necessity. In the chapter on the Will we shall learn that movements themselves are results of images coming before the mind, images sometimes of feelings in the moving part, sometimes of the movement's effects on eye and ear, and sometimes (if the movement be originally reflex or instinctive), of its natural stimulus or exciting cause. It is, in truth, contrary to all wider and deeper analogies to deny that any quality of feeling whatever can directly rise up in the form of an idea, and to assert that only ideas of movement can call other ideas to the mind.

So much for adjustment and preperception. The only third process I can think of as always present is the inhibition of irrele-

[52] See Lange: *loc. cit.*, p. 417, for another proof of his view, drawn from the phenomenon of retinal rivalry.

[53] Many of my students have at my request experimented with imagined letters of the alphabet and syllables, and they tell me that they can see them inwardly as total colored pictures without following their outlines with the eye. I am myself a bad visualizer, and make movements all the while.—M. L. Marillier, in an article of eminent introspective power which appeared after my text was written ("Remarques sur le mécanisme de l'attention," in *Revue Philosophique*, vol. XXVII, p. 566), has contended against Ribot and others for the non-dependence of sensory upon motor images in their relations to attention. I am glad to cite him as an ally.

vant movements and ideas. This seems, however, to be a feature incidental to voluntary attention rather than the essential feature of attention at large,[54] and need not concern us particularly now. Noting merely the intimate connection which our account so far establishes between attention, on the one hand, and imagination, discrimination, and memory, on the other, let us draw a couple of practical inferences, and then pass to the more speculative problem that remains.

The practical inferences are pedagogic. First, *to strengthen attention in children* who care nothing for the subject they are studying and let their wits go wool-gathering. The interest here must be 'derived' from something that the teacher associates with the task, a reward or a punishment if nothing less external comes to mind. Prof. Ribot says:

"A child refuses to read; he is incapable of keeping his mind fixed on the letters, which have no attraction for him; but he looks with avidity upon the pictures contained in a book. 'What do they mean?' he asks. The father replies: 'When you can read, the book will tell you.' After several colloquies like this, the child resigns himself and falls to work, first slackly, then the habit grows, and finally he shows an ardor which has to be restrained. This is a case of the genesis of voluntary attention. An artificial and indirect desire has to be grafted on a natural and direct one. Reading has no immediate attractiveness, but it has a borrowed one, and that is enough. The child is caught in the wheelwork, the first step is made."

I take another example, from M. B. Perez:[55]

"A child of six years, habitually prone to mind-wandering, sat down one day to the piano of his own accord to repeat an air by which his mother had been charmed. His exercises lasted an hour. The same

54 Drs. Ferrier (*Functions of the Brain* (1876), (§§102–3) and Obersteiner (*Brain*, I, 439 ff.) treat it as the essential feature. The author whose treatment of the subject is by far the most thorough and satisfactory is Prof. G. E. Müller, whose little work *Zur Theorie der sinnlichen Aufmerksamkeit*, Inauguraldissertation, Leipzig, Edelmann (1873), is for learning and acuteness a model of what a monograph should be. I should like to have quoted from it, but the Germanism of its composition makes quotation quite impossible. See also G. H. Lewes: *Problems of Life and Mind*, 3d Series, Prob. 2, chap. 10; G. H. Schneider: *Der menschliche Wille*, 294 ff., 309 ff.; C. Stumpf: *Tonpsychologie*, I, 67–75; W. B. Carpenter: *Mental Physiology*, chap. 3; Cappie in *Brain*, July 1886 (hyperæmia-theory); J. Sully in *Brain*, Oct. 1890.

55 *L'Enfant de trois à sept ans*, p. 108.

child at the age of seven, seeing his brother busy with tasks in vacation, went and sat at his father's desk. 'What are you doing there?' his nurse said, surprised at so finding him. 'I am,' said the child, 'learning a page of German; it isn't very amusing, but it is for an agreeable surprise to mamma.' "

Here, again, a birth of voluntary attention, grafted this time on a sympathetic instead of a selfish sentiment like that of the first example. The piano, the German, awaken no spontaneous attention; but they arouse and maintain it by borrowing a force from elsewhere.[56]

Then, take that mind-wandering which at a later age may trouble us *whilst reading or listening to a discourse*. If attention be the reproduction of the sensation from within, the habit of reading not merely with the eye, and of listening not merely with the ear, but of articulating to one's self the words seen or heard, ought to deepen one's attention to the latter. Experience shows that this is the case. I can keep my wandering mind a great deal more closely upon a conversation or a lecture if I actively re-echo to myself the words than if I simply hear them; and I find a number of my students who report benefit from voluntarily adopting a similar course.[57]

Second, *a teacher who wishes to engage the attention of his class must knit his novelties on to things of which they already have preperceptions.* The old and familiar is readily attended to by the mind and helps to hold in turn the new, forming, in Herbartian phraseology, an '*Apperceptionsmasse*' for it. Of course it is in every case a very delicate problem to know what 'Apperceptionsmasse' to use. Psychology can only lay down the general rule.

IS VOLUNTARY ATTENTION A RESULTANT OR A FORCE?

When, a few pages back, I symbolized the 'ideational preparation' element in attention by a brain-cell played upon from within, I added 'by other brain-cells, or by some spiritual force,' without deciding which. The question 'which?' is one of those central psychologic mysteries which part the schools. When we reflect that the turnings of our attention form the nucleus of our inner self; when

56 *Psychologie de l'attention*, p. 53.

57 Repetition of this sort does not confer *intelligence* of what is said, it only keeps the mind from wandering into other channels. The intelligence sometimes comes in beats, as it were, at the end of sentences, or in the midst of words which were mere words until then. See above, pp. 270–271.

we see (as in the chapter on the Will we shall see) that volition is nothing but attention; when we believe that our autonomy in the midst of nature depends on our not being pure effect, but a cause,—

> *Principium quoddam quod fati foedera rumpat,*
> *Ex infinito ne causam causa sequatur—*

we must admit that the question whether attention involve such a principle of spiritual activity or not is metaphysical as well as psychological, and is well worthy of all the pains we can bestow on its solution. It is in fact the pivotal question of metaphysics, the very hinge on which our picture of the world shall swing from materialism, fatalism, monism, towards spiritualism, freedom, pluralism,—or else the other way.

It goes back to the automaton-theory. If feeling is an inert accompaniment, then of course the brain-cell can be played upon only by other brain-cells, and the attention which we give at any time to any subject, whether in the form of sensory adaptation or of 'preperception,' is the fatally predetermined *effect* of exclusively material laws. If, on the other hand, the feeling which coexists with the brain-cells' activity reacts dynamically upon that activity, furthering or checking it, then the attention is in part, at least, a *cause.* It does not necessarily follow, of course, that this reactive feeling should be 'free' in the sense of having its amount and direction undetermined in advance, for it might very well be predetermined in all these particulars. If it were so, our attention would not be *materially* determined, nor yet would it be 'free' in the sense of being spontaneous or unpredictable in advance. The question is of course a purely speculative one, for we have no means of objectively ascertaining whether our feelings react on our nerve-processes or not; and those who answer the question in either way do so in consequence of general analogies and presumptions drawn from other fields. As mere *conceptions,* the effect-theory and the cause-theory of attention are equally clear; and whoever affirms either conception to be true must do so on metaphysical or universal rather than on scientific or particular grounds.

As regards *immediate sensorial attention* hardly anyone is tempted to regard it as anything but an effect.[58] We are 'evolved'

[58] The reader will please observe that I am saying all that can *possibly* be said in

so as to respond to special stimuli by special accommodative acts which produce clear perceptions on the one hand in us, and on the other hand such feelings of inner activity as were above described. The accommodation and the resultant feeling *are* the attention. We don't bestow it, the object draws it from us. The object has the initiative, not the mind.

Derived attention, where there is no voluntary effort, seems also most plausibly to be a mere effect. The object again takes the initiative and draws our attention to itself, not by reason of its own intrinsic interest, but because it is connected with some other interesting thing. Its brain-process is connected with another that is either excited, or tending to be excited, and the liability to share the excitement and become aroused is the liability to 'preperception' in which the attention consists. If I have received an insult, I may not be actively thinking of it all the time, yet the thought of it is in such a state of heightened irritability, that the place where I received it or the man who inflicted it cannot be mentioned in my hearing without my attention bounding, as it were, in that direction, as the imagination of the whole transaction revives. Where such a stirring-up occurs, organic adjustment must exist as well, and the ideas must innervate to some degree the muscles. Thus the whole process of involuntary derived attention is accounted for if we grant that there is something interesting enough to arouse and fix the thought of whatever may be connected with it. This fixing *is* the attention;

favor of the effect-theory, since, inclining as I do myself to the cause-theory, I do not want to undervalue the enemy. As a matter of fact, however, one might begin to take one's stand against the effect-theory at the outset, with the phenomenon of immediate sensorial attention. One might say that attention causes the movements of adjustment of the eyes, for example, and is not merely their effect. Hering writes most emphatically to this effect: "The movements from one point of fixation to another are occasioned and regulated by the changes of place of the attention. When an object, seen at first indirectly, draws our attention to itself, the corresponding movement of the eye follows without further ado, as a consequence of the attention's migration and of our effort to make the object distinct. The wandering of the attention entails that of the fixation point. Before its movement begins, its goal is already in consciousness and grasped by the attention, and the location of this spot in the total space seen is what determines the direction and amount of the movement of the eye." (Hermann's *Handbuch*, p. 534.) I do not here insist on this, because it is hard to tell whether the attention or the movement comes first (Hering's reasons, pp. 535–6, also 544–6, seem to me ambiguous), and because, even if the attention to the object does come first, it may be a mere effect of stimulus and association. Mach's theory that the *will to look* is the *space-feeling itself* may be compared with Hering's in this place. See Mach's *Beiträge zur Analyse der Empfindungen* (1886), pp. 55 ff.

and it carries with it a vague sense of activity going on, and of acquiescence, furtherance, and adoption, which makes us feel the activity to be our own.

This reinforcement of ideas and impressions by the pre-existing contents of the mind was what Herbart had in mind when he gave the name of *apperceptive* attention to the variety we describe. We easily see now why the lover's tap should be heard—it finds a nerve-centre half ready in advance to explode. We see how we can attend to a companion's voice in the midst of noises which pass unnoticed though objectively much louder than the words we hear. Each word is *doubly* awakened; once from without by the lips of the talker, but already before that from within by the premonitory processes irradiating from the previous words, and by the dim arousal of all processes that are connected with the 'topic' of the talk. The irrelevant noises, on the other hand, are awakened only once. They form an unconnected train. The boys at school, inattentive to the teacher except when he begins an anecdote, and then all pricking up their ears, are as easily explained. The words of the anecdote shoot into association with exciting objects which react and fix them; the other words do not. Similarly with the grammar heard by the purist and Herbart's other examples quoted on page 395.

Even where the attention is voluntary, it is possible to conceive of it as an effect, and not a cause, a product and not an agent. The things we attend to *come to us* by their own laws. Attention *creates* no idea; an idea must already be there before we can attend to it. Attention only fixes and retains what the ordinary laws of association bring 'before the footlights' of consciousness. But the moment we admit this we see that the attention *per se*, the *feeling* of attending need no more fix and retain the ideas than it need bring them. The associates which bring them also fix them by the interest which they lend. In short, voluntary and involuntary attention may be essentially the same. It is true that where the ideas are intrinsically very unwelcome and the effort to attend to them is great, it seems to us as if the frequent renewal of the effort were the very cause by which they are held fast, and we naturally think of the effort as an original force. In fact it is only to the *effort to attend*, not to the mere *attending*, that we are seriously tempted to ascribe spontaneous power. We think we can make more of it *if we will*; and the amount which we make does not seem a fixed function of the ideas themselves, as it would necessarily have to be if our effort were an effect and not a spiritual force. But even here it is possible to conceive the facts mechanically and to regard the effort as a mere effect.

Effort is felt only where there is a conflict of interests in the mind. The idea A may be intrinsically exciting to us. The idea Z may derive its interest from association with some remoter good. A may be our sweetheart, Z may be some condition of our soul's salvation. Under these circumstances, if we succeed in attending to Z at all it is always with expenditure of effort. The 'ideational preparation,' the 'preperception' of A keeps going on of its own accord, whilst that of Z needs incessant pulses of voluntary reinforcement—that is, we have the *feeling* of voluntary reinforcement (or effort) at each successive moment in which the thought of Z flares brightly up in our mind. Dynamically, however, that may mean only this: that the associative processes which make Z triumph are really the stronger, and in A's absence would make us give a 'passive' and unimpeded attention to Z; but, so long as A is present, some of their force is used to inhibit the processes concerned with A. Such inhibition is a partial neutralization of the brain-energy which would otherwise be available for fluent thought. But what is lost for thought is converted into feeling, in this case into the peculiar feeling of effort, difficulty, or strain.

The stream of our thought is like a river. On the whole easy simple flowing predominates in it, the drift of things is with the pull of gravity, and effortless attention is the rule. But at intervals an obstruction, a set-back, a log-jam occurs, stops the current, creates an eddy, and makes things temporarily move the other way. If a real river could feel, it would feel these eddies and set-backs as places of effort. "I am here flowing," it would say, "in the direction of greatest resistance, instead of flowing, as usual, in the direction of least. My effort is what enables me to perform this feat." Really, the effort would only be a passive index that the feat was being performed. The agent would all the while be the total downward drift of the rest of the water, forcing *some* of it upwards in this spot; and although, *on the average*, the direction of least resistance is downwards, that would be no reason for its not being upwards now and then. Just so with our voluntary acts of attention. They are momentary arrests, coupled with a peculiar feeling, of portions of the stream. But the arresting force, instead of being this peculiar feeling itself, may be nothing but the processes by which the collision is produced. The feeling of effort may be 'an accompaniment,' as Mr. Bradley says, 'more or less superfluous,' and no more contribute to the result than the pain in a man's finger, when a hammer falls on it, contributes to the hammer's weight. Thus the notion that our effort in attending is an original faculty, a force additional to the others of which brain and mind are the seat, may be an abject superstition. Attention may have to go, like many a faculty once deemed essential, like many a verbal phantom, like many an idol of the tribe. It may be an excrescence on Psychology. No need of it to drag ideas before consciousness or fix them, when we see how perfectly they drag and fix each other there.

I have stated the effect-theory as persuasively as I can.[59] It is a clear, strong, well-equipped conception, and like all such, is fitted to carry conviction, where there is no contrary proof. The feeling of effort certainly *may* be an inert accompaniment and not the active element which it seems. No measurements are as yet performed (it is safe to say none ever will be performed) which can show that it contributes energy to the result. We *may* then regard attention as a superfluity, or a 'Luxus,' and dogmatize against its causal function with no feeling in our hearts but one of pride that we are applying Occam's razor to an entity that has multiplied itself 'beyond necessity.'

But Occam's razor, though a very good rule of method, is certainly no law of nature. The laws of stimulation and of association may well be indispensable actors in all attention's performances, and may even be a good enough 'stock-company' to carry on many performances without aid; and yet they *may* at times simply form the background for a 'star-performer,' who is no more their 'inert accompaniment' or their 'incidental product' than Hamlet is Horatio's and Ophelia's. Such a star-performer would be the voluntary effort to attend, if it were an original psychic force. Nature *may*, I say, indulge in these complications; and the conception that she has done so in this case is, I think, just as clear (if not as 'parsimonious' logically) as the conception that she has not. To justify this assertion, *let us ask just what the effort to attend would effect if it were an original force.*

59 F. H. Bradley: "Is There Any Special Activity of Attention?" in *Mind*, XI, 305, and Lipps: *Grundtatsachen*, chaps. IV and XXIX, have stated it similarly.

It would deepen and prolong the stay in consciousness of innumerable ideas which else would fade more quickly away. The delay thus gained might not be more than a second in duration—but that second might be *critical*; for in the constant rising and falling of considerations in the mind, where two associated systems of them are nearly in equilibrium it is often a matter of but a second more or less of attention at the outset, whether one system shall gain force to occupy the field and develop itself, and exclude the other, or be excluded itself by the other. When developed, it may make us act; and that act may seal our doom. When we come to the chapter on the Will, we shall see that the whole drama of the voluntary life hinges on the amount of attention, slightly more or slightly less, which rival motor ideas may receive. But the whole feeling of reality, the whole sting and excitement of our voluntary life, depends on our sense that in it things are *really being decided* from one moment to another, and that it is not the dull rattling off of a chain that was forged innumerable ages ago. This appearance, which makes life and history tingle with such a tragic zest, *may* not be an illusion. As we grant to the advocate of the mechanical theory that it may be one, so he must grant to us that it may *not*. And the result is two conceptions of possibility face to face with no facts definitely enough known to stand as arbiter between them.

Under these circumstances, one can leave the question open whilst waiting for light, or one can do what most speculative minds do, that is, look to one's general philosophy to incline the beam. The believers in mechanism do so without hesitation, and they ought not to refuse a similar privilege to the believers in a spiritual force. I count myself among the latter, but as my reasons are ethical they are hardly suited for introduction into a psychological work.[60] The last word of psychology here is ignorance, for the 'forces' engaged are certainly too delicate and numerous to be followed in detail. Meanwhile, in view of the strange arrogance with which the wildest materialistic speculations persist in calling themselves 'science,' it is well to recall just what the reasoning is, by which the effect-theory of attention is confirmed. It is an argument from analogy, drawn from rivers, reflex actions and other material phenomena where no consciousness *appears* to exist at all, and extended

60 More will be said of the matter when we come to the chapter on the Will.

to cases where consciousness seems the phenomenon's essential feature. *The consciousness doesn't count,* these reasoners say; it doesn't exist for science, it is *nil*; you mustn't think about it at all. The intensely reckless character of all this needs no comment. It is making the mechanical theory true *per fas aut nefas.* For the sake of that theory we make inductions from phenomena to others that are startlingly *un*like them; and we assume that a complication which Nature has introduced (the presence of feeling and of effort, namely) is not worthy of scientific recognition at all. Such conduct may conceivably be *wise,* though I doubt it; but scientific, as contrasted with metaphysical, it cannot seriously be called.[61]

INATTENTION

Having spoken fully of attention, let me add a word about *inattention.*

We do not notice the ticking of the clock, the noise of the city streets, or the roaring of the brook near the house; and even the din of a foundry or factory will not mingle with the thoughts of its workers, if they have been there long enough. When we first put on spectacles, especially if they be of certain curvatures, the bright reflections they give of the windows, etc., mixing with the field of view, are very disturbing. In a few days we ignore them altogether. Various entoptic images, *muscæ volitantes,* etc., although constantly present, are hardly ever known. The pressure of our clothes and shoes, the beating of our hearts and arteries, our breathing, certain steadfast bodily pains, habitual odors, tastes in the mouth, etc., are examples from other senses, of the same lapse into unconsciousness of any too unchanging content—a lapse which Hobbes has expressed in the well-known phrase, "*Semper idem sentire ac non sentire ad idem revertunt.*"

The cause of the unconsciousness is certainly not the mere blunting of the sense-organs. Were the sensation important, we should notice it well enough; and we can at any moment notice it by expressly throwing our attention upon it,[62] provided it have not be-

61 See, for a defence of the notion of inward activity, Mr. James Ward's searching articles in *Mind,* XII, 45 and 564.

62 It must be admitted that some little time will often elapse before this effort succeeds. As a child, I slept in a nursery with a very loud-ticking clock, and remember my astonishment more than once, on listening for its tick, to find myself unable to

come so inveterate that inattention to it is ingrained in our very constitution, as in the case of the *muscæ volitantes* the double retinal images, etc. But even in these cases artificial conditions of observation and patience soon give us command of the impression which we seek. The inattentiveness must then be a habit grounded on higher conditions than mere sensorial fatigue.

Helmholtz has formulated a general law of inattention which we shall have to study in the next chapter but one. Helmholtz's law is that we leave all impressions unnoticed which are valueless to us as signs by which to *discriminate things*. At most such impressions fuse with their consorts into an aggregate effect. The upper partial tones which make human voices differ make them differ as wholes only—we cannot dissociate the tones themselves. The odors which form integral parts of the characteristic taste of certain substances, meat, fish, cheese, butter, wine, do not come as odors to our attention. The various muscular and tactile feelings that make up the perception of the attributes 'wet,' 'elastic,' 'doughy,' etc., are not singled out separately for what they are. And all this is due to an inveterate habit we have contracted, of passing from them immediately to their import and letting their substantive nature alone. They have formed connections in the mind which it is now difficult to break; they are constituents of processes which it is hard to arrest, and which differ altogether from what the processes of catching the attention would be. In the cases Helmholtz has in mind, not only we but our ancestors have formed these habits. In the cases we started from, however, of the mill-wheel, the spectacles, the factory, din, the tight shoes, etc., the habits of inattention are more recent, and the manner of their genesis seems susceptible, hypothetically at least, of being traced.

How *can* impressions that are not needed by the intellect be thus shunted off from all relation to the rest of consciousness? Professor G. E. Müller has made a plausible reply to this question, and most of what follows is borrowed from him.[63] He begins with the fact that

---

catch it for what seemed a long space of time; then suddenly it would break into my consciousness with an almost startling loudness.—M. Delbœuf somewhere narrates how, sleeping in the country near a mill-dam, he woke in the night and thought the water had ceased to flow, but on looking out of the open window saw it flowing in the moonlight, and then heard it too.

[63] *Zur Theorie der sinnlichen Aufmerksamkeit*, p. 127 foll.

"When we first come out of a mill or factory, in which we have remained long enough to get wonted to the noise, we feel as if something were *lacking*. Our total feeling of existence is different from what it was when we were in the mill. . . . A friend writes to me: 'I have in my room a little clock which does not run quite twenty-four hours without winding. In consequence of this, it often stops. So soon as this happens, I notice it, whereas I naturally fail to notice it when going. When this first began to happen, there was this modification: I suddenly felt an undefined uneasiness or sort of void, without being able to say what was the matter; and only after some consideration did I find the cause in the stopping of the clock.' "

That the stopping of an unfelt stimulus may itself be felt is a well-known fact: the sleeper in church who wakes when the sermon ends; the miller who does the same when his wheel stands still, are stock examples. Now (since every impression falling on the nervous system must propagate itself somewhither), Müller suggests that impressions which come to us when the thought-centres are preoccupied with other matters may thereby be blocked or inhibited from invading these centres, and may then overflow into lower paths of discharge. And he farther suggests that if this process recur often enough, the side-track thus created will grow so permeable as to be used, no matter what may be going on in the centres above. In the acquired inattention mentioned, the constant stimulus always caused disturbance *at first*; and consciousness of it was extruded successfully only when the brain was *strongly excited* about other things. Gradually the extrusion became easier, and at last automatic.

The side-tracks which thus learn to draft off the stimulations that interfere with thought cannot be assigned with any precision. They probably terminate in organic processes, or insignificant muscular contractions which, when stopped by the cessation of their instigating cause, immediately give us the feeling that something is gone from our existence (as Müller says), or (as his friend puts it) the feeling of a void.[64]

Müller's suggestion awakens another. It is a well-known fact that persons striving to keep their attention on a difficult subject will resort to movements of various unmeaning kinds, such as pacing

[64] I have begun to inquire experimentally whether any of the measurable functions of the workmen change after the din of machinery stops at a workshop. So far I have found no constant results as regards either pulse, breathing, or strength of squeeze by the hand. I hope to prosecute the inquiry farther (May, 1890).

the room, drumming with the fingers, playing with keys or watch-chain, scratching head, pulling mustache, vibrating foot, or what not, according to the individual. There is an anecdote of Sir W. Scott, when a boy, rising to the head of his class by cutting off from the jacket of the usual head-boy a button which the latter was in the habit of twirling in his fingers during the lesson.—The button gone, its owner's power of reciting also departed. Now much of this activity is unquestionably due to the overflow of emotional excitement during anxious and concentrated thought. It drains away nerve-currents which if pent up within the thought-centres would very likely make the confusion there worse confounded. But may it not also be a means of drafting off all the irrelevant sensations of the moment, and so keeping the attention more exclusively concentrated upon its inner task? Each individual usually has his own peculiar habitual movement of this sort. A downward nerve-path is thus kept constantly open during concentrated thought; and as it seems to be a law of frequent (if not of universal) application, that incidental stimuli tend to discharge through paths that are already discharging rather than through others, the whole arrangement might protect the thought-centres from interference from without. Were this the true *rationale* of these peculiar movements, we should have to suppose that the sensations produced by each phase of the movement itself are also drafted off immediately by the next phase and help to keep the circular process agoing. I offer the suggestion for what it is worth; the connection of the movements themselves with the continued effort of attention is certainly a genuine and curious fact.

Chapter XII

Conception

THE SENSE OF SAMENESS

In Chapter VIII, p. 216, the distinction was drawn between two kinds of knowledge of things, bare acquaintance with them and knowledge about them. The possibility of two such knowledges depends on a fundamental psychical peculiarity which may be entitled "*the principle of constancy in the mind's meanings,*" and which may be thus expressed: "*The same matters can be thought of in successive portions of the mental stream, and some of these portions can know that they mean the same matters which the other portions meant.*" One might put it otherwise by saying that "*the mind can always intend, and know when it intends, to think of the Same.*"

This *sense of sameness* is the very keel and backbone of our thinking. We saw in Chapter X how the consciousness of personal identity reposed on it, the present thought finding in its memories a warmth and intimacy which it recognizes as the same warmth and intimacy it now feels. This sense of identity of the knowing subject is held by some philosophers to be the only vehicle by which the world hangs together. It seems hardly necessary to say that a sense of identity of the known object would perform exactly the same unifying function, even if the sense of subjective identity were lost. And without the intention to think of the same outer things over and over again, and the sense that we were doing so, our sense of our own personal sameness would carry us but a little way towards making a universe of our experience.

Note, however, that we are in the first instance speaking of the sense of sameness from the point of view of the mind's structure alone, and not from the point of view of the universe. We are psychologizing, not philosophizing. That is, we do not care whether there be any *real* sameness in *things* or not, or whether the mind be true or false in its assumptions of it. Our principle only lays it down that the mind makes continual use of the *notion* of sameness, and if deprived of it, would have a different structure from what it has. In a word, the principle that the mind can mean the Same is true of its *meanings*, but not necessarily of aught besides.[1] The mind must conceive as possible that the Same should be before it, for our experience to be the sort of thing it is. Without the psychological sense of identity, sameness might rain down upon us from the outer world for ever and we be none the wiser. With the psychological sense, on the other hand, the outer world might be an unbroken flux, and yet we should perceive a repeated experience. Even now, the world may be a place in which the same thing never did and never will come twice. The thing we mean to point at may change from top to bottom and we be ignorant of the fact. But in our meaning itself we are not deceived; our intention is to think of the same. The name which I have given to the principle, in calling it the law of constancy in our meanings, accentuates its subjective character, and justifies us in laying it down as the most important of all the features of our mental structure.

Not all psychic life need be assumed to have the sense of sameness developed in this way. In the consciousness of worms and polyps, though the same realities may frequently impress it, the feeling of sameness may seldom emerge. We, however, running back and forth, like spiders on the web they weave, feel ourselves to be work-

[1] There are two other 'principles of identity' in philosophy. The *ontological* one asserts that every real thing is what it is, that *a* is *a*, and *b*, *b*. The *logical* one says that what is once true of the subject of a judgment is always true of that subject. The ontological law is a tautological truism; the logical principle is already more, for it implies subjects unalterable by time. The *psychological* law also implies facts which might not be realized: there might be no succession of thoughts; or if there were, the later ones might not think of the earlier; or if they did, they might not recall the content thereof; or, recalling the content, they might not take it as 'the same' with anything else.

ing over identical materials and thinking them in different ways. And the man who identifies the materials most is held to have the most philosophic human mind.

CONCEPTION DEFINED

The function by which we thus identify a numerically distinct and permanent subject of discourse is called CONCEPTION; and the thoughts which are its vehicles are called *concepts.* But the word 'concept' is often used as if it stood for the object of discourse itself; and this looseness feeds such evasiveness in discussion that I shall avoid the use of the expression concept altogether, and speak of 'conceiving state of mind' or something similar, instead. The word 'conception' is unambiguous. It properly denotes neither the mental state nor what the mental state signifies, but the relation between the two, namely, the *function* of the mental state in signifying just that particular thing. It is plain that one and the same mental state can be the vehicle of many conceptions, can mean a particular thing, and a great deal more besides. If it has such a multiple conceptual function, it may be called an act of compound conception.

We may conceive realities supposed to be extra-mental, as steam-engine; fictions, as mermaid; or mere *entia rationis,* like difference or nonentity. But whatever we do conceive, our conception is of that and nothing else—nothing else, that is, *instead* of that, though it may be of much else *in addition* to that. Each act of conception results from our attention singling out some one part of the mass of matter-for-thought which the world presents, and holding fast to it, without confusion.[2] Confusion occurs when we do not know

[2] In later chapters we shall see that determinate relations exist between the various data thus fixed upon by the mind. These are called *a priori* or axiomatic relations. Simple inspection of the data enables us to perceive them; and one inspection is as effective as a million for engendering in us the conviction that between *those* data that relation must always hold. To change the relation we should have to make the data different. 'The guarantee for the uniformity and adequacy' of the data can only be the mind's own power to fix upon any objective content, and to mean that content as often as it likes. This right of the mind to 'construct' permanent ideal objects for itself out of the data of experience seems, singularly enough, to be a stumbling-block to many. Professor Robertson in his clear and instructive article "Axiom" in the *Encyclopædia Britannica* (9th edition) suggests that it may only be where *movements* enter into the constitution of the ideal object (as they do in geometrical figures) that we can "*make* the ultimate relations to be what for us they must be in all circumstances." He makes, it is true, a concession in favor of conceptions of number abstracted from "subjective occurrences succeeding each other in time" because these

whether a certain object proposed to us is the same with one of our meanings or not; so that the conceptual function requires, to be complete, that the thought should not only say 'I mean this,' but also say 'I don't mean that.'[3]

Each conception thus eternally remains what it is, and never can become another. The mind may change its states, and its meanings, at different times; may drop one conception and take up another: but the dropped conception can in no intelligible sense be said to *change into* its successor. The paper, a moment ago white, I may now see to have been scorched black. But my conception 'white' does not change into my conception 'black.' On the contrary, it stays alongside of the objective blackness, as a different meaning in my mind, and by so doing lets me judge the blackness as the paper's change. Unless it stayed, I should simply say 'blackness' and know no more. Thus, amid the flux of opinions and of physical things, the world of conceptions, or things intended to be thought about, stands stiff and immutable, like Plato's Realm of Ideas.[4]

Some conceptions are of things, some of events, some of qualities. Any fact, be it thing, event, or quality, may be conceived sufficiently for purposes of identification, if only it be singled out and marked so as to separate it from other things. Simply calling it 'this' or 'that' will suffice. To speak in technical language, a subject may be conceived by its *denotation*, with no *connotation*, or a very minimum of connotation, attached. The essential point is that it should be re-identified by us as that which the talk is about; and no full representation of it is necessary for this, even when it is a fully representable thing.

In this sense, creatures extremely low in the intellectual scale

---

also are acts "of construction, dependent on the power we have of voluntarily determining the flow of subjective consciousness." "The content of passive sensation," on the other hand, "may indefinitely vary beyond any control of ours." What if it do vary, so long as we can continue to think of and mean the qualities it varied from? We can 'make' ideal objects for ourselves out of irrecoverable bits of passive experience quite as perfectly as out of easily repeatable active experiences. And when we have got our objects together and compared them, we do not *make*, but *find*, their relations.

[3] Cf. Hodgson: *Time and Space*, § 46. Lotze: *Logic*, § 11.

[4] "For though a man in a fever should from sugar have a bitter taste, which at another time would produce a sweet one, yet the idea of bitter in that man's mind would be as distinct as if he had tasted only gall." (Locke's *Essay*, bk. II, chap. XI, § 3. Read the whole section!)

may have conception. All that is required is that they should recognize the same experience again. A polyp would be a conceptual thinker if a feeling of 'Hollo! thingumbob again!' ever flitted through its mind.

Most of the objects of our thought, however, are to some degree represented as well as merely pointed out. Either they are things and events perceived or imagined, or they are qualities apprehended in a positive way. Even where we have no intuitive acquaintance with the nature of a thing, if we know any of the relations of it at all, anything *about* it, that is enough to individualize and distinguish it from all the other things which we might mean. Many of our topics of discourse are thus *problematical*, or defined by their relations only. We think of a thing *about* which certain facts must obtain. But we do not yet know how the thing will look when it is realized. Thus we conceive of a perpetual-motion machine. It is a *quæsitum* of a perfectly definite kind,—we can tell whether the actual machines offered us do or do not agree with what we mean by it. The natural possibility or impossibility of the thing does not touch the question of its conceivability in this problematic way. 'Round-square,' 'black-white-thing,' are absolutely definite conceptions; it is a mere accident, as far as conception goes, that they happen to stand for things which nature never lets us sensibly perceive.[5]

[5] Black round things, square white things *per contra*, Nature gives us freely enough. But the combinations which she refuses to realize may exist as distinctly, in the shape of postulates, as those which she gives may exist in the shape of positive images, in our mind. As a matter of fact, she *may* realize a warm cold thing whenever two points of the skin, so near together as not to be locally distinguished, are touched, the one with a warm, the other with a cold, piece of metal. The warmth and the cold are then often felt as if in the same objective place. Under similar conditions two objects, one sharp and the other blunt, may feel like one sharp blunt thing. The same space may appear of two colors if, by optical artifice, one of the colors is made to appear as if seen *through* the other.—Whether any two attributes whatever shall be compatible or not, in the sense of appearing or not to occupy the same place and moment, depends simply on *de facto* peculiarities of natural bodies and of our sense-organs. *Logically*, any one combination of qualities is to the full as *conceivable* as any other, and has as distinct a meaning for thought. What necessitates this remark is the confusion deliberately kept up by certain authors (e.g., Spencer: *Psychology*, §§ 426–7) between the inconceivable and the not-distinctly-imaginable. How do we know *which* things we cannot imagine unless by first conceiving them, meaning *them* and not other things?

CONCEPTIONS ARE UNCHANGEABLE

The fact that the same real topic of discourse is at one time conceived as a mere 'that' or 'that which, etc.,' and is at another time conceived with additional specifications, has been treated by many authors as a proof that conceptions themselves are fertile and self-developing. A conception, according to the Hegelizers in philosophy, 'develops its own significance,' 'makes explicit what it implicitly contained,' passes, on occasion, 'over into its opposite,' and in short loses altogether the blankly self-identical character we supposed it to maintain. The figure we viewed as a polygon appears to us now as a sum of juxtaposed triangles; the number hitherto conceived as thirteen is at last noticed to be six plus seven, or prime; the man thought honest is believed a rogue. Such changes of our opinion are viewed by these thinkers as evolutions of our conception, from within.

The facts are unquestionable; our knowledge does grow and change by rational and inward processes, as well as by empirical discoveries. Where the discoveries are empirical, no one pretends that the propulsive agency, the force that makes the knowledge develop, is mere conception. All admit it to be our continued exposure to the *thing*, with its power to impress our senses. Thus strychnin, which tastes bitter, we find will also kill, etc. Now I say that where the new knowledge merely comes from *thinking*, the facts are essentially the same, and that *to talk of self-development on the part of our conceptions is a very bad way of stating the case.* Not new sensations, as in the empirical instance, but new conceptions, are the indispensable conditions of advance.

For if the alleged cases of self-development be examined it will be found, I believe, that the new truth affirms in every case a *relation* between the original subject of conception and some new subject conceived later on. These new subjects of conception arise in various ways. Every one of our conceptions is of something which our attention originally tore out of the continuum of felt experience, and provisionally isolated so as to make of it an individual topic of discourse. Every one of them has a way, if the mind is left alone with it, of suggesting other parts of the continuum from which it was torn, for conception to work upon in a similar way. This 'suggestion' is often no more than what we shall later know as the association of ideas. Often, however, it is a sort of invitation to the mind to play, add lines, break number-groups, etc. Whatever it is, it brings new conceptions into consciousness, which latter thereupon may or may not expressly attend to the relation in which the new stands to the old. Thus I have a conception of equidistant lines. Suddenly, I know not whence, there pops into my head the conception of their meeting. Suddenly again I think of the meeting and the equidistance both together, and perceive them incompatible. "*Those* lines will never meet," I say. Suddenly again the word 'parallel' pops into my head. 'They are parallels,' I continue; and so on. Original conceptions to start with; adventitious conceptions pushed forwards by multifarious psychologic causes; comparisons and combinations of the two; resultant conceptions to end with; which latter may be of either rational or empirical relations.

As regards these relations, they are conceptions of the second degree, as one might say, and their birthplace is the mind itself. In Chapter XXVIII I shall at considerable length defend the mind's claim to originality and fertility in bringing them forth. But no single one of the mind's conceptions is fertile *of itself*, as the opinion which I criticise pretends. When the several notes of a chord are sounded together, we get a new feeling from their combination. This feeling is due to the mind reacting upon that group of sounds in that determinate way, and no one would think of saying of any single note of the chord that it 'developed' of itself into the other notes or into the feeling of harmony. So of Conceptions. No one of them develops into any other. But if two of them are thought at once, their *relation* may come to consciousness, and form matter for a third conception.

Take 'thirteen' for example, which is said to develop into 'prime.' What really happens is that we compare the utterly changeless conception of thirteen with various other conceptions, those of the different multiples of two, three, four, five, and six, and ascertain that it *differs* from them all. Such difference is a freshly ascertained relation. It is only for mere brevity's sake that we call it a property of the original thirteen, the property of being prime. We shall see in the next chapter that (if we count out æsthetic and moral relations between things) the only important relations of which the mere inspection of conceptions makes us aware are relations of comparison, that is, of difference and no-difference, between them. The judgment $6 + 7 = 13$ expresses the relation of *equality* between two ideal objects, 13 on the one hand and $6 + 7$ on the other, successively conceived and compared. The judgments $6 + 7 > 12$, or $6 + 7 < 14$, express in like manner relations of *in*equality between ideal objects. But if it be unfair to say that the conception of $6 + 7$ generates that of 12 or of 14, surely it is as unfair to say that it generates that of 13.

The conceptions of 12, 13, and 14 are each and all generated by individual acts of the mind, playing with its materials. When, comparing two ideal objects, we find them equal, the conception of one of them may be that of a whole and of the other that of all its parts. This particular case is, it seems to me, the only case which makes the notion of one conception evolving into another sound plausible. But even in this case the conception, as such, of the whole does not evolve into the conception, as such, of the parts. Let the conception of some object as a whole be given first. To begin with, it points to and identifies for future thought a certain *that.* The 'whole' in question might be one of those mechanical puzzles of which the difficulty is to unlock the parts. In this case, nobody would pretend that the richer and more elaborate conception which we gain of the puzzle after solving it came directly out of our first crude conception of it, for it is notoriously the outcome of experimenting with our hands. It is true that, as they both mean *that same puzzle,* our earlier thought and our later thought have one conceptual function, are vehicles of one conception. But in addition to being the vehicle of this bald unchanging conception, 'that same puzzle,' the later thought is the vehicle of all those other conceptions which it took the manual experimentation to acquire. Now, it is just the same where the whole is mathematical instead of being mechanical. Let it be a polygonal space, which we cut into triangles, and of which we then affirm that it *is* those triangles. Here the experimentation (although usually done by a pencil in the hands) may be done by the unaided imagination. We hold the space, first conceived as polygonal simply, in our mind's eye until our attention wandering to and fro within it has carved it into the triangles. The triangles are a new conception, the result of this new operation. Having once conceived them, however, and compared them with the old polygon which we originally conceived and which we have never ceased conceiving, we judge them to fit exactly into its area. The earlier and later conceptions, we say, are of one and the same space. But this relation between triangles and polygon which the mind cannot help finding if it compares them at all, is very badly expressed by saying that the old conception has developed into the new. New conceptions come from new sensations, new movements, new emotions, new associations, new acts of attention, and new comparisons of old conceptions, and not in other ways. Endogenous prolification is not a mode of growth to which conceptions can lay claim.

I hope, therefore, that I shall not be accused of huddling mysteries out of sight, when I insist that the psychology of conception is not the place in which to treat of those of continuity and change. Conceptions form the one class of entities that cannot under any circumstances change. They can cease to be, altogether; or they can stay, as what they severally are; but there is for them no middle way. They form an essentially discontinuous system, and translate the process of our perceptual experience, which is naturally a flux, into a set of stagnant and petrified terms. The very conception of flux itself is an absolutely changeless meaning in the mind: it signifies just that one thing, flux, immovably.—And, with this, the doctrine of the flux of the concept may be dismissed, and need not occupy our attention again.[6]

[6] Arguments seldom make converts in matters philosophical; and some readers, I know, who find that they conceive a certain matter differently from what they did, will still prefer saying they have two different editions of the same conception, one evolved from the other, to saying they have two different conceptions of the same thing. It depends, after all, on how we define conception. We ourselves defined it as the function by which a state of mind means to think the same whereof it thought on a former occasion. Two states of mind will accordingly be two editions of the same conception just so far as either does mean to think what the other thought; but no farther. If either mean to think what the other did not think, it is a different conception from the other. And if either mean to think all that the other thought, *and more*, it is a different conception, so far as the *more* goes. In this last case one state of mind has two conceptual functions. Each thought decides, by its own authority, which, out of all the conceptive functions open to it, it shall now renew; with which other thought it shall identify itself as a conceiver, and just how far. "The same A which I once meant," it says, "I shall now mean again, and mean it with C as its predicate (or what not) instead of B, as before." In all this, therefore, there is absolutely no changing, but only uncoupling and recoupling of conceptions. Compound conceptions come, as functions of new states of mind. Some of these functions are the same with previous ones, some not. Any changed opinion, then, *partly* contains new editions (absolutely identical with the old, however) of former conceptions, *partly* absolutely new conceptions. The division is a perfectly easy one to make in each particular case.

'ABSTRACT' IDEAS

We have now to pass to a less excusable mistake. There are philosophers who deny that associated things can be broken asunder at all, even provisionally, by the conceiving mind. The opinion known as Nominalism says that we really never frame any conception of the partial elements of an experience, but are compelled, whenever we think it, to think it in its totality, just as it came.

I will be silent of mediæval Nominalism, and begin with Berkeley, who is supposed to have rediscovered the doctrine for himself. His asseverations against 'abstract ideas' are among the oftenest quoted passages in philosophic literature.

"It is agreed," he says, "on all hands that the qualities or modes of things do never really exist each of them apart by itself, and separated from all others, but are mixed, as it were, and blended together, several in the same object. But, we are told, the mind being able to consider each quality singly, or abstracted from those other qualities with which it is united, does by that means frame to itself abstract ideas. . . . After this manner it is said we come by the abstract idea of man, or, if you please, humanity, or human nature; wherein it is true there is included colour, because there is no man but has some colour, but then it can be neither white, nor black, nor any particular colour, because there is no one particular colour wherein all men partake. So likewise there is included stature, but then it is neither tall stature, nor low stature, nor yet middle stature, but something abstracted from all these. And so of the rest. . . . Whether others have this wonderful faculty of abstracting their ideas, they best can tell: for myself, I find indeed I have a faculty of imagining, or representing to myself, the ideas of those particular things I have perceived, and of variously compounding and dividing them. . . . I can consider the hand, the eye, the nose, each by itself abstracted or separated from the rest of the body. But then whatever hand or eye I imagine, it must have some particular shape and colour. Likewise the idea of man that I frame to myself must be either of a white, or a black, or a tawny, a straight, or a crooked, a tall, or a low, or a middle-sized man. I cannot by any effort of thought conceive the abstract idea above described. And it is equally impossible for me to form the abstract idea of motion distinct from the body moving, and which is neither swift nor slow, curvilinear nor rectilinear; and the like may be said of all other abstract general ideas whatsoever. . . . And there is ground to think most men will acknowledge themselves to be in my case. The generality of men which are simple and illiterate never pretend to abstract notions. It is said they are difficult and not to be attained without pains and study . . . . Now, I would fain know at what time it is men are employed in surmounting that difficulty, and furnishing themselves with those necessary helps for discourse. It cannot be when they are grown up, for then it seems they are not conscious of any such painstaking; it remains therefore to be the business of their childhood. And surely the great and multiplied labour of framing abstract notions will be found a hard task for that tender age. Is it not a hard thing to imagine that a couple of children cannot prate together of their sugar-plums and rattles and the rest of their little trinkets, till they have first tacked together numberless inconsistencies, and so framed in their minds abstract general ideas, and annexed them to every common name they make use of?"[7]

The note, so bravely struck by Berkeley, could not, however, be well sustained in face of the fact patent to every human being that we *can* mean color without meaning any particular color, and stature without meaning any particular height. James Mill, to be sure, chimes in heroically in the chapter on Classification of his *Analysis*; but in his son John the nominalistic voice has grown so weak that, although 'abstract ideas' are repudiated as a matter of traditional form, the opinions uttered are really nothing but a conceptualism ashamed to call itself by its own legitimate name.[8] Conceptualism says the mind can conceive any quality or relation it pleases, and mean nothing but it, in isolation from everything else in the world. This is, of course, the doctrine which we have professed. John Mill says:

"The formation of a Concept, does not consist in separating the attributes which are said to compose it, from all other attributes of the same object, and enabling us to conceive those attributes, disjoined from any others. We neither conceive them, nor think them, nor cognise them in any way, as a thing apart, but solely as forming, in combination with numerous other attributes, the idea of an individual object. But, though thinking them only as part of a larger agglomeration, we have the power of fixing our attention on them, to the neglect of the other attributes with which we think them combined. *While the concentration of attention lasts, if it is sufficiently intense, we may be temporarily unconscious of any of the other attributes, and may really, for a brief interval, have nothing present to our mind but the attributes constituent of the concept.* . . . General concepts, therefore,

[7] *Principles of Human Knowledge*, Introduction, §§ 7, 9, 10, 14.

[8] "Conceptualisme honteux," Rabier: *Psychologie*, 310.

we have, properly speaking, none; we have only complex ideas of objects in the concrete: but we are able to *attend exclusively to certain parts* of the concrete idea: and by that *exclusive attention*, we enable those parts to *determine exclusively the course of our thoughts* as subsequently called up by association; and are in a condition to carry on a train of meditation or reasoning relating to those parts only, *exactly as if* we were able to *conceive* them separately from the rest."[9]

This is a lovely example of Mill's way of holding piously to his general statements, but conceding in detail all that their adversaries ask. If there be a better description extant, of a mind in possession of an 'abstract idea,' than is contained in the words I have italicized, I am unacquainted with it. The Berkeleyan nominalism thus breaks down.

It is easy to lay bare the false assumption which underlies the whole discussion of the question as hitherto carried on. That assumption is that ideas, in order to know, must be cast in the exact likeness of whatever things they know, and that the only things that can be known are those which ideas can resemble. The error has not been confined to nominalists. *Omnis cognitio fit per assimilationem cognoscentis et cogniti* has been the maxim, more or less explicitly assumed, of writers of every school. Practically it amounts to saying that an idea must *be* a duplicate edition of what it knows[10] —in other words, that it can only know itself—or, more shortly still, that knowledge in any strict sense of the word, as a self-transcendent function, is impossible.

Now our own blunt statements about the ultimateness of the cognitive relation, and the difference between the 'object' of the thought and its mere 'topic' or 'subject of discourse' (cf. pp. 265 ff.), are all at variance with any such theory; and we shall find more and more occasion, as we advance in this book, to deny its general truth. All that a state of mind need do, in order to take cognizance of a reality, intend it, or be 'about' it, is to lead to a remoter state of mind which either acts upon the reality or resembles it. The only class of thoughts which can with any show of plausibility be said to

9 *Examination of Hamilton*, p. 393. Cf. also *Logic*, bk. II, chap. V, § 1, and bk. IV, chap. II, § 1.

10 E.g.: "The knowledge of things must mean that the mind finds itself in them, or that, in some way, the difference between them and the mind is dissolved." (E. Caird: *A Critical Account of the Philosophy of Kant*, first edition, p. 553.)

resemble their objects are sensations. The stuff of which all our other thoughts are composed is symbolic, and a thought attests its pertinency to a topic by simply *terminating*, sooner or later, in a sensation which resembles the latter.

But Mill and the rest believe that a thought must *be* what it means, and mean what it *is*, and that if it be a picture of an entire individual, it cannot mean any part of him to the exclusion of the rest. I say nothing here of the preposterously false descriptive psychology involved in the statement that the only things we can mentally picture are individuals completely determinate in all regards. Chapter XVIII will have something to say on that point, and we can ignore it here. For even if it were true that our images were always of concrete individuals, it would not in the least follow that our meanings were of the same.

The sense of our meaning is an entirely peculiar element of the thought. It is one of those evanescent and 'transitive' facts of mind which introspection cannot turn round upon, and isolate and hold up for examination, as an entomologist passes round an insect on a pin. In the (somewhat clumsy) terminology I have used, it pertains to the 'fringe' of the subjective state, and is a 'feeling of tendency,' whose neural counterpart is undoubtedly a lot of dawning and dying processes too faint and complex to be traced. The geometer, with his one definite figure before him, knows perfectly that his thoughts apply to countless other figures as well, and that although he *sees* lines of a certain special bigness, direction, color, etc., he *means* not one of these details. When I use the word *man* in two different sentences, I may have both times exactly the same sound upon my lips and the same picture in my mental eye, but I may mean, and at the very moment of uttering the word and imagining the picture know that I mean, two entirely different things. Thus when I say: "What a wonderful man Jones is!" I am perfectly aware that I mean by man to exclude Napoleon Bonaparte or Smith. But when I say: "What a wonderful thing Man is!" I am equally well aware that I mean to *in*clude not only Jones, but Napoleon and Smith as well. This added consciousness is an absolutely positive sort of feeling, transforming what would otherwise be mere noise or vision into something *understood*; and determining the sequel of my thinking, the later words and images, in a perfectly definite way. We saw in Chapter IX that the image *per se*, the nucleus, is *functionally* the least important part of the thought. *Our doctrine, therefore, of the 'fringe' leads to a perfectly satisfactory decision of the nominalistic and conceptualistic controversy,* so far as it touches psychology. *We must decide in favor of the conceptualists,* and affirm that the power to think things, qualities, relations, or whatever other elements there may be, isolated and abstracted from the total experience in which they appear, is the most indisputable function of our thought.

UNIVERSALS

After abstractions, universals! The 'fringe,' which lets us believe in the one, lets us believe in the other too. An individual conception is of something restricted, in its application, to a single case. A universal or general conception is of an entire class, or of something belonging to an entire class, of things. The conception of an abstract quality is, taken by itself, neither universal nor particular.[11] If I abstract *white* from the rest of the wintry landscape this morning, it is a perfectly definite conception, a self-identical quality which I may mean again; but, as I have not yet individualized it by expressly meaning to restrict it to this particular snow, nor thought at all of the possibility of other things to which it may be applicable, it is so far nothing but a 'that,' a 'floating adjective,' as Mr. Bradley calls it, or a topic broken out from the rest of the world. Properly it is, in this state, a singular—I have 'singled it out'; and when, later, I universalize or individualize its application, and my thought turns to mean either *this* white or *all possible* whites, I am in reality meaning two new things and forming two new conceptions.[12] Such an alteration of my meaning has nothing to do with any change in the image I may have in my mental eye, but solely with the vague consciousness that surrounds the image, of the sphere to which it

[11] The traditional conceptualist doctrine is that an abstract must *eo ipso* be a universal. Even modern and independent authors like Prof. Dewey (*Psychology*, 207) obey the tradition: "The mind seizes upon some one aspect . . . abstracts or prescinds it. This very seizure of some one element generalizes the one abstracted. . . . Attention, in drawing it forth, makes it a distinct content of consciousness, and thus universalizes it; it is considered no longer in its connection with the particular object, but on its own account; that is, as an idea, or what it signifies to the mind; and significance is always universal."

[12] Cf. Reid's *Intellectual Powers*, Essay v, chap. III.—*Whiteness* is one thing, *the whiteness of this sheet of paper* another thing.

is intended to apply. We can give no more definite account of this vague consciousness than has been given on pp. 240–256. But that is no reason for denying its presence.[13]

But the nominalists and traditional conceptualists find matter for an inveterate quarrel in these simple facts. Full of their notion that an idea, feeling, or state of consciousness can at bottom only be aware of its own quality; and agreeing, as they both do, that such an idea or state of consciousness is a perfectly determinate, singular, and transitory thing; they find it impossible to conceive how it should become the vehicle of a knowledge of anything permanent or universal. "To know a universal, it must be universal; for like can only be known by like," etc. Unable to reconcile these incompatibles, the knower and the known, each side immolates one of them to save the other. The nominalists 'settle the hash' of the thing known by denying it to be ever a genuine universal; the conceptualists despatch the knower by denying it to be a state of mind, in the sense of being a perishing segment of thoughts' stream, consubstantial with other facts of sensibility. They invent, instead of it, as the vehicle of the knowledge of universals, an *actus purus intellectûs*, or an Ego, whose function is treated as quasi-miraculous and nothing if not awe-inspiring, and which it is a sort of blasphemy to approach with the intent to explain and make common, or reduce to lower terms. Invoked in the first instance as a vehicle for the knowledge of universals, the higher principle presently is made the indispensable vehicle of all thinking whatever, for, it is contended, "a universal element is present in every thought." The nominalists meanwhile, who dislike *actus puros* and awe-inspiring principles and despise the reverential mood, content themselves with saying that we are mistaken in supposing we ever get sight of the face of an universal; and that what deludes us is nothing but

[13] Mr. F. H. Bradley says the conception or the 'meaning' "consists of a part of the content, cut off, fixed by the mind, and considered apart from the existence of the sign. It would not be correct to add, 'and referred away to another real subject;' for where we think without judging, and where we deny, that description would not be applicable." This seems to be the same doctrine as ours; the application to one or to all subjects of the abstract fact conceived (i.e., its individuality or its universality), constituting a new conception. I am, however, not quite sure that Mr. Bradley steadily maintains this ground. Cf. the first chapter of his *Principles of Logic*. The doctrine I defend is stoutly upheld in Rosmini's *Philosophical System*, Introduction by Thomas Davidson, p. 43 (London, 1882).

the swarm of 'individual ideas' which may at any time be awakened by the hearing of a name.

If we open the pages of either school, we find it impossible to tell, in all the whirl about universal and particular, when the author is talking about universals in the mind, and when about objective universals, so strangely are the two mixed together. James Ferrier, for example, is the most brilliant of anti-nominalist writers. But who is nimble-witted enough to count, in the following sentences from him, the number of times he steps from the known to the knower, and attributes to both whatever properties he finds in either one?

"To think is to pass from the singular or particular to the idea [concept] or the universal. . . . Ideas are necessary, because no thinking can take place without them. They are universal, inasmuch as they are completely divested of the particularity which characterises all the phenomena of mere sensation. To grasp the nature of this universality is not easy. Perhaps the best means by which this end may be compassed is by contrasting it with the particular. It is not difficult to understand that a sensation, a phenomenon of sense, is never more than the particular phenomenon which it is. As such, that is, in its strict particularity, it is absolutely unthinkable. In the very act of being thought something more than it emerges, and this something more cannot be again the particular . . . . Ten particulars, *per se,* cannot be thought of any more than one particular can be thought of . . . there always emerges in thought an additional something, which is the possibility of other particulars to an indefinite extent. . . . The indefinite additional something which they are instances of is a universal. . . . The idea or universal cannot by any possibility be pictured in the imagination, for this would at once reduce it to the particular . . . . This inability to form any sort of picture or representation of an idea does not proceed from any imperfection or limitation of our faculties, but is a quality inherent in the very nature of intelligence. A contradiction is involved in the supposition that an idea or universal can become the object either of sense or of the imagination. An idea is thus diametrically opposed to an image."[14]

The nominalists, on their side, admit a *quasi*-universal, something which we think *as if it were* universal, though it is not; and in all that they say about this something, which they explain to be

[14] *Lectures on Greek Philosophy,* pp. 333–39.

'an indefinite number of particular ideas,' the same vacillation between the subjective and the objective points of view appears. The reader never can tell whether an 'idea' spoken of is supposed to be a knower or a known. The authors themselves do not distinguish. They want to get something in the mind which shall *resemble* what is out of the mind, however vaguely, and they think that when that fact is accomplished, no farther questions will be asked. James Mill writes:[15]

"The word, man, we shall say, is first applied to an individual; it is first associated with the idea of that individual, and acquires the power of calling up the idea of him; it is next applied to another individual, and acquires the power of calling up the idea of him; so of another, and another, till it has become associated with an indefinite number, and has acquired the power of calling up an indefinite number of those ideas indifferently. What happens? It does call up an indefinite number of the ideas of individuals, as often as it occurs; and calling them up in close connexion, it forms them into a species of complex idea. . . . It is also a fact, that when an idea becomes to a certain degree complex, from the multiplicity of the ideas it *comprehends*, it is of necessity indistinct . . . and this indistinctness has, doubtless, been the main cause of the mystery, which has appeared to belong to it. . . . It thus appears, that the word, *man*, is not a word having a very simple idea, as was the opinion of the Realists; nor a word having no idea at all, as was that of the [earlier] Nominalists; but a word calling up an indefinite number of ideas, by the irresistible laws of association, and forming them into one very complex, and indistinct, but not therefore unintelligible, idea."

Berkeley had already said:[16]

"A word becomes general by being made the sign, not of an abstract general idea, but of several particular ideas, any one of which it indifferently suggests to the mind. . . . An idea which, considered in itself, is particular, becomes general by being made to represent or stand for all other particular ideas of the same sort."

'Stand for,' not *know*; 'becomes general,' not becomes *aware of something* general; 'particular ideas,' not particular *things*—everywhere the same timidity about begging the fact of knowing, and the pitifully impotent attempt to foist it in the shape of a mode of

[15] *Analysis*, chap. VIII.

[16] *Principles of Human Knowledge*, Introduction, §§ 11, 12.

being of 'ideas.' If the fact to be conceived be the indefinitely numerous actual and possible members of a class, then it is assumed that if we can only get enough ideas to huddle together for a moment in the mind, the *being* of each several one of them there will be an equivalent for the *knowing*, or *meaning*, of *one* member of the class in question; and their number will be so large as to confuse our tally and leave it doubtful whether all the possible members of the class have thus been satisfactorily told off or not.

Of course this is nonsense. An idea neither is what it knows, nor knows what it is; nor will swarms of copies of the same 'idea,' recurring in stereotyped form, or 'by the irresistible laws of association formed into one idea,' ever be the same thing as a thought of '*all the possible members*' of a class. We must mean *that* by an altogether special bit of consciousness *ad hoc*. But it is easy to translate Berkeley's, Hume's, and Mill's notion of a swarm of ideas into cerebral terms, and so to make them stand for something real; and, in this sense, I think the doctrine of these authors less hollow than the opposite one which makes the vehicle of universal conceptions to be an *actus purus* of the soul. If each 'idea' stand for some special nascent nerve-process, then the aggregate of these nascent processes might have for its conscious correlate a psychic 'fringe,' which should be just that universal meaning, or intention that the name or mental picture employed should mean all the possible individuals of the class. Every peculiar complication of brain-processes must have some peculiar correlate in the soul. To one set of processes will correspond the thought of an indefinite taking of the extent of a word like *man*; to another set that of a particular taking; and to a third set that of a universal taking, of the extent of the same word. The thought corresponding to either set of processes, is always itself a unique and singular event, whose dependence on its peculiar nerve-process I of course am far from professing to explain.[17]

[17] It may add to the effect of the text to quote a passage from the essay in *Mind*, referred to on p. 219.

"Why may we not side with the Conceptualists in saying that the universal sense of a word does correspond to a mental fact of *some* kind, but at the same time, agreeing with the Nominalists that all mental facts are modifications of subjective sensibility, why may we not call that fact a 'feeling'? *Man* meant for *mankind* is in short a different feeling from *man* as a mere noise, or from *man* meant for *that* man, to wit, John Smith alone. Not that the difference consists simply in the fact that, when taken universally, the word has one of Mr. Galton's 'blended' images of man associated with it. Many persons have seemed to think that these blended, or as Prof. Huxley calls them, 'generic,' images, are equivalent to concepts. But, in itself, a blurred thing is just as particular as a sharp thing; and the generic character of either sharp image or blurred image depends on its being felt *with its representative function.* This function is the mysterious *plus*, the understood meaning. But it is nothing applied to the image from above, no pure act of reason inhabiting a supersensible and semi-supernatural plane. It can be diagrammatised as continuous with all the other segments of the subjective stream. It is just that staining, fringe or halo of obscurely felt relation to masses of other imagery about to come, but not yet distinctly in focus, which we have so abundantly set forth [in Chapter IX].

"If the image come unfringed it reveals but a simple quality, thing, or event; if it come fringed it may reveal something expressly taken universally or in a scheme of relations. The difference between thought and feeling thus reduces itself, in the last subjective analysis, to the presence or absence of 'fringe'. And this in turn reduces itself, with much probability, in the last physiological analysis, to the absence or presence of sub-excitements in other convolutions of the brain than those whose discharges underlie the more definite nucleus, the substantive ingredient, of the thought,—in this instance, the word or image it may happen to arouse.

"The contrast is not, then, as the Platonists would have it, between certain subjective facts called images and sensations, and others called acts of relating intelligence; the former being blind perishing things, knowing not even their own existence as such, whilst the latter combine the poles in the mysterious synthesis of their cognitive sweep. The contrast is really between two *aspects*, in which all mental facts without exception may be taken; their structural aspect, as being subjective, and their functional aspect, as being cognitions. In the former aspect, the highest as well as the lowest is a feeling, a peculiarly tinged segment of the stream. This tingeing is its sensitive body, the *wie ihm zu Muthe ist*, the way it feels whilst passing. In the latter aspect, the lowest mental fact as well as the highest may grasp some bit of truth as its content, even though that truth were as relationless a matter as a bare unlocalised and undated quality of pain. From the cognitive point of view, all mental facts are intellections. From the subjective point of view all are feelings. Once admit that the passing and evanescent are as real parts of the stream as the distinct and comparatively abiding; once allow that fringes and haloes, inarticulate perceptions, whereof the objects are as yet unnamed, mere nascencies of cognition, premonitions, awarenesses of direction, are thoughts *sui generis*, as much as articulate imaginings and propositions are; once restore, I say, the *vague* to its psychological rights, and the matter presents no further difficulty.

"And then we see that the current opposition of Feeling to Knowledge is quite a false issue. If every feeling is at the same time a bit of knowledge, we ought no longer to talk of mental states differing by having more or less of the cognitive quality; they only differ in knowing more or less, in having much fact or little fact for their object. The feeling of a broad scheme of relations is a feeling that knows much; the feeling of a simple quality is a feeling that knows little. But the knowing itself, whether of much or of little, has the same essence, and is as good knowing in the one case as in the other. Concept and image, thus discriminated through their objects, are consubstantial in their inward nature, as modes of feeling. The one, as particular, will no longer be held to be a relatively base sort of an entity, to be taken as a matter of course, whilst the other, as universal, is celebrated as a sort of standing miracle, to be adored but not explained. Both concept and image, *quâ* subjective, are singular and particular. Both are moments of the stream which come, and in an instant are no more. The word universality has no meaning as applied to their psychic body or

Truly in comparison with the fact that every conception, whatever it be of, is one of the mind's immutable possessions, the question whether a single thing, or a whole class of things, or only an unassigned quality, be meant by it, is an insignificant matter of detail. Our meanings are of singulars, particulars, indefinites, and universals, mixed together in every way. A singular individual is as much *conceived* when he is isolated and identified away from the rest of the world in my mind, as is the most rarefied and universally applicable quality he may possess—*being*, for example, when treated in the same way.[18] From every point of view, the overwhelming and portentous character ascribed to universal conceptions is surprising. Why, from Plato and Aristotle downwards, philosophers should have vied with each other in scorn of the knowledge of the particular, and in adoration of that of the general, is hard to understand, seeing that the more adorable knowledge ought to be that of the more adorable things, and that the *things* of worth are all concretes and singulars. The only value of universal characters is that they help us, by reasoning, to know new truths about individual things. The restriction of one's meaning, moreover, to an individual thing, probably requires even more complicated brain-processes than its extension to all the instances of a kind; and the mere mystery, as such, of the knowledge, is equally great, whether generals or singulars be the things known. In sum, therefore, the traditional universal-worship can only be called a bit of perverse sentimentalism, a philosophic 'idol of the cave.'

It may seem hardly necessary to add (what follows as a matter of course from pp. 224–230, and what has been implied in our assertions all along) that *nothing can be conceived twice over without being conceived in entirely different states of mind.* Thus, my arm-chair is one of the things of which I have a conception; I knew it yesterday and recognized it when I looked at it. But if I think of it to-day as the same arm-chair which I looked at yesterday, it is

---

structure, which is always finite. It only has a meaning when applied to their use, import, or reference to the kind of object they may reveal. The representation, as such, of the universal object is as particular as that of an object about which we know so little that the interjection 'Ha!' is all it can evoke from us in the way of speech. Both should be weighed in the same scales, and have the same measure meted out to them, whether of worship or of contempt." (*Mind*, IX, pp. 18–19.)

[18] Hodgson: *Time and Space*, p. 404.

obvious that the very conception of it as the same is an additional complication to the thought, whose inward constitution must alter in consequence. In short, it is logically impossible that the same thing should be *known as the same* by two successive copies of the same thought. As a matter of fact, the thoughts by which we know that we mean the same thing are apt to be very different indeed from each other. We think the thing now in one context, now in another; now in a definite image, now in a symbol. Sometimes our sense of its identity pertains to the mere fringe, sometimes it involves the nucleus, of our thought. We never can break the thought asunder and tell just which one of its bits is the part that lets us know which subject is referred to; but nevertheless we always *do* know which of all possible subjects we have in mind. Introspective psychology must here throw up the sponge; the fluctuations of subjective life are too exquisite to be arrested by its coarse means. It must confine itself to bearing witness to the fact that all sorts of different subjective states do form the vehicle by which the same is known; and it must contradict the opposite view.

The ordinary Psychology of 'ideas' constantly talks as if the vehicle of the same thing-known must be the same recurrent state of mind, and as if the having over again of the same 'idea' were not only a necessary but a sufficient condition for meaning the same thing twice. But this recurrence of the same idea would utterly defeat the existence of a repeated knowledge of anything. It would be a simple reversion into a pre-existent state, with nothing gained in the interval, and with complete unconsciousness of the state having existed before. Such is not the way in which we think. As a rule we are fully aware that we have thought before of the thing we think of now. The continuity and permanency of the topic is of the essence of our intellection. We recognize the old problem, and the old solutions; and we go on to alter and improve and substitute one predicate for another without ever letting the subject change.

This is what is meant when it is said that thinking consists in making *judgments*. A succession of judgments may all be about the same thing. The general practical postulate which encourages us to keep thinking at all is that by going on to do so we shall judge better *of the same things* than if we do not.[19] In the successive judgments, all sorts of new operations are performed on the things, and

[19] Compare the admirable passage in Hodgson's *Time and Space*, p. 310.

all sorts of new results brought out, without the sense of the main topic ever getting lost. At the outset, we merely *have* the topic; then we *operate* on it; and finally we have it again in a richer and truer way. A compound conception has been substituted for the simple one, but with full consciousness that both are of the Same.

The distinction between having and operating is as natural in the mental as in the material world. As our hands may hold a bit of wood and a knife, and yet do naught with either; so our mind may simply be aware of a thing's existence, and yet neither attend to it nor discriminate it, neither locate nor count nor compare nor like nor dislike nor deduce it, nor recognize it articulately as having been met with before. At the same time we know that, instead of staring at it in this entranced and senseless way, we may rally our activity in a moment, and locate, class, compare, count, and judge it. There is nothing involved in all this which we did not postulate at the very outset of our introspective work: realities, namely, *extra mentem*, thoughts, and possible relations of cognition between the two. The result of the thoughts' operating on the data given to sense is to transform the order in which experience *comes* into an entirely different order, that of the *conceived* world. There is no spot of light, for example, which I pick out and proceed to define as a pebble, which is not thereby torn from its mere time- and space-neighbors, and thought in conjunction with things physically parted from it by the width of nature. Compare the form in which facts appear in a text-book of physics, as logically subordinated laws, with that in which we naturally make their acquaintance. The conceptual scheme is a sort of sieve in which we try to gather up the world's contents. Most facts and relations fall through its meshes, being either too subtle or insignificant to be fixed in any conception. But whenever a physical reality is caught and identified as the same with something already conceived, it remains on the sieve, and all the predicates and relations of the conception with which it is identified become its predicates and relations too; it is subjected to the sieve's network, in other words. Thus comes to pass what Mr. Hodgson calls the translation of the perceptual into the conceptual order of the world.[20]

In Chapter XXII we shall see how this translation always takes place for the sake of some subjective *interest*, and how the concep-

[20] *Philosophy of Reflection*, I, 273–308.

tion with which we handle a bit of sensible experience is really nothing but a teleological instrument. *This whole function of conceiving, of fixing, and holding fast to meanings, has no significance apart from the fact that the conceiver is a creature with partial purposes and private ends.* There remains, therefore, much more to be said about conception, but for the present this will suffice.

Chapter XIII

Discrimination and Comparison

It is matter of popular observation that some men have sharper senses than others, and that some have acuter minds and are able to 'split hairs' and see two shades of meaning where the majority see but one. Locke long ago set apart the faculty of discrimination as one in which men differ individually. What he wrote is good enough to quote as an introduction to this chapter:

"Another faculty we may take notice of in our minds, is that of discerning and distinguishing between the several ideas it has. It is not enough to have a confused perception of something in general: unless the mind had a distinct perception of different objects and their qualities, it would be capable of very little knowledge; though the bodies that affect us were as busy about us as they are now, and the mind were continually employed in thinking. On this faculty of distinguishing one thing from another, depends the evidence and certainty of several even very general propositions, which have passed for innate truths; because men, overlooking the true cause why those propositions find universal assent, impute it wholly to native uniform impressions: whereas it in truth depends upon this clear discerning faculty of the mind, whereby it perceives two ideas to be the same or different. But of this more hereafter.

"How much the imperfection of accurately discriminating ideas one from another lies either in the dulness or faults of the organs of sense, or want of acuteness, exercise, or attention in the understanding, or hastiness and precipitancy natural to some tempers, I will not here examine: it suffices to take notice, that this is one of the operations that the mind may reflect on and observe in itself. It is of that consequence to its other knowledge, that so far as this faculty is in itself dull, or not rightly made use of for the distinguishing one thing from another, so far our notions are confused, and our reason and judgment disturbed or misled. If in having our ideas in the memory ready at hand consists quickness of parts; in this of having them unconfused, and being able nicely to distinguish one thing from another where there is but the least difference, consists in a great measure the exactness of judgment and clearness of reason which is to be observed in one man above another. And hence, perhaps, may be given some reason of that common observation,—that men who have a great deal of wit and prompt memories, have not always the clearest judgment or deepest reason. For, wit lying most in the assemblage of ideas, and putting those together with quickness and variety wherein can be found any resemblance or congruity, thereby to make up pleasant pictures and agreeable visions in the fancy; judgment, on the contrary, lies quite on the other side, in separating carefully one from another ideas wherein can be found the least difference, thereby to avoid being misled by similitude and by affinity to take one thing for another. This is a way of proceeding quite contrary to metaphor and allusion, wherein for the most part lies that entertainment and pleasantry of wit which strikes so lively on the fancy, and therefore so acceptable to all people; because its beauty appears at first sight, and there is required no labour of thought to examine what truth or reason there is in it." [1]

But Locke's descendants have been slow to enter into the path whose fruitfulness was thus pointed out by their master, and have so neglected the study of discrimination that one might almost say that the classic English psychologists have, as a school, hardly recognized it to exist. 'Association' has proved itself in their hands the one all-absorbing power of the mind. Dr. Martineau, in his review of Bain, makes some very weighty remarks on this onesidedness of the Lockian school. Our mental history, says he, is, in its view,

"a perpetual formation of new compounds: and the words, 'Association,' 'Cohesion,' 'Fusion,' 'Indissoluble Connection,' all express the change from plurality of data to some unity of result. An explanation of the process therefore requires two things;—a true enumeration of the primary constituents, and a correct statement of their laws of combination: just as, in chemistry, we are furnished with a list of the simple elements, and then with the principles of their synthesis. Now the

[1] *Human Understanding*, II, XI, 1, 2.

latter of these two conditions we find satisfied by the Association psychologists: but not the former. They are not agreed upon their catalogue of elements, or the marks by which they may know the simple from the compound. The psychologic unit is not fixed; that which is called *one* impression by Hartley is treated as half-a-dozen or more by Mill: and the tendency of the modern teachers on this point is to recede more and more from the better chosen track of their master. Hartley, for example, regarded the whole present effect upon us of any single object,—say, an orange,—as a single sensation; and the whole vestige it left behind, as a single 'idea of sensation.' His modern disciples, on the other hand, consider this same effect as an aggregate from a plurality of sensations, and the ideal trace it leaves as highly compound. The 'idea of an object,' instead of being an elementary starting-point with them, is one of the elaborate results of repetition and experience; and is continually adduced as remarkably illustrating the fusing power of habitual association. Thus James Mill observes:

"'It is to this great law of association, that we trace the formation of our ideas of what we call external objects; that is, the ideas of a certain number of sensations, received together so frequently that they coalesce as it were, and are spoken of under the idea of unity. Hence, what we call the idea of a tree, the idea of a stone, the idea of a horse, the idea of a man. In using the names, tree, horse, man, the names of what I call objects, I am referring, and can be referring, only to my own sensations; in fact, therefore, only naming a certain number of sensations, regarded as in a particular state of combination; that is, concomitance. Particular sensations of sight, of touch, of the muscles, are the sensations, to the ideas of which, colour, extension, roughness, hardness, smoothness, taste, smell, so coalescing as to appear one idea, I give the name, idea of a tree.'[2]

"To precisely the same effect Mr. Bain remarks:

"'External objects usually affect us through a plurality of senses. The pebble on the sea shore is pictured on the eye as form and colour. We take it up in the hand and repeat the impression of form, with the additional feeling of touch. Knock two together, and there is a characteristic sound. To preserve the impression of an object of this kind, there must be an association of all these different effects. Such association, when matured and firm, is our idea, our intellectual grasp of the pebble. Passing to the organic world, and plucking a rose, we have the same effects of form to the eye and hand, colour and touch, with the new effects of odour and taste. A certain time is requisite for the coherence of all these qualities in one aggregate, so as to give us for all purposes the enduring image of the rose. When fully acquired any one

[2] *Analysis*, vol. I, p. 70.

of the characteristic impressions will revive the others; the odour, the sight, the feeling of the thorny stalk,—each of these by itself will hoist the entire impression into the view.'[3]

"Now, this order of derivation, making our objective knowledge begin with plurality of impression and arrive at unity, we take to be a complete inversion of our psychological history. Hartley, we think, was perfectly right in taking no notice of the number of inlets through which an object delivers its effect upon us, and, in spite of this circumstance, treating the effect as one. . . . Even now, after life has read us so many analytic lessons, in proportion as we can fix the attitude of our scene and ourselves, the sense of plurality in our impressions retreats, and we lapse into an undivided consciousness; losing, for instance, the separate notice of any uniform hum in the ear, or light in the eye, or weight of clothes on the body, though not one of them is inoperative on the complexion of our feeling. This law, once granted, must be carried far beyond Hartley's point. Not only must each object present itself to us integrally before it shells off into its qualities, but the whole scene around us must disengage for us object after object from its still background by emergence and change; and even our self-detachment from the world over-against us must wait for the start of collision between the force we issue and that which we receive. To confine ourselves to the simplest case: when a red ivory-ball, seen for the first time, has been withdrawn, it will leave a mental representation of itself, in which all that it simultaneously gave us will indistinguishably co-exist. Let a white ball succeed to it; now, and not before, will an attribute detach itself, and the color, by force of contrast, be shaken out into the foreground. Let the white ball be replaced by an egg: and this new difference will bring the form into notice from its previous slumber. And thus, that which began by being simply an object, cut out from the surrounding scene, becomes for us first a *red* object, and then a *red round* object; and so on. Instead, therefore, of the qualities, as separately given, subscribing together and adding themselves up to present us with the object as their aggregate, the object is beforehand with them, and from its integrity delivers them out to our knowledge, one by one. In this disintegration, the primary nucleus never loses its substantive character or name; whilst the difference which it throws off appears as a mere attribute, expressed by an adjective. Hence it is that we are compelled to think of the object as *having*, not as *being*, its qualities; and can never heartily admit the belief of any loose lot of attributes really fusing themselves into a *thing*. The unity of the original whole is not felt to go to pieces and be resolved into the properties which it successively gives off; it retains a

[3] *The Senses and the Intellect*, page 411.

residuary existence, which constitutes it a *substance*, as against the emerging quality, which is only its *phenomenal predicate*. Were it not for this perpetual process of differentiation—of self from the world, of object from its scene, of attribute from object, no step of Abstraction could be taken; no qualities could fall under our notice; and had we ten thousand senses, they would all converge and meet in but one consciousness. But if this be so, it is an utter falsification of the order of nature to speak of sensations grouping themselves into aggregates, and so composing for us the objects of which we think; and the whole language of the theory, in regard to the field of synchronous existences, is a direct inversion of the truth. Experience proceeds and intellect is trained, not by Association, but by *Dissociation*, not by reduction of pluralities of impression to one, but by the opening out of one into many; and a true psychological history must expound itself in analytic rather than synthetic terms. Precisely those ideas,—of Substance, of Mind, of Cause, of Space,—which this system treats as infinitely complex, the last result of myriads of confluent elements, are in truth the residuary simplicities of consciousness, whose stability the eddies and currents of phenomenal experience have left undisturbed."[4]

The truth is that Experience is trained by *both* association and dissociation, and that psychology must be writ *both* in synthetic and in analytic terms. Our original sensible totals are, on the one hand, subdivided by discriminative attention, and, on the other, united with other totals,—either through the agency of our own movements, carrying our senses from one part of space to another, or because new objects come successively and replace those by which we were at first impressed. The 'simple impression' of Hume, the 'simple idea' of Locke are both abstractions, never realized in experience. Experience, from the very first, presents us with concreted objects, vaguely continuous with the rest of the world which envelops them in space and time, and potentially divisible into inward elements and parts. These objects we break asunder and reunite. We must treat them in both ways for our knowledge of them to grow; and it is hard to say, on the whole, which way preponderates. But since the elements with which the traditional associationism performs its constructions—'simple sensations,' namely —are all products of discrimination carried to a high pitch, it seems as if we ought to discuss the subject of analytic attention and discrimination first.

[4] *Essays, Philosophical and Theological*, First Series, pp. 268–273.

The noticing of any *part* whatever of our object is an act of discrimination. Already on p. 382 I have described the manner in which we often spontaneously lapse into the undiscriminating state, even with regard to objects which we have already learned to distinguish. Such anæsthetics as chloroform, nitrous oxide, etc., sometimes bring about transient lapses even more total, in which numerical discrimination especially seems gone; for one sees light and hears sound, but whether one or many lights and sounds is quite impossible to tell. Where the parts of an object have already been discerned, and each made the object of a special discriminative act, we can with difficulty feel the object again in its pristine unity; and so prominent may our consciousness of its composition be, that we may hardly believe that it ever could have appeared undivided. But this is an erroneous view, the undeniable fact being that *any number of impressions, from any number of sensory sources, falling simultaneously on a mind* WHICH HAS NOT YET EXPERIENCED THEM SEPARATELY, *will fuse into a single undivided object for that mind.* The law is that all things fuse that *can* fuse, and nothing separates except what must. What makes impressions separate we have to study in this chapter. Although they separate easier if they come in through distinct nerves, yet distinct nerves are not an unconditional ground of their discrimination, as we shall presently see. The baby, assailed by eyes, ears, nose, skin, and entrails at once, feels it all as one great blooming, buzzing confusion; and to the very end of life, our location of all things in one space is due to the fact that the original extents or bignesses of all the sensations which came to our notice at once, coalesced together into one and the same space. There is no other reason than this why "the hand I touch and see coincides spatially with the hand I immediately feel."[5]

It is true that we may sometimes be tempted to exclaim, when once a lot of hitherto unnoticed details of the object lie before us, "How could we ever have been ignorant of these things and yet have felt the object, or drawn the conclusion, as if it were a *continuum*, a *plenum*? There would have been *gaps*—but we felt no gaps; wherefore we must have seen and heard these details, leaned upon these steps; they must have been operative upon our minds, just as they are now, only *unconsciously*, or at least *inattentively*. Our first unanalyzed sensation was really composed of these elementary sen-

[5] Montgomery in *Mind*, x, 527. Cf. also Lipps: *Grundtatsachen des Seelenlebens*, p. 579 ff.; and see below, Chapter XIX.

sations, our first rapid conclusion was really based on these intermediate inferences, all the while, only we failed to note the fact." But this is nothing but the fatal 'psychologist's fallacy' (p. 195) of treating an inferior state of mind as if it must somehow know implicitly all that is explicitly known *about the same topic* by superior states of mind. The thing thought of is unquestionably the same, but it is thought twice over in two absolutely different psychoses,—once as an unbroken unit, and again as a sum of discriminated parts. It is not one thought in two editions, but two entirely distinct thoughts of one thing. And each thought is within itself a *continuum,* a *plenum,* needing no contributions from the other to fill up its gaps. As I sit here, I think objects, and I make inferences, which the future is sure to analyze and articulate and riddle with discriminations, showing me many things wherever I now notice one. Nevertheless, my thought feels quite sufficient unto itself for the time being; and ranges from pole to pole, as free, and as unconscious of having overlooked anything, as if it possessed the greatest discriminative enlightenment. We all cease analyzing the world at some point, and notice no more differences. The last units with which we stop are our objective elements of being. Those of a dog are different from those of a Humboldt; those of a practical man from those of a metaphysician. But the dog's and the practical man's thoughts *feel* continuous, though to the Humboldt or the metaphysician they would appear full of gaps and defects. And they *are* continuous, *as thoughts.* It is only *as mirrors of things* that the superior minds find them full of omissions. And when the omitted things are discovered and the unnoticed differences laid bare, it is not that the old *thoughts* split up, but that *new thoughts supersede* them, which make new judgments about the same objective world.

THE PRINCIPLE OF MEDIATE COMPARISON

When we discriminate an element, we may contrast it with the case of its own absence, of its simply not being there, without reference to what *is* there; or we may also take the latter into account. Let the first sort of discrimination be called *existential,* the latter *differential* discrimination. A peculiarity of differential discriminations is that they result in a perception of differences which are felt as *greater or less* one than the other. Entire groups of differences may be ranged in series: the musical scale, the color scale, are examples. Every department of our experience may have its data written down in an evenly gradated order, from a lowest to a highest member. And any one datum may be a term in several such orders. A given note may have a high place in the pitch-series, a low place in the loudness-series, and a medium place in the series of agreeablenesses. A given tint must, in order to be fully determined, have its place assigned in the series of qualities, in the series of purities (freedom from white), and in the series of intensities or brightnesses. It may be low in one of these respects, but high in another. In passing from term to term in any such series we are conscious not only of each step of difference being equal to (or greater or less than) the last, but we are conscious of proceeding in a *uniform direction*, different from other possible directions. This *consciousness of serial increase of differences* is one of the fundamental facts of our intellectual life. More, *more*, MORE, of the same kind of difference, we say, as we advance from term to term, and realize that the farther on we get the larger grows the breach between the term we are at and the one from which we started. Between any two terms of such a series the difference is greater than that between any intermediate terms, or than that between an intermediate term and either of the extremes. The louder than the loud is louder than the less loud; the farther than the far is farther than the less far; the earlier than the early is earlier than the late; the higher than the high is higher than the low; the bigger than the big is bigger than the small; or, to put it briefly and universally, *the more than the more is more than the less*; such is *the great synthetic principle of mediate comparison which is involved in the possession by the human mind of the sense of serial increase.* In Chapter XXVIII we shall see the altogether overwhelming importance of this principle in the conduct of all our higher rational operations.

ARE ALL DIFFERENCES DIFFERENCES OF COMPOSITION?

Each of the differences in one of these uniform series feels like a definite sensible quantity, and each term seems like the last term with this quantity added. In many concrete objects which differ from one another we can plainly see that the difference does consist simply in the fact that one object is the same as the other *plus* something else, or that they both have an identical part, to which each adds a distinct remainder. Thus two pictures may be struck from the same block, but one of them may differ in having color added; or two carpets may show an identical pattern which in each is woven in distinct hues. Similarly, two classes of sensation may have the same emotional tone but negate each other in remaining respects—a dark color and a deep sound, for example; or two faces may have the same shape of nose but everything else unlike. The similarity of the same note sounded by instruments of different timbre is explained by the coexistence of a fundamental tone common to both, with over-tones in one which the other lacks. Dipping my hand into water and anon into a colder water, I may then observe certain additional feelings, broader and deeper irradiations of the cold, so to speak, which were not in the earlier experience, though for aught I can tell, the feelings may be otherwise the same. 'Hefting' first one weight, and then another, new feelings may start out in my elbow-joint, wrist, and elsewhere, and make me call the second weight the heavier of the twain. In all these cases each of the differing things may be represented by two parts, one that is common to it and the others, and another that is peculiar to itself. If they form a series, A, B, C, D, etc., and the common part be called X, whilst the lowest difference be called d, then the composition of the series would be as follows:

$$A = X + d;$$
$$B = (X + d) + d, \text{ or } X + 2d;$$
$$C = X + 3d;$$
$$D = X + 4d;$$
$$\cdot \quad \cdot \quad \cdot \quad \cdot \quad \cdot \quad \cdot$$

If X itself were ultimately composed of d's we should have the entire series explained as due to the varying combination and recombination with itself of an unvarying element; and all the apparent differences of quality would be translated into differences of quantity alone. This is the sort of reduction which the atomic theory in physics and the mind-stuff theory in psychology regard as their ideal. So that, following the analogy of our instances, one might easily be tempted to generalize and to say that all difference is but addition and subtraction, and that what we called 'differential' discrimination is only 'existential' discrimination in disguise; that is to say, that where A and B differ, we merely discern something in the one which the other is without. *Absolute identity in things up to a certain point, then absolute non-identity,* would on this theory take the place of those ultimate qualitative unlikenesses between them, in which we naturally believe; and the mental function of discrimination, ceasing to be regarded as an ultimate one, would resolve itself into mere logical affirmation and negation, or perception that a feature found in one thing, in another does not exist.

Theoretically, however, this theory is full of difficulty. If all the differences which we feel were *in one direction,* so that all objects could be arranged in one series (however long), it might still work. But when we consider the notorious fact that objects differ from each other in *divergent directions,* it grows well nigh impossible to make it do so. For then, supposing that an object differed from things in one direction by the increment *d,* it would have to differ from things in another direction by a different sort of increment, call it *d′*; so that, after getting rid of qualitative unlikeness between objects, we should have it back on our hands again between their increments. We may of course re-apply our method, and say that the difference between *d* and *d′* is not a qualitative unlikeness, but a fact of composition, one of them being the same as the other *plus* an increment of still higher order, δ for example, added. But when we recollect that everything in the world can be compared with everything else, and that the number of directions of difference is indefinitely great, then we see that the complication of self-compoundings of the ultimate differential increment by which, on this theory, all the innumerable unlikenesses of the world are explained, in order to avoid writing any of them down as ultimate differences of kind, would beggar all conception. It is the mind-dust theory, with all its difficulties in a particularly uncompromising form; and all for the sake of the fantastic pleasure of being able arbitrarily to say that there is between the things in the world and between the 'ideas' in the mind nothing but absolute sameness and absolute not-sameness of elements, the not-sameness admitting no degrees.

To me it seems much wiser to turn away from such transcendental extravagances of speculation, and to abide by the natural appearances. These would leave unlikeness as an indecomposable relation amongst things, and a relation moreover of which there were all degrees. Absolute not-sameness would be the maximal degree, absolute sameness the minimal degree of this unlikeness, the discernment of which would be one of our ultimate cognitive powers.[6] Certainly the natural appearances are dead against the notion that no qualitative differences exist. With the same clearness with which, in certain objects, we do feel a difference to be a mere matter of *plus* and *minus*, in other objects we feel that this is not the case. Contrast our feeling of the difference between the length of two lines with our feeling of the difference between blue and yellow, or with that between right and left. Is right equal to left with something added? Is blue yellow *plus* something? If so, *plus* what?[7] So long as we stick to *verifiable* psychology, *we are forced to admit that differences of simple* KIND *form an irreducible sort of relation* between some of the elements of our experience, and forced to deny that differential discrimination can everywhere be reduced to the mere ascertainment that elements present in one fact, in another fail to exist. The perception that an element exists in one thing and does not exist in another and the perception of qualitative difference are, in short, entirely disconnected mental functions.[8]

But at the same time that we insist on this, we must also admit that differences of quality, however abundant, are not the only distinctions with which our mind has to deal. Differences which seem

[6] Stumpf (*Tonpsychologie*, I, 116 ff.) tries to prove that the theory that all differences are differences of composition leads necessarily to an infinite regression when we try to determine the unit. It seems to me that in his particular reasoning he forgets the ultimate units of the mind-stuff theory. I cannot find the completed infinite to be one of the obstacles to belief in this theory, although I fully accept Stumpf's general reasoning, and am only too happy to find myself on the same side with such an exceptionally clear thinker. The strictures by Wahle in the *Vierteljahrsschrift für wissenschaftliche Philosophie* seem to me to have no force, since the writer does not discriminate between resemblance of things obviously compound and that of things sensibly simple.

[7] The *belief that the causes* of effects felt by us to differ qualitatively are facts which differ only in quantity (e.g., that blue is caused by so many ether-waves, and yellow by a smaller number) must not be confounded with the feeling that the effects differ quantitatively themselves.

[8] Herr G. H. Schneider, in his youthful pamphlet (*Die Unterscheidung*, 1877) has tried to show that there are no positively existent elements of sensibility, no substantive qualities between which differences obtain, but that the terms we call such, the sensations, are but sums of differences, loci or starting points whence many directions of difference proceed. '*Unterschiedsempfindungscomplexe*' are what he calls them. This absurd carrying out of that 'principle of relativity' which we shall have to mention in Chapter XVII may serve as a counterpoise to the mind-stuff theory, which says that there are nothing but substantive sensations, and denies the existence of relations of difference between them at all.

of mere composition, of number, of *plus* and *minus*, also abound.[9] But it will be best for the present to disregard all these quantitative cases and, taking the others (which, by the least favorable calculation, will still be numerous enough), to consider next *the manner in which we come to cognize simple differences of kind.* We cannot *explain* the cognition; we can only ascertain the conditions by virtue of which it occurs.

THE CONDITIONS OF DISCRIMINATION

What, then, are the conditions under which we discriminate things differing in a simple way?

First, *the things must* BE *different,* either in time, or place, or quality. If the difference in any of these regards is sufficiently great, then we cannot overlook it, except by not noticing the things at all. No one can help singling out a black stripe on a white ground, or feeling the contrast between a bass note and a high one sounded immediately after it. Discrimination is here *involuntary*. But where the objective difference is less, discrimination need not so inevitably occur, and may even require considerable effort of attention to be performed at all.

Another condition which then favors it is that the sensations excited by *the differing objects should not come to us simultaneously but fall in immediate* SUCCESSION upon the same organ. It is easier to compare successive than simultaneous sounds, easier to compare two weights or two temperatures by testing one after the other with the same hand, than by using both hands and comparing both at once. Similarly it is easier to discriminate shades of light or color by moving the eye from one to the other, so that they successively stimulate the same retinal tract. In testing the local discrimination of the skin, by applying compass-points, it is found that they are felt to touch different spots much more readily when set down one after the other than when both are applied at once. In the latter case they may be two or three inches apart on the back, thighs, etc., and still feel as if they were set down in one spot. Finally, in the case of smell and taste it is well-nigh impossible to compare simultaneous impressions at all. The reason why successive impression so much favors the result seems to be that there is a real *sensation of difference,*

9 Cf. Stumpf: *Tonpsychologie,* I, 121, and James Ward: *Mind,* I, 464.

aroused by the shock of transition from one perception to another which is unlike the first. This sensation of difference has its own peculiar quality, as difference, which remains sensible, no matter of what sort the terms may be, between which it obtains. It is, in short, one of those transitive feelings, or feelings of relation, of which I treated in a former place (pp. 238 ff.); and, when once aroused, its object lingers in the memory along with the substantive terms which precede and follow, and enables our *judgments of comparison* to be made. We shall soon see reason to believe that no two terms can possibly be *simultaneously* perceived to differ, unless, in a preliminary operation, we have successively attended to each, and, in so doing, had the transitional sensation of difference between them aroused. A field of consciousness, however complex, is never analyzed unless some of its ingredients have changed. We *now* discern, 'tis true, a multitude of coexisting things about us at every moment: but this is because we have had a long education, and each thing we now see distinct has been already differentiated from its neighbors by repeated appearances in successive order. To the infant, sounds, sights, touches, and pains, form probably one unanalyzed bloom of confusion.[10]

Where the difference between the successive sensations is but slight, the transition between them must be made as immediate as possible, and both must be compared *in memory*, in order to get the best results. One cannot judge accurately of the difference between two similar wines whilst the second is still in one's mouth. So of sounds, warmths, etc.—we must get the dying phases of both sensations of the pair we are comparing. Where, however, the difference is strong, this condition is immaterial, and we can then compare a sensation actually felt with another carried in memory only. The longer the interval of time between the sensations, the more uncertain is their discrimination.

The difference, thus immediately felt between two terms, is independent of our ability to identify either of the terms by itself. I can feel two distinct spots to be touched on my skin, yet not know which is above and which below. I can observe two neighboring musical tones to differ, and still not know which of the two is the

[10] The ordinary treatment of this is to call it the result of the *fusion* of a lot of sensations, in themselves separate. This is pure mythology, as the sequel will abundantly show.

higher in pitch. Similarly I may discriminate two neighboring tints, whilst remaining uncertain which is the bluer or the yellower, or *how* either differs from its mate.[11]

With such direct perceptions of difference as this, we must not confound those entirely unlike cases in which we *infer* that two things must differ because we know enough *about* each of them taken by itself to warrant our classing them under distinct heads. It often happens, when the interval is long between two experiences, that our judgments are guided, not so much by a positive image or copy of the earlier one, as by our recollection of certain facts about it. Thus I know that the sunshine to-day is less bright than on a certain day last week, because I then said it was quite dazzling, a remark I should not now care to make. Or I know myself to feel better now than I was last summer, because I can now psychologize, and then I could not. We are constantly busy comparing feelings with whose quality our imagination has no sort of *acquaintance* at the time—pleasures, or pains, for example. It is notoriously hard to conjure up in imagination a lively image of either of these classes of feeling. The associationists may prate of an idea of pleasure being a pleasant idea, of an idea of pain being a painful one, but the unsophisticated sense of mankind is against them, agreeing with Homer that the memory of griefs when past may be a joy, and with Dante that there is no greater sorrow than, in misery, to recollect one's happier time.

Feelings remembered in this imperfect way *must* be compared with present or recent feelings by the aid of what we know about them. We identify the remote experience in such a case by *conceiving it*. The most perfect way of conceiving it is by defining it in terms of some standard scale. If I know the thermometer to stand at zero to-day and to have stood at 32° last Sunday, I know to-day to be colder, and I know just how much colder, than it was last Sunday. If I know that a certain note was *c*, and that this note is *d*, I know that this note must be the higher of the two.

[11] "We often begin to be dimly aware of a difference in a sensation or group of sensations before we can assign any definite character to that which differs. Thus we detect a strange or foreign ingredient of flavour in a familiar dish, or of tone in a familiar tune, and yet are wholly unable for a while to say what the intruder is like. Hence perhaps discrimination may be regarded as the earliest and most primordial mode of intellectual activity." (Sully: *Outlines of Psychology*, p. 142. Cf. also G. H. Schneider: *Die Unterscheidung*, pp. 9–10.)

The inference that two things differ because their concomitants, effects, names, kinds, or—to put it generally—their *signs*, differ, is of course susceptible of unlimited complication. The sciences furnish examples, in the way in which men are led, by noticing differences in effects, to assume new hypothetical causes, differing from any known heretofore. But no matter how many may be the steps by which such inferential discriminations are made, *they all end in a direct intuition of difference somewhere*. The *last* ground for inferring that A and B differ must be that, whilst A is an *m*, B is an *n*, and that *m* and *n* are *seen to differ*. Let us then neglect the complex cases, the A's and the B's, and go back to the study of the unanalyzable perception of difference between their signs, the *m*'s and the *n*'s, when these are seemingly simple terms.

I said that in their immediate succession the shock of their difference was *felt*. It is felt *repeatedly* when we go back and forth from *m* to *n*; and we make a point of getting it thus repeatedly (by alternating our attention at least) whenever the shock is so slight as to be with difficulty perceived. But in addition to being felt at the brief instant of transition, the difference also feels as if incorporated and taken up into the second term, which feels 'different-from-the-first' even while it lasts. It is obvious that the 'second term' of the mind in this case is not bald *n*, but a very complex object; and that the sequence is not simply first '*m*,' then '*difference*,' then '*n*'; but first '*m*,' then '*difference*,' then '*n-different-from-m*.' The several thoughts, however, to which these three several objects are revealed, are three ordinary 'segments' of the mental 'stream.'

As our brains and minds are actually made, it is impossible to get certain *m*'s and *n*'s in immediate sequence and to keep them *pure*. If kept pure, it would mean that they remained uncompared. With us, inevitably, by a mechanism which we as yet fail to understand, the shock of difference is felt between them, and the second object is not *n* pure, but *n-as-different-from-m*.[12] It is no more a paradox that under these conditions this cognition of *m* and *n* in mutual relation should occur, than that under other conditions the cognition of *m*'s or *n*'s simple quality should occur. But

[12] In cases where the difference is slight, we may need, as previously remarked, to get the dying phase of *n* as well as of *m* before *n-different-from-m* is distinctly felt. In that case the inevitably successive feelings (as far as we can sever what is so continuous) would be four, *m, difference, n, n-different-from-m*. This slight additional complication alters not a whit the essential features of the case.

as it has been treated as a paradox, and as a spiritual agent, not itself a portion of the stream, has been invoked to account for it, a word of further remark seems desirable.

My account, it will be noted, is merely a description of the facts as they occur: feelings (or thoughts) each knowing something, but the later one knowing, if preceded by a certain earlier one, a more complicated object than it would have known had the earlier one not been there. I offer no *explanation* of such a sequence of cognitions. The explanation (I devoutly expect) will be found some day to depend on cerebral conditions. Until it is forthcoming, we can only treat the sequence as a special case of the general law that every experience undergone by the brain leaves in it a modification which is one factor in determining what manner of experiences the following ones shall be (cf. pp. 227–230). To anyone who denies the possibility of such a law I have nothing to say, until he brings his proofs.

The sensationalists and the spiritualists meanwhile (filled both of them with their notion that the mind must in some fashion *contain* what it knows) begin by giving a crooked account of the facts. Both admit that for *m* and *n* to be known in any way whatever, little rounded and finished off duplicates of each must be contained in the mind as separate entities. These pure ideas, so called, of *m* and *n* respectively, succeed each other there. And since they *are distinct*, say the sensationalists, they are *eo ipso* distinguished. "To have ideas different and ideas distinguished, are synonymous expressions; different and distinguished, meaning exactly the same thing," says James Mill.[13] "Distinguished!" say the spiritualists, "distinguished *by what*, forsooth?" Truly the respective ideas of *m* and of *n* in the mind are distinct. But for that very reason neither can distinguish itself from the other, for to do that it would have to be aware of the other, and thus for the time being become the other, and that would be to get mixed up with the other and to lose its own distinctness. Distinctness of ideas and idea of distinctness, are not one thing, but two. This last is a *relation*. Only a *relating principle*, opposed in nature to all facts of feeling, an Ego, Soul, or Subject, is competent, by being present to both of the ideas alike, to hold them together and at the same time to keep them distinct."

But if the plain facts be admitted that the *pure* idea of '*n*' is

[13] *Analysis*, J. S. Mill's ed., II, 17. Cf. also pp. 12, 14.

never in the mind at all, when '*m*' has once gone before; and that the feeling '*n-different-from-m*' is itself an absolutely unique pulse of thought, the bottom of this precious quarrel drops out and neither party is left with anything to fight about. Surely such a consummation ought to be welcomed, especially when brought about, as here, by a formulation of the facts which offers itself so naturally and unsophistically.[14]

We may, then, conclude our examination of the manner in which simple involuntary discrimination comes about, by saying, 1) that its vehicle is a thought possessed of a knowledge of both terms compared and of their difference; 2) that the necessary and sufficient condition (as the human mind goes) for arousing this thought is that a thought or feeling of one of the terms discriminated should,

[14] There is only one obstacle, and that is our inveterate tendency to believe that where two things or qualities are compared, it *must* be that exact duplicates of both have got into the mind and have matched themselves against each other there. To which the first reply is the empirical one of "Look into the mind and see." When I recognize a weight which I now lift as *inferior* to the one I just lifted; when, with my tooth now aching, I perceive the pain to be *less* intense than it was a minute ago; the two things in the mind which are compared would, by the authors I criticise, be admitted to be an actual sensation and an image in the memory. An image in the memory, by general consent of these same authors, is admitted to be a weaker thing than a sensation. Nevertheless it is in these instances judged stronger; that is, an object supposed to be known only in so far forth as this image represents it, is judged stronger. Ought not this to shake one's belief in the notion of separate representative 'ideas' weighing themselves, or being weighed by the Ego, against each other in the mind? And let it not be said that what makes us judge the felt pain to be weaker than the imagined one of a moment since is our recollection of the *downward nature of the shock of difference* which we felt as we passed to the present moment from the one before it. That shock does undoubtedly have a different character according as it comes between terms of which the second diminishes or increases; and it may be admitted that in cases where the past term is doubtfully remembered, the memory of the shock, as *plus* or *minus,* might sometimes enable us to establish a relation which otherwise we should not perceive. But one could hardly expect the memory of this shock to overpower our actual comparison of terms, both of which are *present* (as are the image and the sensation in the case supposed), and make us judge the weaker one to be the stronger.—And hereupon comes the second reply: Suppose the mind does compare two realities by comparing two ideas of its own which represent them—what is gained? The same mystery is still there. The ideas must still be *known*; and, as the attention in comparing oscillates from one to the other, past must be known with present just as before. If you must end by simply saying that your 'Ego,' whilst *being* neither the idea of *m* nor the idea of *n*, yet knows and compares both, why not allow your pulse of thought, which *is* neither the thing *m* nor the thing *n*, to know and compare both directly? 'Tis but a question of how to *name* the facts least artificially. The egoist *explains* them, by naming them as an Ego 'combining' or 'synthetizing' two ideas, no more than we do by naming them a pulse of thought knowing two facts.

as immediately as possible, precede that in which the other term is known; and 3) that the thought which knows the second term will then also know the difference (or in more difficult cases will be continuously succeeded by one which does know the difference) and both of the terms between which it holds.

This last thought need, however, not *be* these terms with their difference, nor *contain* them. A man's thought can know and mean all sorts of things without those things getting bodily into it—the distant, for example, the future, and the past.[15] The vanishing term in the case which occupies us vanishes; but because it is the specific term it is and nothing else, it leaves a specific influence behind it when it vanishes, the effect of which is to determine the succeeding pulse of thought in a perfectly characteristic way. Whatever consciousness comes next must know the vanished term and call it different from the one now there.

Here we are at the end of our tether about involuntary discrimination of successively felt simple things; and must drop the subject, hopeless of seeing any deeper into it for the present, and turn to discriminations of a less simple sort.

THE PROCESS OF ANALYSIS

And first, of the discrimination of simultaneously felt impressions! Our first way of looking at a reality is often to suppose it simple, but later we may learn to perceive it as compound. This new way of knowing the same reality may conveniently be called by the name of *Analysis*. It is manifestly one of the most incessantly performed of all our mental processes, so let us examine the conditions under which it occurs.

I think we may safely lay down at the outset this fundamental principle, that *any total impression made on the mind must be unanalyzable, whose elements are never experienced apart*. The com-

[15] I fear that few will be converted by my words, so obstinately do thinkers of all schools refuse to admit the unmediated function of *knowing a thing*, and so incorrigibly do they substitute *being the thing* for it. E.g., in the latest utterance of the spiritualistic philosophy (Bowne's *Introduction to Psychological Theory*, 1887, published only three days before this writing) one of the first sentences which catch my eye is this: "What remembers? The spiritualist says, The soul remembers; it abides across the years and the flow of the body, and *gathering up its past carries it with it*" (p. 28). Why, for heaven's sake, O Bowne, cannot you say '*knows it*'? If there is anything our soul does *not* do to its past, it is to carry it with it.

ponents of an absolutely changeless group of not-elsewhere-occurring attributes could never be discriminated. If all cold things were wet and all wet things cold, if all hard things pricked our skin, and no other things did so; is it likely that we should discriminate between coldness and wetness, and hardness and pungency respectively? If all liquids were transparent and no non-liquid were transparent, it would be long before we had separate names for liquidity and transparency. If heat were a function of position above the earth's surface, so that the higher a thing was the hotter it became, one word would serve for hot and high. We have, in fact, a number of sensations whose concomitants are almost invariably the same, and we find it, accordingly, almost impossible to analyze them out from the totals in which they are found. The contraction of the diaphragm and the expansion of the lungs, the shortening of certain muscles and the rotation of certain joints, are examples. The converging of the eyeballs and the accommodation for near objects are, for each distance of the object (in the common use of the eyes) inseparably linked, and neither can (without a sort of artificial training which shall presently be mentioned) be felt by itself. We learn that the *causes* of such groups of feelings are multiple, and therefore we frame theories about the composition of the feelings themselves, by 'fusion,' 'integration,' 'synthesis,' or what not. But by direct introspection no analysis of them is ever made. A conspicuous case will come to view when we treat of the emotions. Every emotion has its 'expression,' of quick breathing, palpitating heart, flushed face, or the like. The expression gives rise to bodily feelings; and the emotion is thus necessarily and invariably accompanied by these bodily feelings. The consequence is that it is impossible to apprehend it as a spiritual state by itself, or to analyze it away from the lower feelings in question. It is in fact impossible to prove that it exists as a distinct psychic fact. The present writer strongly doubts that it does so exist. But those who are most firmly persuaded of its existence must wait, to prove their point, until they can quote some as yet unfound pathological case of an individual who shall have emotions in a body in which either complete paralysis will have prevented their expression, or complete anæsthesia will have made the latter unfelt.

In general, then, if an object affects us simultaneously in a number of ways, *abcd*, we get a peculiar integral impression, which thereafter characterizes to our mind the individuality of that object, and becomes the sign of its presence; and which is only resolved into *a, b, c, d,* respectively by the aid of farther experiences. These we now may turn to consider.

If any single quality or constituent, a, of such an object have previously been known by us isolatedly, or have in any other manner already become an object of separate acquaintance on our part, so that we have an image of it, distinct or vague, in our mind, disconnected with *bcd, then that constituent a may be analyzed out from the total impression.* Analysis of a thing means separate attention to each of its parts. In Chapter XI we saw that one condition of attending to a thing was the formation from within of a separate image of that thing, which should, as it were, go out to meet the impression received. Attention being the condition of analysis, and separate imagination being the condition of attention, it follows also that separate imagination is the condition of analysis. *Only such elements as we are acquainted with, and can imagine separately, can be discriminated within a total sense-impression.* The image seems to welcome its own mate from out of the compound, and to heighten the feeling thereof; whereas it dampens and opposes the feeling of the other constituents; and thus the compound becomes broken for our consciousness into parts.

All the facts cited in Chapter XI to prove that attention involves inward reproduction go to prove this point as well. In looking for any object in a room, for a book in a library, for example, we detect it the more readily if, in addition to merely knowing its name, etc., we carry in our mind a distinct image of its appearance. The assafœtida in 'Worcestershire sauce' is not obvious to anyone who has not tasted assafœtida *per se*. In a 'cold' color an artist would never be able to analyze out the pervasive presence of *blue*, unless he had previously made acquaintance with the color blue by itself. All the colors we actually experience are mixtures. Even the purest primaries always come to us with some white. Absolutely pure red or green or violet is never experienced, and so can never be discerned in the so-called primaries with which we have to deal: the latter consequently pass for pure.—The reader will remember how an overtone can only be attended to in the midst of its consorts in the voice of a musical instrument, by sounding it previously alone. The imagination, being then full of it, hears the like of it in the compound tone. Helmholtz, whose account of this observation we formerly quoted, goes on to explain the difficulty of the case in a way which beautifully corroborates the point I now seek to prove. He says:

"The ultimate simple elements of the sensation of tone, simple tones themselves, are rarely heard alone. Even those instruments by which they can be produced, as tuning-forks before resonance chambers, when strongly excited, give rise to weak harmonic upper partials, partly within and partly without the ear . . . . Hence the opportunities are very scanty for impressing on our memory an exact and sure image of these simple elementary tones. But if the constituents are only indefinitely and vaguely known, the analysis of their sum into them must be correspondingly uncertain. If we do not know with certainty how much of the musical tone under consideration is to be attributed to its prime, we cannot but be uncertain as to what belongs to the partials. Consequently we must begin by making the individual elements which have to be distinguished, individually audible, so as to obtain an entirely fresh recollection of the corresponding sensation, and the whole business requires undisturbed and concentrated attention. We are even without the ease that can be obtained by frequent repetitions of the experiment, such as we possess in the analysis of musical chords into their individual notes. In that case we hear the individual notes sufficiently often by themselves, whereas we rarely hear simple tones and may almost be said never to hear the building up of a compound from its simple tones."[16]

THE PROCESS OF ABSTRACTION

Very few elements of reality are experienced by us in absolute isolation. The most that usually happens to a constituent *a* of a compound phenomenon *abcd* is that its *strength* relatively to *bcd* varies from a maximum to a minimum; or that it appears linked with *other* qualities, in other compounds, as *aefg* or *ahik*. Either of these vicissitudes in the mode of our experiencing *a* may, under favorable circumstances, lead us to feel the difference between it and its concomitants, and to single it out—not absolutely, it is true, but approximately—and so to analyze the compound of which it is a part. The act of singling out is then called *abstraction*, and the element disengaged is an *abstract*.

Consider the case of fluctuations of relative strength or intensity first. Let there be three grades of the compound, as *Abcd*, *abcd*, and

[16] *Sensations of Tone*, 2d English Ed., p. 65.

abcD. In passing between these compounds, the mind will feel shocks of difference. The differences, moreover, will serially increase, and their direction will be felt as of a distinct sort. The increase from *abcd* to *Abcd* is on the *a* side; that to *abcD* is on the *d* side. And these two differences of direction are differently felt. I do not say that this discernment of the *a*-direction from the *d*-direction will give us an actual intuition either of *a* or of *d* in the abstract. But it leads us to *conceive* or *postulate* each of these qualities, and to define it as the *extreme* of a certain direction. 'Dry' wines and 'sweet' wines, for example, differ, and form a series. It happens that we have an experience of sweetness pure and simple in the taste of sugar, and this we can analyze out of the wine-taste. But no one knows what 'dryness' tastes like, all by itself. It must, however, be something extreme in the dry direction; and we should probably not fail to recognize it as the original of our abstract conception, in case we ever did come across it. In some such way we get to form notions of the flavor of meats, apart from their feeling to the tongue, or of that of fruits apart from their acidity, etc., and we abstract the touch of bodies as distinct from their temperature. We may even apprehend the quality of a muscle's contraction as distinguished from its extent, or one muscle's contraction from another's, as when, by practising with prismatic glasses, and varying our eyes' convergence whilst our accommodation remains the same, we learn the direction in which our feeling of the convergence differs from that of the accommodation.

But the fluctuation in a quality's intensity is a less efficient aid to our abstracting of it than the diversity of the other qualities in whose company it may appear. *What is associated now with one thing and now with another tends to become dissociated from either, and to grow into an object of abstract contemplation by the mind.* One might call this the *law of dissociation by varying concomitants.*[16a] The practical result of it will be to allow the mind which has thus dissociated and abstracted a character to analyze it out of a total whenever it meets with it again. The law has been frequently recognized by psychologists, though I know of none who has given it the emphatic prominence in our mental history which it deserves. Mr. Spencer says:

[16a] Attributed to Hume, by Carveth Read: *Treatise*, Bk. I, pt. I, § 7, especially the last two paragraphs (*Metaphysics of Nature*, p. 260).

"If the property A occurs here along with the properties B, C, D; there along with C, F, H; and again with E, G, B; . . . it must happen that by multiplication of experiences, the impressions produced by these properties on the organism will be disconnected, and rendered so far independent in the organism as the properties are in the environment. Whence must eventually result a power to recognize attributes in themselves, apart from particular bodies."[17]

And still more to the point Dr. Martineau, in the passage I have already quoted, writes:

"When a red ivory-ball, seen for the first time, has been withdrawn, it will leave a mental representation of itself, in which all that it simultaneously gave us will indistinguishably co-exist. Let a white ball succeed to it; now, and not before, will an attribute detach itself, and the *color*, by force of contrast, be shaken out into the foreground. Let the white ball be replaced by an egg: and this new difference will bring the *form* into notice from its previous slumber. And thus, that which began by being simply an object, cut out from the surrounding scene, becomes for us first a *red* object, and then a *red round* object; and so on."

Why the repetition of the character in combination with different wholes will cause it thus to break up its adhesion with any one of them, and roll out, as it were, alone upon the table of consciousness, is a little of a mystery. One might suppose the nerve-processes of the various concomitants to neutralize or inhibit each other more or less and to leave the process of the common term alone distinctly active. Mr. Spencer appears to think that the mere fact that the common term is repeated more often than any one of its associates will, of itself, give it such a degree of intensity that its abstraction must needs ensue.

This has a plausible sound, but breaks down when examined closely. For it is not always the often-repeated character which is first noticed when its concomitants have varied a certain number of times; it is even more likely to be the most novel of all the concomitants, which will arrest the attention. If a boy has seen nothing all his life but sloops and schooners, he will probably never distinctly have singled out in his notion of 'sail' the character of being hung lengthwise. When for the first time he sees a square-rigged

17 *Psychology*, I, 345.

ship, the opportunity of extracting the lengthwise mode of hanging as a special accident, and of dissociating it from the general notion of sail, is offered. But there are twenty chances to one that that will not be the form of the boy's consciousness. What he *notices* will be the new and exceptional character of being hung crosswise. He will go home and speak of that, and perhaps never consciously formulate what the more familiar peculiarity consists in.

This mode of abstraction is realized on a very wide scale, because the elements of the world in which we find ourselves appear, as a matter of fact, here, there, and everywhere, and are changing their concomitants all the while. But on the other hand the abstraction is, so to speak, never complete, the analysis of a compound never perfect, because no element is ever given to us absolutely alone, and we can never therefore approach a compound with the image in our mind of any one of its components in a perfectly pure form. Colors, sounds, smells, are just as much entangled with other matter as are more formal elements of experience, such as extension, intensity, effort, pleasure, difference, likeness, harmony, badness, strength, and even consciousness itself. All are embedded in one world. But by the fluctuations and permutations of which we have spoken, we come to form a pretty good notion of the *direction* in which each element differs from the rest, and so we frame the notion of it as a *terminus,* and continue to mean it as an individual thing. In the case of many elements, the simple sensibles, like heat, cold, the colors, smells, etc., the extremes of the directions are almost touched, and in these instances we have a comparatively exact perception of what it is we mean to abstract. But even this is only an approximation; and in literal mathematical strictness *all* our abstracts must be confessed to be but imperfectly imaginable things. At bottom the process is one of *conception*, and is everywhere, even in the sphere of simple sensible qualities, the same as that by which we are usually understood to attain to the notions of abstract goodness, perfect felicity, absolute power, and the like: the direct perception of a difference between compounds, and the imaginary prolongation of the direction of the difference to an ideal terminus, the notion of which we fix and keep as one of our permanent subjects of discourse.

This is all that I can say usefully about abstraction, or about analysis, to which it leads.

THE IMPROVEMENT OF DISCRIMINATION BY PRACTICE

In all the cases considered hitherto I have supposed the differences involved to be so large as to be flagrant, and the discrimination, where successive, was treated as involuntary. But, so far from being always involuntary, discriminations are often difficult in the extreme, and by most men never performed. Professor De Morgan, thinking, it is true, rather of conceptual than of perceptive discrimination, wrote, wittily enough:

> "The great bulk of the illogical part of the educated community—whether majority or minority I know not; perhaps six of one and half-a-dozen of the other—have not power to make a distinction, cannot be made to take a distinction, and of course, never attempt to shake a distinction. With them all such things are evasions, subterfuges, come-offs, loopholes, &c. They would hang a man for horse-stealing under a statute against sheep-stealing; and would laugh at you if you quibbled about the distinction between a horse and a sheep."[18]

Any personal or practical interest, however, in the results to be obtained by distinguishing, makes one's wits amazingly sharp to detect differences. The culprit himself is not likely to overlook the difference between a horse and a sheep. And long training and practice in distinguishing has the same effect as personal interest. Both of these agencies give to small amounts of objective difference the same effectiveness upon the mind that, under other circumstances, only large ones would have. Let us seek to penetrate the *modus operandi* of their influence—beginning with that of practice and habit.

That 'practice makes perfect' is notorious in the field of motor accomplishments. But motor accomplishments depend in part on sensory discrimination. Billiard-playing, rifle-shooting, tight-rope-dancing, demand the most delicate appreciation of minute disparities of sensation, as well as the power to make accurately graduated muscular response thereto. In the purely sensorial field we have the well-known virtuosity displayed by the professional buyers and testers of various kinds of goods. One man will distinguish by taste between the upper and the lower half of a bottle of old Ma-

18 *A Budget of Paradoxes*, p. 380.

deira. Another will recognize, by feeling the flour in a barrel, whether the wheat was grown in Iowa or Tennessee. The blind deaf-mute, Laura Bridgman, had so improved her touch as to recognize, after a year's interval, the hand of a person who once had shaken hers; and her sister in misfortune, Julia Brace, is said to have been employed in the Hartford Asylum to sort the linen of its multitudinous inmates, after it came from the wash, by her wonderfully educated sense of smell.

The fact is so familiar that few, if any, psychologists have even recognized it as needing explanation. They have seemed to think that practice must, in the nature of things, improve the delicacy of discernment, and have let the matter rest. At most they have said: "Attention accounts for it; we attend more to habitual things, and what we attend to we perceive more minutely." This answer is true, but too general; it seems to me that we can be a little more precise.

There are at least two distinct causes which we can see at work whenever experience improves discrimination:

First, the *terms* whose difference comes to be felt contract disparate associates and these help to drag them apart.

Second, the *difference* reminds us of larger differences of the same sort, and these help us to notice it.

Let us study the first cause first, and begin by supposing two compounds, of ten elements apiece. Suppose no one element of either compound to differ from the corresponding element of the other compound enough to be distinguished from it if the two are compared alone, and let the amount of this imperceptible difference be called equal to 1. The compounds will differ from each other, however, in ten different ways; and, although each difference by itself might pass unperceived, the total difference, equal to 10, may very well be sufficient to strike the sense. In a word, *increasing the number of 'points' involved in a difference may excite our discrimination as effectually as increasing the amount of difference at any one point.* Two men whose mouth, nose, eyes, cheeks, chin, and hair, all differ slightly, will be as little confounded by us, as two appearances of the same man one with, and the other without, a false nose. The only contrast in the cases is that we can easily name the *point* of difference in the one, whilst in the other we cannot.

Two things, then, B and C, indistinguishable when compared

together alone, may each contract adhesions with different associates, and the compounds thus formed may, as wholes, be judged very distinct. *The effect of practice in increasing discrimination must then, in part, be due to the reinforcing effect, upon an original slight difference between the terms, of additional differences between the diverse associates which they severally affect.* Let B and C be the terms: If A contract adhesions with B, and C with D, AB may appear very distinct from CD, though B and C *per se* might have been almost identical.

To illustrate, how does one learn to distinguish claret from burgundy? Probably they have been drunk on different occasions. When we first drank claret we heard it called by that name, we were eating such and such a dinner, etc. Next time we drink it, a dim reminder of all those things chimes through us as we get the taste of the wine. When we try burgundy our first impression is that it is a kind of claret; but something falls short of full identification, and presently we hear it called burgundy. During the next few experiences, the discrimination may still be uncertain—"which," we ask ourselves, "of the two wines is this present specimen?" But at last the claret-flavor recalls pretty distinctly its own name, 'claret,' "that wine I drank at So-and-so's table," etc.; and the burgundy-flavor recalls the name burgundy and someone else's table. *And only when this different* SETTING *has come to each is our discrimination between the two flavors solid and stable.* After a while the tables and other parts of the setting, besides the name, grow so multifarious as not to come up distinctly into consciousness; but *pari passu* with this, the adhesion of each wine with its own *name* becomes more and more inveterate, and at last each flavor suggests instantly and certainly its own name and nothing else. The names differ far more than the flavors, and help to stretch these latter farther apart. Some such process as this must go on in all our experience. Beef and mutton, strawberries and raspberries, odor of rose and odor of violet, contract different adhesions which reinforce the differences already felt in the terms.

The reader may say that this has nothing to do with making us feel the *difference* between the two terms. It is merely fixing, identifying, and so to speak substantializing, the *terms*. But what we feel as their *difference*, we should feel, even though we were unable to name or otherwise identify the terms.

To which I reply that I believe that the difference is always concreted and made to seem *more substantial* by recognizing the terms. I went out for instance the other day and found that the snow just fallen had a very odd look, different from the common appearance of snow. I presently called it a 'micaceous' look; and it seemed to me as if, the moment I did so, the difference grew more distinct and fixed than it was before. The other connotations of the word 'micaceous' dragged the snow farther away from ordinary snow and seemed even to aggravate the peculiar look in question. I think some such effect as this on our way of feeling a difference will be very generally admitted to follow from naming the terms between which it obtains; although I admit myself that it is difficult to show coercively that naming or otherwise identifying any given pair of hardly distinguishable terms is essential to their being felt as different at *first*.[19]

I offer the explanation only as a partial one: it certainly is not

[19] The explanation I offer presupposes that a difference too faint to have any direct effect in the way of making the mind notice it *per se* will nevertheless be strong enough to keep its 'terms' from calling up identical associates. It seems probable from many observations that this is the case. All the facts of 'unconscious' inference are proofs of it. We say a painting 'looks' like the work of a certain artist, though we cannot name the characteristic differentiæ. We see by a man's face that he is sincere, though we can give no definite reason for our faith. The facts of sense-perception quoted from Helmholtz a few pages below will be additional examples. Here is another good one, though it will perhaps be easier understood after reading the chapter on Space-perception than now. Take two stereoscopic slides and represent on each half-slide a pair of spots, a and b, but make their distances such that the a's are equidistant on both slides, whilst the b's are nearer together on slide 1 than on slide 2. Make moreover the distance $ab = ab'''$ and the distance $ab' = ab''$. Then look successively at

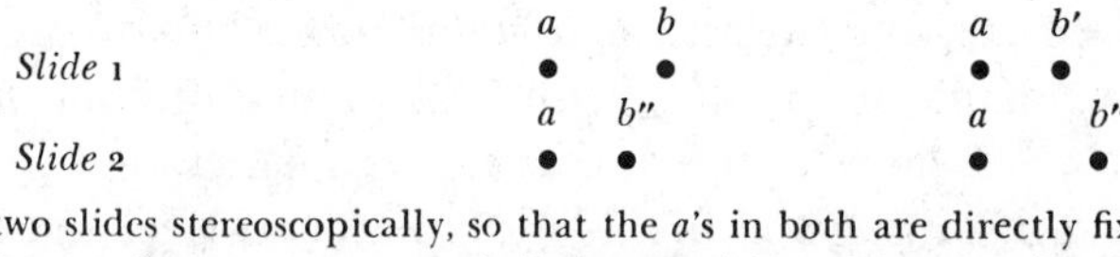

	a	b	a	b'
Slide 1	•	•	•	•
	a	b''	a	b'''
Slide 2	•	•	•	•

the two slides stereoscopically, so that the a's in both are directly fixated (that is, fall on the two foveæ, or centres of distinctest vision). The a's will then appear single, and so probably will the b's. But the now single-seeming b on slide 1 will look nearer, whilst that on slide 2 will look farther than the a. But, if the diagrams are rightly drawn, b and b''' must affect 'identical' spots, spots equally far to the right of the fovea, b in the left eye and b''' in the right eye. The same is true of b' and b''. Identical spots are spots whose sensations cannot possibly be discriminated as such. Since in these two observations, however, they give rise to such opposite perceptions of distance, and prompt such opposite tendencies to movement (since in slide 1 we *converge* in looking from a to b, whilst in slide 2 we *diverge*), it follows that two processes which occasion feelings quite indistinguishable to direct consciousness may nevertheless be each allied with disparate associates both of a sensorial and of a motor kind. Cf. Donders: *Archiv für Ophthalmologie*, Bd. 13 (1867). The basis of his essay is that we

complete. Take the way in which *practice refines our local discrimination on the skin,* for example. Two compass-points touching the palm of the hand must be kept, say, half an inch asunder in order not to be mistaken for one point. But at the end of an hour or so of practice with them we can distinguish them as two, even when less than a quarter of an inch apart. If the same two regions of the skin were constantly touched, in this experience, the explanation we have been considering would perfectly apply. Suppose a line *a b c d e f* of points upon the skin. Suppose the local difference of feeling between *a* and *f* to be so strong as to be instantly recognized when the points are simultaneously touched, but suppose that between *c* and *d* to be at first too small for this purpose. If we began by putting the compasses on *a* and *f* and gradually contracted their opening, the strong doubleness recognized at first would still be *suggested,* as the compass-points approached the positions *c* and *d*; for the point *e* would be so near *f*, and so like it, as not to be aroused without *f* also coming to mind. Similarly *d* would recall *e* and, more remotely, *f*. In such wise *c–d* would no longer be bare *c–d*, but something more like *abc–def*,–palpably differing impressions. But in actual experience the education can take place in a much less methodical way, and we learn at last to discriminate *c* and *d* without any constant adhesion being contracted between one of these spots and *ab*, and the other and *ef*. Volkmann's experiments show this. He and Fechner, prompted by Czermak's observation that the skin of the blind was twice as discriminative as that of seeing folks, sought by experiment to show the effects of practice upon themselves. They discovered that even within the limits of a single sitting the distances at which points were felt double might fall at the end to considerably less than half of their magnitude at the beginning; and that some, though not all, of this improved sensibility was retained next day. But they also found that exercising one part of the skin in this way improved the discrimination not only of the corresponding part of the opposite side of the body, but of the neighboring parts as well. Thus, at the beginning of an experimental sitting, the compass-points had to be a Paris line asunder, in order to be distinguished by the little-finger-tip. But after exercising the *other fingers,* it was found that the little-finger-tip could discriminate

---

cannot *feel* on which eye any particular element of a compound picture falls, but its effects on our total perception differ in the two eyes.

points only half a line apart.[20] The same relation existed betwixt divers points of the arm and hand.[21]

Here it is clear that the cause which I first suggested fails to apply, and that we must invoke another.

What are the exact experimental phenomena? The spots, as such, are not distinctly located, and the difference, as such, between their feelings, is not distinctly felt, until the interval is greater than the minimum required for the mere perception of their *doubleness*. What we first feel is a bluntness, then a suspicion of doubleness, which presently becomes a distinct doubleness, and at last two different-feeling and differently placed spots with a definite tract of space between them. Some of the places we try give us this latest stage of the perception immediately; some only give us the earliest; and between them are intermediary places. But as soon as the *image of the doubleness* as it is felt in the more discriminative places gets lodged in our memory, it helps us to find its like in places where otherwise we might have missed it, much as the recent hearing of an 'overtone' helps us to detect the latter in a compound sound (*supra*, pp. 416–417). A dim doubleness grows clearer by being assimilated to the image of a distincter doubleness felt a moment before. It is interpreted by means of the latter. And so is any difference, like any other sort of impression, more easily perceived when we carry in our mind to meet it a distinct image of what sort of a thing we are to look for, of what its nature is likely to be.[22]

These two processes, the reinforcement of the terms by disparate associates, and the filling of the memory with past differences, of similar direction with the present one, but of more conspicuous amount, *are the only explanations I can offer of the effects of education in this line*. What is accomplished by both processes is essentially the same thing: they make small differences affect us as if they were large ones—that large differences should affect us as they do remains an inexplicable fact. In principle these two processes ought to be sufficient to account for all possible cases. Whether in fact

20 A. W. Volkmann: "Über den Einfluss der Übung," etc., Leipzig *Berichte*, mathematisch-physische Classe, x, 1858, p. 67.

21 *Ibid.*, Tabelle 1, p. 43.

22 Professor Lipps accounts for the tactile discrimination of the blind in a way which (divested of its 'mythological' assumptions) seems to me essentially to agree with this. Stronger ideas are supposed to raise weaker ones over the threshold of consciousness by fusing with them, the tendency to fuse being proportional to the similarity of the ideas. Cf. *Grundtatsachen*, etc., pp. 232–3; also pp. 118, 492, 526–7.

they are sufficient, whether there be no residual factor which we have failed to detect and analyze out, I will not presume to decide.

PRACTICAL INTERESTS LIMIT DISCRIMINATION

It will be remembered that on page 481 personal interest was named as a sharpener of discrimination alongside of practice. But personal interest probably acts through attention and not in any immediate or specific way. A distinction in which we have a practical stake is one which we concentrate our minds upon and which we are on the look-out for. We draw it frequently, and we get all the benefits of so doing, benefits which have just been explained. Where, on the other hand, a distinction has no practical interest, where we gain nothing by analyzing a feature from out of the compound total of which it forms a part, we contract a habit of leaving it unnoticed, and at last grow callous to its presence. Helmholtz was the first psychologist who dwelt on these facts as emphatically as they deserve, and I can do no better than quote his very words.

"We are accustomed," he says, "in a large number of cases where sensations of different kinds or in different parts of the body, exist simultaneously, to recognise that they are distinct as soon as they are perceived, and to direct our attention at will to any one of them separately. Thus at any moment we can be separately conscious of what we see, of what we hear, of what we feel, and distinguish what we feel in a finger or in the great toe, whether pressure or a gentle touch, or warmth. So also in the field of vision. Indeed, as I shall endeavour to shew in what follows, we readily distinguish our sensations from one another *when we have a precise knowledge* that they are composite, as, for example, when we have become certain, by frequently repeated and invariable experience, that our present sensation arises from the simultaneous action of many independent stimuli, each of which usually excites an equally well-known individual sensation."

This, it will be observed, is only another statement of our law, that the only individual components which we can pick out of compounds are those of which we have independent knowledge in a separate form.

"This induces us to think that nothing can be easier, when a number of different sensations are simultaneously excited, than to distinguish them individually from each other, and that this is an innate faculty of our minds.

"Thus we find, among other things, that it is quite a matter of course to hear separately the different musical tones which come to our senses collectively, and we expect that in every case when two of them occur together, we shall be able to do the like.

"The matter becomes very different when we set to work to investigate the more unusual cases of perception, and seek more completely to understand the conditions under which the above-mentioned distinction can or cannot be made, as is the case in the physiology of the senses. We then become aware that *two different kinds or grades must be distinguished in our becoming conscious of a sensation*. The lower grade of this consciousness, is that in which the influence of the sensation in question makes itself felt only in the conceptions we form of external things and processes, and assists in determining them. This can take place without our needing or indeed being able to ascertain to what particular part of our sensations we owe this or that circumstance in our perceptions. In this case we will say that the impression of the sensation in question is *perceived synthetically*. The second and higher grade is when we immediately distinguish the sensation in question as an existing part of the sum of the sensations excited in us. We will say then that the sensation is *perceived analytically*. The two cases must be carefully distinguished from each other."[23]

By the sensation being perceived synthetically, Helmholtz means that it is not discriminated at all, but only felt in a mass with other simultaneous sensations. That it *is* felt there he thinks is proved by the fact that our *judgment* of the total will change if anything occurs to alter the *outer cause* of the sensation.[24] The following pages from an earlier edition show what the concrete cases of synthetic perception and what those of analytic perception are wont to be:

"In the use of our senses, practice and experience play a much larger part than we ordinarily suppose. Our sensations are in the first instance important only in so far as they enable us to judge rightly of the world about us; and our practice in discriminating between them usually goes only just far enough to meet this end. We are, however, too much disposed to think that we must be immediately conscious of every ingredient of our sensations. This natural prejudice is due to the fact that we are indeed conscious, immediately and without effort, of everything in our sensations which has a bearing upon those practi-

23 *Sensations of Tone*, 2d English Edition, p. 62.

24 Compare as to this, however, what I said above, Chapter VI, pp. 173–177.

cal purposes, for the sake of which we wish to know the outer world. Daily and hourly, during our whole life, we keep our senses in training for this end exclusively, and for its sake our experiences are accumulated. But even within the sphere of these sensations, which do correspond to outer things, training and practice make themselves felt. It is well known how much finer and quicker the painter is in discriminating colors and illuminations than one whose eye is not trained in these matters; how the musician and the musical-instrument maker perceive with ease and certainty differences of pitch and tone which for the ear of the layman do not exist; and how even in the inferior realms of cookery and wine-judging it takes a long habit of comparing to make a master. But more strikingly still is seen the effect of practice when we pass to sensations which depend only on inner conditions of our organs, and which, not corresponding at all to outer things or to their effects upon us, are therefore of no value in giving us information about the outer world. The physiology of the sense-organs has, in recent times, made us acquainted with a number of such phenomena, discovered partly in consequence of theoretic speculations and questionings, partly by individuals, like Goethe and Purkinje, specially endowed by nature with talent for this sort of observation. These so-called subjective phenomena are extraordinarily hard to find; and when they are once found, special aids for the attention are almost always required to observe them. It is usually hard to notice the phenomenon again even when one knows already the description of the first observer. The reason is that we are not only unpractised in singling out these subjective sensations, but that we are, on the contrary, most thoroughly trained in abstracting our attention from them, because they would only hinder us in observing the outer world. Only when their intensity is so strong as actually to hinder us in observing the outer world do we begin to notice them; or they may sometimes, in dreaming and delirium, form the starting point of hallucinations.

"Let me give a few well-known cases, taken from physiological optics, as examples. Every eye probably contains *muscæ volitantes*, so called; these are fibres, granules, etc., floating in the vitreous humor, throwing their shadows on the retina, and appearing in the field of vision as little dark moving spots. They are most easily detected by looking attentively at a broad, bright, blank surface like the sky. Most persons who have not had their attention expressly called to the existence of these figures are apt to notice them for the first time when some ailment befalls their eyes and attracts their attention to the subjective state of these organs. The usual complaint then is that the *muscæ volitantes* came in with the malady; and this often makes the patients very anxious about these harmless things, and attentive to all their peculiarities. It is then hard work to make them believe that these figures have existed throughout all their previous life, and that all healthy eyes contain them. I knew an old gentleman who once had occasion to cover one of his eyes which had accidentally become diseased, and who was then in no small degree shocked at finding that his other eye was totally blind; with a sort of blindness, moreover, which must have lasted years, and yet he never was aware of it.

"Who, besides, would believe without performing the appropriate experiments, that when one of his eyes is closed there is a great gap, the so-called 'blind spot,' not far from the middle of the field of the open eye, in which he sees nothing at all, but which he fills out with his imagination? Mariotte, who was led by theoretic speculations to discover this phenomenon, awakened no small surprise when he showed it at the court of Charles II. of England. The experiment was at that time repeated with many variations, and became a fashionable amusement. The gap is, in fact, so large that seven full moons alongside of each other would not cover its diameter, and that a man's face 6 or 7 feet off disappears within it. In our ordinary use of vision this great hole in the field fails utterly to be noticed; because our eyes are constantly wandering, and the moment an object interests us we turn them full upon it. So it follows that the object which at any actual moment excites our attention never happens to fall upon this gap, and thus it is that we never grow conscious of the blind spot in the field. In order to notice it, we must first purposely rivet our gaze upon one object and then move about a second object in the neighborhood of the blind spot, striving meanwhile to *attend* to this latter without moving the direction of our gaze from the first object. This runs counter to all our habits, and is therefore a difficult thing to accomplish. With some people it is even an impossibility. But only when it is accomplished do we see the second object vanish and convince ourselves of the existence of this gap.

"Finally, let me refer to the double images of ordinary binocular vision. Whenever we look at a point with both eyes, all objects on this side of it or beyond it appear double. It takes but a moderate effort of observation to ascertain this fact; and from this we may conclude that we have been seeing the far greater part of the external world double all our lives, although numbers of persons are unaware of it, and are in the highest degree astonished when it is brought to their attention. As a matter of fact, we never *have* seen in this double fashion any particular object upon which our attention was directed at the time; for upon such objects we always converge both eyes. In the habitual use of our eyes, our attention is always withdrawn from such objects as give us double images at the time; this is the reason why we so seldom learn that these images exist. In order to find them we must set our attention a new and unusual task; we must make it explore the lateral parts of the field of vision, not, as usual, to find what objects are there, but to analyze our sensations. Then only do we notice this phenomenon.[25]

"The same difficulty which is found in the observation of subjective sensations to which no external object corresponds is found also in the analysis of compound sensations which correspond to a single object. Of this sort are many of our sensations of sound. When the sound of a violin, no matter how often we hear it, excites over and over again in our ear the same sum of partial tones, the result is that our feeling of this sum of tones ends by becoming for our mind a mere sign for the voice of the violin. Another combination of partial tones becomes the sensible sign of the voice of a clarionet, etc. And the oftener any such combination is heard, the more accustomed we grow to perceiving it as an integral total, and the harder it becomes to analyze it by immediate observation. I believe that this is one of the principal reasons why the analysis of the notes of the human voice in singing is relatively so difficult. Such fusions of many sensations into what, to conscious perception, seems a simple whole, abound in all our senses.

"Physiological optics affords other interesting examples. The perception of the bodily form of a near object comes about through the combination of two diverse pictures which the eyes severally receive from it, and whose diversity is due to the different position of each eye, altering the perspective view of what is before it. Before the invention of the stereoscope this explanation could only be assumed hypothetically; but it can now be proved at any moment by the use of the instrument. Into the stereoscope we insert two flat drawings, representing the two perspective views of the two eyes, in such a manner that each eye sees its own view in the proper place; and we obtain, in consequence, the perception of a single extended solid, as complete and vivid as if we had the real object before us.

"Now we can, it is true, by shutting one eye after the other and attending to the point, recognize the difference in the pictures—at least when it is not too small. But, for the stereoscopic perception of solidity, pictures suffice whose difference is so extraordinarily slight as hardly to be recognized by the most careful comparison; and it is certain that, in our ordinary careless observing of bodily objects, we never dream

25 [When a person squints, double images are formed in the centre of the field. As a matter of fact, most squinters are found blind of one eye, or almost so; and it has long been supposed amongst ophthalmologists that the blindness is a secondary affection superinduced by the voluntary suppression of one of the sets of double images, in other words by the positive and persistent refusal to use one of the eyes. This explanation of the blindness has, however, been called in question of late years. See, for a brief account of the matter, O. F. Wadsworth in *Boston Medical and Surgical Journal*, CXVI, 49 (Jan. 20, '87), and the replies by Derby and others a little later.—W. J.]

that the perception is due to two perspective views fused into one, because it is an entirely different kind of perception from that of either flat perspective view by itself. It is certain, therefore, that two different sensations of our two eyes fuse into a third perception entirely different from either. Just as partial tones fuse into the perception of a certain instrument's voice; and just as we learn to separate the partial tones of a vibrating string by pinching a nodal point and letting them sound in isolation; so we learn to separate the images on the two eyes by opening and closing them alternately.

"There are other much more complex instances of the way in which many sensations may combine to serve as the basis of a quite simple perception. When, for example, we perceive an object in a certain *direction*, we must somehow be impressed by the fact that certain of our optic nerve-fibres, and no others, are impressed by its light. Furthermore, we must rightly judge the position of our eyes in our head, and of our head upon our body, by means of feelings in our eye-muscles and our neck-muscles respectively. If any of these processes is disturbed we get a false perception of the object's position. The nerve-fibres can be changed by a prism before the eye; or the eyeball's position changed by pressing the organ towards one side; and such experiments show that, for the simple seeing of the position of an object, sensations of these two sorts must concur. But it would be quite impossible to gather this directly from the sensible impression which the object makes. Even when we have made experiments and convinced ourselves in every possible manner that such must be the fact, it still remains hidden from our immediate introspective observation.

"These examples" [of 'synthetic perception,' perception in which each contributory sensation is felt *in* the whole, and is a co-determinant of what the whole shall be, but does not attract the attention to its separate self] "may suffice to show the vital part which the direction of attention and practice in observing play in sense-perception. To apply this now to the ear. The ordinary task which our ear has to solve when many sounds assail it at once is to discern the voices of the several sounding bodies or instruments engaged; beyond this it has no objective interest in analyzing. We wish to know, when many men are speaking together, what each one says, when many instruments and voices combine, which melody is executed by each. Any deeper analysis, such as that of each separate note into its partial tones (although it might be performed by the same means and faculty of hearing as the first analysis) would tell us nothing new about the sources of sound actually present, but might lead us astray as to their number. For this reason we confine our attention in analyzing a mass of sound to the several instruments' voices, and expressly abstain, as it were, from discriminating the elementary components of the latter. In this last sort of discrimination we are as unpractised as we are, on the contrary, well trained in the former kind."[26]

[26] *Tonempfindungen*, Dritte Auflage, pp. 102–107.—The reader who has assimilated the contents of our Chapter V, above, will doubtless have remarked that the illustrious physiologist has fallen, in these paragraphs, into that sort of interpretation of the facts which we there tried to prove erroneous. Helmholtz, however, is no more careless than most psychologists in confounding together the object perceived, the organic conditions of the perception, and the sensations which *would* be excited by the several parts of the object, or by the several organic conditions, *provided* they came into action separately or were separately attended to, and in assuming that what is true of any one of these sorts of fact must be true of the other sorts also. If each organic condition or part of the object is there, its sensation, he thinks, must be there also, only in a 'synthetic'—which is indistinguishable from what the authors whom we formerly reviewed called an 'unconscious'—state. I will not repeat arguments sufficiently detailed in the earlier chapter (see especially pp. 172–177), but simply say that what he calls the 'fusion of many *sensations* into one' is really the production of one sensation by the co-operation of many *organic conditions*; and that what perception fails to discriminate (when it is 'synthetic') is not *sensations* already existent but not singled out, but new objective *facts*, judged truer than the facts already synthetically perceived—two views of the solid body, many harmonic tones, instead of one view and one tone, states of the eyeball-muscles thitherto unknown, and the like. These new facts, when first discovered, are known in states of consciousness never till that moment exactly realized before, states of consciousness which at the same time judge them to be determinations of the same *matter of fact* which was previously realized. All that Helmholtz says of the conditions which hinder and further analysis applies just as naturally to the analysis, through the advent of *new* feelings, of *objects* into their elements, as to the analysis of aggregate feelings into elementary feelings supposed to have been hidden in them all the while.

The reader can himself apply this criticism to the following passages from Lotze and Stumpf respectively, which I quote because they are the ablest expressions of the view opposed to my own. Both authors, it seems to me, commit the psychologist's fallacy, and allow their later knowledge of the things felt to be foisted into their account of the primitive way of feeling them.

Lotze says: "It is indubitable that the simultaneous assault of a variety of different stimuli on different senses, or even on the same sense, puts us into a state of confused general feeling in which we are certainly not conscious of clearly distinguishing the different impressions. Still it does not follow that in such a case we have a positive perception of an actual unity of the contents of our ideas, arising from their mixture; our state of mind seems rather to consist in (1) the consciousness of our inability to separate what has really remained diverse, and (2) in the general feeling of the disturbance produced in the economy of our body by the simultaneous assault of the stimuli. . . . Not that the sensations melt into one another, but simply that the act of distinguishing them is absent; and this again certainly not so far that the fact of the difference remains entirely unperceived, but only so far as to prevent us from determining the amount of the difference, and from apprehending other relations between the different impressions. Anyone who is annoyed at one and the same time by glowing heat, dazzling light, deafening noise, and an offensive smell, will certainly not fuse these disparate sensations into a single one with a single content which could be sensuously perceived; they remain for him in separation, and he merely finds it impossible to be conscious of one of them apart from the others. But, further, he will have a feeling of discomfort—what I mentioned above as the *second* constituent

After all we have said, no comment seems called for upon these interesting and important facts and reflections of Helmholtz.

REACTION-TIME AFTER DISCRIMINATION

The *time required for discrimination* has been made a subject of experimental measurement. Wundt calls it *Unterscheidungszeit.* His subjects (whose simple reaction-time—see p. 92 ff.—had previously been determined) were required to make a movement, always the same, the instant they discerned *which* of two or more signals they received. The exact time of the signal and that of the movement were automatically registered by a galvanic chronoscope. The particular signal to be received was unknown in advance, and the excess of time occupied by those reactions in which its character had first to be discerned, over the simple reaction-time, measured,

---

of his whole state. For every stimulus which produces in consciousness a definite content of sensation, is also a definite degree of disturbance and therefore makes a call upon the forces of the nerves; and the sum of these little changes, which in their character as disturbances are not so diverse as the contents of consciousness they give rise to, produce the general feeling which, added to the inability to distinguish, deludes us into the belief in an actual absence of diversity in our sensations. It is only in some such way as this, again, that I can imagine that state which is sometimes described as the beginning of our whole education, a state which in itself is supposed to be simple, and to be afterwards divided into different sensations by an activity of separation. No activity of separation in the world could establish differences where no real diversity existed; for it would have nothing to guide it to the places where it was to establish them, or to indicate the width it was to give them." (*Metaphysic,* § 260, English translation.)

Stumpf writes as follows: "Of coexistent sensations there are always a large number undiscriminated in consciousness (or if one prefer to call what is undiscriminated unconscious, in the soul). They are, however, not fused into a simple quality. When, on entering a room, we receive sensations of odor and warmth together, without expressly attending to either, the two qualities of sensation are not, as it were, an entirely new simple quality, which first at the moment in which attention analytically steps in *changes into* smell and warmth. . . . In such cases we find ourselves in presence of an indefinable, unnamable total of feeling. And when, after successfully analyzing this total, we call it back to memory, as it was in its unanalyzed state, and compare it with the elements we have found, the latter (as it seems to me) may be recognized as real parts contained in the former, and the former seen to be their sum. So, for example, when we clearly perceive that the content of our sensation of oil of peppermint is partly a sensation of taste and partly one of temperature." (*Tonpsychologie,* I, 106.)

I should prefer to say that we perceive that objective fact, known to us as the peppermint taste, to contain those other objective facts known as aromatic or sapid quality, and coldness, respectively. No ground to suppose that the vehicle of this last very complex perception has any identity with the earlier psychosis—least of all is contained in it.

according to Wundt, the time required for the act of discrimination It was found longer when four different signals were irregularly used than when only two were used. In the former case it averaged for three observers respectively (the signals being the sudden appearance of a black or of a white object),

0.050 sec.;
0.047 "
0.079 "

In the latter case, a red and a green signal being added to the former ones, it became, for the same observers,

0.157;
0.073;
0.132.[27]

Later, in Wundt's Laboratory, Herr Tischer made many careful experiments after the same method, where the facts to be discriminated were the different degrees of loudness in the sound which served as a signal. I subjoin Herr Tischer's table of results, explaining that each vertical column after the first gives the average results obtained from a distinct individual, and that the figure in the first column stands for the number of possible loudnesses that might be expected in the particular series of reactions made. The times are expressed in thousandths of a second.

2	6	8.5	10.75	10.7	33	53
3	10	14.4	19.9	22.7	58.5	57.8
4	16.7	20.8	29	29.1	75	84
5	25.6	31	....	40.1	95.5	138[28]

The interesting points here are the great individual variations, and the rapid way in which the time for discrimination increases with the number of possible terms to discriminate. The individual variations are largely due to want of practice in the particular task set, but partly also to discrepancies in the psychic process. One gentleman said, for example, that in the experiments with three sounds, he kept the image of the middle one ready in his mind, and compared what he heard as either louder, lower, or the same. His discrimination among three possibilities became thus very similar to a discrimination between two.[29]

27 *Physiologische Psychologie*, II, 248.
28 Wundt's *Philosophische Studien*, I, 4, 527.
29 *Ibid.*, p. 530.

Mr. J. M. Cattell found he could get no results by this method,[30] and reverted to one used by observers previous to Wundt and which Wundt had rejected. This is the *einfache Wahlmethode,* as Wundt calls it. The reacter awaits the signal and reacts if it is of one sort, but omits to act if it is of another sort. The reaction thus occurs after discrimination; the motor impulse cannot be sent to the hand until the subject knows what the signal is. The nervous impulse, as Mr. Cattell says, must probably travel to the cortex and excite changes there, causing in consciousness the perception of the signal. These changes occupy the time of discrimination (or perception-time, as it is called by Mr. C.). But *then* a nervous impulse must descend from the cortex to the lower motor centre which stands primed and ready to discharge; and this, as Mr. C. says, gives a will-time as well. The total reaction-time thus includes both 'will-time' and 'discrimination-time.' But as the centrifugal and centripetal processes occupying these two times respectively are probably about the same, and the time used in the cortex is about equally divided between the perception of the signal and the preparation of the motor discharge, if we divide it equally between perception (discrimination) and volition, the error cannot be great.[31] We can moreover change the nature of the perception without altering the will-time, and thus investigate with considerable thoroughness the length of the perception-time.

Guided by these principles, Prof. Cattell found the time required for distinguishing a white signal from no signal to be, in two observers:

0.030 sec. and 0.050 sec.;

that for distinguishing one color from another was similarly:

0.100 and 0.110;

that for distinguishing a certain color from ten other colors:

0.105 and 0.117;

that for distinguishing the letter A in ordinary print from the letter Z:

0.142 and 0.137;

30 *Mind,* XI, 377 ff. He says: "I apparently either distinguished the impression and made the motion simultaneously, or if I tried to avoid this by waiting until I had formed a distinct impression before I began to make the motion, I added to the simple reaction, not only a perception, but also a volition."—Which remark may well confirm our doubts as to the strict *psychologic* worth of any of these measurements.

31 *Mind,* XI, 379.

that for distinguishing a given letter from all the rest of the alphabet (not reacting until that letter appeared):

0.119 and 0.116;

that for distinguishing a word from any of twenty-five other words, from

0.118 sec. to 0.158 sec.

—the difference depending on the length of the words and the familiarity of the language to which they belonged.

Prof. Cattell calls attention to the fact that the time for distinguishing a word is often but little more than that for distinguishing a letter:

> "We do not therefore perceive separately the letters of which a word is composed, but the word as a whole. The application of this to teaching children to read is evident."

He also finds a great difference in the time with which various letters are distinguished, E being particularly bad.[32]

I have, in describing these experiments, followed the example of previous writers and spoken as if the process by which the nature of the signal determines the reaction were identical with the ordinary conscious process of discriminative perception and volition. I am convinced, however, that this is not the case; and that although the results are the same, the form of consciousness is quite different. The reader will remember my contention (*supra*, p. 96 ff.) that the simple reaction-time (usually supposed to include a conscious process of perceiving) really measures nothing but a reflex act. Anyone who will perform reactions with discrimination will easily convince himself that the process here also is far more like a reflex, than like a deliberate, operation. I have made, with myself and students, a large number of measurements where the signal expected was in one series a touch *somewhere* on the skin of the back and head, and in another series a spark *somewhere* in the field of view. The hand had to move as quickly as possible towards the place of the touch or the spark. It did so infallibly, and sensibly instantly; whilst both place and movement seemed to be *perceived* only a moment later, in memory. These experiments were undertaken for

[32] For other determinations of discrimination-time by this method cf. von Kries and Auerbach: *Archiv für Physiologie*, 1877, p. 297 ff. (these authors get much smaller figures); Friedrich: *Philosophische Studien*, I, 39. Chapter IX of Buccola's book, *La Legge del tempo*, etc., gives a full account of the subject.

the express purpose of ascertaining whether the movement at the sight of the spark was discharged *immediately* by the visual perception, or whether a 'motor-idea' had to intervene between the perception of the spark and the reaction.[33] The first thing that was manifest to introspection was that no perception or idea of *any* sort preceded the reaction. It jumped of itself, whenever the signal came; and perception was retrospective. We must suppose, then, that the state of eager expectancy of a certain definite range of possible discharges, innervates a whole set of paths in advance, so that when a particular sensation comes it is drafted into its appropriate motor outlet too quickly for the perceptive process to be aroused. In the experiments I describe, the conditions were most favorable for rapidity, for the connection between the signals and their movements might almost be called innate. It is instinctive to move the hand towards a thing seen or a skin-spot touched. But where the movement is *conventionally* attached to the signal, there would be more chance for delay, and the amount of practice would then determine the speed. This is well shown in Tischer's results, quoted on p. 495, where the most practised observer, Tischer himself, reacted in one eighth of the time needed by one of the others.[34] But what all investigators have aimed to determine in these experiments is the *minimum* time. I trust I have said enough to convince the student that this minimum time by no means measures what we consciously know as discrimination. It only measures something which, under the experimental conditions, leads to a similar result. But it is the bane of psychology to suppose that where results are similar, processes must be the same. Psychologists are too apt to reason as geometers would, if the latter were to say that the diameter of a circle is the same thing as its semi-circumference, because, forsooth, they terminate in the same two points.[35]

33 If so, the reactions upon the spark would have to be slower than those upon the touch. The investigation was abandoned because it was found impossible to narrow down the difference between the conditions of the sight-series and those of the touch-series, to nothing more than the possible presence in the latter of the intervening motor-idea. Other disparities could not be excluded.

34 Tischer gives figures from quite unpractised individuals, which I have not quoted. The discrimination-time of one of them is 22 times longer than Tischer's own! (*Philosophische Studien*, I, 527.)

35 Compare Lipps's excellent passage to the same critical effect in his *Grundtatsachen des Seelenlebens*, pp. 390–393.—I leave my text just as it was written before the publication of Lange's and Münsterberg's results cited on pp. 98–99 and 409. Their 'shortened' or 'muscular' times, got when the expectant attention was addressed to the

THE PERCEPTION OF LIKENESS

The perception of likeness is practically very much bound up with that of difference. That is to say, the only differences we note *as* differences, and estimate quantitatively, and arrange along a scale, are those comparatively limited differences which we find between members of a common genus. The force of gravity and the color of this ink are things it never occurred to me to compare until now that I am casting about for examples of the incomparable. Similarly the elastic quality of this india-rubber band, the comfort of last night's sleep, the good that can be done with a legacy, these are things too discrepant to have ever been compared ere now. Their relation to each other is less that of difference than of mere logical negativity. To be found *different*, things must as a rule have some commensurability, some aspect in common, which suggests the possibility of their being treated in the same way. This is of course not a theoretic necessity—for any distinction may be called a 'difference,' if one likes—but a practical and linguistic remark.

The *same things*, then, *which arouse the perception of difference usually arouse that of resemblance also*. And the analysis of them, so as to define wherein the difference and wherein the resemblance respectively consists, is called *comparison*. If we start to deal with the things as simply the same or alike, we are liable to be surprised by the difference. If we start to treat them as merely different, we are apt to discover how much they are alike. *Difference, commonly so called, is thus between species of a genus*. And the faculty by which we perceive the resemblance upon which the genus is based, is just as ultimate and inexplicable a mental endowment as that by which we perceive the differences upon which the species depend. There is a shock of likeness when we pass from one thing to another which in the first instance we merely discriminate numerically, but, at the moment of bringing our attention to bear, perceive to be *similar* to the first; just as there is a shock of difference when we pass between two dissimilars.[36] The objective extent of the likeness, just like that of the difference, determines the magnitude of the shock. The likeness may be so evanescent, or the basis of it so ha-

---

possible reactions rather than to the stimulus, constitute the minimal reaction-time of which I speak, and all that I say in the text falls beautifully into line with their results.

36 Cf. Sully: *Mind*, x, 494–5; Bradley: *ibid.*, xi, 83; Bosanquet: *ibid.*, xi, 405.

bitual and little liable to be attended to, that it will escape observation altogether. Where, however, we find it, there we make a genus of the things compared; and their discrepancies and incommensurabilities in other respects can then figure as the *differentiæ* of so many species. As 'thinkables' or 'existents' even the smoke of a cigarette and the worth of a dollar-bill are comparable—still more so as 'perishables,' or as 'enjoyables.'

Much, then, of what I have said of difference in the course of this chapter will apply, with a simple change of language, to resemblance as well. We go through the world, carrying on the two functions abreast, discovering differences in the like, and likenesses in the different. To abstract the *ground* of either difference or likeness (where it is not ultimate) demands an analysis of the given objects into their parts. So that all that was said of the dependence of analysis upon a preliminary separate acquaintance with the character to be abstracted, and upon its having varied concomitants, finds a place in the psychology of resemblance as well as in that of difference.

But when all is said and done about the conditions which favor our perception of resemblance and our abstraction of its ground, the crude fact remains, that *some people are far more sensitive to resemblances, and far more ready to point out wherein they consist, than others are*. They are the wits, the poets, the inventors, the scientific men, the practical geniuses. *A native talent for perceiving analogies* is reckoned by Prof. Bain, and by others before and after him, as *the leading fact in genius of every order*. But as this chapter is already long, and as the question of genius had better wait till Chapter XXII, where its practical consequences can be discussed at the same time, I will say nothing more at present either about it or about the faculty of noting resemblances. If the reader feels that this faculty is having small justice done it at my hands, and that it ought to be wondered at and made much more of than has been done in these last few pages, he will perhaps find some compensation when that later chapter is reached. I think I emphasize it enough when I call it one of the ultimate foundation-pillars of the intellectual life, the others being Discrimination, Retentiveness, and Association.

THE MAGNITUDE OF DIFFERENCES

On page 463 I spoke of differences being greater or less, and of certain groups of them being susceptible of a linear arrangement exhibiting serial *increase*. A series whose terms grow more and more different from the starting point is one whose terms grow less and less like it. They grow more and more like it if you read them the other way. So that likeness and unlikeness to the starting point are functions inverse to each other, of the position of any term in such a series.

Professor Stumpf introduces the word *distance* to denote the position of a term in any such series. The less like is the term, the more distant it is from the starting point. The ideally regular series of this sort would be one in which the distances—the steps of resemblance or difference—between all pairs of adjacent terms were equal. This would be an evenly gradated series. And it is an interesting fact in psychology that we are able, in many departments of our sensibility, to arrange the terms without difficulty in this evenly gradated way. Differences, in other words, between diverse pairs of terms, *a* and *b*, for example, on the one hand, and *c* and *d* on the other,[37] can be judged equal or diverse in amount. The distances from one term to another in the series are equal. Linear magnitudes and musical notes are perhaps the impressions which we easiest arrange in this way. Next come shades of light or color, which we have little difficulty in arranging by steps of difference of sensibly equal value. Messrs. Plateau and Delbœuf have found it fairly easy to determine what shade of gray will be judged by everyone to hit the exact middle between a darker and a lighter shade.[38]

How now do we so readily recognize the equality of two differences between different pairs of terms? or, more briefly, how do we

[37] The judgment becomes easier if the two couples of terms have one member in common, if *a—b* and *b—c*, for example, are compared. This, as Stumpf says (*Tonpsychologie*, I, 131), is probably because the introduction of the fourth term brings involuntary cross-comparisons with it, *a* and *b* with *d*, *b* with *c*, etc., which confuses us by withdrawing our attention from the relations we ought alone to be estimating.

[38] J. Delbœuf: *Éléments de psychophysique* (Paris, 1883), p. 64. Plateau in Stumpf: *Tonpsychologie*, I, 125. I have noticed a curious enlargement of certain 'distances' of difference under the influence of chloroform. The jingling of the bells on the horses of a horse-car passing the door, for example, and the rumbling of the vehicle itself, which to our ordinary hearing merge together very readily into a *quasi*-continuous body of sound, have seemed so far apart as to require a sort of mental facing in opposite directions to get from one to the other, as if they belonged in different worlds. I am inclined to suspect, from certain data, that the ultimate philosophy of difference and likeness will have to be built upon experiences of intoxication, especially by nitrous oxide gas, which lets us into intuitions the subtlety whereof is denied to the waking state. Cf. B. P. Blood: *The Anæsthetic Revelation, and the Gist of Philosophy* (Amsterdam, N.Y., 1874). Cf. also *Mind*, VII, 206.

recognize the *magnitude* of a difference at all? Prof. Stumpf discusses this question in an interesting way;[39] and comes to the conclusion that our feeling for the size of a difference, and our perception that the terms of two diverse pairs are equally or unequally distant from each other, can be explained by no simpler mental process, but, like the shock of difference itself, must be regarded as for the present an unanalyzable endowment of the mind. This acute author rejects in particular the notion which would make our judgment of the distance between two sensations depend upon our *mentally traversing the intermediary steps.* We may of course do so, and may often find it useful to do so, as in musical intervals, or figured lines. But we need not do so; and nothing more is really *required* for a comparative judgment of the amount of a 'distance' than three or four impressions belonging to a common kind.

The vanishing of all perceptible difference between two numerically distinct things makes them *qualitatively the same* or *equal.* Equality, or *qualitative* (as distinguished from numerical) *identity,* is thus nothing but the *extreme degree of likeness.*[40]

We saw above (pp. 465–466) that some persons consider that the difference between two objects is constituted of two things, viz., their absolute identity in certain respects, *plus* their absolute non-identity in others. We saw that this theory would not apply to all cases (p. 467). So here any theory which would base likeness on identity, and not rather identity on likeness, must fail. It is supposed perhaps, by most people, that two resembling things owe their resemblance to their absolute identity in respect of some attribute or attributes, combined with the absolute non-identity of the rest of their being. This, which may be true of compound things, breaks down when we come to simple impressions.

"When we compare a deep, a middle, and a high note, e.g., *C*, *f* sharp, *a'''*, we remark immediately that the first is less like the third than the second is. The same would be true of *c d e* in the same region of the scale. Our very calling one of the notes a 'middle' note is the expression of a judgment of this sort. But where here is the identical and where the non-identical part? We cannot think of the overtones; for the first-named three notes have none in common, at least not on musical instruments. Moreover, we might take simple tones, and still our

39 *Op. cit.*, p. 126 ff.
40 Stumpf, pp. 111–121.

judgment would be unhesitatingly the same, provided the tones were not chosen too close together. . . . Neither can it be said that the identity consists in their all being sounds, and not a sound, a smell, and a color, respectively. For this identical attribute comes to each of them in equal measure, whereas the first, being less like the third than the second is, ought, on the terms of the theory we are criticising, to have less of the identical quality. . . . It thus appears impracticable to define all possible cases of likeness as partial identity *plus* partial disparity; and it is vain to seek in all cases for identical elements."[41]

And as all compound resemblances are based on simple ones like these, it follows that likeness *überhaupt* must not be conceived as a special complication of identity, but rather that identity must be conceived as a special degree of likeness, according to the proposition expressed at the outset of the paragraph that precedes. Likeness and difference are ultimate relations perceived. As a matter of fact, no two sensations, no two objects of all those we know, are in scientific rigor identical. We call those of them identical whose difference is unperceived. Over and above this we have a *conception* of absolute sameness, it is true, but this, like so many of our conceptions (cf. p. 480), is an ideal construction got by following a certain direction of serial increase to its maximum supposable extreme. It plays an important part, among other permanent meanings possessed by us, in our ideal intellectual constructions. But it plays no part whatever in explaining psychologically how we perceive likenesses between simple things.

THE MEASURE OF DISCRIMINATIVE SENSIBILITY

In 1860, Professor G. T. Fechner of Leipzig, a man of great learning and subtlety of mind, published two volumes entitled *Psycho-*

[41] Stumpf, pp. 116–7. I have omitted, so as not to make my text too intricate, an extremely acute and conclusive paragraph, which I reproduce here: "We may generalize: Wherever a number of sensible impressions are apprehended *as a series*, there in the last instance must perceptions of simple likeness be found. *Proof*: Assume that all the terms of a series, e.g., the qualities of tone, *c d e f g*, have something in common,—*no matter what it is*, call it X; then I say that the differing parts of each of these terms must not only be differently constituted in each, but must *themselves form a series*, whose existence is the ground for our apprehending the original terms in serial form. We thus get instead of the original series *a b c d e f* . . . the equivalent series $X\alpha$, $X\beta$, $X\gamma$, . . . etc. What is gained? The question immediately arises: How is α β γ known as a series? According to the theory, these elements must themselves be made up of a part common to all, and of parts differing in each, which latter parts form a new series, and so on *ad infinitum*, which is absurd."

physik, devoted to establishing and explaining a law called by him the psychophysic law, which he considered to express the deepest and most elementary relation between the mental and the physical worlds. It is a formula for the connection between the amount of our sensations and the amount of their outward causes. Its simplest expression is, that when we pass from one sensation to a stronger one of the same kind, the sensations increase proportionally to the logarithms of their exciting causes. Fechner's book was the starting point of a new department of literature, which it would be perhaps impossible to match for the qualities of thoroughness and subtlety, but of which, in the humble opinion of the present writer, the proper psychological outcome is just *nothing*. The psychophysic law controversy has prompted a good many series of observations on sense-discrimination, and has made discussion of them very rigorous. It has also cleared up our ideas about the best methods for getting average results, when particular observations vary; and beyond this it has done nothing; but as it is a chapter in the history of our science, some account of it is here due to the reader.

Fechner's train of thought has been popularly expounded a great many times. As I have nothing new to add, it is but just that I should quote an existing account. I choose the one given by Wundt in his *Vorlesungen über die Menschen- und Thierseele*, 1863, omitting a good deal:

"How much stronger or weaker one sensation is than another, we are never able to say. Whether the sun be a hundred or a thousand times brighter than the moon, a cannon a hundred or a thousand times louder than a pistol, is beyond our power to estimate. The natural measure of sensation which we possess enables us to judge of the equality, of the 'more' and of the 'less,' but not of 'how many times more or less.' This natural measure is, therefore, as good as no measure at all, whenever it becomes a question of accurately ascertaining intensities in the sensational sphere. Even though it may teach us in a general way that with the strength of the outward physical stimulus the strength of the concomitant sensation waxes or wanes, still it leaves us without the slightest knowledge of whether the sensation varies in exactly the same proportion as the stimulus itself, or at a slower or a more rapid rate. In a word, we know by our natural sensibility nothing of the *law* that connects the sensation and its outward cause together. To find this law we must first find an exact measure for the sensation itself; we must be able to say: A stimulus of strength *one* begets a sensation of strength *one*; a stimulus of strength *two* begets a sensation of strength *two,* or *three,* or *four,* etc. But to do this we must first know what a sensation two, three, or four times greater than another, signifies. . . .

"Space magnitudes we soon learn to determine exactly, because we only measure one space against another. The measure of mental magnitudes is far more difficult. . . . But the problem of measuring the magnitude of *sensations* is the first step in the bold enterprise of making mental magnitudes altogether subject to exact measurement. . . . Were our whole knowledge limited to the fact that the sensation rises when the stimulus rises, and falls when the latter falls, much would not be gained. But even immediate unaided observation teaches us certain facts which, at least in a general way, suggest the law according to which the sensations vary with their outward cause.

"Everyone knows that in the stilly night we hear things unnoticed in the noise of day. The gentle ticking of the clock, the air circulating through the chimney, the cracking of the chairs in the room, and a thousand other slight noises, impress themselves upon our ear. It is equally well known that in the confused hubbub of the streets, or the clamor of a railway, we may lose not only what our neighbor says to us, but even not hear the sound of our own voice. The stars which are brightest at night are invisible by day; and although we see the moon then, she is far paler than at night. Everyone who has had to deal with weights knows that if to a pound in the hand a second pound be added, the difference is immediately felt; whilst if it be added to a hundredweight, we are not aware of the difference at all. . . .

"The sound of the clock, the light of the stars, the pressure of the pound, these are all *stimuli* to our senses, and stimuli whose outward amount remains the same. What then do these experiences teach? Evidently nothing but this, that one and the same stimulus, according to the circumstances under which it operates, will be felt either more or less intensely, or not felt at all. Of what sort now is the alteration in the circumstances, upon which this alteration in the feeling may depend? On considering the matter closely we see that it is everywhere of one and the same kind. The tick of the clock is a feeble stimulus for our auditory nerve, which we hear plainly when it is alone, but not when it is added to the strong stimulus of the carriage-wheels and other noises of the day. The light of the stars is a stimulus to the eye. But if the stimulation which this light exerts be added to the strong stimulus of daylight, we feel nothing of it, although we feel it distinctly when it unites itself with the feebler stimulation of the twilight. The pound-weight is a stimulus to our skin, which we feel when it joins itself to a preceding stimulus of equal strength, but which vanishes when it is combined with a stimulus a thousand times greater in amount.

"We may therefore lay it down as a general rule that a stimulus, in order to be felt, may be so much the smaller if the already pre-existing stimulation of the organ is small, but must be so much the larger, the greater the pre-existing stimulation is. From this in a general way we can perceive the connection between the stimulus and the feeling it excites. At least thus much appears, that the law of dependence is not as simple a one as might have been expected beforehand. The simplest relation would obviously be that the sensation should increase in identically the same ratio as the stimulus, thus that if a stimulus of strength *one* occasioned a sensation *one*, a stimulus of *two* should occasion sensation *two*, stimulus *three*, sensation *three*, etc. But if this simplest of all relations prevailed, a stimulus added to a pre-existing strong stimulus ought to provoke as great an increase of feeling as if it were added to a pre-existing weak stimulus; the light of the stars e.g., ought to make as great an addition to the daylight as it does to the darkness of the nocturnal sky. This we know not to be the case: the stars are invisible by day, the addition they make to our sensation then is unnoticeable, whereas the same addition to our feeling of the twilight is very considerable indeed. So it is clear that the strength of the sensations does not increase in proportion to the amount of the stimuli, but more slowly. And now comes the question, in what proportion does the increase of the sensation grow less as the increase of the stimulus grows greater. To answer this question, every-day experiences do not suffice. We need exact measurements both of the amounts of the various stimuli, and of the intensity of the sensations themselves.

"How to execute these measurements, however, is something which daily experience suggests. To measure the strength of sensations is, as we saw, impossible; we can only measure the difference of sensations. Experience showed us what very unequal differences of sensation might come from equal differences of outward stimulus. But all these experiences expressed themselves in one kind of fact, that the same difference of stimulus could in one case be felt, and in another case not felt at all—a pound felt if added to another pound, but not if added to a hundred-weight. . . . We can quickest reach a result with our observations if we start with an arbitrary strength of stimulus, notice what sensation it gives us, and then *see how much we can increase the stimulus without making the sensation seem to change.* If we carry out such observations with stimuli of varying absolute amounts, we shall be forced to choose in an equally varying way the amounts of addition to the stimulus which are capable of giving us a just barely perceptible feeling of *more.* A light, to be just perceptible in the twilight need not be near as bright as the starlight; it must be far brighter to be just perceived during the day. If now we institute such observations for all possible strengths of the various stimuli, and note for each strength the amount of addition of the latter required to produce a barely perceptible alteration of sensation, we shall have a series of figures in which is immediately expressed the law according to which the sensation alters when the stimulation is increased. . . ."

Observations according to this method are particularly easy to make in the spheres of light-, sound-, and pressure-sensation. . . . Beginning with the latter case,

"We find a surprisingly simple result. The barely sensible addition to the original weight *must stand exactly in the same proportion to it*, be the *same fraction* of it, no matter what the absolute value may be of the weights on which the experiment is made. . . . As the average of a number of experiments, this fraction is found to be about ⅓; that is, no matter what pressure there may already be made upon the skin, an increase or a diminution of the pressure will be *felt*, as soon as the added or subtracted weight amounts to one third of the weight originally there."

Wundt then describes how differences may be observed in the muscular feelings, in the feelings of heat, in those of light, and in those of sound; and he concludes his seventh lecture (from which our extracts have been made) thus:

"So we have found that all the senses whose stimuli we are enabled to measure accurately, obey a uniform law. However various may be their several delicacies of discrimination, *this* holds true of all, that *the increase of the stimulus necessary to produce an increase of the sensation bears a constant ratio to the total stimulus.* The figures which express this ratio in the several senses may be shown thus in tabular form:

Sensation of light,	1/100
Muscular sensation,	1/17
Feeling of pressure, " " warmth, " " sound,	1/3

"These figures are far from giving as accurate a measure as might be desired. But at least they are fit to convey a general notion of the relative discriminative susceptibility of the different senses. . . . The important law which gives in so simple a form the relation of the sensation to the stimulus that calls it forth was first discovered by the physiologist Ernst Heinrich Weber to obtain in special cases. Gustav Theodor Fechner first proved it to be a law for all departments of sensation. Psychology owes to him the first comprehensive investigation of sensations from a physical point of view, the first basis of an exact Theory of Sensibility."

So much for a general account of what Fechner calls Weber's law. The 'exactness' of the theory of sensibility to which it leads consists in the supposed fact that it gives the means of representing sensations by numbers. The *unit* of any kind of sensation will be that increment which, when the stimulus is increased, we can just barely perceive to be added. The total number of units which any given sensation contains will consist of the total number of such increments which may be perceived in passing from no sensation of the kind to a sensation of the present amount. We cannot get at this number directly, but we can, now that we know Weber's law, get at it by means of the physical stimulus of which it is a function. For if we know how much of the stimulus it will take to give a barely perceptible sensation, and then what percentage of addition to the stimulus will constantly give a barely perceptible increment to the sensation, it is at bottom only a question of compound interest to compute, out of the total amount of stimulus which we may be employing at any moment, the number of such increments, or, in other words, of sensational units to which it may give rise. This number bears the same relation to the total stimulus which the time elapsed bears to the capital plus the compound interest accrued.

To take an example: If stimulus A just falls short of producing a sensation, and if r be the percentage of itself which must be added to it to get a sensation which is barely perceptible—call this sensation 1—then we should have the series of sensation-numbers corresponding to their several stimuli as follows:

$$
\begin{array}{llll}
\text{Sensation } 0 & = \text{stimulus A;} & & \\
\text{"} \quad 1 & = & \text{"} & A(1+r); \\
\text{"} \quad 2 & = & \text{"} & A(1+r)^2; \\
\text{"} \quad 3 & = & \text{"} & A(1+r)^3; \\
\ldots & & & \ldots \\
\text{"} \quad n & = & \text{"} & A(1+r)^n.
\end{array}
$$

The sensations here form an arithmetical series, and the stimuli a geometrical series, and the two series correspond term for term. Now, of two series corresponding in this way, the terms of the arithmetical one are called the logarithms of the terms corresponding in rank to them in the geometrical series. A conventional arithmetical series beginning with zero has been formed in the ordinary logarithmic tables, so that we may truly say (assuming our facts to be correct so far) that the *sensations vary in the same proportion as the logarithms of their respective stimuli.* And we can thereupon proceed to compute the number of units in any given sensation (considering the unit of sensation to be equal to the just perceptible increment above zero, and the unit of stimulus to be equal to the increment of stimulus *r*, which brings this about) by multiplying the logarithm of the stimulus by a constant factor which must vary with the particular kind of sensation in question. If we call the stimulus R, and the constant factor C, we get the formula

$$S = C \log R,$$

which is what Fechner calls the *psychophysischer Maasformel.* This, in brief, is Fechner's reasoning, as I understand it.

The *Maasformel* admits of mathematical development in various directions, and has given rise to arduous discussions into which I am glad to be exempted from entering here, since their interest is mathematical and metaphysical and not primarily psychological at all.[42] I must say a word about them metaphysically a few pages later on. Meanwhile it should be understood that no human being, in any investigation into which sensations entered, has ever used the numbers computed in this or any other way in order to test a theory or to reach a new result. The whole notion of measuring sensations numerically, remains in short a mere mathematical speculation about possibilities, which has never been applied to practice. Incidentally to the discussion of it, however, a great many particular facts have been discovered about discrimination which merit a place in this chapter.

In the first place it is found, when the difference of two sensations approaches the limit of discernibility, that at one moment we discern it and at the next we do not. There are accidental fluctuations in our inner sensibility which make it impossible to tell just what the least discernible increment of the sensation is without taking the average of a large number of appreciations. These *accidental errors* are as likely to increase as to diminish our sensibility, and are eliminated in such an average, for those above and those below the line then neutralize each other in the sum, and the normal sensibility, if there be one (that is, the sensibility due to constant

[42] The most important ameliorations of Fechner's formula are Delbœuf's in his "Recherches théoriques et expérimentales sur la mesure des sensations" (1873), p. 35, and Elsas's in his pamphlet *Über die Psychophysik* (1886), p. 16.

causes as distinguished from these accidental ones), stands revealed. The best way of getting at the average sensibility has been very minutely worked over. Fechner discussed three methods, as follows:

(1) *The Method of just-discernible Differences.* Take a standard sensation S, and add to it until you distinctly feel the addition d; then subtract from $S + d$ until you distinctly feel the effect of the subtraction;[43] call the difference here d'. The least discernible difference sought is $\frac{d + d'}{2}$; and the ratio of this quantity to the original S (or rather to $S + d - d'$) is what Fechner calls the difference-threshold. *This difference-threshold should be a constant fraction* (no matter what is the size of S) *if Weber's law holds universally true.* The difficulty in applying this method is that we are *so often in doubt* whether anything has been added to S or not. Furthermore, if we simply take the smallest d about which we are *never* in doubt or in error, we certainly get our least discernible difference larger than it ought theoretically to be.[44]

Of course the *sensibility* is small when the least discernible difference is large, and *vice versâ*; in other words, it and the difference-threshold are inversely related to each other.

(2) *The Method of True and False Cases.* A sensation which is barely greater than another will, on account of accidental errors in a long series of experiments, sometimes be judged equal, and sometimes smaller; i.e., we shall make a certain number of false and a certain number of true judgments about the difference between the two sensations which we are comparing.

"But the larger this difference is, the more the number of the true judgments will increase at the expense of the false ones; or, otherwise expressed, the nearer to unity will be the fraction whose denominator represents the whole number of judgments, and whose numerator represents those which are true. If m is a ratio of this nature, obtained by comparison of two stimuli, A and B, we may seek another couple of stimuli, a and b, which when compared will give the same ratio of true to false cases."[45]

[43] Reversing the order is for the sake of letting the opposite accidental errors due to 'contrast' neutralize each other.

[44] Theoretically it would seem that it ought to be equal to the sum of all the additions which we judge to be increases divided by the total number of judgments made.

[45] J. Delbœuf: *Éléments de psychophysique* (1883), p. 9.

If this were done, and the ratio of *a* to *b* then proved to be equal to that of *A* to *B*, that would prove that pairs of small stimuli and pairs of large stimuli may affect our discriminative sensibility similarly so long as the ratio of the components to each other within each pair is the same. In other words, it would in so far forth prove the Weberian law. Fechner made use of this method to ascertain his own power of discriminating differences of weight, recording no less than 24,576 separate judgments, and computing as a result that his discrimination for the same relative increase of weight was less good in the neighborhood of 500 than of 300 grams, but that after 500 grams it improved up to 3000, which was the highest weight he experimented with.

(3) *The Method of Average Errors* consists in taking a standard stimulus and then trying to make another one of the same sort exactly equal to it. There will in general be an error whose amount is large when the discriminative sensibility called in play is small, and *vice versâ*. The sum of the errors, no matter whether they be positive or negative, divided by their number, gives the average error. This, when certain corrections are made, is assumed by Fechner to be the 'reciprocal' of the discriminative sensibility in question. It should bear a constant proportion to the stimulus, no matter what the absolute size of the latter may be, if Weber's law hold true.

These methods deal with just perceptible differences. Delbœuf and Wundt have experimented with larger differences by means of what Wundt calls the *Methode der mittleren Abstufungen,* and what we may call

(4) *The Method of Equal-appearing Intervals.* This consists in so arranging three stimuli in a series that the interval between the first and the second shall appear equal to that between the second and the third. At first sight there seems to be no direct logical connection between this method and the preceding ones. By them we compare equally *perceptible* increments of stimulus in different regions of the latter's scale; but by the fourth method we compare increments which strike us as equally *big*. But what we can but just notice as an increment need not appear always of the same bigness after it is noticed. On the contrary, it will appear much bigger when we are dealing with stimuli that are already large.

(5) The method of doubling the *stimulus* has been employed by Wundt's collaborator, Merkel, who tried to make one stimulus seem just double the other, and then measured the objective relation of the two. The remarks just made apply also to this case.

So much for the methods. The results differ in the hands of different observers. I will add a few of them, and will take first the *discriminative sensibility to light.*

By the first method, Volkmann, Aubert, Masson, Helmholtz, and Kraepelin find figures varying from $\frac{1}{3}$ or $\frac{1}{4}$ to $\frac{1}{195}$ of the original stimulus. The smaller fractional increments are discriminated when the light is already fairly strong, the larger ones when it is weak or intense. That is, the discriminative sensibility is low when weak or overstrong lights are compared, and at its best with a certain medium illumination. It is thus a function of the light's intensity; but throughout a certain range of the latter it keeps constant, and *in so far forth* Weber's law is verified for light. Absolute figures cannot be given, but Merkel, by method 1, found that Weber's law held good for stimuli (measured by his arbitrary unit) between 96 and 4096, beyond which intensity no experiments were made.[46] König and Brodhun have given measurements by method 1 which cover the most extensive series, and moreover apply to six different colors of light. These experiments (performed in Helmholtz's laboratory, apparently) ran from an intensity called 1 to one which was 100,000 times as great. From intensity 2000 to 20,000 Weber's law held good; below and above this range discriminative sensibility declined. The increment discriminated here was the same for all colors of light, and lay (according to the tables) between 1 and 2 per cent of the stimulus.[47] Delbœuf had verified Weber's law for a certain range of luminous intensities by method 4; that is, he had found that the objective intensity of a light which appeared midway between two others was really the geometrical mean of the latter's intensities. But A. Lehmann and afterwards Neiglick, in Wundt's laboratory, found that effects of contrast played so large a part in experiments performed in this way that Delbœuf's results could not be held conclusive. Merkel, repeating the experiments still later, found that the objective intensity of the light which we judge to stand mid-

46 *Philosophische Studien,* IV, 588.

47 Berlin Academy *Sitzungsberichte,* 1888, p. 917. Other observers (Dobrowolsky, Lamansky) found great differences in different colors.

way between two others neither stands midway nor is a geometric mean. The discrepancy from both figures is enormous, but is least large from the midway figure or arithmetical mean of the two extreme intensities.[48] Finally, the stars have from time immemorial been arranged in 'magnitudes' supposed to differ by equal-seeming intervals. Lately their intensities have been gauged photometrically, and the comparison of the subjective with the objective series has been made. Prof. J. Jastrow is the latest worker in this field. He finds, taking Pickering's Harvard photometric tables as a basis, that the ratio of the average intensity of each 'magnitude' to that below it decreases as we pass from lower to higher magnitudes, showing a uniform departure from Weber's law, if the method of equal-appearing intervals be held to have any direct relevance to the latter.[49]

Sounds are less delicately discriminated in intensity than lights. A certain difficulty has come from disputes as to the measurement of the objective intensity of the stimulus. Earlier inquiries made the perceptible increase of the stimulus to be about $1/3$ of the latter. Merkel's latest results of the method of just perceptible differences make it about $3/10$ for that part of the scale of intensities during which Weber's law holds good, which is from 20 to 5000 of M.'s arbitrary unit.[50] Below this the fractional increment must be larger. Above it no measurements were made.

For *pressure and muscular sense* we have rather divergent results. Weber found by the method of just-perceptible differences that persons could distinguish an increase of weight of $1/40$ when the two weights were successively lifted by the same hand. It took a much larger fraction to be discerned when the weights were laid on a hand which rested on the table. He seems to have verified his results for only two pairs of differing weights,[51] and on this founded his 'law.' Experiments in Hering's laboratory on lifting 11 weights, running from 250 to 2750 grams showed that the least perceptible increment varied from $1/21$ for 250 grams to $1/114$ for 2500. For 2750 it rose to $1/98$ again. Merkel's recent and very careful experiments, in which

48 See Merkel's tables, *loc. cit.*, p. 568.

49 *American Journal of Psychology*, I, 125. The rate of decrease is small but steady, and I cannot well understand what Professor J. means by saying that his figures verify Weber's law.

50 *Philosophische Studien*, V, 514–5.

51 Cf. G. E. Müller: *Zur Grundlegung der Psychophysik*, §§ 68–70.

the finger pressed down the beam of a balance counterweighted by from 25 to 8020 grams, showed that between 200 and 2000 grams a constant fractional increase of about 1/13 was felt when there was no movement of the finger, and of about 1/19 when there was movement. Above and below these limits the discriminative power grew less. It was greater when the pressure was upon one square millimeter of surface than when it was upon seven.[52]

Warmth and taste have been made the subject of similar investigations with the result of verifying something like Weber's law. The determination of the unit of stimulus is, however, so hard here that I will give no figures. The results may be found in Wundt's *Physiologische Psychologie*, 3d Ed., I, 370–2.

The discrimination of lengths by the eye has been found also to obey to a certain extent Weber's law. The figures will all be found in G. E. Müller, *op. cit.*, part II, chap. X, to which the reader is referred. Professor Jastrow has published some experiments, made by what may be called a modification of the method of equal-appearing differences, on our estimation of the length of sticks, by which it would seem that the estimated intervals and the real ones are directly and not logarithmically proportionate to each other. This resembles Merkel's results by that method for weights, lights, and sounds, and differs from Jastrow's own finding about star-magnitudes.[53]

If we look back over these facts as a whole, we see that it is not any fixed amount added to an impression that makes us notice an increase in the latter, but that the amount depends on how large the impression already is. The amount is expressible as a certain fraction of the entire impression to which it is added; and it is found that the fraction is a well-nigh constant figure throughout an entire region of the scale of intensities of the impression in question. Above and below this region the fraction increases in value. This is *Weber's law*, which in so far forth expresses an empirical generalization of practical importance, without involving any theory whatever or seeking any absolute measure of the sensations themselves. It is in the

[52] *Philosophische Studien*, V, 287 ff.
[53] *American Journal of Psychology*, III, 44–7.

that Fechner's originality exclusively consists, in his assumptions, namely, 1) that the just-perceptible increment is the *sensation-unit*, and is in all parts of the scale the same (mathematically expressed, $\Delta s =$ const.); 2) that all our sensations consist of sums of these units; and finally, 3) that the reason why it takes a constant fractional increase of the stimulus to awaken this unit lies in an ultimate law of the connection of mind with matter, whereby the quantities of our feelings are related logarithmically to the quantities of their objects. Fechner seems to find something inscrutably sublime in the existence of an ultimate 'psychophysic' law of this form.

These assumptions are all peculiarly fragile. To begin with, the *mental fact* which in the experiments corresponds to the increase of the stimulus is not an *enlarged sensation*, but a *judgment that the sensation is enlarged*. What Fechner calls the 'sensation' is really what appears to the mind as the *objective phenomenon* of light, warmth, weight, sound, impressed part of body, etc. Fechner tacitly if not openly assumes that such a *judgment of increase* consists in the simple fact that an *increased number* of sensation-units are present to the mind; and that the judgment is thus itself a quantitatively bigger mental thing when it judges large differences, or differences between large terms, than when it judges small ones. But these ideas are really absurd. The hardest sort of judgment, the judgment which strains the attention most (if *that* be any criterion of the judgment's 'size'), is that about the *smallest* things and differences. But really it has no meaning to talk about one judgment being bigger than another. And even if we leave out judgments and talk of sensations only, we have already found ourselves (in Chapter VI) quite unable to read any clear meaning into the notion that they are masses of units combined. To introspection, our feeling of pink is surely not a portion of our feeling of scarlet; nor does the light of an electric arc seem to contain that of a tallow-candle in itself. Compound *things* contain parts; and one such thing may have twice or three times as many parts as another. But when we take a simple sensible quality like light or sound, and say that there is now twice or thrice as much of it present as there was a moment ago, although we seem to mean the same thing as if we were talking of compound objects, we really mean something different. We mean that if we were to arrange the various possible degrees of the quality in a scale of serial increase, the *distance, interval,* or *difference* between the stronger and the weaker specimen before us would seem about as great as that between the weaker one and the beginning of the scale. *It is these* RELATIONS, *these* DISTANCES, *which we are measuring and not the composition of the qualities themselves,* as Fechner thinks. Whilst if we turn to objects which *are* divisible, surely a big object may be known in a little thought. Introspection shows moreover that in most sensations a new *kind* of feeling invariably accompanies our judgment of an increased impression; and this is a fact which Fechner's formula disregards.[54]

But apart from these *a priori* difficulties, and even supposing that sensations did consist of added units, Fechner's assumption that all *equally perceptible* additions are *equally great* additions is entirely arbitrary. Why might not a small addition to a small sensation be as *perceptible* as a large addition to a large one? In this case Weber's law would apply not to the additions themselves, but only to their perceptibility. Our *noticing* of a difference of units in two sensations would depend on the latter being in a fixed ratio. But the *difference itself* would depend directly on that between their respective stimuli. So many units added to the stimulus, so many added to the sensation, and if the stimulus grew in a certain ratio, in exactly the same ratio would the sensation also grow, though its *perceptibility* grew according to the logarithmic law.[55]

If Δ stand for the smallest difference which *we perceive,* then we should have, instead of the formula $\Delta s =$ const., which is Fechner's, the formula $\frac{\Delta s}{s} =$ const., a formula which interprets all the *facts*

[54] Cf. Stumpf: *Tonpsychologie,* pp. 397–9. "One sensation cannot be a multiple of another. If it could, we ought to be able to subtract the one from the other, and to feel the remainder by itself. Every sensation presents itself as an indivisible unit." Professor von Kries, in the *Vierteljahrsschrift für wissenschaftliche Philosophie,* VI, 257 ff., shows very clearly the absurdity of supposing that our stronger sensations contain our weaker ones as parts. They differ as qualitative units. Compare also J. Tannery in Delbœuf's *Éléments de psychophysique* (1883), p. 134 ff.; J. Ward in *Mind,* I, 464; Lotze: *Metaphysic,* § 258.

[55] F. Brentano: *Psychologie,* I, 9, 88 ff.—Merkel thinks that his results with the method of equal-appearing intervals show that we compare considerable intervals with each other by a different law from that by which we notice barely perceptible intervals. The stimuli form an arithmetical series (a pretty wild one according to his figures) in the former case, a geometrical one in the latter—at least so I understand this valiant experimenter but somewhat obscure if acute writer.

of Weber's law, in an entirely different theoretic way from that adopted by Fechner.[56]

The entire superstructure which Fechner rears upon the facts is thus not only seen to be arbitrary and subjective, but in the highest degree improbable as well. The departures from Weber's law in regions where it does not obtain, he explains by the compounding with it of other unknown laws which mask its effects. As if *any* law could not be found in *any* set of phenomena, provided one have the wit to invent enough other coexisting laws to overlap and neutralize it! The whole outcome of the discussion, so far as Fechner's theories are concerned, is indeed *nil. Weber's law alone remains true as an empirical generalization of fair extent*: What we add to a large stimulus we notice less than what we add to a small one, unless it happen *relatively to the stimulus* to be as great.

Weber's law is probably purely physiological

One can express this state of things otherwise by saying that the whole of the stimulus does not seem to be effective in giving us the perception of 'more,' and the simplest interpretation of such a state of things would be *physical*. The loss of effect would take place in the nervous system. If our feelings resulted from a condition of the nerve-molecules which it grew ever more difficult for the stimulus to increase, our feelings would naturally grow at a slower rate than the stimulus itself. An ever larger part of the latter's work would go to overcoming the resistances, and an ever smaller part to the realization of the feeling-bringing state. Weber's law would thus be a sort of *law of friction* in the neural machine.[57] Just how these inner resistances and frictions are to be conceived is a speculative question. Delbœuf has formulated them as fatigue; Bernstein and Ward, as irradiations. The latest, and probably the most 'real,' hypothesis is that of Ebbinghaus, who supposes that the intensity of sensation depends on the *number* of neural molecules which are disintegrated in the unit of time. There are only a certain number at any time which are *capable* of disintegrating; and whilst most of these are in

[56] This is the formula which Merkel thinks he has verified (if I understand him aright) by his experiments by method 4.

[57] Elsas: *Über die Psychophysik* (1886), p. 41. When the pans of a balance are already loaded, but in equilibrium, it takes a proportionally larger weight added to one of them to incline the beam.

an average condition of instability, some are almost stable and some already near to decomposition. The smallest stimuli affect these latter molecules only; and as they are but few, the sensational effect from adding a given quantity of stimulus *at first* is relatively small. Medium stimuli affect the majority of the molecules, but affect fewer and fewer in proportion as they have already diminished their number. The latest additions to the stimuli find all the medium molecules already disintegrated, and only affect the small relatively indecomposable remainder, thus giving rise to increments of feeling which are correspondingly small. (Pflüger's *Archiv*, 45, 113.)

It is surely in some such way as this that Weber's law is to be interpreted, if it ever is. The Fechnerian *Massformel* and the conception of it as an ultimate 'psychophysic law' will remain an 'idol of the den,' if ever there was one. Fechner himself indeed was a German *Gelehrter* of the ideal type, at once simple and shrewd, a mystic and an experimentalist, homely and daring, and as loyal to facts as to his theories. But it would be terrible if even such a dear old man as this could saddle our Science forever with his patient whimsies, and, in a world so full of more nutritious objects of attention, compel all future students to plough through the difficulties, not only of his own works, but of the still drier ones written in his refutation. Those who desire this dreadful literature can find it; it has a 'disciplinary value'; but I will not even enumerate it in a footnote. The only amusing part of it is that Fechner's critics should always feel bound, after smiting his theories hip and thigh and leaving not a stick of them standing, to wind up by saying that nevertheless to him belongs the *imperishable glory* of first formulating them and thereby turning psychology into an *exact science*,

" 'And everybody praised the Duke,
Who this great fight did win.'
'But what good came of it at last?'
Quoth little Peterkin.
'Why, that I cannot tell,' said he;
'But 'twas a famous victory.' "

*Chapter XIV**

Association

After discrimination, association! Already in the last chapter I have had to invoke, in order to explain the improvement of certain discriminations by practice, the 'association' of the objects to be distinguished, with other more widely differing ones. It is obvious that the advance of our knowledge *must* consist of both operations; for objects at first appearing as wholes are analyzed into parts, and objects appearing separately are brought together and appear as new compound wholes to the mind. Analysis and synthesis are thus the incessantly alternating mental activities, a stroke of the one preparing the way for a stroke of the other, much as, in walking, a man's two legs are alternately brought into use, both being indispensable for any orderly advance.

The manner in which trains of imagery and consideration follow each other through our thinking, the restless flight of one idea before the next, the transitions our minds make between things wide as the poles asunder, transitions which at first sight startle us by their abruptness, but which, when scrutinized closely, often reveal intermediating links of perfect naturalness and propriety–all this magical, imponderable streaming has from time immemorial excited the admiration of all whose attention happened to be caught by its omnipresent mystery. And it has furthermore challenged the race of philosophers to banish something of the mystery by formu-

* The theory propounded in this chapter, and a good many pages of the text, were originally published in the *Popular Science Monthly* for March, 1880.

lating the process in simpler terms. The problem which the philosophers have set themselves is that of ascertaining *principles of connection* between the thoughts which thus appear to sprout one out of the other, whereby their peculiar succession or coexistence may be explained.

But immediately an ambiguity arises: which sort of connection is meant? connection *thought-of*, or connection *between thoughts*? These are two entirely different things, and only in the case of one of them is there any hope of finding 'principles.' The jungle of connections *thought of* can never be formulated simply. Every conceivable connection may be thought of—of coexistence, succession, resemblance, contrast, contradiction, cause and effect, means and end, genus and species, part and whole, substance and property, early and late, large and small, landlord and tenant, master and servant,—Heaven knows what, for the list is literally inexhaustible. The only simplification which could possibly be aimed at would be the reduction of the relations to a smaller number of types, like those which such authors as Kant and Renouvier call the 'categories' of the understanding.[1] According as we followed one category or another we should sweep, with our thought, through the world in this way or in that. And all the categories would be logical, would be relations of reason. They would fuse the items into a continuum. Were *this* the sort of connection sought between one moment of our thinking and another, our chapter might end here. For the only summary description of these infinite possibilities of transition, is that they are all *acts of reason*, and that the mind proceeds from one object to another by some rational path of connection. The trueness of this formula is only equalled by its sterility, for psychological purposes. Practically it amounts to simply referring the inquirer to the relations between facts or things, and to telling him that his thinking follows them.

But as a matter of fact, his thinking only sometimes follows them, and these so-called 'transitions of reason' are far from being all alike reasonable. If pure thought runs all our trains, why should she run some so fast and some so slow, some through dull flats and some through gorgeous scenery, some to mountain-heights and jewelled mines, others through dismal swamps and darkness?—and run some off the track altogether, and into the wilderness of lunacy? Why do

1 Compare Renouvier's criticism of associationism in his *Essais de critique générale*: *Logique*, II, p. 493 foll.

we spend years straining after a certain scientific or practical problem, but all in vain—thought refusing to evoke the solution we desire? And why, some day, walking in the street with our attention miles away from that quest, does the answer saunter into our minds as carelessly as if it had never been called for—suggested, possibly, by the flowers on the bonnet of the lady in front of us, or possibly by nothing that we can discover? If reason can give us relief then, why did she not do so earlier?

The truth must be admitted that thought works under conditions imposed *ab extra.* The great law of habit itself—that twenty experiences make us recall a thing better than one, that long indulgence in error makes right thinking almost impossible—seems to have no essential foundation in reason. The business of thought is with truth—the number of experiences ought to have nothing to do with her hold of it; and she ought by right to be able to hug it all the closer, after years wasted out of its presence. The contrary arrangements seem quite fantastic and arbitrary, but nevertheless are part of the very bone and marrow of our minds. Reason is only one out of a thousand possibilities in the thinking of each of us. Who can count all the silly fancies, the grotesque suppositions, the utterly irrelevant reflections he makes in the course of a day? Who can swear that his prejudices and irrational beliefs constitute a less bulky part of his mental furniture than his clarified opinions? It is true that a presiding arbiter seems to sit aloft in the mind, and emphasize the better suggestions into permanence, while it ends by dropping out and leaving unrecorded the confusion. But this is all the difference. The *mode of genesis* of the worthy and the worthless seems the same. The laws of our actual thinking, of the *cogitatum,* must account alike for the bad and the good materials on which the arbiter has to decide, for wisdom and for folly. The laws of the arbiter, of the *cogitandum,* of what we *ought* to think, are to the former as the laws of ethics are to those of history. Who but an hegelian historian ever pretended that reason in action was *per se* a sufficient explanation of the political changes in Europe?

There are, then, mechanical conditions on which thought depends, and which, to say the least, *determine the order in which is presented the content or material for her comparisons, selections, and decisions.* It is a suggestive fact that Locke, and many more recent Continental psychologists, have found themselves obliged to invoke a mechanical process to account for the *aberrations* of thought, the obstructive prepossessions, the frustrations of reason. This they found in the law of habit, or what we now call Association by Contiguity. But it never occurred to these writers that a process which could go the length of actually producing some ideas and sequences in the mind might safely be trusted to produce others too; and that those habitual associations which further thought may also come from the same mechanical source as those which hinder it. Hartley accordingly suggested habit as a sufficient explanation of all connections of our thoughts, and in so doing planted himself squarely upon the properly psychological aspect of the problem of connection, and sought to treat both rational and irrational connections from a single point of view. The problem which he essayed, however lamely, to answer, was that of the connection between our psychic states considered purely as such, regardless of the objective connections of which they might take cognizance. How does a man come, after thinking of A, to think of B the next moment? or how does he come to think A and B always together? These were the phenomena which Hartley undertook to explain by cerebral physiology. I believe that he was, in many essential respects, on the right track, and I propose simply to revise his conclusions by the aid of distinctions which he did not make.

But the whole historic doctrine of psychological association is tainted with one huge error—that of the construction of our thoughts out of the compounding of themselves together of immutable and incessantly recurring 'simple ideas.' It is the cohesion of these which the 'principles of association' are considered to account for. In Chapters VI and IX we saw abundant reasons for treating the doctrine of simple ideas or psychic atoms as mythological; and, in all that follows, our problem will be to keep whatever truths the associationist doctrine has caught sight of without weighing it down with the untenable incumbrance that the association is between 'ideas.'

Association, so far as the word stands for an *effect, is between* THINGS THOUGHT OF—*it is* THINGS, *not ideas, which are associated in the mind.* We ought to talk of the association of *objects,* not of the association of *ideas.* And so far as association stands for a *cause,* it is between *processes in the brain*—it is these which, by being associated in certain ways, determine what successive objects shall be thought. Let us proceed towards our final generalizations by surveying first a few familiar facts.

The laws of motor habit in the lower centres of the nervous system are disputed by no one. A series of movements repeated in a certain order tend to unroll themselves with peculiar ease in that order for ever afterwards. Number one awakens number two, and that awakens number three, and so on, till the last is produced. A habit of this kind once become inveterate may go on automatically. And so it is with the objects with which our thinking is concerned. With some persons each note of a melody, heard but once, will accurately revive in its proper sequence. Small boys at school learn the inflections of many a Greek noun, adjective, or verb, from the reiterated recitations of the upper classes falling on their ear as they sit at their desks. All this happens with no voluntary effort on their part and with no thought of the spelling of the words. The doggerel rhymes which children use in their games, such as the formula

"Ana mana mona mike
Barcelona bona strike,"

used for 'counting out,' form another familiar example of things heard in sequence cohering in the same order in the memory.

In touch we have a smaller number of instances, though probably everyone who bathes himself in a certain fixed manner is familiar with the fact that each part of his body over which the water is squeezed from the sponge awakens a premonitory tingling consciousness in that portion of skin which is habitually the next to be deluged. Tastes and smells form no very habitual series in our experience. But even if they did, it is doubtful whether habit would fix the order of their reproduction quite so well as it does that of other sensations. In vision, however, we have a sense in which the order of reproduced things is very nearly as much influenced by habit as is the order of remembered sounds. Rooms, landscapes, buildings, pictures, or persons with whose look we are very familiar, surge up before the mind's eye with all the details of their appearance complete, so soon as we think of any one of their component parts. Some persons, in reciting printed matter by heart, will seem to see each successive word, before they utter it, appear in its order on an imaginary page. A certain chess-player, one of those heroes who train themselves to play several games at once blindfold, is reported to say that in bed at night after a match the games are played all over again before his mental eye, each board being pictured as passing in turn through each of its successive stages. In this case, of course, the intense previous voluntary strain of the power of visual representation is what facilitated the fixed order of revival.

Association occurs as amply between impressions of different senses as between homogeneous sensations. Seen things and heard things cohere with each other, and with odors and tastes, in representation, in the same order in which they cohered as impressions of the outer world. Feelings of contact reproduce similarly the sights, sounds, and tastes with which experience has associated them. In fact, the 'objects' of our perception, as trees, men, houses, microscopes, of which the real world seems composed, are nothing but clusters of qualities which through simultaneous stimulation have so coalesced that the moment one is excited actually it serves as a sign or cue for the idea of the others to arise. Let a person enter his room in the dark and grope among the objects there. The touch of the matches will instantaneously recall their appearance. If his hand comes in contact with an orange on the table, the golden yellow of the fruit, its savor and perfume will forthwith shoot through his mind. In passing the hand over the sideboard or in jogging the coal-scuttle with the foot, the large glossy dark shape of the one and the irregular blackness of the other awaken like a flash and constitute what we call the recognition of the objects. The voice of the violin faintly echoes through the mind as the hand is laid upon it in the dark, and the feeling of the garments or draperies which may hang about the room is not *understood* till the look correlative to the feeling has in each case been resuscitated. Smells notoriously have the power of recalling the other experiences in whose company they were wont to be felt, perhaps long years ago; and the voluminous emotional character assumed by the images which suddenly pour into the mind at such a time forms one of the staple topics of popular psychologic wonder—

> " 'Lost and gone and lost and gone!'
> A breath, a whisper—some divine farewell—
> Desolate sweetness—far and far away."

We cannot hear the din of a railroad train or the yell of its whistle, without thinking of its long, jointed appearance and its headlong speed, nor catch a familiar voice in a crowd without recalling, with the name of the speaker, also his face. But the most notorious and important case of the mental combination of auditory with optical impressions originally experienced together is furnished by language. The child is offered a new and delicious fruit and is at the same time told that it is called a 'fig.' Or looking out of the window he exclaims, "What a funny horse!" and is told that it is a 'piebald' horse. When learning his letters, the sound of each is repeated to him whilst its shape is before his eye. Thenceforward, long as he may live, he will never see a fig, a piebald horse, or a letter of the alphabet without the name which he first heard in conjunction with each clinging to it in his mind; and inversely he will never hear the name without the faint arousal of the image of the object.[2]

THE RAPIDITY OF ASSOCIATION

Reading exemplifies this kind of cohesion even more beautifully. It is an uninterrupted and protracted recall of sounds by sights which have always been coupled with them in the past. I find that I can name six hundred letters in two minutes on a printed page. Five distinct acts of association between sight and sound (not to speak of all the other processes concerned) must then have occurred in each second in my mind. In reading entire words the speed is much more rapid. Valentin relates in his *Physiology* that the reading of a single page of the proof, containing 2629 letters, took him 1 minute and 32 seconds. In this experiment each letter was *understood* in 1/28 of a second, but owing to the integration of letters into entire words, forming each a single aggregate impression directly associated with a single acoustic image, we need not suppose as many as 28 separate associations in a sound. The figures, however, suffice to show with what extreme rapidity an actual sensation recalls its customary associates. Both in fact seem to our ordinary attention to come into the mind at once.

The time-measuring psychologists of recent days have tried their

2 Unless the name belong to a rapidly uttered sentence, when no substantive image may have time to arise.

hand at this problem by more elaborate methods. Galton, using a very simple apparatus, found that the sight of an unforeseen word would awaken an associated 'idea' in about 5/6 of a second.[3] Wundt next made determinations in which the 'cue' was given by single-syllabled words called out by an assistant. The person experimented on had to press a key as soon as the sound of the word awakened an associated idea. Both word and reaction were chronographically registered, and the total time-interval between the two amounted, in four observers, to 1.009, 0.896, 1.037, and 1.154 seconds respectively. From this the simple physiological reaction-time and the time of merely identifying the word's sound (the 'apperception-time,' as Wundt calls it) must be subtracted, to get the exact time required for the associated idea to arise. These times were separately determined and subtracted. The difference, called by Wundt the *association-time*, amounted, in the same four persons, to 706, 723, 752, and 874 thousandths of a second respectively.[4] The length of the last figure is due to the fact that the person reacting (President G. S. Hall) was an American, whose associations with German words would naturally be slower than those of natives. The shortest association-time noted was when the word 'Sturm' suggested to Prof. Wundt the word 'Wind' in 0.341 second.[5]—Finally, Mr. Cattell made some interesting observations upon the association-time between the look of letters and their names. "I pasted letters," he says, "on a revolving drum, and determined at what rate they could be read aloud, as they passed by a slit in a screen." He found it to vary according as one, or more than one, letter was visible at a time through the slit, and gives half a second as about the time which it takes to see and name a single letter seen alone.

3 In his observations he says that time was lost in mentally taking in the word which was the cue, "owing to the quiet unobtrusive way in which I found it necessary to bring it into view, so as not to distract the thoughts. Moreover, a substantive standing by itself is usually the equivalent of too abstract an idea for us to conceive properly without delay. Thus it is very difficult to get a quick conception of the word 'carriage,' because there are so many different kinds—two-wheeled, four-wheeled, open and closed, and all of them in so many different possible positions, that the mind possibly hesitates amidst an obscure sense of many alternatives that cannot blend together. But limit the idea to say a landau, and the mental association declares itself more quickly." (*Inquiries*, etc., p. 190.)

4 *Physiologische Psychologie*, II, 280 foll.

5 For interesting remarks on the sorts of things associated, in these experiments, with the prompting word, see Galton, *op. cit.*, pp. 185–203, and Trautscholdt in Wundt's *Philosophische Studien*, I, 213.

"When . . . two or more letters are always in view, not only do the processes of seeing and naming overlap, but while the subject is seeing one letter, he begins to see the ones next following, and so can read them more quickly. Of the nine persons experimented on four could read the letters faster when five were in view at once, but were not helped by a sixth letter; three were not helped by a fifth and two not by a fourth letter. This shows that while one idea is in the centre, two, three or four additional ideas may be in the background of consciousness. The second letter in view shortens the time about 1/40, the third 1/60, the fourth 1/100, the fifth 1/200 sec.

"I find it takes about twice as long to read (aloud, as fast as possible) words which have no connexion as words which make sentences, and letters which have no connexion as letters which make words. When the words make sentences and the letters words, not only do the processes of seeing and naming overlap, but by one mental effort the subject can recognise a whole group of words or letters, and by one will-act choose the motions to be made in naming them, so that the rate at which the words and letters are read is really only limited by the maximum rapidity at which the speech-organs can be moved. As the result of a large number of experiments the writer found that he had read words not making sentences at the rate of 1/4 sec., words making sentences (a passage from Swift) at the rate of 1/8 sec. per word. . . . The rate at which a person reads a foreign language is proportional to his familiarity with the language. For example, when reading as fast as possible the writer's rate was, English 138, French 167, German 250, Italian 327, Latin 434 and Greek 484; the figures giving the thousandths of a second taken to read each word. Experiments made on others strikingly confirm these results. The subject does not know that he is reading the foreign language more slowly than his own; this explains why foreigners seem to talk so fast. This simple method of determining a person's familiarity with a language might be used in school-examinations.

"The time required to see and name colours and pictures of objects was determined in the same way. The time was found to be about the same (over 1/2 sec.) for colours as for pictures, and about twice as long as for words and letters. Other experiments I have made show that we can recognise a single colour or picture in a slightly shorter time than a word or letter, but take longer to name it. This is because in the case of words and letters the association between the idea and name has taken place so often that the process has become automatic, whereas in the case of colours and pictures we must by a voluntary effort choose the name."[6]

[6] *Mind*, XI, 64–5.

In later experiments Mr. Cattell studied the time for various associations to be performed, the termini (i.e., cue and answer) being words. A word in one language was to call up its equivalent in another, the name of an author the tongue in which he wrote, that of a city the country in which it lay, that of a writer one of his works, etc. The mean variation from the average is very great in all these experiments; and the interesting feature which they show is the existence of certain constant differences between associations of different sorts. Thus:

From	*country*	to	*city,*	Mr. C.'s time was			0.340 sec.
"	*season*	"	*month,*	"	"	"	0.399
"	*language*	"	*author,*	"	"	"	0.523
"	*author*	"	*work,*	"	"	"	0.596

The average time of two observers, experimenting on eight different types of association, was 0.420 and 0.436 sec. respectively.[7]

[7] This value is much smaller than that got by Wundt as above. No reason for the difference is suggested by Mr. Cattell. Wundt calls attention to the fact that the figures found by him give an average, 0.720″, exactly equal to the *time interval* which in his experiments (*vide infra*, chapter on Time) was reproduced without error either way, and to that required, according to the Webers, for the legs to swing in rapid locomotion. "It is not improbable," he adds, "that this psychic constant, of the mean association-time and of the most correct appreciation of a time-interval, may have been developed under the influence of the most usual bodily movements, which also have determined the manner in which we tend to subdivide rhythmically longer periods of time." (*Physiologische Psychologie,* 2d ed., II, 286.) The *rapprochement* is of that tentative sort which it is no harm for psychologists to make, provided they recollect how very fictitious and incomparable mutually all these averages derived from different observers, working under different conditions, are. Mr. Cattell's figure throws Wundt's ingenious parallel entirely out of line.—The only measurements of association-time which so far seem likely to have much theoretic importance are a few made on insane patients by von Tschisch (Mendel's *Neurologisches Centralblatt,* 15 Mai, 1885, 4 Jhrg., p. 217). The simple reaction time was found about normal in three patients, one with progressive paralysis, one with inveterate mania of persecution, one recovering from ordinary mania. In the convalescent maniac and the paralytic, however, the association-time was hardly half as much as Wundt's normal figure (0.28″ and 0.23″ instead of 0.7″—smaller also than Cattell's), whilst in the sufferer from delusions of persecution and hallucinations it was twice as great as normal (1.39″ instead of 0.7″). This latter patient's time was sixfold that of the paralytic. Herr von Tschisch remarks on the connection of the short times with diminished power for clear and consistent processes of thought, and on that of the long times with the persistent fixation of the attention upon monotonous objects (delusions). Miss Marie Walitzky (*Revue Philosophique,* XXVIII, 583) has carried von Tschisch's observations still farther, making 18,000 measurements in all. She found association-time increased in paralytic dementia and diminished in mania. Choice-time, on the contrary, is increased in mania.

The very wide range of variation is undoubtedly a consequence of the fact that the words used as cues, and the different types of association studied, differ much in their degree of familiarity.

"For example, B is a teacher of mathematics, C has busied himself more with literature, C knows quite as well as B that 5+7=12, yet he needs 1/10 of a second longer to call it to mind; B knows quite as well as C that Dante was a poet, but needs 1/10 of a second longer to think of it. Such experiments lay bare the mental life in a way that is startling and not always gratifying."[8]

THE LAW OF CONTIGUITY

Time-determinations apart, the facts we have run over can all be summed up in the simple statement that *objects once experienced together tend to become associated in the imagination, so that when any one of them is thought of, the others are likely to be thought of also, in the same order of sequence or coexistence as before.* This statement we may name the law of *mental association by contiguity.*[9]

I preserve this name in order to depart as little as possible from tradition, although Mr. Ward's designation of the process as that of association by *continuity*[10] or Wundt's as that of *external* association (to distinguish it from the *internal* association which we shall presently learn to know under the name of association by similarity)[11] are perhaps better terms. Whatever we name the law, since it expresses merely a phenomenon of mental *habit, the most natural way of accounting for it is to conceive it as a result of the laws of habit in the nervous system; in other words, it is to ascribe it*

8 *Mind*, XII, 67–74.

9 Compare Bain's law of Association by Contiguity: "Actions, Sensations, and States of Feeling, occurring together or in close succession, tend to grow together, or cohere, in such a way that, when any one of them is afterwards presented to the mind, the others are apt to be brought up in idea" (*Senses and the Intellect*, p. 327). Compare also Hartley's formulation: "Any Sensations *A*, *B*, *C*, &c. by being associated with one another a sufficient Number of Times, get such a Power over the corresponding Ideas *a*, *b*, *c*, &c. that any one of the Sensations *A*, when impressed alone, shall be able to excite in the Mind *b*, *c*, &c. the Ideas of the rest." (*Observations on Man*, part I, chap. I, § 2, Prop. 10.) The statement in the text differs from these in holding fast to the objective point of view. It is *things*, and objective *properties in things*, which are associated in our thought.

10 *Encyclopædia Britannica*, 9th Ed., article "Psychology," p. 60, col. 2.

11 *Physiologische Psychologie*, 2d ed., II, 300.

to a physiological cause. If it be truly a law of those nerve-centres which co-ordinate sensory and motor processes together that paths once used for coupling any pair of them are thereby made more permeable, there appears no reason why the same law should not hold good of ideational centres and their coupling-paths as well.[12] Parts of these centres which have once been in action together will thus grow so linked that excitement at one point will irradiate through the system. The chances of complete irradiation will be strong in proportion as the previous excitements have been frequent, and as the present points excited afresh are numerous. If all points were originally excited together, the irradiation may be sensibly simultaneous throughout the system, when any single point or group of points is touched off. But where the original impressions were successive—the conjugation of a Greek verb, for example—awakening nerve-tracts in a definite order, they will now, when one of them awakens, discharge into each other in that definite order and in no other way.

The reader will recollect all that has been said of increased tension in nerve-tracts and of the summation of stimuli (p. 89 ff.). We must therefore suppose that in these ideational tracts as well as elsewhere, activity may be awakened, in any particular locality, by

[12] The difficulty here as with habit *überhaupt* is in seeing how new paths come *first* to be formed (cf. above, 113). Experience shows that a new path *is* formed between centres for sensible impressions whenever these vibrate together or in rapid succession. A child sees a certain bottle and hears it called 'milk,' and thenceforward thinks the name when he again sees the bottle. But why the successive or simultaneous excitement of two centres independently stimulated from without, one by sight and the other by hearing, *should* result in a path between them, one does not immediately see. We can only make hypotheses. Any hypothesis of the specific mode of their formation which tallies well with the observed facts of association will be in so far forth credible, in spite of possible obscurity. Herr Münsterberg thinks (*Beiträge zur experimentellen Psychologie*, Heft 1, p. 132) that between centres excited successively from without no path ought to be formed, and that consequently all contiguous association is between *simultaneous* experiences. Mr. Ward (*loc. cit.*) thinks, on the contrary, that it can only be between *successive* experiences: "The association of objects simultaneously presented can be resolved into an association of objects successively attended to. . . . It seems hardly possible to mention a case in which attention to the associated objects could not have been successive. In fact, an aggregate of objects on which attention could be focused at once would be already associated." Between these extreme possibilities, I have refrained from deciding in the text, and have described contiguous association as holding between both successively and coexistently presented objects. The physiological question as to how we may conceive the paths to originate had better be postponed till it comes to us again in the chapter on the Will, where we can treat it in a broader way. It is enough here to have called attention to it as a serious problem.

the summation therein of a number of tensions, each incapable alone of provoking an actual discharge. Suppose for example the locality M to be in functional continuity with four other localities, K, L, N, and O. Suppose moreover that on four previous occasions it has been separately combined with each of these localities in a common activity. M may then be indirectly awakened by any cause which tends to awaken either K, L, N, or O. But if the cause which awakens K, for instance, be so slight as only to increase its tension without arousing it to full discharge, K will only succeed in slightly increasing the tension of M. But if at the same time the tensions of L, N, and O are similarly increased, the combined effects of all four upon M may be so great as to awaken an actual discharge in this latter locality. In like manner if the paths between M and the four other localities have been so slightly excavated by previous experience as to require a very intense excitement in either of the localities before M can be awakened, a less strong excitement than this in any one will fail to reach M. But if all four at once are mildly excited, their compound effect on M may be adequate to its full arousal.

The psychological law of association of objects thought of through their previous contiguity in thought or experience *would thus be an effect, within the mind, of the physical fact that nerve-currents propagate themselves easiest through those tracts of conduction which have been already most in use.* Descartes and Locke hit upon this explanation, which modern science has not yet succeeded in improving.

"Custom," says Locke, "settles habits of thinking in the understanding, as well as of determining in the will, and of motions in the body; all which seem to be but *trains of motion in the animal spirits* [by this Locke meant identically what we understand by *neural processes*], which, once set a-going, continue in the same steps they have been used to, which, by often treading, are worn into a smooth path, and the motion in it becomes easy, and as it were natural."[13]

[13] *Essay*, bk. II, chap. XXXIII, § 6. Compare Hume, who, like Locke, only uses the principle to account for unreasonable and obstructive mental associations:

" 'Twou'd have been easy to have made an imaginary dissection of the brain, and have shewn, why upon our conception of any idea, the animal spirits run into all the contiguous traces, and rouze up the other ideas, that are related to it. But tho' I have neglected any advantage, which I might have drawn from this topic in explaining the relations of ideas, I am afraid I must here have recourse to it, in order to

Hartley was more thorough in his grasp of the principle. The sensorial nerve-currents, produced when objects are fully present, were for him 'vibrations,' and those which produce ideas of objects in their absence were 'miniature vibrations.' And he sums up the cause of mental association in a single formula by saying:

"Any Vibrations, *A, B, C,* &c. by being associated together a sufficient Number of Times, get such a Power over *a, b, c,* &c. the corresponding miniature Vibrations, that any of the Vibrations *A,* when impressed alone, shall be able to excite *b, c,* &c. the Miniatures of the rest."[14]

It is evident that if there be any law of neural habit similar to this, the contiguities, coexistences, and successions, met with in outer experience, must inevitably be copied more or less perfectly in our thought. If A B C D E be a sequence of outer impressions (they may be events or they may be successively experienced properties of an object) which once gave rise to the successive 'ideas,' *a b c d e,* then no sooner will A impress us again and awaken the *a,* than *b c d e* will arise as ideas even before B C D E have come in as impressions. In other words, the order of impressions will the next time be *anticipated;* and the mental order will so far forth copy the order of the outer world. Any object when met again will make us expect its former concomitants, through the overflowing of its brain-tract into the paths which lead to theirs. And all these suggestions will be effects of a material law.

Where the associations are, as here, of successively appearing things, the distinction I made at the outset of the chapter, between

---

account for the mistakes that arise from these relations. I shall therefore observe, that as the mind is endow'd with a power of exciting any idea it pleases; whenever it dispatches the spirits into that region of the brain, in which the idea is plac'd; these spirits always excite the idea, when they run precisely into the proper traces, and rummage that cell, which belongs to the idea. But as their motion is seldom direct, and naturally turns a little to the one side or the other; for this reason the animal spirits, falling into the contiguous traces, present other related ideas in lieu of that, which the mind desir'd at first to survey. This change we are not always sensible of; but continuing still the same train of thought, make use of the related idea, which is presented to us, and employ it in our reasoning, as if it were the same with what we demanded. This is the cause of many mistakes and sophisms in philosophy; as will naturally be imagin'd, and as it wou'd be easy to show, if there was occasion."

[14] *Op. cit.,* prop. 11.

a connection *thought of* and a connection *of thoughts,* is unimportant. For the connection thought of is concomitance or succession; and the connection between the thoughts is just the same. The 'objects' and the 'ideas' fit into parallel schemes, and may be described in identical language, as contiguous things tending to be thought again together, or contiguous ideas tending to recur together.

Now were these cases fair samples of all association, the distinction I drew might well be termed a *Spitzfindigkeit* or piece of pedantic hair-splitting, and be dropped. But as a matter of fact we cannot treat the subject so simply. The same outer object may suggest *either of many* realities formerly associated with it—for in the vicissitudes of our outer experience we are constantly liable to meet the same thing in the midst of differing companions—and a philosophy of association that should merely say that it will suggest one of these, or even of that one of them which it has oftenest accompanied, would go but a very short way into the *rationale* of the subject. This, however, is about as far as most associationists have gone with their 'principle of contiguity.' Granted an object, A, they never tell us beforehand which of its associates it *will* suggest; their wisdom is limited to showing, after it *has* suggested a second object, that that object was once an associate. They have had to supplement their principle of Contiguity by other principles, such as those of Similarity and Contrast, before they could begin to do justice to the richness of the facts.

THE ELEMENTARY LAW OF ASSOCIATION

I shall try to show, in the pages which immediately follow, that there is no other *elementary* causal law of association than the law of neural habit. All the *materials* of our thought are due to the way in which one elementary process of the cerebral hemispheres tends to excite whatever other elementary process it may have excited at some former time. The number of elementary processes at work, however, and the nature of those which at any time are fully effective in rousing the others, determine the character of the total brain-action, and, as a consequence of this, they determine the object thought of at the time. According as this resultant object is one thing or another, we call it a product of association by contiguity or of association by similarity, or contrast, or whatever other sorts we may have recognized as ultimate. Its production, however, is, in each one of these cases, to be explained by a merely quantitative variation in the elementary brain-processes momentarily at work under the law of habit, so that *psychic* contiguity, similarity, etc., are derivatives of a single profounder kind of fact.

My thesis, stated thus briefly, will soon become more clear; and at the same time certain disturbing factors, which co-operate with the law of neural habit, will come to view.

Let us then assume as the *basis* of all our subsequent reasoning this law: *When two elementary brain-processes have been active together or in immediate succession, one of them, on reoccurring, tends to propagate its excitement into the other.*

But, as a matter of fact, every elementary process has found itself at different times excited in conjunction with *many* other processes, and this by unavoidable outward causes. Which of these others it shall awaken now becomes a problem. Shall *b* or *c* be aroused next by the present *a*? We must make a further postulate, based, however, on the fact of *tension* in nerve-tissue, and on the fact of summation of excitements, each incomplete or latent in itself, into an open resultant.[15] The process *b*, rather than *c*, will awake, if in addition to the vibrating tract *a* some other tract *d* is in a state of sub-excitement, and formerly was excited with *b* alone and not with *a*. In short, we may say:

The amount of activity at any given point in the brain-cortex is the sum of the tendencies of all other points to discharge into it, such tendencies being proportionate (1) *to the number of times the excitement of each other point may have accompanied that of the point in question;* (2) *to the intensity of such excitements; and* (3) *to the absence of any rival point functionally disconnected with the first point, into which the discharges might be diverted.*

Expressing the fundamental law in this most complicated way leads to the greatest ultimate simplification. Let us, for the present, only treat of spontaneous trains of thought and ideation, such as occur in revery or musing. The case of voluntary thinking towards a certain end shall come up later.

Take, to fix our ideas, the two verses from "Locksley Hall":

"I the heir of all *the ages,* in the foremost files of time,"

[15] See Chapter III, pp. 89–92.

and—

"Yet I doubt not through *the ages* one increasing purpose runs."

Why is it that when we recite from memory one of these lines, and get as far as *the ages,* that portion of the *other* line which follows and, so to speak, sprouts out of *the ages* does not also sprout out of our memory and confuse the sense of our words? Simply because the word that follows *the ages* has its brain-process awakened not simply by the brain-process of *the ages* alone, but by it *plus* the brain-processes of all the words preceding *the ages.* The word *ages* at its moment of strongest activity would, *per se,* indifferently discharge into either 'in' or 'one.' So would the previous words (whose tension is momentarily much less strong than that of *ages*) each of them indifferently discharge into either of a large number of other words with which they have been at different times combined. But when the processes of '*I the heir of all the ages,*' simultaneously vibrate in the brain, the last one of them in a maximal, the others in a fading phase of excitement; then the strongest line of discharge will be that which they *all alike* tend to take. '*In*' and not '*one*' or any other word will be the next to awaken, for its brain-process has previously vibrated in unison not only with that of *ages,* but with that of all those other words whose activity is dying away. It is a good case of the effectiveness over thought of what we called on p. 249 a 'fringe.'

But if some one of these preceding words—'heir,' for example—had an intensely strong association with some brain-tracts entirely disjoined in experience from the poem of "Locksley Hall"—if the reciter, for instance, were tremulously awaiting the opening of a will which might make him a millionaire—it is probable that the path of discharge through the words of the poem would be suddenly interrupted at the word 'heir.' His *emotional interest in that word* would be such that its *own special associations would prevail* over the combined ones of the other words. He would, as we say, be abruptly reminded of his personal situation, and the poem would lapse altogether from his thoughts.

The writer of these pages has every year to learn the names of a large number of students who sit in alphabetical order in a lecture-room. He finally learns to call them by name, as they sit in their accustomed places. On meeting one in the street, however, early in the year, the face hardly ever recalls the name, but it may recall the place of its owner in the lecture-room, his neighbors' faces, and consequently his general alphabetical position; and then, usually as the common associate of all these combined data, the student's name surges up in his mind.

A father wishes to show to some guests the progress of his rather dull child in Kindergarten instruction. Holding the knife upright on the table, he says, "What do you call that, my boy?" "I calls it a *knife*, I does," is the sturdy reply, from which the child cannot be induced to swerve by any alteration in the form of question, until the father recollecting that in the Kindergarten a pencil was used and not a knife, draws a long one from his pocket, holds it in the same way, and then gets the wished-for answer, "I calls it *vertical.*" All the concomitants of the Kindergarten experience had to recombine their effect before the word 'vertical' could be reawakened.

Professor Bain, in his chapters on "Compound Association," has treated in a minute and exhaustive way of this type of mental sequence, and what he has done so well need not be here repeated.[16]

Impartial Redintegration

The ideal working of the law of compound association, were it unmodified by any extraneous influence, would be such as to keep the mind in a perpetual treadmill of concrete reminiscences from which no detail could be omitted. Suppose, for example, we begin by thinking of a certain dinner-party. The only thing which all the components of the dinner-party could combine to recall would be the first concrete occurrence which ensued upon it. All the details of this occurrence could in turn only combine to awaken the next following occurrence, and so on. If *a, b, c, d, e,* for instance, be the elementary nerve-tracts excited by the last act of the dinner-party, call this act A, and *l, m, n, o, p* be those of walking home through the frosty night, which we may call B, then the thought of A must awaken that of B, because *a, b, c, d, e,* will each and all discharge into *l* through the paths by which their original discharge took place. Similarly they will discharge into *m, n, o,* and *p*; and these latter tracts will also each reinforce the other's action because, in the experience B, they have already vibrated in unison. The lines in Fig. 40, p. 537, symbolize the summation of discharges into each

[16] I strongly advise the student to read his *Senses and the Intellect*, pp. 544–555.

of the components of B, and the consequent strength of the combination of influences by which B in its totality is awakened.

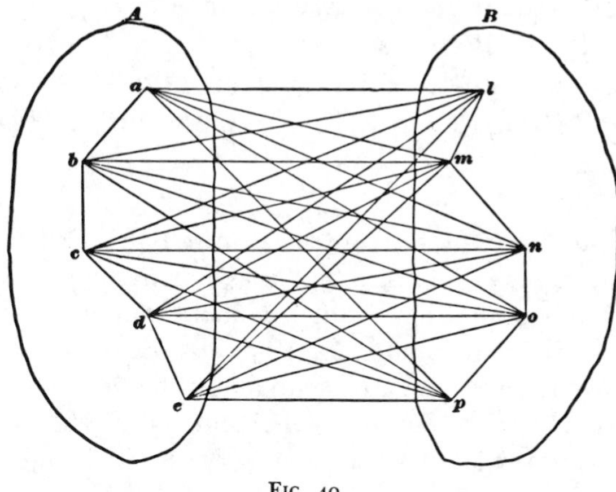

FIG. 40.

Hamilton first used the word 'redintegration' to designate all association. Such processes as we have just described might in an emphatic sense be termed redintegrations, for they would necessarily lead, if unobstructed, to the reinstatement in thought of the *entire* content of large trains of past experience. From this complete redintegration there could be no escape save through the irruption of some new and strong present impression of the senses, or through the excessive tendency of some one of the elementary brain-tracts to discharge independently into an aberrant quarter of the brain. Such was the tendency of the word 'heir' in the verse from "Locksley Hall," which was our first example. How such tendencies are constituted we shall have soon to inquire with some care. Unless they are present, the panorama of the past, once opened, must unroll itself with fatal literality to the end, unless some outward sound, sight, or touch divert the current of thought.

Let us call this process *impartial redintegration.* Whether it ever occurs in an absolutely complete form is doubtful. We all immediately recognize, however, that in some minds there is a much greater tendency than in others for the flow of thought to take this form. Those insufferably garrulous old women, those dry and fanciless beings who spare you no detail, however petty, of the facts they are recounting, and upon the thread of whose narrative all the irrelevant items cluster as pertinaciously as the essential ones, the slaves of literal fact, the stumblers over the smallest abrupt step in thought, are figures known to all of us. Comic literature has made her profit out of them. Juliet's nurse is a classical example. George Eliot's village characters and some of Dickens's minor personages supply excellent instances.

Perhaps as successful a rendering as any of this mental type is the character of Miss Bates in Miss Austen's *Emma*. Hear how she redintegrates:

> " 'But where could *you* hear it?' cried Miss Bates. 'Where could you possibly hear it, Mr. Knightley? For it is not five minutes since I received Mrs. Cole's note—no, it cannot be more than five—or at least ten—for I had got my bonnet and spencer on, just ready to come out—I was only gone down to speak to Patty again about the pork—Jane was standing in the passage—were not you, Jane?—for my mother was so afraid that we had not any salting-pan large enough. So I said, I would go down and see, and Jane said, "Shall I go down instead? for I think you have a little cold, and Patty has been washing the kitchen."—"Oh, my dear," said I—well, and just then came the note. A Miss Hawkins—that's all I know—a Miss Hawkins of Bath. But, Mr. Knightley, how could you possibly have heard it? for the very moment Mr. Cole told Mrs. Cole of it, she sat down and wrote to me. A Miss Hawkins—' "

But in every one of us there are moments when this complete reproduction of all the items of a past experience occurs. What are those moments? They are moments of emotional recall of the past as something which once was, but is gone for ever—moments, the interest of which consists in the feeling that our self was once other than it now is. When this is the case, any detail, however minute, which will make the past picture more complete, will also have its effect in swelling that total contrast between *now* and *then* which forms the central interest of our contemplation.

ORDINARY OR MIXED ASSOCIATION

This case helps us to understand why it is that the ordinary spontaneous flow of our ideas does not follow the law of impartial redintegration. *In no revival of a past experience are all the items of our thought equally operative in determining what the next thought shall be. Always some ingredient is prepotent over the rest.* Its special suggestions or associations in this case will often be different from those which it has in common with the whole group of items; and its tendency to awaken these outlying associates will deflect the path of our revery. Just as in the original sensible experience our attention focalized itself upon a few of the impressions of the scene before us, so here in the reproduction of those impressions an equal partiality is shown, and some items are emphasized above the rest. What these items shall be is, in most cases of spontaneous revery, hard to determine beforehand. In subjective terms we say that *the prepotent items are those which appeal most to our* INTEREST.

Expressed in brain-terms, the law of interest will be: *some one brain-process is always prepotent above its concomitants in arousing action elsewhere.*

"Two processes," says Mr. Hodgson,[17] "are constantly going on in redintegration, the one a process of corrosion, melting, decay, and the other a process of renewing, arising, becoming . . . no object of representation remains long before consciousness in the same state, but fades, decays, and becomes indistinct. Those parts of the object, however, which possess an interest resist this tendency to gradual decay of the whole object. . . . This inequality in the object, some parts, the uninteresting, submitting to decay, others, the interesting parts, resisting it, when it has continued for a certain time, ends in becoming a new object."

Only where the interest is diffused equally over all the parts (as in the emotional memory just referred to, where, as all *past*, they all interest us alike) is this law departed from. It will be least obeyed by those minds which have the smallest variety and intensity of interests—those who, by the general flatness and poverty of their æsthetic nature, are kept for ever rotating among the literal sequences of their local and personal history.

Most of us, however, are better organized than this, and our musings pursue an erratic course, swerving continually into some new direction traced by the shifting play of interest as it ever falls on some partial item in each complex representation that is evoked.

[17] *Time and Space*, p. 266. Compare Coleridge: "The true practical general law of association is this; that whatever makes certain parts of a total impression more vivid or distinct than the rest, will determine the mind to recall these in preference to others equally linked together by the common condition of contemporaneity or . . . of *continuity*. But the will itself, by confining and intensifying the attention, may arbitrarily give vividness or distinctness to any object whatsoever." (*Biographia Literaria*, Chap. VII.)

Thus it so often comes about that we find ourselves thinking at two nearly adjacent moments of things separated by the whole diameter of space and time. Not till we carefully recall each step of our cogitation do we see how naturally we came by Hodgson's law to pass from one to the other. Thus, for instance, after looking at my clock just now (1879), I found myself thinking of a recent resolution in the Senate about our legal-tender notes. The clock had called up the image of the man who had repaired its gong. He had suggested the jeweller's shop where I had last seen him; that shop, some shirt-studs which I had bought there; they, the value of gold and its recent decline; the latter, the equal value of greenbacks, and this, naturally, the question of how long they were to last, and of the Bayard proposition. Each of these images offered various points of interest. Those which formed the turning-points of my thought are easily assigned. The gong was momentarily the most interesting part of the clock, because, from having begun with a beautiful tone, it had become discordant and aroused disappointment. But for this the clock might have suggested the friend who gave it to me, or any one of a thousand circumstances connected with clocks. The jeweller's shop suggested the studs, because they alone of all its contents were tinged with the egoistic interest of possession. This interest in the studs, their value, made me single out the material as its chief source, etc., to the end. Every reader who will arrest himself at any moment and say, "How came I to be thinking of just this?" will be sure to trace a train of representations linked together by lines of contiguity and points of interest inextricably combined. This is the ordinary process of the association of ideas as it spontaneously goes on in average minds. *We may call it* ORDINARY, *or* MIXED, ASSOCIATION.

Another example of it is given by Hobbes in a passage which has been quoted so often as to be classical:

"In a Discourse of our present civill warre, what could seem more impertinent, than to ask (as one did) what was the value of a Roman Penny? Yet the Cohærence to me was manifest enough. For the Thought of the warre, introduced the Thought of the delivering up the King to his Enemies; The Thought of that, brought in the Thought of the delivering up of Christ; and that again the Thought of the 30 pence, which was the price of that treason: and thence easily followed that malicious question; and all this in a moment of time; for Thought is quick."[18]

[18] *Leviathan*, pt. I, chap. III, *init.*

Can we determine, now, when a certain portion of the going thought has, by dint of its interest, become so prepotent as to make its own exclusive associates the dominant features of the coming thought—can we, I say, determine *which* of its own associates shall be evoked? For they are many. As Hodgson says:

"The interesting parts of the decaying object are free to combine again with any objects, or parts of objects, with which they have at any time been combined before. All the former combinations of these parts may come back into consciousness; one must; but which will?"

Mr. Hodgson replies:

"There can be but one answer; That which has been most *habitually* combined with them before. This new object begins at once to form itself in consciousness, and to group its parts round the part still remaining from the former object; part after part comes out and arranges itself in its old position; but scarcely has the process begun, when the original law of interest begins to operate on this new formation, seizes on the interesting parts and impresses them on the attention to the exclusion of the rest, and the whole process is repeated again with endless variety. I venture to propose this as a complete and true account of the whole process of spontaneous redintegration."

In restricting the discharge from the interesting item into that channel which is simply most *habitual* in the sense of most frequent, Hodgson's account is assuredly imperfect. An image by no means always revives its most frequent associate, although frequency is certainly one of the most potent determinants of revival. If I abruptly utter the word *swallow*, the reader, if by habit an ornithologist, will think of a bird; if a physiologist or a medical specialist in throat-diseases, he will think of deglutition. If I say *date*, he will, if a fruit-merchant or an Arabian traveller, think of the produce of the palm; if an habitual student of history, figures with A.D. or B.C. before them will rise in his mind. If I say *bed, bath, morning*, his own daily toilet will be invincibly suggested by the combined names of three of its habitual associates. But frequent lines of transition are often set at naught. The sight of C. Göring's *System der kritischen Philosophie* has most frequently awakened in me thoughts of the opinions therein propounded. The idea of suicide has never been connected with the volume. But a moment since, as my eye fell upon it, suicide was the thought that flashed into my mind.

Why? Because but yesterday I received a letter from Leipzig informing me that this philosopher's recent death by drowning was an act of self-destruction. Thoughts tend, then, to awaken their most recent as well as their most habitual associates. This is a matter of notorious experience, too notorious, in fact, to need illustration. If we have seen our friend this morning, the mention of his name now recalls the circumstances of that interview, rather than any more remote details concerning him. If Shakespeare's plays are mentioned, and we were last night reading *Richard II.*, vestiges of that play rather than of *Hamlet* or *Othello* float through our mind. Excitement of peculiar tracts, or peculiar modes of general excitement in the brain, leave a sort of tenderness or exalted sensibility behind them which takes days to die away. As long as it lasts, those tracts or those modes are liable to have their activities awakened by causes which at other times might leave them in repose. Hence, *recency* in experience is a prime factor in determining revival in thought.[19]

Vividness in an original experience may also have the same effect as habit or recency in bringing about likelihood of revival. If we have once witnessed an execution, any subsequent conversation or reading about capital punishment will almost certainly suggest images of that particular scene. Thus it is that events lived through only once, and in youth, may come in after-years, by reason of their exciting quality or emotional intensity, to serve as types or instances used by our mind to illustrate any and every occurring topic whose interest is most remotely pertinent to theirs. If a man in his boyhood once talked with Napoleon, any mention of great men or historical events, battles or thrones, or the whirligig of fortune, or islands in the ocean, will be apt to draw to his lips the incidents of that one memorable interview. If the word *tooth* now suddenly appears on the page before the reader's eye, there are fifty chances out of a hundred that, if he gives it time to awaken any image, it will be an image of some operation of dentistry in which he has been the sufferer. Daily he has touched his teeth and masticated with them; this very morning he brushed them, chewed his

[19] I refer to a recency of a few hours. Mr. Galton found that experiences from boyhood and youth were more likely to be suggested by words seen at random than experiences of later years. See his highly interesting account of experiments in his *Inquiries into Human Faculty*, pp. 191–203.

breakfast and picked them; but the rarer and remoter associations arise more promptly because they were so much more intense.[20]

A fourth factor in tracing the course of reproduction is *congruity in emotional tone* between the reproduced idea and our mood. The same objects do not recall the same associates when we are cheerful as when we are melancholy. Nothing, in fact, is more striking than our utter inability to keep up trains of joyous imagery when we are depressed in spirits. Storm, darkness, war, images of disease, poverty, and perishing afflict unremittingly the imaginations of melancholiacs. And those of sanguine temperament, when their spirits are high, find it impossible to give any permanence to evil forebodings or to gloomy thoughts. In an instant the train of association dances off to flowers and sunshine, and images of spring and hope. The records of Arctic or African travel perused in one mood awaken no thoughts but those of horror at the malignity of Nature; read at another time they suggest only enthusiastic reflections on the indomitable power and pluck of man. Few novels so overflow with joyous animal spirits as *The Three Guardsmen* of Dumas. Yet it may awaken in the mind of a reader depressed with sea-sickness (as the writer can personally testify) a most dismal and woful consciousness of the cruelty and carnage of which heroes like Athos, Porthos, and Aramis make themselves guilty.

Habit, recency, vividness, and emotional congruity are, then, all reasons why one representation rather than another should be awakened by the interesting portion of a departing thought. We may say with truth that *in the majority of cases the coming representation will have been either habitual, recent, or vivid, and will be congruous.* If all these qualities unite in any one absent associate, we may predict almost infallibly that that associate of the going thought will form an important ingredient in the coming thought. In spite of the fact, however, that the succession of representations is thus redeemed from perfect indeterminism and limited to a few classes whose characteristic quality is fixed by the nature of our past experience, it must still be confessed that an immense number of terms in the linked chain of our representations fall outside of all assignable rule. To take the instance of the clock given on page 540. Why did the jeweller's shop suggest the shirt-studs rather than a

20 For other instances see Wahle, in *Vierteljahrsschrift für wissenschaftliche Philosophie*, IX, 414–417 (1885).

chain which I had bought there more recently, which had cost more, and whose sentimental associations were much more interesting? Both chain and studs had excited brain-tracts simultaneously with the shop. The only reason why the nerve-stream from the shop-tract switched off into the stud-tract rather than into the chain-tract must be that the stud-tract happened at that moment to lie more open, either because of some accidental alteration in its nutrition or because the incipient sub-conscious tensions of the brain as a whole had so distributed their equilibrium that it was more unstable here than in the chain-tract. Any reader's introspection will easily furnish similar instances. It thus remains true that to a certain extent, even in those forms of ordinary mixed association which lie nearest to impartial redintegration, *which* associate of the interesting item shall emerge must be called largely a matter of accident—accident, that is, for our intelligence. No doubt it is determined by cerebral causes, but they are too subtile and shifting for our analysis.

ASSOCIATION BY SIMILARITY

In partial or mixed association we have all along supposed the interesting portion of the disappearing thought to be of considerable extent, and to be sufficiently complex to constitute by itself a concrete object. Sir William Hamilton relates, for instance, that after thinking of Ben Lomond he found himself thinking of the Prussian system of education, and discovered that the links of association were a German gentleman whom he had met on Ben Lomond, Germany, etc. The interesting part of Ben Lomond, as he had experienced it, the part operative in determining the train of his ideas, was the complex image of a particular man. But now let us suppose that that selective agency of interested attention, which may thus convert impartial redintegration into partial association—let us suppose that it refines itself still further and accentuates a portion of the passing thought, so small as to be no longer the image of a concrete thing, but only of an abstract quality or property. Let us moreover suppose that the part thus accentuated persists in consciousness (or, in cerebral terms, has its brain-process continue) after the other portions of the thought have faded. *This small surviving portion will then surround itself with its own associates* after the fashion we have already seen, and the relation between the new thought's object and the object of the faded thought will be a *relation of similarity*. The pair of thoughts will form an instance of what is called '*Association by Similarity*.'[21]

The similars which are here associated, or of which the first is followed by the second in the mind, are seen to be *compounds*. Experience proves that this is always the case. *There is no tendency on the part of* SIMPLE *'ideas,' attributes, or qualities to remind us of their like.*[21a] The thought of one shade of blue does not remind us of that of another shade of blue, etc., unless indeed we have in mind some general purpose like naming the tint, when we should naturally think of other blues of the scale, through 'mixed association' of purpose, names, and tints, together. But there is no elementary tendency of pure qualities to awaken their similars in the mind.[21b]

We saw in the chapter on Discrimination that two compound things are similar when some one quality or group of qualities is shared alike by both, although as regards their other qualities they may have nothing in common. The moon is similar to a gas-jet, it is also similar to a foot-ball; but a gas-jet and a foot-ball are not similar to each other. When we affirm the similarity of two compound things, we should always say *in what respect it obtains*. Moon and gas-jet are similar in respect of luminosity, and nothing else; moon and foot-ball in respect of rotundity, and nothing else. Foot-ball and gas-jet are in no respect similar—that is, they possess no common point, no identical attribute. Similarity, in compounds, is partial identity. When the *same* attribute appears in two phenomena, though it be their only common property, the two phenomena are similar in so far forth. To return now to our associated representations. If the thought of the moon is succeeded by the thought of a foot-ball, and that by the thought of one of Mr. X's railroads, it is because the attribute rotundity in the moon broke

[21] I retain the title of association by similarity in order not to depart from common usage. The reader will observe, however, that my nomenclature is not based on the same principle throughout. Impartial redintegration connotes neural processes; similarity is an objective relation perceived by the mind; ordinary or mixed association is a merely denotative word. *Total recall, partial recall,* and *focalized recall,* of associates, would be better terms. But as the *denotation* of the latter word is almost identical with that of association by similarity, I think it better to sacrifice propriety to popularity, and to keep the latter well-worn phrase.

[21a] Ehrenfels: *Vierteljahrsschrift*, XIV, 282, admits this and suggests that if there *be* any pure Association by similarity it applies to forms of combination only (Gestaltqualitäten) and not to elements. See also Lotze: *Microcosmus*, Eng. tr., I, 217.

[21b] Höffding forgets this passage when in *Philosophische Studien*, VIII, p. 96, he accuses me of inconsistency in maintaining both that there is immediate resemblance and that *association* by resemblance is through a common part. Only such like things as have a common part, or at least a common associate, will call each other up.

away from all the rest and surrounded itself with an entirely new set of companions—elasticity, leathery integument, swift mobility in obedience to human caprice, etc.; and because the last-named attribute in the foot-ball in turn broke away from its companions, and, itself persisting, surrounded itself with such new attributes as make up the notions of a 'railroad king,' of a rising and falling stock-market, and the like.

The gradual passage from impartial redintegration to similar association through what we have called ordinary mixed association may be symbolized by diagrams. Fig. 41 is impartial redintegration, Fig. 42 is mixed, and Fig. 43 similar association. A in each is the passing, B the coming thought. In 'impartial,' all parts of A are

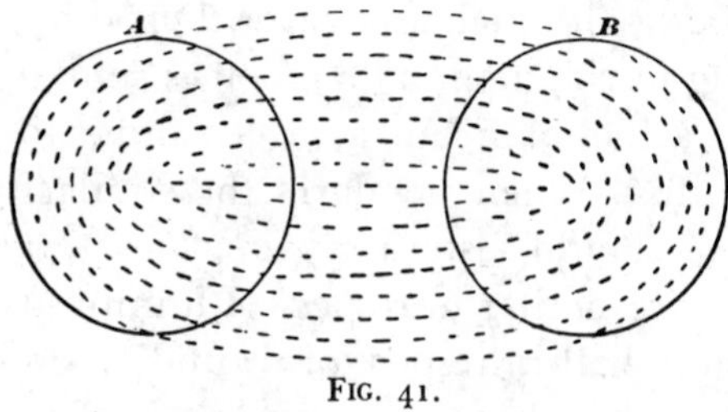

FIG. 41.

equally operative in calling up B. In 'mixed,' most parts of A are inert. The part M alone breaks out and awakens B. In 'similar,' the focalized part M is much smaller than in the previous case, and

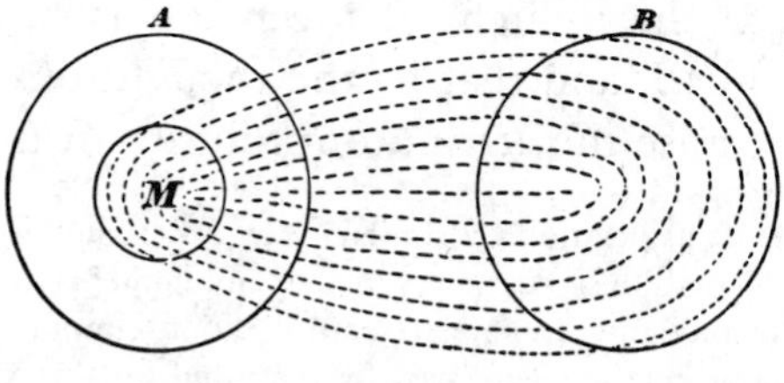

FIG. 42.

after awakening its new set of associates, instead of fading out itself, it continues persistently active along with them, forming an identical part in the two ideas, and making these, *pro tanto*, resemble each other.

Why a single portion of the passing thought should break out from its concert with the rest and act, as we say, on its own hook, why the other parts should become inert, are mysteries which we

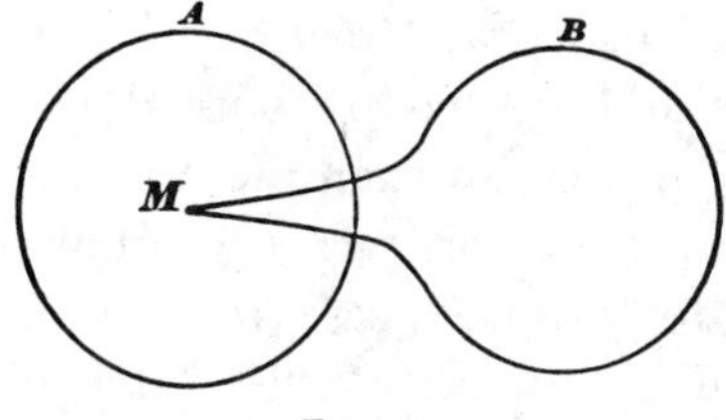

Fig. 43.

can ascertain but not explain. Possibly a minuter insight into the laws of neural action will some day clear the matter up; possibly neural laws will not suffice, and we shall need to invoke a dynamic reaction of the form of consciousness upon its content. But into this we cannot enter now.

To sum up, then, we see that *the difference between the three kinds of association reduces itself to a simple difference in the amount of that portion of the nerve-tract supporting the going thought which is operative in calling up the thought which comes.* But the *modus operandi* of this active part is the same, be it large or be it small. The items constituting the coming object waken in every instance because their nerve-tracts once were excited continuously with those of the going object or its operative part. This ultimate physiological law of habit among the neural elements is what *runs* the train. The direction of its course and the form of its transitions, whether redintegrative, associative, or similar, are due to unknown regulative or determinative conditions which accomplish their effect by opening this switch and closing that, setting the engine sometimes at half-speed, and coupling or uncoupling cars.

This last figure of speech, into which I have glided unwittingly, affords itself an excellent instance of association by similarity. I was thinking of the deflections of the course of ideas. Now, from Hobbes's time downwards, English writers have been fond of speaking of the *train* of our representations. This word happened to stand out in the midst of my complex thought with peculiarly sharp accentuation, and to surround itself with numerous details of railroad imagery. Only such details became clear, however, as had their nerve-tracts besieged by a double set of influences—those from *train* on the one hand, and those from the *movement of thought* on the other. It may possibly be that the prepotency of the suggestions of the word *train* at this moment were due to the recent excitation of the railroad brain-tract by the instance chosen a few pages back of a railroad king playing foot-ball with the stock-market.

It is apparent from such an example how inextricably complex are all the contributory factors whose resultant is the line of our revery. It would be folly in most cases to attempt to trace them out. From an instance like the above, where the pivot of the Similar Association was formed by a definite concrete word, *train*, to those where it is so subtile as utterly to elude our analysis, the passage is unbroken. We can form a series of examples. When Mr. Bagehot says that the mind of the savage, so far from being in a state of nature, is *tattooed* all over with monstrous superstitions, the case is very like the one we have just been considering. When Sir James Stephen compares our belief in the uniformity of nature, the congruity of the future with the past, to a man rowing one way and looking another, and steering his boat by keeping her stern in a line with an object behind him, the operative link becomes harder to dissect out. It is subtler still in Dr. Holmes's phrase, that stories in passing from mouth to mouth make a great deal of lee-way in proportion to their headway; or in Mr. Lowell's description of German sentences, that they have a way of yawing and going sternforemost and not minding the helm for several minutes after it has been put down. And finally, it is a real puzzle when the color pale-blue is said to have feminine and blood-red masculine affinities. And if I hear a friend describe a certain family as having *blotting-paper* voices, the image, though immediately felt to be apposite, baffles the utmost powers of analysis. The higher poets all use abrupt epithets, which are alike intimate and remote, and, as Emerson says, sweetly torment us with invitations to their inaccessible homes.

In these latter instances we must suppose that there is an identical portion in the similar objects, and that its brain-tract is energetically operative, without, however, being sufficiently isolable in its activity as to stand out *per se*, and form the condition of a distinctly discriminated 'abstract idea.' We cannot even by careful search see the bridge over which we passed from the heart of one representation to that of the next. In some brains, however, this mode of transition is extremely common. It would be one of the most important of physiological discoveries could we assign the mechanical or chemical difference which makes the thoughts of one brain cling close to impartial redintegration, while those of another shoot about in all the lawless revelry of similarity. Why, in these latter brains, action should tend to focalize itself in small spots, while in the others it fills patiently its broad bed, it seems impossible to guess. Whatever the difference may be, it is what separates the man of genius from the prosaic creature of habit and routine thinking. In Chapter XXII we shall need to recur again to this point.

ASSOCIATION IN VOLUNTARY THOUGHT

Hitherto we have assumed the process of suggestion of one object by another to be spontaneous. The train of imagery wanders at its own sweet will, now trudging in sober grooves of habit, now with a hop, skip, and jump darting across the whole field of time and space. This is revery, or musing; but great segments of the flux of our ideas consist of something very different from this. They are guided by a distinct purpose or conscious interest. As the Germans say, we *nachdenken,* or think towards a certain end. It is now necessary to examine what modification is made in the trains of our imagery by the having of an end in view. The course of our ideas is then called *voluntary.*

Physiologically considered, we must suppose that a purpose means the persistent activity of certain rather definite brain-processes throughout the whole course of thought. Our most usual cogitations are not pure reveries, absolute driftings, but revolve about some central interest or topic to which most of the images are relevant, and towards which we return promptly after occasional digressions. This interest is subserved by the persistently active brain-tracts we have supposed. In the mixed associations which we have hitherto studied, the parts of each object which form the pivots on which our thoughts successively turn have their interest largely determined by their connection with some *general interest* which for the time has seized upon the mind. If we call Z the brain-tract of general interest, then, if the object *abc* turns up, and *b* has more associations with Z than have either *a* or *c, b* will become the object's interesting, pivotal portion, and will call up its own associates exclusively. For the energy of *b*'s brain-tract will be augmented by Z's activity,—an activity which, from lack of previous connection between Z and *a* or *c,* does not influence *a* or *c.* If, for instance, I think of Paris whilst I am *hungry,* I shall not improbably find that its *restaurants* have become the pivot of my thought, etc., etc.

But in the theoretic as well as in the practical life there are interests of a more acute sort, taking the form of definite images of some achievement, be it action or acquisition, which we desire to effect. The train of ideas arising under the influence of such an interest constitutes usually the thought of the *means* by which the end shall be attained. If the end by its simple presence does not instantaneously suggest the means, the search for the latter becomes an intellectual *problem*. The solution of problems is the most characteristic and peculiar sort of voluntary thinking. Where the end thought of is some outward deed or gain, the solution is largely composed of the actual motor processes, walking, speaking, writing, etc., which lead up to it. Where the end is in the first instance only ideal, as in laying out a place of operations, the steps are purely imaginary. In both of these cases the discovery of the means may form a new sort of end, of an entirely peculiar nature—an end, namely, which we intensely desire before we have attained it, but of the nature of which, even whilst most strongly craving it, we have no distinct imagination whatever. Such an end is a problem.

The same state of things occurs whenever we seek to recall something forgotten, or to state the reason for a judgment which we have made intuitively. The desire strains and presses in a direction which it feels to be right, but towards a point which it is unable to see. In short, the *absence of an item* is a determinant of our representations quite as positive as its presence can ever be. The gap becomes no mere void, but what is called an *aching* void. If we try to explain in terms of brain-action how a thought which only potentially exists can yet be effective, we seem driven to believe that the brain-tract thereof must actually be excited, but only in a minimal and sub-conscious way. Try, for instance, to symbolize what goes on in a man who is racking his brains to remember a thought which occurred to him last week. The associates of the thought are there, many of them at least, but they refuse to awaken the thought itself. We cannot suppose that they do not irradiate *at all* into its brain-tract, because his mind quivers on the very edge of its recovery. Its actual rhythm sounds in his ears; the words seem on the imminent point of following, but fail. What it is that blocks the discharge and keeps the brain-excitement here from passing beyond the nascent into the vivid state cannot be guessed. But we see in the philosophy of desire and pleasure, that such nascent excitements, spontaneously tending to a crescendo, but inhibited or checked by other causes, may become potent mental stimuli and determinants of desire. All questioning, wonder, emotion of curiosity, must be referred to cerebral causes of some such form as this. The great difference between the effort to recall things forgotten and the search after the means to a given end is that the latter have not, whilst the former have, already formed a part of our experience. If we first study *the mode of recalling a thing forgotten,* we can take up with better understanding the voluntary quest of the unknown.

The forgotten thing is felt by us as a gap in the midst of certain other things. If it is a thought, we possess a dim idea of where we were and what we were about when it occurred to us. We recollect the general subject to which it relates. But all these details refuse to shoot together into a solid whole, for the lack of the vivid traits of this missing thought, the relation whereof to each detail forms now the main interest of the latter. We keep running over the details in our mind, dissatisfied, craving something more. From each detail there radiate lines of association forming so many tentative guesses. Many of these are immediately seen to be irrelevant, are therefore void of interest, and lapse immediately from consciousness. Others are associated with the other details present, and with the missing thought as well. When *these* surge up, we have a peculiar feeling that we are 'warm,' as the children say when they play hide and seek; and such associates as these we clutch at and keep before the attention. Thus we recollect successively that when we had the thought in question we were at the dinner-table; then that our friend J. D. was there; then that the subject talked about was so and so; finally, that the thought came *a propos* of a certain anecdote, and then that it had something to do with a French quotation. Now all these added associations *arise independently of the will,* by the spontaneous process we know so well. *All that the will does is to emphasize and linger over those which seem pertinent, and ignore the rest.* Through this hovering of the attention in the neighborhood of the desired object, the accumulation of associates becomes so great that the combined tensions of their neural processes break through the bar, and the nervous wave pours into the tract which has so long been awaiting its advent. And as the expectant, sub-conscious itching there, bursts into the fulness of vivid feeling, the mind finds an inexpressible relief.

The whole process can be rudely symbolized in a diagram. Call the forgotten thing Z, the first facts with which we felt it was related *a*, *b*, and *c*, and the details finally operative in calling it up *l*, *m*, and *n*. Each circle will then stand for the brain-process underlying the thought of the object denoted by the letter contained within it. The activity in Z will at first be a mere tension; but as the activities in *a*, *b*, and *c* little by little irradiate into *l*, *m*, and *n*,

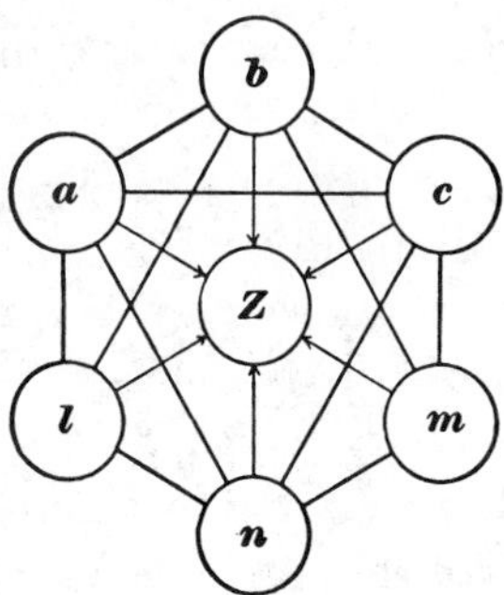

FIG. 44.

and as *all* these processes are somehow connected with Z, their combined irradiations upon Z, represented by the centripetal arrows, succeed in helping the tension there to overcome the resistance, and in rousing Z also to full activity.

The tension present from the first in Z, even though it keep below the threshold of discharge, is probably to some degree co-operative with *a*, *b*, *c* in determining that *l*, *m*, *n* shall awake. Without Z's tension there might be a slower accumulation of objects connected with it. But, as aforesaid, the objects come before us through the brain's own laws, and the Ego of the thinker can only remain on hand, as it were, to recognize their relative values and brood over some of them, whilst others are let drop. As when we have lost a material object we cannot recover it by a direct effort, but only through moving about such neighborhoods wherein it is likely to lie, and trusting that it will then strike our eye; so here, by not letting our attention leave the neighborhood of what we seek, we trust that it will end by speaking to us of its own accord.[22]

[22] No one has described this process better than Hobbes: "Sometimes a man seeks what he hath lost; and from that place, and time, wherein hee misses it, his mind runs back, from place to place, and time to time, to find where, and when he had it; that is to say, to find some certain, and limited time and place, in which to begin a method of seeking. Again, from thence, his thoughts run over the same places and times, to find what action, or other occasion might make him lose it. This we call

Turn now to the case of finding the unknown means to a distinctly conceived end. The end here stands in the place of *a, b, c,* in the diagram. It is the starting-point of the irradiations of suggestion; and here, as in that case, what the voluntary attention does is only to dismiss some of the suggestions as irrelevant, and hold fast to others which are felt to be more pertinent—let these be symbolized by *l, m, n.* These latter at last accumulate sufficiently to discharge all together into Z, the excitement of which process is, in the mental sphere, equivalent to the solution of our problem. The only difference between this case and the last, is that in this one there need be no original sub-excitement in Z, co-operating from the very first. When we seek a forgotten name, we must suppose the name's centre to be in a state of active tension from the very outset, because of that peculiar feeling of *recognition* which we get at the moment of recall. The plenitude of the thought seems here but a maximum degree of something which our mind divined in advance. It instantaneously fills a socket completely moulded to its shape; and it seems most natural to ascribe the identity of quality in our feeling of the gaping socket and our feeling of what comes to fill it, to the sameness of a nerve-tract excited in different degrees. In the solving of a problem, on the contrary, the recognition that we have found the means is much less immediate. Here, what we are aware of in advance seems to be its relations with the items we already know. It must bear a causal relation, or it must be an effect, or it must contain an attribute common to two items, or it must be a uniform concomitant, or what not. We know, in short, a lot *about* it, whilst as yet we have no knowledge of *acquaintance* with it (see p. 216), or in Mr. Hodgson's language, "we know what we want to find beforehand, in a certain sense, in its second intention, and do not know it in another sense, in its first intention."[23] Our intuition that one of the ideas which turn up is, at last, our *quæsitum,* is due to our recognition that its relations are identical with those we had in mind, and this may be a rather slow act of judgment. In fact,

---

Remembrance, or Calling to mind . . . . Sometimes a man knows a place determinate, within the compasse whereof he is to seek; and then his thoughts run over all the parts thereof, in the same manner, as one would sweep a room, to find a jewell; or as a Spaniel ranges the field, till he find a sent; or as a man should run over the Alphabet, to start a rime." (*Leviathan,* 1651, p. 10.)

[23] *Theory of Practice,* vol. I, p. 394.

everyone knows that an object may be for some time present to his mind before its relations to other matters are perceived. To quote Hodgson again:

"The mode of operation is common to voluntary memory and reasoning; . . . but reasoning adds to memory the function of comparing or judging the images which arise . . . . Memory aims at filling the gap with an image which has at some particular time filled it before, reasoning with one which bears certain time and space relations to the images before and after"—

or, to use perhaps clearer language, one which stands in determinate logical relations to those data round about the gap which filled our mind at the start. This feeling of the blank form of relationship before we get the material quality of the thing related will surprise no one who has read Chapter IX.

From the guessing of newspaper enigmas to the plotting of the policy of an empire there is no other process than this. We trust to the laws of cerebral nature to present us spontaneously with the appropriate idea:

"Our only command over it is by the effort we make to keep the painful unfilled gap in consciousness[24]. . . . Two circumstances are important to notice; the first is, that volition has no power of calling up images, but only of rejecting and selecting from those offered by spontaneous redintegration.[25] But the rapidity with which this selection is made, owing to the familiarity of the ways in which spontaneous redintegration runs, gives the process of reasoning the appearance of evoking images that are foreseen to be conformable to the purpose. There is no seeing them before they are offered; there is no summoning them before they are seen. The other circumstance is, that every kind of reasoning is nothing, in its simplest form, but attention."[26]

It is foreign to our purpose here to enter into any detailed analysis of the different classes of mental pursuit. In a scientific

24 *Ibid.*, p. 394.

25 All association is called redintegration by Hodgson.

26 *Ibid.*, p. 400. Compare Bain: *Emotions and the Will*, p. 376. "The outgoings of the mind are necessarily random; the end alone is the thing that is clear to the view, and with that there is a perception of the fitness of every passing suggestion. The volitional energy keeps up the attention, or the active search; and, the moment that anything in point rises before the mind, it springs upon that like a wild beast on its prey."

research we get perhaps as rich an example as can be found. The inquirer starts with a fact of which he seeks the reason, or with an hypothesis of which he seeks the proof. In either case he keeps turning the matter incessantly in his mind until, by the arousal of associate upon associate, some habitual, some similar, one arises which he recognizes to suit his need. This, however, may take years. No rules can be given by which the investigator may proceed straight to his result; but both here and in the case of reminiscence the accumulation of helps in the way of associations may advance more rapidly by the use of certain routine methods. In striving to recall a thought, for example, we may of set purpose run through the successive classes of circumstance with which it may possibly have been connected, trusting that when the right member of the class has turned up it will help the thought's revival. Thus we may run through all the *places* in which we may have had it. We may run through the *persons* whom we remember to have conversed with, or we may call up successively all the *books* we have lately been reading. If we are trying to remember a person we may run through a list of streets or of professions. Some item out of the lists thus methodically gone over will very likely be associated with the fact we are in need of, and may suggest it or help to do so. And yet the item might never have arisen without such systematic procedure. In scientific research this accumulation of associates has been methodized by Mill under the title of "The Four Methods of Experimental Inquiry." By the 'method of agreement,' by that of 'difference,' by those of 'residues' and 'concomitant variations' (which cannot here be more nearly defined), we make certain lists of cases; and by ruminating these lists in our minds the cause we seek will be more likely to emerge. But the final stroke of discovery is only prepared, not effected, by them. The brain-tracts must, of their own accord, shoot the right way at last, or we shall still grope in darkness. That in some brains the tracts *do* shoot the right way much oftener than in others, and that we cannot tell why,—these are ultimate facts to which we must never close our eyes. Even in forming our lists of instances according to Mill's methods, we are at the mercy of the spontaneous workings of Similarity in our brain. How are a number of facts, resembling the one whose cause we seek, to be brought together in a list unless the one will rapidly suggest the other through association by similarity?

SIMILARITY NO ELEMENTARY LAW

Such is the analysis I propose, first of the three main types of spontaneous association, and then of voluntary association. It will be observed that the *object called up may bear any logical relation whatever to the one which suggested it.* The law requires only that one condition should be fulfilled. The fading object must be due to a brain-process some of whose elements awaken through habit some of the elements of the brain-process of the object which comes to view. This awakening is the operative machinery, the causal agency, throughout, quite as much so in the kind of association I have called by the name of Similarity, as in any other sort. The similarity between the objects, or between the thoughts (if similarity there be between these latter), has no causal agency in carrying us from one to the other. It is but a result—the effect of the usual causal agent when this happens to work in a certain particular and assignable way. But ordinary writers talk as if the similarity of the objects were itself an agent, co-ordinate with habit, and independent of it, and like it able to push objects before the mind. This is quite unintelligible. The similarity of two things does not exist till both things are there—it is meaningless to talk of it as an *agent of production* of anything, whether in the physical or the psychical realms.[27] It is a relation which the mind perceives after the fact, just as it may perceive the relations of superiority, of distance, of causality, of container and content, of substance and accident, or of contrast, between an object and some second object which the associative machinery calls up.[28]

There are, nevertheless, able writers who not only insist on preserving association by similarity as a distinct elementary law, but

[27] Compare what is said of the principle of Similarity by F. H. Bradley: *Principles of Logic*, pp. 294 ff.; E. Rabier: *Psychologie*, 187 ff.; Paulhan: *Critique Philosophique*, 2me Série, I, 458; Rabier: *ibid.*, 460; Pillon: *ibid.*, II, 55; B. P. Bowne: *Introduction to Psychological Theory*, 92; Ward: *Encyclopædia Britannica* article "Psychology," p. 60; Wahle: *Vierteljahrsschrift für wissenschaftliche Philosophie*, IX, 426–431.

[28] Dr. McCosh is accordingly only logical when he sinks similarity in what he calls the "*Law of Correlation*, according to which, when we have discovered *a relation between things*, the idea of one tends to bring up the others" (*Psychology: The Cognitive Powers*, p. 130). The relations mentioned by this author are Identity, Whole and Parts, Resemblance, Space, Time, Quantity, Active Property, and Cause and Effect. If perceived relations among objects are to be treated as grounds for their appearance before the mind, similarity has of course no right to an exclusive, or even to a predominant, place.

who make it the most elementary law, and seek to derive contiguous association from it. Their reasoning is as follows: When the present impression A awakens the idea *b* of its past contiguous associate B, how can this occur except through first reviving an image *a* of its own past occurrence. *This* is the term directly connected with *b*; so that the process instead of being simply A—*b* is A—*a*—*b*. Now A and *a* are similars; therefore no association by contiguity can occur except through a previous association by similarity. The most important supposition here made is that every impression on entering the mind must needs awaken an image of its past self, in the light of which it is 'apperceived' or understood, and through the intermediation of which it enters into relation with the mind's other objects. This assumption is almost universally made; and yet it is hard to find any good reason for it. It first came before us when we were reviewing the facts of aphasia and mental blindness (see p. 59 ff.). But we then saw no need of optical and auditory images to interpret optical and auditory sensations by. On the contrary, we agreed that auditory sensations were understood by us only so far as they awakened *non*-auditory images, and optical sensations only so far as they awakened *non*-optical images. In the chapters on Memory, on Reasoning, and on Perception the same assumption will meet us again, and again will have to be rejected as groundless. The sensational process A and the ideational process *a* probably occupy essentially the same tracts. When the outer stimulus comes and those tracts vibrate with the sensation A, they discharge as directly into the paths which lead to B as when there is no outer stimulus and they only vibrate with the idea *a*. To say that the process A can only reach these paths by the help of the weaker process *a* is like saying that we need a candle to see the sun by. A replaces *a*, does all that *a* does and more; and there is no intelligible meaning, to my mind, in saying that the weaker process coexists with the stronger. I therefore consider that these writers are altogether wrong. The only plausible proof they give of the coexistence of *a* with A is when A gives us a *sense of familiarity* but fails to awaken any distinct thought of past contiguous associates. In a later chapter I shall consider this case. Here I content myself with saying that it does not seem conclusive as to the point at issue; and that I still believe association of coexistent or sequent impressions to be the one *elementary* law.

CONTRAST *has also been held to be an independent agent in association*. But the reproduction of an object contrasting with one already in the mind is easily explained on our principles. Recent writers, in fact, all reduce it either to similarity or contiguity. Contrast always presupposes generic similarity; it is only the *extremes of a class* which are contrasted, black and white, not black and sour, or white and prickly. A machinery which reproduces a similar at all, may reproduce the *opposite* similar, as well as any intermediate term. Moreover, the greater number of contrasts are habitually coupled in speech, young and old, life and death, rich and poor, etc., and are, as Dr. Bain says, in everybody's memory.[29]

I trust that the student will now feel that the way to a deeper understanding of the order of our ideas lies in the direction of cerebral physiology. The *elementary* process of revival can be nothing but the law of habit. Truly the day is distant when physiologists shall actually trace from cell-group to cell-group the irradiations which we have hypothetically invoked. Probably it will never arrive. The schematism we have used is, moreover, taken immediately from the analysis of objects into their elementary parts, and only extended by analogy to the brain. And yet it is only as incorporated in the brain that such a schematism can represent anything *causal*. This is, to my mind, the conclusive reason for saying that the order of *presentation of the mind's materials* is due to cerebral physiology alone.

The law of accidental prepotency of certain processes over others falls also within the sphere of cerebral probabilities. Granting such instability as the brain-tissue requires, certain points must always discharge more quickly and strongly than others; and this prepotency would shift its place from moment to moment by accidental causes, giving us a perfect mechanical diagram of the capricious play of similar association in the most gifted mind. The study of dreams confirms this view. The usual abundance of paths of irradiation seems, in the dormant brain, reduced. A few only are pervious, and the most fantastic sequences occur because the currents run—'like sparks in burnt-up paper'—wherever the nutrition of the moment creates an opening, but nowhere else.

29 Cf. Bain: *Senses and the Intellect*, 564 ff.; J. S. Mill: Note 39 to J. Mill's *Analysis*; Lipps: *Grundtatsachen*, 97.

The *effects of interested attention and volition* remain. These activities seem to hold fast to certain elements and, by emphasizing them and dwelling on them, to make their associates the only ones which are evoked. *This* is the point at which an anti-mechanical psychology must, if anywhere, make its stand in dealing with association. Everything else is pretty certainly due to cerebral laws. My own opinion on the question of active attention and spiritual spontaneity is expressed elsewhere. But even though there be a mental spontaneity, it can certainly not create ideas or summon them *ex abrupto*. Its power is limited to *selecting* amongst those which the associative machinery has already introduced or tends to introduce. If it can emphasize, reinforce, or protract for a second either one of these, it can do all that the most eager advocate of free-will need demand; for it then decides the direction of the next associations by making them hinge upon the emphasized term; and determining in this wise the course of the man's thinking, it also determines his acts.

THE HISTORY OF OPINION CONCERNING ASSOCIATION

may be briefly glanced at ere we end the chapter.[30] Aristotle seems to have caught both the facts and the principle of explanation; but he did not expand his views, and it was not till the time of Hobbes that the matter was again touched on in a definite way. Hobbes first formulated the problem of the succession of our thoughts. He writes in *Leviathan*, chapter III, as follows:

"By *Consequence*, or TRAYNE of Thoughts, I understand that succession of one Thought to another, which is called (to distinguish it from Discourse in words) *Mentall Discourse*. When a man thinketh on any thing whatsoever, His next Thought after, is not altogether so casuall as it seems to be. Not every Thought to every Thought succeeds indifferently. But as wee have no Imagination, whereof we have not formerly had Sense, in whole, or in parts; so we have no Transition from one Imagination to another, whereof we never had the like before in our Senses. The reason whereof is this. All Fancies are Motions within us, reliques of those made in the Sense: And those motions that

30 See, for farther details, Hamilton's *Reid*, Appendices D** and D***; and L. Ferri: *La Psychologie de l'association* (Paris, 1883). Also Robertson: article "Association of Ideas" in *Encyclopædia Britannica*.

immediately succeeded one another in the sense, continue also together after Sense: In so much as the former comming again to take place, and be prædominant, the later followeth, by coherence of the matter moved, in such manner, as water upon a plain Table is drawn which way any one part of it is guided by the finger. But because in sense, to one and the same thing perceived, sometimes one thing, sometimes another succeedeth, it comes to passe in time, that in the Imagining of any thing, there is no certainty what we shall Imagine next; Onely this is certain, it shall be something that succeeded the same before, at one time or another. This Trayne of Thoughts, or Mentall Discourse, is of two sorts. The first is *Unguided, without Designe,* and inconstant; Wherein there is no Passionate Thought, to govern and direct those that follow, to it self, as the end and scope of some desire, or other passion . . . . The second is more constant; as being *regulated* by some desire, and designe. For the impression made by such things as wee desire, or feare, is strong, and permanent, or, (if it cease for a time,) of quick return: so strong it is sometimes, as to hinder and break our sleep. From Desire, ariseth the Thought of some means we have seen produce the like of that which we ayme at; and from the thought of that, the thought of means to that mean; and so continually, till we come to some beginning within our own power. And because the End, by the greatnesse of the impression, comes often to mind, in case our thoughts begin to wander, they are quickly again reduced into the way: which observed by one of the seven wise men, made him give men this præcept, which is now worne out, *Respice finem*; that is to say, in all your actions, look often upon what you would have, as the thing that directs all your thoughts in the way to attain it.

"The Trayne of regulated Thoughts is of two kinds; One, when of an effect imagined, wee seek the causes, or means that produce it: and this is common to Man and Beast. The other is, when imagining any thing whatsoever, wee seek all the possible effects, that can by it be produced; that is to say, we imagine what we can do with it, when wee have it. Of which I have not at any time seen any signe, but in man onely; for this is a curiosity hardly incident to the nature of any living creature that has no other Passion but sensuall, such as are hunger, thirst, lust, and anger. In summe, the Discourse of the Mind, when it is governed by designe, is nothing but *Seeking*, or the faculty of Invention, which the Latines call *Sagacitas*, and *Solertia*; a hunting out of the causes, of some effect, present or past; or of the effects, of some present or past cause."

The most important passage after this of Hobbes is Hume's:

"As all simple ideas may be separated by the imagination, and may be united again in what form it pleases, nothing wou'd be more unaccountable than the operations of that faculty, were it not guided by some universal principles, which render it, in some measure, uniform with itself in all times and places. Were ideas entirely loose and unconnected, chance alone wou'd join them; and 'tis impossible the same simple ideas should fall regularly into complex ones (as they commonly do) without some bond of union among them, some associating quality, by which one idea naturally introduces another. This uniting principle among ideas is not to be consider'd as an inseparable connexion; for that has been already excluded from the imagination: Nor yet are we to conclude, that without it the mind cannot join two ideas; for nothing is more free than that faculty: but we are only to regard it as a gentle force, which commonly prevails, and is the cause why, among other things, languages so nearly correspond to each other; nature in a manner pointing out to every one those simple ideas, which are most proper to be united in a complex one. The qualities, from which this association arises, and by which the mind is after this manner convey'd from one idea to another, are three, *viz.* RESEMBLANCE, CONTIGUITY in time or place, and CAUSE and EFFECT.

"I believe it will not be very necessary to prove, that these qualities produce an association among ideas, and upon the appearance of one idea naturally introduce another. 'Tis plain, that in the course of our thinking, and in the constant revolution of our ideas, our imagination runs easily from one idea to any other that *resembles* it, and that this quality alone is to the fancy a sufficient bond and association. 'Tis likewise evident, that as the senses, in changing their objects, are necessitated to change them regularly, and take them as they lie *contiguous* to each other, the imagination must by long custom acquire the same method of thinking, and run along the parts of space and time in conceiving its objects. As to the connexion, that is made by the relation of *cause and effect*, we shall have occasion afterwards to examine it to the bottom, and therefore shall not at present insist upon it. 'Tis sufficient to observe, that there is no relation, which produces a stronger connexion in the fancy, and makes one idea more readily recall another, than the relation of cause and effect betwixt their objects. . . . These are therefore the principles of union or cohesion among our simple ideas, and in the imagination supply the place of that inseparable connexion, by which they are united in our memory. Here is a kind of ATTRACTION, which in the mental world will be found to have as extraordinary effects as in the natural, and to shew itself in as many and as various forms. Its effects are every where conspicuous;

but as to its causes, they are mostly unknown, and must be resolv'd into *original* qualities of human nature, which I pretend not to explain."[31]

Hume did not, however, any more than Hobbes, follow out the effects of which he speaks, and the task of popularizing the notion of association and making an effective school based on association of ideas alone was reserved for Hartley[32] and James Mill.[33] These authors traced minutely the presence of association in all the cardinal notions and operations of the mind. The several 'faculties' of the Mind were dispossessed; the one principle of association between ideas did all their work. As Priestley says:

"Nothing is requisite to make any man whatever he is, but a sentient principle, with this single law . . . . Not only all our intellectual pleasures and pains, but all the phænomena of memory, imagination, volition, reasoning, and every other mental affection and operation, are only different modes, or cases, of the association of ideas."[34]

An eminent French psychologist, M. Ribot, repeats Hume's comparison of the law of association with that of gravitation, and goes on to say:

"It is remarkable that this discovery was made so late. Nothing is simpler, apparently, than to notice that this law of association is the truly fundamental, irreducible phenomenon of our mental life; that it is at the bottom of all our acts; that it permits of no exception; that neither dream, revery, mystic ecstasy, nor the most abstract reasoning can exist without it; that its suppression would be equivalent to that of thought itself. Nevertheless no ancient author understood it, for one cannot seriously maintain that a few scattered lines in Aristotle and the Stoics constitute a theory and clear view of the subject. It is to Hobbes, Hume, and Hartley that we must attribute the origin of these studies on the connection of our ideas. The discovery of the ultimate law of our psychologic acts has this, then, in common with many other discoveries: it came late and seems so simple that it may justly astonish us.

"Perhaps it is not superfluous to ask in what this manner of ex-

31 *Treatise of Human Nature,* part I, § IV.

32 *Observations on Man* (London, 1749).

33 *Analysis of the Phenomena of the Human Mind* (1829).

34 *Hartley's Theory of the Human Mind,* 2d ed. (1790), p. XXVII.

planation is superior to the current theory of Faculties.[35] The most extended usage consists, as we know, in dividing intellectual phenomena into classes, in separating those which differ, in grouping together those of the same nature and in giving to these a common name and in attributing them to the same cause; it is thus that we have come to distinguish those diverse aspects of intelligence which are called judgment, reasoning, abstraction, perception, etc. This method is precisely the one followed in Physics, where the words caloric, electricity, gravity, designate the unknown causes of certain groups of phenomena. If one thus never forgets that the diverse faculties are only the unknown causes of known phenomena, that they are simply a convenient means of classifying the facts and speaking of them, if one does not fall into the common fault of making out of them substantial entities, creations which now agree, now disagree, so forming in the intelligence a little republic; then, we can see nothing reprehensible in this distribution into faculties, conformable as it is to the rules of a sound method and of a good natural classification. In what then is Mr. Bain's procedure superior to the method of the faculties? It is that the latter is simply a *classification* while his is an *explanation*. Between the psychology which traces intellectual facts back to certain faculties, and that which reduces them to the single law of association, there is, according to our way of thinking, the same difference that we find in Physics between those who attribute its phenomena to five or six causes, and those who derive gravity, caloric, light, etc., from motion. The system of the faculties explains nothing because each one of them is only a *flatus vocis* which is of value merely through the phenomena which it contains, and signifies nothing more than these phenomena. The new theory, on the contrary, shows that the different processes of intelligence are only diverse cases of a single law; that imagination, deduction, induction, perception, etc., are but so many determinate ways in which ideas may combine with each other; and that the differences of faculties are only differences of association. It *explains* all intellectual facts, certainly not after the manner of Metaphysics which demands the ultimate and absolute reason of things; but after the manner of Physics which seeks only their secondary and immediate cause."[36]

The inexperienced reader may be glad of a brief indication of the manner in which all the different mental operations may be conceived to consist of images of sensation associated together.

Memory is the association of a present image with others known to belong to the past. *Expectation* the same, with future substituted

35 [Current, that is, in France.—W. J.]

36 *La Psychologie anglaise contemporaine,* p. 242.

for past. *Fancy*, the association of images without temporal order.

Belief in anything *not* present to sense is the very lively, strong, and steadfast association of the image of that thing with some present sensation, so that as long as the sensation persists the image cannot be excluded from the mind.

Judgment is "transferring the idea of *truth*, by association, from one proposition to another that resembles it."[37]

Reasoning is the perception that "whatever has any mark has that which it is a mark of"; in the concrete case the mark or middle term being always *associated* with each of the other terms and so serving as a link by which they are themselves indirectly associated together. This same kind of transfer of a sensible experience associated with another to a third also associated with that other, serves to explain emotional facts. When we are pleased or hurt we express it, and the expression associates itself with the feeling. Hearing the same expression from another revives the associated feeling, and we *sympathize*, i.e., grieve or are glad with him.

The other social affections, *Benevolence*, *Conscientiousness*, *Ambition*, etc., arise in like manner by the transfer of the bodily pleasure experienced as a reward for social service, and hence associated with it, to the act of service itself, the link of reward being dropped out. Just so *Avarice* when the miser transfers the bodily pleasures associated with the spending of money to the money itself, dropping the link of spending.

Fear is a transfer of the bodily hurt associated by experience with the thing feared, to the thought of the thing, with the precise features of the hurt left out. Thus we fear a dog without distinctly imagining his bite.

Love is the association of the agreeableness of certain sensible experiences with the idea of the object capable of affording them. The experiences themselves may cease to be distinctly imagined after the notion of their pleasure has been transferred to the object, constituting our love therefor.

Volition is the association of ideas of muscular motion with the ideas of those pleasures which the motion produces. The motion at first occurs automatically and results in a pleasure unforeseen. The latter becomes so associated with the motion that whenever we think of it the idea of the motion arises; and the idea of the

[37] Priestley: *op. cit.*, p. xxx.

motion when vivid causes the motion to occur. This is an act of will.

Nothing is easier than for a philosopher of this school to explain from experience such a notion as that of infinitude.

"He sees in it an ordinary manifestation of one of the laws of the association of ideas,—the law, that the idea of a thing irresistibly suggests the idea of any other thing which has been often experienced in close conjunction with it, and not otherwise. As we have never had experience of any point of space without other points beyond it, nor of any point of time without others following it, the law of indissoluble association makes it impossible for us to think of any point of space or time, however distant, without having the idea irresistibly realised in imagination, of other points still more remote. And thus the supposed original and inherent property of these two ideas is completely explained and accounted for by the law of association; and we are enabled to see, that if Space or Time were really susceptible of termination, we should be just as unable as we now are to conceive the idea."[38]

These examples of the Associationist Psychology are with the exception of the last, very crudely expressed, but they suffice for our temporary need. Hartley and James Mill[39] improved upon Hume so far as to employ but a single principle of association, that of contiguity or habit. Hartley ignores resemblance, James Mill expressly repudiates it in a passage which is assuredly one of the curiosities of literature:

"I believe it will be found that we are accustomed to see like things together. When we see a tree, we generally see more trees than one; . . . a sheep, more sheep than one; a man, more men than one. From this observation, I think, we may refer resemblance to the law of frequency [i.e., contiguity], of which it seems to form only a particular case."

Mr. Herbert Spencer has still more recently tried to construct a Psychology which ignores Association by Similarity,[40] and in a

38 Review of Bain's *Psychology*, by J. S. Mill, in *Edinburgh Review*, Oct. 1859, p. 293.

39 *Analysis of the Phenomena of the Human Mind*, J. S. Mill's edition, vol. I, p. 111.

40 "The Associability of Relations between Feelings," in *Principles of Psychology*, vol. I, p. 259. It is impossible to regard the "cohering of each feeling with previously-experienced feelings of the same class, order, genus, species, and, so far as may be, the same variety," which Spencer calls (p. 257) "the sole process of association of feelings," as any equivalent for what is commonly known as Association by similarity.

chapter, which also is a curiosity, he tries to explain the association of two ideas by a conscious reference of the first to the point of time when its sensation was experienced, which point of time is no sooner thought of than its content, namely, the second idea, arises. Messrs. Bain and Mill, however, and the immense majority of contemporary psychologists retain both Resemblance and Contiguity as irreducible principles of Association.

Professor Bain's exposition of association is by common consent looked upon as the best expression of the English school. Perception of agreement and difference, retentiveness, and the two sorts of association, contiguity and similarity, are by him regarded as constituting all that is meant by intellect proper. His pages are painstaking and instructive from a descriptive point of view; though, after my own attempt to deal with the subject causally, I can hardly award to them any profound *explanatory* value. Association by Similarity, too much neglected by the British school before Bain, receives from him the most generous exemplification. As an instructive passage, the following, out of many equally good, may be chosen to quote:

"We may have similarity in form with diversity of use, and similarity of use with diversity of form. A rope suggests other ropes and cords, if we look to the appearance; but looking to the *use*, it may suggest an iron cable, a wooden prop, an iron girding, a leather band, or bevelled gear. In spite of diversity of appearance, the suggestion turns on what answers a common end. If we are very much attracted by sensible appearances, there will be the more difficulty in recalling things that agree only in the use; if, on the other hand, we are profoundly sensitive to the one point of practical efficiency as a tool, the peculiarities not essential to this will be little noticed, and we shall be ever ready to revive past objects corresponding in use to some one present, although diverse in all other circumstances. We become oblivious to the difference between a horse, a steam-engine, and a waterfall, when our minds are engrossed with the one circumstance of moving power. The diversity in these had no doubt for a long time the effect of keeping back their first identification; and to obtuse intellects, this identification might have been for ever impossible. A strong concentration of mind upon the single peculiarity of mechanical force, and a degree of indifference to the general aspect of the things themselves, must conspire with the intellectual energy of resuscitation by similars, in order to summon together in the view three structures so different. We can see, by an instance like this, how new adaptations of existing machinery might arise in the mind of a mechanical inventor. When it first occurred to a reflecting mind that moving water had a property identical with human or brute force, namely, the property of setting other masses in motion, overcoming inertia and resistance,—when the sight of the stream suggested through this point of likeness the power of the animal,—a new addition was made to the class of prime movers, and when circumstances permitted, this power could become a substitute for the others. It may seem to the modern understanding, familiar with water wheels and drifting rafts, that the similarity here was an extremely obvious one. But if we put ourselves back into an early state of mind, when running water affected the mind by its brilliancy, its roar, and irregular devastation, we may easily suppose that to identify this with animal muscular energy was by no means an obvious effect. Doubtless when a mind arose, insensible by natural constitution to the superficial aspects of things, and having withal a great stretch of identifying intellect, such a comparison would then be possible. We may pursue the same example one stage further, and come to the discovery of steam power, or the identification of expanding vapour with the previously known sources of mechanical force. To the common eye, for ages, vapour presented itself as clouds in the sky; or as a hissing noise at the spout of a kettle, with the formation of a foggy curling cloud at a few inches' distance. The forcing up of the lid of a kettle may also have been occasionally observed. But how long was it, ere any one was struck with the parallelism of this appearance with a blast of wind, a rush of water, or an exertion of animal muscle? The discordance was too great to be broken through by such a faint and limited amount of likeness. In one mind, however, the identification did take place, and was followed out into its consequences. The likeness had occurred to other minds previously, but not with the same results. Such minds must have been in some way or other distinguished above the millions of mankind; and we are now endeavouring to give the explanation of their superiority. The intellectual character of Watt contained all the elements preparatory to a great stroke of similarity in such a case;—a high susceptibility, both by nature and by education, to the mechanical properties of bodies; ample previous knowledge or familiarity; and indifference to the superficial and sensational effects of things. It is not only possible, however, but exceedingly probable, that many men possessed all these accomplishments; they are of a kind not transcending common abilities. They would in some degree attach to a mechanical education almost as a matter of course. That the discovery was not sooner made, supposes that something farther, and not of common occurrence, was necessary; and this additional endowment appears to be the identifying power of Similarity in general; the tendency to detect likeness in the midst of disparity and disguise. This supposition accounts for the fact; and is consistent with the known intellectual character of the inventor of the steam-engine."[41]

Dr. Hodgson's account of association is by all odds the best yet propounded in English.[42] All these writers hold more or less explicitly to the notion of atomistic 'ideas' which recur. In Germany, the same mythological supposition has been more radically grasped, and carried out to a still more logical, if more repulsive, extreme, by Herbart[43] and his followers, who until recently may be said to have reigned almost supreme in their native country.[44] For Herbart each idea is a permanently existing entity, the entrance whereof into consciousness is but an accidental determination of its being. So far as it succeeds in occupying the theatre of consciousness, it crowds out another idea previously there. This act of inhibition gives it, however, a sort of hold on the other representation which on all later occasions facilitates its following the other into the mind. The ingenuity with which most special cases of association are formulated in this mechanical language of struggle and inhibition, is great, and surpasses in analytic thoroughness anything that has been done by the British school. This, however, is a doubtful merit, in a case where the elements dealt with are artificial; and I must confess that to my mind there is something almost hideous in the glib Herbartian jargon about *Vorstellungsmassen* and their *Hemmungen* and *Hemmungssummen*, and *sinken* and *erheben* and *schweben*, and *Verschmelzungen* and *Complexionen*. Herr Lipps, the most recent systematic German Psychologist, has, I regret to say, carried out the theory of ideas in a way which the great originality, learning, and acuteness he shows make only the more regrettable.[45] Such elaborately artificial constructions are, it seems to me, only a burden and a hindrance, not a help, to our science.[46]

41 *The Senses and the Intellect*, pp. 491–3.

42 See his *Time and Space*, chapter v, and his *Theory of Practice*, §§ 53 to 57.

43 *Psychologie als Wissenschaft* (1824), I, part 2.

44 Prof. Ribot, in chapter I of his *German Psychology of To-day*, has given a good account of Herbart and his school, and of Beneke, his rival and partial analogue. See also two articles on the Herbartian Psychology, by G. F. Stout, in *Mind* for 1888. J. D. Morell's *An Introduction to Mental Philosophy* (London, 1862) largely follows Herbart and Beneke. I know of no other English book which does so.

45 See his *Grundtatsachen des Seelenlebens* (1883), chap. VI *et passim*, especially pp. 106 ff., 364.

46 The most burdensome and utterly gratuitous of them are perhaps Steinthal's, in his *Einleitung in die Psychologie und Sprachwissenschaft*, 2te Aufl. (1881). Cf. also G. Glogau: *Steinthals psychologische Formeln zusammenhängend entwickelt* (1876).

In French, M. Rabier in his chapter on Association,[47] handles the subject more vigorously and acutely than anyone. His treatment of it, though short, seems to me for general soundness to rank second only to Hodgson's.

In the last chapter we already invoked association to account for the effects of use in improving discrimination. In later chapters we shall see abundant proof of the immense part which it plays in other processes, and shall then readily admit that few principles of analysis, in any science, have proved more fertile than this one, however vaguely formulated it often may have been. Our own attempt to formulate it more definitely, and to escape the usual confusion between causal agencies and relations merely known, must not blind us to the immense services of those by whom the confusion was unfelt. From this practical point of view it would be a true *ignoratio elenchi* to flatter one's self that one has dealt a heavy blow at the psychology of association, when one has exploded the theory of atomistic ideas, or shown that contiguity and similarity between ideas can only be there after association is done.[48] The whole body of the associationist psychology remains standing after you have translated 'ideas' into 'objects,' on the one hand, and 'brain-processes' on the other; and the analysis of faculties and operations is as conclusive in these terms as in those traditionally used.

[47] *Leçons de philosophie*, I, *Psychologie*, chap. XVI (1884).

[48] Mr. F. H. Bradley seems to me to have been guilty of something very like this *ignoratio elenchi* in the, of course, subtle and witty but decidedly long-winded critique of the association of ideas, contained in book II, part II, chap. I, of his *Principles of Logic*.

*Chapter XV**

The Perception of Time

In the next two chapters I shall deal with what is sometimes called internal perception, or the perception of *time*, and of events as occupying a date therein, especially when the date is a past one, in which case the perception in question goes by the name of *memory*. To remember a thing as past, it is necessary that the notion of 'past' should be one of our 'ideas.' We shall see in the chapter on Memory that many things come to be thought by us as past, not because of any intrinsic quality of their own, but rather because they are associated with other things which for us signify pastness. But how do these things get *their* pastness? What is the *original* of our experience of pastness, from whence we get the meaning of the term? It is this question which the reader is invited to consider in the present chapter. We shall see that we have a constant feeling *sui generis* of pastness, to which every one of our experiences in turn falls a prey. To think a thing as past is to think it amongst the objects or in the direction of the objects which at the present moment appear affected by this quality. This is the original of our notion of past time, upon which memory and history build their systems. And in this chapter we shall consider this immediate sense of time alone.

If the constitution of consciousness were that of a string of bead-like sensations and images, all separate,

* This chapter is reprinted almost verbatim from the *Journal of Speculative Philosophy*, vol. xx, p. 374.

"we never could have any knowledge, excepting that of the present instant. The moment each of our sensations ceased, it would be gone for ever; and we should be as if we had never been. . . . We should be wholly incapable of acquiring experience . . . . Even if our ideas were associated in trains, but only as they are in Imagination, we should still be without the capacity of acquiring knowledge. One idea, upon this supposition, would follow another. But that would be all. Each of our successive states of consciousness, the moment it ceased, would be gone for ever. Each of those momentary states would be our whole being."[1]

We might, nevertheless, under these circumstances, *act* in a rational way, provided the mechanism which produced our trains of images produced them in a rational order. We should make appropriate speeches, though unaware of any word except the one just on our lips; we should decide upon the right policy without ever a glimpse of the total grounds of our choice. Our consciousness would be like a glow-worm spark, illuminating the point it immediately covered, but leaving all beyond in total darkness. Whether a very highly developed practical life be possible under such conditions as these is more than doubtful; it is, however, conceivable.

I make the fanciful hypothesis merely to set off our real nature by the contrast. Our feelings are not thus contracted, and our consciousness never shrinks to the dimensions of a glow-worm spark. *The knowledge of some other part of the stream, past or future, near or remote, is always mixed in with our knowledge of the present thing.*

A simple sensation, as we shall hereafter see, is an abstraction, and all our concrete states of mind are representations of objects with some amount of complexity. Part of the complexity is the echo of the objects just past, and, in a less degree, perhaps, the foretaste of those just to arrive. Objects fade out of consciousness slowly. If the present thought is of A B C D E F G, the next one will be of B C D E F G H, and the one after that of C D E F G H I—the lingerings of the past dropping successively away, and the incomings of the future making up the loss. These lingerings of old objects, these incomings of new, are the germs of memory and expectation, the retrospective and the prospective sense of time. They give that con-

[1] James Mill: *Analysis*, vol. I, p. 319 (J. S. Mill's Edition).

tinuity to consciousness without which it could not be called a stream.[2]

[2] "What I find, when I look at consciousness at all, is, that what I cannot divest myself of, or not have in consciousness, if I have consciousness at all, is a sequence of different feelings. . . . The simultaneous perception of both sub-feelings, whether as parts of a coexistence or of a sequence, is the total feeling, the minimum of consciousness, and this minimum has duration. . . . Time-duration, however, is inseparable from the minimum, notwithstanding that, in an isolated moment, we could not tell which part of it came first, which last. . . . We do not require to know that the sub-feelings come in sequence, first one, then the other; nor to know what coming in sequence means. But we have, in any artificially isolated minimum of consciousness, the *rudiments* of the perception of former and latter in time, in the sub-feeling that grows fainter, and the sub-feeling that grows stronger, and the change between them. . . .

"In the next place I remark that the rudiments of memory are involved in the minimum of consciousness. The first beginnings of it appear in that minimum, just as the first beginnings of perception do. As each member of the change or difference, which goes to compose that minimum, is the rudiment of a single perception, so the priority of one member to the other, although both are given to consciousness in one empirical present moment, is the rudiment of memory. The fact, that the minimum of consciousness is difference or change in feelings, is the ultimate explanation of memory as well as of single perceptions. A former and a latter are included in the minimum of consciousness; and this is what is meant by saying that all consciousness is in the form of *time*, or that time is the form of feeling, the form of sensibility. Crudely and popularly we divide the course of time into Past, Present, and Future; but, strictly speaking, there is no Present; it is composed of Past and Future divided by an indivisible point or instant. That instant, or time-point, is the strict *present*. What we call loosely the Present is an empirical portion of the course of time, containing at least the minimum of consciousness, in which the instant of change is the present time-point. . . . If we take this as the present time-point, it is clear that the minimum of feeling contains two portions, a sub-feeling that goes and a sub-feeling that comes. One is remembered, the other imagined. The limits of both are indefinite at beginning and end of the minimum, and ready to melt into other minima, proceeding from other stimuli.

"Time and consciousness do not come to us ready marked out into minima; we have to do that by reflection, asking ourselves, What is the least empirical moment of consciousness? That least empirical moment is what we usually call the present moment; and even this is too minute for ordinary use; the present moment is often extended practically to a few seconds, or even minutes; beyond which, we specify what length of time we mean, as the present hour, or day, or year, or century.

"But this popular way of thinking imposes itself on great numbers even of philosophically minded people, and they talk about the *present* as if it was a *datum*, as if time came to us marked into present periods like a measuring-tape." (S. H. Hodgson: *Philosophy of Reflection*, vol. I, pp. 248–254.)

"The representation of time agrees with that of space in that a certain amount of it must be presented together—included between its initial and terminal limit. A continuous ideation, flowing from one point to another, would indeed *occupy* time, but not *represent* it, for it would exchange one element of succession for another instead of grasping the whole succession at once. Both points—the beginning and

THE SENSIBLE PRESENT HAS DURATION

Let anyone try, I will not say to arrest, but to notice or attend to, the *present* moment of time. One of the most baffling experiences occurs. Where is it, this present? It has melted in our grasp, fled ere we could touch it, gone in the instant of becoming. As a poet, quoted by Mr. Hodgson, says,

"Le moment où je parle est déjà loin de moi,"

and it is only as entering into the living and moving organization of a much wider tract of time that the strict present is apprehended at all. It is, in fact, an altogether ideal abstraction, not only never realized in sense, but probably never even conceived of by those unaccustomed to philosophic meditation. Reflection leads us to the conclusion that it *must* exist, but that it *does* exist can never be a fact of our immediate experience. The only fact of our immediate experience is what Mr. E. R. Clay has well called 'the *specious* present.' His words deserve to be quoted in full:[3]

"The relation of experience to time has not been profoundly studied. Its objects are given as being of the present, but the part of time referred to by the datum is a very different thing from the conterminus

---

the end—are equally essential to the conception of time, and must be present with equal clearness together." (Herbart: *Psychologie als Wissenschaft*, § 115.)

"Assume that . . . similar pendulum-strokes follow each other at regular intervals in a consciousness otherwise void. When the first one is over, an image of it remains in the fancy until the second succeeds. This, then, reproduces the first by virtue of the law of association by similarity, but at the same time meets with the aforesaid persisting image . . . . Thus does the simple repetition of the sound provide all the elements of time-perception. The first sound [as it is recalled by association] gives the beginning, the second the end, and the persistent image in the fancy represents the length of the interval. At the moment of the second impression, the entire time-perception exists at once, for then all its elements are presented together, the second sound and the image in the fancy immediately, and the first impression by reproduction. But, in the same act, we are aware of a state in which only the first sound existed, and of another in which only its image existed in the fancy. Such a consciousness as this *is* that of time. . . . *In it no succession of ideas takes place*." (Wundt: *Physiologische Psychologie*, 1st ed., pp. 681–2.) Note here the assumption that the *persistence* and the *reproduction* of an impression are two processes which may go on simultaneously. Also that Wundt's description is merely an *attempt to analyze the 'deliverance'* of a time-perception, and no *explanation of the manner in which it comes about*.

[3] *The Alternative*, p. 167.

of the past and future which philosophy denotes by the name Present. The present to which the datum refers is really a part of the past—a recent past—delusively given as being a time that intervenes between the past and the future. Let it be named the specious present, and let the past that is given as being the past be known as the obvious past. All the notes of a bar of a song seem to the listener to be contained in the present. All the changes of place of a meteor seem to the beholder to be contained in the present. At the instant of the termination of such series no part of the time measured by them seems to be a past. Time, then, considered relatively to human apprehension, consists of four parts, viz. the obvious past, the specious present, the real present, and the future. Omitting the specious present, it consists of three . . . nonentities, the past which does not exist, the future which does not exist, and their conterminus the present: the faculty from which it proceeds lies to us in the fiction of the specious present."

In short, the practically cognized present is no knife-edge, but a saddle-back, with a certain breadth of its own on which we sit perched, and from which we look in two directions into time. The unit of composition of our perception of time is a *duration*, with a bow and a stern, as it were—a rearward- and a forward-looking end.[4] It is only as parts of this *duration-block* that the relation of *succession* of one end to the other is perceived. We do not first feel one end and then feel the other after it, and from the perception of the succession infer an interval of time between, but we seem to feel the interval of time as a whole, with its two ends embedded in it. The experience is from the outset a synthetic datum, not a simple one; and to sensible perception its elements are inseparable,

[4] Locke, in his dim way, derived the sense of duration from reflection on the succession of our ideas (*Essay*, book II, chap. XIV, § 3; chap. XV, § 12). Reid justly remarks that if ten successive elements are to make duration, "then one must make duration, otherwise duration must be made up of parts that have no duration, which is impossible. . . . I conclude, therefore, that there must be duration in every single interval or element of which the whole duration is made up. Nothing indeed is more certain than that every elementary part of duration must have duration, as every elementary part of extension must have extension. Now, it must be observed, that in these elements of duration, or single intervals of successive ideas, there is no succession of ideas, yet we must conceive them to have duration; whence we may conclude with certainty, that *there is a conception of duration, where there is no succession of ideas in the mind*." (*Intellectual Powers*, essay III, chap. V.) "Qu'on ne cherche point," says Royer-Collard in the "Fragments" added to Jouffroy's Translation of Reid, "la durée dans la succession; on ne l'y trouvera jamais; la durée a précédé la succession; la notion de la durée a précédé la notion de la succession. Elle en est donc tout-à-fait indépendante, dira-t-on? Oui, elle en est tout-à-fait indépendante."

although attention looking back may easily decompose the experience, and distinguish its beginning from its end.

When we come to study the perception of Space, we shall find it quite analogous to time in this regard. Date in time corresponds to position in space; and although we now mentally construct large spaces by mentally imagining remoter and remoter positions, just as we now construct great durations by mentally prolonging a series of successive dates, yet the original experience of both space and time is always of something already given as a unit, inside of which attention afterwards discriminates parts in relation to each other. Without the parts already given as *in* a time and *in* a space, subsequent discrimination of them could hardly do more than perceive them as *different* from each other; it would have no motive for calling the difference temporal order in this instance and spatial position in that.

And just as in certain experiences we may be conscious of an extensive space full of objects, without locating each of them distinctly therein; so, when many impressions follow in excessively rapid succession in time, although we may be distinctly aware that they occupy some duration, and are not simultaneous, we may be quite at a loss to tell which comes first and which last; or we may even invert their real order in our judgment. In complicated reaction-time experiments, where signals and motions, and clicks of the apparatus come in exceedingly rapid order, one is at first much perplexed in deciding what the order is, yet of the fact of its occupancy of time we are never in doubt.

ACCURACY OF OUR ESTIMATE OF SHORT DURATIONS

We must now proceed to an account of the *facts* of time-perception in detail as preliminary to our speculative conclusion. Many of the facts are matters of patient experimentation, others of common experience.

First of all, we note a marked *difference between the elementary sensations of duration and those of space*. The former have a much narrower range; the time-sense may be called a myopic organ, in comparison with the eye, for example. The eye sees rods, acres, even miles, at a single glance, and these totals it can afterwards subdivide into an almost infinite number of distinctly identified parts. The units of duration, on the other hand, which the time-sense is able to take in at a single stroke, are groups of a few seconds, and within these units very few subdivisions—perhaps forty at most, as we shall presently see—can be clearly discerned. The durations we have practically most to deal with—minutes, hours, and days—have to be symbolically conceived, and constructed by mental addition, after the fashion of those extents of hundreds of miles and upwards, which in the field of space are beyond the range of most men's practical interests altogether. To 'realize' a quarter of a mile we need only look out of the window and *feel* its length by an act which, though it may in part result from organized associations, yet seems immediately performed. To realize an hour, we must count 'now!—now!—now!—now!—' indefinitely. Each 'now' is the feeling of a separate *bit* of time, and the exact sum of the bits never makes a very clear impression on our mind.

How many bits can we clearly apprehend at once? Very few if they are long bits, more if they are extremely short, most if they come to us in compound groups, each including smaller bits of its own.

Hearing is the sense by which the subdivision of durations is most sharply made. Almost all the experimental work on the time-sense has been done by means of strokes of sound. How long a series of sounds, then, can we group in the mind so as not to confound it with a longer or a shorter series?

Our spontaneous tendency is to break up any monotonously given series of sounds into some sort of a rhythm. We involuntarily accentuate every second, or third, or fourth beat, or we break the series in still more intricate ways. Whenever we thus grasp the impressions in rhythmic form, we can identify a longer string of them without confusion.

Each variety of verse, for example, has its 'law'; and the recurrent stresses and sinkings make us feel with peculiar readiness the lack of a syllable or the presence of one too much. Divers verses may again be bound together in the form of a stanza, and we may then say of another stanza, "Its second verse differs by so much from that of the first stanza," when but for the felt stanza-form the two differing verses would have come to us too separately to be compared at all. But these superposed systems of rhythm soon reach their limit. In music, as Wundt[5] says, "while the measure may easily contain 12 changes of intensity of sound (as in $^{12}\!/_{8}$ time), the rhyth-

[5] *Physiologische Psychologie*, II, 54.

mical group may embrace 6 measures, and the period consist of 4, exceptionally of 5 [8?] groups."

Wundt and his pupil Dietze have both tried to determine experimentally the *maximal extent of our immediate distinct consciousness for successive impressions.*

Wundt found[6] that twelve impressions could be distinguished clearly as a united cluster, provided they were caught in a certain rhythm by the mind, and succeeded each other at intervals not smaller than 0.3 and not larger than 0.5 of a second. This makes the total time distinctly apprehended to be equal to from 3.6 to 6 seconds.

Dietze[7] gives larger figures. The most favorable intervals for clearly catching the strokes were when they came at from 0.3 second to 0.18 second apart. *Forty* strokes might then be remembered as a whole, and identified without error when repeated, provided the mind grasped them in five sub-groups of eight, or in eight sub-groups of five strokes each. When no grouping of the strokes beyond making *couples* of them by the attention was allowed—and practically it was found impossible not to group them in at least this simplest of all ways—16 was the largest number that could be clearly apprehended as a whole.[8] This would make 40 times 0.3 second, or 12 seconds, to be the *maximum filled duration* of which we can be both *distinctly and immediately* aware.

The maximum unfilled, or *vacant duration,* seems to lie within the same objective range. Estel and Mehner, also working in Wundt's laboratory, found it to vary from 5 or 6 to 12 seconds, and perhaps more. The differences seemed due to practice rather than to idiosyncrasy.[9]

6 *Ibid.*, II, 215.

7 *Philosophische Studien*, II, 362.

8 *Counting* was of course not permitted. It would have given a symbolic concept and no intuitive or immediate perception of the totality of the series. With counting we may of course compare together series of any length—series whose beginnings have faded from our mind, and of whose totality we retain no sensible impression at all. To count a series of clicks is an altogether different thing from merely perceiving them as discontinuous. In the latter case we need only be conscious of the bits of empty duration between them; in the former we must perform rapid acts of association between them and as many names of numbers.

9 Estel in Wundt's *Philosophische Studien*, II, 50. Mehner: *ibid.*, II, 571. In Dietze's experiments even numbers of strokes were better caught than odd ones, by the ear. The *rapidity of their sequence* had a great influence on the result. At more than 4 seconds apart it was impossible to perceive series of them as units in all (cf. Wundt:

These figures may be roughly taken to stand for the most important part of what, with Mr. Clay, we called, a few pages back, the *specious present.* The specious present has, in addition, a vaguely vanishing backward and forward fringe; but its nucleus is probably the dozen seconds or less that have just elapsed.

If these are the maximum, what, then, is the *minimum* amount of duration which we can distinctly feel?

The smallest figure experimentally ascertained was by Exner, who distinctly heard the doubleness of two successive clicks of a Savart's wheel, and of two successive snaps of an electric spark, when their interval was made as small as about 1/500 of a second.[10]

With the eye, perception is less delicate. Two sparks, made to fall beside each other in rapid succession on the centre of the retina, ceased to be recognized as successive by Exner when their interval fell below 0.044″.[11]

Where, as here, the succeeding impressions are only two in number, we can easiest perceive the interval between them. President Hall, who experimented with a modified Savart's wheel, which gave clicks in varying number and at varying intervals, says:[12]

"In order that their discontinuity may be clearly perceived, four or even three clicks or beats must be farther apart than two need to be.

Physiologische Psychologie, II, 214). They were simply counted as so many individual strokes. Below 0.21 to 0.11 second, according to the observer, judgment again became confused. It was found that the rate of succession most favorable for grasping long series was when the strokes were sounded at intervals of from 0.3″ to 0.18″ apart. Series of 4, 6, 8, 16 were more easily identified than series of 10, 12, 14, 18. The latter could hardly be clearly grasped at all. Among odd numbers, 3, 5, 7 were the series easiest caught; next, 9, 15; hardest of all, 11 and 13; and 17 was impossible to apprehend.

10 The exact interval of the sparks was 0.00205″. The doubleness of their snap was usually replaced by a single-seeming sound when it fell to 0.00198″, the sound becoming *louder* when the sparks seemed simultaneous. The *difference* between these two intervals is only $\frac{7}{100000}$ of a second; and, as Exner remarks, our ear and brain must be wonderfully efficient organs to get distinct feelings from so slight an objective difference as this. See Pflüger's *Archiv,* Bd. XI.

11 *Ibid.,* p. 407. When the sparks fell so close together that their irradiation-circles overlapped, they appeared like *one spark moving* from the position of the first to that of the second; and they might then follow each other as close as 0.015″ without the *direction of the movement* ceasing to be clear. When one spark fell on the centre, the other on the margin, of the retina, the time-interval for successive apprehension had to be raised to 0.076″.

12 Hall and Jastrow: "Studies of Rhythm," *Mind,* XI, 58.

When two are easily distinguished, three or four separated by the same interval . . . are often confidently pronounced to be two or three respectively. It would be well if observations were so directed as to ascertain, at least up to ten or twenty, the increase [of interval] required by each additional click in a series for the sense of discontinuity to remain constant throughout." [13]

Where the first impression falls on one sense, and the second on another, the perception of the intervening time tends to be less certain and delicate, and it makes a difference which impression comes first. Thus, Exner found[14] the smallest perceptible interval to be, in seconds:

From sight to touch	0.071
From touch to sight	0.053
From sight to hearing	0.16
From hearing to sight	0.06
From one ear to another	0.064

To be conscious of a time-interval at all is one thing; to tell whether it be shorter or longer than another interval is a different thing. A number of experimental data are on hand which give us a measure of the delicacy of this latter perception. The problem is that of the *smallest difference between two times* which we can perceive.

The difference is at its minimum when the times themselves are very short. Exner,[15] reacting as rapidly as possible with his foot,

[13] Nevertheless, multitudinous impressions may be felt as discontinuous, though separated by excessively minute intervals of time. Gruenhagen says (Pflüger's *Archiv*, VI, 175) that 10,000 electric shocks a second are felt as interrupted, by the tongue (!). Von Wittich (*ibid.*, II, 329), that between 1000 and 2000 strokes a second are felt as discrete by the finger. W. Preyer, on the other hand (*Über die Grenzen des Empfindungsvermögens*, etc., 1868, p. 15), makes contacts appear continuous to the finger when 36.8 of them follow in a second. Similarly, Mach (Wiener *Sitzungsberichte*, LI, 2, 142) gives about 36. Lalanne (*Comptes Rendus*, LXXXII, p. 1314) found summation of finger-contacts after 22 repetitions in a second. Such discrepant figures are of doubtful worth. On the retina 20 to 30 impressions a second at the very utmost can be felt as discrete when they fall on the same spot. The ear, which begins to fuse stimuli together into a musical tone when they follow at the rate of a little over 30 a second, can still feel 132 of them a second as discontinuous when they take the shape of 'beats' (Helmholtz: *Tonempfindungen*, 3d ed., p. 270).

[14] Pflüger's *Archiv*, XI, 428. Also in Hermann's *Handbuch der Physiologie*, Bd. 2, Thl. II, pp. 260–262.

[15] Pflüger's *Archiv*, VII, 639. Tigerstedt (*Bihang till Kongliga Svenska Vetenskaps-*

upon a signal seen by the eye (spark), noted all the reactions which seemed to him either slow or fast in the making. He thought thus that deviations of about 1/100 of a second either way from the average were correctly noticed by him at the time. The average was here 0.1840″. Hall and Jastrow listened to the intervals between the clicks of their apparatus. Between two such equal intervals of 4.27″ each, a middle interval was included, which might be made either shorter or longer than the extremes. "After the series had been heard two or even three times, no impression of the relative length of the middle interval would often exist, and only after hearing the fourth and last [repetition of the series] would the judgment incline to the *plus* or *minus* side. Inserting the variable between two invariable and like intervals greatly facilitated judgment, which between two unlike terms is far less accurate."[16] Three observers in these experiments made no error when the middle interval varied 1/60 from the extremes. When it varied 1/120, errors occurred, but were few. This would make the minimum *absolute* difference perceived as large as 0.355″.

This minimum absolute difference, of course, increases as the times compared grow long. Attempts have been made to ascertain what *ratio* it bears to the times themselves. According to Fechner's 'Psychophysic Law' it ought always to bear the same ratio. Various observers, however, have found this not to be the case.[17] On the contrary, very interesting *oscillations* in the accuracy of judgment and in the direction of the error—oscillations dependent upon the absolute amount of the times compared—have been noticed by all who have experimented with the question. Of these a brief account may be given.

Akademiens Handlingar, Bd. 8, Häfte 2, Stockholm, 1884) revises Exner's figures, and shows that his conclusions are exaggerated. According to Tigerstedt, two observers almost always rightly appreciated 0.05″ or 0.06″ of reaction-time difference. Half the time they did it rightly when the difference sank to 0.03″, though from 0.03″ and 0.06″ differences were often not noticed at all. Buccola found (*Le Legge del tempo nei fenomeni del pensiero*, Milano, 1883, p. 371) that, after much practice in making rapid reactions upon a signal, he estimated directly, in figures, his own reaction-time, in 10 experiments, with an error of from 0.010″ to 0.018″; in 6, with one of 0.005″ to 0.009″; in one, with one of 0.002″; and in 3, with one of 0.003″.

16 *Mind*, XI, 61 (1886).

17 Mach: Wiener *Sitzungsberichte*, LI, 2, 133 (1865); Estel: *loc. cit.*, p. 65; Mehner: *loc. cit.*, p. 586; Buccola: *op. cit.*, p. 378. Fechner labors to prove that his law is only overlaid by other interfering laws in the figures recorded by these experimenters; but his case seems to me to be one of desperate infatuation with a hobby. (See Wundt's *Philosophische Studien*, III, 1.)

In the first place, *in every list of intervals experimented with there will be found what Vierordt calls an* 'INDIFFERENCE-POINT'; that is to say, an interval which we judge with maximum accuracy, a time which we tend to estimate as neither longer or shorter than it really is, and away from which, in both directions, errors increase their size.[18] This time varies from one observer to another, but its average is remarkably constant, as the following table shows.[19]

The times, noted by the ear, and the average indifference-points (given in seconds) were, for—

Wundt[20]	0.72
Kollert[21]	0.75
Estel (probably)	0.75
Mehner	0.71
Stevens[22]	0.71
Mach[23]	0.35
Buccola (about)[24]	0.40

18 Curious discrepancies exist between the German and the American observers with respect to the *direction* of the error below and above the point of indifference—differences perhaps due to the *fatigue* involved in the American method. The Germans lengthened intervals below it and shortened those above. With seven Americans experimented on by Stevens this was exactly reversed. The German method was to passively listen to the intervals, then judge; the American was to reproduce them actively by movements of the hand. In Mehner's experiments there was found a second indifference-point at about 5 seconds, beyond which times were judged again too long. Glass, whose work on the subject is the latest (*Philosophische Studien*, IV, 423), found (when corrections were allowed for) that all times except 0.8 sec. were estimated too short. He found a series of points of greatest relative accuracy (viz., at 1.5, 2.5, 3.75, 5, 6.25, etc., seconds respectively), and thought that his observations roughly corroborated Weber's law. As 'maximum' and 'minimum' are printed interchangeably in Glass's article it is hard to follow.

19 With Vierordt and his pupils the indifference-point lay as high as from 1.5 sec. to 4.9 sec., according to the observer (cf. *Der Zeitsinn*, 1868, p. 112). In most of these experiments the time heard was actively reproduced, after a short pause, by movements of the hand, which were recorded. Wundt gives good reasons (*Physiologische Psychologie*, II, 289, 290) for rejecting Vierordt's figures as erroneous. Vierordt's book, it should be said, is full of important matter, nevertheless.

20 *Physiologische Psychologie*, II, 286, 290.

21 *Philosophische Studien*, I, 86.

22 *Mind*, XI, 400.

23 *Loc. cit.*, p. 144.

24 *Op. cit.*, p. 376. Mach's and Buccola's figures, it will be observed, are about *one half* of the rest—sub-multiples, therefore. It ought to be observed, however, that Buccola's figure has little value, his observations not being well fitted to show this particular point.

The odd thing about these figures is the recurrence they show in so many men of about three fourths of a second, as the interval of time most easy to catch and reproduce. Odder still, both Estel and Mehner found that *multiples* of this time were more accurately reproduced than the time-intervals of intermediary length;[25] and Glass found a certain periodicity, with the constant increment of 1.25 sec., in his observations. There would seem thus to exist something like a periodic or rhythmic sharpening of our time-sense, of which the period differs somewhat from one observer to the next.

Our sense of time, like other senses, *seems subject to the law of contrast*. It appeared pretty plainly in Estel's observations that an interval sounded shorter if a long one had immediately preceded it, and longer when the opposite was the case.

Like other senses, too, *our sense of time is sharpened by practice*. Mehner ascribes almost all the discrepancies between other observers and himself to this cause alone.[26]

Tracts of time filled (with clicks of sound) *seem longer than vacant ones* of the same duration, when the latter does not exceed a second or two.[27] This, which reminds one of what happens with spaces seen by the eye, becomes reversed when longer times are taken. It is, perhaps, in accordance with this law that a *loud* sound, limiting a short interval of time, makes it appear longer, a *slight* sound shorter. In comparing intervals marked out by sounds, we must take care to keep the sounds uniform.[28]

There is a certain emotional *feeling* accompanying the intervals of time, as is well known in music. *The sense of haste goes with one measure of rapidity, that of delay with another*; and these two feelings harmonize with different mental moods. Vierordt listened to series of strokes performed by a metronome at rates varying from 40 to 200 a minute, and found that they very naturally fell into seven categories, from 'very slow' to 'very fast.'[29] Each category of

[25] Estel's figures led him to think that *all* the multiples enjoyed this privilege; with Mehner, on the other hand, only the *odd* multiples showed diminution of the average error; thus, 0.71, 2.15, 3.55, 5, 6.4, 7.8, 9.3, and 10.65 seconds were respectively registered with the least error. Cf. *Philosophische Studien*, II, pp. 57, 562–565.

[26] Cf. especially pp. 558–561.

[27] Wundt: *Physiologische Psychologie*, II, 287. Hall and Jastrow: *Mind*, XI, 62.

[28] Mehner: *loc. cit.*, p. 553.

[29] The number of distinguishable *differences* of speed between these limits is, as he takes care to remark, very much larger than 7 (*Der Zeitsinn*, p. 137).

feeling included the intervals following each other within a certain range of speed, and no others. This is a qualitative, not a quantitative judgment—an æsthetic judgment, in fact. The middle category, of speed that was neutral, or, as he calls it, 'adequate,' contained intervals that were grouped about 0.62 second, and Vierordt says that this made what one might almost call an *agreeable* time.[30]

The feeling of time and accent in music, of rhythm, is quite independent of that of melody. Tunes with marked rhythm can be readily recognized when simply drummed on the table with the finger-tips.

WE HAVE NO SENSE FOR EMPTY TIME

Although subdividing the time by beats of sensation aids our accurate knowledge of the amount of it that elapses, such subdivision does not seem at the first glance essential to our perception of its flow. Let one sit with closed eyes and, abstracting entirely from the outer world, attend exclusively to the passage of time, like one who wakes, as the poet says, "to hear time flowing in the middle of the night, and all things creeping to a day of doom." There seems under such circumstances as these no variety in the material content of our thought, and what we notice appears, if anything, to be the pure series of durations budding, as it were, and growing beneath our indrawn gaze. Is this really so or not? The question is important; for, if the experience be what it roughly seems, we have a sort of special sense for pure time—a sense to which empty duration is an adequate stimulus; while if it be an illusion, it must be that our perception of time's flight, in the experiences quoted, is due to the *filling* of the time, and to our *memory* of a content which it had a moment previous, and which we feel to agree or disagree with its content now.

It takes but a small exertion of introspection to show that the latter alternative is the true one, and that *we can no more intuit a duration than we can intuit an extension, devoid of all sensible content.* Just as with closed eyes we perceive a dark visual field in which a curdling play of obscurest luminosity is always going on; so, be we never so abstracted from distinct outward impressions, we are always inwardly immersed in what Wundt has somewhere

[30] P. 19, § 18, p. 112.

called the twilight of our general consciousness. Our heart-beats, our breathing, the pulses of our attention, fragments of words or sentences that pass through our imagination, are what people this dim habitat. Now, all these processes are rhythmical, and are apprehended by us, as they occur, in their totality; the breathing and pulses of attention, as coherent successions, each with its rise and fall; the heart-beats similarly, only relatively far more brief; the words not separately, but in connected groups. In short, empty our minds as we may, some form of *changing process* remains for us to feel, and cannot be expelled. And along with the sense of the process and its rhythm goes the sense of the length of time it lasts. Awareness of *change* is thus the condition on which our perception of time's flow depends; but there exists no reason to suppose that empty time's own changes are sufficient for the awareness of change to be aroused. The change must be of some concrete sort—an outward or inward sensible series, or a process of attention or volition.[31]

[31] I leave the text just as it was printed in the *Journal of Speculative Philosophy* (for 'Oct. 1886') in 1887. Since then Münsterberg in his masterly *Beiträge zur experimentellen Psychologie* (Heft 2, 1889) seems to have made it clear what the sensible changes are by which we measure the lapse of time. When the time which separates two sensible impressions is less than one third of a second, he thinks it is almost entirely the *amount to which the memory-image of the first impression has faded* when the second one overtakes it, which makes us feel how wide they are apart (p. 29). When the time is longer than this, we rely, he thinks, exclusively upon the feelings of muscular tension and relaxation, which we are constantly receiving although we give to them so little of our direct attention. *These feelings are primarily in the muscles by which we adopt our sense-organs in attending to the signals used*, some of the muscles being in the eye and ear themselves, some of them in the head, neck, etc. We here judge two time-intervals to be equal when between the beginning and end of each we feel exactly similar relaxations and subsequent expectant tensions of these muscles to have occurred. In reproducing intervals ourselves we try to make our feelings of this sort just what they were when we passively heard the interval. These feelings by themselves, however, can only be used when the intervals are very short, for the tension anticipatory of the terminal stimulus naturally reaches its maximum very soon. With longer intervals we *take the feeling of our inspirations and expirations into account*. With our expirations all the other muscular tensions in our body undergo a rhythmical decrease; with our inspirations the reverse takes place. When, therefore, we note a time-interval of several seconds with intent to reproduce it, what we seek is to make the earlier and later interval agree in the number and amount of these respiratory changes combined with sense-organ adjustments with which they are filled. Münsterberg has studied carefully in his own case the variations of the respiratory factor. They are many; but he sums up his experience by saying that whether he measured by inspirations that were divided by momentary pauses into six parts, or by inspirations that were continuous; whether with sensory tension during inspiration and relaxation during expiration, or by tension during both inspiration and expiration, separated by a sudden interpolated relaxation; whether

And here again we have an analogy with space. The earliest form of distinct space-perception is undoubtedly that of a movement over some one of our sensitive surfaces, and this movement is originally given as a simple whole of feeling, and is only decomposed into its elements—successive positions successively occupied by the moving body—when our education in discrimination is much advanced. But a movement is a change, a process; so we see that in the time-world and the space-world alike the first known things are not elements, but combinations, not separate units, but wholes already formed. The condition of *being* of the wholes may be the elements; but the condition of our *knowing* the elements is our having already felt the wholes as wholes.

In the experience of watching empty time flow—'empty' to be taken hereafter in the relative sense just set forth—we tell it off in pulses. We say 'now! now! now!' or we count 'more! more! more!' as we feel it bud. This composition out of units of duration is called the law of time's *discrete flow*. The discreteness is, however, merely due to the fact that our successive acts of *recognition* or *apperception* of *what* it is are discrete. The sensation is as continuous as any sensation can be. All continuous sensations are *named* in beats. We notice that a certain finite 'more' of them is passing or already past. To adopt Hodgson's image, the sensation is the measuring-tape, the perception the dividing-engine which stamps its length. As we listen to a steady sound, we *take it in* in

---

with special notice taken of the cephalic tensions, or of those in the trunk and shoulders, in all cases alike and without exception he involuntarily endeavored, whenever he compared two times or tried to make one the same as the other, to get exactly the same respiratory conditions and conditions of tension, *all* the subjective conditions, in short, *exactly* the same during the second interval as they were during the first. Münsterberg corroborated his subjective observations by experiments. The observer of the time had to reproduce as exactly as possible an interval between two sharp sounds given him by an assistant. The only condition imposed upon him was that he should not modify his breathing for the purposes of measurement. It was then found that when the assistant broke in at random with his signals, the judgment of the observer was vastly less accurate than when the assistant carefully watched the observer's breathing and made both the beginning of the time given him and that of the time which he was to give coincide with identical phases thereof.—Finally, Münsterberg with great plausibility tries to explain the discrepancies between the results of Vierordt, Estel, Mehner, Glass, etc., as due to the fact that they *did not all use the same measure*. Some breathe a little faster, some a little slower. Some break their inspirations into two parts, some do not, etc. The coincidence of the objective times measured with definite natural phases of breathing would very easily give periodical maxima of facility in measuring accurately.

discrete pulses of recognition, calling it successively 'the same! the same! the same!' The case stands no otherwise with time.

After a small number of beats our impression of the amount we have told off becomes quite vague. Our only way of knowing it accurately is by counting, or noticing the clock, or through some other symbolic conception.[32] When the times exceed hours or days, the conception is absolutely symbolic. We think of the amount we mean either solely as a *name*, or by running over a few salient *dates* therein, with no pretence of imagining the full durations that lie between them. No one has anything like a *perception* of the greater length of the time between now and the first century than of that between now and the tenth. To an historian, it is true, the longer interval will suggest a host of additional dates and events, and so appear a more *multitudinous* thing. And for the same reason most people will think they directly perceive the length of the past fortnight to exceed that of the past week. But there is properly no comparative time-*intuition* in these cases at all. It is but dates and events *representing* time, their abundance *symbolizing* its length. I am sure that this is so, even where the times compared are no more than an hour or so in length. It is the same with Spaces of many miles, which we always compare with each other by the numbers which measure them.[33]

32 "Any one wishing yet further examples of this mental substitution, will find one on observing how habitually he thinks of the spaces on the clock-face instead of the periods they stand for—how, on discovering it to be half an hour later than he supposed, he does not represent the half-hour in its duration, but scarcely passes beyond the sign of it marked by the finger." (H. Spencer: *Psychology*, § 336.)

33 The only objections to this which I can think of are: (1) The accuracy with which some men judge of the hour of day or night without looking at the clock; (2) the faculty some have of waking at a preappointed hour; (3) the accuracy of time-perception reported to exist in certain trance-subjects. It might seem that in these persons some sort of a sub-conscious record was kept of the lapse of time *per se*. But this cannot be admitted until it is proved that there are no physiological processes, the feeling of whose course may serve as a *sign* of how much time has sped, and so lead us to infer the hour. That there are such processes it is hardly possible to doubt. An ingenious friend of mine was long puzzled to know why each day of the week had such a characteristic physiognomy to him. That of Sunday was soon noticed to be due to the cessation of the city's rumbling, and the sound of people's feet shuffling on the sidewalk; of Monday, to come from the clothes drying in the yard and casting a white reflection on the ceiling; of Tuesday, to a cause which I forget; and I think my friend did not get beyond Wednesday. Probably each hour in the day has for most of us some outer or inner sign associated with it as closely as these signs with the days of the week. It must be admitted, after all, however, that the great improvement of the time-perception during sleep and trance is a mystery not as yet cleared

From this we pass naturally to speak of certain familiar variations in our estimation of lengths of time. *In general, a time filled with varied and interesting experiences seems short in passing, but long as we look back. On the other hand, a tract of time empty of experiences seems long in passing, but in retrospect short.* A week of travel and sight-seeing may subtend an angle more like three weeks in the memory; and a month of sickness hardly yields more memories than a day. The length in retrospect depends obviously on the multitudinousness of the memories which the time affords. Many objects, events, changes, many subdivisions, immediately widen the view as we look back. Emptiness, monotony, familiarity, make it shrivel up. In von Holtei's *Vagabonds* one Anton is described as revisiting his native village.

"Seven years," he exclaims, "seven years since I ran away! More like seventy it seems, so much has happened. I cannot think of it all without becoming dizzy—at any rate not now. And yet again, when I look at the village, at the church-tower, it seems as if I could hardly have been seven days away."

Prof. Lazarus[34] (from whom I borrow this quotation), thus explains both of these contrasted illusions by our principle of the awakened memories being multitudinous or few:

---

up. All my life I have been struck by the accuracy with which I will wake at the same *exact minute* night after night and morning after morning, if only the habit fortuitously begins. The organic registration in me is independent of sleep. After lying in bed a long time awake I suddenly rise without knowing the time, and for days and weeks together will do so at an identical minute by the clock, as if some inward physiological process caused the act by punctually running down.—Idiots are said sometimes to possess the time-measuring faculty in a marked degree. I have an interesting manuscript account of an idiot girl which says: "She was punctual almost to a minute in her demand for food and other regular attentions. Her dinner was generally furnished her at 12.30 P.M., and at that hour she would begin to scream if it were not forthcoming. If on Fast-day or Thanksgiving it were delayed, in accordance with the New England custom, she screamed from her usual dinner-hour until the food was carried to her. On the next day, however, she again made known her wants promptly at 12.30. Any slight attention shown her on one day was demanded on the next at the corresponding hour. If an orange were given her at 4 P.M. on Wednesday, at the same hour on Thursday she made known her expectation, and if the fruit were not given her she continued to call for it at intervals for two or three hours. At four on Friday the process would be repeated but would last less long; and so on for two or three days. If one of her sisters visited her accidentally at a certain hour, the sharp piercing scream was sure to summon her at the same hour the next day," etc., etc.—For these obscure matters consult C. du Prel: *The Philosophy of Mysticism*, chap. III, § 1.

[34] *Ideale Fragen in Reden und Vorträgen* (1878), p. 218 (Essay, "Zeit und Weile").

"The circle of experiences, widely extended, rich in variety, which he had in view on the day of his leaving the village rises now in his mind as its image lies before him. And with it—in rapid succession and violent motion, not in chronologic order, or from chronologic motives, but suggesting each other by all sorts of connections—arise massive images of all his rich vagabondage and roving life. They roll and wave confusedly together, first perhaps one from the first year, then from the sixth, soon from the second, again from the fifth, the first, etc., until it seems as if seventy years must have been there, and he reels with the fulness of his vision. . . . Then the inner eye turns away from all this past. The outer one turns to the village, especially to the church-tower. The sight of it calls back the old sight of it, so that the consciousness is filled with that alone, or almost alone. The one vision compares itself with the other, and looks so near, so unchanged, that it seems as if only a week of time could have come between."

The same space of time seems shorter as we grow older—that is, the days, the months, and the years do so; whether the hours do so is doubtful, and the minutes and seconds to all appearance remain about the same.

"Whoever counts many lustra in his memory need only question himself to find that the last of these, the past five years, have sped much more quickly than the preceding periods of equal amount. Let anyone remember his last eight or ten school years: it is the space of a century. Compare with them the last eight or ten years of life: it is the space of an hour."

So writes Prof. Paul Janet,[35] and gives a solution which can hardly be said to diminish the mystery. There is a law, he says, by which the apparent length of an interval at a given epoch of a man's life is proportional to the total length of the life itself. A child of 10 feels a year as $\frac{1}{10}$ of his whole life—a man of 50 as $\frac{1}{50}$, the whole life meanwhile apparently preserving a constant length. This formula roughly expresses the phenomena, it is true, but cannot possibly be an elementary psychic law; and it is certain that, in great part at least, the foreshortening of the years as we grow older is due to the monotony of memory's content, and the consequent simplification of the backward-glancing view. In youth we may have an

35 *Revue Philosophique*, vol. III, p. 497.

absolutely new experience, subjective or objective, every hour of the day. Apprehension is vivid, retentiveness strong, and our recollections of that time, like those of a time spent in rapid and interesting travel, are of something intricate, multitudinous, and long-drawn-out. But as each passing year converts some of this experience into automatic routine which we hardly note at all, the days and the weeks smooth themselves out in recollection to contentless units, and the years grow hollow and collapse.

So much for the apparent shortening of tracts of time in *retrospect*. They shorten *in passing* whenever we are so fully occupied with their content as not to note the actual time itself. A day full of excitement, with no pause, is said to pass 'ere we know it.' On the contrary, a day full of waiting, of unsatisfied desire for change, will seem a small eternity. *Tædium, ennui, Langweile, boredom,* are words for which, probably, every language known to man has its equivalent. It comes about whenever, from the relative emptiness of content of a tract of time, we grow attentive to the passage of the time itself. Expecting, and being ready for, a new impression to succeed; when it fails to come, we get an empty time instead of it; and such experiences, ceaselessly renewed, make us most formidably aware of the extent of the mere time itself.[36] Close your eyes and simply wait to hear somebody tell you that a minute has elapsed. The full length of your leisure with it seems incredible. You engulf yourself into its bowels as into those of that interminable first week of an ocean voyage, and find yourself wondering that history can have overcome many such periods in its course. All because you attend so closely to the mere feeling of the time *per se*, and because your attention to that is susceptible of such fine-grained successive subdivision. The *odiousness* of the whole experience comes from its insipidity; for *stimulation* is the indispensable requisite for pleasure in an experience, and the feeling of bare time is the least

36 "Empty time is most strongly perceived when it comes as a *pause* in music or in speech. Suppose a preacher in the pulpit, a professor at his desk, to stick still in the midst of his discourse; or let a composer (as is sometimes purposely done) make all his instruments stop at once; we await every instant the resumption of the performance, and, in this awaiting, perceive, more than in any other possible way, the empty time. To change the example, let, in a piece of polyphonic music—a figure, for instance, in which a tangle of melodies are under way—suddenly a single voice be heard, which sustains a long note, while all else is hushed. . . . This one note will appear very protracted—why? Because we *expect* to hear accompanying it the notes of the other instruments, but they fail to come." (Herbart: *Psychologie als Wissenschaft*, § 115.)—Compare also Münsterberg: *Beiträge*, Heft 2, p. 41.

stimulating experience we can have.[37] The sensation of tædium is a *protest*, says Volkmann, against the entire present.

Exactly parallel variations occur in our consciousness of space. A road we walk back over, hoping to find at each step an object we have dropped, seems to us longer than when we walked over it the other way. A space we measure by pacing appears longer than one we traverse with no thought of its length. And in general an amount of space attended to in itself leaves with us more impression of spaciousness than one of which we only note the content.[38]

I do not say that *everything* in these fluctuations of estimate can be accounted for by the time's content being crowded and interesting, or simple and tame. Both in the shortening of time by old age and in its lengthening by *ennui* some deeper cause *may* be at work. This cause can only be ascertained, if it exist, by finding out *why we perceive time at all.* To this inquiry let us, though without much hope, proceed.

THE FEELING OF PAST TIME IS A PRESENT FEELING

If asked why we perceive the light of the sun, or the sound of an explosion, we reply, "Because certain outer forces, ether-waves or air-waves, smite upon the brain, awakening therein changes, to which the conscious perceptions, light and sound, respond." But we hasten to add that neither light nor sound *copy* or *mirror* the ether- or air-waves; they represent them only symbolically. The *only* case, says Helmholtz, in which such copying occurs, and in which

"our perceptions can truly correspond with outer reality, is that of the *time-succession* of phenomena. Simultaneity, succession, and the

37 A night of pain will seem terribly long; we keep looking forward to a moment which never comes—the moment when it shall cease. But the odiousness of this experience is not named *ennui* or *Langweile*, like the odiousness of time that seems long from its emptiness. The more positive odiousness of the pain, rather, is what tinges our memory of the night. What we feel, as Prof. Lazarus says (*op. cit.*, p. 202), is the long time of the suffering, not the suffering of the long time *per se*.

38 On these variations of time-estimate, cf. Romanes: "Consciousness of Time," in *Mind*, vol. III, p. 297; J. Sully: *Illusions*, pp. 245–261, 302–305; W. Wundt: *Physiologische Psychologie*, II, 287, 288; besides the essays quoted from Lazarus and Janet. In German, the successors of Herbart have treated of this subject: compare Volkmann's *Lehrbuch der Psychologie*, § 89, and for references to other authors his note 3 to this section. Lindner (*Lehrbuch der empirischen Psychologie*), as a parallel effect, instances Alexander the Great's life (thirty-three years), which seems to us as if it must be long, because it was so eventful. Similarly the English Commonwealth, etc.

regular return of simultaneity or succession, can obtain as well in sensations as in outer events. Events, like our perceptions of them, take place in time, so that the time-relations of the latter can furnish a true copy of those of the former. The sensation of the thunder follows the sensation of the lightning just as the sonorous convulsing of the air by the electric discharge reaches the observer's place later than that of the luminiferous ether."[39]

One experiences an almost instinctive impulse, in pursuing such reflections as these, to follow them to a sort of crude speculative conclusion, and to think that he has at last got the mystery of cognition where, to use a vulgar phrase, 'the wool is short.' What more natural, we say, than that the sequences and durations of things *should* become known? The succession of the outer forces stamps itself as a like succession upon the brain. The brain's successive changes are copied exactly by correspondingly successive pulses of the mental stream. The mental stream, feeling itself, must feel the time-relations of its own states. But as these are copies of the outward time-relations, so must it know them too. That is to say, these latter time-relations arouse their own cognition; or, in other words, the mere existence of time in those changes out of the mind which affect the mind is a sufficient cause why time is perceived by the mind.

This philosophy is unfortunately too crude. Even though we *were* to conceive the outer successions as forces stamping their image on the brain, and the brain's successions as forces stamping their image on the mind,[40] still, between the mind's own changes *being* successive, and *knowing their own succession*, lies as broad a chasm as between the object and subject of any case of cognition in the world. *A succession of feelings, in and of itself, is not a feeling of succession. And since, to our successive feelings, a feeling of their own succession is added, that must be treated as an additional fact requiring its own special elucidation,* which this talk about outer time-relations stamping copies of themselves within, leaves all untouched.

I have shown, at the outset of the article, that what is past, to be known as past, must be known *with* what is present, and *during* the

39 *Physiologische Optik,* p. 445.

40 Succession, time *per se, is* no force. Our talk about its devouring tooth, etc., is all elliptical. Its *contents* are what devour. The law of inertia is incompatible with time's being assumed as an efficient cause of anything.

'present' spot of time. As the clear understanding of this point has some importance, let me, at the risk of repetition, recur to it again. Volkmann has expressed the matter admirably, as follows:

"One might be tempted to answer the question of the origin of the time-idea by simply pointing to the train of ideas, whose various members, starting from the first, successively attain to full clearness. But against this it must be objected that the successive ideas are not yet the idea of succession, because succession *in* thought is not the thought *of* succession. If idea A follows idea B, consciousness simply exchanges one for another. That B *comes after* A is for our consciousness a non-existent fact; for this *after* is given neither in B nor in A; and no third idea has been supposed. The thinking of the sequence of B upon A is another kind of thinking from that which brought forth A and then brought forth B; and this first kind of thinking is absent so long as merely the thinking of A and the thinking of B are there. In short, when we look at the matter sharply, we come to this antithesis, that if A and B are to be represented *as occurring in succession* they must be *simultaneously represented*; if we are to think *of* them as one after the other, we must *think* them both at once."[41]

If we represent the actual time-stream of our thinking by an horizontal line, the thought *of* the stream or of any segment of its length, past, present, or to come, might be figured in a perpendicular raised upon the horizontal at a certain point. The length of this perpendicular stands for a certain object or content, which in this case is the time thought of, and all of which is thought of together at the actual moment of the stream upon which the perpendicular is raised. Mr. James Ward puts the matter very well in his masterly article "Psychology" in the ninth edition of the *Encyclopædia Britannica*, page 64. He says:

"We may, if we represent succession as a line, represent simultaneity as a second line at right angles to the first; empty time—or time-length without time-breadth, we may say—is a mere abstraction. Now it is with the former line that we have to do in treating of time as it is, and with the latter in treating of our intuition of time, where, just as in a perspective representation of distance, we are confined to lines in a plane at right angles to the actual line of depth. In a succes-

[41] *Lehrbuch der Psychologie*, § 87. Compare also H. Lotze: *Metaphysik*, § 154.

sion of events, say of sense-impressions, *A B C D E* . . . the presence of *B* means the absence of *A* and of *C*, but the presentation of this succession involves the simultaneous presence, in some mode or other, of two or more of the presentations *A B C D*. In reality, past, present, and future are differences in time, but in presentation all that corresponds to these differences is in consciousness simultaneously."

There is thus a sort of *perspective projection* of past objects upon present consciousness, similar to that of wide landscapes upon a camera-screen.

And since we saw a while ago that our maximum distinct *intuition* of duration hardly covers more than a dozen seconds (while our maximum vague intuition is probably not more than that of a minute or so), we must suppose that *this amount of duration is pictured fairly steadily in each passing instant of consciousness* by virtue of some fairly constant feature in the brain-process to which the consciousness is tied. *This feature of the brain-process, whatever it be, must be the cause of our perceiving the fact of time at all.*[42] The duration thus steadily perceived is hardly more than the 'specious present,' as it was called a few pages back. Its *content* is in a constant flux, events dawning into its forward end as fast as they fade out of its rearward one, and each of them changing its time-coefficient from 'not yet,' or 'not quite yet,' to 'just gone,' or 'gone,' as it passes by. Meanwhile, the specious present, the intuited duration, stands permanent, like the rainbow on the waterfall, with its own quality unchanged by the events that stream through it. Each of these, as it slips out, retains the power of being reproduced; and when reproduced, is reproduced with the duration and neighbors which it originally had. Please observe, however, that the reproduction of an event, *after* it has once completely dropped out of the rearward end of the specious present, is an entirely different psychic fact from its direct perception in the specious present as a thing immediately past. A creature might be entirely devoid of *reproductive* memory, and yet have the time-sense; but the latter would be limited, in his case, to the few seconds immediately passing by. Time older than that he would never recall. I assume reproduction in the text, because I am speaking of human beings who notoriously possess it. Thus memory gets strewn with *dated* things—dated in

42 The cause of the perceiving, not the object perceived!

the sense of being before or after each other.[43] The date of a thing is a mere relation of *before* or *after* the present thing or some past or future thing. Some things we date simply by mentally tossing them into the past or future *direction*. So in space we think of England as simply to the eastward, of Charleston as lying south. But, again, we may date an event exactly, by fitting it between two terms of a past or future series explicitly conceived, just as we may accurately think of England or Charleston being just so many miles away.[44]

The things and events thus vaguely or exactly dated become thenceforward those signs and symbols of longer time-spaces, of which we previously spoke. According as we think of a multitude of them, or of few, so we imagine the time they represent to be long or short. But *the original paragon and prototype of all conceived times is the specious present, the short duration of which we are immediately and incessantly sensible.*

TO WHAT CEREBRAL PROCESS IS THE SENSE OF TIME DUE?

Now, to what element in the brain-process may this sensibility be due? It cannot, as we have seen, be due to the mere duration itself of the process; it must be due to an element present at every moment of the process, and this element must bear the same inscrutable *sort* of relation to its correlative feeling which all other elements of neural activity bear to their psychic products, be the latter what they may. Several suggestions have been made as to

43 " 'No more' and 'not yet' are the proper time-feelings, and we are aware of time in no other way than through these feelings," says Volkmann (*Psychologie*, § 87). This, which is not strictly true of our feeling of *time per se*, as an elementary bit of duration, is true of our feeling of *date* in its events.

44 We construct the miles just as we construct the years. Travelling in the cars makes a succession of different fields of view pass before our eyes. When those that have passed from present sight revive in memory, they maintain their mutual order because their contents overlap. We think them as having been before or behind each other; and, from the multitude of the views we can recall behind the one now presented, we compute the total space we have passed through.

It is often said that the perception of time develops later than that of space, because children have so vague an idea of all dates before yesterday and after tomorrow. But no vaguer than they have of extensions that exceed as greatly their unit of space-intuition. Recently I heard my child of four tell a visitor that he had been 'as much as one week' in the country. As he had been there three months, the visitor expressed surprise; whereupon the child corrected himself by saying he had been there 'twelve years.' But the child made exactly the same kind of mistake when he asked if Boston was not one hundred miles from Cambridge, the distance being three miles.

what the element is in the case of time. Treating of them in a note,[45] I will try to express briefly the only conclusion which seems

[45] Most of these explanations simply give the *signs* which, adhering to impressions, lead us to *date* them within a duration, or, in other words, to assign to them their order. Why it should be a *time*-order, however, is not explained. Herbart's would-be explanation is a simple description of time-perception. He says it comes when, with the last member of a series present to our consciousness, we also think of the first; and then the whole series revives in our thought at once, but with strength diminishing in the *backward* direction (*Psychologie als Wissenschaft*, § 115; *Lehrbuch zur Psychologie*, §§ 171, 172, 175). Similarly Drobisch, who adds that the series must appear as one already *elapsed* (*durchlaufene*), a word which shows even more clearly the question-begging nature of this sort of account (*Empirische Psychologie*, § 59). Theodor Waitz is guilty of similar question-begging when he explains our time-consciousness to be engendered by a set of unsuccessful attempts to make our percepts agree with our *expectations* (*Lehrbuch der Psychologie*, § 52). Volkmann's mythological account of past representations striving to drive present ones out of the seat of consciousness, being driven *back* by them, etc., suffers from the same fallacy (*Psychologie*, § 87). But all such accounts agree in implying one fact—viz., that the brain-processes of various events must be active simultaneously, and in varying strength, for a time-perception to be possible. Later authors have made this idea more precise. Thus, Lipps: "Sensations arise, occupy consciousness, fade into images, and vanish. According as two of them, *a* and *b*, go through this process simultaneously, or as one precedes or follows the other, the *phases of their fading* will agree or differ; and the difference will be proportional to the time-difference between their several moments of beginning. Thus there are differences of *quality* in the images, which the mind may *translate* into corresponding differences of their temporal order. There is no other possible middle term between the objective time-relations and those in the mind than these differences of phase." (*Grundtatsachen des Seelenlebens*, p. 588.) Lipps accordingly calls them 'temporal signs,' and hastens explicitly to add that the soul's translation of their order of strength into a time-order is entirely inexplicable (p. 591). M. Guyau's account (*Revue Philosophique*, XIX, 353) hardly differs from that of his predecessors, except in picturesqueness of style. Every change leaves a series of *trainées lumineuses* in the mind like the passage of shooting stars. Each image is in a more fading phase, according as its original was more remote. This group of images gives duration, the mere time-form, the 'bed' of time. The distinction of past, present, and future within the bed comes from our active nature. The future (as with Waitz) is what I want, but have not yet got, and must wait for. All this is doubtless true, but is no *explanation*.

Mr. Ward gives, in his *Encyclopædia Britannica* article ("Psychology," p. 65, col. 1), a still more refined attempt to specify the 'temporal sign.' The problem being, among a number of other things thought as successive, but simultaneously thought, to determine which is first and which last, he says: "After each distinct representation *a*, *b*, *c*, *d* there may intervene the representation of that *movement of attention* of which we are aware in passing from one object to another. In our present reminiscences we have, it must be allowed, little direct proof of this intervention; though there is, I think, indirect evidence of it in the tendency of the flow of ideas to follow the order in which the presentations were at first attended to. With the movement itself when the direction of attention changes, we are familiar enough, though the residua of such movements are not ordinarily conspicuous. These residua, then, are our temporal signs . . . . But temporal signs alone will not furnish all the pictorial exactness of the time-perspective. These give us only a fixed series; but the law of obliviscence, by insuring a progressive variation in intensity as we pass from one member of the series to the other, yields the effect which we call time-distance. By themselves such variations in intensity would leave us liable to confound more vivid representations in the distance with fainter ones nearer the present, but from this mistake the temporal signs save us; where the memory-continuum is imperfect such mistakes continually occur. On the other hand, where these variations are slight and imperceptible, though the memory-continuum preserves the order of events intact, we have still no such distinct appreciation of comparative distance in time as we have nearer to the present, where these perspective effects are considerable. . . . Locke speaks of our ideas succeeding each other 'at certain distances not much unlike the images in the inside of a lantern turned round by the heat of a candle,' and 'guesses' that 'this appearance of theirs in train varies not very much in a waking man.' *Now what is this 'distance' that separates a from b, b from c, and so on*; and what means have we of knowing that it is tolerably constant in waking life? *It is, probably, that, the residuum of which I have called a temporal sign; or, in other words, it is the movement of attention from a to b.*" Nevertheless, Mr. Ward does not call our feeling of this movement of attention the *original* of our feeling of time, or its brain-process the brain-process which directly causes us to perceive time. He says, a moment later, that "though the fixation of attention does of course really occupy time, it is probably not in the first instance perceived as time, *i.e.*, as continuous 'protensity,' to use a term of Hamilton's, but as intensity. Thus, if this supposition be true, there is an element in our concrete time-perceptions which has no place in our abstract conception of Time. In Time physically conceived there is no trace of intensity; in time psychically experienced duration is primarily an intensive magnitude, and so far literally a perception." Its 'original' is, then, if I understand Mr. Ward, something like a *feeling* which accompanies, as pleasure and pain may accompany, the movements of attention. Its brain-process must, it would seem, be assimilated in general type to the brain-processes of pleasure and pain. Such would seem more or less consciously to be Mr. Ward's own view, for he says: "Everybody knows what it is to be distracted by a rapid succession of varied impressions, and equally what it is to be wearied by the slow and monotonous recurrence of the same impressions. Now these 'feelings' of distraction and tedium owe their characteristic qualities to movements of attention. In the first, attention is kept incessantly on the move: before it is accommodated to *a*, it is disturbed by the suddenness, intensity, and novelty of *b*; in the second, it is kept all but stationary by the repeated presentation of the same impression. Such excess and defect of surprises make one realize a fact which in ordinary life is so obscure as to escape notice. But recent experiments have set this fact in a more striking light, and made clear what Locke had dimly before his mind in talking of a certain distance between the presentations of a waking man. In estimating very short periods of time, of a second or less, indicated say by the beats of a metronome, it is found that there is a certain period for which the mean of a number of estimates is correct, while shorter periods are on the whole over-, and longer periods under-estimated. I take this to be evidence of the time occupied in accommodating or fixing attention." Alluding to the fact that a series of experiences, *a b c d e*, may seem short in retrospect, which seemed everlasting in passing, he says: "What tells in retrospect is the series *a b c d e*, &c., what tells in the present is the intervening t_1 t_2 t_3, &c., or rather the original accommodation of which these temporal signs are the residuum." And he concludes thus: "We seem to have proof that our perception of duration rests ultimately upon quasi-motor objects of varying intensity, the duration of which we do not directly experience as duration at all."

Wundt also thinks that the interval of about three fourths of a second, which is

to emerge from a study of them and of the facts—unripe though that conclusion be.

The phenomena of 'summation of stimuli' in the nervous system prove that each stimulus leaves some latent activity behind it which only gradually passes away. (See above, pp. 89–92.) Psychological proof of the same fact is afforded by those 'after-images' which we perceive when a sensorial stimulus is gone. We may read off peculiarities in an after-image, left by an object on the eye, which we failed to note in the original. We may 'hark back' and take in the meaning of a sound several seconds after it has ceased. Delay for a minute, however, and the echo itself of the clock or the question is mute; present sensations have banished it beyond recall. With the feeling of the present thing there must at all times mingle the fad-

---

estimated with the minimum of error, points to a connection between the time-feeling and the succession of distinctly 'apperceived' objects before the mind. The 'association-time' is also equal to about three fourths of a second. This association-time he regards as a sort of internal standard of duration to which we involuntarily assimilate all intervals which we try to reproduce, bringing shorter ones up to it and longer ones down. [In the Stevens results we should have to say *contrast* instead of assimilate, for the longer intervals there seem longer, and the shorter ones shorter still.] "Singularly enough," he adds (*Physiologische Psychologie*, II, 286), "this time is about that in which in rapid walking, according to the Webers, our legs perform their swing. It seems thus not unlikely that both psychical constants, that of the average speed of reproduction and that of the surest estimation of time, have formed themselves under the influence of those most habitual movements of the body which we also use when we try to subdivide rhythmically longer tracts of time."

Finally, Prof. Mach makes a suggestion more specific still. After saying very rightly that we have a real *sensation* of time—how otherwise should we identify two entirely different airs as being played in the same 'time'? how distinguish in memory the first stroke of the clock from the second, unless to each there clove its special time-sensation, which revived with it?—he says "it is probable that this feeling is connected with that organic *consumption* which is necessarily linked with the production of consciousness, and that the time which we feel is probably due to the [mechanical?] *work of* [the process of?] *attention*. When attention is strained, time seems long; during easy occupation, short, etc. . . . The fatigue of the organ of consciousness, as long as we wake, continually increases, and the work of attention augments as continually. Those impressions which are conjoined with a *greater amount* of work of attention appear to us as the *later*." The apparent relative displacement of certain simultaneous events and certain anachronisms of dreams are held by Mach to be easily explicable as effects of a splitting of the attention between two objects, one of which consumes most of it (*Beiträge zur Analyse der Empfindungen*, p. 103 foll.). Mach's theory seems worthy of being better worked out. It is hard to say now whether he, Ward, and Wundt mean at bottom the same thing or not. The theory advanced in my own text, it will be remarked, does not pretend to be an *explanation*, but only an elementary statement of the 'law' which makes us aware of time. The Herbartian mythology purports to *explain*.

ing echo of all those other things which the previous few seconds have supplied. Or, to state it in neural terms, *there is at every moment a cumulation of brain-processes overlapping each other, of which the fainter ones are the dying phases of processes which but shortly previous were active in a maximal degree. The* AMOUNT OF THE OVERLAPPING *determines the feeling of the* DURATION OCCUPIED. WHAT EVENTS *shall appear to occupy the duration depends on just* WHAT PROCESSES *the overlapping processes are.* We know so little of the intimate nature of the brain's activity that even where a sensation monotonously endures, we cannot say that the earlier moments of it do not leave fading processes behind which coexist with those of the present moment. *Duration and events together form our intuition of the specious present with its content.*[46] *Why* such an intuition should result from such a combination of brain-processes I do not pretend to say. All I aim at is to state the most *elemental* form of the psycho-physical conjunction.

I have assumed that the brain-processes are sensational ones. Processes of active attention (see Mr. Ward's account in the long footnote) will leave similar fading brain-processes behind. If the mental processes are conceptual, a complication is introduced of which I will in a moment speak. Meanwhile, still speaking of sensational processes, a remark of Wundt's will throw additional light on the account I give. As is known, Wundt and others have proved that every act of perception of a sensorial stimulus takes an appreciable time. When two different stimuli—e.g., a sight and a sound—are given at once or nearly at once, we have difficulty in attending to both, and may wrongly judge their interval, or even invert their order. Now, as the result of his experiments on such stimuli, Wundt lays down this law:[47] that of the three possible determinations we may make of their order—

46 It would be rash to say definitely just how many seconds long this specious present must needs be, for processes fade 'asymptotically,' and the distinctly intuited present merges into a penumbra of mere dim *recency* before it turns into the past which is simply reproduced and conceived. Many a thing which we do not distinctly date by intercalating it in a place between two other things will, nevertheless, come to us with this feeling of belonging to a *near* past. This sense of recency is a feeling *sui generis,* and may affect things that happened hours ago. It would seem to show that their brain-processes are still in a state modified by the foregoing excitement, still in a 'fading' phase, in spite of the long interval.

47 *Physiologische Psychologie,* II, 263.

"namely, simultaneity, continuous transition, and discontinuous transition—only the first and last are realized, *never the second.* Invariably, when we fail to perceive the impressions as simultaneous, we notice a shorter or longer empty time between them, *which seems to correspond to the sinking of one of the ideas and to the rise of the other.* . . . For our attention may share itself equally between the two impressions, which will then compose one total percept [and be simultaneously felt]; or it may be so adapted to one event as to cause it to be perceived immediately, and then the second event can be perceived only after a certain time of latency, during which the attention reaches its effective maximum for it and diminishes for the first event. In this case the events are perceived as *two,* and in successive order—that is, as separated by a time-interval in which attention is not sufficiently accommodated to either to bring a distinct perception about. . . . While we are hurrying from one to the other, everything between them vanishes in the twilight of general consciousness." [48]

One might call this the *law of discontinuous succession in time, of percepts to which we cannot easily attend at once.* Each percept then requires a separate brain-process; and when one brain-process is at its maximum, the other would appear perforce to be in either

[48] I leave my text as it was printed before Münsterberg's essay appeared (see above page 584, note). He denies that we measure any but minimal durations by the amount of fading in the ideational processes, and talks almost exclusively of our feelings of muscular tension in his account, whereas I have made no mention of such things in mine. I cannot, however, see that there is any conflict between what he and I suggest. I am mainly concerned with the consciousness of duration regarded as a specific sort of object, he is concerned with this object's measurement exclusively. Feelings of tension might be the means of the measurement, whilst overlapping processes of any and every kind gave the object to be measured. The accommodative and respiratory movements from which the feelings of tension come form regularly recurring sensations divided by their 'phases' into intervals as definite as those by which a yardstick is divided by the marks upon its length.

Let a^1, a^2, a^3, a^4, be homologous phases in four successive movements of this kind. If four outer stimuli 1, 2, 3, 4, coincide each with one of these successive phases, then their 'distances apart' are felt as *equal,* otherwise not. But there is no reason whatever to suppose that the mere overlapping of the brain-process of 2 by the fading process of 1, or that of 3 by that of 2, etc., does not give the *characteristic quality of content* which we *call* 'distance apart' in this experience, and which by aid of the muscular feelings gets judged to be equal. Doubtless the muscular feelings can give us the object 'time' as well as its measure, because their earlier phases leave fading sensations which constantly overlap the vivid sensation of the present phase. But it would be contrary to analogy to suppose that they should be the only experiences which give this object. I do not understand Herr Münsterberg to claim this for them. He takes our *sense* of time for granted, and only discusses its measurement.

a waning or a waxing phase. If our theory of the time-feeling be true, empty time *must* then subjectively appear to separate the two percepts, no matter how close together they may objectively be; for, according to that theory, the feeling of a time-duration is the immediate effect of such an overlapping of brain-processes of different phase—wherever and from whatever cause it may occur.

To pass, now, to conceptual processes: Suppose I think of the Creation, then of the Christian era, then of the battle of Waterloo, all within a few seconds. These matters have their dates far outside the specious present. The processes by which I think them, however, all overlap. What events, then, does the specious present seem to contain? Simply my successive *acts of thinking* these long-past things, not the long-past things themselves. As the instantly-present thought may be of a long-past thing, so the just-past thought may be of another long-past thing. When a long-past event is reproduced in memory and conceived with its date, the reproduction and conceiving traverse the specious present. The immediate content of the latter is thus all my *direct experiences*, whether subjective or objective. Some of these meanwhile may be *representative* of other experiences indefinitely remote.

The number of these direct experiences which the specious present and immediately-intuited past may embrace measures the extent of our 'primary,' as Exner calls it, or, as Richet calls it, of our 'elementary' memory.[49] The sensation resultant from the overlapping is that of the duration which the experiences seem to fill. As is the number of any larger set of events to that of these experiences, so we suppose is the length of that duration to this duration. But of the longer duration we have no direct 'realizing sense.' The variations in our appreciation of the same amount of real time may possibly be explained by alterations in the rate of fading in the images, producing changes in the complication of superposed processes, to which changes changed states of consciousness may correspond. But however *long we may conceive* a space of time to be, the objective amount of it which is *directly perceived* at any one moment by us can never exceed the scope of our 'primary memory' at the moment in question.[50]

49 Exner in Hermann's *Handbuch der Physiologie*, Bd. II, Thl. II, p. 281. Richet in *Revue Philosophique*, XXI, 568 (juin 1886). See the next chapter, pp. 606–608.

50 I have spoken of *fading* brain-processes alone, but only for simplicity's sake. *Dawning* processes probably play as important a part in giving the feeling of duration to the specious present.

We have every reason to think that creatures may possibly differ enormously in the amounts of duration which they intuitively feel, and in the fineness of the events that may fill it. Von Baer has indulged[51] in some interesting computations of the effect of such differences in changing the aspect of Nature. Suppose we were able, within the length of a second, to note 10,000 events distinctly, instead of barely 10, as now; if our life were then destined to hold the same number of impressions, it might be 1000 times as short. We should live less than a month, and personally know nothing of the change of seasons. If born in winter, we should believe in summer as we now believe in the heats of the Carboniferous era. The motions of organic beings would be so slow to our senses as to be inferred, not seen. The sun would stand still in the sky, the moon be almost free from change, and so on. But now reverse the hypothesis and suppose a being to get only one 1000th part of the sensations that we get in a given time, and consequently to live 1000 times as long. Winters and summers will be to him like quarters of an hour. Mushrooms and the swifter-growing plants will shoot into being so rapidly as to appear instantaneous creations; annual shrubs will rise and fall from the earth like restlessly boiling-water springs; the motions of animals will be as invisible as are to us the movements of bullets and cannon-balls; the sun will scour through the sky like a meteor, leaving a fiery trail behind him, etc. That such imaginary cases (barring the superhuman longevity) may be realized somewhere in the animal kingdom, it would be rash to deny.

"A gnat's wings," says Mr. Spencer,[52] "make ten or fifteen thousand strokes per second. Each stroke implies a separate nervous action. Each such nervous action, or change in a nervous centre, is probably as appreciable by the gnat as is a quick movement of his arm by a man. And if this, or anything like this, is the fact, then the time occupied by a given external change, measured by many movements in the one case, must seem much longer than in the other case, when measured by one movement."

In hasheesh-intoxication there is a curious increase in the apparent time-perspective. We utter a sentence, and ere the end is reached the beginning seems already to date from indefinitely long ago. We

51 *Reden* (St. Petersburg, 1864), vol. 1, pp. 255–268.
52 *Psychology*, § 91.

enter a short street, and it is as if we should never get to the end of it. This alteration might conceivably result from an approach to the condition of von Baer's and Spencer's short-lived beings. If our discrimination of successions became finer-grained, so that we noted ten stages in a process where previously we only noted one; and if at the same time the processes faded ten times as fast as before; we might have a specious present of the same subjective length as now, giving us the same time-feeling and containing as many distinguishable successive events, but out from the earlier end of it would have dropped nine tenths of the real events it now contains. They would have fallen into the general reservoir of merely dated memories, reproducible at will. The beginning of our sentences would have to be expressly recalled; each word would appear to pass through consciousness at a tenth of its usual speed. The condition would, in short, be exactly analogous to the enlargement of space by a microscope; fewer real things at once in the immediate field of view, but each of them taking up more than its normal room, and making the excluded ones seem unnaturally far away.

Under other conditions, processes seem to fade rapidly without the compensating increase in the subdivisibility of successions. Here the apparent length of the specious present contracts. Consciousness dwindles to a point, and loses all intuitive sense of the whence and whither of its path. Express acts of memory replace rapid bird's-eye views. In my own case, something like this occurs in extreme fatigue. Long illnesses produce it. Occasionally, it appears to accompany aphasia.[53] It would be vain to seek to imagine

[53] "The patient cannot retain the image of an object more than a moment. His memory is as short for sounds, letters, figures, and printed words. If we cover a written or printed word with a sheet of paper in which a little window has been cut, so that only the first letter is visible through the window, he pronounces this letter. If, then, the sheet is moved so as to cover the first letter and make the second one visible, he pronounces the second, but forgets the first, and cannot pronounce the first and second together." And so forth to the end. "If he closes his eyes and draws his finger exploringly over a well-known object like a knife or key, he cannot combine the separate impressions and recognize the object. But if it is put into his hand so that he can simultaneously touch it with several fingers, he names it without difficulty. This patient has thus lost the capacity for grouping successive . . . impressions . . . into a whole and perceiving them as a whole." (Grashey, in *Archiv für Psychiatrie*, Bd. XVI, pp. 672–673.) It is hard to believe that in such a patient the time intuited was not clipped off like the impressions it held, though perhaps not so much of it.

I have myself often noted a curious exaggeration of time-perspective at the moment of a falling asleep. A person will be moving or doing something in the room,

the exact brain-change in any of these cases. But we must admit the possibility that to some extent the variations of time-estimate between youth and age, and excitement and *ennui*, are due to such causes, more immediate than to the one we assigned some time ago.

But whether our feeling of the time which immediately-past[54] *events have filled be of something long or of something short, it is not what it is because those events are past,* but *because they have left behind them processes which are present. To those processes, however caused, the mind would still respond by feeling a specious present, with one part of it just vanishing or vanished into the past.* As the Creator is supposed to have made Adam with a navel—sign of a birth which never occurred—so He might instantaneously make a man with a brain in which were processes just like the 'fading' ones of an ordinary brain. The first real stimulus after creation would set up a process additional to these. The processes would overlap; and the new-created man would unquestionably have the feeling, at the very primal instant of his life, of having been in existence already some little space of time.

Let me sum up, now, by saying that we are constantly conscious of a certain duration—the specious present—varying in length from a few seconds to probably not more than a minute, and that this duration (with its content perceived as having one part earlier and the other part later) is the original intuition of time. Longer times are conceived by adding, shorter ones by dividing, portions of this vaguely bounded unit, and are habitually thought by us symbolically. Kant's notion of an *intuition* of objective time as an infinite necessary continuum has nothing to support it. The *cause* of the intuition which we really have cannot be the *duration* of our brain-

---

and a certain stage of his act (whatever it may be) will be my last waking perception. Then a subsequent stage will wake me to a new perception. The two stages of the act will not be more than a few seconds apart; and yet it always seems to me as if, between the earlier and the later one, a long interval has passed away. I conjecturally account for the phenomenon thus, calling the two stages of the act *a* and *b* respectively: Were I awake, *a* would leave a fading process in my sensorium which would overlap the process of *b* when the latter came, and both would then appear in the same specious present, *a* belonging to its earlier end. But the sudden advent of the brain-change called sleep extinguishes *a*'s fading process abruptly. When *b* then comes and wakes me, *a* comes back, it is true, but not as belonging to the specious present. It has to be specially *revoked* in memory. This mode of revocation usually characterizes long-past things—whence the illusion.

54 Again I omit the future, merely for simplicity's sake.

processes or our mental changes. That duration is rather the *object* of the intuition which, being realized at every moment of such duration, must be due to a permanently present cause. This cause —probably the simultaneous presence of brain-processes of different phase—fluctuates; and hence a certain range of variation in the amount of the intuition, and in its subdivisibility, accrues.

Chapter XVI

Memory

In the last chapter what concerned us was the direct *intuition* of time. We found it limited to intervals of considerably less than a minute. Beyond its borders extends the immense region of *conceived* time, past and future, into one direction or another of which we mentally project all the events which we think of as real, and form a systematic order of them by giving to each a date. The relation of conceived to intuited time is just like that of the fictitious space pictured on the flat back-scene of a theatre to the actual space of the stage. The objects painted on the former (trees, columns, houses in a receding street, etc.) carry back the series of similar objects solidly placed upon the latter, and we think we see things in a continuous perspective, when we really see thus only a few of them and imagine that we see the rest. The chapter which lies before us deals with the way in which we paint the remote past, as it were, upon a canvas in our memory, and yet often imagine that we have direct vision of its depths.

The stream of thought flows on; but most of its segments fall into the bottomless abyss of oblivion. Of some, no memory survives the instant of their passage. Of others, it is confined to a few moments, hours, or days. Others, again, leave vestiges which are indestructible, and by means of which they may be recalled as long as life endures. Can we explain these differences?

PRIMARY MEMORY

The first point to be noticed is that *for a state of mind to survive in memory it must have endured for a certain length of time.* In other words, it must be what I call a substantive state. Prepositional and conjunctival states of mind are not remembered as independent facts—we cannot recall just how we felt when we said 'how' or 'notwithstanding.' Our consciousness of these transitive states is shut up to their own moment—hence one difficulty in introspective psychologizing.

Any state of mind which is shut up to its own moment and fails to become an object for succeeding states of mind, is as if it belonged to another stream of thought. Or rather, it belongs only physically, not intellectually, to its own stream, forming a bridge from one segment of it to another, but not being appropriated inwardly by later segments or appearing as part of the empirical self, in the manner explained in Chapter X. All the intellectual value for us of a state of mind depends on our after-memory of it. Only then is it combined in a system and knowingly made to contribute to a result. Only then does it *count* for us. So that *the* EFFECTIVE *consciousness we have of our states is the after-consciousness*; and the more of this there is, the more influence does the original state have, and the more permanent a factor is it of our world. An indelibly-imprinted pain may color a life; but, as Professor Richet says:

> "To suffer for only a hundredth of a second is not to suffer at all; and for my part I would readily agree to undergo a pain, however acute and intense it might be, provided it should last only a hundredth of a second, and leave after it neither reverberation nor recall."[1]

Not that a momentary state of consciousness need be practically resultless. Far from it: such a state, though absolutely unremembered, might at its own moment determine the transition of our thinking in a vital way, and decide our action irrevocably.[2] But the

[1] *L'Homme et l'intelligence*, p. 32.

[2] Professor Richet has therefore no right to say, as he does in another place (*Revue Philosophique*, XXI, 570): "*Without memory no conscious sensation, without memory no consciousness.*" All he is entitled to say is: "Without memory no consciousness known outside of itself." Of the sort of consciousness that is an object for later states, and becomes as it were permanent, he gives a good example: "Who

idea of it could not *afterwards* determine transition and action, its content could not be conceived as one of the mind's permanent meanings: that is all I mean by saying that its intellectual value lies in after-memory.

As a rule sensations outlast for some little time the objective stimulus which occasioned them. This phenomenon is the ground of those 'after-images' which are familiar in the physiology of the sense-organs. If we open our eyes instantaneously upon a scene, and then shroud them in complete darkness, it will be as if we saw the scene in ghostly light through the dark screen. We can read off details in it which were unnoticed whilst the eyes were open.[3]

In every sphere of sense, an intermittent stimulus, often enough repeated, produces a continuous sensation. This is because the after-image of the impression just gone by blends with the new impression coming in. The effects of stimuli may thus be superposed upon each other many stages deep, the total result in consciousness being an increase in the feeling's intensity, and in all probability, as we saw in the last chapter, an elementary sense of the lapse of time (see pp. 597–598).

Exner writes:

---

of us, alas! has not experienced a bitter and profound grief, the immense laceration caused by the death of some cherished fellow-being? Well, in these great griefs the present endures neither for a minute, for an hour, nor for a day, but for weeks and months. The memory of the cruel moment will not efface itself from consciousness. It disappears not, but remains living, present, coexisting with the multitude of other sensations which are juxtaposed in consciousness alongside of this one persistent emotion which is felt always in the present tense. A long time is needed ere we can attain to forgetting it, ere we can make it enter into the past. *Hæret lateri letalis arundo.*" (*Ibid.*, 583.)

[3] This is the primary positive after-image. According to Helmholtz, one third of a second is the most favorable length of exposure to the light for producing it. Longer exposure, complicated by subsequent admission of light to the eye, results in the ordinary negative and complementary after-images, with their changes, which may (if the original impression was brilliant and the fixation long) last for many minutes. Fechner gives the name of memory-after-images (*Psychophysik*, II, 492) to the instantaneous positive effects, and distinguishes them from ordinary after-images by the following characters: 1) Their originals must have been *attended to*, only such parts of a compound original as have been attended to appearing. This is not the case in common visual after-images. 2) The strain of attention towards them is inwards, as in ordinary remembering, not outwards, as in observing a common after-image. 3) A short fixation of the original is better for the memory-after-image, a long one for the ordinary after-image. 4) The colors of the memory-after-image are never complementary of those of the original.

"Impressions to which we are inattentive leave so brief an image in the memory that it is usually overlooked. When deeply absorbed, we do not hear the clock strike. But our attention may awake after the striking has ceased, and we may then count off the strokes. Such examples are often found in daily life. We can also prove the existence of this *primary memory-image*, as it may be called, in another person, even when his attention is completely absorbed elsewhere. Ask someone, e.g., to count the lines of a printed page as fast as he can, and whilst this is going on walk a few steps about the room. Then, when the person has done counting, ask him where you stood. He will always reply quite definitely that you have walked. Analogous experiments may be made with vision. This primary memory-image is, whether attention have been turned to the impression or not, an extremely lively one, but is subjectively quite distinct from every sort of after-image or hallucination. . . . It vanishes, if not caught by attention, in the course of a few seconds. Even when the original impression is attended to, the liveliness of its image in memory fades fast."[4]

The physical condition in the nerve-tissue of this primary memory is called by Richet 'elementary memory.'[5] I much prefer to reserve the word memory for the conscious phenomenon. What happens in the nerve-tissue is but an example of that plasticity or of semi-inertness, yielding to change, but not yielding instantly or wholly, and never quite recovering the original form, which, in Chapter IV, we saw to be the groundwork of habit. Elementary *habit* would be the better name for what Professor Richet means. Well, the first manifestation of elementary habit is the slow dying away of an impressed movement on the neural matter, and its first effect in consciousness is this so-called elementary memory. But what elementary memory makes us aware of is the *just* past. The objects we feel in this directly intuited past differ from properly recollected objects. An object which is recollected, in the proper sense of that term, is one which has been absent from consciousness altogether, and now revives anew. It is brought back, recalled, fished up, so to speak, from a reservoir in which, with countless other objects, it lay buried and lost from view. But an object of primary memory is not thus brought back; it never was lost; its date was never cut off in consciousness from that of the immediately present moment. In fact it comes to us as belonging to the rearward

4 Hermann's *Handbuch*, Bd. II, Thl. II, 281.

5 *Revue Philosophique*, 562.

portion of the present space of time, and not to the genuine past. In the last chapter we saw that the portion of time which we directly intuit has a breadth of several seconds, a rearward and a forward end, and may be called the specious present. All stimuli whose first nerve-vibrations have not yet ceased seem to be conditions of our getting this feeling of the specious present. They give rise to objects which appear to the mind as events just past.[6]

When we have been exposed to an unusual stimulus for many minutes or hours, a nervous process is set up which results in the haunting of consciousness by the impression for a long time afterwards. The tactile and muscular feelings of a day of skating or riding, after long disuse of the exercise, will come back to us all through the night. Images of the field of view of the microscope will annoy the observer for hours after an unusually long sitting at the instrument. A thread tied around the finger, an unusual constriction in the clothing, will feel as if still there, long after they have been removed. These revivals (called phenomena of *Sinnesgedächtniss* by the Germans) have something periodical in their nature.[7] They show that profound rearrangements and slow settlings into a new equilibrium are going on in the neural substance, and they form the transition to that more peculiar and proper phenomenon of memory, of which the rest of this chapter must treat. The first condition which makes a thing susceptible of recall after it has been forgotten is that the original impression of it should have been prolonged enough to give rise to a *recurrent* image of it, as distinguished from one of those primary after-images which very fleeting impressions may leave behind, and which contain in themselves no guarantee that they will ever come back after having once faded away.[8] A certain length of stimulation seems demanded by

[6] Richet says: "The present has a certain duration, a variable duration, sometimes a rather long one, which comprehends all the time occupied by the after-reverberation [*retentissement*, after-image] of a sensation. For example, if the reverberation of an electric shock within our nerves lasts ten minutes, for that electric shock there is a present of ten minutes. On the other hand, a feebler sensation will have a shorter present. But in every case, for a conscious sensation [I should say for a *remembered* sensation] to occur, there must be a present of a certain duration, of a few seconds at least." We have seen in the last chapter that it is hard to trace the backward limits of this immediately intuited duration, or specious present. The figures which M. Richet supposes appear to be considerably too large.

[7] Cf. Fechner: *Psychophysik*, II, 499.

[8] The primary after-image itself cannot be utilized if the stimulus is too brief. Mr. Cattell found (*Philosophische Studien*, III, p. 93 ff.) that the color of a light must fall

the inertia of the nerve-substance. Exposed to a shorter influence, its modification fails to 'set,' and it retains no effective tendency to fall again into the same form of vibration at which the original feeling was due. This, as I said at the outset, may be the reason why only 'substantive' and not 'transitive' states of mind are as a rule recollected, at least as independent things. The transitive states pass by too quickly.

ANALYSIS OF THE PHENOMENON OF MEMORY

Memory proper, or secondary memory as it might be styled, is the knowledge of a former state of mind after it has already once dropped from consciousness; or rather *it is the knowledge of an event, or fact,* of which meantime we have not been thinking, *with the additional consciousness that we have thought or experienced it before.*

The first element which such a knowledge involves would seem to be the revival in the mind of an image or copy of the original event.[9] And it is an assumption made by many writers[10] that the

upon the eye for a period varying from 0.006 to 0.0275 of a second, in order to be recognized for what it is. Letters of the alphabet and familiar words require from 0.00075 to 0.00175 sec.—truly an interval extremely short. Some letters, E for example, are harder than others. In 1871 Helmholtz and Baxt had ascertained that when an impression was immediately followed by another, the latter quenched the former and prevented it from being known to later consciousness. The first stimulus was letters of the alphabet, the second a bright white disk. "With an interval of 0.0048 sec. between the two excitations [I copy here the abstract in Ladd's *Physiological Psychology,* p. 480], the disk appeared as scarcely a trace of a weak shimmer; with an interval of 0.0096 sec., letters appeared in the shimmer—one or two of which could be partially recognized when the interval increased to 0.0144 sec. When the interval was made 0.0192 sec., the objects were a little more clearly discerned; at 0.0336 sec. four letters could be well recognized; at 0.0432 sec., five letters; and at 0.0528 sec. all the letters could be read." (Pflüger's *Archiv,* IV, 325 ff.)

9 When the past is recalled symbolically, or conceptually only, it is true that no such copy need be there. In no sort of conceptual knowledge is it requisite that definitely resembling images be there (cf. pp. 445 ff.). But as all conceptual knowledge stands for intuitive knowledge, and terminates therein, I abstract from this complication, and confine myself to those memories in which the past is directly imaged in the mind, or, as we say, intuitively known.

10 E.g., Spencer: *Psychology,* I, p. 448. How do the believers in the sufficiency of the 'image' formulate the cases where we remember that something did *not* happen—that we did not wind our watch, did not lock the door, etc.? It is very hard to account for these memories of omission. The image of winding the watch is just as present to my mind now when I remember that I did not wind it as if I remembered that I did. It must be a difference in the mode of feeling the image which leads me to such differ-

revival of an image is all that is needed to constitute the memory of the original occurrence. But such a revival is obviously not a *memory*, whatever else it may be; it is simply a duplicate, a second event, having absolutely no connection with the first event except that it happens to resemble it. The clock strikes to-day; it struck yesterday; and may strike a million times ere it wears out. The rain pours through the gutter this week; it did so last week; and will do so *in sæcula sæculorum*. But does the present clock-stroke become aware of the past ones, or the present stream recollect the past stream, because they repeat and resemble them? Assuredly not. And let it not be said that this is because clock-strokes and gutters are physical and not psychical objects; for psychical objects (sensations, for example) simply recurring in successive editions will remember each other *on that account* no more than clock-strokes do. No memory is involved in the mere fact of recurrence. The successive editions of a feeling are so many independent events, each snug in its own skin. Yesterday's feeling is dead and buried; and the presence of to-day's is no reason why it should resuscitate. A farther condition is required before the present image can be held to stand for a *past original*.

That condition is that the fact imaged be *expressly referred to the past*, thought as *in the past*. But how can we think a thing as in the past, except by thinking of the past together with the thing, and of the relation of the two? And how can we think of the past? In the chapter on Time-perception we have seen that our intuitive or immediate consciousness of pastness hardly carries us more than a few seconds backwards of the present instant of time. Remoter dates are conceived, not perceived; known symbolically by names, such as 'last week,' '1850'; or thought of by events which happened in them, as the year in which we attended such a school, or met with such a loss. So that if we wish to think of a particular past epoch, we must think of a name or other symbol, or else of certain concrete events, associated therewithal. Both must be thought of,

---

ent conclusions in the two cases. When I remember that I did wind it, I feel it grown together with its associates of past date and place. When I remember that I did not, it keeps aloof; the associates fuse with each other, but not with it. This sense of fusion, of the belonging together of things, is a most subtle relation; the sense of non-fusion is an equally subtle one. Both relations demand most complex mental processes to know them, processes quite different from that mere presence or absence of an image which does such service in the cruder books.

to think the past epoch adequately. And to 'refer' any special fact to the past epoch is to think that fact *with* the names and events which characterize its date, to think it, in short, with a lot of contiguous associates.

But even this would not be memory. Memory requires more than mere dating of a fact in the past. It must be dated in *my* past. In other words, I must think that I directly experienced its occurrence. It must have that 'warmth and intimacy' which were so often spoken of in the chapter on the Self, as characterizing all experiences 'appropriated' by the thinker as his own.

A general feeling of the past direction in time, then, a particular date conceived as lying along that direction, and defined by its name or phenomenal contents, an event imagined as located therein, and owned as part of my experience,—such are the elements of every act of memory.

It follows that what we began by calling the 'image,' or 'copy,' of the fact in the mind, is really not there at all in that simple shape, as a separate 'idea.' Or at least, if it be there as a separate idea, no memory will go with it. What memory goes with is, on the contrary, a very complex representation, that of the fact to be recalled *plus* its associates, the whole forming one 'object' (as explained on page 265, Chapter IX), known in one integral pulse of consciousness (as set forth on pp. 266 ff.) and demanding probably a vastly more intricate brain-process than that on which any simple sensorial image depends.

Most psychologists have given a perfectly clear analysis of the phenomenon we describe. Christian Wolff, for example, writes:

"Suppose you have seen Mevius in the temple, but now afresh in Titus' house. I say you *recognize* Mevius, that is, are conscious of having seen him before, because, although now you perceive him with your senses along with Titus' house, your imagination produces an image of him along with one of the temple, and of the acts of your own mind reflecting on Mevius in the temple. Hence the idea of Mevius which is reproduced in sense is contained in another series of perceptions than that which formerly contained it, and this difference is the reason why we are conscious of having had it before. . . . For whilst now you see Mevius in the house of Titus, your imagination places him in the temple, and renders you conscious of the state of mind which you found in yourself when you beheld him there. By this you know that you have seen him before, that is, you recognize him. But you recognize him because his idea is now contained in another series of perceptions from that in which you first saw him."[11]

Similarly James Mill writes:

"In my remembrance of George III., addressing the two Houses of Parliament, there is, first of all, the mere idea, or simple apprehension; the conception as it is sometimes called, of the objects. There is combined with this, to make it memory, my idea of my having seen and heard those objects. And this combination is so close, that it is not in my power to separate them. I cannot have the idea of George III.; his person and attitude, the paper he held in his hand, the sound of his voice while reading from it . . . without having the other idea along with it, that of my having been a witness of the scene. . . . If this explanation of the case in which we remember sensations is understood, the explanation of the case in which we remember ideas cannot occasion much of difficulty. I have a lively recollection of Polyphemus's cave, and the actions of Ulysses and the Cyclops, as described by Homer. In this recollection there is, first of all, the ideas, or simple conceptions of the objects and acts; and along with these ideas, and so closely combined as not to be separable, the idea of my having formerly had those same ideas. And this idea of my having formerly had those ideas, is a very complicated idea; including the idea of myself of the present moment remembering, and that of myself of the past moment conceiving; and the whole series of the states of consciousness, which intervened between myself remembering, and myself conceiving."[12]

Memory is then the feeling of belief in a peculiar complex object; but all the elements of this object may be known to other states of belief; nor is there in the particular combination of them as they appear in memory anything so peculiar as to lead us to oppose the latter to other sorts of thought as something altogether *sui generis*, needing a special faculty to account for it. When later we come to our chapter on Belief we shall see that any represented object which is connected either mediately or immediately with our present sensations or emotional activities tends to be believed in as a reality.

[11] *Psychologia Empirica*, § 174.

[12] *Analysis*, I, 330–1. Mill believed that the various things remembered, the self included, enter consciousness in the form of separate ideas, but so rapidly that they are 'all clustered into one.' "Ideas called up in close conjunction . . . assume, even when there is the greatest complexity, the appearance, not of many ideas, but of one" (vol. II, p. 123). This mythology does not impair the accuracy of his description of memory's *object*.

The sense of a peculiar active relation in it to ourselves is what gives to an object the characteristic quality of reality, and a merely imagined past event differs from a recollected one only in the absence of this peculiar feeling relation. The electric current, so to speak, between it and our present self does not close. But in their other determinations the re-recollected past and the imaginary past may be much the same. In other words, there is nothing unique in the *object* of memory, and no special faculty is needed to account for its formation. It is a synthesis of parts thought of as related together, perception, imagination, comparison and reasoning being analogous syntheses of parts into complex objects. The objects of any of these faculties may awaken belief or fail to awaken it; *the object of memory is only an object imagined in the past* (usually very completely imagined there) *to which the emotion of belief adheres.*

MEMORY'S CAUSES

Such being the *phenomenon* of memory, or the analysis of its object, can we see how it comes to pass? can we lay bare its causes?

Its complete exercise presupposes two things:

1) The *retention* of the remembered fact;

2) Its *reminiscence, recollection, reproduction,* or *recall.*

Now *the cause both of retention and of recollection is the law of habit in the nervous system, working as it does in the 'association of ideas.'*

Associationists have long explained *recollection* by association. James Mill gives an account of it which I am unable to improve upon, unless it might be by translating his word 'idea' into 'thing thought of,' or 'object,' as explained so often before.

"There is," he says, "a state of mind familiar to all men, in which we are said to try to remember. In this state, it is certain that we have not in the mind the idea which we are trying to have in it.[13] How then is it, that we proceed in the course of our endeavour to procure its introduction into the mind? If we have not the idea itself, we have certain ideas connected with it. We run over those ideas, one after another, in hopes that some one of them will suggest the idea we are in quest of; and if any one of them does, it is always one so connected with it, as to

[13] Compare, however, p. 243, Chapter IX.

call it up in the way of association. I meet an old acquaintance, whose name I do not remember, and wish to recollect. I run over a number of names, in hopes that some of them may be associated with the idea of the individual. I think of all the circumstances in which I have seen him engaged; the time when I knew him, the persons along with whom I knew him, the things he did, or the things he suffered; and, if I chance upon any idea with which the name is associated, then immediately I have the recollection; if not, my pursuit of it is in vain.[14] There is another set of cases, very familiar, but affording very important evidence on the subject. It frequently happens, that there are matters which we desire not to forget. What is the contrivance to which we have recourse for preserving the memory; that is, for making sure that it will be called into existence, when it is our wish that it should. All men, invariably employ the same expedient. They endeavour to form an association between the idea of the thing to be remembered, and some sensation, or some idea, which they know beforehand will occur at or near the time when they wish the remembrance to be in their minds. If this association is formed, and the sensation or the idea, with which it has been formed, occurs; the sensation, or idea, calls up the remembrance; and the object of him who formed the association is attained. To use a vulgar instance: a man receives a commission from his friend, and, that he may not forget it, ties a knot on his handkerchief. How is this fact to be explained? First of all, the idea of the commission is associated with the making of the knot. Next, the handkerchief is a thing which it is known beforehand will be frequently seen, and of course at no great distance of time from the occasion on which the memory is desired. The handkerchief being seen, the knot is seen, and this sensation recalls the idea of the commission, between which and itself, the association had been purposely formed." [15]

In short, we make search in our memory for a forgotten idea, just as we rummage our house for a lost object. In both cases we visit what seems to us the probable *neighborhood* of that which we miss. We turn over the things under which, or within which, or alongside of which, it may possibly be; and if it lies near them, it soon comes to view. But these matters, in the case of a mental object sought, are nothing but its *associates*. The machinery of recall is thus the same as the machinery of association, and the machinery

[14] Professor Bain adds, in a note to this passage of Mill's: "This process seems best expressed by laying down a law of Compound or Composite Association; under which a plurality of feeble links of connexion may be a substitute for one powerful and self-sufficing link."

[15] *Analysis*, chap. x.

of association, as we know, is nothing but the elementary law of habit in the nerve-centres.

And this same law of habit is the machinery of retention also. Retention means *liability* to recall, and it means nothing more than such liability. The only proof of there being retention is that recall actually takes place. The retention of an experience is, in short, but another name for the *possibility* of thinking it again, or the *tendency* to think it again, with its past surroundings. Whatever accidental cue may turn this tendency into an actuality, the permanent *ground* of the tendency itself lies in the organized neural paths by which the cue calls up the experience on the proper occasion, together with its past associates, the sense that the self was there, the belief that it really happened, etc., etc., just as previously described. When the recollection is of the 'ready' sort, the resuscitation takes place the instant the occasion arises; when it is slow, resuscitation comes after delay. But be the recall prompt or slow, the condition which makes it possible at all (or, in other words, the 'retention' of the experience) is neither more nor less than the brain-paths which *associate* the experience with the occasion and cue of the recall. *When slumbering, these paths are the condition of retention; when active, they are the condition of recall.*

A simple scheme will now make the whole cause of memory

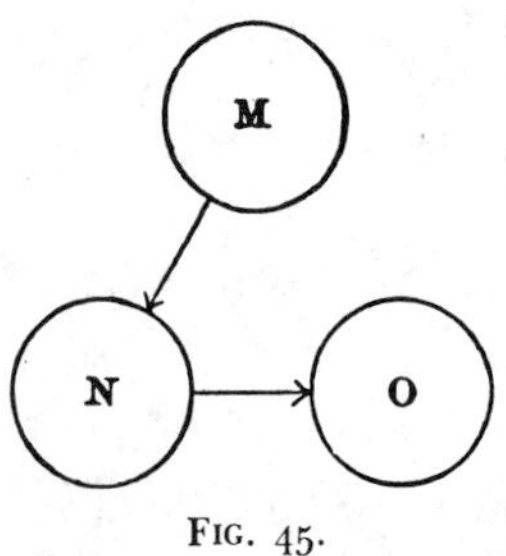

FIG. 45.

plain. Let *n* be a past event; *o* its 'setting' (concomitants, date, self present, warmth and intimacy, etc., etc., as already set forth); and *m* some present thought or fact which may appropriately become the occasion of its recall. Let the nerve-centres, active in the thought of *m*, *n*, and *o*, be represented by M, N, and O, respectively; then the *existence* of the paths M—N and N—O will be the fact indicated by the phrase 'retention of the event *n* in the memory,' and the *ex-*

citement of the brain along these paths will be the condition of the event *n*'s actual recall. The *retention* of *n*, it will be observed, is no mysterious storing up of an 'idea' in an unconscious state. It is not a fact of the mental order at all. It is a purely physical phenomenon, a morphological feature, the presence of these 'paths,' namely, in the finest recesses of the brain's tissue. The recall or recollection, on the other hand, is a *psychophysical* phenomenon, with both a bodily and a mental side. The bodily side is the functional excitement of the tracts and paths in question; the mental side is the conscious vision of the past occurrence, and the belief that we experienced it before.

These habit-worn paths of association are a clear rendering of what authors mean by 'predispositions,' 'vestiges,' 'traces,' etc., left in the brain by past experience. Most writers leave the nature of these vestiges vague; few think of explicitly assimilating them to channels of association. Dr. Maudsley, for example, writes:

> "When an idea which we have once had is excited again, there is a reproduction of the same nervous current, with the conscious addition that it is a reproduction—it is the same idea *plus* the consciousness that it is the same. The question then suggests itself, What is the physical condition of this consciousness? What is the modification of the anatomical substrata of fibres and cells, or of their physiological activity, which is the occasion of this *plus* element in the reproduced idea? It may be supposed that the first activity did leave behind it, when it subsided, some after-effect, some modification of the nerve element, whereby the nerve circuit was disposed to fall again readily into the same action; such disposition appearing in consciousness as *re*cognition or memory. Memory is, in fact, the conscious phase of this physiological disposition when it becomes active or discharges its functions on the recurrence of the particular mental experience. To assist our conception of what may happen, let us suppose the individual nerve-elements to be endowed with their own consciousness, and let us assume them to be, as I have supposed, modified in a certain way by the first experience; it is hard to conceive that when they fall into the same action on another occasion they should not recognise or remember it; for the second action is a reproduction of the first, with the addition of what it contains from the after-effects of the first. As we have assumed the process to be conscious, this reproduction with its addition would be a memory or remembrance." [16]

[16] Maudsley: *The Physiology of Mind* (London, 1876), p. 513.

In this passage Dr. Maudsley seems to mean by the 'nerve element,' or 'anatomical substrata of fibres and cells,' something that corresponds to the N of our diagram. And the 'modification' he speaks of seems intended to be understood as an internal modification of this same particular group of elements. Now the slightest reflection will convince anyone that there is no conceivable ground for supposing that with the mere re-excitation of N there should arise the 'conscious addition' that it is a re-excitation. The two excitations are simply two excitations, their consciousnesses are two consciousnesses, they have nothing to do with each other. And a vague 'modification,' supposed to be left behind by the first excitation, helps us not a whit. For, according to all analogy, such a modification can only result in making the next excitation more smooth and rapid. This might make it less *conscious,* perhaps, but could not endow it with any reference to the past. The gutter is worn deeper by each successive shower, but not for that reason brought into contact with previous showers. Psychology (which Dr. Maudsley in his next sentence says "affords us not the least help in this matter") puts us on the track of an at least possible brain-explanation. As it is the *setting o* of the idea, when it recurs, which makes us conscious of it as past, so it can be no *intrinsic* modification of the 'nerve element' N which is the organic condition of memory, but something extrinsic to it altogether, namely, its connections with those other nerve-elements which we called O—that letter standing in the scheme for the cerebral substratum of a great plexus of things other than the principal event remembered, dates, names, concrete surroundings, realized intervals, and what not. The 'modification' is the formation in the plastic nerve-substance of the system of associative paths between N and O.

The only hypothesis, in short, to which the facts of inward experience give countenance is that *the brain-tracts excited by the event proper, and those excited in its recall, are in part different from each other.* If we could revive the past event without any associates we should exclude the possibility of memory, and simply dream that we were undergoing the experience as if for the first time.[17] Wherever, in fact, the recalled event does appear without a

[17] The only fact which might plausibly be alleged against this view is the familiar one that we may feel the lapse of time in an experience so monotonous that its earlier portions can have no 'associates' different from its later ones. Sit with closed

definite setting, it is hard to distinguish it from a mere creation of fancy. But in proportion as its image lingers and recalls associates which gradually become more definite, it grows more and more distinctly into a remembered thing. For example, I enter a friend's room and see on the wall a painting. At first I have the strange, wondering consciousness, 'surely I have seen that before,' but when or how does not become clear. There only clings to the picture a sort of penumbra of familiarity,—when suddenly I exclaim: "I have it, it is a copy of part of one of the Fra Angelicos in the Florentine Academy—I recollect it there!" But the motive to the recall does *not* lie in the fact that the brain-tract now excited by the painting was once before excited in a similar way; it lies simply and solely in the fact that with that brain-tract other tracts also are excited: those which sustain my friend's room with all its peculiarities, on the one hand; those which sustain the mental image of the Florence Academy, on the other hand, with the circumstances of my visit there; and finally those which make me (more dimly) think of the years I have lived through between these two times. The result of this total brain-disturbance is a thought with a peculiar object, namely, that I who now stand here with this picture before me, stood so many years ago in the Florentine Academy looking at its original.

M. Taine has described the gradual way in which a mental image

---

eyes, for example, and steadily pronounce some vowel-sound, thus, *a—a—a—a—a—* . . . thinking only of the sound. Nothing changes during the time occupied by the experiment, and yet at the end of it you know that its beginning was far away. I think, however, that a close attention to what happens during this experiment shows that it does not violate in the least the conditions of recall laid down in the text; and that if the moment to which we mentally hark back lie many seconds behind the present instant, it always *has* different associates by which we define its date. Thus it was when I had just breathed out, or in; or it was the 'first moment' of the performance, the one 'preceded by silence'; or it was 'one very close to that'; or it was 'one when we were looking forwards instead of back, as now'; or it is simply represented by a number and conceived symbolically with no definite image of its date. It seems to me that I have no really intuitive discrimination of the different past moments after the experience has gone on some little time, but that back of the 'specious present' they all fuse into a single conception of the *kind of thing* that has been going on, with a more or less clear sense of the total time it has lasted, this latter being based on an automatic counting of the successive pulses of thought by which the process is from moment to moment recognized as being always the same. Within the few seconds which constitute the specious present there is an intuitive perception of the successive moments. But these moments, of which we have a primary memory-image, are not properly *recalled* from the past, our knowledge of them is in no way analogous to a memory properly so called. Cf. *supra*, p. 608.

develops into an object of memory, in his usual vivid fashion. He says:

"I meet casually in the street a person whose appearance I am acquainted with, and say to myself at once that I have seen him before. Instantly the figure recedes into the past, and there wavers about vaguely without at once fixing itself in any spot. It persists in me for some time, and surrounds itself with new details. 'When I saw him he was bare-headed, with a working jacket on, painting in a studio; he is so-and-so, of such-and-such a street. But when was it? It was not yesterday, nor this week, nor recently. I have it; he told me that he was waiting for the first leaves to come out to go into the country. It was before the spring. But at what exact date? I saw, the same day, people carrying branches in the streets and omnibuses: it was Palm Sunday!'—Observe the travels of the internal figure, its various shiftings to front and rear along the line of the past; each of these mental sentences has been a swing of the balance. When confronted with the present sensation, and with the latent swarm of indistinct images which repeat our recent life, the figure first recoiled suddenly to an indeterminate distance. Then, completed by precise details, and confronted with all the shortened images by which we sum up the proceedings of a day or a week, it again receded beyond the present day, beyond yesterday, the day before, the week, still further, beyond the ill-defined mass constituted by our recent recollections. Then something said by the painter was recalled, and it at once receded again beyond an almost precise limit, which is marked by the image of the green leaves and denoted by the word spring. A moment afterwards, thanks to a new detail, the recollection of the branches, it has shifted again, but forward this time, not backward; and, by a reference to the calendar, is situated at a precise point, a week further back than Easter, and five weeks nearer than the Carnival, by the double effect of the contrary impulsions, pushing it, one forward and the other backward, and which are, at a particular moment, annulled by one another."[18]

THE CONDITIONS OF GOODNESS IN MEMORY

The remembered fact being *n*, then, the path N—O is what arouses for *n* its setting when it *is* recalled, and makes it other than a mere imagination. The path M—N, on the other hand, gives the cue or occasion of its being recalled at all. *Memory being thus altogether conditioned on brain-paths, its excellence in a given indi-*

[18] *On Intelligence*, I, 258–9.

vidual will depend partly on the number and partly on the persistence of these paths.

The persistence or permanence of the paths is a physiological property of the brain-tissue of the individual, whilst their number is altogether due to the facts of his mental experience. Let the quality of permanence in the paths be called the native tenacity, or physiological retentiveness. This tenacity differs enormously from infancy to old age, and from one person to another. Some minds are like wax under a seal—no impression, however disconnected with others, is wiped out. Others, like a jelly, vibrate to every touch, but under usual conditions retain no permanent mark. These latter minds, before they can recollect a fact, must weave it into their permanent stores of knowledge. They have no *desultory* memory. Those persons, on the contrary, who retain names, dates and addresses, anecdotes, gossip, poetry, quotations, and all sorts of miscellaneous facts, without an effort, have desultory memory in a high degree, and certainly owe it to the unusual tenacity of their brain-substance for any path once formed therein. No one probably was ever effective on a voluminous scale without a high degree of this physiological retentiveness. In the practical as in the theoretic life, the man whose acquisitions *stick* is the man who is always achieving and advancing, whilst his neighbors, spending most of their time in relearning what they once knew but have forgotten, simply hold their own. A Charlemagne, a Luther, a Leibnitz, a Walter Scott, any example, in short, of your quarto or folio editions of mankind, must needs have amazing retentiveness of the purely physiological sort. Men without this retentiveness may excel in the *quality* of their work at this point or at that, but will never do such mighty sums of it, or be influential contemporaneously on such a scale.[19]

[19] Not that *mere* native tenacity will make a man great. It must be coupled with great passions and great intellect besides. Imbeciles sometimes have extraordinary desultory memory. Drobisch describes (*Empirische Psychologie*, p. 95) the case of a young man whom he examined. He had with difficulty been taught to read and speak. "But if two or three minutes were allowed him to peruse an octavo page, he then could spell the single words out from his memory as well as if the book lay open before him. . . . That there was no deception I could test by means of a new Latin law-dissertation which had just come into my hands, which he never could have seen, and of which both subject and language were unknown to him. He read off [mentally] many lines, skipping about too, of the page which had been given him to see, no worse than if the experiment had been made with a child's story." Drobisch describes this case as if it were one of unusual persistence in the visual image ['primary mem-

But there comes a time of life for all of us when we can do no more than hold our own in the way of acquisitions, when the old paths fade as fast as the new ones form in our brain, and when we forget in a week quite as much as we can learn in the same space of time. This equilibrium may last many, many years. In extreme old age it is upset in the reverse direction, and forgetting prevails over acquisition, or rather there is no acquisition. Brain-paths are so transient that in the course of a few minutes of conversation the same question is asked and its answer forgotten half a dozen times. Then the superior tenacity of the paths formed in childhood becomes manifest: the dotard will retrace the facts of his earlier years after he has lost all those of later date.

So much for the permanence of the paths. Now for their number.

It is obvious that the more there are of such paths as M–N in the brain, and the more of such possible cues or occasions for the recall of *n* in the mind, the prompter and surer, on the whole, the memory of *n* will be, the more frequently one will be reminded of it, the more avenues of approach to it one will possess. In mental terms, *the more other facts a fact is associated with in the mind, the better possession of it our memory retains.* Each of its associates be-

---

ory,' *vide supra*, p. 606]. But he adds that the youth 'remembered his pages a long time.' In the *Journal of Speculative Philosophy* for Jan. 1871 (v, 6) is an account by Mr. W. D. Henkle (together with the stock classic examples of preternatural memory) of an almost blind Pennsylvania farmer who could remember the day of the week on which any date had fallen for forty-two years past, and also the kind of weather it was, and what he was doing on each of more than fifteen thousand days. Pity that such a magnificent faculty as this could not have found more worthy application!

What these cases show is that the mere organic retentiveness of a man need bear no definite relation to his other mental powers. Men of the highest general powers will often forget nothing, however insignificant. One of the most generally accomplished men I know has a memory of this sort. He never keeps written note of anything, yet is never at a loss for a fact which he has once heard. He remembers the old addresses of all his New York friends, living in numbered streets, addresses which they themselves have long since moved away from and forgotten. He says that he should probably recognize an individual fly, if he had seen him thirty years previous —he is, by the way, an entomologist. As an instance of his desultory memory, he was introduced to a certain colonel at a club. The conversation fell upon the signs of age in man. The colonel challenged him to estimate his age. He looked at him, and gave the exact day of his birth, to the wonder of all. But the secret of this accuracy was that, having picked up some days previously an army-register, he had idly turned over its list of names, with dates of birth, graduation, promotions, etc., attached, and when the colonel's name was mentioned to him at the club, these figures, on which he had not bestowed a moment's thought, involuntarily surged up in his mind. Such a memory is of course a priceless boon.

comes a hook to which it hangs, a means to fish it up by when sunk beneath the surface. Together, they form a network of attachments by which it is woven into the entire tissue of our thought. The 'secret of a good memory' is thus the secret of forming diverse and multiple associations with every fact we care to retain. But this forming of associations with a fact, what is it but *thinking about* the fact as much as possible? Briefly, then, of two men with the same outward experiences and the same amount of mere native tenacity, *the one who* THINKS *over his experiences most,* and weaves them into systematic relations with each other, *will be the one with the best memory.* We see examples of this on every hand. Most men have a good memory for facts connected with their own pursuits. The college athlete who remains a dunce at his books will astonish you by his knowledge of men's 'records' in various feats and games, and will be a walking dictionary of sporting statistics. The reason is that he is constantly going over these things in his mind, and comparing and making series of them. They form for him not so many odd facts, but a concept-system—so they stick. So the merchant remembers prices, the politician other politicians' speeches and votes, with a copiousness which amazes outsiders, but which the amount of thinking they bestow on these subjects easily explains. The great memory for facts which a Darwin and a Spencer reveal in their books is not incompatible with the possession on their part of a brain with only a middling degree of physiological retentiveness. Let a man early in life set himself the task of verifying such a theory as that of evolution, and facts will soon cluster and cling to him like grapes to their stem. Their relations to the theory will hold them fast; and the more of these the mind is able to discern, the greater the erudition will become. Meanwhile the theorist may have little, if any, desultory memory. Unutilizable facts may be unnoted by him and forgotten as soon as heard. An ignorance almost as encyclopædic as his erudition may coexist with the latter, and hide, as it were, in the interstices of its web. Those who have had much to do with scholars and *savants* will readily think of examples of the class of mind I mean.

In a system, every fact is connected with every other by some thought-relation. The consequence is that every fact is retained by the combined suggestive power of all the other facts in the system, and forgetfulness is well-nigh impossible.

The reason why *cramming* is such a bad mode of study is now made clear. I mean by cramming that way of preparing for examinations by committing 'points' to memory during a few hours or days of intense application immediately preceding the final ordeal, little or no work having been performed during the previous course of the term. Things learned thus in a few hours, on one occasion, for one purpose, cannot possibly have formed many associations with other things in the mind. Their brain-processes are led into by few paths, and are relatively little liable to be awakened again. Speedy oblivion is the almost inevitable fate of all that is committed to memory in this simple way. Whereas, on the contrary, the same materials taken in gradually, day after day, recurring in different contexts, considered in various relations, associated with other external incidents, and repeatedly reflected on, grow into such a system, form such connections with the rest of the mind's fabric, lie open to so many paths of approach, that they remain permanent possessions. This is the *intellectual* reason why habits of continuous application should be enforced in educational establishments. Of course there is no moral turpitude in cramming. If it led to the desired end of secure learning it would be infinitely the best method of study. But it does not; and students themselves should understand the reason why.

ONE'S NATIVE RETENTIVENESS IS UNCHANGEABLE

It will now appear clear that *all improvement of the memory lies in the line of* ELABORATING THE ASSOCIATES of each of the several things to be remembered. *No amount of culture would seem capable of modifying a man's* GENERAL *retentiveness.* This is a physiological quality, given once for all with his organization, and which he can never hope to change. It differs no doubt in disease and health; and it is a fact of observation that it is better in fresh and vigorous hours than when we are fagged or ill. We may say, then, that a man's native tenacity will fluctuate somewhat with his hygiene, and that whatever is good for his tone of health will also be good for his memory. We may even say that whatever amount of intellectual exercise is bracing to the general tone and nutrition of the brain will also be profitable to the general retentiveness. But more than this we cannot say; and this, it is obvious, is far less than most people believe.

It is, in fact, commonly thought that certain exercises, systematically repeated, will strengthen, not only a man's remembrance of the particular facts used in the exercises, but his faculty for remembering facts at large. And a plausible case is always made out by saying that practice in learning words by heart makes it easier to learn new words in the same way.[20] If this be true, then what I have just said is false, and the whole doctrine of memory as due to 'paths' must be revised. But I am disposed to think the alleged fact untrue. I have carefully questioned several mature actors on the point, and all have denied that the practice of learning parts has made any such difference as is alleged. What it has done for them is to improve their power of *studying* a part systematically. Their mind is now full of precedents in the way of intonation, emphasis, gesticulation; the new words awaken distinct suggestions and decisions; are caught up, in fact, into a pre-existing net-work, like the merchant's prices, or the athlete's store of 'records,' and are recollected easier, although the mere native tenacity is not a whit improved, and is usually, in fact, impaired by age. It is a case of better remembering by better *thinking*. Similarly when school-boys improve by practice in ease of learning by heart, the improvement will, I am sure, be always found to reside in the *mode of study of the particular piece* (due to the greater interest, the greater suggestiveness, the generic similarity with other pieces, the more sustained attention, etc., etc.), and not at all to any enhancement of the brute retentive power.

The error I speak of pervades an otherwise useful and judicious book, *How to Strengthen the Memory*, by Dr. Holbrook of New York.[21] The author fails to distinguish between the general physiological retentiveness and the retention of particular things, and talks as if both must be benefited by the same means.

"I am now treating," he says, "a case of loss of memory in a person advanced in years, who did not know that his memory had failed most remarkably till I told him of it. He is making vigorous effort to bring it back again, and with partial success. The method pursued is to spend two hours daily, one in the morning and one in the evening, in exercising this faculty. The patient is instructed to give the closest attention

20 Cf. Ebbinghaus: *Über das Gedächtnis, Untersuchungen zur experimentellen Psychologie* (1885), pp. 67, 45. One may hear a person say: "I have a very poor memory, because I was never systematically made to learn poetry at school."

21 *How to Strengthen the Memory; or, Natural and Scientific Methods of Never Forgetting*. By M. L. Holbrook, M.D., New York (no date).

to all that he learns, so that it shall be impressed on his mind clearly. He is asked to recall every evening all the facts and experiences of the day, and again the next morning. Every name heard is written down and impressed on his mind clearly, and an effort made to recall it at intervals. Ten names from among public men are ordered to be committed to memory every week. A verse of poetry is to be learned, also a verse from the Bible, daily. He is asked to remember the number of the page in any book where any interesting fact is recorded. These and other methods are slowly resuscitating a failing memory."[22]

I find it very hard to believe that the memory of the poor old gentleman is a bit the better for all this torture except in respect of the particular facts thus wrought into it, the occurrences attended to and repeated on those days, the names of those politicians, those Bible verses, etc., etc. In another place Dr. Holbrook quotes the account given by the late Thurlow Weed, journalist and politician, of his method of strengthening his memory.

" 'My memory was a sieve. I could remember nothing. Dates, names, appointments, faces—everything escaped me. I said to my wife, "Catherine, I shall never make a successful politician, for I cannot remember, and that is a prime necessity of politicians. . . ." My wife told me I must train my memory. So when I came home that night I sat down alone and spent fifteen minutes trying silently to recall with accuracy the principal events of the day. I could remember but little at first; now I remember that I could not then recall what I had for breakfast. After a few days' practice I found I could recall more. Events came back to me more minutely, more accurately and more vividly than at first. After a fortnight or so of this, Catherine said, "Why don't you relate to me the events of the day instead of recalling them to yourself? It would be interesting, and my interest in it would be a stimulus to you." Having great respect for my wife's opinion, I began a habit of oral confession, as it were, which was continued for almost fifty years. Every night, the last thing before retiring, I told her everything I could remember that had happened to me or about me during the day. I generally recalled the very dishes I had had for breakfast, dinner and tea; the people I had seen and what they had said; the editorials I had written for my paper, giving her a brief abstract of them; I mentioned all the letters I had sent and received, and the very language used, as nearly as possible; when I had walked or ridden—I told her everything that had come within my observation. I found I

22 Page 38.

could say my lessons better and better every year, and instead of the practice growing irksome, it became a pleasure to go over again the events of the day. I am indebted to this discipline for a memory of somewhat unusual tenacity, and I recommend the practice to all who wish to store up facts, or expect to have much to do with influencing men.' "[23]

I do not doubt that Mr. Weed's practical command of his past experiences was much greater after fifty years of this heroic drill than it would have been without it. Expecting to give his account in the evening, he attended better to each incident of the day, named and conceived it differently, set his mind upon it, and in the evening went over it again. He did *more thinking* about it, and it stayed with him in consequence. But I venture to affirm pretty confidently (although I know how foolish it often is to deny a fact on the strength of a theory) that the same matter, *casually attended to and not thought about,* would have stuck in his memory no better at the end than at the beginning of his years of heroic self-discipline. He had acquired a better method of noting and recording his experiences, but his physiological retentiveness was probably not a bit improved.[24]

23 *Op. cit.*, p. 99.

24 In order to test the opinion so confidently expressed in the text, I have tried to see whether a certain amount of daily training in learning poetry by heart will shorten the time it takes to learn an entirely different kind of poetry. During eight successive days I learned 158 lines of Victor Hugo's "Satyr." The total number of minutes required for this was 131⅚—it should be said that I had learned nothing by heart for many years. I then, working for twenty-odd minutes daily, learned the entire first book of *Paradise Lost*, occupying 38 days in the process. After this training I went back to Victor Hugo's poem, and found that 158 additional lines (divided exactly as on the former occasion) took me 151½ minutes. In other words, I committed my Victor Hugo to memory before the training at the rate of a line in 50 seconds, after the training at the rate of a line in 57 seconds, just the opposite result from that which the popular view would lead one to expect. But as I was perceptibly fagged with other work at the time of the second batch of Victor Hugo, I thought that might explain the retardation; so I persuaded several other persons to repeat the test.

Dr. W. H. Burnham learned 16 lines of *In Memoriam* for 8 days; time, 14–17 minutes—daily average 14¾. He then trained himself on Schiller's translation of the second book of the *Æneid* into German, 16 lines daily for 26 consecutive days. On returning to the same quantity of *In Memoriam* again, he found his maximum time 20 minutes, minimum 10, average 14 27/48. As he feared the outer conditions might not have been as favorable this time as the first, he waited a few days and got conditions as near as possible identical. The result was, minimum time 8 minutes; maximum 19½; average 14 3/48.

Mr. E. S. Drown tested himself on Virgil for 16 days, then again for 16 days, after

All improvement of memory consists, then, in the improvement of one's habitual methods of recording facts. In the traditional terminology methods are divided into the mechanical, the ingenious, and the judicious.

The *mechanical methods* consist in the intensification, prolongation, and *repetition* of the impression to be remembered. The modern method of teaching children to read by blackboard work, in which each word is impressed by the fourfold channel of eye, ear, voice, and hand, is an example of an improved mechanical method of memorizing.

Judicious methods of remembering things are nothing but logical ways of conceiving them and working them into rational systems, classifying them, analyzing them into parts, etc., etc. All the sciences are such methods.

Of *ingenious methods* many have been invented, under the

---

training himself on Scott. Average time before training, 13 minutes 26 seconds; after training, 12 minutes 16 seconds. [Sixteen days is too long for the test, it gives time for training on the test-verse.]

Mr. C. H. Baldwin took 10 lines for 15 days as his test, trained himself on 450 lines 'of an entirely different verse,' and then took 15 days more of the former verse 10 lines a day. Average result: 3 minutes 41 seconds before, 3 minutes 2 seconds after, training. [Same criticism as before.]

Mr. E. A. Pease tested himself on *Idyls of the King*, and trained himself on *Paradise Lost*. Average result of 6 days each time: 14 minutes 34 seconds before, 14 minutes 55 seconds after, training. Mr. Burnham having suggested that to eliminate facilitating effect entirely from the training verses one ought to test one's self *à la* Ebbinghaus on series of nonsense-syllables, having no analogy whatever with any system of expressive verses. I induced two of my students to perform that experiment also. The record is unfortunately lost; but the result was a very considerable shortening of the average time of the second series of nonsense-syllables, learned after training. This seems to me, however, more to show the effects of rapid habituation to the nonsense-verses themselves than those of the poetry used between them. But I mean to prosecute the experiments farther, and will report in another place.

One of my students having quoted a clergyman of his acquaintance who had marvellously improved by practice his power of learning his sermons by heart, I wrote to the gentleman for corroboration. I append his reply, which shows that the increased facility is due rather to a change in his methods of learning than to his native retentiveness having grown by exercise: "As for memory, mine has improved year by year, except when in ill-health, like a gymnast's muscle. Before twenty it took three or four days to commit an hour-long sermon; after twenty, two days, one day, half a day, and now one slow analytic, very attentive or adhesive reading does it. But memory seems to me the most physical of intellectual powers. Bodily ease and freshness have much to do with it. Then there is a great difference of facility in method. I used to commit sentence by sentence. Now I take the idea of the whole, then its leading divisions, then its subdivisions, then its sentences."

name of technical memories. By means of these systems it is often possible to retain entirely disconnected facts, lists of names, numbers, and so forth, so multitudinous as to be entirely unrememberable in a natural way. The method consists usually in a framework learned mechanically, of which the mind is supposed to remain in secure and permanent possession. Then, whatever is to be remembered is deliberately associated by some fanciful analogy or connection with some part of this framework, and this connection thenceforward helps its recall. The best known and most used of these devices is the figure-alphabet. To remember numbers, e.g., a figure-alphabet is first formed, in which each numerical digit is represented by one or more letters. The number is then translated into such letters as will best make a word, if possible a word suggestive of the object to which the number belongs. The word will then be remembered when the numbers alone might be forgotten.

"The most common figure-alphabet is this:

1,	2,	3,	4,	5,	6,	7,	8,	9,	0.
t,	n,	m,	r,	l,	sh,	g,	f,	b,	s,
d,					j,	k,	v,	p,	c,
					ch,	c,			z,
					g,	qu.			

"To briefly show its use, suppose it is desired to fix 1142 feet in a second as the velocity of sound: t, t, r, n, are the letters and order required. Fill up with vowels forming a phrase, like 'tight run,' and connect it by some such flight of the imagination as that if a man tried to keep up with the velocity of sound, he would have a tight run. When you recall this a few days later great care must be taken not to get confused with the velocity of light, nor to think he had a *hard* run, which would be 3000 feet too fast."[25]

Dr. Pick and others use a system which consists in linking together any two ideas to be remembered by means of an intermediate idea which will be suggested by the first and suggest the second, and so on through the list. Thus,

"Let us suppose that we are to retain the following series of ideas: garden, hair, watchman, philosophy, copper etc. . . . We can combine the ideas in this manner: *garden*, plant, hair of plant—*hair*; *hair*,

[25] E. Pick: *Memory and Its Doctors* (1888), p. 7.

bonnet, *watchman*;–*watchman*, wake, study, *philosophy*; *philosophy*, chemistry, *copper*; etc. etc." (Pick.)[26]

It is matter of popular knowledge that an impression is remembered the better in proportion as it is

1) More recent;
2) More attended to; and
3) More often repeated.

The effect of recency is all but absolutely constant. Of two events of equal significance the remoter one will be the one more likely to be forgotten. The memories of childhood which persist in old age can hardly be compared with the events of the day or hour which are forgotten, for these latter are trivial once-repeated things, whilst the childish reminiscences have been wrought into us during the retrospective hours of our entire intervening life. *Other things equal*, at all times of life recency promotes memory. The only exception I can think of is the unaccountable memory of certain moments of our childhood, apparently not fitted by their intrinsic interest to survive, but which are perhaps the only incidents we can remember out of the year in which they occurred. Everybody probably has isolated glimpses of certain hours of his nursery life, the position in which he stood or sat, the light of the room, what his father or mother said, etc. These moments so oddly selected for immunity from the tooth of time probably owe their good fortune to historical peculiarities which it is now impossible to trace. Very likely we were reminded of them again soon after they occurred; that became a reason why we should again recollect them, etc., so that at last they became ingrained.

The *attention* which we lend to an experience is proportional to its vivid or interesting character; and it is a notorious fact that what interests us most vividly at the time is, other things equal, what we remember best. An impression may be so exciting emotionally as almost to leave a *scar* upon the cerebral tissues; and thus originates a pathological delusion. "A woman attacked by robbers takes all the men whom she sees, even her own son, for brigands bent on killing her. Another woman sees her child run over by a horse; no amount of reasoning, not even the sight of the living child, will persuade her that he is not killed. A woman called 'thief' in a dis-

[26] This system is carried out in great detail in a book called *Memory Training*, by William L. Evans (1889).

pute remains convinced that everyone accuses her of stealing (Esquirol). Another, attacked with mania at the sight of the fires in her street during the Commune, still after six months sees in her delirium flames on every side about her (Luys), etc., etc."[27]

On the general effectiveness of both attention and repetition I cannot do better than copy what M. Taine has written:

"If we compare different sensations, images, or ideas, we find that their aptitudes for revival are not equal. A large number of them are obliterated, and never reappear through life; for instance, I drove through Paris a day or two ago, and though I saw plainly some sixty or eighty new faces, I cannot now recall any one of them; some extraordinary circumstance, a fit of delirium, or the excitement of haschich would be necessary to give them a chance of revival. On the other hand, there are sensations with a force of revival which nothing destroys or decreases. Though, as a rule, time weakens and impairs our strongest sensations, these reappear entire and intense, without having lost a particle of their detail, or any degree of their force. M. Brierre de Boismont, having suffered when a child from a disease of the scalp, asserts that 'after fifty-five years have elapsed he can still feel his hair pulled out under the treatment of the *skull-cap*.'— For my own part, after thirty years, I remember feature for feature the appearance of the theatre to which I was taken for the first time. From the third row of boxes, the body of the theatre appeared to me an immense well, red and flaming, swarming with heads; below, on the right, on a narrow floor, two men and a woman entered, went out, and re-entered, made gestures, and seemed to me like lively dwarfs: to my great surprise, one of these dwarfs fell on his knees, kissed the lady's hand, then hid behind a screen; the other, who was coming in, seemed angry, and raised his arm. I was then seven, I could understand nothing of what was going on; but the well of crimson velvet was so crowded, gilded, and bright, that after a quarter of an hour I was, as it were, intoxicated, and fell asleep.

"Every one of us may find similar recollections in his memory, and may distinguish in them a common character. The primitive impression has been accompanied *by an extraordinary degree of attention*, either as being horrible or delightful, or as being new, surprising, and out of proportion to the ordinary run of our life; this it is we express by saying that we have been strongly impressed; that we were absorbed, that we could not think of any thing else; that our other sensations were effaced; that we were pursued all the next day by the re-

[27] Paulhan: *L'Activité mentale et les éléments de l'esprit* (1889), p. 70.

sulting image; that it beset us, that we could not drive it away; that all distractions were feeble beside it. It is by force of this disproportion that impressions of childhood are so persistent; the mind being quite fresh, ordinary objects and events are surprising. At present, after seeing so many large halls and full theatres, it is impossible for me, when I enter one, to feel swallowed up, engulfed, and as it were, lost in a huge dazzling well. The medical man of sixty, who has experienced much suffering, both personally and in imagination, would be less upset now by a surgical operation than when he was a child.

"Whatever may be the kind of attention, voluntary or involuntary, it always acts alike; the image of an object or event is capable of revival, and of complete revival, in proportion to the degree of attention with which we have considered the object or event. We put this rule in practice at every moment in ordinary life. If we are applying ourselves to a book, or are in lively conversation, while an air is being sung in the adjoining room, we do not retain it; we know vaguely that there is singing going on, and that is all. We then stop our reading or conversation, we lay aside all internal pre-occupations and external sensations which our mind or the outer world can throw in our way; we close our eyes, we cause a silence within and about us, and, if the air is repeated, we listen. We say then that we have listened with all our ears, that we have applied our whole minds. If the air is a fine one, and has touched us deeply, we add that we have been transported, uplifted, ravished, that we have forgotten the world and ourselves; that for some minutes our soul was dead to all but sounds. . . .

"This exclusive momentary ascendency of one of our states of mind explains the greater durability of its aptitude for revival and for more complete revival. As the sensation revives in the image, the image reappears with a force proportioned to that of the sensation. What we meet with in the first state is also to be met with in the second, since the second is but a revival of the first. So, in the struggle for life, in which all our images are constantly engaged, the one furnished at the outset with most force, retains in each conflict, by the very law of repetition which gives it being, the capacity of treading down its adversaries; this is why it revives, incessantly at first, then frequently, until at last the laws of progressive decay, and the continual accession of new impressions, take away its preponderance, and its competitors, finding a clear field, are able to develope in their turn.

"A second cause of prolonged revivals is repetition itself. Every one knows that to learn a thing we must not only consider it attentively, but consider it repeatedly. We say as to this in ordinary language, that an impression many times renewed is imprinted more deeply and exactly on the memory. This is how we contrive to retain a language, airs of music, passages of verse or prose, the technical terms and propositions of a science, and still more so the ordinary facts by which our conduct is regulated. When, from the form and color of a currant jelly, we think of its taste, or when tasting it with our eyes shut, we imagine its red tint and the brilliancy of a quivering slice, the images in our mind are brightened by repetition. Whenever we eat, or drink, or walk, or avail ourselves of any of our senses, or commence or continue any action whatever, the same thing happens. Every man and every animal thus possesses at every moment of life a certain stock of clear and easily reviving images, which had their source in the past in a confluence of numerous experiences, and are now fed by a flow of renewed experiences. When I want to go from the Tuileries to the Panthéon, or from my study to the dining-room, I foresee at every turn the colored forms which will present themselves to my sight; it is otherwise in the case of a house where I have spent two hours, or of a town where I have stayed three days; after ten years have elapsed the images will be vague, full of blanks, sometimes they will not exist, and I shall have to seek my way or shall lose myself.—This new property of images is also derived from the first. As every sensation tends to revive in its image, the sensation twice repeated will leave after it a double tendency, that is, provided the attention be as great the second time as the first; usually this is not the case, for the novelty diminishing, the interest diminishes; but if other circumstances renew the interest, or if the will renovates the attention, the incessantly increasing tendency will incessantly increase the chances of the resurrection and integrity of the image."[28]

If a phenomenon is met with, however, too often, and with too great a variety of contexts, although its image is retained and reproduced with correspondingly great facility, it fails to come up with any one particular setting, and the projection of it backwards to a particular past date consequently does not come about. We *recognize* but do not *remember* it—its associates form too confused a cloud. No one is said to remember, says Mr. Spencer,

"that the object at which he looks has an opposite side; or that a certain modification of the visual impression implies a certain distance; or that the thing he sees moving about is a live animal. To ask a man whether he remembers that the sun shines, that fire burns, that iron is hard, would be a misuse of language. Even the almost fortuitous connexions among our experiences, cease to be classed as memories when they have become thoroughly familiar. Though, on hearing the voice

[28] *On Intelligence*, I, 78–82.

of some unseen person slightly known to us, we say we recollect to whom the voice belongs, we do not use the same expression respecting the voices of those with whom we live. The meanings of words which in childhood have to be consciously recalled, seem in adult life to be immediately present."[29]

These are cases where too many paths, leading to too diverse associates, block each other's way, and all that the mind gets along with its object is a fringe of felt familiarity or sense that there *are* associates. A similar result comes about when a definite setting is only nascently aroused. We then feel that we have seen the object already, but when or where we cannot say, though we may seem to ourselves to be on the brink of saying it. That nascent cerebral excitations can effect consciousness with a sort of sense of the imminence of that which stronger excitations would make us definitely feel, is obvious from what happens when we seek to remember a name. It tingles, it trembles on the verge, but does not come. Just such a tingling and trembling of unrecovered associates is the penumbra of recognition that may surround any experience and make it seem familiar, though we know not why.[30]

[29] *Psychology*, § 201.

[30] Professor Höffding considers that the absence of contiguous associates distinctly thought-of is a proof that associative processes are not concerned in these cases of instantaneous recognition where we get a strong sense of familiarity with the object, but no recall of previous time or place. His theory of what happens is that the object before us, A, comes with a sense of familiarity whenever it awakens *a slumbering image, a, of its own past self*, whilst without this image it seems unfamiliar. The *quality of familiarity* is due to the coalescence of the two similar processes A + *a* in the brain (*Psychologie*, p. 188; *Vierteljahrsschrift für wissenschaftliche Philosophie*, XIII, 432 [1889]). This explanation is a very tempting one where the phenomenon of recognition is reduced to its simplest terms. Experiments have been performed in Wundt's laboratory (by Messrs. Wolfe, see below, p. 639, and Lehmann (*Philosophische Studien*, v, 96), in which a person had to tell out of several closely resembling sensible impressions (sounds, tints of color) presented, which of them was the same with one presented a moment before. And it does seem here as if the fading process in the just-excited tract must combine with the process of the new impression to give to the latter a peculiar subjective tinge which should separate it from the impressions which the other objects give. But recognition of this immediate sort is beyond our power after a very short time has intervened. A couple of minutes' interval is generally fatal to it; so that it is impossible to conceive that our frequent instantaneous recognition of a face, e.g., as having been met before, takes place by any such simple process. Where we associate a *head of classification* with the object, the time-interval has much less effect. Dr. Lehmann could identify shades of gray much more successfully and permanently after mentally attaching names or numbers to them. Here it is the recall of the contiguous associate, the number or name, which brings about the recognition. Where an experience is complex, each element of the total object has had

There is a curious experience which everyone seems to have had —the feeling that the present moment in its completeness has been experienced before—we were saying just this thing, in just this place, to just these people, etc. This 'sense of pre-existence' has been treated as a great mystery and occasioned much speculation. Dr. Wigan considered it due to a dissociation of the action of the

---

the *other elements* for its past contiguous associates. Each element thus tends to revive the other elements from within, at the same time that the outward object is making them revive from without. We have thus, whenever we meet a familiar object, that sense of *expectation gratified* which is so large a factor in our æsthetic emotions; and even were there no 'fringe of tendency' towards the arousal of *extrinsic* associates (which there certainly always is), still this *intrinsic* play of mutual association among the parts would give a character of ease to familiar percepts which would make of them a distinct subjective class. A process fills its old bed in a different way from that in which it makes a new bed. One can appeal to introspection for proof. When, for example, I go into a slaughter-house into which I once went years ago, and the horrid din of the screaming hogs strikes me with the overpowering sense of identification, when the blood-stained face of the 'sticker,' whom I had long ceased to think of, is immediately recognized as the face that struck me so before; when the dingy and reddened woodwork, the purple-flowing floor, the smell, the emotion of disgust, and *all* the details, in a word, forthwith re-establish themselves as familiar occupants of my mind; the *extraneous* associates of the past time are anything but prominent. Again, in trying to think of an engraving, say the portrait of Rajah Brooke prefixed to his biography, I can do so only partially; but when I take down the book and, looking at the actual face, am smitten with the intimate sense of its sameness with the one I was striving to resuscitate,—where in the experience is the element of *extrinsic* association? In both these cases it surely *feels* as if the moment when the sense of recall is most vivid were also the moment when all *extraneous* associates were most suppressed. The butcher's face recalls the former walls of the shambles; their thought recalls the groaning beasts, and they the face again, just as I now experience them, with no different past ingredient. In like manner the peculiar deepening of my consciousness of the Rajah's physiognomy at the moment when I open the book and say "Ah! that's the very face!" is so intense as to banish from my mind all collateral circumstances, whether of the present or of former experiences. But here it is the nose preparing tracts for the eye, the eye preparing them for the mouth, the mouth preparing them for the nose again, all these processes involving paths of contiguous association, as defended in the text. I cannot agree, therefore, with Prof. Höffding, in spite of my respect for him as a psychologist, that the phenomenon of instantaneous recognition is only explicable through the recall and comparison of the thing with its own past image. Nor can I see in the facts in question any additional ground for reinstating the general notion which we have already rejected (*supra*, p. 557) that a 'sensation' is ever received into the mind by an 'image' of its own past self. It is received by contiguous associates; or if they form too faint a fringe, its neural currents run into a bed which is still 'warm' from just-previous currents, and which consequently feel different from currents whose bed is cold. I agree, however, with Höffding that Dr. Lehmann's experiments (many of them) do not seem to prove the point which he seeks to establish. Lehmann, indeed, seems himself to believe that we recognize a sensation A by comparing it with its own past image *a* (*loc. cit.*, p. 114), in which opinion I altogether fail to concur.

two hemispheres, one of them becoming conscious a little later than the other, but both of the same fact.[31] I must confess that the quality of mystery seems to me a little strained. I have over and over again in my own case succeeded in resolving the phenomenon into a case of memory, so indistinct that whilst some past circumstances are presented again, the others are not. The dissimilar portions of the past do not arise completely enough at first for the date to be identified. All we get is the present scene with a general suggestion of pastness about it. That faithful observer, Prof. Lazarus, interprets the phenomenon in the same way;[32] and it is noteworthy that just as soon as the past context grows complete and distinct the emotion of weirdness fades from the experience.

EXACT MEASUREMENTS OF MEMORY

have recently been made in Germany. Professor Ebbinghaus, in a really heroic series of daily observations of more than two years' duration, examined the powers of retention and reproduction. He learned lists of meaningless syllables by heart, and tested his recollection of them from day to day. He could not remember more than 7 after a single reading. It took, however, 16 readings to remember 12, 44 readings to remember 24, and 55 readings to remember 26 syllables, the moment of 'remembering' being here reckoned as the first moment when the list could be recited without a fault.[33] When a 16-syllable list was read over a certain number of times on one day, and then studied on the day following until remembered, it was found that the number of seconds saved in the study on the second day was proportional to the number of readings on the first —proportional, that is, within certain rather narrow limits, for which see the text.[34] No amount of repetition spent on nonsense-verses over a certain length enabled Dr. Ebbinghaus to retain them without error for 24 hours. In forgetting such things as these lists of syllables, the loss goes on very much more rapidly at first than

31 *Duality of the Mind*, p. 84. The same thesis is defended by the late Mr. R. A. Proctor, who gives some cases rather hard to reconcile with my own proposed explanation, in *Knowledge* for Nov. 28, 1884. See also Ribot: *Maladies de la mémoire*, p. 149 ff.

32 *Zeitschrift für Völkerpsychologie und Sprachwissenschaft*, Bd. v, p. 146.

33 *Über das Gedächtnis, experimentelle Psychologie* (1885), p. 64.

34 *Ibid.*, § 23.

later on. He measured the loss by the number of seconds required to *relearn* the list after it had been once learned. Roughly speaking, if it took a thousand seconds to learn the list, and five hundred to relearn it, the loss between the two learnings would have been one half. Measured in this way, full half of the forgetting seems to occur within the first half-hour, whilst only four fifths is forgotten at the end of a month. The nature of this result might have been anticipated, but hardly its numerical proportions. Dr. Ebbinghaus says:

> "The initial rapidity, as well as the final slowness, as these were ascertained under certain experimental conditions and for a particular individual, . . . may well surprise us. An hour after the work of learning had ceased, forgetting was so far advanced that more than half of the original work had to be applied again before the series of syllables could once more be reproduced. Eight hours later two thirds of the original labor had to be applied. Gradually, however, the process of oblivion grew slower, so that even for considerable stretches of time the losses were but barely ascertainable. After 24 hours a third, after 6 days a fourth, and after a whole month a good fifth of the original labor remain in the shape of its after-effects, and made the relearning by so much the more speedy."[35]

But the most interesting result of all those reached by this author relates to the question whether ideas are recalled only by those that previously came immediately before them, or whether an idea can possibly recall another idea with which it was never in *immediate* contact, without passing through the intermediate mental links. The question is of theoretic importance with regard to the way in which the process of 'association of ideas' must be conceived; and Dr. Ebbinghaus's attempt is as successful as it is original, in bringing two views, which seem at first sight inaccessible to proof, to a direct practical test, and giving the victory to one of them. His experiments conclusively show that an idea is not only 'associated' directly with the one that follows it, and with the rest *through that,* but that it is *directly* associated with *all* that are near it, though in unequal degrees. He first measured the time needed to impress on the memory certain lists of syllables, and then the time needed to impress lists of the same syllables with gaps between them. Thus,

[35] *Op. cit.*, p. 103.

representing the syllables by numbers, if the first list were 1, 2, 3, 4, . . . 13, 14, 15, 16, the second would be 1, 3, 5, . . . 15, 2, 4, 6, . . . 16, and so forth, with many variations.

Now, if 1 and 3 in the first list were learned in that order merely by 1 calling up 2, and by 2 calling up 3, leaving out the 2 ought to leave 1 and 3 with no tie in the mind; and the second list ought to take as much time in the learning as if the first list had never been heard of. If, on the other hand, 1 has a *direct* influence on 3 as well as on 2, that influence should be exerted even when 2 is dropped out; and a person familiar with the first list ought to learn the second one more rapidly than otherwise he could. This latter case is what actually occurs; and Dr. Ebbinghaus has found that syllables originally separated by as many as seven intermediaries still reveal, by the increased rapidity with which they are learned in order, the strength of the tie that the original learning established between them, over the heads, so to speak, of all the rest. These last results ought to make us careful, when we speak of nervous 'paths,' to use the word in no restricted sense. They add one more fact to the set of facts which prove that association is subtler than consciousness, and that a nerve-process may, without producing consciousness, be effective in the same way in which consciousness would have seemed to be effective if it had been there.[36] Evidently the path from 1 to 3 (omitting 2 from consciousness) is facilitated, broadened perhaps, by the old path from 1 to 3 through 2—only the component which shoots round through this latter way is too feeble to let 2 be thought as a distinct object.

36 All the inferences for which we can give no articulate reasons exemplify this law. In the chapter on Perception we shall have innumerable examples of it. A good pathological illustration of it is given in the curious observations of M. Binet on certain hysterical subjects, with anæsthetic hands, who *saw* what was done with their hands as an independent vision but did not feel it. The hand being hidden by a screen, the patient was ordered to look at another screen and to tell of any visual image which might project itself thereon. Numbers would then come, corresponding to the number of times the insensible member was raised, touched, etc. Colored lines and figures would come, corresponding to similar ones traced on the palm; the hand itself, or its fingers, would come when manipulated; and, finally, objects placed in it would come; but on the hand itself nothing could ever be felt. The whole phenomenon shows how an idea which remains itself below the threshold of a certain conscious self may occasion associative effects therein. The skin-sensations, unfelt by the patient's primary consciousness, awaken, nevertheless, their usual visual associates therein.

Mr. Wolfe, in his experiments on recognition, used vibrating metal tongues.

"These tongues gave tones differing by 2 vibrations only in the two lower octaves, and by 4 vibrations in the three higher octaves. In the first series of experiments a tone was selected, and, after sounding it for one second, a second tone was sounded, which was either the same as the first, or different from it by 4, 8, or 12 vibrations in different series. The person experimented upon was to answer whether the second tone was the same as the first, thus showing that he recognized it, or whether it was different, and, if so, whether it was higher or lower. Of course, the interval of time between the two tones was an important factor. The proportionate number of correct judgments, and the smallness of the difference of the vibration-rates of the two tones, would measure the accuracy of the tone memory. It appeared that one could tell more readily whether the two tones were alike than whether they were different, although in both cases the accuracy of the memory was remarkably good. . . . The main point is the effect of the time-interval between the tone and its reproduction. This was varied from 1 second to 30 seconds, or even to 60 seconds, or 120 seconds in some experiments. The general result is, that the longer the interval, the smaller the chances that the tone will be recognized; and this process of forgetting takes place at first very rapidly, and then more slowly. . . . This law is subject to considerable variations, one of which seems to be constant and is peculiar; namely, there seems to be a rhythm in the memory itself, and, after falling, it recovers slightly, and then fades out again." [37]

This periodical renewal of acoustic memory would seem to be an important element in the production of the agreeableness of certain rates of recurrence in sound.

FORGETTING

In the practical use of our intellect, forgetting is as important a function as recollecting.

Locke says, in a memorable page of his dear old book:

[37] I copy from the abstract of Wolfe's paper in *Science* for Nov. 19, 1886. The original is in *Philosophische Studien*, III, 534 ff.

"The memory in some men, it is true, is very tenacious, even to a miracle: but yet there seems to be a constant decay of all our ideas, even of those which are struck deepest, and in minds the most retentive; so that if they be not sometimes renewed by repeated exercise of the senses, or reflection on those kinds of objects which at first occasioned them, the print wears out, and at last there remains nothing to be seen. Thus the ideas, as well as children, of our youth often die before us; and our minds represent to us those tombs to which we are approaching; where though the brass and marble remain, yet the inscriptions are effaced by time, and the imagery moulders away. The pictures drawn in our minds are laid in fading colours; and if not sometimes refreshed, vanish and disappear. How much the constitution of our bodies, and the make of our animal spirits, are concerned in this; and whether the temper of the brain makes this difference, that in some it retains the characters drawn on it like marble, in others like free-stone, and in others little better than sand, I shall not here inquire: though it may seem probable that the constitution of the body does sometimes influence the memory; since we oftentimes find a disease quite strip the mind of all its ideas, and the flames of a fever in a few days calcine all those images to dust and confusion, which seemed to be as lasting as if graved in marble."[38]

This peculiar mixture of forgetting with our remembering is but one instance of our mind's selective activity. Selection is the very keel on which our mental ship is built. And in this case of memory its utility is obvious. If we remembered everything, we should on most occasions be as ill off as if we remembered nothing. It would take as long for us to recall a space of time as it took the original time to elapse, and we should never get ahead with our thinking. All recollected times undergo, accordingly, what M. Ribot calls foreshortening; and this foreshortening is due to the omission of an enormous number of the facts which filled them.

"As fast as the present enters into the past, our states of consciousness disappear and are obliterated. Passed in review at a few days' distance, nothing or little of them remains: most of them have made shipwreck in that great nonenity from which they never more will emerge, and they have carried with them the quantity of duration which was inherent in their being. This deficit of surviving conscious states is thus a deficit in the amount of represented time. The process of abridgment, of foreshortening, of which we have spoken, presupposes this deficit.

38 *Essay Concerning Human Understanding*, II, X, 5.

If, in order to reach a distant reminiscence, we had to go through the entire series of terms which separate it from our present selves, memory would become impossible on account of the length of the operation. We thus reach the paradoxical result that one condition of remembering is that we should forget. Without totally forgetting a prodigious number of states of consciousness, and momentarily forgetting a large number, we could not remember at all. Oblivion, except in certain cases, is thus no malady of memory, but a condition of its health and its life."[39]

There are many irregularities in the process of forgetting which are as yet unaccounted for. A thing forgotten on one day will be remembered on the next. Something we have made the most strenuous efforts to recall, but all in vain, will, soon after we have given up the attempt, saunter into the mind, as Emerson somewhere says, as innocently as if it had never been sent for. Experiences of bygone date will revive after years of absolute oblivion, often as the result of some cerebral disease or accident which seems to develop latent paths of association, as the photographer's fluid develops the picture sleeping in the collodion film. The oftenest quoted of these cases is Coleridge's:

"In a Roman Catholic town in Germany, a young woman, who could neither read nor write, was seized with a fever, and was said by the priests to be possessed of a devil, because she was heard talking Latin, Greek, and Hebrew. Whole sheets of her ravings were written out, and found to consist of sentences intelligible in themselves, but having slight connection with each other. Of her Hebrew sayings, only a few could be traced to the Bible, and most seemed to be in the Rabbinical dialect. All trick was out of the question; the woman was a simple creature; there was no doubt as to the fever. It was long before any explanation, save that of demoniacal possession, could be obtained. At last the mystery was unveiled by a physician, who determined to trace back the girl's history, and who, after much trouble, discovered that at the age of nine she had been charitably taken by an old Protestant pastor, a great Hebrew scholar, in whose house she lived till his death. On further inquiry it appeared to have been the old man's custom for years to walk up and down a passage of his house into which the kitchen opened, and to read to himself with a loud voice out of his books. The books were ransacked, and among them were found several of the Greek and Latin Fathers, together with a collection of Rab-

39 Théodule Ribot: *Les Maladies de la mémoire*, p. 45.

binical writings. In these works so many of the passages taken down at the young woman's bed-side were identified, that there could be no reasonable doubt as to their source."[40]

Hypnotic subjects as a rule forget all that has happened in their trance. But in a succeeding trance they will often remember the events of a past one. This is like what happens in those cases of 'double personality' in which no recollection of one of the lives is to be found in the other. We have already seen in an earlier chapter that the sensibility often differs from one of the alternate personalities to another, and we have heard M. Pierre Janet's theory that anæsthesias carry amnesias with them (see above, pp. 363 ff.). In certain cases this is evidently so; the throwing of certain functional brain-tracts out of gear with others, so as to dissociate their consciousness from that of the remaining brain, throws them out for both sensorial and ideational service. M. Janet proved in various ways that what his patients forgot when anæsthetic they remembered when the sensibility returned. For instance, he restored their tactile sense temporarily by means of electric currents, passes, etc., and then made them handle various objects, such as keys and pencils, or make particular movements, like the sign of the cross. The moment the anæsthesia returned they found it impossible to recollect the objects or the acts. "They had had nothing in their hands, they had done nothing," etc. The next day, however, sensibility being again restored by similar processes, they remembered perfectly the circumstance, and told what they had handled or had done.

All these pathological facts are showing us that the sphere of possible recollection may be wider than we think, and that in certain matters apparent oblivion is no proof against possible recall under other conditions. They give no countenance, however, to

40 *Biographia Literaria*, ed. 1847, I, 117 (quoted in Carpenter's *Mental Physiology*, chapter x, which see for a number of other cases, all unfortunately deficient, like this one, in the evidence of exact verification which 'psychical research' demands). Compare also Théodule Ribot: *Diseases of Memory*, chap. IV. The knowledge of foreign words, etc., reported in trance-mediums, etc., may perhaps often be explained by exaltation of memory. An hystero-epileptic girl, whose case I quoted in *Proceedings of the American Society for Psychical Research*, automatically writes an "Ingoldsby Legend" in several cantos, which her parents say she 'had never read.' Of course she must have read or heard it, but perhaps never *learned* it. Of some macaronic Latin-English verses about a sea-serpent which her hand also wrote unconsciously, I have vainly sought the original (see *Proceedings*, etc., p. 553).

the extravagant opinion that nothing we experience can be absolutely forgotten. In real life, in spite of occasional surprises, most of what happens actually is forgotten. The only reasons for supposing that if the conditions were forthcoming everything would revive are of a transcendental sort. Sir William Hamilton quotes and adopts them from the German writer Schmid. Knowledge being a 'spontaneous self-energy' on the part of the mind,

"this energy being once determined, it is natural that it should persist, until again annihilated by other causes. This [annihilation] would be the case, were the mind merely passive . . . . But the mental activity, the act of knowledge, of which I now speak, is more than this; it is an energy of the self-active power of a subject one and indivisible: consequently, a part of the ego must be detached or annihilated, if a cognition once existent be again extinguished. Hence it is, that the problem most difficult of solution is not, how a mental activity endures, but how it ever vanishes."[41]

Those whom such an argument persuades may be left happy with their belief. Other positive argument there is none, none certainly of a physiological sort.[42]

When memory begins to decay, proper names are what go first, and at all times proper names are harder to recollect than those of general properties and classes of things.

This seems due to the fact that common qualities and names have contracted an infinitely greater number of associations in our mind than the names of most of the persons whom we know. Their memory is better organized. Proper names as well organized as those of our family and friends are recollected as well as those of any other objects.[43] 'Organization' means numerous associations; and the more numerous the associations, the greater the number of paths of recall. For the same reason adjectives, conjunctions, prepositions, and the cardinal verbs, those words, in short, which form the grammatical framework of all our speech, are the very last to decay. Kussmaul[44] makes the following acute remark on this subject:

41 *Lectures on Metaphysics*, II, 211.

42 Cf. on this point J. Delbœuf: *Le Sommeil et les rêves* (1885), p. 119 ff.; R. Verdon: "Forgetfulness," in *Mind*, II, 437.

43 Cf. A. Maury: *Le Sommeil et les rêves*, p. 442.

44 *Die Störungen der Sprache*, quoted by Ribot: *Les Maladies de la mémoire*, p. 133.

"The concreter a conception is, the sooner is its name forgotten. This is because our ideas of persons and things are less strongly bound up with their names than with such abstractions as their business, their circumstances, their qualities. We easily can imagine persons and things without their names, the sensorial image of them being more important than that other symbolic image, their name. Abstract conceptions, on the other hand, are only acquired by means of the words which alone serve to confer stability upon them. This is why verbs, adjectives, pronouns, and still more adverbs, prepositions, and conjunctions are more intimately connected with our thinking than are substantives."

The disease called Aphasia, of which a little was said in Chapter II, has let in a flood of light on the phenomenon of Memory, by showing the number of ways in which the use of a given object, like a word, may be lost by the mind. We may lose our acoustic idea or our articulatory idea of it; neither without the other will give us proper command of the word. And if we have both, but have lost the paths of association between the brain-centres which support the two, we are in as bad a plight. 'Ataxic' and 'amnesic' aphasia, 'word-deafness,' and 'associative aphasia' are all practical losses of word-memory. We have thus, as M. Ribot says, not memory so much as memories.[45] The visual, the tactile, the muscular, the auditory memory may all vary independently of each other in the same individual; and different individuals may have them developed in different degrees. As a rule, a man's memory is good in the departments in which his interest is strong; but those departments are apt to be those in which his discriminative sensibility is high. A man with a bad ear is not likely to have practically a good musical memory, or a purblind person to remember visual appearances well. In a later chapter we shall see illustrations of the differences in men's imagining power.[46] It is obvious that the machinery of memory must be largely determined thereby.

Mr. Galton, in his work on *English Men of Science*,[47] has given a very interesting collation of cases showing individual variations in the type of memory, where it is strong. Some have it verbal.

45 *Op. cit.*, chap. III.

46 "Those who have a good memory for figures are in general those who know best how to handle them, that is, those who are most familiar with their relations to each other and to things." (A. Maury: *Le Sommeil et les rêves*, p. 443.)

47 Pp. 107–121.

Others have it good for facts and figures, others for form. Most say that what is to be remembered must first be rationally conceived and assimilated.[48]

There is an interesting fact connected with remembering, which, so far as I know, Mr. R. Verdon was the first writer expressly to call attention to. We can *set* our memory as it were to retain things for a certain time, and then let them depart.

"Individuals often remember clearly and well up to the time when they have to use their knowledge, and then when it is no further required, there follows a rapid and extensive decay of the traces. Many schoolboys forget their lessons after they have said them, many barristers forget details got up for a particular case. Thus a boy learns thirty lines of Homer, says them perfectly and then forgets them so that he could not say five consecutive lines the next morning, and a barrister may be one week learned in the mysteries of making cog-wheels, but in the next he may be well acquainted with the anatomy of the ribs instead."[49]

The rationale of this fact is obscure; and the existence of it ought to make us feel how truly subtle are the nervous processes which memory involves. Mr. Verdon adds that

"When the use of a record is withdrawn, and attention is withdrawn from it and we think no more about it, we know that we experience a feeling of relief, and we thus may conclude that energy is in some way liberated. If the . . . attention is not withdrawn so that we keep the record in mind, we know that this feeling of relief does not take place . . . . Also we are well aware not only that after this feeling of relief takes place the record does not seem conserved so well as before, but that we have real difficulty in attempting to remember it."

This shows that we are not as entirely unconscious of a topic as we think, during the time in which we seem to be merely retaining it subject to recall.

"Practically," says Mr. Verdon, "we sometimes keep a matter in mind not exactly by attending to it but by keeping our attention re-

[48] For other examples see Hamilton's *Lectures*, II, 219, and J. Huber: *Das Gedächtniss*, p. 36 ff.

[49] *Mind*, II, 449.

ferred to something connected with it from time to time. Translating this into the language of physiology, we mean that, by referring attention to a part within or closely connected with the system of traces [paths] required to be remembered, we keep it well fed, so that the traces are preserved with the utmost delicacy."

This is perhaps as near as we can get to an explanation. Setting the mind to remember a thing involves a continual minimal irradiation of excitement into paths which lead thereto, involves the continued presence of the thing in the 'fringe' of our consciousness. Letting the thing go involves withdrawal of the irradiation, unconsciousness of the thing, and, after a time, obliteration of the paths.

A curious peculiarity of our memory is that things are impressed better by active than by passive repetition. I mean that in learning by heart (for example), when we almost know the piece, it pays better to wait and recollect by an effort from within, than to look at the book again. If we recover the words in the former way, we shall probably know them the next time; if in the latter way, we shall very likely need the book once more. The learning by heart means the formation of paths from a former set to a later set of cerebral word-processes: call 1 and 2 in the diagram the processes in question; what we need for remembering hereafter is that the path 1—2 should be deepened. Obviously when we remember by inward effort, this is the path that is now used and consequently also deep-

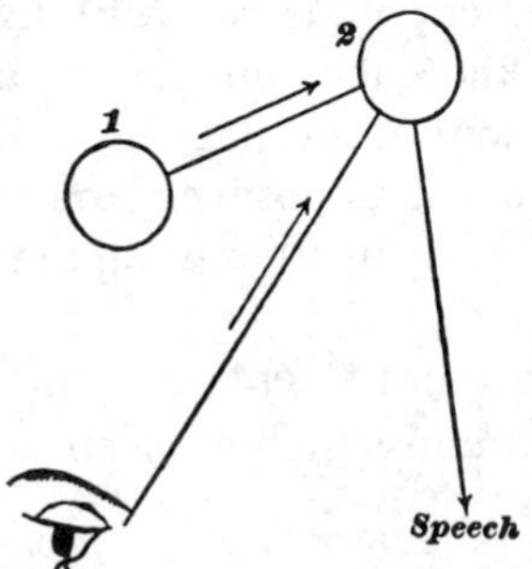

Fig. 46.

ened for future use. But when we excite 2 by the eye, although the path 1—2 doubtless is then shot through also, the phenomenon which we are discussing shows that the direct discharge from 1 into 2, unaided by the eyes, ploughs the deeper and more permanent groove. There is, moreover, a greater amount of tension accumulated in the brain before the discharge from 1 to 2, when the latter takes place unaided by the eye. This is proved by the general feeling of strain in the effort to remember 2; and this also ought to make the discharge more violent and the path more deep. A similar reason doubtless accounts for the familiar fact that we remember our own theories, our own discoveries, combinations, inventions, in short whatever 'ideas' originate in our own brain, a thousand times better than exactly similar things which are communicated to us from without.

A word, in closing, about the metaphysics involved in remembering. According to the assumptions of this book, thoughts accompany the brain's workings, and those thoughts are cognitive of realities. The whole relation is one which we can only write down empirically, confessing that no glimmer of explanation of it is yet in sight. That brains should give rise to a knowing consciousness at all, this is the one mystery which returns, no matter of what sort the consciousness and of what sort the knowledge may be. Sensations, aware of mere qualities, involve the mystery as much as thoughts, aware of complex systems, involve it. To the platonizing tradition in philosophy, however, this is not so. Sensational consciousness is something *quasi*-material, hardly cognitive, which one need not much wonder at. *Relating* consciousness is quite the reverse, and the mystery of it is unspeakable. Professor Ladd, for example, in his usually excellent book,[50] after well showing the matter-of-fact dependence of retention and reproduction on brain-paths, says:

"In the study of perception psycho-physics *can* do much toward a scientific explanation. It can tell what qualities of stimuli produce certain qualities of sensations; it can suggest a principle relating the quantity of the stimuli to the intensity of the sensation; it can investigate the laws under which, by combined action of various excitations, the *sensations are combined* [?] into presentations of sense; it can show how the time-relations of the sensations and percepts in consciousness correspond to the objective relations in time of the stimulations. But for that spiritual activity which actually *puts together* in consciousness the sensations, it cannot even suggest the beginning of a physical

50 *Physiological Psychology*, pt. II, chap. X, § 23.

explanation. Moreover, no cerebral process can be conceived of which —in case it were known to exist—could possibly be regarded as a fitting physical basis for this unifying *actus* of mind. Thus also, and even more emphatically, must we insist upon the complete inability of physiology to suggest an explanation for conscious memory, in so far as it is *memory*—that is, in so far as it most imperatively calls for explanation. . . . The very essence of the act of memory consists in the ability to say: This after-image is the image of a percept I had a moment since; or this image of memory is the image of the percept I had at a certain time—I do not remember precisely how long since. It would, then, be quite contrary to the facts to hold that, when the image of memory appears in consciousness, it is recognized as belonging to a particular original percept on account of its perceived resemblance to this percept. The original percept does not exist, and will never be *reproduced.* Even more palpably false and absurd would it be to hold that any similarity of the impressions or processes in end-organs or central organs explains the act of conscious memory. Consciousness knows nothing of such similarity; knows nothing even of the existence of nervous impressions and processes. Moreover, we could never *know* two impressions or processes that are separated in time to be similar, without implying this same inexplicable act of memory. It is a fact of consciousness, on which all possibility of connected experience and of recorded and cumulative human knowledge is dependent, that certain phases or products of consciousness appear with a claim to stand for (to represent)[51] past experiences to which they are regarded as in some respect similar. It is this peculiar claim in consciousness which constitutes the *essence* of an act of memory; it is this which makes memory wholly inexplicable as a mere persistence or recurrence of similar impressions. It is this which makes conscious memory a spiritual phenomenon, the explanation of which, as arising out of nervous processes and conditions, is not simply undiscovered in fact, but utterly incapable of approach by the imagination. When, then, we speak of a physical basis of memory, recognition must be made of the complete inability of science to suggest any physical process which can be conceived of as correlated with that peculiar and mysterious *actus* of the mind, *connecting* its present and its past, which constitutes the essence of memory."

This passage seems to me characteristic of the reigning half-way modes of thought. It puts the difficulties in the wrong places. At one moment it seems to admit with the cruder sensationalists that the material of our thoughts is independent sensations reproduced,

51 [Why not say 'know'?—W. J.]

and that the 'putting together' of these sensations would be knowledge, if it could only be brought about, the only mystery being as to the what '*actus*' can bring it about. At another moment it seems to contend that even this sort of 'combining' would not be knowledge, because certain of the elements connected must 'claim to represent or stand for' past originals, which is incompatible with their being mere images revived. The result is various confused and scattered mysteries and unsatisfied intellectual desires. But why not 'pool' our mysteries into one great mystery, the mystery that brain-processes occasion knowledge at all? It is surely no different mystery to *feel* myself by means of one brain-process writing at this table now, and by means of a different brain-process a year hence to *remember* myself writing. All that psychology can do is to seek to determine *what* the several brain-processes are; and this, in a wretchedly imperfect way, is what such writings as the present chapter have begun to do. But of 'images reproduced,' and 'claiming to represent,' and 'put together by a unifying *actus*,' I have been silent, because such expressions either signify nothing, or they are only roundabout ways of simply saying that the *past is known* when certain brain-conditions are fulfilled, and it seems to me that the straightest and shortest way of saying that is the best.

For a history of opinion about Memory, and other bibliographic references, I must refer to the admirable little monograph on the subject by Mr. W. H. Burnham in the *American Journal of Psychology*, vol. II. Useful books are: D. Kay's *Memory, What It Is and How to Improve It* (1888); and F. Fauth's *Das Gedächtnis, Studie zu einer Pädagogik*, etc., 1888.

Chapter XVII

Sensation

After inner perception, outer perception! The next three chapters will treat of the processes by which we cognize at all times the present world of space and the material things which it contains. And first, of the process called Sensation.

SENSATION AND PERCEPTION DISTINGUISHED

The words Sensation and Perception do not carry very definitely discriminated meanings in popular speech, and in Psychology also their meanings run into each other. Both of them name processes in which we cognize an objective world; both (under normal conditions) need the stimulation of incoming nerves ere they can occur; Perception always involves Sensation as a portion of itself; and Sensation in turn never takes place in adult life without Perception also being there. They are therefore names for different cognitive *functions,* not for different sorts of mental *fact.* The nearer the object cognized comes to being a simple quality like 'hot,' 'cold,' 'red,' 'noise,' 'pain,' apprehended irrelatively to other things, the more the state of mind approaches pure sensation. The fuller of relations the object is, on the contrary; the more it is something classed, located, measured, compared, assigned to a function, etc., etc.; the more unreservedly do we call the state of mind a perception, and the relatively smaller is the part in it which sensation plays.

Sensation, then, so long as we take the analytic point of view, differs from Perception only in the extreme simplicity of its object or content.[1] Its function is that of mere *acquaintance* with a fact. Perception's function, on the other hand, is knowledge *about*[2] a fact; and this knowledge admits of numberless degrees of complication. But in both sensation and perception we perceive the fact as an *immediately present outward reality,* and this makes them differ from 'thought' and 'conception,' whose objects do not appear present in this immediate physical way. *From the physiological point of view both sensations and perceptions differ from 'thoughts'* (in the narrower sense of the word) *in the fact that nerve-currents coming in from the periphery are involved in their production. In perception these nerve-currents arouse voluminous*

[1] Some persons will say that we never have a really simple object or content. My definition of sensation does not require the simplicity to be absolutely, but only relatively, extreme. It is worth while in passing, however, to warn the reader against a couple of inferences that are often made. One is that because we gradually learn to analyze so many qualities we ought to conclude that there are no really indecomposable feelings in the mind. The other is that because the processes that produce our sensations are multiple, the sensations regarded as subjective facts must also be compound. To take an example, to a child the taste of lemonade comes at first as a simple quality. He later learns both that many stimuli and many nerves are involved in the exhibition of this taste to his mind, and he also learns to perceive separately the sourness, the coolness, the sweet, the lemon aroma, etc., and the several degrees of strength of each and all of these things,—the experience falling into a large number of aspects, each of which is abstracted, classed, named, etc., and all of which appear to be the elementary sensations into which the original 'lemonade flavor' is decomposed. It is argued from this that the latter never was the simple thing which it seemed. I have already criticised this sort of reasoning in Chapter VI (see pp. 172 ff.). The mind of the child enjoying the simple lemonade flavor and that of the same child grown up and analyzing it are in two entirely different conditions. Subjectively considered, the two states of mind are two altogether distinct sorts of fact. The later mental state says 'this is the *same flavor (or fluid)* which that earlier state perceived as simple,' but that does not make the two states themselves identical. It is nothing but a case of learning more and more *about* the same topics of discourse or things.—Many of these topics, however, must be confessed to resist all analysis, the various colors for example. He who sees blue and yellow 'in' a certain green means merely that when green is confronted with these other colors he sees relations of *similarity*. He who sees abstract 'color' in it means merely that he sees a similarity between it and all the other objects known as colors. (Similarity itself cannot ultimately be accounted for by an identical abstract element buried in all the similars, as has been already shown, p. 466 ff.) He who sees abstract paleness, intensity, purity, in the green means other similarities still. These are all outward determinations of that special green, knowledges *about* it, *zufällige Ansichten*, as Herbart would say, not *elements* of its composition. Compare the article by Meinong in the *Vierteljahrsschrift für wissenschaftliche Philosophie*, XII, 324.

[2] See above, p. 216.

associative or reproductive processes in the cortex; but when sensation occurs alone, or with a minimum of perception, the accompanying reproductive processes are at a minimum too.

I shall in this chapter discuss some general questions more especially relative to Sensation. In a later chapter perception will take its turn. I shall entirely pass by the classification and natural history of our special 'sensations,' such matters finding their proper place, and being sufficiently well treated, in all the physiological books.[3]

THE COGNITIVE FUNCTION OF SENSATION

A pure sensation is an abstraction; and when we adults talk of our 'sensations' we mean one of two things: either certain *objects*, namely simple *qualities* or *attributes* like *hard, hot, pain*; or else those of our thoughts in which acquaintance with these objects is least combined with knowledge about the relations of them to other things. As we can only think or talk about the relations of objects with which we have *acquaintance* already, we are forced to postulate a function in our thought whereby we first become aware of the *bare immediate natures* by which our several objects are distinguished. This function is sensation. And just as logicians always point out the distinction between substantive terms of discourse and relations found to obtain between them, so psychologists, as a rule, are ready to admit this function, of the vision of the terms or matters meant, as something distinct from the knowledge about them and of their relations *inter se*. Thought with the former function is sensational, with the latter, intellectual. Our earliest thoughts are almost exclusively sensational. They merely give us a set of *thats*, or *its*, of subjects of discourse, with their relations not brought out. The first time we see *light*, in Condillac's phrase we *are* it rather than see it. But all our later optical knowledge is about what this experience gives. And though we were struck blind from that first moment, our scholarship in the subject would lack no essential feature so long as our memory remained. In training-institutions for the blind they teach the pupils as much *about* light as in ordinary schools. Reflection, refraction, the spectrum, the

[3] Those who wish a fuller treatment than Martin's *Human Body* affords may be recommended to Bernstein's *Five Senses of Man*, in the International Scientific Series, or to Ladd's or Wundt's *Physiological Psychology*. The completest compendium is L. Hermann's *Handbuch der Physiologie*, vol. III.

ether-theory, etc., are all studied. But the best taught born-blind pupil of such an establishment yet lacks a knowledge which the least instructed seeing baby has. They can never show him what light is in its 'first intention'; and the loss of that sensible knowledge no book-learning can replace. All this is so obvious that we usually find sensation 'postulated' as an element of experience, even by those philosophers who are least inclined to make much of its importance, or to pay respect to the knowledge which it brings.[4]

But the trouble is that most, if not all, of those who admit it, admit it as a fractional *part* of the thought, in the old-fashioned atomistic sense which we have so often criticised.

Take the pain called toothache for example. Again and again we feel it and greet it as the same real item in the universe. We must therefore, it is supposed, have a distinct pocket for it in our mind

[4] "The sensations which we *postulate* as the signs or occasions of our perceptions" (A. Seth: *Scottish Philosophy*, p. 89). "Their existence is *supposed* only because, without them, it would be impossible to account for the complex phenomena which are directly present in consciousness" (J. Dewey: *Psychology*, p. 34). Even as great an enemy of Sensation as T. H. Green has to allow it a sort of hypothetical existence under protest. "Perception presupposes feeling" (*Contemporary Review*, vol. XXXI, p. 747). Cf. also such passages as those in his *Prolegomena to Ethics*, §§ 48, 49.—Physiologically, the sensory and the reproductive or associative processes may wax and wane independently of each other. Where the part directly due to stimulation of the sense-organ preponderates, the thought has a sensational character, and differs from other thoughts in the sensational direction. Those thoughts which lie farthest in that direction we call *sensations*, for practical convenience, just as we call *conceptions* those which lie nearer the opposite extreme. But we no more have conceptions pure than we have pure sensations. Our most rarefied intellectual states involve some bodily sensibility, just as our dullest feelings have some intellectual scope. Common-sense and common psychology express this by saying that the mental state is composed of distinct fractional *parts*, one of which is sensation, the other conception. We, however, who believe every mental state to be an integral thing (p. 266) cannot talk thus, but must speak of the degree of sensational or intellectual character, or function, of the mental state. Professor Hering puts, as usual, his finger better upon the truth than anyone else. Writing of visual perception, he says: "It is inadmissible in the present state of our knowledge to assert that first and last the same retinal picture arouses exactly the same *pure sensation*, but that this sensation, in consequence of practice and experience, is differently *interpreted* the last time, and elaborated into a different perception from the first. For the only real *data* are, on the one hand, the physical picture on the retina,—and that is both times the same; and, on the other hand, the resultant state of consciousness (*ausgelöste Empfindungscomplex*)—and that is both times distinct. *Of any third thing, namely, a pure sensation thrust between the retinal and the mental pictures, we know nothing. We can then, if we wish to avoid all hypothesis, only say that the nervous apparatus reacts upon the same stimulus differently the last time from the first, and that in consequence the consciousness is different too.*" (Hermann's *Handbuch*, III, 1, 567–8.)

into which it and nothing else will fit. This pocket, when filled, is the sensation of toothache; and must be either filled or half-filled whenever and under whatever form toothache is present to our thought, and whether much or little of the rest of the mind be filled at the same time. Thereupon of course comes up the paradox and mystery: If the knowledge of toothache be pent up in this separate mental pocket, how can it be known *cum alio* or brought into one view with anything else? This pocket knows nothing else; no other part of the mind knows toothache. The knowing of toothache *cum alio* must be a miracle. And the miracle must have an Agent. And the Agent must be a Subject or Ego 'out of time,'—and all the rest of it, as we saw in Chapter X. And then begins the well-worn round of recrimination between the sensationalists and the spiritualists, from which we are saved by our determination from the outset to accept the psychological point of view, and to admit knowledge whether of simple toothaches or of philosophic systems as an ultimate fact. There are realities and there are 'states of mind,' and the latter know the former; and it is just as wonderful for a state of mind to be a 'sensation' and know a simple pain as for it to be a thought and know a system of related things.[5] But there is no reason to suppose that when different states of mind know different things about the same toothache, they do so by virtue of their all *containing* faintly or vividly the original pain. Quite the reverse. The by-gone sensation of my gout was painful, as Reid somewhere says; the *thought* of the same gout as by-gone is pleasant, and in no respect resembles the earlier mental state.

Sensations, then, first make us acquainted with innumerable things, and then are replaced by thoughts which know the same things in altogether other ways. And Locke's main doctrine remains eternally true, however hazy some of his language may have been, that

> "though there be a great number of considerations wherein things may be compared one with another, and so a multitude of relations; yet they all *terminate in*, and are concerned about, those simple ideas[6]

[5] Yet even writers like Prof. Bain will deny, in the most gratuitous way, that sensations know anything. "It is evident that the lowest or most restricted form of sensation does not contain an element of knowledge. The mere state of mind, called the sensation of scarlet, is not knowledge, although a necessary preparation for it." 'Is not knowledge *about* scarlet' is all that Professor Bain can rightfully say.

[6] By simple ideas of sensation Locke merely means sensations.

either of sensation or reflection, which I think to be the whole materials of all our knowledge. . . . The simple ideas we receive from sensation and reflection are the *boundaries* of our thoughts; beyond which, the mind, whatever efforts it would make, is not able to advance one jot; nor can it make any discoveries, when it would pry into the nature and hidden causes of those ideas."[7]

The nature and hidden causes of ideas will never be unravelled till the *nexus* between the brain and consciousness is cleared up. All we can say now is that *sensations are first things* in the way of consciousness. Before conceptions can come, sensations must have come; but before sensations come, no psychic fact need have existed, a nerve-current is enough. If the nerve-current be not given, nothing else will take its place. To quote the good Locke again:

"It is not in the power of the most exalted wit or enlarged understanding, by any quickness or variety of thoughts, to invent or frame one new simple idea [i.e., sensation] in the mind . . . . I would have any one try to fancy any taste which had never affected his palate, or frame the idea of a scent he had never smelt; and when he can do this, I will also conclude, that a blind man hath ideas of colours, and a deaf man true, distinct notions of sounds."[8]

The brain is so made that all currents in it run one way. Consciousness of some sort goes with all the currents, but it is only when new currents are entering that it has the sensational *tang*. And it is only then that consciousness directly *encounters* (to use a word of Mr. Bradley's) a reality outside itself.

The difference between such encounter and all conceptual knowledge is very great. A blind man may know all *about* the sky's blueness, and I may know all *about* your toothache, conceptually; tracing their causes from primeval chaos, and their consequences to the crack of doom. But so long as he has not felt the blueness, nor I the toothache, our knowledge, wide as it is, of these realities, will be hollow and inadequate. Somebody must *feel* blueness, somebody must *have* toothache, to make human knowledge of these matters real. Conceptual systems which neither began nor left off in sensations would be like bridges without piers. Systems about fact must plunge themselves into sensation as bridges plunge

[7] *Essay Concerning Human Understanding*, bk. II, ch. XXV, § 9; ch. XXIII, § 29.
[8] *Op. cit.*, bk. II, ch. II, § 2.

their piers into the rock. Sensations are the stable rock, the *terminus a quo* and the *terminus ad quem* of thought. To find such termini is our aim with all our theories—to conceive first when and where a certain sensation may be had, and then to have it. Finding it stops discussion. Failure to find it kills the false conceit of knowledge. Only when you deduce a possible sensation for me from your theory, and give it to me when and where the theory requires, do I begin to be sure that your thought has anything to do with truth.

Pure sensations can only be realized in the earliest days of life. They are all but impossible to adults with memories and stores of associations acquired. Prior to all impressions on sense-organs the brain is plunged in deep sleep and consciousness is practically non-existent. Even the first weeks after birth are passed in almost unbroken sleep by human infants. It takes a strong message from the sense-organs to break this slumber. In a new-born brain this gives rise to an absolutely pure sensation. But the experience leaves its 'unimaginable touch' on the matter of the convolutions, and the next impression which a sense-organ transmits produces a cerebral reaction in which the awakened vestige of the last impression plays its part. Another sort of feeling and a higher grade of cognition are the consequence; and the complication goes on increasing till the end of life, no two successive impressions falling on an identical brain, and no two successive thoughts being exactly the same. (See above, p. 224 ff.)

The first sensation which an infant gets is for him the Universe. And the Universe which he later comes to know is nothing but an amplification and an implication of that first simple germ which, by accretion on the one hand and intussusception on the other, has grown so big and complex and articulate that its first estate is unrememberable. In his dumb awakening to the consciousness of *something there*, a mere *this* as yet (or something for which even the term *this* would perhaps be too discriminative, and the intellectual acknowledgment of which would be better expressed by the bare interjection 'lo!'), the infant encounters an object in which (though it be given in a pure sensation) all the 'categories of the understanding' are contained. *It has objectivity, unity, substantiality, causality, in the full sense in which any later object or system of objects has these things.* Here the young knower meets and greets his world; and the miracle of knowledge bursts forth, as

Voltaire says, as much in the infant's lowest sensation as in the highest achievement of a Newton's brain. The physiological condition of this first sensible experience is probably nerve-currents coming in from many peripheral organs at once. Later, the one confused Fact which these currents cause to appear is perceived to be many facts, and to contain many qualities.[9] For as the currents vary, and the brain-paths are moulded by them, other thoughts with other 'objects' come, and the 'same thing' which was apprehended as a present *this* soon figures as a past *that*, about which many unsuspected things have come to light. The principles of this development have been laid down already in Chapters XII and XIII, and nothing more need here be added to that account.

"THE RELATIVITY OF KNOWLEDGE"

To the reader who is tired of so much *Erkenntnisstheorie* I can only say that I am so myself, but that it is indispensable, in the actual state of opinions about Sensation, to try to clear up just what the word means. Locke's pupils seek to do the impossible with sensations, and against them we must once again insist that sensations 'clustered together' cannot build up our more intellectual states of mind. Plato's earlier pupils used to admit Sensation's existence, grudgingly, but they trampled it in the dust as something corporeal, non-cognitive, and vile.[10] His latest followers seem to seek

9 "So far is it from true that we necessarily have as many feelings in consciousness at one time as there are inlets to the sense then played upon, that it is a fundamental law of pure sensation that each momentary state of the organism yields but one feeling, however numerous may be its parts and its exposures. . . . To this original Unity of consciousness it makes no difference that the tributaries to the single feeling are beyond the organism instead of within it, in an outside object with several sensible properties, instead of in the living body with its several sensitive functions. . . . The unity therefore is not made by 'association' of severed components; but the plurality is formed by *dissociation* of unsuspected varieties within the unity; the substantive thing being no product of synthesis, but the residuum of differentiation." (J. Martineau: *A Study of Religion* (1888), pp. 192–4.) Compare also F. H. Bradley: *Logic*, book I, chap. II.

10 Such passages as the following abound in anti-sensationalist literature: "*Sense* is a kind of dull Confused and Stupid Perception obtruded upon the Soul from without, whereby it perceives the Alterations and Motions within its own Body, and takes Cognizance of Individual Bodies existing round about it, but doth not clearly Comprehend what they are, nor penetrate into the Nature of them, it being intended by Nature, as *Plotinus* speaks, not so properly *for Knowledge*, as for the *Use of the Body*. For the Soul suffering under that which it perceives by way of *Passion*, cannot master or conquer it, that is to say, know or understand it. For so *Anaxagoras* in *Aristotle* very fitly expresses the Nature of *Knowledge* and *Intellec-*

to crowd it out of existence altogether. The only reals for the neo-hegelian writers appear to be *relations*, relations without terms, or whose terms are only speciously such and really consist in knots, or snarls of relations finer still *in infinitum*.

"Exclude from what we have considered real all qualities constituted by relation, we find that none are left." "Abstract the many relations from the one thing, and there is nothing. . . . Without the relations it would not exist at all."[11] "The single feeling is nothing real." "On the

---

tion under the Notion of *Conquering. Wherefore it is necessary, since the Mind understands all things, that it should be free from Mixture and Passion, for this end, as* Anaxagoras *speaks, that it may be able to master and conquer its Objects, that is to say, to know or understand them.* In like manner *Plotinus*, in his Book of *Sense and Memory*, makes *to suffer* and *to be conquered* all one, as also to *know and to conquer*; for which Cause he concludes that that which suffers doth not know . . . . *Sense*, that suffers from External Objects, lies as it were prostrate under them, and is overcome by them . . . . *Sense* therefore is a certain kind of drowsy and Somnolent Perception of that Passive Part of the Soul, which is as it were asleep in the Body, and acts concretely with it. . . . It is an Energy arising from the Body, and a certain kind of Drowsy or Sleeping Life of the Soul blended together with it. The Perceptions of which *Compound*, or *of the Soul as it were half asleep and half awake*, are confused, indistinct, turbid and encumbred Cogitations, very different from the Energies of the *Noetical* Part, . . . which are free, clear, serene, Satisfactory and awakened Cogitations, That is to say, Knowledges." Etc., etc., etc. (R. Cudworth: *A Treatise Concerning Eternal and Immutable Morality*, bk. III, chap. II.) Similarly Malebranche: "THÉODORE.—Oh, oh, Ariste! God knows pain, pleasure, warmth, and the rest. But he does not feel these things. He knows pain, since he knows what that modification of the soul is in which pain consists. He knows it because he alone causes it in us (as I shall presently prove), and he knows what he does. In a word, he knows it because his knowledge has no bounds. But he does not feel it, for if so he would be unhappy. To know pain, then, is not to feel it. ARISTE.—That is true. But to feel it is to know it, is it not? THÉODORE.—No indeed, since God does not feel it in the least, and yet he knows it perfectly. But in order not to quibble about terms, if you will have it that to feel pain is to know it, agree at least that it is not to know it clearly, that it is not to know it by light and by evidence—in a word, that it is not to know its nature; in other words and to speak exactly, it is not to know it at all. To feel pain, for example, is to feel ourselves unhappy without well knowing either what we are or what is this modality of our being which makes us unhappy. . . . Impose silence on your senses, your imagination, and your passions, and you will hear the pure voice of inner truth, the clear and evident replies of our common master. Never confound the evidence which results from the comparison of ideas with the liveliness of the sensations which touch and thrill you. The livelier our sensations and feelings (*sentiments*) are, the more darkness do they shed. The more terrible or agreeable are our phantoms, and the more body and reality they appear to have, the more dangerous are they and fit to lead us astray." (*Entretiens sur la métaphysique*, 3me Entretien, *ad init.*) Malebranche's Théodore prudently does not try to explain how God's 'infinite felicity' is compatible with his not feeling joy.

[11] Green: *Prolegomena*, §§ 20, 28.

recognition of relations as constituting the *nature* of ideas rests the possibility of any tenable theory of their reality."

Such quotations as these from the late T. H. Green[12] would be matters of curiosity rather than of importance, were it not that sensationalist writers themselves believe in a so-called 'Relativity of Knowledge,' which, if they only understood it, they would see to be identical with Professor Green's doctrine. They tell us that the relation of sensations to each other is something belonging to their essence, and that no one of them has an absolute content:

"That, e.g., black can only be felt in contrast to white, or at least in distinction from a paler or a deeper black; similarly a tone or a sound only in alternation with others or with silence; and in like manner a smell, a taste, a touch, only, so to speak, *in statu nascendi*, whilst, when the stimulus continues, all sensation disappears. This all seems at first sight to be splendidly consistent both with itself and with the facts. But looked at more closely, it is seen that neither is the case."[13]

12 "Introduction" to Hume, §§ 146, 188. It is hard to tell just what this apostolic human being but strenuously feeble writer means by relation. Sometimes it seems to stand for system of related fact. The ubiquity of the 'psychologist's fallacy' (see p. 195) in his pages, his incessant leaning on the confusion between the thing known, the thought that knows it, and the farther things known about that thing and about that thought by later and additional thoughts, make it impossible to clear up his meaning. Compare, however, with the utterances in the text such others as these: "The waking of self-consciousness from the sleep of sense is an absolute new beginning, and nothing can come within the 'crystal sphere' of intelligence, except as it is determined by intelligence. What sense is to sense is nothing for thought. What sense is to thought, it is as determined *by* thought. There can, therefore, be no 'reality' in sensation to which the world of thought can be referred." (Edward Caird's *Philosophy of Kant*, 1st ed., p. 394.) "When," says Green again, "feeling a pain or pleasure of heat, I perceive it to be connected with the action of approaching the fire, am I not perceiving a relation *of which one constituent, at any rate, is a simple sensation? The true answer is, No.*" "Perception in its simplest form . . . —perception as the first sight or touch of an object in which nothing but what is seen or touched is recognized—*neither is nor contains sensation.*" (*Contemporary Review*, XXXI, pp. 746, 749.) "Mere sensation is in truth a phrase that represents no reality." "Mere feeling, then, as a matter unformed by thought, has no place in the world of facts, in the cosmos of possible experience." (*Prolegomena to Ethics*, §§ 46, 50.)—I have expressed myself a little more fully on this subject in *Mind*, X, 27 ff.

13 Stumpf: *Tonpsychologie*, I, pp. 7, 8. Hobbes's phrase, *sentire semper idem, et non sentire, ad idem recidunt*, is generally treated as the original statement of the relativity doctrine. J. S. Mill (*Examination of Hamilton*, p. 6) and Bain (*Senses and the Intellect*, p. 321; *Emotions and the Will*, pp. 550, 570–2; *Logic*, I, p. 2; *Mind and*

The two leading facts from which the doctrine of universal relativity derives its wide-spread credit are these:

1) The *psychological fact* that so much of our actual knowledge *is* of the relations of things—even our simplest sensations in adult life are habitually referred to classes as we take them in; and

2) The *physiological fact* that our senses and brain must have periods of change and repose, else we cease to feel and think.

Neither of these facts proves anything about the presence or non-presence to our mind of absolute qualities with which we become sensibly acquainted. Surely not the psychological fact; for our inveterate love of relating and comparing things does not alter the intrinsic qualities or nature of the things compared, or undo their absolute givenness. And surely not the physiological fact; for the length of time during which we can feel or attend to a quality is altogether irrelevant to the intrinsic constitution of the quality felt. The time, moreover, is long enough in many instances, as sufferers from neuralgia know.[14] And the doctrine of relativity, not proved by these facts, is flatly disproved by other facts even more patent. So far are we from not knowing (in the words of Professor Bain) "any one thing of itself, but only the difference between it and another thing," that if this were true the whole edifice of our knowledge would collapse. If all we felt were the *difference* between the *C* and *D*, or *c* and *d*, on the musical scale, that being the same in the two pairs of notes, the pairs themselves would be the same, and language could get along without substantives. But Professor Bain does not mean seriously what he says, and we need spend no more time on this vague and popular form of the doctrine.[15] The facts which seem to hover before the minds of its champions are those which are best described under the head of a physiological law.

Body, p. 81) are subscribers to this doctrine. Cf. also J. Mill's *Analysis*, J. S. Mill's edition, II, 11, 12.

[14] We can steadily hear a note for half an hour. The differences between the senses are marked. Smell and taste seem soon to get fatigued.

[15] In the popular mind it is mixed up with that entirely different doctrine of the 'Relativity of Knowledge' preached by Hamilton and Spencer. This doctrine says that our knowledge is relative *to us*, and is not of the object as the latter is in itself. It has nothing to do with the question which we have been discussing, of whether our objects of knowledge contain absolute terms or consist altogether of relations.

THE LAW OF CONTRAST

I will first enumerate the main facts which fall under this law, and then remark upon what seems to me their significance for psychology.[16]

[Nowhere are the phenomena of contrast better exhibited, and their laws more open to accurate study, than in connection with the sense of sight. Here both kinds—simultaneous and successive—can easily be observed, for they are of constant occurrence. Ordinarily they remain unnoticed, in accordance with the general law of economy which causes us to select for conscious notice only such elements of our object as will serve us for æsthetic or practical utility, and to neglect the rest; just as we ignore the double images, the *mouches volantes,* etc., which exist for everyone, but which are not discriminated without careful attention. But by attention we may easily discover the general facts involved in contrast. We find that *in general the color and brightness of one object always apparently affect the color and brightness of any other object seen simultaneously with it or immediately after.*

In the first place, if we look for a moment at any surface and then turn our eyes elsewhere, the complementary color and opposite degree of brightness to that of the first surface tend to mingle themselves with the color and the brightness of the second. This is *successive contrast.* It finds its explanation in the fatigue of the organ of sight, causing it to respond to any particular stimulus less and less readily the longer such stimulus continues to act. This is shown clearly in the very marked changes which occur in case of continued fixation of one particular point of any field. The field darkens slowly, becomes more and more indistinct, and finally, if one is practised enough in holding the eye perfectly steady, slight differences in shade and color may entirely disappear. If we now turn aside the eyes, a negative after-image of the field just fixated at once forms, and mingles its sensations with those which may happen to come from anything else looked at. This influence is distinctly evident only when the first surface has been 'fixated' without movement of the eyes. It is, however, none the less present at all times, even when the eye wanders from point to point, causing each sensation to be modified more or less by that just previous-

16 What follows in brackets, as far as p. 674, is from the pen of my friend and pupil Mr. E. B. Delabarre.

ly experienced. On this account successive contrast is almost sure to be present in cases of simultaneous contrast, and to complicate the phenomena.

A *visual image is modified not only by other sensations just previously experienced, but also by all those experienced simultaneously with it, and especially by such as proceed from contiguous portions of the retina.* This is the phenomenon of *simultaneous contrast.* In this, as in successive contrast, both brightness and hue are involved. A bright object appears still brighter when its surroundings are darker than itself, and darker when they are brighter than itself. Two colors side by side are apparently changed by the admixture, with each, of the complement of the other. And lastly, a gray surface near a colored one is tinged with the complement of the latter.[17]

The phenomena of simultaneous contrast in sight are so complicated by other attendant phenomena that it is difficult to isolate them and observe them in their purity. Yet it is evidently of the greatest importance to do so, if one would conduct his investigations accurately. Neglect of this principle has led to many mistakes being made in accounting for the facts observed. As we have seen, if the eye is allowed to wander here and there about the field as it ordinarily does, successive contrast results and allowance must be made for its presence. It can be avoided only by carefully fixating with the well-rested eye a point of one field, and by then observing the changes which occur in this field when the contrasting field is placed by its side. Such a course will insure pure simultaneous contrast. But even thus it lasts in its purity for a moment only. It reaches its maximum of effect immediately after the introduction of the contrasting field, and then, if the fixation is continued, it

[17] These phenomena have close analogues in the phenomena of contrast presented by the temperature-sense (see W. Preyer in *Archiv für die gesammte Physiologie*, Bd. xxv, p. 79 ff.). Successive contrast here is shown in the fact that a warm sensation appears warmer if a cold one has just previously been experienced; and a cold one colder, if the preceding one was warm. If a finger which has been plunged in hot water, and another which has been in cold water, be both immersed in lukewarm water, the same water appears cold to the former finger and warm to the latter. In simultaneous contrast, a sensation of warmth on any part of the skin tends to induce the sensation of cold in its immediate neighborhood; and *vice versâ.* This may be seen if we press with the palm on two metal surfaces of about an inch and a half square and three-fourths inch apart; the skin between them appears distinctly warmer. So also a small object of exactly the temperature of the palm appears warm if a cold object, and cold if a warm object, touch the skin near it.

begins to weaken rapidly and soon disappears; thus undergoing changes similar to those observed when any field whatever is fixated steadily and the retina becomes fatigued by unchanging stimuli. If one continues still further to fixate the same point, the color and brightness of one field tend to spread themselves over and mingle with the color and brightness of the neighboring fields, thus substituting '*simultaneous induction*' for simultaneous contrast.

Not only must we recognize and eliminate the effects of successive contrast, of temporal changes due to fixation, and of simultaneous induction, in analyzing the phenomena of simultaneous contrast, but we must also take into account *various other influences which modify its effects.* Under favorable circumstances the contrast-effects are very striking, and did they always occur as strongly they could not fail to attract the attention. But they are not always clearly apparent, owing to various disturbing causes which form no exception to the laws of contrast, but which have a modifying effect on its phenomena. When, for instance, the ground observed has many distinguishable features—a *coarse grain, rough surface, intricate pattern,* etc.—the contrast effect appears weaker. This does not imply that the effects of contrast are absent, but merely that the resulting sensations are overpowered by the many other stronger sensations which entirely occupy the attention. On such a ground a faint negative after-image—undoubtedly due to retinal modifications—may become invisible; and even weak objective differences in color may become imperceptible. For example, a faint spot or grease-stain on woollen cloth, easily seen at a distance, when the fibres are not distinguishable, disappears when closer examination reveals the intricate nature of the surface.

Another frequent cause of the apparent absence of contrast is the presence of narrow dark intermediate fields, such as are formed by *bordering a field with black lines, or by the shaded contours of objects.* When such fields interfere with the contrast, it is because black and white can absorb much color without themselves becoming clearly colored; and because such lines separate other fields too far for them to distinctly influence one another. Even weak objective differences in color may be made imperceptible by such means.

A third case where contrast does not clearly appear is where the *color of the contrasting fields is too weak or too intense,* or where there is *much difference in brightness between the two fields.* In the latter case, as can easily be shown, it is the contrast of brightness which interferes with the color-contrast and makes it imperceptible. For this reason contrast shows best between fields of about equal brightness. But the intensity of the color must not be too great, for then its very darkness necessitates a dark contrasting field which is too absorbent of induced color to allow the contrast to appear strongly. The case is similar if the fields are too light.

To obtain the best contrast-effects, therefore, the contrasting fields should be near together, should not be separated by shadows or black lines, should be of homogeneous texture, and should be of about equal brightness and medium intensity of color. Such conditions do not often occur naturally, the disturbing influences being present in case of almost all ordinary objects, thus making the effects of contrast far less evident. To eliminate these disturbances and to produce the conditions most favorable for the appearance of good contrast-effects, various experiments have been devised, which will be explained in comparing the rival theories of explanation.

There are *two theories—the psychological and the physiological*—which attempt to explain the phenomena of contrast.

Of these the *psychological one* was the first to gain prominence. *Its most able advocate has been Helmholtz. It explains contrast as a* DECEPTION OF JUDGMENT. In ordinary life our sensations have interest for us only so far as they give us practical knowledge. Our chief concern is to recognize objects, and we have no occasion to estimate exactly their absolute brightness and color. Hence we gain no facility in so doing, but neglect the constant changes in their shade, and are very uncertain as to the exact degree of their brightness or tone of their color. When objects are near one another "we are inclined to consider those differences which are clearly and surely perceived as greater than those which appear uncertain in perception or which must be judged by aid of memory,"[18] just as we see a medium-sized man taller than he really is when he stands beside a short man. Such deceptions are more easily possible in the judgment of small differences than of large ones; also where there is but one element of difference instead of many. In a large number of cases of contrast, in all of which a whitish spot is surrounded on all sides by a colored surface—Meyer's experi-

[18] Helmholtz: *Physiologische Optik*, p. 392.

ment, the mirror experiment, colored shadows, etc., soon to be described—the contrast is produced, according to Helmholtz, by the fact that "a colored illumination or a transparent colored covering appears to be spread out over the field, and observation does not show directly that it fails on the white spot."[19] We therefore believe that we see the latter through the former color. Now

"Colors have their greatest importance for us in so far as they are properties of bodies and can serve as signs for the recognition of bodies. . . . We have become accustomed, in forming a judgment in regard to the colors of bodies, to eliminate the varying brightness and color of the illumination. We have sufficient opportunity to investigate the same colors of objects in full sunshine, in the blue light of the clear sky, in the weak white light of a cloudy day, in the reddish-yellow light of the sinking sun or of the candle. Moreover the colored reflections of surrounding objects are involved. Since we see the same colored objects under these varying illuminations, we learn to form a correct conception of the color of the object in spite of the difference in illumination, i.e., to judge how such an object would appear in white illumination; and since only the constant color of the object interests us, we do not become conscious of the particular sensations on which our judgment rests. So also we are at no loss, when we see an object through a colored covering, to distinguish what belongs to the color of the covering and what to the object. In the experiments mentioned we do the same also where the covering over the object is not at all colored, because of the deception into which we fall, and in consequence of which we ascribe to the body a false color, the color complementary to the colored portion of the covering."[20]

We think that we see the complementary color through the colored covering,—for these two colors together would give the sensation of white which is actually experienced. If, however, in any way the white spot is recognized as an independent object, or if it is compared with another object known to be white, our judgment is no longer deceived and the contrast does not appear.

"As soon as the contrasting field is recognized as an independent body which lies above the colored ground, or even through an adequate tracing of its outlines is seen to be a separate field, the contrast disappears. Since, then, the judgment of the spatial position, the ma-

[19] *Loc. cit.*, p. 407.
[20] *Loc. cit.*, p. 408.

terial independence, of the object in question is decisive for the determination of its color, it follows that the contrast-color arises not through an act of sensation but through an act of judgment."[21]

In short, the apparent change in color or brightness through contrast is due to no change in excitation of the organ, to no change in sensation; but in consequence of a false judgment the unchanged sensation is wrongly interpreted, and thus leads to a changed *perception* of the brightness or color.

In opposition to this theory has been developed one which attempts to explain all cases of contrast as depending purely on *physiological action of the terminal apparatus of vision. Hering is the most prominent supporter of this view.* By great originality in devising experiments and by insisting on rigid care in conducting them, he has been able to detect the faults in the psychological theory and to practically establish the validity of his own. Every visual sensation, he maintains, is correlated to a physical process in the nervous apparatus. Contrast is occasioned, not by a false idea resulting from unconscious conclusions, but by the fact that the excitation of any portion of the retina—and the consequent sensation—depends not only on its own illumination, but on that of the rest of the retina as well.

"If this psycho-physical process is aroused, as usually happens, by light-rays impinging on the retina, its nature depends not only on the nature of these rays, but also on the constitution of the entire nervous apparatus which is connected with the organ of vision, and on the state in which it finds itself."[22]

When a limited portion of the retina is aroused by external stimuli, the rest of the retina, and especially the immediately contiguous parts, tends to react also, and in such a way as to produce therefrom the sensation of the opposite degree of brightness and the complementary color to that of the directly-excited portion. When a gray spot is seen alone, and again when it appears colored through contrast, the objective light from the spot is in both cases the same. Helmholtz maintains that the neural process and the corresponding *sensation* also remain unchanged, but are different-

21 *Loc. cit.*, p. 406.

22 E. Hering, in Hermann's *Handbuch der Physiologie*, III, 1, p. 565.

ly *interpreted*; Hering, that the neural process and the sensation are themselves changed, and that the 'interpretation' is the direct conscious correlate of the altered retinal conditions. According to the one, the contrast is psychological in its origin; according to the other, it is purely physiological. In the cases cited above where the contrast-color is no longer apparent—on a ground with many distinguishable features, on a field whose borders are traced with black lines, etc.,—the psychological theory, as we have seen, attributes this to the fact that under these circumstances we judge the smaller patch of color to be an independent object on the surface, and are no longer deceived in judging it to be something over which the color of the ground is drawn. The physiological theory, on the other hand, maintains that the contrast-effect is still produced, but that the conditions are such that the slight changes in color and brightness which it occasions become imperceptible.

The two theories, stated thus broadly, may seem equally plausible. Hering, however, has conclusively proved, by experiments with after-images, that the process on one part of the retina does modify that on neighboring portions, under conditions where deception of judgment is impossible.[23] A careful examination of the facts of contrast will show that its phenomena must be due to this

[23] Hering: *Zur Lehre vom Lichtsinne.*—Of these experiments the following (found on p. 24 ff.) may be cited as a typical one: "From dark gray paper cut two strips 3–4 cm. long and ½ cm. wide, and lay them on a background of which one half is white and the other half deep black, in such a way that one strip lies on each side of the border-line and parallel to it, and at least 1 cm. distant from it. Fixate ½ to 1 minute a point on the border-line between the strips. One strip appears much brighter than the other. Close and cover the eyes, and the negative after-image appears. . . . The difference in brightness of the strips in the after-image is in general much greater than it appeared in direct vision. . . . This difference in brightness of the strips by no means always increases and decreases with the difference in brightness of the two halves of the background. . . . A phase occurs in which the difference in brightness of the two halves of the background entirely disappears, and yet both after-images of the strips are still very clear, one of them brighter and one darker than the background, which is equally bright on both halves. Here can no longer be any question of contrast-effect, because the *conditio sine qua non* of contrast, namely, the differing brightness of the ground, is no longer present. This proves that the different brightness of the after-images of the strips must have its ground in a different state of excitation of the corresponding portions of the retina, and from this follows further that both these portions of the retina were differently stimulated during the original observation; for the different after-effect demands here a different fore-effect. . . . In the original arrangement, the objectively similar strips appeared of different brightness, because both corresponding portions of the retina were truly differently excited."

cause. *In all the cases which one may investigate it will be seen that the upholders of the psychological theory have failed to conduct their experiments with sufficient care.* They have not excluded successive contrast, have overlooked the changes due to steady fixation, and have failed to properly account for the various modifying influences which have been mentioned above. We can easily establish this if we examine the most striking experiments in simultaneous contrast.

Of these one of the best known and most easily arranged is that known as *Meyer's experiment.* A scrap of gray paper is placed on a colored background, and both are covered by a sheet of transparent white paper. The gray spot then assumes a contrast-color, complementary to that of the background, which shines with a whitish tinge through the paper which covers it. Helmholtz explains the phenomenon thus:

"If the background is green, the covering-paper itself appears to be of a greenish color. If now the substance of the paper extends without apparent interruption over the gray which lies under it, we think that we see an object glimmering through the greenish paper, and such an object must in turn be rose-red, in order to give white light. If, however, the gray spot has its limits so fixed that it appears to be an independent object, the continuity with the greenish portion of the surface fails, and we regard it as a gray object which lies on this surface."[24]

The contrast-color may thus be made to disappear by tracing in black the outlines of the gray scrap, or by placing above the tissue paper another gray scrap of the same degree of brightness, and comparing together the two grays. On neither of them does the contrast-color now appear.

Hering[25] shows clearly that this interpretation is incorrect, and that the disturbing factors are to be otherwise explained. In the first place, the experiment can be so arranged that we could not possibly be deceived into believing that we see the gray through a colored medium. Out of a sheet of gray paper cut strips 5 mm. wide in such a way that there will be alternately an empty space and a bar of gray, both of the same width, the bars being held together by the uncut edges of the gray sheet (thus presenting an appearance like a gridiron). Lay this on a colored background—e.g.,

[24] Helmholtz: *Physiologische Optik,* p. 407.
[25] In *Archiv für die gesammte Physiologie,* Bd. XLI, S. 1 ff.

green—cover both with transparent paper, and above all put a black frame which covers all the edges, leaving visible only the bars, which are now alternately green and gray. The gray bars appear strongly colored by contrast, although, since they occupy as much space as the green bars, we are not deceived into believing that we see the former through a green medium. The same is true if we weave together into a basket pattern narrow strips of green and gray and cover them with the transparent paper.

Why, then, if it is a true sensation due to physiological causes, and not an error of judgment, which causes the contrast, does the color disappear when the outlines of the gray scrap are traced, enabling us to recognize it as an independent object? In the first place, it does not necessarily do so, as will easily be seen if the experiment is tried. The contrast-color often remains distinctly visible in spite of the black outlines. In the second place, there are many adequate reasons why the effect should be modified. Simultaneous contrast is always strongest at the border-line of the two fields; but a narrow black field now separates the two, and itself by contrast strengthens the whiteness of both original fields, which were already little saturated in color; and on black and on white, contrast-colors show only under the most favorable circumstances. Even weak objective differences in color may be made to disappear by such tracing of outlines, as can be seen if we place on a gray background a scrap of faintly-colored paper, cover it with transparent paper and trace its outlines. Thus we see that it is not the recognition of the contrasting field as an independent object which interferes with its color, but rather a number of entirely explicable physiological disturbances.

The same may be proved in the case of holding above the tissue paper a second gray scrap and comparing it with that underneath. To avoid the disturbances caused by using papers of different brightness, the second scrap should be made exactly like the first by covering the same gray with the same tissue paper, and carefully cutting a piece about 10 mm. square out of both together. To thoroughly guard against successive contrast, which so easily complicates the phenomena, we must carefully prevent all previous excitation of the retina by colored light. This may be done by arranging thus: Place the sheet of tissue paper on a glass pane, which rests on four supports; under the paper put the first gray scrap. By means of a wire, fasten the second gray scrap 2 or 3 cm. above the glass plate. Both scraps appear exactly alike, except at the edges. Gaze now at both scraps, with eyes not exactly accommodated, so that they appear near one another, with a very narrow space between. Shove now a colored field (green) underneath the glass plate, and the contrast appears at once on both scraps. If it appears less clearly on the upper scrap, it is because of its bright and dark edges, its inequalities, its grain, etc. When the accommodation is exact, there is no essential change, although then on the upper scrap the bright edge on the side toward the light, and the dark edge on the shadow side, disturb somewhat. By continued fixation the contrast becomes weaker and finally yields to simultaneous induction, causing the scraps to become indistinguishable from the ground. Remove the green field and both scraps become green, by successive induction. If the eye moves about freely these last-named phenomena do not appear, but the contrast continues indefinitely and becomes stronger. When Helmholtz found that the contrast on the lower scrap disappeared, it was evidently because he then really held the eye fixed. This experiment may be disturbed by holding the upper scrap wrongly and by the differences in brightness of its edges, or by other inequalities, but not by that recognizing of it 'as an independent body lying above the colored ground,' on which the psychological explanation rests.

In like manner the claims of the psychological explanation can be shown to be inadequate in other cases of contrast. Of frequent use are revolving disks, which are especially efficient in showing good contrast-phenomena, because all inequalities of the ground disappear and leave a perfectly homogeneous surface. On a white disk are arranged colored sectors, which are interrupted midway by narrow black fields in such a way that when the disk is revolved the white becomes mixed with the color and the black, forming a colored disk of weak saturation on which appears a gray ring. The latter is colored by contrast with the field which surrounds it. Helmholtz explains the fact thus:

"The difference of the compared colors appears greater than it really is either because this difference, when it is the only existing one and draws the attention to itself alone, makes a stronger impression than when it is one among many, or because the different colors of the surface are conceived as alterations of the one ground-color of the surface such as might arise through shadows falling on it, through colored reflexes, or through mixture with colored paint or dust. In truth, to produce an objectively gray spot on a green surface, a reddish coloring would be necessary."[26]

This explanation is easily proved false by painting the disk with narrow green and gray concentric rings, and giving each a different saturation. The contrast appears though there is no ground-color, and no longer a single difference, but many. The facts which Helmholtz brings forward in support of his theory are also easily turned against him. He asserts that if the color of the ground is too intense, or if the gray ring is bordered by black circles, the contrast becomes weaker; that no contrast appears on a white scrap held over the colored field; and that the gray ring when compared with such scrap loses its contrast-color either wholly or in part. Hering points out the inaccuracy of all these claims. Under favorable conditions it is impossible to make the contrast disappear by means of black enclosing lines, although they naturally form a disturbing element; increase in the saturation of the field, if disturbance through increasing brightness-contrast is to be avoided, demands a darker gray field, on which contrast-colors are less easily perceived; and careful use of the white scrap leads to entirely different results. The contrast-color does appear upon it when it is first placed above the colored field; but if it is carefully fixated, the contrast-color diminishes very rapidly both on it and on the ring, from causes already explained. To secure accurate observation, all complication through successive contrast should be avoided thus: first arrange the white scrap, then interpose a gray screen between it and the disk, rest the eye, set the wheel in motion, fixate the scrap, and then have the screen removed. The contrast at once appears clearly, and its disappearance through continued fixation can be accurately watched.

Brief mention of a few other cases of contrast must suffice. The so-called mirror experiment consists of placing at an angle of 45° a green (or otherwise colored) pane of glass, forming an angle with two white surfaces, one horizontal and the other vertical. On each white surface is a black spot. The one on the horizontal surface is seen through the glass and appears dark green, the other is reflected from the surface of the glass to the eye, and appears by contrast red. The experiment may be so arranged that we are not

[26] Helmholtz: *loc. cit.*, p. 412.

aware of the presence of the green glass, but think that we are looking directly at a surface with green and red spots upon it; in such a case there is no deception of judgment caused by making allowance for the colored medium through which we think that we see the spot, and therefore the psychological explanation does not apply. On excluding successive contrast by fixation the contrast soon disappears as in all similar experiments.[27]

Colored shadows have long been thought to afford a convincing proof of the fact that simultaneous contrast is psychological in its origin. They are formed whenever an opaque object is illuminated from two separate sides by lights of different colors. When the light from one source is white, its shadow is of the color of the other light, and the second shadow is of a color complementary to that of the field illuminated by both lights. If now we take a tube, blackened inside, and through it look at the colored shadow, none of the surrounding field being visible, and then have the colored light removed, the shadow still appears colored, although 'the circumstances which caused it have disappeared.' This is regarded by the psychologists as conclusive evidence that the color is due to deception of judgment. It can, however, easily be shown that the persistence of the color seen through the tube is due to fatigue of the retina through the prevailing light, and that when the colored light is removed the color slowly disappears as the equilibrium of the retina becomes gradually restored. When successive contrast is carefully guarded against, the simultaneous contrast, whether seen directly or through the tube, never lasts for an instant on removal of the colored field. The physiological explanation applies throughout to all the phenomena presented by colored shadows.[28]

If we have a small field whose illumination remains constant, surrounded by a large field of changing brightness, an increase or decrease in brightness of the latter results in a corresponding apparent decrease or increase respectively in the brightness of the former, while the large field seems to be unchanged. Exner says:

> "This illusion of sense shows that we are inclined to regard as constant the dominant brightness in our field of vision, and hence to refer the changing difference between this and the brightness of a limited field to a change in brightness of the latter."

27 See Hering: *Archiv für die gesammte Physiologie*, Bd. XLI, S. 358 ff.

28 Hering: *Archiv für die gesammte Physiologie*, Bd. XL, S. 172 ff.; Delabarre: *American Journal of Psychology*, II, 636.

The result, however, can be shown to depend not on illusion, but on actual retinal changes, which alter the sensation experienced. The irritability of those portions of the retina lighted by the large field becomes much reduced in consequence of fatigue, so that the increase in brightness becomes much less apparent than it would be without this diminution in irritability. The small field, however, shows the change by a change in the contrast-effect induced upon it by the surrounding parts of the retina.[29]

The above cases show clearly that *physiological processes, and not deception of judgment, are responsible for contrast of color.* To say this, however, is not to maintain that our perception of a color is never in any degree modified by our judgment of what the particular colored thing before us may be. We have unquestionable illusions of color due to wrong inferences as to what object is before us. Thus von Kries[30] speaks of wandering through evergreen forests covered with snow, and thinking that through the interstices of the boughs he saw the deep blue of pine-clad mountains, covered with snow and lighted by brilliant sunshine; whereas what he really saw was the white snow on trees near by, lying in shadow.][31]

Such a mistake as this is undoubtedly of psychological origin. It is a wrong *classification* of the appearances, due to the arousal of intricate processes of association, amongst which is the suggestion of a different hue from that really before the eyes. In the ensuing chapters such illusions as this will be treated of in considerable detail. But it is a mistake to interpret the simpler cases of contrast in the light of such illusions as these. These illusions can be rectified in an instant, and we then wonder how they could have been. They come from insufficient attention, or from the fact that the impression which we get is a sign of more than one possible object, and can be interpreted in either way. In none of these points do they resemble simple color-contrast, which *unquestionably is a phenomenon of sensation immediately aroused.*

I have dwelt upon the facts of color-contrast at such great length because they form so good a text to comment on in my struggle against the view that sensations are immutable psychic things which

29 Hering: *Archiv für die gesammte Physiologie,* Bd. XLI, S. 91 ff.

30 *Die Gesichts-Empfindungen und ihre Analyse,* p. 128.

31 Mr. Delabarre's contribution ends here.

coexist with higher mental functions. Both sensationalists and intellectualists agree that such sensations exist. They *fuse*, say the pure sensationalists, and *make* the higher mental function; they *are combined* by activity of the Thinking Principle, say the intellectualists. I myself have contended that they *do not exist* in or alongside of the higher mental function when that exists. The things which arouse them exist; and the higher mental function also knows these same things. But just as its knowledge of the things supersedes and displaces the sensation's knowledge, so it supersedes and displaces them, when it comes, being as much as they are a direct resultant of whatever momentary brain-conditions may obtain. The psychological theory of contrast, on the other hand, holds the sensations still to exist in themselves unchanged before the mind, whilst the 'relating activity' of the latter deals with them freely and settles to its own satisfaction what each shall be, in view of what the others also are. Wundt says expressly that the Law of Relativity is "not a law of sensation but a law of Apperception"; and the word Apperception connotes with him a higher intellectual spontaneity.[32] This way of taking things belongs with the philosophy that looks at the *data* of sense as something earth-born and servile, and the 'relating of them together' as something spiritual and free. Lo! the spirit can even change the intrinsic quality of the sensible facts themselves if by so doing it can relate them better to each other! But (apart from the difficulty of seeing how changing the sensations should relate them better) is it not manifest that the relations are part of the 'content' of consciousness, part of the 'object,' just as much as the sensations are? Why ascribe the former exclusively to the *knower* and the latter to the *known*? The *knower* is in every case a unique pulse of thought corresponding to a unique reaction of the brain upon its conditions. All that the facts of contrast show us is that the *same real thing* may give us quite different sensations when the conditions alter, and that we must therefore be careful which one to select as the thing's truest representative.

[32] *Physiologische Psychologie* (2nd ed.), I, 351, 458–60. The full inanity of the law of relativity is best to be seen in Wundt's treatment, where the great *'allgemeines Gesetz der Beziehung,'* invoked to account for Weber's law as well as for the phenomena of contrast "feeling," and many other matters, can only be defined as a tendency *to feel all things in relation to each other*! Bless its little soul! But why need it change the things so, in order thus to feel them in relation? See *Vorlesungen*, 2nd ed., p. 65, and *Physiologische Psychologie*, 4th ed., I, 397.

There are many other facts beside the phenomena of contrast which prove that *when two objects act together on us the sensation which either would give alone becomes a different sensation.* A certain amount of skin dipped in hot water gives the perception of a certain heat. More skin immersed makes the heat much more intense, although of course the water's heat is the same. A certain extent as well as intensity, in the quantity of the stimulus is requisite for any quality to be felt. Fick and Wunderli could not distinguish heat from touch when both were applied through a hole in a card, and so confined to a small part of the skin. Similarly there is a *chromatic minimum* of size in objects. The image they cast on the retina must needs have a certain extent, or it will give no sensation of color at all. Inversely, more intensity in the outward impression may make the subjective object more extensive. This happens, as will be shown in Chapter XIX, when the illumination is increased: The whole room expands and dwindles according as we raise or lower the gas-jet. It is not easy to explain any of these results as illusions of judgment due to the inference of a wrong objective cause for the sensation which we get. No more is this easy in the case of Weber's observation that a thaler laid on the skin of the forehead feels heavier when cold than when warm; or of Szabadföldi's observation that small wooden disks when heated to 122° Fahrenheit often feel heavier than those which are larger but not thus warmed;[33] or of Hall's observation that a heavy point moving over the skin seems to go faster than a lighter one moving at the same rate of speed.[34]

Bleuler and Lehmann some years ago called attention to a strange idiosyncrasy found in some persons, and consisting in the fact that impressions on the eye, skin, etc., were accompanied by distinct sensations of *sound.*[35] *Colored hearing* is the name sometimes given to the phenomenon, which has now been repeatedly described. Quite lately the Viennese aurist Urbantschitsch has proved that these cases are only extreme examples of a very general law, and that all our sense-organs influence each other's sensations.[36] The hue of patches of color so distant as not to be recognized was immediately, in U.'s patients, perceived when a tuning-fork was

33 Ladd: *Physiological Psychology,* p. 348.

34 *Mind,* X, 567.

35 *Zwangsmässige Lichtempfindungen durch Schall* (Leipzig, 1881).

36 Pflüger's *Archiv,* XLII, 154.

sounded close to the ear. Sometimes, on the contrary, the field was darkened by the sound. The acuity of vision was increased, so that letters too far off to be read could be read when the tuning-fork was heard. Urbantschitsch, varying his experiments, found that their results were mutual, and that sounds which were on the limits of audibility became audible when lights of various colors were exhibited to the eye. Smell, taste, touch, sense of temperature, etc., were all found to fluctuate when lights were seen and sounds were heard. Individuals varied much in the degree and kind of effect produced, but almost everyone experimented on seems to have been in some way affected. The phenomena remind one somewhat of the 'dynamogenic' effects of sensations upon the strength of muscular contraction observed by M. Féré, and later to be described. The most familiar examples of them seem to be the increase of *pain* by noise or light, and the increase of *nausea* by all concomitant sensations. Persons suffering in any way instinctively seek stillness and darkness.

Probably everyone will agree that the best way of formulating all such facts is physiological: it must be that the cerebral process of the first sensation is reinforced or otherwise altered by the other current which comes in. No one, surely, will prefer a psychological explanation *here*. Well, it seems to me that *all* cases of mental reaction to a plurality of stimuli must be like these cases, and that the physiological formulation is everywhere the simplest and the best. When simultaneous red and green light make us see yellow, when three notes of the scale make us hear a chord, it is not because the sensations of red and of green and of each of the three notes enter the mind as such, and there 'combine' or 'are combined by its relating activity' into the yellow and the chord; but it is rather because the larger sum of light-waves and of air-waves arouses new cortical processes, to which the yellow and the chord directly correspond. Even when the sensible qualities of things enter into the objects of our highest thinking, it is surely the same. Their several *sensations* do not continue to exist there tucked away. They are *replaced* by the higher thought which, although a different psychic unit from them, knows the same sensible qualities which they know.

The principles laid down in Chapter VI seem then to be corroborated in this new connection. *You cannot build up one thought or one sensation out of many; and only direct experiment can inform us of what we shall perceive when we get many stimuli at once.*

THE 'ECCENTRIC PROJECTION' OF SENSATIONS

We often hear the opinion expressed that all our sensations at first appear to us as subjective or internal, and are afterwards and by a special act on our part 'extradited' or 'projected' so as to appear located in an outer world. Thus we read in Professor Ladd's valuable work that

"Sensations . . . are psychical states *whose place*—so far as they can be said to have one—*is the mind.* The transference of these sensations from mere mental states to physical processes located in the periphery of the body, or to qualities of things projected in space external to the body, is a mental act. It may rather be said to be a mental *achievement* [cf. Cudworth, above, as to knowledge being *conquering*]; for it is an act which in its perfection results from a long and intricate process of development. . . . Two noteworthy stages, or 'epoch-making' achievements, in the process of elaborating the presentations of sense require a special consideration. These are '*localization,*' or the transference of the composite sensations from mere states of the mind to processes or conditions recognized as taking place at more or less definitely fixed points or areas of the body; and '*eccentric projection*' (sometimes called 'eccentric perception'), or the giving to these sensations an objective existence (in the fullest sense of the word 'objective') as qualities of objects situated within a field of space and in contact with, or more or less remotely distant from, the body."[37]

It seems to me that there is not a vestige of evidence for this view. It hangs together with the opinion that our sensations are originally devoid of all spatial content,[38] an opinion which I confess that I am wholly at a loss to understand. As I look at my bookshelf opposite I cannot frame to myself an idea, however imaginary, of

37 *Physiological Psychology*, 385, 387. See also such passages as that in Bain: *The Senses and the Intellect*, pp. 364–6.

38 "Especially must we avoid all attempts, whether avowed or concealed, to account for the *spatial* qualities of the presentations of sense by merely describing the qualities of the simple sensations and the modes of their combination. It is position and extension in space which constitutes the very peculiarity of the objects as *no longer* mere sensations or affections of the mind. As sensations, they are neither *out* of ourselves nor possessed of the qualities indicated by the word '*spread-out.*'" (Ladd: *op. cit.*, p. 391.)

any feeling which I could ever possibly have got from it except the feeling of the same big extended sort of outward fact which I now perceive. So far is it from being true that our first way of feeling things is the feeling of them as subjective or mental, that the exact opposite seems rather to be the truth. Our earliest, most instinctive, least developed kind of consciousness is the objective kind; and only as reflection becomes developed do we become aware of an inner world at all. Then indeed we enrich it more and more, even to the point of becoming idealists, with the spoils of the outer world which at first was the only world we knew. But subjective consciousness, aware of itself as subjective, does not at first exist. Even an attack of pain is surely felt at first objectively as something in space which prompts to motor reaction, and to the very end it is located, not in the mind, but in some bodily part.

"A sensation which should not awaken an impulse to move, nor any tendency to produce an outward effect, would manifestly be useless to a living creature. On the principles of evolution such a sensation could never be developed. Therefore every sensation originally refers to something external and independent of the sentient creature. Rhizopods (according to Engelmann's observations) retract their pseudopodia whenever these touch foreign bodies, even if these foreign bodies are the pseudopodia of other individuals of their own species, whilst the mutual contact of their own pseudopodia is followed by no such contraction. These low animals can therefore already feel an outer world —even in the absence of innate ideas of causality, and probably without any clear consciousness of space. In truth the conviction that something exists outside of ourselves does not come from thought. It comes from sensation; it rests on the same ground as our conviction of our own existence. . . . If we consider the behavior of new-born animals, we never find them betraying that they are first of all conscious of their sensations as purely subjective excitements. We far more readily incline to explain the astonishing certainty with which they make use of their sensations (and which is an effect of adaptation and inheritance) as the result of an inborn intuition of the outer world. . . . Instead of starting from an original pure subjectivity of sensation, and seeking how this could possibly have acquired an objective signification, we must, on the contrary, begin by the possession of objectivity by the sensation and then show how for reflective consciousness the latter becomes interpreted as an effect of the object, how in short the original immediate objectivity becomes changed into a remote one."[39]

[39] A. Riehl: *Der philosophische Kriticismus,* Bd. II, Theil II, pp. 60–61, 54–55.

Another confusion, much more common than the denial of all objective character to sensations, is the assumption that they are all originally located *inside the body* and are projected outwards by a secondary act. This secondary judgment is always false, according to M. Taine, so far as the place of the sensation itself goes. But it happens to *hit* a real object which is at the point towards which the sensation is projected; so we may call its result, according to this author, a *veridical hallucination*.[40] The word Sensation,

[40] *On Intelligence*, part II, bk. II, chap. II, §§ VII, VIII. Compare such statements as these: "The consequence is that when a sensation has for its usual condition the presence of an object more or less distant from our bodies, and experience has once made us acquainted with this distance, we shall situate our sensation at this distance.—This, in fact, is the case with sensations of hearing and sight. The peripheral extremity of the acoustic nerve is in the deep-seated chamber of the ear. That of the optic nerve is in the most inner recess of the eye. But still, in our present state, we never situate our sensations of sound or color in these places, but without us, and often at a considerable distance from us. . . . All our sensations of color are thus projected out of our body, and clothe more or less distant objects, furniture, walls, houses, trees, the sky, and the rest. This is why, when we afterwards reflect on them, we cease to attribute them to ourselves; they are alienated and detached from us, so far as to appear different from us. Projected from the nervous surface in which we localize the majority of the others, the tie which connected them to the others and to ourselves is undone . . . . Thus, all our sensations are wrongly situated, and the red color is no more extended on the armchair than the sensation of tingling is situated at my fingers' ends. They are all situated in the sensory centres of the encephalon; all appear situated elsewhere, and a common law allots to each of them its apparent situation." (Vol. II, pp. 47–53.)—Similarly Schopenhauer: "I will now show the same by the sense of sight. The immediate *datum* is here limited to the sensation of the retina which, it is true, admits of considerable diversity, but at bottom reverts to the impression of light and dark with their shades, and that of colors. This sensation is through and through subjective, that is, inside of the organism and under the skin." (Schopenhauer: *Satz vom Grunde*, p. 57.) This philosopher then enumerates *seriatim* what the Intellect does to make the originally subjective sensation objective: 1) it turns it bottom side up; 2) it reduces its doubleness to singleness; 3) it changes its flatness to solidity; and 4) it projects it to a distance from the eye. Again: "*Sensations* are what we call the impressions on our senses, in so far as they come to our consciousness as states of our own body, especially of our nervous apparatus; we call them *perceptions* when we form out of them the representation of outer objects." (Helmholtz: *Tonempfindungen*, 1870, p. 101.)—Once more: "Sensation is always accomplished in the psychic centres, but it manifests itself at the excited part of the periphery. In other words, one is conscious of the phenomenon in the nervous centres, . . . but one perceives it in the peripheric organs. This phenomenon depends on the experience of the sensations themselves, in which there is a *reflection* of the subjective phenomenon and a tendency on the part of perception to return as it were to the external cause which has roused the mental state because the latter

to begin with, is constantly, in psychological literature, used as if it meant one and the same thing with the *physical impression* either in the terminal organs or in the centres, which is its antecedent condition, and this notwithstanding that by sensation we mean a mental, not a physical, fact. But those who expressly mean by it a mental fact still leave to it a physical *place*, still think of it as objectively inhabiting the very neural tracts which occasion its appearance when they are excited; and then (going a step farther) they think that it must *place itself* where *they* place it, or be subjectively sensible of that place as its habitat in the first instance, and afterwards have to be *moved* so as to appear elsewhere.

All this seems highly confused and unintelligible. Consciousness, as we saw in an earlier chapter (p. 210) cannot properly be said to *inhabit* any place. It has dynamic relations with the brain, and cognitive relations with everything and anything. From the one point of view *we* may say that a sensation is in the same place with the brain (if we like), just as from the other point of view we may say that it is in the same place with whatever quality it may be cognizing. But the supposition that a sensation primitively *feels either itself or its object to be in the same place with the brain* is absolutely groundless, and neither *a priori* probability nor facts from experience can be adduced to show that such a deliverance forms any part of the original cognitive function of our sensibility.

Where, then, do we feel the objects of our original sensations to be?

Certainly a child newly born in Boston, who gets a sensation from the candle-flame which lights the bedroom, or from his diaper-pin, does not feel either of these objects to be situated in longitude 71° W. and latitude 42° N. He does not feel them to be in the third story of the house. He does not even feel them in any distinct manner to be to the right or the left of any of the other sensations which he may be getting from other objects in the room at the same time. He does not, in short, know anything *about* their space-relations to anything else in the world. The flame fills its own place, the pain fills its own place; but as yet these places are

---

is connected with the former." (Sergi: *La Psychologie physiologique* (Paris, 1888), p. 189.)—The clearest and best passage I know is in Liebmann: *Über den objectiven Anblick* (1869), pp. 67–72, but it is unfortunately too long to quote.

neither identified with, nor discriminated from, any other places. That comes later. For the places thus first sensibly known are elements of the child's space-world which remain with him all his life; and by memory and later experience he learns a vast number of things *about* those places which at first he did not know. But to the end of time certain places of the world remain defined for him as the places *where those sensations were*; and his only possible answer to the question *where anything is* will be to say '*there*,' and to name some sensation or other like those first ones, which shall identify the spot. Space *means* but the aggregate of all our possible sensations. There is no duplicate space known *aliunde*, or created by an 'epoch-making achievement' into which our sensations, originally spaceless, are dropped. They *bring* space and all its places to our intellect, and do not derive it thence.

By his body, then, the child later means simply *that place where* the pain from the pin, and a lot of other sensations like it, were or are felt. It is no more true to say that he locates that pain in his body, than to say that he locates his body in that pain. Both are true: that pain is part of what he *means by the word body*. Just so by the outer world the child means nothing more than *that place where* the candle-flame and a lot of other sensations like it are felt. He no more locates the candle in the outer world than he locates the outer world in the candle. Once again, he does both; for the candle is part of what he *means* by 'outer world.'

This (it seems to me) will be admitted, and will (I trust) be made still more plausible in the chapter on the Perception of Space. But the later developments of this perception are so complicated that these simple principles get easily overlooked. One of the complications comes from the fact that things *move*, and that the original object which we feel them to be splits into two parts, one of which remains as their whereabouts and the other goes off as their quality or nature. We then contrast where they *were* with where they *are*. If *we* do not move, the sensation of *where they were* remains unchanged; but we ourselves presently move, so that that also changes; and 'where they were' becomes no longer the actual sensation which it was originally, but a sensation which we merely conceive as possible. Gradually the system of these possible sensations takes more and more the place of the actual sensations. 'Up' and 'down' become 'subjective' notions; east and west grow more 'correct' than 'right' and 'left' etc.; and things get at last more 'truly' located by their relation to certain ideal fixed co-ordinates than by their relation either to our bodies or to those objects by which their place was originally defined. *Now this revision of our original localizations is a complex affair; and contains some facts which may very naturally come to be described as translocations whereby sensations get shoved farther off than they originally appeared.*

Few things indeed are more striking than the changeable distance which the objects of many of our sensations may be made to assume. A fly's humming may be taken for a distant steam-whistle; or the fly itself, seen out of focus, may for a moment give us the illusion of a distant bird. The same things seem much nearer or much farther, according as we look at them through one end or another of an opera-glass. Our whole optical education indeed is largely taken up with assigning their proper distances to the objects of our retinal sensations. An infant will grasp at the moon; later, it is said, he projects that sensation to a distance which he knows to be beyond his reach. In the much quoted case of the 'young gentleman who was born blind,' and who was 'couched' for the cataract by Mr. Cheselden, it is reported of the patient that "when he first saw, he was so far from making any Judgment about Distances, that he thought all Objects whatever touch'd his Eyes, (as he express'd it) as what he felt, did his Skin." And other patients born blind, but relieved by surgical operation, have been described as bringing their hand close to their eyes to feel for the objects which they at first saw, and only gradually stretching out their hand when they found that no contact occurred. Many have concluded from these facts that our earliest visual objects must seem in immediate contact with our eyes.

But tactile objects also may be affected with a like ambiguity of situation.

If one of the hairs of our head be pulled, we are pretty accurately sensible of the direction of the pulling by the movements imparted to the head.[41] But the feeling of the pull is localized, not in that part of the hair's length which the fingers hold, but in the scalp itself. This seems connected with the fact that our hair hardly serves at all as a tactile organ. In creatures with *vibrissæ*, however,

41 This is proved by Weber's device of causing the head to be firmly pressed against a support by another person, whereupon the direction of traction ceases to be perceived.

and in those quadrupeds whose whiskers are tactile organs, it can hardly be doubted that the feeling is projected out of the root into the shaft of the hair itself. We ourselves have an approach to this when the beard as a whole, or the hair as a whole, is touched. We perceive the contact at some distance from the skin.

When fixed and hard appendages of the body, like the teeth and nails, are touched, we feel the contact where it objectively is, and not deeper in, where the nerve-terminations lie. If, however, the tooth is loose, we feel two contacts, spatially separated, one at its root, one at its top.

From this case to that of a hard body not organically connected with the surface, but only accidentally in contact with it, the transition is immediate. With the point of a cane we can trace letters in the air or on a wall just as with the finger-tip; and in so doing feel the size and shape of the path described by the cane's tip just as immediately as, without a cane, we should feel the path described by the tip of our finger. Similarly the draughtsman's immediate perception seems to be of the point of his pencil, the surgeon's of the end of his knife, the duellist's of the tip of his rapier as it plunges through his enemy's skin. When on the middle of a vibrating ladder, we feel not only our feet on the round, but the ladder's feet against the ground far below. If we shake a locked iron gate we feel the middle, on which our hands rest, move, but we equally feel the stability of the ends where the hinges and the lock are, and we seem to feel all three at once.[42] And yet the place where the contact is *received* is in all these cases the skin, whose sensations accordingly are sometimes interpreted as objects on the surface, and at other times as objects a long distance off.

We shall learn in the chapter on Space that our feelings of our own movement are principally due to the sensibility of our rotating *joints*. Sometimes by fixing the attention, say on our elbow-joint, we can feel the movement in the joint itself; but we always are simultaneously conscious of the path which during the movement our finger-tips describe through the air, and yet these same finger-tips themselves are in no way physically modified by the motion. A blow on our ulnar nerve behind the elbow is felt both there and in the fingers. Refrigeration of the elbow produces pain in the

[42] Lotze: *Medicinische Psychologie*, 428–433; Lipps: *Grundtatsachen des Seelenlebens*, 582.

fingers. Electric currents passed through nerve-trunks, whether of cutaneous or of more special sensibility (such as the optic nerve), give rise to sensations which are vaguely localized beyond the nerve-tracts traversed. Persons whose legs or arms have been amputated are, as is well known, apt to preserve an illusory feeling of the lost hand or foot being there. Even when they do not have this feeling constantly, it may be occasionally brought back. This sometimes is the result of exciting electrically the nerve-trunks buried in the stump.

"I recently faradised," says Dr. Mitchell, "a case of disarticulated shoulder without warning my patient of the possible result. For two years he had altogether ceased to feel the limb. As the current affected the brachial plexus of nerves, he suddenly cried aloud, 'Oh, the hand, the hand!' and attempted to seize the missing member. The phantom I had conjured up swiftly disappeared, but no spirit could have more amazed the man, so real did it seem."[43]

Now the apparent position of the lost extremity varies. Often the foot seems on the ground, or follows the position of the artificial foot, where one is used. Sometimes where the arm is lost the elbow will seem bent, and the hand in a fixed position on the breast. Sometimes, again, the position is non-natural, and the hand will seem to bud straight out of the shoulder, or the foot to be on the same level with the knee of the remaining leg. Sometimes, again, the position is vague; and sometimes it is ambiguous, as in another patient of Dr. Weir Mitchell's who

"lost his leg at the age of eleven, and remembers that the foot by degrees approached, and at last reached, the knee. When he began to wear an artificial leg it reassumed, in time, its old position, and he is never, at present, aware of the leg as shortened, unless for some time he talks and thinks of the stump and of the missing leg, when . . . the direction of attention to the part causes a feeling of discomfort, and the subjective sensation of active and unpleasant movement of the toes. With these feelings returns at once the delusion of the foot as being placed at the knee."

All these facts, and others like them, can easily be described as if our sensations might be induced by circumstances to migrate from their *original locality* near the brain or near the surface of

43 *Injuries of Nerves* (Philadelphia, 1872), p. 349 ff.

the body, and to appear farther off; and (under different circumstances) to return again after having migrated. But a little analysis of what happens shows us that this description is inaccurate.

The objectivity with which each of our sensations originally comes to us, the roomy and spatial character which is a primitive part of its content, is not in the first instance relative to any other sensation. The first time we open our eyes we get an optical object which is *a place,* but which is not yet *placed* in relation to any other object, nor identified with any place otherwise known. It is a place with which so far we are only *acquainted.* When later we know that this same place is in 'front' of us, that only means that we have learned something *about* it, namely, that it is *congruent with that other* place, called 'front,' which is given us by certain sensations of the arm and hand or of the head and body. But at the first moment of our optical experience, even though we already had an acquaintance with our head, hand, and body, we could not possibly know anything about their relations to this new seen object. It could not be immediately located in respect of *them.* How its place agrees with the places which their feelings yield is a matter of which only later experience can inform us; and in the next chapter we shall see with some detail how later experience does this by means of discrimination, association, selection, and other constantly working functions of the mind. When, therefore, the baby grasps at the moon, that does not mean that what he sees fails to give him the sensation which he afterwards knows as distance; it means only that he has not learned at what *tactile or manual distance* things which appear at that *visual distance* are.[44] And when a person just operated for cataract gropes close to his face for far-off objects, that only means the same thing. All the ordinary optical signs of differing distances are absent from the poor creature's sensation anyhow. His vision is monocular (only one eye being operated at a time); the lens is gone, and everything is out of focus; he feels photophobia, lachrymation, and other painful resident sensations of the eyeball itself, whose place he has long since learned to know in tactile terms; what wonder, then, that the first tactile reaction which the new sensations provoke should be one associated with the tactile situation of the organ itself? And as for his assertions about the matter, what wonder, again, if, as Prof. Paul

[44] In reality it probably means only a restless movement of desire, which he might make even after he had become aware of his impotence to touch the object.

Janet says, they are still expressed in the tactile language which is the only one he knows. "*To be touched* means for him to receive an impression without first making a movement." His eye gets such an impression now; so he can only say that the objects are 'touching it.'

"All his language, borrowed from touch, but applied to the objects of his sight, make us think that he perceives differently from ourselves, whereas, at bottom, it is only his different way of talking about the same experience."[45]

The other cases of translocation of our sensations are equally easily interpreted without supposing any 'projection' from a centre at which they are originally perceived. Unfortunately the details are intricate; and what I say now can only be made fully clear when we come to the next chapter. We shall then see that we are constantly selecting certain of our sensations as *realities* and degrading others to the status of *signs* of these. When we get one of the signs we think of the reality signified; and the strange thing is that then the reality (which need not be itself a sensation at all at the time, but only an idea) is so interesting that it acquires an hallucinatory strength, which may even eclipse that of the relatively uninteresting sign and entirely divert our attention from the latter. Thus the sensations to which our joints give rise when they rotate are signs of what, through a large number of other sensations, tactile and optical, we have come to know as the movement of the whole limb. This movement of the whole limb is what we *think of* when the joint's nerves are excited in that way; and *its* place is so much more important than the joint's place that our sense of the latter is taken up, so to speak, into our perception of the former, and the sensation of the movement seems to diffuse itself into our very fingers and toes. But by abstracting our attention from the suggestion of the entire extremity we can perfectly well perceive the same sensation as if it were concentrated in one spot. We can identify it with a differently located tactile and visual image of 'the joint' itself.

Just so when we feel the tip of our cane against the ground. The peculiar sort of movement of the hand (impossible in one direction, but free in every other) which we experience when the tip

45 *Revue Philosophique*, VII, p. 1 ff., an admirable critical article, in the course of which M. Janet gives a bibliography of the cases in question. See also Dunan: *ibid.*, XXV, 165–7. They are also discussed and similarly interpreted by T. K. Abbott: *Sight and Touch* (1864), chapter X.

touches 'the ground,' is a sign to us of the visual and tactile object which we already know under that name. We think of 'the ground' as being there and giving us the sensation of this kind of movement. The sensation, we say, comes *from* the ground. The ground's place seems to be its place; although at the same time, and for very similar practical reasons, we think of another optical and tactile object, 'the hand' namely, and consider that *its* place *also* must be the place of our sensation. In other words, we take an object or sensible content A, and confounding it with another object otherwise known, B, or with two objects otherwise known, B and C, we identify its place with their places. But in all this there is *no 'projecting'* (such as the extradition-philosophers talk of) of A out of an *original* place; no primitive location which it first occupied, *away from* these other sensations, has to be contradicted; no natural 'centre,' from which it is expelled, exists. That would imply that A aboriginally came to us in definite local relations with other sensations, for to be *out* of B and C is to be in local relation with them as much as to be *in* them is so. But it was no more out of B and C than it was in them when it first came to us. It simply had nothing to do with them. To say that we feel a sensation's seat to be 'in the brain' or 'against the eye' or 'under the skin' is to say as much *about* it and to deal with it in as non-primitive a way as to say that it is a mile off. These are all secondary perceptions, ways of defining the sensation's seat *per aliud*. They involve numberless associations, identifications, and imaginations, and admit a great deal of vacillation and uncertainty in the result.[46]

I conclude, then, that there is no truth in the 'eccentric projection' theory. It is due to the confused assumption that the bodily processes which cause a sensation must also be its seat.[47] But sensa-

[46] The intermediary and shortened locations of the lost hand and foot in the amputation cases also show this. It is easy to see why the phantom foot might continue to follow the position of the artificial one. But I confess that I cannot explain its half-way positions.

[47] It is from this confused assumption that the time-honored riddle comes, of how, with an upside-down picture on the retina, we can see things right-side up. Our consciousness is *naïvely* supposed to inhabit the picture and to feel the picture's position as related to other objects of space. But the truth is that the picture is non-existent either as a habitat or as anything else, for immediate consciousness. Our notion of it is an enormously late conception. The outer object is given immediately with all those qualities which later are named and determined in relation to other sensations. The 'bottom' of this object is where we see what by touch we

tions have no seat in this sense. They *become* seats for each other, as fast as experience associates them together; but that violates no primitive seat possessed by any one of them. And though our sensations cannot then so analyze and talk of themselves, yet at their very first appearance quite as much as at any later date are they cognizant of all those qualities which we end by extracting and conceiving under the names of *objectivity*, *exteriority*, and *extent.* It is surely subjectivity and interiority which are the notions *latest* acquired by the human mind.[48]

---

afterwards know as our *feet*, the 'top' is the place in which we see what we know as other people's heads, etc., etc. Berkeley long ago made this matter perfectly clear (see his *Essay towards a New Theory of Vision*, §§ 93–98, 113–118).

[48] For full justification the reader must see the next chapter. He may object, against the summary account given now, that in a babe's immediate field of vision the various things which appear are located *relatively to each other* from the outset. I admit that *if discriminated*, they would appear so located. But they are parts of the content of one sensation, not sensations separately experienced, such as the text is concerned with. The fully developed 'world,' in which all our sensations ultimately find location, is nothing but an imaginary object framed after the pattern of the field of vision, by the addition and continuation of one sensation upon another in an orderly and systematic way. In corroboration of my text I must refer to pp. 57–60 of Riehl's book quoted above on page 679, and to Uphues: *Wahrnehmung und Empfindung* (1888), especially the Einleitung and pp. 51–61.

Chapter XVIII

Imagination

Sensations, once experienced, modify the nervous organism, so that copies of them arise again in the mind after the original outward stimulus is gone. No mental copy, however, can arise in the mind, of any kind of sensation which has never been directly excited from without.

The blind may dream of sights, the deaf of sounds, for years after they have lost their vision or hearing;[1] but the man *born* deaf can never be made to imagine what sound is like, nor can the man *born* blind ever have a mental vision. In Locke's words, already quoted, "the mind can frame unto itself no one new simple idea." The originals of them all must have been given from without. Fantasy, or Imagination, are the names given to the faculty of reproducing copies of originals once felt. The imagination is called 'reproductive' when the copies are literal; 'productive' when elements from different originals are recombined so as to make new wholes.

After-images belong to sensation rather than to imagination; so that the most immediate phenomena of imagination would seem to be those tardier images (due to what the Germans call *Sinnesgedächtniss*) which were spoken of in Vol. I, p. 609,—coercive haunt-

1 Prof. Jastrow has ascertained by statistical inquiry among the blind that if their blindness have occurred before a period embraced between the fifth and seventh years the visual centres seem to decay, and visual dreams and images are gradually outgrown. If sight is lost after the seventh year, visual imagination seems to survive through life. See Prof. J.'s interesting article on the "Dreams of the Blind," in the *New Princeton Review* for January 1888.

ings of the mind by echoes of unusual experiences for hours after the latter have taken place. The phenomena ordinarily ascribed to imagination, however, are those mental pictures of possible sensible experiences, to which the ordinary processes of associative thought give rise.

When represented with surroundings concrete enough to constitute a *date*, these pictures, when they revive, form *recollections.* We have already studied the machinery of recollection in Chapter XVI. When the mental pictures are of data freely combined, and reproducing no past combination exactly, we have acts of imagination properly so called.

OUR IMAGES ARE USUALLY VAGUE

For the ordinary 'analytic' psychology, each sensibly discernible element of the object imagined is represented by its own separate idea, and the total object is imagined by a 'cluster' or 'gang' of ideas. We have seen abundant reason to reject this view (see p. 266 ff.). An imagined object, however complex, is at any one moment thought in one idea, which is aware of all its qualities together. If I slip into the ordinary way of talking, and speak of various ideas 'combining,' the reader will understand that this is only for popularity and convenience, and he will not construe it into a concession to the atomistic theory in psychology.

Hume was the hero of the atomistic theory. Not only were ideas copies of original impressions made on the sense-organs, but they were, according to him, completely adequate copies, and were all so separate from each other as to possess no manner of connection. Hume proves ideas in the imagination to be completely adequate copies, not by appeal to observation, but by *a priori* reasoning, as follows:

"The mind cannot form any notion of quantity or quality without forming a precise notion of the degrees of each," for " 'tis confest, that no object can appear to the senses; or in other words, that no impression[2] can become present to the mind, without being determin'd in its degrees both of quantity and quality. The confusion, in which impressions are sometimes involv'd, proceeds only from their faintness and unsteadiness, not from any capacity in the mind to receive any impression, which in its real existence has no particular degree nor propor-

[2] Impression means sensation for Hume.

tion. That is a contradiction in terms; and even implies the flattest of all contradictions, *viz.* that 'tis possible for the same thing both to be and not to be. Now since all ideas are deriv'd from impressions, and are nothing but copies and representations of them, whatever is true of the one must be acknowledg'd concerning the other. Impressions and ideas differ only in their strength and vivacity. The foregoing conclusion is not founded on any particular degree of vivacity. It cannot therefore be affected by any variation in that particular. An idea is a weaker impression; and as a strong impression must necessarily have a determinate quantity and quality, the case must be the same with its copy or representative."[3]

The slightest introspective glance will show to anyone the falsity of this opinion. Hume surely had images of his own works without seeing distinctly every word and letter upon the pages which floated before his mind's eye. His dictum is therefore an exquisite example of the way in which a man will be blinded by *a priori* theories to the most flagrant facts. It is a rather remarkable thing, too, that the psychologists of Hume's own empiricist school have, as a rule, been more guilty of this blindness than their opponents. The fundamental *facts* of consciousness have been, on the whole, more accurately reported by the spiritualistic writers.[3a] None of Hume's pupils, so far as I know, until Taine and Huxley, ever took the pains to contradict the opinion of their master. Prof. Huxley in his brilliant little work on Hume set the matter straight in the following words:

"When complex impressions or complex ideas are reproduced as memories, it is probable that the copies never give all the details of the originals with perfect accuracy, and it is certain that they rarely do so. No one possesses a memory so good, that if he has only once observed a natural object, a second inspection does not show him something that he has forgotten. Almost all, if not all, our memories are therefore sketches, rather than portraits, of the originals—the salient features are obvious, while the subordinate characters are obscure or unrepresented.

"Now, when several complex impressions which are more or less different from one another—let us say that out of ten impressions in each, six are the same in all, and four are different from all the rest—are successively presented to the mind, it is easy to see what must be the nature of the result. The repetition of the six similar impressions

3 *Treatise of Human Nature*, part I, § VII.

3a Spinoza sets forth the blended image theory in his *Ethics*, II, 40, schol.

will strengthen the six corresponding elements of the complex idea, which will therefore acquire greater vividness; while the four differing impressions of each will not only acquire no greater strength than they had at first, but, in accordance with the law of association, they will all tend to appear at once, and will thus neutralise one another.

"This mental operation may be rendered comprehensible by considering what takes place in the formation of compound photographs—when the images of the faces of six sitters, for example, are each received on the same photographic plate, for a sixth of the time requisite to take one portrait. The final result is that all those points in which the six faces agree are brought out strongly, while all those in which they differ are left vague; and thus what may be termed a *generic* portrait of the six, in contradistinction to a *specific* portrait of any one, is produced.

"Thus our ideas of single complex impressions are incomplete in one way, and those of numerous, more or less similar, complex impressions are incomplete in another way; that is to say, they are *generic*, not *specific*. And hence it follows that our ideas of the impressions in question are not, in the strict sense of the word, copies of those impressions; while, at the same time, they may exist in the mind independently of language.

"The generic ideas which are formed from several similar, but not identical, complex experiences are what are commonly called *abstract* or *general* ideas; and Berkeley endeavoured to prove that all general ideas are nothing but particular ideas annexed to a certain term, which gives them a more extensive signification, and makes them recall, upon occasion, other individuals which are similar to them. Hume says that he regards this as 'one of the greatest and the most valuable discoveries that has been made of late years in the republic of letters,' and endeavours to confirm it in such a manner that it shall be 'put beyond all doubt and controversy.'

"I may venture to express a doubt whether he has succeeded in his object; but the subject is an abstruse one; and I must content myself with the remark, that though Berkeley's view appears to be largely applicable to such general ideas as are formed after language has been acquired, and to all the more abstract sort of conceptions, yet that general ideas of sensible objects may nevertheless be produced in the way indicated, and may exist independently of language. In dreams, one sees houses, trees, and other objects, which are perfectly recognisable as such, but which remind one of the actual objects as seen 'out of the corner of the eye,' or of the pictures thrown by a badly-focussed magic lantern. A man addresses us who is like a figure seen by twilight; or we travel through countries where every feature of the scenery is vague;

the outlines of the hills are ill-marked, and the rivers have no defined banks. They are, in short, generic ideas of many past impressions of men, hills, and rivers. An anatomist who occupies himself intently with the examination of several specimens of some new kind of animal, in course of time acquires so vivid a conception of its form and structure, that the idea may take visible shape and become a sort of waking dream. But the figure which thus presents itself is generic, not specific. It is no copy of any one specimen, but, more or less, a mean of the series; and there seems no reason to doubt that the minds of children before they learn to speak, and of deaf-mutes, are peopled with similarly generated generic ideas of sensible objects."[4]

Are Vague Images 'Abstract Ideas'?

The only point which I am tempted to criticise in this account is Prof. Huxley's *identification of these generic images with 'abstract or general ideas' in the sense of universal conceptions.* Taine gives the truer view. He writes:

"Some years ago I saw in England, in Kew Gardens, for the first time, araucarias, and I walked along the beds looking at these strange plants, with their rigid bark, and compact, short, scaly leaves, of a sombre green, whose abrupt, rough, bristling form cut in upon the fine softly lighted turf of the fresh grass-plat. If I now inquire what this experience has left in me, I find, first, the sensible representation of an araucaria; in fact, I have been able to describe almost exactly the form and color of the plant. But there is a difference between this representation and the former sensations, of which it is the present echo. The internal semblance, from which I have just made my description, is vague, and my past sensations were precise. For, assuredly, each of the araucarias I saw, then excited in me a distinct visual sensation; there are no two absolutely similar plants in nature; I observed perhaps twenty or thirty araucarias; without a doubt each one of them differed from the others in size, in girth, by the more or less obtuse angles of its branches, by the more or less abrupt jutting out of its scales, by the style of its texture; consequently, my twenty or thirty visual sensations were different. But no one of these sensations has completely survived in its echo; the twenty or thirty revivals have blunted one another; thus upset and agglutinated by their resemblance they are confounded together, and my present representation is their residue only. This is the

[4] Huxley's *Hume*, pp. 92–94.

product, or rather the fragment, which is deposited in us, when we have gone through a series of similar facts or individuals. Of our numerous experiences there remain on the following day four or five more or less distinct recollections, which, obliterated themselves, leave behind in us a simple colorless, vague representation, into which enter as components various reviving sensations, in an utterly feeble, incomplete, and abortive state.—*But this representation is not the general and abstract idea. It is but its accompaniment,* and, if I may say so, the ore from which it is extracted. For the representation, though badly sketched, is a sketch, the sensible sketch of a distinct individual . . . . But my abstract idea corresponds to the whole class; it differs, then, from the representation of an individual.—Moreover, my abstract idea is perfectly clear and determinate; now that I possess it, I never fail to recognize an araucaria among the various plants which may be shown me; it differs, then, from the confused and floating representation I have of some particular araucaria."[5]

In other words, a blurred picture is just as much a single mental fact as a sharp picture is; and *the use of either picture by the mind to symbolize a whole class of individuals is a new mental function,* requiring some other modification of consciousness than the mere perception that the picture is distinct or not. I may bewail the indistinctness of my mental image of my absent friend. That does not prevent my thought from meaning *him* alone, however. And I may mean all mankind, with perhaps a very sharp image of one man in my mind's eye. The meaning is a function of the more 'transitive' parts of consciousness, the 'fringe' of relations which we feel surrounding the image, be the latter sharp or dim. This was explained in a previous place (see p. 447 ff., especially the note to page 451), and I would not touch upon the matter at all here but for its historical interest.

Our ideas or images of past sensible experiences may then be either distinct and adequate or dim, blurred, and incomplete. It is likely that the different degrees in which different men are able to make them sharp and complete has had something to do with keeping up such philosophic disputes as that of Berkeley with Locke over abstract ideas. Locke had spoken of our possessing 'the general idea of a triangle' which "must be neither oblique, nor rectangle, neither equilateral, equicrural, nor scalenon; but all and none of these at once." Berkeley says:

[5] *On Intelligence* (N. Y.), vol. II, p. 139.

"If any man has the faculty of framing in his mind such an idea of a triangle as is here described, it is in vain to pretend to dispute him out of it, nor would I go about it. All I desire is that the reader would fully and certainly inform himself whether *he* has such an idea or no."[6]

Until very recent years it was supposed by all philosophers that there was a typical human mind which all individual minds were like, and that propositions of universal validity could be laid down about such faculties as 'the Imagination.' Lately, however, a mass of revelations have poured in which make us see how false a view this is. There are imaginations, not 'the Imagination,' and they must be studied in detail.

INDIVIDUALS DIFFER IN IMAGINATION

The first breaker of ground in this direction was Fechner, in 1860. Fechner was gifted with unusual talent for subjective observation, and in Chapter XLIV of his *Psychophysik* he gave the results of a careful comparison of his own optical after-images, with his optical memory-pictures, together with accounts by several other individuals of their optical memory-pictures.[7] The result was to show a great personal diversity. "It would be interesting," he writes, "to work up the subject statistically; and I regret that other occupations have kept me from fulfilling my earlier intention to proceed in this way."

Fechner's intention was independently executed by Mr. Galton, the publication of whose results in 1880 may be said to have made an era in descriptive Psychology.

"It is not necessary," says Galton, "to trouble the reader with my earlier tentative steps . . . . After the inquiry had been fairly started it took the form of submitting a certain number of printed questions to a large number of persons. There is hardly any more difficult task than that of framing questions which are not likely to be misunderstood, which admit of easy reply, and which cover the ground of inquiry. I did my best in these respects, without forgetting the most important part of all—namely, to tempt my correspondents to write freely in fuller explanation of their replies, and on cognate topics as well. These sepa-

[6] *Principles*, Introduction, § 13. Compare also the passage quoted above, pp. 443–4.

[7] The differences noted by Fechner between after-images and images of imagination proper are as follows:

rate letters have proved more instructive and interesting by far than the replies to the set questions.

"The first group of the rather long series of queries related to the illumination, definition, and colouring of the mental image, and were framed thus:—

" 'Before addressing yourself to any of the Questions on the opposite page, think of some definite object—suppose it is your breakfast-table as you sat down to it this morning—and consider carefully the picture that rises before your mind's eye.

" '1. *Illumination.*—Is the image dim or fairly clear? Is its brightness comparable to that of the actual scene?

After-images	*Imagination-images*
Feel coercive;	Feel subject to our spontaneity;
Seem unsubstantial, vaporous;	Have, as it were, more body;
Are sharp in outline;	Are blurred;
Are bright;	Are darker than even the darkest black of the after-images;
Are almost colorless;	Have lively coloration;
Are continuously enduring;	Incessantly disappear, and have to be renewed by an effort of will. At last even this fails to revive them;
Cannot be voluntarily changed;	Can be exchanged at will for others;
Are exact copies of originals;	Cannot violate the necessary laws of appearance of their originals—e.g., a man cannot be imagined from in front and behind at once. The imagination must walk round him, so to speak;
Are more easily got with shut than with open eyes;	Are more easily had with open than with shut eyes;
Seem to move when the head or eyes move;	Need not follow movements of head or eyes;
The field within which they appear (with closed eyes) is dark, contracted, flat, close to the eyes, in front, and the images have no perspective;	The field is extensive in three dimensions, and objects can be imagined in it above or behind almost as easily as in front;
The attention seems directed forwards towards the sense-organ, in observing after-images.	In imagining, the attention feels as if drawn backwards towards the brain.

Finally, Fechner speaks of the impossibility of attending to both after-images and imagination-images at once, even when they are of the same object and might be expected to combine. All these differences are true of Fechner; but many of them would be untrue of other persons. I quote them as a type of observation which any reader with sufficient patience may repeat. To them may be added, as a universal proposition, that after-images seem larger if we project them on a distant screen, and smaller if we project them on a near one, whilst no such change takes place in mental pictures.

" '2. *Definition.*–Are all the objects pretty well defined at the same time, or is the place of sharpest definition at any one moment more contracted than it is in a real scene?

" '3. *Colouring.*–Are the colours of the china, of the toast, bread-crust, mustard, meat, parsley, or whatever may have been on the table, quite distinct and natural?'

"The earliest results of my inquiry amazed me. I had begun by questioning friends in the scientific world, as they were the most likely class of men to give accurate answers concerning this faculty of visualising, to which novelists and poets continually allude, which has left an abiding mark on the vocabularies of every language, and which supplies the material out of which dreams and the well-known hallucinations of sick people are built.

"To my astonishment, I found that *the great majority of the men of science to whom I first applied protested that mental imagery was unknown to them,* and they looked on me as fanciful and fantastic in supposing that the words 'mental imagery' really expressed what I believed everybody supposed them to mean. They had no more notion of its true nature than a colour-blind man, who has not discerned his defect, has of the nature of colour. They had a mental deficiency of which they were unaware, and naturally enough supposed that those who affirmed they possessed it, were romancing. To illustrate their mental attitude it will be sufficient to quote a few lines from the letter of one of my correspondents, who writes:–

" 'These questions presuppose assent to some sort of a proposition regarding the "mind's eye," and the "images" which it sees. . . . This points to some initial fallacy. . . . It is only by a figure of speech that I can describe my recollection of a scene as a "mental image" which I can "see" with my "mind's eye." . . . I do not see it . . . any more than a man sees the thousand lines of Sophocles which under due pressure he is ready to repeat. The memory possesses it, etc.'

"Much the same result followed inquiries made for me by a friend among members of the French Institute.

"On the other hand, when I spoke to persons whom I met *in general society,* I found an entirely different disposition to prevail. *Many men and a yet larger number of women, and many boys and girls, declared that they habitually saw mental imagery, and that it was perfectly distinct to them and full of colour.* The more I pressed and cross-questioned them, professing myself to be incredulous, the more obvious was the truth of their first assertions. They described their imagery in minute detail, and they spoke in a tone of surprise at my apparent hesitation in accepting what they said. I felt that I myself should have spoken exactly as they did if I had been describing a scene that lay before my eyes, in broad daylight, to a blind man who persisted in doubting the reality of vision. Reassured by this happier experience, I recommenced to inquire among scientific men, and soon found scattered instances of what I sought, though in by no means the same abundance as elsewhere. I then circulated my questions more generally among my friends and through their hands, and obtained the replies . . . from persons of both sexes, and of various ages, and in the end from occasional correspondents in nearly every civilised country.

"I have also received batches of answers from various educational establishments both in England and America, which were made after the masters had fully explained the meaning of the questions, and interested the boys in them. These have the merit of returns derived from a general census, which my other data lack, because I cannot for a moment suppose that the writers of the latter are a haphazard proportion of those to whom they were sent. Indeed I know of some who, disavowing all possession of the power, and of many others who, possessing it in too faint a degree to enable them to express what their experiences really were, in a manner satisfactory to themselves, sent no returns at all. Considerable statistical similarity was, however, observed between the sets of returns furnished by the schoolboys and those sent by my separate correspondents, and I may add that they accord in this respect with the oral information I have elsewhere obtained. The conformity of replies from so many different sources which was clear from the first, the fact of their apparent trustworthiness being on the whole much increased by cross-examination (though I could give one or two amusing instances of break-down), and the evident effort made to give accurate answers, have convinced me that it is a much easier matter than I had anticipated to obtain trustworthy replies to psychological questions. Many persons, especially women and intelligent children, take pleasure in introspection, and strive their very best to explain their mental processes. I think that a delight in self-dissection must be a strong ingredient in the pleasure that many are said to take in confessing themselves to priests.

"Here, then, are two rather notable results: the one is the proved facility of obtaining statistical insight into the processes of other persons' minds, whatever *à priori* objection may have been made as to its possibility; and the other is that scientific men, as a class, have feeble powers of visual representation. There is no doubt whatever on the latter point, however it may be accounted for. My own conclusion is, that an over-ready perception of sharp mental pictures is antagonistic to the acquirement of habits of highly-generalised and abstract thought, especially when the steps of reasoning are carried on by words as symbols, and that if the faculty of seeing the pictures was ever possessed by men who think hard, it is very apt to be lost by disuse. The highest minds are probably those in which it is not lost, but subordinated, and is ready for use on suitable occasions. I am, however, bound to say, that the missing faculty seems to be replaced so serviceably by other modes of conception, chiefly, I believe, connected with the incipient motor sense, not of the eyeballs only but of the muscles generally, that *men who declare themselves entirely deficient in the power of seeing mental pictures can nevertheless give life-like descriptions* of what they have seen, and can otherwise express themselves as if they were gifted with a vivid visual imagination. *They can also become painters of the rank of Royal Academicians.*[8] . . .

"It is a mistake to suppose that sharp sight is accompanied by clear visual memory. I have not a few instances in which the independence of the two faculties is emphatically commented on; and I have at least one clear case where great interest in outlines and accurate appreciation of straightness, squareness, and the like, is unaccompanied by the power of visualising. Neither does the faculty go with dreaming. I have cases where it is powerful, and at the same time where dreams are rare and faint or altogether absent. One friend tells me that his dreams have not the hundredth part of the vigour of his waking fancies.

"The visualising and the identifying powers are by no means necessarily combined. A distinguished writer on metaphysical topics assures me that he is exceptionally quick at recognising a face that he has seen before, but that he cannot call up a mental image of any face with clearness.

"Some persons have the power of combining in a single perception more than can be seen at any one moment by the two eyes. . . .

"I find that a few persons can, by what they often describe as a kind of touch-sight, visualise at the same moment all round the image of a solid body. Many can do so nearly, but not altogether round that of a terrestrial globe. An eminent mineralogist assures me that he is able to imagine simultaneously all the sides of a crystal with which he is familiar. I may be allowed to quote a curious faculty of my own in respect to this. It is exercised only occasionally and in dreams, or rather in nightmares, but under those circumstances I am perfectly conscious of embracing an entire sphere in a single perception. It appears to lie within my mental eyeball, and to be viewed centripetally.

"This power of comprehension is practically attained in many cases

[8] [I am myself a good draughtsman, and have a very lively interest in pictures, statues, architecture and decoration, and a keen sensibility to artistic effects. But I am an extremely poor visualizer, and find myself often unable to reproduce in my mind's eye pictures which I have most carefully examined.—W. J.]

by indirect methods. It is a common feat to take in the whole surroundings of an imagined room with such a rapid mental sweep as to leave some doubt whether it has not been viewed simultaneously. Some persons have the habit of viewing objects as though they were partly transparent; thus, if they so dispose a globe in their imagination as to see both its north and south poles at the same time, they will not be able to see its equatorial parts. They can also perceive all the rooms of an imaginary house by a single mental glance, the walls and floors being as if made of glass. A fourth class of persons have the habit of recalling scenes, not from the point of view whence they were observed, but from a distance, and they visualise their own selves as actors on the mental stage. By one or other of these ways, the power of seeing the whole of an object, and not merely one aspect of it, is possessed by many persons.

"The place where the image appears to lie, differs much. Most persons see it in an indefinable sort of way, others see it in front of the eye, others at a distance corresponding to reality. There exists a power which is rare naturally, but can, I believe, be acquired without much difficulty, of projecting a mental picture upon a piece of paper, and of holding it fast there, so that it can be outlined with a pencil. To this I shall recur.

"Images usually do not become stronger by dwelling on them; the first idea is commonly the most vigorous, but this is not always the case. Sometimes the mental view of a locality is inseparably connected with the sense of its position as regards the points of the compass, real or imaginary. I have received full and curious descriptions from very different sources of this strong geographical tendency, and in one or two cases I have reason to think it allied to a considerable faculty of geographical comprehension.

"The power of visualising is higher in the female sex than in the male, and is somewhat, but not much, higher in public schoolboys than in men. After maturity is reached, the further advance of age does not seem to dim the faculty, but rather the reverse, judging from numerous statements to that effect; but advancing years are sometimes accompanied by a growing habit of hard abstract thinking, and in these cases —not uncommon among those whom I have questioned—the faculty undoubtedly becomes impaired. There is reason to believe that it is very high in some young children, who seem to spend years of difficulty in distinguishing between the subjective and objective world. Language and book-learning certainly tend to dull it.

"The visualising faculty is a natural gift, and, like all natural gifts, has a tendency to be inherited. In this faculty the tendency to inheritance is exceptionally strong, as I have abundant evidence to prove, especially in respect to certain rather rare peculiarities, . . . which, when they exist at all, are usually found among two, three, or more brothers and sisters, parents, children, uncles and aunts, and cousins.

"Since families differ so much in respect to this gift, we may suppose that races would also differ, and there can be no doubt that such is the case. I hardly like to refer to civilised nations, because their natural faculties are too much modified by education to allow of their being appraised in an off-hand fashion. I may, however, speak of the French, who appear to possess the visualising faculty in a high degree. The peculiar ability they show in prearranging ceremonials and *fêtes* of all kinds, and their undoubted genius for tactics and strategy, show that they are able to foresee effects with unusual clearness. Their ingenuity in all technical contrivances is an additional testimony in the same direction, and so is their singular clearness of expression. Their phrase, 'figurez-vous,' or 'picture to yourself,' seems to express their dominant mode of perception. Our equivalent of 'imagine' is ambiguous.

. . . .

"I have many cases of persons mentally reading off scores when playing the pianoforte, or manuscript when they are making speeches. One statesman has assured me that a certain hesitation in utterance which he has at times, is due to his being plagued by the image of his manuscript speech with its original erasures and corrections. He cannot lay the ghost, and he puzzles in trying to decipher it.

"Some few persons see mentally in print every word that is uttered; they attend to the visual equivalent and not to the sound of the words, and they read them off usually as from a long imaginary strip of paper, such as is unwound from telegraphic instruments."

The reader will find further details in Mr. Galton's *Inquiries into Human Faculty*, pp. 83–114.[9] I have myself for many years collected from each and all of my psychology-students descriptions of their own visual imagination; and found (together with some curious idiosyncrasies) corroboration of all the variations which Mr. Galton reports. As examples, I subjoin extracts from two cases near the ends of the scale. The writers are first cousins, grandsons of a distinguished man of science. The one who is a good visualizer says:

[9] See also McCosh and Osborn: *Princeton Review*, Jan. 1884. There are some good examples of high development of the Faculty in the London *Spectator*, Dec. 28, 1878, pp. 1631, 1634, Jan. 4, 11, 25, and March 18, 1879.

"This morning's breakfast-table is both dim and bright; it is dim if I try to think of it when my eyes are open upon any object; it is perfectly clear and bright if I think of it with my eyes closed.—All the objects are clear at once, yet when I confine my attention to any one object it becomes far more distinct.—I have more power to recall color than any other one thing: if, for example, I were to recall a plate decorated with flowers I could reproduce in a drawing the exact tone, etc. The color of anything that was on the table is perfectly vivid.—There is very little limitation to the extent of my images: I can see all four sides of a room, I can see all four sides of two, three, four, even more rooms with such distinctness that if you should ask me what was in any particular place in any one, or ask me to count the chairs, etc., I could do it without the least hesitation.—The more I learn by heart the more clearly do I see images of my pages. Even before I can recite the lines I see them so that I could give them very slowly word for word, but my mind is so occupied in looking at my printed image that I have no idea of what I am saying, of the sense of it, etc. When I first found myself doing this I used to think it was merely because I knew the lines imperfectly; but I have quite convinced myself that I really do see an image. The strongest proof that such is really the fact is, I think, the following:

"I can look down the mentally seen page and see the words that *commence* all the lines, and from any one of these words I can continue the line. I find this much easier to do if the words begin in a straight line than if there are breaks. Example:

Étant fait . . . . .
Tous . . . . .
A des . . . . .
Que fit . . . . .
Céres . . . . .
        Avec . . . . .
Un fleuve . . . . .
        Comme . . . . .
(*La Fontaine* 8, IV.)"

The poor visualizer says:

"My ability to form mental images seems, from what I have studied of other people's images, to be defective, and somewhat peculiar. The process by which I seem to remember any particular event is not by a series of distinct images, but a sort of panorama, the faintest impressions of which are perceptible through a thick fog.—I cannot shut my eyes and get a distinct image of anyone, although I used to be able to a few years ago, and the faculty seems to have gradually slipped away.—In my most vivid dreams, where the events appear like the most real facts, I am often troubled with a dimness of sight which causes the images to appear indistinct.—To come to the question of the breakfast-table, there is nothing definite about it. Everything is vague. I cannot say *what* I see. I could not possibly count the chairs, but I happen to know that there are ten. I see nothing in detail.—The chief thing is a general impression that I cannot tell exactly what I do see. The coloring is about the same, as far as I can recall it, only very much washed out. Perhaps the only color I can see at all distinctly is that of the table-cloth, and I could probably see the color of the wall-paper if I could remember what color it was."

A person whose visual imagination is strong finds it hard to understand how those who are without the faculty can think at all. *Some people undoubtedly have no visual images at all worthy of the name,*[10] and instead of *seeing* their breakfast-table, they tell you that they *remember* it or *know* what was on it. This knowing and remembering takes place undoubtedly by means of verbal images, as was explained already in Chapter IX, p. 256.

The study of Aphasia (see p. 63) *has of late years shown how unexpectedly great are the differences between individuals in respect of imagination.* And at the same time the discrepancies between lesion and symptom in different cases of the disease have been largely cleared up. In some individuals the habitual 'thought-stuff,' if one may so call it, is visual; in others it is auditory, articulatory, or motor; in most, perhaps, it is evenly mixed. The same local cerebral injury must needs work different practical results in persons who differ in this way. In one it will throw a much-used brain-tract out of gear; in the other it may affect an unimportant region. A particularly instructive case was published by Charcot in 1883.[11]

[10] Take the following report from one of my students: "I am unable to form in my mind's eye any visual likeness of the table whatever. After many trials, I can only get a hazy surface, with nothing on it or about it. I can see no variety in color, and no positive limitations in extent, while I cannot see what I see well enough to determine its position in respect to my eye, or to endow it with any quality of size. I am in the same position as to the word *dog*. I cannot see it in my mind's eye at all; and so cannot tell whether I should have to run my eye along it, if I did see it."

[11] *Progrès Médical,* 21 juillet. I abridge from the German report of the case in Wilbrand: *Die Seelenblindheit* (1887).

The patient was

Mr. X., a merchant, born in Vienna, highly educated, master of German, Spanish, French, Greek, and Latin. Up to the beginning of the malady which took him to Professor Charcot, he read Homer at sight. He could, starting from any verse out of the first book of the *Iliad*, repeat the following verses without hesitating, by heart. Virgil and Horace were familiar. He also knew enough of modern Greek for business purposes. Up to within a year (from the time Charcot saw him) he enjoyed an exceptional *visual* memory. He no sooner thought of persons or things, but features, forms, and colors arose with the same clearness, sharpness, and accuracy as if the objects stood before him. When he tried to recall a fact or a figure in his voluminous polyglot correspondence, the letters themselves appeared before him with their entire content, irregularities, erasures and all. At school he recited from a mentally seen page which he read off line by line and letter by letter. In making computations, he ran his mental eye down imaginary columns of figures, and performed in this way the most varied operations of arithmetic. He could never think of a passage in a play without the entire scene, stage, actors, and audience appearing to him. He had been a great traveller. Being a good draughtsman, he used to sketch views which pleased him; and his memory always brought back the entire landscape exactly. If he thought of a conversation, a saying, an engagement, the place, the people, the entire scene rose before his mind.

His *auditory memory* was always deficient, or at least secondary. He had no taste for music.

A year and a half previous to examination, after business-anxieties, loss of sleep, appetite, etc., he noticed suddenly one day an extraordinary change in himself. After complete confusion, there came a violent contrast between his old and his new state. Everything about him seemed so new and foreign that at first he thought he must be going mad. He was nervous and irritable. Although he saw all things distinct, he had entirely lost his memory for forms and colors. On ascertaining this, he became reassured as to his sanity. He soon discovered that he could carry on his affairs by using his memory in an altogether new way. He can now describe clearly the difference between his two conditions.

Every time he returns to A., from which place business often calls him, he seems to himself as if entering a strange city. He views the monuments, houses, and streets with the same surprise as if he saw them for the first time. Gradually, however, his memory returns, and he finds himself at home again. When asked to describe the principal public place of the town, he answered, "I know that it is there, but it is impossible to imagine it, and I can tell you nothing about it." He has often drawn the port of A. To-day he vainly tries to trace its principal outlines. Asked to draw a minaret, he reflects, says it is a square tower, and draws, rudely, four lines, one for ground, one for top, and two for sides. Asked to draw an arcade, he says, "I remember that it contains semi-circular arches, and that two of them meeting at an angle make a vault, but how it *looks* I am absolutely unable to imagine." The profile of a man which he drew by request was as if drawn by a little child; and yet he confessed that he had been helped to draw it by looking at the bystanders. Similarly he drew a shapeless scribble for a tree.

He can no more remember his wife's and children's faces than he can remember the port of A. Even after being with them some time they seem unusual to him. He forgets his own face, and once spoke to his image in a mirror, taking it for a stranger. He complains of his loss of feeling for colors. "My wife has black hair, this I know; but I can no more recall its color than I can her person and features." This visual amnesia extends to objects dating from his childhood's years—paternal mansion, etc., forgotten.

No other disturbances but this loss of visual images. Now when he seeks something in his correspondence, he must rummage among the letters like other men, until he meets the passage. He can recall only the first few verses of the *Iliad*, and must *grope* to read Homer, Virgil, and Horace. Figures which he adds he must now whisper to himself. He realizes clearly that he must help his memory out with auditory images, which he does with effort. *The words and expressions which he recalls seem now to echo in his ear, an altogether novel sensation for him.* If he wishes to learn by heart anything, a series of phrases for example, he must *read them several times aloud*, so as to impress his ear. When later he repeats the thing in question, the sensation of inward hearing which precedes articulation rises up in his mind. This feeling was formerly unknown to him. He speaks French fluently; but affirms that he can no longer think in French; but must get his French words by translating them from Spanish or German, the languages of his childhood. He dreams no more in visual terms, but only in words, usually Spanish words. A certain degree of verbal blindness affects him—he is troubled by the Greek alphabet, etc.[12]

[12] In a letter to Charcot this interesting patient adds that his character also is changed: "I was formerly receptive, easily made enthusiastic, and possessed a rich fancy. Now I am quiet and cold, and fancy never carries my thoughts away. . . . I am much less susceptible than formerly to anger or sorrow. I lately lost my dearly-beloved mother; but felt far less grief at the bereavement than if I had been able

If this patient had possessed the auditory type of imagination from the start, it is evident that the injury, whatever it was, to his centres for optical imagination, would have affected his practical life much less profoundly.

"*The auditory type*," says M. A. Binet,[13] "*appears to be rarer than the visual.* Persons of this type imagine what they think of in the language of sound. In order to remember a lesson they impress upon their mind, not the look of the page, but the sound of the words. They reason, as well as remember, by ear. In performing a mental addition they repeat verbally the names of the figures, and add, as it were, the sounds, without any thought of the graphic signs. Imagination also takes the auditory form. 'When I write a scene,' said Legouvé to Scribe, 'I *hear*; but you *see*. In each phrase which I write, the voice of the personage who speaks strikes my ear. *Vous, qui êtes le théâtre même*, your actors walk, gesticulate before your eyes; I am a *listener*, you a *spectator*.'—'Nothing more true,' said Scribe; 'do you know where I am when I write a piece? In the middle of the parterre.' It is clear that the *pure audile*, seeking to develop only a single one of his faculties, may, like the pure visualizer, perform astounding feats of memory—Mozart, for example, noting from memory the *Miserere* of the Sistine Chapel after two hearings; the deaf Beethoven, composing and inwardly repeating his enormous symphonies. On the other hand, the man of auditory type, like the visual, is exposed to serious dangers; for if he lose his auditory images, he is without resource and breaks down completely.

"It is possible that persons with hallucinations of hearing, and individuals afflicted with the mania that they are victims of persecution, may all belong to the auditory type; and that the predominance of a certain kind of imagination may predispose to a certain order of hallucinations, and perhaps of delirium.

"The *motor type* remains—perhaps the most interesting of all, and certainly the one of which least is known. Persons who belong to this type [*les moteurs*, in French, *motiles*, as Mr. Galton proposes to call them in English] make use, in memory, reasoning, and all their intellectual operations, of images derived from movement. In order to understand this important point, it is enough to remember that 'all our perceptions, and in particular the important ones, those of sight and

---

to see in my mind's eye her physiognomy and the phases of her suffering, and especially less than if I had been able to witness in imagination the outward effects of her untimely loss upon the members of the family."

13 *Psychologie du raisonnement* (1886), p. 25.

touch, contain as integral elements the movements of our eyes and limbs; and that, if movement is ever an essential factor in our really seeing an object, it must be an equally essential factor when we see the same object in imagination' (Ribot).[14] For example, the complex impression of a ball, which is there, in our hand, is the resultant of optical impressions of touch, of muscular adjustments of the eye, of the movements of our fingers, and of the muscular sensations which these yield. When we imagine the ball, its idea must include the images of these muscular sensations, just as it includes those of the retinal and epidermal sensations. They form so many *motor images.* If they were not earlier recognized to exist, that is because our knowledge of the muscular sense is relatively so recent. In older psychologies it never was mentioned, the number of senses being restricted to five.

"There are persons who remember a drawing better when they have followed its outlines with their finger. Lecoq de Boisbaudran used this means in his artistic teaching, in order to accustom his pupils to draw from memory. He made them follow the outlines of figures with a pencil held in the air, forcing them thus to associate muscular with visual memory. Galton quotes a curious corroborative fact. Colonel Moncrieff often observed in North America young Indians who, visiting occasionally his quarters, interested themselves greatly in the engravings which were shown them. One of them followed with care with the point of his knife the outline of a drawing in the Illustrated London News, saying that this was to enable him to carve it out the better on his return home. In this case the motor images were to reinforce the visual ones. The young savage was a *motor.*[15] . . . When one's motor images are destroyed, one loses one's remembrance of movements, and sometimes, more curiously still, one loses the power of executing them. Pathology gives us examples in motor aphasia, agraphia, etc. Take the case of agraphia. An educated man, knowing how to write, suddenly loses this power, as a result of cerebral injury. His hand and arm are in no way paralytic, yet he cannot write. Whence this loss of power? He

14 [I am myself a very poor visualizer, and find that I can seldom call to mind even a single letter of the alphabet in purely retinal terms. I must trace the letter by running my mental eye over its contour in order that the image of it shall have any distinctness at all. On questioning a large number of other people, mostly students, I find that perhaps half of them say they have no such difficulty in seeing letters mentally. Many affirm that they can see an entire word at once, especially a short one like 'dog,' with no such feeling of creating the letters successively by tracing them with the eye.—W. J.]

15 It is hardly needful to say that in modern primary education, in which the blackboard is so much used, the children are taught their letters, etc., by all possible channels at once, sight, hearing, and movement.

tells us himself: he no longer knows how. He has forgotten how to set about it to trace the letters, he has lost the memory of the movements to be executed, he has no longer the motor images which, when formerly he wrote, directed his hand. . . . Other patients, affected with word-blindness, resort to these motor images precisely to make amends for their other deficiency. . . . An individual affected in this way cannot read letters which are placed before his eyes, even although his sight be good enough for the purpose. This loss of the power of reading by sight may, at a certain time, be the only trouble the patient has. Individuals thus mutilated succeed in reading by an ingenious roundabout way which they often discover themselves: it is enough that they should trace the letters with their finger to understand their sense. What happens in such a case? How can the hand supply the place of the eye? The motor image gives the key to the problem. If the patient can read, so to speak, with his fingers, it is because in tracing the letters he gives himself a certain number of muscular impressions which are those of writing. In one word, the patient reads by writing (Charcot): the feeling of the graphic movements suggests the sense of what is being written as well as sight would."[16]

The imagination of a blind-deaf mute like Laura Bridgman must be confined entirely to tactile and motor material. *All blind persons must belong to the 'tactile' and 'motile' types* of the French authors. When the young man whose cataracts were removed by Dr. Franz was shown different geometric figures, he said he "had not been able to form from them the idea of a square and a disc, until he perceived a sensation of what he saw in the points of his fingers, as if he really touched the objects."[17]

Professor Stricker of Vienna, who seems to have the motile form of imagination developed in unusual strength, has given a very careful analysis of his own case in a couple of monographs with which all students should become familiar.[18] His recollections both of his own movements and of those of other things are accompanied invariably by distinct muscular feelings in those parts of his body which would naturally be used in effecting or in following the movement. In thinking of a soldier marching, for example, it is as if he were helping the image to march by marching himself in his

[16] See an interesting case of a similar sort, reported by Farges, in *L'Encéphale*, 7me Année, p. 545.

[17] *Philosophical Transactions*, 1841, p. 65.

[18] *Studien über die Sprachvorstellungen* (1880), and *Studien über die Bewegungsvorstellungen* (1882).

rear. And if he suppresses this sympathetic feeling in his own legs, and concentrates all his attention on the imagined soldier, the latter becomes, as it were, paralyzed. In general his imagined movements, of whatsoever objects, seem paralyzed the moment no feelings of movement either in his own eyes or in his own limbs accompany them.[19] The movements of articulate speech play a predominant part in his mental life.

"When after my experimental work I proceed to its description, as a rule I reproduce in the first instance only words which I had already associated with the perception of the various details of the observation whilst the latter was going on. For speech plays in all my observing so important a part that I ordinarily clothe phenomena in words as fast as I observe them."[20]

Most persons, on being asked *in what sort of terms they imagine words,* will say 'in terms of hearing.' It is not until their attention is expressly drawn to the point that they find it difficult to say whether auditory images or motor images connected with the organs of articulation predominate. A good way of bringing the difficulty to consciousness is that proposed by Stricker: Partly open your mouth and then imagine any word with labials or dentals in it, such as 'bubble,' 'toddle.' Is your image under these conditions distinct? To most people the image is at first 'thick,' as the sound of the word would be if they tried to pronounce it with the lips parted. Many can never imagine the words clearly with the mouth open; others succeed after a few preliminary trials. The experiment proves how dependent our verbal imagination is on actual feelings in lips, tongue, throat, larynx, etc.

"When we recall the impression of a word or a sentence, if we do not speak it out, we feel the twitter of the organs just about to come to that point. The articulating parts,—the larynx, the tongue, the lips,—are all sensibly excited; a *suppressed articulation is in fact the material of our recollection,* the intellectual manifestation, the *idea* of speech."[21]

The open mouth in Stricker's experiment not only prevents actual articulation of the labials, but our feeling of its openness keeps

19 Prof. Stricker admits that by practice he has succeeded in making his eye-movements 'act vicariously' for his leg-movements in imagining men walking.

20 *Bewegungsvorstellungen,* p. 6.

21 Bain: *Senses and the Intellect,* p. 339.

us from imagining their articulation, just as a sensation of glaring light will keep us from strongly imagining darkness. In persons whose auditory imagination is weak, the articulatory image seems to constitute the whole material for verbal thought. Professor Stricker says that in his own case no auditory image enters into the words of which he thinks.[22] Like most psychologists, however, he makes of his personal peculiarities a rule, and says that verbal thinking is normally and universally an exclusively motor representation. *I* certainly get auditory images, both of vowels and of consonants, in addition to the articulatory images or feelings on which this author lays such stress. And I find that numbers of my students, after repeating his experiments, come to this conclusion. There is *at first* a difficulty due to the open mouth. That, however, soon vanishes, as does also the difficulty of thinking of one vowel whilst continuously sounding another. What probably remains true, however, is that most men have a less auditory and a more articulatory verbal imagination than they are apt to be aware of. Professor Stricker himself has acoustic images, and can imagine the sounds of musical instruments, and the peculiar voice of a friend. A statistical inquiry on a large scale, into the variations of acoustic, tactile, and motor imagination, would probably bear less fruit than Galton's inquiry into visual images. A few monographs by competent observers, like Stricker, about their own peculiarities, would give much more valuable information about the diversities which prevail.[23]

[22] *Studien über die Sprachvorstellungen*, 28, 31, etc. Cf. pp. 69–70, etc. Against Stricker, see Stumpf: *Tonpsychologie*, 155–162, and *Revue Philosophique*, XX, 617. See also Paulhan: *Revue Philosophique*, XVI, 405. Stricker replies to Paulhan in vol. XVIII, p. 685. P. retorts in vol. XIX, p. 118. Stricker reports that out of 100 persons questioned he found only *one* who had *no* feeling in his lips when silently thinking the letters M, B, P; and out of 60 only *two* who were conscious of no internal articulation whilst reading (pp. 49–50).

[23] I think it must be admitted that some people have no vivid substantive images in *any* department of their sensibility. One of my students, an intelligent youth, denied so pertinaciously that there was *anything* in his mind *at all* when he thought, that I was much perplexed by his case. I myself certainly have no such vivid play of nascent movements or motor images as Professor Stricker describes. When I seek to represent a row of soldiers marching, all I catch is a view of stationary legs first in one phase of movement and then in another, and these views are extremely imperfect and momentary. Occasionally (especially when I try to stimulate my imagination, as by repeating Victor Hugo's lines about the regiment,

"Leur pas est si correct, sans tarder ni courir,
Qu'on croit voir des ciseaux se fermer et s'ouvrir.")

Touch-images are very strong in some people. The most vivid touch-images come when we ourselves barely escape local injury, or when we see another injured. The place may then actually tingle with the imaginary sensation—perhaps not altogether imaginary, since goose-flesh, paling or reddening, and other evidences of actual muscular contraction in the spot, may result.

"An educated man," says a writer who must always be quoted when it is a question of the powers of imagination,[24] "told me once that on entering his house one day he received a shock from crushing the finger of one of his little children in the door. At the moment of his fright he felt a violent pain in the corresponding finger of his own body, and this pain abode with him three days."

The same author makes the following discrimination, which probably most men could verify:

"On the skin I easily succeed in bringing out suggested sensations wherever I will. But because it is necessary to protract the mental effort I can only awaken such sensations as are in their nature prolonged, as warmth, cold, pressure. Fleeting sensations, as those of a prick, a cut, a blow, etc., I am unable to call up, because I cannot imagine them

---

I seem to get an instantaneous glimpse of an actual movement, but it is to the last degree dim and uncertain. All these images seem at first as if purely retinal. I think, however, that rapid eye-movements accompany them, though these latter give rise to such slight feelings that they are almost impossible of detection. Absolutely no leg-movements of my own are there; in fact, to call such up arrests my imagination of the soldiers. My optical images are in general very dim, dark, fugitive, and contracted. It would be utterly impossible to *draw* from them, and yet I perfectly well distinguish one from the other. My auditory images are excessively inadequate reproductions of their originals. I have *no* images of taste or smell. Touch-imagination is fairly distinct, but comes very little into play with most objects thought of. Neither is all my thought verbalized; for I have shadowy schemes of relation, as apt to terminate in a nod of the head or an expulsion of the breath as in a definite word. On the whole, vague images or sensations of movement inside of my head towards the various parts of space in which the terms I am thinking of either lie or are momentarily symbolized to lie, together with movements of the breath through my pharynx and nostrils, form a by no means inconsiderable part of my *thought-stuff*. I doubt whether my difficulty in giving a clearer account is wholly a matter of inferior power of introspective attention, though that doubtless plays its part. Attention, *ceteris paribus*, must always be inferior in proportion to the feebleness of the internal images which are offered it to hold on to.

[24] Georg Hermann Meyer: *Untersuchungen über die Physiologie der Nervenfaser* (1843), p. 233. For other cases see Tuke's *Influence of the Mind upon the Body*, chaps. II and VII.

ex abrupto with the requisite intensity. The sensations of the former order I can excite upon any part of the skin; and they may become so lively that, whether I will or not, I have to pass my hand over the place just as if it were a real impression on the skin."[25]

Meyer's account of his own visual images is very interesting; and with it we may close our survey of differences between the normal powers of imagining in different individuals.

"With much practice," he says, "I have succeeded in making it possible for me to call up subjective visual sensations at will. I tried all my experiments by day or at night with closed eyes. At first it was very difficult. In the first experiments which succeeded the whole picture was luminous, the shadows being given in a somewhat less strong bluish light. In later experiments I saw the objects dark, with bright outlines, or rather I saw outline drawings of them, bright on a dark ground. I can compare these drawings less to chalk drawings on a blackboard than to drawings made with phosphorus on a dark wall at night, though the phosphorus would show luminous vapors which were absent from my lines. If I wished, for example, to see a face, without intending that of a particular person, I saw the outline of a profile against the dark background. When I tried to repeat an experiment of the elder Darwin I saw only the edges of the die as bright lines on a dark ground. Sometimes, however, I saw the die really white and its edges black; it was then on a paler ground. I could soon at will change between a white die with black borders on a light field, and a black die with white borders on a dark field; and I can do this at any moment now. After long practice . . . these experiments succeeded better still. I can now call before my eyes almost any object which I please, as a subjective appearance, and this in its own natural color and illumination. I see them almost always on a more or less light or dark, mostly dimly changeable ground. Even known faces I can see quite sharp, with the true color of hair and cheeks. It is odd that I see these faces mostly in profile, whereas those described [in the previous extract] were all full-face. Here are some of the final results of these experiments:

"1) Some time after the pictures have arisen they vanish or change into others, without my being able to prevent it.

"2) When the color does not integrally belong to the object, I cannot always control it. A face, e.g., never seems to me blue, but always in its natural color; a red cloth, on the other hand, I can sometimes change to a blue one.

[25] Meyer: *op. cit.*, p. 238.

"3) I have sometimes succeeded in seeing pure colors without objects; they then fill the entire field of view.

"4) I often fail to see objects which are not known to me, mere fictions of my fancy, and instead of them there will appear familiar objects of a similar sort; for instance, I once tried to see a brass sword-hilt with a brass guard, instead of which the more familiar picture of a rapier-guard appeared.

"5) Most of these subjective appearances, especially when they were bright, left after-images behind them when the eyes were quickly opened during their presence. For example, I thought of a silver stirrup, and after I had looked at it a while I opened my eyes and for a long while afterwards saw its after-image.

"These experiments succeeded best when I lay quietly on my back and closed my eyes. I could bear no noise about me, as this kept the vision from attaining the requisite intensity. The experiments succeed with me now so easily that I am surprised they did not do so at first, and I feel as though they ought to succeed with everyone. The important point in them is to get the image sufficiently intense by the exclusive direction of the attention upon it, and by the removal of all disturbing impressions."[26]

The negative after-images which succeeded upon Meyer's imagination when he opened his eyes are a highly interesting, though rare, phenomenon. So far as I know there is only one other published report of a similar experience.[27] It would seem that in such a case the neural process corresponding to the imagination must be the entire tract concerned in the actual sensation, even down as far as the retina. This leads to a new question to which we may now turn—of what is

THE NEURAL PROCESS WHICH UNDERLIES IMAGINATION?

The commonly-received idea is that it is only a milder degree of the same process which took place when the thing now imagined was sensibly perceived. Professor Bain writes:

[26] Meyer: *op. cit.*, pp. 239–41.

[27] That of Dr. Charles Féré in the *Revue Philosophique*, xx, 364. Johannes Müller's account of hypnagogic hallucinations floating before the eyes for a few moments after these had been opened, seems to belong more to the category of spontaneous hallucinations (see his *Elements of Physiology*, London, 1842, p. 1394). It is impossible to tell whether the words in Wundt's *Vorlesungen*, I, 387, refer to a personal experience of his own or not; probably not. *Il va sans dire* that an inferior visualizer like myself can get no such after-images. Nor have I as yet succeeded in getting report of any from my students.

"Since a sensation, in the first instance, diffuses nerve currents through the interior of the brain outwards to the organs of expression and movement,—the persistence of that sensation, after the outward exciting cause is withdrawn, can be but a continuance of the same diffusive currents, perhaps less intense, but not otherwise different. The shock remaining in the ear and in the brain, after the sound of thunder, must pass through the same circles, and operate in the same way, as during the actual sound. We can have no reason for believing that, in this self-sustaining condition, the impression changes its seat, or passes into some new circles that have the special property of retaining it. Every part actuated *after* the shock must have been actuated *by* the shock, only more powerfully. With this single difference of intensity, the mode of existence of a sensation persisting after the fact is essentially the same as its mode of existence during the fact . . . . Now, if this be the case with impressions *persisting* when the cause has ceased, what view are we to adopt concerning impressions *reproduced* by mental causes alone, or without the aid of the original, as in ordinary recollection? What is the manner of occupation of the brain with a resuscitated feeling of resistance, a smell, or a sound? There is only one answer that seems admissible. *The renewed feeling occupies the very same parts, and in the same manner, as the original feeling, and no other parts, nor in any other assignable manner.* I imagine that if our present knowledge of the brain had been present to the earliest speculators, this is the only hypothesis that would have occurred to them. For where should a past feeling be reembodied, if not in the same organs as the feeling when present? It is only in this way that its identity can be preserved; a feeling differently embodied would be a different feeling."[28]

It is not plain from Professor Bain's text whether by the 'same parts' he means only the same parts *inside the brain*, or the same *peripheral* parts also, as those occupied by the original feeling. The examples which he himself proceeds to give are almost all cases of imagination of *movement*, in which the peripheral organs are indeed affected, for actual movements of a weak sort are found to accompany the idea. This is what we should expect. All currents tend to run forwards in the brain and discharge into the muscular system; and the idea of a movement tends to do this with peculiar facility. But the question remains: Do currents run *backwards*, so that if the optical centres (for example) are excited by 'association' and a visual object is imagined, a current runs *down to the retina* also, and excites that sympathetically with the higher tracts? In

[28] *Senses and the Intellect*, p. 337.

other words, *can peripheral sense-organs be excited from above, or only from without? Are they excited in imagination?* Professor Bain's instances are almost silent as to this point. All he says is this:

"We might think of a blow on the hand until the skin were actually irritated and inflamed. The attention very much directed to any part of the body, as the great toe, for instance, is apt to produce a distinct feeling in the part, which we account for only by supposing a revived nerve-current to flow there, making a sort of false sensation, an influence from within mimicking the influences from without in sensation proper.—(See the writings of Mr. Braid, of Manchester, on Hypnotism, etc.)"

If I may judge from my own experience, all feelings of this sort are consecutive upon motor currents invading the skin and producing contraction of the muscles there, the muscles whose contraction gives 'goose-flesh' when it takes place on an extensive scale. I never get a *feeling* in the skin, however strongly I *imagine* it, until some actual change in the condition of the skin itself has occurred. The truth seems to be that the cases where peripheral sense-organs are directly excited in consequence of imagination are exceptional rarities, if they exist at all. *In common cases of imagination it would seem more natural to suppose that the seat of the process is purely cerebral, and that the sense-organ is left out.* Reasons for such a conclusion would be briefly these:

1) In imagination the *starting-point* of the process must be in the brain. Now we know that currents usually flow one way in the nervous system; and for the peripheral sense-organs to be excited in these cases, the current would have to flow backwards.

2) There is between imagined objects and felt objects a difference of conscious quality which may be called almost absolute. It is hardly possible to confound the liveliest image of fancy with the weakest real sensation. The felt object has a plastic reality and outwardness which the imagined object wholly lacks. Moreover, as Fechner says, in imagination the attention feels as if drawn backwards to the brain; in sensation (even of after-images) it is directed forwards towards the sense-organ.[29] The difference between the two processes feels like one of kind, and not like a mere 'more' or 'less' of the same.[30] If a sensation of sound were only a strong imagina-

29 See above, Vol. II, p. 696, note.

30 V. Kandinsky (*Kritische und klinische Betrachtungen im Gebiete der Sinnestäuschungen* (Berlin, 1885), p. 135 ff.) insists that in even the liveliest pseudo-

tion, and an imagination a weak sensation, there ought to be a border-line of experience where we never could tell whether we were hearing a weak sound or imagining a strong one. In comparing a present sensation felt with a past one imagined, it will be remembered that we often judge the imagined one to *have been the stronger* (see above, p. 473, note). This is inexplicable if the imagination be simply a weaker excitement of the sensational process.

To these reasons the following objections may be made:

To 1): The current demonstrably *does* flow backwards down the optic nerve in Meyer's and Féré's negative after-image. Therefore it *can* flow backwards; therefore it *may* flow backwards in some, however slight, degree, in all imagination.[31]

To 2): The difference alleged is not absolute, and sensation and imagination *are* hard to discriminate where the sensation is so weak as to be just perceptible. At night hearing a very faint strik-

---

hallucinations (see below, Chapter XX), which may be regarded as the intensest possible results of the imaginative process, there is no outward objectivity perceived in the thing represented, and that a *ganzer Abgrund* separates these 'ideas' from true hallucination and objective perception.

[31] It seems to also flow backwards in certain hypnotic hallucinations. Suggest to a 'Subject' in the hypnotic trance that a sheet of paper has a red cross upon it, then pretend to remove the imaginary cross, whilst you tell the Subject to look fixedly at a dot upon the paper, and he will presently tell you that he sees a 'bluish-green' cross. The genuineness of the result has been doubted, but there seems no good reason for rejecting M. Binet's account (*Le Magnétisme animal*, 1887, p. 188). M. Binet, following M. Parinaud, and on the faith of a certain experiment, at one time believed, the optical brain-centres and not the retina to be the seat of ordinary negative after-images. The experiment is this: Look fixedly, with one eye open, at a colored spot on a white background. Then close that eye and look fixedly with the *other* eye at a plain surface. A negative after-image of the colored spot will presently appear. (*Psychologie du raisonnement*, 1886, p. 45.) But Mr. Delabarre has proved (*American Journal of Psychology*, II, 326) that this after-image is due, not to a higher cerebral process, but to the fact that the retinal process in the *closed* eye affects consciousness at certain moments, and that its object is then projected into the field seen by the eye which is open. M. Binet informs me that he is converted by the proofs given by Mr. Delabarre.

The fact remains, however, that the negative after-images of Herr Meyer, M. Féré, and the hypnotic subjects, form an exception to all that we know of nerve-currents, if they are due to a refluent centrifugal current to the retina. It may be that they will hereafter be explained in some other way. Meanwhile we can only write them down as a paradox. Sig. Sergi's theory that there is *always* a refluent wave in perception hardly merits serious consideration (*Psychologie physiologique*, pp. 99, 189). Sergi's theory has recently been reaffirmed with almost incredible crudity by Lombroso and Ottolenghi in the *Revue Philosophique*, XXIX, 70 (Jan. 1890).

ing of the hour by a far-off clock, our imagination reproduces both rhythm and sound, and it is often difficult to tell which was the last real stroke. So of a baby crying in a distant part of the house, we are uncertain whether we still hear it, or only imagine the sound. Certain violin-players take advantage of this in diminuendo terminations. After the pianissimo has been reached they continue to bow as if still playing, but are careful not to touch the strings. The listener hears in imagination a degree of sound fainter still than the preceding pianissimo. This phenomenon is not confined to hearing:

"If we slowly approach our finger to a surface of water, we often deceive ourselves about the moment in which the wetting occurs. The apprehensive patient believes himself to feel the knife of the surgeon whilst it is still at some distance."[32]

Visual perception supplies numberless instances in which the same sensation of vision is perceived as one object or another according to the interpretation of the mind. Many of these instances will come before us in the course of the next two chapters; and in Chapter XIX similar illusions will be described in the other senses. Taken together, all these facts would force us to admit that *the subjective difference between imagined and felt objects is less absolute than has been claimed, and that the cortical processes which underlie imagination and sensation are not quite as discrete as one at first is tempted to suppose. That peripheral sensory processes are ordinarily involved in imagination seems improbable; that they may sometimes be aroused from the cortex downwards cannot, however, be dogmatically denied.*

The imagination-process CAN *then pass over into the sensation-process.* In other words, genuine sensations *can* be centrally originated. When we come to study hallucinations in the chapter on Outer Perception, we shall see that this is by no means a thing of rare occurrence. At present, however, we must admit that *normally the two processes do* NOT *pass over into each other*; and we must inquire why. One of two things must be the reason. Either

1. Sensation-processes occupy a different *locality* from imagination-processes; or

2. Occupying the same locality, they have an *intensity* which

[32] Lotze: *Medicinische Psychologie*, p. 509.

under normal circumstances currents from other cortical regions are incapable of arousing, and to produce which currents from the periphery are required.

It seems almost certain (after what was said in Chapter II, pp. 59–60) *that the imagination-process differs from the sensation-process by its intensity rather than by its locality.* However it may be with lower animals, the assumption that ideational and sensorial centres are locally distinct appears to be supported by no facts drawn from the observation of human beings. After occipital destruction, the hemianopsia which results in man is sensorial blindness, not mere loss of optical ideas. Were there centres for crude optical sensation below the cortex, the patients in these cases would still feel light and darkness. Since they do not preserve even this impression on the lost half of the field, we must suppose that there are no centres for vision of any sort whatever below the cortex, and that the corpora quadrigemina and other lower optical ganglia are organs for reflex movement of eye-muscles and not for conscious sight. Moreover there are no facts which oblige us to think that, within the occipital cortex, one part is connected with sensation and another with mere ideation or imagination. The pathological cases assumed to prove this are all better explained by disturbances of conduction between the optical and other centres (see p. 60). In bad cases of hemianopsia the patient's images depart from him together with his sensibility to light. They depart so completely that he does not even know what is the matter with him. To perceive that one is blind to the right half of the field of view one must have an idea of that part of the field's possible existence. But the defect in these patients has to be revealed to them by the doctor, they themselves only knowing that there is 'something wrong' with their eyes. What you have no idea of you cannot miss; and their not definitely missing this great region out of their sight seems due to the fact that their very idea and memory of it is lost along with the sensation. A man blind of his eyes merely, sees *darkness.* A man blind of his visual brain-centres can no more see darkness out of the parts of his retina which are connected with the brain-lesion than he can see it out of the skin of his back. He cannot see at all in that part of the field; and he cannot think of the light which he ought to be feeling *there,* for the very notion of the existence of that particular 'there' is cut out of his mind.[33]

[33] See an important article by Binet in the *Revue Philosophique,* XXVI, 481

Now if we admit that sensation and imagination are due to the activity of the same centres in the cortex, we can see a very good teleological reason why they should correspond to discrete kinds of process in these centres, and why the process which gives the sense that the object is really there ought normally to be arousable only by currents entering from the periphery and not by currents from the neighboring cortical parts. We can see, in short, why *the sensational process* OUGHT TO *be discontinuous with all normal ideational processes, however intense.* For, as Dr. Münsterberg justly observes:

"Were there not this peculiar arrangement we should not distinguish reality and fantasy, our conduct would not be accommodated to the facts about us, but would be inappropriate and senseless, and we could not keep ourselves alive. . . . That our thoughts and memories should be copies of sensations with their intensity greatly reduced is thus a consequence deducible logically from the natural adaptation of the cerebral mechanism to its environment."[34]

Mechanically the discontinuity between the ideational and the sensational kinds of process must mean that when the greatest ideational intensity has been reached, an order of *resistance* presents itself which only a new order of force can break through. The current from the periphery is the new order of force required; and what happens after the resistance is overcome is the sensational process. We may suppose that the latter consists in some new and more violent sort of disintegration of the neural matter, which now explodes at a deeper level than at other times.

Now how shall we conceive of the 'resistance' which prevents this sort of disintegration from taking place, this sort of intensity in the process from being attained, so much of the time? It must be either an intrinsic resistance, some force of cohesion in the neural molecules themselves; or an extrinsic influence, due to other cortical cells. When we come to study the process of hallucination we shall see that both factors must be taken into account. There is a degree of inward molecular cohesion in our brain-cells which it probably takes a sudden inrush of destructive energy to spring apart. Incoming peripheral currents possess this energy from the

(1888); also Dufour, in *Revue Médicale de la Suisse Romande*, 1889, No. 8, cited in the *Neurologisches Centralblatt*, 1890, p. 48.

[34] *Die Willenshandlung* (1888), pp. 139–40.

outset. Currents from neighboring cortical regions might attain to it if they could *accumulate* within the centre which we are supposed to be considering. But since during waking hours every centre communicates with others by association-paths, no such accumulation can take place. The cortical currents which run in run right out again, awakening the next ideas; the level of tension in the cells does not rise to the higher explosion-point; and the latter must be gained by a sudden current from the periphery or not at all.

Chapter XIX

The Perception of 'Things'

PERCEPTION AND SENSATION COMPARED

A pure sensation we saw above, p. 657, to be an abstraction never realized in adult life. Any quality of a thing which affects our sense-organs does also more than that: it arouses processes in the hemispheres which are due to the organization of that organ by past experiences, and the results of which in consciousness are commonly described as ideas which the sensation suggests. The first of these ideas is that of the *thing* to which the sensible quality belongs. *The consciousness of particular material things present to sense* is nowadays called *perception*.[1] The consciousness of such things may be more or less complete; it may be of the mere name of the thing and its other essential attributes, or it may be of the thing's various remoter relations. It is impossible to draw any sharp line of distinction between the barer and the richer consciousness, because the moment we get beyond the first crude sensation all our consciousness is a matter of suggestion, and the various suggestions

[1] The word Perception, however, has been variously used. For historical notices, see Hamilton's *Lectures on Metaphysics*, II, 96. For Hamilton perception is 'the consciousness of external objects' (*ibid.*, 28). Spencer defines it oddly enough as "a discerning of the relation or relations between *states of consciousness*, partly presentative and partly representative; which states of consciousness must be themselves known to the extent involved in the knowledge of their relations" (*Psychology*, § 355).

shade gradually into each other, being one and all products of the same psychological machinery of association. In the directer consciousness fewer, in the remoter more, associative processes are brought into play.

Perception thus differs from sensation by the consciousness of farther facts associated with the object of the sensation:

"When I lift my eyes from the paper on which I am writing, I see the chairs, and tables, and walls of my room, each of its proper shape, and at its proper distance. I see, from my window, trees, and meadows, and horses, and oxen, and distant hills. I see each of its proper size, of its proper form, and at its proper distance; and these particulars appear as immediate informations of the eye, as the colours which I see by means of it. Yet, philosophy has ascertained, that we derive nothing from the eye whatever, but sensations of colour . . . . How, then, is it, that we receive accurate information, by the eye, of size, and shape, and distance? By association merely. The colours upon a body are different, according to its figure, its distance, and its size. But the sensations of colour, and what we may here, for brevity, call the sensations of extension, of figure, of distance, have been so often united, felt in conjunction, that the sensation of the colour is never experienced without raising the ideas of the extension, the figure, the distance, in such intimate union with it, that they not only cannot be separated, but are actually supposed to be seen. The sight, as it is called, of figure, or distance, appearing, as it does, a simple sensation, is in reality a complex state of consciousness; a sequence, in which the antecedent, a sensation of colour; and the consequent, a number of ideas, are so closely combined by association, that they appear not one idea, but one sensation."

This passage from James Mill[2] gives a clear statement of the doctrine which Berkeley in his *Theory of Vision* made for the first time an integral part of Psychology. Berkeley compared our visual sensations to the words of a language, which are but signs or occasions for our intellects to pass to what the speaker means. As the sounds called words have no inward affinity with the ideas they signify, so neither have our visual sensations, according to Berkeley, any inward affinity with the things of whose presence they make us aware. Those things are *tangibles*; their real properties, such as shape, size, mass, consistency, position, reveal themselves only to touch. But the visible signs and the tangible significates are

[2] *Analysis*, I, 94–96.

by long custom so "closely twisted, blended, and incorporated together, and the prejudice is so confirmed and riveted in our thoughts by a long tract of time, by the use of language, and want of reflection,"[3] that we think we *see* the whole object, tangible and visible alike, in one simple indivisible act.

Sensational and reproductive brain-processes combined, then, are what give us the content of our perceptions. Every concrete particular material thing is a conflux of sensible qualities, with which we have become acquainted at various times. Some of these qualities, since they are more constant, interesting, or practically important, we regard as essential constituents of the thing. In a general way, such are the tangible shape, size, mass, etc. Other properties, being more fluctuating, we regard as more or less accidental or inessential. We call the former qualities the reality, the latter its appearances. Thus, I hear a sound, and say 'a horse-car'; but the sound is not the horse-car, it is one of the horse-car's least important manifestations. The real horse-car is a feelable, or at most a feelable and visible, thing which in my imagination the sound calls up. So when I get, as now, a brown eye-picture with lines not parallel, and with angles unlike, and call it my big solid rectangular walnut library-table, that picture is not the table. It is not even like the table as the table is for vision, when rightly seen. It is a distorted perspective view of three of the sides of what I mentally *perceive* (more or less) in its totality and undistorted shape. The back of the table, its square corners, its size, its heaviness, are features of which I am conscious when I look, almost as I am conscious of its name. The suggestion of the name is of course due to mere custom. But no less is that of the back, the size, weight, squareness, etc.

Nature, as Reid says, is frugal in her operations, and will not be at the expense of a particular instinct to give us that knowledge which experience and habit will soon produce. Reproduced sights and contacts tied together with the present sensation in the unity of a *thing* with a name, these are the complex objective stuff out of which my actually perceived table is made. Infants must go through a long education of the eye and ear before they can perceive the realities which adults perceive. *Every perception is an acquired perception.*[4]

3 *An Essay towards a New Theory of Vision,* § 51.

4 The educative process is particularly obvious in the case of the ear, for all sud-

Perception may then be defined, in Mr. Sully's words, as that process by which the mind

"supplements a sense-impression by an accompaniment or escort of revived sensations, the whole aggregate of actual and revived sensations being solidified or 'integrated' into the form of a percept, that is, an apparently immediate apprehension or cognition of an object now present in a particular locality or region of space."[5]

Every reader's mind will supply abundant examples of the process here described; and to write them down would be therefore both unnecessary and tedious. In the chapter on Space we have already discussed some of the more interesting ones; for in our perceptions of shape and position it is really difficult to decide how much of our sense of the object is due to reproductions of past experience, and how much to the immediate sensations of the eye. I shall accordingly confine myself in the rest of this chapter to certain additional generalities connected with the perceptive process.

The first point is relative to that 'solidification' or 'integration,' whereof Mr. Sully speaks, of the present with the absent and merely represented sensations. Cerebrally taken, these words mean no more than this, that the process aroused in the sense-organ has shot into various paths which habit has already organized in the hemispheres, and that instead of our having the sort of consciousness which would be correlated with the simple sensorial process, we have that which is correlated with this more complex process. This, as it turns out, is the consciousness of that more complex 'object,' the whole 'thing,' instead of being the consciousness of that more simple object, the few qualities or attributes which actually impress our peripheral nerves. This consciousness must have the unity which every 'section' of our stream of thought retains so long as its objective content does not sensibly change. More than this we cannot say; we certainly ought not to say what usually is said by psychologists, and treat the perception as a sum of distinct psychic entities, the present sensation namely, *plus* a lot of images from the past, all 'integrated' together in a way impossible to describe. The

den sounds seem alarming to babies. The familiar noises of house and street keep them in constant trepidation until such time as they have either learned the objects which emit them, or have become blunted to them by frequent experience of their innocuity.

[5] *Outlines of Psychology*, p. 153.

perception is one state of mind or nothing—as I have already so often said.

In many cases it is easy to compare the psychic results of the sensational with those of the perceptive process. We then see a marked difference in the way in which the impressed portions of the object are felt, in consequence of being cognized along with the reproduced portion, in the higher state of mind. Their sensible quality changes under our very eye. Take the already-quoted catch, *Pas de lieu Rhône que nous*: one may read this over and over again without recognizing the sounds to be identical with those of the words *paddle your own canoe*. As we seize the English meaning the sound itself appears to change. Verbal sounds are usually perceived with their meaning at the moment of being heard. Sometimes, however, the associative irradiations are inhibited for a few moments (the mind being preoccupied with other thoughts) whilst the words linger on the ear as mere echoes of acoustic sensation. Then, usually, their interpretation suddenly occurs. But at that moment one may often surprise a change in the very *feel* of the word. Our own language would sound very different to us if we heard it without understanding, as we hear a foreign tongue. Rises and falls of voice, odd sibilants and other consonants, would fall on our ear in a way of which we can now form no notion. Frenchmen say that English sounds to them like the *gazouillement des oiseaux*—an impression which it certainly makes on no native ear. Many of us English would describe the sound of Russian in similar terms. All of us are conscious of the strong inflections of voice and explosives and gutturals of German speech in a way in which no German can be conscious of them.

This is probably the reason why, if we look at an isolated printed word and repeat it long enough, it ends by assuming an entirely unnatural aspect. Let the reader try this with any word on this page. He will soon begin to wonder if it can possibly be the word he has been using all his life with that meaning. It stares at him from the paper like a glass eye, with no speculation in it. Its body is indeed there, but its soul is fled. It is reduced, by this new way of attending to it, to its sensational nudity. We never before attended to it in this way, but habitually got it clad with its meaning the moment we caught sight of it, and rapidly passed from it to the other words of the phrase. We apprehended it, in short, with a cloud of associates, and thus perceiving it, we felt it quite otherwise than as we feel it now divested and alone.

Another well-known change is when we look at a landscape with our head upside-down. Perception is to a certain extent baffled by this manœuvre; gradations of distance and other space-determinations are made uncertain; the reproductive or associative processes, in short, decline; and, simultaneously with their diminution, the colors grow richer and more varied, and the contrasts of light and shade more marked. The same thing occurs when we turn a painting bottom-upwards. We lose much of its meaning, but, to compensate for the loss, we feel more freshly the value of the mere tints and shadings, and become aware of any lack of purely sensible harmony or balance which they may show.[6] Just so, if we lie on the floor and look up at the mouth of a person talking behind us. His lower lip here takes the habitual place of the upper one upon our retina, and seems animated by the most extraordinary and unnatural mobility, a mobility which now strikes us because (the associative processes being disturbed by the unaccustomed point of view) we get it as a naked sensation and not as part of a familiar object perceived.

On a later page other instances will meet us. For the present these are enough to prove our point. Once more we find ourselves driven to admit that when qualities of an object impress our sense and we thereupon perceive the object, the sensation as such of those qualities does not still exist inside of the perception and form a constituent thereof. The sensation is one thing and the perception another, and neither can take place at the same time with the other, because their cerebral conditions are not the same. They may *resemble* each other, but in no respect are they identical states of mind.

PERCEPTION IS OF DEFINITE AND PROBABLE THINGS

The chief cerebral conditions of perception are the paths of association irradiating from the sense-impression, which may have been already formed. If a certain sensation be strongly associated with the attributes of a certain thing, that thing is almost sure to

[6] Cf. Helmholtz: *Optik*, pp. 433, 723, 724, 772; and Spencer: *Psychology*, vol. II, p. 249, note.

be perceived when we get the sensation. Examples of such things would be familiar people, places, etc., which we recognize and name at a glance. But *where the sensation is associated with more than one reality*, so that either of two discrepant sets of residual properties may arise, the perception is doubtful and vacillating, and *the most that can then be said of it is that it will be of a* PROBABLE *thing*, of the thing which would most usually have given us that sensation.

In these ambiguous cases it is interesting to note that perception is rarely abortive; *some* perception takes place. The two discrepant sets of associates do not neutralize each other or mix and make a blur. What we more commonly get is first one object in its completeness, and then the other in its completeness. In other words, *all brain-processes are such as give rise to what we may call* FIGURED *consciousness.* If paths are irradiated at all, they are irradiated in consistent systems, and occasion thoughts of definite objects, not mere hodge-podges of elements. Even where the brain's functions are half thrown out of gear, as in aphasia or dropping asleep, this law of figured consciousness holds good. A person who suddenly gets sleepy whilst reading aloud will read wrong; but instead of emitting a mere broth of syllables, he will make such mistakes as to read 'supper-time' instead of 'sovereign,' 'overthrow' instead of 'opposite,' or indeed utter entirely imaginary phrases, composed of several definite words, instead of phrases of the book. So in aphasia: where the disease is mild the patient's mistakes consist in using entire wrong words instead of right ones. It is only in the gravest lesions that he becomes quite inarticulate. These facts show how subtle is the associative link; how delicate yet how strong that connection among brain-paths which makes any number of them, once excited together, thereafter tend to vibrate as a systematic whole. A small group of elements, '*this*,' common to two systems, A and B, may touch off A or B according as accident decides the next step (see Fig. 47). If it happen that a single point leading from '*this*' to B is momentarily a little more pervious than any leading from '*this*' to A, then that little advantage will upset the equilibrium in favor of the entire system B. The currents will sweep first through that point and thence into all the paths of B, each increment of advance making A more and more impossible. The thoughts correlated with A and B, in such a case, will have objects different,

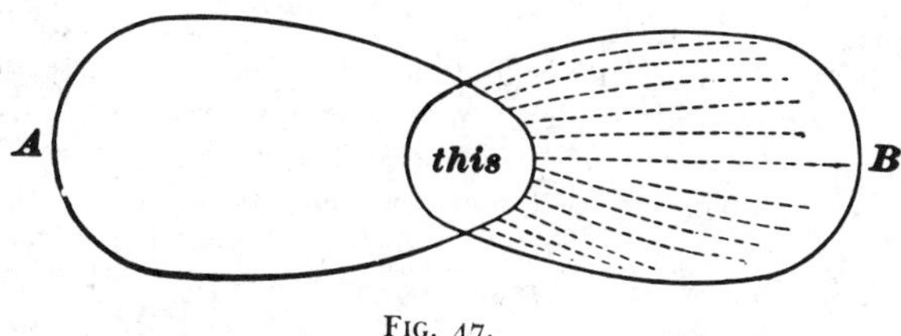

FIG. 47.

though similar. The similarity will, however, consist in some very limited feature if the 'this' be small.

Thus the faintest sensations will give rise to the perception of definite things if only they resemble sensations which the things are wont to arouse. In fact, a sensation must be strong and distinct in order not to suggest an object and, if it is a nondescript feeling, really to seem one. The auræ of epilepsy, globes of light, fiery vision, roarings in the ears, the sensations which electric currents give rise to when passed through the head, these are unfigured because they are strong. Weaker feelings of the same sort would probably suggest objects. Many years ago, after reading Maury's book, *Le Sommeil et les rêves,* I began for the first time to observe those ideas which faintly flit through the mind at all times, words, visions, etc., disconnected with the main stream of thought, but discernible to an attention on the watch for them. A horse's head, a coil of rope, an anchor, are, for example, ideas which have come to me unsolicited whilst I have been writing these latter lines. They can often be explained by subtle links of association, often not at all. But I have not a few times been surprised, after noting some such idea, to find, on shutting my eyes, an after-image left on the retina by some bright or dark object recently looked at, and which had evidently suggested the idea. 'Evidently,' I say, because the general shape, size, and position of object thought-of and of after-image were the same, although the idea had details which the retinal image lacked. We shall probably never know just what part retinal after-images play in determining the train of our thoughts. Judging by my own experiences I should suspect it of being not insignificant.[7]

[7] The more or less geometrically regular phantasms which are produced by pressure on the eyeballs, congestion of the head, inhalation of anæsthetics, etc., might again be cited to prove that faint and vague excitements of sense-organs are transformed into figured objects by the brain, only the facts are not quite clearly interpretable; and the figuring may possibly be due to some retinal peculiarity, as yet unex-

plored. Beautiful patterns, which would do for wall-papers, succeed each other when the eyeballs are long pressed. Goethe's account of his own phantasm of a flower is well known. It came in the middle of his visual field whenever he closed his eyes and depressed his head, "unfolding itself, and developing from its interior new flowers, formed of coloured or sometimes green leaves, not natural but of fantastic forms, and symmetrical as the rosettes of sculptors," etc. (quoted in Müller's *Physiology*, Baly's tr., p. 1397). The fortification- and zigzag-patterns, which are well-known appearances in the field of view in certain functional disorders, have characteristics (steadiness, coerciveness, blotting out of other objects) suggestive of a retinal origin—this is why the entire class of phenomena treated of in this note seem to me still doubtfully connected with the cerebral factor in perception of which the text treats. —I copy from Taine's book, *On Intelligence* (vol. 1, p. 61), the translation of an interesting observation by Prof. M. Lazarus, in which the same effect of an after-image is seen. Lazarus himself proposes the name of 'visionary illusions' for such modifications of ideal pictures by peripheral stimulations (*Zur Lehre von den Sinnestäuschungen*, 1867, p. 19). "I was on the Kaltbad terrace at Rigi, on a very clear afternoon, and attempting to make out the Waldbruder, a rock which stands out from the midst of the gigantic wall of mountains surrounding it, on whose summits we see like a crown the glaciers of Titlis, Uri-Rothsdock, etc. I was looking alternately with the naked eye and with a spy-glass; but could not distinguish it, with the naked eye. For the space of six to ten minutes I had gazed steadfastly upon the mountains, whose color varied according to their several altitudes or declivities between violet, brown, and dark green, and I had fatigued myself to no purpose, when I ceased looking and turned away. At that moment I saw before me (I cannot recollect whether my eyes were shut or open) the figure of an absent friend, like a corpse. . . . I asked myself at once how I had come to think of my absent friend?—In a few seconds I regained the thread of my thoughts, which my looking for the Waldbruder had interrupted, and readily found that the idea of my friend had by a very simple necessity introduced itself among them. My recollecting him was thus naturally accounted for.—But in addition to this, he had appeared as a corpse. How was this?—At this moment, whether through fatigue or in order to think, I closed my eyes, and found at once the whole field of sight, over a considerable extent, covered with the same corpse-like hue, a greenish-yellow gray. I thought at once that I had here the principle of the desired explanation, and attempted to recall to memory the forms of other persons. And, in fact, these forms too appeared like corpses; standing or sitting, as I wished, all had a corpse-like tint. The persons whom I wished to see did not all appear to me as sensible phantoms; and again, when my eyes were open, I did not see phantoms, or at all events only saw them faintly, of no determined color.—I then inquired how it was that phantoms of persons were affected by and colored like the visual field surrounding them, how their outlines were traced, and if their faces and clothes were of the same color. But it was then too late, or perhaps the influence of reflection and examination had been too powerful. All grew suddenly pale, and the subjective phenomenon, which might have lasted some minutes longer, had disappeared.—It is plain that here an inward reminiscence, arising in accordance with the laws of association, had combined with an optical after-image. The excessive excitation of the periphery of the optic nerve, I mean the long-continued preceding sensation of my eyes when contemplating the color of the mountain, had indirectly provoked a subjective and durable sensation, that of the complementary color; and my reminiscence, incorporating itself with this subjective sensation, became the corpse-like phantom I have described."

ILLUSIONS

Let us now, for brevity's sake, treat A and B in Fig. 47 as if they stood for objects instead of brain-processes. And let us furthermore suppose that A and B are, both of them, objects which might probably excite the sensation which I have called '*this*,' but that on the present occasion A and not B is the one which actually does so. If, then, on this occasion '*this*' suggests A and not B, the result is a *correct perception*. But if, on the contrary, 'this' suggests B and not A, the result is a *false perception*, or, as it is technically called, an *illusion*. But the *process* is the same, whether the perception be true or false.

Note that in every illusion what is false is what is inferred, not what is immediately given. The 'this,' if it were felt by itself alone, would be all right; it only becomes misleading by what it suggests. If it is a sensation of sight, it may suggest a tactile object, for example, which later tactile experiences prove to be not there. *The so-called 'fallacy of the senses,' of which the ancient sceptics made so much account, is not fallacy of the senses proper, but rather of the intellect, which interprets wrongly what the senses give.*[8]

So much premised, let us look a little closer at these illusions. They are due to two main causes. *The wrong object is perceived either because*

1) *Although not on this occasion the real cause, it is yet the habitual, inveterate, or most probable cause of 'this'*; or because

2) *The mind is temporarily full of the thought of that object, and therefore 'this' is peculiarly prone to suggest it at this moment.*

I will give briefly a number of examples under each head. The first head is the more important, because it includes a number of constant illusions to which all men are subject, and which can only be dispelled by much experience.

Illusions of the First Type

One of the oldest instances dates from Aristotle. Cross two fingers and roll a pea, penholder, or other small object between them.

[8] Cf. Thomas Reid's *Intellectual Powers*, essay II, chap. XXII, and A. Binet, in *Mind*, IX, 206. M. Binet points out the fact that what is fallaciously inferred is always an object of some other sense than the 'this.' 'Optical illusions' are generally errors of touch and muscular sensibility, and the fallaciously perceived object and the experiences which correct it are both tactile in these cases.

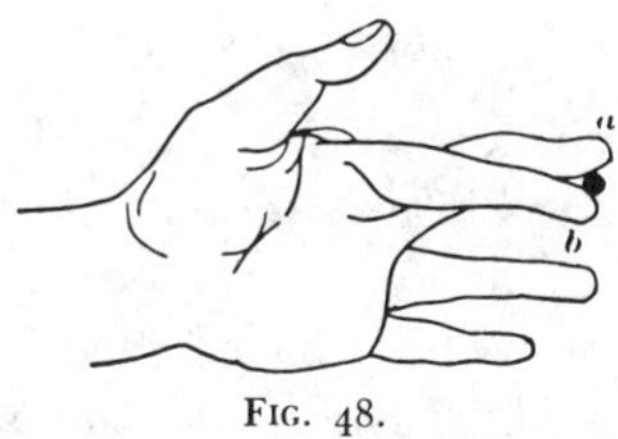

Fig. 48.

It will seem double. Professor Croom Robertson has given the clearest analysis of this illusion. He observes that if the object be brought into contact first with the forefinger and next with the second finger, the two contacts seem to come in at different points of space. The forefinger-touch seems higher, though the finger is really lower; the second-finger-touch seems lower, though the finger is really higher. "We perceive the contacts as double because we refer them to two distinct parts of space." The touched sides of the two fingers are normally not together in space, and customarily never do touch one thing; the one thing which now touches them, therefore, seems in two places, i.e., seems two things.[9]

There is a whole batch of illusions which come from optical sensations interpreted by us in accordance with our usual rule, although they are now produced by an unusual object. The *stereoscope* is an example. The eyes see a picture apiece, and the two pictures are a little disparate, the one seen by the right eye being a view of the object taken from a point slightly to the right of that from which the left eye's picture is taken. Pictures thrown on the two eyes by solid objects present this identical disparity. Whence we react on the sensation in our usual way, and perceive a solid. If the pictures be exchanged we perceive a hollow mould of the object, for a hollow mould would cast just such disparate pictures as these. Wheatstone's instrument, the *pseudoscope*, allows us to look at solid objects and see with each eye the other eye's picture. We then perceive the solid object hollow, *if it be an object which*

[9] The converse illusion is hard to bring about. The points *a* and *b*, being normally in contact, mean to us the same space, and hence it might be supposed that when simultaneously touched, as by a pair of callipers, we should feel but one object, whilst as a matter of fact we feel two. It should be remarked in explanation of this that an object placed between the two fingers in their normal uncrossed position always awakens the sense of *two contacts*. When the fingers are *pressed together* we feel *one object* to be between them. And when the fingers are crossed, and their corresponding points *a* and *b* simultaneously *pressed*, we do get something like the illusion of singleness—that is, we get a very doubtful doubleness.

might probably be hollow, but not otherwise. A human face, e.g., never appears hollow to the pseudoscope. In this irregularity of reaction on different objects, some seem hollow, others not; the perceptive process is true to its law, which is *always to react on the sensation in a determinate and figured fashion if possible, and in as probable a fashion as the case admits.* To couple faces and hollowness violates all our habits of association. For the same reason it is very easy to make an intaglio cast of a face, or the painted inside of a pasteboard mask, look convex, instead of concave as they are.

Our sense of the *position* of things with respect to our eye consists in suggestions of how we must move our hand to touch them. Certain places of the image on the retina, certain actively-produced positions of the eyeballs, are normally linked with the sense of every determinate position which an outer thing may come to occupy. Hence we perceive the usual position, even if the optical sensation be artificially brought from a different part of space. Prisms warp the light-rays in this way, and throw upon the retina the image of an object situated, say, at spot *a* of space in the same manner in which (without the prisms) an object situated at spot *b* would cast its image. Accordingly we feel for the object at *b* instead of *a*. If the prism be before one eye only we see the object at *b* with that eye, and in its right position *a* with the other—in other words, we see it double. If both eyes be armed with prisms with their angle towards the right, we pass our hand to the right of all objects when we try rapidly to touch them. And this illusory sense of their position lasts until a new association is fixed, when on removing the prisms a contrary illusion at first occurs. Passive or unintentional changes in the position of the eyeballs seem to be no more kept account of by the mind than prisms are; so we spontaneously make no allowance for them in our perception of distance and movements. Press one of the eyeballs into a strained position with the finger, and objects move and are translocated accordingly, just as when prisms are used.

Curious *illusions of movement* in objects occur whenever the eyeballs move without our intending it. We shall learn in the following chapter that the original visual feeling of movement is produced by any image passing over the retina. Originally, however, this sensation is definitely referred neither to the object nor to the eyes. Such definite reference grows up later, and obeys certain simple laws. We believe objects to move: 1) whenever we get the retinal movement-feeling, but think our eyes are still; and 2) whenever we think that our eyes move, but fail to get the retinal movement-feeling. We believe objects to be still, on the contrary, 1) whenever we get the retinal movement-feeling, but think our eyes are moving; and 2) whenever we neither think our eyes are moving, nor get the retinal movement-feeling. Thus the perception of the object's state of motion or rest depends on the notion we frame of our own eye's movement. Now many sorts of stimulation make our eyes move without our knowing it. If we look at a waterfall, river, railroad train, or any body which continuously passes in front of us in the same direction, it carries our eyes with it. This movement can be noticed in our eyes by a bystander. If the object keep passing towards our left, our eyes keep following whatever moving bit of it may have caught their attention at first, until that bit disappears from view. Then they jerk back to the right again, and catch a new bit, which again they follow to the left, and so on indefinitely. This gives them an oscillating demeanor, slow involuntary rotations leftwards alternating with rapid voluntary jerks rightwards. But *the oscillations continue* for a while after the object has come to a standstill, or the eyes are carried to a new object, and this produces the illusion that things now move in the opposite direction. For we are unaware of the slow leftward automatic movements of our eyeballs, and think that the retinal movement-sensations thereby aroused must be due to a rightward motion of the object seen; whilst the rapid voluntary rightward movements of our eyeballs we interpret as attempts to pursue and catch again those parts of the object which have been slipping away to the left.

Exactly similar oscillations of the eyeballs are produced in *giddiness*, with exactly similar results. Giddiness is easiest produced by whirling on our heels. It is a feeling of the movement of our own head and body through space, and is now pretty well understood to be due to the irritation of the semi-circular canals of the inner ear.[10] When, after whirling, we stop, we seem to be spinning

10 Purkinje, Mach, and Breuer are the authors to whom we mainly owe the explanation of the feeling of vertigo. I have found (*American Journal of Otology*, Oct. 1882) that in deaf-mutes (whose semi-circular canals or entire auditory nerves must often be disorganized) there very frequently exists no susceptibility to giddiness or whirling.

in the reverse direction for a few seconds, and then objects appear to continue whirling in the same direction in which, a moment previous, our body actually whirled. The reason is that our *eyes normally tend to maintain* their field of view. If we suddenly turn our head leftwards it is hard to make the eyes follow. They roll in their orbits rightwards, by a sort of compensating inertia. Even though we *falsely think* our head to be moving leftwards, this consequence occurs, and our eyes move rightwards—as may be observed in anyone with vertigo after whirling. As these movements are unconscious, the retinal movement-feelings which they occasion are naturally referred to the objects seen. And the intermittent voluntary twitches of the eyes towards the left, by which we ever and anon recover them from the extreme rightward positions to which the reflex movement brings them, simply confirm and intensify our impression of a leftward-whirling field of view: we seem to ourselves to be periodically pursuing and overtaking the objects in their leftward flight. The whole phenomenon fades out after a few seconds. And it often ceases if we voluntarily fix our eyes upon a given point.[11]

Optical vertigo, as these illusions of objective movement are called, results sometimes from brain-trouble, intoxications, paralysis, etc. A man will awaken with a weakness of one of his eye-muscles. An intended orbital rotation will then not produce its expected result in the way of retinal movement-feeling—whence false perceptions, of which one of the most interesting cases will fall to be discussed in later chapters.

There is an illusion of movement of the opposite sort, with which everyone is familiar at *railway stations.* Habitually, when we ourselves move forwards, our entire field of view glides backwards over our retina. When our movement is due to that of the windowed carriage, car, or boat in which we sit, all stationary objects visible through the window give us a sensation of gliding in the opposite direction. Hence, whenever we get this sensation, of a window with *all* objects visible through it moving in one direction,

[11] The involuntary continuance of the eye's motions is not the only cause of the false perception in these cases. There is also a true negative after-image of the original retinal movement-sensations, as we shall see in Chapter XX.

we react upon it in our customary way, and perceive a stationary field of view, over which the window, and we ourselves inside of it, are passing by a motion of our own. Consequently when another train comes alongside of ours in a station, and fills the entire window, and, after standing still awhile, begins to glide away, we judge that it is *our* train which is moving, and that the other train is still. If, however, we catch a glimpse of any part of the station through the windows, or between the cars, of the other train, the illusion of our own movement instantly disappears, and we perceive the other train to be the one in motion. This, again, is but making the usual and probable inference from our sensation.[12]

Another illusion due to movement is explained by Helmholtz. Most wayside objects, houses, trees, etc., look small when seen out of the windows of a swift train. This is because we perceive them in the first instance unduly near. And we perceive them unduly near because of their extraordinarily rapid parallactic flight backwards. When we ourselves move forwards all objects glide backwards, as aforesaid; but the nearer they are, the more rapid is this apparent translocation. Relative rapidity of passage backwards is thus so familiarly associated with nearness that when we feel it we perceive nearness. But with a given size of retinal image the nearer an object is, the smaller do we judge its actual size to be. Hence in the train, the faster we go, the nearer do the trees and houses seem; and the nearer they seem, the smaller do they look.[13]

Other illusions are due to the feeling of convergence being wrongly interpreted. When we converge our eyeballs we perceive an *approximation* of whatever thing we may be looking at. Whatever things do approach whilst we look at them oblige us, so long as they are not very distant, to converge our eyes. Hence approach of the thing is the *probable* objective fact when we feel our eyes converging. Now in most persons the internal recti muscles, to which convergence is due, are weaker than the others; and the entirely passive position of the eyeballs, the position which they assume when covered and looking at nothing in particular, is either that of parallelism or of slight divergence. Make a person look with both eyes at some near object, and then screen the object from *one*

[12] We never, so far as I know, get the converse illusion at a railroad station and believe the other train to move when it is still.

[13] Helmholtz: *Physiologische Optik*, 635.

of his eyes by a card or book. The chances are that you will see the eye thus screened turn just a little outwards. Remove the screen, and you will now see it turn in as it catches sight of the object again. The other eye meanwhile keeps as it was at first. To most persons, accordingly, all objects seem to *come nearer* when, after looking at them with one eye, both eyes are used; and they seem to *recede* during the opposite change. With persons whose external recti muscles are insufficient, the illusions may be of the contrary kind.

The size of the retinal image is a fruitful source of illusions. Normally, the retinal image grows larger as the object draws near. But the sensation yielded by this enlargement is also given by any object which really grows in size without changing its distance. Enlargement of retinal image is therefore an ambiguous sign. An opera-glass enlarges the moon. But most persons will tell you that she looks smaller through it, only a great deal nearer and brighter. They read the enlargement as a sign of approach; and the perception of approach makes them actually reverse the sensation which suggests it—by an exaggeration of our habitual custom of making allowance of the apparent enlargement of whatever object approaches us, and reducing it in imagination to its natural size. Similarly, in the theatre the glass brings the stage near, but hardly seems to magnify the people on it.

The well-known increased *apparent size of the moon on the horizon* is a result of association and probability. It is seen through vaporous air, and looks dimmer and duskier than when it rides on high; and it is seen over fields, trees, hedges, streams, and the like, which break up the intervening space and make us the better realize the latter's extent. Both these causes make the moon seem more distant from us when it is low; and as its visual angle grows no less, we deem that it must be a larger body, and we so perceive it. It looks particularly enormous when it comes up directly behind some well-known large object, as a house or tree, distant enough to subtend an angle no larger than that of the moon itself.[14]

The feeling of accommodation also gives rise to false perceptions of size. Usually we accommodate our eyes for an object as it approaches us. Usually under these circumstances the object throws

[14] Cf. Berkeley's *Theory of Vision*, §§ 67–79; Helmholtz: *Physiologische Optik*, pp. 630–1; Lechalas in *Revue Philosophique*, XXVI, 49.

a larger retinal image. But believing the object to remain the same, we make allowance for this and treat the entire eye-feeling which we receive as significant of nothing but *approach*. When we relax our accommodation and at the same time the retinal image grows smaller, the probable cause is always a *receding* object. The moment we put on convex glasses, however, the accommodation relaxes, but the retinal image grows larger instead of less. This is what would happen if our object, whilst receding, grew. Such a probable object we accordingly perceive, though with a certain vacillation as to the recession, for the growth in apparent size is also a probable sign of approach, and is at moments interpreted accordingly.—Atropin paralyzes the muscles of accommodation. It is possible to get a dose which will weaken these muscles without laming them altogether. When a known near object is then looked at we have to make the same voluntary strain to accommodate, as if it were a great deal nearer; but as its retinal image is not enlarged in proportion to this suggested approach, we deem that it must have grown smaller than usual. In consequence of this so-called *micropsy*, Aubert relates that he saw a man apparently no larger than a photograph. But the small size again made the man seem farther off. The real distance was two or three feet, and he seemed against the wall of the room.[15] Of these vacillations we shall have to speak again in the ensuing chapter.[16]

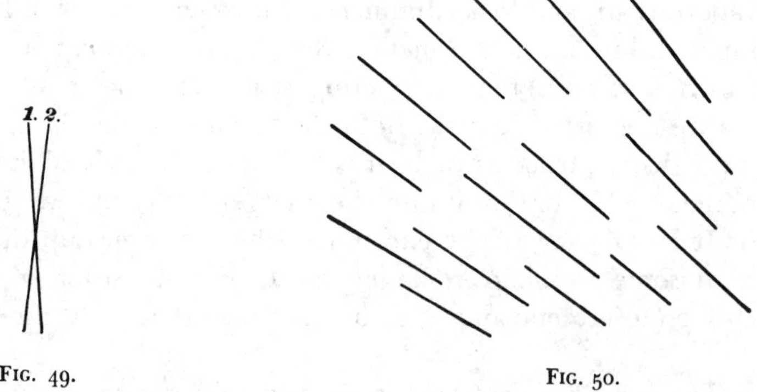

FIG. 49. FIG. 50.

[15] *Physiologische Optik*, p. 602.

[16] It seems likely that the strains in the *recti* muscles have something to do with the vacillating judgment in these atropin cases. The internal recti contract when-

Mrs. C. L. Franklin has recently described and explained with rare acuteness an illusion of which the most curious thing is that it was never noticed before. Take a single pair of crossed lines (Fig. 49), hold them in a horizontal plane before the eyes, and look along them, at such a distance that with the right eye shut, 1, and with the left eye shut, 2, looks like the projection of a vertical line. Look steadily now at the point of intersection of the lines with both eyes open, and you will see a third line sticking up like a pin through the paper at right angles to the plane of the two first lines. The explanation of this illusion is very simple, but so circumstantial that I must refer for it to Mrs. Franklin's own account.[17] Suffice it that images of the two lines fall on 'corresponding' rows of retinal points, and that the illusory vertical line is the only object capable of throwing such images. A variation of the experiment is this:

"In Fig. 50, the lines are all drawn so as to pass through a common point. With a little trouble, one eye can be put in the position of this point,—it is only necessary that the paper be held so that, with one eye shut, the other eye sees all the lines leaning neither to the right nor to the left. After a moment, one can fancy the lines to be vertical staffs standing out of the plane of the paper. . . . This illusion [says Mrs. Franklin] I take to have a purely mental origin. When a line lies anywhere in a plane passing through the apparent vertical meridian of one eye, and is looked at with that eye only . . . we have no very good means of knowing how it is directed in that plane . . . . Now of the lines in nature which lie anywhere within such a plane, by far the greater number . . . are vertical lines; hence we are peculiarly inclined to think that a line which we perceive to be in such a plane is a vertical line. But to see a lot of lines at once, all ready to throw their images upon the apparent vertical meridian, is a thing that has hardly ever happened to us, except when they have all been vertical lines. Hence when that happens, we have a still stronger tendency to think that what we see before us *is* a group of vertical lines."

In other words, we see, as always, the most probable object.

---

ever we accommodate. They squint and produce double vision when the innervation for accommodation is excessive. To see singly, when straining the atropinized accommodation, the contraction of our internal *recti* must be neutralized by a correspondingly excessive contraction of the external *recti*. But this is a sign of the object's recession, etc.

[17] *American Journal of Psychology*, I, 101 ff.

The foregoing may serve as examples of the first type of illusions mentioned on page 731. I could cite of course many others, but it would be tedious to enumerate all the thaumatropes and zoetropes, dioramas, and juggler's tricks in which they are embodied. In the chapter on Sensation we saw that many illusions commonly ranged under this type are, physiologically considered, of another sort altogether, and that associative processes, strictly so called, have nothing to do with their production.

Illusions of the Second Type

We may now turn to illusions of the second of the two types discriminated on page 731. In this type we perceive a wrong object because our mind is full of the thought of it at the time, and any sensation which is in the least degree connected with it touches off, as it were, a train already laid, and gives us a sense that the object is really before us. Here is a familiar example:

"If a sportsman while shooting woodcock in cover sees a bird about the size and colour of a woodcock get up and fly through the foliage, not having time to see more than that it is a bird of such a size and colour, he immediately supplies by inference the other qualities of a woodcock, and is afterwards disgusted to find that he has shot a thrush. I have done so myself, and could hardly believe that the thrush was the bird I had fired at, so complete was my mental supplement to my visual perception."[18]

As with game, so with enemies, ghosts, and the like. Anyone waiting in a dark place and expecting or fearing strongly a certain object will interpret any abrupt sensation to mean that object's presence. The boy playing 'I spy,' the criminal skulking from his pursuers, the superstitious person hurrying through the woods or past the churchyard at midnight, the man lost in the woods, the girl who tremulously has made an evening appointment with her swain, all are subject to illusions of sight and sound which make their hearts beat till they are dispelled. Twenty times a day the lover, perambulating the streets with his preoccupied fancy, will think he perceives his idol's bonnet before him.

The Proof-reader's Illusion. I remember one night in Boston, whilst waiting for a 'Mount Auburn' car to bring me to Cambridge, reading most distinctly that name upon the signboard of a car on

18 Romanes: *Mental Evolution in Animals*, p. 324.

which (as I afterwards learned) 'North Avenue' was painted. The illusion was so vivid that I could hardly believe my eyes had deceived me. All reading is more or less performed in this way.

"Practised novel- or newspaper-readers could not possibly get on so fast if they had to see accurately every single letter of every word in order to perceive the words. More than half of the words come out of their mind, and hardly half from the printed page. Were this not so, did we perceive each letter by itself, typographic errors in well-known words would never be overlooked. Children, whose ideas are not yet ready enough to perceive words at a glance, read them wrong if they are printed wrong, that is, right according to the way of printing. In a foreign language, although it may be printed with the same letters, we read by so much the more slowly as we do not understand, or are unable promptly to perceive, the words. But we notice misprints all the more readily. For this reason Latin and Greek, and still better Hebrew, works are more correctly printed, because the proofs are better corrected, than in German works. Of two friends of mine, one knew much Hebrew, the other little; the latter, however, gave instruction in Hebrew in a gymnasium; and when he called the other to help correct his pupils' exercises, it turned out that he could find out all sorts of little errors better than his friend, because the latter's perception of the words as totals was too swift."[19]

Testimony to personal identity is proverbially fallacious for similar reasons. A man has witnessed a rapid crime or accident, and carries away his mental image. Later he is confronted by a prisoner whom he forthwith perceives in the light of that image, and recognizes or 'identifies' as a participant, although he may never have been near the spot. Similarly at the so-called 'materializing séances' which fraudulent mediums give: in a dark room a man sees a gauze-robed figure who in a whisper tells him she is the spirit of his sister, mother, wife, or child, and falls upon his neck. The darkness, the previous forms, and the expectancy have so filled his mind with premonitory images that it is no wonder he perceives what is sug-

[19] M. Lazarus: *Das Leben der Seele*, II (1857), p. 31. In the ordinary hearing of speech half the words we seem to hear are supplied out of our own head. A language with which we are perfectly familiar is understood, even when spoken in low tones and far off. An unfamiliar language is unintelligible under these conditions. If we do not get a very good seat at a foreign theatre, we fail to follow the dialogue; and what gives trouble to most of us when abroad is not only that the natives speak so fast, but that they speak so indistinctly and so low. The verbal objects for interpreting the sounds by are not alert and ready-made in our minds, as they are in our familiar mother-tongue, and do not start up at so faint a cue.

gested. These fraudulent 'séances' would furnish most precious documents to the psychology of perception, if they could only be satisfactorily inquired into. In the hypnotic trance any suggested object is sensibly perceived. In certain subjects this happens more or less completely after waking from the trance. It would seem that under favorable conditions a somewhat similar susceptibility to suggestion may exist in certain persons who are not otherwise entranced at all.

This suggestibility is greater in the lower senses than in the higher. A German observer writes:

"We know that a weak smell or taste may be very diversely interpreted by us, and that the same sensation will now be named as one thing and the next moment as another. Suppose an agreeable smell of flowers in a room: A visitor will notice it, seek to recognize what it is, and at last perceive more and more distinctly that it is the perfume of roses—until after all he discovers a bouquet of violets. Then suddenly he recognizes the violet-smell, and wonders how he could possibly have hit upon the roses.—Just so it is with taste. Try some meat whose visible characteristics are disguised by the mode of cooking, and you will perhaps begin by taking it for venison, and end by being quite certain that it is venison, until you are told that it is mutton; whereupon you get distinctly the mutton flavor.—In this wise one may make a person taste or smell what one will, if one only makes sure that he shall conceive it beforehand as we wish, by saying to him: 'Doesn't that taste just like, etc.?' or 'Doesn't it smell just like, etc.?' One can cheat whole companies in this way; announce, for instance, at a meal, that the meat tastes 'high,' and almost everyone who is not animated by a spirit of opposition will discover a flavor of putrescence which in reality is not there at all.

"In the sense of *feeling* this phenomenon is less prominent, because we get so close to the object that our sensation of it is never incomplete. Still, examples may be adduced from this sense. On superficially feeling of a cloth, one may confidently declare it for velvet, whilst it is perhaps a long-haired cloth; or a person may perhaps not be able to decide whether he has put on woolen or cotton stockings, and, trying to ascertain this by the feeling on the skin of the feet, he may become aware that he gets the feeling of cotton or wool according as he thinks of the one or the other. When the feeling in our fingers is somewhat blunted by cold, we notice many such phenomena, being then more exposed to confound objects of touch with one another."[20]

[20] G. H. Meyer: *Untersuchungen*, etc., pp. 242–4.

High authorities have doubted this power of imagination to falsify present impressions of sense.[21] Yet it unquestionably exists. Within the past fortnight I have been annoyed by a smell, faint but unpleasant, in my library. My annoyance began by an escape of gas from the furnace below stairs. This seemed to get lodged in my imagination as a sort of standard of perception; for, several days after the furnace had been rectified, I perceived the 'same smell' again. It was traced this time to a new pair of India rubber shoes which had been brought in from the shop and laid on a table. It persisted in coming to me for several days, however, in spite of the fact that no other member of the family or visitor noticed anything unpleasant. My impression during part of this time was one of uncertainty whether the smell was imaginary or real; and at last it faded out. Everyone must be able to give instances like this from the smell-sense. When we have paid the faithless plumber for pretending to mend our drains, the intellect inhibits the nose from perceiving the same unaltered odor, until perhaps several days go by. As regards the ventilation or heating of rooms, we are apt to feel for some time as we think we ought to feel. If we believe the ventilator is shut, we feel the room close. On discovering it open, the oppression disappears.

An extreme instance is given in the following extract:

"A patient called at my office, one day, in a state of great excitement from the effects of an offensive odor in the horse-car she had come in, and which she declared had probably emanated from some very sick person who must have been just carried in it. There could be no doubt that something had affected her seriously for she was very pale, with nausea, difficulty in breathing and other evidences of bodily and mental stress. I succeeded, after some difficulty and time, in quieting her, and she left, protesting that the smell was unlike anything she had ever before experienced and was something dreadful. Leaving my office soon after, it so happened that I found her at the street corner, waiting for a car: we thus entered the car together. She immediately called my attention to the same sickening odor which she had experienced in the other car and began to be affected the same as before, when I pointed out to her that the smell was simply that which always emanates from the straw which has been in stables. She quickly recognized it as the

21 Helmholtz: *Physiologische Optik*, 438. The question will soon come before us again in the chapter on the "Perception of Space."

same, when the unpleasant effects which arose while she was possessed with another perception of its character, at once passed away."[22]

It is the same with touch. Everyone must have felt the sensible quality change under his hand, as sudden contact with something moist or hairy, in the dark, awoke a shock of disgust or fear which faded into calm recognition of some familiar object. Even so small a thing as a crumb of potato on the table-cloth, which we pick up, thinking it a crumb of bread, feels horrible for a few moments to our fancy, and different from what it is.

Weight or muscular feeling is a sensation; yet who has not heard the anecdote of someone to whom Sir Humphry Davy showed the metal sodium which he had just discovered? "Bless me, how heavy it is!" said the man; showing that his idea of what metals as a class ought to be had falsified the sensation he derived from a very light substance.

In the sense of hearing, similar mistakes abound. I have already mentioned the hallucinatory effect of mental images of very faint sounds, such as distant clock-strokes (above, pp. 717–718). But even when stronger sensations of sound have been present, everyone must recall some experience in which they have altered their acoustic character as soon as the intellect referred them to a different source. The other day a friend was sitting in my room, when the clock, which has a rich low chime, began to strike. "Hollo!" said he, "hear that hand-organ in the garden," and was surprised at finding the real source of the sound. I had myself some years ago a very striking illusion of the sort. Sitting reading late one night, I suddenly heard a most formidable noise proceeding from the upper part of the house, which it seemed to fill. It ceased, and in a moment renewed itself. I went into the hall to listen, but it came no more. Resuming my seat in the room, however, there it was again, low, mighty, alarming, like a rising flood or the *avant-courier* of an awful gale. It came from all space. Quite startled, I again went into the hall, but it had already ceased once more. On returning a second time to the room, I discovered that it was nothing but the breathing of a little Scotch terrier which lay asleep on the floor. The noteworthy thing is that as soon as I recognized what it was, I was compelled to think it a different sound, and could not then *hear* it as I had heard it a moment before.

22 C. F. Taylor: *Sensation and Pain*, p. 37 (N. Y., 1881).

In the anecdotes given by Delbœuf and Reid, this was probably also the case, though it is not so stated. Reid says:

"I remember, that once lying a-bed, and having been put into a fright, I heard my own heart beat; but I took it to be one knocking at the door, and arose and opened the door oftener than once, before I discovered that the sound was in my own breast." (*Inquiry*, chap. IV, § 1.)

Delbœuf's story is as follows:

"The illustrious P. J. van Beneden, senior, was walking one evening with a friend along a woody hill near Chaudfontaine. 'Don't you hear,' said the friend, 'the noise of a hunt on the mountain?' M. van Beneden listens and distinguishes in fact the giving-tongue of the dogs. They listen some time, expecting from one moment to another to see a deer bound by; but the voice of the dogs seems neither to recede nor approach. At last a countryman comes by, and they ask him who it is that can be hunting at this late hour. But he, pointing to some puddles of water near their feet, replies: 'Yonder little animals are what you hear.' And there there were in fact a number of toads of the species *Bombinator igneus*. . . . This batrachian emits at the pairing season a silvery or rather crystalline note. . . . Sad and pure, it is a voice in no wise resembling that of hounds giving chase."[23]

The sense of sight, as we have seen in studying Space, is pregnant with illusions of both the types considered. No sense gives such fluctuating impressions of the same object as sight does. With no sense are we so apt to treat the sensations immediately given as mere signs; with none is the invocation from memory of a *thing*, and the consequent perception of the latter, so immediate. The 'thing' which we perceive always resembles, as we have seen, the object of some absent sensation, usually another optical figure which in our mind has come to be the standard of reality; and it is this incessant reduction of our optical objects to more 'real' forms which has led some authors into the mistake of thinking that the sensations which first apprehend them are originally and natively of no form at all.[24]

Of accidental and occasional illusions of sight many amusing examples might be given. Two will suffice. One is a reminiscence of my own. I was lying in my berth in a steamer listening to the sailors

[23] *Examen critique de la loi psychophysique* (1883), p. 61.

[24] Compare A. W. Volkmann's essay "Über Ursprüngliches und Erworbenes in den

holystone the deck outside; when, on turning my eyes to the window, I perceived with perfect distinctness that the chief-engineer of the vessel had entered my state-room, and was standing looking through the window at the men at work upon the guards. Surprised at his intrusion, and also at his intentness and immobility, I remained watching him and wondering how long he would stand thus. At last I spoke; but getting no reply, sat up in my berth, and then saw that what I had taken for the engineer was my own cap and coat hanging on a peg beside the window. The illusion was complete; the engineer was a peculiar-looking man; and I saw him unmistakably; but after the illusion had vanished I found it hard voluntarily to make the cap and coat look like him at all.

The following story, which I owe to my friend Prof. Hyatt, is of a probably not uncommon class:

"During the winter of 1858, while in Venice, I had the somewhat peculiar illusion which you request me to relate. I remember the circumstances very accurately because I have often repeated the story, and have made an effort to keep all the attendant circumstances clear of exaggeration. I was travelling with my mother, and we had taken rooms at a hotel which had been located in an old palace. The room in which I went to bed was large and lofty. The moon was shining brightly, and I remember standing before a draped window, thinking of the romantic nature of the surroundings, remnants of old stories of knights and ladies, and the possibility that even in that room itself love-scenes and sanguinary tragedies might have taken place. The night was so lovely that many of the people were strolling through the narrow lanes or so-called streets, singing as they went, and I laid awake for some time listening to these patrols of serenaders, and of course finally fell asleep. I became aware that some one was leaning over me closely, and that my own breathing was being interfered with; a decided feeling of an unwelcome presence of some sort awakened me. As I opened my eyes I saw, as distinctly as I ever saw any living person, a draped head about a foot or eighteen inches to the right, and just above my bed. The horror which took possession of my young fancy was beyond anything I have ever experienced. The head was covered by a long black veil which floated out into the moonlight, the face itself was pale and beautiful, and the lower part swathed in the white band com-

---

Raumanschauungen," on p. 139 of his *Physiologische Untersuchungen im Gebiete der Optik*; and Chapter XIII of Hering's contribution to Hermann's *Handbuch der Physiologie*, vol. III, Th. 1.

monly worn by the nuns of Catholic orders. My hair seemed to rise up, and a profuse perspiration attested the genuineness of the terror which I felt. For a time I lay in this way, and then gradually gaining more command over my superstitious terrors, concluded to try to grapple with the apparition. It remained perfectly distinct until I reached at it sharply with my hand, and then disappeared, to return again, however, as soon as I sank back into the pillow. The second or third grasp which I made at the head was not followed by a reappearance, and I then saw that the ghost was not a real presence, but depended upon the position of my head. If I moved my eyes either to the left or right of the original position occupied by my head when I awakened, the ghost disappeared, and by returning to about the same position, I could make it reappear with nearly the same intensity as at first. I presently satisfied myself by these experiments that the illusion arose from the effect of the imagination, aided by the actual figure made by a visual section of the moonbeams shining through the lace curtains of the window. If I had given way to the first terror of the situation and covered up my head, I should probably have believed in the reality of the apparition, since I have not by the slightest word, so far as I know, exaggerated the vividness of my feelings."

THE PHYSIOLOGICAL PROCESS IN PERCEPTION

Enough has now been said to prove the general law of perception, which is this, that *whilst part of what we perceive comes through our senses from the object before us, another part* (and it may be the larger part) *always comes* (in Lazarus's phrase) *out of our own head.*

At bottom this is only one case (and that the simplest case) of the general fact that our nerve-centres are an organ for reacting on sense-impressions, and that our hemispheres, in particular, are given us in order that records of our private past experience may co-operate in the reaction. Of course such a general way of stating the fact is vague; and all those who follow the current theory of ideas will be prompt to throw this vagueness at it as a reproach. Their way of describing the process goes much more into detail. The sensation, they say, awakens 'images' of other sensations associated with it in the past. These images either 'fuse,' or are 'combined' by the Ego with the present sensation into a new product, the percept, etc., etc. Something so indistinguishable from this in practical outcome is what really occurs, that one may seem fastidious in objecting to such a statement, specially if he have no rival theory of the elementary processes to propose. And yet, if this notion of images rising and flocking and fusing *be* mythological (and we have all along so considered it), why should we entertain it unless confessedly as a mere figure of speech? As such, of course, it is convenient and welcome to pass. But if we try to put an exact meaning into it, all we find is that the brain reacts by paths which previous experiences have worn, and makes us usually perceive the probable thing, i.e., the thing by which on previous occasions the reaction was most frequently aroused.

But we can, I think, without danger of being too speculative, be a little more exact than this, and conceive of a physiological reason why the felt quality of an object changes when, instead of being apprehended in a mere sensation, the object is perceived as a thing. All consciousness seems to depend on a certain slowness of the process in the cortical cells. The rapider currents are, the less feeling they seem to awaken. If a region A, then, be so connected with another region B that every current which enters A immediately drains off into B, we shall not be very strongly conscious of the sort of object that A can make us feel. But if B in turn have no such copious channel of discharge, the excitement will linger there longer ere it diffuses itself elsewhere, and our consciousness of the sort of object that B makes us feel will be strong. Carrying this to an ideal maximum, we may say that if A offer *no* resistance to the transmission forwards of the current, and if the current *terminate* in B, then, no matter what causes may initiate the current, we shall get no consciousness of the object peculiar to A, but on the contrary a vivid sensation of the object peculiar to B. And this will be true though at other times the connection between A and B might lie less open, and every current *then* entering A might give us a strong consciousness of A's peculiar object. In other words, just in proportion as associations are habitual and fluent, will the qualities of the suggested thing tend to substitute themselves in consciousness for those of the thing immediately there; or, more briefly, *just in proportion as an experience is probable will it tend to be directly felt.* In all such experiences the paths lie wide open from the cells first affected to those concerned with the suggested ideas. A circular after-image on the receding wall or ceiling is actually *seen* as an ellipse, a square after-image of a cross there is seen as slant-legged, etc., because only in the process correlated with the vision of the latter figures do the inward currents find a pause (see the next chapter, p. 864 ff.).

We must remember this when, in dealing with the eye, we come to point out the erroneousness of the principle laid down by Reid and Helmholtz that true sensations can never be changed by the suggestions of experience.

A certain illusion of which I have not yet spoken affords an additional illustration of this. *When we will to execute a movement and the movement for some reason does not occur, unless the sensation of the part's* NOT *moving is a strong one, we are apt to feel as if the movement had actually taken place.* This seems habitually to be the case in anæsthesia of the moving parts. Close the patient's eyes, hold his anæsthetic arm still, and tell him to raise his hand to his head; and when he opens his eyes he will be astonished to find that the movement has not taken place. All reports of anæsthetic cases seem to mention this illusion.[25] Sternberg who wrote on the subject in 1885, lays it down as a law that the intention to move is the same thing as the feeling of the motion. We shall later see that this is false (Chapter XXVI); but it certainly may *suggest* the feeling of the motion with hallucinatory intensity. Sternberg gives the following experiment, which I find succeeds with at least half of those who try it: Rest your palm on the edge of the table with your forefinger hanging over in a position of extreme flexion, and then exert your will to flex it still more. The position of the other fingers makes this impossible, and yet if we do not look to see the finger, we think we feel it move. He quotes from Exner a

[25] In the *Proceedings of the American Society for Psychical Research*, p. 255, I have tried to account for some of the variations in this consciousness. Out of 140 persons whom I found to feel their lost foot, some did so *dubiously*. "Either they only feel it occasionally, or only when it pains them, or only when they try to move it; or they only feel it when they 'think a good deal about it' and make an effort to conjure it up. When they 'grow inattentive,' the feeling 'flies back,' or 'jumps back to the stump.' Every degree of consciousness, from complete and permanent hallucination, down to something hardly distinguishable from ordinary fancy, seems represented in the sense of the missing extremity which these patients say they have. Indeed I have seldom seen a more plausible lot of evidence for the view that imagination and sensation are but differences of vividness in an identical process, than these confessions, taking them altogether, contain. Many patients say they can hardly tell whether they feel or fancy the limb."

similar experiment with the jaws: Put some hard rubber or other unindentable obstacle between your back teeth and bite hard: you think you feel the jaw move and the front teeth approach each other, though in the nature of things no movement can occur.[26]—The visual suggestion of the path traversed by the finger-tip as the *locus* of the movment-feeling in the joint, which we discussed on page 687, is another example of this semi-hallucinatory power of the suggested thing. Amputated people, as we have learned, still feel their lost feet, etc. This is a necessary consequence of the law of specific energies, for if the central region correlated with the foot give rise to any feeling at all it must give rise to the feeling of a foot. But the curious thing is that many of these patients can *will the foot to move,* and when they have done so, distinctly *feel the movement to occur.* They can, to use their own language, 'work' or 'wiggle' their lost toes.[27]

Now in all these various cases we are dealing with data which in normal life are inseparably joined. Of all possible experiences, it is hard to imagine any pair more uniformly and incessantly coupled than the volition to move, on the one hand, and the feeling of the changed position of the parts, on the other. From the earliest ancestors of ours which had feet, down to the present day, the movement of the feet must always have accompanied the will to move them; and here, if anywhere, habit's consequences ought to be found.[28] The process of the willing ought, then, to pour into the process of feeling the command effected, and ought to awaken that feeling in a maximal degree provided no other positively contradictory sensation come in at the same time. In most of us, when the will fails of its effect there is a contradictory sensation. We discern a resistance or the unchanged position of the limb. But neither in anæsthesia nor in amputation can there be any contradictory sensation in the foot to correct us; so imagination has all the force of fact.

'APPERCEPTION'

In Germany since Herbart's time Psychology has always had a great deal to say about a process called *Apperception.*[29] The in-

26 Pflüger's *Archiv,* XXXVII, 1.

27 Not all patients have this additional illusion.

28 I ought to say that in *almost* all cases the volition is followed by actual contraction of muscles in the *stump.*

29 Cf. Herbart: *Psychologie als Wissenschaft,* § 125.

coming ideas or sensations are said to be 'apperceived' by 'masses' of ideas already in the mind. It is plain that the process we have been describing as perception is, at this rate, an apperceptive process. So are all recognition, classing, and naming; and passing beyond these simplest suggestions, all farther thoughts about our percepts are apperceptive processes as well. I have myself not used the word apperception because it has carried very different meanings in the history of philosophy,[30] and 'psychic reaction,' 'interpretation,' 'conception,' 'assimilation,' 'elaboration,' or simply 'thought,' are perfect synonyms for its Herbartian meaning, widely taken. It is, moreover, hardly worth while to pretend to analyze the so-called apperceptive performances beyond the first or perceptive stage, because their variations and degrees are literally innumerable. 'Apperception' is a name for the sum-total of the effects of what we have studied as association; and it is obvious that the things which a given experience will suggest to a man depend on what Mr. Lewes calls his entire psychostatical conditions, his nature and stock of ideas, or, in other words, his character, habits, memory, education, previous experience, and momentary mood. We gain no insight into what really occurs either in the mind or in the brain by calling all these things the 'apperceiving mass,' though of course this may upon occasion be convenient. On the whole I am inclined to think Mr. Lewes's term of 'assimilation' the most fruitful one yet used.[31]

Professor H. Steinthal has analyzed apperceptive processes with a sort of detail which is simply burdensome.[32] His introduction of the matter may, however, be quoted. He begins with an anecdote from a comic paper.

"In the compartment of a railway-carriage six persons unknown to each other sit in lively conversation. It becomes a matter of regret that one of the company must alight at the next station. One of the others says that he of all things prefers such a meeting with entirely unknown persons, and that on such occasions he is accustomed neither to ask who or what his companions may be nor to tell who or what he is. Another thereupon says that he will undertake to decide this question, if they each and all will answer him an entirely disconnected question.

30 Compare the historical reviews by K. Lange: *Über Apperception* (Plauen, 1879), pp. 12–14; by Staude in Wundt's *Philosophische Studien*, I, 149; and by Marty in *Vierteljahrsschrift für wissenschaftliche Philosophie*, x, 347 ff.

31 *Problems*, vol. I, p. 118 ff.

32 See his *Einleitung in die Psychologie und Sprachwissenschaft* (1881), p. 166 ff.

They began. He drew five leaves from his note-book, wrote a question on each, and gave one to each of his companions with the request that he write the answer below. When the leaves were returned to him, he turned, after reading them, without hesitation to the others, and said to the first, 'You are a man of science'; to the second, 'You are a soldier'; to the third, 'You are a philologer'; to the fourth, 'You are a journalist'; to the fifth, 'You are a farmer.' All admitted that he was right, whereupon he got out and left the five behind. Each wished to know what question the others had received; and behold, he had given the same question to each. It ran thus:

" 'What being destroys what it has itself brought forth?'

"To this the naturalist had answered, 'vital force'; the soldier, 'war'; the philologist, 'Kronos'; the publicist, 'revolution'; the farmer, 'a boar'. This anecdote, methinks, if not true, is at least splendidly well invented. Its narrator makes the journalist go on to say: 'Therein consists the joke. Each one answers the first thing that occurs to him,[33] and that is whatever is most nearly related to his pursuit in life. Every question is a hole-drilling experiment, and the answer is an opening through which one sees into our interiors.' . . . So do we all. We are all able to recognize the clergyman, the soldier, the scholar, the business man, not only by the cut of their garments and the attitude of their body, but by what they say and how they express it. We guess the place in life of men by the interest which they show and the way in which they show it, by the objects of which they speak, by the point of view from which they regard things, judge them, conceive them, in short by their mode of *apperceiving*. . . .

"Every man has one group of ideas which relate to his own person and interests, and another which is connected with society. Each has his group of ideas about plants, religion, law, art, etc., and more especially about the rose, epic poetry, sermons, free trade, and the like. Thus the mental content of every individual, even of the uneducated and of children, consists of masses or circles of knowledge of which each lies within some larger circle, alongside of others similarly included, and of which each includes smaller circles within itself. . . . The perception of a thing like a horse . . . is a process between the present horse's picture before our eyes, on the one hand, and those fused or interwoven pictures and ideas of all the horses we have ever seen, on the other; . . . a process between two factors or momenta, of which one

33 [One of my colleagues, asking himself the question after reading the anecdote, tells me that he replied 'Harvard College,' the faculty of that body having voted, a few days previously, to keep back the degrees of members of the graduating class who might be disorderly on class-day night. W. J.]

existed before the process and was an old possession of the mind (the group of ideas, or concept, namely), whilst the other is but just presented to the mind, and is the immediately supervening factor (the sense-impression). The former apperceives the latter; the latter is apperceived by the former. Out of their combination an apperception-product arises: the knowledge of the perceived being as a horse. The earlier factor is relatively to the later one active and *a priori*; the supervening factor is given, *a posteriori*, passive.... We may then define Apperception as the movement of two masses of consciousness (Vorstellungsmassen) against each other so as to produce a cognition.

"The *a priori* factor we called active, the *a posteriori* factor passive, but this is only relatively true. . . . Although the *a priori* moment commonly shows itself to be the more powerful, apperception-processes can perfectly well occur in which the new observation transforms or enriches the apperceiving group of ideas. A child who hitherto has seen none but four-cornered tables apperceives a round one as a table; but by this the apperceiving mass ('table') is enriched. To his previous knowledge of tables comes this new feature that they need not be four-cornered, but may be round. In the history of science it has happened often enough that some discovery, at the same time that it was apperceived, i.e., brought into connection with the system of our knowledge, transformed the whole system. In principle, however, we must maintain that, although either factor is both active and passive, the *a priori* factor is almost always the more active of the two."[34]

This account of Steinthal's brings out very clearly the *difference between our psychological conceptions and what are called concepts in logic.* In logic a concept is unalterable; but what are popularly called our 'conceptions of things' alter by being used. The aim of 'Science' is to attain conceptions so adequate and exact that we shall never need to change them. There is an everlasting struggle in every mind between the tendency to keep unchanged, and the tendency to renovate, its ideas. Our education is a ceaseless compromise between the conservative and the progressive factors. Every new experience must be disposed of under *some* old head. The great point is to find the head which has to be least altered to take it in. Certain Polynesian natives, seeing horses for the first time, called them pigs, that being the nearest head. My child of two played for a week with the first orange that was given him, calling it a 'ball.' He called the first whole eggs he saw 'potatoes,'

34 *Op. cit.*, pp. 167–73.

having been accustomed to see 'eggs' already broken in a glass, and potatoes without the skin. A folding pocket-corkscrew he unhesitatingly called 'bad-scissors.' Hardly any one of us can make new heads easily when fresh experiences come. Most of us grow more and more enslaved to the stock conceptions with which we have once become familiar, and less and less capable of assimilating impressions in any but the old ways. Old-fogyism, in short, is the inevitable terminus to which life sweeps us on. Objects which violate our established habits of 'apperception' are simply not taken account of at all; or, if on some occasion we are forced by dint of argument to admit their existence, twenty-four hours later the admission is as if it were not, and every trace of the unassimilable truth has vanished from our thought. Genius, in truth, means little more than the faculty of perceiving in an unhabitual way.

On the other hand, nothing is more congenial, from babyhood to the end of life, than to be able to assimilate the new to the old, to meet each threatening violator or burster of our well-known series of concepts, as it comes in, see through its unwontedness, and ticket it off as an old friend in disguise. This victorious assimilation of the new is in fact the type of all intellectual pleasure. The lust for it is curiosity. The relation of the new to the old, before the assimilation is performed, is wonder. We feel neither curiosity nor wonder concerning things so far beyond us that we have no concepts to refer them to or standards by which to measure them.[35] The Fuegians, in Darwin's voyage, wondered at the small boats, but took the big ship as a 'matter of course.' Only what we partly know already inspires us with a desire to know more. The more elaborate textile fabrics, the vaster works in metal, to most of us

[35] The great maxim in pedagogy is to knit every new piece of knowledge on to a pre-existing curiosity—i.e., to assimilate its matter in some way to what is already known. Hence the advantage of "comparing all that is far off and foreign to something that is near home, of making the unknown plain by the example of the known, and of connecting all the instruction with the personal experience of the pupil. . . . If the teacher is to explain the distance of the sun from the earth, let him ask . . . 'If anyone there in the sun fired off a cannon straight at you, what should you do?' 'Get out of the way' would be the answer. 'No need of that,' the teacher might reply. 'You may quietly go to sleep in your room, and get up again, you may wait till your confirmation-day, you may learn a trade, and grow as old as I am,—*then* only will the cannon-ball be getting near, *then* you may jump to one side! See, so great as that is the sun's distance!' " (K. Lange: *Über Apperception*, 1879, p. 74—a charming though prolix little work.)

are like the air, the water, and the ground, absolute existences which awaken no ideas. It is a matter of course that an engraving or a copper-plate inscription should possess that degree of beauty. But if we are shown a *pen*-drawing of equal perfection, our personal sympathy with the difficulty of the task makes us immediately wonder at the skill. The old lady admiring the Academician's picture, says to him: "And is it really all done *by hand*?"

IS PERCEPTION UNCONSCIOUS INFERENCE?

A widely-spread opinion (which has been held by such men as Schopenhauer, Spencer, Hartmann, Wundt, Helmholtz, and lately interestingly pleaded for by M. Binet[36]) will have it that *perception should be called a sort of reasoning operation, more or less unconsciously and automatically performed.* The question seems at first a verbal one, depending on how broadly the term reasoning is to be taken. If, every time a present sign suggests an absent reality to our mind, we make an inference; and if every time we make an inference we reason; then perception is indubitably reasoning. Only one sees no room in it for any unconscious part. Both associates, the present sign and the contiguous things which it suggests, are above-board, and no intermediary ideas are required. Most of those who have upheld the thesis in question have, however, made a more complex supposition. What they have meant is that perception is a *mediate* inference, and that the middle term is unconscious. When the sensation which I have called 'this' (p. 728, *supra*) is felt, they think that some process like the following runs through the mind:

'This' is M;
but M is A;
therefore 'this' is A.[37]

36 A. Schopenhauer: *Satz vom Grunde,* chap. IV. H. Spencer: *Psychology,* part VI, chaps. IX, X. E. von Hartmann: *Philosophy of the Unconscious* (B), chaps. VII, VIII. W. Wundt: *Beiträge zur Theorie der Sinneswahrnehmung,* pp. 422 ff.; *Vorlesungen,* IV, XIII. H. Helmholtz: *Physiologische Optik,* pp. 430, 447. A. Binet: *Psychologie du raisonnement,* chaps. III, V. Wundt and Helmholtz have more recently 'recanted.' See above, p. 171, note.

37 When not all M, but only some M, is A, when, in other words, M is 'undistributed' the conclusion is liable to error. Illusions would thus be *logical fallacies,* if true perceptions were valid syllogisms. They would draw false conclusions from undistributed middle terms.

Now there seem no good grounds for supposing this additional wheelwork in the mind. The classification of '*this*' as M is itself an act of perception, and should, if all perception were inference, require a still earlier syllogism for its performance, and so backwards *in infinitum*. The only extrication from this coil would be to represent the process in altered guise, thus:

'This' is *like those*;
Those are A;
Therefore 'this' is A.

The major premise here involves no association by contiguity, no *naming* of *those* as M, but only a suggestion of unnamed similar images, a recall of analogous past sensations with which the characters that make up A were habitually conjoined. But here again, what grounds of fact are there for admitting this recall? We are quite unconscious of any such images of the past. And the conception of all the forms of association as resultants of the elementary fact of habit-worn paths in the brain makes such images entirely superfluous for explaining the phenomena in point. Since the brain-process of 'this,' the sign of A, has repeatedly been aroused in company with the process of the full object A, direct paths of irradiation from the one to the other must be already established. And although roundabout paths may also be possible, as from 'this' to 'those,' and then from 'those' to 'A' (paths which would lead to practically the same conclusion as the straighter ones), yet there is no ground whatever for assuming them to be traversed now, especially since appearances point the other way. In *explicit* reasoning, such paths are doubtless traversed; in perception they are in all probability closed. So far, then, from perception being a species of reasoning properly so called, both it and reasoning are co-ordinate varieties of that deeper sort of process known psychologically as the association of ideas, and physiologically as the law of habit in the brain. *To call perception unconscious reasoning is thus either a useless metaphor, or a positively misleading confusion between two different things.*

One more point and we may leave the subject of Perception. *Sir William Hamilton thought that he had discovered a 'great law'* which had been wholly overlooked by psychologists, and which, 'simple and universal,' is this: "Knowledge and Feeling,—Perception and Sensation, though always coexistent, are always in the inverse ratio of each other." Hamilton wrote as if perception and sensation were two coexistent elements entering into a single state of consciousness. Spencer refines upon him by contending that they are two mutually exclusive *states* of consciousness, not two elements of a single state. If sensation be taken, as both Hamilton and Spencer mainly take it in this discussion, to mean the feeling of *pleasure* or *pain*, there is no doubt that the law, however expressed, is true; and that the mind which is strongly conscious of the pleasantness or painfulness of an experience is *ipso facto* less fitted to observe and analyze its outward cause.[38] Apart from pleasure and pain, however, the law seems but a corollary of the fact that the more concentrated a state of consciousness is, the more vivid it is. When feeling a color, or listening to a tone *per se*, we get it more intensely, notice it better, than when we are aware of it merely as one among many other properties of a total object. The more diffused cerebral excitement of the perceptive state is probably incompatible with quite as strong an excitement of separate parts as the sensational state comports. So we come back here to our own earlier discrimination between the perceptive and the sensational processes, and to the examples which we gave on pp. 726, 727.[39]

HALLUCINATIONS

Between normal perception and illusion we have seen that there is no break, the *process* being identically the same in both. The last illusions we considered might fairly be called hallucinations.

38 See Spencer: *Psychology*, II, p. 250, note, for a physiological hypothesis to account for this fact.

39 Here is another good example, taken from Helmholtz's *Optik*, p. 435: "The sight of a man walking is a familiar spectacle to us. We perceive it as a connected whole, and at most notice the most striking of its peculiarities. Strong attention is required, and a special choice of the point of view, in order to feel the perpendicular and lateral oscillations of such a walking figure. We must choose fitting points or lines in the background with which to compare the positions of its head. But if a distant walking man be looked at through an astronomical telescope (which inverts the object), what a singular hopping and rocking appearance he presents! No difficulty now in seeing the body's oscillations, and many other details of the gait. . . . But, on the other hand, its total character, whether light or clumsy, dignified or graceful, is harder to perceive than in the upright position."

We must now consider the false perceptions more commonly called by that name.[40] In ordinary parlance hallucination is held to differ from illusion in that, whilst there is an object really there in illusion, *in hallucination there is no objective stimulus at all.* We shall presently see that this supposed absence of objective stimulus in hallucination is a mistake, and that hallucinations are often only *extremes* of the perception process, in which the secondary cerebral reaction is out of all normal proportion to the peripheral stimulus which occasions the activity. Hallucinations usually ap-

40 Illusions and hallucinations must both be distinguished from *delusions.* A delusion is a false opinion about a matter of fact, which need not necessarily involve, though it often does involve, false perceptions of sensible things. We may, for example, have religious delusions, medical delusions, delusions about our own importance, about other peoples' characters, etc., *ad libitum.* The delusions of the insane are apt to affect certain typical forms, often very hard to explain. But in many cases they are certainly theories which the patients invent to account for their abnormal bodily sensations. In other cases they are due to hallucinations of hearing and of sight. Dr. Clouston (*Clinical Lectures on Mental Diseases,* lecture III *ad fin.*) gives the following special delusions as having been found in about a hundred melancholy female patients who were afflicted in this way. There were delusions of

general persecution;
general suspicion;
being poisoned;
being killed;
being conspired against;
being defrauded;
being preached against in church;
being pregnant;
being destitute;
being followed by the police;
being very wicked;
impending death;
impending calamity;
the soul being lost;
having no stomach;
having no inside;
having a bone in the throat;
having lost much money;
being unfit to live;
that she will not recover;
that she is to be murdered;
that she is to be boiled alive;
that she is to be starved;
that the flesh is boiling;
that the head is severed from the body;
that children are burning;
that murders take place around;
that it is wrong to take food;
being in hell;
being tempted of the devil;
being possessed of the devil;
having committed an unpardonable sin;
unseen agencies working;
her own identity;
being on fire;
having neither stomach nor brains;
being covered with vermin;
letters being written about her;
property being stolen;
her children being killed;
having committed theft;
the legs being made of glass;
having horns on the head;
being chloroformed;
having committed murder;
fear of being hanged;
being called names by persons;
being acted on by spirits;
being a man;
the body being transformed;
insects coming from the body;
rape being practised on her;
having a venereal disease;
being a fish;
being dead;
having committed 'suicide of the soul.'

pear abruptly and have the character of being forced upon the subject. But they possess various degrees of apparent *objectivity.* One mistake *in limine* must be guarded against. They are often talked of as mental *images* projected outwards by mistake. But where an hallucination is complete, it is much more than a mental image. *An hallucination is a strictly sensational form of consciousness, as good and true a sensation as if there were a real object there.* The object happens not to be there, that is all.

The milder degrees of hallucination have been designated as *pseudo-hallucinations.* Pseudo-hallucinations and hallucinations have been sharply distinguished from each other only within a few years. Dr. Kandinsky writes of their difference as follows:

> "In carelessly questioning a patient we may confound his pseudo-hallucinatory perceptions with hallucinations. But to the unconfused consciousness of the patient himself, even though he be imbecile, the identification of the two phenomena is impossible, at least in the sphere of vision. At the moment of having a pseudo-hallucination of sight, the patient feels himself in an entirely different relation to this subjective sensible appearance, from that in which he finds himself whilst subject to a true visual hallucination. The latter is reality itself; the former, on the contrary, remains always a subjective phenomenon which the individual commonly regards either as sent to him as a sign of God's grace, or as artificially induced by his secret persecutors. . . . If he knows by his *own experience* what a genuine hallucination is, it is quite impossible for him to mistake the pseudo-hallucination for it. . . . A concrete example will make the difference clear:
>
> "Dr. N. L. . . . heard one day suddenly amongst the voices of his persecutors ('coming from a hollow space in the midst of the wall') a rather loud voice impressively saying to him: 'Change your national allegiance.' Understanding this to mean that his only hope consisted in ceasing to be subject to the Czar of Russia, he reflected a moment what allegiance would be better, and resolved to become an English subject. At the same moment he saw a pseudo-hallucinatory lion of natural size, which appeared and quickly laid its fore-paws on his shoulders. He had a lively feeling of these paws as a tolerably painful local pressure (complete hallucination of touch). Then the same voice from the wall said: 'Now you have a lion—now you will rule,' whereupon the patient recollected that the lion was the national emblem of England. The lion appeared to L. very distinct and vivid, but he nevertheless remained conscious, as he afterwards expressed it, that he saw the animal, not with his bodily but with his mental eyes. (After his recovery he called analogous apparitions by the name of 'expressive-plastic

ideas.') Accordingly he felt no terror, even though he felt the contact of the claws. . . . Had the lion been a complete hallucination, the patient, as he himself remarked after recovery, would have felt great fear, and very likely screamed or taken to flight. Had it been a simple image of the fancy he would not have connected it with the voices, of whose objective reality he was at the time quite convinced."[41]

From ordinary images of memory and fancy, pseudo-hallucinations differ in being much more vivid, minute, detailed, steady, abrupt, and spontaneous, in the sense that all feeling of our own activity in producing them is lacking. Dr. Kandinsky had a patient who, after taking opium or hasheesh, had abundant pseudo-hallucinations and hallucinations. As he also had strong visualizing power and was an educated physician, the three sorts of phenomena could be easily compared. Although projected outwards (usually not farther than the limit of distinctest vision, a foot or so) the pseudo-hallucinations *lacked the character of objective reality* which the hallucinations possessed, but, unlike the pictures of imagination, it was almost impossible to produce them at will. Most of the 'voices' which people hear (whether they give rise to delusions or not) are pseudo-hallucinations. They are described as '*inner*' voices, although their character is entirely unlike the inner speech of the subject with himself. I know two persons who hear such inner voices making unforeseen remarks whenever they grow quiet and listen for them. They are a very common incident of delusional insanity, and at last grow into vivid hallucinations. The latter are comparatively frequent occurrences in sporadic form; and certain individuals are liable to have them often. From the results of the *Census of Hallucinations*, which was begun by Edmund Gurney, it would appear that, roughly speaking, one person at least in every ten is likely to have had a vivid hallucination at some time in his life.[42] The following cases from healthy people will give an idea of what these hallucinations are:

"When a girl of eighteen, I was one evening engaged in a very painful discussion with an elderly person. My distress was so great that I took up a thick ivory knitting-needle that was lying on the mantelpiece

[41] V. Kandinsky: *Kritische und klinische Betrachtungen im Gebiete der Sinnestäuschungen* (1885), p. 40.

[42] See *Proceedings of Society for Psychical Research*, Dec. 1889, pp. 7, 183. The International Congress for Experimental Psychology has now charge of the Census, and the present writer is its agent for America.

of the parlor and broke it into small pieces as I talked. In the midst of the discussion I was very wishful to know the opinion of a brother with whom I had an unusually close relationship. I turned round and saw him sitting at the further side of a centre-table, with his arms folded (an unusual position with him), but, to my dismay, I perceived from the sarcastic expression of his mouth that he was not in sympathy with me, was not 'taking my side,' as I should then have expressed it. The surprise cooled me, and the discussion was dropped.

"Some minutes after, having occasion to speak to my brother, I turned towards him, but he was gone. I inquired when he left the room, and was told that he had not been in it, which I did not believe, thinking that he had come in for a minute and had gone out without being noticed. About an hour and a half afterwards he appeared, and convinced me, with some trouble, that he had never been near the house that evening. He is still alive and well."

Here is another case:

"One night in March 1873 or '74, I cannot recollect which year, I was attending on the sick-bed of my mother. About eight o'clock in the evening I went into the dining room to fix a cup of tea, and on turning from the sideboard to the table, on the other side of the table before the fire, which was burning brightly, as was also the gas, I saw standing with his hand clasped to his side in true military fashion a soldier of about thirty years of age, with dark, piercing eyes looking directly into mine. He wore a small cap with standing feather; his costume was also of a soldierly style. He did not strike me as being a spirit, ghost, or anything uncanny, only a living man; but after gazing for fully a minute I realized that it was nothing of earth, for he neither moved his eyes nor his body, and in looking closely I could see the fire beyond. I was of course startled, and yet did not run out of the room. I felt stunned. I walked out rapidly, however, and turning to the servant in the hall asked her if she saw anything. She said not. I went into my mother's room and remained talking for about an hour, but never mentioned the above subject for fear of exciting her, and finally forgot it altogether, returning to the dining-room, still in forgetfulness of what had occurred, but repeating, as above, the turning from sideboard to table in act of preparing more tea. I looked casually towards the fire, and there I saw the soldier again. This time I was entirely alarmed, and fled from the room in haste. I called to my father, but when he came he saw nothing."

Sometimes more than one sense is affected. The following is a case:

"In response to your request to write out my experience of Oct. 30, 1886, I will inflict on you a letter.

"On the day above mentioned, Oct. 30, 1886, I was in ———, where I was teaching. I had performed my regular routine work for the day, and was sitting in my room working out trigonometrical formulæ. I was expecting every day to hear of the confinement of my wife, and naturally my thoughts for some time had been more or less with her. She was, by the way, in B———, some fifty miles from me.

"At the time, however, neither she nor the expected event was in my mind; as I said, I was working out trigonometrical formulæ, and I had been working on trigonometry the entire evening. About eleven o'clock, as I sat there buried in sines, cosines, tangents, cotangents, secants, and cosecants, I felt very distinctly upon my left shoulder a touch, and a slight shake, as if somebody had tried to attract my attention by other means and had failed. Without rising I turned my head, and there between me and the door stood my wife, dressed exactly as I last saw her, some five weeks before. As I turned she said: 'It is a little Herman; he has come.' Something more was said, but this is the only sentence I can recall. To make sure that I was not asleep and dreaming, I rose from the chair, pinched myself and walked toward the figure, which disappeared immediately as I rose. I can give no information as to the length of time occupied by this episode, but I know I was awake, in my usual good health. The touch was very distinct, the figure was absolutely perfect, stood about three feet from the door, which was closed, and had not been opened during the evening. The sound of the voice was unmistakable, and I should have recognized it as my wife's voice even if I had not turned and had not seen the figure at all. The tone was conversational, just as if she would have said the same words had she been actually standing there.

"In regard to myself, I would say, as I have already intimated, I was in my usual good health; I had not been sick before, nor was I after the occurrence, not so much as a headache having afflicted me.

"Shortly after the experience above described, I retired for the night and, as I usually do, slept quietly until morning. I did not speculate particularly about the strange appearance of the night before, and though I thought of it some, I did not tell anybody. The following morning I rose, not conscious of having dreamed anything, but I was very firmly impressed with the idea that there was something for me at the telegraph-office. I tried to throw off the impression, for so far as I knew there was no reason for it. Having nothing to do, I went out for a walk; and to help throw off the impression above noted, I walked away from the telegraph-office. As I proceeded, however, the impression became a conviction, and I actually turned about and went to the very place I had resolved not to visit, the telegraph-office. The first person I saw on arriving at said office was the telegraph-operator, who being on terms of intimacy with me, remarked: 'Hello, papa, I've got a telegram for you.' The telegram announced the birth of a boy, weighing nine pounds, and that all were doing well. Now, then, I have no theory at all about the events narrated above; I never had any such experience before nor since; I am no believer in spiritualism, am not in the least superstitious, know very little about 'thought-transference,' 'unconscious cerebration,' etc., etc., but I am absolutely certain about what I have tried to relate.

"In regard to the remark which I heard, 'It is a little Herman,' etc., I would add that we had previously decided to call the child, if a boy, *Herman*—my own name, by the way."[43]

The hallucination sometimes carries a change of the general consciousness with it, so as to appear more like a sudden lapse into a dream. The following case was given me by a man of 43, who had never anything resembling it before:

"While sitting at my desk this A. M. reading a circular of the Loyal Legion a very curious thing happened to me, such as I have never experienced. It was perfectly real, so real that it took some minutes to recover from. It seems to me like a direct intromission into some other world. I never had anything approaching it before save when dreaming at night. I was wide awake, of course. But this was the feeling. I had only just sat down and become interested in the circular, when I seemed to lose myself for a minute and then found myself in the top story of a high building very white and shining and clean, with a noble window immediately at the right of where I sat. Through this window I looked out upon a marvellous reach of landscape entirely new. I never had before such a sense of infinity in nature, such superb stretches of light and color and *cleanness*. I know that for the space of three minutes I was entirely lost, for when I began to come to, so to speak,—sitting in that other world, I debated for three or four minutes more as to which was dream and which was reality. Sitting there I got a faint sense of C. . . . [the town in which the writer was], away off and dim at first. Then I remember thinking 'Why, I used to live in C. . . . ; perhaps I am going back.' Slowly C. . . . did come back, and I found myself at

[43] This case is of the class which Mr. Myers terms 'veridical.' In a subsequent letter the writer informs me that his vision occurred some five hours *before* the child was born.

my desk again. For a few minutes the process of determining where I was was very funny. But the whole experience was perfectly delightful, there was such a sense of brilliancy and clearness and lightness about it. I suppose it lasted in all about seven minutes or ten minutes."

The hallucinations of fever-delirium are a mixture of pseudo-hallucination, true hallucination, and illusion. Those of opium, hasheesh, and belladonna resemble them in this respect. The following vivid account of a fit of hasheesh-delirium has been given me by a friend:

"I was reading a newspaper, and the indication of the approaching delirium was an inability to keep my mind fixed on the narrative. Directly I lay down upon a sofa there appeared before my eyes several rows of human hands, which oscillated for a moment, revolved and then changed to spoons. The same motions were repeated, the objects changing to wheels, tin soldiers, lamp-posts, brooms, and countless other absurdities. This stage lasted about ten minutes, and during that time it is safe to say that I saw at least a thousand different objects. These whirling images did not appear like the realities of life, but had the character of the secondary images seen in the eye after looking at some brightly-illuminated object. A mere suggestion from the person who was with me in the room was sufficient to call up an image of the thing suggested, while without suggestion there appeared all the common objects of life and many unreal monstrosities, which it is absolutely impossible to describe, and which seemed to be creations of the brain.

"The character of the symptoms changed rapidly. A sort of wave seemed to pass over me, and I became aware of the fact that my pulse was beating rapidly. I took out my watch, and by exercising considerable will-power managed to time the heart-beats, 135 to the minute.

"I could feel each pulsation through my whole system, and a curious twitching commenced, which no effort of the mind could stop.

"There were moments of apparent lucidity, when it seemed as if I could see within myself, and watch the pumping of my heart. A strange fear came over me, a certainty that I should never recover from the effects of the opiate, which was as quickly followed by a feeling of great interest in the experiment, a certainty that the experience was the most novel and exciting that I had ever been through.

"My mind was in an exceedingly impressionable state. Any place thought of or suggested appeared with all the distinctness of the reality. I thought of the Giant's Causeway in Staffa, and instantly I stood within the portals of Fingal's Cave. Great basaltic columns rose on all sides, while huge waves rolled through the chasm and broke in silence upon the rocky shore. Suddenly there was a roar and blast of sound, and the word 'Ishmaral' was echoing up the cave. At the enunciation of this remarkable word the great columns of basalt changed into whirling clothes pins and I laughed aloud at the absurdity.

"(I may here state that the word 'Ishmaral' seemed to haunt my other hallucinations, for I remember that I heard it frequently thereafter.) I next enjoyed a sort of metempsychosis. Any animal or thing that I thought of could be made the being which held my mind. I thought of a fox, and instantly I was transformed into that animal. I could distinctly feel myself a fox, could see my long ears and bushy tail, and by a sort of introvision felt that my complete anatomy was that of a fox. Suddenly the point of vision changed. My eyes seemed to be located at the back of my mouth; I looked out between the parted lips, saw the two rows of pointed teeth, and, closing my mouth with a snap, saw—nothing.

"I was next transformed into a bombshell, felt my size, weight, and thickness, and experienced the sensation of being shot up out of a giant mortar, looking down upon the earth, bursting and falling back in a shower of iron fragments.

"Into countless other objects was I transformed, many of them so absurd that I am unable to conceive what suggested them. For example, I was a little china doll, deep down in a bottle of olive oil, next moment a stick of twisted candy, then a skeleton inclosed in a whirling coffin, and so on *ad infinitum.*

"Towards the end of the delirium the whirling images appeared again, and I was haunted by a singular creation of the brain, which reappeared every few moments. It was an image of a double-faced doll, with a cylindrical body running down to a point like a peg-top.

"It was always the same, having a sort of crown on its head, and painted in two colors, green and brown, on a background of blue. The expression of the Janus-like profiles was always the same, as were the adornments of the body. After recovering from the effects of the drug I could not picture to myself exactly how this singular monstrosity appeared, but in subsequent experiences I was always visited by this phantom, and always recognized every detail of its composition. It was like visiting some long-forgotten spot and seeing some sight that had faded from the memory, but which appeared perfectly familiar as soon as looked upon.

"The effects of the drug lasted about an hour and a half, leaving me a trifle tipsy and dizzy; but after a ten-hour sleep I was myself again, save for a slight inability to keep my mind fixed on any piece of work for any length of time, which remained with me during most of the next day."

THE NEURAL PROCESS IN HALLUCINATION

Examples of these singular perversions of perception might be multiplied indefinitely, but I have no more space. Let us turn to the question of what the physiological process may be to which they are due. It must, of course, consist of an excitement from within of those centres which are active in normal perception, identical in kind and degree with that which real external objects are usually needed to induce. The particular process which currents from the sense-organs arouse would seem under normal circumstances to be arousable in no other way. On p. 718 ff. above, we saw that the centres aroused by incoming peripheral currents are probably identical with the centres used in mere imagination; and that the vividness of the sensational kind of consciousness is probably correlated with a discrete degree of *intensity* in the process therein aroused. Referring the reader back to that passage and to what was more lately said on p. 747 ff., I now proceed to complete my theory of the perceptive process by an analysis of what may most probably be believed to take place in hallucination strictly so called.

We have seen (p. 721) that the free discharge of cells into each other through associative paths is a likely reason why the maximum intensity of function is not reached when the cells are excited by their neighbors in the cortex. At the end of Chapter XXV we shall return to this conception, and whilst making it still more precise, use it for explaining certain phenomena connected with the will. The idea is that the leakage forwards along these paths is too rapid for the inner tension in any centre to accumulate to the maximal explosion-point, unless the exciting currents are greater than those which the various portions of the cortex supply to each other. Currents from the periphery are (as it seems) the only currents whose energy can vanquish the supra-ideational resistance (so to call it) of the cells, and cause the peculiarly intense sort of disintegration with which the sensational quality is linked. *If, however, the leakage forwards were to stop*, the tension inside certain cells might reach the explosion-point, even though the influence which excited them came only from neighboring cortical parts. Let an empty pail with a leak in its bottom, tipped up against a support so that if it ever became full of water it would upset, represent the resting condition of the centre for a certain sort of feeling. Let water poured into it stand for the currents which are its natural stimulus; then the hole in its bottom will, of course, represent the 'paths' by which it transmits its excitement to other associated cells. Now let two other vessels have the function of supplying it with water. One of these vessels stands for the neighboring cortical cells, and can pour in hardly any more water than goes out by the leak. The pail consequently never upsets in consequence of the supply from this source. A current of water passes through it and does work elsewhere, but in the pail itself nothing but what stands for *ideational* activity is aroused. The other vessel, however, stands for the peripheral sense-organs, and supplies a stream of water so copious that the pail promptly fills up in spite of the leak, and presently *upsets*; in other words, *sensational* activity is aroused. But it is obvious that if the leak were plugged, the slower stream of supply would also end by upsetting the pail.

To apply this to the brain and to thought, if we take a series of processes A B C D E, associated together in that order, and suppose that the current through them is very fluent, there will be little intensity anywhere until, perhaps, a pause occurs at E. But the moment the current is blocked anywhere, say between C and D, the process in C must grow more intense, and might even be conceived to explode so as to produce a sensation in the mind instead of an idea.

It would seem that some hallucinations are best to be explained in this way. We have in fact a regular series of facts which can all be formulated under the single law that *the substantive strength of a state of consciousness bears an inverse proportion to its suggestiveness.* It is the halting-places of our thought which are occupied with distinct imagery. Most of the words we utter have no time to awaken images at all; they simply awaken the following words. But when the sentence *stops*, an image dwells for awhile before the mental eye (see Vol. I, p. 236). Again, whenever the associative processes are reduced and impeded by the approach of unconsciousness, as in falling asleep, or growing faint, or becoming narcotized, we find a concomitant increase in the intensity of whatever partial consciousness may survive. In some people what M. Maury has called 'hypnagogic' hallucinations[44] are the regular concomitant of

44 *Le Sommeil et les rêves* (1865), chaps. III, IV.

the process of falling asleep. Trains of faces, landscapes, etc., pass before the mental eye, first as fancies, then as pseudo-hallucinations, finally as full-fledged hallucinations forming dreams. If we regard association-paths as paths of drainage, then the shutting off of one after another of them as the encroaching cerebral paralysis advances ought to act like the plugging of the hole in the bottom of the pail, and make the activity more intense in those systems of cells that retain any activity at all. The level rises because the currents are not drained away, until at last the full sensational explosion may occur.

The usual explanation of hypnagogic hallucinations is that they are ideas deprived of their ordinary *reductives*. In somnolescence, sensations being extinct, the mind, it is said, then having no stronger things to compare its ideas with, ascribes to these the fulness of reality. At ordinary times the objects of our imagination are reduced to the *status* of subjective facts by the ever-present contrast of our sensations with them. Eliminate the sensations, however, this view supposes, and the 'images' are forthwith 'projected' into the outer world and appear as realities. Thus is the illusion of dreams also explained. This, indeed, after a fashion gives an account of the facts.[45] And yet it certainly fails to explain the extraordinary vivacity and completeness of so many of our dream-fantasms. The process of 'imagining' must (in these cases at least[46]) be not merely relatively, but absolutely and in itself more intense than at other times. The fact is, it is not a process of imagining, but a genuine sensational process; and the theory in question is therefore false as far as that point is concerned.

Dr. J. Hughlings Jackson's explanation of the epileptic seizure is acknowledged to be masterly. It involves principles exactly like those which I am bringing forwards here. The 'loss of consciousness' in epilepsy is due to the most highly organized brain-processes being exhausted and thrown out of gear. The less organized (more instinctive) processes, ordinarily inhibited by the others, are then exalted, so that we get as a mere consequence of relief from the in-

[45] This theory of incomplete rectification of the inner images by their usual reductives is most brilliantly stated by M. Taine in his work, *On Intelligence*, book II, chap. I.

[46] Not, of course, in all cases, because the cells remaining active are themselves on the way to be overpowered by the general (unknown) condition to which sleep is due.

hibition, the meaningless or maniacal action which so often follows the attack.[47]

Similarly the *subsultus tendinorum* or jerking of the muscles which so often startles us when we are on the point of falling asleep, may be interpreted as due to the rise (in certain lower motor centres) of the ordinary 'tonic' tension to the explosion-point, when the inhibition commonly exerted by the higher centres falls too suddenly away.

One possible condition of hallucination then stands revealed, whatever other conditions there may be. *When the normal paths of association between a centre and other centres are thrown out of gear, any activity which may exist in the first centre tends to increase in intensity until finally the point may be reached at which the last inward resistance is overcome, and the full sensational*

[47] For a full account of Jackson's theories, see his "Croonian Lectures" published in the *British Medical Journal*, vol. I for 1884. Cf. also his remarks in the Discussion of Dr. Mercier's paper on "Inhibition" in *Brain*, XI, 361.

The loss of vivacity in the images in the process of waking, as well as the gain of it in falling asleep, are both well described by M. Taine, who writes (*On Intelligence*, I, 50, 58) that often in the daytime, when fatigued and seated in a chair, it is sufficient for him to close one eye with a handkerchief, when, "by degrees the sight of the other eye becomes vague, and it closes. All external sensations are gradually effaced, or cease, at all events, to be remarked; the internal images, on the other hand, feeble and rapid during the state of complete wakefulness, become intense, distinct, colored, steady, and lasting; there is a sort of ecstasy, accompanied by a feeling of expansion and of comfort. Warned by frequent experience, I know that sleep is coming on, and that I must not disturb the rising vision; I remain passive and, in a few minutes it is complete. Architecture, landscapes, moving figures, pass slowly by, and sometimes remain, with incomparable clearness of form and fulness of being; sleep comes on, and I know no more of the real world I am in. Many times, like M. Maury, I have caused myself to be gently roused at different moments of this state, and have thus been able to mark its characters.—The intense image which seems an external object is but a more forcible continuation of the feeble image which an instant before I recognized as internal; some scrap of a forest, some house, some person which I vaguely imagined on closing my eyes, has in a minute become present to me with full bodily details, so as to change into a complete hallucination. Then, waking up on a hand touching me, I feel the figure decay, lose color, and evaporate; what had appeared a substance is reduced to a shadow. . . . In such a case, I have often seen, for a passing moment, the image *grow pale*, waste away, and evaporate; sometimes, on opening the eyes, a fragment of landscape or the skirt of a dress appears still to float over the fire-irons or on the black hearth." This persistence of dream-objects for a few moments after the eyes are opened seems to be no extremely rare experience. Many cases of it have been reported to me directly. Compare Müller's *Physiology*, Baly's tr., p. 1394.

process explodes.[48] Thus it will happen that causes of an amount of activity in brain-cells which would ordinarily result in a weak consciousness may produce a very strong consciousness when the overflow of these cells is stopped by the torpor of the rest of the brain. A slight peripheral irritation, then, if it reaches the centres of consciousness at all during sleep, will give rise to the dream of a violent sensation. All the books about dreaming are full of anecdotes which illustrate this. For example, M. Maury's nose and lips are tickled with a feather while he sleeps. He dreams he is being tortured by having a pitch-plaster applied to his face, torn off, lacerating the skin of nose and lips. Descartes, on being bitten by a flea, dreams of being run through by a sword. A friend tells me, as I write this, of his hair changing its position in his forehead just as he 'dozed off' in his chair a few days since. Instantly he dreamed that someone had struck him a blow. Examples can be quoted *ad libitum,* but these are enough.[49]

We seem herewith to have an explanation for a certain number of hallucinations. *Whenever the normal forward irradiation of intra-cortical excitement through association-paths is checked, any accidental spontaneous activity or any peripheral stimulation (however inadequate at other times) by which a brain-centre may be visited, sets up a process of full sensational intensity therein.*

In the hallucinations artificially produced in hypnotic subjects, some degree of peripheral excitement seems usually to be required. The brain is asleep as far as its own spontaneous thinking goes, and the words of the 'magnetizer' then awaken a cortical process which drafts off into itself any currents of a related sort which may come in from the periphery, resulting in a vivid objective perception of the suggested thing. Thus, point to a dot on a sheet of paper, and call it 'General Grant's photograph,' and your subject will see a photograph of the General there instead of the dot. The dot gives

[48] I say the 'normal' paths, because hallucinations are not incompatible with *some* paths of association being left. Some hypnotic patients will not only have hallucinations of objects suggested to them, but will amplify them and act out the situation. But the paths here seem excessively narrow, and the reflections which ought to make the hallucination incredible do not occur to the subject's mind. In general, the narrower a train of 'ideas' is, the vivider the consciousness is of each. Under ordinary circumstances, the entire brain probably plays a part in draining any centre which may be ideationally active. When the drainage is reduced in any way it probably makes the active process more intense.

[49] M. A. Maury gives a number: *op. cit.,* pp. 126–32.

objectivity to the appearance, and the suggested notion of the General gives it form. Then magnify the dot by a lens; double it by a prism or by nudging the eyeball; reflect it in a mirror; turn it upside-down; or wipe it out; and the subject will tell you that the 'photograph' has been enlarged, doubled, reflected, turned about, or made to disappear. In M. Binet's language,[50] the dot is the outward *point de repère* which is needed to give objectivity to your suggestion, and without which the latter will only produce a *conception* in the subject's mind.[51] M. Binet has shown that such a peripheral *point de repère* is used in an enormous number, not only of hypnotic hallucinations, but of hallucinations of the insane. These latter are often *unilateral*; that is, the patient hears the voices always on one side of him, or sees the figure only when a certain one of his eyes is open. In many of these cases it has been distinctly proved that a morbid irritation in the internal ear, or an opacity in the humors of the eye, was the starting point of the current which the patient's diseased acoustic or optical centres clothed with their peculiar products in the way of ideas. *Hallucinations produced in this way are* 'ILLUSIONS'; *and M. Binet's theory, that all hallucinations must start in the periphery, may be called an attempt to reduce hallucination and illusion to one physiological type,* the type, namely, to which normal perception belongs. In every case, according to M. Binet, whether of perception, of hallucination, or of illusion, we get the sensational vividness by means of a current from the peripheral nerves. It may be a mere trace of a current. But that trace is enough to kindle the maximal or supra-ideational process so that the object perceived will have the character of *externality*. What the *nature* of the object shall be will de-

[50] M. Binet's highly important experiments, which were first published in Vol. XVII of the *Revue Philosophique* (1884), are also given in full in Chapter IX of his and Féré's work on *Animal Magnetism* in the International Scientific Series. Where there is no dot on the paper, nor any other visible mark, the subject's judgment about the 'portrait' would seem to be guided by what he sees happening to the entire sheet.

[51] It is a difficult thing to distinguish in a hypnotic patient between a genuine sensorial hallucination of something suggested and a conception of it merely, coupled with belief that it is there. I have been surprised at the vagueness with which such subjects will often trace upon blank paper the outlines of the pictures which they say they 'see' thereupon. On the other hand, you will hear them say that they find no difference between a real flower which you show them and an imaginary flower which you tell them is beside it. When told that one is imaginary and that they must pick out the real one, they sometimes say the choice is impossible, and sometimes they point to the imaginary flower.

pend wholly on the particular system of paths in which the process is kindled. Part of the thing in all cases comes from the sense-organ, the rest is furnished by the mind. But we cannot by introspection distinguish between these parts; and our only formula for the result is that the brain has *reacted on* the impression in the normal way. Just so in the dreams which we have considered, and in the hallucinations of which M. Binet tells, we can only say that the brain has *reacted* in an abnormal way.

M. Binet's theory accounts indeed for a multitude of cases, but certainly not for all. The prism does not always double the false appearance,[52] nor does the latter always disappear when the eyes are closed. Dr. Hack Tuke[53] gives several examples in sane people of well-exteriorized hallucinations which did not respond to Binet's tests; and Mr. Edmund Gurney[54] gives a number of reasons why intensity in a cortical process may be expected to result from local pathological activity just as much as its peculiar nature does. For Binet, an abnormally or exclusively active part of the cortex gives the *nature* of what shall appear, whilst a peripheral sense-organ alone can give the *intensity* sufficient to make it appear projected into real space. But since this intensity is after all but a matter of degree, one does not see why, under rare conditions, the degree in question *might* not be attained by inner causes exclusively. In that case we should have certain hallucinations centrally initiated alongside of the peripherally initiated hallucinations, which are the only sort that M. Binet's theory allows. *It seems probable on the whole, therefore, that centrally initiated hallucinations can exist.* How often they do exist is another question. The existence of hallucinations which affect more than one sense is an argument for central initiation. For grant that the thing seen may have its starting point in the outer world, the voice which it is heard to utter must be due to an influence from the visual region, i.e., must be of central origin.

Sporadic cases of hallucination, visiting people only once in a lifetime (which seem to be by far the most frequent type), are on any theory hard to understand in detail. They are often extraordinarily complete; and the fact that many of them are reported as

52 Only the other day, in three hypnotized girls, I failed to double an hallucination with a prism. Of course it may not have been a fully-developed hallucination.

53 *Brain*, XI, 441.

54 *Mind*, X, 161, 316; and *Phantasms of the Living* (1886), I, 470–488.

veridical, that is, as coinciding with real events, such as accidents, deaths, etc., of the persons seen, is an additional complication of the phenomenon. The first really scientific study of hallucination in all its possible bearings, on the basis of a large mass of empirical material, was begun by Mr. Edmund Gurney and is continued by other members of the Society for Psychical Research; and the Census is now being applied to several countries under the auspices of the International Congress of Experimental Psychology. It is to be hoped that out of these combined labors something solid will eventually grow. The facts shade off into the phenomena of motor automatism, trance, etc.; and nothing but a wide comparative study can give really instructive results.[55]

The part played by the peripheral sense-organ in hallucination is just as obscure as we found it in the case of imagination. The things seen often seem opaque and hide the background upon which they are projected. It does not follow from this, however, that the retina is actually involved in the vision. A contrary process going on in the visual centres would prevent the retinal impression made by the outer realities from being felt, and this would in mental terms be equivalent to the hiding of them by the imaginary figure. The negative after-images of mental pictures reported by Meyer and Féré, and the negative after-images of hypnotic hallucinations reported by Binet and others so far constitute the only evidence there is for the retina being involved. But until these after-images are explained in some other way we must admit the possibility of a centrifugal current from the optical centres downwards into the peripheral organ of sight, paradoxical as the course of such a current may appear.

'PERCEPTION-TIME'

The time which the perceptive process occupies has been inquired into by various experimenters. Some call it perception-time, some choice-time, some discrimination-time. The results have been already given in Chapter XIII (Vol. I, p. 494 ff.), to which the reader is consequently referred.

Dr. Romanes gives an interesting variation of these time-measurements. He found[56]

[55] In Mr. Gurney's work, just cited, a very large number of veridical cases are critically discussed.

[56] *Mental Evolution in Animals*, p. 136.

"an astonishing difference between different individuals with respect to the rate at which they are able to *read*. Of course reading implies enormously intricate processes of perception both of the sensuous and of the intellectual order; but if we choose for these observations persons who have been accustomed to read much, we may consider that they are all very much on a par with respect to the amount of practice which they have had, so that the differences in their rates of reading may fairly be attributed to real differences in their rates of forming complex perceptions in rapid succession, and not to any merely accidental differences arising from greater or less facility acquired by special practice.

"My experiments consisted in marking a brief printed paragraph in a book which had never been read by any of the persons to whom it was to be presented. The paragraph, which contained simple statements of simple facts, was marked on the margin with pencil. The book was then placed before the reader open, the page however being covered with a sheet of paper. Having pointed out to the reader upon this sheet of paper what part of the underlying page the marked paragraph occupied, I suddenly removed the sheet of paper with one hand, while I started a chronograph with the other. Twenty seconds being allowed for reading the paragraph (ten lines octavo), as soon as the time was up I again suddenly placed the sheet of paper over the printed page, passed the book on to the next reader, and repeated the experiment as before. Meanwhile the first reader, the moment after the book had been removed, wrote down all that he or she could remember having read. And so on with all the other readers.

"Now the results of a number of experiments conducted on this method were to show, as I have said, astonishing differences in the *maximum* rate of reading which is possible to different individuals, all of whom have been accustomed to extensive reading. That is to say, the difference may amount to 4 to 1; or, otherwise stated, in a given time one individual may be able to read four times as much as another. Moreover, it appeared that there was no relationship between slowness of reading and power of assimilation; on the contrary, when all the efforts are directed to assimilating as much as possible in a given time, the rapid readers (as shown by their written notes) usually give a better account of the portions of the paragraph which has been compassed by the slow readers than the latter are able to give; and the most rapid reader whom I have found is also the best at assimilating. I should further say that there is no relationship between rapidity of perception as thus tested and intellectual activity as tested by the general results of intellectual work; for I have tried the experiment with several highly distinguished men in science and literature, most of whom I found to be slow readers."[57]

[57] *Literature.* The best treatment of perception with which I am acquainted is that in Mr. James Sully's book on *Illusions* in the International Scientific Series. On hallucinations the literature is large. Gurney, Kandinsky (as already cited), and some articles by Kraepelin in the *Vierteljahrsschrift für wissenschaftliche Philosophie,* vol. v (1881), are the most systematic studies recently made. All works on Insanity treat of them. Dr. W. W. Ireland's works, *The Blot upon the Brain* (1886) and *Through the Ivory Gate* (1889), have much information on the subject. Gurney gives pretty complete references to older literature. The most important thing on the subject from the point of view of theory is the article by Mr. Myers on the "Dæmon of Socrates" in the *Proceedings of the Society for Psychical Research* for 1889, p. 522.

Chapter XX[*]

The Perception of Space

THE FEELING OF CRUDE EXTENSITY

In the sensations of hearing, touch, sight, and pain we are accustomed to distinguish from among the other elements the element of voluminousness. We call the reverberations of a thunderstorm more voluminous than the squeaking of a slate-pencil; the entrance into a warm bath gives our skin a more massive feeling than the prick of a pin; a little neuralgic pain, fine as a cobweb, in the face, seems less extensive than the heavy soreness of a boil or the vast discomfort of a colic or a lumbago; and a solitary star looks smaller than the noonday sky. In the sensation of dizziness or subjective motion, which recent investigation has proved to be connected with stimulation of the semi-circular canals of the ear, the spatial character is very prominent. Whether the 'muscular sense' directly yields us knowledge of space is still a matter of litigation among psychologists. Whilst some go so far as to ascribe our entire cognition of extension to its exclusive aid, others deny to it all extensive quality whatever. Under these circumstances we shall do better to adjourn its consideration; admitting, however, that it seems at first sight as if we felt something decidedly more voluminous when we contract our thigh-muscles than when we twitch an eyelid or some small muscle in the face. It seems, moreover, as if this difference lay in the feeling of the thigh-muscles themselves.

* Reprinted, with considerable revision, from *Mind* for 1887.

In the sensations of smell and taste this element of varying vastness seems less prominent but not altogether absent. Some tastes and smells appear less extensive than complex flavors, like that of roast meat or plum pudding, on the one hand, or heavy odors like musk or tuberose, on the other. The epithet *sharp* given to the acid class would seem to show that to the popular mind there is something narrow and, as it were, streaky, in the impression they make, other flavors and odors being bigger and rounder.

The sensations derived from the inward organs are also distinctly more or less voluminous. Repletion and emptiness, suffocation, palpitation, headache, are examples of this, and certainly not less spatial is the consciousness we have of our general bodily condition in nausea, fever, heavy drowsiness, and fatigue. Our entire cubic content seems then sensibly manifest to us as such, and feels much larger than any local pulsation, pressure, or discomfort. Skin and retina are, however, the organs in which the space-element plays the most active part. Not only does the maximal vastness yielded by the retina surpass that yielded by any other organ, but the intricacy with which our attention can subdivide this vastness and perceive it to be composed of lesser portions simultaneously coexisting alongside of each other is without a parallel elsewhere.[1] The ear gives a greater vastness than the skin, but is considerably less able to subdivide it.[2]

Now my first thesis is that this element, discernible in each and every sensation, though more developed in some than in others, is the original sensation of space, out of which all the exact knowledge about space that we afterwards come to have is woven by processes of discrimination, association, and selection. 'Extensity,' as Mr. James Ward calls it,[3] on this view, becomes an element in each

[1] Prof. Jastrow has found that invariably we tend to *underestimate* the amount of our skin which may be stimulated by contact with an object when we express it in terms of visual space; that is, when asked to mark on paper the extent of skin affected, we always draw it much too small. This shows that the eye gets as much space-feeling from the smaller line as the skin gets from the larger one. Cf. Jastrow: *Mind*, XI, 546–7; *American Journal of Psychology*, III, 53.

[2] Amongst sounds the graver ones seem the most extensive. Stumpf gives three reasons for this: 1) association with bigger causes; 2) wider reverberation of the hand and body when grave notes are sung; 3) audibility at a greater distance. He thinks that these three reasons dispense us from supposing an immanent extensity in the sensation of sound as such. See his remarks in the *Tonpsychologie*, I, 207–211.

[3] *Encyclopædia Britannica*, 9th Edition, article "Psychology," pp. 46, 53.

sensation just as intensity is. The latter everyone will admit to be a distinguishable though not separable ingredient of the sensible quality. In like manner extensity, being an entirely peculiar kind of feeling indescribable except in terms of itself, and inseparable in actual experience from some sensational quality which it must accompany, can itself receive no other name than that of *sensational element.*

It must now be noted that *the vastness hitherto spoken of is as great in one direction as in another.* Its dimensions are so vague that in it there is no question as yet of surface as opposed to depth; 'volume' being the best short name for the sensation in question. *Sensations of different orders are roughly comparable, inter se, with respect to their volumes.* This shows that the spatial quality in each is identical wherever found, for different qualitative elements, e.g., warmth and odor, are incommensurate. Persons born blind are reported surprised at the largeness with which objects appear to them when their sight is restored. Franz says of his patient cured of cataract: "He saw everything much larger than he had supposed from the idea obtained by his sense of touch. Moving, and especially living, objects appeared very large."[4] Loud sounds have a certain enormousness of feeling. It is impossible to conceive of the explosion of a cannon as filling a small space. In general, sounds seem to occupy all the room between us and their source; and in the case of certain ones, the cricket's song, the whistling of the wind, the roaring of the surf, or a distant railway train, to have no definite starting point.

In the sphere of vision we have facts of the same order. 'Glowing' bodies, as Hering says, give us a perception "which seems *roomy* (*raumhaft*) in comparison with that of strictly surface color. A glowing iron looks luminous through and through, and so does a flame."[5] A luminous fog, a band of sunshine, affect us in the same way. As Hering urges:

> "We must distinguish *roomy* from superficial, as well as distinctly from indistinctly bounded, sensations. The dark which with closed eyes one sees before one is, for example, a roomy sensation. We do not see a black surface like a wall in front of us, but a space filled with darkness, and even when we succeed in seeing this darkness as terminated by a black wall there still remains in front of this wall the dark space.

[4] *Philosophical Transactions* (1841), p. 66.

[5] Hermann's *Handbuch der Physiologie,* Bd. III, 1, S. 575.

The same thing happens when we find ourselves with open eyes in an absolutely dark room. This sensation of darkness is also vaguely bounded. An example of a distinctly bounded roomy sensation is that of a clear and colored fluid seen in a glass; the yellow of the wine is seen not only on the bounding surface of the glass; the yellow sensation fills the whole interior of the glass. By day the so-called empty space between us and objects seen appears very different from what it is by night. The increasing darkness settles not only upon the things but also *between* us and the things, so as at last to cover them completely and fill the space alone. If I look into a dark box I find it *filled* with darkness, and this is seen not merely as the dark-colored sides or walls of the box. A shady corner in an otherwise well-lighted room is full of a darkness which is not only *on* the walls and floor but *between* them in the space they include. Every sensation is there where I experience it, and if I have it at once at every point of a certain roomy space, it is then a voluminous sensation. A cube of transparent green glass gives us a spatial sensation; an opaque cube painted green, on the contrary, only sensations of surface."[6]

There are certain quasi-motor sensations in the head when we change the direction of the attention, which equally seem to involve three dimensions. If with closed eyes we think of the top of the house and then of the cellar, of the distance in front of us and then of that behind us, of space far to the right and then far to the left, we have something far stronger than an idea,—an actual feeling, namely, as if something in the head moved into another direction. Fechner was, I believe, the first to publish any remarks on these feelings. He writes as follows:

"When we transfer the attention from objects of one sense to those of another we have an indescribable feeling (though at the same time one perfectly determinate and reproducible at pleasure) of altered direction, or differently localized tension (*Spannung*). We feel a strain forwards in the eyes, one directed sideways in the ears, increasing with the degree of our attention, and changing according as we look at an object carefully, or listen to something attentively; wherefore we speak of *straining the attention*. The difference is most plainly felt when the attention vibrates rapidly between eye and ear. This feeling localizes itself with most decided difference in regard to the various sense-organs according as we wish to discriminate a thing delicately by touch, taste, or smell.

"But now I have, when I try to vividly recall a picture of memory or

[6] *Loc. cit.*, S. 572.

fancy, a feeling perfectly analogous to that which I experience when I seek to grasp a thing keenly by eye or ear; and this analogous feeling is very differently localized. While in sharpest possible attention to real objects (as well as to after-images) the strain is plainly forwards, and, when the attention changes from one sense to another, only alters its direction between the sense-organs, leaving the rest of the head free from strain, the case is different in memory or fancy; for here the feeling withdraws entirely from the external sense-organs, and seems rather to take refuge in that part of the head which the brain fills. If I wish, for example, to recall a place or person, it will arise before me with vividness, not according as I strain my attention forwards, but rather in proportion as I, so to speak, retract it backwards."[7]

It appears probable that the feelings which Fechner describes are in part constituted by imaginary semi-circular canal sensations.[8] These undoubtedly convey the most delicate perception of change in direction; and when, as here, the changes are not perceived as taking place in the external world, they occupy a vague internal space located within the head.[9]

In the skin itself there is a vague form of projection into the third dimension to which Hering has called attention.

"Heat is not felt only against the cutaneous surface, but when communicated through the air may appear extending more or less out from

[7] *Elemente der Psychophysik*, II, 475–6.

[8] See Foster's *Text Book of Physiology*, bk. III, c. VI, § 2.

[9] Fechner, who was ignorant of the but lately discovered function of the semicircular canals, gives a different explanation of the organic seat of these feelings. They are probably highly composite. With me, actual movements in the eyes play a considerable part in them, though I am hardly conscious of the peculiar feelings in the scalp which Fechner goes on to describe thus: "The feeling of strained attention in the different sense-organs seems to be only a muscular one produced in using these various organs by setting in motion, by a sort of reflex action, the set of muscles which belong to them. One can ask, then, with what particular muscular contraction the sense of strained attention in the effort to recall something is associated? On this question my own feeling gives me a decided answer; it comes to me distinctly not as a sensation of tension in the inside of the head, but as a feeling of strain and contraction in the scalp, with a pressure from outwards in over the whole cranium, undoubtedly caused by a contraction of the muscles of the scalp. This harmonizes very well with the expressions, *sich den Kopf zerbrechen, den Kopf zusammennehmen*. In a former illness, when I could not endure the slightest effort after continuous thought, and had no theoretical bias on this question, the muscles of the scalp, especially those of the back-head, assumed a fairly morbid degree of sensibility whenever I tried to think." (*Elemente der Psychophysik*, II, 490–91.)

the surface into the third dimension of surrounding space. . . . We can determine in the dark the place of a radiant body by moving the hand to and fro, and attending to the fluctuation of our feeling of warmth. The feeling itself, however, is not projected fully into the spot at which we localize the hot body, but always remains in the neighborhood of the hand."

The interior of one's mouth-cavity feels larger when explored by the tongue than when looked at. The crater of a newly-extracted tooth, and the movements of a loose tooth in its socket, feel quite monstrous. A midge buzzing against the drum of the ear will often seem as big as a butterfly. The spatial sensibility of the tympanic membrane has hitherto been very little studied, though the subject will well repay much trouble. If we approach it by introducing into the outer ear some small object like the tip of a rolled-up tissue-paper lamplighter, we are surprised at the large radiating sensation which its presence gives us, and at the sense of clearness and openness which comes when it is removed. It is immaterial to inquire whether the far-reaching sensation here be due to actual irradiation upon distant nerves or not. We are considering now, not the objective causes of the spatial feeling, but its subjective varieties, and the experiment shows that the same object gives more of it to the inner than to the outer cuticle of the ear. The pressure of the air in the tympanic cavity upon the membrane gives an astonishingly large sensation. We can increase the pressure by holding our nostrils and closing our mouth and forcing air through our Eustachian tubes by an expiratory effort; and we can diminish it by either inspiring or swallowing under the same conditions of closed mouth and nose. In either case we get a large round tridimensional sensation inside of the head, which seems as if it must come from the affection of an organ much larger than the tympanic membrane, whose surface hardly exceeds that of one's little-finger-nail.

The tympanic membrane is furthermore able to render sensible differences in the pressure of the external atmosphere, too slight to be felt either as noise or in this more violent way. If the reader will sit with closed eyes and let a friend approximate some solid object, like a large book, noiselessly to his face, he will immediately become aware of the object's presence and position—likewise of its departure. A friend of the writer, making the experiment for the first time, discriminated unhesitatingly between the three degrees of solidity of a board, a lattice-frame, and a sieve, held close to his ear. Now as this sensation is never used by ordinary persons as a means of perception, we may fairly assume that its felt quality, in those whose attention is called to it for the first time, belongs to it *quâ* sensation, and owes nothing to educational suggestions. But this felt quality is most distinctly and unmistakably one of vague spatial vastness in three dimensions—quite as much so as is the felt quality of the retinal sensation when we lie on our back and fill the entire field of vision with the empty blue sky. When an object is brought near the ear we immediately feel shut in, contracted; when the object is removed, we suddenly feel as if a transparency, clearness, openness, had been made outside of us. And the feeling will, by anyone who will take the pains to observe it, be acknowledged to involve the third dimension in a vague, unmeasured state.[10]

The reader will have noticed, in this enumeration of facts, that *voluminousness of the feeling seems to bear very little relation to the size of the organ that yields it.* The ear and eye are comparatively minute organs, yet they give us feelings of great volume. The same lack of exact proportion between size of feeling and size of organ affected obtains within the limits of particular sensory organs. An object appears smaller on the lateral portions of the retina than it does on the fovea, as may be easily verified by holding the two forefingers parallel and a couple of inches apart, and transferring the gaze of one eye from one to the other. Then the finger not directly looked at will appear to shrink, and this whatever be the direction of the fingers. On the tongue a crumb, or the calibre of a small tube, appears larger than between the fingers. If two points kept equidistant (blunted compass- or scissors-points, for example) be drawn across the skin so as really to describe a pair of parallel lines, the lines will appear farther apart in some spots than in others. If, for example, we draw them horizontally across the face, so that the mouth falls between them, the person experimented upon will feel as if they began to diverge near the mouth and to include it in a well-marked ellipse. In like manner, if we

[10] That the sensation in question is one of tactile rather than of acoustic sensibility would seem proved by the fact that a medical friend of the writer, both of whose *membranæ tympani* are quite normal, but one of whose ears is almost totally deaf, feels the presence and withdrawal of objects as well at one ear as at the other.

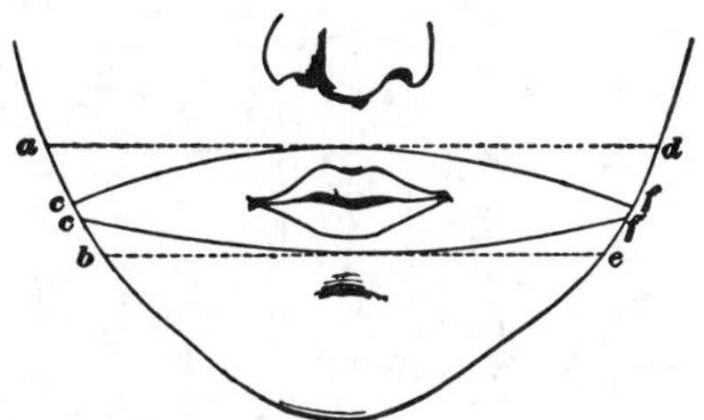

FIG. 51 (after Weber).

keep the compass-points one or two centimetres apart, and draw them down the fore-arm over the wrist and palm, finally drawing one along one finger, the other along its neighbor, the appearance will be that of a single line, soon breaking into two, which become more widely separated below the wrist, to contract again in the palm, and finally diverge rapidly again towards the finger-tips. The dotted lines in Figs. 51 and 52 represent the true path of the compass-points; the full lines their apparent path.

The same length of skin, moreover, will convey a more extensive sensation according to the manner of stimulation. If the edge of a card be pressed against the skin, the distance between its extremities will seem shorter than that between two compass-tips touching the same terminal points.[11]

In the eye, intensity of nerve-stimulation seems to increase the *volume* of the feeling as well as its brilliancy. If we raise and lower the gas alternately, the whole room and all the objects in it seem alternately to enlarge and contract. If we cover half a page of small print with a gray glass, the print seen through the glass appears decidedly smaller than that seen outside of it, and the darker the glass the greater the difference. When a circumscribed opacity in front of the retina keeps off part of the light from the portion which it covers, objects projected on that portion may seem but half as

[11] The skin seems to obey a different law from the eye here. If a given retinal tract be excited, first by a series of points, and next by the two extreme points, with the interval between them unexcited, this interval will seem considerably less in the second case than it seemed in the first. In the skin the unexcited interval feels the larger. The reader may easily verify the facts in this case by taking a visiting-card, cutting one edge of it into a saw-tooth pattern, and from the opposite edge cutting out all but the two corners, and then comparing the feelings aroused by the two edges when held against the skin.

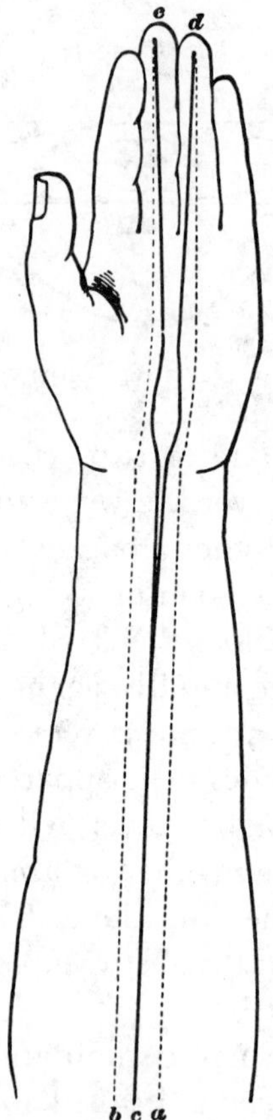

Fig. 52 (after Weber).

large as when their image falls outside of it.[12] The inverse effect seems produced by certain drugs and anæsthetics. Morphine, atropine, daturine, and cold blunt the sensibility of the skin, so that distances upon it seem less. Hasheesh produces strange perversions of the general sensibility. Under its influence one's body may seem either enormously enlarged or strangely contracted. Sometimes a single member will alter its proportion to the rest; or one's back, for instance, will appear entirely absent, as if one were hollow behind. Objects comparatively near will recede to a vast distance, a short street assume to the eye an immeasurable perspective. Ether

[12] Classen: *Physiologie des Gesichtssinnes*, p. 114; see also A. Riehl: *Der philosophische Kriticismus*, vol. II, pt. 1, p. 149.

and chloroform occasionally produce not wholly dissimilar results. Panum, the German physiologist, relates that when, as a boy, he was etherized for neuralgia, the objects in the room grew extremely small and distant, before his field of vision darkened over and the roaring in his ears began. He also mentions that a friend of his in church, struggling in vain to keep awake, saw the preacher grow smaller and smaller and more and more distant. I myself on one occasion observed the same recession of objects during the beginning of chloroformization. In various cerebral diseases we find analogous disturbances.

Can we assign the physiological conditions which make the elementary sensible largeness of one sensation vary so much from that of another? Only imperfectly. One factor in the result undoubtedly is the number of nerve-terminations simultaneously excited by the outward agent that awakens the sensation. When many skin-nerves are warmed, or much retinal surface illuminated, our feeling is larger than when a lesser nervous surface is excited. The single sensation yielded by two compass-points, although it seems simple, is yet felt to be much bigger and blunter than that yielded by one. The touch of a single point may always be recognized by its quality of sharpness. This page looks much smaller to the reader if he closes one eye than if both eyes are open. So does the moon, which latter fact shows that the phenomenon has nothing to do with parallax. The celebrated boy couched for the cataract by Cheselden thought, after his first eye was operated, "the Things he saw, he thought extreamly large," but being couched of his second eye, said "that Objects at first appear'd large to this Eye, but not so large as they did at first to the other; and looking upon the same Object with both Eyes, he thought it look'd about twice as large as with the first couch'd Eye only, but not Double, that we can any Ways discover."

The greater extensiveness that the feeling of certain parts of the same surface has over other parts, and that one order of surface has over another (retina over skin, for example), may also to a certain extent be explained by the operation of the same factor. It is an anatomical fact that the most spatially sensitive surfaces (retina, tongue, finger-tips, etc.) are supplied by nerve-trunks of unusual thickness, which must supply to every unit of surface-area an unusually large number of terminal fibres. But the variations of felt extension obey probably only a very rough law of numerical proportion to the number of fibres. A sound is not twice as voluminous to two ears as to one; and the above-cited variations of feeling, when the same surface is excited under different conditions, show that the feeling is a resultant of several factors of which the anatomical one is only the principal. Many ingenious hypotheses have been brought forwards to assign the co-operating factors where different conditions give conflicting amounts of felt space. Later we shall analyze some of these cases in detail, but it must be confessed here in advance that many of them resist analysis altogether.[13]

THE PERCEPTION OF SPATIAL ORDER

So far, all we have established or sought to establish is the existence of the vague form or *quale* of spatiality as an inseparable element bound up with the other peculiarities of each and every one

[13] It is worth while at this point to call attention with some emphasis to the fact that, though the anatomical condition of the feeling *resembles* the feeling itself, such resemblance cannot be taken by our understanding to explain *why* the feeling should be just what it is. We hear it untiringly reiterated by materialists and spiritualists alike that we can see no possible inward reason why a certain brain-process should produce the feeling of redness and another of anger: the one process is no more red than the other is angry, and the coupling of process and feeling is, as far as our understanding goes, a juxtaposition pure and simple. But in the matter of *spatial* feeling, where the retinal patch that produces a triangle in the mind is itself a triangle, etc., it looks at first sight as if the sensation might be a direct cognition of its own neural condition. Were this true, however, our sensation should be one of *multitude* rather than of continuous extent; for the condition is *number* of optical nerve-termini, and even this is only a remote condition and not an immediate condition. The immediate condition of the feeling is not the process in the retina, but the process in the brain; and the process in the brain may, for aught we know, be as unlike a triangle,—nay, it probably is so,—as it is unlike redness or rage. It is simply a *coincidence* that in the case of space one of the organic conditions, viz., the triangle impressed on the skin or the retina, should lead to a representation in the mind of the subject observed similar to that which it produces in the psychological observer. In no other kind of case is the coincidence found. Even should we admit that we cognize triangles in space because of our immediate cognition of the triangular shape of our excited group of nerve-tips, the matter would hardly be more transparent, for the mystery would still remain, why are we so much better cognizant of triangles on our finger-tips than on the nerve-tips of our back, on our eye than on our ear, and on any of these parts than in our brain? Thomas Brown very rightly rejects the notion of explaining the shape of the space perceived by the shape of the 'nervous expansion affected.' "If this alone were necessary, we should have square inches, and half inches, and various other forms, rectilinear or curvilinear, of fragrance and sound." (*Lectures*, XXII.)

of our sensations. The numerous examples we have adduced of the variations of this extensive element have only been meant to make clear its strictly sensational character. In very few of them will the reader have been able to explain the variation by an added intellectual element, such as the suggestion of a recollected experience. In almost all it has seemed to be the immediate psychic effect of a peculiar sort of nerve-process excited; and all the nerve-processes in question agree in yielding what space they do yield, to the mind, in the shape of a simple total vastness, in which, *primitively* at least, no *order of parts* or of *subdivisions* reigns.

Let no one be surprised at this notion of a space without order. There may be a space without order just as there may be an order without space.[14] And the primitive perceptions of space are certainly of an unordered kind. The order which the spaces first perceived potentially include must, before being distinctly apprehended by the mind, be woven into those spaces by a rather complicated set of intellectual acts. The primordial largenesses which the sensations yield must be *measured and subdivided* by consciousness, and *added* together, before they can form by their synthesis what we know as the real Space of the objective world. In these operations, imagination, association, attention, and selection play a decisive part; and although they nowhere add any new material to the space-data of sense, they so shuffle and manipulate these data and hide present ones behind imagined ones that it is no wonder if some authors have gone so far as to think that the sense-data have no spatial worth at all, and that the intellect, since it makes the subdivisions, also gives the spatial quality to them out of resources of its own.

As for ourselves, having found that all our sensations (however as yet unconnected and undiscriminated) are of extensive objects, *our next problem is: How do we* ARRANGE *these at first chaotically given spaces into the one regular and orderly 'world of space' which we now know?*

14 Musical tones, e.g., have an order of quality independent either of their space- or time-order. Music comes from the time-order of the notes upsetting their quality-order. In general, if *a b c d e f g h i j k*, etc., stand for an arrangement of feelings in the order of their quality, they may assume *any* space-order or time-order, as *d e f a h g*, etc., and still the order of quality will remain fixed and unchanged.

To begin with, there is no reason to suppose that the several sense-spaces of which a sentient creature may become conscious, each filled with its own peculiar content, should tend, simply *because they are many*, to enter into any definite spatial intercourse with each other, or lie in any particular order of positions. Even in ourselves we can recognize this. Different feelings may coexist in us without assuming any particular spatial order. The sound of the brook near which I write, the odor of the cedars, the comfort with which my breakfast has filled me, and my interest in this paragraph, all lie distinct in my consciousness, but in no sense outside or alongside of each other. Their spaces are interfused and at most fill the same vaguely objective world. Even where the qualities are far less disparate, we may have something similar. If we take our subjective and corporeal sensations alone, there are moments when, as we lie or sit motionless, we find it very difficult to feel distinctly the length of our back or the direction of our feet from our shoulders. By a strong effort we can succeed in dispersing our attention impartially over our whole person, and then we feel the real shape of our body in a sort of unitary way. But in general a few parts are strongly emphasized to consciousness and the rest sink out of notice; and it is then remarkable how vague and ambiguous our perception of their relative order of location is. Obviously, for the orderly arrangement of a multitude of sense-spaces in consciousness, something more than their mere separate existence is required. What is this further condition?

If a number of sensible extents are to be perceived alongside of each other and in definite order they must appear as parts in a vaster sensible extent which can enter the mind simply and all at once. I think it will be seen that the difficulty of estimating correctly the form of one's body by pure feeling arises from the fact that it is very hard to feel its totality as a unit at all. The trouble is similar to that of thinking forwards and backwards simultaneously. When conscious of our head we tend to grow unconscious of our feet, and there enters thus an element of time-succession into our perception of ourselves which transforms the latter from an act of intuition to one of construction. This element of constructiveness is present in a still higher degree, and carries with it the same consequences, when we deal with objective spaces too great to be grasped by a single look. The relative positions of the shops in a town, separated by many tortuous streets, have to be thus constructed from data apprehended in succession, and the result is a greater or less degree of vagueness.

That a sensation *be discriminated as a part* from out of a larger enveloping space is then the *conditio sine quâ non* of its being apprehended in a definite spatial order. The problem of ordering our feelings in space is then, in the first instance, a problem of discrimination, but not of discrimination pure and simple; for then not only coexistent sights but coexistent sounds would necessarily assume such order, which they notoriously do not. Whatever is discriminated will appear as a small space within a larger space, it is true, but this is but the very rudiment of order. For the location of it within that space to become precise, other conditions still must supervene; and the best way to study what they are will be to pause for a little and *analyze what the expression 'spatial order' means.*

Spatial order is an abstract term. The concrete perceptions which it covers are figures, directions, positions, magnitudes, and distances. To single out any one of these things from a total vastness is partially to introduce order into the vastness. To subdivide the vastness into a multitude of these things is to apprehend it in a completely orderly way. Now what are these things severally? To begin with, no one can for an instant hesitate to say that some of them are qualities of sensation, just as the total vastness is in which they lie. Take figure: a square, a circle, and a triangle appear in the first instance to the eye simply as three different kinds of impressions, each so peculiar that we should recognize it if it were to return. When Nunneley's patient had his cataracts removed, and a cube and a sphere were presented to his notice, he could at once perceive a difference in their shapes; and though he could not say which was the cube and which the sphere, he saw they were not of the same figure. So of lines: if we can notice lines at all in our field of vision, it is inconceivable that a vertical one should not affect us differently from an horizontal one, and should not be recognized as affecting us similarly when presented again, although we might not yet know the name 'vertical,' or any of its connotations, beyond this peculiar affection of our sensibility. So of angles: an obtuse one affects our feeling immediately in a different way from an acute one. Distance-apart, too, is a simple sensation—the sensation of a line joining the two distant points: lengthen the line, you alter the feeling and with it the distance felt.

Space-relations

But with distance and direction we pass to the category of space-*relations*, and are immediately confronted by an opinion which makes of all relations something *toto cœlo* different from all facts of feeling or imagination whatsoever. A relation, for the Platonizing school in psychology, is an energy of pure thought, and, as such, is quite incommensurable with the data of sensibility between which it may be perceived to obtain.

We may consequently imagine a disciple of this school to say to us at this point: "Suppose you *have* made a separate specific sensation of each line and each angle, what boots it? You have still the order of directions and of distances to account for; you have still the relative magnitudes of all these felt figures to state; you have their respective positions to define before you can be said to have brought order into your space. And not one of these determinations can be effected except through an act of relating thought, so that your attempt to give an account of space in terms of pure sensibility breaks down almost at the very outset. *Position*, for example, can never be a sensation, for it has nothing intrinsic about it; it can only obtain *between* a spot, line, or other figure and *extraneous co-ordinates*, and can never be an element of the sensible datum, the line or the spot, in itself. Let us then confess that Thought alone can unlock the riddle of space, and that Thought is an adorable but unfathomable mystery."

Such a method of dealing with the problem has the merit of shortness. Let us, however, be in no such hurry, but see whether we cannot get a little deeper by patiently considering what these space-relations are.

'Relation' is a very slippery word. It has so many different concrete meanings that the use of it as an abstract universal may easily introduce bewilderment into our thought. We must therefore be careful to avoid ambiguity by making sure, wherever we have to employ it, what its precise meaning is in that particular sphere of application. At present we have to do with space-relations, and no others. Most 'relations' are feelings of an entirely different order from the terms they relate. The relation of similarity, e.g., may equally obtain between jasmine and tuberose, or between Mr. Browning's verses and Mr. Story's; it is itself neither odorous nor poetical, and those may well be pardoned who have denied to it all sensational content whatever. But just as, in the field of quantity, the relation between two numbers is another number, so *in the field of space the relations are facts of the same order with the facts they relate. If these latter be patches in the circle of vision, the former are certain other patches between them.* When we speak of the relation of direction of two points towards each other, we mean simply the sensation of the line that joins the two points together. *The line is the relation*; feel it and you feel the relation, see it and you see the relation; nor can you in any conceivable way think the latter except by imagining the former (however vaguely), or describe or indicate the one except by pointing to the other. And the moment you have imagined the line, the relation stands before you in all its completeness, with nothing further to be done. Just so the relation of *direction* between two lines is identical with the peculiar sensation of shape of the space enclosed between them. This is commonly called an angular relation.

If these relations are sensations, no less so are the relations of position. *The relation of position between the top and bottom points of a vertical line is that line*, and nothing else. The relations of position between a point and a horizontal line below it are potentially numerous. There is one more important than the rest, called its distance. This is the sensation, ideal or actual, of a perpendicular drawn from the point to the line.[15] Two lines, one from each extremity of the horizontal to the point, give us a peculiar sensation of triangularity. This feeling may be said to constitute the *locus* of all the relations of position of the elements in question. *Rightness and leftness, upness and downness, are again pure sensations* differing specifically from each other, and generically from everything else. Like all sensations, they can only be indicated, not described. If we take a cube and label one side *top*, another *bottom*, a third *front*, and a fourth *back*, there remains no form of words by which we can describe to another person which of the remaining sides is *right* and which *left*. We can only point

15 The whole science of geometry may be said to owe its being to the exorbitant interest which the human mind takes in *lines*. We cut space up in every direction in order to manufacture them.

and say *here* is right and *there* is left, just as we should say *this* is red and *that* blue. Of two points seen beside each other at all, one is always affected by one of these feelings, and the other by the opposite; the same is true of the extremities of any line.[16]

Thus it appears indubitable that all space-relations except those of magnitude are nothing more or less than pure sensational objects. But *magnitude* appears to outstep this narrow sphere. We have relations of muchness and littleness between times, numbers, intensities, and qualities, as well as spaces. It is impossible, then, that such relations should form a particular kind of simply spatial feeling. This we must admit: the relation of quantity is generic and occurs in many categories of consciousness, whilst the other relations we have considered are specific and occur in space alone. When our attention passes from a shorter line to a longer, from a smaller spot to a larger, from a feebler light to a stronger, from a paler blue to a richer, from a march tune to a galop, the transition is accompanied in the synthetic field of consciousness by a peculiar feeling of difference which is what we call the sensation of *more,*—more length, more expanse, more light, more blue, more motion. This transitional sensation of *more* must be identical with itself under all these different accompaniments, or we should not give it the same name in every case. We get it when we pass from a short vertical line to a long horizontal one, from a small square to a large circle, as well as when we pass between those figures whose shapes are congruous. But when the shapes are congruous our consciousness of the relation is a good deal more distinct, and it is most distinct of all when, in the exercise of our analytic attention, we notice, first, a *part,* and then the *whole,* of a *single* line or shape.

[16] Kant was, I believe, the first to call attention to this last order of facts. After pointing out that two opposite spherical triangles, two gloves of a pair, two spirals wound in contrary directions, have identical inward determinations, that is, have their parts defined with relation *to each other* by the same law, and so must be *conceived* as identical, he showed that the impossibility of their mutual superposition obliges us to assign to each figure of a symmetrical pair a peculiar difference of its own which can only consist in an *outward* determination or relation of its parts, no longer to each other, but to the whole of an objectively outlying space with its points of the compass given absolutely. This in*con*ceivable difference is perceived only "through the relation to right and left, which is a matter of immediate intuition." In these last words (*welches unmittelbar auf Anschauung geht —Prolegomena,* § 13) Kant expresses all that we have meant by speaking of up and down, right and left, as *sensations.* He is wrong, however, in invoking relation to extrinsic total space as essential to the existence of these contrasts in figures. Relation to our own body is enough.

Then the *more* of the whole actually sticks out, as a separate piece of space, and is so envisaged. The same exact sensation of it is given when we are able to superpose one line or figure on another. This indispensable condition of exact measurement of the *more* has led some to think that the feeling itself arose in every case from original experiences of superposition. This is probably not an absolutely true opinion, but for our present purpose that is immaterial. So far as the subdivisions of a sense-space are to be *measured* exactly against each other, objective forms occupying one subdivision must directly or indirectly be superposed upon the other, and the mind must get the immediate feeling of an outstanding *plus*. And even where we only feel one subdivision to be vaguely larger or less, the mind must pass rapidly between it and the other subdivision, and receive the immediate sensible shock of the *more*.

*We seem thus to have accounted for all space-relations, and made them clear to our understanding. They are nothing but sensations of particular lines, particular angles, particular forms of transition, or (*in the case of a *distinct more) of particular outstanding portions of space after two figures have been superposed.* These relation-sensations may actually be produced as such, as when a geometer draws new lines across a figure with his pencil to demonstrate the relations of its parts, or they may be ideal representations of lines, not really drawn. But in either case their entrance into the mind is equivalent to a more detailed subdivision, cognizance, and measurement of the space considered. *The bringing of subdivisions to consciousness constitutes, then, the entire process by which we pass from our first vague feeling of a total vastness to a cognition of the vastness in detail.* The more numerous the subdivisions are, the more elaborate and perfect the cognition becomes. But inasmuch as all the subdivisions are themselves sensations, and even the feeling of 'more' or 'less' is, where not itself a figure, at least a sensation of transition between two sensations of figure, it follows, for aught we can as yet see to the contrary, that *all spatial knowledge is sensational at bottom*, and that, as the sensations lie together in the unity of consciousness, no new material element whatever comes to them from a supra-sensible source.[17]

[17] In the eyes of many it will have seemed strange to call a relation a mere line, and a line a mere sensation. We may easily learn a great deal *about* any relation,

The bringing of subdivisions to consciousness! This, then, is our next topic. They may be brought to consciousness under three aspects in respect of their *locality*, in respect of their *size*, in respect of their *shape*.

The Meaning of Localization

Confining ourselves to the problem of locality for the present, let us begin with the simple case of a sensitive surface, only two points of which receive stimulation from without. How, first, are these two points felt as alongside of each other with an interval of space between them? We must be conscious of two things for this: of the duality of the excited points, and of the extensiveness of the unexcited interval. The duality alone, although a necessary, is not a sufficient condition of the spatial separation. We may, for instance, discern two sounds in the same place, sweet and sour in the same lemonade, warm and cold, round and pointed contact in the same place on the skin, etc.[18] In all discrimination the recognition of the duality of two feelings by the mind is the easier the more strongly the feelings are contrasted in quality. If our two excited points awaken identical qualities of sensation, they must, perforce, appear to the mind as one; and, not distinguished at all, they are, *a fortiori*, not localized apart. Spots four centimetres dis-

---

say that between two points: we may divide the line which joins these, and distinguish it, and classify it, and find out *its* relations by drawing or representing new lines, and so on. But all this further industry has naught to do with our *acquaintance* with the relation itself, in its first intention. So cognized, the relation *is* the line and nothing more. It would indeed be fair to call it something less; and in fact it is easy to understand how most of us come to feel as if the line were a much grosser thing than the relation. The line is broad or narrow, blue or red, made by this object or by that alternately, in the course of our experience; it is therefore independent of any one of these accidents; and so, from viewing it as no one of *such* sensible qualities, we may end by thinking of it as something which cannot be defined except as the negation of all sensible quality whatever, and which needs to be put *into* the sensations by a mysterious act of 'relating thought.'

Another reason why we get to feel as if a space-relation must be something other than the mere feeling of a line or angle is that between two positions we can potentially make any number of lines and angles, or find, to suit our purposes, endlessly numerous relations. The sense of this indefinite potentiality cleaves to our words when we speak in a general way of 'relations of place,' and misleads us into supposing that not even any single one of them can be exhaustively equated by a single angle or a single line.

18 This often happens when the warm and cold points, or the round and pointed ones, are applied to the skin within the limits of a single 'Empfindungskreis.'

tant on the back have no qualitative contrast at all, and fuse into a single sensation. Points less than three thousandths of a millimetre apart awaken on the retina sensations so contrasted that we apprehend them immediately as two. Now these unlikenesses which arise so slowly when we pass from one point to another in the back, so much faster on the tongue and finger-tips, but with such inconceivable rapidity on the retina, what are they? Can we discover anything about their intrinsic nature?

The most natural and immediate answer to make is that they are unlikeness of *place* pure and simple. In the words of a German physiologist,[19] to whom psychophysics owes much:

> "The sensations are from the outset (*von vornherein*) localized. . . . Every sensation as such is from the very beginning affected with the spatial quality, so that this quality is nothing like an external attribute coming to the sensation from a higher faculty, but must be regarded as something immanently residing in the sensation itself."

And yet the moment we reflect on this answer an insuperable logical difficulty seems to present itself. No single *quale* of sensation can, by itself, amount to a consciousness of *position*. Suppose no feeling but that of a single point ever to be awakened. Could that possibly be the feeling of any special *whereness* or *thereness*? Certainly not. *Only when a second point is felt to arise can the first one acquire a determination of up, down, right or left, and these determinations are all relative to that second point*. Each point, so far as it is *placed, is* then only by virtue of what it *is not*, namely, by virtue of another point. This is as much as to say that position has nothing *intrinsic* about it; and that, although a feeling of absolute bigness may, *a feeling of place cannot, possibly form an immanent element in any single isolated sensation*. The very writer we have quoted has given heed to this objection, for he continues (p. 335) by saying that the sensations thus originally localized "are only so *in themselves*, but not in the representation of consciousness, which is not yet present. . . . They are, in the first instance, devoid of all mutual relations with each other." But such a localization of the sensation 'in itself' would seem to mean nothing more than the susceptibility or *potentiality* of being distinctly localized when the time came and other conditions became fulfilled. Can we now dis-

19 Vierordt: *Grundriss der Physiologie des Menschen*, 5te Auflage (1877), pp. 326, 436.

cover anything about such susceptibility in itself before it has borne its ulterior fruits in the developed consciousness?

'Local Signs'

To begin with, every sensation of the skin and every visceral sensation seems to derive from its topographic seat a peculiar shade of feeling, which it would not have in another place. And this feeling *per se* seems quite another thing from the perception of the place. Says Wundt:[20]

"If with the finger we touch first the cheek and then the palm, exerting each time precisely the same pressure, the sensation shows notwithstanding a distinctly marked difference in the two cases. Similarly, when we compare the palm with the back of the hand, the nape of the neck with its anterior surface, the breast with the back; in short, any two distant parts of the skin with each other. And moreover, we easily remark, by attentively observing, that spots even tolerably close together differ in respect of the quality of their feeling. If we pass from one point of our cutaneous surface to another, we find a perfectly gradual and continuous alteration in our feeling, notwithstanding the objective nature of the contact has remained the same. Even the sensations of corresponding points on opposite sides of the body, though similar, are not identical. If, for instance, we touch first the back of one hand and then of the other, we remark a qualitative unlikeness of sensation. It must not be thought that such differences are mere matters of imagination, and that we take the sensations to be different because we represent each of them to ourselves as occupying a different place. With sufficient sharpening of the attention, we may, confining ourselves to the quality of the feelings alone, entirely abstract from their locality, and yet notice the differences quite as markedly."

Whether these local contrasts shade into each other with absolutely continuous gradations, we cannot say. But we know (continues Wundt) that

"they change, when we pass from one point of the skin to its neighbor, with very different degrees of rapidity. On delicately-feeling parts, used principally for touching, such as the finger-tips, the difference of sensa-

20 *Vorlesungen über die Menschen- und Thierseele* (Leipzig, 1863), I, 214. See also Ladd's *Physiological Psychology*, pp. 396–8, and compare the account by G. Stanley Hall (*Mind*, x, 571) of the sensations produced by moving a blunt point lightly over the skin. Points of cutting pain, quivering, thrilling, whirling, tickling, scratching, and acceleration, alternated with each other along the surface.

tion between two closely approximate points is already strongly pronounced; whilst in parts of lesser delicacy, as the arm, the back, the legs, the disparities of sensation are observable only between distant spots."

The internal organs, too, have their specific *qualia* of sensation. An inflammation of the kidney is different from one of the liver; pains in joints and muscular insertions are distinguished. Pain in the dental nerves is wholly unlike the pain of a burn. But very important and curious similarities prevail throughout these differences. Internal pains, whose seat we cannot see, and have no means of knowing unless the character of the pain itself reveal it, are felt *where* they belong. Diseases of the stomach, kidney, liver, rectum, prostate, etc., of the bones, of the brain and its membranes, are referred to their proper position. Nerve-pains describe the length of the nerve. Such localizations as those of vertical, frontal, or occipital headache of intracranial origin force us to conclude that parts which are neighbors, whether inner or outer, may possess by mere virtue of that fact a common peculiarity of feeling, a respect in which their sensations agree, and which serves as a token of their proximity. These *local* colorings are, moreover, so strong that we cognize them as the same, throughout all contrasts of sensible quality in the accompanying perception. Cold and heat are wide as the poles asunder; yet if both fall on the cheek, there mixes with them something that makes them in *that respect* identical; just as, contrariwise, despite the identity of cold with itself wherever found, when we get it first on the palm and then on the cheek, some difference comes, which keeps the two experiences for ever asunder.[21]

[21] Of the anatomical and physiological conditions of these facts we know as yet but little, and that little need not here be discussed. Two principal hypotheses have been invoked in the case of the retina. Wundt (*Menschen- und Thierseele*, I, 214) called attention to the changes of color-sensibility which the retina displays as the image of the colored object passes from the fovea to the periphery. The color alters and becomes darker, and the change is more rapid in certain directions than in others. This alteration in general, however, is one of which, *as such*, we are wholly unconscious. We see the sky as bright blue all over, the modifications of the blue sensation being interpreted by us, not as differences in the objective color, but as distinctions in its locality. Lotze (*Medicinische Psychologie*, 333, 355), on the other hand, has pointed out the peculiar tendency which each particular point of the retina has to call forth that movement of the eyeball which will carry the image of the exciting object from the point in question to the *fovea*. With each separate tendency to movement (as with each actual movement) we may suppose a peculiar modification of sensibility to be conjoined. This modification would constitute the

And now let us revert to the query propounded a moment since: *Can these differences of mere quality in feeling, varying according to locality yet having each sensibly and intrinsically and by itself nothing to do with position, constitute the 'susceptibilities' we mentioned, the conditions of being perceived in position, of the localities to which they belong?* The numbers on a row of houses, the initial letters of a set of words, have no intrinsic kinship with points of space, and yet they are the conditions of our knowledge of where any house is in the row, or any word in the dictionary. Can the modifications of feeling in question be tags or labels of this kind which in no wise originally reveal the position of the spot to which they are attached, but guide us to it by what Berkeley would call a 'customary tie'? Many authors have unhesitatingly replied in the affirmative; Lotze, who in his *Medicinische Psychologie*[22] first described the sensations in this way, designating them, thus conceived, as *local signs.* This term has obtained wide currency in Germany, and *in speaking of the* 'LOCAL-SIGN THEORY' *hereafter, I shall always mean the theory which denies that there can be in a sensation any element of actual locality, of inherent spatial order,* any tone as it were which cries to us immediately and without further ado, 'I am *here,*' or 'I am *there.*'

If, as may well be the case, we by this time find ourselves tempted to accept the Local-sign theory in a general way, we have to clear up several farther matters. If a sign is to lead us to *the thing* it means, we must have some other source of knowledge of that thing. Either the thing has been given in a previous experience of which the sign also formed part—they are *associated*; or it is what Reid calls a 'natural' sign, that is, a feeling which, the first time it enters the mind, evokes from the native powers thereof a cognition of the thing that hitherto had lain dormant. In both cases, however, the sign is one thing, and the thing another. In the instance that now concerns us, *the sign is a quality of feeling and the thing is a position.* Now we have seen that the position of a point is not only

---

peculiar local tingeing of the image by each point. See also Sully's *Psychology*, pp. 118–121. Prof. B. Erdmann has quite lately (*Vierteljahrsschrift für wissenschaftliche Philosophie,* x, 324–9) denied the existence of all evidence for such immanent *qualia* of feeling characterizing each locality. Acute as his remarks are, they quite fail to convince me. On the skin the *qualia* are evident, I should say. Where, as on the retina, they are less so (Kries and Auerbach), this may well be a mere difficulty of discrimination not yet educated to the analysis.

22 1852, p. 331.

revealed, but created, by the existence of other points to which it stands in determinate *relations. If the sign can by any machinery which it sets in motion evoke a consciousness either of the other points, or of the relations, or of both, it would seem to fulfil its function, and reveal to us the position we seek.*

But such a machinery is already familiar to us. It is neither more nor less than the law of habit in the nervous system. When any point of the sensitive surface has been frequently excited simultaneously with, or immediately before or after, other points, and afterwards comes to be excited alone, there will be a tendency for its perceptive nerve-centre to irradiate into the nerve-centres of the other points. Subjectively considered, this is the same as if we said that *the peculiar feeling of the first point* SUGGESTS *the feeling of the entire region with whose stimulation its own excitement has been habitually* ASSOCIATED.

Take the case of the stomach. When the epigastrium is heavily pressed, when certain muscles contract, etc., the stomach is squeezed, and its peculiar local sign awakes in consciousness simultaneously with the local signs of the other squeezed parts. There is also a sensation of total vastness aroused by the combined irritation, and *somewhere* in this the stomach-feeling seems to lie. Suppose that later a pain arises in the stomach from some non-mechanical cause. It will be tinged by the gastric local sign, and the nerve-centre supporting this latter feeling will excite the centre supporting the dermal and muscular feelings habitually associated with it when the excitement was mechanical. From the combination the same peculiar vastness will again arise. In a word, 'something' in the stomach-sensation 'reminds' us of a total space, of which the diaphragmatic and epigastric sensations also form a part, or, to express it more briefly still, suggests the neighborhood of these latter organs.[23]

23 Maybe the localization of intracranial pain is itself due to such association as this of local signs with each other, rather than to their qualitative similarity in neighboring parts (*supra*, p. 797); though it is conceivable that association and similarity itself should here have one and the same neural basis. If we suppose the sensory nerves from those parts of the body beneath any patch of skin to terminate in the same sensorial brain-tract as those from the skin itself, and if the excitement of any one fibre tends to irradiate through the whole of that tract, the feelings of all fibres going to that tract would presumably both have a similar intrinsic quality, and at the same time tend each to arouse the other. Since the same nerve-trunk in most cases supplies the skin and the parts beneath, the anatomical hypothesis presents nothing improbable.

Revert to the case of two excited points on a surface with an unexcited space between them. The general result of previous experience has been that when either point was impressed by an outward object, the same object also touched the immediately neighboring parts. Each point, together with its local sign, is thus associated with a circle of surrounding points, the association fading in strength as the circle grows larger. Each will revive its own circle; but when both are excited together, the strongest revival will be that due to the *combined* irradiation. Now the tract *joining the two excited points* is the only part common to the two circles. And the feelings of this whole tract will therefore awaken with considerable vividness in the imagination when its extremities are touched by an outward irritant. The mind receives with the impression of the two distinct points the vague idea of a line. The twoness of the points comes from the contrast of their local signs: the line comes from the associations into which experience has wrought these latter. If no ideal line arises we have duality without sense of interval; if the line be excited actually rather than ideally, we have the interval given with its ends, in the form of a single extended object felt. E. H. Weber, in the famous article in which he laid the foundations of all our accurate knowledge of these subjects, *laid it down as the logical requisite for the perception of two separated points, that the mind should, along with its consciousness of them, become aware of an unexcited interval as such. I have only tried to show how the known laws of experience may cause this requisite to be fulfilled.* Of course, if the local signs of the entire region offer but little qualitative contrast *inter se*, the line suggested will be but dimly defined or discriminated in length or direction from other possible lines in its neighborhood. This is what happens in the back, where consciousness can sunder two spots, whilst only vaguely apprehending their distance and direction apart.

The relation of position of the two points *is* the suggested interval or line. Turn now to the simplest case, that of *a single excited spot. How can it suggest its position?* Not by recalling any particular line unless experience have constantly been in the habit of marking or tracing some one line from it towards some one neighboring point. Now on the back, belly, viscera, etc., no such tracing habitually occurs. The consequence is that the only suggestion is that of the whole neighboring circle; i.e., *the spot simply recalls the general region in which it happens to lie.* By a process of successive construction, it is quite true that we can also get the feeling of distance between the spot and some other particular spot. Attention, by reinforcing the local sign of one part of the circle, can awaken a new circle round this part, and so *de proche en proche* we may slide our feeling down from our cheek, say, to our foot. But when we first touched our cheek we had no consciousness of the foot at all.[24] In the extremities, the lips, the tongue and other mobile parts, the case is different. We there have an instinctive tendency, when a part of lesser discriminative sensibility is touched, to move the member so that the touching object glides along it to the place where sensibility is greatest. If a body touches our hand we move the hand over it till the finger-tips are able to explore it. If the sole of our foot touches anything we bring it towards the toes, and so forth. There thus arise lines of habitual passage from all points of a member to its sensitive tip. These are the lines most readily recalled when any point is touched, and their recall is identical with the consciousness of the distance of the touched point from the 'tip.' I think anyone must be aware when he touches a point of his hand or wrist that it is the relation to the finger-tips of which he is usually most conscious. Points on the fore-arm suggest either the finger-tips or the elbow (the latter being a spot of greater sensibility).[25] In the foot it is the toes, and so on. A point can only be cognized in its relations to the entire body at once by awakening a *visual* image of the whole body. Such awakening is even more obviously than the previously considered cases a matter of pure association.

This leads us to the eye. On the retina the fovea and the yellow spot about it form a focus of exquisite sensibility, towards which every impression falling on an outlying portion of the field is moved by an instinctive action of the muscles of the eyeball. Few

[24] Unless, indeed, the foot happen to be spontaneously tingling or something of the sort at the moment. The whole surface of the body is always in a state of semi-conscious irritation which needs only the emphasis of attention, or of some accidental inward irritation, to become strong at any point.

[25] It is true that the inside of the fore-arm, though its discriminative sensibility is often less than that of the outside, usually rises very prominently into consciousness when the latter is touched. Its *æsthetic* sensibility to contact is a good deal finer. We enjoy stroking it from the extensor to the flexor surface around the ulnar side more than in the reverse direction. Pronating movements give rise to contacts in this order, and are frequently indulged in when the back of the fore-arm feels an object against it.

persons, until their attention is called to the fact, are aware how almost impossible it is to keep a conspicuous visible object in the margin of the field of view. The moment volition is relaxed we find that without our knowing it our eyes have turned so as to bring it to the centre. This is why most persons are unable to keep the eyes steadily converged upon a point in space with nothing in it. The objects against the walls of the room invincibly attract the foveæ to themselves. If we contemplate a blank wall or sheet of paper, we always observe in a moment that we are directly looking at some speck upon it which, unnoticed at first, ended by 'catching our eye.' Thus *whenever an image falling on the point P of the retina excites attention, it more habitually moves from that point towards the fovea than in any one other direction.* The line traced thus by the image is not always a straight line. When the direction of the point from the fovea is neither vertical nor horizontal but oblique, the line traced is often a curve, with its concavity directed upwards if the direction is upwards, downwards if the direction is downwards. This may be verified by anyone who will take the trouble to make a simple experiment with a luminous body like a candle-flame in a dark enclosure, or a star. Gazing first at some point remote from the source of light, let the eye be suddenly turned full upon the latter. The luminous image will necessarily fall in succession upon a continuous series of points, reaching from the one first affected to the fovea. But by virtue of the slowness with which retinal excitements die away, the entire series of points will for an instant be visible as an after-image, displaying the above peculiarity of form according to its situation.[26] These radiating lines are neither regular nor invariable in the same person, nor, probably, equally curved in different individuals. We are incessantly drawing them between the fovea and every point of the field of view. Objects remain in their peripheral indistinctness only so long as they are unnoticed. The moment we attend to them they grow distinct through one of these motions—which leads to the idea prevalent among uninstructed persons that we see distinctly all parts of the field of view at once. *The result of this incessant tracing of radii is that whenever a local sign P is awakened by a spot of light falling upon it, it recalls forthwith, even though the eyeball be unmoved, the local signs of all the other points which lie*

[26] These facts were first noticed by Wundt: see his *Beiträge*, pp. 140, 202. See also Lamansky: Pflüger's *Archiv*, II, 418.

between P and the fovea. It recalls them in imaginary form, just as the normal reflex movement would recall them in vivid form; and with their recall is given a consciousness more or less faint of the whole line on which they lie. In other words, no ray of light can fall on any retinal spot without the local sign of that spot revealing to us, by recalling the line of its most habitual associates, its direction and distance from the centre of the field. The fovea acts thus as the origin of a system of polar co-ordinates, in relation to which each and every retinal point has through an incessantly-repeated process of association its distance and direction determined. Were *P* alone illumined and all the rest of the field dark we should still, even with motionless eyes, know whether *P* lay high or low, right or left, through the *ideal streak*, different from all other streaks, which *P* alone has the power of awakening.[27]

27 So far all has been plain sailing, but our course begins to be so tortuous when we descend into minuter detail that I will treat of the more precise determination of locality in a long note. When *P* recalls an ideal line leading to the fovea the line is felt in its entirety and but vaguely; whilst *P*, which we supposed to be a single star of actual light, stands out in strong distinction from it. The ground of the distinction between *P* and the ideal line which it terminates is manifest—*P* being vivid while the line is faint; *but why should P hold the particular position it does, at the end of the line, rather than anywhere else—for example, in its middle?* That seems something not at all manifest.

To clear up our thoughts about this latter mystery, let us take the case of an actual line of light, none of whose parts is ideal. The feeling of the line is produced, as we know, when a multitude of retinal points are excited together, each of which *when excited separately* would give rise to *one* of the feelings called local signs. Each of these signs is the feeling of a small space. From their simultaneous arousal we might well suppose a feeling of larger space to result. But why is it necessary that *in* this larger spaciousness the sign *a* should appear always at one end of the line, *z* at the other, and *m* in the middle? For though the line be a unitary streak of light, its several constituent points can nevertheless break out from it, and become alive, each for itself, under the selective eye of attention.

The uncritical reader, giving his first careless glance at the subject, will say that there is no mystery in this, and that 'of course' local signs must appear alongside of each other, each in its own place;—there is no other way possible. But the more philosophic student, whose business it is to discover difficulties quite as much as to get rid of them, will reflect that it is conceivable that the partial factors might fuse into a larger space, and yet not each be located within it any more than a voice is *located* in a chorus. He will wonder how, after combining into the line, the points *can* become severally alive again: the separate puffs of a 'sirene' no longer strike the ear after they have fused into a certain pitch of sound. He will recall the fact that when, after looking at things with one eye closed, we double, by opening the other eye, the number of retinal points affected, the new retinal sensations do not as a rule appear *alongside* of the old ones and additional to them, but merely make the old ones seem larger and nearer. Why should the affection of new points on the *same* retina have so different a result? In fact, he will see no sort of logical connection between (1) the original separate local signs, (2) the line as a unit, (3) the line with the points discriminated in it, and (4) the various nerve-processes which subserve all these different things. He will suspect our local sign of being a very slippery and ambiguous sort of creature. Positionless at first, it no sooner appears in the midst of a gang of companions than it is found maintaining the strictest position of its own, and assigning place to each of its associates. How is this possible? Must we accept what we rejected a while ago as absurd, and admit the points each to have position *in se*? Or must we suspect that our whole construction has been fallacious, and that we have tried to conjure up, out of association, qualities which the associates never contained?

There is no doubt a real difficulty here; and the shortest way of dealing with it would be to confess it insoluble and ultimate. Even if position be not an intrinsic character of any one of those sensations we have called local signs, we must still admit that there is *something about* every one of them that stands for the potentiality of position, and is the *ground* why the local sign, when it gets placed at all, gets placed *here* rather than *there*. If this 'something' be interpreted as a physiological something, as a mere nerve-process, it is easy to say in a blank way that when it is excited alone, it is an 'ultimate fact' (1) that a positionless spot will appear; that when it is excited together with other similar processes, but *without* the process of discriminative attention, it is another 'ultimate fact' (2) that a unitary line will come; and that the final 'ultimate fact' (3) is that, when the nerve-process is excited *in combination with* that other process which subserves the feeling of attention, what results will be the line with the local sign inside of it determined to a particular place. Thus we should escape the responsibility of explaining, by falling back on the everlasting inscrutability of the psycho-neural nexus. The moment we call the ground of localization physiological, we need only point out *how*, in those cases in which localization occurs, the physiological process *differs* from those in which it does not, to have done all we can possibly do in the matter. This would be unexceptionable logic, and with it we might let the matter drop, satisfied that there was no self-contradiction in it, but only the universal psychological puzzle of how a new mode of consciousness emerges whenever a fundamentally new mode of nervous action occurs.

But, blameless as such tactics would logically be on our part, let us see whether we cannot push our theoretic insight a little farther. It seems to me we can. We cannot, it is true, give a reason why the line we feel when process (2) awakens should have its own peculiar shape; nor can we explain the essence of the process of discriminative attention. But we can see why, if the brute facts be admitted that a line may have one of its parts singled out by attention at all, and that that part may appear in relation to other parts at all, the relation must be *in the line itself*,—for the line and the parts are the only things supposed to be in consciousness. And we can furthermore suggest a reason why parts appearing thus in relation to each other in a line should fall into an immutable order, and each within that order keep its characteristic place.

If a lot of such local signs all have any quality which evenly augments as we pass from one to the other, we can arrange them in an ideal serial order, in which any one local sign must lie below those with more, above those with less, of the quality in question. It must divide the series into two parts,—unless indeed it have a maximum or minimum of the quality, when it either begins or ends it.

Such an ideal series of local signs in the mind is, however, not yet identical with the feeling of a line in space. Touch a dozen points on the skin *successively*, and there seems no necessary reason why the notion of a definite line should emerge,

And with this we can close the first great division of our subject. We have shown that, within the range of every sense, experience takes *ab initio* the spatial form. We have also shown that in the cases of the retina and skin every sensible total may be subdivided by discriminative attention into sensible parts, which are also spaces, and into relations between the parts, these being sensible

---

even though we be strongly aware of a gradation of quality among the touches. We may of course symbolically arrange them in a line in our thought, but we can always distinguish between a line symbolically thought and a line directly felt.

But note now the peculiarity of the nerve-processes of all these local signs: though they may give no line when excited successively, when excited *together* they do give the actual sensation of a line in space. The sum of them is the neural process of that line; the sum of their feelings is the feeling of that line; and if we begin to single out particular points from the line, and notice them by their rank, it is impossible to see how this rank can *appear* except as an actual fixed space-position sensibly felt as a bit of the total line. The scale itself appearing as a line, rank in it must appear as a definite part of the line. If the seven notes of an octave, when heard together, appeared to the sense of hearing as an outspread *line* of sound—which it is needless to say they do not—why then no one note could be discriminated without being localized, according to its pitch, *in* the line, either as one of its extremities or as some part between.

But not alone the gradation of their quality arranges the local-sign feelings in a scale. Our *movements* arrange them also in a *time*-scale. Whenever a stimulus passes from point *a* of the skin or retina to point *f*, it awakens the local-sign feelings in the perfectly definite time-order *abcdef*. It cannot excite *f* until *cde* have been successively aroused. The feeling *c* sometimes is preceded by *ab*, sometimes followed by *ba*, according to the movement's direction; the result of it all being that we never feel either *a*, *c*, or *f*, without there clinging to it faint reverberations of the various time-orders of transition in which, throughout past experience, it has been aroused. To the local sign *a* there clings the tinge or tone, the penumbra or fringe, of the transition *bcd*. To *f*, to *c*, there cling quite different tones. Once admit the principle that a feeling may be tinged by the reproductive consciousness of an habitual transition, even when the transition is not made, and it seems entirely natural to admit that, if the transition be habitually in the order *abcdef*, and if *a*, *c*, and *f* be felt separately at all, *a* will be felt with an essential *earliness*, *f* with an essential *lateness*, and that *c* will fall between. Thus those psychologists who set little store by local signs and great store by movements in explaining space-perception, would have a perfectly definite time-order, due to motion, by which to account for the definite order of positions that appears when sensitive spots are excited all at once. Without, however, the preliminary admission of the 'ultimate fact' that this collective excitement shall feel like a *line* and nothing else, it can never be explained why the new order should needs be an order of *positions*, and not of merely ideal serial rank. We shall hereafter have any amount of opportunity to observe how thoroughgoing is the participation of motion in all our spatial measurements. Whether the local signs have their respective qualities evenly graduated or not, the feelings of transition must be set down as among the *veræ causæ* in localization. But the gradation of the local signs is hardly to be doubted; so we may believe ourselves really to possess two sets of reasons for localizing any point we may happen to distinguish from out the midst of any line or any larger space.

spaces too. Furthermore, we have seen (in a foot-note) that different parts, once discriminated, necessarily fall into a determinate order, both by reason of definite gradations in their quality, and by reason of the fixed order of time-succession in which movements arouse them. But in all this nothing has been said of the comparative *measurement* of one sensible space-total against another, or of the way in which, by summing our divers simple sensible space-experiences together, we end by constructing what we regard as the unitary, continuous, and infinite objective Space of the real world. To this more difficult inquiry we next pass.

THE CONSTRUCTION OF 'REAL' SPACE

The problem breaks into two subordinate problems.

(1) *How is the subdivision and measurement of the several sensorial spaces completely effected?* and

(2) *How do their mutual addition and fusion and reduction to the same scale, in a word, how does their synthesis, occur?*

I think that, as in the investigation just finished, we found ourselves able to get along without invoking any data but those that pure sensibility on the one hand, and the ordinary intellectual powers of discrimination and recollection on the other, were able to yield; so here we shall emerge from our more complicated quest with the conviction that all the facts can be accounted for on the supposition that no other mental forces have been at work save those we find everywhere else in psychology: sensibility, namely, for the data; and discrimination, association, memory, and choice for the rearrangements and combinations which they undergo.

1. *The Subdivision of the Original Sense-spaces*

How are spatial subdivisions brought to consciousness? in other words, How does spatial discrimination occur? The general subject of discrimination has been treated in a previous chapter. Here we need only inquire what are the conditions that make spatial discrimination so much finer in sight than in touch, and in touch than in hearing, smell, or taste.

The first great condition is, that different points of the surface shall differ in the quality of their immanent sensibility, that is, that each shall carry its special local sign. If the skin felt everywhere exactly alike, a foot-bath could be distinguished from a total immersion, as being smaller, but never distinguished from a wet face. The local signs are indispensable; two points which have the same local sign will always be felt as the same point. We do not judge them two unless we have discerned their sensations to be different.[28] Granted none but homogeneous irritants, that organ would then distinguish the greatest multiplicity of irritants—would count most stars or compass-points, or best compare the size of two wet surfaces—whose local sensibility was the least even. A skin whose sensibility shaded rapidly off from a focus, like the apex of a boil, would be better than a homogeneous integument for spatial perception. The retina, with its exquisitely sensitive fovea, has this peculiarity, and undoubtedly owes to it a great part of the minuteness with which we are able to subdivide the total bigness of the sensation it yields. On its periphery the local differences do not shade off very rapidly, and we can count there fewer subdivisions.

But these local differences of feeling, so long as the surface is unexcited from without, are almost null. I cannot feel them by a pure mental act of attention unless they belong to quite distinct parts of the body, as the nose and the lip, the finger-tip and the ear; their contrast needs the reinforcement of outward excitement to be felt. In the spatial muchness of a colic—or, to call it by the more spacious-sounding vernacular, of a 'bellyache'—one can with difficulty distinguish the north-east from the south-west corner, but can do so much more easily if, by pressing one's finger against the former region, one is able to make the pain there more intense.

The local differences require then an adventitious sensation, superinduced upon them, to awaken the attention. After the attention has once been awakened in this way, it may continue to be conscious of the unaided difference; just as a sail on the horizon may be too faint for us to notice until someone's finger, placed against the spot, has pointed it out to us, but may then remain visible after the finger has been withdrawn. But all this is true only on condition that separate points of the surface may be *exclusively* stimulated. If the whole surface at once be excited from without, and homogeneously, as, for example, by immersing the body in

28 M. Binet (*Revue Philosophique*, Sept. 1880, page 291) says we judge them locally different as soon as their sensations differ enough for us to distinguish them as qualitatively different when successively excited. This is not strictly true. Skin-sensations, different enough to be discriminated when *successive*, may still fuse locally if excited both at once.

salt water, local discrimination is not furthered. The local signs, it is true, all awaken at once; but in such multitude that no one of them, with its specific quality, stands out in contrast with the rest. If, however, a single extremity be immersed, the contrast between the wet and dry parts is strong, and, at the surface of the water especially, the local signs attract the attention, giving the feeling of a ring surrounding the member. Similarly, two or three wet spots separated by dry spots, or two or three hard points against the skin, will help to break up our consciousness of the latter's bigness. In cases of this sort, where points receiving an identical kind of excitement are, nevertheless, felt to be locally distinct, and the objective irritants are also judged multiple,—e.g., compass-points on skin or stars on retina,—the ordinary explanation is no doubt just, and we judge the outward causes to be multiple because we have discerned the local feelings of their sensations to be different.

Capacity for partial stimulation is thus the second condition favoring discrimination. A sensitive surface which has to be excited in all its parts at once can yield nothing but a sense of undivided largeness. This appears to be the case with the olfactory, and to all intents and purposes with the gustatory, surfaces. Of many tastes and flavors, even simultaneously presented, each affects the totality of its respective organ, each appears with the whole vastness given by that organ, and appears interpenetrated by the rest.[29]

[29] It may, however, be said that even in the tongue there is a determination of bitter flavors to the back and of acids to the front edge of the organ. Spices likewise affect its sides and front, and a taste like that of alum localizes itself, by its styptic effect on the portion of mucous membrane, which it immediately touches, more sharply than roast pork, for example, which stimulates all parts alike. The pork, therefore, tastes more spacious than the alum or the pepper. In the nose, too, certain smells, of which vinegar may be taken as the type, seem less spatially extended than heavy, suffocating odors, like musk. The reason of this appears to be that the former inhibit inspiration by their sharpness, whilst the latter are drawn into the lungs, and thus excite an objectively larger surface. The ascription of height and depth to certain notes seems due, not to any localization of the sounds, but to the fact that a feeling of vibration in the chest and tension in the gullet accompanies the singing of a bass note, whilst, when we sing high, the palatine mucous membrane is drawn upon by the muscles which move the larynx, and awakens a feeling in the roof of the mouth.

The only real objection to the law of partial stimulation laid down in the text is one that might be drawn from the organ of hearing; for, according to modern theories, the cochlea may have its separate nerve-termini exclusively excited by sounds of differing pitch, and yet the sounds seem all to fill a common space, and not necessarily to be arranged alongside of each other. At most the high note is felt as a thinner, brighter streak against a darker background. In an article on

I should have been willing some years ago to name without hesitation a third condition of discrimination—saying it would be most developed in that organ which is susceptible of the *most various qualities* of feeling. The retina is unquestionably such an organ. The colors and shades it perceives are infinitely more numerous than the diversities of skin-sensation. And it can feel at once white and black, whilst the ear can in no wise so feel sound and silence. But the late researches of Donaldson, Blix, and Goldscheider,[30] on specific points for heat, cold, pressure, and pain in the skin; the older ones of Czermak (repeated later by Klug in Ludwig's laboratory), showing that a hot and a cold compass-point are no more easily discriminated as two than two of equal temperature; and some unpublished experiments of my own—all disincline me to make much of this condition now.[31] There is, however, one quality

---

Space, published in the *Journal of Speculative Philosophy* for January 1879, I ventured to suggest that possibly the auditory nerve-termini might be "excited all at once by sounds of any pitch, as the whole retina would be by every luminous point if there were no dioptric apparatus affixed." And I added: "Notwithstanding the brilliant conjectures of the last few years which assign different acoustic end-organs to different rates of air-wave, we are still greatly in the dark about the subject; and I, for my part, would much more confidently reject a theory of hearing which violated the principles advanced in this article than give up those principles for the sake of any hypothesis hitherto published about either organs of corti or basilar membrane." Professor Rutherford's theory of hearing, advanced at the meeting of the British Association for 1886, already furnishes an alternative view which would make hearing present no exception to the space-theory I defend, and which, whether destined to be proved true or false, ought, at any rate, to make us feel that the Helmholtzian theory is probably not the last word in the physiology of hearing. Stepanoff (Hermann und Schwalbe's *Jahresbericht*, xv, 404, Literature 1886) reports a case in which more than the upper half of one cochlea was lost without any such deafness to deep notes on that side as Helmholtz's theory would require.

30 Donaldson, in *Mind*, x, 399, 557; Goldscheider, in *Archiv für (Anatomie und) Physiologie*; Blix, in *Zeitschrift für Biologie*. A good résumé may be found in Ladd's *Physiological Psychology*, part II, chap. IV, §§ 21–23.

31 I tried on nine or ten people, making numerous observations on each, what difference it made in the discrimination of two points to have them alike or unlike. The points chosen were (1) two large needle-heads, (2) two screw-heads, and (3) a needle-head and a screw-head. The distance of the screw-heads was measured from their centres. I found that when the points gave diverse qualities of feeling (as in 3), this facilitated the discrimination, but much less strongly than I expected. The difference, in fact, would often not be perceptible twenty times running. When, however, one of the points was endowed with a rotary movement, the other remaining still, the doubleness of the points became much more evident than before. To observe this I took an ordinary pair of compasses with one point blunt, and the movable leg replaced by a metallic rod which could, at any moment, be made to rotate *in situ* by a dentist's drilling-machine, to which it was attached. The compass

of sensation which is particularly exciting, and that is the *feeling of motion over any of our surfaces.* The erection of this into a separate elementary quality of sensibility is one of the most recent of psychological achievements, and is worthy of detaining us a while at this point.

The Sensation of Motion over Surfaces

The feeling of motion has generally been assumed by physiologists to be impossible until the positions of *terminus a quo* and *terminus ad quem* are severally cognized, and the successive occupancies of these positions by the moving body are perceived to be separated by a distinct interval of time.[32] As a matter of fact, however, we cognize only the very slowest motions in this way. Seeing the hand of a clock at XII and afterwards at VI, we judge that it has moved through the interval. Seeing the sun now in the east and again in the west, I infer it to have passed over my head. But we can only *infer* that which we already generically know in some more direct fashion, and it is experimentally certain that we have the feeling of motion given us as a direct and simple *sensation.* Czermak long ago pointed out the difference between seeing the motion of the second-hand of a watch, when we look directly at it, and noticing the fact of its having altered its position when we fix our gaze upon some other point of the dial-plate. In the first case we have a specific quality of sensation which is absent in the second. If the reader will find a portion of his skin—the arm, for example—where a pair of compass-points an inch apart are felt as one impression, and if he will then trace lines a tenth of an inch long on that spot with a pencil-point, he will be distinctly aware of the point's motion and vaguely aware of the direction of the motion. The perception of the motion here is certainly not derived from a pre-existing knowledge that its starting and ending points are separate positions in space, because positions in space ten times wider apart fail to be discriminated as such when excited by the dividers. It is the same with the retina. One's fingers when cast upon its periph-

---

had then its points applied to the skin at such a distance apart as to be felt as one impression. Suddenly rotating the drill-apparatus then almost always made them seem as two.

[32] This is only another example of what I call 'the psychologist's fallacy'—thinking that the mind he is studying must necessarily be conscious of the object after the fashion in which the psychologist himself is conscious of it.

eral portions cannot be counted—that is to say, the five retinal tracts which they occupy are not distinctly apprehended by the mind as five separate positions in space—and yet the slightest *movement* of the fingers is most vividly perceived as movement and nothing else. It is thus certain that our sense of movement, being so much more delicate than our sense of position, cannot possibly be derived from it. *A curious observation by Exner*[33] completes the proof that movement is a primitive form of sensibility, by showing it to be much more delicate than our sense of succession in time. This very able physiologist caused two electric sparks to appear in rapid succession, one beside the other. The observer had to state whether the right-hand one or the left-hand one appeared first. When the interval was reduced to as short a time as 0.045″ the discrimination of temporal order in the sparks became impossible. But Exner found that if the sparks were brought so close together in space that their irradiation-circles overlapped, the eye then felt their flashing as if it were the motion of a single spark from the point occupied by the first to the point occupied by the second, and the time-interval might then be made as small as 0.014″ before the mind began to be in doubt as to whether the apparent motion started from the right or from the left. On the skin similar experiments gave similar results.

Vierordt, at almost the same time,[34] *called attention to certain persistent illusions, amongst which are these:* If another person gently trace a line across our wrist or finger, the latter being stationary, it will feel to us as if the member were moving in the opposite direction to the tracing point. If, on the contrary, we move our limb across a fixed point, it will be seen as if the point were moving as well. If the reader will touch his forehead with his forefinger kept motionless, and then rotate the head so that the skin of the forehead passes beneath the finger's tip, he will have an irresistible sensation of the latter being itself in motion in the opposite direction to the head. So in abducting the fingers from each other; some may move and the rest be still, but the still ones will feel as if they were actively separating from the rest. These illusions, according to Vierordt, are survivals of a primitive form of perception, when motion was felt as such, but ascribed to the whole 'content'

33 *Sitzungsberichte der kaiserlichen Akademie der Wissenschaften*, Wien, Bd. LXXII, Abth. 3 (1875).

34 *Zeitschrift für Biologie*, XII, 226 (1876).

of consciousness, and not yet distinguished as belonging exclusively to one of its parts. When our perception is fully developed we go beyond the mere relative motion of thing and ground, and can ascribe absolute motion to one of these components of our total object, and absolute rest to another. When, in vision for example, the whole background moves together, we think that it is ourselves or our eyes which are moving; and any object in the foreground which may move relatively to the background is judged by us to be still. But primitively this discrimination cannot be perfectly made. The sensation of the motion spreads over all that we see and infects it. Any relative motion of object and retina both makes the object seem to move, and makes us feel ourselves in motion. Even now when our whole object moves we still get giddy; and we still see an apparent motion of the entire field of view, whenever we suddenly jerk our head and eyes or shake them quickly to and fro. Pushing our eyeballs gives the same illusion. We *know* in all these cases what really happens, but the conditions are unusual, so our primitive sensation persists unchecked. So it does when clouds float by the moon. We *know* the moon is still; but we *see* it move even faster than the clouds. Even when we slowly move our eyes the primitive sensation persists under the victorious conception. If we notice closely the experience, we find that any object towards which we look appears moving to meet our eye.

But the most valuable contribution to the subject is the paper of G. H. Schneider,[35] who takes up the matter zoologically, and shows by examples from every branch of the animal kingdom that movement is the quality by which animals most easily attract each other's attention. The instinct of 'shamming death' is no shamming of death at all, but rather a paralysis through fear, which saves the insect, crustacean, or other creature from being *noticed at all* by his enemy. It is parallelled in the human race by the breath-holding stillness of the boy playing 'I spy,' to whom the seeker is near; and its obverse side is shown in our involuntary waving of arms, jumping up and down, and so forth, when we wish to attract someone's attention at a distance. Creatures 'stalking' their prey and creatures hiding from their pursuers alike show how immobility diminishes conspicuity. In the woods, if we are quiet, the squirrels and birds will actually touch us. Flies will light on stuffed birds and station-

35 *Vierteljahrsschrift für wissenschaftliche Philosophie*, II, 377.

ary frogs.[36] On the other hand, the tremendous shock of feeling the thing we are sitting on begin to move, the exaggerated start it gives us to have an insect unexpectedly pass over our skin, or a cat noiselessly come and snuffle about our hand, the excessive reflex effects of tickling, etc., show how exciting the sensation of motion is *per se*. A kitten cannot help pursuing a moving ball. Impressions too faint to be cognized at all are immediately felt if they move. A fly sitting is unnoticed,—we feel it the moment it crawls. A shadow may be too faint to be perceived. As soon as it moves, however, we see it. Schneider found that a shadow, with distinct outline, and directly fixated, could still be perceived when moving, although its objective strength might be but half as great as that of a stationary shadow so faint as just to disappear. With a blurred shadow in indirect vision the difference in favor of motion was much greater—namely, 13.8:40.7. If we hold a finger between our closed eyelid and the sunshine we shall not notice its presence. The moment we move it to and fro, however, we discern it. Such visual perception as this reproduces the conditions of sight among the radiates.[37]

36 Exner tries to show that the structure of the faceted eye of articulates adapts it for perceiving motions almost exclusively.

37 Schneider tries to explain why a sensory surface is so much more excited when its impression moves. It has long since been noticed how much more acute is discrimination of successive than of simultaneous differences. But in the case of a moving impression, say on the retina, we have a summation of both sorts of difference; whereof the natural effect must be to produce the most perfect discrimination of all.

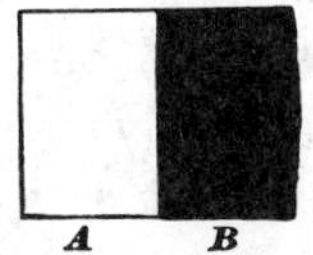

FIG. 53.

In the left-hand figure let the dark spot B move, for example, from right to left. At the outset there is the simultaneous contrast of black and white in B and A. When the motion has occurred so that the right-hand figure is produced, the same contrast remains, the black and the white having changed places. But in addition to it there is a double successive contrast, first in A, which, a moment ago white, has now become black; and second in B, which, a moment ago black, has now become white. If we make each single feeling of contrast = 1 (a supposition far too favorable to the state of rest), the sum of contrasts in the case of motion will be 3, as against 1 in the state of rest. That is, our attention will be called by a treble force to the difference of color, provided the color begin to move.—(Cf. also Fleischl: "Physiologisch-optische Notizen," 2te Mittheilung, Wiener *Sitzungsberichte*, 1882.)

Enough has now been said to show that *in the education of spatial discrimination the motions of impressions across sensory surfaces must have been the principal agent* in breaking up our consciousness of the surfaces into a consciousness of their parts. Even to-day the main function of the peripheral regions of our retina is that of sentinels, which, when beams of light move over them, cry 'Who goes there?' and call the fovea to the spot. Most parts of the skin do but perform the same office for the finger-tips. Of course finger-tips and fovea leave *some* power of direct perception to marginal retina and skin respectively. But it is worthy of note that such perception is best developed on the skin of the most movable parts (the labors of Vierordt and his pupils have well shown this); and that in the blind, whose skin is exceptionally discriminative, it seems to have become so through the inveterate habit which most of them possess of twitching and moving it under whatever object may touch them, so as to become better acquainted with the conformation of the same. Czermak was the first to notice this. It may be easily verified. Of course *movement of surface under object is (for purposes of stimulation) equivalent to movement of object over surface.* In exploring the shapes and sizes of things by either eye or skin the movements of these organs are incessant and unrestrainable. Every such movement draws the points and lines of the object across the surface, imprints them a hundred times more sharply, and drives them home to the attention. The immense part thus played by movements in our perceptive activity is held by many psychologists[38] to prove that the muscles are themselves the space-perceiving organ. Not surface-sensibility, but 'the muscular sense,' is for these writers the original and only revealer of objective extension. But they have all failed to notice with what peculiar intensity muscular contractions call surface-sensibilities into play, and that the mere discrimination of impressions (quite apart from any question of measuring the space between them) largely depends on the mobility of the surface upon which they fall.[39]

38 Brown, Bain, J. S. Mill, and in a modified manner Wundt, Helmholtz, Sully, etc.

39 M. Charles Dunan, in his forcibly written essay "Espace visuel et l'espace tactile" in the *Revue Philosophique* for 1888, endeavors to prove that surfaces alone give no perception of extent, by citing the way in which the blind go to work to gain an idea of an object's shape. If surfaces were the percipient organ, he says, "both the seeing and the blind ought to gain an exact idea of the size (and shape) of an object by merely laying their hand flat upon it (provided of course that it were smaller than the hand), and this because of their direct appreciation of the

2. *The Measurement of the Sense-spaces against Each Other*

What precedes is all we can say in answer to the problem of discrimination. Turn now to that of measurement of the several spaces against each other, that being the first step in our constructing out of our diverse space-experiences the one space we believe in as that of the real world.

The first thing that seems evident is that we have no *immediate* power of comparing together with any accuracy the extents revealed by different sensations. Our mouth-cavity feels indeed to itself smaller, and to the tongue larger, than it feels to the finger or eye, our tympanic membrane feels larger than our finger-tip, our lips feel larger than a surface equal to them on our thigh. So much comparison is immediate; but it is vague; and for anything exact we must resort to other help.

The great agent in comparing the extent felt by one sensory surface with that felt by another, is superposition—superposition of one surface upon another, and superposition of one outer thing upon many surfaces. Thus are exact equivalencies and common measures introduced, and the way prepared for numerical results.

Could we not superpose one part of our skin upon another, or one object on both parts, we should hardly succeed in coming to that knowledge of our own form which we possess. The original differences of bigness of our different parts would remain vaguely

---

amount of tactile surface affected, and with no recourse to the muscular sense. . . . But the fact is that a person born blind never proceeds in this way to measure objective surfaces. The only means which he has of getting at the size of a body is that of running his finger along the lines by which it is bounded. For instance, if you put into the hands of one born blind a book whose dimensions are unknown to him, he will begin by resting it against his chest so as to hold it horizontal; then, bringing his two hands together at the middle of the edge opposite to the one against his body, he will draw them asunder till they reach the ends of the edge in question: and then, and not till then, will he be able to say what the length of the object is" (vol. xxv, p. 148). I think that anyone who will try to appreciate the size and shape of an object by simply 'laying his hand flat upon it' will find that the great obstacle is that he *feels the contours* so imperfectly. The moment, however, the hands move, the contours are emphatically and distinctly felt. All perception of shape and size is perception of contours, and first of all these must be made *sharp*. Motion does this; and the impulse to move our organs in perception is primarily due to the craving which we feel to get our surface-sensations sharp. When it comes to the naming and measuring of objects in terms of some common standard we shall see presently how movements help also; but no more in this case than the other do they help, because the quality of extension itself is contributed by the 'muscular sense.'

operative, and we should have no certainty as to how much lip was equivalent to so much forehead, how much finger to so much back.

But with the power of exploring one part of the surface by another we get a direct perception of cutaneous equivalencies. The primitive differences of bigness are overpowered when we feel by an immediate sensation that a certain length of thigh-surface is in contact with the entire palm and fingers. And when a motion of the opposite finger-tips draws a line first along this same length of thigh and then along the whole of the hand in question, we get a new manner of measurement, less direct but confirming the equivalencies established by the first. In these ways, by superpositions of parts and by tracing lines on different parts by identical movements, a person deprived of sight can soon learn to reduce all the dimensions of his body to a homogeneous scale. By applying the same methods to objects of his own size or smaller, he can with equal ease make himself acquainted with their extension stated in terms derived from his own bulk, palms, feet, cubits, spans, paces, fathoms (armspreads), etc. In these reductions it is to be noticed that *when the resident sensations of largeness of two opposed surfaces conflict, one of the sensations is chosen as the true standard and the other treated as illusory*. Thus an empty tooth-socket is believed to be *really smaller* than the finger-tip which it will not admit, although it may *feel* larger; and in general it may be said that the hand, as the almost exclusive organ of palpation, gives its own magnitude to the other parts, instead of having its size determined by them. In general, it is, as Fechner says, the extent felt by the more sensitive part to which the other extents are reduced.[40]

But even though exploration of one surface by another were impossible, we could always measure our various surfaces against each other by applying the same extended object first to one and then to another. We should of course have the alternative of supposing that the object itself waxed and waned as it glided from one place

40 Fechner describes (*Psychophysik*, I, 132) a 'method of equivalents' for measuring the sensibility of the skin. Two compasses are used, one on the part A, another on the part B, of the surface. The points on B must be adjusted so that their distance apart appears equal to that between the points on A. With the place A constant, the second pair of points must be varied a great deal for every change in the place B, though for the same A and B the relation of the two compasses is remarkably constant, and continues unaltered for months provided but few experiments are made on each day. If, however, we practise daily their difference grows less, in accordance with the law given in the text.

to another (cf. above, p. 782); but the principle of simplifying as much as possible our world would soon drive us out of that assumption into the easier one that objects as a rule keep their sizes, and that most of our sensations are affected by errors for which a constant allowance must be made.

In the retina there is no reason to suppose that the bignesses of two impressions (lines or blotches) falling on different regions are primitively felt to stand in any exact mutual ratio. It is only when the impressions come from the *same object* that we judge their sizes to be the same. And this, too, only when the relation of the object to the eye is believed to be on the whole unchanged. When the object by moving changes its relations to the eye, the sensation excited by its image even on the same retinal region becomes so fluctuating that we end by ascribing no absolute import whatever to the retinal space-feeling which at any moment we may receive. So complete does this overlooking of retinal magnitude become that it is next to impossible to compare the visual magnitudes of objects at different distances without making the experiment of superposition. We cannot say beforehand how much of a distant house or tree our finger will cover. The various answers to the familiar question, How large is the moon?—answers which vary from a cartwheel to a wafer—illustrate this most strikingly. The hardest part of the training of a young draughtsman is his learning to feel directly the retinal (i.e., primitively sensible) magnitudes which the different objects in the field of view subtend. To do this he must recover what Ruskin calls the 'innocence of the eye'—that is, a sort of childish perception of stains of color merely as such, without consciousness of what they mean.

With the rest of us this innocence is lost. *Out of all the visual magnitudes of each known object we have selected one as the* REAL *one to think of, and degraded all the others to serve as its signs.* This 'real' magnitude is determined by æsthetic and practical interests. It is that which we get when the object is at the distance most propitious for exact visual discrimination of its details. This is the distance at which we hold anything we are examining. Farther than this we see it too small, nearer too large. And the larger and the smaller feeling vanish in the act of suggesting this one, their more important *meaning*. As I look along the dining-table I overlook the fact that the farther plates and glasses *feel* so much smaller than my own, for I *know* that they are all equal in size; and the feeling of them, which is a present sensation, is eclipsed in the glare of the knowledge, which is a merely imagined one.

If the inconsistencies of sight-spaces *inter se* can thus be reduced, of course there can be no difficulty in equating sight-spaces with spaces given to touch. In this equation it is probably the touch-feeling which prevails as real and the sight which serves as sign—a reduction made necessary not only by the far greater constancy of felt over seen magnitudes, but by the greater practical interest which the sense of touch possesses for our lives. As a rule, things only benefit or harm us by coming into direct contact with our skin: sight is only a sort of anticipatory touch; the latter is, in Mr. Spencer's phrase, the 'mother tongue of thought,' and the handmaid's idiom must be translated into the language of the mistress before it can speak clearly to the mind.[41]

Later on we shall see that the feelings excited in the joints when a limb moves are used as signs of the path traversed by the extremity. But of this more anon. As for the equating of sound-, smell-, and taste-volumes with those yielded by the more discriminative senses, they are too vague to need any remark. It may be observed of pain, however, that its size has to be reduced to that of the normal tactile size of the organ which is its seat. A finger with a felon on it, and the pulses of the arteries therein, both 'feel' larger than we believe they really 'are.'

It will have been noticed in the account given that *when two sensorial space-impressions, believed to come from the same object, differ, then* THE ONE MOST INTERESTING, *practically or æsthetically,* IS JUDGED TO BE THE TRUE ONE. This law of interest holds throughout—though a permanent interest, like that of touch, may resist a strong but fleeting one like that of pain, as in the case just given of the felon.

[41] Prof. Jastrow gives as the result of his experiments this general conclusion (*American Journal of Psychology*, III, 53): "The space-perceptions of disparate senses are themselves disparate, and whatever harmony there is among them we are warranted in regarding as the result of experience. The spacial notions of one deprived of the sense of sight and reduced to the use of the other space-senses must indeed be different from our own." But he continues: "The existence of the striking disparities between our visual and our other space-perceptions, without confusing us, and, indeed, without usually being noticed, can only be explained by the tendency to interpret all dimensions *into their visual equivalents*." But this author gives no reasons for saying 'visual' rather than 'tactile'; and I must continue to think that probabilities point the other way so far as what we call real magnitudes are concerned.

3. *The Summation of the Sense-spaces*

Now for the next step in our construction of real space: *How are the various sense-spaces added together into a consolidated and unitary continuum?* For they are, in man at all events, incoherent at the start.

Here again the first fact that appears is that *primitively our space-experiences form a chaos, out of which we have no immediate faculty for extricating them. Objects of different sense-organs, experienced together, do not in the first instance appear either inside or alongside or far outside of each other, neither spatially continuous nor discontinuous, in any definite sense of these words.* The same thing is almost as true of objects felt by different parts of the same organ before discrimination has done its finished work. The most we can say is that all our space-experiences together form an *objective total* and that this *objective total* is vast.

Even now the space inside our mouth, which is so intimately known and accurately measured by its inhabitant the tongue, can hardly be said to have its internal directions and dimensions known in any exact relation to those of the larger world outside. It forms almost a little world by itself. Again, when the dentist excavates a small cavity in one of our teeth, we feel the hard point of his instrument scraping, in distinctly differing directions, a surface which seems to our sensibility vaguely larger than the subsequent use of the mirror tells us it 'really' is. And though the directions of the scraping differ so completely *inter se*, not one of them can be identified with the particular direction in the outer world to which it corresponds. The space of the tooth-sensibility is thus really a little world by itself, which can only become congruent with the outer space-world by farther experiences which shall alter its bulk, identify its directions, fuse its margins, and finally imbed it as a definite part within a definite whole. And even though every joint's rotations should be felt to vary *inter se* as so many differences of direction in a common room; even though the same were true of diverse tracings on the skin, and of diverse tracings on the retina respectively, it would still not follow that feelings of direction, on these different surfaces, are intuitively comparable among each other, or with the other directions yielded by the feelings of the semi-circular canals. It would not follow that we should immediately judge the relations of them all to each other in one space-world.

If with the arms in an unnatural attitude we 'feel' things, we are perplexed about their shape, size, and position. Let the reader lie on his back with his arms stretched above his head, and it will astonish him to find how ill able he is to recognize the geometrical relations of objects placed within reach of his hands. But the geometrical relations here spoken of are nothing but identities recognized between the directions and sizes perceived in this way and those perceived in the more usual ways. The two ways do not fit each other intuitively.

How lax the connection between the system of visual and the system of tactile directions is in man, appears from the facility with which microscopists learn to reverse the movements of their hand in manipulating things on the stage of the instrument. To move the slide to the *seen* left they must draw it to the *felt* right. But in a very few days the habit becomes a second nature. So in tying our cravat, shaving before a mirror, etc., the right and left sides are inverted, and the directions of our hand movements are the opposite of what they seem. Yet this never annoys us. Only when by accident we try to tie the cravat of another person do we learn that there are two ways of combining sight and touch perceptions. Let anyone try for the first time to write or draw while looking at the image of his hand and paper in a mirror, and he will be utterly bewildered. But a very short training will teach him to undo in this respect the associations of his previous lifetime.

Prisms show this in an even more striking way. If the eyes be armed with spectacles containing slightly prismatic glasses with their bases turned, for example, towards the right, every object looked at will be apparently translocated to the left; and the hand put forth to grasp any such object will make the mistake of passing beyond it on the left side. But less than an hour of practice in wearing such spectacles rectifies the judgment so that no more mistakes are made. In fact the new-formed associations are already so strong, that when the prisms are first laid aside again the opposite error is committed, the habits of a lifetime violated, and the hand now passed to the right of every object which it seeks to touch.

The primitive chaos thus subsists to a great degree through life so far as our immediate sensibility goes. We feel our various objects and their bignesses, together or in succession; but so soon as it is a question of the order and relations of many of them at once our intuitive apprehension remains to the very end most vague and incomplete. Whilst we are attending to one, or at most to two or three objects, all the others *lapse*, and the most we feel of them is that they still linger on the outskirts and can be caught again by turning in a certain way. Nevertheless *throughout all this confusion we conceive of a world spread out in a perfectly fixed and orderly fashion, and we believe in its existence. The question is: How do this conception and this belief arise? How is the chaos smoothed and straightened out?*

Mainly by two operations: Some of the experiences are apprehended to exist out- and alongside of each other, and others are apprehended to interpenetrate each other, and to occupy the same room. In this way what was incoherent and irrelative ends by being coherent and definitely related; nor is it hard to trace the principles, by which the mind is guided in this arrangement of its perceptions, in detail.

In the first place, following the great intellectual law of economy, we simplify, unify, and identify as much as we possibly can. *Whatever sensible data can be attended to together we locate together. Their several extents seem one extent. The place at which each appears is held to be the same with the place at which the others appear. They become, in short, so many properties of* ONE AND THE SAME REAL THING. This is the first and great commandment, the fundamental 'act' by which our world gets spatially arranged.

In this *coalescence in a 'thing,'* one of the coalescing sensations is held to *be* the thing, the other sensations are taken for its more or less accidental *properties*, or modes of appearance.[42] The sensation chosen to be the thing essentially is the most constant and practically important of the lot; most often it is hardness or weight. But the hardness or weight is never without tactile bulk; and as we can always see something in our hand when we feel something there, we equate the bulk felt with the bulk seen, and thenceforward this common bulk is also apt to figure as of the essence of the 'thing.' Frequently a shape so figures, sometimes a temperature, a taste, etc.; but for the most part temperature, smell, sound, color, or whatever other phenomena may vividly impress us simultaneously with the bulk felt or seen, figure among the accidents. Smell and

[42] Cf. Lipps on "Complication," *Grundtatsachen*, etc., p. 579.

sound impress us, it is true, when we neither see nor touch the thing; but they are strongest when we see or touch, so we locate the *source* of these properties within the touched or seen space, whilst the properties themselves we regard as overflowing in a weakened form into the spaces filled by other things. *In all this, it will be observed, the sense-data whose spaces coalesce into one are yielded by different sense-organs.* Such data have no tendency to displace each other from consciousness, but can be attended to together all at once. Often indeed they vary concomitantly and reach a maximum together. We may be sure, therefore, that the general rule of our mind is to locate IN *each other all* sensations which are associated in simultaneous experience, and do not interfere with each other's perception.[43]

Different impressions on the same sense-organ do interfere with each other's perception, and cannot well be attended to at once. Hence *we do not locate them in each other's spaces, but arrange them in a serial order of exteriority, each alongside of the rest, in a space larger than that which any one sensation brings.* This larger space, however, is an object of conception rather than of direct intuition, and bears all the marks of being constructed piecemeal by the mind. The blind man forms it out of tactile, locomotor, and auditory experiences, the seeing man out of visual ones almost exclusively. As the visual construction is the easiest to understand, let us consider that first.

Every single visual sensation or 'field of view' is limited. To get a new field of view for our object the old one must disappear. But the disappearance may be only partial. Let the first field of view be A B C. If we carry our attention to the limit C, it ceases to be the limit, and becomes the centre of the field, and beyond it appear fresh parts where there were none before:[44] A B C changes, in short, to C D E. But although the parts A B are lost to sight, yet their

[43] Ventriloquism shows this very prettily. The ventriloquist talks without moving his lips, and at the same time draws our attention to a doll, a box, or some other object. We forthwith locate the voice within this object. On the stage an actor ignorant of music sometimes has to sing, or play on the guitar or violin. He goes through the *motions* before our eyes, whilst in the orchestra or elsewhere the music is performed. But because as we listen we see the actor, it is almost impossible not to *hear* the music as if coming from where he sits or stands.

[44] Cf. Shand, in *Mind*, XIII, 340.

image abides in the memory; and if we think of our first object A B C as having existed or as still existing at all, we must think of it as it was originally presented, namely, as spread out from C in one direction just as C D E is spread out in another. A B and D E can never coalesce in one place (as they could were they objects of different senses) because they can never be perceived at once: we must lose one to see the other. So (the letters standing now for 'things') we get to conceive of the successive fields of things after the analogy of the several things which we perceive in a single field. They must be out- and alongside of each other, and we conceive that their juxtaposed spaces must make a larger space. A B C + C D E must, in short, be imagined to exist in the form of A B C D E or not imagined at all.

We can usually recover anything lost from sight by moving our attention and our eyes back in its direction; and through these constant changes every field of seen things comes at last to be thought of as always having a fringe of *other things possible to be seen* spreading in all directions round about it. Meanwhile the movements concomitantly with which the various fields alternate are also felt and remembered; and gradually (through association) this and that movement come in our thought to suggest this or that extent of fresh objects introduced. Gradually, too, since the objects vary indefinitely in kind, we abstract from their several natures and think separately of their mere extents, of which extents the various movements remain as the only constant introducers and associates. More and more, therefore, do we think of movement and seen extent as mutually involving each other, until at last (with Bain and J. S. Mill) we may get to regard them as synonymous, and say, "What is the *meaning of the word extent,* unless it be possible movement?"[45] We forget in this conclusion that (whatever intrinsic extensiveness the movements may appear endowed with) that seen spreadoutness which is the pattern of the abstract extensiveness which we imagine came to us originally from the retinal sensation.

The muscular sensations of the eyeball *signify* this sort of visible spreadoutness, just as this visible spreadoutness may come in later experience to *signify* the 'real' bulks, distances, lengths and breadths known to touch and locomotion.[46] To the very end, how-

45 See, e.g., Bain's *Senses and the Intellect*, pp. 366–7, 371.

46 When, for example, a baby looks at its own moving hand, it sees one object

ever, in us seeing men, the quality, the nature, the *sort of thing we mean* by extensiveness, would seem to be the sort of feeling which our retinal stimulations bring.

In one deprived of sight the principles by which the notion of real space is constructed are the same. Skin-feelings take in him the place of retinal feelings in giving the quality of lateral spreadoutness, as our attention passes from one extent of them to another, awakened by an object sliding along. Usually the moving object is our hand; and feelings of movement in our joints invariably accompany the feelings in the skin. But the feeling of the skin is what the blind man *means* by his skin; so the size of the skin-feelings stands as the absolute or real size, and the size of the joint-feelings becomes a sign of these. Suppose, for example, a blind baby with (to make the description shorter) a blister on his toe, exploring his leg with his finger-tip and feeling a pain shoot up sharply the instant the blister is touched. The experiment gives him four different kinds of sensation—two of them protracted, two sudden. The first pair are the movement-feeling in the joints of the upper limb, and the movement-feeling on the skin of the leg and foot. These, attended to together, have their extents identified as one objective space—the hand moves through the same space in which the leg lies. The second pair of objects are the pain in the blister, and the peculiar feeling the blister gives to the finger. Their spaces also fuse; and as each marks the end of a peculiar movement-series (arm moved, leg stroked), the movement-spaces are *emphatically* identified with each other at *that* end. Were there other small blisters distributed down the leg, there would be a number of these emphatic points; the movement-spaces would be identified, not only as totals, but point for point.[47]

---

at the same time that it feels another. Both interest its attention, and it locates them together. But the felt object's size is the more constant size, just as the felt object is, on the whole, the more interesting and important object; and so the retinal sensations become regarded as its signs and have their 'real space-values' interpreted in tangible terms.

47 The incoherence of the different primordial sense-spaces *inter se* is often made a pretext for denying to the primitive bodily feelings any spatial quality at all. Nothing is commoner than to hear it said: "Babies have originally no spatial perception; for when a baby's toe aches he does not place the pain in the toe. He makes no definite movements of defence, and may be vaccinated without being

Just so with spaces beyond the body's limits. Continuing the joint-feeling beyond the toe, the baby hits another object, which he can still think of when he brings his hand back to its blister again. That object at the end of that joint-feeling means a new place for him, and the more such objects multiply in his experience the wider does the space of his conception grow. If, wandering through the woods to-day by a new path, I find myself suddenly in a glade which affects my senses exactly as did another I reached last week at the end of a different walk, I believe the two identical affections to present the same persisting glade, and infer that I have attained it by two differing roads. The spaces walked over grow congruent by their extremities; though apart from the common sensation which those extremities give me, I should be under no necessity of connecting one walk with another at all. The case in no whit differs when shorter movements are concerned. If, moving first one arm and then another, the blind child gets the same kind of sensation upon the hand, and gets it again as often as he repeats either process, he judges that he has touched the same object by both motions, and concludes that the motions terminate in a common place. From place to place marked in this way he moves, and adding the places moved through, one to another, he builds up his notion of the extent of the outer world. The seeing man's process is identical; only his units, which may be successive bird's-eye views, are much larger than in the case of the blind.

---

held." The facts are true enough; but the interpretation is all wrong. What really happens is that *the baby does not place his 'toe' in the pain*; for he knows nothing of his 'toe' as yet. He has not attended to it as a visual object; he has not handled it with his fingers; nor have its normal organic sensations or contacts yet become interesting enough to be discriminated from the whole massive feeling of the foot, or even of the leg to which it belongs. In short, the toe is neither a member of the babe's optical space, of his hand-movement space, nor an independent member of his leg-and-foot space. It has actually no mental existence yet save as this little pain-space. What wonder, then, if the pain seem a little space-world all by itself? But let the pain once associate itself with these other space-worlds, and its space will become part of their space. Let the baby feel the nurse stroking the limb and awakening the pain every time her finger passes towards the toe; let him look on and see her finger on the toe every time the pain shoots up; let him handle his foot himself and get the pain whenever the toe comes into his fingers or his mouth; let moving the leg exacerbate the pain,—and all is changed. The space of the pain becomes identified with that part of each of the other spaces which gets felt when it awakens; and by their identity with *it* these parts are identified with each other, and grow systematically connected as members of a larger extensive whole.

FEELINGS IN JOINTS AND FEELINGS IN MUSCLES

1. *Feelings of Movement in Joints*

I have been led to speak of feelings which arise in joints. As these feelings have been too much neglected in Psychology hitherto, in entering now somewhat minutely into their study I shall probably at the same time freshen the interest of the reader, which under the rather dry abstractions of the previous pages may presumably have flagged.

When, by simply flexing my right forefinger on its metacarpal joint, I trace with its tip an inch on the palm of my left hand, is my feeling of the size of the inch purely and simply a feeling in the skin of the palm, or have the muscular contractions of the right hand and fore-arm anything to do with it? In the preceding pages I have constantly assumed spatial sensibility to be an affair of surfaces. At first starting, the consideration of the 'muscular sense' as a space-measurer was postponed to a later stage. Many writers, of whom the foremost was Thomas Brown, in his *Lectures on the Philosophy of the Human Mind*, and of whom the latest is no less a Psychologist than Prof. Delbœuf,[48] hold that the consciousness of active muscular motion, aware of its own amount, is the *fons et origo* of all spatial measurement. It would seem to follow, if this theory were true, that two skin-feelings, one of a large patch, one of a small one, possess their difference of spatiality, not as an immediate element, but solely by virtue of the fact that the large one, to get its points *successively* excited, demands more muscular contraction than the small one does. Fixed associations with the several amounts of muscular contraction required in this particular experience would thus explain the apparent sizes of the skin-patches, which sizes would consequently not be primitive data but derivative results.

It seems to me that no evidence of the muscular measurements in question exists; but that all the facts may be explained by sur-

[48] "Pourquoi les sensations visuelles sont étendues?" in *Revue Philosophique*, IV, 167.—As the proofs of this chapter are being corrected, I receive the third 'Heft' of Münsterberg's *Beiträge zur experimentellen Psychologie*, in which that vigorous young psychologist reaffirms (if I understand him after so hasty a glance) more radically than ever the doctrine that muscular sensation proper is our one means of measuring extension. Unable to reopen the discussion here, I am in duty bound to call the attention of the reader to Herr M.'s work.

face-sensibility, provided we take that of the joint-surfaces also into account.

The most striking argument, and the most obvious one, which an upholder of the muscular theory is likely to produce is undoubtedly this fact: if, with closed eyes, we trace figures in the air with the extended forefinger (the motions may occur from the metacarpal-, the wrist-, the elbow-, or the shoulder-joint indifferently), what we are *conscious of* in each case, and indeed most acutely conscious of, is the geometric path described by the finger-*tip*. Its angles, its subdivisions, are all as distinctly felt as if seen by the eye; and yet the surface of the finger-tip receives no impression at all.[49] But with each variation of the figure, the muscular contractions vary, and so do the feelings which these yield. Are not these latter the sensible data that make us aware of the lengths and directions we discern in the traced line?

Should we be tempted to object to this supposition of the advocate of perception by muscular feelings, that we have *learned* the spatial significance of these feelings by reiterated experiences of *seeing* what figure is drawn when each special muscular grouping is felt, so that in the last resort the muscular space-feelings would be derived from retinal-surface feelings, our opponent might immediately hush us by pointing to the fact that in persons born blind the phenomenon in question is even more perfect than in ourselves.

If we suggest that the blind may have originally traced the figures on the cutaneous surface of cheek, thigh, or palm, and may now remember the specific figure which each present movement formerly caused the skin-surface to perceive, he may reply that the delicacy of the motor perception far exceeds that of most of the cutaneous surfaces; that, in fact, we can feel a figure traced only in its differentials, so to speak,—a figure which we merely *start* to trace by our finger-tip, a figure which, traced in the same way *on* our finger-tip by the hand of another, is almost if not wholly unrecognizable.

The champion of the muscular sense seems likely to be triumphant *until we invoke the articular cartilages*, as internal surfaces

49 Even if the figure be drawn on a board instead of in the air, the variations of contact on the finger's surface will be much simpler than the peculiarities of the traced figure itself.

whose sensibility is called in play by every movement we make, however delicate the latter may be.

To establish the part they play in our geometrizing, it is necessary to review a few facts. It has long been known by medical practitioners that, in patients with cutaneous anæsthesia of a limb, whose muscles also are insensible to the thrill of the faradic current, a very accurate sense of the way in which the limb may be flexed or extended by the hand of another may be preserved.[50] On the other hand, we may have this sense of movement impaired when the tactile sensibility is well preserved. That the pretended feeling of outgoing innervation can play in these cases no part, is obvious from the fact that the movements by which the limb changes its position are passive ones, imprinted on it by the experimenting physician. The writers who have sought a *rationale* of the matter have consequently been driven by way of exclusion to assume the articular surfaces to be the seat of the perception in question.[51]

That the joint-surfaces are sensitive appears evident from the fact that in inflammation they become the seat of excruciating pains, and from the perception by everyone who lifts weights or presses against resistance, that every increase of the force opposing him betrays itself to his consciousness principally by the starting-out of new feelings or the increase of old ones, in or about the joints. If the structure and mode of mutual application of two articular surfaces be taken into account, it will appear that, granting the surfaces to *be* sensitive, no more favorable mechanical conditions could be possible for the delicate calling of the sensibility into play than are realized in the minutely graduated rotations and firmly resisted variations of pressure involved in every act of extension or flexion. Nevertheless it is a great pity that we have as yet no direct testimony, no expressions from patients with healthy joints accidentally laid open, of the impressions they experience when the cartilage is pressed or rubbed.

The first approach to direct evidence, so far as I know, is contained in the paper of Lewinski,[52] published in 1879. This observer had a patient the inner half of whose leg was anæsthetic. When

50 See for example Duchenne: *Électrisation localisée*, pp. 767, 770; Leyden: Virchow's *Archiv*, Bd. XLVII (1869).

51 E.g., Eulenburg: *Lehrbuch der Nervenkrankheiten* (Berlin), 1878, I, 3.

52 "Über den Kraftsinn," Virchow's *Archiv*, Bd. LXXVII, 134.

this patient stood up, he had a curious illusion about the position of his limb, which disappeared the moment he lay down again: he thought himself *knock-kneed.* If, as Lewinski says, we assume the inner half of the joint to share the insensibility of the corresponding part of the skin, then he *ought* to feel, when the joint-surfaces pressed against each other in the act of standing, the outer half of the joint most strongly. But this is the feeling he would also get whenever it was by any chance sought to force his leg into a knock-kneed attitude. Lewinski was led by this case to examine the feet of certain ataxic patients with imperfect sense of position. He found in every instance that when the toes were flexed *and drawn upon* at the same time (the joint-surfaces drawn asunder) all sense of the amount of flexion disappeared. On the contrary, when he pressed a toe *in*, whilst flexing it, the patient's appreciation of the amount of flexion was much improved, evidently because the artificial increase of articular pressure made up for the pathological insensibility of the parts.

Since Lewinski's paper an important experimental research by A. Goldscheider[53] has appeared, which completely establishes our point. This patient observer caused his fingers, arms, and legs to be passively rotated upon their various joints in a mechanical apparatus which registered both the velocity of movement impressed and the amount of angular rotation. No active muscular contraction took place. The minimal felt amounts of rotation were in all cases surprisingly small, being much less than a single angular degree in all the joints except those of the fingers. Such displacements as these, the author says (p. 490), can hardly be detected by the eye. The point of application of the force which rotated the limb made no difference in the result. Rotations round the hip-joint, for example, were as delicately felt when the leg was hung by the heel as when it was hung by the thigh whilst the movements were performed. Anæsthesia of the skin produced by induction-currents also had no disturbing effect on the perception, nor did the various degrees of pressure of the moving force upon the skin affect it. It became, in fact, all the more distinct in proportion as the concomitant pressure-feelings were eliminated by artificial anæsthesia. When the joints themselves, however, were made artificially anæsthetic the perception of the movement grew obtuse and the angular rotations had to be much increased before they were

53 *Archiv für (Anatomie und) Physiologie* (1889), pp. 369, 540.

perceptible. All these facts prove, according to Herr Goldscheider, that *the joint-surfaces and these alone are the starting point of the impressions by which the movements of our members are immediately perceived.*

Applying this result, which seems invulnerable, to the case of the tracing finger-tip, we see that our perception of the latter gives no countenance to the theory of the muscular sense. *We indubitably localize the finger-tip at the successive points of its path by means of the sensations which we receive from our joints.* But if this is so, it may be asked, why do we feel the figure to be traced, not within the joint itself, but in such an altogether different place? And why do we feel it so much larger than it really is?

I will answer these questions by asking another: Why do we move our joints at all? Surely to gain something more valuable than the insipid joint-feelings themselves. And these more interesting feelings are in the main produced upon the *skin* of the moving part, or of some other part over which it passes, or upon the eye. With movements of the fingers we explore the configuration of all real objects with which we have to deal, our own body as well as foreign things. Nothing that interests us is located in the joint; everything that interests us either *is* some part of our skin, or is something that we see as we handle it. The cutaneously felt and the seen extents come thus to figure as the important things for us to concern ourselves with. Every time the joint moves, even though we neither see, nor feel cutaneously, the reminiscence of skin-events and sights which formerly coincided with that extent of movement, ideally awaken as the movement's import, and the mind drops the present sign to attend to the import alone. The joint-sensation itself, as such, does not disappear in the process. A little attention easily detects it, with all its fine peculiarities, hidden beneath its vaster suggestions; so that really the mind has two space-perceptions before it, congruent in form but different in scale and place, either of which exclusively it may notice, or both at once,—the joint-space which it *feels* and the real space which it *means.*

The joint-spaces serve so admirably as signs because of their capacity for *parallel variation* to all the peculiarities of external motion. There is not a direction in the real world nor a ratio of distance which cannot be matched by some direction or extent of joint-rotation. Joint-feelings, like all feelings, are roomy. Specific ones are contrasted *inter se* as different directions are contrasted within the same extent. If I extend my arm straight out at the shoulder, the rotation of the shoulder-joint will give me one feeling of movement; if then I sweep the arm forwards, the same joint will give me another feeling of movement. Both these movements are felt to happen in space, and differ in specific quality. Why shall not the specificness of the quality just consist in the feeling of a peculiar *direction?*[54] Why may not the several joint-feelings *be* so many perceptions of movement in so many different directions? That we cannot explain why they *should* is no presumption that they *do* not, for we never can explain why any sense-organ should awaken the sensation it does.

But if the joint-feelings are directions and extents, standing in relation to each other, the task of association in interpreting their import in eye- or skin-terms is a good deal simplified. Let the movement *bc*, of a certain joint, derive its absolute space-value from the cutaneous feeling it is always capable of engendering; then the longer movement *abcd* of the same joint will be judged to have a greater space-value, even though it may never have wholly merged with a skin-experience. So of differences of direction: so much joint-difference = so much skin-difference; therefore, more joint-difference = more skin-difference. *In fact, the joint-feeling can excellently serve as a map on a reduced scale, of a reality which the imagination can identify at its pleasure with this or that sensible extension simultaneously known in some other way.*

When the joint-feeling in itself acquires an emotional interest,—which happens whenever the joint is inflamed and painful,—the secondary suggestions fail to arise, and the movement is felt where it is, and in its intrinsic scale of magnitude.[55]

54 Direction in its 'first intention,' of course; direction with which so far we merely become *acquainted*, and *about* which we know nothing save perhaps its difference from another direction a moment ago experienced in the same way!

55 I have said hardly anything about associations with visual space in the foregoing account, because I wished to represent a process which the blind and the seeing man might equally share. It is to be noticed that the space suggested to the imagination when the joint moves, and projected to the distance of the finger-tip, is not represented as any *specific* skin-tract. What the seeing man imagines is a visible path; what the blind man imagines is rather a generic image, an abstraction from many skin-spaces whose local signs have neutralized each other, and left nothing but their common vastness behind. We shall see as we go on that this generic abstraction of space-magnitude from the various local peculiarities of feeling which accompanied it when it was for the first time felt, occurs on a considerable scale in the acquired perceptions of blind as well as of seeing men.

The localization of the joint-feeling in a space simultaneously known otherwise (i.e., to eye or skin), is what is commonly called the *extradition or eccentric projection of the feeling*. In the preceding chapter I said a good deal on this subject; but we must now see a little more closely just what happens in this instance of it. The content of the joint-feeling, to begin with, is an object, and *is* in itself a place. For it to be *placed*, say *in the elbow*, the elbow as seen or handled must already have become another object for the mind, and with its place as thus known, the place which the joint-feeling fills must coalesce. That the latter should be felt 'in the elbow' is therefore a 'projection' of it into the place of another object as much as its being felt in the finger-tip or at the end of a cane can be. But when we say 'projection' we generally have in our mind the notion of a *there* as contrasted with a *here*. What is the *here* when we say that the joint-feeling is *there*? The 'here' seems to be the spot which the mind has chosen for its own post of observation, usually some place within the head, but sometimes within the throat or breast—not a rigorously fixed spot, but a region from any portion of which it may send forth its various acts of attention. Extradition from either of *these* regions is the common law under which we perceive the whereabouts of the north star, of our own voice, of the contact of our teeth with each other, of the tip of our finger, of the point of our cane on the ground, or of a movement in our elbow-joint.

But *for the distance between the 'here' and the 'there' to be felt, the entire intervening space must be itself an object of perception.* The consciousness of this intervening space is the *sine quâ non* of the joint-feeling's projection to the farther end of it. When it is filled by our own bodily tissues (as where the projection only goes as far as the elbow or finger-tip) we are sensible of its extent alike by our eye, by our exploring movements, and by the resident sensations which fill its length. When it reaches beyond the limits of our body, the resident sensations are lacking, but limbs and hand and eye suffice to make it known. Let me, for example, locate a feeling of motion coming from my elbow-joint in the point of my cane a yard beyond my hand. Either I see this yard as I flourish the cane, and the seen end of it then absorbs my sensation just as my seen elbow might absorb it, or I am blind and imagine the cane as an object continuing my arm, either because I have explored both arm and cane with the other hand, or because I have pressed them both along my body and leg. If I project my joint-feeling farther still, it is by a conception rather than a distinct imagination of the space. I *think*: 'farther,' 'thrice as far,' etc.; and thus get a symbolic image of a distant path at which I point.[56] But the 'absorption' of the joint-feeling by the distant spot, in whatever terms the latter may be apprehended, is never anything but that coalescence into one 'thing' already spoken of on page 821, of whatever different sensible objects interest our attention at once.

2. *Feelings of Muscular Contraction*

Readers versed in psychological literature will have missed, in our account thus far, the usual invocation of 'the muscular sense.' This word is used with extreme vagueness to cover all resident sensations, whether of motion or position, in our members, and even to designate the supposed feeling of efferent discharge from the brain. We shall later see good reason to deny the existence of the latter feeling. We have accounted for the better part at least of the resident feelings of motion in limbs by the sensibility of the articular surfaces. The skin and ligaments also must have feelings awakened as they are stretched or squeezed in flexion or extension. And I am inclined to think that *the sensations of our contracting muscles themselves probably play as small a part in building up our exact knowledge of space as any class of sensations which we possess.* The muscles, indeed, play an all-important part, but it is through the remote effect of their contractions on other sensitive parts, not through their own resident sensations being aroused. In other words, *muscular contraction is only indirectly instrumental, in giving us space-perceptions, by its effects on surfaces.* In skin and retina it produces a motion of the stimulus upon the surface; in joints it produces a motion of the surfaces upon each other—such motion being by far the most delicate manner of exciting the surfaces in question. One is tempted to doubt whether the muscular

[56] The ideal enlargement of a system of sensations by the mind is nothing exceptional. Vision is full of it; and in the manual arts, where a workman gets a tool larger than the one he is accustomed to and has suddenly to adapt all his movements to its scale, or where he has to execute a familiar set of movements in an unnatural position of body; where a piano-player meets an instrument with unusually broad or narrow keys; where a man has to alter the size of his handwriting —we see how promptly the mind multiplies once for all, as it were, the whole series of its operations by a constant factor, and has not to trouble itself after that with further adjustment of the details.

sensibility as such plays even a subordinate part as *sign* of these more immediately geometrical perceptions which are so uniformly associated with it as effects of the contraction objectively viewed.

For this opinion many reasons can be assigned. First, it seems *a priori* improbable that such organs as muscles should give us feelings whose variations bear any exact proportion to the spaces traversed when they contract. As G. E. Müller says,[57] their sensory nerves must be excited either chemically or by mechanical compression whilst the contractions last, and in neither case can the excitement be proportionate to the position into which the limb is thrown. The chemical state of the muscle depends on the *previous* work more than on the actually present contraction; and the internal pressure of it depends on the resistance offered more than on the shortening attained. *The intrinsic muscular sensations are likely therefore to be merely those of massive strain or fatigue, and to carry no accurate discrimination with them of lengths of path moved through.*

Empirically we find this probability confirmed by many facts. The judicious A. W. Volkmann observes[58] that:

> "Muscular feeling gives tolerably fine evidence as to the *existence* of movement, but hardly any direct information about its extent or direction. We are not aware that the contractions of a *supinator longus* have a wider range than those of a *supinator brevis*; and that the fibres of a bipenniform muscle contract in opposite directions is a fact of which the muscular feeling itself gives not the slightest intimation. Muscle-feeling belongs to that class of general sensations which tell us of our inner states, but not of outer relations; it does not belong among the space-perceiving senses."

E. H. Weber in his article "Tastsinn" called attention to the fact that muscular movements as large and strong as those of the diaphragm go on continually without our perceiving them as motion.

G. H. Lewes makes the same remark. When we think of our muscular sensations as movements in space, it is because we have ingrained with them in our imagination a movement on a surface simultaneously felt.

57 Pflüger's *Archiv*, XLV, 65.

58 *Physiologische Untersuchungen im Gebiete der Optik*, Leipzig (1863), p. 188.

"Thus, whenever we breathe, there is a contraction of the muscles of the ribs and the diaphragm. Since we *see* the chest expanding, we know it as a movement, and can only think of it as such. But the diaphragm itself is not seen, and consequently by no one who is not physiologically enlightened on the point, is this diaphragm thought of in movement. Nay, even when told by a physiologist that the diaphragm moves at each breathing, every one, who has not seen it moving downward, pictures it as an upward movement, because the chest moves upward."[59]

A personal experience of my own seems strongly to corroborate this view. For years I have been familiar, during the act of gaping, with a large, round, smooth sensation in the region of the throat, a sensation characteristic of gaping and nothing else, but which, although I had often wondered about it, never suggested to my mind the motion of anything. The reader probably knows from his own experience exactly what feeling I mean. It was not till one of my students told me, that I learned its objective cause. If we look into the mirror while gaping, we see that at the moment we have this feeling the hanging palate *rises* by the contraction of its intrinsic muscles. The contraction of these muscles and the compression of the palatine mucous membrane are what occasion the feeling; and I was at first astonished that, coming from so small an organ, it could appear so voluminous. Now the curious point is this—that no sooner had I learned by the eye its objective space-significance, than I found myself enabled mentally to *feel* it as a movement upwards of a body in the situation of the uvula. When I now have it, my fancy *injects* it, so to speak, with the image of the rising uvula; and it *absorbs* the image easily and naturally. In a word, a muscular contraction gave me a sensation whereof I was unable during forty years to interpret a motor meaning, of which two glances of the eye made me permanently the master. To my mind no further proof is needed of the fact that muscular contraction, merely as such, need not be perceived directly as so much motion through space.

Take again the contractions of the muscles which make the eyeball rotate. The feeling of these is supposed by many writers to play the chief part in our perceptions of extent. The space seen between two things *means*, according to these authors, nothing but

[59] *Problems of Life and Mind*, prob. VI, chap. IV, § 45.

the amount of contraction which is needed to carry the *fovea* from the first thing to the second. But close the eyes and note the contractions in themselves (even when coupled as they still are with the delicate surface sensations of the eyeball rolling under the lids), and we are surprised at finding how vague their space-import appears. Shut the eyes and roll them, and you can with no approach to accuracy tell the outer object which shall first be seen when you open them again.[60] Moreover, if our eye-muscle-contractions had much to do with giving us our sense of seen extent, we ought to have a natural illusion of which we find no trace. Since the feeling in the muscles grows disproportionately intense as the eyeball is rolled into an extreme eccentric position, all places on the extreme *margin* of the field of view ought to appear farther from the centre than they really are, for the fovea cannot get to them without an amount of this feeling altogether in excess of the amount of actual rotation.[61] When we turn to the muscles of the body at large we

[60] Volkmann: *op. cit.*, p. 189. Compare also what Hering says of the inability in his own case to make after-images seem to move when he rolls his closed eyes in their sockets; and of the insignificance of his feelings of convergence for the sense of distance (*Beiträge zur Physiologie*, 1861–2, pp. 31, 141). Helmholtz also allows to the muscles of convergence a very feeble share in producing our sense of the third dimension (*Physiologische Optik*, 649–59).

[61] Compare Lipps: *Psychologische Studien* (1885), p. 18, and the other arguments given on pp. 12 to 27. The most plausible reasons *for* contractions of the eyeball-muscles being admitted as original contributors to the perception of extent, are those of Wundt: *Physiologische Psychologie* (2nd ed.), II, 96–100. They are drawn from certain constant errors in our estimate of lines and angles; which, however, are susceptible, all of them, of different interpretations (see some of them further on).—Just as my MS. goes to the printer, Herr Münsterberg's *Beiträge zur experimentellen Psychologie*, Heft 2, comes into my hands with experiments on the measurement of space recorded in it, which, in the author's view, prove the feeling of muscular strain to be a principal factor in our vision of extent. As Münsterberg worked three hours a day for a year and a half at comparing the length of lines, seen with his eyes in different positions; and as he carefully averaged and 'percented' 20,000 observations, his conclusion must be listened to with great respect. Briefly it is this, that "our judgments of size depend on a comparison of the intensity of the feelings of movement which arise in our eyeball-muscles as we glance over the distance, and which fuse with the sensations of light" (p. 142). The facts upon which the conclusion is based are certain constant errors which Münsterberg found according as the standard or given interval was to the right or the left of the interval to be marked off as equal to it, or as it was above or below it, or stood in some more complicated relation still. He admits that he cannot explain all the errors in detail, and that we "stand before results which seem surprising and not to be unravelled, because we cannot analyze the elements which enter into the complex sensation which we receive." But he has no doubt whatever of the general fact "that the movements of the eyes and the sense of their position when fixed exert so

find the same vagueness. Goldscheider found that the minimal perceived rotation of a limb about a joint was no less when the movement was 'active' or produced by muscular contraction than when it was 'passively' impressed.[62] The consciousness of active movement became so blunt when the joint (alone!) was made anæsthetic by faradization, that it became evident that the feeling of contraction could never be used for *fine* discrimination of extents. And that it was not used for coarse discriminations appeared clear to Goldscheider from certain other results which are too circumstantial for me to quote in detail.[63] His general conclusion is that we

---

decisive an influence on our estimate of the spaces seen, that the errors cannot possibly be explained by anything else than the movement-feelings and their reproductions in the memory" (pp. 166, 167). It is presumptuous to doubt a man's opinion when you haven't had his experience; and yet there are a number of points which make me feel like suspending judgment in regard to Herr M.'s *dictum.* He found, for example, a constant tendency to underestimate intervals lying to the right, and to overestimate intervals lying to the left. He ingeniously explains this as a result of the habit of *reading,* which trains us to move our eyes easily along straight lines from left to right, whereas in looking from right to left we move them in curved lines across the page. As we *measure intervals as straight lines,* it costs more muscular effort to measure from right to left than the other way, and an interval lying to the left seems to us consequently longer than it really is. Now I have been a reader for more years than Herr Münsterberg; and yet with me there is a strongly pronounced error the other way. It is the rightward-lying interval which to me seems longer than it really is. Moreover, Herr M. wears concave spectacles, and looked through them with his *head fixed.* May it not be that some of the errors were due to distortion of the retinal image, as the eye looked no longer through the centre but through the margin of the glass? In short, with all the presumptions which we have seen against muscular contraction being definitely felt as length, I think that there may be explanations of Herr M.'s results which have escaped even his sagacity; and I call for a suspension of judgment until they shall have been confirmed by other observers. I do not myself doubt that our feeling of seen extent may be *altered* by concomitant muscular feelings. In Chapter XVII (pp. 676–677) we saw many examples of similar alterations, interferences with, or exaltations of, the sensory effect of one nerve-process by another. I do not see why currents from the muscles or eyelids, coming in at the same time with a retinal impression, might not make the latter seem bigger, in the same way that a greater *intensity* in the retinal stimulation makes it seem bigger; or in the way that a greater extent of surface excited makes the color of the surface seem stronger, or if it be a skin-surface, makes its heat seem greater; or in the way that the coldness of the dollar on the forehead (in Weber's old experiments) made the dollar seem heavier. But this is a *physiological* way; and the bigness gained is that of the retinal image after all. If I understand Münsterberg's meaning, it is quite different from this: the bigness belongs to the muscular feelings, as such, and is merely *associated* with those of the retina. *This* is what I deny.

62 *Archiv für (Anatomie und) Physiologie* (1889), p. 542.

63 *Ibid.*, p. 496.

feel our movements exclusively in our articular surfaces, and that our muscular contractions in all probability hardly occasion this sort of perception at all.[64]

My conclusion is that the 'muscular sense' must fall back to the humble position from which Charles Bell raised it, and no longer figure in Psychology as the leading organ in space-perception which it has been so long 'cracked up' to be.

Before making a minuter study of Space as apprehended by the eye, we must turn to see what we can discover of space as known to the blind. But as we do so, let us cast a glance upon the results of the last pages, and ask ourselves once more whether the building up of orderly space-perceptions out of primitive incoherency requires any mental powers beyond those displayed in ordinary intellectual operations. I think it is obvious—granting the spatial *quale* to exist in the primitive sensations—that discrimination, association, addition, multiplication, and division, blending into generic images, substitution of similars, selective emphasis, and abstraction from uninteresting details, are quite capable of giving us all the space-perceptions we have so far studied, without the aid of any mysterious 'mental chemistry' or power of 'synthesis' to create elements absent from the original data of feeling. It cannot be too strongly urged in the face of mystical attempts, however learned, that there is not a landmark, not a length, not a point of the compass in real space which *is* not some *one* of our feelings, either experienced directly as a presentation or ideally suggested by another feeling which has come to serve as its sign. In degrading some sensations to the rank of signs and exalting others to that of realities signified, we smooth out the wrinkles of our first chaotic impressions and make a continuous order of what was a rather incoherent multiplicity. But the *content* of the order remains identical with that of the multiplicity—sensational both, through and through.

HOW THE BLIND PERCEIVE SPACE

The blind man's construction of real space differs from that of the seeing man most obviously in the larger part which synthesis plays in it, and the relative subordination of analysis. The seeing

64 *Ibid.*, p. 497. Goldscheider thinks that our muscles do not even give us the feeling of *resistance*, that being also due to the articular surfaces; whilst *weight* is due to the tendons. *Ibid.*, p. 541.

baby's eyes take in the whole room at once, and discriminative attention must arise in him before single objects are visually discerned. The blind child, on the contrary, must form his mental image of the room by the addition, piece to piece, of parts which he learns to know successively. With our eyes we may apprehend instantly, in an enormous bird's-eye view, a landscape which the blind man is condemned to build up bit by bit after weeks perhaps of exploration. We are exactly in his predicament, however, for spaces which exceed our visual range. We think the ocean as a whole by multiplying mentally the impression we get at any moment when at sea. The distance between New York and San Francisco is computed in days' journeys; that from earth to sun is so many times the earth's diameter, etc.; and of longer distances still we may be said to have no adequate mental image whatever, but only numerical verbal symbols.

But the symbol will often give us the emotional effect of the perception. Such expressions as the abysmal vault of heaven, the endless expanse of ocean, etc., summarize many computations to the imagination, and give the sense of an enormous horizon. So it seems with the blind. They multiply mentally the amount of a distinctly felt freedom to move, and gain the immediate sense of a vaster freedom still. Thus it is that blind men are never without the consciousness of their horizon. They all enjoy travelling, especially with a companion who can describe to them the objects they pass. On the prairies they feel the great openness; in valleys they feel closed in; and one has told me that he thought few seeing people could enjoy the view from a mountain-top more than he. A blind person on entering a house or room immediately receives, from the reverberations of his voice and steps, an impression of its dimensions, and to a certain extent of its arrangement. The tympanic sense noticed on p. 781, *supra*, comes in to help here, and possibly other forms of tactile sensibility not yet understood. Mr. W. Hanks Levy, the blind author of *Blindness and the Blind* (London), gives the following account of his powers of perception:

"Whether within a house or in the open air, whether walking or standing still, I can tell, although quite blind, when I am opposite an object, and can perceive whether it be tall or short, slender or bulky. I can also detect whether it be a solitary object or a continuous fence, whether it be a close fence or composed of open rails, and often whether it be a wooden fence, a brick or stone wall, or a quickset hedge. I cannot usually perceive objects if much lower than my shoulder, but sometimes very low objects can be detected. This may depend on the nature of the objects, or on some abnormal state of the atmosphere. The currents of air can have nothing to do with this power, as the state of the wind does not directly affect it; the sense of hearing has nothing to do with it, as when snow lies thickly on the ground objects are more distinct, although the footfall cannot be heard. I seem to perceive objects through the skin of my face, and to have the impressions immediately transmitted to the brain. The only part of my body possessing this power is my face; this I have ascertained by suitable experiments. Stopping my ears does not interfere with it, but covering my face with a thick veil destroys it altogether. None of the five senses have anything to do with the existence of this power, and the circumstances above named induce me to call this unrecognized sense by the name of 'facial perception.' . . . When passing along a street I can distinguish shops from private houses, and even point out the doors and windows, etc. and this whether the doors be shut or open. When a window consists of one entire sheet of glass, it is more difficult to discover than one composed of a number of small panes. From this it would appear that glass is a bad conductor of sensation, or at any rate of the sensation specially connected with this sense. When objects below the face are perceived, the sensation seems to come in an oblique line from the object to the upper part of the face. While walking with a friend in Forest Lane, Stratford, I said, pointing to a fence which separated the road from a field, 'Those rails are not quite as high as my shoulder.' He looked at them and said they were higher. We, however, measured and found them about three inches lower than my shoulder. At the time of making this observation I was about four feet from the rails. Certainly in this instance facial perception was more accurate than sight. When the lower part of a fence is brick-work, and the upper part rails, the fact can be detected, and the line where the two meet easily perceived. Irregularities in height and projections, and indentations in walls, can also be discovered."

According to Mr. Levy, this power of seeing with the face is diminished by a fog, but not by ordinary darkness. At one time he could tell when a cloud obscured the horizon, but he has now lost that power, which he has known several persons to possess who are totally blind. These effects of aqueous vapor suggest immediately that fluctuations in the heat radiated by the objects may be the source of the perception. One blind gentleman, Mr. Kilbourne, an instructor in the Perkins Institution in South Boston, who has the power spoken of in an unusual degree, proved, however, to have no more delicate a sense of temperature in his face than ordinary persons. He himself supposed that his ears had nothing to do with the faculty until a complete stoppage of them, not only with cotton but with putty on top of it, by abolishing the perception entirely, proved his first impression to be erroneous. Many blind men say immediately that their ears are concerned in the matter.

Sounds certainly play a far more prominent part in the mental life of the blind than in our own. In taking a walk through the country, the mutations of sound, far and near, constitute their chief delight. And to a great extent their imagination of distance and of objects moving from one distant spot to another seems to consist in thinking how a certain sonority would be modified by the change of place. It is unquestionable that the semi-circular-canal feelings play a great part in defining the points of the compass and the direction of distant spots, in the blind as in us. We *start* towards them by feelings of this sort; and so many directions, so many different-feeling starts.[65]

The only point that offers any theoretic difficulty is the prolongation into space of the direction, after the start. We saw, nine pages back, that for extradition to occur beyond the skin, the portion of skin in question *and* the space beyond must form a common object for some other sensory surface. The eyes are for most of us this sensory surface; for the blind it can only be other parts of the skin, coupled or not with motion. But the mere gropings of the hands in every direction must end by surrounding the whole body with a sphere of felt space. And this sphere must become enlarged with every movement of locomotion, these movements gaining their space-values from the semi-circular-canal feelings which accompany them, and from the farther and farther parts of large fixed objects (such as the bed, the wainscoting, or a fence) which they bring within the grasp. It might be supposed that a knowledge of space acquired by so many successive discrete acts would always retain a somewhat jointed and so to speak, granulated character. When we who are gifted with sight think of a space too large to come into a single field of view, we are apt to imagine it as composite, and filled with more or less jerky stoppings and startings

65 "Whilst the memories which we seeing folks preserve of a man all centre round a certain exterior form composed of his image, his height, his gait, in the blind all these memories are referred to something quite different, namely, *the sound of his voice*." (Dunan: *Revue Philosophique*, xxv, 357.)

(think, for instance, of the space from here to San Francisco), or else we reduce the scale symbolically and imagine how much larger on a map the distance would look than others with whose totality we are familiar.

I am disposed to believe, after interrogating many blind persons, that the use of imaginary maps on a reduced scale is less frequent with them than with the rest of us. Possibly the extraordinary changeableness of the visual magnitudes of things makes this habit natural to us, while the fixity of tactile magnitudes keeps them from falling into it. (When the blind young man operated on by Dr. Franz was shown a portrait in a locket, he was vastly surprised that the face could be put into so small a compass: it would have seemed to him, he said, as impossible as to put a bushel into a pint.) Be this as it may, however, the space which each blind man feels to extend beyond his body is felt by him as one smooth continuum—all trace of those muscular startings and stoppings and reversals which presided over its formation having been eliminated from the memory. It seems, in other words, a generic image of the space-element common to all these experiences, with the unessential particularities of each left out. In truth, *where* in this space a start or a stop may have occurred was quite accidental. It may never occur just there again, and so the attention lets it drop altogether. Even as long a space as that traversed in a several-mile walk will not necessarily appear to a blind man's thought in the guise of a series of locomotor acts. Only where there is some distinct locomotor difficulty, such as a step to ascend, a difficult crossing, or a disappearance of the path, will distinct locomotor images constitute the idea. Elsewhere the space seems continuous, and its parts may even all seem coexistent; though, as a very intelligent blind friend once remarked to me, "To think of such distances involves probably more mental wear and tear and brain-waste in the blind than in the seeing." This seems to point to a greater element of successive addition and construction in the blind man's idea.

Our own visual explorations go on by means of innumerable stoppings and startings of the eyeballs. Yet these are all effaced from the final space-sphere of our visual imagination. They have neutralized each other. We can even distribute our attention to the right and left sides simultaneously, and think of those two quarters of space as coexistent. Does the smoothing out of the locomotor interruptions from the blind man's tactile space-sphere offer any greater paradox? Surely not. And it is curious to note that both in him and in us there is one particular locomotor feeling that is apt to assert itself obstinately to the last. We and he alike spontaneously imagine space as lying *in front* of us, for reasons too obvious to enumerate. If we think of the space behind us, we, as a rule, have to *turn round* mentally, and in doing so the front space vanishes. But in this, as in the other things of which we have been talking, individuals differ widely. Some, in imagining a room, can think of all its six surfaces at once. Others mentally turn round, or, at least, imagine the room in several successive and mutually exclusive acts (cf. p. 701, above).

Sir William Hamilton, and J. S. Mill after him, have quoted approvingly an opinion of Platner (an eighteenth-century philosopher) regarding the space-perceptions of the blind. Platner says:

"The attentive observation of a person born blind . . . has convinced me, that the sense of touch, by itself, is altogether incompetent to afford us the representation of extension and space . . . . In fact, to those born blind, time serves instead of space. Vicinity and distance means in their mouths nothing more than the shorter or longer time . . . necessary to attain from some one feeling to some other."

After my own observation of blind people, I should hardly have considered this as anything but an eccentric opinion, worthy to pair off with that other belief that color is primitively seen without extent, had it not been for the remarkable Essay on Tactile and Visual Space by M. Charles Dunan, which appeared in the *Revue Philosophique* for 1888. This author quotes[66] three very competent witnesses, all officials in institutions for the blind [it does not appear from the text that more than one of them was blind himself], who say that blind people *only live in time.* M. Dunan himself does not share exactly this belief, but he insists that the blind man's and the seeing man's representation of space have *absolutely naught* in common, and that we are deceived into believing that what they mean by space is analogous to what we mean, by the fact that so many of them are but semi-blind and still think in visual terms, and from the farther fact that they all *talk* in visual terms just like ourselves. But on examining M. Dunan's reasons one finds that they all rest on the groundless logical assumption that the percep-

[66] Vol. xxv, pp. 357–8.

tion of a geometrical form which we get with our eyes, and that which a blind man gets with his fingers, must either be absolutely identical or absolutely unlike. They cannot be similar in diversity, "for they are simple notions, and it is of the essence of such to enter the mind or leave it all at once, so that one who has a simple notion at all, possesses it in all its completeness. . . . Therefore, since it is impossible that the blind should have of the forms in question ideas *completely identical* with our seeing ones, it follows that their ideas must be *radically different from and wholly irreducible to our own*."[67] Hereupon M. Dunan has no difficulty in finding a blind man who still preserves a crude sensation of diffused light, and who says when questioned that *this light has no extent*. Having 'no extent' appears, however, on farther questioning, to signify merely not enveloping any particular tactile objects, nor being located within their outline; so that (allowing for latitude of expression) the result tallies perfectly with our own view. A relatively stagnant retinal sensation of diffused light, not varying when different objects are handled, would naturally remain an object quite apart. If the word 'extent' were habitually used to denote tactile extent, this sensation, having no tactile associates whatever, would naturally have 'extent' denied of it. And yet all the while it would be *analogous* to the tactile sensations in having the quality of bigness. Of course it would have no *other* tactile qualities, just as the tactile objects have no other optical qualities than bigness. All sorts of analogies obtain between the spheres of sensibility. Why are 'sweet' and 'soft' used so synonymously in most languages? and why are both these adjectives applied to objects of so many sensible kinds? Rough sounds, heavy smells, hard lights, cold colors, are other examples. Nor does it follow from such analogies as these that the sensations compared need be composite and have some of their parts identical. We saw in Chapter XIII that likeness and difference are an elementary relation, not to be resolved in every case into a mixture of absolute identity and absolute heterogeneity of content (cf. Vol. I, pp. 465–466).

I conclude, then, that although in its more superficial determinations the blind man's space is very different from our space, yet a deep analogy remains between the two. 'Big' and 'little,' 'far' and 'near,' are similar contents of consciousness in both of us. But the *measure* of the bigness and the farness is very different in him and

67 P. 135.

in ourselves. He, for example, can have no notion of what we mean by objects appearing smaller as they move away, because he must always conceive of them as of their constant tactile size. Nor, whatever analogy the two extensions involve, should we expect that a blind man receiving sight for the first time should recognize his new-given optical objects by their familiar tactile names. Molyneux wrote to Locke:

" 'Suppose a man born blind, and now adult, and taught by his touch to distinguish between a cube and a sphere . . . so as to tell, when he felt one and the other, which is the cube, which the sphere. Suppose then the cube and sphere placed on a table, and the blind man to be made to see; query, Whether by his sight, before he touched them, he could now distinguish and tell which is the globe, which the cube?' "

This has remained in literature as 'Molyneux's query.' Molyneux answered 'No.' And Locke says:[68]

"I agree with this thinking gentleman, whom I am proud to call my friend . . . and am of opinion, that the blind man, at first sight, would not be able to say which was the globe, which the cube, whilst he only saw them; though he could unerringly name them by his touch, and certainly distinguish them by the difference of their figures felt."

This opinion has not lacked experimental confirmation. From Cheselden's case downwards, patients operated for congenital cataract have been unable to name at first the things they saw. "So, puss! I shall know you another time," said Cheselden's patient, after catching the cat, looking at her steadfastly, and setting her down. Some of this incapacity is unquestionably due to general mental confusion at the new experience, and to the excessively unfavorable conditions for perception which an eye with its lens just extirpated affords. That the analogy of inner nature between the retinal and tactile sensations goes beyond mere extensity is proved by the cases where the patients were the most intelligent, as in the young man operated on by Dr. Franz, who named circular, triangular, and quadrangular figures at first sight.[69]

68 *Essay Concerning Human Understanding*, bk. II, chap. IX, § 8.

69 *Philosophical Transactions*, 1841. In T. K. Abbott's *Sight and Touch* there is a good discussion of these cases. Obviously, positive cases are of more importance than negative. An under-witted peasant, Noé M., whose case is described by Dr. Dufour of Lausanne (*Guérison d'un aveugle-né*, 1876) is much made of by MM. Naville and Dunan; but it seems to me only to show how little *some* people can deal with new experiences in which others find themselves quickly at home. This

VISUAL SPACE

It is when we come to analyze minutely the conditions of *visual* perception that difficulties arise which have made psychologists appeal to new and *quasi*-mythical mental powers. But I firmly believe that even here exact investigation will yield the same verdict as in the cases studied hitherto. This subject will close our survey of the facts; and if it give the result I foretell, we shall be in the best of positions for a few final pages of critically historical review.

If a common person is asked how he is enabled to see things as they are, he will simply reply, by opening his eyes and looking. This innocent answer has, however, long since been impossible for science. There are various paradoxes and irregularities about *what* we appear to perceive under seemingly identical optical conditions, which immediately raise questions. To say nothing now of the time-honored conundrums of why we see upright with an inverted retinal picture, and why we do not see double; and to leave aside the whole field of color-contrasts and ambiguities, as not directly relevant to the space-problem,—it is certain that the same retinal image makes us see quite differently-sized and differently-shaped objects at different times, and it is equally certain that the same ocular movement varies in its perceptive import. It ought to be possible, were the act of perception completely and *simply* intelligible, to assign for every distinct judgment of size, shape, and position a distinct optical modification of some kind as its occasion. And the connection between the two ought to be so constant that, given the same modification, we should always have the same judgment. But if we study the facts closely *we soon find no such constant connection between either judgment and retinal modification, or judgment and muscular modification, to exist.* The judgment seems to result frcm the combination of retinal, muscular and intellectual factors with each other; and any one of them may occasionally overpower the rest in a way which seems to leave the matter subject to no simple law.

The scientific study of the subject, if we omit Descartes, began with Berkeley, and the particular perception he analyzed in his *New Theory of Vision* was that of distance or depth. Starting with the physical assumption that a difference in the distance of a point

---

man could not even tell whether one of his first objects of sight moved or stood still (p. 9).

can make no difference in the nature of its retinal image, since "distance being a line directed endwise to the eye, it projects only one point in the fund of the eye—which point remains invariably the same, whether the distance be longer or shorter," he concluded that distance could not possibly be a visual sensation, but must be an intellectual 'suggestion' from 'custom' of some non-visual experience. According to Berkeley this experience was tactile. His whole treatment of the subject was excessively vague—no shame to him, as a breaker of fresh ground—but as it has been adopted and enthusiastically hugged in all its vagueness by nearly the whole line of British psychologists who have succeeded him, it will be well for us to begin our study of vision by refuting his notion that depth cannot possibly be perceived in terms of purely visual feeling.

The Third Dimension

Berkeleyans unanimously assume that no retinal sensation can primitively be of volume; if it be of extension at all (which they are barely disposed to admit), it can be only of two-, not of three-, dimensional extension. At the beginning of the present chapter we denied this, and adduced facts to show that all objects of sensation are voluminous in three dimensions (cf. p. 778 ff.). It is impossible to lie on one's back on a hill, to let the empty abyss of blue fill one's whole visual field, and to sink deeper and deeper into the merely sensational mode of consciousness regarding it, without feeling that an indeterminate, palpitating, circling depth is as indefeasibly one of its attributes as its breadth. We may artificially exaggerate this sensation of depth. Rise and look from the hill-top at the distant view; represent to yourself as vividly as possible the distance of the uttermost horizon; and then *with inverted head* look at the same. There will be a startling increase in the perspective, a most sensible recession of the maximum distance; and as you raise the head you can actually see the horizon-line again draw near.[70]

[70] What may be the physiological process connected with this increased sensation of depth is hard to discover. It seems to have nothing to do with the parts of the retina affected, since the mere inversion of the picture (by mirrors, reflecting prisms, etc.), without inverting the head, does not seem to bring it about; nothing with sympathetic axial rotation of the eyes, which might enhance the perspective through exaggerated disparity of the two retinal images (see J. J. Müller: "Raddrehung und Tiefendimension," Leipzig Academy *Berichte*, 1871, page 125), for one-eyed persons get it as strongly as those with two eyes. I cannot find it to be connected with any alteration in the pupil or with any ascertainable strain in the muscles of the eye,

Mind, I say nothing as yet about our estimate of the 'real' amount of this depth or distance. I only want to confirm its existence as a natural and inevitable optical consort of the two other optical dimensions. The field of view is always a *volume*-unit. Whatever be supposed to be its absolute and 'real' size, the relative sizes of its dimensions are functions of each other. Indeed, it happens perhaps most often that the breadth- and height-feeling take their absolute measure from the depth-feeling. If we plunge our head into a wash-basin, the felt nearness of the bottom makes us feel the lateral expanse to be small. If, on the contrary, we are on a mountain-top, the distance of the horizon carries with it in our judgment a proportionate height and length in the mountain-chains that bound it to our view. But as aforesaid, let us not consider the question of absolute size now,—it must later be taken up in a thorough way. Let us confine ourselves to the way in which the three dimensions which are seen, get their values fixed *relatively to each other.*

Reid, in his *Inquiry into the Human Mind*, has a section "Of the Geometry of Visibles," in which he assumes to trace what the perceptions would be of a race of 'Idomenians' reduced to the sole sense of sight. Agreeing with Berkeley that sight alone can give no knowledge of the third dimension, he humorously deduces various ingenious absurdities in their interpretations of the material appearances before their eyes.

Now I firmly believe, on the contrary, that one of Reid's Idomenians would frame precisely the same conception of the external world that we do, if he had our intellectual powers.[71] Even were

---

sympathizing with those of the body. The exaggeration of distance is even greater when we throw the head over backwards and contract our superior recti in getting the view, than when we bend forwards and contract the inferior recti. Making the eyes diverge slightly by weak prismatic glasses has no such effect. To me, and to all whom I have asked to repeat the observation, the result is so marked that I do not well understand how such an observer as Helmholtz, who has carefully examined vision with inverted head, can have overlooked it. (See his *Physiologische Optik*, pp. 433, 723, 724, 772.) I cannot help thinking that anyone who can explain the exaggeration of the depth-sensation in this case will at the same time throw much light on its normal constitution.

[71] "In Froriep's *Notizen* (1838, July), No. 133, is to be found a detailed account, with a picture, of an Esthonian girl, Eva Lauk, then fourteen years old, born with neither arms nor legs, which concludes with the following words: 'According to the mother, her intellect developed quite as fast as that of her brother and sisters; in particular, she came as quickly to a right judgment of the size and distance of visible objects, although, of course, she had no use of hands.'" (Schopenhauer: *Welt als Wille*, II, 44.)

his very eyeballs fixed and not movable like ours, that would only retard, not frustrate, his education. For the *same object,* by alternately covering in its lateral movements different parts of his retina, would determine the mutual equivalencies of the first two dimensions of the field of view; and by exciting the physiological cause of his perception of depth in various degrees, it would establish a scale of equivalency between the first two and the third.

First of all, one of the sensations given by the object is chosen to represent its 'real' size and shape, in accordance with the principles laid down on pp. 816 and 817. *One sensation measures the 'thing' present, and the 'thing' then measures the other sensations.* The peripheral parts of the retina are equated with the central by receiving the image of the same object. This needs no elucidation in case the object does not change its distance or its front. But suppose, to take a more complicated case, that the object is a stick, seen first in its whole length, and then rotated round one of its ends; let this fixed end be the one near the eye. In this movement the stick's image will grow progressively shorter; its farther end will appear less and less separated laterally from its fixed near end; soon it will be screened by the latter, and then reappear on the opposite side, and finally on that side resume its original length. Suppose this movement to become a familiar experience; the mind will presumably react upon it after its usual fashion (which is that of unifying all data which it is in any way possible to unify), and consider it the movement of a constant object rather than the transformation of a fluctuating one. Now, the *sensation of depth* which it receives during the experience is awakened more by the far than by the near end of the object. But how much depth? What shall measure its amount? Why, at the moment the far end is ready to be eclipsed, the difference of its distance from the near end's distance must be judged equal to the stick's whole length; but that length has already been judged equal to a certain optical sensation of breadth. *Thus we find that given amounts of the visual depth-feeling become signs of fixed amounts of the visual breadth-feeling. The measurement of distance is, as Berkeley truly said, a result of suggestion and experience. But visual experience alone is adequate to produce it, and this he erroneously denied.*

Suppose a colonel in front of his regiment at dress-parade, and suppose he walks at right angles towards the midmost man of the line. As he advances, and surveys the line in either direction, he looks more and more *down* it and less and less *at* it, until, when abreast of the midmost man, he feels the end men to be *most* distant; then when the line casts hardly any lateral image on his retina at all, what distance shall he judge to be that of the end men? Why, half the length of the regiment as it was originally seen, of course; but this length was a moment ago a retinal object spread out laterally before his sight. He has now merely equated a retinal depth-feeling with a retinal breadth-feeling. If the regiment moved, and the colonel stood still, the result would be the same. In such ways as these a creature endowed with eyes alone could hardly fail of measuring out all three dimensions of the space he inhabited. And we ourselves, I think, although we *may* often 'realize' distance in locomotor terms (as Berkeley says we must always do), yet do so no less often in terms of our retinal map, and always in this way the more spontaneously. Were this not so, the three visual dimensions could not possibly feel to us as homogeneous as they do, nor as commensurable *inter se*.

Let us then admit distance to be at least as genuinely optical a content of consciousness as either height or breadth. The question immediately returns, Can any of them be said in any strictness to be optical sensations? We have contended all along for the affirmative reply to this question, but must now cope with difficulties greater than any that have assailed us hitherto.

Helmholtz and Reid on Sensations

A sensation is, as we have seen in Chapter XVII, the mental affection that follows most immediately upon the stimulation of the sense-tract. Its antecedent is directly physical, no psychic links, no acts of memory, inference, or association intervening. Accordingly, if we suppose the nexus between neural process in the sense-organ, on the one hand, and conscious affection, on the other, to be by nature uniform, *the same process ought always to give the same sensation*; and conversely, *if what seems to be a sensation varies whilst the process in the sense-organ remains unchanged, the reason is presumably that it is really not a sensation but a higher mental product, whereof the variations depend on events occurring in the system of higher cerebral centres.*

Now the *size* of the field of view varies enormously in all three dimensions, without our being able to assign with any definiteness the process in the visual tract on which the variation depends. We just saw how impossible such assignment was in the case where turning down the head produces the enlargement. In general, the maximum feeling of depth or distance seems to take the lead in determining the apparent magnitude of the whole field, and the two other dimensions seem to follow. If, to use the former instance, I look close into a wash-basin, the lateral extent of the field shrinks proportionately to its nearness. If I look from a mountain, the things seen are vast in height and breadth, in proportion to the farness of the horizon. But *when we ask what changes in the eye determine how great this maximum feeling of depth or distance* (which is undoubtedly felt as a unitary vastness) *shall be, we find ourselves unable to point to any one of them as being its absolutely regular concomitant.* Convergence, accommodation, double and disparate images, differences in the parallactic displacement when we move our head, faintness of tint, dimness of outline, and smallness of the retinal image of objects named and known, are all processes that have *something to do* with the perception of 'far' and of 'near'; but the effect of each and any one of them in determining such a perception at one moment may at another moment be reversed by the presence of some other sensible quality in the object, that makes us, evidently by reminding us of past experience, judge it to be at a different distance and of another shape. If we paint the inside of a pasteboard-mask like the outside, and look at it with one eye, the accommodation- and parallax-feelings are there, but fail to make us see it hollow, as it is. Our mental knowledge of the fact that human faces are always convex overpowers them, and we directly perceive the nose to be nearer to us than the cheek instead of farther off.

The other organic tokens of farness and nearness are proved by similar experiments (of which we shall ere long speak more in detail) to have an equally fluctuating import. They lose all their value whenever the collateral circumstances favor a strong intellectual conviction that the object presented to the gaze is *improbable*—cannot be either *what* or *where* they would make us perceive it to be.

Now the query immediately arises: *Can the feelings of these processes in the eye, since they are so easily neutralized and reversed by intellectual suggestions, ever have been direct sensations of distance at all?* Ought we not rather to assume, since the distances which we see *in spite* of them are conclusions from past experience, that the distances which we see *by means* of them are equally such conclusions? Ought we not, in short, to say unhesitatingly that distance must be an intellectual and not a sensible content of consciousness? and that each of these eye-feelings serves as a mere signal to awaken this content, our intellect being so framed that sometimes it notices one signal more readily and sometimes another?

Reid long ago (*Inquiry*, Ch. VI, sec. 17) said:

"It may be taken for a general rule, That things which are produced by custom, may be undone or changed by disuse, or by a contrary custom. On the other hand, it is a strong argument, that an effect is not owing to custom, but to the constitution of nature, when a contrary custom is found neither to change nor to weaken it."

More briefly, a way of seeing things that can be unlearned was presumably learned, and only what we cannot unlearn is instinctive.

This seems to be Helmholtz's view, for he confirms Reid's maxim by saying in emphatic print:

"No elements in our perception can be sensational which may be overcome or reversed by factors of demonstrably experimental origin. Whatever can be overcome by suggestions of experience must be regarded as itself a product of experience and custom. If we follow this rule it will appear that only *qualities* are sensational, whilst almost all *spatial* attributes are results of habit and experience."[72]

This passage of Helmholtz's has obtained, it seems to me, an almost deplorable celebrity. The reader will please observe its very radical import. Not only would he, and does he, for the reasons we have just been ourselves considering, deny distance to be an optical sensation; but, extending the same method of criticism to judgments of size, shape, and direction, and finding no single retinal or muscular process in the eyes to be indissolubly linked with any one of these, he goes so far as to say that all optical space-perceptions whatsoever must have an intellectual origin, and a content that no items of visual sensibility can account for.[73]

[72] *Physiologische Optik*, p. 438. Helmholtz's reservation of 'qualities' is inconsistent. Our judgments of light and color vary as much as our judgments of size, shape, and place, and ought by parity of reasoning to be called intellectual products and not sensations. In other places he does treat color as if it were an intellectual product.

[73] It is needless at this point to consider what Helmholtz's views of the nature

As Wundt and others agree with Helmholtz here, and as their conclusions, if true, are irreconcilable with all the sensationalism which I have been teaching hitherto, it clearly devolves upon me to defend my position against this new attack. But as this chapter on Space is already so overgrown with episodes and details, I think it best to reserve the refutation of their general principle for the next chapter, and simply to assume at this point its untenability. This has of course an arrogant look; but if the reader will bear with me for not very many pages more, I shall hope to appease his mind. Meanwhile I affirm confidently that *the same outer objects actually* FEEL *different to us according as our brain reacts on them in one way or another by making us perceive them as this or as that sort of thing*. So true is this that one may well, with Stumpf,[74] reverse Helmholtz's query, and ask: "What would become of our sense-perceptions in case experience were *not* able so to transform them?" Stumpf adds: "All wrong perceptions that depend on peculiarities in the organs are more or less perfectly corrected by the influence of imagination following the guidance of experience."

If, therefore, among the facts of optical space-perception (which we must now proceed to consider in more detail) we find instances of an identical organic eye-process, giving us different perceptions at different times, in consequence of different collateral circumstances suggesting different objective facts to our imagination, we must not hastily conclude, with the school of Helmholtz and Wundt, that the organic eye-process pure and simple, without the collateral circumstances, is incapable of giving us any sensation of a spatial kind at all. We must rather seek to discover *by what means* the circumstances can so have transformed a space-sensation, which, but for their presence, would probably have been felt in its natural purity. And I may as well say now in advance that we shall find the means to be nothing more or less than association—*the suggestion to the mind of optical objects not actually present*, but more habitually associated with the 'collateral circumstances' than the sensation which they now displace and being imagined now with a quasi-hallucinatory strength. But before this conclusion emerges, it will be necessary to have reviewed the most important facts of optical space-perception, in relation to the organic conditions on

of the intellectual space-yielding process may be. He vacillates—we shall later see how.

[74] *Op. cit.*, p. 214.

which they depend. Readers acquainted with German optics will excuse what is already familiar to them in the following section.[75]

[75] Before embarking on this new topic it will be well to shelve, once for all, the problem of what is the physiological process that underlies the distance-feeling. Since one-eyed people have it, and are inferior to the two-eyed only in measuring its gradations, it can have no exclusive connection with the double and disparate images produced by binocular parallax. Since people with closed eyes, looking at an after-image, do not usually see it draw near or recede with varying convergence, it cannot be simply constituted by the convergence-feeling. For the same reason it would appear non-identical with the feeling of accommodation. The differences of apparent parallactic movement between far and near objects as we move our head cannot constitute the distance-sensation, for such differences may be easily reproduced experimentally (in the movements of visible spots against a background) without engendering any illusion of perspective. Finally, it is obvious that visible faintness, dimness, and smallness *are* not *per se* the feeling of visible distance, however much in the case of well-known objects they may serve as signs to suggest it.

A certain maximum distance-value, however, being given to the field of view of the moment, whatever it be, the feelings that accompany the processes just enumerated become so many *local signs* of the gradation of distances within this maximum depth. They help us to subdivide and measure it. Itself, however, is felt as a unit, a total distance-value, determining the vastness of the whole field of view, which accordingly appears as an abyss of a certain volume. And the question still persists, what neural process is it that underlies the sense of this distance-value?

Hering, who has tried to explain the gradations within it by the interaction of certain native distance-values belonging to each point of the two retinæ, seems willing to admit that the *absolute* scale of the space-volume within which the natively fixed relative distances shall appear is *not* fixed, but determined each time by 'experience in the widest sense of the word' (*Beiträge*, p. 344). What he calls the *Kernpunkt* of this space-volume is the point we are momentarily fixating. The absolute scale of the whole volume depends on the absolute distance at which this *Kernpunkt* is judged to lie from the person of the looker. "By an alteration of the localization of the *Kernpunkt*, the *inner* relations of the seen space are no wise altered; this space in its totality is as a fixed unit, so to speak, displaced with respect to the self of the looker" (p. 345). But what constitutes the localization of the *Kernpunkt* itself at any given time, except 'Experience,' i.e., higher cerebral and intellectual processes, involving memory, Hering does not seek to define.

Stumpf, the other sensationalist writer who has best realized the difficulties of the problem, thinks that the primitive sensation of distance must have an immediate physical antecedent, either in the shape of "an organic alteration accompanying the process of accommodation, or else given directly in the specific energy of the optic nerve." In contrast with Hering, however, he thinks that it is the *absolute* distance of the spot fixated which is thus primitively, immediately, and physiologically given, and not the relative distances of other things about this spot. These, he thinks, are originally seen in what, broadly speaking, may be termed one plane with it. Whether the distance of this plane, considered as a phenomenon of our primitive sensibility, be an invariable datum, or susceptible of fluctuation, he does not, if I understand him rightly, undertake dogmatically to decide, but inclines to the former view. For him then, as for Hering, higher cerebral processes of association,

Let us begin the long and rather tedious inquiry by the most important case. Physiologists have long sought for a simple law by which to connect the seen direction and distance of objects with the retinal impressions they produce. Two principal theories have been held of this matter, the 'theory of identical points,' and the

---

under the name of 'Experience,' are the authors of fully one-half part of the distance-perceptions which we at any given time may have.

Hering's and Stumpf's theories are reported for the English reader by Mr. Sully (in *Mind,* III, pp. 172–6). Mr. Abbott, in his *Sight and Touch* (pp. 96–8), gives a theory which is to me so obscure that I only refer the reader to its place, adding that it seems to make of distance a fixed function of retinal sensation as modified by focal adjustment. Besides these three authors I am ignorant of any, except Panum, who may have attempted to define distance as in any degree an immediate sensation. And with them the direct sensational share is reduced to a very small proportional part, in our completed distance judgments.

Professor Lipps, in his singularly acute *Psychologische Studien* (p. 69 ff.), argues, as Ferrier, in his review of Berkeley (*Philosophical Remains,* II, 330 ff.), had argued before him, that it is *logically impossible* we should perceive the distance of anything from the eye by sight; for a *seen* distance can only be between *seen* termini; and one of the termini, in the case of distance from the eye, is the eye itself, which is not seen. Similarly of the distance of two points behind each other: the near one *hides* the far one, no space is seen between them. For the space between two objects to be *seen,* both must appear *beside* each other, then the space in question will be *visible.* On no other condition is its visibility possible. The conclusion is that things can properly be seen only in what Lipps calls a surface, and that our knowledge of the third dimension must needs be conceptual, not sensational or visually intuitive.

But no arguments in the world can prove a feeling which actually exists to be impossible. The feeling of depth or distance, of farness or awayness, does actually exist as a fact of our visual sensibility. All that Professor Lipps's reasonings prove concerning it is that it is not linear in its character, or in its immediacy fully homogeneous and consubstantial with the feeling of lateral distance between two seen termini; in short, that there are *two* sorts of optical sensation, each inexplicably due to a peculiar neural process. The neural process is easily discovered, in the case of lateral extension or spreadoutness, to be the number of retinal nerve-ends affected by the light; in the case of protension or mere farness it is more complicated and, as we have concluded, is still to seek. The two sensible qualities unite in the primitive visual bigness. The measurement of their various amounts against each other obeys the general laws of all such measurements. We discover their equivalencies by means of objects, apply the same units to both, and translate them into each other so habitually that at last they get to seem to us even quite similar in kind. This final appearance of homogeneity may perhaps be facilitated by the fact that in binocular vision two points situated on the prolongation of the optical axis of *one* of the eyes, so that the near one hides the far one, are by the *other* eye seen laterally apart. Each eye has in fact a foreshortened lateral view of the other's line of sight. In the London *Times* for Feb. 8, 1884, is an interesting letter by J. D. Dougall, who tries to explain by this reason why two-eyed rifle-shooting has such advantages over shooting with one eye closed.

'theory of projection,'—each incompatible with the other, and each beyond certain limits becoming inconsistent with the facts.

The Theory of Identical Points

This theory starts from the truth that on both retinæ an impression on the upper half makes us perceive an object as below, on the lower half as above, the horizon; and on the right half an object

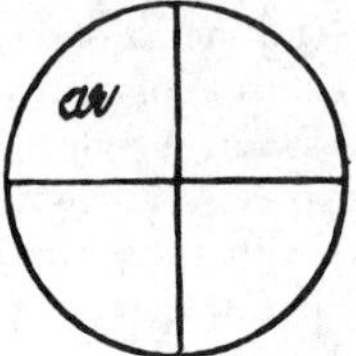

FIG. 54.

to the left, on the left half one to the right, of the median line. Thus each quadrant of one retina corresponds as a whole to the *similar* quadrant of the other; and within two similar quadrants, *al* and *ar* for example, there should, if the correspondence were consistently carried out, be geometrically similar points which, if impressed at the same time by light emitted from the same object, should cause that object to appear in the same direction to either eye. Experiment verifies this surmise. If we look at the starry vault with parallel eyes, the stars all seem single; and the laws of perspective show that under the circumstances the parallel light-rays coming from each star must impinge on points within either retina which *are* geometrically similar to each other. The same result may be more artificially obtained. If we take two exactly similar pictures, smaller, or at least no larger, than those on an ordinary stereoscopic slide, and if we look at them as stereoscopic slides are looked at, that is, at one with each eye (a median partition confining the view of either eye to the picture opposite it), we shall see but one flat picture, all of whose parts appear sharp and single.[76]

[76] Just so, a pair of spectacles held an inch or so from the eyes seem like one large median glass. The faculty of seeing stereoscopic slides single without an instrument is of the utmost utility to the student of physiological optics, and persons with strong eyes can easily acquire it. The only difficulty lies in dissociating the degree of accommodation from the degree of convergence which it usually accompanies. If the right picture is focussed by the right eye, the left by the left eye, the optic axes must either be parallel or converge upon an imaginary point some distance

Identical points being impressed, both eyes see their object in the same direction, and the two objects consequently coalesce into one.

The same thing may be shown in still another way. With fixed head converge the eyes upon some conspicuous objective point behind a pane of glass; then close either eye alternately and make a little ink-mark on the glass, 'covering' the object as seen by the eye which is momentarily open. On looking now with both eyes the ink-marks will seem single, and in the same direction as the objective point. Conversely, let the eyes converge on a single ink-spot on the glass, and then by alternate shutting of them let it be noted what objects behind the glass the spot covers to the right and left eye respectively. Now with both eyes open, both these objects and the spot will appear in the same place, one or other of the three becoming more distinct according to the fluctuations of retinal attention.[77]

Now what is the direction of this common place? The only way of defining the direction of an object is by *pointing to it.* Most people, if asked to look at an object over the horizontal edge of a sheet of paper which conceals their hand and arm, and then to point their finger at it (raising the hand gradually so that at last a finger-tip will appear above the sheet of paper), are found to place the finger not between either eye and the object, but between the latter and the root of the nose, and this whether both eyes or either alone be used. Hering and Helmholtz express this by saying that we judge of the direction of objects as they would appear to an imaginary cyclopean eye, situated between our two real eyes, and with its optical axis bisecting the angle of convergence of the latter. Our two retinæ act, according to Hering, as if they were superposed in the place of this imaginary double-eye; we see by the corresponding points of each, situated far asunder as they really are, just as we *should* see if they were superposed and could both be excited together.

The judgment of objective singleness and that of identical di-

---

behind the plane of the pictures, according to the size and distance apart of the pictures. The accommodation, however, has to be made for the plane of the pictures itself, and a near accommodation with a far-off convergence is something which the ordinary use of our eyes never teaches us to effect.

77 These two observations prove the law of identical direction only for objects which excite the foveæ or lie in the line of direct looking. Observers skilled in indirect vision can, however, more or less easily verify the law for outlying retinal points.

rection seem to hang necessarily together. And that of identical direction seems to carry with it the necessity of a common origin, between the eyes or elsewhere, from which all the directions felt may seem to be estimated. This is why the cyclopean eye is really a fundamental part of the formulation of the theory of identical retinal points, and why Hering, the greatest champion of this theory, lays so much stress upon it.

It is an immediate consequence of the law of identical projection of images on geometrically similar points that images which fall upon geometrically DISPARATE *points of the two retinæ should be projected in* DISPARATE *directions, and that their objects should consequently appear in* TWO *places, or* LOOK DOUBLE. Take the parallel rays from a star falling upon two eyes which converge upon a near object, O, instead of being parallel, as in the previously instanced case. If SL and SR in Fig. 55 be the parallel rays, each of them will fall upon the nasal half of the retina which it strikes.

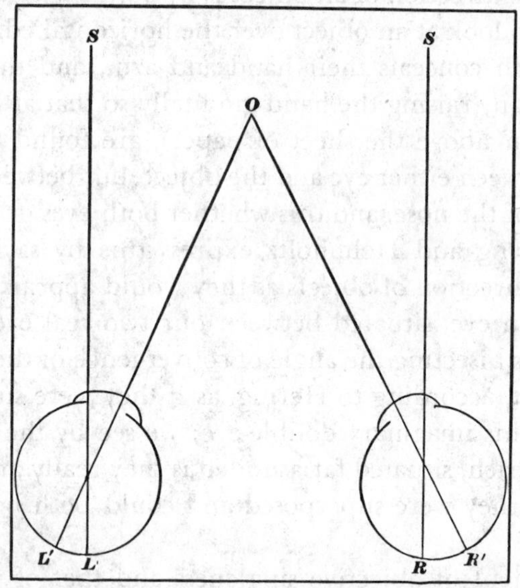

FIG. 55.

But the two nasal halves are disparate, geometrically *symmetrical*, not geometrically *similar*. The image on the left one will therefore appear as if lying in a direction leftwards of the cyclopean eye's line of sight; the image of the right one will appear far to the right of the same direction. The star will, in short, be seen double,—'homonymously' double.

Conversely, if the star be looked at directly with parallel axes, O will be seen double, because its images will affect the outer or cheek halves of the two retinæ, instead of one outer and one nasal half. The position of the images will here be reversed from that of the previous case. The right eye's image will now appear to the left, the left eye's to the right—the double images will be 'heteronymous.'

The same reasoning and the same result ought to apply where the object's place with respect to the direction of the two optic axes is such as to make its images fall not on non-similar retinal halves, but on non-similar parts of similar halves. Here, of course, the directions of projection will be less widely disparate than in the other case, and the double images will appear to lie less widely apart.

Careful experiments made by many observers according to the so-called haploscopic method confirm this law, and show that *corresponding points, of single visual direction,* exist upon the two retinæ. For the detail of these one must consult the special treatises.

Note now an important consequence. If we take a stationary object and allow the eyes to vary their direction and convergence, a purely geometrical study will show that there will be some positions in which its two images impress corresponding retinal points, but more in which they impress disparate points. The former constitute the so-called horopter, and their discovery has been attended with great mathematical difficulty. Objects or parts of objects which lie in the eyes' horopter at any given time cannot appear double. *Objects lying out of the horopter would seem, if the theory of identical points were strictly true, necessarily and always to appear double.*

Here comes the first great conflict of the identity-theory with experience. Were the theory true, we ought all to have an intuitive knowledge of the horopter as the line of distinctest vision. Objects placed elsewhere ought to seem, if not actually double, at least blurred. And yet no living man makes any such distinction between the parts of his field of vision. To most of us the whole field appears single, and it is only by rare accident or by special education that we ever catch a glimpse of a double image. In 1838, Wheatstone, in his truly classical memoir on binocular vision and the stereoscope,[78] showed that the disparateness of the points on which the

78 This essay, published in the *Philosophical Transactions,* contains the germ of

two images of an object fall does not within certain limits affect its seen singleness at all, but rather the *distance* at which it shall appear. Wheatstone made an observation, moreover, which subsequently became the bone of much hot contention, in which he strove to show that not only might disparate images fuse, but images on corresponding or identical points might be seen double.[79]

I am unfortunately prevented by the weakness of my own eyes from experimenting enough to form a decided personal opinion on the matter. It seems to me, however, that the balance of evidence is against the Wheatstonian interpretation, and that disparate points may fuse, without identical points for that reason ever giving double images. The two questions, "Can we see single with disparate points?" and "Can we see double with identical points?" although at the first blush they may appear, as to Helmholtz they appear, to be but two modes of expressing the same inquiry, are in reality distinct. The first may quite well be answered affirmatively and the second negatively.

Add to this that the experiment quoted from Helmholtz above by no means always succeeds, but that many individuals place their finger between the object and *one* of their eyes, oftenest the right;[80] finally, observe that the identity-theory, with its Cyclopean starting point for all lines of direction, gives by itself no ground for the *distance* on any line at which an object shall appear, and has to be helped out in this respect by subsidiary hypotheses, which, in the hands of Hering and others, have become so complex as easily to

---

almost all the methods applied since to the study of optical perception. It seems a pity that England, leading off so brilliantly the modern epoch of this study, should so quickly have dropped out of the field. Almost all subsequent progress has been made in Germany, Holland, and, *longo intervallo*, America.

[79] This is no place to report this controversy, but a few bibliographic references may not be inappropriate. Wheatstone's own experiment is in section 12 of his memoir. In favor of his interpretation see Helmholtz: *Physiologische Optik*, pp. 736–9; Wundt: *Physiologische Psychologie*, 2te Aufl., II, p. 144; Nagel: *Das Sehen mit zwei Augen*, pp. 78–82. Against Wheatstone see Volkmann: *Archiv für Ophthalmologie*, V, 2–74, and *Untersuchungen*, p. 266; Hering: *Beiträge zur Physiologie*, §§ 29–45, also in Hermann's *Handbuch der Physiologie*, Bd. III, 1 Th., p. 435; Aubert: *Physiologie der Netzhaut*, p. 322; Schoen: *Archiv für Ophthalmologie*, XXIV, 1, pp. 56–65; and Donders: *ibid.*, XIII, 1, p. 15 and note.

[80] When we see the finger the whole time, we usually put it in the line joining object and left eye if it be the left finger, joining object and right eye if it be the right finger. Microscopists, marksmen, or persons one of whose eyes is much better than the other, almost always refer directions to a single eye, as may be seen by the position of the shadow on their face when they point at a candle-flame.

fall a prey to critical attacks; and it will soon seem as if *the law of identical seen directions by corresponding points, although a simple formula for expressing concisely many fundamental phenomena, is by no means an adequate account of the whole matter of retinal perception.*[81]

The Projection-Theory

Does the theory of projection fare any better? This theory admits that each eye sees the object in a different direction from the other, along the line, namely, passing from the object through the middle of the pupil to the retina. A point directly fixated is thus seen on the optical axes of both eyes. There is only one point, however, which these two optical axes have in common, and that is the point to which they converge. Everything directly looked at is seen at this point, and is thus seen both single and at its proper distance. It is easy to show the incompatibility of this theory with the theory of identity. Take an objective point (like O in Fig. 55, when the star is looked at) casting its images R′ and L′ on geometrically dissimilar parts of the two retinæ and affecting the outer half of each eye. On the identity-theory it ought necessarily to appear double, whilst on the projection-theory there is no reason whatever why it should not appear single, provided only it be located by the judgment on each line of visible direction, neither nearer nor farther than its point of intersection with the other line.

Every point in the field of view ought, in truth, if the projection-theory were uniformly valid, to appear single, entirely irrespective of the varying positions of the eyes, for from every point of space two lines of visible direction pass to the two retinæ; and at the intersection of these lines, or just where the point is, there, according to the theory, it should appear. *The objection to this theory is thus precisely the reverse of the objection to the identity-theory. If the latter ruled, we ought to see most things double all the time. If the*

81 Professor Joseph Le Conte, who believes strongly in the identity-theory, has embodied the latter in a pair of laws of the relation between positions seen single and double, near or far, on the one hand, and convergences and retinal impressions, on the other, which, though complicated, seems to me by far the best descriptive formulation yet made of the normal facts of vision. His account is easily accessible to the reader in his volume *Sight* in the International Scientific Series, bk. II, c. 3, so I say no more about it now, except that it does not solve any of the difficulties we are noting in the identity-theory, nor account for the other fluctuating perceptions of which we go on to treat.

projection-theory ruled, we ought never to see anything double. As a matter of fact we get too few double images for the identity-theory, and too many for the projection-theory.

The partisans of the projection-theory, beginning with Aguilonius, have always explained double images as the result of an erroneous judgment of the *distance* of the object, the images of the latter being projected by the imagination along the two lines of visible direction either nearer or farther than the point of intersection of the latter. A diagram will make this clear.

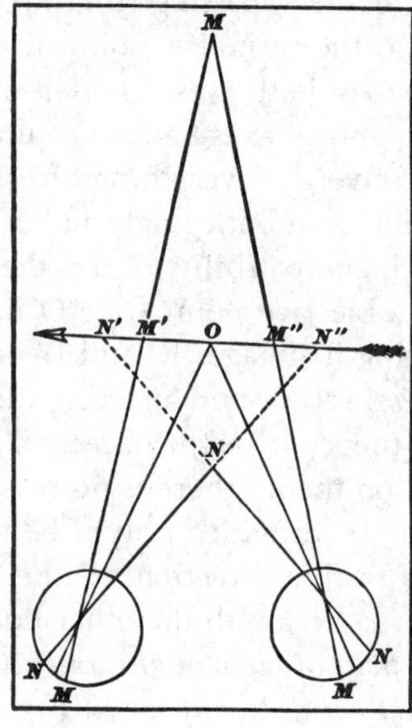

FIG. 56.

Let O be the point looked at, M an object farther, and N an object nearer, than it. Then M and N will send the lines of visible direction MM and NN to the two retinæ. If N be judged as far as O, it must necessarily lie where the two lines of visible direction NN intersect the plane of the arrow, or in two places, at N′ and at N″. If M be judged as near as O, it must for the same reason form two images at M′ and M″.

It is, as a matter of fact, true that we often misjudge the distance in the way alleged. If the reader will hold his forefingers, one beyond the other, in the median line, and fixate them alternately, he will see the one not looked at, double; and he will also notice that it appears nearer to the plane of the one looked at, whichever the latter may be, than it really is. Its changes of apparent size, as the convergence of the eyes alters, also prove the change of apparent distance. The distance at which the axes converge seems, in fact, to exert a sort of attraction upon objects situated elsewhere. Being the distance of which we are most acutely sensible, it invades, so to speak, the whole field of our perception. If two half-dollars be laid on the table an inch or two apart, and the eyes fixate steadily the point of a pen held in the median line at varying distances between the coins and the face, there will come a distance at which the pen stands between the left half-dollar and the right eye, and the right half-dollar and the left eye. The two half-dollars will then coalesce into one; and this one will show its apparent approach to the pen-point by seeming suddenly much reduced in size.[82]

Yet, in spite of this tendency to inaccuracy, we are never actually mistaken about the half-dollar being behind the pen-point. It may not seem far enough off, but still it is farther than the point. In general it may be said that where the objects are known to us, no such illusion of distance occurs in any one as the theory would require. And in some observers, Hering for example, it seems hardly to occur at all. If I look into infinite distance and get my finger in double images, they do not seem infinitely far off. To make objects at different distances seem equidistant, careful precautions must be taken to have them alike in appearance, and to exclude all outward reasons for ascribing to the one a different location from that ascribed to the other. Thus Donders tries to prove the law of projection by taking two similar electric sparks, one behind the other on a dark ground, one seen double; or an iron rod placed so near to the eyes that its double images seem as broad as that of a fixated stove-pipe, the top and bottom of the objects being cut off by screens, so as to prevent all suggestions of perspective, etc. The three objects in each experiment seem in the same plane.[83]

Add to this the impossibility, recognized by *all* observers, of ever seeing double with the *foveæ*, and the fact that authorities as able as those quoted in the note on Wheatstone's observation deny that they can see double then with identical points, and we are forced

[82] Naturally it takes a smaller object at a less distance to cover by its image a constant amount of retinal surface.

[83] *Archiv für Ophthalmologie,* Bd. XVII, Abth. 2, pp. 44–6 (1877).

to conclude that *the projection-theory, like its predecessor, breaks down. Neither formulates exactly or exhaustively a law for all our perceptions.*

Ambiguity of Retinal Impressions

What does each theory try to do? To make of seen location a fixed function of retinal impression. Other facts may be brought forwards to show how far from fixed are the perceptive functions of retinal impressions. We alluded a while ago to the extraordinary ambiguity of the retinal image as a revealer of magnitude. Produce an after-image of the sun and look at your finger-tip: it will be smaller than your nail. Project it on the table, and it will be as big as a strawberry; on the wall, as large as a plate; on yonder mountain, bigger than a house. And yet it is an unchanged retinal impression. Prepare a sheet with the figures shown in Fig. 57 strongly marked upon it, and get by direct fixation a distinct after-image of each.

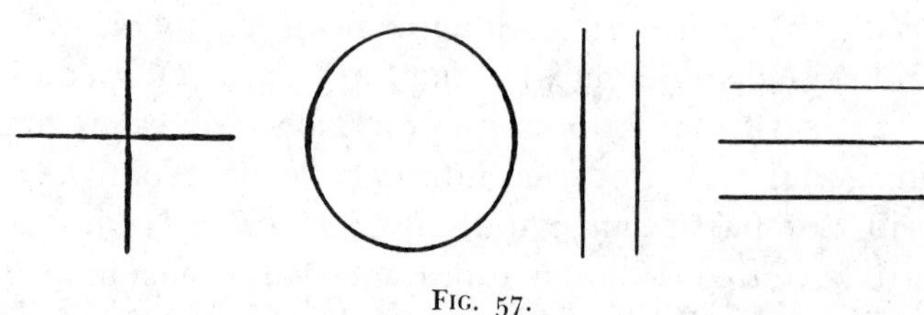

Fig. 57.

Project the after-image of the cross upon the upper left-hand part of the wall, it will appear as in Fig. 58; on the upper right-hand it will appear as in Fig. 59. The circle similarly projected will be

Fig. 58. Fig. 59.

distorted into two different ellipses. If the two parallel lines be projected upon the ceiling or floor far in front, the farther ends will diverge; and if the three parallel lines be thrown on the same surfaces, the upper pair will seem farther apart than the lower.

Adding certain lines to others has the same distorting effect. In what is known as Zöllner's pattern (Fig. 60), the long parallels tip towards each other the moment we draw the short slanting lines

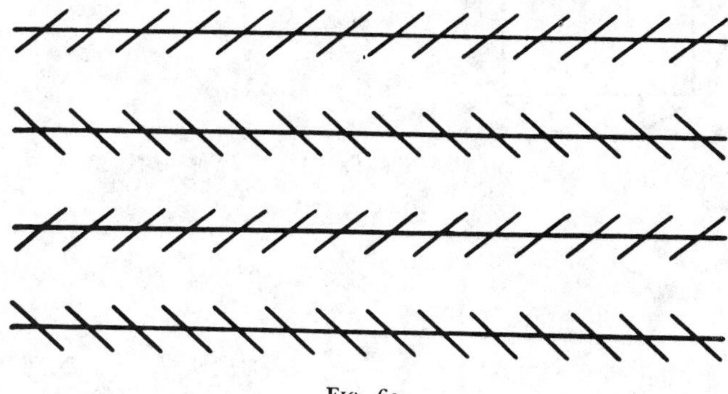

Fig. 60.

over them yet their retinal images are the same they always were. A similar distortion of parallels appears in Fig. 61.

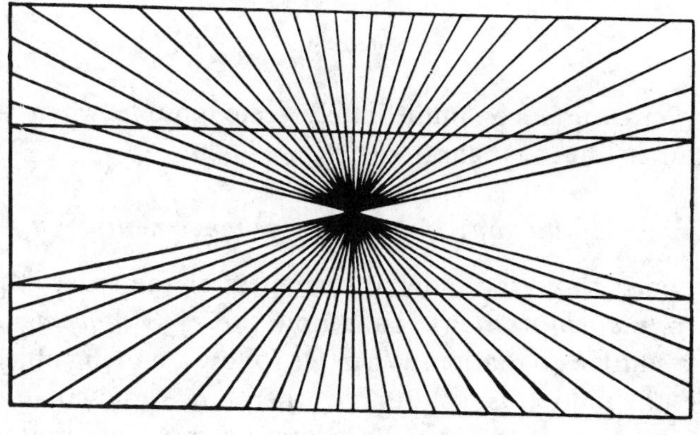

Fig. 61.

Drawing a square inside the circle (Fig. 62) gives to the outline of the latter an indented appearance where the square's corners touch it. Drawing the radii inside of one of the right angles in the same figure makes it seem larger than the other. In Fig. 63, the retinal image of the space between the extreme dots is in all three lines the same, yet it seems much larger the moment it is filled up with other dots.

In the stereoscope certain pairs of lines which look single under

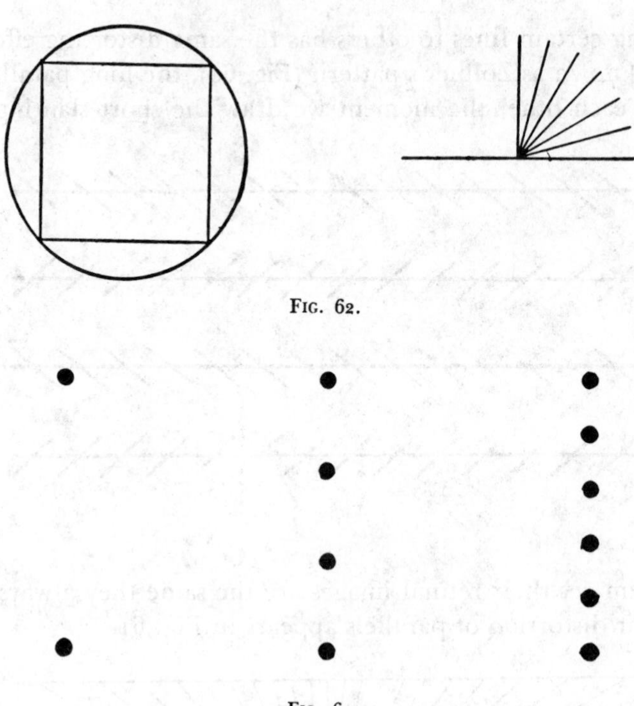

FIG. 62.

FIG. 63.

ordinary circumstances immediately seem double when we add certain other lines to them.[84]

Ambiguous Import of Eye-movements

These facts show the indeterminateness of the space-import of various *retinal impressions.* Take now the *eye's movements,* and we find a similar vacillation. When we follow a moving object with our gaze, the motion is 'voluntary'; when our eyes oscillate to and fro after we have made ourselves dizzy by spinning around, it is 'reflex'; and when the eyeball is pushed with the finger, it is 'passive.' Now, in all three of these cases we get a feeling from the movement as it effects itself. But the objective perceptions to which the feeling assists us are by no means the same. In the first case we may see a stationary field of view with one moving object in it; in the second, the total field swimming more or less steadily in one direction; in the third, a sudden jump or twist of the same total field.

[84] A. W. Volkmann: *Untersuchungen,* p. 253.

The feelings of convergence of the eyeballs permit of the same ambiguous interpretation. When objects are near we converge strongly upon them in order to see them; when far, we set our optic axes parallel. But the exact degree of convergence fails to be felt; or rather, being felt, fails to tell us the absolute distance of the object we are regarding. Wheatstone arranged his stereoscope in such a way that the size of the retinal images might change without the convergence altering; or conversely, the convergence might change without the retinal image altering. Under these circumstances, he says,[85] the object seemed to approach or recede in the first case, without altering its size; in the second, to change its size without altering its distance—just the reverse of what might have been expected. Wheatstone adds, however, that 'fixing the attention' converted each of these perceptions into its opposite. The same perplexity occurs in looking through prismatic glasses, which alter the eyes' convergence. We cannot decide whether the object has come nearer, or grown larger, or both, or neither; and our judgment vacillates in the most surprising way. We may even make our eyes diverge, and the object will none the less appear at a finite distance. When we look through the stereoscope, the picture seems at no determinate distance. These and other facts have led Helmholtz to deny that the feeling of convergence has any very exact value as a distance-measurer.[86]

With *the feelings of accommodation* it is very much the same. Donders has shown[87] that the apparent magnifying power of spectacles of moderate convexity hardly depends at all upon their enlargement of the retinal image, but rather on the relaxation they permit of the muscle of accommodation. This suggests an object farther off, and consequently a much larger one, since its retinal size rather increases than diminishes. But in this case the same vacillation of judgment as in the previously mentioned case of convergence takes place. The recession made the object seem larger, but the apparent growth in size of the object now makes it look as if it came nearer instead of receding. The effect thus contradicts its own cause. Everyone is conscious, on first putting on a pair of

85 *Philosophical Transactions*, 1852, p. 4.

86 *Physiologische Optik*, 649–664. Later this author is led to value convergence more highly. *Archiv für (Anatomie und) Physiologie* (1878), p. 322.

87 *On the Anomalies of Accommodation and Refraction of the Eye* (New Sydenham Society Translation, London, 1864), p. 155.

spectacles, of a doubt whether the field of view draws near or retreats.[88]

There is still *another deception, occurring in persons who have had one eye-muscle suddenly paralyzed.* This deception has led Wundt to affirm that the eyeball-feeling proper, the incoming sensation of effected rotation, tells us only of the direction of our eye-movements, but not of their whole extent.[89] For this reason, and because not only Wundt, but many other authors, think the phenomena in these partial paralyses demonstrate the existence of a feeling of innervation, a feeling of the outgoing nervous current, opposed to every afferent sensation whatever, it seems proper to note the facts with a certain degree of detail.

Suppose a man wakes up some morning with the external rectus muscle of his right eye half paralyzed, what will be the result? He will be enabled only with great effort to rotate the eye so as to look at objects lying far off to the right. Something in the effort he makes will make him feel as if the object lay much farther to the right than it really is. If the left and sound eye be closed, and he be asked to touch rapidly with his finger an object situated towards his right, he will point the finger to the right of it. The current explanation of the 'something' in the effort which causes this deception is that it is the sensation of the outgoing discharge from the nervous centres, the 'feeling of innervation,' to use Wundt's expression, requisite for bringing the open eye with its weakened muscle to bear upon the object to be touched. If that object be situated 20 degrees to the right, the patient has now to innervate as powerfully to turn the eye those 20 degrees as formerly he did to turn the eye 30 degrees. He consequently believes as before that he *has* turned it 30 degrees; until, by a newly-acquired custom, he learns the altered spatial import of all the discharges his brain makes into his right abducens nerve. The 'feeling of innervation,' maintained to exist by this and other observations, plays an immense part in the space-theories of certain philosophers, especially Wundt. I shall else-

88 These strange contradictions have been called by Aubert 'secondary' deceptions of judgment. See *Grundzüge der physiologischen Optik* (Leipzig, 1876), pp. 601, 615, 627. One of the best examples of them is the small size of the moon as first seen through a telescope. It is larger and brighter, so we see its details more distinctly and judge it nearer. But because we judge it so much nearer we think it must have grown smaller. Cf. Charpentier in *Jahresberichte über die Fortschritte der Anatomie und Physiologie*, x, 430.

89 *Revue Philosophique*, vi, p. 220.

where try to show that the observations by no means warrant the conclusions drawn from them, and that the feeling in question is probably a wholly fictitious entity.[90] Meanwhile it suffices to point out that even those who set most store by it are compelled, by the readiness with which the translocation of the field of view becomes corrected and further errors avoided, to admit that the precise space-import of *the supposed sensation of outgoing energy is as ambiguous and indeterminate as that of any other of the eye-feelings we have considered hitherto.*

I have now given what no one will call an understatement of the facts and arguments by which it is sought to banish the credit of directly revealing space from each and every kind of eye-sensation taken by itself. The reader will confess that they make a very plausible show, and most likely wonder whether my own theory of the matter can rally from their damaging evidence. But the case is far from being hopeless; and the introduction of a discrimination hitherto unmade will, if I mistake not, easily vindicate the view adopted in these pages, whilst at the same time it makes ungrudging allowance for all the ambiguity and illusion on which so much stress is laid by the advocates of the intellectualist-theory.

The Choice of the Visual Reality

We *have* native and fixed optical space-sensations; *but experience leads us to select certain ones from among them to be the exclusive bearers of reality: the rest become mere signs and suggesters of these.* The factor of *selection,* on which we have already laid so much stress, here as elsewhere is the solving word of the enigma. If Helmholtz, Wundt, and the rest, with an ambiguous retinal sensation before them, meaning now one size and distance, and now another, had not contented themselves with merely saying:—The size and distance are not this sensation, they are something beyond it which it merely calls up, and whose own birthplace is afar—in 'synthesis' (Wundt) or in 'experience' (Helmholtz) as the case may be; if they had gone on definitely to ask and definitely to answer the question, What are the size and distance in their proper selves? they would not only have escaped the present deplorable vagueness of their space-theories, but they would have seen that the objective spatial attributes 'signified' are simply and solely *certain*

[90] See Chapter XXVI.

other optical sensations now absent, but which the present sensations suggest.

What, for example, is the slant-legged cross which we think we see on the wall when we project the rectangular after-image high up towards our right or left (Figs. 58 and 59)? Is it not in very sooth a retinal sensation itself? An imagined sensation, not a felt one, it is true, but none the less essentially and originally sensational or retinal for that,—the sensation, namely, which we should receive if a 'real' slant-legged cross stood on the wall *in front of us* and threw its image on our eye. That image is not the one our retina now holds. Our retina now holds the image which a cross of square shape throws when in front, but which a cross of the slant-legged pattern *would* throw, provided it were actually on the wall in the distant place at which we look. Call this actual retinal image the 'square' image. The square image is then one of the innumerable images the slant-legged cross can throw. Why should another one, and that an absent one, of those innumerable images be picked out to represent exclusively the slant-legged cross's 'true' shape? Why should that absent and imagined slant-legged image displace the present and felt square image from our mind? Why, when the objective cross gives us so many shapes, as it varies its position, should we think we feel the true shape only when the cross is directly in front? And when that question is answered, how can the absent and represented feeling of a slant-legged figure so successfully intrude itself into the place of a presented square one?

Before answering either question, let us be doubly sure about our facts, and see how true it is that *in our dealings with objects we always do pick out one of the visual images they yield, to constitute the real form or size.*

The matter of size has been already touched upon, so that no more need be said of it here. As regards shape, almost all the retinal shapes that objects throw are perspective 'distortions.' Square table-tops constantly present two acute and two obtuse angles; circles drawn on our wall-papers, our carpets, or on sheets of paper, usually show like ellipses; parallels approach as they recede; human bodies are foreshortened; and the transitions from one to another of these altering forms are infinite and continual. Out of the flux, however, one phase always stands prominent. It is the form the object has when we see it easiest and best: and that is when our eyes and the object both are in what may be called *the normal po-*

sition. In this position our head is upright and our optic axes either parallel or symmetrically convergent; the plane of the object is perpendicular to the visual plane; and if the object is one containing many lines it is turned so as to make them, as far as possible, either parallel or perpendicular to the visual plane. In this situation it is that we compare all shapes with each other; here every exact measurement and decision is made.[91]

It is very easy to see why the normal situation should have this extraordinary pre-eminence. First, it is the position in which we easiest hold anything we are examining in our hands; second, it is a turning-point between all right- and all left-hand perspective views of a given object; third, it is the only position in which symmetrical figures seem symmetrical and equal angles seem equal; fourth, it is often that starting point of movements from which the eye is least troubled by axial rotations, by which *superposition*[92] of the retinal images of different lines and different parts of the same line is easiest produced, and consequently by which the eye can make the best comparative measurements in its sweeps. All these merits single the normal position out to be chosen. No other point of view offers so many æsthetic and practical advantages. Here we believe we see the object as it *is*; elsewhere, only as it seems. Experience and custom soon teach us, however, that the seeming appearance passes into the real one by continuous gradations. They teach us, moreover, that seeming and being may be strangely interchanged. Now a real circle may slide into a seeming ellipse; now an ellipse may, by sliding in the same direction, become a seeming circle; now a rectangular cross grows slant-legged; now a slant-legged one grows rectangular.

Almost any form in oblique vision may be thus a derivative of almost any other in 'primary' vision; and we must learn, when we get one of the former appearances, to translate it into the appropriate one of the latter class; we must learn of what optical 'reality' it is one of the optical signs. Having learned this, we do but obey that law of economy or simplification which dominates our whole psychic life, when we attend exclusively to the 'reality' and ignore as much as our consciousness will let us the 'sign' by which we came

91 The only exception seems to be when we expressly wish to abstract from particulars, and to judge of the general 'effect.' Witness ladies trying on new dresses with their heads inclined and their eyes askance; or painters in the same attitude judging of the 'values' in their pictures.

92 The importance of Superposition will appear later on.

to apprehend it. The signs of each probable real thing being multiple and the thing itself one and fixed, we gain the same mental relief by abandoning the former for the latter that we do when we abandon mental images, with all their fluctuating characters, for the definite and unchangeable *names* which they suggest. The selection of the several 'normal' appearances from out of the jungle of our optical experiences, to serve as the real sights of which we shall think, is psychologically a parallel phenomenon to the habit of thinking in words, and has a like use. Both are substitutions of terms few and fixed for terms manifold and vague.

Sensations which we Ignore

This service of sensations as mere signs, to be ignored when they have evoked the other sensations which are their significates, was noticed first by Berkeley and remarked in many passages, as the following:

"Signs, being little considered in themselves, or for their own sake, but only in their relative capacity, and for the sake of those things whereof they are signs, it comes to pass that the mind overlooks them, so as to carry its attention immediately on to the things signified . . . which, in truth and strictness, are not *seen*, but only *suggested* and *apprehended* by means of the proper objects of sight, which alone are seen." (*Alciphron: Or, the Minute Philosopher*, Fourth Dialogue, § 12.)

Berkeley of course erred in supposing that the thing suggested was not even *originally* an object of sight, as the sign now is which calls it up. Reid expressed Berkeley's principle in yet clearer language:

"The visible appearances of objects are intended by nature only as signs or indications; and the mind passes instantly to the things signified, without making the least reflection upon the sign, or even perceiving that there is any such thing. . . . The mind has acquired a confirmed and inveterate habit of inattention to them [the signs]; for they no sooner appear, than quick as lightning the thing signified succeeds, and engrosses all our regard. They have no name in language; and, although we are conscious of them when they pass through the mind, yet their passage is so quick and so familiar, that it is absolutely unheeded; nor do they leave any footsteps of themselves, either in the memory or imagination." (*Inquiry*, chap. VI, §§ 2, 3.)

If we review the facts we shall find every grade of non-attention between the extreme form of overlooking mentioned by Reid (or forms even more extreme still) and complete conscious perception of the sensation present. Sometimes it is literally impossible to become aware of the latter. Sometimes a little artifice or effort easily leads us to discern it together, or in alternation, with the 'object' it reveals. Sometimes the present sensation is held to *be* the object or to reproduce its features in undistorted shape, and *then*, of course, it receives the mind's full glare.

The deepest inattention is to subjective optical sensations, strictly so called, or those which are not signs of outer objects at all. Helmholtz's treatment of these phenomena, *muscæ volitantes*, negative after-images, double images, etc., is very satisfactory. He says:

"We only attend with any ease and exactness to our sensations in so far forth as they can be utilized for the knowledge of outward things; and we are accustomed to neglect all those portions of them which have no significance as regards the external world. So much is this the case that for the most part special artifices and practice are required for the observation of these latter more subjective feelings. Although it might seem that nothing should be easier than to be conscious of one's own sensations, experience nevertheless shows that often enough either a special talent like that showed in eminent degree by Purkinje, or accident or theoretic speculation, is a necessary condition for the discovery of subjective phenomena. Thus, for example, the blind spot on the retina was discovered by Mariotte by the theoretic way; similarly by me the existence of 'summation'-tones in acoustics. In the majority of cases accident is what first led observers whose attention was especially exercised on subjective phenomena to discover this one or that; only where the subjective appearances are so intense that they interfere with the perception of objects are they noticed by all men alike. But if they have once been discovered it is for the most part easy for subsequent observers who place themselves in proper conditions and bend their attention in the right direction to perceive them. But in many cases—for example, in the phenomena of the blind spot, in the discrimination of over-tones and combination-tones from the ground-tone of musical sounds, etc.—such a strain of the attention is required, even with appropriate instrumental aids, that most persons fail. The very after-images of bright objects are by most men perceived only under exceptionally favorable conditions, and it takes steady practice to see the fainter images of this kind. It is a commonly recurring experience that persons smitten with some eye-disease which impairs vision suddenly remark for the first time the *muscæ volitantes* which all through life their vitreous humor has contained, but which they now firmly believe to have arisen since their malady; the truth being that the latter has only made them more observant of all their visual sensations. There are also cases where one eye has gradually grown blind, and the patient lived for an indefinite time without knowing it, until, through the accidental closure of the healthy eye alone, the blindness of the other was brought to attention.

"Most people, when first made aware of binocular double images, are uncommonly astonished that they should never have noticed them before, although all through their life they had been in the habit of seeing singly only those few objects which were about equally distant with the point of fixation, and the rest, those nearer and farther, which constitute the great majority, had always been double.

"We must then *learn* to turn our attention to our particular sensations, and we learn this commonly only for such sensations as are means of cognition of the outer world. Only so far as they serve this end have our sensations any importance for us in ordinary life. Subjective feelings are mostly interesting only to scientific investigators; were they remarked in the ordinary use of the senses, they could only cause disturbance. Whilst, therefore, we reach an extraordinary degree of firmness and security in objective observation, we not only do not reach this where subjective phenomena are concerned, but we actually attain in a high degree the faculty of overlooking these altogether, and keeping ourselves independent of their influence in judging of objects, even in cases where their strength might lead them easily to attract our attention." (*Physiologische Optik*, pp. 431–2.)

Even where the sensation is not merely subjective, as in the cases of which Helmholtz speaks, but is a sign of something outward, we are also liable, as Reid says, to overlook its intrinsic quality and attend exclusively to the image of the 'thing' it suggests. But here everyone *can* easily notice the sensation itself if he will. Usually we see a sheet of paper as uniformly white, although a part of it may be in shadow. But we can in an instant, if we please, notice the shadow as local color. A man walking towards us does not usually seem to alter his size; but we can, by setting our attention in a peculiar way, make him appear to do so. The whole education of the artist consists in his learning to see the presented signs as well as the represented things. No matter what the field of view *means*, he sees it also as it *feels*—that is, as a collection of patches of color bounded by lines—the whole forming an optical diagram of whose intrinsic proportions one who is not an artist has hardly a conscious inkling. The ordinary man's attention passes *over* them to their import; the artist's turns back and dwells *upon* them for their own sake. "Don't draw the thing as it *is*, but as it *looks*!" is the endless advice of every teacher to his pupil; forgetting that what it 'is' is what it would also 'look,' provided it were placed in what we have called the 'normal' situation for vision. In this situation the sensation as 'sign' and the sensation as 'object' coalesce into one, and there is no contrast between them.

Sensations which seem Suppressed

But a great difficulty has been made of certain peculiar cases which we must now turn to consider. They are *cases in which a present sensation, whose existence is supposed to be proved by its outward conditions being there, seems absolutely suppressed or changed by the image of the 'thing' it suggests.*

This matter carries us back to what was said on p. 852. The passage there quoted from Helmholtz refers to these cases. He thinks they conclusively disprove the original and intrinsic spatiality of any of our retinal sensations; for if such a one, actually present, had an immanent and essential space-determination of its own, that might well be added to and overlaid or even momentarily eclipsed by suggestions of its signification, but how could it possibly be altered or completely *suppressed* thereby? Of actually present sensations, he says, being *suppressed* by suggestions of experience—

"We have not a single well-attested example. In all those illusions which are provoked by *sensations* in the absence of their usually exciting objects, the mistake never vanishes by the better understanding of the object really present, and by insight into the cause of deception. Phosphenes provoked by pressure on the eyeball, by traction on the entrance of the optic nerve, after-images, etc., remain projected into their apparent place in the field of vision, just as the image projected from a mirror's surface continues to be seen *behind* the mirror, although we *know* that to all these appearances no outward reality corresponds. True enough, we can remove our attention, and keep it removed, from sensations that have no reference to the outer world, those, e.g., of the weaker after-images, and of entoptic objects, etc. . . . But what would become of our perceptions at all if we had the power not only of ignoring, but of *transforming into their opposites*, any part of them that differed from that outward experience, the image of which, as that of a present reality, accompanies them in the mind?"[93]

And again:

"On the analogy of all other experience, we should expect that the conquered feelings would persist to our perception, even if only in the shape of recognized illusions. But this is not the case. One does not see how the assumption of originally spatial sensations can explain our optical cognitions, when in the last resort those who believe in these very sensations find themselves obliged to assume that they are *overcome* by our better judgment, based on experience."

These words, coming from such a quarter, necessarily carry great weight. But the authority even of a Helmholtz ought not to shake one's critical composure. And the moment one abandons abstract generalities and comes to close quarters with the particulars, I think one easily sees that no such conclusions as those we have quoted follow from the latter. But profitably to conduct the discussion *we must divide the alleged instances into groups.*

(*a*) With Helmholtz, *color-perception* is equally with space-perception an intellectual affair. The so-called simultaneous color-contrast, by which one color modifies another alongside of which it is laid, is explained by him as an unconscious inference. In Chapter XVII we discussed the color-contrast problem; the principles which applied to its solution will prove also applicable to part of the present problem. In my opinion, Hering has definitively proved that, when one color is laid beside another, it modifies the sensation of the latter, not by virtue of any mere mental suggestion, as Helmholtz would have it, but by actually exciting a new nerve-process, to which the modified feeling of color immediately corresponds. The explanation is physiological, not psychological. The transformation of the original color by the inducing color is due to the disappearance of the physiological conditions under which the first color was produced, and to the induction, under the new conditions, of a genuine new sensation, with which the 'suggestions of experience' have naught to do.

That processes in the visual apparatus propagate themselves laterally, if one may so express it, is also shown by the *phenomena of*

[93] *Physiologische Optik*, p. 817.

contrast which occur after looking upon motions of various kinds. Here are a few examples. If, over the rail of a moving vessel, we look at the water rushing along the side, and then transfer our gaze to the deck, a band of planks will appear to us, moving in the opposite direction to that in which, a moment previously, we had been seeing the water move, whilst on either side of this band another band of planks will move as the water did. Looking at a waterfall, or at the road from out of a car-window in a moving train, produces the same illusion, which may be easily verified in the laboratory by a simple piece of apparatus. A board with a win-

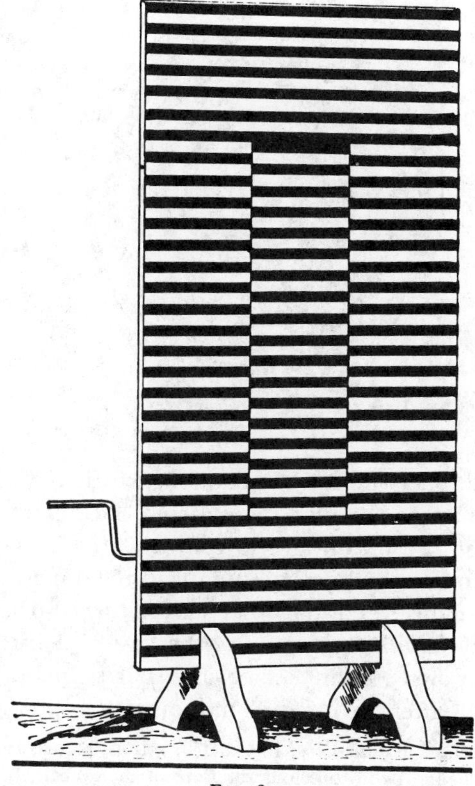

Fig. 64.

dow five or six inches wide and of any convenient length is supported upright on two feet. On the back side of the board, above and below the window, are two rollers, one of which is provided with a crank. An endless band of any figured stuff is passed over these rollers (one of which can be so adjusted on its bearings as to keep the stuff always taut and not liable to slip), and the surface of the front board is also covered with stuff or paper of a nature to catch the eye. Turning the crank now sets the central band in continuous motion, whilst the margins of the field remain really at rest, but after a while appear moving in the contrary way. Stopping the crank results in an illusory appearance of motion in reverse directions all over the field.

A disk with an Archimedean spiral drawn upon it, whirled round on an ordinary rotating machine, produces still more startling effects.

Fig. 65.

"If the revolution is in the direction in which the spiral line approaches the centre of the disk the entire surface of the latter seems to expand during revolution and to contract after it has ceased; and *vice versâ* if the movement of revolution is in the opposite direction. If in the former case the eyes of the observers are turned from the rotating disk towards any familiar object, *e.g.*, the face of a friend, the latter seems to contract or recede in a somewhat striking manner, and to expand or approach after the opposite motion of the spiral."[94]

[94] Bowditch and Hall, in *Journal of Physiology*, vol. III, p. 299. Helmholtz tries to explain this phenomenon by unconscious rotations of the eyeball. But movements of the eyeball can only explain such appearances of movement as are the same over the whole field. In the windowed board one part of the field seems to move in one way, another part in another. The same is true when we turn from the spiral to look at the wall—the *centre* of the field alone swells out or contracts, the margin does the reverse or remains at rest. Dvořák has beautifully proved the impossibility of eye-rotations in this case (*Sitzungsberichte* der Wiener Akademie, Bd. LXI). See also Bowditch and Hall's paper as above, p. 300.

An elementary form of these motor illusions seems to be the one described by Helmholtz on pp. 568–571 of his *Optik*. The motion of anything in the field of vision along an acute angle towards a straight line sensibly distorts that line. Thus in Fig. 66: Let AB

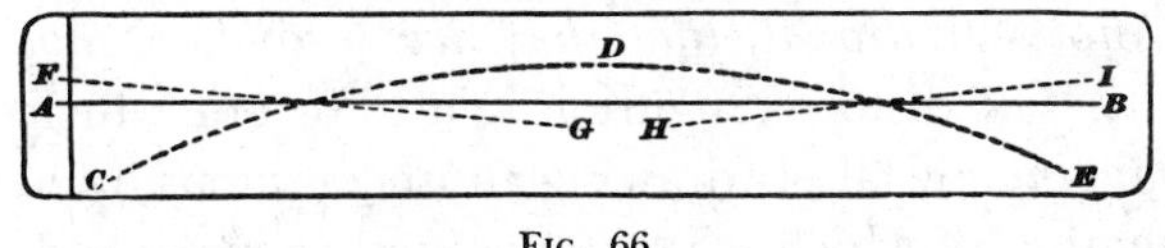

FIG. 66.

be a line drawn on paper, CDE the tracing made over this line by the point of a compass steadily followed by the eye, as it moves. As the compass-point passes from C to D, the line appears to move downwards; as it passes from D to E, the line appears to move upwards; at the same time the whole line seems to incline itself in the direction FG during the first half of the compass's movement; and in the direction HI during its last half; the change from one inclination to another being quite distinct as the compass-point passes over D.

Any line across which we draw a pencil-point appears to be animated by a rapid movement of its own towards the pencil-point. This apparent movement of both of two things in relative motion to each other, even when one of them is absolutely still, reminds us of the instances quoted from Vierordt on page 811, and seems to take us back to a primitive stage of perception, in which the discriminations we now make when we feel a movement have not yet been made. If we draw the point of a pencil through 'Zöllner's pattern' (Fig. 60, p. 865), and follow it with the eye, the whole figure becomes the scene of the most singular apparent unrest, of which Helmholtz has very carefully noted the conditions. The illusion of Zöllner's figure vanishes entirely, or almost so, with most people, if they steadily look at one point of it with an unmoving eye; and the same is the case with many other illusions.

Now all these facts taken together seem to show—vaguely it is true, but certainly—*that present excitements and after-effects of former excitements may alter the result of processes occurring simultaneously at a distance from them in the retina* or other portions of the apparatus for optical sensation. In the cases last considered, the moving eye, as it sweeps the fovea over certain parts of the figure, seems thereby to determine a modification in the feeling which the *other* parts confer, which modification is the figure's 'distortion.' It is true that this statement explains nothing. It only keeps the cases to which it applies from being explained spuriously. *The spurious account of these illusions is that they are intellectual, not sensational, that they are secondary, not primary, mental facts.* The distorted figure is said to be one which the mind is led to *imagine*, by falsely drawing an unconscious inference from certain premises of which it is not distinctly aware. And the imagined figure is supposed to be strong enough to suppress the perception of whatever real sensations there may be. But Helmholtz, Wundt, Delbœuf, Zöllner, and all the advocates of unconscious inference are at variance with each other when it comes to the question what these unconscious premises and inferences may be.

That small angles look proportionally larger than larger ones is, in brief, the fundamental illusion to which almost all authors would reduce the peculiarity of Fig. 67, as of Figs. 60, 61, 62 (pp. 865, 866). This peculiarity of small angles is by Wundt treated as

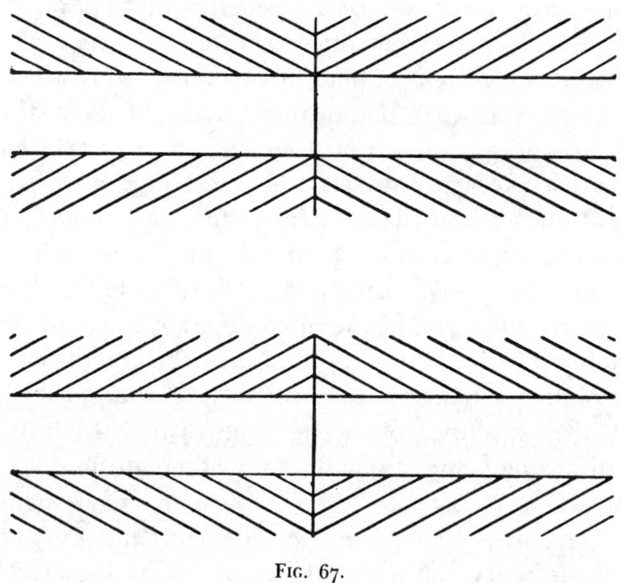

Fig. 67.

the case of a filled space seeming larger than an empty one, as in Fig. 68; and this, according to both Delbœuf and Wundt, is owing

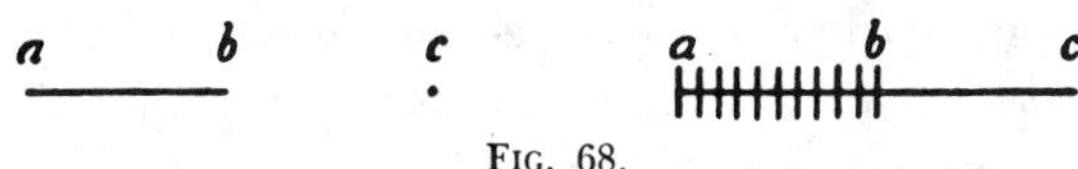

FIG. 68.

to the fact that more muscular innervation is needed for the eye to traverse a filled space than an empty one, because the points and lines in the filled space inevitably arrest and constrain the eye, and this makes us feel as if it were doing more work, i.e., traversing a longer distance.[95] When, however, we recollect that muscular movements are positively proved to have *no* share in the waterfall and revolving-spiral illusions, and that it is hard to see how Wundt's and Delbœuf's particular form of muscle-explanation can possibly apply to the compass-point illusion considered a moment ago, we must conclude that these writers have probably exaggerated, to say the least, the reach of their muscle-explanation in the case of the subdivided angles and lines. Never do we get such strong muscular feelings as when, against the course of nature, we oblige our eyes to be still; but fixing the eyes on one point of the figure, so far from making that part of the latter seem larger, dispels, in most persons, the illusion of these diagrams altogether.

As for Helmholtz, he invokes, to explain the enlargement of small angles,[96] what he calls a '*law of contrast*' between directions and distances of lines, analogous to that between colors and intensities of light. Lines cutting another line make the latter seem more inclined away from them than it really is. Moreover, clearly recognizable magnitudes appear greater than equal magnitudes which we but vaguely apprehend. But this is surely a sensationalistic law, a native function of our seeing-apparatus. Quite as little as the negative after-image of the revolving spiral could such contrast be deduced from any association of ideas or recall of past objects. The principle of contrast is criticised by Wundt,[97] who says that by it small spaces ought to appear to us smaller, and not larger, than they really are. Helmholtz might have retorted (had not the retort been as fatal to the uniformity of his own principle as to Wundt's) that if the muscle-explanation were true, it ought not to give rise

95 *Bulletin de l'Académie de Belgique*, XIX, 2; *Revue Philosophique*, VI, pp. 223–5; *Physiologische Psychologie*, 2te Aufl., Bd. II, p. 103. Compare Münsterberg's views, *Beiträge*, Heft 2, p. 174.

96 *Physiologische Optik*, pp. 562–71.

97 *Physiologische Psychologie*, 2nd ed., vol. II, pp. 107–8.

to just the opposite illusions in the skin. We saw on p. 783 that subdivided spaces appear shorter than empty ones upon the skin. To the instances there given add this: Divide a line on paper into equal halves, puncture the extremities, and make punctures all along one of the halves; then, with the finger-tip on the opposite side of the paper, follow the line of punctures; the empty half will seem much longer than the punctured half. This seems to bring things back to unanalyzable laws, by reason of which our feeling of size is determined differently in the skin and in the retina, even when the objective conditions are the same. Hering's explanation of Zöllner's figure is to be found in Hermann's *Handbuch der Physiologie,* III, 1, p. 579. Lipps[98] gives another reason why lines cutting another line make the latter seem to bend away from them more than is really the case. If, he says, we draw (Fig. 69) the line *pm* upon the line *ab*, and follow the latter with our eye, we shall,

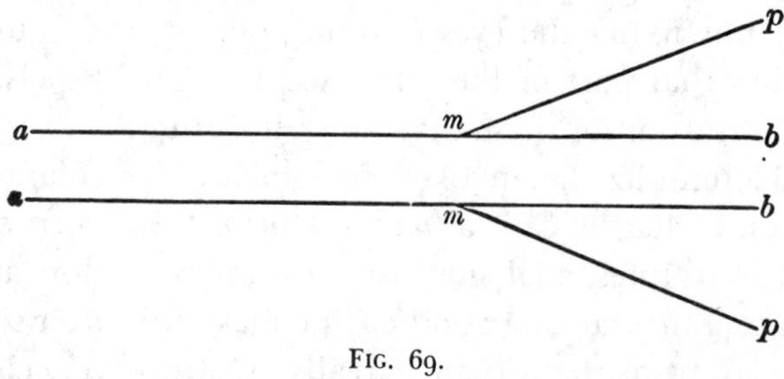

Fig. 69.

on reaching the point *m*, tend for a moment to slip off *ab* and to follow *mp*, without distinctly realizing that we are not still on the main line. This makes us feel as if the remainder *mb* of the main line were bent a little away from its original direction. The illusion is apparent in the shape of a seeming approach of the ends *b*, *b*, of the two main lines. This to my mind would be a more satisfactory explanation of this class of illusions than any of those given by previous authors, were it not again for what happens in the skin.

Considering all the circumstances, I feel justified in discarding this entire batch of illusions as irrelevant to our present inquiry. Whatever they may prove, they do not prove that our visual percepts of form and movement may not be sensations strictly so called. They much more probably fall into line with the phenome-

98 *Grundtatsachen des Seelenlebens,* pp. 526–30.

na of irradiation and of color-contrast, and with Vierordt's primitive illusions of movement. They show us, if anything, a realm of sensations in which our habitual experience has not yet made traces, and which persist in spite of our better knowledge, *un*suggestive of those other space-sensations which we all the time know from extrinsic evidence to constitute the real space-determinations of the diagram. Very likely, if these sensations were as frequent and as practically important as they now are insignificant and rare, we should end by substituting their significates—the real space-values of the diagrams—for them. These latter we should then seem to see directly, and the illusions would disappear like that of the size of a tooth-socket when the tooth has been out a week.

(*b*) *Another batch of cases which we may discard is that of double images.* A thoroughgoing anti-sensationalist ought to deny all native tendency to see double images when disparate retinal points are stimulated, because, he should say, most people never get them, but *see* all things single which experience has led them to believe to *be* single. "Can a doubleness, so easily neutralized by our knowledge, ever be a datum of sensation at all?" such an anti-sensationalist might ask.

To which the answer is that it *is* a datum of sensation, but a datum which, like many other data, must first be *discriminated.* As a rule, no sensible qualities are discriminated without a motive.[99] And those that later we learn to discriminate were originally felt confused. As well pretend that a voice, or an odor, which we have learned to pick out, is no sensation now. One may easily acquire skill in discriminating double images, though, as Hering somewhere says, it is an art of which one cannot become master in one year or in two. For masters like Hering himself, or Le Conte, the ordinary stereoscopic diagrams are of little use. Instead of combining into one solid appearance, they simply cross each other with their doubled lines. Volkmann has shown a great variety of ways in which the addition of secondary lines, differing in the two fields, helps us to see the primary lines double. The effect is analogous to that shown in the cases which we despatched a moment ago, where given lines have their space-value changed by the addition of new lines, without our being able to say why, except that a certain mu-

[99] Cf. *supra*, p. 487 ff.

tual adhesion of the lines and modification of the resultant feeling takes place by psychophysiological laws. Thus, if in Fig. 70, *l* and *r* be crossed by an horizontal line at the same level, and viewed stereoscopically, they appear as a single pair of lines, *s*, in space. But if the horizontal be at different levels, as in *l′*, *r′*, three lines appear, as in *s′*.[100]

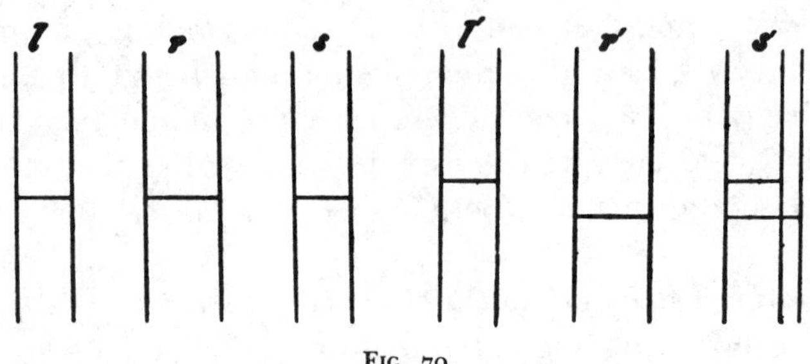

FIG. 70.

Let us then say no more about double images. All that the facts prove is what Volkmann says,[101] that, although there may be sets of retinal fibres so organized as to give an impression of two separate spots, yet the excitement of other retinal fibres may inhibit the effect of the first excitement, and prevent us from actually making the discrimination. Still farther retinal processes may, however, bring the doubleness to the eye of attention; and, once there, it is as genuine a sensation as any that our life affords.[102]

(*c*) *These groups of illusions being eliminated*, either as cases of defective discrimination, or as changes of one space-sensation into another when the total retinal process changes, *there remain but two other groups to puzzle us.* The first is that of the after-images distorted by projection on to oblique planes; the second relates to the instability of our judgments of relative distance and size by the

100 See *Archiv für Ophthalmologie*, vol. v, pt. 2, 1 (1859), where many more examples are given.

101 *Untersuchungen*, p. 250; see also p. 242.

102 I pass over certain difficulties about double images, drawn from the perceptions of a few squinters (e.g., by Schweigger: *Klinische Untersuchungen über das Schielen*, Berlin, 1881; by Javal: *Annales d'Oculistique*, LXXXV, p. 217), because the facts are exceptional at best and very difficult of interpretation. In favor of the sensationalistic or nativistic view of one such case, see the important paper by von Kries: *Archiv für Ophthalmologie*, XXIV, 4, p. 117.

eye, and includes especially what are known as pseudoscopic illusions.

The phenomena of the first group were described on page 864. A. W. Volkmann has studied them with his accustomed clearness and care.[103] Even an imaginarily inclined wall, in a picture, will, if an after-image be thrown upon it, distort the shape thereof, and make us *see* a form of which our after-image would be the natural projection on the retina, were that form laid upon the wall. Thus a signboard is painted in perspective on a screen, and the eye, after steadily looking at a rectangular cross, is turned to the painted signboard. The after-image appears as an oblique-legged cross upon the signboard. It is the converse phenomenon of a perspective drawing

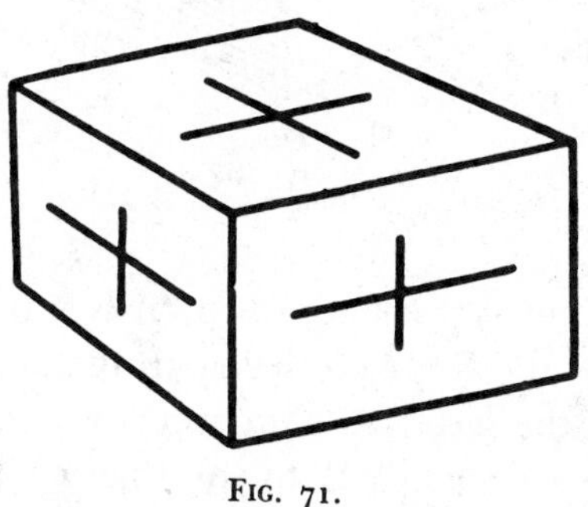

FIG. 71.

like Fig. 71, in which really oblique-legged figures are seen as rectangular crosses.

The unstable judgments of relative distance and size were also mentioned on pp. 864–865. Whatever the size may be of the retinal image which an object makes, the object is seen as of its own normal size. A man moving towards us is not sensibly perceived to *grow*, for example; and my finger, of which a single joint may more than conceal him from my view, is nevertheless seen as a much smaller object than the man. As for distances, it is often possible to make the farther part of an object seem near and the nearer part far. A human profile in intaglio, looked at steadily with one eye, or even both, soon appears irresistibly as a bas-relief. The inside of a common pasteboard mask, painted like the outside, and viewed with one eye in a direct light, also looks convex instead of

103 *Physiologische Untersuchungen im Gebiete der Optik*, v.

hollow. So strong is the illusion, after long fixation, that a friend who painted such a mask for me told me it soon became difficult to see how to apply the brush. Bend a visiting-card across the middle, so that its halves form an angle of 90° more or less; set it upright on the table, as in Fig. 72, and view it with one eye. You can

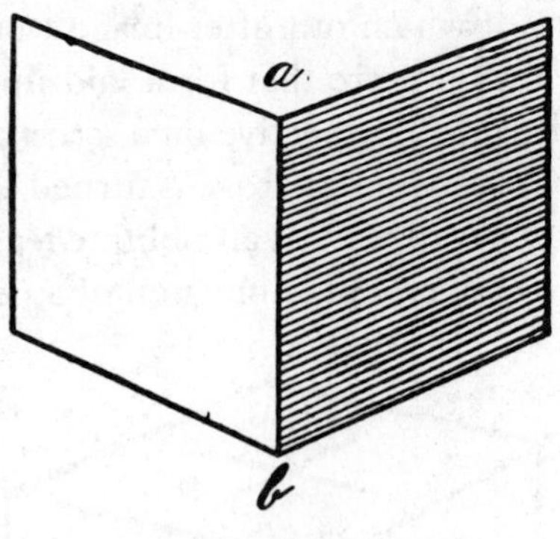

FIG. 72.

make it appear either as if it opened towards you or away from you. In the former case, the angle *ab* lies upon the table, *b* being nearer to you than *a*; in the latter case *ab* seems vertical to the table—as indeed it really is—with *a* nearer to you than *b*.[104] Again, look, with either one or two eyes, at the opening of a wine-glass or tumbler (Fig. 73), held either above or below the eye's level. The retinal

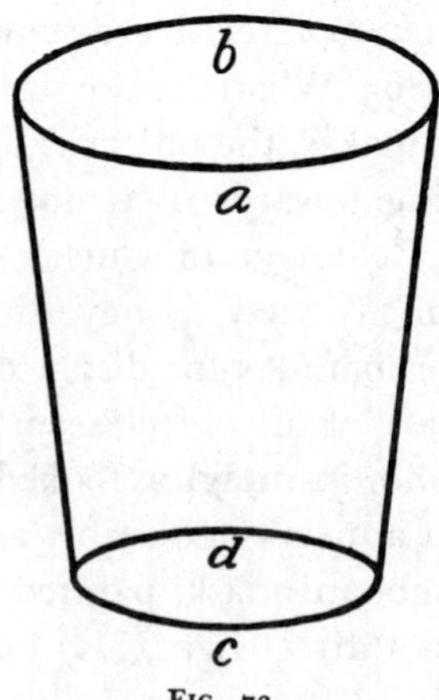

FIG. 73.

104 Cf. E. Mach: *Beiträge zur Analyse der Empfindungen*, p. 87.

image of the opening is an oval, but we can see the oval in either of two ways,—as if it were the perspective view of a circle whose edge *b* were farther from us than its edge *a* (in which case we should seem to be looking down on the circle), or as if its edge *a* were the more distant edge (in which case we should be looking up at it through the *b* side of the glass). As the manner of seeing the edge changes, the glass itself alters its form in space and looks straight or seems bent towards or from the eye,[105] according as the latter is placed beneath or above it.

Plane diagrams also can be conceived as solids, and that in more than one way. Figs. 74, 75, 76, for example, are ambiguous per-

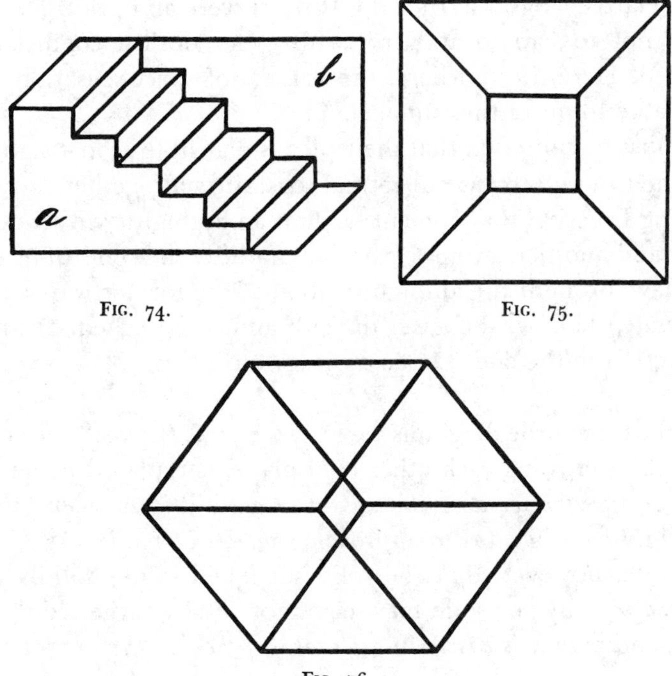

Fig. 74.

Fig. 75.

Fig. 76.

spective projections, and may each of them remind us of two different natural objects. Whichever of these objects we conceive clearly at the moment of looking at the figure, we seem to *see* in all its solidity before us. A little practice will enable us to flap the figures, so to speak, backwards and forwards from one object to the other

[105] Cf. V. Egger: *Revue Philosophique*, xx, 488.

at will. We need only attend to one of the angles represented, and imagine it either solid or hollow—pulled towards us out of the plane of the paper, or pushed back behind the same—and the whole figure obeys the cue and is instantaneously transformed beneath our gaze.[106]

The peculiarity of all these cases is the ambiguity of the perception to which the fixed retinal impression gives rise. With our retina excited in exactly the same way, whether by after-image, mask or diagram, we *see* now this object and now that, as if the retinal image *per se* had no essential space-import. Surely if form and length were originally retinal sensations, retinal rectangles ought not to become acute or obtuse, and lines ought not to alter their relative lengths as they do. If *relief* were an optical feeling, it ought not to flap to and fro, with every optical condition unchanged. Here, if anywhere, the deniers of space-sensation ought to be able to make their final stand.[107]

It must be confessed that their plea is plausible at first sight. But it is one thing to throw out retinal sensibility altogether as a space-yielding function the moment we find an ambiguity in its deliverances, and another thing to examine candidly the conditions which may have brought the ambiguity about. The former way is cheap, wholesale, shallow; the latter difficult and complicated, but full of instruction in the end. Let us try it for ourselves.

In the case of the diagrams 72, 73, 74, 75, 76, the real object, lines meeting or crossing each other on a plane, is replaced by an *imagined solid which we describe as seen. Really it is not seen but only so vividly conceived as to approach a vision of reality.* We feel all the while, however, that the solid suggested is not solidly there. *The reason* why one solid may seem more easily suggested than another, and *why it is easier in general to perceive the diagram solid*

106 Loeb (Pflüger's *Archiv*, XL, 274) has proved that muscular changes of adaptation in the eye for near and far distance are what determine the form of the relief.

107 The strongest passage in Helmholtz's argument against sensations of space is relative to these fluctuations of seen relief: "Ought one not to conclude that if sensations of relief exist at all, they must be so faint and vague as to have no influence compared with that of past experience? Ought we not to believe that the perception of the third dimension may have arisen *without* them, since we now see it taking place as well *against* them as *with* them?" (*Physiologische Optik*, p. 817.)

than flat, seems due to probability.[108] Those lines have countless times in our past experience been drawn on our retina by solids for once that we have seen them flat on paper. And hundreds of times we have looked down upon the upper surface of parallelopipeds, stairs and glasses, for once that we have looked upwards at their bottom—hence we see the solids easiest as if from above.

Habit or probability seems also to govern the illusion of the intaglio profile, and of the hollow mask. We have *never* seen a human face except in relief—hence the ease with which the present sensation is overpowered. Hence, too, the obstinacy with which human faces and forms, and other extremely familiar convex objects, refuse to appear hollow when viewed through Wheatstone's pseudoscope. Our perception seems wedded to certain total ways of seeing certain objects. The moment the object is suggested at all, it takes possession of the mind in the fulness of its stereotyped habitual form. This explains the suddenness of the transformations when the perceptions change. The object shoots back and forth completely from this to that familiar thing, and doubtful, indeterminate, and composite things are excluded, apparently because we are *unused* to their existence.

When we turn from the diagrams to the actual folded visiting-card and to the real glass, the imagined form seems fully as real as the correct one. The card flaps over; the glass rim tilts this way or that, as if some inward spring suddenly became released in our eye. In these changes the actual retinal image receives different *complements from the mind.* But the remarkable thing is that the complement and the image combine so completely that the twain are one flesh, as it were, and cannot be discriminated in the result. If the complement be, as we have called it (on pp. 869–870), a set of imaginary absent eye-sensations, they seem no whit less vividly there than the sensation which the eye now receives from without.

The case of the after-images distorted by projection upon an oblique plane is even more strange, for the imagined perspective figure, lying in the plane, seems less to combine with the one a moment previously seen by the eye than to suppress it and take its place.[109] The point needing explanation, then, in all this, is how it

108 Cf. E. Mach: *Beiträge*, etc., p. 90, and the preceding chapter of the present work, p. 731 ff.

109 I ought to say that I seem always able to see the cross rectangular at will.

comes to pass that, when imagined sensations are usually so inferior in vivacity to real ones, they should in these few experiences prove to be almost or quite their match.

The mystery is solved when we note the class to which all these experiences belong. They are 'perceptions' of definite 'things,' definitely situated in tridimensional space. The mind uniformly uses its sensations to *identify things by.* The sensation is invariably apperceived by the idea, name, or 'normal' aspect (p. 870) of the *thing.* The peculiarity of the *optical* signs of things is their extraordinary mutability. A 'thing' which we follow with the eye, never doubting of its physical identity, will change its retinal image incessantly. A cross, a ring, waved about in the air, will pass through every conceivable angular and elliptical form. All the while, however, as we look at them, we hold fast to the perception of their 'real' shape, by mentally combining the pictures momentarily received with the notion of peculiar positions in space. It is not the cross and ring pure and simple which we perceive, but the cross *so held,* the ring *so held.* From the day of our birth we have sought every hour of our lives to *correct* the apparent form of things, and translate it into the real form by keeping note of the way they are placed or held. In no other class of sensations does this incessant correction occur. What wonder, then, that the notion 'so placed' should invincibly exert its habitual corrective effect, even when the object with which it combines is only an after-image, and make us perceive the latter under a changed but more 'real' form? The 'real' form is also a sensation conjured up by memory; but it is one so *probable,* so *habitually* conjured up when we have just this combination of optical experiences, that it partakes of the invincible freshness of reality, and seems to break through that law which elsewhere condemns reproductive processes to being so much fainter than sensations.

Once more, *these cases form an extreme. Somewhere, in the list of our imaginations of absent feelings, there must be found the vividest of all. These optical reproductions of real form are the*

But this appears to come from an imperfect absorption of the rectangular after-image by the inclined plane at which the eyes look. The cross, with me, is apt to detach itself from this and then look square. I get the illusion better from the circle, whose after-image becomes in various ways elliptical on being projected upon the different surfaces of the room, and cannot then be easily made to look circular again.

vividest of all. It is foolish to reason from cases lower in the scale, to prove that the scale can contain no such extreme cases as these; and particularly foolish since we can definitely see why these imaginations ought to be more vivid than any others, whenever they recall the forms of habitual and probable things. These latter, by incessantly repeated presence and reproduction, will plough deep grooves in the nervous system. There will be developed, to correspond to them, paths of least resistance, of unstable equilibrium, liable to become active in their totality when any point is touched off. Even when the objective stimulus is imperfect, we shall still *see* the full convexity of a human face, the correct inclination of an angle or sweep of a curve, or the distance of two lines. Our mind will be like a polyhedron, whose facets are the attitudes of perception in which it can most easily rest. These are worn upon it by *habitual* objects, and from one of these it can pass only by tumbling over into another.[110]

Hering has well accounted for the sensationally vivid character of these habitually reproduced forms. He says, after reminding us that every visual sensation is correlated to a physical process in the nervous apparatus:

"If this psychophysical process is aroused, as usually happens, by light-rays impinging on the retina, its form depends not only on the nature of these rays, but on the constitution of the entire nervous apparatus which is connected with the organ of vision, and on the *state* in which it finds itself. The same stimulus may excite widely different sensations according to this state.

"The constitution of the nervous apparatus depends naturally in part upon innate predisposition; but the *ensemble* of effects wrought by stimuli upon it in the course of life, whether these come through the eyes or from elsewhere, is a co-factor of its development. To express it otherwise, involuntary and voluntary experience and exercise assist in determining the material structure of the nervous organ of vision, and hence the ways in which it may react on a retinal image as an outward stimulus. That experience and exercise should be possible at all in vision is a consequence of the reproductive power, or memory, of its nerve-substance. Every particular activity of the organ makes it more suited to a repetition of the *same*; ever slighter touches are required to

[110] In Chapter XVIII, p. 720, I gave a reason why imaginations *ought* not to be as vivid as sensations. It should be borne in mind that that reason does not apply to these complemental imaginings of the real shape of things actually before our eyes.

make the repetition occur. The organ habituates itself to the repeated activity. . . .

"Suppose now that, in the first experience of a complex sensation produced by a particular retinal image, certain portions were made the special objects of attention. In a repetition of the sensible experience it will happen that notwithstanding the identity of the outward stimulus these portions will be more easily and strongly reproduced; and when this happens a hundred times the inequality with which the various constituents of the complex sensation appeal to consciousness grows ever greater.

"Now in the present state of our knowledge we cannot assert that in both the first and the last occurrence of the retinal image in question the same *pure sensation* is provoked, but that the mind *interprets* it differently the last time in consequence of experience; for the only *given* things we know are on the one hand the retinal image which is both times the same, and on the other the mental percept which is both times different; of a third thing, such as a pure sensation, interpolated between image and percept, we know nothing. We ought, therefore, if we wish to avoid hypotheses, simply to say that the nervous apparatus reacts the last time differently from the first, and gives us in consequence a different group of sensations.

"But not only by repetition of the same retinal image, but by that of similar ones, will the law obtain. Portions of the image common to the successive experiences will awaken, as it were, a stronger echo in the nervous apparatus than other portions. Hence it results that *reproduction is usually elective*: the more strongly reverberating parts of the picture yield stronger feelings than the rest. This may result in the latter being quite overlooked and, as it were, eliminated from perception. It may even come to pass that instead of these parts eliminated by election a feeling of entirely different elements comes to consciousness—elements not objectively contained in the stimulus. A group of sensations, namely, for which a strong tendency to reproduction has become, by frequent repetition, ingrained in the nervous system will easily revive as a *whole* when, not its whole retinal image, but only an essential part thereof, returns. In this case we get some sensations to which no adequate stimulus exists in the retinal image, and which owe their being solely to the reproductive power of the nervous apparatus. This is *complementary (ergänzende) reproduction.*

"Thus a few points and disconnected strokes are sufficient to make us see a human face, and without specially directed attention we fail to note that we see much that really is not drawn on the paper. Attention will show that the outlines were deficient in spots where we thought them complete. . . . The portions of the percept supplied by complementary reproduction depend, however, just as much as its other portions, on the reaction of the nervous apparatus upon the retinal image, indirect though this reaction may, in the case of the supplied portions, be. And so long as they are present, we have a perfect right to call them sensations, for they differ in no wise from such sensations as correspond to an actual stimulus in the retina. Often, however, they are not persistent; many of them may be expelled by more close observation, but this is not proved to be the case with all. . . . In vision with one eye . . . the distribution of parts within the third dimension is essentially the work of this complementary reproduction, i.e., of former experience. . . . When a certain way of localizing a particular group of sensations has become with us a second nature, our better knowledge, our judgment, our logic, are of no avail. . . . Things actually diverse may give similar or almost identical retinal images; e.g., an object extended in three dimensions, and its flat perspective picture. In such cases it often depends on small accidents, and especially on our will, whether the one or the other group of sensations shall be excited. . . . We can see a relief hollow, as a mould, or *vice versâ*; for a relief illuminated from the left can look just like its mould illuminated from the right. Reflecting upon this, one may infer from the direction of the shadows that one has a relief before one, and the idea of the relief will guide the nerve-processes into the right path, so that the *feeling* of the relief is suddenly aroused. . . . Whenever the retinal image is of such a nature that two diverse modes of reaction on the part of the nervous apparatus are, so to speak, equally, or nearly equally, imminent, it must depend on small accidents whether the one or the other reaction is realized. In these cases our previous knowledge often has a decisive effect, and helps the correct perception to victory. The bare idea of the right object is itself a feeble reproduction which with the help of the proper retinal picture develops into clear and lively sensation. But if there be not already in the nervous apparatus a disposition to the production of that percept which our judgment tells us is right, our knowledge strives in vain to conjure up the feeling of it; we then know that we see something to which no reality corresponds, but we see it all the same."[111]

Note that no object not probable, no object which we are not incessantly practised in reproducing, can acquire this vividness in imagination. Objective corners are ever changing their angles to the eyes, spaces their apparent size, lines their distance. But by no transmutation of position in space does an objective straight line

111 Hermann's *Handbuch der Physiologie,* III, 1, p. 565–71.

appear bent, and only in one position out of an infinity does a broken line look straight. Accordingly, it is impossible by projecting the after-image of a straight line upon two surfaces which make a solid angle with each other to give the line itself a sensible 'kink.' Look with it at the corner of your room: the after-image, which may overlap all three surfaces of the corner, still continues straight. Volkmann constructed a complicated surface of projection like that drawn in Fig. 77, but he found it impossible so to throw a straight after-image upon it as to alter its visible form.

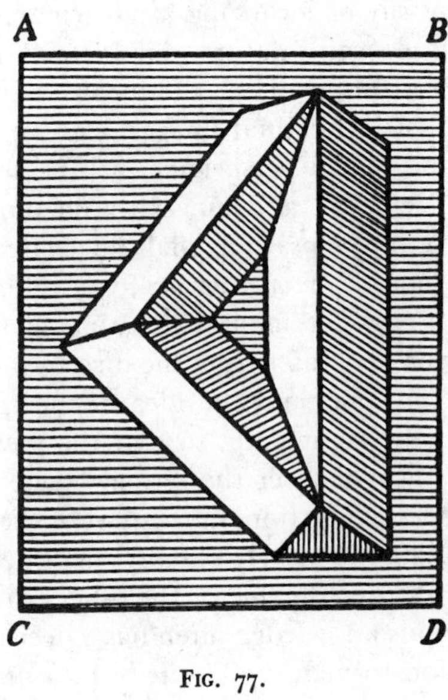

FIG. 77.

One of the situations in which we oftenest see things is spread out on the ground before us. We are incessantly drilled in making allowance for *this* perspective, and reducing things to their real form in spite of optical foreshortening. Hence if the preceding explanations are true, we ought to find this habit inveterate. The *lower* half of the retina, which habitually sees the *farther* half of things spread out on the ground, ought to have acquired a habit of enlarging its pictures by imagination, so as to make them more than equal to those which fall on the upper retinal surface; and this habit ought to be hard to escape from, even when both halves of the object are equidistant from the eye, as in a vertical line on paper. Delbœuf has found, accordingly, that if we try to bisect such a line we place the point of division about $\frac{1}{16}$ of its length too high.[112]

Similarly, a square cross, or a square, drawn on paper, should look higher than it is broad. And that this is actually the case, the reader may verify by a glance at Fig. 78. For analogous reasons the

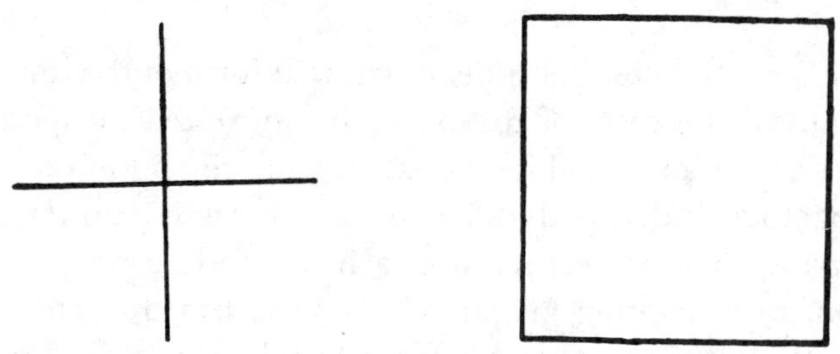

Fig. 78.

upper and lower halves of the letter S, or of the figure 8, hardly seem to differ. But when turned upside down, as S, 8, the upper half looks much the larger.[113]

Hering has tried to explain our exaggeration of small angles in the same way. We have more to do with right angles than with any others: right angles, in fact, have an altogether unique sort of interest for the human mind. Nature almost never begets them, but we think space by means of them and put them everywhere. Consequently obtuse and acute ones, liable always to be the images of right ones foreshortened, particularly easily revive right ones in memory. It is hard to look at such figures as *a, b, c,* in Fig. 79, without seeing them in perspective, as approximations, at least, to foreshortened rectangular forms.[114]

112 *Bulletin de l'Académie de Belgique*, 2me Série, xix, 2.

113 Wundt seeks to explain all these illusions by the relatively stronger 'feeling of innervation' needed to move the eyeballs upwards,—a careful study of the muscles concerned is taken to prove this,—and a consequently greater estimate of the distance traversed. It suffices to remark, however, with Lipps, that were the innervation all, a column of S's placed on top of each other should look each larger than the one below it, and a weather-cock on a steeple gigantic, neither of which is the case. Only the halves of *the same object* look different in size, because the customary correction for foreshortening bears only on the relations of the parts of special *things* spread out before us. Cf. Wundt: *Physiologische Psychologie*, 2te Aufl., ii, 96–8; Theodor Lipps: *Grundtatsachen*, etc., p. 535.

114 Hering would partly solve in this way the mystery of Figs. 60, 61, and 67. No doubt the explanation partly applies; but the strange cessation of the illusion when we fix the gaze fails to be accounted for thereby.

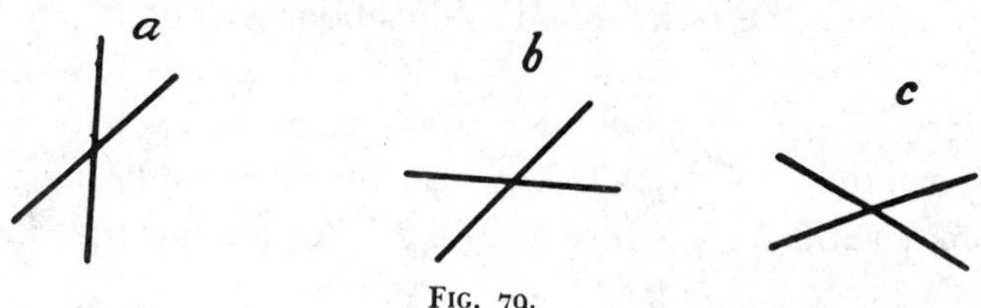

FIG. 79.

At the same time the genuine sensational form of the lines before us can, in all the cases of distortion by suggested perspective, be felt correctly by a mind able to abstract from the notion of perspective altogether. Individuals differ in this abstracting power. Artistic training improves it, so that after a little while errors in vertical bisection, in estimating height relatively to breadth, etc., become impossible. In other words, we learn to take the optical sensation before us *pure.*[115]

We may then sum up our study of illusions by saying that they in no wise undermine our view that every spatial determination of things is originally given in the shape of a sensation of the eyes. They only show how very potent certain *imagined* sensations of the eyes may become.

These sensations, so far as they bring definite forms to the mind, appear to be retinal exclusively. The movements of the eyeballs play a great part in educating our perception, it is true; but they have nothing to do with *constituting* any one feeling of form. Their function is limited to *exciting* the various feelings of form, by tracing retinal streaks; and to *comparing* them, and *measuring*

[115] Helmholtz has sought (*Physiologische Optik*, p. 715) to explain the divergence of the apparent vertical meridians of the two retinæ, by the manner in which an identical line drawn on the ground before us in the median plane will throw its images on the two eyes respectively. The matter is too technical for description here; the unlearned reader may be referred for it to J. Le Conte's *Sight* in the International Scientific Series, p. 198 ff. But, for the benefit of those to whom *verbum sat*, I cannot help saying that it seems to me that the *exactness* of the relation of the two meridians—whether divergent or not, for their divergence differs in individuals and often in one individual at diverse times—precludes its being due to the mere habitual falling-off of the image of one objective line on both. Le Conte, e.g., measures their position down to a sixth of a degree, others to tenths. This indicates an organic identity in the sensations of the two retinæ, which the experience of median perspective horizontals may roughly have agreed with, but hardly can have engendered. Wundt explains the divergence as usual, by the *Innervationsgefühl* (*op. cit.*, II, 99 ff.).

them off against each other, by applying different parts of the retinal surface to the same objective thing. Helmholtz's analysis of the facts of our '*measurement of the field of view*' is, bating a lapse or two, masterly, and seems to prove that the movements of the eye have had some part in bringing our sense of retinal equivalencies about—*equivalencies*, mind, of different retinal forms and sizes, not forms and sizes themselves. *Superposition* is the way in which the eye-movements accomplish this result. An object traces the line AB on a peripheral tract of the retina. Quickly we move the eye so that the same object traces the line *ab* on a central tract. Forthwith, to our mind, AB and *ab* are judged equivalent. But, as Helmholtz admits, the equivalence-judgment is independent of the way in which we may feel the form and length of the several retinal pictures themselves:

> "The retina is like a pair of compasses, whose points we apply in succession to the ends of several lines to see whether they agree or not in length. All we need know meanwhile about the compasses is that the distance of their points remains unchanged. What that distance is, and what is the shape of the compasses, is a matter of no account."[116]

Measurement implies a stuff to measure. Retinal sensations give the stuff; objective things form the yard-stick; motion does the measuring operation; which can, of course, be well performed only where it is possible to make the same object fall on many retinal tracts. This is practically impossible where the tracts make a wide angle with each other. But there are certain directions in the field of view, certain retinal lines, along which it is particularly easy to make the image of an object slide. The object then becomes a 'ruler' for these lines, as Helmholtz puts it,[117] making them seem

[116] *Physiologische Optik*, p. 547.

[117] "We can with a short ruler draw a line as long as we please on a plane surface by first drawing one as long as the ruler permits, and then sliding the ruler somewhat along the drawn line and drawing again, etc. If the ruler is exactly straight, we get in this way a straight line. If it is somewhat curved we get a circle. Now, instead of the sliding ruler we use in the field of sight the central spot of distinctest vision impressed with a linear sensation of sight, which at times may be intensified till it becomes an after-image. We follow, in looking, the direction of this line, and in so doing we slide the line along itself and get a prolongation of its length. On a plane surface we can carry on this procedure on any sort of a straight or curved ruler, but in the field of vision there is for each direction and movement of the eye only one sort of line which it is possible for us to slide along in its own direction continually." These are what Helmholtz calls the 'circles of direction' of

straight throughout if the object looked straight to us in that part of them at which it was most distinctly seen.

But all this need of superposition shows how devoid of exact space-import the feelings of movement are *per se*. As we compare the space-value of two retinal tracts by superposing them successively upon the same objective line, so we also have to compare the space-value of objective angles and lines by superposing them on the same retinal tract. Neither procedure would be required if our eye-movements were apprehended immediately, by pure muscular feeling or innervation, for example, as distinct lengths and directions in space. To compare retinal tracts, it would then suffice simply to notice how it feels to move *any* image over them. And two objective lines could be compared as well by moving different retinal tracts along them as by laying them along the same. It would be as easy to compare non-parallel figures as it now is to judge of those which are parallel.[118] Those which it took the same amount of movement to traverse would be equal, in whatever direction the movement occurred.

GENERAL SUMMARY

With this we may end our long and, I fear to many readers, tediously minute survey. The facts of vision form a jungle of intricacy; and those who penetrate deeply into physiological optics will be more struck by our omissions than by our abundance of detail. But for students who may have lost sight of the forest for the trees, I will recapitulate briefly the points of our whole argument from the beginning, and then proceed to a short historical survey, which will set them in relief.

All our sensations are positively and inexplicably extensive wholes.

The sensations contributing to space-*perception* seem exclusively to be the surface of skin, retina, and joints. 'Muscular' feelings play no appreciable part in the generation of our feelings of form, direction, etc.

The total bigness of a cutaneous or retinal feeling soon becomes subdivided by discriminative attention.

---

the visual field—lines which he has studied with his usual care. Cf. *Physiologische Optik*, p. 548 ff.

118 Cf. Hering in Hermann's *Handbuch der Physiologie*, III, 1, pp. 553–4.

Movements assist this discrimination by reason of the peculiarly exciting quality of the sensations which stimuli moving over surfaces arouse.

Subdivisions, once discriminated, acquire definite relations of position towards each other within the total space. These 'relations' are themselves feelings of the subdivisions that intervene. When these subdivisions are not the seat of stimuli, the relations are only reproduced in imaginary form.

The various sense-spaces are, in the first instance, incoherent with each other; and primitively both they and their subdivisions are but vaguely comparable in point of bulk and form.

The *education* of our space-perception consists largely of two processes—reducing the various sense-feelings to a common *measure,* and *adding them together* into the single all-including space of the real world.

Both the measuring and the adding are performed by the aid of *things.*

The imagined aggregate of positions occupied by all the actual or possible, moving or stationary, things which we know, is our notion of 'real' space—a very incomplete and vague conception in all minds.

The *measuring* of our space-feelings against each other mainly comes about through the successive arousal of different ones by the same *thing,* by our selection of certain ones as feelings of its *real* size and shape, and by the degradation of others to the status of being merely *signs* of these.

For the successive application of the same thing to different space-giving surfaces motion is indispensable, and hence plays a great part in our space-education, especially in that of the eye. Abstractly considered, the motion of the object over the sensitive surface would educate us quite as well as that of the surface over the object. But the self-mobility of the organ carrying the surface *accelerates* immensely the result.

In completely educated space-perception, the present sensation is usually just what Helmholtz (*Physiologische Optik,* p. 797) calls it, "a sign, the interpretation of whose meaning is left to the understanding." But the understanding is exclusively reproductive and never productive in the process; and its function is limited to the recall of previous space-sensations with which the present one has been associated and which may be judged more real than it.

Finally, this reproduction may in the case of certain visual forms be as vivid, or almost so, as actual sensation is.

The third dimension forms an original element of all our space-sensations. In the eye it is subdivided by various discriminations. The more distant subdivisions are often shut out altogether, and, in being suppressed, have the effect of diminishing the absolute space-value of the total field of view.[119]

HISTORICAL

Let us now close with a brief historical survey. The first achievement of note in the study of space-perception was Berkeley's theory of vision. This undertook to establish two points, first that *distance* was not a visual but a tactile form of consciousness, suggested by visual signs; secondly, that there is no one quality or 'idea' common to the sensations of touch and sight, such that prior to experience one might possibly anticipate from the look of an object anything about its felt size, shape, or position, or from the touch of it anything about its look.

In other words, that primitively chaotic or semi-chaotic condition of our various sense-spaces which we have demonstrated, was established for good by Berkeley; and he bequeathed to psychology the problem of describing the manner in which the deliverances are harmonized so as all to refer to one and the same extended world.

His disciples in Great Britain have solved this problem after Berkeley's own fashion, and to a great extent as we have done ourselves, by the ideas of the various senses suggesting each other in consequence of Association. But, either because they were intoxicated with the principle of association, or because in the number of details they lost their general bearings, they have forgotten, as a rule, to state *under what sensible form the primitive spatial experiences are found* which later became associated with so many other sensible signs. Heedless of their master Locke's precept, that the

119 This shrinkage and expansion of the absolute space-value of the total optical sensation remains to my mind the most obscure part of the whole subject. It is a real optical sensation, seeming introspectively to have nothing to do with locomotor or other suggestions. It is easy to say that 'the Intellect produces it,' but what does that mean? The investigator who will throw light on this one point will probably clear up other difficulties as well.

mind can frame unto itself no one new simple idea, they seem for the most part to be trying to *explain the extensive quality itself*, account for it, and evolve it, by the mere association together of feelings which originally possessed it not. They first evaporate the nature of extension by making it tantamount to mere 'coexistence,' and then they explain coexistence as being the same thing as *succession*, provided it be an extremely rapid or a reversible succession. Space-perception thus emerges without being anywhere postulated. The only things postulated are unextended feelings and time. Says Thomas Brown (lecture XXIII): "I am inclined to reverse exactly the process commonly supposed; and, instead of deriving the measure of time from extension, to derive the knowledge and the original measure of extension from time." Brown and both the Mills think that retinal sensations, colors, in their primitive condition, are felt with no extension and that the latter merely becomes inseparably associated with them. John Mill says: "Whatever may be the retinal impression conveyed by a line which bounds two colours, I see no ground for thinking that by the eye alone we could acquire the conception of what we now mean when we say that one of the colours is outside [beside] the other." [120]

Whence does the extension come which gets so inseparably associated with these non-extended colored sensations? From the 'sweep and movements' of the eye—from muscular feelings. But, as Prof. Bain says, if movement-feelings give us any property of things, "it would seem to be not space, but time." [121] And John Mill says that "the idea of space is, at bottom, one of time." [122] Space, then, is not to be found in any elementary sensation, but, in Bain's words, "as a quality, it has no other origin and no other meaning than the *association* of these different [non-spatial] sensitive and motor effects." [123]

This phrase is mystical-sounding enough to one who understands association as *producing* nothing, but only as knitting together things already produced in separate ways. The truth is that the English Associationist school, in trying to show how much their principle can accomplish, have altogether overshot the mark and espoused a kind of theory in respect to space-perception which the

120 *Examination of Hamilton*, 4th ed., p. 295.

121 *Senses and the Intellect*, 3d ed., p. 183.

122 *Examination of Hamilton*, 4th ed., p. 283.

123 *Senses and the Intellect*, p. 372.

general tenor of their philosophy should lead them to abhor. Really there are but three possible kinds of theory concerning space. Either (1) there is no spatial *quality* of sensation at all, and space is a mere symbol of succession; or (2) there is an *extensive quality given* immediately in certain particular sensations; or, finally, (3) there is a *quality produced* out of the inward resources of the mind, to envelop sensations which, as given originally, are not spatial, but which, on being cast into the spatial form, become united and orderly. This last is the Kantian view. Stumpf admirably designates it as the 'psychic stimulus' theory, the crude sensations being considered as goads to the mind to put forth its slumbering power.

Brown, the Mills, and Bain, amid these possibilities, seem to have gone astray like lost sheep. With the 'mental chemistry' of which the Mills speak—precisely the same thing as the 'psychical synthesis' of Wundt, which, as we shall soon see, is a principle expressly intended to do what Association can never perform—they hold the third view, but again in other places imply the first. And, between the impossibility of getting from mere association anything not contained in the sensations associated and the dislike to allow spontaneous mental productivity, they flounder in a dismal dilemma. Mr. Sully joins them there in what I must call a vague and vacillating way. Mr. Spencer of course is bound to pretend to 'evolve' all mental qualities out of antecedents different from themselves, so that we need perhaps not wonder at his refusal to accord the spatial quality to any of the several elementary sensations out of which our space-perception grows. Thus (*Psychology*, II, 168, 172, 218):

> "No idea of extension can arise from a *simultaneous* excitation" of a multitude of nerve-terminations like those of the skin or the retina, since this would imply a "knowledge of their relative positions"—that is, "a pre-existent idea of a special extension: which is absurd." "No relation between *successive* states of consciousness gives in itself any idea of extension." "The muscular sensations accompanying motion are quite distinct from the notions of space and time associated with them."

Mr. Spencer none the less inveighs vociferously against the Kantian position that space is produced by the mind's own resources. And yet he nowhere denies space to be a specific affection of consciousness different from time!

Such incoherency is pitiful. The fact is that, at bottom, all these authors are really 'psychical stimulists,' or Kantists. The space they speak of is a super-sensational mental product. This position appears to me thoroughly mythological. But let us see how it is held by those who know more definitely what they mean. Schopenhauer expresses the Kantian view with more vigor and clearness than anyone else. He says:

"A man must be forsaken by all the gods to dream that the world we see outside of us, filling space in its three dimensions, moving down the inexorable stream of time, governed at each step by Causality's invariable law,—but in all this only following rules which we may prescribe for it in advance of all experience,—to dream, I say, that such a world should stand there outside of us, quite objectively real with no complicity of ours, and thereupon by a subsequent *act*, through the instrumentality of mere sensation, that it should enter our head and reconstruct a duplicate of itself as it was outside. For what a poverty-stricken thing is this mere sensation! Even in the noblest organs of sense it is nothing more than a local and specific feeling, susceptible within its kind of a few variations, but always strictly subjective and containing in itself nothing objective, nothing resembling a perception. For sensation of every sort is and remains a process in the organism itself. As such it is limited to the territory inside the skin and can never, accordingly, *per se* contain anything that lies outside the skin or outside ourselves. . . . Only when the Understanding . . . is roused to activity and brings its sole and only form, the *law of Causality*, into play, only then does the mighty transformation take place which makes out of subjective sensation objective intuition. The Understanding, namely, grasps by means of its innate, *a priori*, ante-experiential form, the given sensation of the body as an *effect* which as such must necessarily have a *cause*. At the same time the Understanding summons to its aid the form of the outer sense which similarly lies already preformed in the intellect (or brain), and which is Space, in order to locate that cause outside of the organism. . . . In this process the Understanding, as I shall soon show, takes note of the most minute peculiarities of the given sensation in order to construct in the outer space a cause which shall completely account for them. This operation of the Understanding is, however, not one that takes place discursively, reflectively, *in abstracto*, by means of words and concepts; but is intuitive and immediate. . . . Thus the Understanding must first create the objective world; never can the latter, already complete *in se*, simply promenade into our heads through the senses and organic apertures. For the senses yield us nothing further than the raw material which must be first elaborated into the objective conception of an orderly physical world-system by means of the aforesaid simple forms of Space, Time, and Causality. . . . Let me show the great chasm between sensation and perception by showing how raw the material is out of which the fair structure is upreared. Only two senses serve objective perception: touch and sight. They alone furnish the data on the basis whereof the Understanding, by the process indicated, erects the objective world. . . . These data in themselves are still no perception; that is the Understanding's work. If I press with my hand against the table, the sensation I receive has no analogy with the idea of the firm cohesion of the parts of this mass: only when my Understanding passes from the sensation to its cause does it create for itself a body with the properties of solidity, impenetrability, and hardness. When in the dark I lay my hand on a surface, or grasp a ball of three inches diameter, in either case the same parts of the hand receive the impression: but out of the different contraction of the hand in the two cases my Understanding constructs the form of the body whose contact caused the feeling, and confirms its construction by leading me to move my hand over the body. If one born blind handles a cubical body, the sensations of his hand are quite uniform on all sides and in all directions,–only the corners press upon a smaller part of his skin. In these sensations, as such, there is nothing whatever analogous to a cube. But from the felt resistance his Understanding infers immediately and intuitively a cause thereof, which now presents itself as a solid body; and from the movements of exploration which the arms made whilst the feelings of the hands remained constant he constructs, in the space known to him *a priori*, the body's cubical shape. Did he not bring with him ready-made the idea of a cause and of a space, with the laws thereof, there never could arise, out of those successive feelings in his hand, the image of a cube. If we let a string run through our closed hand, we immediately construct as the cause of the friction and its duration in such an attitude of the hand, a long cylindrical body moving uniformly in one direction. But never out of the pure sensation in the hand could the idea of movement, that is, of change of position in space by means of time, arise: such a content can never lie in sensation, nor come out of it. Our Intellect, antecedently to all experience, must bear in itself the intuitions of Space and Time, and therewithal of the possibility of motion, and no less the idea of Causality, to pass from the empirically given feeling to its cause, and to construct the latter as a so moving body of the designated shape. For how great is the abyss between the mere sensation in the hand and the ideas of causality, materiality, and movement through Space, occurring in Time! The feeling in the hand, even with different contacts and positions, is something far too uniform and poor in content for it to be possible to construct out of *it* the idea of Space with its three dimensions, of the action of bodies on each other, with the properties of extension, impenetrability, cohesion, shape, hardness, softness, rest, and motion—in short, the foundations of the objective world. This is only possible through Space, Time, and Causality . . . being preformed in the Intellect itself . . . from whence it again follows that the perception of the external world is essentially an intellectual process, a work of the Understanding, *to which sensation furnishes merely the occasion*, and the data to be interpreted in each particular case."[124]

I call this view mythological, because I am conscious of no such Kantian machine-shop in my mind, and feel no call to disparage the powers of poor sensation in this merciless way. I have no introspective experience of mentally producing or creating space. My space-intuitions occur not in two times but in one. There is not one moment of passive inextensive sensation, succeeded by another of active extensive perception, but the form I see is as immediately felt as the color which fills it out. That the higher parts of the mind come in, who can deny? They add and subtract, they compare and measure, they reproduce and abstract. They inweave the space-sensations with intellectual relations; but *these* relations are the same when they obtain between the elements of the space-system as when they obtain between any of the other elements of which the world is made.

The essence of the Kantian contention is that there are not *spaces*, but *Space*—one infinite continuous *Unit*—and that our knowledge of *this* cannot be a piecemeal sensational affair, produced by summation and abstraction. To which the obvious reply is that, if any known thing bears on its front the *appearance* of piecemeal construction and abstraction, it is this very notion of the infinite unitary space of the world. It is a *notion*, if ever there was one; and no intuition. Most of us apprehend it in the barest symbolic abridgment: and if perchance we ever do try to make it more adequate, we just add one image of sensible extension to another until we are tired. Most of us are obliged to turn round and drop the thought of the space in front of us when we think of that behind. And the space represented as near to us seems more minutely subdivisible than that we think of as lying far away.

124 *Vierfache Wurzel des Satzes vom zureichenden Grunde*, pp. 52–7.

The other prominent German writers on space are also 'psychical stimulists.' Herbart, whose influence has been widest, says "the resting eye sees no space,"[125] and ascribes visual extension to the influence of movements combining with the non-spatial retinal feelings so as to form gradated series of the latter. A given sensation of such a series reproduces the idea of its associates in regular order, and its idea is similarly reproduced by any one of them with the order reversed. Out of the fusion of these two contrasted reproductions comes the form of space[126]—Heaven knows how.

The obvious objection is that mere serial order is a *genus*, and space-order a very peculiar species of that *genus*; and that, if the terms of reversible series became by that fact coexistent terms in space, the musical scale, the degrees of warmth and cold, and all other ideally graded series ought to appear to us in the shape of extended corporeal aggregates,—which they notoriously do not, though we may of course *symbolize* their order by a spatial scheme. W. Volkmann von Volkmar, the Herbartian, takes the bull here by the horns, and says the musical scale *is* spatially extended, though he admits that its space does not belong to the real world.[127] I am unacquainted with any other Herbartian so bold.

To Lotze we owe the much-used term 'local sign.' He insisted that space could not emigrate directly into the mind from without, but must be *reconstructed* by the soul; and he seemed to think that the first reconstructions of it by the soul must be super-sensational. But why sensations themselves might not be the soul's *original* spatial reconstructive acts Lotze fails to explain.

Wundt has all his life devoted himself to the elaboration of a space-theory, of which the neatest and most final expression is to be found in his *Logik* (I, 457–60). He says:

"In the eye, space-perception has certain constant peculiarities which prove that no single optical sensation by itself possesses the extensive form, but that everywhere in our perception of space heterogeneous feelings combine. If we simply suppose that luminous sensations

125 *Psychologie als Wissenschaft*, § 111.

126 *Psychologie als Wissenschaft*, § 113.

127 *Lehrbuch der Psychologie*, 2te Auflage, Bd. II, p. 66. Volkmann's fifth chapter contains a really precious collection of historical notices concerning space-perception theories.

per se feel extensive, our supposition is shattered by that influence of movement in vision which is so clearly to be traced in many normal errors in the measurement of the field of view. If we assume, on the other hand, that the movements and their feelings are alone possessed of the extensive quality, we make an unjustified hypothesis, for the phenomena compel us, it is true, to accord an influence to movement, but give us no right to call the retinal sensations indifferent, for there are no visual ideas without retinal sensations. If then we wish rigorously to express the given facts, we can ascribe a spatial constitution only to *combinations* of retinal sensations with those of movement."

Thus Wundt, dividing theories into 'nativistic' and 'genetic,' calls his own a genetic theory. To distinguish it from other theories of the same class, he names it a 'theory of complex local signs.'

"It supposes two systems of local signs, whose relations—taking the eye as an example—we may think as . . . the measuring of the manifold local-sign system of the retina by the simple local-sign system of the movements. In its psychological nature this is a process of associative synthesis: it consists in the fusion of both groups of sensations into a product, whose elementary components are no longer separable from each other in idea. In melting wholly away into the product which they create they become consciously undistinguishable, and the mind apprehends only their resultant, the intuition of space. Thus there obtains a certain analogy between this psychic synthesis and that chemical synthesis which out of simple bodies generates a compound that appears to our immediate perception as a homogeneous whole with new properties."

Now let no modest reader think that if this sounds obscure to him it is because he does not know the full context; and that if a wise professor like Wundt can talk so fluently and plausibly about 'combination' and 'psychic synthesis,' it must surely be because those words convey a so much greater fulness of positive meaning to the scholarly than to the unlearned mind. Really it is quite the reverse; *all* the virtue of the phrase lies in its mere sound and skin. Learning does but make one the more sensible of its inward unintelligibility. Wundt's 'theory' is the flimsiest thing in the world. It starts by an untrue assumption, and then corrects it by an unmeaning phrase. Retinal sensations *are* spatial; and were they not, no amount of 'synthesis' with equally spaceless motor sensations could intelligibly make them so. Wundt's theory is, in short, but an avowal of impotence, and an appeal to the inscrutable powers of the soul.[128] It confesses that we cannot analyze the constitution or give the genesis of the spatial quality in consciousness. But at the same time it says the *antecedents* thereof are psychical and not cerebral facts. In calling the quality in question a *sensational* quality, our own account equally disclaimed ability to analyze it, but said its antecedents were cerebral, not psychical—in other words, that it was a *first* psychical thing. This is merely a question of probable fact, which the reader may decide.

And now what shall be said of Helmholtz? Can I find fault with a book which, on the whole, I imagine to be one of the four or five greatest monuments of human genius in the scientific line? If truth impels I must fain try, and take the risks. It seems to me that Helmholtz's genius moves most securely when it keeps close to particular facts. At any rate, it shows least strong in purely speculative passages, which in the *Optics*, in spite of many beauties, seem to me fundamentally vacillating and obscure. The 'empiristic' view which Helmholtz defends is that the space-determinations we perceive are in every case products of a process of unconscious inference.[129] The inference is similar to one from induction or analogy.[130] We always see that form before us which *habitually* would have caused the sensation we now have.[131] But the latter sensation can never be intrinsically spatial, or its intrinsic space-determinations would never be overcome as they are so often by the 'illusory' space-determinations it so often suggests.[132] Since the illusory determination can be traced to a suggestion of Experience, the 'real' one must also be such a suggestion: so that *all* space intuitions are due solely to Experience.[133] The only psychic activity required for this is the association of ideas.[134]

But how, it may be asked, can association produce a space-quality

128 Why talk of 'genetic theories'? when we have in the next breath to write as Wundt does: "If then we must regard the intuition of space as a product that simply emerges from the conditions of our mental and physical organization, nothing need stand in the way of our designating it as one of the *a priori* functions with which consciousness is endowed." (*Logik*, I, 460.)

129 P. 430.

130 Pp. 430, 449.

131 P. 428.

132 P. 442.

133 Pp. 442, 818.

134 P. 798. Cf. also *Popular Scientific Lectures*, pp. 301–3.

not in the things associated? How can we by induction or analogy infer what we do not already generically know? Can 'suggestions of experience' reproduce elements which no particular experience originally contained? This is the point by which Helmholtz's 'empiristic' theory, as a *theory*, must be judged. No theory is worthy of the name which leaves such a point obscure.

Well, Helmholtz does so leave it. At one time he seems to fall back on inscrutable powers of the soul, and to range himself with the 'psychical stimulists.' He speaks of Kant as having made the essential step in the matter in distinguishing the content of experience from that form—space, of course—which is given it by the peculiar faculties of the mind.[135] But elsewhere, again,[136] speaking of sensationalistic theories which would connect spatially determinate feelings *directly* with certain neural events, he says it is better to assume only such simple psychic activities as we *know* to exist, and gives the association of ideas as an instance of what he means. Later,[137] he reinforces this remark by confessing that he does not see how any neural process *can* give rise without antecedent experience to a ready-made (*fertige*) perception of space. And, finally, in a single momentous sentence, he speaks of sensations of *touch* as if they might be the original material of our space-percepts—which thus, from the optical point of view, 'may be assumed as *given*.'[138]

Of course the eye-man has a right to fall back on the skin-man for help at a pinch. But doesn't this mean that he is a mere eye-man and not a complete psychologist? In other words, Helmholtz's *Optics* and the 'empiristic theory' therein professed must not be understood as attempts at answering the *general* question of how space-consciousness enters the mind. They simply deny that it enters with the first optical sensations.[139] Our own account has affirmed stoutly that it enters *then*; but no more than Helmholtz have we pretended to show *why*. Who calls a thing a first sensation

135 P. 456; see also 428, 441.

136 P. 797.

137 P. 812.

138 Bottom of page 797.

139 In fact, to borrow a simile from Prof. G. E. Müller (*Zur Theorie der sinnlichen Aufmerksamkeit*, p. 38), the various senses bear in the Helmholtzian philosophy of perception the same relation to the 'object' perceived by their means that a troop of jolly drinkers bear to the landlord's bill, when no one has any money, but each hopes that one of the rest will pay.

admits he has no theory of its production. Helmholtz, though all the while without an articulate theory, makes the world think he has one. He beautifully traces the immense part which reproductive processes play in our vision of space, and never—except in that one pitiful little sentence about touch—does he tell us just what it is they reproduce. He limits himself to denying that they reproduce originals of a visual sort. And so difficult is the subject, and so magically do catch-words work on the popular-scientist ear, that most likely, had he written 'physiological' instead of 'nativistic,' and 'spiritualistic' instead of 'empiristic' (which synonyms Hering suggests), numbers of his present empirical evolutionary followers would fail to find in his teaching anything worthy of praise. But since he wrote otherwise, they hurrah for him as a sort of second Locke, dealing another death-blow at the old bugaboo of 'innate ideas.' His 'nativistic' adversary Hering they probably imagine—Heaven save the mark!—to be a scholastic in modern disguise.

After Wundt and Helmholtz, the most important anti-sensationalist space-philosopher in Germany is Professor Lipps, whose deduction of space from an order of non-spatial differences, continuous yet separate, is a wonderful piece of subtlety and logic. And yet he has to confess that continuous differences form in the first instance only a logical series, which *need* not appear spatial, and that wherever it does so appear, this must be accounted a 'fact,' due merely 'to the nature of the soul.'[140]

Lipps, and almost all the anti-sensationalist theorists except Helmholtz, seem guilty of that confusion which Mr. Shadworth Hodgson has done so much to clear away, viz., the confounding the analysis of an idea with the means of its production. Lipps, for example, finds that every space we think of can be broken up into positions, and concludes that in some undefined way the several positions must have pre-existed in thought before the aggregate space could have appeared to perception. Similarly Mr. Spencer, defining extension as an 'aggregate of relations of coexistent position,' says "every cognition of magnitude is a cognition of relations of position,"[141] and "no idea of extension can arise from the simultaneous excitation" of many nerves "unless there is a knowl-

140 *Grundtatsachen des Seelenlebens* (1883), pp. 480, 591–2. *Psychologische Studien* (1885), p. 14.

141 *Psychology*, II, p. 174.

edge of their relative positions."[142] Just so Prof. Bain insists that the very *meaning* of space is scope for movement,[143] and that therefore distance and magnitude *can* be no original attributes of the eye's sensibility. Similarly because movement is analyzable into positions occupied at successive moments by the mover, philosophers (e.g., Schopenhauer, as quoted above) have repeatedly denied the possibility of *its* being an immediate sensation. We have, however, seen that it is the most immediate of all our space-sensations. Because it can only occur in a definite direction the impossibility of perceiving it without perceiving its direction has been decreed—a decree which the simplest experiment overthrows.[144] It is a case of what I have called the 'psychologist's fallacy': mere acquaintance with space is treated as tantamount to every sort of knowledge about it, the conditions of the latter are demanded of the former state of mind, and all sorts of mythological processes are brought in to help.[145] As well might one say that because the world consists of all its parts, therefore we can only apprehend it at all by having unconsciously summed these up in our head. It is the old idea of our actual knowledge being drawn out from a pre-existent potentiality, an idea which, whatever worth it may metaphysically possess, does no good in psychology.

My own sensationalistic account has derived most aid and comfort from the writings of Hering, A. W. Volkmann, Stumpf, Le Conte, and Schoen. All these authors allow ample scope to that Experience which Berkeley's genius saw to be a present factor in all our visual acts. But they give Experience some grist to grind, which the *soi-disant* 'empiristic' school forgets to do. Stumpf seems to me the most philosophical and profound of all these writers; and I owe him much. I should doubtless have owed almost as much to Mr. James Ward, had his article on Psychology in the *Encyclopædia Britannica* appeared before my own thoughts were written down. The literature of the question is in all languages very vo-

142 *Ibid.*, p. 168.

143 *Senses and the Intellect*, 3d ed., pp. 366–75.

144 Cf. Hall and Donaldson in *Mind*, x, 559.

145 As other examples of the confusion, take Mr. Sully: "The *fallacious assumption* that there can be an idea of distance in general apart from particular distances" (*Mind*, III, p. 177); and Wundt: "An indefinite localization, which waits for experience to give it its reference to real space, stands in contradiction with the very idea of localization, which means the reference to a determinate point of space" (*Physiologische Psychologie*, 1te Aufl., p. 480).

luminous. I content myself with referring to the bibliography in Helmholtz's and Aubert's works on Physiological Optics for the visual part of the subject, and with naming in a note the ablest works in the English tongue which have treated of the subject in a *general* way.[146]

[146] G. Berkeley: *Essay towards a New Theory of Vision*; Samuel Bailey: *A Review of Berkeley's Theory of Vision* (1842); J. S. Mill's Review of Bailey, in his *Dissertations and Discussions*, vol. II; James Ferrier: Review of Bailey, in *Philosophical Remains*, vol. II; A. Bain: *Senses and the Intellect*, "Intellect," chap. I; H. Spencer: *Principles of Psychology*, pt. VI, chaps. XIV, XVI; J. S. Mill: *Examination of Hamilton*, chap. XIII (the best statement of the so-called English empiricist position); T. K. Abbott: *Sight and Touch*, 1864 (the first English book to go at all minutely into *facts*; Mr. Abbott maintaining retinal sensations to be originally of space in three dimensions); A. C. Fraser: Review of Abbott, in *North British Review* for Aug. 1864; another review in *Macmillan's Magazine*, March 1866; J. Sully: *Outlines of Psychology*, chap. VI; J. Ward: *Encyclopædia Britannica*, 9th Ed., article "Psychology," pp. 53–5; J. E. Walter: *The Perception of Space and Matter* (1879)—I may also refer to a 'discussion' between Prof. G. Croom Robertson, Mr. J. Ward, and the present writer, in *Mind*, vol. XIII.—The present chapter is only the filling out with detail of an article entitled "The Spatial Quale," which appeared in the *Journal of Speculative Philosophy* for January 1879 (XIII, 64).

Chapter XXI[*]

The Perception of Reality

BELIEF

Everyone knows the difference between imagining a thing and believing in its existence, between supposing a proposition and acquiescing in its truth. In the case of acquiescence or belief, the object is not only apprehended by the mind, but is held to have reality. Belief is thus the mental state or function of cognizing reality. As used in the following pages, 'Belief' will mean every degree of assurance, including the highest possible certainty and conviction.

There are, as we know, two ways of studying every psychic state. First, the way of analysis: What does it consist in? What is its inner nature? Of what sort of mind-stuff is it composed? Second, the way of history: What are its conditions of production, and its connection with other facts?

Into the first way we cannot go very far. *In its inner nature belief, or the sense of reality, is a sort of feeling more allied to the emotions than to anything else.* Mr. Bagehot distinctly calls it the 'emotion' of conviction. I just now spoke of it as acquiescence. It resembles more than anything what in the psychology of volition we know as consent. Consent is recognized by all to be a manifestation of our active nature. It would naturally be described by such terms as 'willingness' or the 'turning of our disposition.' What characterizes both consent and belief is the cessation of theoretic

* Reprinted, with additions, from *Mind* for July 1889.

agitation, through the advent of an idea which is inwardly stable, and fills the mind solidly to the exclusion of contradictory ideas. When this is the case, motor effects are apt to follow. Hence the states of consent and belief, characterized by repose on the purely intellectual side, are both intimately connected with subsequent practical activity. This inward stability of the mind's content is as characteristic of disbelief as of belief. But we shall presently see that we never disbelieve anything except for the reason that we believe something else which contradicts the first thing.[1] Disbelief is thus an incidental complication to belief, and need not be considered by itself.

The true opposites of belief, psychologically considered, *are doubt and inquiry, not disbelief.* In both these states the content of our mind is in unrest, and the emotion engendered thereby is, like the emotion of belief itself, perfectly distinct, but perfectly indescribable in words. Both sorts of emotion may be pathologically exalted. One of the charms of drunkenness unquestionably lies in the deepening of the sense of reality and truth which is gained therein. In whatever light things may then appear to us, they seem more utterly what they are, more 'utterly utter' than when we are sober. This goes to a fully unutterable extreme in the nitrous oxide intoxication, in which a man's very soul will sweat with conviction, and he be all the while unable to tell what he is convinced of at all.[2] The pathological state opposed to this solidity and deepening has been called the questioning mania (*Grübelsucht* by the Germans). It is sometimes found as a substantive affection, paroxysmal or chronic, and consists in the inability to rest in any conception, and the need of having it confirmed and explained. 'Why do I stand here where I stand?' 'Why is a glass a glass, a chair a chair?' 'How is it that men are only of the size they are? Why not as big as houses,' etc., etc.[3] There is, it is true, another pathological state

1 Compare this psychological fact with the corresponding logical truth that all negation rests on covert assertion of something else than the thing denied. (See Bradley's *Principles of Logic*, bk. I, ch. 3.)

2 See that very remarkable little work, *The Anæsthetic Revelation and the Gist of Philosophy*, by Benjamin P. Blood (Amsterdam, N. Y., 1874). Compare also *Mind*, VII, 206.

3 "To one whose mind is healthy thoughts come and go unnoticed, with me they have to be faced, thought about in a peculiar fashion, and then disposed of as finished, and this often when I am utterly wearied and would be at peace; but the call is imperative. This goes on to the hindrance of all natural action. If I were

which is as far removed from doubt as from belief, and which some may prefer to consider the proper contrary of the latter state of mind. I refer to the feeling that everything is hollow, unreal, dead. I shall speak of this state again upon a later page. The point I wish to notice here is simply that belief and disbelief are but two aspects of one psychic state.

John Mill, reviewing various opinions about belief, comes to the conclusion that no account of it can be given:

"What," he says, "is the difference *to our minds* between thinking of a reality, and representing to ourselves an imaginary picture? I confess that I can perceive no escape from the opinion that the distinction is ultimate and primordial. There is no more difficulty in holding it to be so, than in holding the difference between a sensation and an idea to be primordial. It seems almost another aspect of the same difference. . . . I cannot help thinking, therefore, that there is in the remembrance of a real fact, as distinguished from that of a thought, an element which does not consist . . . in a difference between the mere ideas which are present to the mind in the two cases. This element, howsoever we define it, constitutes Belief, and is the difference between Memory and Imagination. From whatever direction we approach, this difference seems to close our path. When we arrive at it, we seem to have reached, as it were, the central point of our intellectual nature, presupposed and built upon in every attempt we make to explain the more recondite phenomena of our mental being."[4]

If the words of Mill be taken to apply to the mere subjective analysis of belief—to the question, What does it feel like when we

---

told the staircase was on fire and I had only a minute to escape, and the thought arose—'Have they sent for fire engines? It is probable the man who has the key is at hand. Is the man a careful sort of person? Will the key be hanging on a peg? Am I thinking rightly? Perhaps they don't lock the depot.' My foot would be lifted to go down. I should be conscious to excitement that I was losing my chance—but I should be unable to stir, until all these absurdities were entertained and disposed of. In the most critical moments of my life, when I ought to have been so *engrossed as to leave no room for any secondary thoughts,* I have been oppressed by the inability to be at peace. And in the most ordinary circumstances it is all the same. Let me instance the other morning I went to walk. The day was biting cold, but I was unable to proceed except by jerks. Once I got arrested—my feet in a muddy pool. One foot was lifted to go, knowing that it was not good to be standing in water, but there I was fast, the cause of detention being the discussing with myself the reasons why I should not stand in that pool." (T. S. Clouston: *Clinical Lectures on Mental Diseases,* 1883, p. 43. See also Berger, in *Archiv für Psychiatrie,* VI, 217.)

[4] Note to James Mill's *Analysis,* I, 412–423.

have it?—they must be held, on the whole, to be correct. Belief, the sense of reality, feels like itself—that is about as much as we can say.

Prof. Brentano, in an admirable chapter of his *Psychologie*, expresses this by saying that conception and belief (which he names *judgment*) are two different fundamental psychic phenomena. What I myself have called (Vol. I, p. 265) the 'object' of thought may be comparatively simple, like "Ha! what a pain," or "It-thunders"; or it may be complex, like "Columbus-discovered-America-in-1492," or "There-exists-an-all-wise-Creator-of-the-world." In either case, however, the mere thought of the object may exist as something quite distinct from the belief in its reality. The belief, as Brentano says, presupposes the mere thought:

"Every object comes into consciousness in a twofold way, as simply thought of [*vorgestellt*] and as admitted [*anerkannt*] or denied. The relation is analogous to that which is assumed by most philosophers (by Kant no less than by Aristotle) to obtain between mere thought and desire. Nothing is ever desired without being thought of; but the desiring is nevertheless a second quite new and peculiar form of relation to the object, a second quite new way of receiving it into consciousness. No more is anything judged [i.e., believed or disbelieved] which is not thought of too. But we must insist that, so soon as the object of a thought becomes the object of an assenting or rejecting judgment, our consciousness steps into an entirely new relation towards it. It is then twice present in consciousness, as thought of, and as held for real or denied; just as when desire awakens for it, it is both thought and simultaneously desired" (P. 266).

The commonplace doctrine of 'judgment' is that it consists in the combination of 'ideas' by a 'copula' into a 'proposition,' which may be of various sorts, as affirmative, negative, hypothetical, etc. But who does not see that in a disbelieved or doubted or interrogative or conditional proposition, the ideas are combined in the same identical way in which they are in a proposition which is solidly believed? *The way in which the ideas are combined is a part of the inner constitution of the thought's object or content.* That object is sometimes an articulated whole with relations between its parts, amongst which relations, that of predicate to subject may be one. But when we have got our object with its inner constitution thus defined in a proposition, then the question comes up regarding the object as a whole: 'Is it a real object? is this proposition a true proposition or not?' And in the answer *Yes* to *this* question lies that new psychic act which Brentano calls 'judgment,' but which I prefer to call 'belief.'

In every proposition, then, so far as it is believed, questioned, or disbelieved, four elements are to be distinguished, the subject, the predicate, and their relation (of whatever sort it be)—these form the *object* of belief—and finally the psychic attitude in which our mind stands towards the proposition taken as a whole—and this is the belief itself.[5]

Admitting, then, that this attitude is a state of consciousness *sui generis*, about which nothing more can be said in the way of internal analysis, let us proceed to the second way of studying the subject of belief: *Under what circumstances do we think things real?* We shall soon see how much matter this gives us to discuss.

THE VARIOUS ORDERS OF REALITY

Suppose a new-born mind, entirely blank and waiting for experience to begin. Suppose that it begins in the form of a visual impression (whether faint or vivid is immaterial) of a lighted candle against a dark background, and nothing else, so that whilst this image lasts it constitutes the entire universe known to the mind in question. Suppose, moreover (to simplify the hypothesis), that the candle is only imaginary, and that no 'original' of it is recognized by us psychologists outside. Will this hallucinatory candle be believed in, will it have a real existence for the mind?

What possible sense (for that mind) would a suspicion have that the candle was not real? What would doubt or disbelief of it imply? When *we*, the onlooking psychologists, say the candle is unreal, we mean something quite definite, viz., that there is a world known to *us* which *is* real, and to which we perceive that the candle does not belong; it belongs exclusively to that individual mind, has no *status* anywhere else, etc. It exists, to be sure, in a fashion, for it forms the content of that mind's hallucination; but the hallucination itself, though unquestionably it is a sort of existing fact, has no knowledge of *other* facts; and since those *other* facts are the realities *par excellence* for us, and the only things we believe in, the candle is simply outside of our reality and belief altogether.

By the hypothesis, however, the *mind which sees the candle* can

[5] For an excellent account of the history of opinion on this subject see A. Marty, in *Vierteljahrsschrift für wissenschaftliche Philosophie*, VIII, 161 ff. (1884).

spin no such considerations as these about it, for of other facts, actual or possible, it has no inkling whatever. That candle is its all, its absolute. Its entire faculty of attention is absorbed by it. It *is*, it is *that*; it is *there*; no other possible candle, or quality of this candle, no other possible place, or possible object in the place, no alternative, in short, suggests itself as even conceivable; so how can the mind help believing the candle real? The supposition that it might possibly not do so is, under the supposed conditions, unintelligible.[6]

This is what Spinoza long ago announced:

> "Let us conceive a boy," he said, "imagining to himself a horse, and taking note of nothing else. As this imagination involves the existence of the horse, *and the boy has no perception which annuls its existence*, he will necessarily contemplate the horse as present, nor will he be able to doubt of its existence, however little certain of it he may be. I deny that a man in so far as he imagines [*percipit*] affirms nothing. For what is it to imagine a winged horse but to affirm that the horse [that horse, namely] has wings? For if the mind had nothing before it but the winged horse it would contemplate the same as present, would have no cause to doubt of its existence, nor any power of dissenting from its existence, unless the imagination of the winged horse were joined to an idea which contradicted [*tollit*] its existence." (*Ethics*, II, 49, Scholium.)

The sense that anything we think of is unreal can only come, then, when that thing is contradicted by some other thing of which we think. *Any object which remains uncontradicted is ipso facto believed and posited as absolute reality.*

Now, how comes it that one thing thought of can be contradicted by another? It cannot unless it begins the quarrel by saying something inadmissible about that other. Take the mind with the candle, or the boy with the horse. If either of them say, "That candle or that horse, even when I don't see it, exists in *the outer world*," he pushes into 'the outer world' an object which may be incompatible with everything which he otherwise knows of that world. If so, he must take his choice of which to hold by, the present perceptions or the other knowledge of the world. If he holds to the

[6] We saw near the end of Chapter XIX that a candle-image taking exclusive possession of the mind in this way would probably acquire the sensational vividness. But this physiological accident is logically immaterial to the argument in the text, which ought to apply as well to the dimmest sort of mental image as to the brightest sensation.

other knowledge, the present perceptions are contradicted, *so far as their relation to that world goes.* Candle and horse, whatever they may be, are not existents in outward space. They are existents, of course; they are mental objects; mental objects have existence as mental objects. But they are situated in their own spaces, the space in which they severally appear, and neither of those spaces is the space in which the realities called 'the outer world' exist.

Take again the horse with wings. If I merely dream of a horse with wings, my horse interferes with nothing else and has not to be contradicted. That horse, its wings, and its place, are all equally real. That horse exists no otherwise than as winged, and is moreover really there, for that place exists no otherwise than as the place of that horse, and claims as yet no connection with the other places of the world. But if with this horse I make an inroad into the *world otherwise known,* and say, for example, "That is my old mare Maggie, having grown a pair of wings where she stands in her stall," the whole case is altered; for now the horse and place are identified with a horse and place otherwise known, and *what* is known of the latter objects is incompatible with what is perceived with the former. "Maggie in her stall with wings! Never!" The wings are unreal, then, visionary. I have dreamed a lie about Maggie in her stall.

The reader will recognize in these two cases the two sorts of judgment called in the logic-books existential and attributive respectively. 'The candle exists as an outer reality' is an existential, 'My Maggie has got a pair of wings' is an attributive, proposition;[7] and it follows from what was first said that *all propositions, whether attributive or existential, are believed through the very fact of being conceived, unless they clash with other propositions believed at the same time, by affirming that their terms are the same with*

[7] In both existential and attributive judgments a synthesis is represented. The syllable *ex* in the word Existence, *da* in the word *Dasein,* express it. 'The candle exists' is equivalent to 'The candle is *over there.*' And the 'over there' means real space, space related to other reals. The proposition amounts to saying: 'The candle is in the same space with other reals.' It affirms of the candle a very concrete predicate—namely, this relation to other particular concrete things. *Their* real existence, as we shall later see, resolves itself into their peculiar relation to *ourselves.* Existence is thus no substantive quality when we predicate it of any object; it is a relation, ultimately terminating in ourselves, and at the moment when it terminates, becoming a *practical* relation. But of this more anon. I only wish now to indicate the superficial nature of the distinction between the existential and the attributive proposition.

the terms of these other propositions. A dream-candle has existence, true enough; but not the same existence (existence for itself, namely, or *extra mentem meam*) which the candles of waking perception have. A dream-horse has wings; but then neither horse nor wings are the same with any horses or wings known to memory. That we can at any moment think of the same thing which at any former moment we thought of is the ultimate law of our intellectual constitution. But when we now think of it incompatibly with our other ways of thinking it, then we must choose which way to stand by, for we cannot continue to think in two contradictory ways at once. *The whole distinction of real and unreal, the whole psychology of belief, disbelief, and doubt, is thus grounded on two mental facts—first, that we are liable to think differently of the same; and second, that when we have done so, we can choose which way of thinking to adhere to and which to disregard.*

The subjects adhered to become real subjects, the attributes adhered to real attributes, the existence adhered to real existence; whilst the subjects disregarded become imaginary subjects, the attributes disregarded erroneous attributes, and the existence disregarded an existence in no man's land, in the limbo "where footless fancies dwell." The real things are, in M. Taine's terminology, the *reductives* of the things judged unreal.

THE MANY WORLDS

Habitually and practically we do not *count* these disregarded things as existents at all. For them *Væ victis* is the law in the popular philosophy; they are not even treated as appearances; they are treated as if they were mere waste, equivalent to nothing at all. To the genuinely philosophic mind, however, they still have existence, though not the same existence, as the real things. *As* objects of fancy, *as* errors, *as* occupants of dreamland, etc., they are in their way as indefeasible parts of life, as undeniable features of the Universe, as the realities are in their way. The total world of which the philosophers must take account is thus composed of the realities *plus* the fancies and illusions.

Two sub-universes, at least, connected by relations which philosophy tries to ascertain! Really there are more than two sub-universes of which we take account, some of us of this one, and others of that. For there are various categories both of illusion and of reality, and alongside of the world of absolute error (i.e., error confined to single individuals) but still within the world of absolute reality (i.e., reality believed by the complete philosopher) there is the world of collective error, there are the worlds of abstract reality, of relative or practical reality, of ideal relations, and there is the supernatural world. The popular mind conceives of all these sub-worlds more or less disconnectedly; and when dealing with one of them, forgets for the time being its relations to the rest. The complete philosopher is he who seeks not only to assign to every given object of his thought its right place in one or other of these sub-worlds, but he also seeks to determine the relation of each sub-world to the others in the total world which *is*.

The most important sub-universes commonly discriminated from each other and recognized by most of us as existing, each with its own special and separate style of existence, are the following:

(1) The world of sense, or of physical 'things' as we instinctively apprehend them, with such qualities as heat, color, and sound, and such 'forces' as life, chemical affinity, gravity, electricity, all existing as such within or on the surface of the things.

(2) The world of science, or of physical things as the learned conceive them, with secondary qualities and 'forces' (in the popular sense) excluded, and nothing real but solids and fluids and their 'laws' (i.e., customs) of motion.[8]

(3) The world of ideal relations, or abstract truths believed or believable by all, and expressed in logical, mathematical, metaphysical, ethical, or æsthetic propositions.

(4) The world of 'idols of the tribe,' illusions or prejudices common to the race. All educated people recognize these as forming one sub-universe. The motion of the sky round the earth, for example, belongs to this world. That motion is not a recognized item of any of the other worlds; but as an 'idol of the tribe' it really exists. For certain philosophers 'matter' exists only as an idol of the tribe. For science, the 'secondary qualities' of matter are but 'idols of the tribe.'

(5) The various supernatural worlds, the Christian heaven and hell, the world of the Hindoo mythology, the world of Swedenborg's *visa et audita*, etc. Each of these is a consistent system, with definite relations among its own parts. Neptune's trident, e.g., has

[8] I define the scientific universe here in the radical mechanical way. Practically, it is oftener thought of in a mongrel way and resembles in more points the popular physical world.

no status of reality whatever in the Christian heaven; but within the classic Olympus certain definite things are true of it, whether one believe in the reality of the classic mythology as a whole or not. The various worlds of deliberate fable may be ranked with these worlds of faith—the world of the *Iliad*, that of *King Lear*, of the *Pickwick Papers*, etc.[9]

(6) The various worlds of individual opinion, as numerous as men are.

(7) The worlds of sheer madness and vagary, also indefinitely numerous.

Every object we think of gets at last referred to one world or another of this or of some similar list. It settles into our belief as a common-sense object, a scientific object, an abstract object, a mythological object, an object of someone's mistaken conception, or a madman's object; and it reaches this state sometimes immediately, but often only after being hustled and bandied about amongst other objects until it finds some which will tolerate its presence and stand in relations to it which nothing contradicts. The molecules and ether-waves of the scientific world, for example, simply kick the object's warmth and color out, they refuse to have any relations with them. But the world of 'idols of the tribe' stands ready to take them in. Just so the world of classic myth takes up the winged horse; the world of individual hallucination, the vision of the candle; the world of abstract truth, the proposition that justice is kingly, though no actual king be just. The various worlds themselves, however, appear (as aforesaid) to most men's minds in no very definitely conceived relation to each other, and our attention, when it turns to one, is apt to drop the others for the time being out of its account. Propositions concerning the different worlds are made from 'different points of view'; and in this more or less chaotic state the consciousness of most thinkers remains to

[9] It thus comes about that we can say such things as that Ivanhoe did not *really* marry Rebecca, as Thackeray *falsely* makes him do. The real Ivanhoe-world is the one which Scott wrote down for us. *In that world* Ivanhoe does *not* marry Rebecca. The objects within that world are knit together by perfectly definite relations, which can be affirmed or denied. Whilst absorbed in the novel, we turn our backs on all other worlds, and, for the time, the Ivanhoe-world remains our absolute reality. When we wake from the spell, however, we find a still more real world, which reduces Ivanhoe, and all things connected with him, to the fictive status, and relegates them to one of the sub-universes grouped under No. 5.

the end. Each world *whilst it is attended to* is real after its own fashion; only the reality lapses with the attention.

THE WORLD OF 'PRACTICAL REALITIES'

Each thinker, however, has dominant habits of attention; and these *practically elect from among the various worlds some one to be for him the world of ultimate realities.* From this world's objects he does not appeal. Whatever positively contradicts them must get into another world or die. The horse, e.g., may have wings to its heart's content, so long as it does not pretend to be the real world's horse—*that* horse is absolutely wingless. For most men, as we shall immediately see, the 'things of sense' hold this prerogative position, and are the absolutely real world's nucleus. Other things, to be sure, may be real for this man or for that—things of science, abstract moral relations, things of the Christian theology, or what not. But even for the special man, these things are usually real with a less real reality than that of the things of sense. They are taken less seriously; and the very utmost that can be said for anyone's belief in them is that it is as strong as his 'belief in his own senses.'[10]

In all this the everlasting partiality of our nature shows itself, our inveterate propensity to choice. For, in the strict and ultimate sense of the word existence, everything which can be thought of at all exists as *some* sort of object, whether mythical object, individual thinker's object, or object in outer space and for intelligence at large. Errors, fictions, tribal beliefs, are parts of the whole great

[10] The world of dreams is our real world whilst we are sleeping, because our attention then lapses from the sensible world. Conversely, when we wake the attention usually lapses from the dream-world and that becomes unreal. But if a dream haunts us and compels our attention during the day it is very apt to remain figuring in our consciousness as a sort of sub-universe alongside of the waking world. Most people have probably had dreams which it is hard to imagine not to have been glimpses into an actually existing region of being, perhaps a corner of the 'spiritual world.' And dreams have accordingly in all ages been regarded as revelations, and have played a large part in furnishing forth mythologies and creating themes for faith to lay hold upon. The 'larger universe,' here, which helps us to believe both in the dream and in the waking reality which is its immediate reductive, is the *total* universe, of Nature *plus* the Supernatural. The dream holds true, namely, in one half of that universe; the waking perceptions in the other half. Even to-day dream-objects figure among the realities in which some 'psychic-researchers' are seeking to rouse our belief. All our theories, not only those about the supernatural, but our philosophic and scientific theories as well, are like our dreams in rousing such different degrees of belief in different minds.

Universe which God has made, and He must have meant all these things to be in it, each in its respective place. But for us finite creatures, " 'tis to consider too curiously to consider so." The mere fact of appearing as an object at all is not enough to constitute reality. That may be metaphysical reality, reality for God; but what we need is practical reality, reality for ourselves; and, to have that, an object must not only appear, but it must appear both *interesting* and *important*. The worlds whose objects are neither interesting nor important we treat simply negatively, we brand them as *un*real.

In the relative sense, then, the sense in which we contrast reality with simple *un*reality, and in which one thing is said to have *more* reality than another, and to be more believed, *reality means simply relation to our emotional and active life.* This is the only sense which the word ever has in the mouths of practical men. *In this sense, whatever excites and stimulates our interest is real*; whenever an object so appeals to us that we turn to it, accept it, fill our mind with it, or practically take account of it, so far it is real for us, and we believe it. Whenever, on the contrary, we ignore it, fail to consider it or act upon it, despise it, reject it, forget it, so far it is unreal for us and disbelieved. Hume's account of the matter was then essentially correct, when he said that belief in anything was simply the having the idea of it in a lively and active manner:

"I say then, that belief is nothing but a more vivid, lively, forcible, firm, steady conception of an object, than what the imagination alone is ever able to attain. . . . It consists not in the peculiar nature or order of ideas, but in the *manner* of their conception, and in their *feeling* to the mind. I confess, that it is impossible perfectly to explain this feeling or manner of conception. . . . Its true and proper name . . . is *belief*; which is a term, that every one sufficiently understands in common life. And in philosophy, we can go no farther than assert, that *belief* is something felt by the mind, which distinguishes the ideas of the judgment from the fictions of the imagination.[11] It gives them more weight and influence; makes them appear of greater importance; inforces them in the mind; gives them a superior influence on the passions, and renders them the governing principle of our actions."[12]

11 Distinguishes realities from unrealities, the essential from the rubbishy and neglectable.

12 *Inquiry Concerning Human Understanding*, sec. v, pt. 2 (slightly transposed in my quotation).

Or as Prof. Bain puts it: "In its essential character, Belief is a phase of our active nature,—otherwise called the Will."[13]

The object of belief, then, reality or real existence, is something quite different from all the other predicates which a subject may possess. Those are properties intellectually or sensibly intuited. When we add any one of them to the subject, we increase the intrinsic content of the latter, we enrich its picture in our mind. But adding reality does not enrich the picture in any such inward way; it leaves it inwardly as it finds it, and only fixes it and stamps it in to *us*.

"The real," as Kant says, "contains no more than the possible. A hundred real dollars do not contain a penny more than a hundred possible dollars. . . . By whatever and by however many predicates I may think a thing . . . nothing is added to it, if I add that the thing exists. . . . Whatever therefore our concept of an object may contain, we must always step outside of it, in order to attribute to it existence."[14]

The 'stepping outside' of it is the establishment either of immediate practical relations between it and ourselves, or of relations between it and other objects with which we have immediate practical relations. Relations of this sort, which are as yet not transcended or superseded by others, are *ipso facto* real relations, and confer reality upon their objective term. *The fons et origo of all reality, whether from the absolute or the practical point of view, is thus subjective, is ourselves.* As bare logical thinkers, without emotional reaction, we give reality to whatever objects we think of, for they are really phenomena, or objects of our passing thought, if nothing more. But, *as thinkers with emotional reaction, we give*

[13] Note to James Mill's *Analysis*, I, 394.

[14] *Critique of Pure Reason*, trans. Müller, II, 515–16. Hume also: "When after the simple conception of any thing we wou'd conceive it as existent, we in reality make no addition to or alteration on our first idea. Thus when we affirm, that God is existent, we simply form the idea of such a being, as he is represented to us; nor is the existence, which we attribute to him, conceiv'd by a particular idea, which we join to his other qualities, and can again separate and distinguish from them. . . . The belief of the existence joins no new ideas to those, which compose the idea of the object. When I think of God, when I think of him as existent, and when I believe him to be existent, my idea of him neither encreases nor diminishes. But as 'tis certain there is a great difference betwixt the simple conception of the existence of an object, and the belief of it, and as this difference lies not in the parts or composition of the idea, which we conceive; it follows, that it must lie in the *manner*, in which we conceive it." (*Treatise of Human Nature*, pt. III, sec. 7.)

what seems to us a still higher degree of reality to whatever things we select and emphasize and turn to WITH A WILL. These are our *living* realities; and not only these, but all the other things which are intimately connected with these. Reality, starting from our Ego, thus sheds itself from point to point—first, upon all objects which have an immediate sting of interest for our Ego in them, and next, upon the objects most continuously related with these. It only fails when the connecting thread is lost. A whole system may be real, if it only hang to our Ego by one immediately *stinging* term. But what contradicts any such stinging term, even though it be another stinging term itself, is either not believed, or only believed after settlement of the dispute.

We reach thus the important conclusion that *our own reality, that sense of our own life which we at every moment possess, is the ultimate of ultimates for our belief.* 'As sure as I exist!'—this is our uttermost warrant for the being of all other things. As Descartes made the indubitable reality of the *cogito* go bail for the reality of all that the *cogito* involved, so we all of us, feeling our own present reality with absolutely coercive force, ascribe an all but equal degree of reality, first to whatever things we lay hold on with a sense of personal need, and second, to whatever farther things continuously belong with these. "Mein Jetzt und Hier," as Prof. Lipps says, "ist der letzte Angelpunkt für alle Wirklichkeit, also alle Erkenntniss."

The world of living realities as contrasted with unrealities is thus anchored in the Ego, considered as an active and emotional term.[15] That is the hook from which the rest dangles, the absolute support. And as from a painted hook it has been said that one can only hang a painted chain, so conversely, from a real hook only a real chain can properly be hung. *Whatever things have intimate and continuous connection with my life are things of whose reality I cannot doubt.* Whatever things fail to establish this connection are things which are practically no better for me than if they existed not at all.

In certain forms of melancholic perversion of the sensibilities and reactive powers, nothing touches us intimately, rouses us, or

[15] I use the notion of the Ego here, as common-sense uses it. Nothing is prejudged as to the results (or absence of results) of ulterior attempts to analyze the notion.

wakens natural feeling. The consequence is the complaint so often heard from melancholic patients, that nothing is believed in by them as it used to be, and that all sense of reality is fled from life. They are sheathed in india-rubber; nothing penetrates to the quick or draws blood, as it were. According to Griesinger, "I see, I hear!" such patients say, "but the objects do not reach me, it is as if there were a wall between me and the outer world!"

"In such patients there often is an alteration of the cutaneous sensibility, such that things feel indistinct or sometimes rough and woolly. But even were this change always present, it would not completely explain the psychic phenomenon . . . which reminds us more of the alteration in our psychic relations to the outer world which advancing age on the one hand, and on the other emotions and passions, may bring about. In childhood we feel ourselves to be closer to the world of sensible phenomena, we live immediately with them and in them; an intimately vital tie binds us and them together. But with the ripening of reflection this tie is loosened, the warmth of our interest cools, things look differently to us, and we act more as foreigners to the outer world, even though we know it a great deal better. Joy and expansive emotions in general draw it nearer to us again. Everything makes a more lively impression, and with the quick immediate return of this warm receptivity for sense-impressions, joy makes us feel young again. In depressing emotions it is the other way. Outer things, whether living or inorganic, suddenly grow cold and foreign to us, and even our favorite objects of interest feel as if they belonged to us no more. Under these circumstances, receiving no longer from anything a lively impression, we cease to turn towards outer things, and the sense of inward loneliness grows upon us. . . . Where there is no strong intelligence to control this *blasé* condition, this psychic coldness and lack of interest, the issue of these states in which all seems so cold and hollow, the heart dried up, the world grown dead and empty, is often suicide or the deeper forms of insanity."[16]

THE PARAMOUNT REALITY OF SENSATIONS

But now we are met by questions of detail. What does this stirring, this exciting power, this interest, consist in, which some ob-

[16] Griesinger: *Die Pathologie und Therapie der psychischen Krankheiten*, §§ 50, 98. See also Lotze: *Medicinische Psychologie*, p. 251. The neologism we so often hear, that an experience 'gives us a *realizing sense*' of the truth of some proposition or other, illustrates the dependence of the sense of reality upon *excitement*. Only what stirs us is 'realized.'

jects have? which *are* those 'intimate relations' with our life which give reality? And what things stand in these relations immediately, and what others are so closely connected with the former that (in Hume's language) we 'carry our disposition' also on to them?

In a simple and direct way these questions cannot be answered at all. The whole history of human thought is but an unfinished attempt to answer them. For what have men been trying to find out, since men were men, but just those things: "Where do our true interests lie—which relations shall we call the intimate and real ones—which things shall we call living realities and which not?" A few psychological points can, however, be made clear.

Any relation to our mind at all, in the absence of a stronger contradicting relation, suffices to make an object real. The barest appeal to our attention is enough for that. Revert to the beginning of the chapter, and take the candle entering the vacant mind. The mind was waiting for just some such object to make its spring upon. It makes its spring and the candle is believed. But when the candle appears at the same time with other objects, it must run the gauntlet of their rivalry, and then it becomes a question which of the various candidates for attention shall compel belief. As a rule we believe as much as we can. We would believe everything if we only could. When objects are represented by us quite unsystematically they conflict but little with each other, and the number of them which in this chaotic manner we can believe is limitless. The primitive savage's mind is a jungle in which hallucinations, dreams, superstitions, conceptions, and sensible objects all flourish alongside of each other, unregulated except by the attention turning in this way or in that. The child's mind is the same. It is only as objects become permanent and their relations fixed that discrepancies and contradictions are felt and must be settled in some stable way. As a rule, the success with which a contradicted object maintains itself in our belief is proportional to several qualities which it must possess. Of these the one which would be put first by most people, because it characterizes objects of sensation, is its—

(1) Coerciveness over attention, or the mere power to possess consciousness: then follow—

(2) Liveliness, or sensible pungency, especially in the way of exciting pleasure or pain;

(3) Stimulating effect upon the will, i.e., capacity to arouse active impulses, the more instinctive the better;

(4) Emotional interest, as object of love, dread, admiration, desire, etc.;

(5) Congruity with certain favorite forms of contemplation—unity, simplicity, permanence, and the like;

(6) Independence of other causes, and its own causal importance.

These characters run into each other. Coerciveness is the result of liveliness or emotional interest. What is lively and interesting stimulates *eo ipso* the will; congruity holds of active impulses as well as of contemplative forms; causal independence and importance suit a certain contemplative demand, etc. I will therefore abandon all attempt at a formal treatment, and simply proceed to make remarks in the most convenient order of exposition.

As a whole, sensations are more lively and are judged more real than conceptions; things met with every hour more real than things seen once; attributes perceived when awake, more real than attributes perceived in a dream. But, owing to the *diverse relations contracted by the various objects with each other*, the simple rule that the lively and permanent is the real is often enough disguised. A conceived thing may be deemed more real than a certain sensible thing, if it only be intimately related to other sensible things more vivid, permanent, or interesting than the first one. Conceived molecular vibrations, e.g., are by the physicist judged more real than felt warmth, because so intimately related to all those other facts of motion in the world which he has made his special study. Similarly, a rare thing may be deemed more real than a permanent thing if it be more widely related to other permanent things. All the occasional crucial observations of science are examples of this. A rare experience, too, is likely to be judged more real than a permanent one, if it be more interesting and exciting. Such is the sight of Saturn through a telescope; such are the occasional insights and illuminations which upset our habitual ways of thought.

But no mere floating conception, no mere disconnected rarity, ever displaces vivid things or permanent things from our belief. A conception, to prevail, must *terminate* in the world of orderly sensible experience. A rare phenomenon, to displace frequent ones, must belong with others more frequent still. The history of science is strewn with wrecks and ruins of theory—essences and principles, fluids and forces—once fondly clung to, but found to hang together with no facts of sense. And exceptional phenomena solicit our belief in vain until such time as we chance to conceive them as of kinds already admitted to exist. What science means by 'verification' is no more than this, that no object of conception shall be believed which sooner or later has not some permanent and vivid object of sensation for its *term*. Compare what was said on pages 653–657, above.

Sensible objects are thus either our realities or the tests of our realities. Conceived objects must show sensible effects or else be disbelieved. And the effects, even though reduced to relative unreality when their causes come to view (as heat, which molecular vibrations make unreal), are yet the things on which our knowledge of the causes rests. Strange mutual dependence this, in which the appearance needs the reality in order to exist, but the reality needs the appearance in order to be known!

Sensible vividness or pungency is then the vital factor in reality when once the conflict between objects, and the connecting of them together in the mind, has begun. No object which neither possesses this vividness in its own right nor is able to borrow it from anything else has a chance of making headway against vivid rivals, or of rousing in us that reaction in which belief consists. On the vivid objects we *pin*, as the saying is, our faith in all the rest; and our belief returns instinctively even to those of them from which reflection has led it away. Witness the obduracy with which the popular world of colors, sounds, and smells holds its own against that of molecules and vibrations. Let the physicist himself but nod, like Homer, and the world of sense becomes his absolute reality again.[17]

[17] The way in which sensations are pitted against systematized conceptions, and in which the one or the other then prevails according as the sensations are felt by ourselves or merely known by report, is interestingly illustrated at the present day by the state of public belief about 'spiritualistic' phenomena. There exist numerous narratives of movement without contact on the part of articles of furniture and other material objects, in the presence of certain privileged individuals called mediums. Such movement violates our memories, and the whole system of accepted physical 'science.' Consequently those who have not seen it either brand the narratives immediately as lies or call the phenomena 'illusions' of sense, produced by fraud or due to hallucination. But one who has actually seen such a phenomenon, under what seems to him sufficiently 'test-conditions,' will hold to his sensible experience through thick and thin, even though the whole fabric of 'science' should be rent in twain. That man would be a weak-spirited creature indeed who should allow any fly-blown generalities about 'the liability of the senses to be deceived' to bully him out of his adhesion to what for him was an indubitable experience of sight. A man may err in this obstinacy, sure enough, in any particular case. But the

That things originally devoid of this stimulating power should be enabled, by association with other things which have it, to compel our belief as if they had it themselves, is a remarkable psychological fact, which since Hume's time it has been impossible to overlook.

"The vividness of the first conception," he writes, "diffuses itself along the relations, and is convey'd, as by so many pipes or canals, to every idea that has any communication with the primary one. . . . Superstitious people are fond of the relicks of saints and holy men, for the same reason that they seek after types and images, in order to inliven their devotion, and give them a more intimate and strong conception of those exemplary lives. . . . Now 'tis evident, one of the best relicks a devotee cou'd procure, wou'd be the handywork of a saint; and if his cloaths and furniture are ever to be consider'd in this light, 'tis because they were once at his disposal, and were mov'd and affected by him; in which respect they are . . . connected with him by a shorter chain of consequences than any of those, from which we learn the reality of his existence. This phænomenon clearly proves, that a present impression with a relation of causation may inliven any idea, and consequently produce belief or assent, according to the precedent definition of it. . . . It has been remark'd among the *Mahometans* as well as *Christians*, that those *pilgrims*, who have seen MECCA or the HOLY LAND, are ever after more faithful and zealous believers, than those who have not had that advantage. A man, whose memory presents him with a lively image of the *Red-Sea, and the Desert, and Jerusalem, and Galilee* can never doubt of any miraculous events, which are related either by *Moses or the Evangelists.* The lively idea of the places passes by an easy transition to the facts, which are suppos'd to have been related to them by contiguity, and encreases the belief by encreasing the vivacity of the conception. The remembrance of these fields and rivers has the same influence as a new argument. . . . The ceremonies of the *Catholic* religion may be consider'd as instances of the same nature. The devotees of that strange superstition usually plead in excuse of the mummeries, with which they are upbraided, that they feel the good effect of those external motions, and postures, and actions, in inlivening their devotion, and quickening their fervour, which otherwise wou'd decay away, if directed entirely to distant and immaterial objects. We shadow out the objects of our faith, say they, in sensible types and images, and render them more present to us by the immediate presence of these

---

spirit that animates him is that on which ultimately the very life and health of Science rest.

types, than 'tis possible for us to do, merely by an intellectual view and contemplation."[18]

Hume's cases are rather trivial; and the things which associated sensible objects make us believe in are supposed by him to be unreal. But all the more manifest for that is the fact of their psychological influence. Who does not 'realize' more the fact of a dead or distant friend's existence, at the moment when a portrait, letter, garment or other material reminder of him is found? The whole notion of him then grows pungent and speaks to us and shakes us, in a manner unknown at other times. In children's minds, fancies and realities live side by side. But however lively their fancies may be, they still gain help from association with reality. The imaginative child identifies its *dramatis personæ* with some doll or other material object, and this evidently solidifies belief, little as it may resemble what it is held to stand for. A thing not too interesting by its own real qualities generally does the best service here. The most useful doll I ever saw was a large cucumber in the hands of a little Amazonian-Indian girl; she nursed it and washed it and rocked it to sleep in a hammock, and talked to it all day long—there was no part in life which the cucumber did not play. Says Mr. Tylor:

"An imaginative child will . . . make a dog do duty for a horse, or a soldier for a shepherd, till at last the objective resemblance almost disappears, and a bit of wood may be dragged about, representing a ship on the sea, or a coach on the road. Here the likeness of the bit of wood to a ship or a coach is very slight indeed; but it is a thing, and can be moved about . . . and is an evident assistance to the child in enabling it to arrange and develop its ideas . . . . Of how much use . . . may be seen by taking it away and leaving the child nothing to play with. . . . In later years, and among highly educated people, the mental process which goes on in a child playing with wooden soldiers and horses, though it never disappears, must be sought for in more complex phenomena. Perhaps nothing in after life more closely resembles the effect of a doll upon a child, than the effect of the illustrations of a tale upon a grown-up reader. Here the objective resemblance is very indefinite . . . yet what reality is given to the scene by a good picture. . . . Mr. Backhouse one day noticed in Van Diemen's Land a woman arranging several stones that were flat, oval, and about two inches wide, and marked in various directions with black and red lines. These he learned represented absent friends, and one larger than the rest stood for a fat native

[18] *Treatise of Human Nature,* bk. I, pt. III, sec. 8.

woman on Flinders Island, known by the name of Mother Brown. Similar practices are found among far higher races than the ill-fated Tasmanians. Among some North American tribes, a mother who has lost a child keeps its memory ever present to her by filling its cradle with black feathers and quills, and carrying it about with her for a year or more. When she stops anywhere, she sets up the cradle and talks to it as she goes about her work, just as she would have done if the dead baby had been still alive within it. Here we have no image; but in Africa we find a rude doll, representing the child, kept as a memorial. . . . Bastian saw Indian women in Peru, who had lost an infant, carrying about on their backs a wooden doll to represent it."[19]

To many persons among us, photographs of lost ones seem to be fetishes. They, it is true, resemble; but the fact that the mere materiality of the reminder is almost as important as its resemblance is shown by the popularity a hundred years ago of the black taffeta 'silhouettes' which are still found among family relics, and of one of which Fichte could write to his affianced: "*Die Farbe fehlt, das Auge fehlt, es fehlt der himmlische Ausdruck deiner lieblichen Züge*"—and yet go on worshipping it all the same. The opinion so stoutly professed by many, that language is essential to thought, seems to have this much of truth in it, that all our inward images tend invincibly to attach themselves to something sensible, so as to gain in corporeity and life. Words serve this purpose, gestures serve it, stones, straws, chalk-marks, anything will do. As soon as any one of these things stands for the idea, the latter seems to be more real. Some persons, the present writer among the number, can hardly lecture without a black-board: the abstract conceptions must be symbolized by letters, squares or circles, and the relations between them by lines. All this symbolism, linguistic, graphic, and dramatic, has other uses too, for it abridges thought and fixes terms. But one of its uses is surely to rouse the believing reaction and give to the ideas a more living reality. As, when we are told a story, and shown the very knife that did the murder, the very ring whose hiding-place the clairvoyant revealed, the whole thing passes from fairy-land to mother-earth, so here we believe all the more, if only we see that 'the bricks are alive to tell the tale.'

So much for the prerogative position of sensations in regard to our belief. But among the sensations themselves all are not deemed

[19] *Researches into the Early History of Mankind*, p. 108.

equally real. The more practically important ones, the more permanent ones, and the more æsthetically apprehensible ones are selected from the mass, to be believed in most of all; the others are degraded to the position of mere signs and suggesters of these. This fact has already been adverted to in former chapters.[20] The real color of a thing is that one color-sensation which it gives us when most favorably lighted for vision. So of its real size, its real shape, etc.—these are but optical sensations selected out of thousands of others, because they have æsthetic characteristics which appeal to our convenience or delight. But I will not repeat what I have already written about this matter, but pass on to our treatment of tactile and muscular sensations, as 'primary qualities,' more real than those 'secondary' qualities which eye and ear and nose reveal. Why do we thus so markedly select the *tangible* to be the real? Our motives are not far to seek. The tangible qualities are the least fluctuating. When we get them at all we get them the same. The other qualities fluctuate enormously as our relative position to the object changes. Then, more decisive still, the tactile properties are those most intimately connected with our weal or woe. A dagger hurts us only when in contact with our skin, a poison only when we take it into our mouths, and we can only use an object for our advantage when we have it in our muscular control. It is as tangibles, then, that things concern us most; and the other senses, so far as their practical use goes, do but warn us of what tangible things to expect. They are but organs of anticipatory touch, as Aristotle and Berkeley have with perfect clearness explained.[21]

Among all sensations, the *most* belief-compelling are those productive of pleasure or of pain. Locke expressly makes the *pleasure-* or *pain*-giving quality to be the ultimate human criterion of anything's reality. Discussing (with a supposed Berkeleyan before Berkeley) the notion that all our perceptions may be but a dream, he says:

"He may please to dream that I make him this answer . . . that I believe he will allow a very manifest difference between dreaming of being in the fire, and being actually in it. But yet if he be resolved to appear so sceptical as to maintain, that what I call 'being actually in the fire' is nothing but a dream; and that we cannot thereby certainly know

20 See Vol. I, pp. 274–5; Vol. II, pp. 869 ff.

21 See *An Essay towards a New Theory of Vision*, § 59.

that any such thing as fire actually exists without us: I answer, that we certainly finding that pleasure or pain [or emotion of any sort] follows upon the application of certain objects to us, whose existence we perceive, or dream that we perceive, by our senses; *this certainly is as great as our happiness or misery,* beyond which we have no concernment to know or to be."[22]

THE INFLUENCE OF EMOTION AND ACTIVE IMPULSE ON BELIEF

The quality of arousing emotion, of shaking, moving us or inciting us to action, has as much to do with our belief in an object's reality as the quality of giving pleasure or pain. In Chapter XXV I shall seek to show that our emotions probably owe their pungent quality to the bodily sensations which they involve. Our tendency to believe in emotionally exciting objects (objects of fear, desire, etc.) is thus explained without resorting to any fundamentally new principle of choice. Speaking generally, the more a conceived object *excites* us, the more reality it has. The same object excites us differently at different times. Moral and religious truths come 'home' to us far more on some occasions than on others. As Emerson says, "There is a difference between one and another hour of life, in their authority and subsequent effect. Our faith comes in moments . . . . Yet there is a depth in those brief moments which constrains us to ascribe more reality to them than to all other experiences." The 'depth' is partly, no doubt, the insight into wider systems of unified relation, but far more often than that it is the emotional thrill. Thus, to descend to more trivial examples, a man who has no belief in ghosts by daylight will temporarily believe in them when, alone at midnight, he feels his blood curdle at a mysterious sound or vision, his heart thumping, and his legs impelled

[22] *Essay*, bk. IV, chap. 2, § 14. In another place: "He that sees a candle burning, and hath experimented the force of its flame by putting his finger in it, will little doubt that this is something existing without him, which does him harm and puts him to great pain . . . . And if our dreamer pleases to try whether the glowing heat of a glass-furnace be barely a wandering imagination in a drowsy man's fancy, by putting his hand into it, he may, perhaps, be awakened into a certainty, greater than he could wish, that it is something more than bare imagination. So that this evidence is as great as we can desire, being as certain to us as our pleasure or pain, i.e. happiness or misery; beyond which we have no concernment either of knowing or being. Such an assurance of the existence of things without us is sufficient to direct us in the attaining the good and avoiding the evil which is caused by them, which is the important concernment we have of being made acquainted with them." (*Ibid.*, bk. IV, chap. 11, § 8.)

to flee. The thought of falling when we walk along a curbstone awakens no emotion of dread; so no sense of reality attaches to it, and we are sure we shall not fall. On a precipice's edge, however, the sickening emotion which the notion of a possible fall engenders makes us believe in the latter's imminent reality, and quite unfits us to proceed.

The greatest proof that a man is *sui compos* is his ability to suspend belief in presence of an emotionally exciting idea. To give this power is the highest result of education. In untutored minds the power does not exist. *Every exciting thought in the natural man carries credence with it. To conceive with passion is eo ipso to affirm.* As Bagehot says:

"The Caliph Omar . . . burnt the Alexandrian Library, saying, 'All books which contain what is not in the Koran are dangerous; all those which contain what is in the Koran are useless!' Probably no one ever had an intenser belief in anything than Omar had in this. Yet it is impossible to imagine it preceded by an argument. His belief in Mahomet, in the Koran, and in the sufficiency of the Koran, came to him probably in spontaneous rushes of emotion; there may have been little vestiges of argument floating here and there, but they did not justify the strength of the emotion, still less did they create it, and they hardly even excused it. . . . Probably, when the subject is thoroughly examined, 'conviction' will be proved to be one of the intensest of human emotions, and one most closely connected with the bodily state . . . accompanied or preceded by the sensation that Scott makes his seer describe as the prelude to a prophecy:—

'At length the fatal answer came,
In characters of living flame—
Not spoke in word, nor blazed in scroll,
But borne and branded on my soul.'

A hot flash seems to burn across the brain. Men in these intense states of mind have altered all history, changed for better or worse the creed of myriads, and desolated or redeemed provinces and ages. Nor is this intensity a sign of truth, for it is precisely strongest in those points in which men differ most from each other. John Knox felt it in his anti-Catholicism; Ignatius Loyola in his anti-Protestantism; and both, I suppose, felt it as much as it is possible to feel it."[23]

The reason of the belief is undoubtedly the bodily commotion which the exciting idea sets up. 'Nothing which I can feel like *that* can be false.' All our religious and supernatural beliefs are of this

[23] W. Bagehot: "On the Emotion of Conviction," *Literary Studies*, II, 412–14.

order. The surest warrant for immortality is the yearning of our bowels for our dear ones; for God, the sinking sense it gives us to imagine no such Providence or help. So of our political or pecuniary hopes and fears, and things and persons dreaded and desired. "A grocer has a full creed as to foreign policy, a young lady a complete theory of the sacraments, as to which neither has any doubt . . . . A girl in a country parsonage will be sure 'that Paris never can be taken,' or that 'Bismarck is a wretch,' "—all because they have either conceived these things at some moment with passion, or associated them with other things which they have conceived with passion.

M. Renouvier calls this belief of a thing for no other reason than that we conceive it with passion, by the name of *mental vertigo*.[24] Other objects whisper doubt or disbelief; but the object of passion makes us deaf to all but itself, and we affirm it unhesitatingly. Such objects are the delusions of insanity, which the insane person can at odd moments steady himself against, but which again return to sweep him off his feet. Such are the revelations of mysticism. Such, particularly, are the sudden beliefs which animate mobs of men when frenzied impulse to action is involved. Whatever be the action in point—whether the stoning of a prophet, the hailing of a conqueror, the burning of a witch, the baiting of a heretic or Jew, the starting of a forlorn hope, or the flying from a foe—the fact that to believe a certain object will *cause that action to explode* is a sufficient reason for that belief to come. The motor impulse sweeps it unresisting in its train.

The whole history of witchcraft and early medicine is a commentary on the facility with which anything which chances to be conceived is believed the moment the belief chimes in with an emotional mood. 'The cause of sickness?' When a savage asks the cause of anything he means to ask exclusively 'What is to blame?' The theoretic curiosity starts from the practical life's demands. Let someone then accuse a necromancer, suggest a charm or spell which has been cast, and no more 'evidence' is asked for. What evidence is required beyond this intimate sense of the culprit's responsibility, to which our very viscera and limbs reply?[25]

24 *Psychologie rationnelle*, ch. 12.

25 Two examples out of a thousand:

Reid: *Inquiry*, ch. II, § 9: "I remember, many years ago, a white ox was brought into this country, of so enormous a size that people came many miles to see him.

There happened, some months after, an uncommon fatality among women in child-bearing. Two such uncommon events, following one another, gave a suspicion of their connection, and occasioned a common opinion among the country-people that the white ox was the cause of this fatality."

H. M. Stanley: *Through the Dark Continent*, II, 384: "On the third day of our stay at Mowa, feeling quite comfortable amongst the people, on account of their friendly bearing, I began to write down in my note-book the terms for articles in order to improve my already copious vocabulary of native words. I had proceeded only a few minutes when I observed a strange commotion amongst the people who had been flocking about me, and presently they ran away. In a short time we heard war-cries ringing loudly and shrilly over the table-land. Two hours afterwards, a long line of warriors were seen descending the table-land and advancing towards our camp. There may have been between five and six hundred of them. We, on the other hand, had made but few preparations except such as would justify us replying to them in the event of the actual commencement of hostilities. But I had made many firm friends amongst them, and I firmly believed that I would be able to avert an open rupture. When they had assembled at about a hundred yards in front of our camp, Safeni and I walked up towards them, and sat down midway. Some half-dozen of the Mowa people came near, and the shauri began.

" 'What is the matter, my friends?' I asked. 'Why do you come with guns in your hands in such numbers, as though you were coming to fight? Fight! Fight us, your friends! Tut! this is some great mistake, surely.'

" 'Mundelé,' replied one of them, . . . 'our people saw you yesterday make marks on some tara-tara (paper). This is very bad. Our country will waste, our goats will die, our bananas will rot, and our women will dry up. What have we done to you, that you should wish to kill us? We have sold you food, and we have brought you wine, each day. Your people are allowed to wander where they please, without trouble. Why is the Mundelé so wicked? We have gathered together to fight you if you do not burn that tara-tara now before our eyes. If you burn it we go away, and shall be friends as heretofore.'

"I told them to rest there, and left Safeni in their hands as a pledge that I should return. My tent was not fifty yards from the spot, but while going towards it my brain was busy in devising some plan to foil this superstitious madness. My note-book contained a vast number of valuable notes . . . . I could not sacrifice it to the childish caprice of savages. As I was rummaging my book box, I came across a volume of Shakespeare (Chandos edition), much worn and well thumbed, and which was of the same size as my field-book; its cover was similar also, and it might be passed for the note-book provided that no one remembered its appearance too well. I took it to them. 'Is this the tara-tara, friends, that you wish burnt?'

" 'Yes, yes, that is it!'

" 'Well, take it, and burn it or keep it.'

" 'M—m. No, no, no. We will not touch it. It is fetish. You must burn it.'

" 'I! Well, let it be so. I will do anything to please my good friends of Mowa.'

"We walked to the nearest fire. I breathed a regretful farewell to my genial companion, which during many weary hours of night had assisted to relieve my mind when oppressed by almost intolerable woes, and then gravely consigned the innocent Shakespeare to the flames, heaping the brush-fuel over it with ceremonious care.

" 'Ah-h-h,' breathed the poor deluded natives, sighing their relief. . . . 'There is no trouble now.' . . . And something approaching to a cheer was shouted among them, which terminated the episode of the Burning of Shakespeare."

Human credulity in the way of therapeutics has similar psychological roots. If there is anything intolerable (especially to the heart of a woman), it is to do nothing when a loved one is sick or in pain. To do anything is a relief. Accordingly, whatever remedy may be suggested is a spark on inflammable soil. The mind makes its spring towards action on that cue, sends for that remedy, and for a day at least believes the danger past. Blame, dread, and hope are thus the great belief-inspiring passions, and cover among them the future, the present, and the past.

These remarks illustrate the earlier heads of the list on page 921. Whichever represented objects give us sensations, especially interesting ones, or incite our motor impulses, or arouse our hate, desire, or fear, are real enough for us. Our requirements in the way of reality terminate in our own acts and emotions, our own pleasures and pains. These are the ultimate fixities from which, as we formerly observed, the whole chain of our beliefs depends, object hanging to object, as the bees, in swarming, hang to each other until, *de proche en proche,* the supporting branch, the Self, is reached and held.

BELIEF IN OBJECTS OF THEORY

Now the merely conceived or imagined objects which our mind represents as hanging to the sensations (causing them, etc.), filling the gaps between them, and weaving their interrupted chaos into order are innumerable. Whole systems of them conflict with other systems, and our choice of which system shall carry our belief is governed by principles which are simple enough, however subtle and difficult may be their application to details. *The conceived system, to pass for true, must at least include the reality of the sensible objects in it, by explaining them as effects on us, if nothing more. The system which includes the most of them, and definitely explains or pretends to explain the most of them, will, ceteris paribus, prevail.* It is needless to say how far mankind still is from having excogitated such a system. But the various materialisms, idealisms, and hylozoisms show with what industry the attempt is forever made. It is conceivable that several rival theories should equally well include the actual order of our sensations in their scheme, much as the one-fluid and two-fluid theories of electricity formulated all the common electrical phenomena equally well. The sciences are full of these alternatives. Which theory is then to be believed? *That theory will be most generally believed which, besides offering us objects able to account satisfactorily for our sensible experience, also offers those which are most interesting, those which appeal most urgently to our æsthetic, emotional, and active needs.* So here, in the higher intellectual life, the same selection among general conceptions goes on which went on among the sensations themselves. First, a word of their relation to our emotional and active needs—and here I can do no better than quote from an article published some years ago:[26]

"A philosophy may be unimpeachable in other respects, but either of two defects will be fatal to its universal acceptance. First, its ultimate principle must not be one that essentially baffles and disappoints our dearest desires and most cherished powers. A pessimistic principle like Schopenhauer's incurably vicious Will-substance, or Hartmann's wicked jack-at-all-trades, the Unconscious, will perpetually call forth essays at other philosophies. Incompatibility of the future with their desires and active tendencies is, in fact, to most men a source of more fixed disquietude than uncertainty itself. Witness the attempts to overcome the 'problem of evil,' the 'mystery of pain.' There is no 'problem of good.'

"But a second and worse defect in a philosophy than that of contradicting our active propensities is to give them no Object whatever to press against. A philosophy whose principle is so incommensurate with our most intimate powers as to deny them all relevancy in universal affairs, as to annihilate their motives at one blow, will be even more unpopular than pessimism. Better face the enemy than the eternal Void! This is why materialism will always fail of universal adoption, however well it may fuse things into an atomistic unity, however clearly it may prophesy the future eternity. For materialism denies reality to the objects of almost all the impulses which we most cherish. The real *meaning* of the impulses, it says, is something which has no emotional interest for us whatever. But what is called extradition is quite as characteristic of our emotions as of our senses. Both point to an Object as the cause of the present feeling. What an intensely objective reference lies in fear! In like manner an enraptured man, a dreary-feeling man, are not simply aware of their subjective states; if they were, the force of their feelings would evaporate. Both believe there is outward cause *why* they should feel as they do: either 'It is a glad world! how good is life!' or 'What a loathsome tedium is existence!' Any philosophy which annihilates the validity of the reference by ex-

[26] "Rationality, Activity and Faith" (*Princeton Review*, July 1882, pp. 64–9).

plaining away its objects or translating them into terms of no emotional pertinency leaves the mind with little to care or act for. This is the opposite condition from that of nightmare, but when acutely brought home to consciousness it produces a kindred horror. In nightmare we have motives to act, but no power; here we have powers, but no motives. A nameless *Unheimlichkeit* comes over us at the thought of there being nothing eternal in our final purposes, in the objects of those loves and aspirations which are our deepest energies. The monstrously lopsided equation of the universe and its knower, which we postulate as the ideal of cognition, is perfectly paralleled by the no less lopsided equation of the universe and the *doer*. We demand in it a *character* for which our emotions and active propensities shall be a match. Small as we are, minute as is the point by which the Cosmos impinges upon each one of us, each one desires to feel that his reaction at that point is congruous with the demands of the vast whole, that he balances the latter, so to speak, and is able to do what it expects of him. But as his abilities to 'do' lie wholly in the line of his natural propensities; as he enjoys reaction with such emotions as fortitude, hope, rapture, admiration, earnestness, and the like; and as he very unwillingly reacts with fear, disgust, despair, or doubt,—a philosophy which should legitimate only emotions of the latter sort would be sure to leave the mind a prey to discontent and craving.

"It is far too little recognized how entirely the intellect is built up of practical interests. The theory of Evolution is beginning to do very good service by its reduction of all mentality to the type of reflex action. Cognition, in this view, is but a fleeting moment, a cross-section at a certain point of what in its totality is a motor phenomenon. In the lower forms of life no one will pretend that cognition is anything more than a guide to appropriate action. The germinal question concerning things brought for the first time before consciousness is not the theoretic 'What is that?' but the practical 'Who goes there?' or rather, as Horwicz has admirably put it, 'What is to be done?'—'*Was fang' ich an?*' In all our discussions about the intelligence of lower animals the only test we use is that of their *acting* as if for a purpose. Cognition, in short, is incomplete until discharged in act. And although it is true that the later mental development, which attains its maximum through the hypertrophied cerebrum of man, gives birth to a vast amount of theoretic activity over and above that which is immediately ministerial to practice, yet the earlier claim is only postponed, not effaced, and the active nature asserts its rights to the end. . . .

"If there be any truth at all in this view, it follows that however vaguely a philosopher may define the ultimate universal datum, he cannot be said to leave it unknown to us so long as he in the slightest degree pretends that our emotional or active attitude towards it should be of one sort rather than another. He who says, 'Life is real, life is earnest,' however much he may speak of the fundamental mysteriousness of things, gives a distinct definition to that mysteriousness by ascribing to it the right to claim from us the particular mood called seriousness, which means the willingness to live with energy, though energy bring pain. The same is true of him who says that all is vanity. Indefinable as the predicate vanity may be *in se*, it is clearly enough something which permits anæsthesia, mere escape from suffering, to be our rule of life. There is no more ludicrous incongruity than for agnostics to proclaim with one breath that the substance of things is unknowable, and with the next that the thought of it should inspire us with admiration of its glory, reverence, and a willingness to add our coöperative push in the direction towards which its manifestations seem to be drifting. The unknowable may be unfathomed, but if it make such distinct demands upon our activity, we surely are not ignorant of its essential quality.

"If we survey the field of history and ask what feature all great periods of revival, of expansion of the human mind, display in common, we shall find, I think, simply this: that each and all of them have said to the human being, 'The inmost nature of the reality is congenial to *powers* which you possess.' In what did the emancipating message of primitive Christianity consist, but in the announcement that God recognizes those weak and tender impulses which paganism had so rudely overlooked? Take repentance: the man who can do nothing rightly can at least repent of his failures. But for paganism this faculty of repentance was a pure supernumerary, a straggler too late for the fair. Christianity took it and made it the one power within us which appealed straight to the heart of God. And after the night of the Middle Ages had so long branded with obloquy even the generous impulses of the flesh, and defined the Reality to be such that only slavish natures could commune with it, in what did the *Sursum corda!* of the Renaissance lie but in the proclamation that the archetype of verity in things laid claim on the widest activity of our whole æsthetic being? What were Luther's mission and Wesley's but appeals to powers which even the meanest of men might carry with them, faith and self-despair, but which were personal, requiring no priestly intermediation, and which brought their owner face to face with God? What caused the wildfire influence of Rousseau but the assurance he gave that man's nature was in harmony with the nature of things, if only the paralyzing corruptions of custom would stand from between? How did Kant and Fichte, Goethe and Schiller, inspire their time with cheer, except by saying, 'Use all your powers; that is the only obedience which the universe exacts'?

And Carlyle with his gospel of Work, of Fact, of Veracity, how does he move us except by saying that the universe imposes no tasks upon us but such as the most humble can perform? Emerson's creed that everything that ever was or will be is here in the enveloping Now; that man has but to obey himself—'He who will rest in what he *is,* is a part of Destiny'—is in like manner nothing but an exorcism of all scepticism as to the pertinency of one's natural faculties.

"In a word, 'Son of Man, *stand upon thy feet* and I will speak unto thee!' is the only revelation of truth to which the solving epochs have helped the disciple. But that has been enough to satisfy the greater part of his rational need. *In se* and *per se* the universal essence has hardly been more defined by any of these formulæ than by the agnostic *x*; but the mere assurance that my powers, such as they are, are not irrelevant to it, but pertinent, that it speaks to them and will in some way recognize their reply, that I can be a match for it if I will, and not a footless waif, suffices to make it rational to my feeling in the sense given above. Nothing could be more absurd than to hope for the definitive triumph of any philosophy which should refuse to legitimate, and to legitimate in an emphatic manner, the more powerful of our emotional and practical tendencies. Fatalism, whose solving word in all crises of behavior is 'All striving is vain,' will never reign supreme, for the impulse to take life strivingly is indestructible in the race. Moral creeds which speak to that impulse will be widely successful in spite of inconsistency, vagueness, and shadowy determination of expectancy. Man needs a rule for his will, and will invent one if one be not given him."

After the emotional and active needs come the intellectual and æsthetic ones. The two great æsthetic principles, of richness and of ease, dominate our intellectual as well as our sensuous life. And, *ceteris paribus,* no system which should not be rich, simple, and harmonious would have a chance of being chosen for belief, if rich, simple, and harmonious systems were also there. Into the latter we should unhesitatingly settle, with that welcoming attitude of the will in which belief consists. To quote from a remarkable book:

"This law, that our consciousness constantly tends to the minimum of complexity and to the maximum of definiteness, is of great importance for all our knowledge. . . . Our own activity of attention will thus determine what we are to know and what we are to believe. If things have more than a certain complexity, not only will our limited powers of attention forbid us to unravel this complexity, but we shall strongly desire to believe the things actually much simpler than they are. For our thoughts about them will have a constant tendency to become as simple and definite as possible. Put a man into a perfect chaos of phenomena, sights, sounds, feelings; and if the man continued to exist, and to be rational at all, his attention would doubtless soon find for him a way to make up some kind of rhythmic regularity, which he would impute to the things about him, so as to imagine that he had discovered some law of sequence in this mad new world. And thus, in every case where we fancy ourselves sure of a simple law of Nature, we must remember that a good deal of the fancied simplicity may be due in the given case not to Nature, but to the ineradicable prejudice of our own minds in favor of regularity and simplicity. All our thought is determined, in great measure, by this law of least effort, as it is found exemplified in our activity of attention. . . . The aim of the whole process seems to be to reach as complete and united a conception of reality as is possible, a conception wherein the greatest fullness of data shall be combined with the greatest simplicity of conception. The effort of consciousness seems to be to combine the greatest richness of content with the greatest definiteness of organization."[27]

The richness is got by including all the facts of sense in the scheme; the simplicity, by deducing them out of the smallest possible number of permanent and independent primordial entities: the definite organization, by assimilating these latter to ideal objects between which relations of an inwardly rational sort obtain. What these ideal objects and rational relations are will require a separate chapter to show.[28] Meanwhile, enough has surely been said to justify the assertion made above that no general offhand answer can be given as to which objects mankind shall choose as its realities. The fight is still under way. Our minds are yet chaotic; and at best we make a mixture and a compromise, as we yield to the claim of this interest or that, and follow first one and then another principle in turn. It is undeniably true that materialistic, or so-called 'scientific,' conceptions of the universe have so far gratified the purely intellectual interests more than the mere sentimental conceptions have. But, on the other hand, as already remarked, they leave the emotional and active interests cold. *The perfect object of belief would be a God or 'Soul of the World,' represented both optimistically and moralistically (if such a combination could be), and withal so definitely conceived as to show us*

[27] J. Royce: *The Religious Aspect of Philosophy* (Boston, 1885), pp. 316–17, 357.
[28] Chapter XXVIII.

why our phenomenal experiences should be sent to us by Him in just the very way in which they come. All Science and all History would thus be accounted for in the deepest and simplest fashion. The very room in which I sit, its sensible walls and floor, and the feeling the air and fire within it give me, no less than the 'scientific' conceptions which I am urged to frame concerning the mode of existence of all these phenomena when my back is turned, would then all be corroborated, not de-realized, by the ultimate principle of my belief. The World-soul sends me just those phenomena in order that I may react upon them; and among the reactions is the intellectual one of spinning these conceptions. What is *beyond* the crude experiences is not an *alternative* to them, but something that *means* them for me here and now. It is safe to say that, if ever such a system is satisfactorily excogitated, mankind will drop all other systems and cling to that one alone as real. Meanwhile the other systems coexist with the attempts at that one, and, all being alike fragmentary, each has its little audience and day.

I have now, I trust, shown sufficiently what the psychologic sources of the sense of reality are. Certain postulates are given in our nature; and whatever satisfies those postulates is treated as if real.[29] I might therefore finish the chapter here, were it not that a few additional words will set the truth in a still clearer light.

[29] Prof. Royce puts this well in discussing idealism and the reality of an 'external' world. "If the history of popular speculation on these topics could be written, how much of cowardice and shuffling would be found in the behavior of the natural mind before the question: 'How dost thou know of an external reality?' Instead of simply and plainly answering: 'I mean by the external world in the first place something that I accept or demand, that I posit, postulate, actively construct on the basis of sense-data,' the natural man gives us all kinds of vague compromise answers . . . . Where shall these endless turnings and twistings have an end? . . . All these lesser motives are appealed to, and the one ultimate motive is neglected. The ultimate motive with the man of every-day life is the *will to have an external world.* Whatever consciousness contains, reason will persist in spontaneously adding the thought: 'But there *shall be* something beyond this.' . . . The popular assurance of an external world is the *fixed determination to make one,* now and henceforth." (*Religious Aspect of Philosophy*, pp. 303–4—the italics are my own.) This immixture of the will appears most flagrantly in the fact that although external matter is doubted commonly enough, minds external to our own are never doubted. We need them too much, are too essentially social to dispense with them. Semblances of matter may suffice to react upon, but not semblances of communing souls. A psychic solipsism is too hideous a mockery of our wants, and, so far as I know, has never been seriously entertained.—Chapters IX and X of Prof. Royce's work are on the whole the clearest account of the psychology of belief with which I am acquainted.

DOUBT

There is hardly a common man who (if consulted) would not say that things come to us in the first instance *as ideas*; and that if we take them for realities, it is because we *add something to them*, namely, the predicate of having also *'real existence outside of our thought.'* This notion that a higher faculty than the mere *having* of a conscious content is needed to make us know anything real by its means has pervaded psychology from the earliest times, and is the tradition of Scholasticism, Kantism, and Common-sense. Just as sensations must come as inward affections and then be 'extradited'; as objects of memory must appear at first as present unrealities, and subsequently be 'projected' backwards as past realities; so conceptions must be *entia rationis* till a higher faculty uses them as windows to look beyond the ego, into the real *extra*-mental world;—so runs the orthodox and popular account.

And there is no question that this is a true account of the way in which many of our later beliefs come to pass. The logical distinction between the bare thought of an object and belief in the object's reality is often a chronological distinction as well. The having and the crediting of an idea do not always coalesce; for often we first suppose and then believe; first play with the notion, frame the hypothesis, and then affirm the existence, of an object of thought. And we are quite conscious of the succession of the two mental acts. But these cases are none of them *primitive* cases. They only occur in minds long schooled to doubt by the contradictions of experience. *The primitive impulse is to affirm immediately the reality of all that is conceived.*[30] When we do doubt, however, in what does

[30] "The leading fact in Belief, according to my view of it, is our Primitive Credulity. We begin by believing everything; whatever is, is true. . . . The animal born in the morning of a summer day, proceeds upon the fact of daylight; assumes the perpetuity of that fact. Whatever it is disposed to do, it does without misgivings. If in the morning it began a round of operations continuing for hours, under the full benefit of daylight, it would unhesitatingly begin the same round in the evening. Its state of mind is practically one of unbounded confidence; but, as yet, it does not understand what confidence means.

"The pristine assurance is soon met by checks; a disagreeable experience leading to new insight. To be thwarted and opposed is one of our earliest and most frequent pains. It develops the sense of a distinction between free and obstructed impulses; the unconsciousness of an open way is exchanged for consciousness; we are now said properly to believe in what has never been contradicted, as we disbelieve in what has been contradicted. We believe that, after the dawn of day, there is before us a continuance of light; we do not believe that this light is to continue for ever.

the subsequent resolution of the doubt consist? It either consists in a purely verbal performance, the coupling of the adjectives 'real' or 'outwardly existing' (as predicates) to the thing originally conceived (as subject); or it consists in the perception in the given case of *that for which these adjectives,* abstracted from other similar concrete cases, *stand.* But what these adjectives stand for, we now know well. They stand for certain relations (immediate, or through intermediaries) to ourselves. Whatever concrete objects have hitherto stood in those relations have been for us 'real,' 'outwardly existing.' So that when we now abstractly admit a thing to be 'real' (without perhaps going through any definite perception of its relations), it is as if we said "it belongs in the same world with those other objects." Naturally enough, we have hourly opportunities for this summary process of belief. All remote objects in space or time are believed in this way. When I believe that some prehistoric savage chipped this flint, for example, the reality of the savage and of his act makes no direct appeal either to my sensation, emotion, or volition. What I mean by my belief in it is simply my dim sense of a *continuity* between the long dead savage and his doings and the present world of which the flint forms part. It is pre-eminently a case for applying our doctrine of the 'fringe' (see Vol. I, p. 249). When I think the savage with one fringe of relationship, I believe in him; when I think him without that fringe, or with another one (as, e.g., if I should class him with 'scientific vagaries' in general), I disbelieve him. The word 'real' itself is, in short, a fringe.

RELATIONS OF BELIEF AND WILL

We shall see in Chapter XXVI that will consists in nothing but a manner of attending to certain objects, or consenting to their stable presence before the mind. The objects, in the case of will, are those whose existence depends on our thought, movements of our own body for example, or facts which such movements executed in future may make real. Objects of belief, on the contrary, are those which do not change according as we think regarding them. I *will* to get up early tomorrow morning; I *believe* that I got up late yesterday morning; I *will* that my foreign bookseller in Boston shall

"Thus, the vital circumstance in belief is never to be contradicted—never to lose *prestige.* The number of repetitions counts for little in the process: we are as much convinced after ten as after fifty; we are more convinced by ten unbroken, than by fifty for and one against." (Bain: *The Emotions and the Will,* pp. 511, 512.)

procure me a German book and write to him to that effect. I *believe* that he will make me pay three dollars for it when it comes, etc. Now the important thing to notice is that this difference between the objects of will and belief is entirely immaterial, as far as the relation of the mind to them goes. All that the mind does is in both cases the same; it looks at the object and consents to its existence, espouses it, says 'it shall be my reality.' It turns to it, in short, in the interested active emotional way. The rest is done by nature, which in some cases *makes* the objects real which we think of in this manner, and in other cases does not. Nature cannot change the past to suit our thinking. She cannot change the stars or the winds; but she *does* change our bodies to suit our thinking, and through their instrumentality changes much besides; so the great practical distinction between objects which we may will or unwill, and objects which we can merely believe or disbelieve, grows up, and is of course one of the most important distinctions in the world. Its roots, however, do not lie in psychology, but in physiology; as the chapter on Volition will abundantly make plain. *Will and Belief, in short, meaning a certain relation between objects and the Self, are two names for one and the same* PSYCHOLOGICAL *phenomenon.* All the questions which arise concerning one are questions which arise concerning the other. The causes and conditions of the peculiar relation must be the same in both. The free-will question arises as regards belief. If our wills are indeterminate, so must our beliefs be, etc. The first act of free-will, in short, would naturally be to believe in free-will, etc. In Chapter XXVI, I shall mention this again.

A practical observation may end this chapter. If belief consists in an emotional reaction of the entire man on an object, how *can* we believe at will? We cannot control our emotions. Truly enough, a man cannot believe at will abruptly. Nature sometimes, and indeed not very infrequently, produces instantaneous conversions for us. She suddenly puts us in an active connection with objects of which she had till then left us cold. "I realize for the first time," we then say, "what that means!" This happens often with moral propositions. We have often heard them; but now they shoot into our lives; they move us; we feel their living force. Such instantaneous beliefs are truly enough not to be achieved by will. But *gradually* our will can lead us to the same results by a very simple method: *we need only in cold blood* ACT *as if the thing in question were real, and keep acting as if it were real, and it will infallibly end by growing into such a connection with our life that it will become real.* It will become so knit with habit and emotion that our interests in it will be those which characterize belief. Those to whom 'God' and 'Duty' are now mere names can make them much more than that, if they make a little sacrifice to them every day. But all this is so well known in moral and religious education that I need say no more.[31]

[31] *Literature.* D. Hume: *Treatise of Human Nature,* part III, §§ VII–X. A. Bain: *Emotions and the Will,* chapter on Belief (also pp. 20 ff.). J. Sully: *Sensation and Intuition,* essay IV. J. Mill: *Analysis of the Human Mind,* chapter XI. Charles Renouvier: *Psychologie rationnelle,* vol. II, pt. II; and *Esquisse d'une classification systématique des doctrines philosophiques,* part VI. J. H. Newman: *A Grammar of Assent.* J. Venn: *On Some of the Characteristics of Belief.* V. Brochard: *De l'erreur,* part II, chap. VI, IX; and *Revue Philosophique,* XVIII, 1. E. Rabier: *Psychologie,* chap. XXI, Appendix. Ollé-Laprune: *De la certitude morale* (1880). G. F. Stout: "The Genesis of the Cognition of Physical Reality," in *Mind,* Jan. 1890. J. Pikler: *The Psychology of the Belief in Objective Existence* (London, 1890).—Mill says that we believe present sensations; and makes our belief in all other things a matter of *association* with these. So far so good; but as he makes no mention of emotional or volitional reaction, Bain rightly charges him with treating belief as a purely intellectual state. For Bain belief is rather an incident of our active life. When a thing is such as to make us *act* on it, then we believe it, according to Bain. "But how about past things, or remote things, upon which no reaction of ours is possible? And how about belief in things which *check* action?" says Sully, who considers that we believe a thing only when "the idea of it has an inherent tendency to approximate in character and intensity to a sensation." It is obvious that each of these authors emphasizes a true aspect of the question. My own account has sought to be more complete, sensation, association, and active reaction all being acknowledged to be concerned. The most compendious possible formula perhaps would be that *our belief and attention* are the same fact. For the moment, what we attend to is reality; Attention is a motor reaction; and we are so made that sensations force attention from us. On Belief and Conduct see an article by Leslie Stephen, *Nineteenth Century,* Sept. 1888.

A set of facts have been recently brought to my attention which I hardly know how to treat, so I say a word about them in this footnote. I refer to a type of experience which has frequently found a place amongst the 'Yes' answers to the Census of Hallucinations, and which is generally described by those who report it as an 'impression of the presence' of someone near them, although no sensation either of sight, hearing, or touch is involved. From the way in which this experience is spoken of by those who have had it, it would appear to be an extremely definite and positive state of mind, coupled with a belief in the reality of its object quite as strong as any direct sensation ever gives. And yet *no* sensation seems to be connected with it at all. Sometimes the person whose nearness is thus impressed is a known person, dead or living, sometimes an unknown one. His attitude and situation are often very definitely impressed, and so, sometimes (though not by way of hearing), are words which he wishes to say.

The phenomenon would seem to be due to a pure *conception* becoming saturated with the sort of stinging urgency which ordinarily only sensations bring. But I cannot yet persuade myself that the urgency in question consists in concomitant emotional and motor impulses. The 'impression' may come quite suddenly and depart quickly; it may carry no emotional suggestions, and wake no motor consequences beyond those involved in attending to it. Altogether, the matter is somewhat paradoxical, and no conclusion can be come to until more definite data are obtained.

Perhaps the most curious case of the sort which I have received is the following. The subject of the observation, Mr. P., is an exceptionally intelligent witness, though the words of the narrative are his wife's.

"Mr. P. has all his life been the occasional subject of rather singular delusions or impressions of various kinds. If I had belief in the existence of latent or embryo faculties, other than the five senses, I should explain them on that ground. Being totally blind, his other perceptions are abnormally keen and developed, and given the existence of a rudimentary sixth sense, it would be only natural that this also should be more acute in him than in others. One of the most interesting of his experiences in this line was the frequent apparition of a corpse some years ago, which may be worth the attention of your Committee on that subject. At the time Mr. P. had a music-room in Boston on Beacon Street, where he used to do severe and protracted practice with little interruption. Now, all one season it was a very familiar occurrence with him while in the midst of work to feel a cold draft of air suddenly upon his face, with a prickling sensation at the roots of his hair, when he would turn from the piano, and a figure which he knew to be dead would come sliding under the crack of the door from without, flattening itself to squeeze through and rounding out again to the human form. It was of a middle-aged man, and drew itself along the carpet on hands and knees, but with head thrown back till it reached the sofa, upon which it stretched itself. It remained some moments, but vanished always if Mr. P. spoke or made a decided movement. The most singular point in the occurrence was its frequent repetition. He might expect it on any day between two and four o'clock, and it came always heralded by the same sudden cold shiver, and was invariably the same figure which went through the same movements. He afterwards traced the whole experience to strong tea. He was in the habit of taking cold tea, which always stimulates him, for lunch, and on giving up this practice he never saw this or any other apparition again. However, even allowing, as is doubtless true, that the event was a delusion of nerves first fatigued by overwork and then excited by this stimulant, there is one point which is still wholly inexplicable and highly interesting to me. Mr. P. has no memory whatever of sight, nor conception of it. It is impossible for him to form any idea of what we mean by light or color, consequently he has no cognizance of any object which does not reach his sense of hearing or of touch, though these are so acute as to give a contrary impression sometimes to other people. When he becomes aware of the presence of a person or an object, by means which seem mysterious to outsiders, he can always trace it naturally and legitimately to slight echoes, perceptible only to his keen ears, or to differences in atmospheric pressure, perceptible only to his acute nerves of touch; but with the apparition described, for the only time in his experience, he was aware of presence, size, and appearance, without the use of either of these mediums. The figure never produced the least sound nor came within a number of feet of his person, yet he knew that it was a man, that it moved, and in what direction, even that it wore a full beard, which, like the thick curly hair, was partially gray; also that it was dressed in the style of suit known as 'pepper and salt.'

These points were all perfectly distinct and invariable each time. If asked how he perceived them, he will answer he cannot tell, he simply knew it, and so strongly and so distinctly that it is impossible to shake his opinion as to the exact details of the man's appearance. It would seem that in this delusion of the senses he really *saw,* as he has never done in the actual experiences of life, except in the first two years of childhood."

On cross-examining Mr. P., I could not make out that there was anything like visual imagination involved, although he was quite unable to describe in just what terms the false perception was carried on. It seemed to be more like an intensely definite *conception* than anything else, a conception to which the feeling of *present reality* was attached, but in no such shape as easily to fall under the heads laid down in my text.

Chapter XXII[*]

Reasoning

We talk of man being the rational animal; and the traditional intellectualist philosophy has always made a great point of treating the brutes as wholly irrational creatures. Nevertheless, it is by no means easy to decide just what is meant by reason, or how the peculiar thinking process called reasoning differs from other thought-sequences which may lead to similar results.

Much of our thinking consists of trains of images suggested one by another, of a sort of spontaneous revery of which it seems likely enough that the higher brutes should be capable. This sort of thinking leads nevertheless to rational conclusions, both practical and theoretical. The links between the terms are either 'contiguity' or 'similarity,' and with a mixture of both these things we can hardly be very incoherent. As a rule, in this sort of irresponsible thinking, the terms which fall to be coupled together are empirical concretes, not abstractions. A sunset may call up the vessel's deck from which I saw one last summer, the companions of my voyage, my arrival into port, etc.; or it may make me think of solar myths, of Hercules' and Hector's funeral pyres, of Homer and whether he could write, of the Greek alphabet, etc. If habitual contiguities predominate, we have a prosaic mind; if rare contiguities or simi-

* The substance of this chapter, and a good many pages of the text, originally appeared in an article entitled "Brute and Human Intellect," in the *Journal of Speculative Philosophy* for July 1878 (vol. XII, p. 236).

larities have free play, we call the person fanciful, poetic, or witty. But the thought as a rule is of matters taken in their entirety. Having been thinking of one, we find later that we are thinking of another, to which we have been lifted along, we hardly know how. If an abstract quality figures in the procession, it arrests our attention but for a moment, and fades into something else; and is never very abstract. Thus, in thinking of the sun-myths, we may have a gleam of admiration at the gracefulness of the primitive human mind, or a moment of disgust at the narrowness of modern interpreters. But, in the main, we think less of qualities than of whole things, real or possible, just as we may experience them.

The upshot of it may be that we are reminded of some practical duty: we write a letter to a friend abroad, or we take down the lexicon and study our Greek lesson. Our thought is rational, and leads to a rational act, but it can hardly be called reasoning in a strict sense of the term.

There are other shorter flights of thought, single couplings of terms which suggest one another by association, which approach more to what would commonly be classed as acts of reasoning proper. Those are where a present sign suggests an unseen, distant, or future reality. Where the sign and what it suggests are both concretes which have been coupled together on previous occasions, the inference is common to both brutes and men, being really nothing more than association by contiguity. A and B, dinner-bell and dinner, have been experienced in immediate succession. Hence A no sooner falls upon the sense than B is anticipated, and steps are taken to meet it. The whole education of our domestic beasts, all the cunning added by age and experience to wild ones, and the greater part of our human knowingness consists in the ability to make a mass of inferences of this simplest sort. Our 'perceptions,' or recognitions of what objects are before us, are inferences of this kind. We feel a patch of color, and we say 'a distant house,' a whiff of odor crosses us, and we say 'a skunk,' a faint sound is heard, and we call it 'a railroad train.' Examples are needless; for such inferences of sensations not presented form the staple and tissue of our perceptive life, and our Chapter XIX was full of them, illusory or veracious. They have been called *unconscious inferences.* Certainly we are commonly unconscious that we are inferring at all. The sign and the signified melt into what seems to us the object of a single pulse of thought. *Immediate inferences* would be a good name for these simple acts of reasoning requiring but two terms,[1] were it not that formal logic has already appropriated the expression for a more technical use.

'RECEPTS'

In these first and simplest inferences the conclusion may follow so continuously upon the 'sign' that the latter is not discriminated or attended to as a separate object by the mind. Even now we can seldom define the optical signs which lead us to infer the shapes and distances of the objects which by their aid we so unhesitatingly perceive. The objects, too, when thus inferred, are *general* objects. The dog crossing a scent thinks of a deer in general, or of another dog in general, not of a particular deer or dog. To these most primitive abstract objects Dr. G. J. Romanes gives the name of *recepts* or *generic* ideas, to distinguish them from concepts and general ideas properly so called.[2] They are not analyzed or defined, but only imagined.

"It requires but a slight analysis of our ordinary mental processes to prove that all our simpler ideas are group-arrangements, which have been formed spontaneously, or without any of that intentionally comparing, sifting, and combining process which is required in the higher departments of ideational activity. The comparing, sifting, and combining is here done, as it were, *for* the conscious agent; not *by* him. Recepts are *received*: it is only concepts that require to be *conceived*. . . . If I am crossing a street and hear behind me a sudden shout, I do not require to wait in order to predicate to myself that there is probably a hansom cab just about to run me down: a cry of this kind, and in those circumstances, is so intimately associated in my mind with its purpose, that the idea which it arouses need not rise above the level of a recept; and the adaptive movements on my part which that idea im-

[1] I see no need of assuming more than two terms in this sort of reasoning—first, the sign, and second, the thing inferred from it. Either may be complex, but essentially it is but A calling up B, and no middle term is involved. M. Binet, in his most intelligent little book, *La Psychologie du raisonnement*, maintains that there are three terms. The present sensation or sign must, according to him, first evoke from the past an image which resembles it and fuses with it, and the things suggested or inferred are always the contiguous associates of this intermediate image, and not of the immediate sensation. The reader of Chapter XIX will see why I do not believe in the 'image' in question as a distinct psychic fact.

[2] *Mental Evolution in Man* (1889), chapters III and IV. See especially pp. 68–80, and later 353, 396.

mediately prompts, are performed without any intelligent reflection. Yet, on the other hand, they are neither reflex actions nor instinctive actions: they are what may be termed receptual actions, or actions depending on recepts."[3]

"How far can this kind of unnamed or non-conceptional ideation extend?" Dr. Romanes asks; and answers by a variety of examples taken from the life of brutes, for which I must refer to his book. One or two of them, however, I will quote:

" 'Houzeau relates that, whilst crossing a wide and arid plain in Texas, his two dogs suffered greatly from thirst, and that between thirty and forty times they rushed down the hollows to search for water. These hollows were not valleys, and there were no trees in them, or any other difference in the vegetation, and as they were absolutely dry there could have been no smell of damp earth. The dogs behaved as if they knew that a dip in the ground offered them the best chance of finding water, and Houzeau has often witnessed the same behaviour in other animals.' . . .

"Mr. Darwin writes:—'When I say to my terrier, in an eager voice (and I have made the trial many times), "Hi, hi, where is it?" she at once takes it as a sign that something is to be hunted, and generally first looks quickly all around, and then rushes into the nearest thicket, to scent for any game, but finding nothing, she looks up into any neighbouring tree for a squirrel. Now do not these actions clearly shew that she had in her mind a general idea or concept that some animal is to be discovered and hunted?' "[4]

They certainly show this. But the idea in question is of an object *about* which nothing farther may be articulately known. The thought of it prompts to activity, but to no theoretic consequence. Similarly in the following example:

"Water-fowl adopt a somewhat different mode of alighting upon land, or even upon ice, from that which they adopt when alighting upon water; and those kinds which dive from a height (such as terns and gannets) never do so upon land or upon ice. These facts prove that the animals have one recept answering to a solid substance, and another answering to a fluid. Similarly, a man will not dive from a height over hard ground or over ice, nor will he jump into water in the same way as he jumps upon dry land. In other words, like the water-fowl, he has two distinct recepts, one of which answers to solid ground, and

[3] *Loc. cit.*, p. 49.

[4] P. 51.

the other to an unresisting fluid. But, unlike the water-fowl, he is able to bestow upon each of these recepts a name, and thus to raise them both to the level of concepts. So far as the practical purposes of locomotion are concerned, it is of course immaterial whether or not he thus raises his recepts into concepts; but . . . for many other purposes it is of the highest importance that he is able to do this."[5]

IN REASONING, WE PICK OUT ESSENTIAL QUALITIES

The chief of these purposes is *predication*, a theoretic function which, though it always leads eventually to some kind of action, yet tends as often as not to inhibit the immediate motor response to which the simple inferences of which we have been speaking give rise. In reasoning, A may suggest B; but B, instead of being an idea which is simply *obeyed* by us, is an idea which suggests the distinct additional idea C. And where the train of suggestion is one of reasoning distinctively so called as contrasted with mere revery or 'associative' sequence, the ideas bear certain inward relations to each other which we must proceed to examine with some care.

The result C yielded by a true act of reasoning is apt to be a thing voluntarily *sought*, such as the means to a proposed end, the ground for an observed effect, or the effect of an assumed cause. All these results may be thought of as concrete things, but they are *not suggested immediately by other concrete things*, as in the trains of simply associative thought. They are linked to the concretes which precede them by intermediate steps, and these steps are formed by *general characters* articulately denoted and expressly analyzed out. A thing inferred by reasoning need neither have been an habitual associate of the datum from which we infer it, nor need it be similar to it. It may be a thing entirely unknown to our previous experience, something which no simple association of concretes could ever have evoked. The great difference, in fact, between that simpler kind of rational thinking which consists in the concrete objects of past experience merely suggesting each other, and reasoning distinctively so called, is this: that whilst the empirical thinking is only reproductive, reasoning is productive. An empirical, or 'rule-of-thumb,' thinker can deduce nothing from data with whose behavior and associates in the concrete he is unfamiliar. But put a reasoner amongst a set of concrete objects

[5] *Loc. cit.*, p. 74.

which he has neither seen nor heard of before, and with a little time, if he is a good reasoner, he will make such inferences from them as will quite atone for his ignorance. Reasoning helps us out of unprecedented situations—situations for which all our common associative wisdom, all the 'education' which we share in common with the beasts, leaves us without resource.

Let us make this ability to deal with NOVEL *data the technical differentia of reasoning.* This will sufficiently mark it out from common associative thinking, and will immediately enable us to say just what peculiarity it contains.

It contains analysis and abstraction. Whereas the merely empirical thinker stares at a fact in its entirety, and remains helpless, or gets 'stuck,' if it suggests no concomitant or similar, the reasoner breaks it up and notices some one of its separate attributes. This attribute he takes to be the essential part of the whole fact before him. This attribute has properties or consequences which the fact until then was not known to have, but which, now that it is noticed to contain the attribute, it must have.

Call the fact or concrete datum S;
the essential attribute M;
the attribute's property P.

Then the reasoned inference of P from S cannot be made without M's intermediation. The 'essence' M is thus that third or middle term in the reasoning which a moment ago was pronounced essential. *For his original concrete S the reasoner substitutes its abstract property M.* What is true of M, what is coupled with M, then holds true of S, is coupled with S. As M is properly one of the *parts* of the entire S, *reasoning may then be very well defined as the substitution of parts and their implications or consequences for wholes.* And the art of the reasoner will consist of two stages:

First, *sagacity,*[6] or the ability to discover what part, M, lies embedded in the whole S which is before him;

Second, *learning,* or the ability to recall promptly M's consequences, concomitants, or implications.[7]

[6] J. Locke: *Essay Concerning Human Understanding,* bk. IV, chap. II, § 3.

[7] To be sagacious is to be a good observer. J. S. Mill has a passage which is so much in the spirit of the text that I cannot forbear to quote it. "The observer is not he who merely sees the thing which is before his eyes, but he who sees what parts that thing is composed of. To do this well is a rare talent. One person, from in-

If we glance at the ordinary syllogism—

M is P;

S is M;

∴ S is P

—we see that the second or minor premise, the 'subsumption' as it is sometimes called, is the one requiring the sagacity; the first or major the one requiring the fertility, or fulness of learning. Usually the learning is more apt to be ready than the sagacity, the ability to seize fresh aspects in concrete things being rarer than the ability to learn old rules; so that, in most actual cases of reasoning, the minor premise, or the way of conceiving the subject, is the one that makes the novel step in thought. This is, to be sure, not always the case; for the fact that M carries P with it may also be unfamiliar and now formulated for the first time.

The perception that S is M is a *mode of conceiving S*. The statement that M is P is an *abstract or general proposition*. A word about both is necessary.

---

attention, or attending only in the wrong place, overlooks half of what he sees; another sets down much more than he sees, confounding it with what he imagines, or with what he infers; another takes note of the *kind* of all the circumstances, but being inexpert in estimating their degree, leaves the quantity of each vague and uncertain; another sees indeed the whole, but makes such an awkward division of it into parts, throwing things into one mass which require to be separated, and separating others which might more conveniently be considered as one, that the result is much the same, sometimes even worse, than if no analysis had been attempted at all. It would be possible to point out what qualities of mind, and modes of mental culture, fit a person for being a good observer: that, however, is a question not of Logic, but of the Theory of Education, in the most enlarged sense of the term. There is not properly an Art of Observing. There may be rules for observing. But these, like rules for inventing, are properly instructions for the preparation of one's own mind; for putting it into the state in which it will be most fitted to observe, or most likely to invent. They are, therefore, essentially rules of self-education, which is a different thing from Logic. They do not teach how to do the thing, but how to make ourselves capable of doing it. They are an art of strengthening the limbs, not an art of using them. The extent and minuteness of observation which may be requisite, and the degree of decomposition to which it may be necessary to carry the mental analysis, depend on the particular purpose in view. To ascertain the state of the whole universe at any particular moment is impossible, but would also be useless. In making chemical experiments, we do not think it necessary to note the position of the planets; because experience has shown, as a very superficial experience is sufficient to show, that in such cases that circumstance is not material to the result: and accordingly, in the ages when men believed in the occult influences of the heavenly bodies, it might have been unphilosophical to omit ascertaining the precise condition of those bodies at the moment of the experiment." (*Logic*, bk. III, chap. VII, § 1. Cf. also bk. IV, chap. II.)

WHAT IS MEANT BY A MODE OF CONCEIVING

When we conceive of S merely as M (of vermilion merely as a mercury-compound, for example), we neglect all the other attributes which it may have, and attend exclusively to this one. We mutilate the fulness of S's reality. Every reality has an infinity of aspects or properties. Even so simple a fact as a line which you trace in the air may be considered in respect to its form, its length, its direction, and its location. When we reach more complex facts, the number of ways in which we may regard them is literally endless. Vermilion is not only a mercury-compound, it is vividly red, heavy, and expensive, it comes from China, and so on, *ad infinitum*. All objects are well-springs of properties, which are only little by little developed to our knowledge, and it is truly said that to know one thing thoroughly would be to know the whole universe. Mediately or immediately, that one thing is related to everything else; and to know *all* about it, all its relations need be known. But each relation forms one of its attributes, one angle by which someone may conceive it, and while so conceiving it may ignore the rest of it. A man is such a complex fact. But out of the complexity all that an army commissary picks out as important for his purposes is his property of eating so many pounds a day; the general, of marching so many miles; the chair-maker, of having such a shape; the orator, of responding to such and such feelings; the theatre-manager, of being willing to pay just such a price, and no more, for an evening's amusement. Each of these persons singles out the particular side of the entire man which has a bearing on *his* concerns, and not till this side is distinctly and separately conceived can the proper practical conclusions *for that reasoner* be drawn; and when they are drawn the man's other attributes may be ignored.

All ways of conceiving a concrete fact, if they are true ways at all, are equally true ways. *There is no property* ABSOLUTELY *essential to any one thing*. The same property which figures as the essence of a thing on one occasion becomes a very inessential feature upon another. Now that I am writing, it is essential that I conceive my paper as a surface for inscription. If I failed to do that, I should have to stop my work. But if I wished to light a fire, and no other materials were by, the essential way of conceiving the paper would be as combustible material; and I need then have no thought of any of its other destinations. It is really *all* that it is: a combustible, a writing surface, a thin thing, a hydrocarbonaceous thing, a thing eight inches one way and ten another, a thing just one furlong east of a certain stone in my neighbor's field, an American thing, etc., etc., *ad infinitum.* Whichever one of these aspects of its being I temporarily class it under, makes me unjust to the other aspects. But as I always am classing it under one aspect or another, I am always unjust, always partial, always exclusive. My excuse is necessity—the necessity which my finite and practical nature lays upon me. My thinking is first and last and always for the sake of my doing, and I can only do one thing at a time. A God who is supposed to drive the whole universe abreast may also be supposed, without detriment to his activity, to see all parts of it at once and without emphasis. But were our human attention so to disperse itself we should simply stare vacantly at things at large and forfeit our opportunity of doing any particular act. Mr. Warner, in his Adirondack story, shot a bear by aiming, not at his eye or heart, but 'at him generally.' But we cannot aim 'generally' at the universe; or if we do, we miss our game. Our scope is narrow, and we must attack things piecemeal, ignoring the solid fulness in which the elements of Nature exist, and stringing one after another of them together in a serial way, to suit our little interests as they change from hour to hour. In this, the partiality of one moment is partly atoned for by the different sort of partiality of the next. To me now, writing these words, emphasis and selection seem to be the essence of the human mind. In other chapters other qualities have seemed, and will again seem, more important parts of psychology.

Men are so ingrainedly partial that, for common-sense and scholasticism (which is only common-sense grown articulate), the notion that there is no one quality genuinely, absolutely, and exclusively essential to anything is almost unthinkable. "A thing's essence makes it *what* it is. Without an exclusive essence it would be nothing in particular, would be quite nameless, we could not say it was this rather than that. What you write on, for example,—why talk of its being combustible, rectangular, and the like, when you know that these are mere accidents, and that what it really is, and was made to be, is just *paper* and nothing else?" The reader is pretty sure to make some such comment as this. But he is himself merely insisting on an aspect of the thing which suits his own petty purpose, that of *naming* the thing; or else on an aspect which suits the manufacturer's purpose, that of *producing an article for which there is a vulgar demand.* Meanwhile the reality overflows these purposes at every pore. Our usual purpose with it, our commonest title for it, and the properties which this title suggests, have in reality nothing sacramental. They characterize *us* more than they characterize the thing. But we are so stuck in our prejudices, so petrified intellectually, that to our vulgarest names, with their suggestions, we ascribe an eternal and exclusive worth. The thing must be, essentially, what the vulgarest name connotes; what less usual names connote, it can be only in an 'accidental' and relatively unreal sense.[8]

Locke undermined the fallacy. But none of his successors, so far as I know, have radically escaped it, or seen that *the only meaning of essence is teleological, and that classification and conception are purely teleological weapons of the mind.* The essence of a thing is that one of its properties which is so *important for my interests* that in comparison with it I may neglect the rest. Amongst those other things which have this important property I class it, after this property I name it, as a thing endowed with this property I conceive it; and whilst so classing, naming, and conceiving it, all other truths about it become to me as naught.[9] The properties which are important vary from man to man and from hour to hour.[10] Hence divers appellations and conceptions for the same

[8] Readers brought up on Popular Science may think that the molecular structure of things is their real essence in an absolute sense, and that water is H–O–H more deeply and truly than it is a solvent of sugar or a slaker of thirst. Not a whit! It is *all* of these things with equal reality, and the only reason why *for the chemist* it is H–O–H primarily, and only secondarily the other things, is that *for his purpose of deduction and compendious definition* the H–O–H aspect of it is the more useful one to bear in mind.

[9] "We find that we take for granted irresistibly that each class [of thing] has some character which distinguishes it from other classes. . . . What is the foundation of this postulate? What is the ground of this assumption, that there must exist a definition which we have never seen, and which perhaps no one has seen in a satisfactory form? . . . I reply, that our persuasion that there must needs be characteristic marks by which things can be defined in words, is founded on the assumption of *the necessary possibility of reasoning.*" (W. Whewell: *History of Scientific Ideas,* bk. VIII, chap. I, § 9.)

[10] I may quote a passage from an article entitled "The Sentiment of Rationality," published in vol. IV of *Mind,* 1879: "What is a *conception*? It is a *teleological instrument.* It is a partial aspect of a thing which *for our purpose* we regard as its

thing. But many objects of daily use—as paper, ink, butter, horse-car—have properties of such constant unwavering importance, and have such stereotyped names, that we end by believing that to conceive them in those ways is to conceive them in the only true way. Those are no truer ways of conceiving them than any others; they are only more important ways, more frequently serviceable ways.[11]

---

essential aspect, as the representative of the entire thing. In comparison with this aspect, whatever other properties and qualities the thing may have, are unimportant accidents which we may without blame ignore. But the essence, the ground of conception, varies with the end we have in view. A substance like oil has as many different essences as it has uses to different individuals. One man conceives it as a combustible, another as a lubricator, another as a food; the chemist thinks of it as a hydro-carbon; the furniture-maker as a darkener of wood; the speculator as a commodity whose market price to-day is this and to-morrow that. The soap-boiler, the physicist, the clothes-scourer severally ascribe to it other essences in relation to their needs. Ueberweg's doctrine that the essential quality of a thing is the quality of most *worth*, is strictly true; but Ueberweg has failed to note that the worth is wholly relative to the temporary interests of the conceiver. And, even, when his interest is distinctly defined in his own mind, the discrimination of the quality in the object which has the closest connexion with it, is a thing which no rules can teach. The only *à priori* advice that can be given to a man embarking on life with a certain purpose is the somewhat barren counsel: Be sure that in the circumstances that meet you, you attend to the *right* ones for your purpose. To pick out the right ones is the measure of the man. 'Millions,' says Hartmann, 'stare at the phenomenon before a *genialer Kopf* pounces on the concept.' The genius is simply he to whom, when he opens his eyes upon the world, the 'right' characters are the prominent ones. The fool is he who, with the same purposes as the genius, infallibly gets his attention tangled amid the accidents."

11 Only if one of our purposes were itself truer than another, could one of our conceptions become the truer conception. To be a truer purpose, however, our purpose must conform more to some absolute standard of purpose in things to which our purposes ought to conform. This shows that the whole doctrine of essential characters is intimately bound up with a teleological view of the world. Materialism becomes self-contradictory when it denies teleology, and yet in the same breath calls atoms, etc., the *essential* facts. The world contains consciousness as well as atoms—and the one must be written down as just as essential as the other, in the absence of any declared purpose regarding them on the creator's part, or in the absence of any creator. As far as we ourselves go, the atoms are worth more for purposes of deduction, the consciousness for purposes of inspiration. We may fairly write the Universe in either way, thus: ATOMS-producing-consciousness; or CONSCIOUSNESS-produced-by-atoms. Atoms alone, or consciousness alone, are precisely equal mutilations of the truth. If, without believing in a God, I still continue to talk of what the world 'essentially is,' I am just as much entitled to define it as a place in which my nose itches, or as a place where at a certain corner I can get a mess of oysters for twenty cents, as to call it an evolving nebula differentiating and integrating itself. It is hard to say which of the three abstractions is the more rotten or miserable substitute for the world's concrete fulness. To conceive it merely as 'God's work' would be a similar mutilation of it, so long as we said not what

So much for what is implied, when the reasoner conceives of the fact S before him as a case of which the essence is to be M. One word now as to what is involved in M's having properties, consequences, or implications, and we can go back to the study of the reasoning process again.

WHAT IS INVOLVED IN GENERAL PROPOSITIONS

M is not a concrete, or 'self-sufficient,' as Mr. Clay would say. It is an abstract character which may exist, embedded with other characters, in many concretes. Whether it be the character of being a writing surface, of being made in America or China, of being eight inches square, or of being in a certain part of space, this is always true of it. Now we might conceive of this being a world in which all such general characters were independent of each other, so that if any one of them were found in a subject S, we never could be sure what others would be found alongside of it. On one occasion there might be P with M, on another Q, and so on. In such a world there would be no *general* sequences or coexistences, and no universal laws. Each grouping would be *sui generis*; from the experience of the past no future could be predicted; and reasoning, as we shall presently see, would be an impossibility.

But the world we live in is not one of this sort. Though many general characters seem indifferent to each other, there remain a number of them which affect constant habits of mutual concomitance or repugnance. They involve or imply each other. One of them is a sign to us that the other will be found. They hunt in couples, as it were; and such a proposition as that M is P, or includes P, or precedes or accompanies P, if it prove to be true in one instance, may very likely be true in every other instance which we meet. This is, in fact, a world in which general laws obtain, in which universal propositions *are* true, and in which reasoning is therefore possible. Fortunately for us: for since we cannot handle things as wholes, but only by conceiving them through some general character which for the time we call their essence, it would be a great pity if the matter ended there, and if the general character, once picked out and in our possession, helped us to no farther advance. In Chapter XXVIII we shall have again to consider this

God, or what kind of work. The only real truth about the world, apart from particular purposes, is the *total* truth.

harmony between our reasoning faculty and the world in which its lot is cast.[12]

To revert now to our symbolic representation of the reasoning process:

$$\begin{array}{l} \text{M is P} \\ \text{S is M} \\ \hline \text{S is P} \end{array}$$

M is discerned and picked out for the time being to be the essence of the concrete fact, phenomenon, or reality, S. But M in this world of ours is inevitably conjoined with P; so that P is the next thing that we may expect to find conjoined with the fact S. We may conclude or infer P, through the intermediation of the M which our sagacity began by discerning, when S came before it, to be the essence of the case.

Now note that if P have any value or importance for us, M was a very good character for our sagacity to pounce upon and abstract. If, on the contrary, P were of no importance, some other character than M would have been a better essence for us to conceive of S by. Psychologically, as a rule, P overshadows the process from the start. We are *seeking* P, or something like P. But the bare totality of S does not yield it to our gaze; and casting about for some point in S to take hold of which will lead us to P, we hit, if we are sagacious, upon M, because M happens to be just the character which is knit up with P. Had we wished Q instead of P, and were N a property of S conjoined with Q, we ought to have ignored M, noticed N, and conceived of S as a sort of N exclusively.

Reasoning is always for a subjective interest, to attain some particular conclusion, or to gratify some special curiosity. It not only breaks up the datum placed before it and conceives it abstractly; it must conceive it *rightly* too; and conceiving it rightly means conceiving it by that one particular abstract character which leads to the one sort of conclusion which it is the reasoner's temporary interest to attain.[13]

[12] Compare Lotze: *Metaphysik*, §§ 58, 67, for some instructive remarks on ways in which the world's constitution might differ from what it actually is. Compare also Chapter XXVIII.

[13] Sometimes, it must be confessed, the conceiver's purpose falls short of reasoning and the only conclusion he cares to reach is the bare naming of the datum. "What is that?" is our first question relative to any unknown thing. And the ease with which our curiosity is quenched as soon as we are supplied with any sort of a name to call the object by, is ridiculous enough. To quote from an unpublished es-

The *results* of reasoning may be hit upon by accident. The stereoscope was actually a result of reasoning; it is conceivable, however, that a man playing with pictures and mirrors might accidentally have hit upon it. Cats have been known to open doors by pulling latches, etc. But no cat, if the latch got out of order, could open the door again, unless some new accident of random fumbling taught her to associate some new total movement with the total phenomenon of the closed door. A reasoning man, however, would open the door by first analyzing the hindrance. He would ascertain what particular feature of the door was wrong. The lever, e.g., does not raise the latch sufficiently from its slot—case of insufficient elevation: raise door bodily on hinges! Or door sticks at bottom by friction against sill: raise it bodily up! Now it is obvious that a child or an idiot might without this reasoning learn the *rule* for opening that particular door. I remember a clock which the maid-servant had discovered would not go unless it were supported so as to tilt slightly forwards. She had stumbled on this method after many weeks of groping. The reason of the stoppage was the friction of the pendulum-bob against the back of the clock-case, a reason which an educated man would have analyzed out in five minutes. I have a student's lamp of which the flame vibrates most unpleasantly unless the collar which bears the chimney be raised about a sixteenth of an inch. I learned the remedy after much torment by accident, and now always keep the collar up with a small wedge. But my procedure is a mere association of two totals, diseased object and remedy. One learned in pneumatics could have named the *cause* of the disease, and thence inferred the remedy immediately. By many measurements of triangles one might find their area always equal to their height multiplied by half their base, and one might formulate an empirical law to that effect. But a

---

say by a former student of mine, Mr. R. W. Black: "The simplest end which a thing's predicate can serve is the satisfaction of the desire for unity itself, the mere desire that the thing shall be the same with *something* else. Why, the other day, when I mistook a portrait of Shakespeare for one of Hawthorne, was I not, on psychological principles, as right as if I had correctly named it?—the two pictures had a common essence, bald forehead, mustache, flowing hair. Simply because the only end that could possibly be served by naming it Hawthorne was my desire to have it so. With reference to any other end that classification of it would not serve. And every unity, every identity, every classification is rightly called fanciful unless it serves some other end than the mere satisfaction, emotion, or inspiration caught by momentarily believing in it."

reasoner saves himself all this trouble by seeing that it is the essence (*pro hac vice*) of a triangle to be the half of a parallelogram whose area is the height into the entire base. To see this he must invent additional lines; and the geometer must often draw such to get at the essential property he may require in a figure. The essence consists in some *relation of the figure to the new lines,* a relation not obvious at all until they are put in. The geometer's sagacity lies in the invention of special new lines which serve his purpose.

THUS, THERE ARE TWO GREAT POINTS IN REASONING

First, an extracted character is taken as equivalent to the entire datum from which it comes; and,

Second, the character thus taken suggests a certain consequence more obviously than it was suggested by the total datum as it originally came. Take them again, successively.

1. Suppose I say, when offered a piece of cloth, "I won't buy that; it looks as if it would fade," meaning merely that something about it suggests the idea of fading to my mind,—my judgment, though possibly correct, is not reasoned, but purely empirical; but if I can say that into the color there enters a certain dye which I know to be chemically unstable, and that *therefore* the color will fade, my judgment is reasoned. The notion of the dye, which is one of the parts of the cloth, is the connecting link between the latter and the notion of fading. So, again, an uneducated man will expect from past experience to see a piece of ice melt if placed near the fire, and the tip of his finger look coarse if he views it through a convex glass. In neither of these cases could the result be anticipated without full previous acquaintance with the entire phenomenon. It is not a result of reasoning.

But a man who should conceive heat as a mode of motion, and liquefaction as identical with increased motion of molecules; who should know that curved surfaces bend light-rays in special ways, and that the apparent size of anything is connected with the amount of the 'bend' of its light-rays as they enter the eye,—such a man would make the right inferences for all these objects, even though he had never in his life had any concrete experience of them; and he would do this because the ideas which we have above supposed him to possess would mediate in his mind between the phenomena he starts with and the conclusions he draws. But these ideas or reasons for his conclusions are all mere extracted portions or circumstances singled out from the mass of characters which make up the entire phenomena. The motions which form heat, the bending of the light-waves, are, it is true, excessively recondite ingredients; the hidden pendulum I spoke of above is less so; and the sticking of a door on its sill in the earlier example would hardly be so at all. But each and all agree in this, that they bear a *more evident relation* to the conclusion than did the immediate data in their full totality.

The difficulty is, in each case, to extract from the immediate data that particular ingredient which shall have this very evident relation to the conclusion. Every phenomenon or so-called 'fact' has an infinity of aspects or properties, as we have seen, amongst which the fool, or man with little sagacity, will inevitably go astray. But no matter for this point now. The first thing is to have seen that every possible case of reasoning involves the extraction of a particular partial aspect of the phenomena thought about, and that whilst Empirical Thought simply associates phenomena in their entirety, Reasoned Thought couples them by the conscious use of this extract.

2. And now to prove the second point: Why are the couplings, consequences, and implications of extracts more evident and obvious than those of entire phenomena? For two reasons.

First, the extracted characters are more general than the concretes, and the connections they may have are, therefore, more familiar to us, having been more often met in our experience. Think of heat as motion, and whatever is true of motion will be true of heat; but we have had a hundred experiences of motion for every one of heat. Think of the rays passing through this lens as bending towards the perpendicular, and you substitute for the comparatively unfamiliar lens the very familiar notion of a particular change in direction of a line, of which notion every day brings us countless examples.

The other reason why the relations of the extracted characters are so evident is that their properties are so *few*, compared with the properties of the whole, from which we derived them. In every concrete total the characters and their consequences are so inexhaustibly numerous that we may lose our way among them before noticing the particular consequence it behooves us to draw. But, if we are lucky enough to single out the proper character, we take in, as it were, by a single glance all its possible consequences. Thus the character of scraping the sill has very few suggestions, prominent among which is the suggestion that the scraping will cease if we raise the door; whilst the entire refractory door suggests an enormous number of notions to the mind.

Take another example. I am sitting in a railroad-car, waiting for the train to start. It is winter, and the stove fills the car with pungent smoke. The brakeman enters, and my neighbor asks him to "stop that stove smoking." He replies that it will stop entirely as soon as the car begins to move. "Why so?" asks the passenger. "It *always* does," replies the brakeman. It is evident from this 'always' that the connection between car moving and smoke stopping was a purely empirical one in the brakeman's mind, bred of habit. But, if the passenger had been an acute reasoner, he, with no experience of what that stove always did, might have anticipated the brakeman's reply, and spared his own question. Had he singled out of all the numerous points involved in a stove's not smoking the one special point of smoke pouring freely out of the stove-pipe's mouth, he would, probably, owing to the few associations of that idea, have been immediately reminded of the law that a fluid passes more rapidly out of a pipe's mouth if another fluid be at the same time streaming over that mouth; and then the rapid draught of air over the stove-pipe's mouth, which is one of the points involved in the car's motion, would immediately have occurred to him.

Thus a couple of extracted characters, with a couple of their few and obvious connections, would have formed the reasoned link in the passenger's mind between the phenomena, smoke stopping and car moving, which were only linked as wholes in the brakeman's mind. Such examples may seem trivial, but they contain the essence of the most refined and transcendental theorizing. The reason why physics grows more deductive the more the fundamental properties it assumes are of a mathematical sort, such as molecular mass or wave-length, is that the immediate consequences of these notions are so few that we can survey them all at once, and promptly pick out those which concern us.

Sagacity; or the Perception of the Essence

To reason, then, we must be able to extract characters,—not *any* characters, but the right characters for our conclusion. If we extract the wrong character, it will not lead to that conclusion. Here, then, is the difficulty: *How are characters extracted, and why does it require the advent of a genius in many cases before the fitting character is brought to light?* Why cannot anybody reason as well as anybody else? Why does it need a Newton to notice the law of the squares, a Darwin to notice the survival of the fittest? To answer these questions we must begin a new research, and see how our insight into facts naturally grows.

All our knowledge at first is vague. When we say that a thing is vague, we mean that it has no subdivisions *ab intra,* nor precise limitations *ab extra*; but still all the forms of thought may apply to it. It may have unity, reality, externality, extent, and what not—*thinghood,* in a word, but thinghood only as a whole.[14] In this vague way, probably, does the room appear to the babe who first begins to be conscious of it as something other than his moving nurse. It has no subdivisions in his mind, unless, perhaps, the window is able to attract his separate notice. In this vague way, certainly, does every entirely new experience appear to the adult. A library, a museum, a machine-shop, are mere confused wholes to the uninstructed, but the machinist, the antiquary, and the bookworm perhaps hardly notice the whole at all, so eager are they to pounce upon the details. Familiarity has in them bred discrimination. Such vague terms as 'grass,' 'mould,' and 'meat' do not exist for the botanist or the anatomist. They know too much about grasses, moulds, and muscles. A certain person said to Charles Kingsley, who was showing him the dissection of a caterpillar, with its exquisite viscera, "Why, I thought it was nothing but skin and squash!" A layman present at a shipwreck, a battle, or a fire is helpless. Discrimination has been so little awakened in him by experience that his consciousness leaves no single point of the complex situation accented and standing out for him to begin to act upon. But the sailor, the fireman, and the general know directly at what corner to take up the business. They 'see into the situation'—that is, they analyze it—with their first glance. It is full of delicately differenced ingredients which their education has little by little brought to their consciousness, but of which the novice gains no clear idea.

How this power of analysis was brought about we saw in our chapters on Discrimination and Attention. We dissociate the ele-

14 See above, p. 657.

ments of originally vague totals by attending to them or noticing them alternately, of course. But what determines which element we shall attend to first? There are two immediate and obvious answers: first, our practical or instinctive interests; and, second, our æsthetic interests. The dog singles out of any situation its smells, and the horse its sounds, because they may reveal facts of practical moment, and are instinctively exciting to these several creatures. The infant notices the candle-flame or the window, and ignores the rest of the room, because those objects give him a vivid pleasure. So, the country boy dissociates the blackberry, the chestnut, and the wintergreen, from the vague mass of other shrubs and trees, for their practical uses, and the savage is delighted with the beads, the bits of looking-glass, brought by an exploring vessel, and gives no heed to the features of the vessel itself, which is too much beyond his sphere. These æsthetic and practical interests, then, are the weightiest factors in making particular ingredients stand out in high relief. What they lay their accent on, that we notice; but what they are in themselves, we cannot say. We must content ourselves here with simply accepting them as irreducible ultimate factors in determining the way our knowledge grows.

Now, a creature which has few instinctive impulses, or interests practical or æsthetic, will dissociate few characters, and will, at best, have limited reasoning powers; whilst one whose interests are very varied will reason much better. Man, by his immensely varied instincts, practical wants, and æsthetic feelings, to which every sense contributes, would, by dint of these alone, be sure to dissociate vastly more characters than any other animal; and accordingly we find that the lowest savages reason incomparably better than the highest brutes. The diverse interests lead, too, to a diversification of experiences, whose accumulation becomes a condition for the play of that *law of dissociation by varying concomitants* of which I treated in a former chapter (see Vol. I, p. 478).

The Help given by Association by Similarity

It is probable, also, that man's *superior association by similarity* has much to do with those discriminations of character on which his higher flights of reasoning are based. As this latter is an important matter, and as little or nothing was said of it in the chapter on Discrimination, it behooves me to dwell a little upon it here.

What does the reader do when he wishes to see in what the precise likeness or difference of two objects lies? He transfers his attention as rapidly as possible, backwards and forwards, from one to the other. The rapid alteration in consciousness shakes out, as it were, the points of difference or agreement, which would have slumbered forever unnoticed if the consciousness of the objects compared had occurred at widely distant periods of time. What does the scientific man do who searches for the reason or law embedded in a phenomenon? He deliberately accumulates all the instances he can find which have any analogy to that phenomenon; and, by simultaneously filling his mind with them all, he frequently succeeds in detaching from the collection the peculiarity which he was unable to formulate in one alone; even though that one had been preceded in his former experience by all of those with which he now at once confronts it. These examples show that the mere general fact of having occurred at some time in one's experience, with varying concomitants, is not by itself a sufficient reason for a character to be dissociated now. We need something more; we need that the varying concomitants should in all their variety be brought into consciousness *at once*. Not till then will the character in question escape from its adhesion to each and all of them and stand alone. This will immediately be recognized by those who have read Mill's *Logic* as the ground of Utility in his famous 'four methods of experimental inquiry,' the methods of agreement, of difference, of residues, and of concomitant variations. Each of these gives a list of analogous instances out of the midst of which a sought-for character may roll and strike the mind.

Now it is obvious that any mind in which association by similarity is highly developed is a mind which will spontaneously form lists of instances like this. Take a present case A, with a character *m* in it. The mind may fail at first to notice this character *m* at all. But if A calls up C, D, E, and F,—these being phenomena which resemble A in possessing *m*, but which may not have entered for months into the experience of the animal who now experiences A, why, plainly, such association performs the part of the reader's deliberately rapid comparison referred to above, and of the systematic consideration of like cases by the scientific investigator, and may lead to the noticing of *m* in an abstract way. Certainly this is obvious; and no conclusion is left to us but to assert that, after the few most powerful practical and æsthetic interests, our chief help towards noticing those special characters of phenomena, which, when once possessed and named, are used as reasons, class names, essences, or middle terms, *is this association by similarity*. Without it, indeed, the deliberate procedure of the scientific man would be impossible: he could never collect his analogous instances. But it operates of itself in highly-gifted minds without any deliberation, spontaneously collecting analogous instances, uniting in a moment what in nature the whole breadth of space and time keeps separate, and so permitting a perception of identical points in the midst of different circumstances, which minds governed wholly by the law of contiguity could never begin to attain.

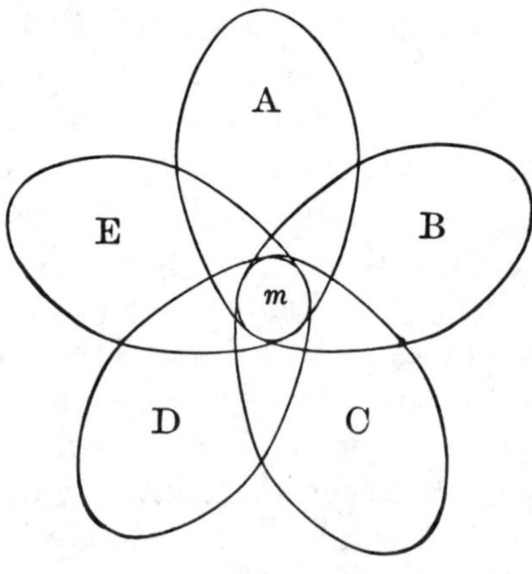

FIG. 80.

Figure 80 shows this. If *m*, in the present representation A, calls up B, C, D, and E, which are similar to A in possessing it, and calls them up in rapid succession, then *m*, being associated almost simultaneously with such varying concomitants, will 'roll out' and attract our separate notice.

If so much is clear to the reader, he will be willing to admit that the mind *in which this mode of association most prevails* will, from its better opportunity of extricating characters, be the one most prone to reasoned thinking; whilst, on the other hand, a mind in which we do not detect reasoned thinking will probably be one in which association by contiguity holds almost exclusive sway.

Geniuses are, by common consent, considered to differ from ordinary minds by an unusual development of association by similarity. One of Professor Bain's best strokes of work is the exhibition of this truth.[15] It applies to geniuses in the line of reasoning as well as in other lines. And as the genius is to the vulgarian, so the vulgar human mind is to the intelligence of a brute. Compared with men, it is probable that brutes neither attend to abstract characters, nor have associations by similarity. Their thoughts probably pass from one concrete object to its habitual concrete successor far more uniformly than is the case with us. In other words, their associations of ideas are almost exclusively by contiguity. It will clear up still farther our understanding of the reasoning process, if we devote a few pages to

THE INTELLECTUAL CONTRAST BETWEEN BRUTE AND MAN

I will first try to show, by taking the best stories I can find of animal sagacity, that the mental process involved may as a rule be perfectly accounted for by mere contiguous association, based on experience. Mr. Darwin, in his *Descent of Man*, instances the Arctic dogs, described by Dr. Hayes, who scatter, when drawing a sledge, as soon as the ice begins to crack. This might be called by some an exercise of reason. The test would be, Would the most intelligent Eskimo dogs that ever lived act so when placed upon ice for the first time together? A band of men from the tropics might do so easily. Recognizing cracking to be a sign of breaking, and seizing immediately the partial character that the point of rupture is the point of greatest strain, and that the massing of weight at a given point concentrates there the strain, a Hindoo might quickly infer that scattering would stop the cracking, and, by crying out to his comrades to disperse, save the party from immersion. But in the dog's case we need only suppose that they have individually experienced wet skins after cracking, that they have often noticed cracking to begin when they were huddled together, and that they have observed it to cease when they scattered. Naturally, therefore, the sound would redintegrate all these former experiences, including that of scattering, which latter they would promptly renew. It would be a case of immediate suggestion or of that 'Logic of Recepts' as Mr. Romanes calls it, of which we spoke above on p. 954.

A friend of the writer gave as a proof of the almost human intelligence of his dog that he took him one day down to his boat on the shore, but found the boat full of dirt and water. He remembered

[15] See his *On the Study of Character*, chap. XV; also *Senses and the Intellect*, "Intellect," chap. II, the latter half.

that the sponge was up at the house, a third of a mile distant; but, disliking to go back himself, he made various gestures of wiping out the boat and so forth, saying to his terrier, "Sponge, sponge; go fetch the sponge." But he had little expectation of a result, since the dog had never received the slightest training with the boat or the sponge. Nevertheless, off he trotted to the house, and, to his owner's great surprise and admiration, brought the sponge in his jaws. Sagacious as this was, it required nothing but ordinary contiguous association of ideas. The terrier was only exceptional in the minuteness of his spontaneous observation. Most terriers would have taken no interest in the boat-cleaning operation, nor noticed what the sponge was for. This terrier, in having picked those details out of the crude mass of his boat-experience distinctly enough to be reminded of them, was truly enough ahead of his peers on the line which leads to human reason. But his act was not yet an act of reasoning proper. It might fairly have been called so if, unable to find the sponge at the house, he had brought back a dipper or a mop instead. Such a substitution would have shown that, embedded in the very different appearances of these articles, he had been able to discriminate the identical partial attribute of capacity to take up water, and had reflected, "For the present purpose they are identical." This, which the dog did not do, any man but the very stupidest could not fail to do.

If the reader will take the trouble to analyze the best dog and elephant stories he knows, he will find that, in most cases, this simple contiguous calling up of one whole by another is quite sufficient to explain the phenomena. Sometimes, it is true, we have to suppose the recognition of a property or character as such, but it is then always a character which the peculiar practical interests of the animal may have singled out. A dog, noticing his master's hat on its peg, may possibly infer that he has not gone out. Intelligent dogs recognize by the tone of the master's voice whether the latter is angry or not. A dog will perceive whether you have kicked him by accident or by design, and behave accordingly. The character inferred by him, the particular mental state in you, however it be represented in his mind—it is represented probably by a 're-cept' (p. 954) or set of practical tendencies, rather than by a definite concept or idea—is still a partial character extracted from the totality of your phenomenal being, and is his reason for crouching and skulking, or playing with you. Dogs, moreover, seem to have the feeling of the value of their master's personal property, or at least a particular *interest* in objects which their master uses. A dog left with his master's coat will defend it, though never taught to do so. I know of a dog accustomed to swim after sticks in the water, but who always refused to dive for stones. Nevertheless, when a fish-basket, which he had never been trained to carry, but merely knew as his master's, fell over, he immediately dived after it and brought it up. Dogs thus discern, at any rate so far as to be able to act, this partial character of *being valuable*, which lies hidden in certain things.[16] Stories are told of dogs carrying coppers to pastry-cooks to

[16] Whether the dog has the notion of your being angry or of your property being valuable in any such abstract way as *we* have these notions is more than doubtful. The conduct is more likely an impulsive result of a conspiracy of outward stimuli; the beast *feels like* acting so when these stimuli are present, though conscious of no definite reason why. The distinction of recept and concept is useful here. Some breeds of dogs, e.g., collies, seem instinctively to defend their master's property. The case is similar to that of a dog's barking at people after dark, at whom he would not bark in daylight. I have heard this quoted as evidence of the dog's reasoning power. It is only, as Chapter III has shown us, the impulsive result of a summation of stimuli, and has no connection with reasoning.

In certain stages of the hypnotic trance the subject seems to lapse into the non-analytic state. If a sheet of ruled foolscap paper, or a paper with a fine monotonous ornamental pattern printed on it, be shown to the subject, and *one* of the ruled lines or elements of the pattern be pointed to for an instant, and the paper immediately removed, he will then almost always, when after a short interval the paper is presented to him again, pick out the indicated line or element with infallible correctness. The operator, meanwhile, has either to keep his eye fixed upon it, or to make sure of its position by counting, in order not to lose its place. Just so we may remember a friend's house in a street by the single character of its number rather than by its general look. The trance-subject would seem, in these instances, to surrender himself to the general look. He disperses his attention impartially over the sheet. The place of the particular line touched is part of a 'total effect' which he gets in its entirety, and which would be distorted if another line were touched instead. This total effect is lost upon the normal looker-on, bent as he is on concentration, analysis, and emphasis. What wonder, then, that, under these experimental conditions, the trance-subject excels him in touching the right line again? If he has time given him to count the line, he will excel the trance-subject; but if the time be too short to count, he will best succeed by following the trance-method, abstaining from analysis, and being guided by the 'general look' of the line's place on the sheet. One is surprised at one's success in this the moment one gives up one's habitually analytic state of mind.

Is it too much to say that we have in this dispersion of the attention and subjection to the 'general effect' something like a relapse into the state of mind of brutes? The trance-subject never gives any other reason for his optical discriminations, save that 'it looks so.' So a man, on a road once traversed inattentively before, takes a certain turn for no reason except that he *feels* as if it must be right. He is guided by a sum of impressions, not one of which is emphatic or distinguished

get buns, and it is said that a certain dog, if he gave two coppers, would never leave without two buns. This was probably mere contiguous association, but it is *possible* that the animal noticed the character of duality, and identified it as the same in the coin and the cake. If so, it is the maximum of canine abstract thinking. Another story told to the writer is this: a dog was sent to a lumber-camp to fetch a wedge, with which he was known to be acquainted. After half an hour, not returning, he was sought and found biting and tugging at the handle of an axe which was driven deeply into a stump. The wedge could not be found. The teller of the story thought that the dog must have had a clear perception of the common character of serving to split which was involved in both the instruments, and, from their identity in this respect, inferred their identity for the purposes required.

It cannot be denied that this interpretation is a possible one, but it seems to me far to transcend the limits of ordinary canine abstraction. The property in question was not one which had direct personal interest for the dog, such as that of belonging to his master is in the case of the coat or the basket. If the dog in the sponge story had returned to the boat with a dipper it would have been no more remarkable. It seems more probable, therefore, that this wood-cutter's dog had also been accustomed to carry the axe, and now, excited by the vain hunt for the wedge, had discharged his carrying powers upon the former instrument in a sort of confusion—just as a man may pick up a sieve to carry water in, in the excitement of putting out a fire.[17]

---

from the rest, not one of which is essential, not one of which is *conceived*, but all of which together drive him to a conclusion to which nothing but *that* sum-total leads. Are not some of the wonderful discriminations of animals explicable in the same way? The cow finds her own stanchions in the long stable, the horse stops at the house he has once stopped at in the monotonous street, because no other stanchions, no other house, yield impartially *all* the impressions of the previous experience. The man, however, by seeking to make some one impression characteristic and essential, prevents the rest from having their effect. So that, if the (for him) essential feature be forgotten or changed, he is too apt to be thrown off altogether, and then the brute or the trance-subject may seem to outstrip him in sagacity.

Dr. Romanes's already quoted distinction between 'receptual' and 'conceptual' thought (published since the body of my text and my note were written) connotes conveniently the difference which I seek to point out. See also his *Mental Evolution in Man*, p. 197 ff., for proofs of the fact that in a receptual way brutes cognize the mental states of other brutes and men.

[17] This matter of confusion is important and interesting. Since confusion is mistaking the wrong part of the phenomenon for the whole, whilst reasoning is, ac-

Thus, then, the characters extracted by animals are very few, and always related to their immediate interests or emotions. That dissociation by varying concomitants, which in man is based so largely on association by similarity, hardly seems to take place at all in the mind of brutes. One total thought suggests to them another total thought, and they find themselves acting with propriety, they know not why. The great, the fundamental, defect of their minds seems to be the inability of their groups of ideas to break across in unaccustomed places. They are enslaved to routine, to cut-and-dried thinking; and if the most prosaic of human beings could be transported into his dog's mind, he would be appalled at the utter absence of fancy which reigns there.[18] Thoughts will not be found to call up their similars, but only their habitual successors. Sunsets will not suggest heroes' deaths, but supper-time. This is why man is the only metaphysical animal. To wonder why the universe should be as it is presupposes the notion of its being different, and a brute, which never reduces the actual to fluidity by breaking up its literal sequences in his imagination, can never form such a notion. He takes the world simply for granted, and never wonders at it at all.

Professor Strümpell quotes a dog-story which is probably a type of many others. The feat performed looks like abstract reasoning; but an acquaintance with all the circumstances shows it to have been a random trick learned by habit. The story is as follows:

"I have two dogs, a small, long-legged pet dog and a rather large watch-dog. Immediately beyond the house-court is the garden, into which one enters through a low lattice-gate which is closed by a latch on the yard-side. This latch is opened by lifting it. Besides this, moreover, the gate is fastened on the garden-side by a string nailed to the

---

cording to our definition, based on the substitution of the right part for the whole, it might be said that confusion and reasoning are generically the same process. I believe that they are so, and that the only difference between a muddle-head and a genius is that between extracting wrong characters and right ones. In other words, a muddle-headed person is a genius spoiled in the making. I think it will be admitted that all *eminently* muddle-headed persons have the temperament of genius. They are constantly breaking away from the usual consecutions of concretes. A common associator by contiguity is too closely tied to routine to get muddle-headed.

[18] The horse is a densely stupid animal, as far as everything goes except contiguous association. We reckon him intelligent, partly because he looks so handsome, partly because he has such a wonderful faculty of contiguous association and can be so quickly moulded into a mass of set habits. Had he anything of reasoning intelligence, he would be a less faithful slave than he is.

gate-post. Here, as often as one wished, could the following sight be observed. If the little dog was shut in the garden and he wished to get out, he placed himself before the gate and barked. Immediately the large dog in the court would hasten to him and raise the latch with his nose while the little dog on the garden-side leaped up and, catching the string in his teeth, bit it through; whereupon the big one wedged his snout between the gate and the post, pushed the gate open, and the little dog slipped through. Certainly reasoning seems here to prevail. In face of it, however, and although the dogs arrived of themselves, and without human aid, at their solution of the gate question, I am able to point out that the complete action was pieced together out of accidental experiences which the dogs followed, I might say, unconsciously. While the large dog was young, he was allowed, like the little one, to go into the garden, and therefore the gate was usually not latched, but simply closed. Now if he saw anyone go in, he would follow by thrusting his snout between gate and post, and so pushing the gate open. When he was grown I forbade his being taken in, and had the gate kept latched. But he naturally still tried to follow when anyone entered and tried in the old fashion to open it, which he could no longer do. Now it fell out that once, while making the attempt, he raised his nose higher than usual and hit the latch from below so as to lift it off its hook, and the gate unclosed. From thenceforth he made the same movement of the head when trying to open it, and, of course, with the same result. He now knew how to open the gate when it was latched.

"The little dog had been the large one's teacher in many things, especially in the chasing of cats and the catching of mice and moles; so when the little one was heard barking eagerly, the other always hastened to him. If the barking came from the garden, he opened the gate to get inside. But meanwhile the little dog, who wanted to get out the moment the gate opened, slipped out between the big one's legs, and so the appearance of his having come with the intention of letting him out arose. And that it was simply an appearance transpired from the fact that when the little dog did not succeed at once in getting out, the large one ran in and nosed about the garden, plainly showing that he had expected to find something there. In order to stop this opening of the gate I fastened a string on the garden-side which, tightly drawn, held the gate firm against the post, so that if the yard dog raised the latch and let go, it would every time fall back on to the hook. And this device was successful for quite a time, until it happened one day that on my return from a walk upon which the little dog had accompanied me I crossed the garden, and in passing through the gate the dog remained behind, and refused to come to my whistle. As it was beginning to rain, and I knew how he disliked to get wet, I closed the gate in order to punish him in this manner. But I had hardly reached the house ere he was before the gate, whining and crying most piteously, for the rain was falling faster and faster. The big dog, to whom the rain was a matter of perfect indifference, was instantly on hand and tried his utmost to open the gate, but naturally without success. Almost in despair the little dog bit at the gate, at the same time springing into the air in the attempt to jump over it, when he chanced to catch the string in his teeth; it broke, and the gate flew open. Now he knew the secret and thenceforth bit the string whenever he wished to get out, so that I was obliged to change it.

"That the big dog in raising the latch did not in the least *know* that the latch closed the gate, that the raising of the same opened it, but that he merely repeated the automatic blow with his snout which had once had such happy consequences, transpires from the following: the gate leading to the barn is fastened with a latch precisely like the one on the garden-gate, only placed a little higher, still easily within the dog's reach. Here, too, occasionally the little dog is confined, and when he barks the big one makes every possible effort to open the gate, but it has never occurred to him to push the latch up. The brute cannot draw conclusions, that is, he cannot think."[19]

Other classical *differentiæ* of man besides that of being the only reasoning animal, also seem consequences of his unrivalled powers of similar association. He has, e.g., been called 'the laughing animal.' But humor has often been defined as the recognition of identities in things different. When the man in *Coriolanus* says of that hero that "there is no more mercy in him than there is milk in a male tiger," both the invention of the phrase and its enjoyment by the hearer depend on a peculiarly perplexing power to associate ideas by similarity.

[19] Th. Schumann: Journal *Daheim*, No. 19, 1878. Quoted by Strümpell: *Die Geisteskräfte der Menschen verglichen mit denen der Thiere* (Leipzig, 1878), p. 39. Cats are notorious for the skill with which they will open latches, locks, etc. Their feats are usually ascribed to their reasoning powers. But Dr. Romanes well remarks (*Mental Evolution in Animals*, p. 351, note) that we ought first to be sure that the actions are not due to mere association. A cat is constantly playing with things with her paws; a trick accidentally hit upon may be retained. Romanes notes the fact that the animals most skilled in this way need not be the most generally intelligent, but those which have the best corporeal members for handling things, cat's paws, horse's lips; elephant's trunk, cow's horns. The monkey has both the corporeal and the intellectual superiority. And my deprecatory remarks on animal reasoning in the text apply far less to the quadrumana than to quadrupeds.—On the possible fallacies in interpreting animals' minds, compare C. L. Morgan in *Mind*, XI, 174 (1886).

Man is known again as 'the talking animal'; and language is assuredly a capital distinction between man and brute. But it may readily be shown how this distinction merely flows from those we have pointed out, easy dissociation of a representation into its ingredients, and association by similarity.

Language is a system of *signs*, different from the things signified, but able to suggest them.

No doubt brutes have a number of such signs. When a dog yelps in front of a door, and his master, understanding his desire, opens it, the dog may, after a certain number of repetitions, get to repeat in cold blood a yelp which was at first the involuntary interjectional expression of strong emotion. The same dog may be taught to 'beg' for food, and afterwards come to do so deliberately when hungry. The dog also learns to understand the signs of men, and the word 'rat' uttered to a terrier suggests exciting thoughts of the rat-hunt. If the dog had the varied impulse to vocal utterance which some other animals have, he would probably repeat the word 'rat' whenever he spontaneously happened to think of a rat-hunt—he no doubt does have it as an auditory image, just as a parrot calls out different words spontaneously from its repertory, and having learned the name of a given dog will utter it on the sight of a different dog. In each of these separate cases the particular sign *may* be consciously noticed by the animal, as distinct from the particular thing signified, and will thus, so far as it goes, be a true manifestation of language. But when we come to man we find a great difference. *He has a deliberate intention to apply a sign to everything.* The linguistic impulse is with him generalized and systematic. For things hitherto unnoticed or unfelt, he *desires* a sign before he has one. Even though the dog should possess his 'yelp' for this thing, his 'beg' for that, and his auditory image 'rat' for a third thing, the matter with him rests there. If a fourth thing interests him for which no sign happens already to have been learned, he remains tranquilly without it and goes no further. But the man *postulates* it, its absence irritates him, and he ends by inventing it. *This* GENERAL PURPOSE *constitutes, I take it, the peculiarity of human speech, and explains its prodigious development.*

How, then, does the general purpose arise? It arises as soon as the notion of a *sign as such*, apart from any particular import, is born; and this notion is born by dissociation from the outstanding portions of a number of concrete cases of signification. The 'yelp,' the 'beg,' the 'rat,' differ as to their several imports and natures. They agree only in so far as they have the same *use*—to *be signs*, to stand for something more important than themselves. The dog whom this similarity could strike would have grasped the sign *per se* as such, and would probably thereupon become a general sign-maker, or speaker in the human sense. But how can the similarity strike him? Not without the juxtaposition of the similars (in virtue of the law we have laid down (p. 478), that in order to be segregated an experience must be repeated with varying concomitants)—not unless the 'yelp' of the dog at the moment it occurs *recalls* to him his 'beg,' by the delicate bond of their subtle similarity of use—not till then can this thought flash through his mind: "Why, yelp and beg, in spite of all their unlikeness, are yet alike in this: that they are actions, signs, which lead to important boons. Other boons, *any* boons, may then be got by other signs!" This reflection made, the gulf is passed. Animals probably never make it, because the bond of similarity is not delicate enough. Each sign is drowned in *its* import, and never awakens other signs and other imports in juxtaposition. The rat-hunt idea is too absorbingly interesting in itself to be interrupted by anything so uncontiguous to it as the idea of the 'beg for food,' or of 'the door-open yelp,' nor in their turn do these awaken the rat-hunt idea.

In the human child, however, these ruptures of contiguous association are very soon made; far off cases of sign-using arise when we make a sign now; and soon language is launched. The child in each case makes the discovery for himself. No one can help him except by furnishing him with the conditions. But as he is constituted, the conditions will sooner or later shoot together into the result.[20]

[20] There are two other conditions of language in the human being, additional to association by similarity, that assist its action, or rather pave the way for it. These are: first, the great natural loquacity; and, second, the great imitativeness of man. The first produces the original reflex interjectional sign; the second (as Bleek has well shown) fixes it, stamps it, and ends by multiplying the number of determinate specific signs which are a requisite preliminary to the general conscious purpose of sign-making, which I have called the characteristic human element in language. The way in which imitativeness fixes the meaning of signs is this: When a primeval man has a given emotion, he utters his natural interjection; or when (to avoid supposing that the reflex sounds are exceedingly determinate by nature) a group of such men experience a common emotion, and one takes the lead in the cry, the others cry like him from sympathy or imitativeness. Now, let one of the group hear another, who is in presence of the experience, utter the cry; he, even

The exceedingly interesting account which Dr. Howe gives of the education of his various blind-deaf mutes illustrates this point admirably. He began to teach Laura Bridgman by gumming raised letters on various familiar articles. The child was taught by mere contiguity to pick out a certain number of particular articles when made to feel the letters. But this was merely a collection of particular signs, out of the mass of which the general purpose of *signification* had not yet been extracted by the child's mind. Dr. Howe compares his situation at this moment to that of one lowering a line to the bottom of the deep sea in which Laura's soul lay, and waiting until she should spontaneously take hold of it and be raised into the light. The moment came, "accompanied by a radiant flash of intelligence and glow of joy"; she seemed suddenly to become aware of the general purpose embedded in the different details of all these signs, and from that moment her education went on with extreme rapidity.

Another of the great capacities in which man has been said to differ fundamentally from the animal is that of possessing self-consciousness or reflective knowledge of himself as a thinker. But this capacity also flows from our criterion, for (without going into the matter very deeply) we may say that the brute never reflects on himself as a thinker, because he has never clearly dissociated, in the full concrete act of thought, the element of the thing thought of and the operation by which he thinks it. They remain always fused, conglomerated—just as the interjectional vocal sign of the brute almost invariably merges in his mind with the thing signified, and is not independently attended to *in se*.[21]

---

without the experience, will repeat the cry from pure imitativeness. But, as he repeats the sign, he will be reminded by it of his own former experience. Thus, first, he has the sign with the emotion; then, without it; then, with it again. It is "dissociated by change of concomitants"; he feels it as a separate entity and yet as having a connection with the emotion. Immediately it becomes possible for him to couple it deliberately with the emotion, in cases where the latter would either have provoked no interjectional cry or not the same one. In a word, his mental procedure tends to *fix* this cry on *that* emotion; and when this occurs, in many instances, he is provided with a stock of signs, like the yelp, beg, rat of the dog, each of which suggests a determinate image. On this stock, then, similarity works in the way above explained.

21 See the "Evolution of Self-Consciousness" in *Philosophical Discussions*, by Chauncey Wright (New York: Henry Holt & Co., 1877). Dr. Romanes, in the book from which I have already quoted, seeks to show that the 'consciousness of truth as truth' and the deliberate intention to predicate (which are the characteristics

Now, the dissociation of these two elements probably occurs first in the child's mind on the occasion of some error or false expectation which would make him experience the shock of difference between merely imagining a thing and getting it. The thought experienced once with the concomitant reality, and then without it or with opposite concomitants, reminds the child of other cases in which the same provoking phenomenon occurred. Thus the general ingredient of error may be dissociated and noticed *per se*, and from the notion of his error or wrong thought to that of his thought in general the transition is easy. The brute, no doubt, has plenty of instances of error and disappointment in his life, but the similar shock is in him most likely always swallowed up in the accidents of the actual case. An expectation disappointed may breed dubiety as to the realization of that particular thing when the dog next expects it. But that disappointment, that dubiety, while they are present in the mind, will *not* call up other cases, in which the material details were different, but this feature of possible error was the same. The brute will, therefore, stop short of dissociating the general notion of error *per se*, and *a fortiori* will never attain the conception of Thought itself as such.

We may then, we think, consider it proven that *the most elementary single difference between the human mind and that of brutes lies in this deficiency on the brute's part to associate ideas by similarity*—characters, the abstraction of which depends on this sort of association, must in the brute always remain drowned, swamped in the total phenomenon which they help constitute, and never used to reason from. If a character stands out alone, it is always some obvious sensible quality like a sound or a smell which is instinctively exciting and lies in the line of the animal's propensities; or it is some obvious sign which experience has habitually coupled with a consequence, such as, for the dog, the sight of his master's hat on and the master's going out.

---

of higher human reasoning) presuppose a consciousness of ideas as such, as things distinct from their objects; and that this consciousness depends on our having made signs for them by language. My text seems to me to include Dr. Romanes's facts, and formulates them in what to me is a more elementary way, though the reader who wishes to understand the matter better should go to his clear and patient exposition also.

DIFFERENT ORDERS OF HUMAN GENIUS

But, now, since nature never makes a jump, it is evident that we should find the lowest men occupying in this respect an intermediate position between the brutes and the highest men. And so we do. Beyond the analogies which their own minds suggest by breaking up the literal sequence of their experience, there is a whole world of analogies which they can appreciate when imparted to them by their betters, but which they could never excogitate alone. This answers the question why Darwin and Newton had to be waited for so long. The flash of similarity between an apple and the moon, between the rivalry for food in nature and the rivalry for man's selection, was too recondite to have occurred to any but exceptional minds. *Genius, then,* as has been already said, *is identical with the possession of similar association to an extreme degree.* Professor Bain says: "This I count the leading fact of genius . . . I consider it quite impossible to afford any explanation of intellectual originality, except on the supposition of an unusual energy on this point." Alike in the arts, in literature, in practical affairs, and in science, association by similarity is the prime condition of success.

But as, according to our view, there are two stages in reasoned thought, one where similarity merely *operates* to call up cognate thoughts, and another farther stage, where the bond of identity between the cognate thoughts is *noticed*; so *minds of genius may be divided into two main sorts, those who notice the bond and those who merely obey it.* The first are the abstract reasoners, properly so called, the men of science, and philosophers—the analysts, in a word; the latter are the poets, the critics—the artists, in a word, the men of intuitions. These judge rightly, classify cases, characterize them by the most striking analogic epithets, but go no further. At first sight it might seem that the analytic mind represented simply a higher intellectual stage, and that the intuitive mind represented an arrested stage of intellectual development; but the difference is not so simple as this. Professor Bain has said that a man's advance to the scientific stage (the stage of noticing and abstracting the bond of similarity) may often be due to an *absence* of certain emotional sensibilities. The sense of color, he says, may no less determine a mind away from science than it determines it towards painting. There must be a penury in one's interest in the details of particular forms in order to permit the forces of the intellect to be concentrated on what is common to many forms.[22] In other words, supposing a mind fertile in the suggestion of analogies, but, at the same time, keenly interested in the particulars of each suggested image, that mind would be far less apt to single out the particular character which called up the analogy than one whose interests were less generally lively. A certain richness of the æsthetic nature may, therefore, easily keep one in the intuitive stage. All the poets are examples of this. Take Homer:

"Ulysses, too, spied round the house to see if any man were still alive and hiding, trying to get away from gloomy death. He found them all fallen in the blood and dirt, and in such number as the fish which the fishermen to the low shore, out of the foaming sea, drag with their meshy nets. These all, sick for the ocean water, are strewn around the sands, while the blazing sun takes their life from them. So there the suitors lay strewn round on one another."

Or again:

"And as when a Mæonian or a Carian woman stains ivory with purple to be a cheek-piece for horses, and it is kept in the chamber, and many horsemen have prayed to bear it off; but it is kept a treasure for a king, both a trapping for his horse and a glory to the driver—in such wise were thy stout thighs, Menelaos, and legs and fair ankles stained with blood."[23]

A man in whom all the accidents of an analogy rise up as vividly as this, may be excused for not attending to the ground of the analogy. But he need not on that account be deemed intellectually the inferior of a man of drier mind, in whom the ground is not as liable to be eclipsed by the general splendor. Rarely are both sorts of intellect, the splendid and the analytic, found in conjunction. Plato among philosophers, and M. Taine, who cannot quote a child's saying without describing the '*voix chantante, étonnée, heureuse*' in which it is uttered, are only exceptions whose strangeness proves the rule.

An often-quoted writer has said that Shakespeare possessed more *intellectual power* than anyone else that ever lived. If by this he meant the power to pass from given premises to right or congruous conclusions, it is no doubt true. The abrupt transitions in Shakespeare's thought astonish the reader by their unexpectedness no less than they delight him by their fitness. Why, for instance, does

[22] *Study of Character*, p. 317.

[23] Translated by my colleague, Professor G. H. Palmer.

the death of Othello so stir the spectator's blood and leave him with a sense of reconcilement? Shakespeare himself could very likely not say why; for his invention, though rational, was not ratiocinative. Wishing the curtain to fall upon a reinstated Othello, that speech about the turbaned Turk suddenly simply flashed across him as the right end of all that went before. The dry critic who comes after can, however, point out the subtle bonds of identity that guided Shakespeare's pen through that speech to the death of the Moor. Othello is sunk in ignominy, lapsed from his height at the beginning of the play. What better way to rescue him at last from this abasement than to make him for an instant identify himself in memory with the old Othello of better days, and then execute justice on his present disowned body, as he used then to smite all enemies of the State? But Shakespeare, whose mind supplied these means, could probably not have told why they were so effective.

But though this is true, and though it would be absurd in an absolute way to say that a given analytic mind was superior to any intuitional one, yet it is none the less true that the former *represents* the higher stage. Men, taken historically, reason by analogy long before they have learned to reason by abstract characters. Association by similarity and true reasoning may have identical results. If a philosopher wishes to prove to you why you should do a certain thing, he may do so by using abstract considerations exclusively; a savage will prove the same by reminding you of a similar case in which you notoriously do as he now proposes, and this with no ability to state the *point* in which the cases are similar. In all primitive literature, in all savage oratory, we find persuasion carried on exclusively by parables and similes, and travellers in savage countries readily adopt the native custom. Take, for example, Dr. Livingstone's argument with the negro conjuror. The missionary was trying to dissuade the savage from his fetichistic ways of invoking rain. "You see," said he, "that, after all your operations, sometimes it rains and sometimes it does not, exactly as when you have not operated at all." "But," replied the sorcerer, "it is just the same with you doctors; you give your remedies, and sometimes the patient gets well and sometimes he dies, just as when you do nothing at all." To that the pious missionary replied: "The doctor does his duty, after which God performs the cure if it pleases Him." "Well," rejoined the savage, "it is just so with me. I do what is necessary to procure rain, after which God sends it or withholds it according to His pleasure."[24]

This is the stage in which proverbial philosophy reigns supreme. "An empty sack can't stand straight" will stand for the reason why a man with debts may lose his honesty; and "a bird in the hand is worth two in the bush" will serve to back up one's exhortations to prudence. Or we answer the question: "Why is snow white?" by saying, "For the same reason that soap-suds or whipped eggs are white"—in other words, instead of giving the *reason* for a fact, we give another *example* of the same fact. This offering a similar instance, instead of a reason, has often been criticised as one of the forms of logical depravity in men. But manifestly it is not a perverse act of thought, but only an incomplete one. Furnishing parallel cases is the necessary first step towards abstracting the reason embedded in them all.

As it is with reasons, so it is with words. The first words are probably always names of entire things and entire actions, of extensive coherent groups. A new experience in the primitive man can only be talked about by him in terms of the old experiences which have received names. It reminds him of certain ones from among them, but the *points* in which it agrees with them are neither named nor dissociated. Pure similarity must work before the abstraction can work which is based upon it. The first adjectives will therefore probably be total nouns embodying the striking character. The primeval man will say, not 'the bread is hard,' but 'the bread is stone'; not 'the face is round,' but 'the face is moon'; not 'the fruit is sweet,' but 'the fruit is sugar-cane.' The first words are thus neither particular nor general, but *vaguely* concrete; just as we speak of an 'oval' face, a 'velvet' skin, or an 'iron' will, without meaning to connote any other attributes of the adjective-noun than those in which it *does* resemble the noun it is used to qualify. After a while certain of these adjectively-used nouns come only to signify the particular quality for whose sake they are oftenest used; the *entire thing* which they originally meant receives another name, and they become true abstract and general terms. Oval, for example, with us suggests *only* shape. The first abstract qualities thus formed are, no doubt, qualities of one and the same sense found in different objects—as big, sweet; next analogies between different senses, as 'sharp' of taste, 'high' of sound, etc.; then analo-

[24] Quoted by Renouvier: *Critique Philosophique*, October 19, 1876.

giès of motor combinations, or form of relation, as simple, confused, difficult, reciprocal, relative, spontaneous, etc. The extreme degree of subtlety in analogy is reached in such cases as when we say certain English art critics' writing reminds us of a close room in which pastilles have been burning, or that the mind of certain Frenchmen is like old Roquefort cheese. Here language utterly fails to hit upon the basis of resemblance.

Over immense departments of our thought we are still, all of us, in the savage state. Similarity operates in us, but abstraction has not taken place. We know what the present case is like, we know what it reminds us of, we have an intuition of the right course to take, if it be a practical matter. But analytic thought has made no tracks, and we cannot justify ourselves to others. In ethical, psychological, and æsthetic matters, to give a clear reason for one's judgment is universally recognized as a mark of rare genius. The helplessness of uneducated people to account for their likes and dislikes is often ludicrous. Ask the first Irish girl why she likes this country better or worse than her home, and see how much she can tell you. But if you ask your most educated friend why he prefers Titian to Paul Veronese, you will hardly get more of a reply; and you will probably get absolutely none if you inquire why Beethoven reminds him of Michael Angelo, or how it comes that a bare figure with unduly flexed joints, by the latter, can so suggest the moral tragedy of life. His thought obeys a *nexus*, but cannot name it. And so it is with all those judgments of *experts*, which even though unmotived are so valuable. Saturated with experience of a particular class of materials, an expert intuitively feels whether a newly-reported fact is probable or not, whether a proposed hypothesis is worthless or the reverse. He instinctively knows that, in a novel case, this and not that will be the promising course of action. The well-known story of the old judge advising the new one never to give reasons for his decisions, "the decisions will probably be right, the reasons will surely be wrong," illustrates this. The doctor will feel that the patient is doomed, the dentist will have a premonition that the tooth will break, though neither can articulate a reason for his foreboding. The reason lies embedded, but not yet laid bare, in all the countless previous cases dimly suggested by the actual one, all calling up the same conclusion, which the adept thus finds himself swept on to, he knows not how or why.

A physiological conclusion remains to be drawn. If the principles laid down in Chapter XIV are true, then it follows that the great cerebral difference between habitual and reasoned thinking must be this: that in the former an entire system of cells vibrating at any one moment discharges in its totality into another entire system, and that the order of the discharges tends to be a constant one in time; whilst in the latter a part of the prior system still keeps vibrating in the midst of the subsequent system, and the order—which part this shall be, and what shall be its concomitants in the subsequent system—has little tendency to fixedness in time. This physical selection, so to call it, of one part to vibrate persistently whilst the others rise and subside, we found, in the chapter in question, to be the basis of similar association. (See especially pp. 544–547.) It would seem to be but a minor degree of that still more urgent and importunate localized vibration which we can easiest conceive to underlie the mental fact of interest, attention, or dissociation. In terms of the brain-process, then, all these mental facts resolve themselves into a single peculiarity: that of indeterminateness of connection between the different tracts, and tendency of action to focalize itself, so to speak, in small localities which vary infinitely at different times, and from which irradiation may proceed in countless shifting ways. (Compare figure 80, p. 972.) To discover, or (what more befits the present stage of nerve-physiology) to adumbrate by some possible guess, on what chemical or molecular-mechanical fact this instable equilibrium of the human brain may depend, should be the next task of the physiologist who ponders over the passage from brute to man. Whatever the physical peculiarity in question may be, *it* is the cause why a man, whose brain has it, reasons so much, whilst his horse, whose brain lacks it, reasons so little. We can but bequeath the problem to abler hands than our own.

But, meanwhile, this mode of stating the matter suggests a couple of other inferences. The first is brief. If *focalization* of brain-activity be the fundamental fact of reasonable thought, we see why intense interest or concentrated passion makes us think so much more truly and profoundly. The persistent *focalization* of motion in certain tracts is the cerebral fact corresponding to the persistent domination in consciousness of the important feature of the subject. When not 'focalized,' we are scatter-brained; but when thoroughly impassioned, we never wander from the point. None but congruous and relevant images arise. When roused by indignation or moral enthusiasm, how trenchant are our reflections, how smiting are our words! The whole network of petty scruples and by-considerations which, at ordinary languid times, surrounded the matter like a cobweb, holding back our thought, as Gulliver was pinned to the earth by the myriad Lilliputian threads, are dashed through at a blow, and the subject stands with its essential and vital lines revealed.

The last point is relative to the theory that what was acquired habit in the ancestor may become congenital tendency in the offspring. So vast a superstructure is raised upon this principle that the paucity of empirical evidence for it has alike been matter of regret to its adherents, and of triumph to its opponents. In Chapter XXVIII we shall see what we may call the whole beggarly array of proof. In the human race, where our opportunities for observation are the most complete, we seem to have no evidence whatever which would support the hypothesis, unless it possibly be the law that city-bred children are more apt to be near-sighted than country children. In the mental world we certainly do not observe that the children of great travellers get their geography lessons with unusual ease, or that a baby whose ancestors have spoken German for thirty generations will, on that account, learn Italian any the less easily from its Italian nurse. But if the considerations we have been led to are true, they explain perfectly well why this law *should not* be verified in the human race, and why, therefore, in looking for evidence on the subject, we should confine ourselves exclusively to lower animals. In them fixed habit is the essential and characteristic law of nervous action. The brain grows to the exact modes in which it has been exercised, and the inheritance of these modes—then called instincts—would have in it nothing surprising. But in man the negation of all fixed modes is the essential characteristic. He owes his whole pre-eminence as a reasoner, his whole human quality of intellect, we may say, to the facility with which a given mode of thought in him may suddenly be broken up into elements, which recombine anew. Only at the price of inheriting no settled instinctive tendencies is he able to settle every novel case by the fresh discovery by his reason of novel principles. He is, *par excellence*, the *educable* animal. If, then, the law that habits are inherited were found exemplified in him, he would, in so far forth, fall short of his human perfections; and, when we survey the human races, we actually do find that those which are most instinctive at the outset are those which, on the whole, are least educated in the end. An untutored Italian is, to a great extent, a man of the world; he has instinctive perceptions, tendencies to behavior, reactions, in a word, upon his environment, which the untutored German wholly lacks. If the latter be not drilled, he is apt to be a thoroughly loutish personage; but, on the other hand, the mere absence in his brain of definite innate tendencies enables him to advance by the development, through education, of his purely reasoned thinking, into complex regions of consciousness that the Italian may probably never approach.

We observe an identical difference between men as a whole and women as a whole. A young woman of twenty reacts with intuitive promptitude and security in all the usual circumstances in which she may be placed.[25] Her likes and dislikes are formed; her opinions, to a great extent, the same that they will be through life. Her character is, in fact, finished in its essentials. How inferior to her is a boy of twenty in all these respects! His character is still gelatinous, uncertain what shape to assume, 'trying it on' in every direction. Feeling his power, yet ignorant of the manner in which he shall express it, he is, when compared with his sister, a being of no definite contour. But this absence of prompt tendency in his brain to set into particular modes is the very condition which insures that it shall ultimately become so much more efficient than the woman's. The very lack of preappointed trains of thought is the ground on which general principles and heads of classification grow up; and the masculine brain deals with new and complex matter indirectly by means of these, in a manner which the feminine method of direct intuition, admirably and rapidly as it performs within its limits, can vainly hope to cope with.

25 Social and domestic circumstances, that is, not material ones. Perceptions of social relations seem very keen in persons whose dealings with the material world are confined to knowing a few useful objects, principally animals, plants, and weapons. Savages and boors are often as tactful and astute socially as trained diplomatists. In general, it is probable that the consciousness of how one stands with other people occupies a relatively larger and larger part of the mind, the lower one goes in the scale of culture. Woman's intuitions, so fine in the sphere of personal relations, are seldom first-rate in the way of mechanics. All boys teach themselves how a clock goes; few girls. Hence Dr. Whately's jest, "Woman is the unreasoning animal, and pokes the fire from on top."

In looking back over the subject of reasoning, one feels how intimately connected it is with conception; and one realizes more than ever the deep reach of that principle of selection on which so much stress was laid towards the close of Chapter IX. As the art of reading (after a certain stage in one's education) is the art of skipping, so the art of being wise is the art of knowing what to overlook. The first effect on the mind of growing cultivated is that processes once multiple get to be performed by a single act. Lazarus has called this the progressive 'condensation' of thought. But in the psychological sense it is less a condensation than a loss, a genuine dropping out and throwing overboard of conscious content. Steps really sink from sight. An advanced thinker sees the relations of his topics in such masses and so instantaneously that when he comes to explain to younger minds it is often hard to say which grows the more perplexed, he or the pupil. In every university there are admirable investigators who are notoriously bad lecturers. The reason is that they never spontaneously see the subject in the minute articulate way in which the student needs to have it offered to his slow reception. They grope for the links, but the links do not come. Bowditch, who translated and annotated Laplace's *Mécanique céleste,* said that whenever his author prefaced a proposition by the words 'it is evident,' he knew that many hours of hard study lay before him.

When two minds of a high order, interested in kindred subjects, come together, their conversation is chiefly remarkable for the summariness of its allusions and the rapidity of its transitions. Before one of them is half through a sentence the other knows his meaning and replies. Such genial play with such massive materials, such an easy flashing of light over far perspectives, such careless indifference to the dust and apparatus that ordinarily surround the subject and seem to pertain to its essence, make these conversations seem true feasts for gods to a listener who is educated enough to follow them at all. His mental lungs breathe more deeply, in an atmosphere more broad and vast than is their wont. On the other hand, the excessive explicitness and short-windedness of a common man are as wonderful as they are tedious to the man of genius. But we need not go as far as the ways of genius. Ordinary social intercourse will do. There the charm of conversation is in direct proportion to the possibility of abridgment and elision, and in inverse ratio to the need of explicit statement. With old friends a word stands for a whole story or set of opinions. With new-comers everything must be gone over in detail. Some persons have a real mania for completeness, they must express every step. They are the most intolerable of companions, and although their mental energy may in its way be great, they always strike us as weak and second-rate. In short, the essence of plebianism, that which separates vulgarity from aristocracy, is perhaps less a defect than an excess, the constant need to animadvert upon matters which for the aristocratic temperament do not exist. To ignore, to disdain to consider, to overlook, are the essence of the 'gentleman.' Often most provokingly so; for the things ignored may be of the deepest moral consequence. But in the very midst of our indignation with the gentleman, we have a consciousness that his preposterous inertia and negativeness in the actual emergency is, somehow or other, *allied* with his general superiority to ourselves. It is not only that the gentleman ignores considerations relative to conduct, sordid suspicions, fears, calculations, etc., which the vulgarian is fated to entertain; it is that he is silent where the vulgarian talks; that he gives nothing but results where the vulgarian is profuse of reasons; that he does not explain or apologize; that he uses one sentence instead of twenty; and that, in a word, there is an amount of *interstitial* thinking, so to call it, which it is quite impossible to get him to perform, but which is nearly all that the vulgarian mind performs at all. All this suppression of the secondary leaves the field *clear*,—for higher flights, should they choose to come. But even if they never came, what thoughts there were would still manifest the aristocratic type and wear the well-bred form. So great is our sense of harmony and ease in passing from the company of a philistine to that of an aristocratic temperament, that we are almost tempted to deem the falsest views and tastes as held by a man of the world, truer than the truest as held by a common person. In the latter the best ideas are choked, obstructed, and contaminated by the redundancy of their paltry associates. The negative conditions, at least, of an atmosphere and a free outlook are present in the former.

I may appear to have strayed from psychological analysis into æsthetic criticism. But the principle of selection is so important that no illustrations seem redundant which may help to show how great is its scope. The upshot of what I say simply is that selection implies rejection as well as choice; and that the function of ignoring, of *in*attention, is as vital a factor in mental progress as the function of attention itself.

Chapter XXIII

The Production of Movement

The reader will not have forgotten, in the jungle of purely inward processes and products through which the last chapters have borne him, that the final result of them all must be some form of bodily activity due to the escape of the central excitement through outgoing nerves. The whole neural organism, it will be remembered, is, physiologically considered, but a machine for converting stimuli into reactions; and the intellectual part of our life is knit up with but the middle or 'central' portion of the machine's operations. Let us now turn to consider the final or emergent operations, the bodily activities, and the forms of consciousness connected therewithal.

Every impression which impinges on the incoming nerves produces some discharge down the outgoing ones, whether we be aware of it or not. Using sweeping terms and ignoring exceptions, *we might say that every possible feeling produces a movement, and that the movement is a movement of the entire organism, and of each and all its parts.* What happens patently when an explosion or a flash of lightning startles us, or when we are tickled, happens latently with every sensation which we receive. The only reason why we do not feel the startle or tickle in the case of insignificant sensations is partly its very small amount, partly our obtuseness. Professor Bain many years ago gave the name of the Law of Diffusion to this phenomenon of general discharge, and expressed it thus: "According as an impression is accompanied with Feeling, the aroused currents diffuse themselves freely over the brain, leading to a general agitation of the moving organs, as well as affecting the viscera."

In cases where the feeling is strong the law is too familiar to require proof. As Prof. Bain says:

"Each of us knows in our own experience that a sudden shock of feeling is accompanied with movements of the body generally, and with other effects. When no emotion is present, we are quiescent; a slight feeling is accompanied with slight manifestations; a more intense shock has a more intense outburst. Every pleasure and every pain, and every mode of emotion, has a definite wave of effects, which our observation makes known to us: and we apply the knowledge to infer other men's feelings from their outward display. . . . The organs first and prominently affected, in the diffused wave of nervous influence, are the moving members, and of these, by preference, the features of the face (with the ears in animals), whose movements constitute the *expression* of the countenance. But the influence extends to all the parts of the moving system, voluntary and involuntary; while an important series of effects are produced on the glands and viscera—the stomach, lungs, heart, kidneys, skin, together with the sexual and mammary organs. . . . The circumstance is seemingly universal, the proof of it does not require a citation of instances in detail; on the objectors is thrown the burden of adducing unequivocal exceptions to the law."[1]

There are probably no exceptions to the diffusion of every impression through the *nerve-centres*. The *effect* of the wave through the centres may, however, often be to interfere with processes, and to diminish tensions already existing there; and the outward consequences of such inhibitions may be the arrest of discharges from the inhibited regions and the checking of bodily activities already in process of occurrence. When this happens it probably is like the draining or siphoning of certain channels by currents flowing through others. When, in walking, we suddenly stand still because a sound, sight, smell, or thought catches our attention, something like this occurs. But there are cases of arrest of peripheral activity which depend, not on central inhibition, but on stimulation of centres which discharge outgoing currents of an inhibitory sort. Whenever we are startled, for example, our heart momentarily stops or slows its beating, and then palpitates with accelerated speed. The brief arrest is due to an outgoing current down the pneumogastric nerve. This nerve, when stimulated, stops or slows

[1] *Emotions and the Will*, pp. 4, 5.

the heart-beats, and this particular effect of startling fails to occur if the nerve be cut.

In general, however, the stimulating effects of a sense-impression preponderate over the inhibiting effects, so that we may roughly say, as we began by saying, that the wave of discharge produces an activity in all parts of the body. The task of tracing out *all* the effects of any one incoming sensation has not yet been performed by physiologists. Recent years have, however, begun to enlarge our information; and although I must refer to special treatises for the full details, I can briefly string together here a number of separate observations which prove the truth of the law of diffusion.

First take *effects upon the circulation.* Those upon the heart we have just seen. Haller long ago recorded that the blood from an open vein flowed out faster at the beat of a drum.[2] In Chapter III (p. 103) we learned how instantaneously, according to Mosso, the circulation in the brain is altered by changes of sensation and of the course of thought. The effect of objects of fear, shame, and anger upon the blood-supply of the skin, especially the skin of the face, are too well known to need remark. Sensations of the higher senses produce, according to Couty and Charpentier, the most varied effects upon the pulse-rate and blood-pressure in dogs. Fig. 81, a pulse-tracing from these authors, shows the tumultuous effect on a dog's heart of hearing the screams of another dog. The changes of blood-pressure still occurred when the pneumogastric nerves were cut, showing the vaso-motor effect to be direct and not dependent on the heart. When Mosso invented that simple instrument, the *plethysmograph,* for recording the fluctuations in volume of the members of the body, what most astonished him, he says, "in the first experiments which he made in Italy, was the extreme unrest of the blood-vessels of the hand, which at every smallest emotion, whether during waking or during sleep, changed their volume in surprising fashion."[3] Figure 82 (from Féré[4]) shows the way in which the pulse of one subject was modified by the exhibition of a red light lasting from the moment marked *a* to that marked *b.*

The effects upon respiration of sudden sensory stimuli are also too well known to need elaborate comment. We 'catch our breath' at every sudden sound. We 'hold our breath' whenever our atten-

[2] Cf. Féré: *Sensation et mouvement* (1887), p. 56.

[3] *La Paura* (1884), p. 117. Compare Féré: *Sensation et mouvement,* chap. XVII.

[4] *Revue Philosophique,* XXIV, 570.

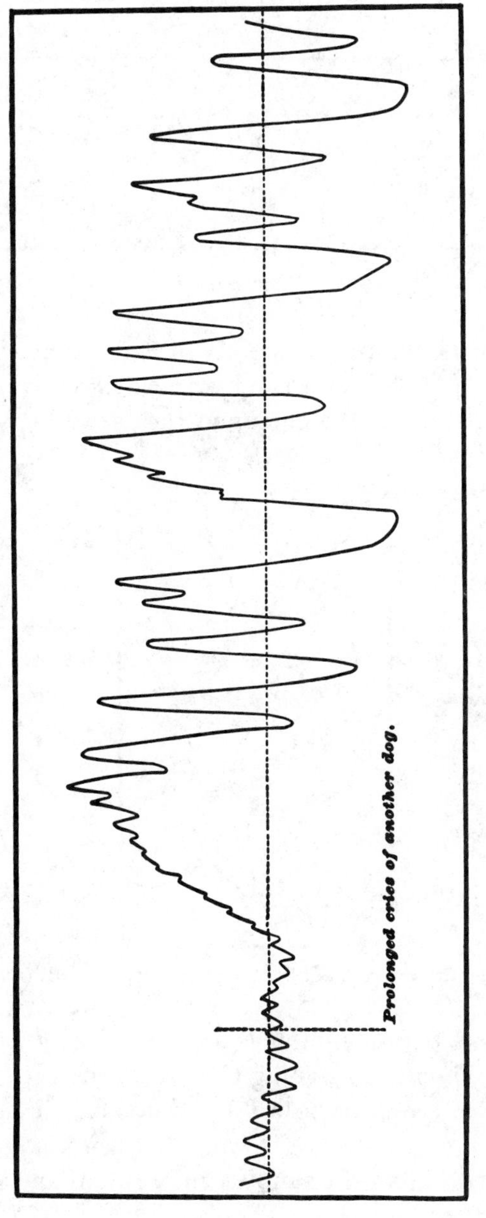

FIG. 81.

tion and expectation are strongly engaged, and we sigh when the tension of the situation is relieved. When a fearful object is before us we pant and cannot deeply inspire; when the object makes us

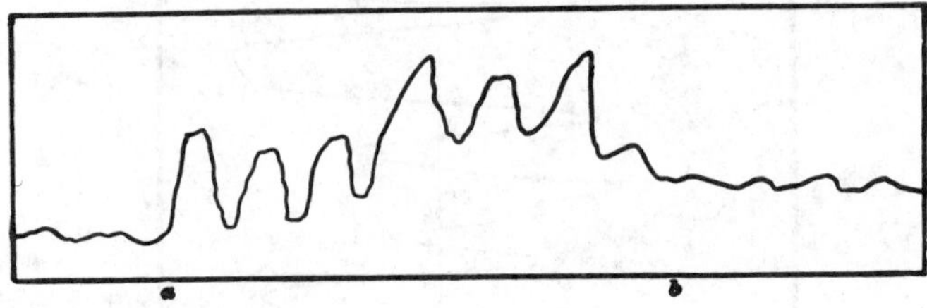

FIG. 82.

angry it is, on the contrary, the act of expiration which is hard. I subjoin a couple of figures from Féré which explain themselves. They show the effects of light upon the breathing of two of his hysteric patients.[5]

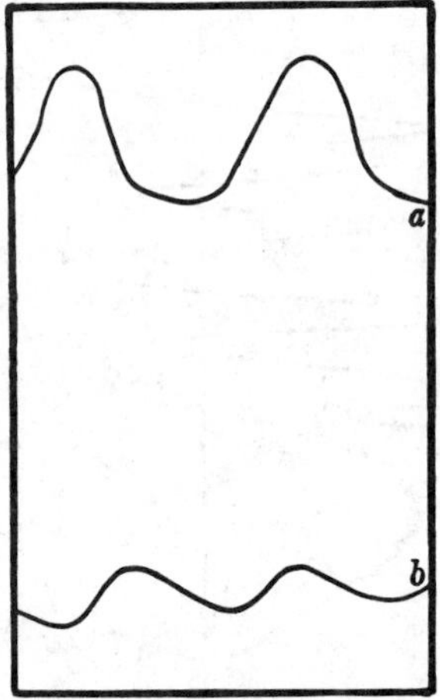

FIG. 83.—Respiratory curve of B: *a*, with eyes open; *b*, with eyes closed.

On the sweat-glands, similar consequences of sensorial stimuli are observed. Tarchanoff, testing the condition of the sweat-glands by the power of the skin to start a galvanic current through electrodes applied to its surface, found that "nearly every kind of nervous activity,—from the simplest impressions and sensations, to

[5] *Revue Philosophique*, XXIV, pp. 566–7.—For further information about the relations between the brain and respiration, see Danilewsky's Essay in the *Biologisches Centralblatt*, II, 690.

voluntary motions and the highest forms of mental exertion,—is accompanied by an increased activity in the glands of the skin."[6] *On the pupil* observations are recorded by Sander which show that

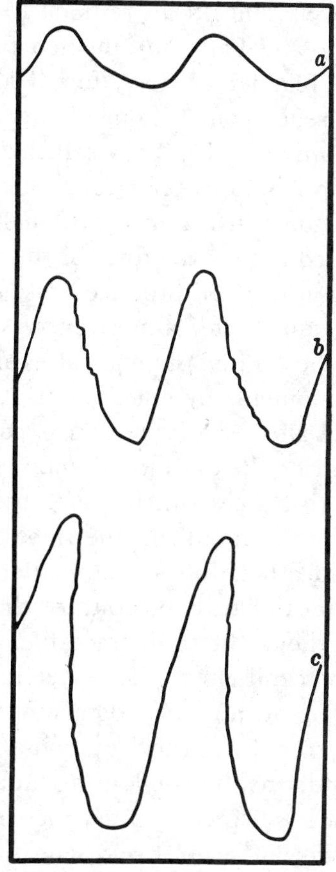

FIG. 84.—Respiratory curve of L: *a*, with yellow light; *b*, with green light; *c*, with red light. The red has the strongest effect.

a transitory dilatation follows every sensorial stimulus applied *during sleep*, even if the stimulus be not strong enough to wake the subject up. At the moment of awaking there is a dilatation, even if strong light falls on the eye.[7] The pupil of children can easily be observed to dilate enormously under the influence of

[6] Quoted from the report of Tarchanoff's paper (in Pflüger's *Archiv*, XLVI, 46) in the *American Journal of Psychology*, II, 653.

[7] *Archiv für Psychiatrie*, VII, 652; IX, 129.

fear. It is said to dilate in pain and fatigue; and to contract, on the contrary, in rage.

As regards *effects on the abdominal viscera,* they unquestionably exist, but very few accurate observations have been made.[8]

The bladder, bowels, and uterus respond to sensations, even indifferent ones. Mosso and Pellacani, in their plethysmographic investigations on the bladder of dogs, found all sorts of sensorial stimuli to produce reflex contractions of this organ, independent of those of the abdominal walls. They call the bladder 'as good an æsthesiometer as the iris,' and refer to the not uncommon reflex effects of psychic stimuli in the human female upon this organ.[9] M. Féré has registered the contractions of the sphincter ani which even indifferent sensations will produce. In some pregnant women the fœtus is felt to move after almost every sensorial excitement received by the mother. The only natural explanation is that it is stimulated at such moments by reflex contractions of the womb.[10] That the glands are affected in emotion is patent enough in the case of the tears of grief, the dry mouth, moist skin, or diarrhœa of fear, the biliary disturbances which sometimes follow upon rage, etc. The watering of the mouth at the sight of succulent food is well known. It is difficult to follow the smaller degrees of all these reflex changes, but it can hardly be doubted that they exist in some degree, even where they cease to be traceable, and that all our sensations have some visceral effects. The sneezing produced by sunshine, the roughening of the skin (gooseflesh) which certain strokings, contacts, and sounds, musical or non-musical, provoke, are facts of the same order as the shuddering and standing up of the hair in fear, only of less degree.

Effects on Voluntary Muscles. Every sensorial stimulus not only sends a special discharge into certain particular muscles dependent on the special nature of the stimulus in question—some of these special discharges we have studied in Chapter XI, others we shall examine under the heads of Instinct and Emotion—but it innervates the muscles generally. M. Féré has given very curious experimental proofs of this. The strength of contraction of the subject's hand was measured by a self-registering dynamometer. Ordinarily

[8] *Sensation et mouvement,* 57–8.

[9] *Reale Accademia dei Lincei* (1881–2). I follow the report in Hofmann und Schwalbe's *Jahresbericht,* x, II, 93.

[10] Cf. Féré: *Sensation et mouvement,* chap. XIV.

the maximum strength, under simple experimental conditions, remains the same from day to day. But if simultaneously with the contraction the subject received a sensorial impression, the contraction was sometimes weakened, but more often increased. This reinforcing effect has received the name of *dynamogeny*. The dynamogenic value of simple *musical notes* seems to be proportional to their loudness and height. Where the notes are compounded into sad strains, the muscular strength diminishes. If the strains are gay, it is increased.—The dynamogenic value of *colored lights* varies with the color. In a subject[11] whose normal strength was expressed by 23, it became 24 when a blue light was thrown on the eyes, 28 for green, 30 for yellow, 35 for orange, and 42 for red. Red is thus the most exciting color. Among *tastes*, sweet has the lowest value, next comes salt, then bitter, and finally sour, though, as M. Féré remarks, such a sour as acetic acid excites the nerves of pain and smell as well as of taste. The stimulating effects of tobacco-smoke, alcohol, beef-extract (which is innutritious), etc., etc., may be partly due to a dynamogenic action of this sort.—Of *odors*, that of musk seems to have a peculiar dynamogenic power. Fig. 85 is a copy of one of M. Féré's dynamographic tracings, which explains itself. The smaller contractions are those without stimulus; the stronger ones are due to the influence of red rays of light.

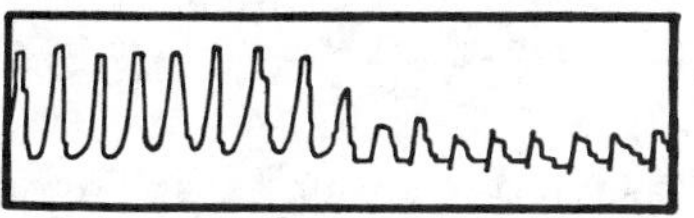

Fig. 85.

Everyone is familiar with the *patellar reflex*, or jerk upwards of the foot, which is produced by smartly tapping the tendon below the knee-pan when the leg hangs over the other knee. Drs. Weir Mitchell and Lombard have found that when other sensations come in simultaneously with the tap, the jerk is increased.[12] Heat,

[11] The figures given are from an hysterical subject, and the differences are greater than normal. M. Féré considers that the unstable nervous system of the hysteric ('les grenouilles de la psychologie') shows the law on a quantitatively exaggerated scale, without altering the qualitative relations. The effects remind us a little of the influence of sensations upon minimal sensations of other orders discovered by Urbantschitsch, and reported on page 676 of this volume.

[12] Mitchell in (Philadelphia) *Medical News* (Feb. 13 and 20, 1886); Lombard in *American Journal of Psychology* (Nov. 1887).

cold, pricking, itching, or faradic stimulation of the skin, sometimes strong optical impressions, music, all have this dynamogenic effect, which also results whenever voluntary movements are set up in other parts of the body, simultaneously with the tap.[13]

These 'dynamogenic' effects, in which one stimulation simply reinforces another already under way, must not be confounded with reflex acts properly so called, in which new activities are originated by the stimulus. All instinctive performances and manifestations of emotion are reflex acts. But underneath those of which we are conscious there seem to go on continually others smaller in amount, which probably in most persons might be called fluctuations of muscular *tone*, but which in certain neurotic subjects can be demonstrated ocularly. M. Féré figures some of them in the article to which I have already referred.[14]

Looking back over all these facts, it is hard to doubt the truth of the law of diffusion, even where verification is beyond reach. *A process set up anywhere in the centres reverberates everywhere, and in some way or other affects the organism throughout, making its activities either greater or less.* We are brought again to the assimilation which was expressed on a previous page of the nerve-central mass to a good conductor charged with electricity, of which the tension cannot be changed anywhere without changing it everywhere.

Herr Schneider has tried to show, by an ingenious and suggestive zoological review,[15] that all the *special* movements which highly evolved animals make are differentiated from the two originally simple movements of contraction and expansion in which the entire body of simple organisms takes part. The tendency to contract is the source of all the self-protective impulses and reactions which are later developed, including that of flight. The tendency to expand splits up, on the contrary, into the impulses and instincts of

13 Prof. H. P. Bowditch has made the interesting discovery that if the reinforcing movement be as much as 0.4 of a second late, the reinforcement fails to occur, and is transformed into a positive inhibition of the knee-jerk for retardations of between 0.4′ and 1.7′. The knee-jerk fails to be modified at all by voluntary movements made later than 1.7′ after the patellar ligament is tapped (see *Boston Medical and Surgical Journal*, May 31, 1888).

14 *Revue Philosophique*, XXIV, 572 ff.

15 In the *Vierteljahrsschrift für wissenschaftliche Philosophie*, III, 294.

an aggressive kind, feeding, fighting, sexual intercourse, etc. Schneider's articles are well worth reading, if only for the careful observations on animals which they embody. I cite them here as a sort of evolutionary reason to add to the mechanical *a priori* reason why there *ought* to be the diffusive wave which our *a posteriori* instances have shown to exist.

I will now proceed to a detailed study of the more important classes of movement consequent upon cerebro-mental change. They may be enumerated as—

1) Instinctive or Impulsive Performances;
2) Expressions of Emotion; and
3) Voluntary Deeds;

and each shall have a chapter to itself.

Chapter XXIV[*]

Instinct

Instinct is usually defined as the faculty of acting in such a way as to produce certain ends, without foresight of the ends, and without previous education in the performance. That instincts, as thus defined, exist on an enormous scale in the animal kingdom needs no proof. They are the functional correlatives of structure. With the presence of a certain organ goes, one may say, almost always a native aptitude for its use.

"Has the bird a gland for the secretion of oil? She knows instinctively how to press the oil from the gland and apply it to the feather. Has the rattlesnake the grooved tooth and gland of poison? He knows without instruction how to make both structure and function most effective against his enemies. Has the silk-worm the function of secreting the fluid silk? At the proper time, she winds the cocoon such as she has never seen, as thousands before have done; and thus without instruction, pattern or experience, forms a safe abode for herself in the period of transformation. Has the hawk talons? She knows by instinct how to wield them effectively against the helpless quarry."[1]

A very common way of talking about these admirably definite tendencies to act is by naming abstractly the purpose they sub-

[*] This chapter has already appeared (almost exactly as now printed) in the form of magazine articles in *Scribner's Magazine* and in the *Popular Science Monthly* for 1887.

[1] P. A. Chadbourne: *Instinct*, p. 28 (New York, 1872).

serve, such as self-preservation, or defence, or care for eggs and young—and saying the animal has an instinctive fear of death or love of life, or that she has an instinct of self-preservation, or an instinct of maternity and the like. But this represents the animal as obeying abstractions which not once in a million cases is it possible it can have framed. The strict physiological way of interpreting the facts leads to far clearer results. *The actions we call instinctive all conform to the general reflex type*; they are called forth by determinate sensory stimuli in contact with the animal's body, or at a distance in his environment. The cat runs after the mouse, runs or shows fight before the dog, avoids falling from walls and trees, shuns fire and water, etc., not because he has any notion either of life or of death, or of self, or of preservation. He has probably attained to no one of these conceptions in such a way as to react definitely upon it. He acts in each case separately, and simply because he cannot help it; being so framed that when that particular running thing called a mouse appears in his field of vision he *must* pursue; that when that particular barking and obstreperous thing called a dog appears there he *must* retire, if at a distance, and scratch if close by; that he *must* withdraw his feet from water and his face from flame, etc. His nervous system is to a great extent a preorganized bundle of such reactions—they are as fatal as sneezing, and as exactly correlated to their special excitants as it is to its own. Although the naturalist may, for his own convenience, class these reactions under general heads, he must not forget that in the animal it is a particular sensation or perception or image which calls them forth.

At first this view astounds us by the enormous number of special adjustments it supposes animals to possess ready-made in anticipation of the outer things among which they are to dwell. *Can* mutual dependence be so intricate and go so far? Is each thing born fitted to particular other things, and to them exclusively, as locks are fitted to their keys? Undoubtedly this must be believed to be so. Each nook and cranny of creation, down to our very skin and entrails, has its living inhabitants, with organs suited to the place, to devour and digest the food it harbors and to meet the dangers it conceals; and the minuteness of adaptation thus shown in the way of *structure* knows no bounds. Even so are there no bounds to the minuteness of adaptation in the way of *conduct* which the several inhabitants display.

The older writings on instinct are ineffectual wastes of words, because their authors never came down to this definite and simple point of view, but smothered everything in vague wonder at the clairvoyant and prophetic power of the animals—so superior to anything in man—and at the beneficence of God in endowing them with such a gift. But God's beneficence endows them, first of all, with a nervous system; and, turning our attention to this, makes instinct immediately appear neither more nor less wonderful than all the other facts of life.

Every instinct is an impulse. Whether we shall call such impulses as blushing, sneezing, coughing, smiling, or dodging, or keeping time to music, instincts or not, is a mere matter of terminology. The process is the same throughout. In his delightfully fresh and interesting work, *Der thierische Wille*, Herr G. H. Schneider subdivides impulses (*Triebe*) into sensation-impulses, perception-impulses, and idea-impulses. To crouch from cold is a sensation-impulse; to turn and follow, if we see people running one way, is a perception-impulse; to cast about for cover, if it begins to blow and rain, is an imagination-impulse. A single complex instinctive action may involve successively the awakening of impulses of all three classes. Thus a hungry lion starts to *seek* prey by the awakening in him of imagination coupled with desire; he begins to *stalk* it when, on eye, ear, or nostril, he gets an impression of its presence at a certain distance; he *springs* upon it, either when the booty takes alarm and flees, or when the distance is sufficiently reduced; he proceeds to *tear* and *devour* it the moment he gets a sensation of its contact with his claws and fangs. Seeking, stalking, springing, and devouring are just so many different kinds of muscular contraction, and neither kind is called forth by the stimulus appropriate to the other.

Schneider says of the hamster, which stores corn in its hole:

"If we analyze the propensity of storing, we find that it consists of three impulses: First, an impulse to *pick up* the nutritious object, due to perception; second, an impulse to *carry it off* into the dwelling-place, due to the idea of this latter; and third, an impulse to *lay it down* there, due to the sight of the place. It lies in the nature of the hamster that it should never see a full ear of corn without feeling a desire to strip it; it lies in its nature to feel, as soon as its cheek-pouches are filled, an irresistible desire to hurry to its home; and finally, it lies in its nature that the sight of the storehouse should awaken the impulse to empty the cheeks" (p. 208).

In certain animals of a low order the feeling of having executed one impulsive step is such an indispensable part of the stimulus of the next one, that the animal cannot make any variation in the order of its performance.

Now, why do the various animals do what seem to us such strange things, in the presence of such outlandish stimuli? Why does the hen, for example, submit herself to the tedium of incubating such a fearfully uninteresting set of objects as a nestful of eggs, unless she have some sort of a prophetic inkling of the result? The only answer is *ad hominem.* We can only interpret the instincts of brutes by what we know of instincts in ourselves. Why do men always lie down, when they can, on soft beds rather than on hard floors? Why do they sit round the stove on a cold day? Why, in a room, do they place themselves, ninety-nine times out of a hundred, with their faces towards its middle rather than to the wall? Why do they prefer saddle of mutton and champagne to hard-tack and pond-water? Why does the maiden interest the youth so that everything about her seems more important and significant than anything else in the world? Nothing more can be said than that these are human ways, and that every creature *likes* its own ways, and takes to the following them as a matter of course. Science may come and consider these ways, and find that most of them are useful. But it is not for the sake of their utility that they are followed, but because at the moment of following them we feel that that is the only appropriate and natural thing to do. Not one man in a billion, when taking his dinner, ever thinks of utility. He eats because the food tastes good and makes him want more. If you ask him *why* he should want to eat more of what tastes like that, instead of revering you as a philosopher he will probably laugh at you for a fool. The connection between the savory sensation and the act it awakens is for him absolute and *selbstverständlich,* an '*a priori* synthesis' of the most perfect sort, needing no proof but its own evidence. It takes, in short, what Berkeley calls a mind debauched by learning to carry the process of making the natural seem strange, so far as to ask for the *why* of any instinctive human act. To the metaphysician alone can such questions occur as: Why do we smile, when pleased, and not scowl? Why are we unable to talk to a crowd as we talk to a single friend? Why does a particular maiden turn our wits so upside-down? The common man can only say, "*Of course* we smile, *of course* our heart palpitates at the sight of the crowd, *of course* we love the maiden, that beautiful soul clad in that perfect form, so palpably and flagrantly made from all eternity to be loved!"

And so, probably, does each animal feel about the particular things it tends to do in presence of particular objects. They, too, are *a priori* syntheses. To the lion it is the lioness which is made to be loved; to the bear, the she-bear. To the broody hen the notion would probably seem monstrous that there should be a creature in the world to whom a nestful of eggs was not the utterly fascinating and precious and never-to-be-too-much-sat-upon object which it is to her.[2]

Thus we may be sure that, however mysterious some animals' instincts may appear to us, our instincts will appear no less mysterious to them. And we may conclude that, to the animal which obeys it, every impulse and every step of every instinct shines with its own sufficient light, and seems at the moment the only eternally right and proper thing to do. It is done for its own sake exclusively. What voluptuous thrill may not shake a fly, when she at last discovers the one particular leaf, or carrion, or bit of dung, that out of all the world can stimulate her ovipositor to its discharge? Does not the discharge then seem to her the only fitting thing? And need she care or know anything about the future maggot and its food?

Since the *egg-laying instincts* are simple examples to consider, a few quotations about them from Schneider may be serviceable:

"The phenomenon so often talked about, so variously interpreted, so surrounded with mystification, that an insect should always lay her

[2] "It would be very simple-minded to suppose that bees follow their queen, and protect her and care for her, because they are aware that without her the hive would become extinct. The odor or the aspect of their queen is manifestly agreeable to the bees—that is why they love her so. Does not all true love base itself on agreeable perceptions much more than on representations of utility?" (G. H. Schneider: *Der thierische Wille*, p. 187.) *A priori*, there is no reason to suppose that *any* sensation might not in *some* animal cause *any* emotion and *any* impulse. To us it seems unnatural that an odor should directly excite anger or fear; or a color, lust. Yet there are creatures to which some smells are quite as frightful as any sounds, and very likely others to which color is as much a sexual irritant as form.

eggs in a spot appropriate to the nourishment of her young, is no more marvellous than the phenomenon that every animal pairs with a mate capable of bearing posterity, or feeds on materials capable of affording him nourishment. . . . Not only the choice of a place for laying the eggs, but all the various acts for depositing and protecting them, are occasioned by the perception of the proper object, and the relation of this perception to the various stages of maternal impulse. When the burying beetle perceives a carrion, she is not only impelled to approach it and lodge her eggs in it, but also to go through the movements requisite for burying it; just as a bird who sees his hen-bird is impelled to caress her, to strut around her, dance before her, or in some other way to woo her; just as a tiger, when he sees an antelope, is impelled to stalk it, to pounce upon it, and to strangle it. When the tailor-bee cuts out pieces of rose-leaf, bends them, carries them into a caterpillar- or mouse-hole in trees or in the earth, covers their seams again with other pieces, and so makes a thimble-shaped case—when she fills this with honey and lays an egg in it, all these various appropriate expressions of her will are to be explained by supposing that at the time when the eggs are ripe within her, the appearance of a suitable caterpillar- or mouse-hole and the perception of rose-leaves are so correlated in the insect with the several impulses in question, that the performances follow as a matter of course when the perceptions take place. . . .

"The perception of the empty nest, or of a single egg, seems in birds to stand in such a close relation to the physiological functions of oviparation, that it serves as a direct stimulus to these functions, while the perception of a sufficient number of eggs has just the opposite effect. It is well known that hens and ducks lay more eggs if we keep removing them than if we leave them in the nest. The impulse to sit arises, as a rule, when a bird sees a certain number of eggs in her nest. If this number is not yet to be seen there, the ducks continue to lay, although they perhaps have laid twice as many eggs as they are accustomed to sit upon. . . . That sitting, also, is independent of any idea of purpose and is a pure perception-impulse is evident, among other things, from the fact that many birds, e.g., wild ducks, steal eggs from each other. . . . The bodily disposition to sit is, it is true, one condition [since broody hens will sit where there are no eggs], but the perception of the eggs is the other condition of the activity of the incubating impulse. The propensity of the cuckoo and of the cow-bird to lay their eggs in the nests of other species must also be interpreted as a pure perception-impulse. These birds have no bodily disposition to become broody, and there is therefore in them no connection between the perception of an egg and the impulse to sit upon it. Eggs ripen, however, in their oviducts, and the body tends to get rid of them. And since the two birds just named do not drop their eggs anywhere on the ground, but in nests, which are the only places where they may preserve the species, it might easily appear that such preservation of the species was what they had in view, and that they acted with full consciousness of the purpose. But this is not so. . . . The cuckoo is simply excited by the perception of quite determinate sorts of nest, which already contain eggs, to drop her own into them, and throw the others out, because this perception is a direct stimulus to these acts. It is impossible that she should have any notion of the other bird coming and sitting on her egg."[3]

INSTINCTS NOT ALWAYS BLIND OR INVARIABLE

Remember that nothing is said yet of the origin of instincts, but only of the constitution of those that exist fully formed. How stands it with the instincts of mankind?

Nothing is commoner than the remark that Man differs from lower creatures by the almost total absence of instincts, and the assumption of their work in him by 'reason.' A fruitless discussion might be waged on this point by two theorizers who were careful not to define their terms. 'Reason' might be used, as it often has been, since Kant, not as the mere power of 'inferring,' but also as a name for the *tendency to obey impulses* of a certain lofty sort, such as duty, or universal ends. And 'instinct' might have its significance so broadened as to cover all impulses whatever, even the impulse to act from the idea of a distant fact, as well as the impulse to act from a present sensation. Were the word instinct used in this broad way, it would of course be impossible to restrict it, as we began by doing, to actions done with no prevision of an end. We must of course avoid a quarrel about words, and the facts of the case are really tolerably plain. Man has a far greater variety of *impulses* than any lower animal; and any one of these impulses, taken in itself, is as 'blind' as the lowest instinct can be; but, owing to man's memory, power of reflection, and power of inference, they come each one to be felt by him, after he has once yielded to them and experienced their results, in connection with a *foresight* of those results. In this condition an impulse acted out may be said to be acted out, in part at least, *for the sake* of its results. It is obvious that *every instinctive act, in an animal with memory, must cease to be 'blind' after being once repeated*, and must be accompanied with foresight of its 'end' just so far as that end may have fallen under

3 *Der thierische Wille*, pp. 280–3.

the animal's cognizance. An insect that lays her eggs in a place where she never sees them hatch must always do so 'blindly'; but a hen who has already hatched a brood can hardly be assumed to sit with perfect 'blindness' on her second nest. Some expectation of consequences must in every case like this be aroused; and this expectation, according as it is that of something desired or of something disliked, must necessarily either re-enforce or inhibit the mere impulse. The hen's idea of the chickens would probably encourage her to sit; a rat's memory, on the other hand, of a former escape from a trap would neutralize his impulse to take bait from anything that reminded him of that trap. If a boy sees a fat hopping-toad, he probably has incontinently an impulse (especially if with other boys) to smash the creature with a stone, which impulse we may suppose him blindly to obey. But something in the expression of the dying toad's clasped hands suggests the meanness of the act, or reminds him of sayings he has heard about the sufferings of animals being like his own; so that, when next he is tempted by a toad, an idea arises which, far from spurring him again to the torment, prompts kindly actions, and may even make him the toad's champion against less reflecting boys.

It is plain, then, that, *no matter how well endowed an animal may originally be in the way of instincts, his resultant actions will be much modified if the instincts combine with experience,* if in addition to impulses he have memories, associations, inferences, and expectations, on any considerable scale. An object O, on which he has an instinctive impulse to react in the manner A, would *directly* provoke him to that reaction. But O has meantime become for him a *sign* of the nearness of P, on which he has an equally strong impulse to react in the manner B, quite unlike A. So that when he meets O, the immediate impulse A and the remote impulse B struggle in his breast for the mastery. The fatality and uniformity said to be characteristic of instinctive actions will be so little manifest that one might be tempted to deny to him altogether the possession of any instinct about the object O. Yet how false this judgment would be! The instinct about O is there; only by the complication of the associative machinery it has come into conflict with another instinct about P.

Here we immediately reap the good fruits of our simple physiological conception of what an instinct is. If it be a mere excito-motor impulse, due to the pre-existence of a certain 'reflex arc' in the nerve-centres of the creature, of course it must follow the law of all such reflex arcs. One liability of such arcs is to have their activity 'inhibited' by other processes going on at the same time. It makes no difference whether the arc be organized at birth, or ripen spontaneously later, or be due to acquired habit; it must take its chances with all the other arcs, and sometimes succeed, and sometimes fail, in drafting off the currents through itself. The mystical view of an instinct would make it invariable. The physiological view would require it to show occasional irregularities in any animal in whom the number of separate instincts, and the possible entrance of the same stimulus into several of them, were great. And such irregularities are what every superior animal's instincts do show in abundance.[4]

Wherever the mind is elevated enough to discriminate; wherever several distinct sensory elements must combine to discharge the reflex arc; wherever, instead of plumping into action instantly at the first rough intimation of what *sort* of a thing is there, the agent waits to see which *one* of its kind it is and what the *circumstances* are of its appearance; wherever different individuals and different circumstances can impel him in different ways; wherever these are the conditions—we have a masking of the elementary constitution of the instinctive life. The whole story of our dealings with the lower wild animals is the history of our taking advantage of the way in which they judge of everything by its mere label, as it were, so as to ensnare or kill them. Nature, in them, has left matters in this rough way, and made them act *always* in the manner which would be *oftenest* right. There are more worms unattached to hooks than impaled upon them; therefore, on the whole, says Nature to her fishy children, bite at *every* worm and take your chances. But as her children get higher, and their lives more precious, she reduces the risks. Since what seems to be the same object

[4] In the instincts of mammals, and even of lower creatures, the uniformity and infallibility which, a generation ago, were considered as essential characters do not exist. The minuter study of recent years has found continuity, transition, variation, and mistake, wherever it has looked for them, and decided that what is called an instinct is usually only a tendency to act in a way of which the *average* is pretty constant, but which need not be mathematically 'true.' Cf. on this point Darwin's *Origin of Species*; Romanes's *Mental Evolution in Animals*, chaps. XI to XVI incl., and Appendix; W. L. Lindsay's *Mind in the Lower Animals*, vol. I, 133–141; II, chaps. V, XX; and K. Semper's *Animal Life As Affected by the Natural Conditions of Existence*, where a great many instances will be found.

may be now a genuine food and now a bait; since in gregarious species each individual may prove to be either the friend or the rival, according to the circumstances, of another; since any entirely unknown object may be fraught with weal or woe, *Nature implants contrary impulses to act on many classes of things,* and leaves it to slight alterations in the conditions of the individual case to decide which impulse shall carry the day. Thus, greediness and suspicion, curiosity and timidity, coyness and desire, bashfulness and vanity, sociability and pugnacity, seem to shoot over into each other as quickly, and to remain in as unstable equilibrium, in the higher birds and mammals as in man. They are all impulses, congenital, blind at first, and productive of motor reactions of a rigorously determinate sort. *Each one of them then is an instinct,* as instincts are commonly defined. *But they contradict each other*—'experience' in each particular opportunity of application usually deciding the issue. *The animal that exhibits them loses the 'instinctive' demeanor* and appears to lead a life of hesitation and choice, an intellectual life; *not, however, because he has no instincts—rather because he has so many that they block each other's path.*

Thus, then, without troubling ourselves about the words instinct and reason, we may confidently say that however uncertain man's reactions upon his environment may sometimes seem in comparison with those of lower creatures, the uncertainty is probably not due to their possession of any principles of action which he lacks. *On the contrary, man possesses all the impulses that they have, and a great many more besides.* In other words, there is no material antagonism between instinct and reason. Reason, *per se,* can inhibit no impulses; the only thing that can neutralize an impulse is an impulse the other way. Reason may, however, make an *inference which will excite the imagination so as to set loose* the impulse the other way; and thus, though the animal richest in reason might be also the animal richest in instinctive impulses too, he would never seem the fatal automaton which a *merely* instinctive animal would be.

Let us now turn to human impulses with a little more detail. All we have ascertained so far is that impulses of an originally instinctive character may exist, and yet not betray themselves by automatic fatality of conduct. But in man what impulses do exist? In the light of what has been said, it is obvious that an existing impulse may not always be superficially apparent even when its object is there. And we shall see that some impulses may be masked by causes of which we have not yet spoken.

TWO PRINCIPLES OF NON-UNIFORMITY IN INSTINCTS

Were one devising an abstract scheme, nothing would be easier than to discover from an animal's actions just how many instincts he possessed. He would react in one way only upon each class of objects with which his life had to deal; he would react in identically the same way upon every specimen of a class; and he would react invariably during his whole life. There would be no gaps among his instincts; all would come to light without perversion or disguise. But there are no such abstract animals, and nowhere does the instinctive life display itself in such a way. Not only, as we have seen, may objects of the same class arouse reactions of opposite sorts in consequence of slight changes in the circumstances, in the individual object, or in the agent's inward condition; but two other principles of which we have not yet spoken, may come into play and produce results so striking that observers as eminent as Messrs. D. A. Spalding and Romanes do not hesitate to call them 'derangements of the mental constitution,' and to conclude that the instinctive machinery has got out of gear.

These principles are those

1. Of the *inhibition of instincts by habits*; and
2. Of the *transitoriness of instincts.*

Taken in conjunction with the two former principles—that the same object may excite ambiguous impulses, or *suggest* an impulse different from that which it *excites,* by suggesting a remote object—they explain any amount of departure from uniformity of conduct, without implying any getting out of gear of the elementary impulses from which the conduct flows.

1. The law of inhibition of instincts by habits is this: *When objects of a certain class elicit from an animal a certain sort of reaction, it often happens that the animal becomes partial to the first specimen of the class on which it has reacted, and will not afterwards react on any other specimen.*

The selection of a particular hole to live in, of a particular mate, of a particular feeding-ground, a particular variety of diet, a particular anything, in short, out of a possible multitude, is a very wide-spread tendency among animals, even those low down in the scale. The limpet will return to the same sticking-place in its rock, and the lobster to its favorite nook on the sea-bottom. The rabbit will deposit its dung in the same corner; the bird makes its nest on the same bough. But each of these preferences carries with it an insensibility to *other* opportunities and occasions—an insensibility which can only be described physiologically as an inhibition of new impulses by the habit of old ones already formed. The possession of homes and wives of our own makes us strangely insensible to the charms of those of other people. Few of us are adventurous in the matter of food; in fact, most of us think there is something disgusting in a bill of fare to which we are unused. Strangers, we are apt to think, cannot be worth knowing, especially if they come from distant cities, etc. The original impulse which got us homes, wives, dietaries, and friends at all, seems to exhaust itself in its first achievements and to leave no surplus energy for reacting on new cases. And so it comes about that, witnessing this torpor, an observer of mankind might say that no *instinctive* propensity towards certain objects existed at all. It existed, but it existed *miscellaneously,* or as an instinct pure and simple, only before habit was formed. A habit, once grafted on an instinctive tendency, restricts the range of the tendency itself, and keeps us from reacting on any but the habitual object, although other objects might just as well have been chosen had they been the first-comers.

Another sort of arrest of instinct by habit is where the same class of objects awakens contrary instinctive impulses. Here the impulse first followed towards a given individual of the class is apt to keep him from ever awakening the opposite impulse in us. In fact, the whole class may be protected by this individual specimen from the application to it of the other impulse. Animals, for example, awaken in a child the opposite impulses of fearing and fondling. But if a child, in his first attempts to pat a dog, gets snapped at or bitten, so that the impulse of fear is strongly aroused, it may be that for years to come no dog will excite in him the impulse to fondle again. On the other hand, the greatest natural enemies, if carefully introduced to each other when young and guided at the outset by superior authority, settle down into those 'happy families' of friends which we see in our menageries. Young animals, immediately after birth, have no instinct of fear, but show their dependence by allowing themselves to be freely handled. Later, however, they grow 'wild,' and, if left to themselves, will not let man approach them. I am told by farmers in the Adirondack wilderness that it is a very serious matter if a cow wanders off and calves in the woods and is not found for a week or more. The calf, by that time, is as wild and almost as fleet as a deer, and hard to capture without violence. But calves rarely show any particular wildness to the men who have been in contact with them during the first days of their life, when the instinct to attach themselves is uppermost, nor do they dread strangers as they would if brought up wild.

Chickens give a curious illustration of the same law. Mr. Spalding's wonderful article on instinct shall supply us with the facts. These little creatures show opposite instincts of attachment and fear, either of which may be aroused by the same object, man. If a chick is born in the absence of the hen, it

"will follow any moving object. And, when guided by sight alone, they seem to have no more disposition to follow a hen than to follow a duck, or a human being. Unreflecting on-lookers, when they saw chickens a day old running after me," says Mr. Spalding, "and older ones following me miles and answering to my whistle, imagined that I must have some occult power over the creatures, whereas I simply allowed them to follow me from the first. There is the instinct to follow; and . . . their ear prior to experience attaches them to the right object."[5]

But if a man presents himself for the first time when the instinct of *fear* is strong, the phenomena are altogether reversed. Mr. Spalding kept three chickens hooded until they were nearly four days old, and thus describes their behavior:

"Each of these on being unhooded evinced the greatest terror of me, dashing off in the opposite direction whenever I sought to approach it. The table on which they were unhooded stood before a window, and each in its turn beat against the glass like a wild bird. One of them darted behind some books, and squeezing itself into a corner, remained cowering for a length of time. We might guess at the meaning of this strange and exceptional wildness; but the odd fact is enough for my present purpose. Whatever might have been the meaning of this marked change in their mental constitution—had they been unhooded on the previous day they would have run to me instead of from me—it could not have been the effect of experience; it must have resulted wholly from changes in their own organization."[6]

[5] Spalding: *Macmillan's Magazine*, Feb. 1873, p. 287.

[6] *Ibid.*, p. 289.

Their case was precisely analogous to that of the Adirondack calves. The two opposite instincts relative to the same object ripen in succession. If the first one engenders a habit, that habit will inhibit the application of the second instinct to that object. All animals are tame during the earliest phase of their infancy. Habits formed then limit the effects of whatever instincts of wildness may later be evolved.

Mr. Romanes gives some very curious examples of the way in which instinctive tendencies may be altered by the habits to which their first 'objects' have given rise. The cases are a little more complicated than those mentioned in the text, inasmuch as the object reacted on not only starts a habit which inhibits other kinds of impulse towards it (although such other kinds might be natural), but even modifies by its own peculiar conduct the constitution of the impulse which it actually awakens.

Two of the instances in question are those of hens who hatched out broods of chicks after having (in three previous years) hatched ducks. They strove to coax or to compel their new progeny to enter the water, and seemed much perplexed at their unwillingness. Another hen adopted a brood of young ferrets which, having lost their mother, were put under her. During all the time they were left with her she had to sit on the nest, for they could not wander like young chicks. She obeyed their hoarse growling as she would have obeyed her chickens' peep. She combed out their hair with her bill, and "used frequently to stop and look with one eye at the wriggling nest-full with an enquiring gaze expressive of astonishment." At other times she would fly up with a loud scream, doubtless because the orphans had nipped her in their search for teats. Finally, a Brahma hen nursed a young peacock during the enormous period of *eighteen months*, and never laid any eggs during all this time. The abnormal degree of pride which she showed in her wonderful chicken is described by Dr. Romanes as ludicrous.[7]

2. This leads us to the *law of transitoriness*, which is this: *Many instincts ripen at a certain age and then fade away*. A consequence of this law is that if, during the time of such an instinct's vivacity, objects adequate to arouse it are met with, a *habit* of acting on them is formed, which remains when the original instinct has passed away; but that if no such objects are met with, then no habit will be formed; and, later on in life, when the animal meets the

[7] For the cases in full see *Mental Evolution in Animals*, pp. 213–217.

objects, he will altogether fail to react, as at the earlier epoch he would instinctively have done.

No doubt such a law is restricted. Some instincts are far less transient than others—those connected with feeding and 'self-preservation' may hardly be transient at all—and some, after fading out for a time, recur as strong as ever, e.g., the instincts of pairing and rearing young. The law, however, though not absolute, is certainly very widespread, and a few examples will illustrate just what it means.

In the chickens and calves above mentioned it is obvious that the instinct to follow and become attached fades out after a few days, and that the instinct of flight then takes its place, the conduct of the creature towards man being decided by the formation or non-formation of a certain habit during those days. The transiency of the chicken's instinct to follow is also proved by its conduct towards the hen. Mr. Spalding kept some chickens shut up till they were comparatively old, and, speaking of these, he says:

"A chicken that has not heard the call of the mother until eight or ten days old then hears it as if it heard it not. I regret to find that on this point my notes are not so full as I could wish, or as they might have been. There is, however, an account of one chicken that could not be returned to the mother when ten days old. The hen followed it, and tried to entice it in every way; still it continually left her and ran to the house or to any person of whom it caught sight. This it persisted in doing, though beaten back with a small branch dozens of times, and indeed cruelly maltreated. It was also placed under the mother at night, but it again left her in the morning."

The instinct of sucking is ripe in all mammals at birth, and leads to that habit of taking the breast which, in the human infant, may be prolonged by daily exercise long beyond its usual term of a year or a year and a half. But the instinct itself is transient, in the sense that if, for any reason, the child be fed by spoon during the first few days of its life and not put to the breast, it may be no easy matter after that to make it suck at all. So of calves. If their mother die, or be dry, or refuse to let them suck for a day or two, so that they are fed by hand, it becomes hard to get them to suck at all when a new nurse is provided. The ease with which sucking creatures are weaned, by simply breaking the habit and giving them food in a new way, shows that the instinct, purely as such, must be entirely extinct.

Assuredly the simple fact that instincts are transient, and that the effect of later ones may be altered by the habits which earlier ones have left behind, is a far more philosophical explanation than the notion of an instinctive constitution vaguely 'deranged' or 'thrown out of gear.'

I have observed a Scotch terrier, born on the floor of a stable in December, and transferred six weeks later to a carpeted house, make, when he was less than four months old, a very elaborate pretence of burying things, such as gloves, etc., with which he had played till he was tired. He scratched the carpet with his fore-feet, dropped the object from his mouth upon the spot, and then scratched all about it (with both fore- and hind-feet, if I remember rightly), and finally went away and let it lie. Of course, the act was entirely useless. I saw him perform it at that age, some four or five times, and never again in his life. The conditions were not present to fix a habit which should last when the prompting instinct died away. But suppose meat instead of a glove, earth instead of a carpet, hunger-pangs instead of a fresh supper a few hours later, and it is easy to see how this dog might have got into a habit of burying superfluous food, which might have lasted all his life. Who can swear that the strictly instinctive part of the food-burying propensity in the wild *Canidæ* may not be as short-lived as it was in this terrier?

A similar instance is given by Dr. H. D. Schmidt[8] of New Orleans:

"I may cite the example of a young squirrel which I had tamed, a number of years ago, when serving in the army, and when I had sufficient leisure and opportunity to study the habits of animals. In the autumn before the winter sets in, adult squirrels bury as many nuts as they can collect separately in the ground. Holding the nut firmly between their teeth, they first scratch a hole in the ground, and after pointing their ears in all directions to convince themselves that no enemy is near, they ram—the head, with the nut still between the front teeth, serving as a sledge-hammer—the nut into the ground, and then fill up the hole by means of their paws. The whole process is executed with great rapidity, and, as it appeared to me, always with exactly the same movements; in fact, it is done so well that I could never discover the traces of the burial-ground. Now, as regards the young squirrel, which of course never had been present at the burial of a nut, I observed that,

[8] *Transactions of the American Neurological Association*, vol. 1, p. 129 (1875).

after having eaten a number of hickory nuts to appease its appetite, it would take one between its teeth, then sit upright and listen in all directions. Finding all right, it would scratch upon the smooth blanket, on which I was playing with it, as if to make a hole, then hammer with the nut between its teeth upon the blanket, and, finally, perform all the motions required to fill up a hole—*in the air*; after which it would jump away, leaving the nut of course uncovered."

The anecdote, of course, illustrates beautifully the close relation of instinct to reflex action—a particular perception calls forth particular movements, and that is all. Dr. Schmidt writes me that the squirrel in question soon passed away from his observation. It may fairly be presumed that, if he had been long retained prisoner in a cage, he would soon have forgotten his gesticulations over the hickory-nuts.

One might, indeed, go still further with safety, and expect that, if such a captive squirrel were then set free, he would never afterwards acquire this peculiar instinct of his tribe.[9]

Leaving lower animals aside, and turning to human instincts, we see the law of transiency corroborated on the widest scale by the alternation of different interests and passions as human life goes on. With the child, life is all play and fairy-tales and learning the external properties of 'things'; with the youth, it is bodily exercises of a more systematic sort, novels of the real world, boon-fellowship and song, friendship and love, nature, travel and adventure, science and philosophy; with the man, ambition and policy, acquisitiveness, responsibility to others, and the selfish zest of the battle of life. If a boy grows up alone at the age of games and sports, and learns neither to play ball, nor row, nor sail, nor ride, nor skate, nor fish, nor shoot, probably he will be sedentary to the end of his days; and, though the best of opportunities be afforded him for learning these things later, it is a hundred to one but he will pass them by and shrink back from the effort of taking those necessary first steps the prospect of which, at an earlier age, would have

[9] "Mr. Spalding," says Mr. Lewes (*Problems of Life and Mind*, prob. I, chap. II, § 22, note), "tells me of a friend of his who reared a gosling in the kitchen away from all water; when this bird was some months old, and was taken to a pond, it not only refused to go into the water, but when thrown in scrambled out again as a hen would have done. Here was an instinct entirely suppressed." See a similar observation on ducklings in T. R. R. Stebbing: *Essays on Darwinism* (London, 1871), p. 73.

filled him with eager delight. The sexual passion expires after a protracted reign; but it is well known that its peculiar manifestations in a given individual depend almost entirely on the habits he may form during the early period of its activity. Exposure to bad company then makes him a loose liver all his days; chastity kept at first makes the same easy later on. In all pedagogy the great thing is to strike the iron while hot, and to seize the wave of the pupil's interest in each successive subject before its ebb has come, so that knowledge may be got and a habit of skill acquired—a headway of interest, in short, secured, on which afterwards the individual may float. There is a happy moment for fixing skill in drawing, for making boys collectors in natural history, and presently dissectors and botanists; then for initiating them into the harmonies of mechanics and the wonders of physical and chemical law. Later, introspective psychology and the metaphysical and religious mysteries take their turn; and, last of all, the drama of human affairs and worldly wisdom in the widest sense of the term. In each of us a saturation-point is soon reached in all these things; the impetus of our purely intellectual zeal expires, and unless the topic be one associated with some urgent personal need that keeps our wits constantly whetted about it, we settle into an equilibrium, and live on what we learned when our interest was fresh and instinctive, without adding to the store. Outside of their own business, the ideas gained by men before they are twenty-five are practically the only ideas they shall have in their lives. They *cannot* get anything new. Disinterested curiosity is past, the mental grooves and channels set, the power of assimilation gone. If by chance we ever do learn anything about some entirely new topic we are afflicted with a strange sense of insecurity, and we fear to advance a resolute opinion. But with things learned in the plastic days of instinctive curiosity we never lose entirely our sense of being at home. There remains a kinship, a sentiment of intimate acquaintance, which, even when we know we have failed to keep abreast of the subject, flatters us with a sense of power over it, and makes us feel not altogether out of the pale.

Whatever individual exceptions might be cited to this are of the sort that 'prove the rule.'

To detect the moment of the instinctive readiness for the subject is, then, the first duty of every educator. As for the pupils, it would probably lead to a more earnest temper on the part of college students if they had less belief in their unlimited future intellectual potentialities, and could be brought to realize that whatever physics and political economy and philosophy they are now acquiring are, for better or worse, the physics and political economy and philosophy that will have to serve them to the end.

The natural conclusion to draw from this transiency of instincts is that *most instincts are implanted for the sake of giving rise to habits, and that, this purpose once accomplished, the instincts themselves, as such, have no raison d'être in the psychical economy, and consequently fade away.* That occasionally an instinct should fade before circumstances permit of a habit being formed, or that, if the habit be formed, other factors than the pure instinct should modify its course, need not surprise us. Life is full of the imperfect adjustment to individual cases, of arrangements which, taking the species as a whole, are quite orderly and regular. Instinct cannot be expected to escape this general risk.

SPECIAL HUMAN INSTINCTS

Let us now test our principles by turning to human instincts in more detail. We cannot pretend in these pages to be minute or exhaustive. But we can say enough to set all the above generalities in a more favorable light. But first, what kind of motor reactions upon objects shall we count as instincts? This, as aforesaid, is a somewhat arbitrary matter. Some of the actions aroused in us by objects go no further than our own bodies. Such is the bristling up of the attention when a novel object is perceived, or the 'expression' on the face or the breathing apparatus of an emotion it may excite. These movements merge into ordinary reflex actions like laughing when tickled, or making a wry face at a bad taste. Other actions take effect upon the outer world. Such are flight from a wild beast, imitation of what we see a comrade do, etc. On the whole it is best to be catholic, since it is very hard to draw an exact line; and call both of these kinds of activity instinctive, so far as either may be *naturally* provoked by the presence of specific sorts of outward fact.

Professor Preyer, in his careful little work, *Die Seele des Kindes*, says "instinctive acts are in man few in number, and, apart from those connected with the sexual passion, difficult to recognize after early youth is past." And he adds, "so much the more attention should we pay to the instinctive movements of new-born babies, sucklings, and small children." That instinctive acts should be easiest *recognized* in childhood would be a very natural effect of our principles of transitoriness, and of the restrictive influence of habits once acquired; but we shall see how far they are from being 'few in number' in man. Professor Preyer divides the movements of infants into *impulsive, reflex,* and *instinctive.* By impulsive movements he means *random* movements of limbs, body, and voice, with no aim, and before perception is aroused. Among the first reflex movements are crying on contact with the air, *sneezing, snuffling, snoring, coughing, sighing, sobbing, gagging, vomiting, hiccuping, starting, moving the limbs when tickled, touched, or blown upon,* etc., etc.

Of the movements called by him instinctive in the child, Professor Preyer gives a full account. Herr Schneider does the same; and as their descriptions agree with each other and with what other writers about infancy say, I will base my own very brief statement on theirs.

Sucking: almost perfect at birth; not coupled with any congenital tendency to *seek* the breast, this being a later acquisition. As we have seen, sucking is a transitory instinct.

Biting an object placed in the mouth, *chewing* and *grinding the teeth*; *licking* sugar; making characteristic *grimaces* over bitter and sweet tastes; *spitting*-out.

Clasping an object which touches the fingers or toes. Later, attempts to *grasp* at an object seen at a distance. *Pointing at* such objects, and making a peculiar *sound expressive of desire,* which, in my own three children, was the first manifestation of speech, occurring many weeks before other significant sounds.

Carrying to the mouth of the object, when grasped. This instinct, guided and inhibited by the sense of taste, and combined with the instincts of biting, chewing, sucking, spitting-out, etc., and with the reflex act of swallowing, leads in the individual to a set of habits which constitute his *function of alimentation,* and which may or may not be gradually modified as life goes on.

Crying at bodily discomfort, hunger, or pain, and at solitude. *Smiling* at being noticed, fondled, or smiled at by others. It seems very doubtful whether young infants have any instinctive fear of a terrible or scowling face. I have been unable to make my own children, under a year old, change their expression when I changed mine; at most they manifested attention or curiosity. Preyer instances a *protrusion of the lips,* which, he says, may be so great as to remind one of that in the chimpanzee, as an instinctive expression of concentrated attention in the human infant.

Turning the head aside as a gesture of rejection, a gesture usually accompanied with a frown and a bending back of the body, and with holding the breath.

Holding head erect.

Sitting up.

Standing.

Locomotion. The early movements of children's limbs are more or less symmetrical. Later a baby will move his legs in alternation if suspended in the air. But until the impulse to walk awakens by the natural ripening of the nerve-centres, it seems to make no difference how often the child's feet may be placed in contact with the ground; the legs remain limp, and do not respond to the sensation of contact in the soles by muscular contractions *pressing downwards.* No sooner, however, is the standing impulse born, than the child stiffens his legs and presses downwards as soon as he feels the floor. In some babies this is the first locomotory reaction. In others it is preceded by the instinct to *creep,* which arises, as I can testify, often in a very sudden way. Yesterday the baby sat quite contentedly wherever he was put; to-day it has become impossible to keep him sitting at all, so irresistible is the impulse, aroused by the sight of the floor, to throw himself forwards upon his hands. Usually the arms are too weak, and the ambitious little experimenter falls on his nose. But his perseverance is dauntless, and he ends in a few days by learning to travel rapidly around the room in the quadrupedal way. The position of the legs in 'creeping' varies much from one child to another. My own child, when creeping, was often observed to pick up objects from the floor with his mouth, a phenomenon which, as Dr. O. W. Holmes has remarked, like the early tendency to grasp with the toes, easily lends itself to interpretation as a reminiscence of prehuman ancestral habits.

The walking instinct may awaken with no less suddenness, and its entire education be completed within a week's compass, barring, of course, a little 'grogginess' in the gait. Individual infants vary enormously; but on the whole it is safe to say that the mode of development of these locomotor instincts is inconsistent with the account given by the older English associationist school, of their being results of the individual's education, due altogether to the gradual association of certain perceptions with certain haphazard movements and certain resultant pleasures. Mr. Bain has tried,[10] by describing the demeanor of new-born lambs, to show that locomotion is *learned* by a very rapid experience. But the observation recorded proves the faculty to be almost perfect from the first; and all others who have observed new-born calves, lambs, and pigs agree that in these animals the powers of standing and walking, and of interpreting the topographical significance of sights and sounds, are all but fully developed at birth. Often in animals who seem to be 'learning' to walk or fly the semblance is illusive. The awkwardness shown is not due to the fact that 'experience' has not yet been there to associate the successful movements and exclude the failures, but to the fact that the animal is beginning his attempts before the co-ordinating centres have quite ripened for their work. Mr. Spalding's observations on this point are conclusive as to birds.

"Birds," he says, "do not *learn* to fly. Two years ago I shut up five unfledged swallows in a small box not much larger than the nest from which they were taken. The little box, which had a wire front, was hung on the wall near the nest, and the young swallows were fed by their parents through the wires. In this confinement, where they could not even extend their wings, they were kept until after they were fully fledged. . . . On going to set the prisoners free, one was found dead . . . . The remaining four were allowed to escape one at a time. Two of these were perceptibly wavering and unsteady in their flight. One of them, after a flight of about ninety yards, disappeared among some trees." No. 3 and No. 4 "never flew against anything, nor was there, in their avoiding objects, any appreciable difference between them and the old birds. No. 3 swept round the Wellingtonia, and No. 4 rose over the hedge just as we see the old swallows doing every hour of the day. I have this summer verified these observations. Of two swallows I had similarly confined, one, on being set free, flew a yard or two too close to the ground, rose in the direction of a beech-tree, which it gracefully avoided; it was seen for a considerable time sweeping round the beeches and performing magnificent evolutions in the air high above them. The other, which was observed to beat the air with its wings more than usual, was soon lost to sight behind some trees. Titmice, tomtits, and wrens I have made the subjects of a similar experiment and with similar results."[11]

10 *Senses and the Intellect*, 3d ed., pp. 412–413, 675–676.
11 *Nature*, XII, 507 (1875).

In the light of this report, one may well be tempted to make a prediction about the human child, and say that if a baby were kept from getting on his feet for two or three weeks after the first impulse to walk had shown itself in him,—a small blister on each sole would do the business,—he might then be expected to walk about as well, through the mere ripening of his nerve-centres, as if the ordinary process of 'learning' had been allowed to occur during all the blistered time. It is to be hoped that some scientific widower, left alone with his offspring at the critical moment, may ere long test this suggestion on the living subject. *Climbing* on trees, fences, furniture, banisters, etc., is a well-marked instinctive propensity which ripens after the fourth year.

Vocalization. This may be either musical or significant. Very few weeks after birth the baby begins to express its spirits by emitting vowel sounds, as much during inspiration as during expiration, and will lie on its back cooing and gurgling to itself for nearly an hour. But this singing has nothing to do with speech. Speech is sound *significant.* During the second year a certain number of significant sounds are gradually acquired; but talking proper does not set in till the instinct to *imitate sounds* ripens in the nervous system; and this ripening seems in some children to be quite abrupt. Then speech grows rapidly in extent and perfection. The child imitates every word he hears uttered, and repeats it again and again with the most evident pleasure at his new power. At this time it is quite impossible to talk *with* him, for his condition is that of 'Echolalia,'—instead of answering the question, he simply reiterates it. The result is, however, that his vocabulary increases very fast; and little by little, with teaching from above, the young prattler understands, puts words together to express his own wants and perceptions, and even makes intelligent replies. From a speechless, he has become a speaking, animal. The interesting point with regard to this instinct is the oftentimes very sudden birth of the impulse to imitate sounds. Up to the date of its awakening the child may have been as devoid of it as a dog. Four days later his whole energy may be poured into this new channel. The habits of articulation formed during the plastic age of childhood are in most persons sufficient to inhibit the formation of new ones of a fundamentally different sort—witness the inevitable 'foreign accent' which distinguishes the speech of those who learn a language after early youth.

Imitation. The child's first words are in part vocables of his own invention, which his parents adopt, and which, as far as they go, form a new human tongue upon the earth; and in part they are his more or less successful imitations of words he hears the parents use. But the instinct of *imitating gestures* develops earlier than that of imitating sounds,—unless the sympathetic crying of a baby when it hears another cry may be reckoned as imitation of a sound. Professor Preyer speaks of his child imitating the protrusion of the father's lips in its fifteenth week. The various accomplishments of infancy, making 'pat-a-cake,' saying 'bye-bye,' 'blowing out the candle,' etc., usually fall well inside the limits of the first year. Later come all the various imitative games in which childhood revels, playing 'horse,' 'soldiers,' etc., etc. And from this time onwards man is essentially *the* imitative animal. His whole educability and in fact the whole history of civilization depend on this trait, which his strong tendencies to rivalry, jealousy, and acquisitiveness reinforce. '*Humani nihil a me alienum puto*,' is the motto of each individual of the species; and makes him, whenever another individual shows a power or superiority of any kind, restless until he can exhibit it himself. But apart from this kind of imitation, of which the psychological roots are complex, there is the more direct propensity to speak and walk and behave like others, usually without any conscious intention of so doing. And there is the imitative tendency which shows itself in large masses of men, and produces panics, and orgies, and frenzies of violence, and which only the rarest individuals can actively withstand. This sort of imitativeness is possessed by man in common with other gregarious animals, and is an instinct in the fullest sense of the term, being a blind impulse to act as soon as a certain perception occurs. It is particularly hard not to imitate gaping, laughing, or looking and running in a certain direction, if we see others doing so. Certain mesmerized subjects must automatically imitate whatever motion their operator makes before their eyes.[12] A successful piece of mimicry gives to both bystanders and mimic a peculiar kind of æsthetic pleasure. The dramatic impulse, the tendency to pretend one is someone else, contains this pleasure of mimicry as one of its elements. Another element seems to be a peculiar sense of power in stretching one's

12 See, for some excellent pedagogic remarks about *doing yourself* what you want to get your pupils to do, and not simply telling them to do it, Baumann, *Handbuch der Moral* (1879), p. 32 ff.

own personality so as to include that of a strange person. In young children this instinct often knows no bounds. For a few months in one of my children's third year, he literally hardly ever appeared in his own person. It was always, "Play I am So-and-so, and you are So-and-so, and the chair is such a thing, and then we'll do this or that." If you called him by his name, H., you invariably got the reply, "I'm not H., I'm a hyena, or a horse-car," or whatever the feigned object might be. He outwore this impulse after a time; but while it lasted, it had every appearance of being the automatic result of ideas, often suggested by perceptions, working out irresistible motor effects. Imitation shades into

Emulation or Rivalry, a very intense instinct, especially rife with young children, or at least especially undisguised. Everyone knows it. Nine-tenths of the work of the world is done by it. We know that if we do not do the task someone else will do it and get the credit, so we do it. It has very little connection with sympathy, but rather more with pugnacity, which we proceed in turn to consider.

Pugnacity; anger; resentment. In many respects man is the most ruthlessly ferocious of beasts. As with all gregarious animals, 'two souls,' as Faust says, 'dwell within his breast,' the one of sociability and helpfulness, the other of jealousy and antagonism to his mates. Though in a general way he cannot live without them, yet, as regards certain individuals, it often falls out that he cannot live with them either. Constrained to be a member of a tribe, he still has a right to decide, as far as in him lies, of which other members the tribe shall consist. Killing off a few obnoxious ones may often better the chances of those that remain. And killing off a neighboring tribe from whom no good thing comes, but only competition, may materially better the lot of the whole tribe. Hence the gory cradle, the *bellum omnium contra omnes*, in which our race was reared; hence the fickleness of human ties, the ease with which the foe of yesterday becomes the ally of to-day, the friend of to-day the enemy of tomorrow; hence the fact that we, the lineal representatives of the successful enactors of one scene of slaughter after another, must, whatever more pacific virtues we may also possess, still carry about with us, ready at any moment to burst into flame, the smouldering and sinister traits of character by means of which they lived through so many massacres, harming others, but themselves unharmed.

Sympathy is an emotion as to whose instinctiveness psychologists have held hot debate, some of them contending that it is no primitive endowment, but, originally at least, the result of a rapid calculation of the good consequences to ourselves of the sympathetic act. Such a calculation, at first conscious, would grow more unconscious as it became more habitual, and at last, tradition and association aiding, might prompt to actions which could not be distinguished from immediate impulses. It is hardly needful to argue against the falsity of this view. Some forms of sympathy, that of mother with child, for example, are surely primitive, and not intelligent forecasts of board and lodging and other support to be reaped in old age. Danger to the child blindly and instantaneously stimulates the mother to actions of alarm or defence. Menace or harm to the adult beloved or friend excites us in a corresponding way, often against all the dictates of prudence. It is true that sympathy does not necessarily follow from the mere fact of gregariousness. Cattle do not help a wounded comrade; on the contrary, they are more likely to dispatch him. But a dog will lick another sick dog, and even bring him food; and the sympathy of monkeys is proved by many observations to be strong. In man, then, we may lay it down that the sight of suffering or danger to others is a direct exciter of interest, and an immediate stimulus, if no complication hinders, to acts of relief. There is nothing unaccountable or pathological about this—nothing to justify Professor Bain's assimilation of it to the 'fixed ideas' of insanity, as 'clashing with the regular outgoings of the will.' It may be as primitive as any other 'outgoing,' and may be due to a random variation selected, quite as probably as gregariousness and maternal love are, even in Spencer's opinion, due to such variations.

It is true that sympathy is peculiarly liable to inhibition from other instincts which its stimulus may call forth. The traveller whom the good Samaritan rescued may well have prompted such instinctive fear or disgust in the priest and Levite who passed him by, that their sympathy could not come to the front. Then, of course, habits, reasoned reflections, and calculations may either check or reinforce one's sympathy; as may also the instincts of love or hate, if these exist, for the suffering individual. The hunting and pugnacious instincts, when aroused, also inhibit our sympathy absolutely. This accounts for the cruelty of collections of men hounding each other on to bait or torture a victim. The blood mounts to the eyes, and sympathy's chance is gone.[13]

The hunting instinct has an equally remote origin in the evolution of the race.[14] The hunting and the fighting instinct combine in many manifestations. They both support the emotion of anger; they combine in the fascination which stories of atrocity have for most minds; and the utterly blind excitement of giving the rein to our fury when our blood is up (an excitement whose intensity is greater than that of any other human passion save one) is only explicable as an impulse aboriginal in character, and having more to do with immediate and overwhelming tendencies to muscular discharge than to any possible reminiscences of effects of experience, or association of ideas. I say this here, because the pleasure of disinterested cruelty has been thought a paradox, and writers have sought to show that it is no primitive attribute of our nature, but rather a resultant of the subtile combination of other less malignant elements of mind. This is a hopeless task. If evolution and the survival of the fittest be true at all, the destruction of prey and of human rivals *must* have been among the most important of man's primitive functions, the fighting and the chasing instincts *must* have become ingrained. Certain perceptions *must* immediately, and without the intervention of inferences and ideas, have

13 Sympathy has been enormously written about in books on Ethics. A very good recent chapter is that by Thomas Fowler: *The Principles of Morals*, part II, chap. II.

14 "I must now refer to a very general passion which occurs in boys who are brought up naturally, especially in the country. Everyone knows what pleasure a boy takes in the sight of a butterfly, fish, crab or other animal, or of a bird's nest, and what a strong propensity he has for pulling apart, breaking, opening, and destroying all complex objects, how he delights in pulling out the wings and legs of flies, and tormenting one animal or another, how greedy he is to steal secret dainties, with what irresistible strength the plundering of birds' nests attracts him without his having the least intention of eating the eggs or the young birds. This fact has long been familiar, and is daily remarked by teachers; but an explanation of these impulses which follow upon a mere perception of the objects, without in most cases any representation being aroused of a future pleasure to be gained, has as yet been given by no one, and yet the impulses are very easy to explain. In many cases it will be said that the boy pulls things apart from curiosity. Quite correct: but whence comes this curiosity, this irresistible desire to open everything and see what is inside? What makes the boy take the eggs from the nest and destroy them when he never thinks of eating them? These are effects of an hereditary instinct, so strong that warnings and punishments are unable to counteract it." (Schneider: *Der menschliche Wille*, p. 224. See also *Der thierische Wille*, pp. 180–2.)

prompted emotions and motor discharges; and both the latter must, from the nature of the case, have been very violent, and therefore, when unchecked, of an intensely pleasurable kind. It is just because human bloodthirstiness is such a primitive part of us that it is so hard to eradicate, especially where a fight or a hunt is promised as part of the fun.[15]

As Rochefoucauld says, there is something in the misfortunes of our very friends that does not altogether displease us; and an apostle of peace will feel a certain vicious thrill run through him, and enjoy a vicarious brutality, as he turns to the column in his newspaper at the top of which 'Shocking Atrocity' stands printed in large capitals. See how the crowd flocks round a street-brawl! Consider the enormous annual sale of revolvers to persons, not one in a thousand of whom has any serious intention of using them, but of whom each one has his carnivorous self-consciousness agreeably tickled by the notion, as he clutches the handle of his weapon, that he will be rather a dangerous customer to meet. See the ignoble crew that escorts every great pugilist—parasites who feel as if the glory of his brutality rubbed off upon them, and whose darling hope, from day to day, is to arrange some set-to of which they may

[15] It is not surprising, in view of the facts of animal history and evolution, that the very special object blood should have become the stimulus for a very special interest and excitement. That the sight of it should make people faint is strange. Less so that a child who sees his blood flow should forthwith become much more frightened than by the mere feeling of the cut. Horned cattle often, though not always, become furiously excited at the smell of blood. In some abnormal human beings the sight or thought of it exerts a baleful fascination. "B. and his father were at a neighbour's one evening, and while paring apples, the old man accidentally cut his hand so severely as to cause the blood to flow profusely. B. was observed to become restless, nervous, pale, and to have undergone a peculiar change in demeanour. Taking advantage of the distraction produced by the accident, B. escaped from the house and proceeded to a neighbouring farm-yard, where he cut the throat of a horse, killing it." Dr. D. H. Tuke, commenting on this man's case (*Journal of Mental Science*, October 1885), speaks of the influence of blood upon him—his whole life had been one chain of cowardly atrocities—and continues: "There can be no doubt that with some individuals it constitutes a fascination. . . . We might speak of a *mania sanguinis*. Dr. Savage admitted a man from France into Bethlem Hospital some time ago, . . . one of whose earliest symptoms of insanity was the thirst for blood, which he endeavoured to satisfy by going to an abattoir in Paris. The man whose case I have brought forward had the same passion for gloating over blood, but had no attack of acute mania. The sight of blood . . . was distinctly a delight to him, and at any time blood aroused in him the worst elements of his nature. Instances will easily be recalled in which murderers, undoubtedly insane, have described the intense pleasure they experienced in the warm blood of children."

share the rapture without enduring the pains! The first blows at a prize-fight are apt to make a refined spectator sick; but his blood is soon up in favor of one party, and it will then seem as if the other fellow could not be banged and pounded and mangled enough—the refined spectator would like to reinforce the blows himself. Over the sinister orgies of blood of certain depraved and insane persons let a curtain be drawn, as well as over the ferocity with which otherwise fairly decent men may be animated, when (at the sacking of a town, for instance), the excitement of victory long delayed, the sudden freedom of rapine and of lust, the contagion of a crowd, and the impulse to imitate and outdo, all combine to swell the blind drunkenness of the killing-instinct, and carry it to its extreme. No! those who try to account for this from above downwards, as if it resulted from the consequences of the victory being rapidly inferred, and from the agreeable sentiments associated with them in the imagination, have missed the root of the matter. Our ferocity is blind, and can only be explained from *below*. Could we trace it back through our line of descent, we should see it taking more and more the form of a fatal reflex response, and at the same time becoming more and more the pure and direct emotion that it is.[16]

In childhood it takes this form. The boys who pull out grasshoppers' legs and butterflies' wings, and disembowel every frog they catch, have no *thought* at all about the matter. The creatures tempt their hands to a fascinating occupation, to which they have to yield. It is with them as with the 'boy-fiend' Jesse Pomeroy, who cut a little girl's throat, 'just to see how she'd act.' The normal provocatives of the impulse are all living beasts, great and small, towards which a contrary habit has not been formed—all human beings in whom we perceive a certain *intent* towards *us*, and a

16 "Bombonnel, having rolled with a panther to the border of a ravine, gets his head away from the open mouth of the animal, and by a prodigious effort rolls her into the abyss. He gets up, blinded, spitting a mass of blood, not knowing exactly what the situation is. He thinks only of one thing, that he shall probably die of his wounds, but that before dying he must take vengeance on the panther. 'I didn't think of my pain,' he tells us. 'Possessed entirely by the fury with which I was transported, I drew my hunting-knife, and not understanding what had become of the beast, I sought for her on every side in order to continue the struggle. It was in this plight that the Arabs found me when they arrived.'" (Quoted by Guyau: *Esquisse d'une morale sans obligation*, etc., p. 210.)

large number of human beings who offend us peremptorily, either by their look, or gait, or by some circumstance in their lives which we dislike. Inhibited by sympathy, and by reflection calling up impulses of an opposite kind, civilized men lose the habit of acting out their pugnacious instincts in a perfectly natural way, and a passing feeling of anger, with its comparatively faint bodily expressions, may be the limit of their physical combativeness. Such a feeling as this may, however, be aroused by a wide range of objects. Inanimate things, combinations of color and sound, bad bills of fare, may in persons who combine fastidious taste with an irascible temperament produce real ebullitions of rage. Though the female sex is often said to have less pugnacity than the male, the difference seems connected more with the extent of the motor consequences of the impulse than with its frequency. Women take offence and get angry, if anything, more easily than men, but their anger is inhibited by fear and other principles of their nature from expressing itself in blows. The hunting-instinct proper seems to be decidedly weaker in them than in men. The latter instinct is easily restricted by habit to certain objects, which become legitimate 'game,' while other things are spared. If the hunting-instinct be not exercised at all, it may even entirely die out, and a man may enjoy letting a wild creature live, even though he might easily kill it. Such a type is now becoming frequent; but there is no doubt that in the eyes of a child of nature such a personage would seem a sort of moral monster.

Fear is a reaction aroused by the same objects that arouse ferocity. The antagonism of the two is an interesting study in instinctive dynamics. We both fear, and wish to kill, anything that may kill us; and the question which of the two impulses we shall follow is usually decided by some one of those *collateral circumstances* of the particular case, to be moved by which is the mark of superior mental natures. Of course this introduces uncertainty into the reaction; but it is an uncertainty found in the higher brutes as well as in men, and ought not to be taken as proof that we are less instinctive than they. Fear has bodily expressions of an extremely energetic kind, and stands, beside lust and anger, as one of the three most exciting emotions of which our nature is susceptible. The progress from brute to man is characterized by nothing so much as by the decrease in frequency of proper occasions for fear.

In civilized life, in particular, it has at last become possible for large numbers of people to pass from the cradle to the grave without ever having had a pang of genuine fear. Many of us need an attack of mental disease to teach us the meaning of the word. Hence the possibility of so much blindly optimistic philosophy and religion. The atrocities of life become 'like a tale of little meaning tho' the words are strong'; we doubt if anything like *us* ever really was within the tiger's jaws, and conclude that the horrors we hear of are but a sort of painted tapestry for the chambers in which we lie so comfortably at peace with ourselves and with the world.

Be this as it may, fear is a genuine instinct, and one of the earliest shown by the human child. *Noises* seem especially to call it forth. Most noises from the outer world, to a child bred in the house, have no exact significance. They are simply startling. To quote a good observer, M. Perez:

"Children between three and ten months are less often alarmed by visual than by auditory impressions. In cats, from the fifteenth day, the contrary is the case. A child, three and a half months old, in the midst of the turmoil of a conflagration, in presence of the devouring flames and ruined walls, showed neither astonishment nor fear, but smiled at the woman who was taking care of him, while his parents were busy. The noise, however, of the trumpet of the firemen, who were approaching, and that of the wheels of the engine, made him start and cry. At this age I have never yet seen an infant startled at a flash of lightning, even when intense; but I have seen many of them alarmed at the voice of the thunder. . . . Thus fear comes rather by the ears than by the eyes, to the child without experience. It is natural that this should be reversed, or reduced, in animals organized to perceive danger afar. Accordingly, although I have never seen a child frightened at his first sight of fire, I have many a time seen young dogs, young cats, young chickens, and young birds frightened thereby. . . . I picked up some years ago a lost cat about a year old. Some months afterwards at the onset of cold weather I lit the fire in the grate of my study, which was her reception-room. She first looked at the flame in a very frightened way. I brought her near to it. She leaped away and ran to hide under the bed. Although the fire was lighted every day, it was not until the end of the winter that I could prevail upon her to stay upon a chair near it. The next winter, however, all apprehension had disappeared. . . . Let us, then, conclude that there are hereditary dispositions to fear, which are independent of experience, but which experiences may end by attenuating very considerably. In the human infant I believe them to be particularly connected with the ear."[17]

The effect of noise in heightening any terror we may feel in adult years is very marked. The *howling* of the storm, whether on sea or land, is a principal cause of our anxiety when exposed to it. The writer has been interested in noticing in his own person, while lying in bed, and kept awake by the wind outside, how invariably each loud gust of it arrested momentarily his heart. A dog, attacking us, is much more dreadful by reason of the noises he makes.

Strange men, and *strange animals*, either large or small, excite fear, but especially men or animals advancing towards us in a threatening way. This is entirely instinctive and antecedent to experience. Some children will cry with terror at their very first sight of a cat or dog, and it will often be impossible for weeks to make them touch it. Others will wish to fondle it almost immediately. Certain kinds of 'vermin,' especially spiders and snakes, seem to excite a fear unusually difficult to overcome. It is impossible to say how much of this difference is instinctive and how much the result of stories heard about these creatures. That the fear of 'vermin' ripens gradually, seemed to me to be proved in a child of my own to whom I gave a live frog once, at the age of six to eight months, and again when he was a year and a half old. The first time he seized it promptly, and holding it, in spite of its struggling, at last got its head into his mouth. He then let it crawl up his breast, and get upon his face, without showing alarm. But the second time, although he had seen no frog and heard no story about a frog between-whiles, it was almost impossible to induce him to touch it. Another child, a year old, eagerly took some very large spiders into his hand. At present he is afraid, but has been exposed meanwhile to the teachings of the nursery. One of my children from her birth upwards saw daily the pet pug-dog of the house, and never betrayed the slightest fear until she was (if I recollect rightly) about

[17] *La Psychologie de l'enfant*, pp. 72–75. In an account of a young gorilla quoted from Falkenstein, by R. Hartmann (*Anthropoid Apes*, International Scientific Series, vol. LII (New York, 1886), p. 265), it is said: "He very much disliked strange noises. Thunder, the rain falling on the skylight, and especially the long-drawn note of a pipe or trumpet threw him into such agitation as to cause a sudden affection of the digestive organs, and it became expedient to keep him at a distance. When he was slightly indisposed, we made use of this kind of music with results as successful as if we had administered purgative medicine."

eight months old. Then the instinct suddenly seemed to develop, and with such intensity that familiarity had no mitigating effect. She screamed whenever the dog entered the room, and for many months remained afraid to touch him. It is needless to say that no change in the pug's unfailingly friendly conduct had anything to do with this change of feeling in the child.

Preyer tells of a young child screaming with fear on being carried near to the *sea*. The great source of terror to infancy is solitude. The teleology of this is obvious, as is also that of the infant's expression of dismay—the never-failing cry—on waking up and finding himself alone.

Black things, and especially *dark places*, holes, caverns, etc., arouse a peculiarly gruesome fear. This fear, as well as that of solitude, of being 'lost,' are explained after a fashion by ancestral experience. Says Schneider:

"It is a fact that men, especially in childhood, fear to go into a dark cavern or a gloomy wood. This feeling of fear arises, to be sure, partly from the fact that we easily suspect that dangerous beasts may lurk in these localities—a suspicion due to stories we have heard and read. But, on the other hand, it is quite sure that this fear at a certain perception is also directly inherited. Children who have been carefully guarded from all ghost-stories are nevertheless terrified and cry if led into a dark place, especially if sounds are made there. Even an adult can easily observe that an uncomfortable timidity steals over him in a lonely wood at night, although he may have the fixed conviction that not the slightest danger is near.

"This feeling of fear occurs in many men even in their own house after dark, although it is much stronger in a dark cavern or forest. The fact of such instinctive fear is easily explicable when we consider that our savage ancestors through innumerable generations were accustomed to meet with dangerous beasts in caverns, especially bears, and were for the most part attacked by such beasts during the night and in the woods, and that thus an inseparable association between the perceptions of darkness, caverns, woods, and fear took place, and was inherited."[18]

High places cause fear of a peculiarly sickening sort, though here, again, individuals differ enormously. The utterly blind instinctive character of the motor impulses here is shown by the fact

[18] *Der menschliche Wille*, p. 224.

that they are almost always entirely unreasonable, but that reason is powerless to suppress them. That they are a mere incidental peculiarity of the nervous system, like liability to sea-sickness, or love of music, with no teleological significance, seems more than probable. The fear in question varies so much from one person to another, and its detrimental effects are so much more obvious than its uses, that it is hard to see how it could be a selected instinct. Man is anatomically one of the best fitted of animals for climbing about high places. The best psychical complement to this equipment would seem to be a 'level head' when there, not a dread of going there at all. In fact, the teleology of fear, beyond a certain point, is very dubious. Professor Mosso, in his interesting monograph, *La Paura* (which has been translated into French), concludes that many of its manifestations must be considered pathological rather than useful; Bain, in several places, expresses the same opinion; and this, I think, is surely the view which any observer without *a priori* prejudices must take. A certain amount of timidity obviously adapts us to the world we live in, but the *fear-paroxysm* is surely altogether harmful to him who is its prey.

Fear of the supernatural is one variety of fear. It is difficult to assign any normal object for this fear, unless it were a genuine ghost. But, in spite of psychical-research societies, science has not yet adopted ghosts; so we can only say that certain *ideas* of supernatural agency, associated with real circumstances, produce a peculiar kind of horror. This horror is probably explicable as the result of a combination of simpler horrors. To bring the ghostly terror to its maximum, many usual elements of the dreadful must combine, such as loneliness, darkness, inexplicable sounds, especially of a dismal character, moving figures half discerned (or, if discerned, of dreadful aspect), and a vertiginous baffling of the expectation. This last element, which is *intellectual*, is very important. It produces a strange emotional 'curdle' in our blood to see a process with which we are familiar deliberately taking an unwonted course. Anyone's heart would stop beating if he perceived his chair sliding unassisted across the floor. The lower animals appear to be sensitive to the mysteriously exceptional as well as ourselves. My friend Professor W. K. Brooks, of the Johns Hopkins University, told me of his large and noble dog being frightened into a sort of epileptic fit by a bone being drawn across the floor by a thread which the dog did not see. Darwin and Romanes have given similar experiences.[19] The idea of the supernatural involves that the usual should be set at naught. In the witch and hobgoblin supernatural, other elements still of fear are brought in—caverns, slime and ooze, vermin, corpses, and the like.[20] A human corpse seems normally to produce an instinctive dread, which is no doubt somewhat due to its mysteriousness, and which familiarity rapidly dispels. But, in view of the fact that cadaveric, reptilian, and underground horrors play so specific and constant a part in many nightmares and forms of delirium, it seems not altogether unwise to ask whether these forms of dreadful circumstance may not at a former period have been more normal objects of the environment than now. The ordinary cock-sure evolutionist ought to have no difficulty in explaining these terrors, and the scenery that provokes them, as relapses into the consciousness of the cave-men, a consciousness usually overlaid in us by experiences of more recent date.

There are certain other pathological fears, and certain peculiarities in the expression of ordinary fear, which might receive an explanatory light from ancestral conditions, even infra-human ones. In ordinary fear, one may either run, or remain semi-paralyzed. The latter condition reminds us of the so-called death-shamming instinct shown by many animals. Dr. Lindsay, in his work *Mind in the Lower Animals*, says this must require great self-command in those that practise it. But it is really no feigning of death at all, and requires no self-command. It is simply a terror-paralysis which has been so useful as to become hereditary. The beast of prey does not think the motionless bird, insect, or crustacean dead. He simply

19 Cf. Romanes: *Mental Evolution in Animals*, p. 156.

20 In the *Overland Monthly* for 1886, a most interesting article on Laura Bridgman's writings has been published by Mr. E. C. Sanford. Among other reminiscences of her early childhood, while she still knew nothing of the sign-language, the wonderful blind deaf-mute records the following item in her quaint language: " 'My Father [he was a farmer and probably did his own butchering] used to enter his kitchen bringing some killed animals in, and deposited them on one of sides of the room many times. as I perceived it, it make me shudder with terror because I did not know what the matter was. I hated to approach the dead. One morning I went to take a short walk with my Mother. I went into a snug house for some time. they took me into a room where there was a coffin. I put my hand in the coffin and felt something so queer; it frightened me unpleasantly. I found something dead wrapped in a silk h'd'k'f so carefully. It must have been a body that [had] had vitality. I did not like to venture to examine the body for I was confounded.' "

fails to notice them at all; because his senses, like ours, are much more strongly excited by a moving object than by a still one. It is the same instinct which leads a boy playing 'I spy' to hold his very breath when the seeker is near, and which makes the beast of prey himself in many cases motionlessly lie in wait for his victim or silently 'stalk' it, by rapid approaches alternated with periods of immobility. It is the opposite of the instinct which makes us jump up and down and move our arms when we wish to attract the notice of someone passing far away, and makes the shipwrecked sailor frantically wave a cloth upon the raft where he is floating when a distant sail appears. Now, may not the statue-like, crouching immobility of some melancholiacs, insane with general anxiety and fear of everything, be in some way connected with this old instinct? They can give no *reason* for their fear to move; but immobility makes them feel safer and more comfortable. Is not this the mental state of the 'feigning' animal?

Again, take the strange symptom which has been described of late years by the rather absurd name of *agoraphobia*. The patient is seized with palpitation and terror at the sight of any open place or broad street which he has to cross alone. He trembles, his knees bend, he may even faint at the idea. Where he has sufficient self-command he sometimes accomplishes the object by keeping safe under the lee of a vehicle going across, or joining himself to a knot of other people. But usually he slinks round the sides of the square, hugging the houses as closely as he can. This emotion has no utility in a civilized man, but when we notice the chronic agoraphobia of our domestic cats, and see the tenacious way in which many wild animals, especially rodents, cling to cover, and only venture on a dash across the open as a desperate measure—even then making for every stone or bunch of weeds which may give a momentary shelter—when we see this we are strongly tempted to ask whether such an odd kind of fear in us be not due to the accidental resurrection, through disease, of a sort of instinct which may in some of our ancestors have had a permanent and on the whole a useful part to play?

Appropriation or *Acquisitiveness.* The beginnings of acquisitiveness are seen in the impulse which very young children display, to snatch at, or beg for, any object which pleases their attention. Later, when they begin to speak, among the first words they emphasize are 'me' and 'mine.'[21] Their earliest quarrels with each other are about questions of ownership; and parents of twins soon learn that it conduces to a quiet house to buy all presents in impartial duplicate. Of the later evolution of the proprietary instinct I need not speak. Everyone knows how difficult a thing it is not to covet whatever pleasing thing we see, and how the sweetness of the thing often is as gall to us so long as it is another's. When another is in possession, the impulse to appropriate the thing often turns into the impulse to harm him—what is called *envy*, or *jealousy*, ensues. In civilized life the impulse to own is usually checked by a variety of considerations, and only passes over into action under circumstances legitimated by habit and common consent, an additional example of the way in which one instinctive tendency may be inhibited by others. A variety of the proprietary instinct is the impulse to form collections of the same sort of thing. It differs much in individuals, and shows in a striking way how instinct and habit interact. For, although a collection of any given thing—like postage-stamps—need not be begun by any given person, yet the chances are that if accidentally it *be* begun by a person with the collecting instinct, it will probably be continued. The chief interest of the objects, in the collector's eyes, is that they are a collection, and that they are his. Rivalry, to be sure, inflames this, as it does every other passion, yet the objects of a collector's mania need not be necessarily such as are generally in demand. Boys will collect anything that they see another boy collect, from pieces of chalk and peach-pits up to books and photographs. Out of a hundred students whom I questioned, only four or five had never collected anything.[22]

The associationist psychology denies that there is any blind primitive instinct to appropriate, and would explain all acquisitiveness, in the first instance, as a desire to secure the 'pleasures' which

[21] I lately saw a boy of five (who had been told the story of Hector and Achilles) teaching his younger brother, aged three, how to play Hector, while he himself should play Achilles, and chase him round the walls of Troy. Having armed themselves, Achilles advanced, shouting "Where's my Patroklos?" Whereupon the would-be Hector piped up, quite distracted from his *rôle*, "Where's *my* Patroklos? I want a Patroklos! I want a Patroklos!"—and broke up the game. Of what kind of a thing a Patroklos might be he had, of course, no notion—enough that his brother had one, for him to claim one too.

[22] In *The Nation* for September 3, 1885, President G. S. Hall has given some account of a statistical research on Boston school-boys, by Miss Wiltse, from which it appears that only nineteen out of two hundred and twenty-seven had made no collections.

the objects possessed may yield; and, secondly, as the association of the idea of pleasantness with the *holding* of the thing, even though the pleasure originally got by it was only gained through its expense or destruction. Thus the miser is shown to us as one who has transferred to the gold by which he may buy the goods of this life all the emotions which the goods themselves would yield; and who thereafter loves the gold for its own sake, preferring the means of pleasure to the pleasure itself. There can be little doubt that much of this analysis a broader view of the facts would have dispelled. 'The miser' is an abstraction. There are all kinds of misers. The common sort, the excessively niggardly man, simply exhibits the psychological law that the potential has often a far greater influence over our mind than the actual. A man will not marry now, because to do so puts an end to his indefinite potentialities of choice of a partner. He prefers the latter. He will not use open fires or wear his good clothes, because the day may come when he will have to use the furnace or dress in a worn-out coat, 'and then where will he be?' For him, better the actual evil than the fear of it; and so it is with the common lot of misers. Better to live poor now, with the *power* of living rich, than to live rich at the risk of losing the power. These men value their gold, not for its own sake, but for its powers. Demonetize it, and see how quickly they will get rid of it! The associationist theory is, as regards them, entirely at fault: they care nothing for the gold *in se*.

With other misers there combines itself with this preference of the power over the act the far more instinctive element of the simple collecting propensity. Everyone collects money, and when a man of petty ways is smitten with the collecting mania for this object he necessarily becomes a miser. Here again the associationist psychology is wholly at fault. The hoarding instinct prevails widely among animals as well as among men. Professor Silliman has thus described one of the hoards of the California wood-rat, made in an empty stove of an unoccupied house:

"'I found the outside to be composed entirely of spikes, all laid with symmetry, so as to present the points of the nails outward. In the centre of this mass was the nest, composed of finely divided fibres of hemp-packing. Interlaced with the spikes were the following:—About two dozen knives, forks, and spoons, all the butcher's knives, three in number; a large carving knife, fork, and steel, several large plugs of tobacco . . . an old purse containing some silver, matches and tobacco;

nearly all the small tools from the tool closets, among them several large augers . . . all of which must have been transported some distance, as they were originally stored in different parts of the house. . . . The outside casing of a silver watch was disposed of in one part of the pile, the glass of the same watch in another, and the works in still another.' "[23]

In every lunatic asylum we find the collecting instinct developing itself in an equally absurd way. Certain patients will spend all their time picking pins from the floor and hoarding them. Others collect bits of thread, buttons, or rags, and prize them exceedingly. Now, 'the Miser' *par excellence* of the popular imagination and of melodrama, the monster of squalor and misanthropy, is simply one of these mentally deranged persons. His intellect may in many matters be clear, but his instincts, especially that of ownership, are insane, and their insanity has no more to do with the association of ideas than with the precession of the equinoxes. As a matter of fact his hoarding usually is directed to money; but it also includes almost anything besides. Lately in a Massachusetts town there died a miser who principally hoarded newspapers. These had ended by so filling all the rooms of his good-sized house from floor to ceiling that his living-space was restricted to a few narrow channels between them. Even as I write, the morning paper gives an account of the emptying of a miser's den in Boston by the City Board of Health. What the owner hoarded is thus described:

"He gathered old newspapers, wrapping-paper, incapacitated umbrellas, canes, pieces of common wire, cast-off clothing, empty barrels, pieces of iron, old bones, battered tin-ware, fractured pots, and bushels of such miscellany as is to be found only at the city 'dump.' The empty barrels were filled, shelves were filled, every hole and corner was filled, and in order to make more storage-room, 'the hermit' covered his store-room with a network of ropes, and hung the ropes as full as they could hold of his curious collections. There was nothing one could think of that wasn't in that room. As a wood-sawyer, the old man had never thrown away a saw-blade or a wood-buck. The bucks were rheumatic and couldn't stand up, and the saw-blades were worn down to almost nothing in the middle. Some had been actually worn in two, but the ends were carefully saved and stored away. As a coal-heaver, the old man had never cast off a worn-out basket, and there were dozens of the remains of the old things, patched up with canvas and rope-yarns, in

[23] Quoted in Lindsay: *Mind in the Lower Animals*, vol. II, p. 151.

the store-room. There were at least two dozen old hats, fur, cloth, silk, and straw," etc.

Of course there may be a great many 'associations of ideas' in the miser's mind about the things he hoards. He is a thinking being, and must associate things; but, without an entirely blind impulse in this direction behind all his ideas, such practical results could never be reached.[24]

Kleptomania, as it is called, is an uncontrollable impulse to appropriate, occurring in persons whose 'associations of ideas' would naturally all be of a counteracting sort. Kleptomaniacs often promptly restore, or permit to be restored, what they have taken; so the impulse need not be to keep, but only to take. But elsewhere hoarding complicates the result. A gentleman, with whose case I am acquainted, was discovered, after his death, to have a hoard in his barn of all sorts of articles, mainly of a trumpery sort, but including pieces of silver which he had stolen from his own dining-room, and utensils which he had stolen from his own kitchen, and for which he had afterwards bought substitutes with his own money.

Constructiveness is as genuine and irresistible an instinct in man as in the bee or the beaver. Whatever things are plastic to his hands, those things he must remodel into shapes of his own, and the result of the remodelling, however useless it may be, gives him more pleasure than the original thing. The mania of young children for breaking and pulling apart whatever is given them is more often the expression of a rudimentary constructive impulse than of a destructive one. 'Blocks' are the playthings of which they are least apt to tire. Clothes, weapons, tools, habitations, and works of art are the result of the discoveries to which the plastic instinct leads, each individual starting where his forerunners left off, and tradition preserving all that once is gained. Clothing, where not necessitated by cold, is nothing but a sort of attempt to remodel the human body itself—an attempt still better shown in the various tattooings, tooth-filings, scarrings, and other mutilations that are practised by savage tribes. As for habitation, there can be no doubt that the instinct to seek a sheltered nook, open only on one side,

[24] Cf. Flint: *Mind,* vol. I, pp. 330–333; Sully: *ibid.,* p. 567. Most people probably have the *impulse* to keep bits of useless finery, old tools, pieces of once useful apparatus, etc.; but it is normally either inhibited at the outset by reflection, or, if yielded to, the objects soon grow displeasing and are thrown away.

into which he may retire and be safe, is in man quite as specific as the instinct of birds to build a nest. It is not necessarily in the shape of a shelter from wet and cold that the need comes before him, but he feels less *exposed* and more at home when not altogether unin-closed than when lying all abroad. Of course the utilitarian origin of this instinct is obvious. But to stick to bare facts at present and not to trace origins, we must admit that this instinct now exists, and probably always has existed, since man was man. Habits of the most complicated kind are reared upon it. But even in the midst of these habits we see the blind instinct cropping out; as, for example, in the fact that we feign a shelter within a shelter, by backing up beds in rooms with their heads against the wall, and never lying in them the other way—just as dogs prefer to get under or upon some piece of furniture to sleep, instead of lying in the middle of the room. The first habitations were caves and leafy grottoes, bettered by the hands; and we see children to-day, when playing in wild places, take the greatest delight in discovering and appropriating such retreats and 'playing house' there.

Play. The impulse to play in special ways is certainly instinctive. A boy can no more help running after another boy who runs provokingly near him, than a kitten can help running after a rolling ball. A child trying to get into its own hand some object which it sees another child pick up, and the latter trying to get away with the prize, are just as much slaves of an automatic prompting as are two chickens or fishes, of which one has taken a big morsel into its mouth and decamps with it, while the other darts after in pursuit. All simple active games are attempts to gain the excitement yielded by certain primitive instincts, through feigning that the occasions for their exercise are there. They involve imitation, hunting, fighting, rivalry, acquisitiveness, and construction, combined in various ways; their special rules are habits, discovered by accident, selected by intelligence, and propagated by tradition; but unless they were founded in automatic impulses, games would lose most of their zest. The sexes differ somewhat in their play-impulses. As Schneider says:

"The little boy imitates soldiers, models clay into an oven, builds houses, makes a wagon out of chairs, rides on horseback upon a stick, drives nails with the hammer, harnesses his brethren and comrades together and plays the stage-driver, or lets himself be captured as a wild horse by someone else. The girl, on the contrary, plays with her doll, washes and dresses it, strokes it, clasps and kisses it, puts it to bed and tucks it in, sings it a cradle-song, or speaks with it as if it were a living being. . . . This fact that a sexual difference exists in the play-impulse, that a boy gets more pleasure from a horse and rider and a soldier than from a doll, while with the girl the opposite is the case, is proof that an hereditary connection exists between the perception of certain things (horse, doll, etc.), and the feeling of pleasure, as well as between this latter and the impulse to play."[25]

There is another sort of human play, into which higher æsthetic feelings enter. I refer to that love of festivities, ceremonies, ordeals, etc., which seems to be universal in our species. The lowest savages have their dances, more or less formally conducted. The various religions have their solemn rites and exercises, and civic and military power symbolize their grandeur by processions and celebrations of divers sorts. We have our operas and parties and masquerades. An element common to all these ceremonial games, as they may be called, is the excitement of concerted action as one of an organized crowd. The same acts, performed with a crowd, seem to mean vastly more than when performed alone. A walk with the people on a holiday afternoon, an excursion to drink beer or coffee at a popular 'resort,' or an ordinary ball-room, are examples of this. Not only are we amused at seeing so many strangers, but there is a distinct stimulation at feeling our share in their collective life. The perception of them is the stimulus; and our reaction upon it is our tendency to join them and do what they are doing, and our unwillingness to be the first to leave off and go home alone. This seems a primitive element in our nature, as it is difficult to trace any association of ideas that could lead up to it; although, once granting it to exist, it is very easy to see what its uses to a tribe might be in facilitating prompt and vigorous collective action. The formation of armies and the undertaking of military expeditions would be among its fruits. In the ceremonial games it is but the impulsive starting point. What particular things the crowd then shall do, depends for the most part on the initiative of individuals, fixed by imitation and habit, and continued by tradition. The co-operation of other æsthetic pleasures with games, ceremonial or other, has a great deal to do with the selection of such as shall become stereotyped and habitual. The peculiar form of excitement called by Professor Bain the emotion of *pursuit*, the pleasure of a

[25] *Der menschliche Wille*, p. 205.

crescendo, is the soul of many common games. The immense extent of the play-activities in human life is too obvious to be more than mentioned.[26]

Curiosity. Already pretty low down among vertebrates we find that any object may excite attention, provided it be only *novel,* and that attention may be followed by approach and exploration by nostril, lips, or touch. Curiosity and fear form a couple of antagonistic emotions liable to be awakened by the same outward thing, and manifestly both useful to their possessor. The spectacle of their alternation is often amusing enough, as in the timid approaches and scared wheelings which sheep or cattle will make in the presence of some new object they are investigating. I have seen alligators in the water act in precisely the same way towards a man seated on the beach in front of them—gradually drawing near as long as he kept still, frantically careering back as soon as he made a movement. Inasmuch as new objects *may* always be advantageous, it is better that an animal should not *absolutely* fear them. But, inasmuch as they may also possibly be harmful, it is better that he should not be quite indifferent to them either, but on the whole remaining on the *qui vive,* ascertain as much about them, and what they may be likely to bring forth, as he can, before settling down to rest in their presence. Some such susceptibility for being excited and irritated by the mere novelty, as such, of any movable feature of the environment must form the instinctive basis of all human curiosity; though, of course, the superstructure absorbs contributions from so many other factors of the emotional life that the original root may be hard to find. With what is called scientific curiosity, and with metaphysical wonder, the practical instinctive root has probably nothing to do. The stimuli here are not objects, but ways of conceiving objects; and the emotions and actions they give rise to are to be classed, with many other æsthetic manifestations, sensitive and motor, as *incidental* features of our mental life. The philosophic brain responds to an inconsistency or a gap in its knowledge, just as the musical brain responds to a discord in what it hears. At certain ages the sensitiveness to particular gaps and the

26 Professor Lazarus (*Über die Reize des Spiels,* Berlin, 1883, p. 44) denies that we have an *instinct* to play, and says the root of the matter is the *aversion to remain unoccupied,* which substitutes a sham occupation when no real one is ready. No doubt this is true; but why the particular forms of sham occupation? The *elements* of all bodily games and of ceremonial games are given by direct excito-motor stimulations—just as when puppies chase one another and swallows have a parliament.

pleasure of resolving particular puzzles reach their maximum, and then it is that stores of scientific knowledge are easiest and most naturally laid in. But these effects may have had nothing to do with the uses for which the brain was originally given; and it is probably only within a few centuries, since religious beliefs and economic applications of science have played a prominent part in the conflicts of one race with another, that they may have helped to 'select' for survival a particular type of brain. I shall have to consider this matter of incidental and supernumerary faculties in Chapter XXVIII.

Sociability and Shyness. As a gregarious animal, man is excited both by the absence and by the presence of his kind. To be alone is one of the greatest of evils for him. Solitary confinement is by many regarded as a mode of torture too cruel and unnatural for civilized countries to adopt. To one long pent up on a desert island, the sight of a human footprint or a human form in the distance would be the most tumultuously exciting of experiences. In morbid states of mind, one of the commonest symptoms is the fear of being alone. This fear may be assuaged by the presence of a little child, or even of a baby. In a case of hydrophobia known to the writer, the patient insisted on keeping his room *crowded* with neighbors all the while, so intense was his fear of solitude. In a gregarious animal, the perception that he is alone excites him to vigorous activity. Mr. Galton thus describes the behavior of the South African cattle whom he had such good opportunities for observing:

> "Although the ox has little affection for, or individual interest in, his fellows, he cannot endure even a momentary severance from his herd. If he be separated from it by stratagem or force, he exhibits every sign of mental agony; he strives with all his might to get back again, and when he succeeds, he plunges into its middle to bathe his whole body with the comfort of closest companionship."[27]

Man is also excited by the presence of his kind. The *bizarre* actions of dogs meeting strange dogs are not altogether without a parallel in our own constitution. We cannot meet strangers without a certain tension, or talk to them exactly as to our familiars. This is particularly the case if the stranger be an important per-

[27] *Inquiries into Human Faculty,* p. 72.

sonage. It may then happen that we not only shrink from meeting his eye, but actually cannot collect our wits or do ourselves any sort of justice in his presence.

"This odd state of mind," says Darwin,[28] "is chiefly recognized by the face reddening, by the eyes being averted or cast down, and by awkward, nervous movements of the body. . . . Shyness seems to depend on sensitiveness to the opinion, whether good or bad, of others, more especially with respect to external appearance. Strangers neither know nor care anything about our conduct or character, but they may, and often do, criticize our appearance . . . . The consciousness of anything peculiar, or even new, in the dress, or any slight blemish on the person, and more especially on the face—points which are likely to attract the attention of strangers—makes the shy intolerably shy.[29] On the other hand, in those cases in which conduct and not personal appearance is concerned, we are much more apt to be shy in the presence of acquaintances, whose judgment we in some degree value, than in that of strangeers. . . . Some persons, however, are so sensitive, that the mere act of speaking to almost any one is sufficient to rouse their self-consciousness, and a slight blush is the result. Disapprobation . . . causes shyness and blushing much more readily than does approbation . . . . Persons who are exceedingly shy are rarely shy in the presence of those with whom they are quite familiar, and of whose good opinion and sympathy they are perfectly assured;—for instance, a girl in the presence of her mother. . . . Shyness . . . is closely related to fear; yet it is distinct from fear in the ordinary sense. A shy man dreads the notice of strangers, but can hardly be said to be afraid of them; he may be as bold as a hero in battle, and yet have no self-confidence about trifles in the presence of strangers. Almost every one is extremely nervous when first addressing a public assembly, and most men remain so throughout their lives."

As Mr. Darwin observes, a real dread of definite consequences may enter into this 'stage-fright' and complicate the shyness. Even so our shyness before an important personage may be complicated by what Professor Bain calls 'servile terror,' based on representation of definite dangers if we fail to please. But both stage-fright and servile terror may exist with the most indefinite apprehensions of danger, and, in fact, when our reason tells us there is no occasion for alarm. We must, therefore, admit a certain amount of purely

28 *The Expression of the Emotions in Man and Animals* (New York, 1873), p. 330.

29 "The certainty that we are well dressed," a charming woman has said, "gives us a peace of heart compared to which that yielded by the consolations of religion is as nothing."

instinctive perturbation and constraint, due to the consciousness that we have become objects for other people's eyes. Mr. Darwin goes on to say: "Shyness comes on at a very early age. In one of my own children, when two years and three months old, I saw a trace of what certainly appeared to be shyness, directed towards myself after an absence from home of only a week." Every parent has noticed the same sort of thing. Considering the despotic powers of rulers in savage tribes, respect and awe must, from time immemorial, have been emotions excited by certain individuals; and stage-fright, servile terror, and shyness, must have had as copious opportunities for exercise as at the present time. Whether these impulses could ever have been useful, and selected for usefulness, is a question which, it would seem, can only be answered in the negative. Apparently they are pure hindrances, like fainting at sight of blood or disease, sea-sickness, a dizzy head on high places, and certain squeamishnesses of æsthetic taste. They are *incidental* emotions, in spite of which we get along. But they seem to play an important part in the production of two other propensities, about the instinctive character of which a good deal of controversy has prevailed. I refer to cleanliness and modesty, to which we must proceed, but not before we have said a word about another impulse closely allied to shyness. I mean—

Secretiveness, which, although often due to intelligent calculation and the dread of betraying our interests in some more or less definitely foreseen way, is quite as often a blind propensity, serving no useful purpose, and is so stubborn and ineradicable a part of the character as fully to deserve a place among the instincts. Its natural stimuli are unfamiliar human beings, especially those whom we respect. Its reactions are the arrest of whatever we are saying or doing when such strangers draw nigh, coupled often with the pretense that we were not saying or doing that thing, but possibly something different. Often there is added to this a disposition to mendacity when asked to give an account of ourselves. With many persons the first impulse, when the door-bell rings, or a visitor is suddenly announced, is to scuttle out of the room, so as not to be 'caught.' When a person at whom we have been looking becomes aware of us, our immediate impulse may be to look the other way, and pretend we have not seen him. Many friends have confessed to me that this is a frequent phenomenon with them in meeting acquaintances in the street, especially unfamiliar ones.

The bow is a secondary correction of the primary feint that we do not see the other person. Probably most readers will recognize in themselves, at least, the *start*, the nascent disposition, on many occasions, to act in each and all of these several ways. That the 'start' is neutralized by second thought proves it to come from a deeper region than thought. There is unquestionably a native impulse in everyone to conceal love-affairs, and the acquired impulse to conceal pecuniary affairs seems in many to be almost equally strong. It is to be noted that even where a given habit of concealment is reflective and deliberate, its motive is far less often definite prudence than a vague aversion to have one's sanctity invaded and one's personal concerns fingered and turned over by other people. Thus, some persons will never leave anything with their name written on it, where others may pick it up—even in the woods, an old envelope must not be thrown on the ground. Many cut all the leaves of a book of which they may be reading a single chapter, so that no one shall know which one they have singled out, and all this with no *definite* notion of harm. The impulse to conceal is more apt to be provoked by superiors than by equals or inferiors. How differently do boys talk together when their parents are not by! Servants see more of their masters' characters than masters of servants'.[30] Where we conceal from our equals and familiars, there is probably always a definite element of prudential prevision involved. *Collective* secrecy, mystery, enters into the emotional interest of many games, and is one of the elements of the importance men attach to freemasonries of various sorts, being delightful apart from any end.

Cleanliness. Seeing how very filthy savages and exceptional individuals among civilized people may be, philosophers have

30 Thackeray, in his exquisite *Roundabout Paper*, "On a Chalk-Mark on the Door," says: "You get truth habitually from equals only; so my good Mr. Holyshade, don't talk to me about the habitual candour of the young Etonian of high birth, or I have my own opinion of *your* candour or discernment when you do. No. Tom Bowling is the soul of honour and has been true to Black-eyed Syousan since the last time they parted at Wapping Old Stairs; but do you suppose Tom is perfectly frank, familiar, and above-board in his conversation with Admiral Nelson, K.C.B.? There are secrets, prevarications, fibs, if you will, between Tom and the Admiral —between your crew (of servants) and *their* captain. I know I hire a worthy, clean, agreeable, and conscientious male or female hypocrite, at so many guineas a year, to do so and so for me. Were he other than hypocrite I would send him about his business."

doubted whether any genuine instinct of cleanliness exists, and whether education and habit be not responsible for whatever amount of it is found. Were it an instinct, its stimulus would be dirt, and its characteristic reaction the shrinking from contact therewith, and the cleaning of it away after contact had occurred. Now, if some animals are cleanly, men *may* be so, and there can be no doubt that some kinds of matter *are* natively repugnant, both to sight, touch, and smell—excrementitious and putrid things, blood, pus, entrails, and diseased tissues, for example. It is true that the shrinking from contact with these things may be inhibited very easily, as by a medical education; and it is equally true that the impulse to clean them away may be inhibited by so slight an obstacle as the thought of the coldness of the ablution, or the necessity of getting up to perform it. It is also true that an impulse to cleanliness, habitually checked, will become obsolete fast enough. But none of these facts prove the impulse never to have been there.[31] It seems to be there in all cases; and then to be particularly amenable to outside influences, the child having his own degree of squeamishness about what he shall touch or eat, and later being either hardened or made more fastidious still by the habits he is forced to acquire and the examples among which he lives.

Examples get their hold on him in this way, that a particularly evil-smelling or catarrhal or lousy comrade is rather offensive to him, and that he sees the odiousness in another of an amount of dirt to which he would have no spontaneous objection if it were on his own skin. That *we dislike in others things which we tolerate in ourselves* is a law of our æsthetic nature about which there can be no doubt. But as soon as generalization and reflection step in, this judging of others leads to a new way of regarding ourselves. "Who taught you politeness? The impolite," is, I believe, a Chinese proverb. The concept, 'dirty fellow,' which we have formed, becomes one under which we personally shrink from being classed; and so we 'wash up,' and set ourselves right, at moments when our social self-consciousness is awakened, in a manner towards which no strictly instinctive native prompting exists. But the standard of

31 The insane symptom called "mysophobia," or dread of foulness, which leads a patient to wash his hands perhaps a hundred times a day, hardly seems explicable without supposing a primitive impulse to clean one's self of which it is, as it were, the convulsive exaggeration.

cleanliness attained in this way is not likely to go beyond the mutual tolerance for one another of the members of the tribe, and hence may comport a good deal of actual filth.

Modesty, Shame. Whether there be an instinctive impulse to hide certain parts of the body and certain acts is perhaps even more open to doubt than whether there be an instinct of cleanliness. Anthropologists have denied it, and in the utter shamelessness of infancy and of many savage tribes have seemed to find a good basis for their views. It must, however, be remembered that infancy proves nothing, and that, as far as sexual modesty goes, the sexual impulse itself works directly against it at times of excitement, and with reference to certain people; and that habits of immodesty contracted with those people may forever afterwards inhibit any impulse to be modest towards *them*. This would account for a great deal of actual immodesty, even if an original modest impulse were there. On the other hand, the modest impulse, if it do exist, must be admitted to have a singularly ill-defined sphere of influence, both as regards the presences that call it forth, and as regards the acts to which it leads. Ethnology shows it to have very little backbone of its own, and to follow easily fashion and example. Still, it is hard to see the ubiquity of *some* sort of tribute to shame, however perverted—as where female modesty consists in covering the face alone, or immodesty in appearing before strangers unpainted—and to believe it to have no impulsive root whatever. Now, what may the impulsive root be? I believe that, for one thing, it is shyness, the feeling of dread that unfamiliar persons, as explained above, may inspire us withal. Such persons are the original stimuli to our modesty.[32] But the actions of modesty are quite different from the actions of shyness. They consist of the restraint of certain bodily functions, and of the covering of certain parts; and why do such particular actions necessarily ensue? That there *may* be in the human animal, as such, a 'blind' and immediate automatic impulse to such restraints and coverings in respect-inspiring presences is a possibility difficult of actual disproof. But it seems more likely, from the facts, that the actions of modesty are suggested to us in a

32 "We often find modesty coming in only in the presence of foreigners, especially of clothed Europeans. Only before these do the Indian women in Brazil cover themselves with their girdle, only before these do the women on Timor conceal their bosom. In Australia we find the same thing happening." (Theodor Waitz: *Anthropologie der Naturvölker*, vol. I, p. 358.) The author gives bibliographical references, which I omit.

roundabout way; and that, even more than those of cleanliness, they arise from the application in the second instance to ourselves of judgments primarily passed upon our mates. It is not easy to believe that, even among the nakedest savages, an unusual degree of cynicism and indecency in an individual should not beget a certain degree of contempt, and cheapen him in his neighbor's eyes. Human nature is sufficiently homogeneous for us to be sure that everywhere reserve must inspire some respect, and that persons who suffer every liberty are persons whom others disregard. Not to be like such people, then, would be one of the first resolutions suggested by social self-consciousness to a child of nature just emerging from the unreflective state. And the resolution would probably acquire effective pungency for the first time when the social self-consciousness was sharpened into a real fit of shyness by some person being present whom it was important not to disgust or displease. Public opinion would of course go on to build its positive precepts upon this germ; and, through a variety of examples and experiences, the ritual of modesty would grow, until it reached the New England pitch of sensitiveness and range, making us say stomach instead of belly, limb instead of leg, retire instead of go to bed, and forbidding us to call a female dog by name.

At bottom this amounts to the admission that, though in some shape or other a natural and inevitable feature of human life, modesty need not necessarily be an instinct in the pure and simple excito-motor sense of the term.

Love. Of all propensities, the sexual impulses bear on their face the most obvious signs of being instinctive, in the sense of blind, automatic, and untaught. The teleology they contain is often at variance with the wishes of the individuals concerned; and the actions are performed for no assignable reason but because Nature urges just that way. Here, if ever, then, we ought to find those characters of fatality, infallibility, and uniformity, which, we are told, make of actions done from instinct a class so utterly apart. But is this so? The facts are just the reverse: the sexual instinct is particularly liable to be checked and modified by slight differences in the individual stimulus, by the inward condition of the agent himself, by habits once acquired, and by the antagonism of contrary impulses operating on the mind. One of these is the ordinary shyness recently described; another is what might be called the *anti-sexual instinct*, the instinct of personal isolation, the actual repulsiveness to us of the idea of intimate contact with most of the persons we meet, especially those of our own sex.[33] Thus it comes about that this strongest passion of all, so far from being the most 'irresistible,' may, on the contrary, be the hardest one to give rein to, and that individuals in whom the inhibiting influences are potent may pass through life and never find an occasion to have it gratified. There could be no better proof of the truth of that proposition with which we began our study of the instinctive life in man, that irregularity of behavior may come as well from the possession of too many instincts as from the lack of any at all.

The instinct of personal isolation, of which we have spoken, exists more strongly in men with respect to one another, and more strongly in women with respect to men. In women it is called coyness, and has to be positively overcome by a process of wooing before the sexual instinct inhibits it and takes its place. As Darwin has shown in his book on the *Descent of Man and Sexual Selection*, it has played a vital part in the amelioration of all higher animal types, and is to a great degree responsible for whatever degree of chastity the human race may show. It illustrates strikingly, however, the law of the inhibition of instincts by habits—for, once broken through with a given person, it is not apt to assert itself again; and habitually broken through, as by prostitutes, with various persons, it may altogether decay. Habit also fixes it in us towards certain individuals: nothing is so particularly displeasing as the notion of close personal contact with those whom we have long known in a respectful and distant way. The fondness of the ancients and of modern Orientals for forms of unnatural vice, of which the notion affects us with horror, is probably a mere case of the way in which this instinct may be inhibited by habit. We can hardly suppose that the ancients had by gift of Nature a propensity of which we are devoid, and were all victims of what is now a pathological aberration limited to individuals. It is more probable that with them the instinct of physical aversion towards a certain class of objects was inhibited early in life by *habits*, formed under the influence of *example*; and that then a kind of sexual appetite, of which very likely most men possess the germinal possibility, developed itself in an unrestricted way. That the development of it in an abnormal way may check its development in the normal way,

[33] To most of us it is even unpleasant to sit down in a chair still warm from occupancy by another person's body. To many, hand-shaking is disagreeable.

seems to be a well-ascertained medical fact. And that the direction of the sexual instinct towards one individual tends to inhibit its application to other individuals, is a law, upon which, though it suffers many exceptions, the whole *régime* of monogamy is based. These details are a little unpleasant to discuss, but they show so beautifully the correctness of the general principles in the light of which our review has been made, that it was impossible to pass them over unremarked.

Jealousy is unquestionably instinctive.

Parental Love is an instinct stronger in woman than in man, at least in the early childhood of its object. I need do little more than quote Schneider's lively description of it as it exists in her:

"As soon as a wife becomes a mother her whole thought and feeling, her whole being, is altered. Until then she had only thought of her own well-being, of the satisfaction of her vanity; the whole world appeared made only for her; everything that went on about her was only noticed so far as it had personal reference to herself; she asked of everyone that he should appear interested in her, pay her the requisite attention, and as far as possible fulfil her wishes. Now, however, the centre of the world is no longer herself, but her child. She does not think of her own hunger, she must first be sure that the child is fed. It is nothing to her that she herself is tired and needs rest, so long as she sees that the child's sleep is disturbed; the moment it stirs she awakes, though far stronger noises fail to arouse her now. She, who formerly could not bear the slightest carelessness of dress, and touched everything with gloves, allows herself to be soiled by the infant, and does not shrink from seizing its clouts with her naked hands. Now, she has the greatest patience with the ugly, piping cry-baby (*Schreihals*), whereas until now every discordant sound, every slightly unpleasant noise, made her nervous. Every limb of the still hideous little being appears to her beautiful, every movement fills her with delight. She has, in one word, transferred her entire egoism to the child, and lives only in it. Thus, at least, it is in all unspoiled, naturally-bred mothers, who, alas! seem to be growing rarer; and thus it is with all the higher animal-mothers. The maternal joys of a cat, for example, are not to be disguised. With an expression of infinite comfort she stretches out her fore-legs to offer her teats to her children, and moves her tail with delight when the little hungry mouths tug and suck. . . . But not only the contact, the bare look of the offspring affords endless delight, not only because the mother thinks that the child will some day grow great and handsome and bring her many joys, but because she has received from Nature an instinctive love for her children. She does not herself know why she is so happy, and why the look of the child and the care of it are so agreeable, any more than the young man can give an account of why he loves a maiden, and is so happy when she is near. Few mothers, in caring for their child, think of the proper purpose of maternal love for the preservation of the species. Such a thought may arise in the father's mind; seldom in that of the mother. The latter feels only . . . that it is an everlasting delight to hold the being which she has brought forth protectingly in her arms, to dress it, to wash it, to rock it to sleep, or to still its hunger."

So far the worthy Schneider, to whose words may be added this remark, that the passionate devotion of a mother—ill herself, perhaps—to a sick or dying child is perhaps the most simply beautiful moral spectacle that human life affords. Contemning every danger, triumphing over every difficulty, outlasting all fatigue, woman's love is here invincibly superior to anything that man can show.

These are the most prominent of the tendencies which are worthy of being called instinctive in the human species.[34] It will be observed that *no other mammal, not even the monkey, shows so large an array.* In a perfectly-rounded development every one of these instincts would start a habit towards certain objects and inhibit a habit towards certain others. Usually this is the case; but, in

[34] Some will, of course, find the list too large, others too small. With the boundaries of instinct fading into reflex action below, and into acquired habit or suggested activity above, it is likely that there will always be controversy about just what to include under the class-name. Shall we add the propensity to walk along a curbstone, or any other narrow path, to the list of instincts? Shall we subtract secretiveness, as due to shyness or to fear? Who knows? Meanwhile our physiological method has this inestimable advantage, that such questions of limit have neither theoretical nor practical importance. The facts once noted, it matters little how they are named. Most authors give a shorter list than that in the text. The phrenologists add adhesiveness, inhabitiveness, love of approbation, etc., etc., to their list of 'sentiments,' which in the main agree with our list of instincts. Fortlage, in his *System der Psychologie*, classes among the *Triebe* all the vegetative physiological functions. Santlus (*Zur Psychologie der menschlischen Triebe*, Leipzig, 1864) says there are at bottom but three instincts, that of 'Being,' that of 'Function,' and that of 'Life.' The 'Instinct of Being' he subdivides into *animal*, embracing the activities of all the senses; and *psychical*, embracing the acts of the intellect and of the 'transempiric consciousness.' The 'Instinct of Function' he divides into *sexual*, *inclinational* (friendship, attachment, honor); and *moral* (religion, philanthropy, faith, truth, moral freedom, etc.). The 'Instinct of Life' embraces *conservation* (nutrition, motion); *sociability* (imitation, juridical and ethical arrangements); and *personal interest* (love of independence and freedom, acquisitiveness, self-defence). Such a muddled list as this shows how great are the advantages of the physiological analysis we have used.

the one-sided development of civilized life, it happens that the timely age goes by in a sort of starvation of objects, and the individual then grows up with gaps in his psychic constitution which future experiences can never fill. Compare the accomplished gentleman with the poor artisan or tradesman of a city: during the adolescence of the former, objects appropriate to his growing interests, bodily and mental, were offered as fast as the interests awoke, and, as a consequence, he is armed and equipped at every angle to meet the world. Sport came to the rescue and completed his education where real things were lacking. He has tasted of the essence of every side of human life, being sailor, hunter, athlete, scholar, fighter, talker, dandy, man of affairs, etc., all in one. Over the city poor boy's youth no such golden opportunities were hung, and in his manhood no desires for most of them exist. Fortunate it is for him if gaps are the only anomalies his instinctive life presents; perversions are too often the fruit of his unnatural bringing-up.

Chapter XXV[*]

The Emotions

In speaking of the instincts it has been impossible to keep them separate from the emotional excitements which go with them. Objects of rage, love, fear, etc., not only prompt a man to outward deeds, but provoke characteristic alterations in his attitude and visage, and affect his breathing, circulation, and other organic functions in specific ways. When the outward deeds are inhibited, these latter emotional expressions still remain, and we read the anger in the face, though the blow may not be struck, and the fear betrays itself in voice and color, though one may suppress all other sign. *Instinctive reactions and emotional expressions thus shade imperceptibly into each other. Every object that excites an instinct excites an emotion as well.* Emotions, however, fall short of instincts, in that the emotional reaction usually terminates in the subject's own body, whilst the instinctive reaction is apt to go farther and enter into practical relations with the exciting object.

Emotional reactions are often excited by objects with which we have no practical dealings. A ludicrous object, for example, or a beautiful object are not necessarily objects to which we *do* anything; we simply laugh, or stand in admiration, as the case may be. The class of emotional, is thus rather larger than that of instinctive, impulses, commonly so called. Its stimuli are more numerous, and its expressions are more internal and delicate, and often less

* Parts of this chapter have already appeared in an article published in 1884 in *Mind*.

practical. The physiological plan and essence of the two classes of impulse, however, is the same.

As with instincts, so with emotions, the mere memory or imagination of the object may suffice to liberate the excitement. One may get angrier in thinking over one's insult than at the moment of receiving it; and we melt more over a mother who is dead than we ever did when she was living. In the rest of the chapter I shall use the word *object* of emotion indifferently to mean one which is physically present or one which is merely thought of.

It would be tedious to go through a complete list of the reactions which characterize the various emotions. For that the special treatises must be referred to. A few examples of their variety, however, ought to find a place here. Let me begin with the manifestations of Grief as a Danish physiologist, C. Lange, describes them:[1]

"The chief feature in the physiognomy of grief is perhaps its paralyzing effect on the voluntary movements. This effect is by no means as extreme as that which fright produces, being seldom more than that degree of weakening which makes it cost an effort to perform actions usually done with ease. It is, in other words, a feeling of weariness; and (as in all weariness) movements are made slowly, heavily, without strength, unwillingly, and with exertion, and are limited to the fewest possible. By this the grieving person gets his outward stamp: he walks slowly, unsteadily, dragging his feet and hanging his arms. His voice is weak and without resonance, in consequence of the feeble activity of the muscles of expiration and of the larynx. He prefers to sit still, sunk in himself and silent. The tonicity or 'latent innervation' of the muscles is strikingly diminished. The neck is bent, the head hangs ('bowed down' with grief), the relaxation of the cheek- and jaw-muscles makes the face look long and narrow, the jaw may even hang open. The eyes appear large, as is always the case where the *orbicularis* muscle is paralyzed, but they may often be partly covered by the upper lid which droops in consequence of the laming of its own *levator*. With this condition of weakness of the voluntary nerve- and muscle-apparatus of the whole body, there coexists, as aforesaid, just as in all states of similar motor weakness, a subjective feeling of weariness and heaviness, of something which weighs upon one; one feels 'downcast,' 'oppressed,' 'laden,' one speaks of his 'weight of sorrow,' one must 'bear up' under it, just as one must 'keep down' his anger. Many there are who 'succumb' to sorrow to such a degree that they literally cannot stand upright, but sink or lean against surrounding objects, fall on their knees,

[1] *Über Gemüthsbewegungen*, übersetzt von H. Kurella (Leipzig, 1887).

or, like Romeo in the monk's cell, throw themselves upon the earth in their despair.

"But this weakness of the entire voluntary motor apparatus (the so-called apparatus of 'animal' life) is only one side of the physiology of grief. Another side, hardly less important, and in its consequences perhaps even more so, belongs to another subdivision of the motor apparatus, namely, the involuntary or 'organic' muscles, especially those which are found in the walls of the blood-vessels, and the use of which is, by contracting, to diminish the latter's calibre. These muscles and their nerves, forming together the 'vaso-motor apparatus,' act in grief contrarily to the voluntary motor apparatus. Instead of being paralyzed, like the latter, the vascular muscles are more strongly contracted than usual, so that the tissues and organs of the body become anæmic. The immediate consequence of this bloodlessness is pallor and shrunkenness, and the pale color and collapsed features are the peculiarities which, in connection with the relaxation of the visage, give to the victim of grief his characteristic physiognomy, and often give an impression of emaciation which ensues too rapidly to be possibly due to real disturbance of nutrition, or waste uncompensated by repair. Another regular consequence of the bloodlessness of the skin is a feeling of cold, and shivering. A constant symptom of grief is sensitiveness to cold, and difficulty in keeping warm. In grief, the inner organs are unquestionably anæmic as well as the skin. This is of course not obvious to the eye, but many phenomena prove it. Such is the diminution of the various secretions, at least of such as are accessible to observation. The mouth grows dry, the tongue sticky, and a bitter taste ensues which, it would appear, is only a consequence of the tongue's dryness. [The expression 'bitter sorrow' may possibly arise from this.] In nursing women the milk diminishes or altogether dries up. There is one of the most regular manifestations of grief, which apparently contradicts these other physiological phenomena, and that is the weeping, with its profuse secretion of tears, its swollen reddened face, red eyes, and augmented secretion from the nasal mucous membrane."

Lange goes on to suggest that this may be a reaction from a previously contracted vaso-motor state. The explanation seems a forced one. The fact is that there are changeable expressions of grief. The weeping is as apt as not to be immediate, especially in women and children. Some men can never weep. The tearful and the dry phases alternate in all who can weep, sobbing storms being followed by periods of calm; and the shrunken, cold, and pale condition which Lange describes so well is more characteristic of a severe settled sorrow than of an acute mental pain. Properly we have two distinct emotions here, both prompted by the same object, it is true, but affecting different persons, or the same person at different times, and *feeling* quite differently whilst they last, as anyone's consciousness will testify. There is an excitement during the crying fit which is not without a certain pungent pleasure of its own; but it would take a genius for felicity to discover any dash of redeeming quality in the feeling of dry and shrunken sorrow.—Our author continues:

"If the smaller vessels of the lungs contract so that these organs become anæmic, we have (as is usual under such conditions) the feeling of insufficient breath, and of oppression of the chest, and these tormenting sensations increase the sufferings of the griever, who seeks relief by long-drawn sighs, instinctively, like everyone who lacks breath from whatever cause.[2]

[2] The bronchial tubes may be contracted as well as the ramifications of the pulmonary artery. Professor J. Henle has, amongst his *Anthropologische Vorträge*, an exquisite one on the "Natural History of the Sigh," in which he represents our inspirations as the result of a battle between the red muscles of our skeleton, ribs, and diaphragm, and the white ones of the lungs, which seek to narrow the calibre of the air-tubes. "In the normal state the former easily conquer, but under other conditions they either conquer with difficulty or are defeated. . . . The contrasted emotions express themselves in similarly contrasted wise, by spasm and paralysis of the unstriped muscles, and for the most part alike in all the organs which are provided with them, as arteries, skin, and bronchial tubes. The contrast among the emotions is generally expressed by dividing them into exciting and depressing ones. It is a remarkable fact that the depressing emotions, like fear, horror, disgust, increase the contraction of these smooth muscles, whilst the exciting emotions, like joy, anger, etc., make them relax. Contrasts of temperature act similarly, cold like the depressing, and warmth like the exciting, emotions. Cold produces pallor and goose-flesh, warmth smooths out the skin and widens the vessels. If one notices the uncomfortable mood brought about by strained expectation, anxiety before a public address, vexation at an unmerited affront, etc., one finds that the suffering part of it concentrates itself principally in the chest, and that it consists in a soreness, hardly to be called pain, felt in the middle of the breast and due to an unpleasant resistance which is offered to the movements of inspiration, and sets a limit to their extent. The insufficiency of the diaphragm is obtruded upon consciousness, and we try by the aid of the external voluntary chest-muscles to draw a deeper breath. [This is the sigh.] If we fail, the unpleasantness of the situation is increased, for then to our mental distress is added the corporeally repugnant feeling of lack of air, a slight degree of suffocation. If, on the contrary, the outer muscles overcome the resistance of the inner ones, the oppressed breast is lightened. We think we speak symbolically when we speak of a stone weighing on our heart, or of a burden rolled from off our breast. But really we only express the exact fact, for we should have to raise the entire weight of the atmosphere (about 820 kilog.) at each inspiration, if the air did not balance it by streaming into our lungs." (P. 54.) It must not be forgotten that an inhibition of the inspiratory centre similar to that produced by exciting the superior laryngeal nerve may possibly play a part in these phenomena. For a very interesting discussion of

"The anæmia of the brain in grief is shown by intellectual inertia, dullness, a feeling of mental weariness, effort, and indisposition to work, often by sleeplessness. Indeed it is the anæmia of the motor centres of the brain which lies at the bottom of all that weakening of the voluntary powers of motion which we described in the first instance."

My impression is that Dr. Lange simplifies and universalizes the phenomena a little too much in this description, and in particular that he very likely overdoes the anæmia-business. But such as it is, his account may stand as a favorable specimen of the sort of descriptive work to which the emotions have given rise.

Take next another emotion, Fear, and read what Mr. Darwin says of its effects:

"Fear is often preceded by astonishment, and is so far akin to it, that both lead to the senses of sight and hearing being instantly aroused. In both cases the eyes and mouth are widely opened, and the eyebrows raised. The frightened man at first stands like a statue motionless and breathless, or crouches down as if instinctively to escape observation. The heart beats quickly and violently, so that it palpitates or knocks against the ribs; but it is very doubtful whether it then works more efficiently than usual, so as to send a greater supply of blood to all parts of the body; for the skin instantly becomes pale, as during incipient faintness. This paleness of the surface, however, is probably in large part, or exclusively, due to the vaso-motor centre being affected in such a manner as to cause the contraction of the small arteries of the skin. That the skin is much affected under the sense of great fear, we see in the marvellous manner in which perspiration immediately exudes from it. This exudation is all the more remarkable, as the surface is then cold, and hence the term a cold sweat; whereas, the sudorific glands are properly excited into action when the surface is heated. The hairs also on the skin stand erect; and the superficial muscles shiver. In connection with the disturbed action of the heart, the breathing is hurried. The salivary glands act imperfectly; the mouth becomes dry, and is often opened and shut. I have also noticed that under slight fear there is a strong tendency to yawn. One of the best-marked symptoms is the trembling of all the muscles of the body; and this is often first seen in the lips. From this cause, and from the dryness of the mouth, the voice becomes husky or indistinct, or may altogether fail. 'Obstupui, steteruntque comae et vox faucibus haesit.' . . . As fear increases into an

---

the respiratory difficulty and its connection with anxiety and fear, see "A Case of Hydrophobia" by the lamented Thomas B. Curtis in the *Boston Medical and Surgical Journal*, Nov. 7 and 14, 1878, and remarks thereon by James J. Putnam, *ibid.*, Nov. 21.

agony of terror, we behold, as under all violent emotions, diversified results. The heart beats wildly, or may fail to act and faintness ensue; there is a death-like pallor; the breathing is laboured; the wings of the nostrils are widely dilated; 'there is a gasping and convulsive motion of the lips, a tremor on the hollow cheek, a gulping and catching of the throat'; the uncovered and protruding eyeballs are fixed on the object of terror; or they may roll restlessly from side to side, *huc illuc volvens oculos totumque pererrat.* The pupils are said to be enormously dilated. All the muscles of the body may become rigid, or may be thrown into convulsive movements. The hands are alternately clenched and opened, often with a twitching movement. The arms may be protruded, as if to avert some dreadful danger, or may be thrown wildly over the head. The Rev. Mr. Hagenauer has seen this latter action in a terrified Australian. In other cases there is a sudden and uncontrollable tendency to headlong flight; and so strong is this, that the boldest soldiers may be seized with a sudden panic."[3]

Finally take Hatred, and read the synopsis of its possible effects as given by Sig. Mantegazza:[4]

"Withdrawal of the head backwards, withdrawal of the trunk; projection forwards of the hands, as if to defend one's self against the hated object; contraction or closure of the eyes; elevation of the upper lip and closure of the nose,—these are all elementary movements of turning away. Next threatening movements, as: intense frowning; eyes wide open; display of teeth; grinding teeth and contracting jaws; opened mouth with tongue advanced; clenched fists; threatening action of arms; stamping with the feet; deep inspirations—panting; growling and various cries; automatic repetition of one word or syllable; sudden weakness and trembling of voice; spitting. Finally, various miscellaneous reactions and vaso-motor symptoms: general trembling; convulsions of lips and facial muscles, of limbs and of trunk; acts of violence to one's self, as biting fist or nails; sardonic laughter; bright redness of face; sudden pallor of face; extreme dilatation of nostrils; standing up of hair on head."

Were we to go through the whole list of emotions which have been named by men, and study their organic manifestations, we should but ring the changes on the elements which these three typical cases involve. Rigidity of this muscle, relaxation of that, constriction of arteries here, dilatation there, breathing of this sort or that, pulse slowing or quickening, this gland secreting and that

[3] *Expression of the Emotions*, Darwin, pp. 290–2.

[4] *La Physionomie et l'expression des sentiments* (Paris, 1885), p. 140.

one dry, etc., etc. We should, moreover, find that our descriptions had no absolute truth; that they only applied to the average man; that every one of us, almost, has some personal idiosyncrasy of expression, laughing or sobbing differently from his neighbor, or reddening or growing pale where others do not. We should find a like variation in the objects which excite emotion in different persons. Jokes at which one explodes with laughter nauseate another, and seem blasphemous to a third; and occasions which overwhelm me with fear or bashfulness are just what give you the full sense of ease and power. The internal shadings of emotional feeling, moreover, merge endlessly into each other. Language has discriminated some of them, as hatred, antipathy, animosity, dislike, aversion, malice, spite, vengefulness, abhorrence, etc., etc.; but in the dictionaries of synonyms we find these feelings distinguished more by their severally appropriate objective stimuli than by their conscious or subjective tone.

The result of all this flux is that the merely descriptive literature of the emotions is one of the most tedious parts of psychology. And not only is it tedious, but you feel that its subdivisions are to a great extent either fictitious or unimportant, and that its pretences to accuracy are a sham. But unfortunately there is little psychological writing about the emotions which is not merely descriptive. As emotions are described in novels, they interest us, for we are made to share them. We have grown acquainted with the concrete objects and emergencies which call them forth, and any knowing touch of introspection which may grace the page meets with a quick and feeling response. Confessedly literary works of aphoristic philosophy also flash lights into our emotional life, and give us a fitful delight. But as far as "scientific psychology" of the emotions goes, I may have been surfeited by too much reading of classic works on the subject, but I should as lief read verbal descriptions of the shapes of the rocks on a New Hampshire farm as toil through them again. They give one nowhere a central point of view, or a deductive or generative principle. They distinguish and refine and specify *in infinitum* without ever getting on to another logical level. Whereas the beauty of all truly scientific work is to get to ever deeper levels. Is there no way out from this level of individual description in the case of the emotions? I believe there is a way out, but I fear that few will take it.

The trouble with the emotions in psychology is that they are regarded too much as absolutely individual things. So long as they are set down as so many eternal and sacred psychic entities, like the old immutable species in natural history, so long all that *can* be done with them is reverently to catalogue their separate characters, points, and effects. But if we regard them as products of more general causes (as 'species' are now regarded as products of heredity and variation), the mere distinguishing and cataloguing becomes of subsidiary importance. Having the goose which lays the golden eggs, the description of each egg already laid is a minor matter. Now the general causes of the emotions are indubitably physiological. Prof. C. Lange, of Copenhagen, in the pamphlet from which I have already quoted, published in 1885 a physiological theory of their constitution and conditioning, which I had already broached the previous year in an article in *Mind*. None of the criticisms which I have heard of it have made me doubt its essential truth. I will therefore devote the next few pages to explaining what it is. I shall limit myself in the first instance to what may be called the *coarser* emotions, grief, fear, rage, love, in which everyone recognizes a strong organic reverberation, and afterwards speak of the *subtler* emotions, or of those whose organic reverberation is less obvious and strong—and which Lotze had to all practical intents and purposes fully expressed in his *Medicinische Psychologie* in 1852 (see p. 518 of that work). Aristotle also, *De Anima*, Bk. I, ch. 1, and Descartes, *Des passions*, Art. XLVI.

EMOTION FOLLOWS UPON THE BODILY EXPRESSION IN THE COARSER EMOTIONS AT LEAST

Our natural way of thinking about these coarser emotions is that the mental perception of some fact excites the mental affection called the emotion, and that this latter state of mind gives rise to the bodily expression. My theory, on the contrary, is that *the bodily changes follow directly the perception of the exciting fact, and that our feeling of the same changes as they occur* is *the emotion*. Common-sense says, we lose our fortune, are sorry and weep; we meet a bear, are frightened and run; we are insulted by a rival, are angry and strike. The hypothesis here to be defended says that this order of sequence is incorrect, that the one mental state is not immediately induced by the other, that the bodily manifestations must first be interposed between, and that the more rational statement is that we feel sorry because we cry, angry because we strike, afraid because we tremble, and not that we cry, strike, or tremble, because we are sorry, angry, or fearful, as the case may be. Without the bodily states following on the perception, the latter would be purely cognitive in form, pale, colorless, destitute of emotional warmth. We might then see the bear and judge it best to run, receive the insult and deem it right to strike, but we should not actually *feel* afraid or angry.

Stated in this crude way, the hypothesis is pretty sure to meet with immediate disbelief. And yet neither many nor far-fetched considerations are required to mitigate its paradoxical character, and possibly to produce conviction of its truth.

To begin with, no reader of the last two chapters will be inclined to doubt the fact that *objects do excite bodily changes* by a preorganized mechanism, or the farther fact that *the changes are so indefinitely numerous and subtle that the entire organism may be called a sounding-board*, which every change of consciousness, however slight, may make reverberate. The various permutations and combinations of which these organic activities are susceptible make it abstractly possible that no shade of emotion, however slight, should be without a bodily reverberation as unique, when taken in its totality, as is the mental mood itself. The immense number of parts modified in each emotion is what makes it so difficult for us to reproduce in cold blood the total and integral expression of any one of them. We may catch the trick with the voluntary muscles, but fail with the skin, glands, heart, and other viscera. Just as an artificially imitated sneeze lacks something of the reality, so the attempt to imitate an emotion in the absence of its normal instigating cause is apt to be rather 'hollow.'

The next thing to be noticed is this, that *every one of the bodily changes, whatsoever it be, is* FELT, *acutely or obscurely, the moment it occurs.* If the reader has never paid attention to this matter, he will be both interested and astonished to learn how many different local bodily feelings he can detect in himself as characteristic of his various emotional moods. It would be perhaps too much to expect him to arrest the tide of any strong gust of passion for the sake of any such curious analysis as this; but he can observe more tranquil states, and that may be assumed here to be true of the greater which is shown to be true of the less. Our whole cubic capacity is sensibly alive; and each morsel of it contributes its pulsations of feeling, dim or sharp, pleasant, painful, or dubious, to that sense of personality that every one of us unfailingly carries with him. It is surprising what little items give accent to these complexes of sensibility. When worried by any slight trouble, one may find that the focus of one's bodily consciousness is the contraction, often quite inconsiderable, of the eyes and brows. When momentarily embarrassed, it is something in the pharynx that compels either a swallow, a clearing of the throat, or a slight cough; and so on for as many more instances as might be named. Our concern here being with the general view rather than with the details, I will not linger to discuss these, but, assuming the point admitted that every change that occurs must be felt, I will pass on.

I now proceed to urge the vital point of my whole theory, which is this: *If we fancy some strong emotion, and then try to abstract from our consciousness of it all the feelings of its bodily symptoms, we find we have nothing left behind,* no 'mind-stuff' out of which the emotion can be constituted, and that a cold and neutral state of intellectual perception is all that remains. It is true that, although most people, when asked, say that their introspection verifies this statement, some persist in saying theirs does not. Many cannot be made to understand the question. When you beg them to imagine away every feeling of laughter and of tendency to laugh from their consciousness of the ludicrousness of an object, and then to tell you what the feeling of its ludicrousness would be like, whether it be anything more than the perception that the object belongs to the class 'funny,' they persist in replying that the thing proposed is a physical impossibility, and that they always *must* laugh if they see a funny object. Of course the task proposed is not the practical one of seeing a ludicrous object and annihilating one's tendency to laugh. It is the purely speculative one of subtracting certain elements of feeling from an emotional state supposed to exist in its fulness, and saying what the residual elements are. I cannot help thinking that all who rightly apprehend this problem will agree with the proposition above laid down. What kind of an emotion of fear would be left if the feeling neither of quickened heart-beats nor of shallow breathing, neither of trembling lips nor of weakened limbs, neither of goose-flesh nor of visceral stirrings, were present, it is quite impossible for me to think. Can one fancy the state of rage and picture no ebullition in the chest, no flushing of the face, no dilatation of the nostrils, no clenching of the teeth, no impulse to vigorous action, but in their stead limp muscles, calm breathing, and a placid face? The present writer, for one, certainly cannot. The rage is as completely evaporated as the sensation of its so-called manifestations, and the only thing that can possibly be supposed to take its place is some cold-blooded and dispassionate judicial sentence, confined entirely to the intellectual realm, to the effect that a certain person or persons merit chastisement for their sins. In like manner of grief: what would it be without its tears, its sobs, its suffocation of the heart, its pang in the breast-bone? A feelingless cognition that certain circumstances are deplorable, and nothing more. Every passion in turn tells the same story. A purely disembodied human emotion is a nonentity. I do not say that it is a contradiction in the nature of things, or that pure spirits are necessarily condemned to cold intellectual lives; but I say that for *us*, emotion dissociated from all bodily feeling is inconceivable. The more closely I scrutinize my states, the more persuaded I become that whatever moods, affections, and passions I have are in very truth constituted by, and made up of, those bodily changes which we ordinarily call their expression or consequence; and the more it seems to me that if I were to become corporeally anæsthetic, I should be excluded from the life of the affections, harsh and tender alike, and drag out an existence of merely cognitive or intellectual form. Such an existence, although it seems to have been the ideal of ancient sages, is too apathetic to be keenly sought after by those born after the revival of the worship of sensibility, a few generations ago.

Let not this view be called materialistic. It is neither more nor less materialistic than any other view which says that our emotions are conditioned by nervous processes. No reader of this book is likely to rebel against such a saying so long as it is expressed in general terms; and if anyone still finds materialism in the thesis now defended, that must be because of the special processes invoked. They are *sensational* processes, processes due to inward currents set up by physical happenings. Such processes have, it is true, always been regarded by the platonizers in psychology as having something peculiarly base about them. But our emotions must always be *inwardly* what they are, whatever be the physiological ground of their apparition. If they are deep pure worthy spiritual facts on any conceivable theory of their physiological source, they remain no less deep pure spiritual and worthy of regard on this present sensational theory. They carry their own inner measure of worth with them; and it is just as logical to use the present theory of the emotions for proving that sensational processes need not be vile and material, as to use their vileness and materiality as a proof that such a theory cannot be true.

If such a theory is true, then each emotion is the resultant of a sum of elements, and each element is caused by a physiological process of a sort already well known. The elements are all organic changes, and each of them is the reflex effect of the exciting object. Definite questions now immediately arise—questions very different from those which were the only possible ones without this view. Those were questions of classification: "Which are the proper genera of emotion, and which the species under each?"—or of description: "By what expression is each emotion characterized?" The questions now are *causal*: "Just what changes does this object and what changes does that object excite?" and "How come they to excite these particular changes and not others?" We step from a superficial to a deep order of inquiry. Classification and description are the lowest stage of science. They sink into the background the moment questions of genesis are formulated, and remain important only so far as they facilitate our answering these. Now the moment the genesis of an emotion is accounted for, as the arousal by an object of a lot of reflex acts which are forthwith felt, *we immediately see why there is no limit to the number of possible different emotions which may exist, and why the emotions of different individuals may vary indefinitely*, both as to their constitution and as to objects which call them forth. For there is nothing sacramental or eternally fixed in reflex action. Any sort of reflex effect is possible, and reflexes actually vary indefinitely, as we know.

"We have all seen men dumb, instead of talkative, with joy; we have seen fright drive the blood into the head of its victim, instead of making him pale; we have seen grief run restlessly about lamenting, instead of sitting bowed down and mute; etc., etc., and this naturally enough, for one and the same cause can work differently on different men's blood-vessels (since these do not always react alike), whilst moreover the impulse on its way through the brain to the vaso-motor centre is differently influenced by different earlier impressions in the form of recollections or associations of ideas."[5]

[5] Lange: *op. cit.*, p. 75.

In short, *any classification of the emotions is seen to be as true and as 'natural' as any other,* if it only serves some purpose; and such a question as "What is the 'real' or 'typical' expression of anger, or fear?" is seen to have no objective meaning at all. Instead of it we now have the question as to how any given 'expression' of anger or fear may have come to exist; and that is a real question of physiological mechanics on the one hand, and of history on the other, which (like all real questions) is in essence answerable, although the answer may be hard to find. On a later page I shall mention the attempts to answer it which have been made.

DIFFICULTY OF TESTING THE THEORY EXPERIMENTALLY

I have thus fairly propounded what seems to me the most fruitful way of conceiving of the emotions. It must be admitted that it is so far only a hypothesis, only *possibly* a true conception, and that much is lacking to its definitive proof. The only way coercively to *dis*prove it, however, would be to take some emotion, and then exhibit qualities of feeling in it which should be *demonstrably* additional to all those which could possibly be derived from the organs affected at the time. But to detect with certainty such purely spiritual qualities of feeling would obviously be a task beyond human power. We have, as Professor Lange says, absolutely no immediate criterion by which to distinguish between spiritual and corporeal feelings; and, I may add, the more we sharpen our introspection, the more *localized* all our qualities of feeling become (see above, Vol. I, p. 287) and the more difficult the discrimination consequently grows.[6]

A positive proof of the theory would, on the other hand, be given if we could find a subject absolutely anæsthetic inside and out, but not paralytic, so that emotion-inspiring objects might evoke the usual bodily expressions from him, but who, on being consulted, should say that no subjective emotional affection was felt. Such a man would be like one who, because he eats, appears to bystanders to be hungry, but who afterwards confesses that he had no appetite at all. Cases like this are extremely hard to find. Medical literature

[6] Professor Höffding, in his excellent treatise on Psychology, admits (p. 342) the mixture of bodily sensation with purely spiritual affection in the emotions. He does not, however, discuss the difficulties of discerning the spiritual affection (nor even show that he has fairly considered them) in his contention that it exists.

contains reports, so far as I know, of but three. In the famous one of Remigius Leins no mention is made by the reporters of his emotional condition. In Dr. G. Winter's case[7] the patient is said to be inert and phlegmatic, but no particular attention, as I learn from Dr. W., was paid to his psychic condition. In the extraordinary case reported by Professor Strümpell (to which I must refer later in another connection)[8] we read that the patient, a shoemaker's apprentice of fifteen, entirely anæsthetic, inside and out, with the exception of one eye and one ear, had shown *shame* on the occasion of soiling his bed, and *grief*, when a formerly favorite dish was set before him, at the thought that he could no longer taste its flavor. Dr. Strümpell is also kind enough to inform me that he manifested *surprise, fear,* and *anger* on certain occasions. In observing him, however, no such theory as the present one seems to have been thought of; and it always remains possible that, just as he satisfied his natural appetites and necessities in cold blood, with no inward feeling, so his emotional expressions may have been accompanied by a quite cold heart.[9] Any new case which turns up of generalized anæsthesia ought to be carefully examined as to the inward emotional sensibility as distinct from the 'expressions' of emotion which circumstances may bring forth.

7 *Ein Fall von allgemeiner Anaesthesie* (Heidelberg, 1882).

8 Ziemssen's *Deutsches Archiv für klinische Medicin*, XXII, 321.

9 The not very uncommon cases of hysterical hemianæsthesia are not complete enough to be utilized in this inquiry. Moreover, the recent researches, of which some account was given in Chapter IV, tend to show that hysterical anæsthesia is not a real absence of sensibility, but a 'dissociation,' as M. Pierre Janet calls it, or splitting-off of certain sensations from the rest of the person's consciousness, this *rest* forming the self which remains connected with the ordinary organs of expression. The split-off consciousness forms a secondary self; and M. Janet writes me that he sees no reason why sensations whose 'dissociation' from the body of consciousness makes the patient practically anæsthetic, might not, nevertheless, contribute to the emotional life of the patient. They do still contribute to the function of locomotion; for in his patient L. there was no ataxia in spite of the anæsthesia. M. Janet writes me, apropos of his anæsthetic patient L., that she seemed to 'suffer by hallucination.' "I have often pricked or burned her without warning, and when she did not see me. She never moved, and evidently perceived nothing. But if afterwards in her movements she caught sight of her wounded arm, and *saw* on her skin a little drop of blood resulting from a slight cut, she would begin to cry out and lament as if she suffered a great deal. 'My blood flows,' she said one day; 'I *must be* suffering a great deal!' She suffered by hallucination. This sort of suffering is very general in hysterics. It is enough for them to receive the slightest hint of a modification in their body, when their imagination fills up the rest and invents changes that were not felt." See the remarks published at a later date in Janet's *Automatisme psychologique*, pp. 214–15.

Objections Considered

Let me now notice a few objections. The replies will make the theory still more plausible.

First Objection. There is no real evidence, it may be said, for the assumption that particular perceptions *do* produce wide-spread bodily effects by a sort of immediate physical influence, antecedent to the arousal of an emotion or emotional idea.

Reply. There is most assuredly such evidence. In listening to poetry, drama, or heroic narrative we are often surprised at the cutaneous shiver which like a sudden wave flows over us, and at the heart-swelling and the lachrymal effusion that unexpectedly catch us at intervals. In listening to music the same is even more strikingly true. If we abruptly see a dark moving form in the woods, our heart stops beating, and we catch our breath instantly and before any articulate idea of danger can arise. If our friend goes near to the edge of a precipice, we get the well-known feeling of 'all-overishness,' and we shrink back, although we positively *know* him to be safe, and have no distinct imagination of his fall. The writer well remembers his astonishment, when a boy of seven or eight, at fainting when he saw a horse bled. The blood was in a bucket, with a stick in it, and, if memory does not deceive him, he stirred it round and saw it drip from the stick with no feeling save that of childish curiosity. Suddenly the world grew black before his eyes, his ears began to buzz, and he knew no more. He had never heard of the sight of blood producing faintness or sickness, and he had so little repugnance to it, and so little apprehension of any other sort of danger from it, that even at that tender age, as he well remembers, he could not help wondering how the mere physical presence of a pailful of crimson fluid could occasion in him such formidable bodily effects.

Professor Lange writes:

"No one has ever thought of separating the emotion produced by an unusually loud sound from the true inward affections. No one hesitates to call it a sort of fright, and it shows the ordinary signs of fright. And yet it is by no means combined with the idea of danger, or in any way occasioned by associations, memories, or other mental processes. The phenomena of fright follow the noise immediately without a trace of 'spiritual' fear. Many men can never grow used to standing beside a cannon when it is fired off, although they perfectly know that there is danger neither for themselves nor for others—the bare sound is too much for them."[10]

Imagine two steel knife-blades with their keen edges crossing each other at right angles, and moving to and fro. Our whole nervous organization is 'on-edge' at the thought; and yet what emotion can be there except the unpleasant nervous feeling itself, or the dread that more of it may come? The entire fund and capital of the emotion here is the senseless bodily effect which the blades immediately arouse. This case is typical of a class: where an ideal emotion seems to precede the bodily symptoms, it is often nothing but an anticipation of the symptoms themselves. One who has already fainted at the sight of blood may witness the preparations for a surgical operation with uncontrollable heart-sinking and anxiety. He anticipates certain feelings, and the anticipation precipitates their arrival. In cases of morbid terror the subjects often confess that what possesses them seems, more than anything, to be fear of the fear itself. In the various forms of what Professor Bain calls 'tender emotion,' although the appropriate object must usually be directly contemplated before the emotion can be aroused, yet sometimes thinking of the symptoms of the emotion itself may have the same effect. In sentimental natures the thought of 'yearning' will produce real 'yearning.' And, not to speak of coarser examples, a mother's imagination of the caresses she bestows on her child may arouse a spasm of parental longing.

In such cases as these we see plainly how the emotion both begins and ends with what we call its effects or manifestations. It has no mental *status* except as either the vivid feeling of the manifestations, or the idea of them; and the latter thus constitute its entire material, and sum and substance. And these cases ought to make us see how in all cases the feeling of the manifestations may play a much deeper part in the constitution of the emotion than we are wont to suppose.

The best proof that the immediate cause of emotion is a physical effect on the nerves is furnished by *those pathological cases in which the emotion is objectless.* One of the chief merits, in fact, of the view which I propose seems to be that we can so easily formulate by its means pathological cases and normal cases under a common

10 *Op. cit.*, p. 63.

scheme. In every asylum we find examples of absolutely unmotived fear, anger, melancholy, or conceit; and others of an equally unmotived apathy which persists in spite of the best of outward reasons why it should give way. In the former cases we must suppose the nervous machinery to be so 'labile' in some one emotional direction that almost every stimulus (however inappropriate) causes it to upset in that way, and to engender the particular complex of feelings of which the psychic body of the emotion consists. Thus, to take one special instance, if inability to draw deep breath, fluttering of the heart, and that peculiar epigastric change felt as 'precordial anxiety,' with an irresistible tendency to take a somewhat crouching attitude and to sit still, and with perhaps other visceral processes not now known, all spontaneously occur together in a certain person; his feeling of their combination *is* the emotion of dread, and he is the victim of what is known as morbid fear. A friend who has had occasional attacks of this most evil of all maladies tells me that in his case the whole drama seems to centre about the region of the heart and respiratory apparatus, that his main effort during the attacks is to get control of his inspirations and to slow his heart, and that the moment he attains to breathing deeply and to holding himself erect, the dread, *ipso facto*, seems to depart.[11]

The emotion here is nothing but the feeling of a bodily state, and it has a purely bodily cause.

"All physicians who have been much engaged in general practice have seen cases of dyspepsia in which constant low spirits and occasional attacks of terror rendered the patient's condition pitiable in the extreme. I have observed these cases often, and have watched them closely, and I have never seen greater suffering of any kind than I have witnessed during these attacks. . . . Thus, a man is suffering from what

[11] It must be confessed that there are cases of morbid fear in which objectively the heart is not much perturbed. These, however, fail to prove anything against our theory, for it is of course possible that the cortical centres normally percipient of dread as a complex of cardiac and other organic sensations due to real bodily change, should become *primarily* excited in brain-disease, and give rise to an hallucination of the changes being there,—an hallucination of dread, consequently, coexistent with a comparatively calm pulse, etc. I say it is possible, for I am ignorant of observations which might test the fact. Trance, ecstasy, etc., offer analogous examples,—not to speak of ordinary dreaming. Under all these conditions one may have the liveliest subjective feelings, either of eye or ear, or of the more visceral and emotional sort, as a result of pure nerve-central activity, and yet, as I believe, with complete peripheral repose.

we call nervous dyspepsia. Some day, we will suppose in the middle of the afternoon, without any warning or visible cause, one of these attacks of terror comes on. The first thing the man feels is great but vague discomfort. Then he notices that his heart is beating much too violently. At the same time, shocks or flashes as of electrical discharges, so violent as to be almost painful, pass one after another through his body and limbs. Then in a few minutes he falls into a condition of the most intense fear. He is not afraid of anything; he is simply afraid. His mind is perfectly clear. He looks for a cause of his wretched condition, but sees none. Presently his terror is such that he trembles violently and utters low moans; his body is damp with perspiration; his mouth is perfectly dry; and at this stage there are no tears in his eyes, though his suffering is intense. When the climax of the attack is reached and passed there is a copious flow of tears, or else a mental condition in which the person weeps upon the least provocation. At this stage a large quantity of pale urine is passed. Then the heart's action becomes again normal, and the attack passes off."[12]

Again:

"There are outbreaks of rage so groundless and unbridled that all must admit them to be expressions of disease. For the medical layman hardly anything can be more instructive than the observation of such a pathological attack of rage, especially when it presents itself pure and unmixed with other psychical disturbances. This happens in that rather rare disease named transitory mania. The patient predisposed to this—otherwise an entirely reasonable person—will be attacked suddenly without the slightest outward provocation, and thrown (to use the words of the latest writer on the subject, O. Schwartzer, *Die transitorische Tobsucht*, Wien, 1880), 'into a paroxysm of the wildest rage, with a fearful and blindly furious impulse to do violence and destroy.' He flies at those about him; strikes, kicks, and throttles whomever he can catch; dashes every object about which he can lay his hands on; breaks and crushes what is near him; tears his clothes; shouts, howls, and roars, with eyes that flash and roll, and shows meanwhile all those symptoms of vaso-motor congestion which we have learned to know as the concomitants of anger. His face is red, swollen, his cheeks hot, his eyes protuberant and their whites bloodshot, the heart beats violently, the pulse marks 100–120 strokes a minute. The arteries of the neck are full and pulsating, the veins are swollen, the saliva flows. The fit lasts only a few hours, and ends suddenly with a sleep of from 8 to 12 hours, on waking from which the patient has entirely forgotten what has happened."[13]

[12] R. M. Bucke: *Man's Moral Nature* (N. Y., 1879), p. 96.

[13] Lange: *op. cit.*, p. 60.

In these (outwardly) causeless emotional conditions the particular paths which are explosive are discharged by any and every incoming sensation. Just as, when we are seasick, every smell, every taste, every sound, every sight, every movement, every sensible experience whatever, augments our nausea, so the morbid terror or anger is increased by each and every sensation which stirs up the nerve-centres. Absolute quiet is the only treatment for the time. It seems impossible not to admit that in all this the bodily condition takes the lead, and that the mental emotion follows. The *intellect* may, in fact, be so little affected as to play the cold-blooded spectator all the while, and note the absence of a real object for the emotion.[14]

A few words from Henle may close my reply to this first objection:

"Does it not seem as if the excitations of the bodily nerves met the ideas half way, in order to raise the latter to the height of emotions? [Note how justly this expresses our theory!] That they do so is proved by the cases in which particular nerves, when specially irritable, share in the emotion and determine its quality. When one is suffering from an open wound, any grievous or horrid spectacle will cause pain in the wound. In sufferers from heart-disease there is developed a psychic excitability, which is often incomprehensible to the patients themselves, but which comes from the heart's liability to palpitate. I said that the very quality of the emotion is determined by the organs disposed to participate in it. Just as surely as a dark foreboding, rightly grounded on inference from the constellations, will be accompanied by a feeling of oppression in the chest, so surely will a similar feeling of oppression, when due to disease of the thoracic organs, be accompanied by groundless forebodings. So small a thing as a bubble of air rising from the stomach through the œsophagus, and loitering on its way a few minutes

[14] I am inclined to think that in some hysteriform conditions of grief, rage, etc., the visceral disturbances are less strong than those which go to outward expression. We have then a tremendous verbal display with a hollow inside. Whilst the bystanders are wrung with compassion, or pale with alarm, the subject all the while lets himself go, but feels his insincerity, and wonders how long he can keep up the performance. The attacks are often surprisingly sudden in their onset. The treatment here is to intimidate the patient by a stronger will. Take out your temper, if he takes out his—"Nay, if thou'lt mouth, I'll rant as well as thou." These are the cases of apparently great bodily manifestation with comparatively little real subjective emotion, which may be used to throw discredit on the theory advanced in the text.—It is probable that the *visceral* manifestations in these cases are quite disproportionately slight, compared with those of the vocal organs. The subject's state is somewhat similar to that of an actor who does not feel his part.

and exerting pressure on the heart, is able during sleep to occasion a nightmare, and during waking to produce a vague anxiety. On the other hand, we see that joyous thoughts dilate our blood-vessels, and that a suitable quantity of wine, because it dilates the vessels, also disposes us to joyous thoughts. If both the jest and the wine work together, they supplement each other in producing the emotional effect, and our demands on the jest are the more modest in proportion as the wine takes upon itself a larger part of the task."[15]

Second Objection. If our theory be true, a necessary corollary of it ought to be this: that any voluntary and cold-blooded arousal of the so-called manifestations of a special emotion ought to give us the emotion itself. Now this (the objection says) is not found to be the case. An actor can perfectly simulate an emotion and yet be inwardly cold; and we can all pretend to cry and not feel grief; and feign laughter without being amused.

Reply. In the majority of emotions this test is inapplicable; for many of the manifestations are in organs over which we have no voluntary control. Few people in pretending to cry can shed real tears, for example. But, within the limits in which it can be verified, experience corroborates rather than disproves the corollary from our theory, upon which the present objection rests. Everyone knows how panic is increased by flight, and how the giving way to the symptoms of grief or anger increases those passions themselves. Each fit of sobbing makes the sorrow more acute, and calls forth another fit stronger still, until at last repose only ensues with lassitude and with the apparent exhaustion of the machinery. In rage, it is notorious how we 'work ourselves up' to a climax by repeated outbreaks of expression. Refuse to express a passion, and it dies. Count ten before venting your anger, and its occasion seems ridiculous. Whistling to keep up courage is no mere figure of speech. On the other hand, sit all day in a moping posture, sigh, and reply to everything with a dismal voice, and your melancholy lingers. There is no more valuable precept in moral education than this, as all who have experience know: if we wish to conquer undesirable emotional tendencies in ourselves, we must assiduously, and in the first instance cold-bloodedly, go through the *outward movements* of those contrary dispositions which we prefer to cul-

[15] *Op. cit.*, p. 71.—Lange lays great stress on the neurotic drugs, as parts of his proof that influences of a physical nature upon the body are the first thing in order in the production of emotions.

tivate. The reward of persistency will infallibly come, in the fading out of the sullenness or depression, and the advent of real cheerfulness and kindliness in their stead. Smooth the brow, brighten the eye, contract the dorsal rather than the ventral aspect of the frame, and speak in a major key, pass the genial compliment, and your heart must be frigid indeed if it do not gradually thaw!

This is recognized by all psychologists, only they fail to see its full import. Professor Bain writes, for example:

"We find that a feeble [emotional] wave . . . is suspended inwardly by being arrested outwardly; the currents of the brain, and the agitation of the centres, die away if the external vent is resisted at every point. It is by such restraint that we are in the habit of suppressing pity, anger, fear, pride—on many trifling occasions. If so, it is a fact that the suppression of the actual movements has a tendency to suppress the nervous currents that incite them, so that the external quiescence is followed by the internal. The effect would not happen in any case, *if there were not some dependence of the cerebral wave upon the free outward vent or manifestation*. . . . By the same interposition, we may summon up a dormant feeling. By acting out the external manifestations, we gradually infect the nerves leading to them, and finally waken up the diffusive current by a sort of induction *ab extra*. . . . Thus it is that we are sometimes able to assume a cheerful tone of mind by forcing a hilarious expression.[16]

We have a mass of other testimony of similar effect. Burke, in his treatise on the *Sublime and Beautiful*, writes as follows of the philosopher Campanella:

"This man, it seems, had not only made very accurate observations on human faces, but was very expert in mimicking such as were any way remarkable. When he had a mind to penetrate into the inclinations of those he had to deal with, he composed his face, his gesture, and his whole body, as nearly as he could, into the exact similitude of the person he intended to examine; and then carefully observed what turn of mind he seemed to acquire by this change. So that, says my author, he was able to enter into the dispositions and thoughts of people, as effectually as if he had been changed into the very men. I have often observed [Burke now goes on in his own person], that, on mimicking the looks and gestures of angry, or placid, or frightened, or daring men, I have involuntarily found my mind turned to that passion whose appearance I endeavoured to imitate; nay, I am convinced it is hard to

16 *Emotions and the Will*, pp. 361–3.

avoid it, though one strove to separate the passion from its corresponding gestures."[17]

Against this it is to be said that many actors who perfectly mimic the outward appearances of emotion in face, gait, and voice declare that they feel no emotion at all. Others, however, according to Mr. William Archer, who has made a very instructive statistical inquiry among them, say that the emotion of the part masters them whenever they play it well.[18] Thus:

" 'I often turn pale,' writes Miss Isabel Bateman, 'in scenes of terror or great excitement. I have been told this many times, and I can feel myself getting very cold and shivering and pale in thrilling situations.' 'When I am playing rage or terror,' Mr. Lionel Brough writes, 'I believe I do turn pale. My mouth gets dry, my tongue cleaves to my palate. In Bob Acres, for instance (in the last act), I have to continually moisten my mouth or I should become inarticulate. I have to "swallow the lump," as I call it.' . . . All artists who have had much experience of emotional parts are absolutely unanimous. . . . 'Playing with the brain,' says Miss Alma Murray, 'is far less fatiguing than playing with the heart. An adventuress taxes the physique far less than a sympathetic heroine. Muscular exertion has comparatively little to do with it.' . . . 'Emotion while acting,' writes Mr. Howe, 'will induce perspiration much more than physical exertion. I always perspired profusely while acting Joseph Surface, which requires little or no exertion.' . . . 'I suffer from fatigue,' writes Mr. Forbes Robertson, 'in proportion to the amount of emotion I may have been called upon to go through, and not from physical exertion.' . . . 'Though I have played Othello,' writes Mr. Coleman, 'ever since I was seventeen (at nineteen I had the honour of acting the Moor to Macready's Iago), husband my resources as I may, this is the one part, the part of parts, which always leaves me physically prostrate. I have never been able to find a pigment that would stay on my face, though I have tried every preparation in existence. Even the titanic Edwin Forrest told me that he was always knocked over in Othello, and I have heard Charles Kean, Phelps,

[17] Quoted by Dugald Stewart: *Elements*, etc. (Hamilton's ed.), III, 140. Fechner (*Vorschule der Aesthetik*, 156) says almost the same thing of himself: "One may find by one's own observation that the *imitation* of the bodily expression of a mental condition makes us understand it much better than the merely looking on. . . . When I walk behind someone whom I do not know, and imitate as accurately as possible his gait and carriage, I get the most curious impression of feeling as the person himself must feel. To go tripping and mincing after the fashion of a young woman puts one, so to speak, in a feminine mood of mind."

[18] "The Anatomy of Acting," in *Longman's Magazine*, vol. XI, pp. 266, 375, 498 (1888), since republished in book form.

Brooke, Dillon, say the same thing. On the other hand I have frequently acted Richard III. without turning a hair.' "[19]

The explanation for the discrepancy amongst actors is probably that which these quotations suggest. The *visceral and organic* part of the expression can be suppressed in some men, but not in others, and on this it is probable that the chief part of the felt emotion depends. Coquelin and the other actors who are inwardly cold are probably able to affect the dissociation in a complete way. Prof. Sikorsky of Kieff has contributed an important article on the facial expression of the insane to the *Neurologisches Centralblatt* for 1887. Having practised facial mimicry himself a great deal, he says:

"When I contract my facial muscles in any mimetic combination, *I feel no emotional excitement*, so that the mimicry is in the fullest sense of the word artificial, although quite irreproachable from the expressive point of view."[20]

We find, however, from the context that Prof. S.'s practice before the mirror has developed in him such a virtuosity in the control of his facial muscles that he can entirely disregard their natural association and contract them in any order of grouping, on either side of the face isolatedly, and each one alone. Probably in him the facial mimicry is an entirely restricted and localized thing, without sympathetic changes of any sort elsewhere.

Third Objection. Manifesting an emotion, so far from increasing it, makes it cease. Rage evaporates after a good outburst; it is *pent-up* emotions that "work like madness in the brain."

Reply. The objection fails to discriminate between what is felt *during* and what is felt *after* the manifestation. *During* the manifestation the emotion is always felt. In the normal course of things this, being the natural channel of discharge, exhausts the nerve-centres, and emotional calm ensues. But if tears or anger are simply suppressed, whilst the object of grief or rage remains unchanged before the mind, the current which would have invaded the normal channels turns into others, for it must find some outlet of escape. It may then work different and worse effects later on. Thus vengeful brooding may replace a burst of indignation; a dry heat may consume the frame of one who fain would weep, or he may, as

19 P. 392.
20 P. 496.

Dante says, turn to stone within; and then tears or a storming fit may bring a grateful relief. This is when the current is strong enough to strike into a pathological path when the normal one is dammed. When this is so, an immediate outpour may be best. But here, to quote Prof. Bain again:

> "There is nothing more implied than the fact that an emotion may be too strong to be resisted, and we only waste our strength in the endeavour. If we are really able to stem the torrent, there is no more reason for refraining from the attempt than in the case of weaker feelings. And, undoubtedly, the *habitual* control of the emotions is not to be attained without a systematic restraint extended to weak and strong."

When we teach children to repress their emotional talk and display, it is not that they may *feel* more—quite the reverse. It is that they may *think* more; for, to a certain extent, whatever currents are diverted from the regions below, must swell the activity of the thought-tracts of the brain. In apoplexies and other brain injuries we get the opposite condition—an obstruction, namely, to the passage of currents among the thought-tracts, and with this an increased tendency of objects to start downward currents into the organs of the body. The consequence is tears, laughter, and temper-fits, on the most insignificant provocation, accompanying a proportional feebleness in logical thought and the power of volitional attention and decision,—just the sort of thing from which we try to wean our child. It is true that we say of certain persons that "they would feel more if they expressed less." And in another class of persons the explosive energy with which passion manifests itself on critical occasions seems correlated with the way in which they bottle it up during the intervals. But these are only eccentric types of character, and within each type the law of the last paragraph prevails. The sentimentalist is so constructed that 'gushing' is his or her normal mode of expression. Putting a stopper on the 'gush' will only to a limited extent cause more 'real' activities to take its place; in the main it will simply produce listlessness. On the other hand, the ponderous and bilious 'slumbering volcano,' let him repress the expression of his passions as he will, will find them expire if they get no vent at all; whilst if the rare occasions multiply which he deems worthy of their outbreak, he will find them grow in intensity as life proceeds. On the whole, I cannot see that this third objection carries any weight.

If our hypothesis is true, it makes us realize more deeply than ever how much our mental life is knit up with our corporeal frame, in the strictest sense of the term. Rapture, love, ambition, indignation, and pride, considered as feelings, are fruits of the same soil with the grossest bodily sensations of pleasure and of pain. But the reader will remember that we agreed at the outset to affirm this only of what we then called the 'coarser' emotions, and that those inward states of emotional sensibility which appeared devoid at first sight of bodily results should be left out of our account. We must now say a word or two about these latter feelings, the 'subtler' emotions, as we then agreed to call them.

THE SUBTLER EMOTIONS

These are the moral, intellectual, and æsthetic feelings. Concords of sounds, of colors, of lines, logical consistencies, teleological fitnesses, affect us with a pleasure that seems ingrained in the very form of the representation itself, and to borrow nothing from any reverberation surging up from the parts below the brain. The Herbartian psychologists have distinguished feelings due to the *form* in which ideas may be arranged. A mathematical demonstration may be as 'pretty,' and an act of justice as 'neat,' as a drawing or a tune, although the prettiness and neatness seem to have nothing to do with sensation. We have, then, or some of us seem to have, genuinely *cerebral* forms of pleasure and displeasure, apparently not agreeing in their mode of production with the 'coarser' emotions we have been analyzing. And it is certain that readers whom our reasons have hitherto failed to convince will now start up at this admission, and consider that by it we give up our whole case. Since musical perceptions, since logical ideas, can immediately arouse a form of emotional feeling, they will say, is it not more natural to suppose that in the case of the so-called 'coarser' emotions, prompted by other kinds of objects, the emotional feeling is equally immediate, and the bodily expression something that comes later and is added on?

In reply to this we must immediately insist that æsthetic emotion, *pure and simple*, the pleasure given us by certain lines and masses, and combinations of colors and sounds, is an absolutely sensational experience, an optical or auricular feeling that is primary, and not due to the repercussion backwards of other sensations elsewhere consecutively aroused. To this simple primary and immediate pleasure in certain pure sensations and harmonious combinations of them, there may, it is true, be *added* secondary pleasures; and in the practical enjoyment of works of art by the masses of mankind these secondary pleasures play a great part. The more *classic* one's taste is, however, the less relatively important are the secondary pleasures felt to be in comparison with those of the primary sensation as it comes in.[21] Classicism and romanticism

[21] Even the feelings of the lower senses may have this secondary escort, due to the arousing of associational trains which reverberate. A flavor may fairly shake us by the ghosts of 'banquet halls deserted,' which it suddenly calls up; or a smell may make us feel almost sick with the waft it brings over our memory of 'gardens that are ruins, and pleasure-houses that are dust.' "In the Pyrenees," says M. Guyau, "after a summer-day's tramp carried to the extreme of fatigue, I met a shepherd and asked him for some milk. He went to fetch from his hut, under which a brook ran, a jar of milk plunged in the water and kept at a coldness which was almost icy. In drinking this fresh milk *into which all the mountain had put its perfume*, and of which each savory swallow seemed to give new life, I certainly experienced a series of feelings which the word *agreeable* is insufficient to designate. It was like a pastoral symphony, apprehended by the taste instead of by the ear" (quoted by F. Paulhan from *Les Problèmes de l'esthétique contemporaine*, p. 63).—Compare the dithyrambic about whiskey of Col. R. Ingersoll, to which the presidential campaign of 1888 gave such notoriety: "I send you some of the most wonderful whiskey that ever drove the skeleton from a feast or painted landscapes in the brain of man. It is the mingled souls of wheat and corn. In it you will find the sunshine and shadow that chase each other over the billowy fields, the breath of June, the carol of the lark, the dews of the night, the wealth of summer, and autumn's rich content—all golden with imprisoned light. Drink it, and you will hear the voice of men and maidens singing the 'Harvest Home,' mingled with the laughter of children. Drink it, and you will feel within your blood the star-lit dawns, the dreamy, tawny dusks of many perfect days. For forty years this liquid joy has been within the happy staves of oak, longing to touch the lips of man."—It is in this way that I should reply to Mr. Gurney's criticism on my theory. My "view," this writer says (*Mind*, IX, 425), "goes far to confound the two things which, in my opinion, it is the prime necessity of musical psychology to distinguish—the effect, chiefly sensuous, of mere streams or masses of finely-coloured sound, and the distinctive musical emotion to which the *form* of a sequence of sound, its melodic and harmonic individuality, even realised in complete silence, is the vital and essential object. It is with the former of these two very different things that the physical reactions—the stirring of the hair, the tingling and the shiver—are by far most markedly connected. . . . If I may speak of myself, there is plenty of music from which I have received as much emotion in silent representation as when presented by the finest orchestra; but it is with the latter condition that I almost exclusively associate the cutaneous tingling and hair-stirring. But to call my enjoyment of the *form*, of the *note-after-note*ness, of a melody a mere critical 'judgment of right,' [see below, p. 1086] would really be to deny me the power of expressing a fact of simple and intimate experience in English. It is quintessentially emotion . . . . Now there are hundreds of other bits of music . . . which I judge to be *right* with-

have their battles over this point. Complex suggestiveness, the awakening of vistas of memory and association, and the stirring of our flesh with picturesque mystery and gloom, make a work of art *romantic*. The classic taste brands these effects as coarse and tawdry, and prefers the naked beauty of the optical and auditory sensations, unadorned with frippery or foliage. To the romantic mind, on the contrary, the immediate beauty of these sensations seems dry and thin. I am of course not discussing which view is right, but only showing that the discrimination between the primary feeling of beauty, as a pure incoming sensible quality, and the secondary emotions which are grafted thereupon, is one that must be made.

These secondary emotions themselves are assuredly for the most part constituted of other incoming sensations aroused by the diffusive wave of reflex effects which the beautiful object sets up. A glow, a pang in the breast, a shudder, a fulness of the breathing, a flutter of the heart, a shiver down the back, a moistening of the eyes, a stirring in the hypogastrium, and a thousand unnamable symptoms besides, may be felt the moment the beauty *excites* us. And these symptoms also result when we are excited by moral perceptions, as of pathos, magnanimity, or courage. The voice breaks and the sob rises in the struggling chest, or the nostril dilates and the fingers tighten, whilst the heart beats, etc., etc.

As far as *these ingredients* of the subtler emotions go, then, the latter form no exception to our account, but rather an additional illustration thereof. In all cases of intellectual or moral rapture we find that, unless there be coupled a bodily reverberation of some kind with the mere thought of the object and cognition of its quality; unless we actually laugh at the neatness of the demonstration or witticism; unless we thrill at the case of justice, or tingle at the act of magnanimity; our state of mind can hardly be called

out receiving an iota of the emotion. For purposes of emotion, they are to me like geometrical demonstrations, or like acts of integrity performed in Peru." The Beethoven-rightness of which Gurney then goes on to speak, as something different from the Clementi-rightness (even when the respective pieces are only heard in idea), is probably a purely *auditory-sensational* thing. The Clementi-rightness also; only, for reasons impossible to assign, the Clementi form does not give the same sort of purely auditory satisfaction as the Beethoven form, and might better be described perhaps negatively as *non-wrong*, i.e., free from positively unpleasant acoustic quality. In organizations as musical as Mr. Gurney's, purely acoustic form gives so intense a degree of sensible pleasure that the lower bodily reverberation is of no account. But I repeat that I see nothing in the facts which Mr. Gurney cites, to lead one to believe in an emotion divorced from *sensational processes* of any kind.

emotional at all. It is in fact a mere intellectual perception of how certain things are to be called—neat, right, witty, generous, and the like. Such a judicial state of mind as this is to be classed among awarenesses of truth; it is a *cognitive* act. As a matter of fact, however, the moral and intellectual cognitions hardly ever do exist thus unaccompanied. The bodily sounding-board is at work, as careful introspection will show, far more than we usually suppose. Still, where long familiarity with a certain class of effects, even æsthetic ones, has blunted mere emotional excitability as much as it has sharpened taste and judgment, we do get the intellectual emotion, if such it can be called, pure and undefiled. And the dryness of it, the paleness, the absence of all glow, as it may exist in a thoroughly expert critic's mind, not only shows us what an altogether different thing it is from the 'coarser' emotions we considered first, but makes us suspect that almost the entire difference lies in the fact that the bodily sounding-board, vibrating in the one case, is in the other mute. "Not so very bad" is, in a person of consummate taste, apt to be the highest limit of approving expression. "*Rien ne me choque*" is said to have been Chopin's superlative of praise of new music. A sentimental layman would feel, and ought to feel, horrified, on being admitted into such a critic's mind, to see how cold, how thin, how void of human significance, are the motives for favor or disfavor that there prevail. The capacity to make a nice spot on the wall will outweigh a picture's whole content; a foolish trick of words will preserve a poem; an utterly meaningless fitness of sequence in one musical composition set at naught any amount of 'expressiveness' in another.

I remember seeing an English couple sit for more than an hour on a piercing February day in the Academy at Venice before the celebrated 'Assumption' by Titian; and when I, after being chased from room to room by the cold, concluded to get into the sunshine as fast as possible and let the pictures go, but before leaving drew reverently near to them to learn with what superior forms of susceptibility they might be endowed, all I overheard was the woman's voice murmuring: "What a *deprecatory* expression her face wears! What self-abneg*ation*! How *unworthy* she feels of the honor she is receiving!" Their honest hearts had been kept warm all the time by a glow of spurious sentiment that would have fairly made old Titian sick. Mr. Ruskin somewhere makes the (for him terrible) admission that religious people as a rule care little for pictures, and that when they do care for them they generally prefer the worst ones to the best. Yes! in every art, in every science, there is the keen perception of certain relations being *right* or not, and there is the emotional flush and thrill consequent thereupon. And these are two things, not one. In the former of them it is that experts and masters are at home. The latter accompaniments are bodily commotions that they may hardly feel, but that may be experienced in their fulness by *crétins* and philistines in whom the critical judgment is at its lowest ebb. The 'marvels' of Science, about which so much edifying popular literature is written, are apt to be 'caviare' to the men in the laboratories. And even divine Philosophy itself, which common mortals consider so 'sublime' an occupation, on account of the vastness of its data and outlook, is too apt to the practical philosopher himself to be but a sharpening and tightening business, a matter of 'points,' of screwing down things, of splitting hairs, and of the 'intent' rather than the 'extent' of conceptions. Very little emotion here!—except the effort of setting the attention fine, and the feeling of ease and relief (mainly in the breathing apparatus) when the inconsistencies are overcome and the thoughts run smoothly for a while. Emotion and cognition seem then parted even in this last retreat; and cerebral processes are almost feelingless, so far as we can judge, until they summon help from parts below.

NO SPECIAL BRAIN-CENTRES FOR EMOTION

If the neural process underlying emotional consciousness be what I have now sought to prove it, the physiology of the brain becomes a simpler matter than has been hitherto supposed. Sensational, associational, and motor elements are all that the organ need contain. The physiologists who, during the past few years, have been so industriously exploring the brain's functions, have limited their explanations to its cognitive and volitional performances. Dividing the brain into sensory and motor centres, they have found their division to be exactly paralleled by the analysis made by empirical psychology of the perceptive and volitional parts of the mind into their simplest elements. But the emotions have been so ignored in all these researches that one is tempted to suppose that if these investigators were asked for a theory of them in brain-terms, they would have to reply, either that they had as yet bestowed no thought upon the subject, or that they had found it so difficult to make distinct hypotheses that the matter lay among the problems of the future, only to be taken up after the simpler ones of the present should have been definitively solved.

And yet it is even now certain that of two things concerning the emotions, one must be true. Either separate and special centres, affected to them alone, are their brain-seat, or else they correspond to processes occurring in the motor and sensory centres already assigned, or in others like them, not yet known. If the former be the case, we must deny the view that is current, and hold the cortex to be something more than the surface of 'projection' for every sensitive spot and every muscle in the body. If the latter be the case, we must ask whether the emotional *process* in the sensory or motor centre be an altogether peculiar one, or whether it resembles the ordinary perceptive processes of which those centres are already recognized to be the seat. Now if the theory I have defended be true, the latter alternative is all that it demands. Supposing the cortex to contain parts, liable to be excited by changes in each special sense-organ, in each portion of the skin, in each muscle, each joint, and each viscus, and to contain absolutely nothing else, we still have a scheme capable of representing the process of the emotions. An object falls on a sense-organ, affects a cortical part, and is perceived; or else the latter, excited inwardly, gives rise to an idea of the same object. Quick as a flash, the reflex currents pass down through their preordained channels, alter the condition of muscle, skin, and viscus; and these alterations, perceived, like the original object, in as many portions of the cortex, combine with it in consciousness and transform it from an object-simply-apprehended into an object-emotionally-felt. No new principles have to be invoked, nothing postulated beyond the ordinary reflex circuits, and the local centres admitted in one shape or another by all to exist.

EMOTIONAL DIFFERENCES BETWEEN INDIVIDUALS

The revivability in memory of the emotions, like that of all the feelings of the lower senses, is very small. We can remember that we underwent grief or rapture, but not just how the grief or rapture felt. This difficult *ideal* revivability is, however, more than compensated in the case of the emotions by a very easy *actual* revivability. That is, we can produce, not remembrances of the old grief or rapture, but new griefs and raptures, by summoning up a lively thought of their exciting cause. The cause is now only an idea, but this idea produces the same organic irradiations, or almost the same, which were produced by its original, so that the emotion is again a reality. We have 'recaptured' it. Shame, love, and anger are particularly liable to be thus revived by ideas of their object. Professor Bain admits[22] that "in their strict character of Emotion proper, they [the emotions] have the minimum of revivability; but being always incorporated with the sensations of the higher senses, they share in the superior revivability of sights and sounds." But he fails to point out that the revived sights and sounds may be *ideal* without ceasing to be distinct; whilst the emotion, to be distinct, must become real again. Prof. Bain seems to forget that an 'ideal emotion' and a real emotion prompted by an ideal object are two very different things.

An emotional temperament on the one hand, and a lively imagination for objects and circumstances on the other, are thus the conditions, necessary and sufficient, for an abundant emotional life. No matter how emotional the temperament may be, if the imagination be poor, the occasions for touching off the emotional trains will fail to be realized, and the life will be *pro tanto* cold and dry. This is perhaps a reason why it may be better that a man of thought should not have too strong a visualizing power. He is less likely to have his trains of meditation disturbed by emotional interruptions. It will be remembered that Mr. Galton found the members of the Royal Society and of the French Academy of Sciences to be below par in visualizing power. If I may speak of myself, I am far less able to visualize now, at the age of 46, than in my earlier years; and I am strongly inclined to believe that the relative sluggishness of my emotional life at present is quite as much connected with this fact as it is with the invading torpor of hoary eld, or with the omnibus-horse routine of settled professional and domestic life. I say this because I occasionally have a flash of the old stronger visual imagery, and I notice that the emotional commentary, so to call it, is then liable to become much more acute than is its present wont. Charcot's patient, whose case is given above on p. 705 ff., complained of his incapacity for emotional feeling after his optical images were gone. His mother's death, which in former times would

[22] In his chapter on "Ideal Emotion," to which the reader is referred for farther details on this subject.

have wrung his heart, left him quite cold; largely, as he himself suggests, because he could form no definite visual image of the event, and of the effect of the loss on the rest of the family at home.

One final generality about the emotions remains to be noted: *They blunt themselves by repetition more rapidly than any other sort of feeling.* This is due not only to the general law of 'accommodation' to their stimulus which we saw to obtain of all feelings whatever, but to the peculiar fact that the 'diffusive wave' of reflex effects tends always to become more narrow. It seems as if it were essentially meant to be a provisional arrangement, on the basis of which precise and determinate reactions might arise. The more we exercise ourselves at anything, the fewer muscles we employ; and just so, the oftener we meet an object, the more definitely we think and behave about it; and the less is the organic perturbation to which it gives rise. The first time we saw it we could perhaps neither act nor think at all, and had no reaction but organic perturbation. The emotions of startled surprise, wonder, or curiosity were the result. Now we look on with absolutely no emotion.[23] This tendency to economy in the nerve-paths through which our sensations and ideas discharge, is the basis of all growth in efficiency, readiness, and skill. Where would the general, the surgeon, the presiding chairman, be, if their nerve-currents kept running down into their viscera, instead of keeping up amid their convolutions? But what they gain for practice by this law, they lose, it must be confessed, for feeling. For the world-worn and experienced man, the sense of pleasure which he gets from the free and powerful flow of thoughts, overcoming obstacles as they arise, is the only compensation for that freshness of the heart which he once enjoyed. This free and powerful flow means that brain-paths of association and memory have more and more organized themselves in him,

[23] Those feelings which Prof. Bain calls 'emotions of relativity,' excitement of novelty, wonder, rapture of freedom, sense of power, hardly survive any repetition of the experience. But as the text goes on to explain, and as Goethe as quoted by Prof. Höffding says, this is because "the soul is inwardly grown larger without knowing it, and can no longer be filled by that first sensation. The man thinks that he has lost, but really he has gained. What he has lost in rapture, he has gained in inward growth." "It is," as Prof. Höffding himself adds, in a beautiful figure of speech, "with our virgin feelings, as with the first breath drawn by the new-born child, in which the lung expands itself so that it can never be emptied to the same degree again. No later breath can feel just like that first one." On this whole subject of emotional blunting, compare Höffding's *Psychologie*, VI, E., and Bain's *Emotions and the Will*, chapter IV, of the first part.

and that through them the stimulus is drafted off into nerves which lead merely to the writing finger or the speaking tongue.[24] The trains of *intellectual* association, the memories, the logical relations, may, however, be voluminous in the extreme. Past emotions may be among the things remembered. The more of all these trains an object can set going in us, the richer our cognitive intimacy with it is. This cerebral sense of richness seems itself to be a source of pleasure, possibly even apart from the *euphoria* which from time to time comes up from respiratory organs.[24a] If there *be* such a thing as a purely spiritual emotion, I should be inclined to restrict it to this cerebral sense of abundance and ease, this feeling, as Sir W. Hamilton would call it, of unimpeded and not overstrained activity of thought. Under ordinary conditions, it is a fine and serene but not an excited state of consciousness. In certain intoxications it becomes exciting, and it may be intensely exciting. I can hardly imagine a more frenzied excitement than that which goes with the consciousness of seeing absolute truth, which characterizes the coming to from nitrous-oxide drunkenness. Chloroform, ether, and alcohol all produce this deepening sense of insight into truth; and with all of them it may be a 'strong' emotion; but then there also come with it all sorts of strange bodily feelings and changes in the incoming sensibilities. I cannot see my way to affirming that the emotion is independent of these. I will concede, however, that if its independence is anywhere to be maintained, these theoretic raptures seem the place at which to begin the defence.

THE GENESIS OF THE VARIOUS EMOTIONS

On a former page (p. 1069) I said that two questions, and only two, are important, if we regard the emotions as constituted by feelings due to the diffusive wave.

24 M. Frédéric Paulhan, in a little work full of accurate observations of detail (*Les Phénomènes affectifs et les lois de leur apparition*), seems to me rather to turn the truth upside down by his formula that emotions are due to an inhibition of impulsive tendencies. *One* kind of emotion, namely, uneasiness, annoyance, distress, does occur when any definite impulsive tendency is checked, and all of M. P.'s illustrations are drawn from this sort. The other emotions are themselves primary impulsive tendencies, of a diffusive sort (involving, as M. P. rightly says, a *multiplicité des phénomènes*); and just in proportion as more and more of these multiple tendencies are checked, and replaced by some few narrow forms of discharge, does the original emotion tend to disappear.

24a Cf. Meynert: *Psychiatrie*, pp. 180–1.

(1) *What special diffusive effects do the various special objective and subjective experiences excite?* and

(2) *How come they to excite them?*

The works on physiognomy and expression are all of them attempts to answer question 1. As is but natural, the effects upon the face have received the most careful attention. The reader who wishes details additional to those given above on pp. 1059–1063 is referred to the works mentioned in the note below.[25]

As regards question 2, some little progress has of recent years been made in answering it. Two things are certain:

a. The facial muscles of expression are not given us simply for expression's sake;[26]

b. Each muscle is not affected to some one emotion exclusively, as certain writers have thought.

Some movements of expression can be accounted for as *weakened repetitions of movements which formerly* (when they were stronger) *were of utility to the subject.* Others are similarly weakened repetitions of movements which under other conditions were *physiologically necessary effects.* Of the latter reactions the respiratory disturbances in anger and fear might be taken as examples—organic reminiscences, as it were, reverberations in imagination of the blowings of the man making a series of combative efforts, of the pantings of one in precipitate flight. Such at least is a suggestion made by Mr. Spencer which has found approval. And he also was the first, so far as I know, to suggest that other movements in anger and fear could be explained by the nascent excitation of formerly useful acts.

"To have in a slight degree," he says, "such psychical states as accompany the reception of wounds, and are experienced during flight, is to be in a state of what we call fear. And to have in a slight degree such psychical states as the processes of catching, killing, and eating imply, is to have the desires to catch, kill, and eat. That the propensities to

25 A list of the older writings on the subject is given in Mantegazza's work, *La Physionomie et l'expression*, chap. I; others in Darwin's first chapter. Bell's *Anatomy of Expression*, Mosso's *La Paura*, Piderit's *Wissenschaftliches System der Mimik und Physiognomik*, Duchenne's *Mécanisme de la physionomie humaine*, are, besides Lange and Darwin, the most useful works with which I am acquainted. Compare also Sully: *Sensation and Intuition*, essay II.

26 One must remember, however, that just in so far forth as sexual selection may have played a part in determining the human organism, selection of expressive faces must have increased the average mobility of the human countenance.

the acts are nothing else than nascent excitations of the psychical state involved in the acts, is proved by the natural language of the propensities. Fear, when strong, expresses itself in cries, in efforts to escape, in palpitations, in tremblings; and these are just the manifestations that go along with an actual suffering of the evil feared. The destructive passion is shown in a general tension of the muscular system, in gnashing of teeth and protrusion of the claws, in dilated eyes and nostrils, in growls; and these are weaker forms of the actions that accompany the killing of prey. To such objective evidences, every one can add subjective evidences. Every one can testify that the psychical state called fear, consists of mental representations of certain painful results; and that the one called anger, consists of mental representations of the actions and impressions which would occur while inflicting some kind of pain."[27]

About fear I shall have more to say presently. Meanwhile the principle of *revival in weakened form of reactions useful in more violent dealings with the object inspiring the emotion*, has found many applications. So slight a symptom as the snarl or sneer, the one-sided uncovering of the upper teeth, is accounted for by Darwin as a survival from the time when our ancestors had large canines, and unfleshed them (as dogs now do) for attack. Similarly the raising of the eyebrows in outward attention, the opening of the mouth in astonishment, come, according to the same author, from the utility of these movements in extreme cases. The raising of the eyebrows goes with the opening of the eye for better vision; the opening of the mouth with the intensest listening, and with the rapid catching of the breath which precedes muscular effort. The distention of the nostrils in anger is interpreted by Spencer as an echo of the way in which our ancestors had to breathe when, during combat, their "mouth was filled up by a part of an antagonist's body that had been seized"(!). The trembling of fear is supposed by Mantegazza to be for the sake of warming the blood(!). The reddening of the face and neck is called by Wundt a compensatory arrangement for relieving the brain of the blood-pressure which the simultaneous excitement of the heart brings with it. The effusion of tears is explained both by this author and by Darwin to be a blood-withdrawing agency of a similar sort. The contraction of the muscles around the eyes, of which the primitive use is to protect those organs from being too much gorged with blood dur-

27 *Psychology*, § 213.

ing the screaming fits of infancy, survives in adult life in the shape of the frown, which instantly comes over the brow when anything difficult or displeasing presents itself either to thought or action.

"As the habit of contracting the brows has been followed by infants during innumerable generations, at the commencement of every crying or screaming fit," says Darwin, "it has become firmly associated with the incipient sense of something distressing or disagreeable. Hence under similar circumstances it would be apt to be continued during maturity, although never then developed into a crying-fit. Screaming or weeping begins to be voluntarily restrained at an early period of life, whereas frowning is hardly ever restrained at any age."[28]

The intermittent expirations which constitute laughter have, according to Dr. Hecker, the purpose of counteracting the anæmia of the brain, which he supposes to be brought about by the action of the joyous or comic stimulus upon the vaso-motor nerves.[29] A smile is the weak vestige of a laugh. The tight closure of the mouth in all effort is useful for retaining the air in the lungs so as to fix the chest and give a firm basis of insertion for the muscles of the flanks. Accordingly, we see the lips compress themselves upon every slight occasion of resolve. The blood-pressure has to be high during the sexual embrace; hence the palpitations, and hence also the tendency to caressing action, which accompanies tender emotion in its fainter forms. Other examples might be given; but these are quite enough to show the scope of the principle of revival of useful action in weaker form.

[28] Weeping in childhood is almost as regular a symptom of anger as it is of grief, which would account (on Darwin's principles) for the frown of anger. Mr. Spencer has an account of the angry frown as having arisen through the survival of the fittest, by its utility in keeping the sun out of one's eyes when engaged in mortal combat(!). (*Principles of Psychology*, II, 546.) Professor Mosso objects to any explanation of the frown by its utility for vision, that it is coupled, during emotional excitement, with a dilatation of the pupil which is very unfavorable for distinct vision, and that this ought to have been weeded out by natural selection, if natural selection had the power to fix the frown (see *La Peur*, French 1st ed., chap. IX, § VI). Unfortunately this very able author speaks as if all the emotions affected the pupil in the same way. Fear certainly does make it dilate. But Gratiolet is quoted by Darwin and others as saying that the pupils *contract* in anger. I have made no observations of my own on the point, and Mosso's earlier paper on the pupil (Turin, 1875) I have not seen. I must repeat, with Darwin, that we need more minute observations on this subject.

[29] *Die Physiologie und Psychologie des Lachens und des Komischen* (Berlin, 1873), pp. 13–15.

Another principle, to which Darwin perhaps hardly does sufficient justice, may be called the principle of *reacting similarly to analogous-feeling stimuli.* There is a whole vocabulary of descriptive adjectives common to impressions belonging to different sensible spheres—experiences of all classes are *sweet,* impressions of all classes *rich* or *solid,* sensations of all classes *sharp.* Wundt and Piderit accordingly explain many of our most expressive reactions upon moral causes as symbolic gustatory movements. As soon as any experience arises which has an affinity with the feeling of sweet, or bitter, or sour, the same movements are executed which would result from the taste in point.[30] "All the states of mind which language designates by the metaphors bitter, harsh, sweet, combine themselves, therefore, with the corresponding mimetic movements of the mouth." Certainly the emotions of disgust and satisfaction do express themselves in this mimetic way. Disgust is an incipient regurgitation or retching, limiting its expression often to the grimace of the lips and nose; satisfaction goes with a sucking smile, or tasting motion of the lips. In Mantegazza's loose if learned work, the attempt is made, much less successfully, to bring in the eye and ear as additional sources of symbolically expressive reaction. The ordinary gesture of negation—among us, moving the head about its axis from side to side—is a reaction originally used by babies to keep disagreeables from getting into their mouth, and may be observed in perfection in any nursery.[31] It is now evoked where the stimulus is only an unwelcome idea. Similarly the nod forwards in affirmation is after the analogy of taking food into the mouth. The connection of the expression of moral or social disdain or dislike, especially in women, with movements having a perfectly definite original olfactory function, is too obvious for comment. Winking is the effect of any threatening surprise, not only of what puts the eyes in danger; and a momentary aversion of the eyes is very apt to

30 These movements are explained teleologically, in the first instance, by the efforts which the tongue is forced to make to adapt itself to the better perception or avoidance of the sapid body. (Cf. *Physiologische Psychologie,* II, 423.)

31 Professor Henle derives the negative wag of the head from an incipient shudder, and remarks how fortunate is the abbreviation, as when a lady declines a partner in the ballroom. The clapping of the hands for applause he explains as a symbolic abridgment of an embrace. The protrusion of the lips (*der prüfende Zug*) which goes with all sorts of dubious and questioning states of mind is derived by Dr. Piderit from the *tasting* movement which we can see on anyone's mouth when deciding whether a wine is good or not.

be one's first symptom of response to an unexpectedly unwelcome proposition.—These may suffice as examples of movements expressive from analogy.

But if certain of our emotional reactions can be explained by the two principles invoked—and the reader will himself have felt how conjectural and fallible in some of the instances the explanation is—there remain many reactions which cannot so be explained at all, and these we must write down for the present as purely idiopathic effects of the stimulus. Amongst them are the effects on the viscera and internal glands, the dryness of the mouth and diarrhœa and nausea of fear, the liver-disturbances which sometimes produce jaundice after excessive rage, the urinary secretion of sanguine excitement, and the bladder-contraction of apprehension, the gaping of expectancy, the 'lump in the throat' of grief, the tickling there and the swallowing of embarrassment, the 'precordial anxiety' of dread, the changes in the pupil, the various sweatings of the skin, cold or hot, local or general, and its flushings, together with other symptoms which probably exist but are too hidden to have been noticed or named. It seems as if even the changes of blood-pressure and heart-beat during emotional excitement might, instead of being teleologically determined, prove to be purely mechanical or physiological outpourings through the easiest drainage-channels—the pneumogastrics and sympathetic nerves happening under ordinary circumstances to be such channels.

Mr. Spencer argues that the *smallest* muscles must be such channels; and instances the tail in dogs, cats, and birds, the ears in horses, the crest in parrots, the face and fingers in man, as the first organs to be moved by emotional stimuli.[32] This principle (if it be one) would apply still more easily to the muscles of the smaller arteries (though not exactly to the heart); whilst the great variability of the circulatory symptoms would also suggest that they are determined by causes into which utility does not enter. The quickening of the heart lends itself, it is true, rather easily to explanation

[32] *Loc. cit.*, § 497. Why a dog's face-muscles are not more mobile than they are Mr. Spencer fails to explain, as also why different stimuli should innervate these small muscles in such different ways, if easy drainage be the only principle involved. Charles Bell accounted for the special part played by the facial muscles in expression by their being *accessory muscles of respiration*, governed by nerves whose origin is close to the respiratory centre in the medulla oblongata. They are an adjuvant of *voice*, and like it their function is *communication*. (See Bell's *Anatomy of Expression*, Appendix by Alexander Shaw.)

by inherited habit, organic memory of more violent excitement; and Darwin speaks in favor of this view (see his *Expression*, etc., pp. 74–5). But, on the other hand, we have so many cases of reaction which are indisputably pathological, as we may say, and which could never be serviceable or derived from what was serviceable, that I think we should be cautious about pushing our explanations of the varied heart-beat too far in the teleological direction. Trembling, which is found in many excitements besides that of terror, is, *pace* Mr. Spencer and Sig. Mantegazza, quite pathological. So are terror's other strong symptoms. Professor Mosso, as the total result of his study, writes as follows:

"We have seen that the graver the peril becomes, the more do the reactions which are positively harmful to the animal prevail in number and in efficacy. We already saw that the trembling and the palsy make it incapable of flight or defence; we have also convinced ourselves that in the most decisive moments of danger we are less able to see [or to think] than when we are tranquil. In face of such facts we must admit that the phenomena of fear cannot all be accounted for by 'selection.' Their extreme degrees are morbid phenomena which show an imperfection in the organism. We might almost say that Nature had not been able to frame a substance which should be excitable enough to compose the brain and spinal marrow, and yet which should not be so excited by exceptional stimulation as to overstep in its reactions those physiological bounds which are useful to the conservation of the creature."[33]

Professor Bain, if I mistake not, had long previously commented upon fear in a similar way.

Mr. Darwin accounts for many emotional expressions by what he calls the principle of antithesis. In virtue of this principle, if a certain stimulus prompted a certain set of movements, then a contrary-feeling stimulus would prompt exactly the opposite movements, although these might otherwise have neither utility nor significance. It is in this wise that Darwin explains the expression of impotence, raised eyebrows, and shrugged shoulders, dropped arms and open palms, as being the antithesis of the frowning brow, the thrown-back shoulders, and clenched fists of rage, which is the emotion of power. No doubt a certain number of movements can be formulated under this law; but whether it expresses a *causal* principle is more than doubtful. It has been by most critics con-

[33] *La Paura*, Appendice, p. 295.

sidered the least successful of Darwin's speculations on this subject.

To sum up, we see the reason for a few emotional reactions; for others a possible species of reason may be guessed; but others remain for which no plausible reason can even be conceived. These may be reactions which are purely mechanical results of the way in which our nervous centres are framed, reactions which, although permanent in us now, may be called accidental as far as their origin goes. In fact, in an organism as complex as the nervous system there *must* be many such reactions, incidental to others evolved for utility's sake, but which would never themselves have been evolved independently, for any utility they might possess. Sea-sickness, the love of music, of the various intoxicants, nay, the entire æsthetic life of man, we shall have to trace to this accidental origin.[33a] It would be foolish to suppose that none of the reactions called emotional could have arisen in this *quasi*-accidental way.

This is all I have to say about the emotions. If one should seek to name each particular one of them of which the human heart is the seat, it is plain that the limit to their number would lie in the introspective vocabulary of the seeker, each race of men having found names for some shade of feeling which other races have left undiscriminated. If then we should seek to break the emotions, thus enumerated, into groups, according to their affinities, it is again plain that all sorts of groupings would be possible, according as we chose this character or that as a basis, and that all groupings would be equally real and true. The only question would be, does this grouping or that suit our purpose best? The reader may then class the emotions as he will, as sad or joyous, sthenic or asthenic, natural or acquired, inspired by animate or inanimate things, formal or material, sensuous or ideal, direct or reflective, egoistic or non-egoistic, retrospective, prospective or immediate, organismally or environmentally initiated, or what more besides. All these are divisions which have been actually proposed. Each of them has its merits, and each one brings together some emotions which the others keep apart. For a fuller account, and for other classificatory schemes, I refer to the Appendix to Bain's *Emotions and the Will*, and to Mercier's, Stanley's, and Read's articles on the Emotions, in *Mind*, Vols. IX, X, and XI. In Vol. IX, p. 421 there is also an article by the lamented Edmund Gurney in criticism of the view which in this chapter I continue to defend.

[33a] *Vide infra*, p. 1225.

Chapter XXVI[*]

Will

Desire, wish, will, are states of mind which everyone knows, and which no definition can make plainer. We desire to feel, to have, to do, all sorts of things which at the moment are not felt, had, or done. If with the desire there goes a sense that attainment is not possible, we simply *wish*; but if we believe that the end is in our power, we *will* that the desired feeling, having, or doing shall be real; and real it presently becomes, either immediately upon the willing or after certain preliminaries have been fulfilled.

The only ends which follow *immediately* upon our willing seem to be movements of our own bodies. Whatever *feelings* and *havings* we may will to get, come in as results of preliminary movements which we make for the purpose. This fact is too familiar to need illustration; so that we may start with the proposition that the only *direct* outward effects of our will are bodily movements. The mechanism of production of these voluntary movements is what befalls us to study now. The subject involves a good many separate points which it is difficult to arrange in any continuous logical order. I will treat of them successively in the mere order of convenience; trusting that at the end the reader will gain a clear and connected view.

* Parts of this chapter have appeared in an essay called "The Feeling of Effort," published in the *Anniversary Memoirs of the Boston Society of Natural History*, 1880; and parts in *Scribner's Magazine* for Feb. 1888.

The movements we have studied hitherto have been automatic and reflex, and (on the first occasion of their performance, at any rate) unforeseen by the agent. The movements to the study of which we now address ourselves, being desired and intended beforehand, are of course done with full prevision of what they are to be. It follows from this that *voluntary movements must be secondary, not primary functions of our organism.* This is the first point to understand in the psychology of Volition. Reflex, instinctive, and emotional movements are all primary performances. The nerve-centres are so organized that certain stimuli pull the trigger of certain explosive parts; and a creature going through one of these explosions for the first time undergoes an entirely novel experience. The other day I was standing at a railroad station with a little child, when an express-train went thundering by. The child, who was near the edge of the platform, started, winked, had his breathing convulsed, turned pale, burst out crying, and ran frantically towards me and hid his face. I have no doubt that this youngster was almost as much astonished by his own behavior as he was by the train, and more than I was, who stood by. Of course if such a reaction has many times occurred we learn what to expect of ourselves, and can then foresee our conduct, even though it remain as involuntary and uncontrollable as it was before. But if, in voluntary action properly so called, the act must be foreseen, it follows that no creature not endowed with divinatory power can perform an act voluntarily for the first time. Well, we are no more endowed with prophetic vision of what movements lie in our power than we are endowed with prophetic vision of what sensations we are capable of receiving. As we must wait for the sensations to be given us, so we must wait for the movements to be performed involuntarily,[1] before we can frame ideas of what either of these things are. We learn all our possibilities by the way of experience. When a particular movement, having once occurred in a random, reflex, or involuntary way, has left an image of itself in the memory, then the movement can be desired again, proposed as an end, and deliberately willed. But it is impossible to see how it could be willed before.

A supply of ideas of the various movements that are possible,

[1] I am abstracting at present for simplicity's sake, and so as to keep to the elements of the matter, from the learning of acts by seeing others do them.

left in the memory by experiences of their involuntary performance, is thus the first prerequisite of the voluntary life.

Now the same movement involuntarily performed may leave many different kinds of ideas of itself in the memory. If performed by another person, we of course *see* it, or we *feel* it if the moving part strikes another part of our own body. Similarly we have an auditory image of its effects if it produces sounds, as for example when it is one of the movements made in vocalization, or in playing on a musical instrument. All these *remote* effects of the movement, as we may call them, are also produced by movements which we ourselves perform; and they leave innumerable ideas in our mind by which we distinguish each movement from the rest. It *looks* distinct; it *feels* distinct to some distant part of the body which it strikes; or it *sounds* distinct. These remote effects would then, rigorously speaking, suffice to furnish the mind with the supply of ideas required.

But in addition to these impressions upon remote organs of sense, we have, whenever we perform a movement ourselves, another set of impressions, those, namely, which come up from the parts that are actually moved. These *kinæsthetic* impressions, as Dr. Bastian has called them, are so many *resident* effects of the motion. Not only are our muscles supplied with afferent as well as with efferent nerves, but the tendons, the ligaments, the articular surfaces, and the skin about the joints are all sensitive, and, being stretched and squeezed in ways characteristic of each particular movement, give us as many distinctive feelings as there are movements possible to perform.

It is by these resident impressions that we are made conscious of *passive movements*—movements communicated to our limbs by others. If you lie with closed eyes, and another person noiselessly places your arm or leg in any arbitrarily chosen attitude, you receive an accurate feeling of what attitude it is, and can immediately reproduce it yourself in the arm or leg of the opposite side. Similarly a man waked suddenly from sleep in the dark is aware of how he finds himself lying. At least this is what happens when the nervous apparatus is normal. But in cases of disease we sometimes find that the resident impressions do not normally excite the centres, and that then the sense of attitude is lost. It is only recently that pathologists have begun to study these anæsthesias with the delicacy which they require; and we have doubtless yet a great deal to learn about them. The skin may be anæsthetic, and the muscles may not feel the cramp-like pain which is produced by faradic currents sent through them, and yet the sense of passive movement may be retained. It seems, in fact, to persist more obstinately than the other forms of sensibility, for cases are comparatively common in which all the other feelings in the limb but this one of attitude are lost. In Chapter XX I have tried to make it appear that the articular surfaces are probably the most important source of the resident kinæsthetic feelings. But the determination of their special organ is indifferent to our present quest. It is enough to know that the existence of these feelings cannot be denied.

When the feelings of passive movement as well as all the other feelings of a limb are lost, we get such results as are given in the following account by Professor A. Strümpell of his wonderful anæsthetic boy, whose only sources of feeling were the right eye and the left ear:[2]

"Passive movements could be imprinted on all the extremities to the greatest extent, without attracting the patient's notice. Only in violent forced hyperextension of the joints, especially of the knees, there arose a dull vague feeling of strain, but this was seldom precisely localized. We have often, after bandaging the eyes of the patient, carried him about the room, laid him on a table, given to his arms and legs the most fantastic and apparently the most inconvenient attitudes, without his having a suspicion of it. The expression of astonishment in his face, when all at once the removal of the handkerchief revealed his situation, is indescribable in words. Only when his head was made to hang away down he immediately spoke of dizziness, but could not assign its ground. Later he sometimes inferred from the sounds connected with the manipulation that something special was being done with him . . . . He had no feelings of muscular fatigue. If, with his eyes shut, we told him to raise his arm and to keep it up, he did so without trouble. After one or two minutes, however, the arm began to tremble and sink without his being aware of it. He asserted still his ability to keep it up. . . . Passively holding still his fingers did not affect him. He thought constantly that he opened and shut his hand, whereas it was really fixed."

Or we read of cases like this:

"Voluntary movements cannot be estimated the moment the patient ceases to take note of them by his eyes. Thus, after having made him close his eyes, if one asks him to move one of his limbs either wholly or

[2] *Deutsches Archiv für klinische Medicin*, XXII, 321.

in part, he does it but cannot tell whether the effected movement is large or small, strong or weak, or even if it has taken place at all. And when he opens his eyes after moving his leg from right to left, for example, he declares that he had a very inexact notion of the extent of the effected movement. . . . If, having the intention of executing a certain movement, *I prevent him*, he does not perceive it, and supposes the limb to have taken the position he intended to give it."[3]

Or this:

"The patient, when his eyes were closed in the middle of an unpractised movement, remained with the extremity in the position it had when the eyes closed and did not complete the movement properly. Then after some oscillations the limb gradually sank by reason of its weight (the sense of fatigue being absent). Of this the patient was not aware, and wondered, when he opened his eyes, at the altered position of his limb."[4]

A similar condition can be readily reproduced experimentally in many hypnotic subjects. All that is needed is to tell a suitably predisposed person during the hypnotic trance that he cannot feel his limb, and he will be quite unaware of the attitudes into which you may throw it.[5]

All these cases, whether spontaneous or experimental, show the absolute need of *guiding sensations* of some kind for the successful carrying out of a concatenated series of movements. It is, in fact, easy to see that, just as where the chain of movements is automatic (see above, Vol. I, p. 120), each later movement of the chain has to be discharged by the impression which the next earlier one makes in being executed, so also, where the chain is voluntary, we need to know at each movement just *where we are in it*, if we are to will intelligently what the next link shall be. A man with no feeling of his movements might lead off never so well, and yet be sure to get lost soon and go astray.[6] But patients like those described, who get

3 Landry: "Mémoire sur la paralysie du sens musculaire," *Gazette des Hôpitaux*, 1855, p. 270.

4 Takács: "Untersuchungen über die Verspätung der Empfindungsleitung," *Archiv für Psychiatrie*, Bd. x, Heft 2, p. 533. Concerning all such cases see the remarks made above on pp. 840–841.

5 *Proceedings of the American Society for Psychical Research*, I (July 1885), p. 95.

6 In reality the movement cannot even be *started* correctly in some cases without the kinæsthetic impression. Thus Dr. Strümpell relates how turning over the boy's hand made him bend the little finger instead of the forefinger, when his eye was closed. "Ordered to point, e.g., towards the left with his left arm, the arm was usually raised

no kinæsthetic impressions, can still be guided by the sense of sight. Thus Strümpell says of his boy:

"One could always observe how his eye was directed first to the object held before him, then to his own arm; and how it never ceased to follow the latter during its entire movement. All his voluntary movements took place under the unremitting lead of the eye, which as an indispensable guide, was never untrue to its functions."

So in the Landry case:

"With his eyes open, he easily opposes the thumb to each of the other fingers; with his eyes closed, the movement of opposition occurs, but the thumb only by chance meets the finger which it seeks. With his eyes open he is able, without hesitation, to bring his two hands together; but when his eyes are closed his hands seek one another in space, and only meet by chance."

In Charles Bell's well-known old case of anæsthesia the woman could only hold her baby safely in her arms so long as she looked at it. I have myself reproduced a similar condition in two hypnotic

---

straight forwards, and then wandered about in groping uncertainty, sometimes getting the right position and then leaving it again. Similarly with the lower limbs. If the patient, lying in bed, had, immediately after the tying of his eyes, to lay the left leg over the right, it often happened that he moved it farther over towards the left, and that it lay over the side of the bed in apparently the most intolerably-uncomfortable position. The turning of the head, too, from right to left, or towards certain objects known to the patient, only ensued correctly when the patient, immediately before his eye was bandaged, specially refreshed his perception as to what the required movement was to be." In another anæsthetic of Dr. Strümpell's (described in the same essay) the arm could not be moved *at all* unless the eyes were opened, however energetic the volition. The variations in these hysteric cases are great. Some patients cannot move the anæsthetic part *at all* when the eyes are closed. Others move it perfectly well, and can even write continuous sentences with the anæsthetic hand. The causes of such differences are as yet incompletely explored. M. Binet suggests (*Revue Philosophique*, XXV, 478) that in those who cannot move the hand at all the sensation of light is required as a 'dynamogenic' agent (see above, p. 1001); and that in those who can move it skilfully the anæsthesia is only a pseudo-insensibility and that the limb is in reality governed by a dissociated or secondary consciousness. This latter explanation is certainly correct. Professor G. E. Müller (Pflüger's *Archiv*, XLV, 90) invokes the fact of individual differences of imagination to account for the cases who cannot write at all. Their kinæsthetic images properly so called may be weak, he says, and their optical images insufficiently powerful to supplement them without a 'fillip' from sensation. Janet's observation that hysteric anæsthesias may carry amnesias with them would perfectly legitimate Müller's supposition. What we now want is a minute examination of the individual cases. Meanwhile Binet's article above referred to, and Bastian's paper in *Brain* for April 1887, contain important discussions of the question. In a later note I shall return to the subject again (see p. 1129).

subjects whose arm and hand were made anæsthetic without being paralyzed. They could write their names when looking, but not when their eyes were closed. The modern mode of teaching deaf mutes to articulate consists in making them attentive to certain laryngeal, labial, thoracic, and other sensations, the reproduction of which becomes a guide to their vocalization. Normally it is the remoter sensations which we receive by the ear which keep us from going astray in our speech. The phenomena of aphasia show this to be the usual case.[7]

This is perhaps all that need be said about the existence of passive sensations of movement and their indispensableness for our voluntary activity. We may consequently set it down as certain that, *whether or no there be anything else in the mind at the moment when we consciously will a certain act, a mental conception made up of memory-images of these sensations, defining which special act it is, must be there.*

Now *is there anything else in the mind when we will to do an act?* We must proceed in this chapter from the simpler to the more complicated cases. My first thesis accordingly is, that *there need be nothing else,* and that *in perfectly simple voluntary acts there is nothing else, in the mind but the kinæsthetic idea, thus defined, of what the act is to be.*

A powerful tradition in Psychology will have it that something additional to these images of passive sensation is essential to the mental determination of a voluntary act. There must, of course, be a special current of energy going out from the brain into the appropriate muscles during the act; and this outgoing current (it is supposed) must have in each particular case a feeling *sui generis* attached to it, or else (it is said) the mind could never tell which particular current, the current to this muscle or the current to that one, was the right one to use. This feeling of the current of outgoing energy has received from Wundt the name of the *feeling of innervation. I disbelieve in its existence,* and must proceed to criticise the notion of it, at what I fear may to some prove tedious length.

[7] Professor Beaunis found that the accuracy with which a certain tenor sang was not lost when his vocal cords were made anæsthetic by cocain. He concludes that the guiding sensations here are resident in the laryngeal muscles themselves. They are much more probably in the ear. (Beaunis, *Les Sensations internes* (1889), p. 253.)

At first sight there is something extremely plausible in the feeling of innervation. The passive feelings of movement with which we have hitherto been dealing all come after the movement's performance. But wherever a movement is difficult and precise, we become, as a matter of fact, acutely aware *in advance* of the amount and direction of energy which it is to involve. One has only to play ten-pins or billiards, or throw a ball, to catch his will in the act, as it were, of balancing tentatively its possible efforts, and ideally rehearsing various muscular contractions nearly correct, until it gets just the right one before it, when it says 'Now go!' This premonitory weighing feels so much like a succession of tentative sallyings forth of power into the outer world, followed by correction just in time to avoid the irrevocable deed, that the notion that *outgoing* nerve-currents rather than mere vestiges of former passive sensibility accompany it, is a most natural one to entertain.

We find accordingly that most authors have taken the existence of feelings of innervation as a matter of course. Bain, Wundt, Helmholtz, and Mach defend them most explicitly. But in spite of the authority which such writers deservedly wield, I cannot help thinking that they are in this instance wrong,—that the discharge into the motor nerves is insentient, and that *all our ideas of movement,* including those of the effort which it requires, as well as those of its direction, its extent, its strength, and its velocity, *are images of peripheral sensations, either 'remote,' or resident in the moving parts, or in other parts which sympathetically act with them in consequence of the 'diffusive wave.'*

A priori, as I shall show, there is no reason why there should be a consciousness of the motor discharge, and there is a reason why there should not be such a consciousness. The *presumption* is thus against the existence of the feeling of innervation; and the burden of proving it falls upon those who believe in it. If the positive empirical evidence which they offer prove also insufficient, then their case falls to the ground, and the feeling in question must be ruled out of court.

In the first place, then, let me show that *the assumption of the feeling of innervation is unnecessary.*

I cannot help suspecting that the scholastic prejudice that 'the effect must be already in some way *contained in* the cause' has had something to do with making psychologists so ready to admit the feeling of innervation. The outgoing current being the effect, what psychic antecedent could contain or prefigure it better than a feeling of it? But if we take a wide view, and consider the psychic antecedents of our activities at large, we see that the scholastic maxim breaks down everywhere, and that its verification in this instance would rather violate than illustrate the general rule. In the diffusive wave, in reflex action, and in emotional expression, the movements which are the effects are in no manner contained by anticipation in the stimuli which are their cause. The latter are subjective sensations or objective perceptions, which do not in the slightest degree resemble or prefigure the movements. But we get them, and, presto! there the movements are! They are knocked out of us, they surprise us. It is just cause for wonder, as our chapter on Instinct has shown us, that such bodily consequences should follow such mental antecedents. We explain the mystery *tant bien que mal* by our evolutionary theories, saying that lucky variations and heredity have gradually brought it about that this particular pair of terms should have grown into a uniform sequence. Meanwhile why any state of consciousness *at all* should precede a movement, we know not—the two things seem so essentially discontinuous. But if a state of consciousness there must be, why then it may, for aught we can see, as easily be one sort of a state as another. It is swallowing a camel and straining at a gnat for a man (all of whose muscles will on certain occasions contract at a sudden touch or sound) to suppose that on another occasion the idea of the feelings about to be produced by their contraction is an insufficient mental signal for the latter, and to insist that an additional antecedent is needed in the shape of 'a feeling of the outgoing discharge.'

No! for aught we can see, and in the light of general analogy, the kinæsthetic ideas, as we have defined them, or images of incoming feelings of attitude and motion, are as *likely* as any feelings of innervation are, to be the last psychic antecedents and determiners of the various currents downwards into the muscles from the brain. The question "What *are* the antecedents and determinants?" is a question of fact, to be decided by whatever empirical evidence may be found.[8]

[8] As the feeling of heat, for example, is the last psychic antecedent of sweating, as the feeling of bright light is that of the pupil's contraction, as the sight or smell of carrion is that of the movements of disgust, as the remembrance of a blunder may be that of a blush, so the idea of a movement's sensible effects might be that of the

But before considering the empirical evidence, let me go on to show that there is *a certain a priori reason why the kinæsthetic images* OUGHT *to be the last psychic antecedents of the outgoing currents, and why we should expect these currents to be insentient; why, in short, the soi-disant feelings of innervation should* NOT *exist.*

It is a general principle in Psychology that consciousness deserts all processes where it can no longer be of use. The tendency of consciousness to a minimum of complication is in fact a dominating law. The law of parsimony in logic is only its best known case. We grow unconscious of every feeling which is useless as a sign to lead us to our ends, and where one sign will suffice others drop out, and

---

movement itself. It is true that the idea of sweating will not commonly make us sweat, nor that of blushing make us blush. But in certain nauseated states the idea of vomiting will make us vomit; and a kind of sequence which is in this case realized only exceptionally might be the rule with the so-called voluntary muscles. It all depends on the nervous connections between the centres of ideation and the discharging paths. These may differ from one sort of centre to another. They do differ somewhat from one individual to another. Many persons never blush at the idea of their blunders, but only when the actual blunder is committed; others blush at the idea; and some do not blush at all. According to Lotze, with some persons "It is possible to weep at will by trying to recall that peculiar feeling in the trigeminal nerve which habitually precedes tears. Some can even succeed in sweating voluntarily, by the lively recollection of the characteristic skin-sensations, and the voluntary reproduction of an indescribable sort of feeling of relaxation, which ordinarily precedes the flow of perspiration." (*Medicinische Psychologie*, p. 303.) The commoner type of exceptional case is that in which the idea of the *stimulus*, not that of the effects, provokes the effects. Thus we read of persons who contract their pupils at will by strongly imagining a brilliant light. A gentleman once informed me (strangely enough I cannot recall who he was, but I have an impression of his being a medical man) that he could sweat at will by imagining himself on the brink of a precipice. The sweating palms of fear are sometimes producible by imagining a terrible object (cf. Manouvrier in *Revue Philosophique*, XXII, 203). One of my students, whose eyes were made to water by sitting in the dentist's chair before a bright window, can now shed tears by imagining that situation again. One might doubtless collect a large number of idiosyncratic cases of this sort. They teach us how greatly the centres vary in their power to discharge through certain channels. All that we need, now, to account for the differences observed between the psychic antecedents of the voluntary and involuntary movements is that centres producing ideas of the movement's sensible effects should be able to instigate the former, but be out of gear with the latter, unless in exceptional individuals. The famous case of Col. Townsend, who could stop his heart at will, is well known. See, on this whole matter, D. H. Tuke: *Illustrations of the Influence of the Mind upon the Body*, chap. XIV, § 3; also J. Braid: *Observations on Trance: Or, Human Hybernation* (1850). The latest reported case of voluntary control of the heart is by Dr. E. A. Pease, in *Boston Medical and Surgical Journal*, May 30, 1889.

that one remains, to work alone. We observe this in the whole history of sense-perception, and in the acquisition of every art. We ignore which eye we see with, because a fixed mechanical association has been formed between our motions and each retinal image. Our motions are the ends of our seeing, our retinal images the signals to these ends. If each retinal image, whichever it be, can suggest automatically a motion in the right direction, what need for us to know whether it be in the right eye or the left? That knowledge would be superfluous complication. So in acquiring any art or voluntary function. The marksman ends by thinking only of the exact position of the goal, the singer only of the perfect sound, the balancer only of the point of the pole whose oscillations he must counteract. The associated mechanism has become so perfect in all these persons that each variation in the thought of the end is functionally correlated with the one movement fitted to bring the latter about. Whilst they were tyros, they thought of their means as well as their end: the marksman of the position of his gun or bow, or the weight of his stone; the pianist of the visible position of the note on the keyboard; the singer of his throat or breathing; the balancer of his feet on the rope, or his hand or chin under the pole. But little by little they succeeded in dropping all this supernumerary consciousness, and they became secure in their movements exactly in proportion as they did so.

Now if we analyze the nervous mechanism of voluntary action, we shall see that by virtue of this principle of parsimony in consciousness the motor discharge *ought* to be devoid of sentience. If we call the immediate psychic antecedent of a movement the latter's *mental cue*, all that is needed for invariability of sequence on the movement's part is a *fixed connection* between each several mental cue, and one particular movement. For a movement to be produced with perfect precision, it suffices that it obey instantly its own mental cue and nothing else, and that this mental cue be incapable of awakening any other movement. Now the *simplest* possible arrangement for producing voluntary movements would be that the memory-images of the movement's distinctive peripheral effects, whether resident or remote,[9] themselves should severally constitute the mental cues, and that no other psychic facts should

[9] Prof. Harless, in an article which in many respects forestalls what I have to say ("Der Apparat des Willens," in Fichte's *Zeitschrift für Philosophie und philosophische Kritik*, Bd. 38, 1861), uses the convenient word *Effektbild* to designate these images.

intervene or be mixed up with them. For a million different voluntary movements, we should then need a million distinct processes in the brain-cortex (each corresponding to the idea or memory-image of one movement), and a million distinct paths of discharge. Everything would then be unambiguously determined, and if the idea were right, the movement would be right too. Everything *after* the idea might then be quite insentient, and the motor discharge itself could be unconsciously performed.

The partisans of the feeling of innervation, however, say that the motor discharge itself must be felt, and that it, and not the idea of the movement's distinctive effects, must be the proper mental cue. Thus the principle of parsimony is sacrificed, and all economy and simplicity are lost. For what can be gained by the interposition of this relay of feeling between the idea of the movement and the movement? Nothing on the score of economy of nerve-tracts; for it takes just as many of them to associate a million ideas of movement with a million motor centres, each with a specific feeling of innervation attached to its discharge, as to associate the same million ideas with a million insentient motor centres. And nothing on the score of precision; for the only conceivable way in which the feelings of innervation might further precision would be by giving to a mind whose idea of a movement was vague, a sort of halting stage with sharper imagery on which to collect its wits before uttering its *fiat*. But not only are the conscious discriminations between our kinæsthetic ideas much sharper than anyone pretends the shades of difference between feelings of innervation to be, but even were this not the case, it is impossible to see how a mind with its idea vaguely conceived could tell out of a lot of *Innervationsgefühle*, were they never so sharply differentiated, which one fitted that idea exactly, and which did not. A sharply conceived idea will, on the other hand, *directly* awaken a distinct movement as easily as it will awaken a distinct feeling of innervation. If feelings can go astray through vagueness, surely the fewer steps of feeling there are interposed the more securely we shall act. We ought then, on *a priori* grounds alone, to regard the *Innervationsgefühl* as a pure encumbrance, and to presume that the peripheral ideas of movement are sufficient mental cues.

The presumption being thus against the feelings of innervation, those who defend their existence are bound to prove it by positive evidence. The evidence might be direct or indirect. If we could introspectively feel them as something plainly distinct from the peripheral feelings and ideas of movement which nobody denies to be there, that would be evidence both direct and conclusive. Unfortunately it does not exist.

There is no introspective evidence of the feeling of innervation. Wherever we look for it and think we have grasped it, we find that we have really got a peripheral feeling or image instead—an image of the way in which we feel when the innervation is over, and the movement is in process of doing or is done. Our idea of raising our arm, for example, or of crooking our finger, is a sense, more or less vivid, of how the raised arm or the crooked finger feels. There is no other mental material out of which such an idea might be made. We cannot possibly have any idea of our ears' motion until our ears have moved; and this is true of every other organ as well.

Since the time of Hume it has been a commonplace in psychology that we are only conversant with the outward results of our volition, and not with the hidden inner machinery of nerves and muscles which are what it primarily sets at work.[10] The believers in the feeling of innervation readily admit this, but seem hardly alive to its consequences. It seems to me that one immediate consequence ought to be to make us doubt the existence of the feeling in dispute. Whoever says that in raising his arm he is ignorant of how many muscles he contracts, in what order of sequence, and in what degrees of intensity, expressively avows a colossal amount of unconsciousness of the processes of motor discharge. Each separate muscle at any rate cannot have its distinct feeling of innervation. Wundt,[11] who makes such enormous use of these hypothetical feelings in his psychologic construction of space, is himself led to admit that they have no differences of quality, but feel alike in all muscles, and vary only in their degrees of intensity. They are used by the mind as guides, not of *which* movement, but of *how strong* a movement, it is making, or shall make. But does not this virtually surrender their existence altogether?[12]

[10] The best modern statement I know is by Jaccoud: *Les Paraplégies et de l'ataxie du mouvement* (Paris, 1864), p. 591.

[11] Leidesdorf und Meynert's *Vierteljahrsschrift für Psychiatrie*, Bd. I, Heft I, S. 36–7 (1867). *Physiologische Psychologie*, 1st ed., S. 316.

[12] Professor Fouillée, who defends them in the *Revue Philosophique*, XXVIII, 561 ff., also admits (p. 574) that they are the same whatever be the movement, and that all our discrimination of *which* movement we are innervating is afferent, consisting of sensations after, and of sensory images before, the act.

For if anything be obvious to introspection, it is that the degree of strength of our muscular contractions is completely revealed to us by afferent feelings coming from the muscles themselves and their insertions, from the vicinity of the joints, and from the general fixation of the larynx, chest, face, and body, in the phenomenon of effort, objectively considered. When a certain degree of energy of contraction rather than another is thought of by us, this complex aggregate of afferent feelings, forming the material of our thought, renders absolutely precise and distinctive our mental image of the exact strength of movement to be made, and the exact amount of resistance to be overcome.

Let the reader try to direct his will towards a particular movement, and then notice what *constituted* the direction of the will. Was it anything over and above the notion of the different feelings to which the movement when effected would give rise? If we abstract from these feelings, will any sign, principle, or means of orientation be left by which the will may innervate the right muscles with the right intensity, and not go astray into the wrong ones? Strip off these images of result, and so far from leaving us with a complete assortment of directions into which our will may launch itself, you leave our consciousness in an absolute and total vacuum. If I will to write "Peter" rather than "Paul," it is the thought of certain digital sensations, of certain alphabetic sounds, of certain appearances on the paper, and of no others, which immediately precedes the motion of my pen. If I will to utter the word *Paul* rather than *Peter*, it is the thought of my voice falling on my ear, and of certain muscular feelings in my tongue, lips, and larynx, which guide the utterance. All these are incoming feelings, and between the thought of them, by which the act is mentally specified with all possible completeness, and the act itself, there is no room for any third order of mental phenomenon.

There is indeed the *fiat*, the element of consent, or resolve that the act shall ensue. This, doubtless, to the reader's mind, as to my own, constitutes the essence of the voluntariness of the act. This *fiat* will be treated of in detail farther on. It may be entirely neglected here, for it is a constant coefficient, affecting all voluntary actions alike, and incapable of serving to distinguish them. No one will pretend that its quality varies according as the right arm, for example, or the left is used.

An anticipatory image, then, of the sensorial consequences of a movement, plus (on certain occasions) the fiat that these consequences shall become actual, is the only psychic state which introspection lets us discern as the forerunner of our voluntary acts. There is no introspective evidence whatever of any still later or concomitant feeling attached to the efferent discharge. The various degrees of difficulty with which the fiat is given form a complication of the utmost importance, to be discussed farther on.

Now the reader may still shake his head and say: "But can you seriously mean that all the wonderfully exact adjustment of my action's strength to its ends is not a matter of outgoing innervation? Here is a cannon-ball, and here a pasteboard box: instantly and accurately I lift each from the table, the ball not refusing to rise because my innervation was too weak, the box not flying abruptly into the air because it was too strong. Could representations of the movement's different sensory effects in the two cases be so delicately foreshadowed in the mind? or being there, is it credible that they should, all unaided, so delicately graduate the stimulation of the unconscious motor centres to their work?" Even so! I reply to both queries. We have a most extremely delicate foreshadowing of the sensory effects. Why else the start of surprise that runs through us if someone has filled the light-seeming box with sand before we try to lift it, or has substituted for the cannon-ball which we know a painted wooden imitation? *Surprise* can only come from getting a sensation which differs from the one we expect. But the truth is that when we know the objects well, the very slightest difference from the expected weight will surprise us, or at least attract our notice. With unknown objects we begin by expecting the weight made probable by their appearance. The expectation of this sensation innervates our lift, and we 'set' it rather small at first. An instant verifies whether it is too small. Our expectation rises, i.e., we think in a twinkling of a setting of the chest and teeth, a bracing of the back, and a more violent feeling in the arms. Quicker than thought we have them, and with them the burden ascends into the air.[13] Bernhardt[14] has shown in a rough experimental way

[13] Cf. Souriau in *Revue Philosophique*, XXII, 454.— Professor G. E. Müller thus describes some of his experiments with weights: If, after lifting a weight of 3000 grams a number of times we suddenly get a weight of only 500 grams to lift, "this latter weight is then lifted with a velocity which strikes every onlooker, so that the receptacle for the weight with all its contents often flies high up as if it carried the arm along with it, and the energy with which it is raised is sometimes so entirely out of proportion to the weight itself, that the contents of the receptacle are slung out

that our estimation of the amount of a resistance is as delicately graduated when our wills are passive, and our limbs made to contract by direct local faradization, as when we ourselves innervate them. Ferrier[15] has repeated and verified the observations. They admit of no great precision, and too much stress should not be laid upon them either way; but at the very least they tend to show that no added delicacy would accrue to our perception from the consciousness of the efferent process, even if it existed.

Since there is no direct introspective evidence for the feelings of innervation, is there any indirect or circumstantial evidence? Much is offered; but on critical examination it breaks down. Let us see what it is. Wundt says that were our motor feelings of an afferent nature,

"it ought to be expected that they would increase and diminish with the amount of outer or inner work actually effected in contraction. This, however, is not the case, but the strength of the motor sensation is purely proportional to the strength of the *impulse* to movement, which starts from the central organ innervating the motor nerves. This may be proved by observations made by physicians in cases of morbid alteration in the muscular effect. A patient whose arm or leg is half paralyzed, so that he can only move the limb with great effort, has a distinct feeling of this effort: the limb seems to him heavier than before, appearing as if weighted with lead; he has, therefore, a sense of more work effected than formerly, and yet the effected work is either the same or even less. Only he must, to get even this effect, exert a stronger innervation, a stronger motor impulse, than formerly."[16]

In complete paralysis, also, patients will be conscious of putting forth the greatest exertion to move a limb which remains absolute-

---

upon the table in spite of the mechanical obstacles which such a result has to overcome. A more palpable proof that the trouble here is a wrong adaptation of the motor impulse could not be given." Pflüger's *Archiv*, XLV, 46. Compare also p. 57, and the quotation from Hering on pp. 58–59.

14 *Archiv für Psychiatrie*, III, 618–635. Bernhardt strangely enough seems to think that what his experiments disprove is the existence of afferent muscular feelings, not those of efferent innervation—apparently because he deems that the peculiar thrill of the electricity ought to overpower all other afferent feelings from the part. But it is far more natural to interpret his results the other way, even aside from the certainty yielded by other evidence that passive muscular feelings exist. This other evidence, after being compendiously summed up by Sachs in Reichert und Du Bois-Reymond's *Archiv* (1874), pp. 175–195, is, as far as the anatomical and physiological grounds go, again thrown into doubt by Mays: *Zeitschrift für Biologie*, Bd. XX.

15 *Functions of the Brain* (Am. ed.), p. 228.

16 *Vorlesungen über die Menschen- und Thierseele*, I, 222.

ly still upon the bed, and from which of course no afferent muscular or other feelings can come.[17]

But Dr. Ferrier in his *Functions of the Brain* (Am. Ed., pp. 222–4) disposes very easily of this line of argument. He says:

"It is necessary, however, to exclude movements *altogether* before such an explanation [as Wundt's] can be adopted. Now, though the hemiplegic patient cannot move his paralysed limb though he is conscious of trying hard, yet he will be found to be making powerful muscular exertion of some kind. Vulpian has called attention to the fact, and I have repeatedly verified it, that when a hemiplegic patient is desired to close his paralysed fist, in his endeavours to do so he unconsciously performs this action with the sound one. It is, in fact, almost impossible to exclude such a source of complication, and unless this is taken into account very erroneous conclusions as to the cause of the sense of effort may be drawn. In the fact of muscular contraction and the concomitant centripetal impressions, even though the action is not such as is desired, the conditions of the consciousness of effort exist without our being obliged to regard it as depending on central innervation or outgoing currents.

"It is, however, easy to make an experiment of a simple nature, which will satisfactorily account for the sense of effort, even when these unconscious contractions of the other side, such as hemiplegics make, are entirely excluded.

"If the reader will extend his right arm and hold his forefinger in the position required for pulling the trigger of a pistol, he may without actually moving his finger, but by simply making believe, experience a consciousness of energy put forth. Here, then, is a clear case of consciousness of energy without actual contraction of the muscles either of the one hand or the other, and without any perceptible bodily strain. If the reader will again perform the experiment, and pay careful attention to the condition of his respiration, he will observe that his consciousness of effort coincides with a fixation of the muscles of his chest, and that in proportion to the amount of energy he feels he is putting

17 In some instances we get an opposite result. Dr. H. Charlton Bastian (*British Medical Journal* (1869), p. 461, note), says:

"Ask a man, whose lower extremities are completely paralysed, whether, when he ineffectually wills to move either of these limbs, he is conscious of an expenditure of energy in any degree proportionate to that which he would have experienced if his muscles had naturally responded to his volition. He will tell us rather that he has a sense only of his own utter powerlessness, and that his volition is a mere mental act, carrying with it no feelings of expended energy, such as he is accustomed to experience when his muscles are in powerful action, and from which action and its consequences alone, as I think, he can derive any adequate notion of resistance."

forth, he is keeping his glottis closed and actively contracting his respiratory muscles. Let him place his finger as before, and *continue breathing* all the time, and he will find that however much he may direct his attention to his finger, he will experience not the slightest trace of consciousness of effort until he has actually moved the finger itself, and then it is referred locally to the muscles in action. It is only when this essential and ever present respiratory factor is, as it has been, overlooked, that the consciousness of effort can with any degree of plausibility be ascribed to the outgoing current. In the contraction of the respiratory muscles there are the necessary conditions of centripetal impressions, and these are capable of originating the general sense of effort. When these active efforts are withheld, no consciousness of effort ever arises, except in so far as it is conditioned by the local contraction of the group of muscles towards which the attention is directed, or by other muscular contractions called unconsciously into play in the attempt.

"I am unable to find a single case of consciousness of effort which is not explicable in one or other of the ways specified. In all instances the consciousness of effort is conditioned by the actual fact of muscular contraction. That it is dependent on centripetal impressions generated by the act of contraction, I have already endeavoured to show. When the paths of the centripetal impressions, or the cerebral centres of the same, are destroyed, there is no vestige of a muscular sense. That the central organs, for the apprehension of the impressions originating from muscular contraction, are different from those which send out the motor impulse, has already been established. But when Wundt argues that this cannot be so, because then the sensation would always keep pace with the energy of muscular contraction, he overlooks the important factor of the fixation of the respiratory muscles, which is the basis of the general sense of effort in all its varying degrees."

To these remarks of Ferrier's I have nothing to add.[18] Anyone may verify them, and they prove conclusively that the conscious-

[18] Münsterberg's words may be added: "In lifting an object in the hand I can discover no sensation of volitional energy. I perceive in the first place a slight tension about the head, but that this results from a contraction in the head muscles, and not from a feeling of the brain-discharge, is shown by the simple fact that I get the tension on the right side of the head when I move the right arm, whereas the motor discharge takes place in the opposite side of the brain. . . . In maximal contractions of body- and limb-muscles there occur, as if it were to reinforce them, those special contractions of the muscles of the face [especially frowning and clenching teeth] and those tensions of the skin of the head. These sympathetic movements, felt particularly on the side which makes the effort, are perhaps the immediate ground why we ascribe our awareness of maximal contraction to the region of the head, and call it a consciousness of force, instead of a peripheral sensation." (*Die Willenshandlung* (1888),

ness of muscular exertion, being impossible without movement *effected somewhere*, must be an afferent and not an efferent sensation; a consequence, and not an antecedent, of the movement itself. An idea of the amount of muscular exertion requisite to perform a certain movement can consequently be nothing other than an anticipatory image of the movement's sensible effects.

Driven thus from the body at large, where next shall the circumstantial evidence for the feeling of innervation lodge itself? Where but in the muscles of the eye, from which small retreat it judges itself inexpugnable. Nevertheless, that fastness too must fall, and by the lightest of bombardments. But, before trying the bombardment, let us recall our general principles about optical vertigo, or illusory appearance of movement in objects.

We judge that an object moves under two distinct sets of circumstances:

1. When its image moves on the retina, and we know that the eye is still.

2. When its image is stationary on the retina, and we know that the eye is moving. In this case we feel that we *follow* the object.

In either of these cases a mistaken judgment about the state of the eye will produce optical vertigo.

If in case 1 we think our eye is still when it is really moving, we get a movement of the retinal image which we judge to be due to a real outward motion of the object. This is what happens after looking at rushing water, or through the windows of a moving railroad car, or after turning on one's heel to giddiness. The eyes, without our intending to move them, go through a series of involuntary rotations, continuing those they were previously obliged to make to keep objects in view. If the objects had been whirling by to our right, our eyes when turned to stationary objects will still move slowly towards the right. The retinal image upon them will then move like that of an object passing to the left. We then try to catch it by voluntarily and rapidly rotating the eyes to the left, when the involuntary impulse again rotates the eyes to the right, continuing the apparent motion; and so the game goes on. (See above, pp. 734–736.)

---

pp. 73, 82.) Herr Münsterberg's work is a little masterpiece, which appeared after my text was written. I shall have repeatedly to refer to it again, and cordially recommend to the reader its most thorough refutation of the Innervationsgefühl-theory.

If in case 2 we think our eyes moving when they are in reality still, we shall judge that we are following a moving object when we are but fixating a steadfast one. Illusions of this kind occur after sudden and complete paralysis of special eye muscles, and the partisans of feelings of efferent innervation regard them as *experimenta crucis.* Helmholtz writes:[19]

"When the external rectus muscle of the right eye, or its nerve, is paralyzed, the eye can no longer be rotated to the right side. So long as the patient turns it only to the nasal side it makes regular movements, and he perceives correctly the position of objects in the visual field. So soon, however, as he tries to rotate it outwardly, i.e., towards the right, it ceases to obey his will, stands motionless in the middle of its course, and the objects appear flying to the right, although position of eye and retinal image are unaltered.[20]

"In such a case the exertion of the will is followed neither by actual movement of the eye, nor by contraction of the muscle in question, nor even by increased tension in it. The act of will *produced absolutely no effects* beyond the nervous system, and yet we judge of the direction of the line of vision as if the will had exercised its normal effects. We believe it to have moved to the right, and since the retinal image is unchanged, we attribute to the object the same movement we have erroneously ascribed to the eye. . . . These phenomena leave no room for doubt that we only judge the direction of the line of sight by the effort of will with which we strive to change the position of our eyes. There are also certain weak feelings in our eyelids, . . . and furthermore in excessive lateral rotations we feel a fatiguing strain in the muscles. But all these feelings are too faint and vague to be of use in the perception of direction. We feel then what impulse of the will, and how strong a one, we apply to turn our eye into a given position."

Partial paralysis of the same muscle, *paresis,* as it has been called, seems to point even more conclusively to the same inference, that the will to innervate is felt independently of all its afferent results. I will quote the account given by a recent authority,[21] of the effects of this accident:

"When the nerve going to an eye muscle, e.g., the external rectus of one side, falls into a state of paresis, the first result is that the same

[19] *Physiologische Optik,* p. 600.

[20] [The left and sound eye is here supposed covered. If both eyes look at the same field there are double images which still more perplex the judgment. The patient, however, learns to see correctly before many days or weeks are over.—W. J.]

[21] Alfred Graefe, in *Handbuch der gesammten Augenheilkunde,* Bd. VI, pp. 18–21.

volitional stimulus, which under normal circumstances would have perhaps rotated the eye to its extreme position outwards, now is competent to effect only a moderate outward rotation, say of 20°. If now, shutting the sound eye, the patient looks at an object situated just so far outwards from the paretic eye that this latter must turn 20° in order to see it distinctly, the patient will feel as if he had moved it not only 20° towards the side, but into its extreme lateral position, for the impulse of innervation requisite for bringing it into view is a perfectly conscious act, whilst the diminished state of contraction of the paretic muscle lies for the present out of the ken of consciousness. The test proposed by von Graefe, of localization by the sense of touch, serves to render evident the error which the patient now makes. If we direct him to touch rapidly the object looked at, with the forefinger of the hand of the same side, the line through which the finger moves will not be the line of sight directed 20° outwards, but will approach more nearly to the extreme possible outward line of vision."

A stone-cutter with the external rectus of the left eye paralyzed, will strike his hand instead of his chisel with his hammer, until experience has taught him wisdom.

It appears as if here the judgment of direction *could* only arise from the excessive innervation of the rectus when the object is looked at. All the afferent feelings must be identical with those experienced when the eye is sound and the judgment is correct. The eyeball is rotated just 20° in the one case as in the other, the image falls on the same part of the retina, the pressures on the eyeball and the tensions of the skin and conjunctiva are identical. There is only one feeling which *can* vary, and lead us to our mistake. That feeling must be the effort which the will makes, moderate in the one case, excessive in the other, but in both cases an efferent feeling, pure and simple.

Beautiful and clear as this reasoning seems to be, it is based on an incomplete inventory of the afferent data. The writers have all omitted to consider what is going on in the *other eye*. This is kept covered during the experiments, to prevent double images, and other complications. But if its condition under these circumstances be examined, it will be found to present changes which must result in strong afferent feelings. And the taking account of these feelings demolishes in an instant all the conclusions which the authors from whom I have quoted base upon their supposed absence. This I will now proceed to show.[22]

22 Professor G. E. Müller (*Zur Grundlegung der Psychophysik* (1878), p. 318), was

Take first the case of complete paralysis and assume the right eye affected. Suppose the patient desires to rotate his gaze to an object situated in the extreme right of the field of vision. As Hering has so beautifully shown, both eyes move by a common act of innervation, and in this instance both move towards the right. But the paralyzed right eye stops short in the middle of its course, the object still appearing far to the right of its fixation point. The left sound eye, meanwhile, although covered, continues its rotation until the extreme rightward limit thereof has been reached. To an observer looking at both eyes the left will seem to squint. Of course this continued and extreme rotation produces afferent feelings of rightward motion in the eyeball, which momentarily overpower the faint feelings of central position in the diseased and uncovered eye. The patient feels by his left eyeball as if he were following an object which by his right retina he perceives he does not overtake. All the conditions of optical vertigo are here present: the image stationary on the retina, and the erroneous conviction that the eyes are moving.

The objection that a feeling in the left eyeball ought not to produce a conviction that the right eye moves, will be considered in a moment. Let us meanwhile turn to the case of simple paresis with apparent translocation of the field.

Here the right eye succeeds in fixating the object, but observation of the left eye will reveal to an observer the fact that it squints just as violently inwards as in the former case. The direction which

---

the first to explain the phenomenon after the manner advocated in the text. Still unacquainted with his book, I published my own similar explanation two years later.

Professor Mach in his wonderfully original little work *Beiträge zur Analyse der Empfindungen*, p. 57, describes an artificial way of getting translocation, and explains the effect likewise by the feeling of innervation. "Turn your eyes," he says, "as far as possible towards the left and press against the right sides of the orbits two large lumps of putty. If you then try to look as quickly as possible towards the right, this succeeds, on account of the incompletely spherical form of the eyes, only imperfectly, and the objects consequently appear translocated very considerably towards the right. The *bare will* to look rightwards gives to all images on the retina a greater *rightwards value*, to express it shortly. The experiment is at first surprising."—I regret to say that I cannot myself make it succeed—I know not for what reason. But even where it does succeed it seems to me that the conditions are much too complicated for Professor Mach's theoretic conclusions to be safely drawn. The putty squeezed into the orbit, and the pressure of the eyeball against it must give rise to peripheral sensations *strong* enough, at any rate (if only of the right kind), to justify any amount of false perception of our eyeball's position, quite apart from the innervation feelings which Professor Mach supposes to coexist.

the finger of the patient takes in pointing to the object, is the direction of this squinting and covered left eye. As Graefe says (although he fails to seize the true import of his own observation), "It appears to have been by no means sufficiently noticed how significantly the direction of the line of sight of the secondarily deviating eye [i.e., of the left], and the line of direction of the pointed finger agree."

The translocation would, in a word, be perfectly explained could we suppose that the sensation of a certain degree of rotation in the left eyeball were able to suggest to the patient the position of an object whose image falls on the right retina alone.[23] Can, then, a feeling in one eye be confounded with a feeling in the other? It most assuredly can, for not only Donders and Adamük, by their vivisections, but Hering by his exquisite optical experiments, have proved that the apparatus of innervation for both eyes is single, and that they act as one organ—a double eye, according to Hering, or what Helmholtz calls a *Cyclopenauge*. The retinal feelings of this double organ, singly innervated, are naturally undistinguished as respects our knowing whether they belong to the left retina or to the right. We use them only to tell us where their objects lie. It

23 An illusion in principle exactly analogous to that of the patient under discussion can be produced experimentally in anyone in a way which Hering has described in his *Lehre vom binocularen Sehen*, pp. 12–14. I will quote Helmholtz's account of it, which is especially valuable as coming from a believer in the *Innervationsgefühl*: "Let the two eyes first look parallel, then let the right eye be closed whilst the left still looks at the infinitely distant object *a*. The directions of both eyes will thus remain unaltered, and *a* will be seen in its right place. Now accommodate the left eye for a point *f* [a needle in Hering's experiment] lying on the optical axis between it and *a*, only very near. The position of the left eye and its optical axis, as well as the place of the retinal image upon it . . . are wholly unaltered by this movement. But the consequence is that an apparent movement of the object occurs—a movement towards the left. As soon as we accommodate again for distance the object returns to its old place. Now what alters itself in this experiment is only the position of the closed right eye: its optical axis, when the effort is made to accommodate for the point *f*, also converges towards this point. . . . Conversely it is possible for me to make my optical axes diverge, even with closed eyes, so that in the above experiment the right eye should turn far to the right of *a*. This divergence is but slowly reached, and gives me therefore no illusory movement. But when I suddenly relax my effort to make it, and the right optical axis springs back to the parallel position, I immediately see the object which the left eye fixates shift its position towards the left. Thus not only the position of the seeing eye *a*, but also that of the closed eye *b*, influences our judgment of the direction in which the seen object lies. The open eye remaining fixed, and the closed eye moving towards the right or left, the object seen by the open eye appears also to move towards the right or left." (*Physiologische Optik*, pp. 607–8.)

takes long practice directed specially *ad hoc* to teach us on which retina the sensations severally fall. Similarly the different sensations which arise from the positions of the eyeballs are used exclusively as signs of the position of objects; an object directly fixated being localized habitually at the intersection of the two optical axes, but without any separate consciousness on our part that the position of one axis is different from another. All we are aware of is a consolidated feeling of a certain 'strain' in the eyeballs, accompanied by the perception that just so far in front and so far to the right or to the left there is an object which we see. So that a 'muscular' process in one eye is as likely to combine with a retinal process in the other eye to effect a perceptive judgment, as two processes in one eye are likely so to combine.

Another piece of circumstantial evidence for the feelings of innervation is that adduced by Professor Mach, as follows:

"If we stand on a bridge, and look at the water flowing beneath, we usually feel ourselves at rest, whilst the water seems in motion. Prolonged looking at the water, however, commonly has for its result to make the bridge with the observer and surroundings suddenly seem to move in the direction opposed to that of the water, whilst the water itself assumes the appearance of standing still. The *relative* motion of the objects is in both cases the same, and there must therefore be some adequate *physiological* ground why sometimes one, sometimes the other part of them is felt to move. In order to investigate the matter con-

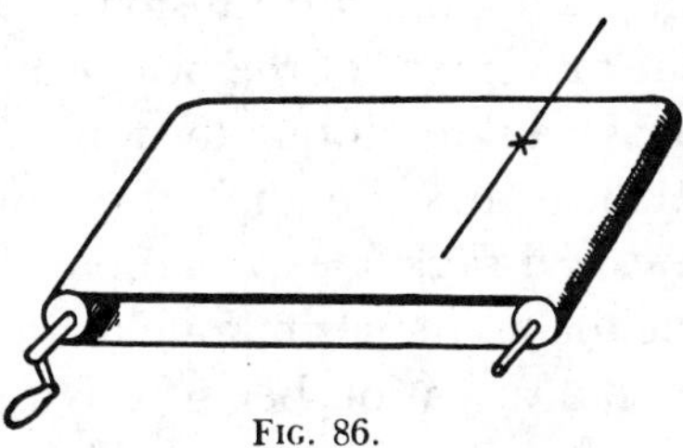

FIG. 86.

veniently, I had the simple apparatus constructed which is represented in Fig. 86. An oil-cloth with a simple pattern is horizontally stretched over two cylinders (each 2 metres long and 3 feet apart) and kept in uniform motion by the help of a crank. Across the cloth, and some 30 cm. above it, is stretched a string, with a knot *x*, which serves as a fixation-point for the eye of the observer. If the observer *follow* with his eyes the pattern of the cloth as it moves, he sees it in movement, himself and the surroundings at rest. But if he looks at the *knot*, he soon feels as if the entire room were moving contrary to the direction of the cloth, whilst the latter seems to stand still. This change in the mode of looking comes about in more or less time according to one's momentary disposition, but usually it takes but a few seconds. If one once understands the point, one can make the two appearances alternate at will. Every following of the oil-cloth makes the observer stationary; every fixation of the knot or *inattention to the oil-cloth, so that its pattern becomes blurred*, sets him in apparent motion."[24]

Professor Mach proceeds to explain the phenomenon as follows:

"Moving objects exert, as is well known, a peculiar motor stimulation upon the eye, they draw our attention and our look after them. If the look really follows them . . . we assume that they move. But if the eye, instead of following the moving objects, remains steadfastly at rest, it must be that the constant stimulus to motion which it receives is neutralized by an equally constant current of innervation flowing into its motor apparatus. But this is just what would happen if the steadfastly fixated point were itself moving uniformly in the other direction, and we were following it with our eyes. When this comes about, whatever motionless things are looked at must appear in motion."[25]

The knot *x*, the string, we ourselves, and all our stationary surroundings thus appear in movement, according to Mach, because we are constantly innervating our eyeballs to resist the *drag* exerted upon them by the pattern or the flowing waves. I have myself repeated the observation many times above flowing streams, but have never succeeded in getting the full illusion as described by Mach. I gain a sense of the movement of the bridge and of my own body, but the river never seems absolutely to stop: it still moves in one direction, whilst I float away in the other. But, be the illusion partial or complete, a different explanation of it from Professor Mach's seems to me the more natural one to adopt. The illusion is said to cease when, our attention being fully fixed on the moving oil-cloth, we perceive the latter for what it is; and to recommence, on the contrary, when we perceive the oil-cloth as a vaguely moving background behind an object which we directly fixate and whose position with regard to our own body is unchanged. This, however, is the sort of consciousness which we have whenever we are ourselves borne in a vehicle, on horseback, or in a boat. As we and our

24 *Beiträge zur Analyse der Empfindungen*, p. 65.

25 P. 68.

belongings go one way, the *whole background* goes the other. I should rather, therefore, explain Professor Mach's illusion as similar to the illusion at railroad-stations described above on page 735. The other train moves, but it makes ours seem to move, because, filling the window as it does, it stands for the time being as the total background. So here, the water or oil-cloth stands for us as background *überhaupt* whenever we seem to ourselves to be moving over it. The relative motion felt by the retina is assigned to that one of its components which we look at more in itself and less as a mere *repoussoir*. This may be the knot above the oil-cloth or the bridge beneath our feet, or it may be, on the other hand, the oil-cloth's pattern or the surface of the swirling stream. Similar changes may be produced in the apparent motion of the moon and the clouds through which it shines, by similarly altering the attention. Such alterations, however, in our conception of which part of the visual field is substantive object and which part background, seem to have no connection with feelings of innervation. I cannot, therefore, regard the observation of Prof. Mach as any proof that the latter feelings exist.[26]

The circumstantial evidence for the feeling of innervation thus seems to break down like the introspective evidence. But not only can we rebut experiments intended to prove it, we can also adduce experiments which disprove it. A person who moves a limb voluntarily must innervate it in any case, and if he feels the innervation he ought to be able to use the feeling to define what his limb is about, even though the limb itself were anæsthetic. If, however,

[26] I owe the interpretation in the text to my friend and former student, Mr. E. S. Drown, whom I set to observe the phenomenon before I had observed it myself. Concerning the vacillations in our interpretation of relative motion over retina and skin, see above, p. 812.

Herr Münsterberg gives additional reasons against the feeling of innervation, of which I will quote a couple. First, our ideas of movement are all *faint* ideas, resembling in this the copies of sensations in memory. Were they feelings of the outgoing discharge, they would be original states of consciousness, not copies; and ought by analogy to be *vivid* like other original states.—Second, our unstriped muscles yield no feelings in contracting, nor can they be contracted at will, differing thus in *two* peculiarities from the voluntary muscles. What more natural than to suppose that the two peculiarities hang together, and that the reason why we cannot contract our intestines, for example, at will, is, that we have no memory-images of how their contraction feels? Were the supposed innervation-feeling always the 'mental cue,' one doesn't see why we might not have it even where, as here, the contractions themselves are unfelt, and why it might not bring the contractions about. (*Die Willenshandlung*, pp. 87–8.)

the limb be totally anæsthetic, it turns out that he does not know at all how much work it performs in its contraction—in other words, he has no perception of the amount of innervation which he exerts. A patient examined by Messrs. Gley and Marillier beautifully showed this. His entire arms, and his trunk down to the navel, were insensible both superficially and deeply, but his arms were not paralyzed:

"We take three stone bottles—two of them are empty and weigh each 250 grams; the third is full of mercury and weighs 1850 grams. We ask L . . . to estimate their weight and tell us which is heaviest. He declares that he finds them all three alike. With many days of interval we made two series of six experiments each. The result was always the same. The experiment, it need hardly be said, was arranged in such wise that he could be informed neither by sight nor by hearing. He even declared, holding in his hand the bottleful of mercury, that he found it to have no weight. . . . We place successively in his hand (his eyes being still bandaged) a piece of modelling wax, a stick of hard wood, a thick India-rubber tube, a newspaper folded up lengthwise and rumpled, and we make him squeeze these several objects. He feels no difference of resistance and does not even perceive that anything is in his hand."[27]

M. Gley in another place[28] quotes experiments by Dr. Bloch which prove that the sense which we have of our limbs' position owes absolutely nothing to the feeling of innervation put forth. Dr. Bloch stood opposite the angle of a screen whose sides made an angle of about 90°, and tried to place his hands symmetrically, or so that both should fall on corresponding spots of the two screen-sides, which were marked with squares for the purpose. The average error being noted, one hand was then passively carried by an assistant to a spot on its screen-side, and the other actively sought the corresponding spot on the opposite side. The accuracy of the correspondence proved to be as great as when both arms were innervated voluntarily, showing that the consciousness of innervation in the first of the two experiments added nothing to the sense of the limbs' position. Dr. Bloch then tried, pressing a certain number of pages of a book between the thumb and forefinger of one hand, to press an equal number between the same fingers of the other hand. He did this just as well when the fingers in question were drawn apart by India-rubber bands as when they were unin-

27 *Revue Philosophique*, XXIII, 442.

28 *Ibid.*, XX, 604.

terfered with, showing that the physiologically much greater innervation-current required in the former case had no effect upon the consciousness of the movement made, so far as its spatial character at any rate was concerned.[29]

29 Herr Sternberg (Pflüger's *Archiv,* XXXVII, p. 1) thinks that he proves the feeling of innervation by the fact that when we have willed to make a movement we generally think that it is made. We have already seen some of the facts on pp. 749–750, above. S. cites from Exner the fact that if we put a piece of hard rubber between our back teeth and bite, our front teeth seem actually to approach each other, although it is physically impossible for them to do so. He proposes the following experiment: Lay the palm of the hand on a table with the forefinger overlapping its edge and flexed back as far as possible, whilst the table keeps the other fingers extended; then try to flex the terminal joint of the forefinger without looking. You do not do it, and yet you think that you do. Here again the innervation, according to the author, is felt as an executed movement. It seems to me, as I said in the previous place, that the illusion is in all these cases due to the inveterate association of ideas. Normally our will to move has always been followed by the sensation that we *have* moved, except when the simultaneous sensation of an external resistance was there. The result is that where we feel no external resistance, and the muscles and tendons tighten, the invariably associated idea is intense enough to be hallucinatory. In the experiment with the teeth, the resistance customarily met with when our masseters contract is a soft one. We do not close our teeth on a thing like hard rubber once in a million times; so when we do so, we imagine the habitual result.—Persons with *amputated limbs* more often than not continue to feel them as if they were still there, and can, moreover, give themselves the feeling of moving them at will. The life-long sensorial associate of the idea of 'working one's toes,' e.g. (uncorrected by any opposite sensation, since no real sensation of non-movement can come from non-existing toes), follows the idea and swallows it up. The man thinks that his toes are 'working' (cf. *Proceedings of American Society for Psychical Research,* p. 249).

Herr Loeb also comes to the rescue of the feeling of innervation with observations of his own made after my text was written, but they convince me no more than the arguments of others. Loeb's facts are these (Pflüger's *Archiv,* XLVI, p. 1): If we stand before a vertical surface, and if, with our hands *at different heights,* we *simultaneously* make with them what seem to us equally extensive movements, that movement always turns out really shorter which is made with the arm whose muscles (in virtue of the arm's position) are already the more contracted. The same result ensues when the arms are laterally unsymmetrical. Loeb assumes that both arms contract by virtue of a common innervation, but that although this innervation is relatively less effective upon the more contracted arm, our *feeling* of its equal strength overpowers the disparity of the incoming sensations of movement which the two limbs send back, and makes us think that the spaces they traverse are the same. "The sensation of the extent and direction of our voluntary movements depends accordingly upon the impulse of our will to move, and not upon the feelings set up by the motion in the active organ." Now if this is the elementary law which Loeb calls it, why does it only manifest its effect when both hands are moving simultaneously? Why not when the *same* hand makes *successive* movements? and especially why not when both hands move symmetrically or at the same level, but *one of them is weighted*? A weighted hand surely requires a stronger innervation than an unweighted one to move an equal distance upwards; and yet, as Loeb confesses, we do not tend to overestimate the path which it traverses under these circumstances. The fact is that the illusion

On the whole, then, it seems as probable as anything can well be, that these feelings of innervation do not exist. If the motor cells are distinct structures, they are as insentient as the motor nerve-trunks are after the posterior roots are cut. If they are not distinct structures, but are only the last sensory cells, those at the 'mouth of the funnel,'[30] then their consciousness is that of kinæsthetic ideas and sensations merely, and this consciousness accompanies the *rise* of activity in them rather than its discharge. The entire content and material of our consciousness—consciousness of movement, as of all things else—is thus of peripheral origin, and came to us in the first instance through the peripheral nerves. If it be asked what we gain by this sensationalistic conclusion, I reply that we gain at any rate simplicity and uniformity. In the chapters on Space, on Belief, on the Emotions, we found sensation to be a much richer thing than is commonly supposed; and this chapter seems at this point to fall into line with those. Then, as for sensationalism being a degrading belief, which abolishes all inward originality and spontaneity, there is this to be said, that the advocates of inward spontaneity may be turning their backs on its real citadel, when they make a fight, on its behalf, for the consciousness of energy put forth in the outgoing discharge. Let there be no such

---

which Loeb has studied is a complex resultant of many factors. One of them, it seems to me, is an instinctive tendency to *revert to the type of the bilateral movements of childhood*. In adult life we move our arms for the most part in alternation; but at a certain period of infancy the free movements of the arms are almost always similar on both sides, symmetrical when the direction of motion is horizontal, and with the hands on the same level when it is vertical. The most natural innervation, when the movements are rapidly performed, is one which takes the movement back to this form. Our *estimation* meanwhile of the lengths severally traversed by the two hands is mainly based, as such estimations with closed eyes usually are (see Loeb's own earlier paper, "Untersuchungen über den Fühlraum der Hand," in Pflüger's *Archiv*, XLI, 107), upon the apparent velocity and duration of the movement. The duration is the same for both hands, since the movements begin and end simultaneously. The velocities of the two hands are under the experimental conditions almost impossible of comparison. It is well known how imperfect a discrimination of *weights* we have when we 'heft' them simultaneously, one in either hand; and G. E. Müller has well shown (Pflüger's *Archiv*, XLV, 57) that the velocity of the lift is the main factor in determining our judgment of weight. It is hardly possible to conceive of more unfavorable conditions for making an accurate comparison of the length of two movements than those which govern the experiments which are under discussion. The only prominent sign is the duration, which would lead us to infer the equality of the two movements. We consequently deem them equal, though a native tendency in our motor centres keeps them from being so.

[30] This is by no means an unplausible opinion. See Vol. I, p. 73.

consciousness; let all our thoughts of movements be of sensational constitution; still in the emphasizing, choosing, and espousing of one of them rather than another, in the saying to it, 'be thou the reality for me,' there is ample scope for our inward initiative to be shown. Here, it seems to me, the true line between the passive materials and the activity of the spirit should be drawn. It is certainly false strategy to draw it between such ideas as are connected with the outgoing and such as are connected with the incoming neural wave.[31]

If the ideas by which we discriminate between one movement and another, at the instant of deciding in our mind which one we shall perform, are always of sensorial origin, then the question arises, "Of which sensorial order need they be?" It will be remembered that we distinguished two orders of kinæsthetic impression, the *remote* ones, made by the movement on the eye or ear or distant skin, etc., and the *resident* ones, made on the moving parts themselves, muscles, joints, etc. Now do 'resident' images, exclusively, form what I have called the mental cue, or will 'remote' ones equally suffice?

There can be no doubt whatever that the mental cue may be either an image of the resident or of the remote kind. Although, at the outset of our learning a movement, it would seem that the resident feelings must come strongly before consciousness (cf. p. 1099), later this need not be the case. The rule, in fact, would seem to be that they tend to lapse more and more from consciousness, and that the more practised we become in a movement, the more 'remote' do the ideas become which form its mental cue. What we are *interested* in is what sticks in our consciousness; everything else we get rid of as quickly as we can. Our resident feelings of movement have no substantive interest for us at all, as a rule. What interest us are the ends which the movement is to attain. Such an end is generally an outer impression on the eye or ear, or sometimes on

31 Maine de Biran, Royer-Collard, Sir John Herschel, Dr. Carpenter, Dr. Martineau, all seem to posit a force-sense by which, in becoming aware of an outer resistance to our will, we are taught the existence of an outer world. I hold that every peripheral sensation gives us an outer world. An insect crawling on our skin gives us as 'outward' an impression as a hundred pounds weighing on our back.—I have read M. A. Bertrand's criticism of my views (*La Psychologie de l'effort,* 1889); but as he seems to think that I deny the *feeling* of effort altogether, I can get no profit from it, despite his charming way of saying things.

the skin, nose, or palate. Now let the idea of the end associate itself definitely with the right motor innervation, and the thought of the innervation's *resident* effects will become as great an encumbrance as we formerly concluded that the feeling of the innervation itself would be. The mind does not need it; the end alone is enough.

The idea of the end, then, tends more and more to make itself all-sufficient. Or, at any rate, if the kinæsthetic ideas are called up at all, they are so swamped in the vivid kinæsthetic feelings by which they are immediately overtaken that we have no time to be aware of their separate existence. As I write, I have no anticipation, as a thing distinct from my sensation, of either the look or the digital feel of the letters which flow from my pen. The words chime on my mental *ear*, as it were, before I write them, but not on my mental eye or hand. This comes from the rapidity with which often-repeated movements follow on their mental cue. An end consented to as soon as conceived innervates directly the centre of the first movement of the chain which leads to its accomplishment, and then the whole chain rattles off *quasi*-reflexly, as was described on pp. 120–121 of Vol. I.

The reader will certainly recognize this to be true in all fluent and unhesitating voluntary acts. The only special fiat there is at the outset of the performance. A man says to himself, "I must change my shirt," and involuntarily he has taken off his coat, and his fingers are at work in their accustomed manner on his waistcoat-buttons, etc.; or we say, "I must go downstairs," and ere we know it we have risen, walked, and turned the handle of the door;—all through the idea of an end coupled with a series of guiding sensations which successively arise. It would seem indeed that we fail of accuracy and certainty in our attainment of the end whenever we are preoccupied with much ideal consciousness of the means. We walk a beam the better the less we think of the position of our feet upon it. We pitch or catch, we shoot or chop the better the less tactile and muscular (the less resident), and the more exclusively optical (the more remote), our consciousness is. Keep your *eye* on the place aimed at, and your hand will fetch it; think of your hand, and you will very likely miss your aim. Dr. Southard found that he could touch a spot with a pencil-point more accurately with a visual than with a tactile mental cue. In the former case he looked at a small object and closed his eyes before trying to touch it. In the latter case he *placed* it with closed eyes, and then after removing his hand tried to touch it again. The average error with touch (when the results were most favorable) was 17.13 mm. With sight it was only 12.37 mm.[32]—All these are plain results of introspection and observation. By what neural machinery they are made possible we need not, at this present stage, inquire.

In Chapter XVIII we saw how enormously individuals differ in respect to their mental imagery. In the type of imagination called *tactile* by the French authors, it is probable that the kinæsthetic ideas are more prominent than in my account. We must not expect too great a uniformity in individual accounts, nor wrangle overmuch as to which one 'truly' represents the process.[33]

[32] Bowditch and Southard in *Journal of Physiology*, vol. III, No. 3. It was found in these experiments that the maximum of accuracy was reached when two seconds of time elapsed between locating the object by eye or hand and starting to touch it. When the mark was located with one hand, and the other hand had to touch it, the error was considerably greater than when the same hand both located and touched it.

[33] The same caution must be shown in discussing pathological cases. There are remarkable discrepancies in the effects of peripheral anæsthesia upon the voluntary power. Such cases as I quoted in the text (p. 1101) are by no means the only type. In those cases the patients could move their limbs accurately when the eyes were open, and inaccurately when they were shut. In other cases, however, the anæsthetic patients *cannot move their limbs at all* when the eyes are shut. (For reports of two such cases see Bastian in *Brain*, Binet in *Revue Philosophique*, XXV, 478.) M. Binet explains these (hysterical) cases as requiring the 'dynamogenic' stimulus of light (see above, p. 998). They *might*, however, be cases of such congenitally defective optical imagination that the 'mental cue' was normally 'tactile'; and that when this tactile cue failed through functional inertness of the kinæsthetic centres, the only optical cue strong enough to determine the discharge had to be an actual *sensation* of the eye.—There is still a third class of cases in which the limbs have lost all sensibility, even for movements passively imprinted, but in which voluntary movements can be accurately executed even when the eyes are closed. MM. Binet and Féré have reported some of these interesting cases, which are found amongst the hysterical hemianæsthetics. They can, for example, write accurately at will, although their eyes are closed and they have no feeling of the writing taking place, and many of them do not know when it begins or stops. Asked to write repeatedly the letter *a*, and then say how many times they have written it, some are able to assign the number and some are not. Some of them admit that they are guided by visual imagination of what is being done. Cf. *Archives de Physiologie*, Oct. 1887, pp. 363–5. Now it would seem at first sight that feelings of outgoing innervation must exist in these cases and be kept account of. There are no other guiding impressions, either immediate or remote, of which the patient is conscious; and unless feelings of innervation be there, the writing would seem miraculous. But if such feelings are present in these cases, and suffice to direct accurately the succession of movements, why do they not suffice in those other anæsthetic cases in which movement becomes disorderly when the eyes are closed. *Innervation* is there, or there would be no movement; why is the *feeling* of the innervation gone? The truth seems to be, as M. Binet supposes (*Revue Phi-*

I trust that I have now made clear what that 'idea of a movement' is which must precede it in order that it be voluntary. It is not the thought of the innervation which the movement requires. It is the anticipation of the movement's sensible effects, resident or remote, and sometimes very remote indeed. Such anticipations, to say the least, determine *what* our movements shall be. I have spoken all along as if they also might determine *that* they shall be. This, no doubt, has disconcerted many readers, for it certainly seems as if a special fiat, or consent to the movement, were required in addition to the mere conception of it, in many cases of volition; and this fiat I have altogether left out of my account. This leads us to the next point in the psychology of the Will. It can be the more easily treated now that we have got rid of so much tedious preliminary matter.

IDEO-MOTOR ACTION

The question is this: *Is the bare idea of a movement's sensible effects its sufficient mental cue* (p. 1108), *or must there be an additional mental antecedent, in the shape of a fiat, decision, consent, volitional mandate, or other synonymous phenomenon of consciousness, before the movement can follow?*

I answer: Sometimes the bare idea is sufficient, but sometimes an additional conscious element, in the shape of a fiat, mandate, or express consent, has to intervene and precede the movement. The cases without a fiat constitute the more fundamental, because the more simple, variety. The others involve a special complication, which must be fully discussed at the proper time. For the present let us turn to *ideo-motor action*, as it has been termed, or the sequence of movement upon the mere thought of it, as the type of the process of volition.

Wherever movement follows *unhesitatingly and immediately* the notion of it in the mind, we have ideo-motor action. We are then aware of nothing between the conception and the execution. All sorts of neuro-muscular processes come between, of course, but

losophique, XXV, p. 479), that these cases are not arguments for the feeling of innervation. They are pathological curiosities; and the patients are not really anæsthetic, but are victims of that curious dissociation or splitting-off of one part of their consciousness from the rest which we are just beginning to understand, thanks to Messrs. Janet, Binet, and Gurney, and in which the split-off part (in this case the kinæsthetic sensations) may nevertheless remain to produce its usual effects. Compare what was said above, p. 1103.

we know absolutely nothing of them. We think the act, and it is done; and that is all that introspection tells us of the matter. Dr. Carpenter, who first used, I believe, the name of ideo-motor action, placed it, if I mistake not, among the curiosities of our mental life. The truth is that it is no curiosity, but simply the normal process stripped of disguise. Whilst talking I become conscious of a pin on the floor, or of some dust on my sleeve. Without interrupting the conversation I brush away the dust or pick up the pin. I make no express resolve, but the mere perception of the object and the fleeting notion of the act seem of themselves to bring the latter about. Similarly, I sit at table after dinner and find myself from time to time taking nuts or raisins out of the dish and eating them. My dinner properly is over, and in the heat of the conversation I am hardly aware of what I do; but the perception of the fruit, and the fleeting notion that I may eat it, seem fatally to bring the act about. There is certainly no express fiat here; any more than there is in all those habitual goings and comings and rearrangements of ourselves which fill every hour of the day, and which incoming sensations instigate so immediately that it is often difficult to decide whether not to call them reflex rather than voluntary acts. We have seen in Chapter IV that the intermediary terms of an habitual series of acts leading to an end are apt to be of this *quasi*-automatic sort. As Lotze says:

"We see in writing or piano-playing a great number of very complicated movements following quickly one upon the other, the instigative representations of which remained scarcely a second in consciousness, certainly not long enough to awaken any other volition than the general one of resigning one's self without reserve to the passing over of representation into action. All the acts of our daily life happen in this wise: Our standing up, walking, talking, all this never demands a distinct impulse of the will, but is adequately brought about by the pure flux of thought."[34]

34 *Medicinische Psychologie*, p. 293. In his admirably acute chapter on the Will this author has most explicitly maintained the position that what we call muscular exertion is an afferent and not an efferent feeling; "We must affirm universally that in the muscular feeling we are not sensible of the *force* on its way to produce an effect, but only of the *sufferance* already produced in our movable organs, the muscles, after the force has, in a manner unobservable by us, exerted upon them its causality" (p. 311). How often the battles of psychology have to be fought over again, each time with heavier armies and bigger trains, though not always with such able generals!

In all this the determining condition of the unhesitating and resistless sequence of the act seems to be *the absence of any conflicting notion in the mind.* Either there is nothing else at all in the mind, or what is there does not conflict. The hypnotic subject realizes the former condition. Ask him what he is thinking about, and ten to one he will reply 'nothing.' The consequence is that he both believes everything he is told, and performs every act that is suggested. The suggestion may be a vocal command, or it may be the performance before him of the movement required. Hypnotic subjects in certain conditions repeat whatever they hear you say, and imitate whatever they see you do. Dr. Féré says that certain waking persons of neurotic type, if one repeatedly close and open one's hand before their eyes, soon begin to have corresponding feelings in their own fingers, and presently begin irresistibly to execute the movements which they see. Under these conditions of 'preparation' Dr. Féré found that his subjects could squeeze the hand-dynamometer much more strongly than when abruptly invited to do so. A few *passive* repetitions of a movement will enable many enfeebled patients to execute it actively with greater strength. These observations beautifully show how the mere quickening of kinæsthetic ideas is equivalent to a certain amount of tension towards discharge in the centres.[35]

We know what it is to get out of bed on a freezing morning in a room without a fire, and how the very vital principle within us protests against the ordeal. Probably most persons have lain on certain mornings for an hour at a time unable to brace themselves to the resolve. We think how late we shall be, how the duties of the day will suffer; we say, "I *must* get up, this is ignominious," etc.; but still the warm couch feels too delicious, the cold outside too cruel, and resolution faints away and postpones itself again and again just as it seemed on the verge of bursting the resistance and passing over into the decisive act. Now how do we *ever* get up under such circumstances? If I may generalize from my own experience, we more often than not get up without any struggle or decision at all. We suddenly find that we *have* got up. A fortunate lapse of consciousness occurs; we forget both the warmth and the cold; we fall into some revery connected with the day's life, in the course of which the idea flashes across us, "Hollo! I must lie here

[35] Charles Féré: *Sensation et mouvement* (1887), chapter III.

no longer"—an idea which at that lucky instant awakens no contradictory or paralyzing suggestions, and consequently produces immediately its appropriate motor effects. It was our acute consciousness of both the warmth and the cold during the period of struggle, which paralyzed our activity then and kept our idea of rising in the condition of *wish* and not of *will*. The moment these inhibitory ideas ceased, the original idea exerted its effects.

This case seems to me to contain in miniature form the data for an entire psychology of volition. It was in fact through meditating on the phenomenon in my own person that I first became convinced of the truth of the doctrine which these pages present, and which I need here illustrate by no farther examples.[36] The reason why that doctrine is not a self-evident truth is that we have so many ideas which *do not* result in action. But it will be seen that in every such case, without exception, that is because other ideas simultaneously present rob them of their impulsive power. But even here, and when a movement is inhibited from *completely* taking place by contrary ideas, it will *incipiently* take place. To quote Lotze once more:

> "The spectator accompanies the throwing of a billiard-ball, or the thrust of the swordsman, with slight movements of his arm; the untaught narrator tells his story with many gesticulations; the reader while absorbed in the perusal of a battle-scene feels a slight tension run through his muscular system, keeping time as it were with the actions he is reading of. These results become the more marked the more we are absorbed in thinking of the movements which suggest them; they grow fainter exactly in proportion as a complex consciousness, under the dominion of a crowd of other representations, withstands the passing over of mental contemplation into outward action."

The 'willing-game,' the exhibitions of so-called 'mind-reading,' or more properly muscle-reading, which have lately grown so fashionable, are based on this incipient obedience of muscular contraction to idea, even when the deliberate intention is that no contraction shall occur.[37]

36 Professor A. Bain (*Senses and the Intellect*, pp. 336–48) and Dr. W. B. Carpenter (*Mental Physiology*, chap. VI) give examples in abundance.

37 For a full account, by an expert, of the 'willing-game,' see Mr. Stuart Cumberland's article: "A Thought-Reader's Experiences" in the *Nineteenth Century*, XX, 867. M. Gley has given a good example of ideo-motor action in the *Bulletins de la Société de Psychologie Physiologique* for 1890. Tell a person to think intently of a

We may then lay it down for certain that *every representation of a movement awakens in some degree the actual movement which is its object; and awakens it in a maximum degree whenever it is not kept from so doing by an antagonistic representation present simultaneously to the mind.*

The express fiat, or act of mental consent to the movement, comes in when the neutralization of the antagonistic and inhibitory idea is required. But that there is no express fiat needed when the conditions are simple, the reader ought now to be convinced. Lest, however, he should still share the common prejudice that voluntary action without 'exertion of will-power' is *Hamlet* with the prince's part left out, I will make a few farther remarks. The first point to start from, in understanding voluntary action and the possible occurrence of it with no fiat or express resolve, is the fact that consciousness is *in its very nature impulsive.*[38] We do not have a sensation or a thought, and then have to *add* something dynamic to it to get a movement. Every pulse of feeling which we have is the correlate of some neural activity that is already on its way to instigate a movement. Our sensations and thoughts are but cross-sections, as it were, of currents whose essential consequence is motion, and which no sooner run in at one nerve than they run out again at another. The popular notion that mere consciousness as such is not essentially a forerunner of activity, that the latter must result from some superadded 'will-force,' is a very natural inference from those special cases in which we think of an act for an indefinite length of time without the action taking place. These cases, however, are not the norm; they are cases of inhibition by antagonistic thoughts. When the blocking is released we feel as if

certain name, and saying that you will then force her to write it, let her hold a pencil, and do you yourself hold her hand. She will then probably trace the name involuntarily, believing that you are forcing her to do it.

38 I abstract here from the fact that a certain *intensity* of the consciousness is required for its impulsiveness to be effective in a complete degree. There is an inertia in the motor processes as in all other natural things. In certain individuals, and at certain times (disease, fatigue), the inertia is unusually great, and we may then have ideas of action which produce no visible act, but discharge themselves into merely nascent dispositions to activity or into emotional expression. The inertia of the motor parts here plays the same rôle as is elsewhere played by antagonistic ideas. We shall consider this restrictive inertia later on; it obviously introduces no essential alteration into the law which the text lays down.

an inward spring were let loose, and this is the additional impulse or *fiat* upon which the act effectively succeeds. We shall study anon the blocking and its release. Our higher thought is full of it. But where there is no blocking, there is naturally no hiatus between the thought-process and the motor discharge. *Movement is the natural immediate effect of feeling, irrespective of what the quality of the feeling may be. It is so in reflex action, it is so in emotional expression, it is so in the voluntary life.* Ideo-motor action is thus no paradox, to be softened or explained away. It obeys the type of all conscious action, and from it one must start to explain action in which a special fiat is involved.

It may be remarked in passing, that the inhibition of a movement no more involves an express effort or command than its execution does. Either of them *may* require it. But in all simple and ordinary cases, just as the bare presence of one idea prompts a movement, so the bare presence of another idea will prevent its taking place. Try to feel as if you were crooking your finger, whilst keeping it straight. In a minute it will fairly tingle with the imaginary change of position; yet it will not sensibly move, because *its not really moving* is also a part of what you have in mind. Drop *this* idea, think of the movement purely and simply, with all brakes off; and, presto! it takes place with no effort at all.

A waking man's behavior is thus at all times the resultant of two opposing neural forces. With unimaginable fineness some currents among the cells and fibres of his brain are playing on his motor nerves, whilst other currents, as unimaginably fine, are playing on the first currents, damming or helping them, altering their direction or their speed. The upshot of it all is, that whilst the currents must always end by being drained off through *some* motor nerves, they are drained off sometimes through one set and sometimes through another; and sometimes they keep each other in equilibrium so long that a superficial observer may think they are not drained off at all. Such an observer must remember, however, that from the physiological point of view a gesture, an expression of the brow, or an expulsion of the breath are movements as much as an act of locomotion is. A king's breath slays as well as an assassin's blow; and the outpouring of those currents which the magic imponderable streaming of our ideas accompanies need not always be of an explosive or otherwise physically conspicuous kind.

ACTION AFTER DELIBERATION

We are now in a position to describe *what happens in deliberate action*, or when the mind is the seat of many ideas related to each other in antagonistic or in favorable ways.[39] One of the ideas is that of an act. By itself this idea would prompt a movement; some of the additional considerations, however, which are present to consciousness block the motor discharge, whilst others, on the contrary, solicit it to take place. The result is that peculiar feeling of inward unrest known as *indecision*. Fortunately it is too familiar to need description, for to describe it would be impossible. As long as it lasts, with the various objects before the attention, we are said to *deliberate*; and when finally the original suggestion either prevails and makes the movement take place, or gets definitively quenched by its antagonists, we are said to *decide*, or to *utter our voluntary fiat* in favor of one or the other course. The reinforcing and inhibiting ideas meanwhile are termed the *reasons* or *motives* by which the decision is brought about.

The process of deliberation contains endless degrees of complication. At every moment of it our consciousness is of an extremely complex object, namely the existence of the whole set of motives and their conflict, as explained on p. 265 of Vol. I. Of this object, the totality of which is realized more or less dimly all the while, certain parts stand out more or less sharply at one moment in the foreground, and at another moment other parts, in consequence of the oscillations of our attention, and of the 'associative' flow of our ideas. But no matter how sharp the foreground-reasons may be, or how imminently close to bursting through the dam and carrying the motor consequences their own way, the background, however dimly felt, is always there; and its presence (so long as the indecision actually lasts) serves as an effective check upon the irrevocable discharge. The deliberation may last for weeks or months, occupying at intervals the mind. The motives which yesterday seemed full of urgency and blood and life to-day feel strangely

[39] I use the common phraseology here for mere convenience' sake. The reader who has made himself acquainted with Chapter IX will always understand, when he hears of many ideas simultaneously present to the mind and acting upon each other, that what is really meant is a mind with one idea before it, of many objects, purposes, reasons, motives, related to each other, some in a harmonious and some in an antagonistic way. With this caution I shall not hesitate from time to time to fall into the popular Lockian speech, erroneous though I believe it to be.

weak and pale and dead. But as little to-day as tomorrow is the question finally resolved. Something tells us that all this is provisional; that the weakened reasons will wax strong again, and the stronger weaken; that equilibrium is unreached; that testing our reasons, not obeying them, is still the order of the day, and that we must wait awhile, patiently or impatiently, until our mind is made up 'for good and all.' This inclining, first to one then to another future, both of which we represent as possible, resembles the oscillations to and fro of a material body within the limits of its elasticity. There is inward strain, but no outward rupture. And this condition, plainly enough, is susceptible of indefinite continuance, as well in the physical mass as in the mind. If the elasticity give way, however, if the dam ever do break, and the currents burst the crust, vacillation is over and decision is irrevocably there.

The decision may come in any one of many modes. I will try briefly to sketch the most characteristic types of it, merely warning the reader that this is only an introspective account of symptoms and phenomena, and that all questions of causal agency, whether neural or spiritual, are relegated to a later page.

The particular reasons for or against action are of course infinitely various in concrete cases. But certain motives are more or less constantly in play. One of these is *impatience of the deliberative state*; or to express it otherwise, proneness to act or to decide merely because action and decision are, as such, agreeable, and relieve the tension of doubt and hesitancy. Thus it comes that we will often take any course whatever which happens to be most vividly before our minds, at the moment when this impulse to decisive action becomes extreme.

Against this impulse we have the *dread of the irrevocable,* which often engenders a type of character incapable of prompt and vigorous resolve, except perhaps when surprised into sudden activity. These two opposing motives twine round whatever other motives may be present at the moment when decision is imminent, and tend to precipitate or retard it. The conflict of these motives so far as they alone affect the matter of decision is a conflict as to *when* it shall occur. One says 'now,' the other says 'not yet.'

Another constant component of the web of motivation is the impulse to persist in a decision once made. There is no more remarkable difference in human character than that between resolute and irresolute natures. Neither the physiological nor the psychical grounds of this difference have yet been analyzed. Its symptom is that whereas in the irresolute all decisions are provisional and liable to be reversed, in the resolute they are settled once for all and not disturbed again. Now into everyone's deliberations the representation of one alternative will often enter with such sudden force as to carry the imagination with itself exclusively, and to produce an apparently settled decision in its own favor. These premature and spurious decisions are of course known to everyone. They often seem ridiculous in the light of the considerations that succeed them. But it cannot be denied that in the resolute type of character the accident that one of them has once been made does afterwards enter as a motive additional to the more genuine reasons why it should not be revoked, or if provisionally revoked, why it should be made again. How many of us persist in a precipitate course which, but for a moment of heedlessness, we might never have entered upon, simply because we hate to 'change our mind.'

FIVE TYPES OF DECISION

Turning now to the form of the decision itself, we may distinguish five chief types. The first may be called *the reasonable type*. It is that of those cases in which the arguments for and against a given course seem gradually and almost insensibly to settle themselves in the mind and to end by leaving a clear balance in favor of one alternative, which alternative we then adopt without effort or constraint. Until this rational balancing of the books is consummated we have a calm feeling that the evidence is not yet all in, and this keeps action in suspense. But some day we wake with the sense that we see the thing rightly, that no new light will be thrown on the subject by farther delay, and that the matter had better be settled *now*. In this easy transition from doubt to assurance we seem to ourselves almost passive; the 'reasons' which decide us appearing to flow in from the nature of things, and to owe nothing to our will. We have, however, a perfect sense of being *free*, in that we are devoid of any feeling of coercion. The conclusive reason for the decision in these cases usually is the discovery that we can refer the case to a *class* upon which we are accustomed to act unhesitatingly in a certain stereotyped way. It may be said in general that a great part of every deliberation consists in the turning over of all the possible modes of *conceiving* the doing or not doing of the act in point. The moment we hit upon a conception which lets us apply some principle of action which is a fixed and stable part of our Ego, our state of doubt is at an end. Persons of authority, who have to make many decisions in the day, carry with them a set of heads of classification, each bearing its motor consequence, and under these they seek as far as possible to range each new emergency as it occurs. It is where the emergency belongs to a species without precedent, to which consequently no cut-and-dried maxim will apply, that we feel most at a loss, and are distressed at the indeterminateness of our task. As soon, however, as we see our way to a familiar classification, we are at ease again. *In action as in reasoning, then, the great thing is the quest of the right conception.* The concrete dilemmas do not come to us with labels gummed upon their backs. We may name them by many names. The wise man is he who succeeds in finding the name which suits the needs of the particular occasion best. A 'reasonable' character is one who has a store of stable and worthy ends, and who does not decide about an action till he has calmly ascertained whether it be ministerial or detrimental to any one of these.

In the next two types of decision, the final fiat occurs before the evidence is all 'in.' It often happens that no paramount and authoritative reason for either course will come. Either seems a case of a Good, and there is no umpire as to which good should yield its place to the other. We grow tired of long hesitation and inconclusiveness, and the hour may come when we feel that even a bad decision is better than no decision at all. Under these conditions it will often happen that some accidental circumstance, supervening at a particular moment upon our mental weariness, will upset the balance in the direction of one of the alternatives, to which then we feel ourselves committed, although an opposite accident at the same time might have produced the opposite result.

In the *second type* of case our feeling is to a certain extent that of letting ourselves drift with a certain indifferent acquiescence in a direction accidentally determined *from without*, with the conviction that, after all, we might as well stand by this course as by the other, and that things are in any event sure to turn out sufficiently right.

In the *third type* the determination seems equally accidental, but it comes from within, and not from without. It often happens, when the absence of imperative principle is perplexing and suspense distracting, that we find ourselves acting, as it were, automatically, and as if by a spontaneous discharge of our nerves, in the direction of one of the horns of the dilemma. But so exciting is this sense of motion after our intolerable pent-up state that we eagerly throw ourselves into it. 'Forward now!' we inwardly cry, 'though the heavens fall.' This reckless and exultant espousal of an energy so little premeditated by us that we feel rather like passive spectators cheering on the display of some extraneous force than like voluntary agents is a type of decision too abrupt and tumultuous to occur often in humdrum and cool-blooded natures. But it is probably frequent in persons of strong emotional endowment and unstable or vacillating character. And in men of the world-shaking type, the Napoleons, Luthers, etc., in whom tenacious passion combines with ebullient activity, when by any chance the passion's outlet has been dammed by scruples or apprehensions, the resolution is probably often of this catastrophic kind. The flood breaks quite unexpectedly through the dam. That it should so often do so is quite sufficient to account for the tendency of these characters to a fatalistic mood of mind. And the fatalistic mood itself is sure to reinforce the strength of the energy just started on its exciting path of discharge.

There is a *fourth form* of decision, which often ends deliberation as suddenly as the third form does. It comes when, in consequence of some outer experience or some inexplicable inward charge, *we suddenly pass from the easy and careless to the sober and strenuous mood,* or possibly the other way. The whole scale of values of our motives and impulses then undergoes a change like that which a change of the observer's level produces on a view. The most sobering possible agents are objects of grief and fear. When one of these affects us, all 'light fantastic' notions lose their motive power, all solemn ones find theirs multiplied many-fold. The consequence is an instant abandonment of the more trivial projects with which we had been dallying, and an instant practical acceptance of the more grim and earnest alternative which till then could not extort our mind's consent. All those 'changes of heart,' 'awakenings of conscience,' etc., which make new men of so many of us may be classed under this head. The character abruptly rises to another 'level,' and deliberation comes to an immediate end.[40]

In the *fifth and final type* of decision, the feeling that the evidence is all in, and that reason has balanced the books, may be either present or absent. But in either case we feel, in deciding, as if we ourselves by our own wilful act inclined the beam: in the former case by adding our living effort to the weight of the logical reason which, taken alone, seems powerless to make the act discharge; in the latter by a kind of creative contribution of something instead of a reason which does a reason's work. The slow dead heave of the will that is felt in these instances makes of them a class altogether different subjectively from all the four preceding classes. What the heave of the will betokens metaphysically, what the effort might lead us to infer about a will-power distinct from motives, are not matters that concern us yet. Subjectively and phenomenally, the *feeling of effort*, absent from the former decisions, accompanies these. Whether it be the dreary resignation for the sake of austere and naked duty of all sorts of rich mundane delights; or whether it be the heavy resolve that of two mutually exclusive trains of future fact, both sweet and good and with no strictly objective or imperative principle of choice between them, one shall forevermore become impossible, while the other shall become reality; it is a desolate and acrid sort of act, an excursion into a lonesome moral wilderness. If examined closely, its chief difference from the former cases appears to be that in those cases the mind at the moment of deciding on the triumphant alternative dropped the other one wholly or nearly out of sight, whereas here both alternatives are steadily held in view, and in the very act of murdering the vanquished possibility the chooser realizes how much in that instant he is making himself lose. It is deliberately driving a thorn into one's flesh; and the sense of *inward effort* with which the act is accompanied is an element which sets the fifth type of decision in strong contrast with the previous four varieties, and makes of it an altogether peculiar sort of mental phenomenon. The immense majority of human decisions are decisions without effort. In comparatively few of them, in most people, does effort accompany the final act. We are, I think, misled into supposing that effort is more frequent than it is, by the fact that *during de-*

40 My attention was first emphatically called to this class of decisions by my colleague, Professor C. C. Everett.

liberation we so often have a feeling of how great an effort it would take to make a decision *now*. Later, after the decision has made itself with ease, we recollect this and erroneously suppose the effort also to have been made then.

The existence of the effort as a phenomenal fact in our consciousness cannot of course be doubted or denied. Its significance, on the other hand, is a matter about which the gravest difference of opinion prevails. Questions as momentous as that of the very existence of spiritual causality, as vast as that of universal predestination or free-will, depend on its interpretation. It therefore becomes essential that we study with some care the conditions under which the feeling of volitional effort is found.

THE FEELING OF EFFORT

When, awhile back (p. 1134), I said that *consciousness* (or the neural process which goes with it) *is in its very nature impulsive*, I added in a note the proviso that *it must be sufficiently intense*. Now there are remarkable differences in the power of different sorts of consciousness to excite movement. The intensity of some feelings is practically apt to be below the discharging point, whilst that of others is apt to be above it. By practically apt, I mean apt under ordinary circumstances. These circumstances may be habitual inhibitions, like that comfortable feeling of the *dolce far niente* which gives to each and all of us a certain dose of laziness only to be overcome by the acuteness of the impulsive spur; or they may consist in the native inertia, or internal resistance, of the motor centres themselves making explosion impossible until a certain inward tension has been reached and overpassed. These conditions may vary from one person to another, and in the same person from time to time. The neural inertia may wax or wane, and the habitual inhibitions dwindle or augment. The intensity of particular thought-processes and stimulations may also change independently, and particular paths of association grow more pervious or less so. There thus result great possibilities of alteration in the actual impulsive efficacy of particular motives compared with others. It is where the normally less efficacious motive becomes more efficacious and the normally more efficacious one less so that actions ordinarily effortless, or abstinences ordinarily easy, either become impossible or are effected (if at all) by the expenditure of effort. A little more description will make it plainer what these cases are.

There is a certain normal ratio in the impulsive power of different sorts of motive, which characterizes what may be called ordinary healthiness of will, and which is departed from only at exceptional times or by exceptional individuals. The states of mind which normally possess the most impulsive quality are either those which represent objects of passion, appetite, or emotion—objects of instinctive reaction, in short; or they are feelings or ideas of pleasure or of pain; or ideas which for any reason we have grown accustomed to obey, so that the habit of reacting on them is ingrained; or finally, in comparison with ideas of remoter objects, they are ideas of objects present or near in space and time. Compared with these various objects, all far-off considerations, all highly abstract conceptions, unaccustomed reasons, and motives foreign to the instinctive history of the race, have little or no impulsive power. They prevail, when they ever do prevail, *with effort; and the normal,* as distinguished from the pathological, *sphere of effort is thus found wherever non-instinctive motives to behavior are to rule the day.*

Healthiness of will moreover requires a certain amount of complication in the process which precedes the fiat or the act. Each stimulus or idea, at the same time that it wakens its own impulse, must arouse other ideas (associated and consequential) with their impulses, and action must follow, neither too slowly nor too rapidly, as the resultant of all the forces thus engaged. Even when the decision is very prompt, there is thus a sort of preliminary survey of the field and a vision of which course is best before the fiat comes. And where the will is healthy, *the vision must be right* (i.e., the motives must be on the whole in a normal or not too unusual ratio to each other), *and the action must obey the vision's lead.*

Unhealthiness of will may thus come about in many ways. The action may follow the stimulus or idea too rapidly, leaving no time for the arousal of restraining associates—*we then have a precipitate will.* Or, although the associates may come, the ratio which the impulsive and inhibitive forces normally bear to each other may be distorted, and we then have *a will which is perverse.* The perversity, in turn, may be due to either of many causes—too much intensity, or too little, here; too much or too little inertia there; or elsewhere too much or too little inhibitory power. *If we compare the outward symptoms of perversity together, they fall into two groups,* in one of which normal actions are impossible, and in the other abnormal ones are irrepressible. Briefly, *we may call them respectively the obstructed and the explosive will.*

It must be kept in mind, however, that since the resultant action is always due to the *ratio* between the obstructive and the explosive forces which are present, we never can tell by the mere outward symptoms to what *elementary* cause the perversion of a man's will may be due, whether to an increase of one component or a diminution of the other. One may grow explosive as readily by losing the usual brakes as by getting up more of the impulsive steam; and one may find things impossible as well through the enfeeblement of the original desire as through the advent of new lions in the path. As Dr. Clouston says, "The driver may be so weak that he cannot control well-broken horses, or the horses may be so hard-mouthed that no driver can pull them up." In some concrete cases (whether of explosive or of obstructed will) it is difficult to tell whether the trouble is due to inhibitory or to impulsive change. Generally, however, we can make a plausible guess at the truth.

THE EXPLOSIVE WILL

There is a normal type of character, for example, in which impulses seem to discharge so promptly into movements that inhibitions get no time to arise. These are the 'dare-devil' and 'mercurial' temperaments, overflowing with animation, and fizzling with talk, which are so common in the Latin and Celtic races, and with which the cold-blooded and long-headed English character forms so marked a contrast. Monkeys these people seem to us, whilst we seem to them reptilian. It is quite impossible to judge, as between an obstructed and an explosive individual, which has the greater sum of vital energy. An explosive Italian with good perception and intellect will cut a figure as a perfectly tremendous fellow, on an inward capital that could be tucked away inside of an obstructed Yankee and hardly let you know that it was there. He will be the king of his company, sing all the songs and make all the speeches, lead the parties, carry out the practical jokes, kiss all the girls, fight the men, and, if need be, lead the forlorn hopes and enterprises, so that an onlooker would think he has more life in his little finger than can exist in the whole body of a correct judicious fellow. But the judicious fellow all the while may have all these possibilities and more besides, ready to break out in the same or even a more violent way, if only the brakes were taken off. It is the absence of scruples, of consequences, of considerations, the extraordinary simplification of each moment's mental outlook, that gives to the explosive individual such motor energy and ease; it need not be the greater intensity of any of his passions, motives, or thoughts. As mental evolution goes on, the complexity of human consciousness grows ever greater, and with it the multiplication of the inhibitions to which every impulse is exposed. But this predominance of inhibition has a bad as well as a good side; and if a man's impulses are in the main orderly as well as prompt, if he has courage to accept their consequences, and intellect to lead them to a successful end, he is all the better for his hair-trigger organization, and for not being 'sicklied o'er with the pale cast of thought.' Many of the most successful military and revolutionary characters in history have belonged to this simple but quick-witted impulsive type. Problems come much harder to reflective and inhibitive minds. They can, it is true, solve much vaster problems; and they can avoid many a mistake to which the men of impulse are exposed. But when the latter do not make mistakes, or when they are always able to retrieve them, theirs is one of the most engaging and indispensable of human types.[41]

In infancy, and in certain conditions of exhaustion, as well as in peculiar pathological states, the inhibitory power may fail to arrest the explosions of the impulsive discharge. We have then an explosive temperament temporarily realized in an individual who at

[41] In an excellent article on "The Mental Qualities of an Athlete" in the *Harvard Monthly*, vol. VI, p. 43, Mr. A. T. Dudley assigns the first place to the rapidly impulsive temperament. "Ask him how, in some complex trick, he performed a certain act, why he pushed or pulled at a certain instant, and he will tell you he does not know; he did it by instinct; or rather his nerves and muscles did it of themselves. . . . Here is the distinguishing feature of the good player. The good player, confident in his training and his practice, in the critical game trusts entirely to his impulse, and does not think out every move. The poor player, unable to trust his impulsive actions, is compelled to think carefully all the time. He thus not only loses his opportunities through his slowness in comprehending the whole situation; but being compelled to think rapidly all the time, at critical points becomes confused: while the first-rate player, not trying to reason but acting as impulse directs, is continually distinguishing himself and plays the better under the greater pressure."

other times may be of a relatively obstructed type. I cannot do better here than copy a few pages from Dr. Clouston's excellent work:[42]

"Take a child of six months, and there is absolutely no such brain power existent as mental inhibition; no desire or tendency is stopped by a mental act. At a year old the rudiments of the great faculty of self-control are clearly apparent in most children. They will resist the desire to seize the gas flame, they will not upset the milk jug, they will obey orders to sit still when they want to run about, all through a higher mental inhibition. But the power of control is just as gradual a development as the motions of the hands. . . . Look at a more complicated act, that will be recognised by any competent physiologist to be automatic and beyond the control of any ordinary inhibitory power, *e.g.*, irritate and tease a child of one or two years sufficiently, and it will strike out at you; suddenly strike at a man, and he will either perform an act of defence or offence, or both, quite automatically, and without power of controlling himself. Place a bright tempting toy before a child of a year and it will be instantly appropriated. Place cold water before a man dying of thirst, and he will take and drink it without power of doing otherwise. Exhaustion of nervous energy always lessens the inhibitory power. Who is not conscious of this? ' Irritability ' is one manifestation of this. Many persons have so small a stock of reserve brain power—that most valuable of all brain qualities—that it is soon used up, and you see at once that they lose their power of self-control very soon. They are angels or demons just as they are fresh or tired. That surplus store of energy or resistive force which provides in persons normally constituted that moderate excesses in all directions shall do no great harm, so long as they are not too often repeated, not being present in these people, over-work, over-drinking, or small debauches, leave them at the mercy of their morbid impulses without power of resistance. . . . Woe to the man who uses up his surplus stock of brain inhibition too near the bitter end, or too often! . . . The physiological word inhibition can be used synonymously with the psychological and ethical expression self-control, or with the will when exercised in certain directions. It is the characteristic of most forms of mental disease for self-control to be lost, but this loss is usually part of a general mental affection with melancholic, maniacal, demented, or delusional symptoms as the chief manifestations of the disease. There are other cases, not so numerous, where the loss of the power of inhibition is the chief and by far the most marked symptom. . . . I shall call this form 'Inhibitory Insanity.' Some of these cases have uncontrollable impulses to violence and destruction, others to homicide, others to suicide prompted by no depressed feelings, others

[42] T. S. Clouston: *Clinical Lectures on Mental Diseases* (London, 1883), pp. 310–318.

to acts of animal gratification (satyriasis, nymphomania, erotomania, bestiality), others to drinking too much alcohol (dipsomania), others towards setting things on fire (pyromania), others to stealing (kleptomania), and others towards immoralities of all sorts. The impulsive tendencies and morbid desires are innumerable in kind. Many of these varieties of insanity have been distinguished by distinct names. To dig up and eat dead bodies (necrophilism), to wander from home and throw off the restraints of society (planomania), to act like a wild beast (lycanthropia) &c. Action from impulse in all these directions may take place from a loss of controlling power in the higher regions of the brain, or from an over-development of energy in certain portions of the brain, which the normal power of inhibition cannot control. The driver may be so weak that he cannot control well-broken horses, or the horses may be so hard-mouthed that no driver can pull them up. Both conditions may arise from purely cerebral disorder . . . or may be reflex . . . . The *ego,* the man, the will, may be non-existent for the time. The most perfect examples of this are murders done during somnambulism or epileptic unconsciousness, or acts done in the hypnotic state. There is no conscious desire to attain the object at all in such cases. In other cases there is consciousness and memory present, but no power of restraining action. The simplest example of this is where an imbecile or a dement, seeing something glittering, appropriates it to himself, or when he commits indecent sexual acts. Through disease a previously sane and vigorous minded person may get into the same state. The motives that would lead other persons not to do such acts do not operate in such persons. I have known a man steal who said he had no intense longing for the article he appropriated at all, at least consciously, but his will was in abeyance, and he could not resist the ordinary desire of possession common to all human nature."

It is not only those technically classed imbeciles and dements who exhibit this promptitude of impulse and tardiness of inhibition. Ask half the common drunkards you know why it is that they fall so often a prey to temptation, and they will say that most of the time they cannot tell. It is a sort of vertigo with them. Their nervous centres have become a sluice-way pathologically unlocked by every passing conception of a bottle and a glass. They do not thirst for the beverage; the taste of it may even appear repugnant; and they perfectly foresee the morrow's remorse. But when they think of the liquor or see it, they find themselves preparing to drink, and do not stop themselves: and more than this they cannot say. Similarly a man may lead a life of incessant love-making or sexual indulgence, though what spurs him thereto seems rather to be suggestions and notions of possibility than any overweening strength in his affections or lusts. He may even be physically impotent all the while. The paths of natural (or it may be unnatural) impulse are so pervious in these characters that the slightest rise in the level of innervation produces an overflow. It is the condition recognized in pathology as 'irritable weakness.' The phase known as nascency or latency is so short in the excitement of the neural tissues that there is no opportunity for strain or tension to accumulate within them; and the consequence is that with all the agitation and activity, the amount of real feeling engaged may be very small. The hysterical temperament is the playground *par excellence* of this unstable equilibrium. One of these subjects will be filled with what seems the most genuine and settled aversion to a certain line of conduct, and the very next *instant* follow the stirring of temptation and plunge in it up to the neck. Professor Ribot well gives the name of "Le Règne des caprices" to the chapter in which he describes the hysterical temperament in his interesting little monograph *The Diseases of the Will.*

Disorderly and impulsive conduct may, on the other hand, come about where the neural tissues preserve their proper inward tone, and where the inhibitory power is normal or even unusually great. In such cases *the strength of the impulsive idea is preternaturally exalted,* and what would be for most people the passing suggestion of a possibility becomes a gnawing, craving urgency to act. Works on insanity are full of examples of these morbid insistent ideas, in obstinately struggling against which the unfortunate victim's soul often sweats with agony, ere at last it gets swept away. One instance will stand for many; M. Ribot quotes it from Calmeil:[43]

"Glénadal, having lost his father in infancy, was brought up by his mother, who adored him. At sixteen, his character, till then good and docile, changed. He became gloomy and taciturn. Pressed with questions by his mother, he decided at last to make a confession. 'To you,' said he, 'I owe everything; I love you with all my soul; yet for some time past an incessant idea drives me to kill you. Prevent so terrible a misfortune from happening, in case some day the temptation should overpower me: allow me to enlist.' Notwithstanding pressing solicitations, he was firm in his resolve, went off, and was a good soldier. Still a secret impulse stimulated him without cessation to desert in order to

[43] In his *Maladies de la volonté,* p. 77.

come home and kill his mother. At the end of his term of service the idea was as strong as on the first day. He enlisted for another term. The murderous instinct persisted, but substituted another victim. He no longer thought of killing his mother—the horrible impulse pointed day and night towards his sister-in-law. In order to resist the second impulse, he condemned himself to perpetual exile. At this time one of his old neighbors arrived in the regiment. Glénadal confesses all his trouble. 'Be at rest,' said the other. 'Your crime is impossible; your sister-in-law has just died.' At these words Glénadal rises like a delivered captive. Joy fills his heart. He travels to the home of his childhood, unvisited for so many years. But as he arrives he sees his sister-in-law living. He gives a cry, and the terrible impulse seizes him again as a prey. That very evening he makes his brother tie him fast. 'Take a solid rope, bind me like a wolf in the barn, and go and tell Dr. Calmeil. . . .' From him he got admission to an insane asylum. The evening before his entrance he wrote to the director of the establishment: 'Sir, I am to become an inmate of your house. I shall behave there as if I were in the regiment. You will think me cured. At moments perhaps I shall pretend to be so. Never believe me. Never let me out on any pretext. If I beg to be released, double your watchfulness; the only use I shall make of my liberty will be to commit a crime which I abhor.' "[44]

The craving for drink in real dipsomaniacs, or for opium or chloral in those subjugated, is of a strength of which normal persons can form no conception. "Were a keg of rum in one corner of a room and were a cannon constantly discharging balls between me and it, I could not refrain from passing before that cannon in order to get at the rum"; "If a bottle of brandy stood at one hand, and the pit of hell yawned at the other, and I were convinced that I would be pushed in as sure as I took one glass, I could not refrain": such statements abound in dipsomaniacs' mouths. Dr. Mussey of Cincinnati relates this case:

"A few years ago a tippler was put into an almshouse in this State. Within a few days he had devised various expedients to procure rum, but failed. At length, however, he hit upon one which was successful. He went into the wood-yard of the establishment, placed one hand upon the block, and with an axe in the other, struck it off at a single blow. With the stump raised and streaming, he ran into the house and cried, 'Get some rum! get some rum! my hand is off.' In the confusion

[44] For other cases of 'impulsive insanity,' see H. Maudsley's *Responsibility in Mental Disease*, pp. 133–170, and Forbes Winslow's *Obscure Diseases of the Mind and Brain*, chapters VI, VII, VIII.

and bustle of the occasion a bowl of rum was brought, into which he plunged the bleeding member of his body; then raising the bowl to his mouth, drank freely, and exultingly exclaimed, 'Now I am satisfied!' Dr. J. E. Turner tells of a man, who while under treatment for inebriety, during four weeks secretly drank the alcohol from six jars containing morbid specimens. On asking him why he had committed this loathsome act, he replied, 'Sir, it is as impossible for me to control this diseased appetite as it is for me to control the pulsations of my heart.' "[45]

The passion of love may be called a monomania to which all of us are subject, however otherwise sane. It can coexist with contempt and even hatred for the 'object' which inspires it, and whilst it lasts the whole life of the man is altered by its presence. Alfieri thus describes the struggles of his unusually powerful inhibitive power with his abnormally excited impulses towards a certain lady:

"Contemptible in my own eyes, I fell into such a state of melancholy as would, if long continued, inevitably have led to insanity or death. I continued to wear my disgraceful fetters till toward the end of January, 1775, when my rage, which had hitherto so often been restrained within bounds, broke forth with the greatest violence. On returning one evening from the opera, the most insipid and tiresome amusement in Italy, where I had passed several hours in the box of the woman who was by turns the object of my antipathy and my love, I took the firm determination of emancipating myself forever from her yoke. Experience had taught me that flight, so far from enabling me to persevere in my resolutions, tended, on the contrary, to weaken, and destroy them; I was inclined, therefore, to subject myself to a still more severe trial, imagining, from the obstinacy and peculiarity of my character, that I should succeed most certainly by the adoption of such measures as would compel me to make the greatest efforts. I determined never to leave the house, which, as I have already said, was exactly opposite that of this lady; to gaze at her windows, to see her go in and out every day, to listen to the sound of her voice, though firmly resolved that no advances on her part either direct or indirect, no tender remembrances, nor, in short, any other means which might be employed, should ever again tempt me to a renewal of our friendship. I was determined to die or liberate myself from my disgraceful thraldom. In order to give stability to my purpose, and to render it impossible for me to waver without the imputation of dishonor, I communicated my determina-

[45] Quoted by G. Burr, in an article "On the Insanity of Inebriety" in the New York *Psychological and Medico-Legal Journal*, Dec. 1874.

tion to one of my friends, who was greatly attached to me, and whom I highly esteemed. He had lamented the state of mind into which I had fallen, but, not wishing to give countenance to my conduct, and seeing the impossibility of inducing me to abandon it, he had for some time ceased to visit at my house. In the few lines which I addressed to him, I briefly stated the resolution I had adopted, and as a pledge of my constancy I sent him a long tress of my ugly red hair. I had purposely caused it to be cut off in order to prevent my going out, as no one but clowns and sailors then appeared in public with short hair. I concluded my billet by conjuring him to strengthen and aid my fortitude by his presence and example. Isolated, in this manner, in my own house, I prohibited all species of intercourse, and passed the first fifteen days in uttering the most frightful lamentations and groans. Some of my friends came to visit me, and appeared to commiserate my situation, perhaps because I did not myself complain; but my figure and whole appearance bespoke my sufferings. Wishing to read something, I had recourse to the Gazettes, whole pages of which I frequently ran over without understanding a single word. . . . I passed more than two months, till the end of March, 1775, in a state almost bordering on frenzy; but about this period a new idea darted into my mind, which tended to assuage my melancholy."

This was the idea of poetical composition, at which Alfieri describes his first attempts, made under these diseased circumstances, and goes on:

"The only good that occurred to me from this new whim was, that of gradually detaching me from love, and of awakening my reason, which had so long lain dormant. I no longer found it necessary to cause myself to be tied with cords to a chair, in order to prevent me from leaving my house and returning to that of my lady. This had been one of the expedients I devised to render myself wise by force. The cords were concealed under a large mantle, in which I was enveloped, and only one hand remained at liberty. Of all those who came to see me, not one suspected I was bound down in this manner. I remained in this situation for whole hours; Elias, who was my jailer, was alone intrusted with the secret. He always liberated me, as he had been enjoined, whenever the paroxysms of my rage subsided. Of all the whimsical methods, however, which I employed, the most curious was that of appearing in masquerade at the theatre towards the end of the carnival. Habited as Apollo, I ventured to present myself with a lyre, on which I played as well as I was able, and sang some bad verses of my own composing. Such effrontery was diametrically opposite to my natural character. The only excuse I can offer for similar scenes was my inability to resist an imperious passion. I felt that it was necessary to place an insuperable barrier between its object and me; and I saw that the strongest of all was the shame to which I should expose myself by renewing an attachment which I had so publicly turned into ridicule."[46]

Often the insistent idea is of a trivial sort, but it may wear the patient's life out. His hands feel dirty, they must be washed. He *knows* they are not dirty; yet to get rid of the teasing idea he washes them. The idea, however, returns in a moment, and the unfortunate victim, who is not in the least deluded *intellectually*, will end by spending the whole day at the wash-stand. Or his clothes are not 'rightly' put on; and to banish the thought he takes them off and puts them on again, till his toilet consumes two or three hours of time. Most people have the potentiality of this disease. To few has it not happened to conceive, after getting into bed, that they may have forgotten to lock the front door, or to turn out the entry gas. And few of us have not on some occasion got up to repeat the performance, less because they believed in the reality of its omission than because only so could they banish the worrying doubt and get to sleep.[47]

THE OBSTRUCTED WILL

In striking contrast with the cases in which inhibition is insufficient or impulsion in excess are those in which impulsion is insufficient or inhibition in excess. We all know the condition described on p. 382 of Vol. I, in which the mind for a few moments seems to lose its focussing power and to be unable to rally its attention to any determinate thing. At such times we sit blankly staring and do nothing. The objects of consciousness fail to touch the quick or break the skin. They are there, but do not reach the level of effectiveness. This state of non-efficacious presence is the normal condition of *some* objects, in all of us. Great fatigue or exhaustion may make it the condition of almost all objects; and an apathy resembling that then brought about is recognized in asylums under the name of *abulia* as a symptom of mental disease. The healthy state of the will requires, as aforesaid, both that vision should be right, and that action should obey its lead. But in the morbid con-

46 *Life*, Howells' edition (1877), pp. 192–6.

47 See a paper on "Insistent and Fixed Ideas" by Dr. Cowles in *American Journal of Psychology*, I, 222; and another on the so-called "Insanity of Doubt" by Dr. Knapp, *ibid.*, III, 1. The latter contains a partial bibliography of the subject.

dition in question the vision may be wholly unaffected, and the intellect clear, and yet the act either fails to follow or follows in some other way. "*Video meliora proboque, deteriora sequor*" is the classic expression of the latter condition of mind. The former it is to which the name *abulia* peculiarly applies. The patients, says Guislain,

> "are able to will inwardly, mentally, according to the dictates of reason. They experience the desire to act, but they are powerless to act as they should. . . . Their will cannot overpass certain limits: one would say that the force of action within them is blocked up: the *I will* does not transform itself into impulsive volition, into active determination. Some of these patients wonder themselves at the impotence with which their will is smitten. If you abandon them to themselves, they pass whole days in their bed or on a chair. If one speaks to them or excites them, they express themselves properly though briefly; and judge of things pretty well."[48]

In Chapter XXI, as will be remembered, it was said that the sentiment of reality with which an object appealed to the mind is proportionate (amongst other things) to its efficacy as a stimulus to the will. Here we get the obverse side of the truth. Those ideas, objects, considerations, which (in these lethargic states) fail to *get to* the will, fail to draw blood, seem, in so far forth, distant and unreal. The connection of the reality of things with their effectiveness as motives is a tale that has never yet been fully told. The moral tragedy of human life comes almost wholly from the fact that the link is ruptured which normally should hold between vision of the truth and action, and that this pungent sense of effective reality will not attach to certain ideas. Men do not differ so much in their mere feelings and conceptions. Their notions of possibility and their ideals are not as far apart as might be argued from their differing fates. No class of them have better sentiments or feel more constantly the difference between the higher and the lower path in life than the hopeless failures, the sentimentalists, the drunkards, the schemers, the 'dead-beats,' whose life is one long contradiction between knowledge and action, and who, with full command of theory, never get to holding their limp characters erect. No one eats of the fruit of the tree of knowledge as they do; so far as moral insight goes, in comparison with them the orderly and

48 Quoted by Ribot: *op. cit.*, p. 38.

prosperous philistines whom they scandalize are sucking babes. And yet their moral knowledge, always there grumbling and rumbling in the background,—discerning, commenting, protesting, longing, half resolving,—never wholly resolves, never gets its voice out of the minor into the major key, or its speech out of the subjunctive into the imperative mood, never breaks the spell, never takes the helm into its hands. In such characters as Rousseau and Restif it would seem as if the lower motives had all the impulsive efficacy in their hands. Like trains with the right of way, they retain exclusive possession of the track. The more ideal motives exist alongside of them in profusion, but they never get switched on, and the man's conduct is no more influenced by them than an express train is influenced by a wayfarer standing by the roadside and calling to be taken aboard. They are an inert accompaniment to the end of time; and the consciousness of inward hollowness that accrues from habitually seeing the better only to do the worse, is one of the saddest feelings one can bear with him through this vale of tears.

We now see at one view when it is that effort complicates volition. It does so whenever a rarer and more ideal impulse is called upon to neutralize others of a more instinctive and habitual kind; it does so whenever strongly explosive tendencies are checked, or strongly obstructive conditions overcome. The *âme bien née*, the child of the sunshine, at whose birth the fairies made their gifts, does not need much of it in his life. The hero and the neurotic subject, on the other hand, do. Now our spontaneous way of conceiving the effort, under all these circumstances, is as an active force adding its strength to that of the motives which ultimately prevail. When outer forces impinge upon a body, we say that the resultant motion is in the line of least resistance, or of greatest traction. But it is a curious fact that our spontaneous language never speaks of volition with effort in this way. Of course if we proceed *a priori* and define the line of least resistance as the line that is followed, the physical law must also hold good in the mental sphere. But we *feel*, in all hard cases of volition, as if the line taken, when the rarer and more ideal motives prevail, were the line of greater resistance, and as if the line of coarser motivation were the more pervious and easy one, even at the very moment when we refuse to follow it. He who under the surgeon's knife represses cries of pain, or he who exposes himself to social obloquy for duty's sake, feels as if he were following the line of greatest temporary resistance. He speaks of conquering and overcoming his impulses and temptations.

But the sluggard, the drunkard, the coward, never talk of their conduct in that way, or say they resist their energy, overcome their sobriety, conquer their courage, and so forth. If in general we class all springs of action as propensities on the one hand and ideals on the other, the sensualist never says of his behavior that it results from a victory over his ideals, but the moralist always speaks of his as a victory over his propensities. The sensualist uses terms of inactivity, says he forgets his ideals, is deaf to duty, and so forth; which terms seem to imply that the ideal motives *per se* can be annulled without energy or effort, and that the strongest mere traction lies in the line of the propensities. The ideal impulse appears, in comparison with this, a still small voice which must be artificially reinforced to prevail. Effort is what reinforces it, making things seem as if, while the force of propensity were essentially a fixed quantity, the ideal force might be of various amount. But what determines the amount of the effort when, by its aid, an ideal motive becomes victorious over a great sensual resistance? The very greatness of the resistance itself. If the sensual propensity is small, the effort is small. The latter is *made great* by the presence of a great antagonist to overcome. And if a brief definition of ideal or moral action were required, none could be given which would better fit the appearances than this: *It is action in the line of the greatest resistance.*

The facts may be most briefly symbolized thus, P standing for the propensity, I for the ideal impulse, and E for the effort:

$$I \textit{ per se} < P.$$
$$I + E > P.$$

In other words, if E adds itself to I, P immediately offers the least resistance, and motion occurs in spite of it.

But the E does not seem to form an integral part of the I. It appears adventitious and indeterminate in advance. We can make more or less as we please, and *if* we make enough we can convert the greatest mental resistance into the least. Such, at least, is the impression which the facts spontaneously produce upon us. But we will not discuss the truth of this impression at present; let us rather continue our descriptive detail.

PLEASURE AND PAIN AS SPRINGS OF ACTION

Objects and thoughts of objects start our action, but the pleasures and pains which action brings modify its course and regulate it; and later the thoughts of the pleasures and the pains acquire themselves impulsive and inhibitive power. Not that the thought of a pleasure need be itself a pleasure, usually it is the reverse—*nessun maggior dolore*—as Dante says—and not that the thought of pain need be a pain, for, as Homer says, "griefs are often afterwards an entertainment." But as present pleasures are tremendous reinforcers, and present pains tremendous inhibitors of whatever action leads to them, so the thoughts of pleasures and pains take rank amongst the thoughts which have most impulsive and inhibitive power. The precise relation which these thoughts hold to other thoughts is thus a matter demanding some attention.

If a movement feels agreeable, we repeat and repeat it as long as the pleasure lasts. If it hurts us, our muscular contractions at the instant stop. So complete is the inhibition in this latter case that it is almost impossible for a man to cut or mutilate himself slowly and deliberately—his hand invincibly refusing to bring on the pain. And there are many pleasures which, when once we have begun to taste them, make it all but obligatory to keep up the activity to which they are due. So widespread and searching is this influence of pleasures and pains upon our movements that a premature philosophy has decided that these are our only spurs to action, and that wherever they seem to be absent, it is only because they are so far on among the 'remoter' images that prompt the action that they are overlooked.

This is a great mistake, however. Important as is the influence of pleasures and pains upon our movements, they are far from being our only stimuli. With the manifestations of instinct and emotional expression, for example, they have absolutely nothing to do. Who smiles for the pleasure of the smiling, or frowns for the pleasure of the frown? Who blushes to escape the discomfort of not blushing? Or who in anger, grief, or fear is actuated to the movements which he makes by the pleasures which they yield? In all these cases the movements are discharged fatally by the *vis a tergo* which the stimulus exerts upon a nervous system framed to respond in just that way. The objects of our rage, love, or terror, the occasions of our tears and smiles, whether they be present to our senses, or whether they be merely represented in idea, have this peculiar sort of impulsive power. The *impulsive quality* of mental states is an attribute behind which we cannot go. Some states of mind have more of it than others, some have it in this direction, and some in that. Feelings of pleasure and pain have it, and perceptions and imaginations of fact have it, but neither have it exclusively or peculiarly. It is of the essence of all consciousness (or of the neural process which underlies it) to instigate movement of some sort. That with one creature and object it should be of one sort, with others of another sort, is a problem for evolutionary history to explain. However the actual impulsions may have arisen, they must now be described as they exist; and those persons obey a curiously narrow teleological superstition who think themselves bound to interpret them in every instance as effects of the secret solicitancy of pleasure and repugnancy of pain.[49]

[49] The silliness of the old-fashioned pleasure-philosophy *saute aux yeux*. Take, for example, Prof. Bain's explanation of sociability and parental love by the pleasures of touch: "Touch is the fundamental and generic sense . . . . Even after the remaining senses are differentiated, the primary sense continues to be a leading susceptibility of the mind. The soft warm touch, if not a first-class influence, is at least an approach to that. The combined power of soft contact and warmth amounts to a considerable pitch of massive pleasure; while there may be subtle influences not reducible to these two heads, such as we term, from not knowing anything about them, magnetic or electric. The sort of thrill from taking a baby in arms is something beyond mere warm touch; and it may rise to the ecstatic height, in which case, however, there may be concurring sensations and ideas. . . . In mere tender emotion, not sexual, there is nothing but the sense of touch to gratify, unless we assume the occult magnetic influences. . . . In a word, our love pleasures begin and end in sensual contact. Touch is both the alpha and the omega of affection. As the terminal and satisfying sensation, the *ne plus ultra*, it must be a pleasure of the highest degree. . . . Why should a more lively feeling grow up towards a fellow-being, than towards a perennial fountain? [This 'should' is simply delicious from the more modern evolutionary point of view.] It must be that there is a source of pleasure in the companionship of other sentient creatures, over and above the help afforded by them in obtaining the necessaries of life. To account for this, I can suggest nothing but the primary and independent pleasure of the animal embrace." [Mind, this is said not of the sexual interest, but of 'Sociability at Large.'] "For this pleasure every creature is disposed to pay something, even when it is only fraternal. A certain amount of material benefit imparted is a condition of the full heartiness of a responding embrace, the complete fruition of this primitive joy. In the absence of those conditions, the pleasure of giving . . . can scarcely be accounted for; we know full well that, without these helps, it would be

It might be that to *reflection* such a narrow teleology would justify itself, that pleasures and pains might seem the only *comprehensible and reasonable* motives for action, the only motives on which we *ought* to act. That is an *ethical* proposition, in favor of which a good deal may be said. But it is not a *psychological* proposition; and nothing follows from it as to the motives upon which as a matter of fact we *do* act. These motives are supplied by innumerable objects, which innervate our voluntary muscles by a process as automatic as that by which they light a fever in our breasts. If the thought of pleasure can impel to action, surely other thoughts may. Experience only can decide which thoughts do. The chapters on Instinct and Emotion have shown us that their name is legion; and with this verdict we ought to remain contented, and not seek an illusory simplification at the cost of half the facts.

If in these our *first* acts pleasures and pains bear no part, as little do they bear in our last acts, or those artificially acquired performances which have become habitual. All the daily routine of life, our dressing and undressing, the coming and going from our work or carrying through of its various operations, is utterly without mental reference to pleasure and pain, except under rarely realized conditions. It is ideo-motor action. As I do not breathe for the pleasure of the breathing, but simply find that I *am* breathing, so I do not write for the pleasure of the writing, but simply because I have once begun, and being in a state of intellectual excitement which keeps venting itself in that way, find that I *am* writing still. Who will pretend that when he idly fingers his knife-handle at the

---

a very meagre sentiment in beings like ourselves. . . . It seems to me that there must be at the [parental instinct's] foundation that intense pleasure in the embrace of the young which we find to characterize the parental feeling throughout. . . . Such a pleasure once created would associate itself with the prevailing features and aspects of the young, and give to all of these their very great interest. For the sake of the pleasure, the parent discovers the necessity of nourishing the subject of it, and comes to regard the ministering function as a part or condition of the delight" (*Emotions and the Will*, pp. 126, 127, 132, 133, 140). Prof. Bain does not explain why a satin cushion kept at about 98° F. would not on the whole give us the pleasure in question more cheaply than our friends and babies do. It is true that the cushion might lack the 'occult magnetic influences.' Most of us would say that neither a baby's nor a friend's skin would possess them, were not a tenderness already there. The youth who feels ecstasy shoot through him when by accident the silken palm or even the 'vesture's hem' of his idol touches him, would hardly feel it were he not hard hit by Cupid in advance. The love creates the ecstasy, not the ecstasy the love. And for the rest of us can it possibly be that all our social virtue springs from an appetite for the sensual pleasure of having our hand shaken, or being slapped on the back?

table, it is for the sake of any pleasure which it gives him, or pain which he thereby avoids? We do all these things because at the moment we cannot help it; our nervous systems are so shaped that they overflow in just that way; and for many of our idle or purely 'nervous' and fidgety performances we can assign absolutely no *reason* at all.

Or what shall be said of a shy and unsociable man who receives point-blank an invitation to a small party? The thing is to him an abomination; but your presence exerts a compulsion on him, he can think of no excuse, and so says yes, cursing himself the while for what he does. He is unusually *sui compos* who does not every week of his life fall into some such blundering act as this. Such instances of *voluntas invita* show not only that our acts cannot all be conceived as effects of represented pleasure, but that they cannot even be classed as cases of represented *good*. The class 'goods' contains many more generally influential motives to action than the class 'pleasants.' Pleasures often attract us only because we deem them goods. Mr. Spencer, e.g., urges us to court pleasures for their influence upon health, which comes to us as a good. But almost as little as under the form of pleasures do our acts invariably appear to us under the form of *goods*. All diseased impulses and pathological fixed ideas are instances to the contrary. It is the very badness of the act that gives it then its vertiginous fascination. Remove the prohibition, and the attraction stops. In my university days a student threw himself from an upper entry window of one of the college buildings and was nearly killed. Another student, a friend of my own, had to pass the window daily in coming and going from his room, and experienced a dreadful temptation to imitate the deed. Being a Catholic, he told his director, who said, 'All right! if you must, you must,' and added, 'Go ahead and do it,' thereby instantly quenching his desire. This director knew how to minister to a mind diseased. But we need not go to minds diseased for examples of the occasional tempting-power of simple badness and unpleasantness as such. Everyone who has a wound or hurt anywhere, a sore tooth, e.g., will ever and anon press it just to bring out the pain. If we are near a new sort of stink, we must sniff it again just to verify once more how bad it is. This very day I have been repeating over and over to myself a verbal jingle whose mawkish silliness was the secret of its haunting power. I loathed yet could not banish it.

Believers in the pleasure-and-pain theory must thus, if they are candid, make large exceptions in the application of their creed. Action from 'fixed ideas' is accordingly a terrible stumbling-block to the candid Professor Bain. Ideas have in his psychology no impulsive but only a 'guiding' function, whilst

"The proper stimulus of the will, namely, some variety of pleasure or pain, is needed to give the impetus. . . . The intellectual link is not sufficient for causing the deed to rise at the beck of the idea (except in case of an 'idée fixe')"; but "should any *pleasure* spring up, or be continued, by performing an action that we clearly conceive, the causation is then complete; both the directing and the moving powers are present."[50]

Pleasures and pains are for Professor Bain the '*genuine* impulses of the will.'[51]

"Without an antecedent of pleasurable, or painful, feeling—actual or ideal, primary or derivative—the will cannot be stimulated. Through all the disguises that wrap up what we call motives, something of one or other of these two grand conditions can be detected."[52]

Accordingly, where Professor Bain finds an exception to this rule, he refuses to call the phenomenon a 'genuinely voluntary impulse.' The exceptions, he admits, "are those furnished by never-dying spontaneity, habits and fixed ideas."[53] Fixed ideas "traverse the proper course of volition."[54]

"*Disinterested impulses* are wholly distinct from the attainment of pleasure and the avoidance of pain. . . . The theory of disinterested action, in the only form that I can conceive it, supposes that the action of the will and the attainment of happiness do not square throughout."[55]

Sympathy "has this in common with the Fixed Idea, that it clashes with the regular outgoings of the Will in favour of our pleasures."[56]

Prof. Bain thus admits all the essential facts. Pleasure and pain

50 *Emotions and the Will*, p. 352. But even Bain's own description belies his formula, for the idea appears as the 'moving' and the pleasure as the 'directing' force.

51 P. 398.

52 P. 354.

53 P. 355.

54 P. 390.

55 Pp. 295–6.

56 P. 121.

are motives of only part of our activity. But he prefers to give to that part of the activity exclusively which these feelings prompt the name of '*regular* outgoings' and '*genuine* impulses' of the will,[57] and to treat all the rest as mere paradoxes and anomalies, of which nothing rational can be said. This amounts to taking one species of a genus, calling it alone by the generic name, and ordering the other co-ordinate species to find what names they may. At bottom this is only verbal play. How much more conducive to clearness and insight it is to take the *genus* 'springs of action' and treat it as a whole; and then to distinguish within it the species 'pleasure and pain' from whatever other species may be found!

There is, it is true, a complication in the relation of pleasure to action, which partly excuses those who make it the exclusive spur. This complication deserves some notice at our hands.

An impulse which discharges itself immediately is generally quite *neutral* as regards pleasure or pain—the breathing impulse, for example. If such an impulse is arrested, however, by an extrinsic force, a great feeling of *uneasiness* is produced—for instance, the dyspnœa of asthma. And in proportion as the arresting force is then overcome, *relief* accrues—as when we draw breath again after the asthma subsides. The relief is a pleasure and the uneasiness a pain; and thus it happens that round all our impulses, merely as such, there twine, as it were, secondary possibilities of pleasant and painful feeling, involved in the manner in which the act is allowed to occur. These *pleasures and pains of achievement, discharge, or fruition* exist, no matter what the original spring of action be. We are glad when we have successfully got ourselves out of a danger, though the thought of the gladness was surely not what suggested to us to escape. To have compassed the steps towards a proposed sensual indulgence also makes us glad, and this gladness is a pleasure additional to the pleasure originally proposed. On the other hand, we are chagrined and displeased when any activity, however instigated, is hindered whilst in process of actual discharge. We are 'uneasy' till the discharge starts up again. And this is just as true when the action is neutral, or has nothing but pain in view as its result, as when it was undertaken for pleasure's express sake. The moth is probably as annoyed if hindered from getting into the lamp-flame as the *roué* is if interrupted in his debauch; and we are

[57] Cf. also Bain's note to James Mill's *Analysis*, vol. II, p. 305.

chagrined if prevented from doing some quite unimportant act which would have given us no noticeable pleasure if done, merely because the prevention itself is disagreeable.

Let us now call the pleasure *for the sake* of which the act may be done the *pursued pleasure*. It follows that, even when no pleasure is pursued by an act, the act itself may be the *pleasantest line* of conduct when once the impulse has begun, on account of the incidental pleasure which then attends its successful achievement and the pain which would come of interruption. A *pleasant act* and an act *pursuing a pleasure* are in themselves, however, two perfectly distinct conceptions, though they coalesce in one concrete phenomenon whenever a pleasure is deliberately pursued. I cannot help thinking that it is the *confusion of pursued pleasure with mere pleasure of achievement* which makes the pleasure-theory of action so plausible to the ordinary mind. We feel an impulse, no matter whence derived; we proceed to act; if hindered, we feel displeasure; and if successful, relief. Action *in the line of the present impulse* is always for the time being the pleasant course; and the ordinary hedonist expresses this fact by saying that we act for the *sake* of the pleasantness involved. But who does not see that for this sort of pleasure to be possible, *the impulse must be there already as an independent fact*? The pleasure of successful performance is the *result* of the impulse, not its *cause*. You cannot have your pleasure of achievement unless you have managed to get your impulse under headway beforehand by some previous means.

It is true that on special occasions (so complex is the human mind) *the pleasure of achievement may itself become a pursued pleasure*; and these cases form another point on which the pleasure-theory is apt to rally. Take a foot-ball game or a fox-hunt. Who in cold blood wants the fox for its own sake, or cares whether the ball be at this goal or that? We know, however, by experience, that if we can once rouse a certain impulsive excitement in ourselves, whether to overtake the fox, or to get the ball to one particular goal, the successful venting of it over the counteracting checks will fill us with exceeding joy. We therefore get ourselves deliberately and artificially into the hot impulsive state. It takes the presence of various instinct-arousing conditions to excite it; but little by little, once we are in the field, it reaches its paroxysm; and we reap the reward of our exertions in that pleasure of successful achievement which, far more than the dead fox or the goal-got ball, was the object we originally pursued. So it often is with duties. Lots of actions are done with heaviness all through, and not till they are completed does pleasure emerge, in the joy of being done with them. Like Hamlet we say of each such successive task,

> "O cursed spite
> That ever I was born to set it right!"

and then we often add to the original impulse that set us on, this additional one, that "we shall feel so glad when well through with it," that thought also having its impulsive spur. But because a pleasure of achievement *can* thus become a pursued pleasure upon occasion, it does not follow that everywhere and always that pleasure must be what is pursued. This, however, is what the pleasure-philosophers seem to suppose. As well might they suppose, because no steamer can go to sea without incidentally consuming coal, and because some steamers may occasionally go to sea to *try* their coal, that therefore no steamer *can* go to sea for any other motive than that of coal-consumption.[58]

As we need not act for the sake of gaining the pleasure of achievement, so neither need we act for the sake of escaping the uneasiness of arrest. This uneasiness is altogether due to the fact that the act is *already tending to occur* on other grounds. And these original grounds are what impel to its continuance, even though the uneasiness of the arrest may upon occasion add to their impulsive power.

To conclude, I am far from denying the exceeding prominence and importance of the part which pleasures and pains, both felt and represented, play in the motivation of our conduct. But I must insist that it is no exclusive part, and that co-ordinately with these mental objects innumerable others have an exactly similar impulsive and inhibitive power.[59]

58 How much clearer Hume's head was than those of his disciples! "It has been prov'd, beyond all Controversy, that even the Passions, commonly esteem'd selfish, carry the Mind beyond Self, directly to the Object; that tho' the Satisfaction of these Passions gives us Enjoyment, yet the Prospect of this Enjoyment is not the Cause of the Passion, but on the contrary the Passion is antecedent to the Enjoyment, and without the former, the latter could never possibly exist," etc. ("Essay on the Different Species of Philosophy," § I, note near the end, in *An Enquiry Concerning Human Understanding*.)

59 In favor of the view in the text, one may consult H. Sidgwick: *Methods of Ethics*, book I, chap. IV; T. H. Green: *Prolegomena to Ethics*, bk. III, chap. I, p. 179; Carpenter: *Mental Physiology*, chap. VI; J. Martineau: *Types of Ethical Theory*, part II, bk. I, chap. II, i, and bk. II, branch I, chap. I, i, § 3. Against it see Leslie Stephen:

If one must have a single name for the condition upon which the impulsive and inhibitive quality of objects depends, one had better call it their *interest*. 'The interesting' is a title which covers not only the pleasant and the painful, but also the morbidly fascinating, the tediously haunting, and even the simply habitual, inasmuch as the attention usually travels on habitual lines, and what-we-attend-to and what-interests-us are synonymous terms. It seems as if we ought to look for the secret of an idea's impulsiveness, not in any peculiar relations which it may have with paths of motor discharge,—for *all* ideas have relations with some such paths,—but rather in a preliminary phenomenon, the *urgency, namely, with which it is able to compel attention and dominate in consciousness.* Let it once so dominate, let no other ideas succeed in displacing it, and whatever motor effects belong to it by nature will inevitably occur—its impulsion, in short, will be given to boot, and will manifest itself as a matter of course. This is what we have seen in instinct, in emotion, in common ideo-motor action, in hypnotic suggestion, in morbid impulsion, and in *voluntas invita*,—the impelling idea is simply the one which possesses the attention. It is the same where pleasure and pain are the motor spurs—they drive other thoughts from consciousness at the same time that they instigate their own characteristic 'volitional' effects. And this is also what happens at the moment of the *fiat*, in all the five types of 'decision' which we have described. In short, one does not see any case in which the steadfast occupancy of consciousness does not appear to be the prime condition of impulsive power. It is still more obviously the prime condition of inhibitive power. What checks our impulses is the mere thinking of reasons to the contrary—it is their bare presence to the mind which gives the veto, and makes acts, otherwise seductive, impossible to perform. If we could only *forget* our scruples, our doubts, our fears, what exultant energy we should for a while display!

WILL IS A RELATION BETWEEN THE MIND AND ITS 'IDEAS'

In closing in, therefore, after all these preliminaries, upon the more *intimate* nature of the volitional process, we find ourselves driven more and more exclusively to consider the conditions which

---

Science of Ethics, chap. II, § 11; H. Spencer: *Data of Ethics*, §§ 9–15; D. G. Thompson: *System of Psychology*, part IX, and *Mind*, VI, 62. Also Bain: *Senses and the Intellect*, 338–44; *Emotions and the Will*, 436.

make ideas prevail in the mind. With the prevalence, once there as a fact, of the motive idea the *psychology* of volition properly stops. The movements which ensue are exclusively physiological phenomena, following according to physiological laws upon the neural events to which the idea corresponds. The *willing* terminates with the prevalence of the idea; and whether the act then follows or not is a matter quite immaterial, so far as the willing itself goes. I will to write, and the act follows. I will to sneeze, and it does not. I will that the distant table slide over the floor towards me; it also does not. My willing representation can no more instigate my sneezing-centre than it can instigate the table to activity. But in both cases it is as true and good willing as it was when I willed to write.[60] In a word, volition is a psychic or moral fact pure and simple, and is absolutely completed when the stable state of the idea is there. The supervention of motion is a supernumerary phenomenon depending on executive ganglia whose function lies outside the mind.

In St. Vitus' dance, in locomotor ataxy, the representation of a movement and the consent to it take place normally. But the inferior executive centres are deranged, and although the ideas discharge them, they do not discharge them so as to reproduce the precise sensations anticipated. In aphasia the patient has an image of certain words which he wishes to utter, but when he opens his mouth he hears himself making quite unintended sounds. This may fill him with rage and despair—which passions only show how intact his will remains. Paralysis only goes a step farther. The associated mechanism is not only deranged but altogether broken through. The volition occurs, but the hand remains as still as the table. The paralytic is made aware of this by the absence of the expected change in his afferent sensations. He tries harder, i.e., he

60 This sentence is written from the author's own consciousness. But many persons say that where they disbelieve in the effects ensuing, as in the case of the table, they cannot will it. They "cannot exert a volition that a table should move." This personal difference may be partly verbal. Different people may attach different connotations to the word 'will.' But I incline to think that we differ psychologically as well. When one knows that he has no power, one's desire of a thing is called a *wish* and not a will. The sense of impotence inhibits the volition. Only by abstracting from the thought of the impossibility am I able to imagine strongly the table sliding over the floor, to make the bodily 'effort' which I do, and to will it to come towards me. It may be that some people are unable to perform this abstraction, and that the image of the table stationary on the floor inhibits the contradictory image of its moving, which is the object to be willed.

mentally frames the sensation of muscular 'effort,' with consent that it shall occur. It does so: he frowns, he heaves his chest, he clenches his other fist, but the palsied arm lies passive as before.[61]

We thus find that *we reach the heart of our inquiry into volition when we ask by what process it is that the thought of any given object comes to prevail stably in the mind.* Where thoughts prevail without effort, we have sufficiently studied in the several chapters on Sensation, Association, and Attention, the laws of their advent before consciousness and of their stay. We will not go over that ground again, for we know that interest and association are the words, let their worth be what it may, on which our explanations must perforce rely. Where, on the other hand, the prevalence of the thought is accompanied by the phenomenon of effort, the case is much less clear. Already in the chapter on Attention we postponed the final consideration of voluntary attention with effort to a later place. We have now brought things to a point at which we see that attention with effort is all that any case of volition implies. *The essential achievement of the will, in short, when it is most 'voluntary,' is to* ATTEND *to a difficult object and hold it fast before the mind.* The so-doing *is* the *fiat*; and it is a mere physiological incident that when the object is thus attended to, immediate motor consequences should ensue. A *resolve,* whose contemplated motor consequences are not to ensue until some possibly far distant future condition shall have been fulfilled, involves all the psychic elements of a motor fiat except the word '*now*'; and it is the same with many of our purely theoretic beliefs. We saw in effect in the appropriate chapter, how in the last resort belief means only a peculiar sort of occupancy of the mind, and relation to the self felt in the thing believed; and we know in the case of many beliefs how constant an effort of the attention is required to keep them in this situation and protect them from displacement by contradictory ideas.[62] (Compare above, p. 948.)

61 A normal palsy occurs during sleep. We will all sorts of motions in our dreams, but seldom perform any of them. In nightmare we become conscious of the non-performance, and make a muscular 'effort.' This seems then to occur in a restricted way, limiting itself to the occlusion of the glottis and producing the respiratory anxiety which wakes us up.

62 Both resolves and beliefs have of course immediate motor consequences of a quasi-emotional sort, changes of breathing, of attitude, internal speech movements, etc.; but these movements are not the *objects* resolved on or believed. The movements in common volition are the objects willed.

Effort of attention is thus the essential phenomenon of will.[63] Every reader must know by his own experience that this is so, for every reader must have felt some fiery passion's grasp. What constitutes the difficulty for a man laboring under an unwise passion of acting as if the passion were wise? Certainly there is no physical difficulty. It is as easy physically to avoid a fight as to begin one, to pocket one's money as to squander it on one's cupidities, to walk away from as towards a coquette's door. The difficulty is mental: it is that of getting the idea of the wise action to stay before our mind at all. When any strong emotional state whatever is upon us, the tendency is for no images but such as are congruous with it to come up. If others by chance offer themselves, they are instantly smothered and crowded out. If we be joyous, we cannot keep thinking of those uncertainties and risks of failure which abound upon our path; if lugubrious, we cannot think of new triumphs, travels, loves, and joys; nor if vengeful, of our oppressor's community of nature with ourselves. The cooling advice which we get from others when the fever-fit is on us is the most jarring and exasperating thing in life. Reply we cannot, so we get angry; for by a sort of self-preserving instinct which our passion has, it feels that these chill objects, if they once but gain a lodgment, will work and work until

[63] This *volitional* effort pure and simple must be carefully distinguished from the *muscular* effort with which it is usually confounded. The latter consists of all those peripheral feelings to which a muscular 'exertion' may give rise. These feelings, whenever they are massive and the body is not 'fresh,' are rather disagreeable, especially when accompanied by stopped breath, congested head, bruised skin of fingers, toes, or shoulders, and strained joints. And it is only *as thus disagreeable* that the mind must make its *volitional* effort in stably representing their reality and consequently bringing it about. That they happen to be made real by muscular activity is a purely accidental circumstance. A soldier standing still to be fired at expects disagreeable sensations from his muscular passivity. The action of his will, in sustaining the expectation, is identical with that required for a painful muscular effort. What is hard for both is *facing an idea as real.*

Where much muscular effort is not needed or where the 'freshness' is very great, the volitional effort is not required to sustain the idea of movement, which comes then and stays in virtue of association's simpler laws. More commonly, however, muscular effort involves volitional effort as well. Exhausted with fatigue and wet and watching, the sailor on a wreck throws himself down to rest. But hardly are his limbs fairly relaxed, when the order 'To the pumps!' again sounds in his ears. Shall he, can he, obey it? Is it not better just to let his aching body lie, and let the ship go down if she will? So he lies on, till, with a desperate heave of the will, at last he staggers to his legs, and to his task again. Again, there are instances where the fiat demands great volitional effort though the muscular exertion be insignificant, e.g., the getting out of bed and bathing one's self on a cold morning.

they have frozen the very vital spark from out of all our mood and brought our airy castles in ruin to the ground. Such is the inevitable effect of reasonable ideas over others—*if they can once get a quiet hearing*; and passion's cue accordingly is always and everywhere to prevent their still small voice from being heard at all. "Let me not think of that! Don't speak to me of that!" This is the sudden cry of all those who in a passion perceive some sobering considerations about to check them in mid-career. There is something so icy in this cold-water bath, something which seems so hostile to the movement of our life, so purely negative, in Reason, when she lays her corpse-like finger on our heart and says "Halt! give up! leave off! go back! sit down!" that it is no wonder that to most men the steadying influence seems, for the time being, a very minister of death.

The strong-willed man, however, is the man who hears the still small voice unflinchingly, and who, when the death-bringing consideration comes, looks at its face, consents to its presence, clings to it, affirms it, and holds it fast, in spite of the host of exciting mental images which rise in revolt against it and would expel it from the mind. Sustained in this way by a resolute effort of attention, the difficult object erelong begins to call up its own congeners and associates and ends by changing the disposition of the man's consciousness altogether. And with his consciousness, his action changes, for the new object, once stably in possession of the field of his thoughts, infallibly produces its own motor effects. The difficulty lies in the gaining possession of that field. Though the spontaneous drift of thought is all the other way, the attention must be kept strained on that one object until at last it *grows*, so as to maintain itself before the mind with ease. This strain of the attention is the fundamental act of will. And the will's work is in most cases practically ended when the bare presence to our thought of the naturally unwelcome object has been secured. For the mysterious tie between the thought and the motor centres next comes into play, and, in a way which we cannot even guess at, the obedience of the bodily organs follows as a matter of course.

In all this one sees how the immediate point of application of the volitional effort lies exclusively within the mental world. The whole drama is a mental drama. The whole difficulty is a mental difficulty, a difficulty with an object of our thought. If I may use the word *idea* without suggesting associationist or Herbartian fables, I will say that it is an idea to which our will applies itself, an idea which if we let it go would slip away, but which we will not let go. Consent to the idea's undivided presence, this is effort's sole achievement. Its only function is to get this feeling of consent into the mind. And for this there is but one way. The idea to be consented to must be kept from flickering and going out. It must be held steadily before the mind until it *fills* the mind. Such filling of the mind by an idea, with its congruous associates, *is* consent to the idea and to the fact which the idea represents. If the idea be that, or include that, of a bodily movement of our own, then we call the consent thus laboriously gained a motor volition. For Nature here 'backs' us instantaneously and follows up our inward willingness by outward changes on her own part. She does this in no other instance. Pity she should not have been more generous, nor made a world whose other parts were as immediately subject to our will!

On page 1138, in describing the 'reasonable type' of decision, it was said that it usually came when the right conception of the case was found. Where, however, the right conception is an anti-impulsive one, the whole intellectual ingenuity of the man usually goes to work to crowd it out of sight, and to find names for the emergency, by the help of which the dispositions of the moment may sound sanctified, and sloth or passion may reign unchecked. How many excuses does the drunkard find when each new temptation comes! It is a new brand of liquor which the interests of intellectual culture in such matters oblige him to test; moreover it is poured out and it is sin to waste it; or others are drinking and it would be churlishness to refuse. Or it is but to enable him to sleep, or just to get through this job of work; or it isn't drinking, it is because he feels so cold; or it is Christmas-day; or it is a means of stimulating him to make a more powerful resolution in favor of abstinence than any he has hitherto made; or it is just this once, and once doesn't count, etc., etc., *ad libitum*—it is, in fact, anything you like except *being a drunkard. That* is the conception that will not stay before the poor soul's attention. But if he once gets able to pick out that way of conceiving, from all the other possible ways of conceiving the various opportunities which occur, if through thick and thin he holds to it that this is being a drunkard and is nothing else, he is not likely to remain one long. The effort by which he succeeds in keeping the right *name* unwaveringly present to his mind proves to be his saving moral act.[64]

Everywhere, then, the function of the effort is the same: to keep affirming and adopting a thought which, if left to itself, would slip away. It may be cold and flat when the spontaneous mental drift is towards excitement, or great and arduous when the spontaneous drift is towards repose. In the one case the effort has to inhibit an explosive, in the other to arouse an obstructed will. The exhausted sailor on a wreck has a will which is obstructed. One of his ideas is that of his sore hands, of the nameless exhaustion of his whole frame which the act of farther pumping involves, and of the deliciousness of sinking into sleep. The other is that of the hungry sea ingulfing him. "Rather the aching toil!" he says; and it becomes reality then, in spite of the inhibiting influence of the relatively luxurious sensations which he gets from lying still. But exactly similar in form would be his consent to lie and sleep. Often it is the thought of sleep and what leads to it which is the hard one to keep before the mind. If a patient afflicted with insomnia can only control the whirling chase of his thoughts so far as to think of *nothing at all* (which can be done), or so far as to imagine one letter after another of a verse of scripture or poetry spelt slowly and monotonously out, it is almost certain that here, too, specific bodily effects will follow, and that sleep will come. The trouble is to keep the mind upon a train of objects naturally so insipid. *To sustain a representation, to think,* is, in short, the only moral act, for the impulsive and the obstructed, for sane and lunatics alike. Most maniacs know their thoughts to be crazy, but find them too pressing to be withstood. Compared with them the sane truths are so deadly sober, so cadaverous, that the lunatic cannot bear to look them in the face and say, "Let these alone be my reality!" But with sufficient effort, as Dr. Wigan says,

"Such a man can for a time *wind himself up*, as it were, and determine that the notions of the disordered brain shall not be manifested. Many instances are on record similar to that told by Pinel, where an inmate of the Bicêtre, having stood a long cross-examination, and given every mark of restored reason, signed his name to the paper authorizing

64 Cf. Aristotle's *Nicomachean Ethics*, VII, 3; also a discussion of the doctrine of "The Practical Syllogism" in Sir A. Grant's edition of this work, 2d ed., vol. I, p. 212 ff.

his discharge, 'Jesus Christ,' and then went off into all the vagaries connected with that delusion. In the phraseology of the gentleman whose case is related in an early part of this [Wigan's] work, he had 'held himself tight' during the examination, in order to attain his object; this once accomplished, he 'let himself down' again, and, if even *conscious* of his delusion, could not control it. I have observed with such persons that it requires a considerable time to wind themselves up to the pitch of complete self-control, and that the effort is a painful tension of the mind. When thrown off their guard by any accidental remark, or worn out by the length of the examination, they *let themselves go,* and cannot gather themselves up again without preparation. Lord Erskine relates the story of a man, who brought an action against Dr. Munro for confining him without cause. He underwent the most rigid examination by the counsel for the defendant, without discovering any appearance of insanity, till a gentleman asked him about a princess with whom he corresponded in cherry juice, and he became instantly insane."[65]

To sum it all up in a word, *the terminus of the psychological process in volition, the point to which the will is directly applied, is always an idea.* There are at all times *some* ideas from which we shy away like frightened horses the moment we get a glimpse of their forbidding profile upon the threshold of our thought. *The only resistance which our will can possibly experience is the resistance which such an idea offers to being attended to at all.* To at-

[65] *The Duality of the Mind,* pp. 141–2. Another case from the same book (p. 122): "A gentleman of respectable birth, excellent education, and ample fortune, engaged in one of the highest departments of trade, . . . [and being] induced to embark in one of the plausible speculations of the day . . . was utterly ruined. Like other men, he could bear a sudden overwhelming reverse better than a long succession of petty misfortunes, and the way in which he conducted himself on the occasion met with unbounded admiration from his friends. He withdrew however into rigid seclusion, and, being no longer able to exercise the generosity and indulge the benevolent feelings which had formed the happiness of his life, made himself a substitute for them by day-dreams, gradually fell into a state of irritable despondency, from which he only gradually recovered with the loss of reason. He now fancied himself possessed of immense wealth, and gave without stint his imaginary riches. He has ever since been under gentle restraint, and leads a life not merely of happiness, but of bliss; converses rationally, reads the newspapers, where every tale of distress attracts his notice, and being furnished with an abundant supply of blank checks, he fills up one of them with a munificent sum, sends it off to the sufferer, and sits down to his dinner with a happy conviction that he has earned the right to a little indulgence in the pleasures of the table; and yet, on a serious conversation with one of his old friends, he is quite conscious of his real position, but the conviction is so exquisitely painful that *he will not let himself believe it.*"

tend to it is the volitional act, and the only inward volitional act which we ever perform.

I have put the thing in this ultra-simple way because I want more than anything else to emphasize the fact that volition is primarily a relation, not between our Self and extra-mental matter (as many philosophers still maintain), but between our Self and our own states of mind. But when, a short while ago, I spoke of the filling of the mind with an idea as being equivalent to consent to the idea's object, I said something which the reader doubtless questioned at the time, and which certainly now demands some qualification ere we pass beyond.

It is unqualifiedly true that if any thought *do* fill the mind exclusively, such filling is consent. The thought, for that time at any rate, carries the man and his will with it. But it is not true that the thought *need* fill the mind exclusively for consent to be there; for we often consent to things whilst thinking of other things, even of hostile things; and we saw in fact that precisely what distinguishes our 'fifth type' of decision from the other types (see p. 1141) is just this coexistence with the triumphant thought of other thoughts which would inhibit it but for the effort which makes it prevail. The effort to *attend* is therefore only a part of what the word 'will' covers; it covers also the effort to *consent* to something to which our attention is not quite complete. Often, when an object has gained our attention exclusively, and its motor results are just on the point of setting in, it seems as if the sense of their imminent irrevocability were enough of itself to start up the inhibitory ideas and to make us pause. Then we need a new stroke of effort to break down the sudden hesitation which seizes upon us, and to persevere. So that although attention is the first and fundamental thing in volition, *express consent to the reality of what is attended to* is often an additional and quite distinct phenomenon involved.

The reader's own consciousness tells him of course just what these words of mine denote. And I freely confess that I am impotent to carry the analysis of the matter any farther, or to explain in other terms of what this consent consists. It seems a subjective experience *sui generis,* which we can designate but not define. We stand here exactly where we did in the case of belief. When an idea *stings* us in a certain way, makes as it were a certain electric connection with our Self, we believe that it *is* a reality. When it stings us in another way, makes another connection with our Self, we say, *let it be* a reality. To the word 'is' and to the words 'let it be' there correspond peculiar attitudes of consciousness which it is vain to seek to explain. The indicative and the imperative moods are as much ultimate categories of thinking as they are of grammar. The 'quality of reality' which these moods attach to things is not like other qualities. It is a relation to our life. It means *our* adoption of the things, *our* caring for them, *our* standing by them. This at least is what it practically means for us; what it may mean beyond that we do not know. And the transition from merely considering an object as possible, to deciding or willing it to be real; the change from the fluctuating to the stable personal attitude concerning it; from the 'don't care' state of mind to that in which 'we mean business,' is one of the most familiar things in life. We can partly enumerate its conditions; and we can partly trace its consequences, especially the momentous one that when the mental object is a movement of our own body, it realizes itself outwardly when the mental change in question has occurred. But the change itself as a subjective phenomenon is something which we can translate into no simpler terms.

THE QUESTION OF 'FREE-WILL'

Especially must we, when talking about it, rid our mind of the fabulous warfare of separate agents called 'ideas.' The brain-processes may be agents, and the thought as such may be an agent. But what the ordinary psychologies call 'ideas' are nothing but parts of the total *object* of representation. All that is before the mind at once, no matter how complex a system of things and relations it may be, is one object for the thought. Thus, 'A-and-B-and-their-mutual-incompatibility-and-the-fact-that-only-one-can-be-true-or-can-become-real-notwithstanding-the-probability-or-desirability-of-both' may be such a complex object; and where the thought is deliberative its object has always some such form as this. When, now, we pass from deliberation to decision, that total object undergoes a change. We either dismiss A altogether and its relations to B, and think of B exclusively; or after thinking of both as possibilities, we next think that A is impossible, and that B is or forthwith shall be real. In either case a *new* object is before our thought; and where effort exists, it is where the change from the first object to the second one is hard. Our thought seems to turn in this case like a heavy door on rusty hinges; only, so far as the effort feels spontaneous, it turns, not as if by someone helping, but as if by an inward activity, born for the occasion, of its own.

The psychologists who discussed 'the muscular sense' at the international congress at Paris in 1889 agreed at the end that they needed to come to a better understanding in regard to this appearance of internal activity at the moment when a decision is made. M. Fouillée, in an article which I find more interesting and suggestive than coherent or conclusive,[66] seems to resolve our sense of activity into that of our very *existence as thinking entities*. At least so I translate his words.[67] But we saw in Chapter X how hard it is to lay a verifying finger plainly upon the thinking process as such, and to distinguish it from certain objects of the stream. M. Fouillée admits this; but I do not think he fully realizes how strong would be the position of a man who should suggest (see Vol. I, p. 288) that the feeling of moral activity itself which accompanies the advent of certain 'objects' before the mind is nothing but certain other objects,—constrictions, namely, in the brows, eyes, throat, and breathing apparatus, present then, but absent from other pulses of subjective change. Were this the truth, then a part, at any rate, of the activity of which we become aware in effort would seem merely to be that of our body; and many thinkers would probably thereupon conclude that this 'settles the claims' of inner activity, and dismisses the whole notion of such a thing as a superfluity in psychological science.

I cannot see my way to so extreme a view; even although I must repeat the confession made on p. 284 of Vol. I, that I do not *fully* understand how we come to our unshakable belief that thinking exists as a special kind of immaterial process alongside of the material processes of the world. It is certain, however, that only by *postulating* such thinking do we make things currently intelligible; and it is certain that no psychologist has as yet denied the *fact* of thinking, the utmost that has been denied being its dynamic power. But if we postulate the fact of the thinking at all, I believe that we must postulate its power as well; nor do I see how we can rightly equalize its power with its mere existence, and say (as M. Fouillée

66 "Le Sentiment de l'effort et la conscience de l'action," in *Revue Philosophique*, XXVIII, 561.

67 P. 577.

seems to say) that for the thought-process to *go on at all* is an activity, and an activity everywhere the same; for certain steps forwards in this process seem *prima facie* to be passive, and other steps (as where an object comes with effort) seem *prima facie* to be active in a supreme degree. If we admit, therefore, that our thoughts *exist,* we ought to admit that they exist after the fashion in which they appear, as things, namely, that supervene upon each other, sometimes with effort and sometimes with ease; the only questions being, is the effort where it exists a fixed function of the *object,* which the latter imposes on the thought? or is it such an independent 'variable' that with a constant object more or less of it may be made?

It certainly appears to us indeterminate, and as if, even with an unchanging object, we might make more or less, as we choose. If it be really indeterminate, our future acts are ambiguous or unpredestinate: in common parlance, *our wills are free.* If the amount of effort be not indeterminate, but be related in a fixed manner to the objects themselves, in such wise that whatever object at any time fills our consciousness was from eternity bound to fill it then and there, and compel from us the exact effort, neither more nor less, which we bestow upon it,—then our wills are not free, and all our acts are foreordained. *The question of fact in the free-will controversy is thus extremely simple.* It relates solely to the amount of effort of attention or consent which we can at any time put forth. Are the duration and intensity of this effort fixed functions of the object, or are they not? Now, as I just said, it *seems* as if the effort were an independent variable, as if we might exert more or less of it in any given case. When a man has let his thoughts go for days and weeks until at last they culminate in some particularly dirty or cowardly or cruel act, it is hard to persuade him, in the midst of his remorse, that he might not have reined them in; hard to make him believe that this whole goodly universe (which his act so jars upon) required and exacted it of him at that fatal moment, and from eternity made aught else impossible. But, on the other hand, there is the certainty that all his *effortless* volitions are resultants of interests and associations whose strength and sequence are mechanically determined by the structure of that physical mass, his brain; and the general continuity of things and the monistic conception of the world may lead one irresistibly to postulate that a little fact like effort can form no real exception to the overwhelming reign of deterministic law. Even in effortless volition we have the consciousness of the alternative being also possible. This is surely a delusion here; why is it not a delusion everywhere?

My own belief is that the question of free-will is insoluble on strictly psychologic grounds. After a certain amount of effort of attention has been given to an idea, it is manifestly impossible to tell whether either more or less of it *might* have been given or not. To tell that, we should have to ascend to the antecedents of the effort, and defining them with mathematical exactitude, prove, by laws of which we have not at present even an inkling, that the only amount of sequent effort which could *possibly* comport with them was the precise amount which actually came. Measurements, whether of psychic or of neural quantities, and deductive reasonings such as this method of proof implies, will surely be forever beyond human reach. No serious psychologist or physiologist will venture even to suggest a notion of how they might be practically made. We are thrown back therefore upon the crude evidences of introspection on the one hand, with all its liabilities to deception, and, on the other hand, upon *a priori* postulates and probabilities. He who loves to balance nice doubts need be in no hurry to decide the point. Like Mephistopheles to Faust, he can say to himself, "*dazu hast du noch eine lange Frist*," for from generation to generation the reasons adduced on both sides will grow more voluminous, and the discussion more refined. But if our speculative delight be less keen, if the love of a *parti pris* outweighs that of keeping questions open, or if, as a French philosopher of genius says, "*l'amour de la vie qui s'indigne de tant de discours*," awakens in us, craving the sense of either peace or power,—then, taking the risk of error on our head, we must project upon one of the alternative views the attribute of reality for us; we must so fill our mind with the idea of it that it becomes our settled creed. The present writer does this for the alternative of freedom, but since the grounds of his opinion are ethical rather than psychological, he prefers to exclude them from the present book.[68]

A few words, however, may be permitted about the logic of the question. The most that any argument can do for determinism is

[68] They will be found indicated, in somewhat popular form, in a lecture on "The Dilemma of Determinism," published in the *Unitarian Review* (of Boston) for September 1884 (vol. XXII, p. 193).

to make it a clear and seductive conception, which a man is foolish not to espouse, so long as he stands by the great scientific postulate that the world must be one unbroken fact, and that prediction of all things without exception must be ideally, even if not actually, possible. It is a *moral* postulate about the Universe, the postulate that *what ought to be can be, and that bad acts cannot be fated, but that good ones must be possible in their place,* which would lead one to espouse the contrary view. But when scientific and moral postulates war thus with each other and objective proof is not to be had, the only course is voluntary choice, for scepticism itself, if systematic, is also voluntary choice. If, meanwhile, the will *be* undetermined, it would seem only fitting that the belief in its indetermination should be voluntarily chosen from amongst other possible beliefs. Freedom's first deed should be to affirm itself. We ought never to hope for any other method of getting at the truth if indeterminism be a fact. Doubt of this particular truth will therefore probably be open to us to the end of time, and the utmost that a believer in free-will can *ever* do will be to show that the deterministic arguments are not coercive. That they are seductive, I am the last to deny; nor do I deny that effort may be needed to keep the faith in freedom, when they press upon it, upright in the mind.

There is a *fatalistic argument* for determinism, however, which is radically vicious. When a man has let himself go time after time, he easily becomes impressed with the enormously preponderating influence of circumstances, hereditary habits, and temporary bodily dispositions over what might seem a spontaneity born for the occasion. "All is fate," he then says; "all is resultant of what pre-exists. Even if the moment seems original, it is but the instable molecules passively tumbling in their preappointed way. It is hopeless to resist the drift, vain to look for any new force coming in; and less, perhaps, than anywhere else under the sun is there anything really mine in the decisions which I make." This is really no argument for simple determinism. There runs throughout it the sense of a force which might make things otherwise from one moment to another, if it were only strong enough to breast the tide. A person who feels the *impotence* of free effort in this way has the acutest notion of what is meant by it, and of its possible independent power. How else could he be so conscious of its absence and of that of its effects? But genuine determinism occupies a totally different ground; not the *impotence* but the *unthinkability* of free-will is what it affirms. It admits something phenomenal *called* free effort, which *seems* to breast the tide, but it claims this as a *portion of the tide*. The variations of the effort cannot be independent, it says; they cannot originate *ex nihilo*, or come from a fourth dimension; they are mathematically fixed functions of the ideas themselves, which are the tide. Fatalism, which conceives of effort clearly enough as an independent variable that might come from a fourth dimension if it *would* come, but that does *not* come, is a very dubious ally for determinism. It strongly imagines that very possibility which determinism denies.

But what, quite as much as the inconceivability of absolutely independent variables, persuades modern men of science that their efforts must be predetermined, is the continuity of the latter with other phenomena whose predetermination no one doubts. Decisions with effort merge so gradually into those without it that it is not easy to say where the limit lies. Decisions without effort merge again into ideo-motor, and these into reflex, acts; so that the temptation is almost irresistible to throw the formula which covers so many cases over absolutely all. Where there is effort just as where there is none, the ideas themselves which furnish the matter of deliberation are brought before the mind by the machinery of association. And this machinery is essentially a system of arcs and paths, a reflex system, whether effort be amongst its incidents or not. The reflex way is, after all, the universal way of conceiving the business. The feeling of *ease* is a passive result of the way in which the thoughts unwind themselves. Why is not the feeling of effort the same? Professor Lipps, in his admirably clear deterministic statement, so far from admitting that the feeling of effort testifies to an increment of force exerted, explains it as a sign that force is lost. We speak of effort, according to him, whenever a force expends itself (wholly or partly) in neutralizing another force, and so fails of its own possible outward effect. The outward effect of the antagonistic force, however, also fails in corresponding measure, "so that there is no effort without counter-effort, . . . and effort and counter-effort signify only that causes are mutually robbing each other of effectiveness."[69] Where the forces are ideas, both sets of them, strictly speaking, are the seat of effort—both those which tend to explode, and those which tend to check them. We, how-

[69] See *Grundtatsachen des Seelenlebens*, pp. 594–5; and compare the conclusion of our own chapter on Attention, Vol. I, pp. 424–430.

ever, call the more abundant mass of ideas *ourselves*; and, talking of its effort as *our* effort, and of that of the smaller mass of ideas as the *resistance*,[70] we say that our effort sometimes overcomes the resistances offered by the inertias of an obstructed, and sometimes those presented by the impulsions of an explosive, will. Really both effort and resistance are ours, and the identification of our *self* with one of these factors is an illusion and a trick of speech. I do not see how anyone can fail (especially when the mythologic dynamism of separate 'ideas,' which Professor Lipps cleaves to, is translated into that of brain-processes) to recognize the fascinating simplicity of some such view as his. Nor do I see why *for scientific purposes* one need give it up even if indeterminate amounts of effort really do occur. Before their indeterminism, science simply *stops*. She can abstract from it altogether, then; for in the impulses and inhibitions with which the effort has to cope there is already a larger field of uniformity than she can ever practically cultivate. Her prevision will never foretell, even if the effort be completely predestinate, the actual way in which each individual emergency is resolved. Psychology will be Psychology,[71] and Science Science, as much as ever (as much and no more) in this world, whether free-will be true in it or not. Science, however, must be constantly reminded that her purposes are not the only purposes, and that the order of uniform causation which she has use for, and is therefore right in postulating, may be enveloped in a wider order, on which she has no claims at all.

We can therefore leave the free-will question altogether out of our account. As we said in Chapter XI (p. 429), the operation of free effort, if it existed, could only be to hold some one ideal object, or part of an object, a little longer or a little more intensely before the mind. Amongst the alternatives which present them-

70 Thus at least I interpret Prof. Lipps's words: "Wir wissen uns naturgemäss in jedem Streben umsomehr aktiv, je mehr unser *ganzes* Ich bei dem Streben beteiligt ist," u. s. w. (p. 601).

71 Such ejaculations as Mr. Spencer's: "Psychical changes either conform to law or they do not. If they do not, this work, in common with all works on the subject, is sheer nonsense: no science of Psychology is possible" (*Principles of Psychology*, I, 503),—are beneath criticism. Mr. Spencer's work, like all the other 'works on the subject,' treats of those general conditions of *possible* conduct within which all our real decisions must fall no matter whether their effort be small or great. However closely psychical changes may conform to law, it is safe to say that individual histories and biographies will never be written in advance no matter how 'evolved' psychology may become.

selves as *genuine possibles*, it would thus make one effective.[72] And although such quickening of one idea might be *morally and historically momentous*, yet, if considered *dynamically*, it would be an operation amongst those physiological infinitesimals which calculation must forever neglect.

But whilst eliminating the question about the amount of our effort as one which psychology will never have a practical call to decide, I must say one word about the extraordinarily intimate and important character which the phenomenon of effort assumes in our own eyes as individual men. Of course we measure ourselves

[72] *Caricatures* of the kind of supposition which free-will demands abound in deterministic literature. The following passage from John Fiske's *Cosmic Philosophy* (pt. II, chap. XVII) is an example: "If volitions arise without cause, it necessarily follows that we cannot infer from them the character of the antecedent states of feeling. If, therefore, a murder has been committed, we have *a priori* no better reason for suspecting the worst enemy than the best friend of the murdered man. If we see a man jump from a fourth-story window, we must beware of too hastily inferring his insanity, since he may be merely exercising his free-will; the intense love of life implanted in the human breast being, as it seems, unconnected with attempts at suicide or at self-preservation. We can thus frame no theory of human actions whatever. The countless empirical maxims of every-day life, the embodiment as they are of the inherited and organized sagacity of many generations, become wholly incompetent to guide us; and nothing which any one may do, ought ever to occasion surprise. The mother may strangle her first-born child, the miser may cast his long-treasured gold into the sea, the sculptor may break in pieces his lately-finished statue, in the presence of no other feelings than those which before led them to cherish, to hoard, and to create.

"To state these conclusions is to refute their premise. Probably no defender of the doctrine of free-will could be induced to accept them, even to save the theorem with which they are inseparably wrapped-up. Yet the dilemma cannot be avoided. Volitions are either caused, or they are not. If they are not caused, an inexorable logic brings us to the absurdities just mentioned. If they are caused, the free-will doctrine is annihilated. . . . In truth, the immediate corollaries of the free-will doctrine are so shocking not only to philosophy but to common-sense, that were not accurate thinking a somewhat rare phenomenon, it would be inexplicable how any credit should ever have been given to such a dogma. This is but one of the many instances, in which by the force of words alone, men have been held subject to chronic delusion. . . . Attempting, as the free-will philosophers do, to destroy the science of history, they are compelled by an inexorable logic to pull down with it the cardinal principles of ethics, politics, and jurisprudence. Political economy, if rigidly dealt with on their theory, would fare little better; and psychology would become chaotic jargon. . . . The denial of causation is the affirmation of chance, and 'between the theory of Chance and the theory of Law, there can be no compromise, no reciprocity, no borrowing and lending.' To write history on any method furnished by the free-will doctrine, would be utterly impossible."—All this comes from Mr. Fiske's not distinguishing between the possibles which really tempt a man and those which tempt him not at all. Free-will, like psychology, deals with the former possibles exclusively.

by many standards. Our strength and our intelligence, our wealth and even our good luck, are things which warm our heart and make us feel ourselves a match for life. But deeper than all such things, and able to suffice unto itself without them, is the sense of the amount of effort which we can put forth. Those are, after all, but effects, products, and reflections of the outer world within. But the effort seems to belong to an altogether different realm, as if it were the substantive thing which we *are*, and those were but externals which we *carry*. If the 'searching of our heart and reins' be the purpose of this human drama, then what is sought seems to be what effort we can make. He who can make none is but a shadow; he who can make much is a hero. The huge world that girdles us about puts all sorts of questions to us, and tests us in all sorts of ways. Some of the tests we meet by actions that are easy, and some of the questions we answer in articulately formulated words. But the deepest question that is ever asked admits of no reply but the dumb turning of the will and the tightening of our heart-strings as we say, "*Yes, I will even have it so!*" When a dreadful object is presented, or when life as a whole turns up its dark abysses to our view, then the worthless ones among us lose their hold on the situation altogether, and either escape from its difficulties by averting their attention, or if they cannot do that, collapse into yielding masses of plaintiveness and fear. The effort required for facing and consenting to such objects is beyond their power to make. But the heroic mind does differently. To it, too, the objects are sinister and dreadful, unwelcome, incompatible with wished-for things. But it can face them if necessary, without for that losing its hold upon the rest of life. The world thus finds in the heroic man its worthy match and mate; and the effort which he is able to put forth to hold himself erect and keep his heart unshaken is the direct measure of his worth and function in the game of human life. He can *stand* this Universe. He can meet it and keep up his faith in it in presence of those same features which lay his weaker brethren low. He can still find a zest in it, not by 'ostrich-like forgetfulness,' but by pure inward willingness to take the world with those deterrent objects there. And hereby he becomes one of the masters and the lords of life. He must be counted with henceforth; he forms a part of human destiny. Neither in the theoretic nor in the practical sphere do we care for, or go for help to, those who have no head for risks, or sense for living on the perilous edge. Our religious life lies more, our practical life lies less, than it used to, on the perilous edge. But just as our courage is so often a reflex of another's courage, so our faith is apt to be, as Max Müller somewhere says, a faith in someone else's faith. We draw new life from the heroic example. The prophet has drunk more deeply than anyone of the cup of bitterness, but his countenance is so unshaken and he speaks such mighty words of cheer that his will becomes our will, and our life is kindled at his own.

Thus not only our morality but our religion, so far as the latter is deliberate, depend on the effort which we can make. "*Will you or won't you have it so?*" is the most probing question we are ever asked; we are asked it every hour of the day, and about the largest as well as the smallest, the most theoretical as well as the most practical, things. We answer by *consents or non-consents* and not by words. What wonder that these dumb responses should seem our deepest organs of communication with the nature of things! What wonder if the effort demanded by them be the measure of our worth as men! What wonder if the amount which we accord of it be the one strictly underived and original contribution which we make to the world!

THE EDUCATION OF THE WILL

The education of the will may be taken in a broader or a narrower sense. In the broader sense, it means the whole of one's training to moral and prudential conduct, and of one's learning to adapt means to ends, involving the 'association of ideas,' in all its varieties and complications, together with the power of inhibiting impulses irrelevant to the ends desired, and of initiating movements contributory thereto. It is the acquisition of these latter powers which I mean by the education of the will in the narrower sense. And it is in this sense alone that it is worth while to treat the matter here.[73]

Since a willed movement is a movement preceded by an idea of itself, the problem of the will's education is the problem of how the idea of a movement can arouse the movement itself. This, as we have seen, is a secondary kind of process; for framed as we are, we can have no *a priori* idea of a movement, no idea of a move-

[73] On the education of the Will from a pedagogic point of view, see an article by G. Stanley Hall in the *Princeton Review* for November 1882, and some bibliographic references there contained.

ment which we have not already performed. Before the idea can be generated, the movement must have occurred in a blind, unexpected way, and left its idea behind. *Reflex, instinctive,* or *random execution* of a *movement* must, in other words, precede its voluntary execution. Reflex and instinctive movements have already been considered sufficiently for the purposes of this book. 'Random' movements are mentioned so as to include *quasi*-accidental reflexes from inner causes, or movements possibly arising from such overflow of nutrition in special centres as Prof. Bain postulates in his explanation of those 'spontaneous discharges' by which he sets such great store in his derivation of the voluntary life.[74]

Now *how can the sensory process which a movement has previously produced, discharge, when excited again, into the centre for the movement itself?* On the movement's original occurrence the motor discharge came first and the sensory process second; now in the voluntary repetition the sensory process (excited in weak or 'ideational' form) comes first, and the motor discharge comes second. To tell how this comes to pass would be to answer the problem of the education of the will in physiological terms. Evidently the problem is that of the formation of *new paths*; and the only thing to do is to make hypotheses, till we find some which seem to cover all the facts.

How is a fresh path ever formed? All paths are paths of discharge, and the discharge always takes place in the direction of least resistance, whether the cell which discharges be 'motor' or 'sensory.' The *connate* paths of least resistance are the paths of instinctive reaction; and I submit as my first hypothesis that *these paths all run one way, that is from 'sensory' cells into 'motor' cells and from motor cells into muscles, without ever taking the reverse direction.* A motor cell, for example, never awakens a sensory cell directly, but only through the incoming current caused by the bodily movements to which its discharge gives rise. And a sensory cell *always* discharges or normally tends to discharge towards the motor region. Let this direction be called the 'forward' direction. I call the law an hypothesis, but really it is an indubitable truth. No impression or idea of eye, ear, or skin comes to us without occasioning a movement, even though the movement be no more than the accommodation of the sense-organ; and all our trains of sensation

74 See his *Emotions and the Will,* "The Will," chap. I. I take the name of random movements from Sully: *Outlines of Psychology,* p. 593.

and sensational imagery have their terms alternated and interpenetrated with motor processes, of most of which we practically are unconscious. Another way of stating the rule is to say that, primarily or connately, all currents through the brain run towards the Rolandic region, and that there they run out, and never return upon themselves. From this point of view the distinction of sensory and motor cells has no fundamental significance. All cells are motor; we simply call those of the Rolandic region, those nearest the mouth of the funnel, the motor cells *par excellence*.

A corollary of this law is that 'sensory' cells do not awaken each other connately; that is, that no one sensible property of things has any tendency, in advance of experience, to awaken in us the idea of any other sensible properties which in the nature of things may go with it. *There is no a priori calling up of one 'idea' by another*; the only *a priori* couplings are of ideas with movements. All suggestions of one sensible fact by another take place by secondary paths which experience has formed.

The diagram (Fig. 87) shows what happens in a nervous system ideally reduced to the fewest possible terms. A stimulus reaching the sense-organ awakens the sensory cell, S; this by the connate or instinctive path discharges the motor cell, M, which makes the muscle contract; and the contraction arouses the second sensory

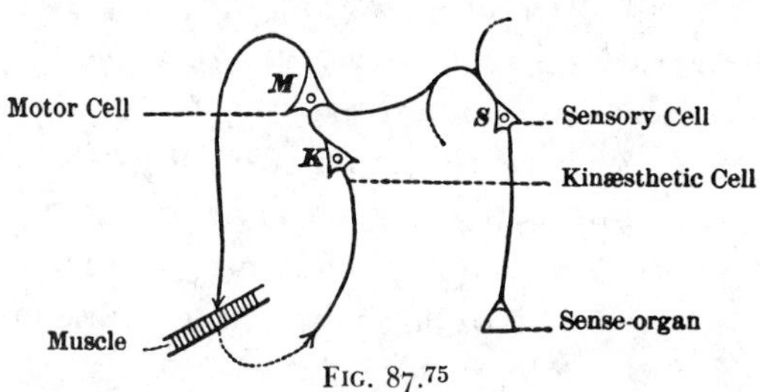

FIG. 87.[75]

cell, K, which may be the organ either of a 'resident' or 'kinæsthetic,' or of a 'remote,' sensation. (See above, p. 1100.) This cell K again

[75] This figure and the following ones are purely schematic, and must not be supposed to involve any theory about protoplasmatic and axis-cylinder processes. The latter, according to Golgi and others, emerge from the base of the cell, and each cell has but one. They alone form a nervous network. The reader will of course also understand that none of the hypothetical constructions which I make from now to the end of the chapter are proposed as definite accounts of what happens. All I aim at is to make it clear in some more or less symbolic fashion that the formation of new paths, the learning of habits, etc., is in *some* mechanical way conceivable. Compare what was said in Vol. I, p. 88, note.

discharges into M. If this were the entire nervous mechanism, the movement, once begun, would be self-maintaining, and would stop only when the parts were exhausted. And this, according to M. Pierre Janet, is what actually happens in *catalepsy*. A cataleptic patient is anæsthetic, speechless, motionless. Consciousness, so far as we can judge, is abolished. Nevertheless the limbs will retain whatever position is impressed upon them from without, and retain it so long that if it be a strained and unnatural position, the phenomenon is regarded by Charcot as one of the few conclusive tests against hypnotic subjects shamming, since hypnotics can be made cataleptic, and then keep their limbs outstretched for a length of time quite unattainable by the waking will. M. Janet thinks that in all these cases the outlying ideational processes in the brain are temporarily thrown out of gear. The kinæsthetic sensation of the raised arm, for example, is produced in the patient when the operator raises the arm, this sensation discharges into the motor cell, which through the muscle reproduces the sensation, etc., the currents running in this closed circle until they grow so weak, by exhaustion of the parts, that the member slowly drops. We may call this circle from the muscle to K, from K to M, and from M to the muscle again, the 'motor circle.' *We should all be cataleptics and never stop a muscular contraction once begun, were it not that other processes simultaneously going on inhibit the contraction. Inhibition is therefore not an occasional accident; it is an essential and unremitting element of our cerebral life.* It is interesting to note that Dr. Mercier, by a different path of reasoning, is also led to conclude that we owe to outside inhibitions exclusively our power to arrest a movement once begun.[76]

One great inhibiter of the discharge of K into M seems to be the painful or otherwise displeasing quality of the sensation itself of K; and conversely, when this sensation is distinctly pleasant, that fact tends to further K's discharge into M, and to keep the primordial motor circle agoing. Tremendous as the part is which pleasure and pain play in our psychic life, we must confess that absolutely nothing is known of their cerebral conditions. It is hard to imagine them as having special centres; it is harder still to invent peculiar forms of process in each and every centre, to which these feelings may be due. And let one try as one will to represent the cerebral activity in exclusively mechanical terms, I, for one, find

[76] *The Nervous System and the Mind* (1888), pp. 75–6.

it quite impossible to enumerate what seem to be the facts and yet to make no mention of the psychic side which they possess. However it be with other drainage currents and discharges, the drainage currents and discharges of the brain are not purely physical facts. They are *psycho-physical* facts, and the spiritual quality of them seems a codeterminant of their mechanical effectiveness. If the mechanical activities in a cell, as they increase, give pleasure, they seem to increase all the more rapidly for that fact; if they give displeasure, the displeasure seems to damp the activities. The psychic side of the phenomenon thus seems, somewhat like the applause or hissing at a spectacle, to be an encouraging or adverse *comment* on what the machinery brings forth. The soul *presents* nothing herself; *creates* nothing; is at the mercy of the material forces for all *possibilities*; but amongst these possibilities she *selects*; and by reinforcing one and checking others, she figures not as an 'epiphenomenon,' but as something from which the play gets moral support. I shall therefore never hesitate to invoke the efficacy of the conscious comment, where no strictly mechanical reason appears why a current escaping from a cell should take one path rather than another.[77] But the *existence* of the current, and its *tendency* towards either path, I feel bound to account for by mechanical laws.

Having now considered a nervous system reduced to its lowest possible terms, in which all the paths are connate, and the possibilities of inhibition not extrinsic, but due solely to the agreeableness or disagreeableness of the feeling aroused, let us turn to the conditions under which new paths may be formed. Potentialities of new paths are furnished by the fibres which connect the sensory cells amongst themselves; but these fibres are not originally pervious, and have to be made so by a process which I proceed hypothetically to state as follows: *Each discharge from a sensory cell in the forward direction*[78] *tends to drain the cells lying behind the discharging one of whatever tension they may possess. The drainage from the rearward cells is what for the first time makes the fibres pervious. The result is a new-formed 'path,' running from the cells which were 'rearward' to the cell which was 'forward' on that occasion; which path, if on future occasions the rearward cells are*

77 Compare Vol. I, pp. 140, 144–145.

78 That is, the direction towards the motor cells.

independently excited, will tend to carry off their activity in the same direction so as to excite the forward cell, and will deepen itself more and more every time it is used.

Now the 'rearward cells,' so far, stand for all the sensory cells of the brain other than the one which is discharging; but such an indefinitely broad path would practically be no better than no path, so here I make a third hypothesis, which, taken together with the others, seems to me to cover all the facts. It is that *the deepest paths are formed from the most drainable to the most draining cells*; that *the most drainable cells are those which have just been discharging*; and that *the most draining cells are those which are now discharging or in which the tension is rising towards the point of discharge.*[79] Another diagram, Fig. 88, will make the matter

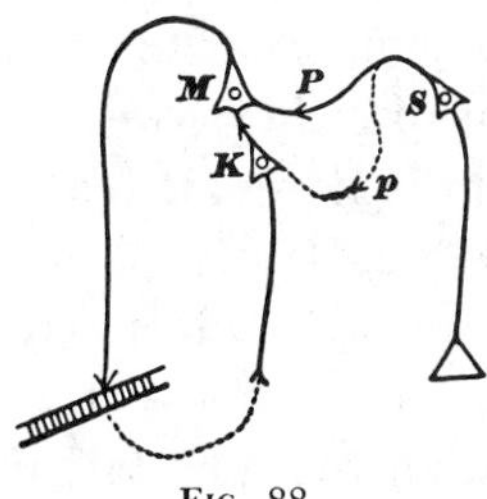

FIG. 88.

clear. Take the operation represented by the previous diagram at the moment when, the muscular contraction having occurred, the cell K is discharging forwards into M. Through the dotted line *p* it will, according to our third hypothesis, drain S (which, in the supposed case, has just discharged into M by the connate path P, and caused the muscular contraction), and the result is that *p* will now remain as a new path open from S to K. When next S is excited from without it will tend not only to discharge into M, but into K as well. K thus gets excited directly by S *before* it gets excited by the incoming current from the muscle; or, translated into psychic terms: *when a sensation has once produced a movement in*

[79] This brain-scheme seems oddly enough to give a certain basis of reality to those hideously fabulous performances of the Herbartian *Vorstellungen*. Herbart says that when one idea is inhibited by another it fuses with that other and thereafter helps it to ascend into consciousness. Inhibition is thus the basis of association in both schemes, for the 'draining' of which the text speaks is tantamount to an inhibition of the activity of the cells which are drained, which inhibition makes the inhibited revive the inhibiter on later occasions.

us, the next time we have the sensation, it tends to suggest the idea of the movement, even before the movement occurs.[80]

The same principles also apply to the relations of K and M. M, lying in the forward direction, drains K, and the path KM, even though it be no primary or connate path, becomes a secondary or habitual one. Hereafter K may be aroused in any way whatsoever (not as before from S or from without) and still it will tend to discharge into M; or, to express it again in psychic terms, *the idea of the movement M's sensory effects will have become an immediately antecedent condition to the production of the movement itself.*

Here, then, we have the answer to our original question of how a sensory process which, the first time it occurred, was the effect of a movement, can later figure as the movement's cause.

It is obvious on this scheme that the cell which we have marked K may stand for the seat of either a resident or a remote sensation occasioned by the motor discharge. It may indifferently be a tactile, a visual, or an auditory cell. The idea of how the arm *feels* when raised may cause it to rise; but no less may the idea of some *sound* which it makes in rising, or of some *optical* impression which it produces. Thus we see that the 'mental cue' may belong to either of various senses; and that what our diagrams lead us to infer is what really happens; namely, that in our movements, such as that of speech, for example, in some of us it is the tactile, in others the acoustic, *Effektbild,* or memory-image, which seems most concerned in starting the articulation (Vol. I, pp. 63–64). The *primitive* 'starters,' however, of all our movements are not *Effektbilder* at all, but sensations and objects, and subsequently ideas derived therefrom.

Let us now turn to the more complex and serially concatenated movements which oftenest meet us in real life. The object of our will is seldom a single muscular contraction; it is almost always an orderly sequence of contractions, ending with a sensation which tells us that the goal is reached. But the several contractions of the sequence are not each distinctly willed; each earlier one seems rather, by the sensation it produces, to call its follower up, after the fashion described in Chapter IV, where we spoke of habitual concatenated movements being due to a series of secondarily organized

80 See the luminous passage in Münsterberg: *Die Willenshandlung,* pp. 144–5.

reflex arcs (Vol. I, p. 120). The first contraction is the one distinctly willed, and after willing it we let the rest of the chain rattle off of its own accord. How now is such an orderly concatenation of movements originally learned? or in other words, how are paths formed for the first time between one motor centre and another, so that the discharge of the first centre makes the others discharge in due order all along the line?

The phenomenon involves a rapid alternation of motor discharges and resultant afferent impressions, for as long a time as it lasts. They must be associated in one definite order; and the order must once have been *learned*, i.e., it must have been picked out and held to more and more exclusively out of the many other random orders which first presented themselves. The random afferent impressions fell out, those that felt right were selected and grew together in the chain. A chain which we actively teach ourselves by stringing a lot of right-feeling impressions together differs in no essential respect from a chain which we passively learn from someone else who gives us impressions in a certain order. So to make our ideas more precise, let us take a particular concatenated movement for an example, and let it be the recitation of the alphabet, which someone in our childhood taught us to say by heart.

What we have seen so far is how the idea of the sound or articulatory feeling of A may make us say 'A,' that of B, 'B,' and so on. But what we now want to see is *why the sensation that A is uttered should make us say 'B,' why the sensation that B is uttered should make us say 'C,' and so on.*

To understand this we must recall what happened when we first learned the letters in their order. Someone repeated A, B, C, D to us over and over again, and we imitated the sounds. Sensory cells corresponding to each letter were awakened in succession in such wise that each one of them (by virtue of our second law) must have 'drained' the cell just previously excited and left a path by which that cell tended ever afterwards to discharge into the cell that drained it. Let S^a, S^b, S^c in figure 89 stand for three of these cells. Each later one of them, as it discharges motorwards, draws a current from the previous one, S^b from S^a, and S^c from S^b. Cell S^b having thus drained S^a, if S^a ever gets excited again, it tends to discharge into S^b; whilst S^c having drained S^b, S^b later discharges into S^c, etc., etc.—all through the dotted lines. Let now the idea of the letter A arise in the mind, or, in other words, let S^a be aroused:

what happens? A current runs from S^a not only into the motor cell M^a for pronouncing that letter, but also into the cell S^b. When, a

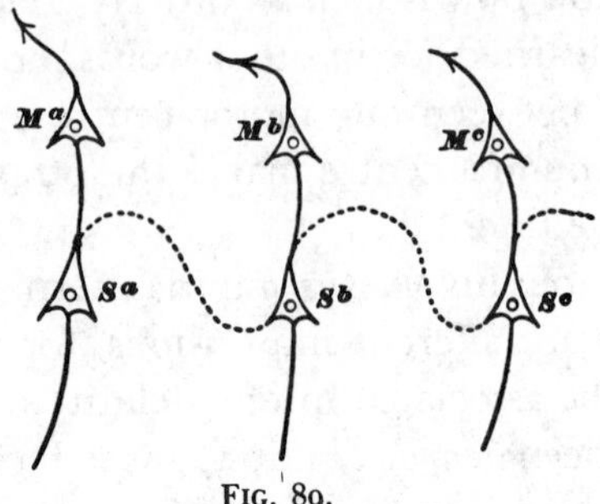

FIG. 89.

moment later, the effect of M^a's discharge comes back by the afferent nerve and re-excites S^a, this latter cell is inhibited from discharging again into M^a and reproducing the 'primordial motor

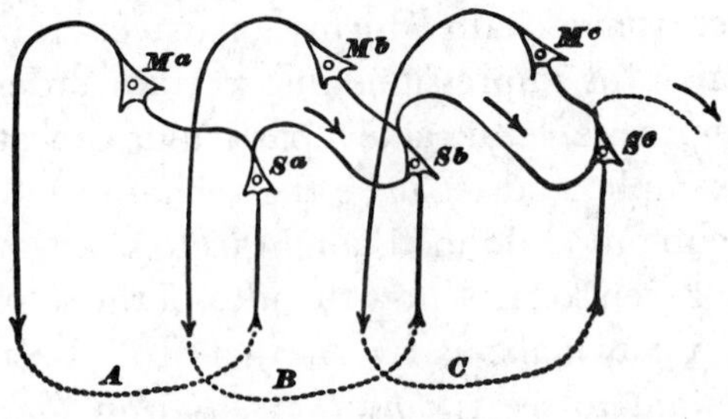

FIG. 90.

circle' (which in this case would be the continued utterance of the letter A), by the fact that the process in S^b, already under headway and tending to discharge into its own motor associate M^b, is, *under the existing conditions,* the stronger drainage-channel for S^a's excitement. The result is that M^b discharges and the letter B is pronounced; whilst at the same time S^c receives some of S^b's overflow; and, a moment later when the sound of B enters the ear, discharges into the motor cell for pronouncing C, by a repetition of the same mechanism as before; and so on *ad libitum.* Figure 90 represents the entire set of processes involved.

The only thing that one does not immediately see is the reason why 'under the existing conditions' the path from S^a to S^b should be the stronger drainage-channel for S^a's excitement. If the cells and fibres in the figure constituted the entire brain we might suppose either a mechanical or a psychical reason. The mechanical reason might lie in a general law that cells like S^b and M^b, whose excitement is in a rising phase, are stronger drainers than cells like M^a, which have just discharged; or it might lie in the fact that an irradiation of the current beyond S^b into S^c and M^c has already begun also; and in a still farther law that drainage tends in the direction of the widest irradiations. Either of these suppositions would be a sufficient mechanical reason why, having once said A, we should not say it again. But we must not forget that the process has a psychical side, nor close our eyes to the possibility that the *sort of feeling* aroused by incipient currents may be the reason why certain of them are instantly inhibited and others helped to flow. There is no doubt that before we have uttered a single letter, the general intention to recite the alphabet is already there; nor is there any doubt that to that intention corresponds a widespread premonitory rising of tensions along the entire system of cells and fibres which are later to be aroused. So long as this rise of tensions *feels good*, so long every current which increases it is furthered, and every current which diminishes it is checked; and this may be the chief one of the 'existing conditions' which make the drainage-channel from S^a to S^b temporarily so strong.[81]

The new paths between the sensory cells of which we have studied the formation are paths of 'association,' and we now see why associations run always in the forward direction; why, for example, we cannot say the alphabet backwards, and why, although S^b discharges into S^c, there is no tendency for S^c to discharge into S^b, or at least no more than for it to discharge into S^a.[82] The first-formed paths had, according to the principles which we invoked, to run from cells that had just discharged to those that were discharging; and now, to get currents to run the other way, we must go through a new learning of our letters with their order reversed. There will *then* be two sets of association-pathways, either of them possible,

[81] L. Lange's and Münsterberg's experiments with 'shortened' or 'muscular' reaction-time (see Vol. I, p. 409) show how potent a fact dynamically this anticipatory preparation of a whole set of possible drainage-channels is.

[82] Even as the proofs of these pages are passing through my hands, I receive Heft 2 of the *Zeitschrift für Psychologie und Physiologie der Sinnesorgane*, in which the irrepressible young Münsterberg publishes experiments to show that there is no association between successive ideas, apart from intervening movements. As my explanations have assumed that an earlier excited *sensory* cell drains a later one, his experiments and inferences would, if sound, upset all my hypotheses. I therefore can (at this late moment) only refer the reader to Herr M.'s article, hoping to review the subject again myself in another place.

between the sensible cells. I represent them in Fig. 91, leaving out the motor features for simplicity's sake. The dotted lines are the paths in the backward direction, newly organized from the reception by the ear of the letters in the order C B A.

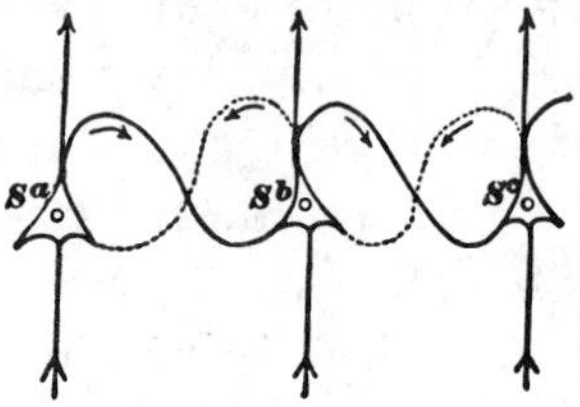

FIG. 91.

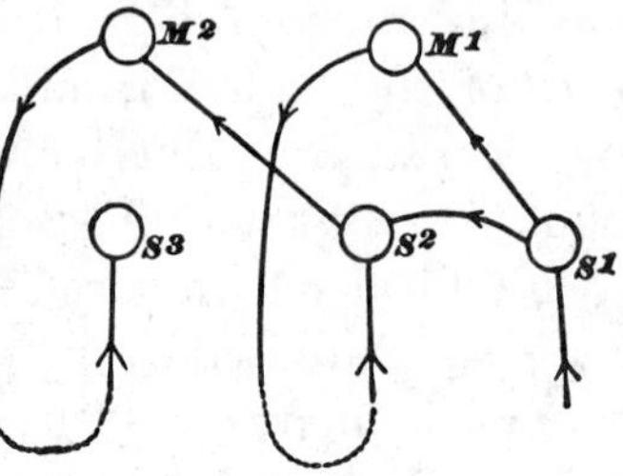

FIG. 92.

The same principles will explain the formation of new paths successively concatenated to no matter how great an extent, but it would obviously be folly to pretend to illustrate by more intricate examples. I will therefore only bring back the case of the child and flame (Vol. I, p. 37), to show how easily it admits of explanation as a 'purely cortical transaction' (*ibid.*, p. 86). The sight of the flame stimulates the cortical centre S^1 which discharges by an instinctive reflex path into the centre M^1 for the grasping-movement. This movement produces the feeling of burn, as its effects come back to the centre S^2; and this centre by a second connate path discharges into M^2, the centre for withdrawing the hand. The movement of withdrawal stimulates the centre S^3, and this, as far as we are concerned, is the last thing that happens. Now the next time the child sees the candle, the cortex is in possession of the secondary paths which the first experience left behind. S^2, having been stimulated immediately after S^1, drained the latter, and now S^1 discharges into S^2 before the discharge of M^1 has had time to occur; in other words, the sight of the flame suggests the idea of the burn before it produces its own natural reflex effects. The result is an inhibition of M^1, or an overtaking of it before it is completed, by M^2.—The characteristic physiological feature in all these acquired systems of paths lies in the fact that the new-formed sensory irradiations keep *draining things forwards*, and so breaking up the 'motor circles' which would otherwise accrue. But, even apart from catalepsy, we see the 'motor circle' every now and then come back. An infant learning to execute a simple movement at will, without regard to other movements beyond it, keeps repeating it till tired. How reiteratively they babble each new-learned word! And we adults often catch ourselves reiterating some meaningless word over and over again, if by chance we once begin to utter it 'absent-mindedly,' that is, without thinking of any ulterior train of words to which it may belong.

One more observation before closing these already too protracted physiological speculations. Already (Vol. I, p. 79) I have tried to shadow forth a reason why collateral innervation should establish itself after loss of brain-tissue, and why incoming stimuli should find their way out again, after an interval, by their former paths. I can now explain this a little better. Let S^1 be the dog's hearing-centre when he receives the command 'Give your paw.' This *used* to discharge into the motor centre M^1, of whose discharge S^2 represents the kinæsthetic effect; but now M^1 has been destroyed by an operation, so that S^1 discharges as it can, into other movements of the body, whimpering, raising the wrong paw, etc. The kinæsthetic

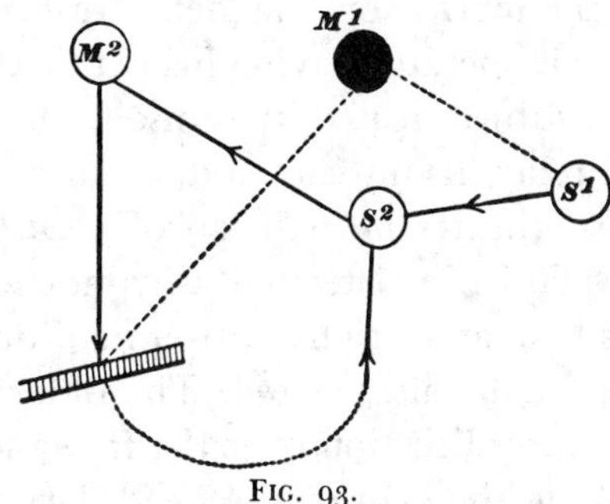

FIG. 93.

centre S^2 meanwhile has been awakened by the order S^1, and the poor animal's mind tingles with expectation and desire of certain incoming sensations which are entirely at variance with those which the really executed movements give. None of the latter sensations arouse a 'motor circle,' for they are displeasing and inhibitory. But when, by random accident, S^1 and S^2 *do* discharge into a path leading through M^2, by which the *paw is again given*, and S^2 is excited at last from without as well as from within, there are no inhibitions and the 'motor circle' is formed: S^1 discharges into M^2 over and over again, and the path from the one spot to the other is so much deepened that at last it becomes organized as the regular channel of efflux when S^1 is aroused. No other path has a chance of being organized in like degree.

Chapter XXVII

Hypnotism

MODES OF OPERATING, AND SUSCEPTIBILITY

The 'hypnotic,' 'mesmeric,' or 'magnetic' trance *can be induced in various ways,* each operator having his pet method. The simplest one is to leave the subject seated by himself, telling him that if he close his eyes and relax his muscles and, as far as possible, think of vacancy, in a few minutes he will 'go off.' On returning in ten minutes you may find him effectually hypnotized. Braid used to make his subjects look at a bright button held near their forehead until their eyes spontaneously closed. The older mesmerists made 'passes' in a downward direction over the face and body, but without contact. Stroking the skin of the head, face, arms and hands, especially that of the region round the brows and eyes, will have the same effect. Staring into the eyes of the subject until the latter droop; making him listen to a watch's ticking; or simply making him close his eyes for a minute whilst you describe to him the feeling of falling into sleep, 'talk sleep' to him, are equally efficacious methods in the hands of some operators; whilst with trained subjects any method whatever from which they have been led by previous suggestion to expect results will be successful.[1] The touching

[1] It should be said that the methods of leaving the patient to himself, and that of the simple verbal suggestion of sleep (the so-called Nancy method introduced by Dr. Liébeault of that place), seem, wherever applicable, to be the best, as they entail none of the after-inconveniences which occasionally follow upon straining his eyes. A new patient should not be put through a great variety of different suggestions in immediate succession. He should be waked up from time to time, and then rehypno-

of an object which they are told has been 'magnetized,' the drinking of 'magnetized' water, the reception of a letter ordering them to sleep, etc., are means which have been frequently employed. Recently M. Liégeois has hypnotized some of his subjects at a distance of $1\frac{1}{2}$ kilometres by giving them an intimation to that effect through a telephone. With some subjects, if you tell them in advance that at a certain hour of a certain day they will become entranced, the prophecy is fulfilled. Certain hysterical patients are immediately thrown into hypnotic catalepsy by any violent sensation, such as a blow on a gong or the flashing of an intense light in their eyes. Pressure on certain parts of the body (called *zones hypnogènes* by M. Pitres) rapidly produces hypnotic sleep in some hysterics. These regions, which differ in different subjects, are oftenest found on the forehead and about the root of the thumbs. Finally, persons in ordinary sleep may be transferred into the hypnotic condition by verbal intimation or contact, performed so gently as not to wake them up.

Some operators appear to be more successful than others in getting control of their subjects. I am informed that Mr. Gurney (who made valuable contributions to the theory of hypnotism) was never able himself to hypnotize, and had to use for his observations the subjects of others. On the other hand, Dr. Liébeault claims that he hypnotizes 92 per cent of all comers, and Wetterstrand in Stockholm says that amongst 718 persons there proved to be only 19 whom he failed to influence. Some of this disparity is unquestionably due to differences in the personal 'authority' of the operator, for the prime condition of success is that the subject should confidently *expect* to be entranced. Much also depends on the operator's tact in interpreting the physiognomy of his subjects, so as to give the right commands, and 'crowd it on' to the subject, at just the propitious moments. These conditions account for the fact that operators grow more successful the more they operate. Bernheim says that whoever does not hypnotize 80 per cent of the persons

tized to avoid mental confusion and excitement. Before finally waking a subject you should *undo* whatever delusive suggestions you may have implanted in him, by telling him that they are all gone, etc., and that you are now going to restore him to his natural state. Headache, languor, etc., which sometimes follow the first trance or two, must be banished at the outset, by the operator strongly assuring the subject that such things *never* come from hypnotism, that the subject *must not* have them, etc.

whom he tries has not yet learned to operate as he should. Whether certain operators have over and above this a peculiar 'magnetic power' is a question which I leave at present undecided.[2] Children under three or four, and insane persons, especially idiots, are unusually hard to hypnotize. This seems due to the impossibility of getting them to fix their attention continuously on the idea of the coming trance. All ages above infancy are probably equally hypnotizable, as are all races and both sexes. A certain amount of mental training, sufficient to aid concentration of the attention, seems a favorable condition, and so does a certain momentary indifference or passivity as to the result. Native strength or weakness of 'will' have absolutely nothing to do with the matter. Frequent trances enormously increase the susceptibility of a subject, and many who resist at first succumb after several trials. Dr. Moll says he has more than once succeeded after forty fruitless attempts. Some experts are of the opinion that everyone is hypnotizable essentially, the only difficulty being the more habitual presence in some individuals of hindering mental preoccupations, which, however, may suddenly at some moment be removed.

The trance may be dispelled instantaneously by saying in a rousing voice, 'All right, wake up!' or words of similar purport. At the Salpêtrière they awaken subjects by blowing on their eyelids. Upward passes have an awakening effect; sprinkling cold water ditto. Anything will awaken a patient who expects to be awakened by that thing. Tell him that he will wake after counting five, and he will do so. Tell him to waken in five minutes, and he is very likely to do so punctually, even though he interrupt thereby some exciting histrionic performance which you may have suggested.—As Dr. Moll says, any theory which pretends to explain the physiology of the hypnotic state must keep account of the fact that so simple a thing as hearing the word 'wake!' will end it.

THEORIES ABOUT THE HYPNOTIC STATE

The intimate nature of the hypnotic condition, when once induced, can hardly be said to be understood. Without entering into details of controversy, one may say that three main opinions

[2] Certain facts would seem to point that way. Cf., e.g., the case of the man described by P. Despine: *Étude scientifique sur le somnambulisme,* p. 286 ff.

have been held concerning it, which we may call respectively the theories of

1. Animal magnetism;
2. of Neurosis; and finally of
3. Suggestion.

According to the *animal-magnetism theory* there is a direct passage of force from the operator to the subject, whereby the latter becomes the former's puppet. This theory is nowadays given up as regards all the ordinary hypnotic phenomena, and is only held to by some persons as an explanation of a few effects exceptionally met with.

According to the *neurosis-theory,* the hypnotic state is a peculiar pathological condition into which certain predisposed patients fall, and in which special physical agents have the power of provoking special symptoms, quite apart from the subjects mentally expecting the effect. Professor Charcot and his colleagues at the Salpêtrière hospital admit that this condition is rarely found in typical form. They call it then *le grand hypnotisme,* and say that it accompanies the disease hystero-epilepsy. If a patient subject to this sort of hypnotism hear a sudden loud noise, or look at a bright light unexpectedly, she falls into the *cataleptic* trance. Her limbs and body offer no resistance to movements communicated to them, but retain permanently the attitudes impressed. The eyes are staring, there is insensibility to pain, etc., etc. If the eyelids be forcibly closed, the cataleptic gives place to the *lethargic* condition, characterized by apparent abolition of consciousness, and absolute muscular relaxation except where the muscles are kneaded or the tendons struck by the operator's hand, or certain nerve-trunks are pressed upon. Then the muscles in question, or those supplied by the same nerve-trunk enter into a more or less steadfast tonic contraction. Charcot calls this symptom by the name of neuro-muscular hyperexcitability. The lethargic state may be *primarily* brought on by fixedly looking at anything, or by pressure on the closed eyeballs. Friction on the top of the head will make the patient pass from either of the two preceding conditions into the *somnambulic* state, in which she is alert, talkative, and susceptible to all the suggestions of the operator. The somnambulic state may also be induced primarily, by fixedly looking at a small object. In this state the accurately limited muscular contractions characteristic of lethargy do not follow upon the above-described manipulations, but instead of them there is a tendency to rigidity of entire regions of the body, which may upon occasion develop into general tetanus, and which is brought about by gently touching the skin or blowing upon it. M. Charcot calls this by the name of cutaneo-muscular hyperexcitability.

Many other symptoms, supposed by their observers to be independent of mental expectation, are described, of which I only will mention the more interesting. Opening the eyes of a patient in lethargy causes her to pass into catalepsy. If one eye only be opened, the corresponding half of the body becomes cataleptic, whilst the other half remains in lethargy. Similarly, rubbing one side of the head may result in a patient becoming hemilethargic or hemicataleptic and hemisomnambulic. The approach of a magnet (or certain metals) to the skin causes these half-states (and many others) to be transferred to the opposite sides. Automatic repetition of every sound heard ('*echolalia*') is said to be produced by pressure on the lower cervical vertebræ or on the epigastrium. *Aphasia* is brought about by rubbing the head over the region of the speech-centre. Pressure behind the occiput determines *movements of imitation.* Heidenhain describes a number of curious automatic tendencies to movement, which are brought about by stroking various portions of the vertebral column. Certain other symptoms have been frequently noticed, such as a flushed face and cold hands, brilliant and congested eyes, dilated pupils. Dilated retinal vessels and spasm of the accommodation are also reported.

The theory of Suggestion denies that there is any special hypnotic *state* worthy of the name of trance or neurosis. All the symptoms above described, as well as those to be described hereafter, are results of that mental susceptibility which we all to some degree possess, of yielding assent to outward suggestion, of affirming what we strongly conceive, and of acting in accordance with what we are made to expect. The bodily symptoms of the Salpêtrière patients are all of them results of expectation and training. The first patients accidentally did certain things which their doctors thought typical and caused to be repeated. The subsequent subjects 'caught on' and followed the established tradition. In proof of this the fact is urged that the classical three stages and their grouped symptoms have *only* been reported as spontaneously occurring, so far, at the

Salpêtrière, though they may be superinduced by deliberate suggestion, in patients anywhere found. The ocular symptoms, the flushed face, accelerated breathing, etc., are said not to be symptoms of the passage into the hypnotic state as such, but merely consequences of the strain on the eyes when the method of looking at a bright object is used. They are absent in the subjects at Nancy, where simple verbal suggestion is employed. The various reflex effects (aphasia, echolalia, imitation, etc.) are but habits induced by the influence of the operator, who unconsciously urges the subject into the direction in which he would prefer to have him go. The influence of the magnet, the opposite effects of upward and downward passes, etc., are similarly explained. Even that sleepy and inert condition, the advent of which seems to be the prime condition of farther symptoms being developed, is said to be merely due to the fact that the mind expects it to come; whilst its influence on the other symptoms is not physiological, so to speak, but psychical, its own easy realization by suggestion simply encouraging the subject to expect that ulterior suggestions will be realized with equal ease. The radical defenders of the suggestion-theory are thus led to deny the very existence of the hypnotic state, in the sense of a peculiar trance-like condition which deprives the patient of spontaneity and makes him passive to suggestion from without. The trance itself is only one of the suggestions, and many subjects in fact can be made to exhibit the other hypnotic phenomena without the preliminary induction of this one.

The theory of suggestion may be said to be quite triumphant at the present day over the neurosis-theory as held at the Salpêtrière, with its three states, and its definite symptoms supposed to be produced by physical agents apart from co-operation of the subject's mind. But it is one thing to say this, and it is quite another thing to say that there is no peculiar physiological condition whatever worthy of the name of hypnotic trance, no peculiar state of nervous equilibrium, 'hypotaxy,' 'dissociation,' or whatever you please to call it, during which the subject's susceptibility to outward suggestion is greater than at ordinary times. All the facts seem to prove that, until this trance-like state is assumed by the patient, suggestion produces very insignificant results, but that, when it is once assumed, there are no limits to suggestion's power. The state in question has many affinities with ordinary sleep. It is probable, in fact, that we all pass through it transiently whenever we fall asleep; and one might most naturally describe the usual relation of operator and subject by saying that the former keeps the latter suspended between waking and sleeping by talking to him enough to keep his slumber from growing profound, and yet not in such a way as to wake him up. A hypnotized patient, *left to himself*, will either fall sound asleep or wake up entirely. The difficulty in hypnotizing refractory persons is that of catching them at the right moment of transition and making it permanent. Fixing the eyes and relaxing the muscles of the body produce the hypnotic state just as they facilitate the advent of sleep. The first stages of ordinary sleep are characterized by a peculiar dispersed attitude of the attention. Images come before consciousness which are entirely incongruous with our ordinary beliefs and habits of thought. The latter either vanish altogether or withdraw, as it were, inertly into the background of the mind, and let the incongruous images reign alone. These images acquire, moreover, an exceptional vivacity; they become first 'hypnagogic hallucinations,' and then, as the sleep grows deeper, dreams. Now the 'mono-ideism,' or else the impotency and failure to 'rally' on the part of the background-ideas, which thus characterize somnolescence, are unquestionably the result of a special physiological change occurring in the brain at that time. Just so that similar mono-ideism, or dissociation of the reigning fancy from those other thoughts which might possibly act as its 'reductives,' which characterize the hypnotic consciousness, must equally be due to a special cerebral change. The term 'hypnotic trance,' which I employ, tells us nothing of what the change is, but it marks the fact that it exists, and is consequently a useful expression. The great vivacity of the hypnotic images (as gauged by their motor effects), the oblivion of them when normal life is resumed, the abrupt awakening, the recollection of them again in subsequent trances, the anæsthesia and hyperæsthesia which are so frequent, all point away from our simple waking credulity and 'suggestibility' as the type by which the phenomena are to be interpreted, and make us look rather towards sleep and dreaming, or towards those deeper alterations of the personality known as automatism, double consciousness, or 'second' personality for the true analogues of the hypnotic trance.[3] Even the best hypnotic subjects

[3] The state is not *identical* with sleep, however analogous in certain respects. The lighter stages of it, particularly, differ from sleep and dreaming, inasmuch as they are

pass through life without anyone suspecting them to possess such a remarkable susceptibility, until by deliberate experiment it is made manifest. The operator fixes their eyes or their attention a short time to develop the propitious phase, holds them in it by his talk, and *the state being there*, makes them the puppets of all his suggestions. But no ordinary suggestions of waking life ever took such control of their mind.

The suggestion-theory may therefore be approved as correct, provided we grant the trance-state as its prerequisite. The three states of Charcot, the strange reflexes of Heidenhain, and all the other bodily phenomena which have been called direct consequences of the trance-state itself, are not such. They are products of suggestion, the trance-state having no particular outward symptoms of its own; but without the trance-state there, those particular suggestions could never have been successfully made.[4]

THE SYMPTOMS OF THE TRANCE

This accounts for the altogether indefinite array of symptoms which have been gathered together as characteristic of the hypnotic state. The law of habit dominates hypnotic subjects even more than it does waking ones. Any sort of personal peculiarity, any trick accidentally fallen into in the first instance by some one subject, may, by attracting attention, become stereotyped, serve as a pattern for imitation, and figure as the type of a school. The first subject trains the operator, the operator trains the succeeding subjects, all of them in perfect good faith conspiring together to evolve a perfectly arbitrary result. With the extraordinary perspicacity and subtlety of perception which subjects often display for all that concerns the operator with whom they are *en rapport*, it is hard to keep them ignorant of anything which he expects. Thus it happens that

---

characterized almost exclusively by *muscular* inabilities and compulsions, which are not noted in ordinary somnolescence, and the *mind*, which is confused in somnolescence, may be quite clearly conscious, in the lighter state of trance, of all that is going on.

[4] The word 'suggestion' has been bandied about too much as if it explained all mysteries: When the subject obeys it is by reason of the 'operator's suggestion'; when he proves refractory it is in consequence of an 'auto-suggestion' which he has made to himself, etc., etc. What explains everything explains nothing; and it must be remembered that what *needs* explanation here is the fact that in a certain condition of the subject suggestions operate as they do *at no other time*; that through them functions are affected which ordinarily elude the action of the waking will; and that usually all this happens in a condition of which no after-memory remains.

one easily verifies on new subjects what one has already seen on old ones, or any desired symptom of which one may have heard or read.

The symptoms earliest observed by writers were all thought to be typical. But with the multiplication of observed phenomena, the importance of most particular symptoms as marks of the state has diminished. This lightens very much our own immediate task. Proceeding to enumerate the symptoms of the hypnotic trance, I may confine myself to those which are intrinsically interesting, or which differ considerably from the normal functions of man.

First of all comes *amnesia*. In the earlier stages of hypnotism the patient remembers what has happened, but with successive sittings he sinks into a deeper condition, which is commonly followed by complete loss of memory. He may have been led through the liveliest hallucinations and dramatic performances, and have exhibited the intensest apparent emotion, but on waking he can recall nothing at all. The same thing happens on waking from sleep in the midst of a dream—it quickly eludes recall. But just as we may be *reminded* of it, or of parts of it, by meeting persons or objects which figured therein, so on being adroitly prompted, the hypnotic patient will often remember what happened in his trance. One cause of the forgetfulness seems to be the disconnection of the trance performances with the system of waking ideas. Memory requires a continuous train of association. M. Delbœuf, reasoning in this way, woke his subjects in the midst of an action begun during trance (washing the hands, e.g.), and found that they then remembered the trance. The act in question bridged over the two states. But one can often make them remember by merely telling them during the trance that they *shall* remember. Acts of one trance, moreover, are usually recalled, either spontaneously or at command, during another trance, provided that the contents of the two trances be not mutually incompatible.

Suggestibility. The patient believes everything which his hypnotizer tells him, and does everything which the latter commands. Even results over which the will has normally no control, such as sneezing, secretion, reddening and growing pale, alterations of temperature and heart-beat, menstruation, action of the bowels, etc., may take place in consequence of the operator's firm assertions during the hypnotic trance, and the resulting conviction on the part of the subject, that the effects will occur. Since almost all the phenomena yet to be described are effects of this heightened suggestibility, I will say no more under the general head, but proceed to illustrate the peculiarity in detail.

Effects on the voluntary muscles seem to be those most easily got; and the ordinary routine of hypnotizing consists in provoking them first. Tell the patient that he cannot open his eyes or his mouth, cannot unclasp his hands or lower his raised arm, cannot rise from his seat, or pick up a certain object from the floor, and he will be immediately smitten with absolute impotence in these regards. The effect here is generally due to the *involuntary contraction* of antagonizing muscles. But one can equally well suggest *paralysis*, of an arm for example, in which case it will hang perfectly placid by the subject's side. Cataleptic and tetanic rigidity are easily produced by suggestion, aided by handling the parts. One of the favorite shows at public exhibitions is that of a subject stretched stiff as a board with his head on one chair and his heels on another. The cataleptic retention of impressed attitudes differs from voluntary assumption of the same attitude. An arm voluntarily held out straight will drop from fatigue after a quarter of an hour at the utmost, and before it falls the agent's distress will be made manifest by oscillations in the arm, disturbances in the breathing, etc. But Charcot has shown that an arm held out in hypnotic catalepsy, though it may as soon descend, yet does so slowly and with no accompanying vibration, whilst the breathing remains entirely calm. He rightly points out that this shows a profound physiological change, and is proof positive against simulation, as far as this symptom is concerned. A cataleptic attitude, moreover, may be held for many hours.—Sometimes an expressive attitude, clenching of the fist, contraction of the brows, will gradually set up a sympathetic action of the other muscles of the body, so that at last a *tableau vivant* of fear, anger, disdain, prayer, or other emotional condition, is produced with rare perfection. This effect would seem to be due to the suggestion of the mental state by the first contraction. Stammering, aphasia, or inability to utter certain words, pronounce certain letters, are readily producible by suggestion.

Hallucinations of all the senses and *delusions* of every conceivable kind can be easily suggested to good subjects. The emotional effects are then often so lively, and the pantomimic display so expressive, that it is hard not to believe in a certain 'psychic hyperexcitability,' as one of the concomitants of the hypnotic condition. You can make the subject think that he is freezing or burning, itching or covered with dirt, or wet; you can make him eat a potato for a peach, or drink a cup of vinegar for a glass of champagne;[5] ammonia will smell to him like cologne water; a chair will be a lion, a broom-stick a beautiful woman, a noise in the street will be an orchestral music, etc., etc., with no limit except your powers of invention and the patience of the lookers on.[6] Illusions and hallucinations form the *pièces de résistance* at public exhibitions. The comic effect is at its climax when it is successfully suggested to the subject that his personality is changed into that of a baby, of a street boy, of a young lady dressing for a party, of a stump orator, or of Napoleon the Great. He may even be transformed into a beast, or an inanimate thing like a chair or a carpet, and in every case will act out all the details of the part with a sincerity and intensity seldom seen at the theatre. The excellence of the performance is in these cases the best reply to the suspicion that the subject may be shamming—so skilful a shammer must long since have found his true function in life upon the stage. Hallucinations and histrionic delusions generally go with a certain depth of the trance, and are followed by complete forgetfulness. The subject awakens from them at the command of the operator with a sudden start of surprise, and may seem for a while a little dazed.

Subjects in this condition will receive and execute suggestions of crime, and act out a theft, forgery, arson, or murder. A girl will believe that she is married to her hypnotizer, etc. It is unfair, however, to say that in these cases the subject is a pure puppet with no spontaneity. His spontaneity is certainly not in abeyance so far as things go which are harmoniously associated with the suggestion given him. He takes the text from his operator; but he may amplify and develop it enormously as he acts it out. His spontaneity is lost only for those systems of ideas which *conflict* with the suggested

[5] A complete fit of drunkenness may be the consequence of the suggested champagne. It is even said that real drunkenness has been cured by suggestion.

[6] The suggested hallucination may be followed by a negative after-image, just as if it were a real object. This can be very easily verified with the suggested hallucination of a colored cross on a sheet of white paper. The subject, on turning to another sheet of paper, will see a cross of the complementary color. Hallucinations have been shown by MM. Binet and Féré to be doubled by a prism or mirror, magnified by a lens, and in many other ways to behave optically like real objects. These points have been discussed already on p. 771 ff.

delusion. The latter is thus 'systematized'; the rest of consciousness is shut off, excluded, dissociated from it. In extreme cases the rest of the mind would seem to be actually abolished and the hypnotic subject to be literally a changed personality, a being in one of those 'second' states which we studied in Chapter X. But the reign of the delusion is often not as absolute as this. If the thing suggested be too intimately repugnant, the subject may strenuously resist and get nervously excited in consequence, even to the point of having an hysterical attack. The conflicting ideas slumber in the background and merely permit those in the foreground to have their way until a *real* emergency arises; then they assert their rights. As M. Delbœuf says, the subject surrenders himself good-naturedly to the performance, stabs with the pasteboard dagger you give him because he knows what it is, and fires off the pistol because he knows it has no ball; but for a real murder he would not be your man. It is undoubtedly true that subjects are often well aware that they are acting a part. They know that what they do is absurd. They know that the hallucination which they see, describe, and act upon, is not really there. They may laugh at themselves; and they always recognize the abnormality of their state when asked about it, and call it 'sleep.' One often notices a sort of mocking smile upon them, as if they were playing a comedy, and they may even say on 'coming to' that they were shamming all the while. These facts have misled ultra-skeptical people so far as to make them doubt the genuineness of any hypnotic phenomena at all. But, save the consciousness of 'sleep,' they do not occur in the deeper conditions; and when they do occur they are only a natural consequence of the fact that the 'monoideism' is incomplete. The background-thoughts still exist, and have the power of *comment* on the suggestions, but no power to inhibit their motor and associative effects. A similar condition is frequent enough in the waking state, when an impulse carries us away and our 'will' looks on wonderingly like an impotent spectator. These 'shammers' continue to sham in just the same way, every new time you hypnotize them, until at last they are forced to admit that if shamming there be, it is something very different from the free voluntary shamming of waking hours.

Real sensations may be abolished as well as false ones suggested. Legs and breasts may be amputated, children born, teeth extracted, in short the most painful experiences undergone, with no other anæsthetic than the hypnotizer's assurance that no pain shall be felt. Similarly morbid pains may be annihilated, neuralgias, toothaches, rheumatisms cured. The sensation of hunger has thus been abolished, so that a patient took no nourishment for fourteen days. The most interesting of these suggested anæsthesias are those limited to certain objects of perception. Thus a subject may be made blind to a certain person and to him alone, or deaf to certain words but to no others.[7] In this case the anæsthesia (or *negative hallucination*, as it has been called) is apt to become *systematized*. Other things related to the person to whom one has been made blind may also be shut out of consciousness. What he says is not heard, his contact is not felt, objects which he takes from his pocket are not seen, etc. Objects which he screens are seen as if he were transparent. Facts about him are forgotten, his name is not recognized when pronounced. Of course there is great variety in the completeness of this systematic extension of the suggested anæsthesia, but one may say that some tendency to it always exists. When one of the subjects' own limbs is made anæsthetic, for example, memories as well as sensations of its movements often seem to depart. An interesting degree of the phenomenon is found in the case related by M. Binet of a subject to whom it was suggested that a certain M. C. was invisible. She still saw M. C., but saw him as a stranger, having lost the memory of his name and his existence.—Nothing is easier than to make subjects forget their own name and condition in life. It is one of the suggestions which most promptly succeed, even with quite fresh ones. A systematized amnesia of certain periods of one's life may also be suggested, the subject placed, for instance, where he was a decade ago with the intervening years obliterated from his mind.

The mental condition which accompanies these systematized anæsthesias and amnesias is a very curious one. The anæsthesia is not a genuine sensorial one, for if you make a real red cross (say) on a sheet of white paper invisible to an hypnotic subject, and yet cause him to look fixedly at a dot on the paper on or near the cross, he will, on transferring his eye to a blank sheet, see a bluish-green after-image of the cross. This proves that it has impressed his sensibility. He has *felt* it, but not *perceived* it. He has actively ignored it, refused to recognize it, as it were. Another experiment proves

[7] M. Liégeois explains the common exhibition-trick of making the subject unable to get his arms into his coat-sleeves again after he has taken his coat off, by an anæsthesia to the necessary parts of the coat.

that he must *distinguish* it first in order thus to ignore it. Make a stroke on paper or blackboard, and tell the subject it is not there, and he will see nothing but the clean paper or board. Next, he not looking, surround the original stroke with other strokes exactly like it, and ask him what he sees. He will point out one by one all the new strokes and omit the original one every time, no matter how numerous the new strokes may be, or in what order they are arranged. Similarly, if the original single stroke to which he is blind be *doubled* by a prism of sixteen degrees placed before one of his eyes (both being kept open), he will say that he now sees *one* stroke, and point in the direction in which the image seen through the prism lies.

Obviously, then, he is not blind to the *kind* of stroke in the least. He is blind only to one individual stroke of that kind in a particular position on the board or paper,—that is, to a particular complex object; and, paradoxical as it may seem to say so, he must distinguish it with great accuracy from others like it, in order to remain blind to it when the others are brought near. He 'apperceives' it, as a preliminary to not seeing it at all! How to conceive of this state of mind is not easy. It would be much simpler to understand the process, if adding new strokes made the first one visible. There would then be two different objects apperceived as totals,—paper with one stroke, paper with two strokes; and, blind to the former, he would see all that was *in* the latter, because he would have apperceived it as a different total in the first instance.

A process of this sort occurs sometimes (not always) when the new strokes, instead of being mere repetitions of the original one, are lines which combine with it into a total object, say a human face. The subject of the trance then may regain his sight of the line to which he had previously been blind, by seeing it as part of the face.

When by a prism before one eye a previously invisible line has been made visible to that eye, and the other eye is closed or screened, *its* closure makes no difference; the line still remains visible. But if *then* the prism is removed, the line will disappear even to the eye which a moment ago saw it, and both eyes will revert to their original blind state.

We have, then, to deal in these cases neither with a sensorial anæsthesia, nor with a mere failure to notice, but with something much more complex; namely, an active counting out and positive exclusion of certain objects. It is as when one 'cuts' an acquaintance, 'ignores' a claim, or 'refuses to be influenced' by a consideration of whose existence one remains aware. Thus a lover of Nature in America finds himself able to overlook and ignore entirely the board- and rail-fences and general roadside raggedness, and revel in the beauty and picturesqueness of the other elements of the landscape, whilst to a newly-arrived European the fences are so aggressively present as to spoil enjoyment.

Messrs. Gurney, Janet, and Binet have shown that the ignored elements are preserved in a split-off portion of the subjects' consciousness which can be tapped in certain ways, and made to give an account of itself (see Vol. I, p. 206).

Hyperæsthesia of the senses is as common a symptom as anæsthesia. On the skin two points can be discriminated at less than the normal distance. The sense of touch is so delicate that (as M. Delbœuf informs me) a subject after simply poising on her finger-tips a blank card drawn from a pack of similar ones can pick it out from the pack again by its 'weight.' We approach here the line where, to many persons, it seems as if something more than the ordinary senses, however sharpened, were required in explanation. I have seen a coin from the operator's pocket repeatedly picked out by the subject from a heap of twenty others,[8] by its greater 'weight' in the subject's language.—Auditory hyperæsthesia may enable a subject to hear a watch tick, or his operator speak, in a distant room.—One of the most extraordinary examples of visual hyperæsthesia is that reported by Bergson, in which a subject who seemed to be reading through the back of a book held and looked at by the operator, was really proved to be reading the image of the page reflected on the latter's cornea. The same subject was able to discriminate with the naked eye details in a microscopic preparation. Such cases of 'hyperæsthesia of vision' as that reported by Taguet and Sauvaire, where subjects could see things mirrored by non-reflecting bodies, or through opaque pasteboard, would seem rather to belong to 'psychical research' than to the present category.—The ordinary test of visual hyperacuteness in hypnotism is the favorite trick of giving a subject the hallucination of a picture on a blank sheet of card-board, and then mixing the latter with a lot of

[8] Precautions being taken against differences of temperature and other grounds of suggestion.

other similar sheets. The subject will always find the picture on the original sheet again, and recognize infallibly if it has been turned over, or upside down, although the bystanders have to resort to artifice to identify it again. The subject notes peculiarities on the card, too small for waking observation to detect.[9] If it be said that the spectators guide him by their manner, their breathing, etc., that is only another proof of his hyperæsthesia; for he undoubtedly *is* conscious of subtler personal indications (of his operator's mental states especially) than he could notice in his waking state. Examples of this are found in the so-called 'magnetic *rapport*.' This is a name for the fact that in deep trance, or in lighter trance whenever the suggestion is made, the subject is deaf and blind to everyone but the operator or those spectators to whom the latter expressly awakens his senses. The most violent appeals from anyone else are for him as if non-existent, whilst he obeys the faintest signals on the part of his hypnotizer. If in catalepsy, his limbs will retain their attitude only when the operator moves them; when others move them they fall down, etc. A more remarkable fact still is that the patient will often answer anyone whom his operator touches, or at whom he even points his finger, in however concealed a manner. All which is rationally explicable by expectation and suggestion, if only it be farther admitted that his senses are acutely sharpened for all the operator's movements.[10] He often shows great anxiety and restlessness if the latter is out of the room. A favorite experiment of Mr. E. Gurney's was to put the subject's hands through an opaque screen, and cause the operator to point at one finger. *That* finger presently grew insensible or rigid. A bystander pointing simultaneously at another finger, never made that insensible or rigid. Of course the elective *rapport* with their operator had been developed in these trained subjects during the hypnotic state, but the phenomenon then occurred in some of them during the waking state, even when their consciousness was absorbed in ani-

9 It should be said, however, that the bystander's ability to discriminate unmarked cards and sheets of paper from each other is much greater than one would naturally suppose.

10 I must repeat, however, that we are here on the verge of possibly unknown forces and modes of communication. Hypnotization at a distance, with no grounds for expectation on the subject's part that it was to be tried, seems pretty well established in certain very rare cases. See in general, for information on these matters, the *Proceedings of the Society for Psychical Research, passim.*

mated conversation with a fourth party.[11] I confess that when I saw these experiments I was impressed with the necessity for admitting between the *emanations* from different people differences for which we have no name, and a discriminative sensibility for them of the nature of which we can form no clear conception, but which seems to be developed in certain subjects by the hypnotic trance.—The enigmatic reports of the effect of magnets and metals, even if they be due, as many contend, to unintentional suggestion on the operator's part, certainly involve hyperæsthetic perception, for the operator seeks as well as possible to conceal the moment when the magnet is brought into play, and yet the subject not only finds out that moment in a way difficult to understand, but may develop effects which (in the first instance certainly) the operator did not expect to find. Unilateral contractures, movements, paralyses, hallucinations, etc., are made to pass to the other side of the body, hallucinations to disappear, or to change to the complementary color, suggested emotions to pass into their opposites, etc. Many Italian observations agree with the French ones; and the upshot is that if unconscious suggestion lie at the bottom of this matter, the patients show an enormously exalted power of divining what it is they are expected to do. This hyperæsthetic perception is what concerns us now.[12] Its *modus* cannot yet be said to be defined.

Changes in the nutrition of the tissues may be produced by suggestion. These effects lead into therapeutics—a subject which I do not propose to treat of here. But I may say that there seems no reasonable ground for doubting that in certain chosen subjects the suggestion of a congestion, a burn, a blister, a raised papule, or a bleeding from the nose or skin, may produce the effect. Messrs. Beaunis, Berjon, Bernheim, Bourru, Burot, Charcot, Delbœuf, Dumontpallier, Focachon, Forel, Jendrássik, Krafft-Ebing, Liébeault, Liégeois, Lipp, Mabille, and others have recently vouched for

[11] Here again the perception in question must take place below the threshold of ordinary consciousness, possibly in one of those split-off selves or 'second' states whose existence we have so often to recognize.

[12] I myself verified many of the above effects of the magnet on a blindfolded subject on whom I was trying them for the first time, and whom I believe to have never heard of them before. The moment, however, an opaque screen was added to the blindfolding, the effects ceased to coincide with the approximation of the magnet, so that it looks as if visual perception had been instrumental in producing them. The subject passed from my observation, so that I never could clear up the mystery. Of course I gave him consciously no hint of what I was looking for.

one or other of these effects. Messrs. Delbœuf and Liégeois have annulled by suggestion, one the effects of a burn, the other of a blister. Delbœuf was led to his experiments, after seeing a burn on the skin produced by suggestion at the Salpêtrière, by reasoning that if the idea of a pain could produce inflammation it must be because pain was itself an inflammatory irritant, and that the abolition of it from a real burn ought therefore to entail the absence of inflammation. He applied the actual cautery (as well as vesicants) to symmetrical places on the skin, affirming that no pain should be felt on one of the sides. The result was a dry scorch on that side, with (as he assures me) no after-mark, but on the other side a regular blister with suppuration and a subsequent scar. This explains the innocuity of certain assaults made on subjects during trance. To test simulation, recourse is often had to sticking pins under their finger-nails or through their tongue, to inhalations of strong ammonia, and the like. These irritations, when not felt by the subject, seem to leave no after-consequences. One is reminded of the reported non-inflammatory character of the wounds made on themselves by dervishes in their pious orgies. On the other hand, the reddenings and bleedings of the skin along certain lines, suggested by tracing lines or pressing objects thereupon, put the accounts handed down to us of the stigmata of the cross appearing on the hands, feet, sides, and forehead of certain Catholic mystics in a new light. As so often happens, a fact is denied until a welcome interpretation comes with it. Then it is admitted readily enough; and evidence judged quite insufficient to back a claim, so long as the church had an interest in making it, proves to be quite sufficient for modern scientific enlightenment, the moment it appears that a reputed saint can thereby be classed as 'a case of hystero-epilepsy.'

There remain two other topics, viz., post-hypnotic effects of suggestion, and effects of suggestion in the waking state.

Post-hypnotic, or deferred, suggestions are such as are given to the patients during trance, to take effect after waking. They succeed with a certain number of patients even when the execution is named for a remote period—months or even a year, in one case reported by M. Liégeois. In this way one can make the patient feel a pain, or be paralyzed, or be hungry or thirsty, or have an hallucination, positive or negative, or perform some fantastic action after emerging from his trance. The effect in question may be ordered to take place not immediately, but after an interval of time has elapsed, and the interval may be left to the subject to measure, or may be marked by a certain signal. The moment the signal occurs, or the time is run out, the subject, who until then seems in a perfectly normal waking condition, will experience the suggested effect. In many instances, whilst thus obedient to the suggestion, he seems to fall into the hypnotic condition again. This is proved by the fact that the moment the hallucination or suggested performance is over he forgets it, denies all knowledge of it, and so forth; and by the further fact that he is 'suggestible' during its performance, that is, will receive new hallucinations, etc., at command. A moment later and this suggestibility has disappeared. It cannot be said, however, that relapse into the trance is an absolutely necessary condition for the post-hypnotic carrying out of commands, for the subject may be neither suggestible nor amnesic, and may struggle with all the strength of his will against the absurdity of this impulse which he feels rising in him, he knows not why. In these cases, as in most cases, he forgets the circumstance of the impulse having been suggested to him in a previous trance; regards it as arising within himself; and often improvises, as he yields to it, some more or less plausible or ingenious motive by which to justify it to the lookers-on. He acts, in short, with his usual sense of personal spontaneity and freedom; and the disbelievers in the freedom of the will have naturally made much of these cases in their attempts to show it to be an illusion.

The only really mysterious feature of these deferred suggestions is the patient's absolute ignorance during the interval preceding their execution that they have been deposited in his mind. They will often surge up at the preappointed time, even though you have vainly tried a while before to make him recall the circumstances of their production. The most important class of post-hypnotic suggestions are, of course, those relative to the patient's health—bowels, sleep, and other bodily functions. Among the most *interesting* (apart from the hallucinations) are those relative to future trances. One can determine the hour and minute, or the signal, at which the patient will of his own accord lapse into trance again. One can make him susceptible in future to another operator who may have been unsuccessful with him in the past. Or more important still in certain cases, one can, by suggesting that certain persons shall never be able hereafter to put him to sleep, remove him for all future time from hypnotic influences which might be dangerous. This, indeed, is the simple and natural safeguard against those 'dangers of hypnotism' of which uninstructed persons talk so vaguely. A subject who knows himself to be ultra-susceptible should never allow himself to be entranced by an operator in whose moral delicacy he lacks complete confidence; and he can use a trusted operator's suggestions to protect himself against liberties which others, knowing his weakness, might be tempted to take with him.

The mechanism by which the command is retained until the moment for its execution arrives is a mystery which has given rise to much discussion. The experiments of Gurney and the observations of M. Pierre Janet and others on certain hysterical somnambulists seem to prove that it is stored up in consciousness; not simply organically registered, but that *the consciousness which thus retains it is split off, dissociated from the rest of the subject's mind.* We have here, in short, an experimental production of one of those 'second' states of the personality of which we have spoken so often. Only here the second state coexists as well as alternates with the first. Gurney had the brilliant idea of *tapping* this second consciousness by means of the planchette. He found that certain persons, who were both hypnotic subjects and automatic writers, would if their hands were placed on a planchette (after being wakened from a trance in which they had received the suggestion of something to be done at a later time) write out unconsciously the order, or something connected with it. This shows that something inside of them, which could express itself through the hand alone, was continuing to think of the order, and possibly of it alone. These researches have opened a new vista of possible experimental investigations into the so-called 'second' states of the personality.

Some subjects seem almost as obedient to suggestion in the waking state as in sleep, or even more so, according to certain observers. Not only muscular phenomena, but changes of personality and hallucinations are recorded as the result of simple affirmation on the operator's part, without the previous ceremony of 'magnetizing' or putting into the 'mesmeric sleep.' These are all trained subjects, however, so far as I know, and the affirmation must apparently be accompanied by the patient concentrating his attention and gazing, however briefly, into the eyes of the operator. It is probable therefore that an extremely rapidly induced condition of trance is a prerequisite for success in these experiments.

I have now made mention of all the more important phenomena of the hypnotic trance. Of their therapeutic or forensic bearings this is not the proper place to speak. The recent literature of the subject is quite voluminous, but much of it consists in repetition. The best compendious work on the subject is *Der Hypnotismus*, by Dr. A. Moll (Berlin, 1889; and just translated into English, N. Y., 1890), which is extraordinarily complete and judicious. The other writings most recommendable are subjoined in the note.[13] Most of them contain a historical sketch and much bibliography. A complete bibliography has been published by M. Dessoir (Berlin, 1888).

[13] Binet and Féré: *Animal Magnetism*, in the International Scientific Series; H. Bernheim: *Suggestive Therapeutics* (N.Y., 1889); J. Liégeois: *De la suggestion* (1889); E. Gurney: two articles in *Mind*, vol. IX. To which may be added J. Cadwell, *How to Mesmerize*; C. Lloyd Tackey, *Psycho-Therapeutics*, Second Edition, 1890; Björnström, *Hypnotism: Its History and Present Development*, 1889; J. G. McKendrick, article "Animal Magnetism" in *Encyclopædia Britannica*, 9th Edition (Reprinted).—In the recent revival of interest in the history of this subject, it seems a pity that the admirably critical and scientific work of Dr. John Kearsley Mitchell of Philadelphia should remain relatively so unknown. It is quite worthy to rank with Braid's investigations. See *Five Essays* by the above author, edited by S. Weir Mitchell, Philadelphia, 1859, pp. 141–274.

Chapter XXVIII

Necessary Truths and the Effects of Experience

In this final chapter I shall treat of what has sometimes been called *psychogenesis,* and try to ascertain just how far the connections of things in the outward environment can account for our tendency to think of, and to react upon, certain things in certain ways and in no others, even though personally we have had of the things in question no experience, or almost no experience, at all. It is a familiar truth that some propositions are *necessary.* We *must* attach the predicate 'equal' to the subject 'opposite sides of a parallelogram' if we think those terms together at all, whereas we need not in any such way attach the predicate 'rainy,' for example, to the subject 'tomorrow.' The dubious sort of coupling of terms is universally admitted to be due to 'experience'; the certain sort is ascribed to the 'organic structure' of the mind. This structure is in turn supposed by the so-called *apriorists* to be of transcendental origin, or at any rate not to be explicable by experience; whilst by evolutionary empiricists it is supposed to be also due to experience, only not to the experience of the individual, but to that of his ancestors as far back as one may please to go. Our emotional and instinctive tendencies, our irresistible impulses to couple certain movements with the perception or thought of certain things, are also features of our connate mental structure, and like the necessary judgments, are interpreted by the apriorists and the empiricists in the same warring ways.

I shall try in the course of the chapter to make plain three things:

1) That, taking the word experience as it is universally understood, the experience of the race can no more account for our necessary or *a priori* judgments than the experience of the individual can;

2) That there is no good evidence for the belief that our instinctive reactions are fruits of our ancestors' education in the midst of the same environment, transmitted to us at birth.

3) That the features of our organic mental structure cannot be explained at all by our conscious intercourse with the outer environment, but must rather be understood as congenital variations, 'accidental'[1] in the first instance, but then transmitted as fixed features of the race.

On the whole, then, the account which the apriorists give of the *facts* is that which I defend; although I should contend (as will hereafter appear) for a naturalistic view of their *cause.*

The first thing I have to say is that all schools (however they otherwise differ) must allow that the *elementary qualities* of cold, heat, pleasure, pain, red, blue, sound, silence, etc., are original, innate, or *a priori* properties of our subjective nature, even though they should require the touch of experience to waken them into actual consciousness, and should slumber, to all eternity, without it.

This is so on either of the two hypotheses we may make concerning the relation of the feelings to the realities at whose touch they become alive. For in the first place, if a feeling do *not* mirror the reality which wakens it and to which we say it corresponds, if it mirror no reality whatever outside of the mind, it of course is a purely mental product. By its very definition it can be nothing else. But in the second place, even if it *do* mirror the reality exactly, still it *is* not that reality itself, it is a duplication of it, the result of a mental reaction. And that the mind should have the power of reacting in just that duplicate way can only be stated as a *harmony* between its nature and the nature of the truth outside of it, a harmony whereby it follows that the qualities of both parties match.

The originality of these *elements* is not, then, a question for dispute. *The warfare of philosophers is exclusively relative to their* FORMS OF COMBINATION. The empiricist maintains that these forms can only follow the order of combination in which the elements

[1] 'Accidental' in the Darwinian sense, as belonging to a cycle of causation inaccessible to the present order of research.

were originally awakened by the impressions of the external world; the apriorists insist, on the contrary, that *some* modes of combination, at any rate, follow from the natures of the elements themselves, and that no amount of experience can modify this result.

WHAT IS MEANT BY EXPERIENCE?

The phrase 'organic mental structure' names the matter in dispute. Has the mind such a structure or not? Are its contents *arranged* from the start, or is the arrangement they may possess simply due to the shuffling of them by experience in an absolutely plastic bed? Now the first thing to make sure of is that when we talk of 'experience,' we attach a definite meaning to the word. *Experience means experience of something foreign supposed to impress us,* whether spontaneously or in consequence of our own exertions and acts. Impressions, as we well know, affect certain orders of sequence and coexistence, and the mind's habits copy the habits of the impressions, so that our images of things assume a time- and space-arrangement which resembles the time- and space-arrangements outside. To uniform outer coexistences and sequences correspond constant conjunctions of ideas, to fortuitous coexistences and sequences casual conjunctions of ideas. We are sure that fire will burn and water wet us, less sure that thunder will come after lightning, not at all sure whether a strange dog will bark at us or let us go by. In these ways experience moulds us every hour, and makes of our minds a mirror of the time- and space-connections between the things in the world. The principle of habit within us so *fixes* the copy at last that we find it difficult even to imagine how the outward order could possibly be different from what it is, and we continually divine from the present what the future is to be. These habits of transition, from one thought to another, are features of mental structure which were lacking in us at birth; we can see their growth under experience's moulding finger, and we can see how often experience undoes her own work, and for an earlier order substitutes a new one. '*The order of experience*,' in this matter of the time- and space-conjunctions of things, is thus an indisputably *vera causa* of our forms of thought. It is our educator, our sovereign helper and friend; and its name, standing for something with so real and definite a use, ought to be kept sacred and encumbered with no vaguer meaning.

If *all* the connections among ideas in the mind could be interpreted as so many combinations of sense-data wrought into fixity in this way from without, then experience in the common and legitimate sense of the word would be the sole fashioner of the mind.

The empirical school in psychology has in the main contended that they can be so interpreted. Before our generation, it was the experience of the individual only which was meant. But when one nowadays says that the human mind owes its present shape to experience, he means the experience of ancestors as well. Mr. Spencer's statement of this is the earliest emphatic one, and deserves quotation in full:[2]

"The supposition that the inner cohesions are adjusted to the outer persistences by *accumulated* experience of those outer persistences, is in harmony with all our actual knowledge of mental phenomena. Though in so far as reflex actions and instincts are concerned, the experience-hypothesis seems insufficient; yet, its seeming insufficiency occurs only where the evidence is beyond our reach. Nay, even here, such few facts as we can get point to the conclusion that automatic psychical connexions result from the registration of *experiences continued for numberless generations.*

"In brief, the case stands thus:—It is agreed that all psychical relations save the absolutely indissoluble are determined by experiences. Their various strengths are admitted, other things equal, to be proportionate to the *multiplication of experiences.* It is an unavoidable corollary that an *infinity of experiences* will produce a psychical relation that is indissoluble. Though such infinity of experiences cannot be received by a single individual, yet it may be received by the succession of individuals forming a race. And if there is a transmission of induced tendencies in the nervous system, it is inferable that *all psychical relations whatever,* from the necessary to the fortuitous, result from the experiences of the corresponding external relations; and are so brought into harmony with them. . . .

"Thus, the experience-hypothesis furnishes an adequate solution. The genesis of instinct, the development of memory and reason out of it, and the consolidation of rational actions and inferences into instinctive ones, are alike explicable on the *single principle,* that the

[2] The passage is in §§ 189, 205, and 208 of the *Principles of Psychology,* at the end of the chapter entitled "Reason." I italicize certain words in order to show that the essence of this explanation is to demand *numerically frequent* experiences. The bearing of this remark will later appear. (Cf. pp. 1237–1238, *infra.*)

cohesion between psychical states is proportionate to the *frequency* with which the relation between the answering external phenomena has been *repeated in experience*. . . .

"The *universal law* that, other things equal, the cohesion of psychical states is proportionate to the *frequency* with which they have followed one another in experience, supplies an explanation of the so-called 'forms of thought,' as soon as it is supplemented by the law that *habitual* psychical successions entail some hereditary tendency to such successions, which, under persistent conditions, will become cumulative in generation after generation. We saw that the establishment of those compound reflex actions called instincts, is comprehensible on the principle that inner relations are, by *perpetual repetition*, organized into correspondence with outer relations. We have now to observe that the establishment of those consolidated, those indissoluble, those instinctive mental relations constituting our ideas of Space and Time, is comprehensible on the same principle. For if even to external relations that are *often* experienced during the life of a single organism, answering internal relations are established that become next to automatic—if such a combination of psychical changes as that which guides a savage in hitting a bird with an arrow, becomes, by constant repetition, so organized as to be performed almost without thought of the processes of adjustment gone through—and if skill of this kind is so far transmissible that particular races of men become characterized by particular aptitudes, which are nothing else than partially-organized psychical connexions; then, if there exist certain external relations which are experienced by all organisms at all instants of their waking lives—relations which are absolutely constant, absolutely universal—there will be established answering internal relations that are absolutely constant, absolutely universal. Such relations we have in those of Space and Time. The organization of subjective relations adjusted to these objective relations has been cumulative, not in each race of creatures only, but throughout successive races of creatures; and such subjective relations have, therefore, become more consolidated than all others. Being experienced in every perception and every action of each creature, these connexions among outer existences must, for this reason too, be responded to by connexions among inner feelings, that are, above all others, indissoluble. As the substrata of all other relations in the *non-ego*, they must be responded to by conceptions that are the substrata of all other relations in the *ego*. Being the *constant and infinitely-repeated* elements of thought, they must become the automatic elements of thought—the elements of thought which it is impossible to get rid of —the 'forms of intuition.'

"Such, it seems to me, is the only possible reconciliation between the experience-hypothesis and the hypothesis of the transcendentalists; neither of which is tenable by itself. Insurmountable difficulties are presented by the Kantian doctrine (as we shall hereafter see); and the antagonist doctrine, taken alone, presents difficulties that are equally insurmountable. To rest with the unqualified assertion that, antecedent to experience, the mind is a blank, is to ignore the questions—whence comes the power of organizing experiences? whence arise the different degrees of that power possessed by different races of organisms, and different individuals of the same race? If, at birth, there exists nothing but a passive receptivity of impressions, why is not a horse as educable as a man? Should it be said that language makes the difference, then why do not the cat and the dog, reared in the same household, arrive at equal degrees and kinds of intelligence? Understood in its current form, the experience-hypothesis implies that the presence of a definitely-organized nervous system is a circumstance of no moment—a fact not needing to be taken into account! Yet it is the all-important fact—the fact to which, in one sense, the criticisms of Leibnitz and others pointed—the fact without which an assimilation of experiences is inexplicable. Throughout the animal kingdom in general, the actions are dependent on the nervous structure. The physiologist shows us that each reflex movement implies the agency of certain nerves and ganglia; that a development of complicated instincts is accompanied by complication of the nervous centres and their commissural connexions; that the same creature in different stages, as larva and imago for example, changes its instincts as its nervous structure changes; and that as we advance to creatures of high intelligence, a vast increase in the size and in the complexity of the nervous system takes place. What is the obvious inference? It is that the ability to co-ordinate impressions and to perform the appropriate actions, always implies the pre-existence of certain nerves arranged in a certain way. What is the meaning of the human brain? It is that the many *established* relations among its parts, stand for so many *established* relations among the psychical changes. Each of the constant connexions among the fibres of the cerebral masses, answers to some *constant connexion* of phenomena in the experiences of the race. Just as the organized arrangement subsisting between the sensory nerves of the nostrils and the motor nerves of the respiratory muscles, not only makes possible a sneeze, but also, in the newly-born infant, implies sneezings to be hereafter performed; so, all the organized arrangements subsisting among the nerves of the infant's brain, not only make possible certain combinations of impressions, but also imply that such combinations will hereafter be made—imply that there are answering combinations in the outer world—imply a preparedness to cognize these combinations—imply faculties of comprehending them. It is true that the resulting compound psychical changes, do not take place with the same readiness and automatic precision as the simple reflex action instanced—it is true that some individual experiences seem required to establish them. But while this is partly due to the fact that these combinations are highly involved, extremely varied in their modes of occurrence, made up therefore of psychical relations less completely coherent, and hence need further repetitions to perfect them; it is in a much greater degree due to the fact that at birth the organization of the brain is incomplete, and does not cease its spontaneous progress for twenty or thirty years afterwards. Those who contend that knowledge results wholly from the experiences of the individual, ignoring as they do the mental evolution which accompanies the autogenous development of the nervous system, fall into an error as great as if they were to ascribe all bodily growth and structure to exercise, forgetting the innate tendency to assume the adult form. Were the infant born with a full-sized and completely-constructed brain, their position would be less untenable. But, as the case stands, the gradually-increasing intelligence displayed throughout childhood and youth, is more attributable to the completion of the cerebral organization, than to the individual experiences—a truth proved by the fact that in adult life there is sometimes displayed a high endowment of some faculty which, during education, was never brought into play. Doubtless, experiences received by the individual furnish the concrete materials for all thought. Doubtless, the organized and semi-organized arrangements existing among the cerebral nerves, can give no knowledge until there has been a presentation of the external relations to which they correspond. And doubtless, the child's daily observations and reasonings aid the formation of those involved nervous connexions that are in process of spontaneous evolution; just as its daily gambols aid the development of its limbs. But saying this is quite a different thing from saying that its intelligence is wholly *produced* by its experiences. That is an utterly inadmissible doctrine—a doctrine which makes the presence of a brain meaningless—a doctrine which makes idiotcy unaccountable.

"In the sense, then, that there exist in the nervous system certain pre-established relations answering to relations in the environment, there is truth in the doctrine of 'forms of intuition'—not the truth which its defenders suppose, but a parallel truth. Corresponding to absolute external relations, there are established in the structure of the nervous system absolute internal relations—relations that are potentially present before birth in the shape of definite nervous connexions; that are antecedent to, and independent of, individual experiences; and that are automatically disclosed along with the first cognitions. And, as here understood, it is not only these fundamental relations which are thus pre-determined; but also hosts of other relations of a more or less constant kind, which are congenitally represented by more or less complete nervous connexions. But these pre-determined internal relations, though independent of the experiences of the individual, are not independent of experiences in general: they have been determined by the experiences of preceding organisms. The corollary here drawn from the general argument is, that the human brain is an organized register of *infinitely-numerous* experiences received during the evolution of life, or rather, during the evolution of that series of organisms through which the human organism has been reached. The effects of the most *uniform and frequent* of these experiences have been successively bequeathed, principal and interest; and have slowly amounted to that high intelligence which lies latent in the brain of the infant—which the infant in after life exercises and perhaps strengthens or further complicates—and which, with minute additions, it bequeaths to future generations. And thus it happens that the European inherits from twenty to thirty cubic inches more brain than the Papuan. Thus it happens that faculties, as of music, which scarcely exist in some inferior human races, become congenital in superior ones. Thus it happens that out of savages unable to count up to the number of their fingers, and speaking a language containing only nouns and verbs, arise at length our Newtons and Shakspeares."

This is a brilliant and seductive statement, and it doubtless includes a good deal of truth. Unfortunately it fails to go into details; and when the details are scrutinized, as they soon must be by us, many of them will be seen to be inexplicable in this simple way, and the choice will then remain to us either of denying the experiential origin of certain of our judgments, or of enlarging the meaning of the word experience so as to include these cases among its effects.

TWO MODES OF ORIGIN OF BRAIN STRUCTURE

If we adopt the former course we meet with a controversial difficulty. The 'experience-philosophy' has from time immemorial been the opponent of theological modes of thought. The word experience has a halo of anti-supernaturalism about it; so that if anyone express dissatisfaction with any function claimed for it, he is liable to be treated as if he could only be animated by loyalty to the catechism, or in some way have the interests of obscurantism at heart. I am entirely certain that, on this ground alone, what I have erelong to say will make this a sealed chapter to many of my readers. "He denies experience!" they will exclaim, "denies science; believes the mind created by miracle; is a regular old partisan of innate ideas! That is enough! we'll listen to such antediluvian twaddle no more." Regrettable as is the loss of readers capable of such wholesale discipleship, I feel that a definite meaning for the word experience is even more important than their company. 'Experience' does not mean every natural, as opposed to every supernatural, cause. It means a particular sort of natural agency, alongside of which other more recondite natural agencies may perfectly well exist. With the scientific animus of anti-supernaturalism we ought to agree, but we ought to free ourselves from its verbal idols and bugbears.

Nature has many methods of producing the same effect. She may make a 'born' draughtsman or singer by tipping in a certain direction at an opportune moment the molecules of some human ovum; or she may bring forth a child ungifted and make him spend laborious but successful years at school. She may make our ears ring by the sound of a bell, or by a dose of quinine; make us see yellow by spreading a field of buttercups before our eyes, or by mixing a little santonine powder with our food; fill us with terror of certain surroundings by making them really dangerous, or by a blow which produces a pathological alteration of our brain. It is obvious that we need two words to designate these two modes of operating. *In the one case the natural agents produce perceptions which take cognizance of the agents themselves; in the other case, they produce perceptions which take cognizance of something else.* What is taught to the mind by the 'experience,' in the first case, is the *order of the experience itself*—the 'inner relation' (in Spencer's phrase) 'corresponds' to the 'outer relation' which produced it, by remembering and knowing the latter. But in the case of the *other* sort of natural agency, what is taught to the mind has nothing to do with the agency itself, but with some different outer relation altogether. A diagram will express the alternatives. B stands for our human brain in the midst of the world. All the little *o*'s with arrows proceeding from them are natural objects (like sunsets, etc.), which impress it through the senses, and in the strict sense of the word give it *experience*, teaching it by habit and association what is the order of their ways. All the little *x*'s inside the brain and all the little *x*'s outside of it are other natural objects and processes (in the ovum, in the blood, etc.), which equally modify the brain, but

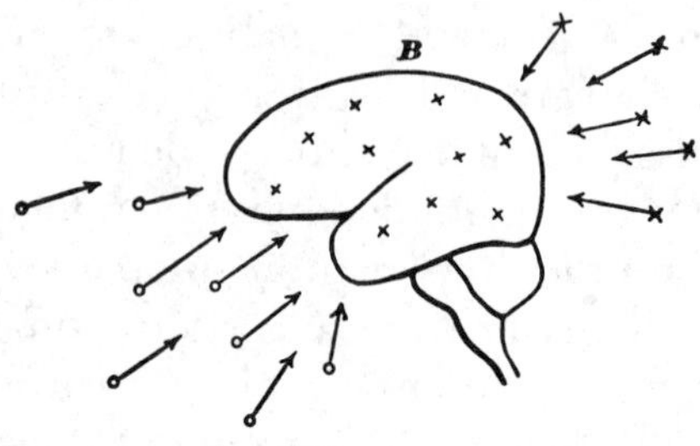

FIG. 94.

mould it to no cognition of *themselves.* The *tinnitus aurium* discloses no properties of the quinine; the musical endowment teaches no embryology; the morbid dread (of solitude, perhaps) no brain-pathology; but the way in which a dirty sunset and a rainy morrow hang together in the mind copies and teaches the sequences of sunsets and rainfall in the outer world.

In zoological evolution we have two modes in which an animal race may grow to be a better match for its environment.

First, the so-called way of 'adaptation,' in which the environment may itself modify its inhabitant by exercising, hardening, and habituating him to certain sequences, and these habits may, it is often maintained, become hereditary.

Second, the way of 'accidental variation,' as Mr. Darwin termed it, in which certain young are born with peculiarities that help them and their progeny to survive. That variations of *this* sort tend to become hereditary, no one doubts.

The first mode is called by Mr. Spencer direct, the second indirect, equilibration. Both equilibrations must of course be natural and physical processes, but they belong to entirely different physical spheres. The direct influences are obvious and accessible things. The causes of variation in the young are, on the other hand, molecular and hidden. The direct influences are the animal's 'experiences,' in the widest sense of the term. Where what is influenced by them is the *mental* organism, they are *conscious* experiences, and become the *objects* as well as the causes of their effects. That is, the effect consists in a tendency of the experience itself to be remembered, or to have its elements thereafter coupled in imagination just as they were coupled in the experience. In the diagram these experiences are represented by the *o*'s exclusively. The *x*'s, on the other hand, stand for the indirect causes of mental modification—causes of which we are not immediately conscious as such, and which are not the direct *objects* of the effects they produce. Some of them are molecular accidents before birth; some of them are collateral and remote combinations, unintended combinations, one might say, of more direct effects wrought in the unstable and intricate brain-tissue. Such a result is unquestionably the susceptibility to music, which some individuals possess at the present day. It has no zoological utility; it corresponds to no object in the natural environment; it is a pure *incident* of having a hearing organ, an incident depending on such instable and inessential conditions that one brother may have it and another brother not. Just so with the susceptibility to sea-sickness, which, so far from being engendered by long experience of its 'object' (if a heaving deck can be called its object) is erelong annulled thereby. Our higher æsthetic, moral, and intellectual life seems made up of affections of this collateral and incidental sort, which have entered the mind by the back stairs, as it were, or rather have not entered the mind at all, but got surreptitiously born in the house. No one can successfully treat of psychogenesis, or the factors of mental evolution, without distinguishing between these two ways in which the mind is assailed. The way of 'experience' proper is the front door, the door of the five senses. The agents which affect the brain in this way immediately become the mind's *objects.* The other agents do not. It would be simply silly to say of two men with perhaps equal effective skill in drawing, one an untaught natural genius, the other a mere obstinate plodder in the studio, that both alike owe their skill to their 'experience.' The reasons of their several skills lie in wholly disparate natural cycles of causation.[3]

[3] *Principles of Biology*, part III, chaps. XI, XII.—Goltz and Loeb have found that dogs become mild in character when their occipital, and fierce when their frontal, brain-lobes are cut off. "A dog which originally was cross in an extreme degree, never suffering himself to be touched, and even refusing, after two days' fasting, to take a piece of bread from my hand, became, after a bilateral operation on the occipital lobes, perfectly trustful and harmless. He underwent five operations on these parts. . . . Each one of them made him more good-natured; so that at last (just as Goltz observed of his dogs) he would let other dogs take away the very bones which he was gnawing" (Loeb: Pflüger's *Archiv*, XXXIX, 300). A course of kind treatment and training might have had a similar effect. But how absurd to call two such different causes by the same name, and to say both times that the beast's 'experience of outer relations' is what educates him to good-nature. This, however, is virtually what all writers do

I will then, with the reader's permission, *restrict the word 'experience' to processes which influence the mind by the front-doorway of simple habits and association.* What the back-door-effects may be will probably grow clearer as we proceed; so I will pass right on to a scrutiny of the actual mental structure which we find.

THE GENESIS OF THE ELEMENTARY MENTAL CATEGORIES

We find: 1. Elementary sorts of sensation, and feelings of personal activity;

2. Emotions; desires; instincts; ideas of worth; æsthetic ideas;

3. Ideas of time and space and number;

4. Ideas of difference and resemblance, and of their degrees.

5. Ideas of causal dependence among events; of end and means; of subject and attribute.

6. Judgments affirming, denying, doubting, supposing any of the above ideas.

7. Judgments that the former judgments logically involve, exclude, or are indifferent to, each other.

Now we may postulate at the outset that all these forms of thought have a *natural* origin, if we could only get at it. That assumption must be made at the outset of every scientific investigation, or there is no temptation to proceed. But the first account of their origin which we are likely to hit upon is a snare. All these mental affections are ways of knowing objects. Most psychologists nowadays believe that the objects first, in some natural way, engendered a brain from out of their midst, and then imprinted these various cognitive affections upon it. But how? The ordinary evolu-

---

who ignore the distinction between the 'front-door' and the 'back-door' manners of producing mental change.

One of the most striking of these back-door affections is *susceptibility to the charm of drunkenness.* This (taking drunkenness in the broadest sense, as teetotalers use the word) is one of the deepest functions of human nature. Half of both the poetry and the tragedy of human life would vanish if alcohol were taken away. As it is, the thirst for it is such that in the United States the cash-value of its sales amounts to that of the sales of meat and of bread put together. And yet what ancestral 'outer relation' is responsible for this peculiar reaction of ours? The only 'outer relation' could be the alcohol itself, which, comparatively speaking, came into the environment but yesterday, and which, so far from creating, is tending to eradicate, the love of itself from our mental structure, by letting only those families of men survive in whom it is not strong. The love of drunkenness is a purely accidental susceptibility of a brain, evolved for entirely different uses, and its causes are to be sought in the molecular realm, rather than in any possible order of 'outer relations.'

tionist answer to this question is exceedingly simple-minded. The idea of most speculators seems to be that, since it suffices *now* for us to become acquainted with a complex object, that it should be simply *present* to us often enough, so it must be fair to assume universally that, with time enough given, the *mere presence* of the various objects and relations to be known must end by bringing about the latter's cognition, and that in this way all mental structure was from first to last evolved. Any ordinary Spencerite will tell you that just as the experience of blue objects wrought into our mind the color blue, and hard objects got it to feel hardness, so the presence of large and small objects in the world gave it the notion of size, moving objects made it aware of motion, and objective successions taught it time. Similarly in a world with different impressing things, the mind had to acquire a sense of difference, whilst the like parts of the world as they fell upon it kindled in it the perception of similarity. Outward sequences which sometimes held good, and sometimes failed, naturally engendered in it doubtful and uncertain forms of expectation, and ultimately gave rise to the disjunctive forms of judgment; whilst the hypothetic form, 'if *a*, then *b*,' was sure to ensue from sequences that were invariable in the outer world. On this view, if the outer order suddenly were to change its elements and modes, we should have no faculties to cognize the new order by. At most we should feel a sort of frustration and confusion. But little by little the new presence would work on us as the old one did; and in course of time another set of psychic categories would arise, fitted to take cognizance of the altered world.

This notion of the outer world inevitably building up a sort of mental duplicate of itself if we only give it time, is so easy and natural in its vagueness that one hardly knows how to start to criticise it. One thing, however, is obvious, namely that *the manner in which we now become acquainted with complex objects need not in the least resemble the manner in which the original elements of our consciousness grew up.* Now, it is true, a new sort of animal need only be present to me, to impress its image permanently on my mind; but this is because I am already in possession of categories for knowing each and all of its several attributes, and of a memory for retracing the order of their conjunction. I now have preformed categories for all possible objects. The objects need only awaken these from their slumber. But it is a very different matter to account for the categories themselves. I think we must admit that the origin of the various elementary feelings is a recondite history, even after some sort of neural tissue is there for the outer world to begin its work on. The mere existence of things to be known is even now not, as a rule, sufficient to bring about a knowledge of them. Our abstract and general discoveries usually come to us as lucky fancies; and it is only *après coup* that we find that they correspond to some reality. What immediately produced them were previous thoughts, with which, and with the brain-processes of which, that reality had naught to do.

Why may it not have been so of the original elements of consciousness, sensation, time, space, resemblance, difference, and other relations? Why may they not have come into being by the back-door method, by such physical processes as lie more in the sphere of morphological accident, of inward summation of effects, than in that of the 'sensible presence' of objects? Why may they not, in short, be pure *idiosyncrasies*, spontaneous variations, fitted by good luck (those of them which have survived) to take cognizance of objects (that is, to steer us in our active dealings with them), without being in any intelligible sense immediate derivatives from them? I think we shall find this view gain more and more plausibility as we proceed.[4]

All these elements are subjective duplicates of outer objects. They *are* not the outer objects. The secondary qualities among them are not supposed by any educated person even to resemble the objects. Their *nature* depends more on the reacting brain than on the stimuli which touch it off. This is even more palpably true of the natures of pleasure and pain, effort, desire and aversion, and of such feelings as those of cause and substance, of denial and of

[4] Mr. Grant Allen, in a brilliant article entitled "Idiosyncrasy" (*Mind*, VIII, 493), seeks to show that accidental morphological changes in the brain cannot possibly be imagined to result in any mental change of a sort which would *fit the animal to its environment.* If spontaneous variation ever works on the brain, its product, says Mr. Allen, ought to be an idiot or a raving madman, not a minister and interpreter of Nature. Only the environment can change us in the direction of accommodation *to itself.* But I think we ought to know a little better just what the molecular changes in the brain are on which thought depends, before we talk so confidently about what the effect can be of their possible variations. Mr. Allen, it should be said, has made a laudable effort to conceive them distinctly. To me his conception remains too purely anatomical. Meanwhile this essay and another by the same author in the *Atlantic Monthly* are probably as serious attempts as any that have been made towards applying the Spencerian theory in a radical way to the facts of human history.

doubt. Here then is a native wealth of inner forms whose origin is shrouded in mystery, and which at any rate were not simply 'impressed' from without, in any intelligible sense of the verb 'to impress.'

Their *time- and space-relations,* however, *are* impressed from without—for two outer things at least the evolutionary psychologist must believe to resemble our thoughts of them, these are the time and space in which the objects lie. *The time- and space-relations between things do stamp copies of themselves within.* Things juxtaposed in space impress us, continue to be thought of *as* thus juxtaposed. Things sequent in time impress their sequence on our memory. And thus, through experience in the legitimate sense of the word, there can be truly explained an immense number of our mental habitudes, many of our abstract beliefs, and all our ideas of concrete things, and of their ways of behavior. Such truths as that fire burns and water wets, that glass refracts, heat melts snow, fishes live in water and die on land, and the like, form no small part of the most refined education, and are the all-in-all of education amongst the brutes and lowest men. Here the mind is passive and tributary, a servile copy, fatally and unresistingly fashioned from without. It is the merit of the associationist school to have seen the wide scope of these effects of neighborhood in time and space; and their exaggerated applications of the principle of mere neighborhood ought not to blind us to the excellent service it has done to Psychology in their hands. As far as a large part of our thinking goes, then, it can intelligibly be formulated as a mere lot of *habits* impressed upon us from without. The degree of cohesion of our inner relations, is, in this part of our thinking, proportionate, in Mr. Spencer's phrase, to the degree of cohesion of the outer relations; the causes and the objects of our thought are one; and we are, in so far forth, what the materialistic evolutionists would have us altogether, mere offshoots and creatures of our environment, and naught besides.[5]

But now the plot thickens, for the images impressed upon our memory by the outer stimuli are not restricted to the mere time- and space-relations, in which they originally came, but revive in various manners (dependent on the intricacy of the brain-paths

[5] In my own previous chapters on habit, memory, association, and perception, justice has been done to all these facts.

and the instability of the tissue thereof), and form secondary combinations such as the *forms of judgment*, which, taken *per se*, are not congruent either with the forms in which reality exists or in those in which experiences befall us, but which may nevertheless be explained by the way in which experiences befall in a mind gifted with memory, expectation, and the possibility of feeling doubt, curiosity, belief, and denial. The conjunctions of experience befall more or less invariably, variably, or never. The idea of one term will then engender a fixed, a wavering, or a negative expectation of another, giving affirmative, the hypothetical, disjunctive, interrogative, and negative judgments, and judgments of actuality and possibility about certain things. The separation of attribute from subject in all judgments (which violates the way in which nature exists) may be similarly explained by the piecemeal order in which our perceptions come to us, a vague nucleus growing gradually more detailed as we attend to it more and more. These particular secondary mental forms have had ample justice done them by associationists from Hume downwards.

Associationists have also sought to account for discrimination, abstraction, and generalization by the rates of frequency in which attributes come to us conjoined. With much less success, I think. In the chapter on Discrimination, I have, under the "law of dissociation by varying concomitants," sought to explain as much as possible by the passive order of experience. But the reader saw how much was left for active interest and unknown forces to do. In the chapter on Imagination I have similarly striven to do justice to the 'blended image' theory of generalization and abstraction. So I need say no more of these matters here.

THE GENESIS OF THE NATURAL SCIENCES

Our 'scientific' ways of thinking the outer reality are highly abstract ways. The essence of things for science is not to be what they seem, but to be atoms and molecules moving to and from each other according to strange laws. Nowhere does the account of inner relations produced by outer ones in proportion to the frequency with which the latter have been met, more egregiously break down than in the case of scientific conceptions. The order of scientific thought is quite incongruent either with the way in which reality exists or with the way in which it comes before us. Scientific thought goes by selection and emphasis exclusively. We break the solid plenitude of fact into separate essences, conceive generally what only exists particularly, and by our classifications leave nothing in its natural neighborhood, but separate the contiguous, and join what the poles divorce. The reality *exists* as a *plenum*. All its parts are contemporaneous, each is as real as any other, and each as essential for making the whole just what it is and nothing else. But we can neither experience nor think this *plenum*. What we experience, what *comes before us*, is a chaos of fragmentary impressions interrupting each other;[6] what we *think* is an abstract system of hypothetical data and laws.[7]

[6] "The order of nature, as perceived at a first glance, presents at every instant a chaos followed by another chaos. We must decompose each chaos into single facts. We must learn to see in the chaotic antecedent a multitude of distinct antecedents, in the chaotic consequent a multitude of distinct consequents. This, supposing it done, will not of itself tell us on which of the antecedents each consequent is invariably attendant. To determine that point, we must endeavour to effect a separation of the facts from one another, not in our minds only, but in nature. The mental analysis, however, must take place first. And every one knows that in the mode of performing it, one intellect differs immensely from another." (J. S. Mill: *Logic*, bk. III, chap. VII, § 1.)

[7] I quote from an address entitled "Reflex Action and Theism," published in the *Unitarian Review* for November 1881, and translated in the *Critique Philosophique* for January and February 1882. "The conceiving or theorizing faculty works exclusively for the sake of ends that do not exist at all in the world of the impressions received by way of our senses, but are set by our emotional and practical subjectivity. It is a transformer of the world of our impressions into a totally different world, the world of our conception; and the transformation is effected in the interests of our volitional nature, and for no other purpose whatsoever. Destroy the volitional nature, the definite subjective purposes, preferences, fondness for certain effects, forms, orders, and not the slightest motive would remain for the brute order of our experience to be remodelled at all. But, as we have the elaborate volitional constitution we do have, the remodelling must be effected, there is no escape. The world's contents are *given* to each of us in an order so foreign to our subjective interests that we can hardly by an effort of the imagination picture to ourselves what it is like. We have to break that order altogether, and by picking out from it the items that concern us, and connecting them with others far away, which we say 'belong' with them, we are able to make out definite threads of sequence and tendency, to foresee particular liabilities and get ready for them, to enjoy simplicity and harmony in the place of what was chaos. Is not the sum of your actual experience taken at this moment and impartially added together an utter chaos? The strains of my voice, the lights and shades inside the room and out, the murmur of the wind, the ticking of the clock, the various organic feelings you may happen individually to possess, do these make a whole at all? Is it not the only condition of your mental sanity in the midst of them that most of them should become non-existent for you, and that a few others—the sounds, I hope, which I am uttering—should evoke from places in your memory, that have nothing to do with this scene, associates fitted to combine with them in what we

This sort of scientific algebra, little as it immediately resembles the reality given to us, turns out (strangely enough) applicable to it. That is, it yields expressions which, at given places and times, can be translated into real values, or interpreted as definite portions of the chaos that falls upon our sense. It becomes thus a practical guide to our expectations as well as a theoretic delight. But I do not see how anyone with a sense for the facts can possibly call our systems immediate results of 'experience' in the ordinary sense. Every scientific conception is in the first instance a 'spontaneous variation' in someone's brain.[8] For one that proves useful and applicable there are a thousand that perish through their worthlessness. Their genesis is strictly akin to that of the flashes of poetry

---

call a rational train of thought?—rational because it leads to a conclusion we have some organ to appreciate. We have no organ or faculty to appreciate the simply given order. The real world as it is given at this moment is the sum total of all its beings and events now. But can we think of such a sum? Can we realize for an instant what a cross-section of all existence at a definite point of time would be? While I talk and the flies buzz, a sea-gull catches a fish at the mouth of the Amazon, a tree falls in the Adirondack wilderness, a man sneezes in Germany, a horse dies in Tartary, and twins are born in France. What does that mean? Does the contemporaneity of these events with each other and with a million more as disjointed as they form a rational bond between them, and unite them into anything that means for us a world? Yet just such a collateral contemporaneity, and nothing else is the *real* order of the world. It is an order with which we have nothing to do but to get away from it as fast as possible. As I said, we break it: we break it into histories, and we break it into arts, and we break it into sciences; and then we begin to feel at home. We make ten thousand separate serial orders of it. On any one of these, we may react as if the rest did not exist. We discover among its parts relations that were never given to sense at all,—mathematical relations, tangents, squares, and roots and logarithmic functions,—and out of an infinite number of these we call certain ones essential and lawgiving, and ignore the rest. Essential these relations are, but only *for our purpose*, the other relations being just as real and present as they; and our purpose is to *conceive simply* and to *foresee*. Are not simple conception and prevision subjective ends, pure and simple? They are the ends of what we call science; and the miracle of miracles, a miracle not yet exhaustively cleared up by any philosophy, is that the given order lends itself to the remodelling. It shows itself plastic to many of our scientific, to many of our æsthetic, to many of our practical purposes and ends." Cf. also Hodgson: *Philosophy of Reflection*, ch. v; Lotze: *Logik*, §§ 342–351; Sigwart: *Logik*, §§ 60–63, 105.

8 In an article entitled "Great Men, Great Thoughts, and the Environment," published in the *Atlantic Monthly* for October 1880, the reader will find some ampler illustrations of these remarks. I have there tried to show that both mental and social evolution are to be conceived after the Darwinian fashion, and that the function of the environment properly so called is much more that of *selecting* forms, produced by invisible forces, than *producing* of such forms,—producing being the only function thought of by the pre-Darwinian evolutionists, and the only one on which stress is laid by such contemporary ones as Mr. Spencer and Mr. Allen.

and sallies of wit to which the instable brain-paths equally give rise. But whereas the poetry and wit (like the science of the ancients) are their 'own excuse for being,' and have to run the gauntlet of no farther test, the 'scientific' conceptions must prove their worth by being 'verified.' This test, however, is the cause of their *preservation*, not that of their production; and one might as well account for the origin of Artemus Ward's jokes by the 'cohesion' of subjects with predicates in proportion to the 'persistence of the outer relations' to which they 'correspond' as to treat the genesis of scientific conceptions in the same ponderously unreal way.

The most persistent outer relations which science believes in are never matters of experience at all, but have to be disengaged from under experience by a process of elimination, that is, by ignoring conditions which are always present. The *elementary* laws of mechanics, physics, and chemistry are all of this sort. The principle of uniformity in nature is of this sort; it has to be *sought* under and in spite of the most rebellious appearances; and our conviction of its truth is far more like a religious faith than like assent to a demonstration. The only cohesions which experience in the literal sense of the word produces in our mind are, as we contended some time back, the proximate laws of nature, and habitudes of concrete things, that heat melts ice, that salt preserves meat, that fish die out of water, and the like.[9] Such 'empirical truths' as these we ad-

9 "It is perfectly true that our world of experience begins with such associations as lead us to expect that what has happened to us will happen again. These associations lead the babe to look for milk from its nurse and not from its father, the child to believe that the apple he sees will taste good; and whilst they make him wish for it, they make him fear the bottle which contains his bitter medicine. But whereas a part of these associations grows confirmed by frequent repetition, another part is destroyed by contradictory experiences; and the world becomes divided for us into two provinces, one in which we are at home and anticipate with confidence always the same sequences; another filled with alternating, variable, accidental occurrences.

". . . Accident is, in a wide sphere, such an every-day matter that we need not be surprised if it sometimes invades the territory where order is the rule. And one personification or another of the capricious power of chance easily helps us over the difficulties which further reflection might find in the exceptions. Yes, indeed, Exception has a peculiar fascination; it is a subject of astonishment, a θαῦμα, and the credulity with which in this first stage of pure association we adopt our supposed rules is matched by the equal credulity with which we adopt the miracles that interfere with them.

"The whole history of popular beliefs about nature refutes the notion that the thought of an universal physical order can possibly have arisen through the purely passive reception and association of particular perceptions. Indubitable as it is that all men infer from known cases to unknown, it is equally certain that this procedure,

mitted to form an enormous part of human wisdom. The 'scientific' truths have to harmonize with these truths, or be given up as useless; but they arise in the mind in no such passive associative way as that in which the simpler truths arise. Even those experiences which are used to prove a scientific truth are for the most part artificial experiences of the laboratory gained after the truth itself has been conjectured. Instead of experiences engendering the 'inner relations,' the inner relations are what engender the experiences here.

What happens in the brain after experience has done its utmost is what happens in every material mass which has been fashioned by an outward force,—in every pudding or mortar, for example, which I may make with my hands. The fashioning from without brings the elements into collocations which set new internal forces free to exert their effects in turn. And the random irradiations and resettlements of our ideas, which *supervene upon experience,* and constitute our free mental play, are due entirely to these secondary internal processes, which vary enormously from brain to brain, even though the brains be exposed to exactly the same 'outer relations.' The higher thought-processes owe their being to causes which correspond far more to the sourings and fermentations of dough, the setting of mortar, or the subsidence of sediments in mixtures, than to the manipulations by which these physical aggre-

---

if restricted to the phenomenal materials that spontaneously offer themselves, would never have led to the belief in a general uniformity, but only to the belief that law and lawlessness rule the world in motley alternation. From the point of view of strict empiricism nothing exists but the sum of particular perceptions with their coincidences on the one hand, their contradictions on the other.

"That there is more order in the world than appears at first sight is not discovered till the order is looked for. The first impulse to look for it proceeds from practical needs: where ends must be attained, we must know trustworthy means which infallibly possess a property or produce a result. But the practical need is only the first occasion for our reflection on the conditions of a true knowledge; even were there no such need, motives would still be present to carry us beyond the stage of mere association. For not with an equal interest, or rather with an equal lack of interest, does man contemplate those natural processes in which like is joined to like, and those in which like and unlike are joined; the former processes harmonize with the conditions of his thinking, the latter do not; in the former his concepts, judgments, inferences apply to realities, in the latter they have no such application. And thus the intellectual satisfaction which at first comes to him without reflection, at last excites in him the conscious wish to find realized throughout the entire phenomenal world those rational continuities, uniformities, and necessities which are the fundamental element and guiding principle of his own thought." (C. Sigwart: *Logik,* II, 380–2.)

gates came to be compounded. Our study of similar association and reasoning taught us that the whole superiority of man depended on the facility with which in his brain the paths worn by the most frequent outer cohesions could be ruptured. The causes of the instability, the reasons why now this point and now that become in him the seat of rupture, we saw to be entirely obscure. (Vol. I, p. 546; Vol. II, p. 987.) The only clear thing about the peculiarity seems to be its interstitial character, and the certainty that no mere appeal to man's 'experience' suffices to explain it.

When we pass from scientific to æsthetic and ethical systems, everyone readily admits that, although the elements are matters of experience, the peculiar forms of relation into which they are woven are incongruent with the order of passively received experience. The world of æsthetics and ethics is an ideal world, a Utopia, a world which the outer relations persist in contradicting, but which we as stubbornly persist in striving to make actual. Why do we thus invincibly crave to alter the given order of nature? Simply because other relations among things are far more interesting to us and more charming than the mere rates of frequency of their time- and space-conjunctions. These other relations are all secondary and brain-born, 'spontaneous variations' most of them, of our sensibility, whereby certain elements of experience, and certain arrangements in time and space, have acquired an agreeableness which otherwise would not have been felt. It is true that habitual arrangements may also become agreeable. But this agreeableness of the merely habitual is felt to be a mere ape and counterfeit of real inward fitness; and one sign of intelligence is never to mistake the one for the other.

There are then ideal and inward relations amongst the objects of our thought which can in no intelligible sense whatever be interpreted as reproductions of the order of outer experience. In the æsthetic and ethical realms they conflict with its order—the early Christian with his kingdom of heaven, and the contemporary anarchist with his abstract dream of justice, will tell you that the existing order must perish, root and branch, ere the true order can come. Now the peculiarity of those relations among the objects of our thought which are dubbed 'scientific' is this, that although they no more are inward *reproductions* of the outer order than the ethical and æsthetic relations are, yet they do not conflict with that order, but, once having sprung up by the play of the inward forces, are found—some of them at least, namely the only ones which have survived long enough to be matters of record—to be *congruent* with the time- and space-relations which our impressions affect.

In other words, though nature's materials lend themselves slowly and discouragingly to our translation of them into ethical forms, but more readily into æsthetic forms; to translation into scientific forms they lend themselves with relative ease and completeness. The translation, it is true, will probably never be ended. The perceptive order does not give way, nor the right conceptive substitute for it arise, at our bare word of command.[10] It is often a deadly fight; and many a man of science can say, like Johannes Müller, after an investigation, '*Es klebt Blut an der Arbeit.*' But victory after victory makes us sure that the essential doom of our enemy is defeat.[11]

[10] Cf. Hodgson: *Philosophy of Reflection*, book II, chap. V.

[11] The aspiration to be 'scientific' is such an idol of the tribe to the present generation, is so sucked in with his mother's milk by every one of us, that we find it hard to conceive of a creature who should not feel it, and harder still to treat it freely as the altogether peculiar and one-sided subjective interest which it is. But as a matter of fact, few even of the cultivated members of the race have shared it; it was invented but a generation or two ago. In the middle ages it meant only impious magic; and the way in which it even now strikes orientals is charmingly shown in the letter of a Turkish cadi to an English traveller asking him for statistical information, which Sir A. Layard prints at the end of his *Discoveries among the Ruins of Nineveh and Babylon*. The document is too full of edification not to be given in full. It runs thus:

"*My Illustrious Friend, and Joy of my Liver!*

"The thing you ask of me is both difficult and useless. Although I have passed all my days in this place, I have neither counted the houses nor have I inquired into the number of the inhabitants; and as to what one person loads on his mules and the other stows away in the bottom of his ship, that is no business of mine. But, above all, as to the previous history of this city, God only knows the amount of dirt and confusion that the infidels may have eaten before the coming of the sword of Islam. It were unprofitable for us to inquire into it.

"Oh, my soul! oh, my lamb! seek not after the things which concern thee not. Thou camest unto us, and we welcomed thee: go in peace.

"Of a truth, thou hast spoken many words; and there is no harm done, for the speaker is one and the listener is another. After the fashion of thy people thou hast wandered from one place to another until thou art happy and content in none. We (praise be to God) were born here, and never desire to quit it. Is it possible then that the idea of a general intercourse between mankind should make any impression on our understandings? God forbid!

"Listen, oh my son! There is no wisdom equal unto the belief in God! He created the world, and shall we liken ourselves unto him in seeking to penetrate into the mysteries of his creation? Shall we say, behold this star spinneth round that star, and

THE GENESIS OF THE PURE SCIENCES

I have now stated in general terms the relation of the natural sciences to experience strictly so called, and shall complete what I have to say by reverting to the subject on a later page. At present I will pass to the so-called *pure* or *a priori sciences* of Classification, Logic, and Mathematics. My thesis concerning these is that they are even less than the natural sciences effects of the order of the world as it comes to our experience. THE PURE SCIENCES EXPRESS RESULTS OF COMPARISON *exclusively; comparison is not a conceivable effect of the order in which outer impressions are experienced —it is one of the house-born* (p. 1225) *portions of our mental structure; therefore the pure sciences form a body of propositions with whose genesis experience has nothing to do.*

First, consider the nature of comparison. *The relations of resemblance and difference among things have nothing to do with the time- and space-order in which we may experience the latter.* Suppose a hundred beings created by God and gifted with the faculties of memory and comparison. Suppose that upon each of them the same lot of sensations are imprinted, but in different orders. Let some of them have no single sensation more than once. Let some have this one and others that one repeated. Let every conceivable permutation prevail. And then let the magic-lantern show die out, and keep the creatures in a void eternity, with naught but their memories to muse upon. Inevitably in their long leisure they will begin to play with the items of their experience and rearrange them, make classificatory series of them, place gray between white and black, orange between red and yellow, and trace all other degrees of resemblance and difference. And this new con-

---

this other star with a tail goeth and cometh in so many years! Let it go! He from whose hand it came will guide and direct it.

"But thou wilt say unto me, Stand aside, oh man, for I am more learned than thou art, and have seen more things. If thou thinkest that thou art in this respect better than I am, thou art welcome. I praise God that I seek not that which I require not. Thou art learned in the things I care not for; and as for that which thou hast seen, I defile it. Will much knowledge create thee a double belly, or wilt thou seek Paradise with thine eyes?

"Oh, my friend! If thou wilt be happy, say, There is no God but God! Do no evil, and thus wilt thou fear neither man nor death; for surely thine hour will come!

"The meek in spirit (El Fakir),

"IMAUM ALI ZADÈ."

struction will be absolutely identical in all the hundred creatures, the diversity of the sequence of the original experiences having no effect as regards this rearrangement. Any and every form of sequence will give the same result, because the result expresses the relation between the *inward natures* of the sensations; and to that the question of their outward succession is quite irrelevant. Black will differ from white just as much in a world in which they always come close together as in one in which they always come far apart; just as much in one in which they appear rarely as in one in which they appear all the time.

But the advocate of 'persistent outer relations' may still return to the charge: These *are* what make us so sure that white and black differ, he may say; for in a world where sometimes black resembled white and sometimes differed from it, we could never be so sure. It is because in this world black and white have *always* differed that the sense of their difference has become a necessary form of thought. The pair of colors on the one hand and the sense of difference on the other, inseparably experienced, not only by ourselves but by our ancestors, have become inseparably connected in the mind. Not through any essential structure of the mind, which made difference the only possible feeling which they could arouse; no, but because they simply *did* differ so often that at last they begat in us an impotency to imagine them doing anything else, and made us accept such a fabulous account as that just presented, of creatures to whom a single experience would suffice to make us feel the necessity of this relation.

I know not whether Mr. Spencer would subscribe to this or not; —nor do I care, for there are mysteries which press more for solution than the meaning of this vague writer's words. But to me such an explanation of our difference-judgment is absolutely unintelligible. We now find black and white different, the explanation says, *because we always have so found them*. But why should we always have so found them? Why should difference have popped into our heads so invariably with the thought of them? There must have been either a subjective or an objective reason. The subjective reason can only be that our minds were so constructed that a sense of difference was the only sort of conscious transition possible between black and white; the objective reason can only be that difference was always there, with these colors, outside the mind as an objective fact. The subjective reason explains outer frequency by inward structure, not inward structure by outer frequency; and so surrenders the experience-theory. The objective reason simply says that if an outer difference is there the mind must needs know it—which is no explanation at all, but a mere appeal to the fact that somehow the mind does know what is there.

The only clear thing to do is to give up the sham of a pretended explanation, and to fall back on the fact that the sense of difference *has* arisen, in some natural manner doubtless, but in a manner which we do not understand. It was by the back-stairs way, at all events; and, from the very first, happened to be the only mode of reaction by which consciousness could feel the transition from one term to another of what (in *consequence* of this very reaction) we now call a contrasted pair.

In noticing the differences and resemblances of things, and their degrees, the mind feels its own activity, and has given the name of *comparison* thereto. It need not compare its materials, but if once roused to do so, it can compare them with but one result, and this a fixed consequence of the nature of the materials themselves. Difference and resemblance are thus relations between ideal objects, or conceptions as such. To learn whether black and white differ, I need not consult the world of experience at all; the mere ideas suffice. *What I mean* by black differs from *what I mean* by white, whether such colors exist *extra mentem meam* or not. If they ever do so exist, they *will* differ. White things may blacken, but the black of them will differ from the white of them, so long as I mean anything definite by these three words.[12]

I shall now in what follows call all propositions which express time- and space-relations empirical propositions; and I shall give the name of rational propositions to all propositions which express

12 "Though a man in a fever should from sugar have a bitter taste, which at another time would produce a sweet one, yet the idea of bitter in that man's mind would be as clear and distinct from the idea of sweet as if he had tasted only gall. Nor does it make any more confusion between the two ideas of sweet and bitter, that the same sort of body produces at one time one and at another time another idea by the taste, than it makes a confusion in two ideas of white and sweet, or white and round, that the same piece of sugar produces them both in the mind at the same time." Locke's *Essay*, bk. II, ch. XI, § 3.

the results of a comparison. The latter denomination is in a sense arbitrary, for resemblance and difference are not usually held to be the only rational relations between things. I will next proceed to show, however, how many other rational relations commonly supposed distinct can be resolved into these, so that my definition of rational propositions will end, I trust, by proving less arbitrary than it now appears to be.

SERIES OF EVEN DIFFERENCE AND MEDIATE COMPARISON

In Chapter XII we saw that the mind can at successive moments *mean the same,* and that it gradually comes into possession of a stock of permanent and fixed meanings, ideal objects, or conceptions, some of which are universal qualities, like the black and white of our example, and some, individual things. We now see that not only are the objects permanent mental possessions, but the results of their comparison are permanent too. The objects and their differences together form an immutable system. *The same objects, compared in the same way, always give the same results*; if the result be not the same, then the objects are not those originally meant.

This last principle, which we may call the *axiom of constant result,* holds good throughout all our mental operations, not only when we compare, but when we add, divide, class, or infer a given matter in any conceivable way. Its most general expression would be "*the Same operated on in the same way gives the Same.*" In mathematics it takes the form of "equals added to, or subtracted from, equals give equals," and the like. We shall meet with it again.

The next thing which we observe is that *the operation of comparing may be repeated on its own results*; in other words, that we can think of the various resemblances and differences which we find and compare them with each other, making differences and resemblances of a higher order. *The mind thus becomes aware of sets of similar differences, and forms series of terms with the same kind and amount of difference between them, terms which, as they succeed each other, maintain a constant direction of serial increase.* This sense of constant direction in a series of operations we saw in Chapter XIII (p. 464) to be a cardinal mental fact. "A differs from B differs from C differs from D, etc.," makes a *series* only when the differences are in the same direction. In any such difference-series all terms differ in just the same way from their predecessors. The numbers 1, 2, 3, 4, 5, . . . the notes of the chromatic scale in music, are familiar examples. As soon as the mind grasps such a series as a whole, it perceives that *two terms taken far apart differ more than two terms taken near together*, and that any one term differs more from a remote than from a near successor, and this no matter what the terms may be, or what the sort of difference may be, provided it is always the same sort.

This PRINCIPLE OF MEDIATE COMPARISON might be briefly (though obscurely) expressed by the formula "*more than the more is more than the less*"—the words *more* and *less* standing simply for degrees of increase along a constant direction of differences. Such a formula would cover all possible cases, as, earlier than early is earlier than late, worse than bad is worse than good, east of east is east of west; etc., etc., *ad libitum*.[13] Symbolically, we might write it as $a < b < c < d$ . . . and say that any number of intermediaries may be expunged without obliging us to alter anything in what remains written.

The principle of mediate comparison is only one form of a law which holds in many series of homogeneously related terms, the law that *skipping intermediary terms leaves relations the same.* This AXIOM OF SKIPPED INTERMEDIARIES or of TRANSFERRED RELATIONS occurs, as we soon shall see, in logic as the fundamental principle of inference, in arithmetic as the fundamental property of the number-series, in geometry as that of the straight line, the plane and the parallel. *It seems to be on the whole the broadest and deepest law of man's thought.*

In certain lists of terms the result of comparison may be to find no-difference, or equality in place of difference. Here also intermediaries may be skipped, and mediate comparison be carried on with the general result expressed by the *axiom of mediate equality*, "equals of equals are equal," which is the great principle of the mathematical sciences. This too as a result of the mind's mere acuteness, and in utter independence of the order in which experiences come associated together. Symbolically, again: $a = b = c = d$ . . . with the same consequence as regards expunging terms which we saw before.

13 Cf. Bradley: *Logic*, p. 226.

CLASSIFICATORY SERIES

Thus we have a rather intricate system of necessary and immutable *ideal truths of comparison,* a system applicable to terms *experienced* in any order of sequence or frequency, or even to terms never experienced or to be experienced, such as the mind's imaginary constructions would be. These truths of comparison result in *Classifications.* It is, for some unknown reason, a great æsthetic delight for the mind to break the order of experience, and class its materials in serial orders, proceeding from step to step of difference, and to contemplate untiringly the crossings and inosculations of the series among themselves. The first steps in most of the sciences are purely classificatory. Where facts fall easily into rich and intricate series (as plants and animals and chemical compounds do), the mere sight of the series fills the mind with a satisfaction *sui generis;* and a world whose *real* materials naturally lend themselves to serial classification is *pro tanto* a more rational world, a world with which the mind will feel more intimate, than with a world in which they do not. By the pre-evolutionary naturalists, whose generation has hardly passed away, classifications were supposed to be ultimate insights into God's mind, filling us with adoration of his ways. The fact that Nature lets us make them was a proof of the presence of his Thought in her bosom. So far as the facts of experience can *not* be serially classified, therefore, so far experience fails to be rational in *one* of the ways, at least, which we crave.

THE LOGIC-SERIES

Closely akin to the function of comparison is that of *judging, predicating, or subsuming.* In fact, these elementary intellectual functions run into each other so, that it is often only a question of practical convenience whether we shall call a given mental operation by the name of one or of the other. Comparisons result in groups of like things; and presently (through discrimination and abstraction) in conceptions of the *respects* in which the likenesses obtain. The groups are *genera* or *classes,* the respects are *characters* or *attributes.* The attributes again may be compared, forming genera of higher orders, and their characters singled out; so that we have a new sort of series, *that of predication, or of kind including kind.* Thus horses are quadrupeds, quadrupeds animals, animals machines, machines liable to wear out, etc. In such a series as this the several couplings of terms may have been made out originally at widely different times and under different circumstances. But memory may bring them together afterwards; and whenever it does so, our faculty of apprehending serial increase makes us conscious of them as a single system of successive terms united by the same relation.[14]

Now whenever we become thus conscious, we may become aware of an additional relation which is of the highest intellectual importance, inasmuch as upon it the whole structure of logic is reared. *The principle of mediate predication or subsumption* is only the axiom of skipped intermediaries applied to a series of successive predications. It expresses the fact that any earlier term in the series stands to any later term in the same relation in which it stands to any intermediate term; in other words, that *whatever has an attribute has all the attributes of that attribute*; or more briefly still, that *whatever is of a kind is of that kind's kind*. A little explanation of this statement will bring out all that it involves.

We learned in the chapter on Reasoning what our great motive is for abstracting attributes and predicating them. It is that our varying practical purposes require us to lay hold of different angles of the reality at different times. But for these we should be satisfied to 'see it whole,' and always alike. The purpose, however, makes one aspect essential; so, to avoid dispersion of the attention, we treat the reality as if for the time being it were nothing but that aspect, and we let its supernumerary determinations go. In short, we substitute the aspect for the whole real thing. *For our purpose* the aspect *can* be substituted for the whole, and the two treated as the same; and the word *is* (which couples the whole with its aspect or attribute in the categoric judgment) expresses (among other things) the identifying operation performed. The predication-series a is b, b is c, c is d, . . . closely resembles for certain practical purposes the equation-series $a = b$, $b = c$, $c = d$, etc.

But what is our purpose in predicating? Ultimately, it may be anything we please; but proximately and immediately, it is always

14 This apprehension of them as forming a single system is what Mr. Bradley means by the act of *construction* which underlies all reasoning. The awareness, which then supervenes, of the additional relation of which I speak in the next paragraph of my text, is what this author calls the act of *inspection*. Cf. *Principles of Logic,* bk. II, pt. I, chap. III.

the gratification of a certain curiosity as to whether the object in hand is or is not *of a kind* connected with that ultimate purpose. Usually the connection is not obvious, and we only find that the object S is of a kind connected with P, after first finding that it is of a kind M, which itself is connected with P. Thus, to fix our ideas by an example, we have a curiosity (our ultimate purpose being conquest over nature) as to how Sirius may move. It is not obvious whether Sirius is a kind of thing which moves in the line of sight or not. When, however, we find it to be a kind of thing in whose spectrum the hydrogen-line is shifted, and when we reflect that *that* kind of thing is a kind of thing which moves in the line of sight; we conclude that Sirius does so move. Whatever Sirius's attribute is, Sirius is; its adjective's adjective can supersede its own adjective in our thinking, and this with no loss to our knowledge, *so long as we stick to the definite purpose in view.*

Now please note that this elimination of intermediary kinds and transfer of *is*'s along the line, results from our insight into the very meaning of the word *is*, and into the constitution of any series of terms connected by that relation. It has naught to do with what any particular thing is or is not; but, *whatever* any given thing may be, we see that it also is whatever *that* is, indefinitely. To grasp in one view a succession of *is*'s is to apprehend this relation between the terms which they connect; just as to grasp a list of successive equals is to apprehend their *mutual* equality throughout. The principle of mediate subsumption thus expresses relations of ideal objects as such. It can be discovered by a mind left at leisure with any set of meanings (however originally obtained), of which some are predicable of others. The moment we string them in a serial line, that moment we see that we can drop intermediaries, treat remote terms just like near ones, and put a genus in the place of a species. This shows that *the principle of mediate subsumption has nothing to do with the particular order of our experiences, or with the outer coexistences and sequences of terms.* Were it a mere outgrowth of habit and association, we should be forced to regard it as having no universal validity; for every hour of the day we meet things which we consider to be of this kind or of that, but later learn that they have none of the kind's properties, that they *do not* belong to the kind's kind. Instead, however, of correcting the principle by these cases, we correct the cases by the principle. We say that if the thing we named an M has not M's properties, then we were either mistaken in calling it an M, or mistaken about M's properties; or else that it is no longer M, but has changed. But we never say that it is an M without M's properties; for by conceiving a thing as of the kind M I mean that it *shall* have M's properties, be of M's kind, even though I should never be able to find in the real world anything which is an M. The principle emanates from my perception of what a lot of successive is's *mean*. This perception can no more be confirmed by one set, or weakened by another set, of outer facts, than the perception that black is not white can be confirmed by the fact that snow never blackens, or weakened by the fact that photographer's paper blackens as soon as you lay it in the sun.

The abstract scheme of successive predications, extended indefinitely, with all the possibilities of substitution which it involves, is thus an immutable system of truth which flows from the very structure and form of our thinking. *If* any real terms ever do fit into such a scheme, they will obey its laws; *whether* they do is a question as to nature's facts, the answer to which can only be empirically ascertained. *Formal logic* is the name of the Science which traces in skeleton form all the remote relations of terms connected by successive *is*'s with each other, and enumerates their possibilities of mutual substitution. To our principle of mediate subsumption she has given various formulations, of which the best is perhaps this broad expression, that *the same can be substituted for the same in any mental operation.*[15]

The ordinary logical series contains but three terms—"Socrates, man, mortal." But we also have 'Sorites'—Socrates, man, animal, machine, run down, mortal, etc.—and it violates psychology to represent these as syllogisms with terms suppressed. The ground of there being any logic at all is our power to grasp any series as a whole, and the more terms it holds the better. This synthetic consciousness of an uniform direction of advance through a multiplicity of terms is, apparently, what the brutes and lower men cannot accomplish, and what gives to us our extraordinary power of ratiocinative thought. The mind which can grasp a string of *is*'s as

15 Realities fall under this only so far as they prove to *be* the same. So far as they cannot be substituted for each other, for the purpose in hand, so far they are not the same; though for other purposes and in other respects they might be substituted, and then be treated as the same. Apart from purpose, of course, no realities ever are absolutely and exactly the same.

a whole—the objects linked by them may be ideal or real, physical, mental, or symbolic, indifferently—can also apply to it the principle of skipped intermediaries. *The logic-list is thus in its origin and essential nature just like those graded classificatory lists which we erewhile described.* The 'rational proposition' which lies at the basis of all reasoning, the *dictum de omni et nullo* in all the various forms in which it may be expressed, the fundamental law of thought, is thus *only the result of the function of comparison* in a mind which has come by some lucky variation to apprehend a series of more than two terms at once.[16] So far, then, *both Systematic Classification and Logic are seen to be incidental results of the mere capacity for discerning difference and likeness,* which capacity is a thing with which the *order of experience,* properly so styled, has absolutely nothing to do.

But how comes it (it may next be asked) when systematic classifications have so little ultimate theoretic importance—for the conceiving of things according to their mere degrees of resemblance always yields to other modes of conceiving when these can be obtained—that the logical relations among things should form such a mighty engine for dealing with the facts of life?

Chapter XXII already gave the reason (see p. 961, above). This world *might* be a world in which all things differed, and in which what properties there were were ultimate and had no farther predicates. In such a world there would be as many kinds as there were separate things. We could never subsume a new thing under an old kind; or if we could, no consequences would follow. Or, again, this might be a world in which innumerable things were of a kind, but in which no concrete thing remained of the same kind long, but all objects were in a flux. Here again, though we could subsume and infer, our logic would be of no practical use to us, for the subjects of our propositions would have changed whilst we were talking. In such worlds, logical relations would obtain, and be known (doubtless) as they are now, but they would form a merely theoretic scheme and be of no use for the conduct of life. But our world is no such world. It is a very peculiar world, and plays right into logic's hands. *Some* of the things, at least, which it contains are of

16 A mind, in other words, which has got *beyond* the merely *dichotomic* style of thought which Wundt alleges to be the essential form of human thinking (*Physiologische Psychologie*, II, 312).

the same kind as other things; *some* of them remain always of the kind of which they once were; and some of the properties of them cohere indissolubly and are always found together. *Which* things these latter things are we learn by experience in the strict sense of the word, and the results of the experience are embodied in 'empirical propositions.' Whenever such a thing is met with by us now, our sagacity notes it to be of a certain kind; our learning immediately recalls that kind's kind, and then *that* kind's kind, and so on; so that a moment's thinking may make us aware that the thing is of a kind so remote that we could never have directly perceived the connection. The flight to this last kind *over the heads of the intermediaries* is the essential feature of the intellectual operation here. Evidently it is a pure outcome of our sense for apprehending serial increase; and, unlike the several propositions themselves which make up the series (and which may all be empirical), it has nothing to do with the time- and space-order in which the things have been experienced.

MATHEMATICAL RELATIONS

So much for the *a priori* necessities called systematic classification and logical inference. The other couplings of data which pass for *a priori* necessities of thought are the *mathematical* judgments, and certain metaphysical propositions. These latter we shall consider farther on. As regards the mathematical judgments, they are all 'rational propositions' in the sense defined on p. 1239, for they express results of comparison and nothing more. The mathematical sciences deal with similarities and equalities exclusively, and not with coexistences and sequences. Hence they have, in the first instance, no connection with the order of experience. The comparisons of mathematics are between numbers and extensive magnitudes, giving rise to arithmetic and geometry respectively.

Number seems to signify primarily the strokes of our attention in discriminating things. These strokes remain in the memory in groups, large or small, and the groups can be compared. The discrimination is, as we know, psychologically facilitated by the mobility of the thing as a total (p. 812). But within each thing we discriminate parts; so that the number of things which any one given phenomenon may be depends in the last instance on our way of taking it. A globe is one, if undivided; two, if composed of hemispheres. A sand-heap is one thing, or twenty thousand things, as we may choose to count it. We amuse ourselves by the counting of *mere* strokes, to form rhythms, and these we compare and name. Little by little in our minds the number-series is formed. This, like all lists of terms in which there is a direction of serial increase, carries with it the sense of those mediate relations between its terms which we expressed by the axiom "the more than the more is more than the less." That axiom seems, in fact, only a way of stating that the terms do form an increasing series. But, in addition to this, we are aware of certain other relations among our strokes of counting. We may interrupt them where we like, and go on again. All the while we feel that the interruption does not alter the strokes themselves. We may count 12 straight through; or count 7 and pause, and then count 5, but still the strokes will be the same. We thus distinguish between our acts of counting and those of interrupting or grouping, as between an unchanged matter and an operation of mere shuffling performed on it. The matter is the original units or strokes; which all modes of grouping or combining simply give us back unchanged. In short, *combinations of numbers are combinations of their units,* which is the fundamental axiom of arithmetic,[17] leading to such consequences as that $7 + 5 = 8 + 4$ because both $= 12$. The general axiom of mediate equality, that equals of equals are equal, comes in here.[18] The principle of constancy in our meanings, when applied to strokes of counting, also gives rise to the axiom that the same number, operated on (interrupted, grouped) in the same way will always give the same result or be the same. How shouldn't it? Nothing is supposed changed.

Arithmetic and its fundamental principles are thus independent of our experiences or of the order of the world. The matter of arithmetic is *mental matter*; its principles flow from the fact that the matter forms a series, which can be cut into by us wherever we like without the matter changing. The empiricist school has strangely tried to interpret the truths of number as results of coexistences among outward things. John Mill calls number a physical property of things. 'One,' according to Mill, means one sort of

[17] Said to be expressed by Grassman in the fundamental Axiom of Arithmetic $(a + b) + 1 = a + (b + 1)$.

[18] Compare Helmholtz's more technically expressed Essay "Zählen und Messen," in the *Philosophische Aufsätze. Eduard Zeller zu seinem fünfzigjährigen Doctor-Jubiläum gewidmet* (Leipzig, 1887), p. 17.

passive sensation which we receive, 'two' another, 'three' a third. The same things, however, can give us different number-sensations. Three things arranged thus, o o o , for example, impress us differently from three things arranged thus, $^{\circ}{}_{\circ}{}^{\circ}$. But experience tells us that every real object-group which can be arranged in one of these ways can always be arranged in the other also, and that 2 + 1 and 3 are thus modes of numbering things which 'coexist' invariably with each other. The indefeasibility of our belief in their 'coexistence' (which is Mill's word for their equivalence) is due solely to the enormous amount of experience we have of it. For all things, whatever other sensations they may give us, give us at any rate number-sensations. Those number-sensations which the same thing may be successively made to arouse are the numbers which we deem equal to each other; those which the same thing refuses to arouse are those which we deem unequal.

This is as clear a restatement as I can make of Mill's doctrine.[19] And its failure is written upon its front. Woe to arithmetic, were such the only grounds for its validity! The same real things are countable in numberless ways, and pass from one numerical form, not only to its equivalent (as Mill implies), but to its other, as the sport of physical accidents or of our mode of attending may decide. How could our notion that one and one are eternally and necessarily two ever maintain itself in a world where every time we add one drop of water to another we get not two but one again? in a world where every time we add a drop to a crumb of quicklime we get a dozen or more?—had it no better warrant than such experiences? At most we could then say that one and one are *usually* two. Our arithmetical propositions would never have the confident tone which they now possess. That confident tone is due to the fact that they deal with abstract and ideal numbers exclusively. *What we mean* by one plus one *is* two; we *make* two out of it; and it would mean two still even in a world where *physically* (according to a conceit of Mill's) a third thing was engendered every time one thing came together with another. We are masters of our meanings, and discriminate between the things we mean and our ways of taking them, between our strokes of numeration themselves, and our bundlings and separatings thereof.

[19] For the original statements, cf. J. S. Mill's *Logic*, bk. II, chap. VI, §§ 2, 3; and bk. III, chap. XXIV, § 5.

Mill ought not only to have said, "All things are numbered." He ought, in order to prove his point, to have shown that they are *unequivocally* numbered, which they notoriously are not. Only the abstract numbers themselves are unequivocal, only those which we create mentally and hold fast to as ideal objects always the same. A concrete natural thing can always be numbered in a great variety of ways. "We need only conceive a thing divided into four equal parts, (and all things may be conceived as so divided,)" as Mill is himself compelled to say, to find the number four in it, and so on.

The relation of numbers to experience is just like that of 'kinds' in logic. So long as an experience will keep its kind we can handle it by logic. So long as it will keep its number we can deal with it by arithmetic. *Sensibly,* however, things are constantly changing their numbers, just as they are changing their kinds. They are forever breaking apart and fusing. Compounds and their elements are never numerically identical, for the elements are sensibly many and the compounds sensibly one. Unless our arithmetic is to remain without application to life, we must somehow *make* more numerical continuity than we spontaneously find. Accordingly Lavoisier discovers his weight-units which remain the same in compounds and elements, though volume-units and quality-units all have changed. A great discovery! And modern science outdoes it by denying that compounds exist at all. There is no such thing as 'water' for 'science'; that is only a handy name for H_2 and O when they have got into the position H-O-H, and then affect our senses in a novel way. The modern theories of atoms, of heat, and of gases are, in fact, only intensely artificial devices for gaining that constancy in the numbers of things which sensible experience will not show. "Sensible things are not the things for me," says Science, "because in their changes they will not keep their numbers the same. Sensible qualities are not the qualities for me, because they can with difficulty be numbered at all. These hypothetic atoms, however, are the things, these hypothetic masses and velocities are the qualities for me; they will stay numbered all the time."

By such elaborate inventions, and at such a cost to the imagination, do men succeed in making for themselves a world in which real things shall be coerced *per fas aut nefas* under arithmetical law.

The other branch of mathematics is *geometry*. Its objects are also ideal creations. Whether nature contain circles or not, I can know what I mean by a circle and can stick to my meaning; and when I mean two circles I mean two things of an identical kind. The axiom of constant results (see above, p. 1240) holds in geometry. The same forms, treated in the same way (added, subtracted, or compared), give the same results—how shouldn't they? The axioms of mediate comparison (p. 1241), of logic (p. 1243), and of number (p. 1248) all apply to the forms which we imagine in space, inasmuch as these resemble or differ from each other, form kinds, and are numerable things. But in addition to these general principles, which are true of space-forms only as they are of other mental conceptions, there are certain axioms relative to space-forms exclusively, which we must briefly consider.

Three of them give marks of identity among straight lines, planes, and parallels. Straight lines which have two points, planes which have three points, parallels to a given line which have one point, in common, coalesce throughout. Some say that the certainty of our belief in these axioms is due to repeated experiences of their truth; others that it is due to an intuitive acquaintance with the properties of space. It is neither. We experience lines enough which pass through two points only to separate again, only we won't call them straight. Similarly of planes and parallels. We have a definite idea of what we mean by each of these words; and when something different is offered us, we see the difference. Straight lines, planes, and parallels, as they figure in geometry, are mere inventions of our faculty for apprehending serial increase. The farther continuations of these forms, we say, *shall* bear the same relation to their last visible parts which these did to still earlier parts. It thus follows (from that axiom of skipped intermediaries which obtains in all regular series) that parts of these figures separated by other parts must agree in direction, just as contiguous parts do. This uniformity of direction throughout is, in fact, all that makes us care for these forms, gives them their beauty, and stamps them into fixed conceptions in our mind. But obviously if two lines, or two planes, with a common segment, were to part company beyond the segment, it could only be because the direction of at least one of them had changed. Parting company in lines and planes *means* changing direction, means assuming a new relation to the parts that pre-exist; and assuming a new relation means ceasing to be straight or plane. If we mean by a parallel a line that will never meet a second line; and if we have one such line drawn through a point, any new line drawn through that point which does not coalesce with the first must be inclined to it, and if inclined to it must approach the second, i.e., cease to be parallel with it. No properties of outlying space need come in here: only a definite conception of uniform direction, and constancy in sticking to one's point.

The other two axioms peculiar to geometry are that figures can be moved in space without change, and that no variation in the way of subdividing a given amount of space alters its total quantity.[20] This last axiom is similar to what we found to obtain in numbers. 'The whole is equal to its parts' is an abridged way of expressing it. A man is not the same biological whole if we cut him in two at the neck as if we divide him at the ankles; but geometrically he is the same whole, no matter in which place we cut him. The axiom about figures being movable in space is rather a postulate than an axiom. *So far as they are* so movable, then certain fixed equalities and differences obtain between forms, *no matter where placed.* But if translation through space warped or magnified forms, then the relations of equality, etc., would always have to be expressed with a position-qualification added. A geometry as absolutely certain as ours could be invented on the supposition of such a space, if the laws of its warping and deformation were fixed. It would, however, be much more complicated than our geometry, which makes the simplest possible supposition; and finds, luckily enough, that it is a supposition with which the space of our experience seems to agree.

By means of these principles, all playing into each other's hands, the mutual equivalences of an immense number of forms can be traced, even of such as at first sight bear hardly any resemblance to each other. We move and turn them mentally, and find that parts of them will superpose. We add imaginary lines which subdivide or enlarge them, and find that the new figures resemble each other in ways which show us that the old ones are equivalent too. We

20 The subdivision itself consumes none of the space. In all practical experience our subdivisions do consume space. They consume it in our geometrical figures. But for simplicity's sake, in geometry we postulate subdivisions which violate experience and consume none of it.

thus end by expressing all sorts of forms in terms of other forms, enlarging our knowledge of the kinds of things which certain other kinds of things are, or to which they are equivalent.

The result is a new system of mental objects which can be treated as identical for certain purposes, a new series of *is*'s almost indefinitely prolonged, just like the series of equivalencies among numbers, part of which the multiplication-table expresses. And all this is in the first instance regardless of the coexistences and sequences of nature, and regardless of whether the figures we speak of have ever been outwardly experienced or not.

CONSCIOUSNESS OF SERIES IS THE BASIS OF RATIONALITY

Classification, logic, and mathematics all result, then, from the mere play of the mind comparing its conceptions, no matter whence the latter may have come. The essential condition for the formation of all these sciences is that we should have grown capable of apprehending series as such, and of distinguishing them as homogeneous or heterogeneous, and as possessing definite directions of what I have called 'increase.' This consciousness of series is a human perfection which has been gradually evolved, and which varies greatly from man to man. There is no accounting for it as a result of habitual associations among outward impressions, so we must simply ascribe it to the factors, whatever they be, of inward cerebral growth. Once this consciousness attained to, however, *mediate* thought becomes possible; with our very awareness of a series may go an awareness that dropping terms out of it will leave identical relations between the terms that remain; and thus arises a perception of relations between things so naturally separate that we should otherwise never have compared them together at all.

The axiom of skipped intermediaries applies, however, only to certain particular series, and among them to those which we have considered, in which the recurring relation is either of difference, of likeness, of kind, of numerical addition, or of prolongation in the same linear or plane direction. It is therefore not a purely formal law of thinking, but flows from the nature of the matters thought about. It will not do to say universally that in all series of homogeneously related terms the remote members are related to each other as the near ones are; for that will often be untrue. The series A is not B is not C is not D . . . does not permit the relation to be traced between remote terms. From two negations no inference can be drawn. Nor, to become more concrete, does the lover of a woman generally love her beloved, or the contradictor of a contradictor contradict whomever he contradicts. The slayer of a slayer does not slay the latter's victim; the acquaintances or enemies of a man need not be each other's acquaintances or enemies; nor are two things which are on top of a third thing necessarily on top of each other.

All skipping of intermediaries and transfer of relations occurs within homogeneous series. But not all homogeneous series allow of intermediaries being skipped and relations transferred. It depends on which series they are, on what relations they contain.[21] Let it not be said that it is a mere matter of verbal association, due to the fact that language sometimes permits us to transfer the *name* of a relation over skipped intermediaries, and sometimes does not; as where we call men 'progenitors' of their remote as well as of their immediate posterity, but refuse to call them 'fathers' thereof. There are relations which are *intrinsically* transferable, whilst others are not. The relation of *condition*, e.g., is intrinsically transferable. What conditions a condition conditions what it conditions—"cause of cause is cause of effect." The relations of negation and *frustration*, on the other hand, are not transferable: what frustrates a frustration does not frustrate what it frustrates. No changes of terminology would annul the intimate difference between these two cases.

Nothing but the clear sight of the ideas themselves shows whether the axiom of skipped intermediaries applies to them or not. Their connections, immediate and remote, flow from their inward natures. We try to consider them in certain ways, to bring them into certain relations, and we find that sometimes we can and sometimes we cannot. *The question whether there are or are not inward and essential connections between conceived objects as such, really is the same thing as the question whether we can get any new perception from mentally coupling them together, or pass from one to another by a mental operation which gives a result.* In the case of some ideas and operations we get a result; but no result in the case of others. Where a result comes, it is due exclusively to the *nature* of the ideas and of the operation. Take blueness and yellowness, for example. We can operate on them in some ways,

[21] Cf. A. De Morgan: *Syllabus of a Proposed System of Logic* (1860), pp. 46–56.

but not in other ways. We can compare them; but we cannot add one to or subtract it from the other. We can refer them to a common kind, color; but we cannot make one a kind of the other, or infer one from the other. This has nothing to do with experience. For we *can* add blue *pigment* to yellow *pigment*, and subtract it again, and get a result both times. Only we know perfectly that this is no addition or subtraction of the blue and yellow qualities or natures themselves.[22]

There is thus no denying the fact that *the mind is filled with necessary and eternal relations which it finds between certain of its ideal conceptions, and which form a determinate system, independent of the order of frequency in which experience may have associated the conception's originals in time and space.*

Shall we continue to call these sciences 'intuitive,' 'innate,' or '*a priori*' bodies of truth, or not?[23] Personally I should like to do so. But I hesitate to use the terms, on account of the odium which controversial history has made the whole of their connotation for many worthy persons. The most politic way not to alienate these readers is to flourish the name of the immortal Locke. For in truth

22 Cf. Locke's *Essay*, bk. II, chap. XVII, § 6.

23 Some readers may expect me to plunge into the old debate as to whether the *a priori* truths are 'analytic' or 'synthetic.' It seems to me that the distinction is one of Kant's most unhappy legacies, for the reason that it is impossible to make it sharp. No one will say that such analytic judgments as "equidistant lines can nowhere meet" are *pure* tautologies. The predicate is a somewhat new way of conceiving as well as of naming the subject. There is *something* 'ampliative' in our greatest truisms, our state of mind is richer after than before we have uttered them. This being the case, the question "at what point does the new state of mind cease to be *implicit* in the old?" is too vague to be answered. The only sharp way of defining synthetic propositions would be to say that they express a relation between *two data* at least. But it is hard to find any proposition which cannot be construed as doing this. Even verbal definitions do it. Such painstaking attempts as that latest one by Mr. D. G. Thompson to prove all necessary judgments to be analytic (*System of Psychology*, II, pp. 232 ff.) seem accordingly but *nugæ difficiles*, and little better than wastes of ink and paper. All philosophic interest vanishes from the question, the moment one ceases to ascribe to *any a priori* truths (whether analytic or synthetic) that "legislative character for all possible experience" which Kant believed in. We ourselves have denied such legislative character, and contended that it was for experience itself to prove whether its data can or cannot be assimilated to those ideal terms between which *a priori* relations obtain. The analytic-synthetic debate is thus for us devoid of all significance. On the whole, the best recent treatment of the question known to me is in one of A. Spir's works, his *Denken und Wirklichkeit*, I think, but I cannot now find the page.

I have done nothing more in the previous pages than to make a little more explicit the teachings of Locke's fourth book:

"The immutability of the same relations between the same immutable things is now the idea that shows him, that if the three angles of a triangle were once equal to two right angles, they will always be equal to two right ones. And hence he comes to be certain, that what was once true in the case is always true; what ideas once agreed will always agree .... Upon this ground it is that particular demonstrations in mathematics afford general knowledge. If, then, the perception that the same ideas will eternally have the same habitudes and relations be not a sufficient ground of knowledge, there could be no knowledge of general propositions in mathematics .... All general knowledge lies only in our own thoughts, and consists barely in the contemplation of our own abstract ideas. Wherever we perceive any agreement or disagreement amongst them, there we have general knowledge; and, by putting the names of those ideas together accordingly in propositions, can with certainty pronounce general truths.... What is once known of such ideas will be perpetually and for ever true. So that, as to all general knowledge, we must search and find it only in our own minds, and it is only the examining of our own ideas that furnisheth us with that. Truths belonging to essences of things (that is, to abstract ideas) are eternal, and are to be found out by the contemplation only of those essences .... Knowledge is the consequence of the ideas (be they what they will) that are in our minds, producing there certain general propositions.... Such propositions are therefore called 'eternal truths,' ... because, being once made about abstract ideas so as to be true, they will, whenever they can be supposed to be made again at any time past or to come, by a mind having those ideas, always actually be true. For, names being supposed to stand perpetually for the same ideas, and the same ideas having immutably the same habitudes one to another, propositions concerning any abstract ideas that are once true must needs be eternal verities."

But what are these eternal verities, these 'agreements,' which the mind discovers by barely considering its own fixed meanings, except what I have said?—relations of likeness and difference, immediate or mediate, between the terms of certain series. Classification is serial comparison, logic mediate subsumption, arithmetic mediate equality of different bundles of attention-strokes, geometry mediate equality of different ways of carving space. None of these eternal verities has anything to say about facts, about what is or is not in the world. Logic does not say whether Socrates, men, mortals or immortals *exist*; arithmetic does not tell us where her 7's, 5's, and 12's are to be *found*; geometry affirms not that circles and rectangles are *real*. All that these sciences make us sure of is, that *if* these things are anywhere to be found, the eternal verities will obtain of them. Locke accordingly never tires of telling us that the

"universal propositions, of whose truth or falsehood we can have certain knowledge, concern not existence . . . . These universal and self-evident principles, being only our constant, clear, and distinct knowledge of our own ideas more general or comprehensive, can assure us of nothing that passes without the mind; their certainty is founded only upon the knowledge we have of each idea by itself, and of its distinction from others; about which we cannot be mistaken whilst they are in our minds . . . . The mathematician considers the truth and properties belonging to a rectangle or circle, only as they are in idea in his own mind. For it is possible he never found either of them existing mathematically, i.e. precisely true, in his life. But yet the knowledge he has of any truths or properties belonging to a circle, or any other mathematical figure, are never the less true and certain even of real things existing: because real things are no farther concerned, nor intended to be meant by any such propositions, than as things really agree to those archetypes in his mind. Is it true of the idea of a triangle, that its three angles are equal to two right ones? It is true also of a triangle wherever it really exists. Whatever other figure exists that is not exactly answerable to that idea of a triangle in his mind, is not at all concerned in that proposition. And therefore he is certain all his knowledge concerning such ideas is real knowledge: because, intending things no farther than they agree with those his ideas, he is sure what he knows concerning those figures when they have barely an ideal existence in his mind, will hold true of them also when they have a real existence in matter." But "that any or what bodies do exist: for that, we are left to our senses to discover to us as far as they can."[24]

Locke accordingly distinguishes between 'mental truth' and 'real truth.'[25] The former is intuitively certain; the latter dependent on experience. Only *hypothetically* can we affirm intuitive truths of real things—by *supposing*, namely, that real things exist which correspond exactly with the ideal subjects of the intuitive propositions.

If our senses corroborate the supposition all goes well. But note

24 Book IV, chaps. IX, § 1; VII, 14; IV, 6; VII, 14.

25 Book IV, chap. V, §§ 6, 8.

the strange descent in Locke's hands of the dignity of *a priori* propositions. By the ancients they were considered, without farther question, to reveal the constitution of Reality. Archetypal things existed, it was assumed, in the relations in which we had to think them. The mind's necessities were a warrant for those of Being; and it was not till Descartes' time that scepticism had so advanced (in 'dogmatic' circles) that the warrant must itself be warranted, and the veracity of the Deity invoked as a reason for holding fast to our natural beliefs.

But the intuitive propositions of Locke leave us as regards outer reality none the better for their possession. We still have to "go to our senses" to find what the reality is. The vindication of the intuitionist position is thus a barren victory. The eternal verities which the very structure of our mind lays hold of do not necessarily themselves lay hold on extra-mental being, nor have they, as Kant pretended later,[26] a legislating character even for all possible experience. They are primarily interesting only as subjective facts. They stand waiting in the mind, forming a beautiful ideal network; and the most we can say is that we *hope* to discover outer realities over which the network may be flung so that ideal and real may coincide.

And this brings us back to 'science' from which we diverted our attention so long ago (see p. 1236). Science thinks that she has discovered the outer realities in question. Atoms and ether, with no properties but masses and velocities expressible by numbers, and paths expressible by analytic formulas, these at last are things over which the mathematico-logical network may be flung, and by supposing which instead of supposing sensible phenomena science becomes yearly more able to manufacture for herself a world about which rational propositions may be framed. Sensible phenomena are pure delusions for the mechanical philosophy. The 'things' and

26 Kant, by the way, made a strange tactical blunder in his way of showing that the forms of our necessary thought are underived from experience. He insisted on thought-forms with which experience largely *agrees*, forgetting that the only forms which could not by any possibility be the results of experience would be such as experience *violated*. The first thing a Kantian ought to do is to discover forms of judgment to which *no* order in 'things' runs parallel. These would indeed be features native to the mind. I owe this remark to Herr A. Spir, in whose *Denken und Wirklichkeit* it is somewhere contained. I have myself already to some extent proceeded, and in the pages which follow shall proceed still farther, to show the originality of the mind's structure in this way.

qualities we instinctively believe in do not exist. The only realities are swarming solids in everlasting motion, undulatory or continued, whose expressionless and meaningless changes of position form the history of the world, and are deducible from initial collocations and habits of movement hypothetically assumed. Thousands of years ago men started to cast the chaos of nature's sequences and juxtapositions into a form that might seem intelligible. Many were their ideal prototypes of rational order: teleological and æsthetic ties between things, causal and substantial bonds, as well as logical and mathematical relations. The most promising of these ideal systems at first were of course the richer ones, the sentimental ones. The baldest and least promising were the mathematical ones; but the history of the latter's application is a history of steadily advancing successes, whilst that of the sentimentally richer systems is one of relative sterility and failure.[27] Take those aspects of phenomena which interest you as a human being most, and class the phenomena as perfect and imperfect, as ends and means to ends, as high and low, beautiful and ugly, positive and negative, harmonious and discordant, fit and unfit, natural and unnatural, etc., and barren are all your results. In the ideal world the kind 'precious' has characteristic properties. What is precious should be preserved; unworthy things should be sacrificed for its sake; exceptions made on its account; its preciousness is a reason for other things' actions, and the like. But none of these things need happen to your 'precious' object in the real world. Call the things of nature as much as you like by sentimental, moral, and æsthetic names, no natural consequences follow from the naming. They may be of the kinds you allege, but they are not of '*the kind's kind*'; and the last great system-maker of this sort, Hegel, was obliged explicitly to repudiate logic in order to make any inferences at all from the names he called things by.

27 Yet even so late as Berkeley's time one could write: "As in reading other books a wise man will choose to fix his thoughts on the sense and apply it to use, rather than lay them out in grammatical remarks on the language; so, in perusing the volume of nature, methinks it is beneath the dignity of the mind to affect an exactness in reducing each particular phenomenon to general rules, or shewing how it follows from them. We should propose to ourselves nobler views, namely, to recreate and exalt the mind with a prospect of the beauty, order, extent, and variety of natural things: hence, by proper inferences, to enlarge our notions of the grandeur, wisdom and beneficence of the Creator," etc., etc., etc. (*Principles of Human Knowledge*, § 109.)

But when you give things mathematical and mechanical names and call them just so many solids in just such positions, describing just such paths with just such velocities, all is changed. Your sagacity finds its reward in the verification by nature of all the deductions which you may next proceed to make. Your 'things' realize all the *consequences* of the names by which you classed them. The modern mechanico-physical philosophy of which we are all so proud, because it includes the nebular cosmogony, the conservation of energy, the kinetic theory of heat and gases, etc., etc., begins by saying that the only facts are collocations and motions of primordial solids, and the only laws the changes of motion which changes in collocation bring. The ideal which this philosophy strives after is a mathematical world-formula, by which, if all the collocations and motions at a given moment were known, it would be possible to reckon those of any wished-for future moment, by simply considering the necessary geometrical, arithmetical, and logical implications. Once we have the world in this bare shape, we can fling our net of *a priori* relations over all its terms, and pass from one of its phases to another by inward thought-necessity. Of course it is a world with a very minimum of rational *stuff*. The sentimental facts and relations are butchered at a blow. But the rationality yielded is so superbly complete in *form* that to many minds this atones for the loss, and reconciles the thinker to the notion of a purposeless universe, in which all the things and qualities men love, *dulcissima mundi nomina*, are but illusions of our fancy attached to accidental clouds of dust which will be dissipated by the eternal cosmic weather as carelessly as they were formed.

The popular notion that 'Science' is forced on the mind *ab extra*, and that our interests have nothing to do with its constructions, is utterly absurd. The craving to believe that the things of the world belong to kinds which are related by inward rationality together, is the parent of Science as well as of sentimental philosophy; and the original investigator always preserves a healthy sense of how plastic the materials are in his hands.

"Once for all," says Helmholtz in beginning that little work of his which laid the foundations of the 'conservation of energy,' "it is the task of the physical sciences to seek for laws by which particular processes in nature may be referred to general rules, and deduced from such again. Such rules (for example the laws of reflection or refraction of light, or that of Mariotte and Gay-Lussac for gas-volumes) are evidently nothing but generic-concepts for embracing whole classes of phenomena. The search for them is the business of the experimental division of our Science. Its theoretic division, on the other hand, tries to discover the unknown causes of processes from their visible effects; tries to understand them by the law of causality. . . . The ultimate goal of theoretic physics is to find the last *unchanging* causes of the processes in Nature. Whether all processes be really ascribable to such causes, whether, in other words, *nature be completely intelligible*, or whether there be changes which would elude the law of a necessary causality, and fall into a realm of spontaneity or freedom, is not here the place to determine; but at any rate it is clear that the Science whose aim it is to make nature appear intelligible [*die Natur zu begreifen*] must start with the *assumption* of her intelligibility, and draw consequences in conformity with this assumption, until irrefutable facts show the limitations of this method. . . . The postulate that natural phenomena must be reduced to changeless ultimate causes next shapes itself so that *forces unchanged by time* must be found to be these causes. Now in Science we have already found portions of matter with changeless forces (indestructible qualities), and called them (chemical) elements. If, then, we imagine the world composed of elements with inalterable qualities, the only changes that can remain possible in such a world are spatial changes, i.e., movements, and the only outer relations which can modify the action of the forces are spatial too, or, in other words, the forces are motor forces dependent for their effect only on spatial relations. More exactly still: The phenomena of nature must be reduced to [*zurückgeführt*, conceived as, classed as] motions of material points with inalterable motor forces acting according to space-relations alone. . . . But points have no mutual space-relations except their distance, . . . and a motor force which they exert upon each other can cause nothing but a change of distance—i.e., be an attractive or a repulsive force. . . . And its intensity can only depend on distance. So that at last the task of Physics resolves itself into this, to refer phenomena to inalterable attractive and repulsive forces whose intensity varies with distance. The solution of this task would at the same time be the condition of Nature's complete intelligibility."[28]

The subjective interest leading to the assumption could not be more candidly expressed. What makes the assumption 'scientific' and not merely poetic, what makes a Helmholtz and his kin *discoverers*, is that the things of Nature turn out to act as if they *were* of the kind assumed. They behave as such mere drawing and driv-

[28] *Über die Erhaltung der Kraft* (1847), pp. 2–6.

ing atoms would behave; and so far as they have been distinctly enough translated into molecular terms to test the point, so far a certain fantastically ideal object, namely, the mathematical sum containing their mutual distances and velocities, is found to be constant throughout all their movements. This sum is called the total energy of the molecules considered. Its constancy or 'conservation' gives the name to the hypothesis of molecules and central forces from which it was logically deduced.

Take any other mathematico-mechanical theory and it is the same. They are all translations of sensible experiences into other forms, substitutions of items between which ideal relations of kind, number, form, equality, etc., obtain, for items between which no such relations obtain; coupled with declarations that the experienced form is false and the ideal form true, declarations which are justified by the appearance of new sensible experiences at just those times and places at which we logically infer that their ideal correlates ought to be. Wave-hypotheses thus make us predict rings of darkness and color, distortions, dispersions, changes of pitch in sonorous bodies moving from us, etc.; molecule-hypotheses lead to predictions of vapor-density, freezing point, etc.,—all which predictions fall true.

Thus the world grows more orderly and rational to the mind, which passes from one feature of it to another by deductive necessity, as soon as it conceives it as made up of so few and so simple phenomena as bodies with no properties but number and movement to and fro.

METAPHYSICAL AXIOMS

But alongside of these ideal relations between terms which the world verifies, there are other ideal relations not as yet so verified. I refer to those propositions (no longer expressing mere results of comparison) which are formulated in such metaphysical and æsthetic axioms as "The Principle of things is one"; "The quantity of existence is unchanged"; "Nature is simple and invariable"; "Nature acts by the shortest ways"; "*Ex nihilo nihil fit*"; "Nothing can be evolved which was not involved"; "Whatever is in the effect must be in the cause"; "A thing can only work where it is"; "A thing can only affect another of its own kind"; "*Cessante causa, cessat et effectus*"; "Nature makes no leaps"; "Things belong to discrete and permanent kinds"; "Nothing is or happens without a reason"; "The world is throughout rationally intelligible"; etc., etc., etc. Such principles as these, which might be multiplied to satiety,[29] are properly to be called *postulates of rationality*, not propositions of fact. If nature *did* obey them, she *would* be *pro tanto* more intelligible; and we seek meanwhile so to conceive her phenomena as to show that she does obey them. To a certain extent we succeed. For example, instead of the 'quantity of existence' so vaguely postulated as unchanged, Nature allows us to suppose that curious sum of distances and velocities which for want of a better term we call 'energy.' For the effect being 'contained in the cause,' nature lets us substitute 'the effect *is* the cause,' so soon as she lets us conceive both effect and cause as the same molecules, in two successive positions.—But all around these incipient successes (as all around the molecular world, so soon as we add to it as its 'effects' those illusory 'things' of common-sense which we had to butcher for its sake), there still spreads a vast field of irrationalized fact whose items simply *are* together, and from one to another of which we can pass by no ideally 'rational' way.

It is not that these more metaphysical postulates of rationality are absolutely barren—though barren enough they were when used, as the scholastics used them, as immediate propositions of fact.[30]

29 Perhaps the most influential of all these postulates is that the nature of the world must be such that sweeping statements may be made about it.

30 Consider, e.g., the use of the axioms '*nemo potest supra seipsum,*' and '*nemo dat quod non habet,*' in this refutation of 'Darwinism,' which I take from the much-used scholastic compendium of *Logic and Metaphysics* of Liberatore, 3d ed. (Rome, 1880): "Hæc hypothesis . . . aperte contradicit principiis Metaphysicæ, quæ docent essentias rerum esse immutabiles, et effectum non posse superare causam. Et sane, quando, juxta Darwin, species inferior se evolvit in superiorem, unde trahit maiorem illam nobilitatem? Ex ejus carentia. At nihil dat quod non habet; et minus gignere nequit plus, aut negatio positionem. Præterea in transformatione quæ fingitur, natura prioris speciei, servatur aut destruitur? Si primum, mutatio erit tantum accidentalis, qualem reapse videmus in diversis stirpibus animantium. Sin alterum asseritur, ut reapse fert hypothesis darwiniana, res tenderet ad seipsam destruendam; cum contra omnia naturaliter tendant ad sui conservationem, et nonnisi per actionem contrarii agentis corruant." It is merely a question of fact whether these ideally proper relations do or do not obtain between animal and vegetable ancestors and descendants. If they do not, what happens? simply this, that we cannot continue to class animal and vegetal facts under the *kinds* between which those ideal relations obtain. Thus, we can no longer call animal breeds by the name of 'species'; cannot call generating a kind of 'giving,' or treat a descendant as an 'effect' of his ancestor. The ideal scheme of terms and relations can remain, if you like; but it must remain purely mental, and without application to life, which 'gangs its ain gait' regardless of ideal schemes. Most

They have a fertility as ideals, and keep us uneasy and striving always to recast the world of sense until its lines become more congruent with theirs. Take for example the principle that 'nothing can happen without a cause.' We have no definite idea of what we mean by cause, or of what causality consists in. But the principle expresses a demand for *some* deeper sort of inward connection between phenomena than their merely habitual time-sequence seems to us to be. The word 'cause' is, in short, an altar to an unknown god; an empty pedestal still marking the place of a hoped-for statue. *Any* really inward belonging-together of the sequent terms, if discovered, would be accepted as what the word cause was meant to stand for. So we seek, and seek; and in the molecular systems we find a sort of inward belonging in the notion of identity of matter with change of collocation. Perhaps by still seeking we may find other sorts of inward belonging, even between the molecules and those 'secondary qualities,' etc., which they produce upon our minds.

It cannot be too often repeated that the triumphant application of any one of our ideal systems of rational relations to the real world justifies our hope that other systems may be found also applicable. Metaphysics should take heart from the example of physics, simply confessing that hers is the longer task. Nature *may* be remodelled, nay, certainly will be remodelled, far beyond the point at present reached. Just how far?—is a question which only the whole future history of Science and Philosophy can answer.[31] Our task being Psychology, we cannot even cross the threshold of that larger problem.

Besides the mental structure which results in such metaphysical principles as those just considered, there is a mental structure which expresses itself in

ÆSTHETIC AND MORAL PRINCIPLES

The æsthetic principles are at bottom such axioms as that a note sounds good with its third and fifth, or that potatoes need salt. We are once for all so made that when certain impressions come be-

---

of us, however, would prefer to doubt whether such abstract axioms as that 'a thing cannot tend to its own destruction' express ideal relations of an important sort at all.

31 Compare A. Riehl: *Der philosophische Kriticismus*, Bd. II, Thl. I, Abschn. I, Cap. III, § 6.

fore our mind, one of them will seem to call for or repel the others as its companions. To a certain extent the principle of habit will explain these æsthetic connections. When a conjunction is repeatedly experienced, the cohesion of its terms grows grateful, or at least their disruption grows unpleasant. But to explain *all* æsthetic judgments in this way would be absurd; for it is notorious how seldom natural experiences come up to our æsthetic demands. Many of the so-called metaphysical principles are at bottom only expressions of æsthetic feeling. Nature is simple and invariable; makes no leaps, or makes nothing but leaps; is rationally intelligible; neither increases nor diminishes in quantity; flows from one principle, etc., etc.,—what do all such principles express save our sense of how pleasantly our intellect would feel if it had a Nature of that sort to deal with? The subjectivity of which feeling is of course quite compatible with Nature also turning out objectively to be of that sort, later on.

The *moral* principles which our mental structure engenders are quite as little explicable *in toto* by habitual experiences having bred inner cohesions. Rightness is not *mere* usualness, wrongness not *mere* oddity, however numerous the facts which might be invoked to prove such identity. Nor are the moral judgments those most invariably and emphatically impressed on us by public opinion. The most characteristically and peculiarly moral judgments that a man is ever called on to make are in unprecedented cases and lonely emergencies, where no popular rhetorical maxims can avail, and the hidden oracle alone can speak; and it speaks often in favor of conduct quite unusual, and suicidal as far as gaining popular approbation goes. The forces which conspire to this resultant are subtle harmonies and discords between the elementary ideas which form the data of the case. Some of these harmonies, no doubt, have to do with habit; but in respect to most of them our sensibility must assuredly be a phenomenon of supernumerary order, correlated with a brain-function quite as secondary as that which takes cognizance of the diverse excellence of elaborate musical compositions. No more than the higher musical sensibility can the higher moral sensibility be accounted for by the frequency with which outer relations have cohered.[32] Take judgments of justice or equity,

32 As one example out of a thousand of exceptionally delicate idiosyncrasy in this regard, take this: "I must quit society. I would rather undergo twice the danger from beasts and ten times the danger from rocks. It is not pain, it is not death, that I

for example. Instinctively, one judges everything differently, according as it pertains to one's self or to someone else. Empirically one notices that everybody else does the same. But little by little there dawns in one the judgment "nothing can be right for me which would not be right for another similarly placed"; or "the fulfilment of my desires is intrinsically no more imperative than that of anyone else's"; or "what it is reasonable that another should do for me, it is also reasonable that I should do for him";[33] and forthwith the whole mass of the habitual gets overturned. It gets *seriously* overturned only in a few fanatical heads. But its overturning is due to a back-door and not to a front-door process. Some minds are preternaturally sensitive to logical consistency and inconsistency. When they have ranked a thing under a kind, they *must* treat it as of that kind's kind, or feel all out of tune. In many respects we do class ourselves with other men, and call them and ourselves by a common name. They agree with us in having the same Heavenly Father, in not being consulted about their birth, in not being themselves to thank or blame for their natural gifts, in having the same desires and pains and pleasures, in short in a host of fundamental relations. Hence, *if these things be our essence,* we should be substitutable for other men, and they for us, in any proposition in which either of us is involved. The more fundamental and common the essence chosen, and the more simple the reasoning,[34] the more wildly radical and unconditional will the justice be which is aspired to. Life is one long struggle between conclusions based on abstract ways of conceiving cases, and opposite conclusions prompted by our instinctive perception of them as individual facts. The logical stickler for justice always seems

---

dread,—it is the hatred of a man; there is something in it so shocking that I would rather submit to any injury than incur or increase the hatred of a man by revenging it . . . . Another sufficient reason for suicide is, that I was this morning out of temper with Mrs. Douglas (for no fault of hers). I did not betray myself in the least, but I reflected that to be exposed to the possibility of such an event once a year was evil enough to render life intolerable. The disgrace of using an impatient word is to me overpowering." (Elton Hamond, quoted in Henry Crabb Robinson's *Diary, Reminiscences, and Correspondence*, vol. I, p. 424.)

33 Compare H. Sidgwick: *Methods of Ethics*, bk. III, chap. XIII, § 3.

34 A gentleman told me that he had a conclusive argument for opening the Harvard Medical School to women. It was this: "Are not women human?"—which major premise of course had to be granted. "Then are they not entitled to all the rights of humanity?" My friend said that he had never met anyone who could successfully meet this reasoning.

pedantic and mechanical to the man who goes by tact and the particular instance, and who usually makes a poor show at argument. Sometimes the abstract conceiver's way is better, sometimes that of the man of instinct. But just as in our study of reasoning we found it impossible to lay down any mark whereby to distinguish *right* conception of a concrete case from *confusion* (see pp. 962, 974), so here we can give no general rule for deciding when it is morally useful to treat a concrete case as *sui generis*, and when to lump it with others in an abstract class.[35]

An adequate treatment of the way in which we come by our æsthetic and moral judgments would require a separate chapter, which I cannot conveniently include in this book. Suffice it that these judgments express inner harmonies and discords between ob-

35 You reach the Mephistophelian point of view as well as the point of view of justice by treating cases as if they belonged rigorously to abstract classes. Pure rationalism, complete immunity from prejudice, consists in refusing to see that the case before one is absolutely unique. It is always possible to treat the country of one's nativity, the house of one's fathers, the bed in which one's mother died, nay, the mother herself if need be, on a naked equality with all other specimens of so many respective genera. It shows the world in a clear frosty light from which all fuliginous mists of affection, all swamp-lights of sentimentality, are absent. Straight and immediate action becomes easy then—witness a Napoleon's or a Frederick's career. But the question always remains, "Are not the mists and vapors *worth* retaining?" The illogical refusal to treat certain concretes by the mere law of their genus has made the drama of human history. The obstinate insisting that tweedledum is *not* tweedledee is the bone and marrow of life. Look at the Jews and the Scots, with their miserable factions and sectarian disputes, their loyalties and patriotisms and exclusions,—their annals now become a classic heritage, because men of genius took part and sang in them. A thing is important if anyone *think* it important. The process of history consists in certain folks becoming possessed of the mania that certain special things are important infinitely, whilst other folks cannot agree in the belief. The Shah of Persia refused to be taken to the Derby Day, saying "It is already known to me that one horse can run faster than another." He made the question "*which* horse?" immaterial. Any question can be made immaterial by subsuming all its answers under a common head. Imagine what college ball-games and races would be if the teams were to forget the absolute distinctness of Harvard from Yale and think of both as One in the higher genus College. The sovereign road to indifference, whether to evils or to goods, lies in the thought of the higher genus. "When we have meat before us," says Marcus Aurelius, seeking indifference to *that* kind of good, "we must receive the impression, that this is the dead body of a fish, and this is the dead body of a bird or of a pig; and again, that this Falernian is only a little grape juice, and this purple robe some sheeps' wool dyed with the blood of a shell-fish: such then are these impressions, and they reach the things themselves and penetrate them, and so we see what kind of things they are. Just in the same way ought we to act all through life, and where there are things which appear most worthy of our approbation, we ought to lay them bare and look at their worthlessness and strip them of all the words by which they are exalted." (Long's Translation, VI, 13.)

jects of thought; and that whilst outer cohesions frequently repeated will often seem harmonious, all harmonies are not thus engendered, but our feeling of many of them is a secondary and incidental function of the mind. Where harmonies are asserted of the real world, they are obviously mere postulates of rationality, so far as they transcend experience. Such postulates are exemplified by the ethical propositions that the individual and universal good are one, and that happiness and goodness are bound to coalesce in the same subject.

SUMMARY OF WHAT PRECEDES

I will now sum up our progress so far by a short summary of the most important conclusions which we have reached.

The mind has a native structure in this sense, that certain of its objects, if considered together in certain ways, give definite results; and that no other ways of considering, and no other results, are possible if the same objects be taken.

The results are 'relations' which are all expressed by judgments of subsumption and of comparison.

The judgments of subsumption are themselves subsumed under the *laws of logic.*

Those of comparison are expressed in *classifications,* and in the *sciences of arithmetic and geometry.*

Mr. Spencer's opinion that our consciousness of classificatory, logical, and mathematical relations between ideas is due to the frequency with which the corresponding 'outer relations' have impressed our minds, is unintelligible.

Our consciousness of these relations, no doubt, has a natural genesis. But it is to be sought rather in the inner forces which have made the brain grow, than in any mere paths of 'frequent' association which outer stimuli may have ploughed in that organ.

But let our sense for these relations have arisen as it may, the relations themselves form a fixed system of lines of cleavage, so to speak, in the mind, by which we naturally pass from one object to another; and the objects connected by these lines of cleavage are often not connected by any regular time- and space-associations. We distinguish, therefore, between the empirical order of things, and this their rational order of comparison; and, so far as possible, we seek to translate the former into the latter, as being the more congenial of the two to our intellect.

Any classification of things into kinds (especially if the kinds form series, or if they successively involve each other) is a more rational way of conceiving the things than is that mere juxtaposition or separation of them as individuals in time and space which is the order of their crude perception. Any assimilation of things to terms between which such classificatory relations, with their remote and mediate transitions, obtain, is a way of bringing the things into a more rational scheme.

Solids in motion are such terms; and the mechanical philosophy is only a way of conceiving nature so as to arrange its items along some of the more natural lines of cleavage of our mental structure.

Other natural lines are the moral and æsthetic relations. Philosophy is still seeking to conceive things so that these relations also may seem to obtain between them.

As long as things have not successfully been so conceived, the moral and æsthetic relations obtain only between *entia rationis*, terms in the mind; and the moral and æsthetic principles remain but postulates, not propositions, with regard to the real world outside.

There is thus a large body of *a priori* or intuitively necessary truths. As a rule, these are truths of *comparison* only, and in the first instance they express relations between merely mental terms. Nature, however, acts as if some of her realities were identical with these mental terms. So far as she does this, we can make *a priori* propositions concerning natural fact. The aim of both science and philosophy is to make the identifiable terms more numerous. So far it has proved easier to identify nature's things with mental terms of the mechanical than with mental terms of the sentimental order.

The widest postulate of rationality is that the world *is* rationally intelligible throughout, after the pattern of *some* ideal system. The whole war of the philosophies is over that point of faith. Some say they can see their way already to the rationality; others that it is hopeless in any other but the mechanical way. To some the very fact that there is a world at all seems irrational. Nonentity would be a more natural thing than existence, for these minds. One philosopher at least says that the relatedness of things to each other is irrational anyhow, and that a world of relations can never be made intelligible.[36]

With this I may be assumed to have completed the programme which I announced at the beginning of the chapter, so far as the *theoretic* part of our organic mental structure goes. It can be due neither to our own nor to our ancestors' experience. I now pass to those practical parts of our organic mental structure. Things are a little different here; and our conclusion, though it lies in the same direction, can be by no means as confidently expressed.

To be as short and simple as possible, I will take the case of instincts, and, supposing the reader to be familiar with Chapter XXIV, I will plunge *in medias res.*

THE ORIGIN OF INSTINCTS

Instincts must have been either

1) Each specially created in complete form, or

2) Gradually evolved.

As the first alternative is nowadays obsolete, I proceed directly to the second. The two most prominent suggestions as to the way in which instincts may have been evolved are associated with the names of Lamarck and Darwin.

Lamarck's statement is that animals have *wants,* and contract, to satisfy them, *habits* which transform themselves gradually into so many propensities which they can neither resist nor change. These *propensities,* once acquired, propagate themselves by way of transmission to the young, so that they come to exist in new individuals, anteriorly to all exercise. Thus are the same emotions, the same habits, the same *instincts,* perpetuated without variation from one generation to another, so long as the outward conditions of existence remain the same.[37] Mr. Lewes calls this the theory of 'lapsed intelligence.' Mr. Spencer's words are clearer than Lamarck's so that I will quote from him:[38]

36 "*An sich, in seinem eigenen Wesen ist jedes reale Object mit sich selbst identisch und unbedingt*"—that is, the "*allgemeinste Einsicht a priori,*" and the "*allgemeinste Einsicht aus Erfahrung*" is "*Alles Erkennbare ist bedingt.*" (A. Spir: *Denken und Wirklichkeit.* Compare also Herbart and Hegel.)

37 *Philosophie zoölogique,* 3me partie, chap. v, "De l'instinct des animaux."

38 It should be said that Mr. Spencer's most formal utterance about instinct is in his *Principles of Psychology,* in the chapter under that name. Dr. Romanes has reformulated and criticised the doctrine of this chapter in his *Mental Evolution in*

"Setting out with the unquestionable assumption, that every new form of emotion making its appearance in the individual or the race, is a modification of some pre-existing emotion, or a compounding of several pre-existing emotions; we should be greatly aided by knowing what always are the pre-existing emotions. When, for example, we find that very few if any of the lower animals show any love of accumulation, and that this feeling is absent in infancy—when we see that an infant in arms exhibits anger, fear, wonder, while yet it manifests no desire of permanent possession, and that a brute which has no acquisitive emotion can nevertheless feel attachment, jealousy, love of approbation; we may suspect that the feeling which property satisfies, is compounded out of simpler and deeper feelings. We may conclude that as, when a dog hides a bone, there must exist in him a prospective gratification of hunger; so there must similarly at first, in all cases where anything is secured or taken possession of, exist an ideal excitement of the feeling which that thing will gratify. We may further conclude that when the intelligence is such that a variety of objects come to be utilized for different purposes—when, as among savages, divers wants are satisfied through the articles appropriated for weapons, shelter, clothing, ornament; the act of appropriating comes to be one constantly involving agreeable associations, and one which is therefore pleasurable, irrespective of the end subserved. And when, as in civilized life, the property acquired is of a kind not conducing to one order of gratifications, but is capable of administering to all gratifications, the pleasure of acquiring property grows more distinct from each of the various pleasures subserved—is more completely differentiated into a separate emotion.[39] . . . It is well-known that on newly-discovered lands

Animals, chapter XVII. I must confess my inability to state its vagueness in intelligible terms. It treats instincts as a further development of reflex actions, and as forerunners of intelligence,—which is probably true of many. But when it ascribes their formation to the mere 'multiplication of experiences,' which, at first simple, mould the nervous system to 'correspond to outer relations' by simple reflex actions, and, afterwards complex, make it 'correspond' by 'compound reflex actions,' it becomes too mysterious to follow without more of a key than is given. The whole thing becomes perfectly simple if we suppose the reflex actions to be accidental inborn idiosyncrasies preserved.

39 This account of acquisitiveness differs from our own. Without denying the associationist account to be a true description of a great deal of our proprietary feeling, we admitted in addition an entirely primitive form of desire. (See above, p. 1039 ff.) The reader must decide as to the plausibilities of the case. Certainly appearances are in favor of there being in us *some* cupidities quite disconnected with the ulterior uses of the things appropriated. The source of their fascination lies in their appeal to our æsthetic sense, and we wish thereupon simply to *own* them. Glittering, hard, metallic, odd, pretty things; curious things especially; natural objects that look as if they were artificial, or that mimic other objects,—these form a class of things

not inhabited by man, birds are so devoid of fear as to allow themselves to be knocked over with sticks; but that in the course of generations, they acquire such a dread of man as to fly on his approach; and that this dread is manifested by young as well as old. Now unless this change be ascribed to the killing-off of the least fearful, and the preservation and multiplication of the more fearful, which, considering the comparatively small number killed by man, is an inadequate cause; it must be ascribed to accumulated experiences; and each experience must be held to have a share in producing it. We must conclude that in each bird that escapes with injuries inflicted by man, or is alarmed by the outcries of other members of the flock . . . there is established an association of ideas between the human aspect and the pains, direct and indirect, suffered from human agency. And we must further conclude, that the state of consciousness which impels the bird to take flight, is at first nothing more than an ideal reproduction of those painful impressions which before followed man's approach; that such ideal reproduction becomes more vivid and more massive as the painful experiences, direct or sympathetic, increase; and that thus the emotion in its incipient state, is nothing else than an aggregation of the revived pains before experienced. As, in the course of generations, the young birds of this race begin to display a fear of man before yet they have been injured by him; it is an unavoidable inference that the nervous system of the race has been organically modified by these experiences: we have no choice but to conclude that when a young bird is thus led to fly, it is because the impression produced on its senses by the approaching man, entails, through an incipiently-reflex action, a partial excitement of all those nerves which in its ancestors had been excited under the like conditions; that this partial excitement has its accompanying painful consciousness; and that the vague painful consciousness thus arising, constitutes emotion proper—*emotion undecomposable into specific experiences, and therefore seemingly homogeneous. If such be the explanation of the fact in this case, then it is in all cases. If emotion is so generated here, then it is so generated throughout.* If so, we must perforce conclude that the emotional modifications displayed by different nations, and those higher emotions by which civilized are distinguished from savage, are to be accounted for on the same principle. And con-

---

which human beings snatch at as magpies snatch rags. They simply fascinate us. What house does not contain some drawer or cupboard full of senseless odds and ends of this sort, with which nobody knows what to do, but which a blind instinct saves from the ash-barrel? Witness people returning from a walk on the sea-shore or in the woods, each carrying some *lusus naturæ* in the shape of stone or shell, or strip of bark or odd-shaped fungus, which litter the house and grow daily more unsightly, until at last reason triumphs over blind propensity and sweeps them away.

cluding this, we are led strongly to suspect that the emotions in general have severally thus originated."[40]

Obviously the word 'emotion' here means instinct as well,—the actions we call instinctive are expressions or manifestations of the emotions whose genesis Mr. Spencer describes. Now if habit could thus bear fruit outside the individual life, and if the modifications so painfully acquired by the parents' nervous systems could be found ready-made at birth in those of the young, it would be hard to overestimate the importance, both practical and theoretical, of such an extension of its sway. In principle, instincts would then be assimilated to 'secondarily-automatic' habits, and the origin of many of them out of tentative experiments made during ancestral lives, perfected by repetition, addition, and association through successive generations, would be a comparatively simple thing to understand.

Contemporary students of instinct have accordingly been alert to discover all the facts which would seem to establish the possibility of such an explanation. The list is not very long, considering what a burden of conclusions it has to bear. Let acquisitiveness and fear of man, as just argued for by Spencer, lead it off. Other cases of the latter sort are the increased shyness of the woodcock noticed to have occurred within sixty years' observation by Mr. T. A. Knight, and the greater shyness everywhere shown by large than by small birds, to which Darwin has called attention. Then we may add—

The propensities of 'pointing,' 'retrieving,' etc., in sporting dogs, which seem partly, at any rate, to be due to training, but which in well-bred stock are all but innate. It is in these breeds considered bad for a litter of young if its sire or dam have not been trained in the field.

Docility of domestic breeds of horses and cattle.

Tameness of young of tame rabbit—young wild rabbits being invincibly timid.

Young foxes are most wary in those places where they are most severely hunted.

Wild ducks, hatched out by tame ones, fly off. But if kept close for some generations, the young are said to become tame.[41]

40 Review of Bain in H. Spencer: *Illustrations of Universal Progress* (New York, 1864), pp. 310, 315.

41 Ribot: *L'Hérédité psychologique*, 2me éd., p. 26.

Young savages at a certain age will revert to the woods.

English greyhounds taken to the high plateau of Mexico could not at first run well, on account of rarefied air. Their whelps entirely got over the difficulty.

Mr. Lewes somewhere[42] tells of a terrier pup whose parents had been taught to 'beg,' and who constantly threw himself spontaneously into the begging attitude. Darwin tells of a French orphan-child, brought up out of France, yet *shrugging* like his ancestors.[43]

Musical ability often increases from generation to generation in the families of musicians.

In the hereditarily epileptic guinea-pigs of Brown-Séquard, whose parents had become epileptic through surgical operations on the spinal cord or sciatic nerve, the adults often lose some of their hind toes, and the young, in addition to being epileptic, are frequently born with the corresponding toes lacking. The offspring of guinea-pigs whose cervical sympathetic nerve has been cut on one side will have the ear larger, the eyeball smaller, etc., just like their parents after the operation. Puncture of the 'restiform body' of the medulla will, in the same animal, congest and enlarge one eye, and cause gangrene of one ear. In the young of such parents the same symptoms occur.

Physical refinement, delicate hands and feet, etc., appear in families well-bred and rich for several generations.

The 'nervous' temperament also develops in the descendants of sedentary brain-working people.

Inebriates produce offspring in various ways degenerate.

Nearsightedness is produced by indoor occupation for generations. It has been found in Europe much more frequent among schoolchildren in towns than among children of the same age in the country.

These latter cases are of the inheritance of structural rather than of functional peculiarities. But as structure gives rise to function it may be said that the principle is the same. Amongst other inheritances of adaptive[44] structural change may be mentioned:

The 'Yankee' type.

42 Quoted (without reference) in Spencer's *Biology*, vol. I, p. 247.

43 *Expression of Emotions* (N. Y.), p. 267.

44 'Adaptive' changes are those produced by the direct effect of outward conditions on an organ or organism. Sunburned complexion, horny hands, muscular toughness, are illustrations.

Scrofula, rickets, and other diseases of bad conditions of life.

The udders and permanent milk of the domestic breeds of cow.

The 'fancy' rabbit's ears, drooping through lack of need to erect them. Dog's, ass's, etc., in some breeds ditto.

The obsolete eyes of mole and various cave-dwelling animals.

The diminished size of the wing-bones of domesticated ducks, due to ancestral disuse of flight.[45]

These are about all the facts which, by one author or another, have been invoked as evidence in favor of the 'lapsed intelligence' theory of the origin of instincts.

Mr. Darwin's theory is that of the natural selection of accidentally produced tendencies to action.

"It would," says he, "be the most serious error to suppose that the greater number of instincts have been acquired by habit in one generation, and then transmitted by inheritance to succeeding generations. It can be clearly shown that the most wonderful instincts with which we are acquainted, namely, those of the hive-bee and of many ants, could not possibly have been thus acquired.[46] It will be universally admitted that instincts are as important as corporeal structure for the welfare of each species, under its present conditions of life. Under changed conditions of life, it is at least possible that slight modifications of instinct might be profitable to a species; and if it can be shown that instincts do vary ever so little, then I can see no difficulty in natural selection preserving and continually accumulating variations of instinct to any extent that may be profitable. It is thus, as I believe, that all the most complex and wonderful instincts have originated. . . . I believe that the effects of habit are of quite subordinate importance to the effects of the natural selection of what may be called accidental variations of instincts;—that is of variations produced by the same unknown causes which produce slight deviations of bodily structure."[47]

The evidence for Mr. Darwin's view is too complex to be given in this place. To my own mind it is quite convincing. If, with the

45 For these and other facts cf. Théodule Ribot: *L'Hérédité*; W. B. Carpenter: *Contemporary Review*, vol. 21, p. 295, 779, 867; H. Spencer: *Principles of Biology*, pt. II, ch. V, VIII, IX, X; pt. III, ch. XI, XII; C. Darwin: *Animals and Plants under Domestication*, ch. XII, XIII, XIV; Samuel Butler: *Life and Habit*; T. A. Knight: *Philosophical Transactions*, 1837; E. Dupuy: *Popular Science Monthly*, vol. XI, p. 332; F. Papillon: *Nature and Life*, p. 330; Crothers, in *Popular Science Monthly*, Feb. 1889.

46 [Because, being exhibited by neuter insects, the effects of mere practice cannot accumulate from one generation to another.—W.J.]

47 *Origin of Species*, chap. VII.

Darwinian theory in mind, one re-reads the list of examples given in favor of the Lamarckian theory, one finds that many of the cases are irrelevant, and that some make for one side as well as for the other. This is so obvious in many of the cases that it is needless to point it out in detail. The shrugging child and the begging pup, e.g., prove somewhat too much. They are examples so unique as to suggest spontaneous variation rather than inherited habit. In other cases the observations much need corroboration, e.g., the effects of not training for a generation in sporting dogs and race-horses, the difference between young wild rabbits born in captivity and young tame ones, the cumulative effect of many generations of captivity on wild ducks, etc.

Similarly, the increased wariness of the large birds, of those on islands frequented by men, of the woodcock, of the foxes, may be due to the fact that the bolder families have been killed off, and left none but the naturally timid behind, or simply to the individual experience of older birds being imparted by example to the young so that a new *educational tradition* has occurred.—The cases of physical refinement, nervous temperament, Yankee type, etc., also need much more discriminating treatment than they have yet received from the Lamarckians. There is no real evidence that physical refinement and nervosity tend to accumulate from generation to generation in aristocratic or intellectual families; nor is there any that the change in that direction which Europeans transplanted to America undergo is not all completed in the first generation of children bred on our soil. To my mind, the facts all point that way. Similarly the better breathing of the greyhounds born in Mexico was surely due to a post-natal adaptation of the pups' thorax to the rarer air, an adaptation which the stiffer thorax of the first imported adult dogs could not undergo.

Distinct neurotic *degeneration* may undoubtedly accumulate from parent to child, and as the parent usually in this case grows worse by his own irregular habits of life, the temptation lies near to ascribe the child's deterioration to this cause. This, again, is a hasty conclusion. For neurotic degeneration is unquestionably a disease whose original causes are unknown; and like other 'accidental variations' it is hereditary. But it ultimately ends in sterility; and it seems to me quite unfair to draw any conclusions from its natural history in favor of the transmission of acquired peculiarities. Nor does the degeneration of the children of alcoholics prove anything in favor of their having inherited the shattered nervous system which the alcohol has induced in their parents: because the poison usually has a chance to directly affect their own bodies before birth, by acting on the germinal matter from which they are formed whilst it is still nourished by the alcoholized blood of the parent. In many cases, moreover, the parental alcoholics are themselves degenerates neurotically, and the drink-habit is only a symptom of their disease, which in some form or other they also propagate to their children.

There remain the inherited mutilations of the guinea-pig. But these are such startling exceptions to the ordinary rule with animals that they should hardly be used as examples of a typical process. The docility of domestic cattle is certainly in part due to man's selection, etc., etc. In a word, the proofs form rather a beggarly array.

Add to this that the writers who have tried to carry out the theory of transmitted habit with any detail are always obliged *somewhere* to admit inexplicable variation. Thus Spencer allows that

> "Sociality can begin only where, through some slight variation, there is less tendency than usual for the individuals to disperse . . . . That slight variations of mental nature sufficient to initiate this process may be fairly assumed, all our domestic animals show us: differences in their characters and likings are conspicuous. Sociality having thus commenced, and survival of the fittest tending ever to maintain and increase it, it will be further strengthened by the inherited effects of habit."[48] Again, in writing of the pleasure of pity, Mr. Spencer says: "This feeling is not one that has arisen through the inherited effects of experiences, but belongs to a quite different group, traceable to the survival of the fittest simply—to the natural selection of incidental variations. In this group are included all the bodily appetites, together with those simpler instincts, sexual and parental, by which every race is maintained; and which must exist before the higher processes of mental evolution can commence."[49]

The inheritance of tricks of manner and trifling peculiarities, such as handwriting, certain odd gestures when pleased, peculiar movements during sleep, etc., has also been quoted in favor of the theory of transmission of acquired habits. Strangely enough; for of all things in the world these tricks seem most like idiosyncratic

48 *Principles of Psychology,* II, 560.

49 *Ibid.,* p. 623.

variations. They are usually defects or oddities which the education of the individual, the pressure of what is really *acquired* by him, would counteract, but which are too native to be repressed, and break through all artificial barriers, in his children as well as in himself.

I leave my text practically just as it was written in 1885. I proceeded at that time to draw a tentative conclusion to the effect that the origin of *most* of our instincts must certainly be deemed fruits of the back-door method of genesis, and not of ancestral experience in the proper meaning of the term. Whether acquired ancestral habits played any part at all in their production was still an open question in which it would be as rash to affirm as to deny. Already before that time, however, Professor Weismann of Freiburg had begun a very serious attack upon the Lamarckian theory,[50] and his polemic has at last excited such a widespread interest among naturalists that the whilom almost unhesitatingly accepted theory seems almost on the point of being abandoned.

I will therefore add some of Weismann's criticisms of the supposed evidence to my own. In the first place, he has a captivating theory of descent of his own,[51] which makes him think it *a priori* impossible that any peculiarity acquired during lifetime by the parent should be transmitted to the germ. Into the nature of that theory this is not the place to go. Suffice to say that it has made him a keener critic of Lamarck's and Spencer's theory than he otherwise might have been. The only way in which the germinal products can be influenced whilst in the body of the parent is, according to Weismann, by good or bad nutrition. Through this they may degenerate in various ways or lose vitality altogether. They may also be infected through the blood by small-pox, syphilis, or other virulent diseases, and otherwise be poisoned. But peculiarities of neural structure and habit in the parents *which the parents themselves were not born with*, they can never acquire unless perhaps accidentally through some coincidental variation of their own. *Accidental* variations develop of course into idiosyncrasies

50 *Über die Vererbung* (Jena, 1883). Prof. Weismann's *Essays upon Heredity* have recently (1889) been published in English in a collected form.

51 Best expressed in the Essay on the *Continuität des Keimplasmas als Grundlage einer Theorie der Vererbung* (1885).

which tend to pass to later generations in virtue of the well-known law which no one doubts.

Referring to the often-heard assertion that the increase of talent found in certain families from one generation to another is due to the transmitted effects of *exercise* of the faculty concerned (the Bachs, the Bernoullis, Mozart, etc.), he sensibly remarks, that the talent being kept in exercise, it ought to have gone on growing for an indefinite number of generations. As a matter of fact, it quickly reaches a maximum, and then we hear no more of it, which is what happens always when an idiosyncrasy is exposed to the effects of miscellaneous intermarriage.

The hereditary epilepsy and other degenerations of the operated guinea-pigs are explained by Professor Weismann as results of *infection* of the young by the parent's blood. The latter he supposes to undergo a pathologic change in consequence of the original traumatic injury. The obsolescence of disused organs he explains very satisfactorily, without invoking any transmission of the direct effects of disuse, by his theory of *panmixy*, for which I must refer to his own writings. Finally, he criticises searchingly the stories we occasionally hear of inherited mutilations in animals (dogs' ears and tails, etc.), and cites a prolonged series of experiments of his own on mice, which he bred for many generations, cutting off both parental tails each time, without interfering in the least with the length of tail with which the young continued to be born.

The strongest argument, after all, in favor of the Lamarckian theory remains the *a priori* one urged by Spencer in his little work (much the solidest thing, by the way, which he has ever written) *The Factors of Organic Evolution*. Since, says Mr. Spencer, the accidental variations of all parts of the body are independent of each other, if the entire organization of animals were due to such accidental variations alone, the amount of mutual adaptation and harmony that we now find there could hardly possibly have come about in any finite time. We must rather suppose that the divers varying parts *brought* the other parts into harmony with themselves by *exercising them ad hoc*, and that the effects of the exercise remained and were passed on to the young. This forms, of course, a great *presumption* against the all-sufficiency of the view of selection of accidental variations exclusively. But it must be admitted that in favor of the contrary view, that adaptive changes are inherited, we have as yet perhaps not one single unequivocal item of positive proof.

I must therefore end this chapter on the genesis of our mental structure by reaffirming my conviction that the so-called Experience-philosophy has failed to prove its point. No more if we take ancestral experiences into account than if we limit ourselves to those of the individual after birth, can we believe that the couplings of terms within the mind are simple copies of corresponding couplings impressed upon it by the environment. This indeed is true of a small part of our cognitions. But so far as logical and mathematical, ethical, æsthetical, and metaphysical propositions go, such an assertion is not only untrue but altogether unintelligible; for these propositions say nothing about the time- and space-order of things, and it is hard to understand how such shallow and vague accounts of them as Mill's and Spencer's could ever have been given by thinking men.

The causes of our mental structure are doubtless natural, and connected, like all our other peculiarities, with those of our nervous structure. Our interests, our tendencies of attention, our motor impulses, the æsthetic, moral, and theoretic combinations we delight in, the extent of our power of apprehending schemes of relation, just like the elementary relations themselves, time, space, difference and similarity, and the elementary kinds of feeling, have all grown up in ways of which at present we can give no account. Even in the clearest parts of Psychology our insight is insignificant enough. And the more sincerely one seeks to trace the actual course of *psychogenesis*, the steps by which as a race we may have come by the peculiar mental attributes which we possess, the more clearly one perceives "the slowly gathering twilight close in utter night."

THE END

Index

Key to the Pagination of Editions

James's Index for *The Principles of Psychology* has been rekeyed to the pages of the present edition with the result that the original volume and page numbers are omitted. Anomalies in accidental matters have been corrected silently. These include mechanical errors of typography, punctuation, and alphabetizing.

Approximately eighty errors of varying kinds which could be considered substantive were found and also corrected silently in the Index. Page numbers were often off by a digit or more as with 'Lazarus, I. 626' which should have been '627' (rekeyed to 590). Page numbers were also occasionally transposed as with 'Calmeil, II. 524' which should have been '542' (rekeyed to 1148). In some entries a reference was wrongly attributed to a page as in 'Lewes, on begging in pup, II. 400'—the reference on that page is actually to Lewes's remarks on the loss of instinct in a gosling; the whole entry was put in brackets and not rekeyed. Sometimes a name was spelled wrong—'Bridgeman, Laura' was corrected to 'Bridgman' as it appeared in the text. Similarly, an initial for a first name could be incorrect as in 'Bergson, J.' which was changed to 'H.' Volume numbers were often not used when they were needed or were wrong; 'Strumpell, A., I. 376, 445, 489, 491' should have been 'I. 376; II. 445 (an error for 455), 489, 491' (rekeyed to 355, 1071, 1101, 1103). In one case a chapter number was incorrect—'Movement, Production of, Chap. XXII' should have been 'XXIII'.

Four changes made by James in his private copy of the book have also been made: 'their facial perception, 204;' has been added under 'Blind, the'; under 'Darwinism' the word 'reputation' has been changed to 'refutation'; an umlaut has been added to 'Grübelsucht'; and the addition of 'II, 49' rekeyed to 695 has been added to ''Fringe' of object'. These have been rekeyed accordingly.

Brackets are put around references which could not be located in the text; the page listings are left as they appeared in the original Index.

Index

Authors the titles only of whose works are cited are not, as a rule, referred to in this index.

Index

Index

Key to the Pagination of Editions

The plates of the Henry Holt first edition of *The Principles of Psychology* have been reprinted a number of times, but always with the same numbering regardless of the date. Since the original edition has been widely used in scholarly reference, a key is here provided by which the pagination of the original Holt printing can be readily equated with the text in the present ACLS edition. In the list that follows, the first number refers to the page of the September 1890 original edition and its printings of different date. The number to the right after the colon represents the page(s) of the present edition on which the corresponding text will be found.

Volume I
v:5–6
vi:6
vii:6–7
ix:9
x:9–10
xi:10–11
xii:11
[1]:15
2:15–16
3:16–17
4:17–18
5:18–19
6:19–20
7:20–21
8:21
9:21–22
10:22–23
11:23–24
12:25–26
13:26–27
14:27–28
15:28–29
16:29
17:29–30
18:30–31
19:31–32
20:32–33
21:33–34
22:34–35
23:35
24:36
25:36–37
26:37–38
27:38–39
28:39–40
29:40–41
30:41–42
31:42–43
32:43–44
33:44
34:45
35:45–46
36:46–47
37:46–49
38:48–49
39:49–50
40:50–51
41:51–52
42:52–53
43:53
44:53–54
45:54–55
46:55–56
47:56–57
48:57–59
49:58–59
50:59–60
51:60–61
52:61–62
53:62–63
54:63
55:63–64
56:64–65
57:65–66
58:66–67
59:67–68
60:68–69
61:69–70
62:70
63:70–71
64:71–73
65:73–74
66:74–75
67:75–76
68:76
69:76–77
70:77–78
71:78–79
72:79–80
73:80–81
74:81–82
75:82–83
76:83
77:83–84
78:84–85
79:85–86
80:86–87
81:88–89
82:89–90
83:90
84:90–91
85:91–92
86:92–93
87:93–94
88:94–95
89:95–96
90:96–97
91:97–98
92:98–99
93:99
94:99–100
95:100–101
96:101–102
97:102–103
98:103–104
99:104–105
100:105–106
101:106–107
102:107–108
103:108
104:109–110
105:110
106:110–111
107:111–112
108:112–113
109:113–114
110:114–115
111:115–116
112:116–117
113:117–118
114:118–119
115:119–120
116:120–121
117:121–122
118:122–123
119:123–124
120:124–125
121:125–126
122:126–127
123:127–128
124:128
125:129
126:129–130
127:130–131
128:132–133
129:133
130:133–134
131:134–135
132:135–136
133:136–137
134:137–138
135:138–139
136:139–140
137:140–141
138:141–142
139:142–143
140:143
141:143–144
142:144–145
143:145–146
144:146–147
145:148
146:149
147:149–150
148:150–152
149:151–152
150:152–153
151:153–154
152:154–155
153:155–156
154:156–157
155:157–158
156:158–159

157:159–160
158:160–161
159:161–162
160:162–163
161:163–164
162:164–165
163:165–166
164:166–167
165:167
166:167–168
167:168–169
168:169–170
169:170–171
170:171–172
171:172–173
172:173–174
173:174–175
174:175–176
175:176
176:176–177
177:177–178
178:178–179
179:179–180
180:180–181
181:181–182
182:182
183:183–184
184:184
185:184–185
186:185–186
187:186–187
188:187–188
189:188–189
190:189–190
191:190–191
192:191–192
193:192–193
194:193–194
195:194
196:194–195
197:195–196
198:196
199:197–198
200:198
201:198–199
202:199–200
203:200–201
204:201–202
205:202–203
206:203–204
207:204–205
208:205–206
209:206
210:206–207
211:207–208
212:208–209
213:209–210
214:210–211
215:211–212
216:212–213
217:213
218:213–214
219:214–215
220:215–216
221:216–217
222:217–218
223:218
224:219–220
225:220
226:220–221
227:221–222
228:222–223
229:223–224
230:224–225
231:225–226
232:226–227
233:227–228
234:228
235:228–229
236:229–230
237:230–231
238:231–232
239:232–233
240:233–234
241:234–235
242:235–236
243:236
244:236–237
245:237–238
246:238–239
247:239–240
248:239–241
249:240–242
250:240–243
251:243
252:243–244
253:244–245
254:245–246
255:246–247
256:247–248
257:248–249
258:249
259:249–250
260:250–251
261:251–252
262:252–253
263:253–254
264:254–255
265:255–256
266:256–257
267:257–258
268:258–259
269:259–260
270:260–261
271:261–262
272:262–263
273:263–264
274:264–265
275:265–266
276:266
277:267
278:267–268
279:268–269
280:269–270
281:270–271
282:271–272
283:272–273
284:273–274
285:274–275
286:275
287:275–276
288:276–277
289:277–278
290:278
291:279–280
292:280
293:280–281
294:281–282
295:282–283
296:283–284
297:284–285
298:285–286
299:286–287
300:287–288
301:288
302:288–289
303:289–290
304:290–291
305:291–292
306:292–293
307:293–294
308:294
309:294–295
310:295–296
311:296–297
312:297–298
313:298–299
314:299–300
315:300–301
316:301
317:301–302
318:302–303
319:303–304
320:304–305
321:305–306
322:306–307
323:307–308
324:308
325:309
326:309–310
327:310–312
328:312
329:312–314
330:313–314
331:314–315
332:315–316
333:316–317
334:317–318
335:318–319
336:319
337:319–320
338:320–321
339:321–322
340:322–323
341:323–324
342:323–325
343:325–326
344:326–327
345:327
346:327–328
347:328–329
348:329–330
349:330–331
350:331–332
351:332–333
352:333–334
353:334–335
354:335–336
355:336–337
356:337–338
357:338–339
358:339–340
359:339–340
360:340–341
361:341–342
362:342–343
363:343–344
364:344–345
365:345–346
366:346
367:346–347
368:347–348
369:348–349
370:349–350
371:350–351
372:351–352
373:352–353
374:353–354
375:354–355
376:355–356
377:356–357
378:357–358
379:358
380:358–359

Key to the Pagination of Editions

381:359-360
382:360-361
383:361-362
384:362-363
385:363-364
386:364-365
387:365-366
388:366-367
389:367-368
390:368-369
391:369-370
392:370-371
393:371-372
394:372-373
395:373-374
396:374-375
397:375-376
398:376-377
399:377-378
400:378-379
401:379
402:380-381
403:381
404:381-382
405:382-383
406:383-384
407:384-385
408:385-386
409:386-387
410:387-388
411:388-389
412:389-390
413:390-391
414:391-392
415:392-393
416:392-394
417:394-395
418:395-396
419:396-397
420:397-398
421:398
422:398-399
423:399-400
424:400-401
425:401-402
426:402-403
427:403-404
428:404-405
429:405-406
430:406-407
431:407-408
432:408-409
433:409-410
434:410-411
435:411-412
436:412-413
437:413-414
438:414-415
439:415-416
440:416-417
441:417-418
442:418-419
443:419-420
444:420-421
445:421-422
446:422-423
447:423-424
448:424-425
449:424-425
450:425-426
451:426-427
452:427-428
453:428-429
454:429-430
455:430-431
456:431-432
457:432-433
458:433
459:434-435
460:435-436
461:436
462:436-437
463:437-438
464:438-439
465:439-440
466:440-441
467:441-442
468:442-443
469:443-444
470:444-445
471:445-446
472:446-447
473:447-448
474:448
475:448-449
476:449-451
477:451
478:451-453
479:452-453
480:453-454
481:454-455
482:455-456
483:457-458
484:458-459
485:459-460
486:460-461
487:461-462
488:462-463
489:463-464
490:464
491:464-465
492:465-466
493:466-467
494:467-468
495:468-469
496:469-470
497:470-471
498:471-472
499:472
500:472-473
501:473-474
502:474-475
503:475-476
504:476-477
505:477-478
506:478-479
507:479-480
508:480-481
509:481-482
510:482-483
511:483
512:483-484
513:484-485
514:485-486
515:486-487
516:487-488
517:488-489
518:489-490
519:490-491
520:491-492
521:492-493
522:493-494
523:494-495
524:495-496
525:496
526:497
527:497-498
528:498-499
529:499-500
530:500-501
531:501-502
532:501-503
533:503-504
534:501
535:504-506
536:506-507
537:507-508
538:508-509
539:509
540:509-510
541:510-511
542:511-512
543:512-513
544:513-514
545:514-515
546:515-516
547:516-517
548:517-518
549:518
550:519-520
551:520
552:520-521
553:521-522
554:522-523
555:523-524
556:524-525
557:525-526
558:526-527
559:527-528
560:528-529
561:529
562:529-530
563:530-531
564:531-532
565:532-533
566:533-534
567:534-535
568:535-536
569:536-537
570:537
571:537-538
572:538-539
573:539-540
574:540-541
575:541-542
576:542-543
577:543-544
578:544-545
579:545-546
580:546-547
581:547-548
582:548-549
583:549
584:549-550
585:550-551
586:551-552
587:552-553
588:553-554
589:554-555
590:555-556
591:556-557
592:557
593:557-558
594:558-559
595:559-560
596:560-561
597:561-563
598:563-564
599:564
600:564-566
601:565-566
602:566-567
603:568
604:568-569

605:570-571
606:571-572
607:572
608:572-573
609:573-574
610:574-575
611:575-576
612:576-577
613:577-578
614:578-579
615:579-580
616:580-581
617:581-582
618:582
619:582-583
620:583-584
621:584-585
622:585-586
623:586-587
624:587-588
625:588-589
626:589-590
627:590
628:590-591
629:591-592
630:592-593
631:593-594
632:594-595
633:595-597
634:596-597
635:597-598
636:598-599
637:599-600
638:600
639:601
640:601-602
641:602-603
642:603-604
643:605-606
644:606-607
645:607
646:607-608
647:608-609
648:609-610
649:610-611
650:611-612
651:612-613
652:613-614
653:614-615
654:615-616
655:616-617
656:617-618
657:618-619
658:618-620
659:620-621
660:621-622
661:622
662:622-623
663:623-624
664:624-625
665:625-626
666:626-627
667:627-628
668:628-629
669:629-630
670:630-631
671:631-632
672:632-633
673:633-634
674:634-635
675:635-636
676:636-637
677:637-638
678:638
679:638-640
680:640-641
681:641-642
682:642-643
683:643
684:643-644
685:644-645
686:645-647
687:647-648
688:648-649
689:649

Volume II

iii:11-12
iv:12-13
v:13
vi:13
[1]:651
2:651-652
3:652-653
4:653-654
5:654-655
6:655-656
7:656-657
8:657-658
9:658-659
10:658-659
11:659-660
12:660-661
13:661-662
14:662-663
15:663-664
16:664-665
17:665-666
18:666-667
19:667-668
20:668-669
21:669-670
22:670
23:670-671
24:671-672
25:672-673
26:673-674
27:674-675
28:675-676
29:676-677
30:677-678
31:678-679
32:679
33:680-681
34:680-681
35:681-682
36:682-683
37:683-684
38:684-685
39:685-686
40:686-687
41:687-688
42:688-689
43:688-689
44:690-691
45:691-692
46:692-693
47:693-694
48:694-695
49:695-696
50:696-697
51:696-698
52:698-699
53:699-700
54:700-701
55:701-702
56:702-703
57:703-704
58:704-705
59:705-706
60:706-707
61:707-708
62:708-709
63:709-710
64:710-711
65:711-712
66:712-713
67:713-714
68:714-715
69:715-716
70:716-717
71:717-718
72:718-719
73:719-720
74:720
75:720-721
76:722-723
77:723-724
78:724-725
79:725
80:725-726
81:726-727
82:727-728
83:728-729
84:729-730
85:730-731
86:731-732
87:732-733
88:733-734
89:734
90:734-735
91:735-736
92:736-737
93:737-738
94:738-739
95:738-740
96:740-741
97:741-742
98:742-743
99:743-744
100:744-745
101:745-746
102:746-747
103:747-748
104:748-749
105:749-750
106:750
107:750-751
108:751-752
109:752-753
110:753-754
111:754-755
112:755-756
113:756-757
114:757-758
115:758-759
116:759-760
117:760-761
118:761-762
119:762-763
120:763-764
121:764-765
122:765-766
123:766-767
124:767-768
125:768
126:768-769
127:769-770
128:770-771
129:771-772
130:772-773
131:773
132:773-774
133:774-775

134:776–777
135:777
136:777–778
137:778–779
138:779–780
139:780–781
140:781–782
141:782–783
142:783–785
143:785
144:785–786
145:786–787
146:787–788
147:788–789
148:789–790
149:790–791
150:791–792
151:792–793
152:793–794
153:794
154:794–795
155:795–796
156:796–797
157:797–798
158:798–799
159:799–800
160:800–801
161:801–802
162:802–803
163:803
164:803–805
165:804–805
166:805–806
167:806–807
168:807–808
169:808–809
170:809–810
171:810
172:810–811
173:811–812
174:812–813
175:813–814
176:814–815
177:815–816
178:816–817
179:817
180:817–818
181:818–819
182:819–820
183:820–821
184:821–822
185:822–823
186:823–824
187:824–825
188:825
189:826
190:826–827
191:827–828
192:828–829
193:829–830
194:830–831
195:831–832
196:832–833
197:833
198:833–834
199:834–835
200:835–836
201:836–837
202:837–838
203:838–839
204:839–840
205:840–841
206:841–842
207:842–843
208:843–844
209:844
210:844–845
211:845–846
212:846–847
213:847–848
214:848–849
215:849–850
216:850–851
217:851–852
218:852
219:852–853
220:853–854
221:854–855
222:855–856
223:856–857
224:857–858
225:858–859
226:859–860
227:859–860
228:860–861
229:861–862
230:862–863
231:863–864
232:864–865
233:865–866
234:865–867
235:867–868
236:868–869
237:869
238:870
239:870–871
240:871–872
241:872–873
242:873–874
243:874–875
244:875–876
245:876–877
246:877–878
247:878–879
248:879–880
249:880–881
250:881–882
251:882–883
252:883–884
253:883–885
254:885–886
255:886
256:886–887
257:887–888
258:888–889
259:889–890
260:890–891
261:891–892
262:892–893
263:893–894
264:894–895
265:895–896
266:896–897
267:897–898
268:898–899
269:899–900
270:900–901
271:901–902
272:902
273:903–904
274:904–905
275:905–906
276:906
277:906–907
278:907–908
279:908–909
280:909–910
281:910–911
282:911–912
283:913–914
284:914
285:914–915
286:915–916
287:916–917
288:917–918
289:918–919
290:919–920
291:920–921
292:921–922
293:922–923
294:923–924
295:924
296:925
297:925–926
298:926–927
299:927–928
300:928–929
301:929–930
302:930–931
303:931–932
304:932–933
305:933–934
306:934–935
307:935–936
308:936–937
309:937
310:937–939
311:938–939
312:939–940
313:940–941
314:941–942
315:942–943
316:943–944
317:944–945
318:945–946
319:946–947
320:947–948
321:948–949
322:949–950
323:950
324:950–951
325:952–953
326:953–954
327:954
328:954–955
329:955–956
330:956–957
331:957–958
332:958–959
333:959–960
334:960–961
335:961–962
336:961–963
337:963
338:963–964
339:964–965
340:965–966
341:966–967
342:967–968
343:968–969
344:969–970
345:970–971
346:971
347:971–972
348:972–973
349:973–974
350:974–975
351:975–976
352:976–977
353:977
354:977–979
355:979–980
356:980
357:980–981

358:981-982
359:982-983
360:983-984
361:984-985
362:985-986
363:986-987
364:987-988
365:988
366:988-989
367:989-990
368:990-991
369:991-992
370:992-993
371:993
372:994-995
373:995-996
374:996
375:997
376:996,998
377:998-999
378:998-1000
379:1000-1001
380:1001-1002
381:1002-1003
382:1003
383:1004-1005
384:1005-1006
385:1006
386:1006-1007
387:1007-1008
388:1008-1009
389:1009-1010
390:1010-1011
391:1011-1012
392:1012-1013
393:1013-1014
394:1014-1015
395:1015-1016
396:1016
397:1017
398:1017-1018
399:1018-1019
400:1019-1020
401:1020-1021
402:1021-1022
403:1022-1023
404:1023-1024
405:1024-1025
406:1025-1026
407:1026
408:1026-1027
409:1027-1028
410:1028-1029
411:1029-1030
412:1030-1031
413:1031-1032
414:1032-1033
415:1033-1034
416:1034-1035
417:1035
418:1035-1037
419:1037
420:1037-1038
421:1038-1039
422:1039-1040
423:1040-1041
424:1041-1042
425:1042-1043
426:1043-1044
427:1044-1045
428:1045
429:1045-1046
430:1046-1047
431:1047-1048
432:1048-1049
433:1049-1050
434:1050-1051
435:1051-1052
436:1052-1053
437:1053-1054
438:1054
439:1054-1055
440:1055-1056
441:1056-1057
442:1058-1059
443:1059-1060
444:1060-1061
445:1061-1062
446:1062-1063
447:1063-1064
448:1064
449:1064-1065
450:1065-1066
451:1066-1067
452:1067-1068
453:1068-1069
454:1069-1070
455:1070-1071
456:1071-1072
457:1072-1073
458:1073
459:1073-1074
460:1074-1075
461:1075-1076
462:1076-1077
463:1077-1078
464:1078-1079
465:1079-1080
466:1080-1081
467:1081-1082
468:1082-1083
469:1083-1084
470:1084
471:1084-1085
472:1085-1086
473:1086-1087
474:1087-1088
475:1088-1089
476:1089-1090
477:1090-1091
478:1091-1092
479:1092
480:1092-1093
481:1093-1094
482:1094-1095
483:1095-1096
484:1096-1097
485:1097
486:1098-1099
487:1099
488:1099-1100
489:1100-1101
490:1101-1102
491:1102-1103
492:1103-1104
493:1104-1105
494:1105-1106
495:1106-1107
496:1107-1108
497:1108-1109
498:1109
499:1109-1110
500:1110-1111
501:1111-1112
502:1112-1113
503:1113-1114
504:1114-1115
505:1115-1116
506:1116-1117
507:1117-1118
508:1118-1119
509:1119
510:1119-1120
511:1120-1121
512:1121-1122
513:1122-1123
514:1123-1124
515:1124-1125
516:1125-1126
517:1126
518:1126-1127
519:1127-1128
520:1128-1129
521:1129-1130
522:1130-1131
523:1131-1132
524:1132-1133
525:1133-1134
526:1134
527:1134-1135
528:1135-1136
529:1136-1137
530:1137-1138
531:1138-1139
532:1139-1140
533:1140-1141
534:1141
535:1141-1142
536:1142-1143
537:1143-1144
538:1144-1145
539:1145-1146
540:1146-1147
541:1147-1148
542:1148-1149
543:1149-1150
544:1150-1151
545:1151-1152
546:1152-1153
547:1153-1154
548:1154-1155
549:1155-1156
550:1156-1157
551:1157
552:1157-1158
553:1158-1159
554:1159-1160
555:1160-1161
556:1161-1162
557:1162-1163
558:1163-1164
559:1164-1165
560:1165
561:1165-1166
562:1166-1167
563:1167-1168
564:1168-1169
565:1169-1170
566:1170-1171
567:1171-1172
568:1172-1173
569:1173
570:1173-1174
571:1174-1175
572:1175-1176
573:1176-1177
574:1177-1178
575:1178-1179
576:1179-1180
577:1180
578:1180-1181
579:1181-1182
580:1182-1183
581:1183-1184